BRITISH
HIT
SINGLES

11th Edition

acknowledgements

We would like to thank Jon Kutner, Alan Jones and Neil Warwick for their contributions to this edition.

© Guinness Publishing Ltd

First edition 1977. Second edition 1979. Third edition 1981. Fourth edition 1983. Fifth edition 1985. Sixth edition 1987. Seventh edition 1989. Eighth edition 1991. Ninth edition 1993. Tenth edition 1995.

Reprint 10 9 8 7 6 5 4 3 2 1

Published in Great Britain by Guinness Publishing Ltd, 338 Euston Road, London, NW1 3BD.

Printed and bound in Great Britain by The Bath Press.

'Guinness' is a registered trade mark of Guinness Publishing Ltd.

Editor:	Helen Weller
Consultant Editor:	Tony Brown
Picture Research:	Richard Philpott
Design:	Town Group Creative
Cover Design:	Ron Callow at Design 23
Page Make-up:	John Eley and Ian Hall
Proof Reading:	Caroline Lucas

Joint Publishing Directors:	Ian Castello-Cortes
	Michael Feldman

A catalogue record for this book is available from The British Library.

ISBN 0-85112-027-X

contents

All statistics and information cover the period 14 November 1952 to 31 December 1996, and are arranged as follows:

1. alphabetical by artist

Chart acts listed alphabetically with chronological title list showing date disc first hit the chart, title, label, catalogue number, highest position reached and number of weeks on chart. Top Ten placings and number ones are indicated.

2. alphabetical by title

Hits listed alphabetically by title, with artists' names and year of initial chart entry. Different versions of the same song and different songs with the same title are indicated.

3. facts and feats

All you need to know and more about the record charts record breakers.

introduction by Mark Lamarr

Believe me, if I had the statistics to hand I'd be ramming 'em at ya by now and your head would be reeling with plenty of market share information and trade weighted averages regarding the relative financial merits of, say, Upside Down as opposed to Funkadelic. Well, for one thing I'm no music insider worrying about economic trends rather than turning the volume up to eleven and getting on down, and for two thing, I figured you just bought a book of statistics and nothing I can add to its magnificence is as important as Chicory Tip reaching number one in 1972 or indeed Westworld reaching number 72 in 1988. However, as my purpose here is to provide a fan's eye view of developments over the past couple of years I'm obliged to note a few salient points with which to establish my credentials and prove to you I'm not some bozo who doesn't know his Four Seasons from his Five Star.

Did you know that in 1967 at the absolute peak of the singles career, an old 45 had to sell at least 100 million copies to even reach the bottom half of the chart? That's right, every Briton had to buy at least two copies of their favourite song before it had even a slim chance of appearing on Ready, Steady, Go!. Whereas today, if only a quarter of the members of a medium-sized Teeside youth club bought their favourite CD, it would

be number one for a good two and a half months. A fascinating fact I'm sure you'll agree but one based only on wilful falsehood.

So, there you go, a quick lesson on how statistics can blur the bigger picture, especially when I make them up. The great surf guitarist Dick Dale once told me, and with a straight face too, that an album he sold 88,000 copies of in 1962 was equivalent to selling four million today. You see how easy it is to be blinded by numbers?

The singles chart is the soundtrack to all our lives. Sure, there are incredible moments in our personal soundtracks that wouldn't be seen dead rubbing shoulders with Dickie Valentine or the Singing Sheep, but if you're looking for some kind of definition of a collective consciousness, you're holding its details in your paws right now. And I'll betcha by golly wow (Prince or the Stylistics) that an eighteen year old of 1996 could care less that Firestarter sold 56,871 units to get to number one.

From very limited experience as a part-time occasional amateur DJ, it's easy to tell that the whole music industry, perhaps shortsightedly, still hangs its hopes on Radio One and Top Of The Pops exposure, and it's to the credit of both these institutions that they've kept pace artistically and led rather than followed. Radio One in particular,

due, it seems to blind panic, has at last got a rap show, a reggae show, a jungle show and more indie music than you can shake a malnutritioned leg at in order to complement its occasionally insipid daytime playlist of Euro-style pop. Not that Jeru The Damaga, the Ganga Kru or Cutty Ranks are in any danger of tearing about at the Radio One Roadshow, but it's doubtful that recent classic pop moments such as Placebo, Kenickie or Rocket From The Crypt would have had chart and thus Top Of The Pops exposure without adventurous playlisting. Obviously, the threat of the independent radio stations has kept the BBC on its toes, and maybe without this threat Radio One would still be best known for Our Tune and Newsbeat. While wonderful One FM could be seen as the dog chasing its own ratings, it does, due to its unique position of having to justify its own existence to the public without being accountable stylistically to its investors, stabilise the environment it dominates.

Televisually though, we're treated like Dickensian orphans peeking through the master's window. Music on TV is treated either as high art (where you might find a Polish orchestra sandwiched in-between B.B. King and Sinead O'Connor) or teenie trash (and we find out what Peter Andre has for breakfast). According to the highest ranking TV commissioners, there's no market for music on the box, though there's obviously a huge market crying out for *Call My Bluff* and *Saved By The Bell*. Never mind where you were when Kennedy was assassinated, I vividly remember where I was when I first witnessed Thin Lizzy, Public Enemy, James Brown, The Only Ones and the Sugarcubes; I was watching telly. Of course I grew up in Swindon so what else would I be doing? But if Jimi Hendrix could appear on the Lulu Show, the Jam on Mark Bolan's show, and Elvis Costello could guest on Mavis Nicholson's, is it too much to ask for the Butthole Surfers on Ant and Dec or Bounty Killa on Richard and Judy? I suspect it is.

So what's up doc since the last edition of this here tome? I'm sure you know as well as me but maybe you're picking this up a few decades down the shuffle, so to refresh your memory the biggest deals pop-wise over the past two years are pretty easy to sum up by checking out the enclosed listings beginning SP, OA and TA (if between me writing this introduction and you purchasing this book a group called Spoata have hit the charts, I apologise for the confusion). Of course no period can be fully covered by only three bands. The 60s weren't just the Beatles, Stones and Kinks y'know, there were also the Bachelors and Topol, but these three have certainly column-inched the

bejeesus out of the competition.

Oasis, minorish chart entrants in the last issue, managed to play the biggest live gigs in U.K. history, have eight entries simultaneously in the Irish Top 40, grabbed headlines on a daily basis and picked up every major critical award in 1996 despite not having released a single record throughout that year. The Blur v. Oasis debate soon turned into a Beatles v. Oasis toss up, and is all set to develop into a heated Big Bang v. Oasis argy-bargy by the millennium.

Take That finally bought the farm after nearly five years of teenie supremacy, and if you think cutesie appeal and novelty factor alone can account for their reign of terror, go and check the chart history of Alessi or Flintlock and think again. The passing of the Takers or the Thatters, or however they were fondly regarded, spawned not only the unlikeliest indie star in Mark Owen but also the TT races; is every teenage boy in the country now choreographing in his bedroom in a bid to topple the troubled East 17 and Boyzone wannabes currently cluttering up *Smash Hits*? It feels like the second skiffle boom.

What else? Depeche Mode returned; U2 returned with a whole new sound; Blur returned after being written off and went straight in at number one; the Pistols reformed and nobody could remember what

the fuss was about; Robson and Jerome presumably wound up even those who consumed their CDs and every waking moment was consumed with Spice mania, fever and dyspepsia. Naughty Spice, Sporty Spice, Haughty Spice and the other ones who sadly don't rhyme, kept the tabloids in a frenzy, conquered America, politically-punditted and zigazigged all over the national psyche leaving no man, woman, child or beast unscarred in their quest for a society with no class.

I'll save my personal Spice opinion 'til the day psychotherapy can deal with public embarrassment adequately, and let you get on with your thirst for knowledge. No matter how many Camel albums you own, Timebox 45s you guard religiously or Manic Street Preachers demos you covet, at some point, I promise you'll use this tome to check out the chart history of the Macarena. Go and get it over with.

the charts

In compiling this book, we have used the charts published by the *New Musical Express* from the date of their first chart, which was the first UK record sales chart, for the week ending 14 November 1952. We continue to use the *NME* chart, as the longest established and most complete chart available, until the appearance of the first UK top 50 in what was then called the *Record Retailer* (now *Music Week*), on 10 March 1960.

It is possible to argue that the *Record Retailer* chart in the first few years of its existence was not the most widely accepted chart, and we often receive angry letters from people wondering why, for example 'Please Please Me' by the Beatles or 'Are You Sure' by the Allisons are not listed as number ones, because they were on other charts. However, the *Record Retailer* was certainly no less accurate than any other available chart. By the mid-1960s, it was accepted as the national chart of record, something which no other chart since the earliest days of the *NME* chart could claim.

The size of the chart has varied over the years:

14 Nov 52
First ever chart, a Top 12 containing 15 hits

1 Oct 54
Chart becomes a Top 20

30 Dec 55
Top 25 published, for this week only

13 Apr 56
Chart becomes a Top 30

26 Feb 60
Last NME Top 30 used by British Hit Singles

10 Mar 60
Record Retailer chart inaugurated. This is a publication date, the chart date being week ending 5 March

3 Jan 63
Top 50 now independently audited

13 Feb 69
Top 50 now compiled for *Record Retailer* and the BBC by the British Market Research Bureau

6 Feb 71
Top 40 only for seven weeks as postal strikes limit the collection of chart sales information

27 Mar 71
Top 50 resumes

6 Jan 73
Top 30 only, for one week

22 Dec 73
Top 30 only, for one week

6 May 78
Top 75 begins

8 Jan 83
Chart compilation taken over by Gallup

12 Feb 94
Chart compilation taken over by Millward Brown. Charts are now © CIN, produced in co-operation with the BPI and BARD, based on a sample of more than 1,000 record outlets, incorporating 7 inch, 12 inch, cassette and CD singles sales

31 Dec 96
The final chart to be incorporated in this edition of The Guinness Book Of British Hit Singles.

Occasionally a week went by with no chart being compiled (this often happened at Christmas in the early years of the chart). In these cases, the previous week's chart has been used again. If a chart was compiled but not published, or if a chart was published incorrectly, the correct chart has been found and used.

1. alphabetically by artist

In this first section of *The Guinness Book Of British Hit Singles*, we list every record that has hit the UK singles chart from 14 November 1952 to the final chart of 1994. The information is presented alphabetically by artist, and then chronologically for each artist. Each hit single is catalogued with the following information: *date disc first hit the chart, title of hit, label and catalogue number, highest position the hit reached on the chart, total number of weeks spent on the chart.*

Records which were not hits are not listed. A record is a hit if it appears in the charts even for just one week at number 75, the lowest position listed.

It should be noted that the date given for the entry of a disc into the chart is the week ending date, which is the way charts have historically been dated. For example,

Abba's 'Waterloo' entered the chart in the week ending 20 April 1974, which means that their first day of chart action could have been any day of that week.

Number one records are indicated by a star, other top ten records by a dot. A dagger indicates hits still on the chart at the end of 1996.

In this edition once again we have credited hits in combination with other acts to each participating artists' lists. So, for example, you will find George Michael and Elton

John's number one hit 'Don't Let The Sun Go Down On Me' listed twice, once under Elton John and once under George Michael. There is no separate entry for them as a duo, and the weeks that this record spent on the chart are credited to both singers. A box after the catalogue number of any hit indicates that the credit on the label of the hit is different to the other hits of that artist. At the foot of each act's list there is an explanation of the details of each of these alternative label credits.

how to use this section

1 — date of chart entry

2 — top ten single

3 — act description

4 — total and individual weeks on chart

5 — highest position

6 — still on chart at end of 1996

7 — alternative billing

8 — catalogue number

9 — label

10 — number one single

EAST 17 *UK, male vocal group*   **144 wks**

29 Aug 92	● **HOUSE OF LOVE** *London LON 325*	**10** 9
14 Nov 92	**GOLD** *London LON 331*	**28** 4
19 Dec 92	**GOLD (re-entry)** *London LON 331*	**64** 4
30 Jan 93	● **DEEP** *London LOCDP 334*	**5** 10
10 Apr 93	**SLOW IT DOWN** *London LONCD 339*	**13** 7
26 Jun 93	**WEST END GIRLS** *London LONCD 344*	**11** 7
4 Dec 93	● **IT'S ALRIGHT** *London LONCD 345*	**3** 14
14 May 94	● **AROUND THE WORLD** *London LONCD 349*	**3** 13
1 Oct 94	● **STEAM** *London LONCD 353*	**7** 8
3 Dec 94	★ **STAY ANOTHER DAY** *London LONCD 354*	**1** 15
25 Mar 95	● **LET IT RAIN** *London LONCD 363*	**10** 7
6 May 95	**STAY ANOTHER DAY (re-entry)** *London LONCD 354*	**64** 1
17 Jun 95	**HOLD MY BODY TIGHT** *London LONCD 367*	**12** 7
4 Nov 95	● **THUNDER** *London LONCD 373*	**4** 14
10 Feb 96	● **DO U STILL** *London LONCD 379*	**7** 7
10 Aug 96	**SOMEONE TO LOVE** *London LONCD 385*	**16** 8
2 Nov 96	● **IF YOU EVER** *London LONCD 388* 1	**21** 9

1 East 17 featuring Gabrielle

We have attempted to describe each act in as concise a manner as possible above their list of hits. Although we are aware that many of the 'vocalists' thus described also play an instrument, we have only mentioned this fact where the artist's instrumental skills were an important factor in their chart success.

Once more we have calculated the total weeks spent on the chart by every single act, and this total appears at the top right of each act's entry.

Alert readers will note that the grand total of weeks on chart for some acts (e.g. Elvis Presley and Cliff Richard) is slightly less than the figure obtained by adding up each individual hits weeks on chart. This is because in the early days of the charts both sides of the same record were sometimes listed simultaneously in different positions (e.g. Elvis Presley's 'Party' and 'Got A Lot O'Livin' To Do'). In these instances the two sides score only one week towards the act's total, not two.

Catalogue numbers are generally those of the 7-inch version of the single, but where there is a good reason for using an alternative (if, for example, the record was not issued on a 7-inch single), the catalogue number for the best-selling alternative format is given.

AALIYAH US, female vocalist — 18 wks

2 Jul 94	**BACK AND FORTH** Jive JIVECD 357	**16**	5
15 Oct 94	**(AT YOUR BEST) YOU ARE LOVE** Jive JIVECD 359	**27**	2
11 Mar 95	**AGE AIN'T NOTHING BUT A NUMBER** Jive JIVECD 369	**32**	2
13 May 95	**DOWN WITH THE CLIQUE** Jive JIVECD 377	**33**	2
9 Sep 95	**THE THING I LIKE** Jive JIVECD 382	**33**	2
3 Feb 96	**I NEED YOU TONIGHT** Big Beat A 8130CD ①	**66**	1
24 Aug 96	**IF YOUR GIRL ONLY KNEW** Atlantic A 5669CD	**21**	2
23 Nov 96	**GOT TO GIVE IT UP** Atlantic A 5632CD	**37**	2

① Junior MAFIA featuring Aaliyah

ABBA
Sweden / Norway, male / female vocal / instrumental group — 252 wks

20 Apr 74	★ **WATERLOO** Epic EPC 2240	**1**	9
13 Jul 74	**RING RING** Epic EPC 2452	**32**	5
12 Jul 75	**I DO I DO I DO I DO I DO** Epic EPC 3229	**38**	4
20 Sep 75	● **S.O.S.** Epic EPC 3576	**6**	10
13 Dec 75	★ **MAMMA MIA** Epic EPC 3790	**1**	14
27 Mar 76	★ **FERNANDO** Epic EPC 4036	**1**	15
21 Aug 76	★ **DANCING QUEEN** Epic EPC 4499	**1**	15
20 Nov 76	● **MONEY MONEY MONEY** Epic EPC 4713	**3**	12
26 Feb 77	★ **KNOWING ME KNOWING YOU** Epic EPC 4955	**1**	13
22 Oct 77	★ **THE NAME OF THE GAME** Epic EPC 5750	**1**	12
4 Feb 78	★ **TAKE A CHANCE ON ME** Epic EPC 5950	**1**	12
16 Sep 78	● **SUMMER NIGHT CITY** Epic EPC 6595	**5**	9
3 Feb 79	● **CHIQUITITA** Epic EPC 7030	**2**	9
5 May 79	● **DOES YOUR MOTHER KNOW** Epic EPC 7316	**4**	9
14 Jul 79	● **ANGELEYES / VOULEZ-VOUS** Epic EPC 7499	**3**	11
20 Oct 79	● **GIMME GIMME GIMME (A MAN AFTER MIDNIGHT)** Epic EPC 7914	**3**	12
15 Dec 79	● **I HAVE A DREAM** Epic EPC 8088	**2**	10
2 Aug 80	★ **THE WINNER TAKES IT ALL** Epic EPC 8835	**1**	10
15 Nov 80	● **SUPER TROUPER** Epic EPC 9089	**1**	12
18 Jul 81	● **LAY ALL YOUR LOVE ON ME** Epic EPC A 1314	**7**	7
12 Dec 81	● **ONE OF US** Epic EPC A 1740	**3**	10
20 Feb 82	**HEAD OVER HEELS** Epic EPC A 2037	**25**	7
23 Oct 82	**THE DAY BEFORE YOU CAME** Epic EPC A 2847	**32**	6
11 Dec 82	**UNDER ATTACK** Epic EPC A 2971	**26**	8
12 Nov 83	**THANK YOU FOR THE MUSIC** CBS A 3894	**33**	6
5 Sep 92	**DANCING QUEEN (re-issue)** Polydor PO 231	**16**	5

ABBACADABRA
UK, male / female, vocal / instrumental group — 1 wk

5 Sep 92	**DANCING QUEEN** PWL International PWL 246	**57**	1

Russ ABBOT UK, male vocalist — 22 wks

6 Feb 82	**A DAY IN THE LIFE OF VINCE PRINCE** EMI 5249	**61**	1
20 Feb 82	**A DAY IN THE LIFE OF VINCE PRINCE (re-entry)** EMI 5249	**75**	1
29 Dec 84	● **ATMOSPHERE** Spirit FIRE 4	**7**	13
13 Jul 85	**ALL NIGHT HOLIDAY** Spirit FIRE 6	**20**	7

Gregory ABBOTT US, male vocalist — 13 wks

22 Nov 86	● **SHAKE YOU DOWN** CBS A 7326	**6**	13

ABC UK, male vocal / instrumental duo — 92 wks

31 Oct 81	**TEARS ARE NOT ENOUGH** Neutron NT 101	**19**	8
20 Feb 82	● **POISON ARROW** Neutron NT 102	**6**	11
15 May 82	● **THE LOOK OF LOVE** Neutron NT 103	**4**	11
4 Sep 82	● **ALL OF MY HEART** Neutron NT 104	**5**	8
15 Jan 83	**THE LOOK OF LOVE (re-entry)** Neutron NT 103	**71**	1
5 Nov 83	**THAT WAS THEN BUT THIS IS NOW** Neutron NT 105	**18**	4
21 Jan 84	**S.O.S.** Neutron NT 106	**39**	5
10 Nov 84	**HOW TO BE A MILLIONAIRE** Neutron NT 107	**49**	4
6 Apr 85	**BE NEAR ME** Neutron NT 108	**26**	4
15 Jun 85	**VANITY KILLS** Neutron NT 109	**70**	1
18 Jan 86	**OCEAN BLUE** Neutron NT 110	**51**	3
6 Jun 87	**WHEN SMOKEY SINGS** Neutron NT 111	**11**	10
5 Sep 87	**THE NIGHT YOU MURDERED LOVE** Neutron NT 112	**31**	8
28 Nov 87	**KING WITHOUT A CROWN** Neutron NT 113	**44**	3
27 May 89	**ONE BETTER WORLD** Neutron NT 114	**32**	4
23 Sep 89	**THE REAL THING** Neutron NT 115	**68**	1
14 Apr 90	**THE LOOK OF LOVE (re-mix)** Neutron NT 116	**68**	1
27 Jul 91	**LOVE CONQUERS ALL** Parlophone R 6292	**47**	2
11 Jan 92	**SAY IT** Parlophone R 6298	**42**	3

The act were a UK, male vocal / instrumental group for first six hits, and a UK / US, male / female vocal / instrumental group for the next four.

Paula ABDUL US, female vocalist — 67 wks

4 Mar 89	● **STRAIGHT UP** Siren SRN 111	**3**	13
3 Jun 89	**FOREVER YOUR GIRL** Siren SRN 112	**24**	6
19 Aug 89	**KNOCKED OUT** Siren SRN 92	**45**	3
2 Dec 89	**(IT'S JUST) THE WAY THAT YOU LOVE ME** Siren SRN 101	**74**	1
7 Apr 90	● **OPPOSITES ATTRACT** Siren SRN 124 ①	**2**	13
21 Jul 90	**KNOCKED OUT (re-mix)** Virgin America VUS 23	**21**	5
29 Sep 90	**COLD HEARTED** Virgin America VUS 27	**46**	2
22 Jun 91	● **RUSH RUSH** Virgin America VUS 38	**6**	11
31 Aug 91	**THE PROMISE OF A NEW DAY** Virgin America VUS 44	**52**	2
18 Jan 92	**VIBEOLOGY** Virgin America VUS 53	**19**	6
8 Aug 92	**WILL YOU MARRY ME** Virgin America VUS 58	**73**	1
17 Jun 95	**MY LOVE IS FOR REAL** Virgin America VUSCD 91	**28**	3

① Paula Abdul with the Wild Pair

ABIGAIL UK, female vocalist — 4 wks

16 Jul 94	**SMELLS LIKE TEEN SPIRIT** Klone CDKLONE 25	**29**	4

Colonel ABRAMS US, male vocalist — 35 wks

17 Aug 85	● **TRAPPED** MCA MCA 997	**3**	23
7 Dec 85	**THE TRUTH** MCA MCA 1022	**53**	3
8 Feb 86	**I'M NOT GONNA LET YOU (GET THE BEST OF ME)** MCA MCA 1031	**24**	4
15 Aug 87	**HOW SOON WE FORGET** MCA MCA 1179	**75**	2

ABSOLUTELY FABULOUS – See PET SHOP BOYS

AC/DC Australia / UK, male vocal / instrumental group — 125 wks

10 Jun 78	**ROCK 'N' ROLL DAMNATION** Atlantic K 11142	**24**	9
1 Sep 79	**HIGHWAY TO HELL** Atlantic K 11321	**56**	4
2 Feb 80	**TOUCH TOO MUCH** Atlantic K 11435	**29**	9
28 Jun 80	**DIRTY DEEDS DONE DIRT CHEAP** Atlantic HM 2	**47**	3
28 Jun 80	**HIGH VOLTAGE (LIVE VERSION)** Atlantic HM 1	**48**	3
28 Jun 80	**IT'S A LONG WAY TO THE TOP (IF YOU WANNA ROCK 'N' ROLL)** Atlantic HM 3	**55**	3
28 Jun 80	**WHOLE LOTTA ROSIE** Atlantic HM 4	**36**	8
13 Sep 80	**YOU SHOOK ME ALL NIGHT LONG** Atlantic K 11600	**38**	6
29 Nov 80	**ROCK 'N' ROLL AIN'T NOISE POLLUTION** Atlantic K 11630	**15**	8
6 Feb 82	**LET'S GET IT UP** Atlantic K 11706	**13**	6

3 Jul 82	**FOR THOSE ABOUT TO ROCK (WE SALUTE YOU)** *Atlantic K 11721*	**15**	6
29 Oct 83	**GUNS FOR HIRE** *Atlantic A 9774*	**37**	4
4 Aug 84	**NERVOUS SHAKEDOWN** *Atlantic A 9651*	**35**	5
6 Jul 85	**DANGER** *Atlantic A 9532*	**48**	4
18 Jan 86	**SHAKE YOUR FOUNDATIONS** *Atlantic A 9474*	**24**	5
24 May 86	**WHO MADE WHO** *Atlantic A 9425*	**16**	5
30 Aug 86	**YOU SHOOK ME ALL NIGHT LONG (re-issue)** *Atlantic A 9377*	**46**	4
16 Jan 88	**HEATSEEKER** *Atlantic A 9136*	**12**	6
2 Apr 88	**THAT'S THE WAY I WANNA ROCK 'N' ROLL** *Atlantic A 9098*	**22**	4
22 Sep 90	**THUNDERSTRUCK** *Atco B 8907*	**13**	5
24 Nov 90	**MONEYTALKS** *Atco B 8886*	**36**	3
27 Apr 91	**ARE YOU READY** *Atco B 8830*	**34**	3
17 Oct 92	**HIGHWAY TO HELL (LIVE)** *Atco B 8479*	**14**	4
6 Mar 93	**DIRTY DEEDS DONE DIRT CHEAP (LIVE)** *Atco B 6073CD*	**68**	1
10 Jul 93	**BIG GUN** *Atco B 8396CD*	**23**	3
30 Sep 95	**HARD AS A ROCK** *Atlantic A 4368CD*	**33**	2
11 May 96	**HAIL CAESAR** *East West 7559660512*	**56**	1

Richard ACE *Jamaica, male vocalist*   **2 wks**

2 Dec 78	**STAYIN' ALIVE** *Blue Inc. INC 2*	**66**	2

ACE *UK, male vocal / instrumental group*   **10 wks**

9 Nov 74	**HOW LONG** *Anchor ANC 1002*	**20**	10

ACE OF BASE
Sweden, male / female vocal / instrumental group   **70 wks**

8 May 93	★ **ALL THAT SHE WANTS** *London 8612702*	**1**	16
28 Aug 93	**WHEEL OF FORTUNE** *London 8615452*	**20**	6
13 Nov 93	**HAPPY NATION** *London 8619272*	**42**	3
26 Feb 94	● **THE SIGN** *London ACECD 1*	**2**	16
11 Jun 94	**DON'T TURN AROUND** *London ACECD 2*	**5**	11
15 Oct 94	**HAPPY NATION (re-issue)** *London 8610972*	**40**	3
14 Jan 95	**LIVING IN DANGER** *London ACECD 3*	**18**	4
11 Nov 95	**LUCKY LOVE** *London ACECD 4*	**20**	5
27 Jan 96	**BEAUTIFUL LIFE** *London ACECD 5*	**15**	6

ACEN *UK, male producer*   **4 wks**

8 Aug 92	**TRIP II THE MOON** *Production House PNT 042*	**38**	3
10 Oct 92	**TRIP II THE MOON (re-mix)** *Production House PNT 042RX*	**71**	1

ACES – *See Desmond DEKKER and the ACES*

Tracy ACKERMAN – *See Q*

ACT *UK / Germany, male / female vocal / instrumental group*   **2 wks**

23 May 87	**SNOBBERY AND DECAY** *ZTT ZTAS 28*	**60**	2

ACT ONE *US, male / female vocal / instrumental group*   **6 wks**

18 May 74	**TOM THE PEEPER** *Mercury 6008 005*	**40**	6

A.D.A.M. featuring AMY
France, male / female vocal / instrumental duo   **11 wks**

1 Jul 95	**ZOMBIE** *Eternal YZ 951CD*	**16**	11

Arthur ADAMS *US, male vocalist*   **5 wks**

24 Oct 81	**YOU GOT THE FLOOR** *RCA 146*	**38**	5

Bryan ADAMS
Canada, male vocalist / instrumentalist – guitar   **164 wks**

12 Jan 85	**RUN TO YOU** *A & M AM 224*	**11**	12
16 Mar 85	**SOMEBODY** *A & M AM 236*	**35**	7
25 May 85	**HEAVEN** *A & M AM 256*	**38**	5
10 Aug 85	**SUMMER OF '69** *A & M AM 267*	**42**	7
2 Nov 85	**IT'S ONLY LOVE** *A & M AM 285* 1	**29**	6
21 Dec 85	**CHRISTMAS TIME** *A & M AM 297*	**55**	2
22 Feb 86	**THIS TIME** *A & M AM 295*	**41**	7
12 Jul 86	**STRAIGHT FROM THE HEART** *A & M AM 322*	**51**	3
28 Mar 87	**HEAT OF THE NIGHT** *A & M ADAM 2*	**50**	2
20 Jun 87	**HEARTS ON FIRE** *A & M ADAM 3*	**57**	3
17 Oct 87	**VICTIM OF LOVE** *A & M AM 407*	**68**	2
29 Jun 91	★ **(EVERYTHING I DO) I DO IT FOR YOU** *A & M AM 789*	**1**	24
14 Sep 91	**CAN'T STOP THIS THING WE STARTED** *A & M AM 612*	**12**	6
23 Nov 91	**THERE WILL NEVER BE ANOTHER TONIGHT** *A & M AM 838*	**32**	3
28 Dec 91	**(EVERYTHING I DO) I DO IT FOR YOU (re-entry)** *A & M AM 789*	**73**	1
22 Feb 92	● **THOUGHT I'D DIED AND GONE TO HEAVEN** *A & M AM 848*	**8**	7
18 Jul 92	**ALL I WANT IS YOU** *A & M AM 879*	**22**	5
26 Sep 92	**DO I HAVE TO SAY THE WORDS** *A & M AM 0068*	**30**	3
30 Oct 93	● **PLEASE FORGIVE ME** *A & M 5804232*	**2**	16
15 Jan 94	● **ALL FOR LOVE** *A & M 5804772* 2	**2**	13
22 Apr 95	● **HAVE YOU EVER REALLY LOVED A WOMAN** *A & M 5810282*	**4**	9
11 Nov 95	**ROCK STEADY** *Capitol CDCL 763* 3	**50**	2
1 Jun 96	● **THE ONLY THING THAT LOOKS GOOD ON ME IS YOU** *A & M 5816392*	**6**	7
24 Aug 96	● **LET'S MAKE A NIGHT TO REMEMBER** *A & M 5818672*	**10**	8
23 Nov 96	**STAR** *A & M 5820252*	**13**	4

1 Bryan Adams and Tina Turner   2 Bryan Adams, Rod Stewart and Sting   3 Bonnie Raitt and Bryan Adams

Cliff ADAMS *UK, orchestra*   **2 wks**

28 Apr 60	**LONELY MAN THEME** *Pye International 7N 25056*	**39**	2

Gayle ADAMS *US, female vocalist*   **1 wk**

26 Jul 80	**STRETCHIN' OUT** *Epic EPC 8791*	**64**	1

Marie ADAMS – *See Johnny OTIS SHOW*

Oleta ADAMS *US, female vocalist*   **36 wks**

24 Mar 90	**RHYTHM OF LIFE** *Fontana OLETA 1*	**52**	2
3 Nov 90	**RHYTHM OF LIFE (re-entry)** *Fontana OLETA 1*	**56**	3
12 Jan 91	● **GET HERE** *Fontana OLETA 3*	**4**	12
13 Apr 91	**YOU'VE GOT TO GIVE ME ROOM / RHYTHM OF LIFE (re-issue)** *Fontana OLETA 4*	**49**	3
29 Jun 91	**CIRCLE OF ONE** *Fontana OLETA 5*	**73**	1
28 Sep 91	**DON'T LET THE SUN GO DOWN ON ME** *Fontana TRIBO 1*	**33**	5
25 Apr 92	**WOMAN IN CHAINS (re-issue)** *Fontana IDEA 16* 1	**57**	1
10 Jul 93	**I JUST HAD TO HEAR YOUR VOICE** *Fontana OLECD 6*	**42**	3
7 Oct 95	**NEVER KNEW LOVE** *Fontana OLECD 9*	**22**	3
16 Dec 95	**RHYTHM OF LIFE (re-mix)** *Fontana OLECD 10*	**38**	2
10 Feb 96	**WE WILL MEET AGAIN** *Mercury OLECD 11*	**51**	1

1 Tears For Fears featuring Oleta Adams

The original release of Woman In Chains credited Tears For Fears only.

ADAMSKI *UK, male instrumentalist / producer*   **38 wks**

20 Jan 90	**N-R-G** *MCA MCA 1386*	**12**	6

7 Apr 90	★ **KILLER** MCA MCA 1400	**1**	18
8 Sep 90	● **THE SPACE JUNGLE** MCA MCA 1435	**7**	8
17 Nov 90	**FLASHBACK JACK** MCA MCA 1459	**46**	2
9 Nov 91	**NEVER GOIN' DOWN / BORN TO BE ALIVE** MCA MCS 1578 [1]	**51**	2
4 Apr 92	**GET YOUR BODY** MCA MCS 1613 [2]	**68**	1
4 Jul 92	**BACK TO FRONT** MCA MCS 1644	**63**	1

[1] Adamski featuring Jimi Polo/Adamski featuring Soho [2] Adamski featuring Nina Hagen

Featured vocalist on Killer was Seal.

ADDAMS and GEE UK, male instrumental duo   1 wk

20 Apr 91	**CHUNG KUO (REVISITED)** Debut DEBT 3108	**72**	1

ADDIS BLACK WIDOW US, male rap duo   2 wks

3 Feb 96	**INNOCENT** Mercury Black Vinyl MBVCD 1	**42**	2

ADDRISI BROTHERS US, male vocal duo   3 wks

6 Oct 79	**GHOST DANCER** Scotti Brothers K 11361	**57**	3

ADEVA US, female vocalist   64 wks

14 Jan 89	**RESPECT** Cooltempo COOL 179	**17**	9
25 Mar 89	**MUSICAL FREEDOM (MOVING ON UP)** Cooltempo COOL 182 [1]	**22**	8
12 Aug 89	**WARNING** Cooltempo COOL 185	**17**	8
21 Oct 89	**I THANK YOU** Cooltempo COOL 192	**17**	7
16 Dec 89	**BEAUTIFUL LOVE** Cooltempo COOL 195	**57**	2
28 Apr 90	**TREAT ME RIGHT** Cooltempo COOL 200	**62**	2
6 Apr 91	**RING MY BELL** Cooltempo COOL 224 [2]	**20**	5
19 Oct 91	**IT SHOULD'VE BEEN ME** Cooltempo COOL 236	**48**	3
29 Feb 92	**DON'T LET IT SHOW ON YOUR FACE** Cooltempo COOL 248	**34**	4
6 Jun 92	**UNTIL YOU COME BACK TO ME** Cooltempo COOL 254	**45**	3
17 Oct 92	**I'M THE ONE FOR YOU** Cooltempo COOL 264	**51**	2
11 Dec 93	**RESPECT** (re-mix) Network NWKCD 79	**65**	1
27 May 95	**TOO MANY FISH** Virgin America VUSCD 89 [3]	**34**	2
18 Nov 95	**WHADDA U WANT (FROM ME)** Virgin America VUSCD 98 [3]	**36**	2
6 Apr 96	**DO WATCHA DO** Avex UK AVEXCD 24 [4]	**54**	1
4 May 96	**I THANK YOU** (re-mix) Cooltempo CDCOOLS 318	**37**	2

[1] Paul Simpson featuring Adeva [2] Monie Love vs Adeva [3] Frankie Knuckles featuring Adeva [4] Hyper Go Go and Adeva

ADICTS UK, male vocal / instrumental group   1 wk

14 May 83	**BAD BOY** Razor RZS 104	**75**	1

ADIEMUS UK, male instrumental duo   2 wks

14 Oct 95	**ADIEMUS** Venture VEND 4	**48**	2

Larry ADLER – See Kate BUSH

ADONIS featuring 2 PUERTO RICANS, A BLACK MAN AND A DOMINICAN
US, male vocal / instrumental group   4 wks

13 Jun 87	**DO IT PROPERLY ('NO WAY BACK') / NO WAY BACK** London LON 136	**47**	4

ADRENALIN M.O.D.
US, male vocal / instrumental group   5 wks

8 Oct 88	**O-O-O** MCA RAGAT 2	**49**	5

ADULT NET
UK / US, male / female vocal / instrumental group   2 wks

10 Jun 89	**WHERE WERE YOU** Fontana BRX 2	**66**	2

ADVENTURES UK, male vocal / instrumental group   24 wks

15 Sep 84	**ANOTHER SILENT DAY** Chrysalis CHS 2000	**71**	2
1 Dec 84	**SEND MY HEART** Chrysalis CHS 2001	**62**	4
13 Jul 85	**FEEL THE RAINDROPS** Chrysalis AD 1	**58**	3
9 Apr 88	**BROKEN LAND** Elektra EKR 69	**20**	10
2 Jul 88	**DROWNING IN THE SEA OF LOVE** Elektra EKR 76	**44**	4
13 Jun 92	**RAINING ALL OVER THE WORLD** Polydor PO 211	**68**	1

ADVENTURES OF STEVIE V
US, male producer and vocalist   21 wks

21 Apr 90	● **DIRTY CASH** Mercury MER 311	**2**	13
29 Sep 90	**BODY LANGUAGE** Mercury MER 331	**29**	5
2 Mar 91	**JEALOUSY** Mercury MER 337	**58**	3

ADVERTS UK, male / female vocal / instrumental group   11 wks

27 Aug 77	**GARY GILMORE'S EYES** Anchor ANC 1043	**18**	7
4 Feb 78	**NO TIME TO BE 21** Bright BR 1	**34**	4

AEROSMITH US, male vocal / instrumental group   51 wks

17 Oct 87	**DUDE (LOOKS LIKE A LADY)** Geffen GEF 29	**45**	5
16 Apr 88	**ANGEL** Geffen GEF 34	**69**	2
9 Sep 89	**LOVE IN AN ELEVATOR** Geffen GEF 63	**13**	8
24 Feb 90	**DUDE (LOOKS LIKE A LADY)** (re-issue) Geffen GEF 72	**20**	5
14 Apr 90	**RAG DOLL** Geffen GEF 76	**42**	4
1 Sep 90	**THE OTHER SIDE** Geffen GEF 79	**46**	2
10 Apr 93	**LIVIN' ON THE EDGE** Geffen GFSTD 35	**19**	4
3 Jul 93	**EAT THE RICH** Geffen GFSTD 46	**34**	3
30 Oct 93	**CRYIN'** Geffen GFSTD 56	**17**	6
18 Dec 93	**AMAZING** Geffen GFSTD 63	**57**	3
2 Jul 94	**SHUT UP AND DANCE** Geffen GFSTD 75	**24**	4
20 Aug 94	**SWEET EMOTION** Columbia 6604492	**74**	1
5 Nov 94	**CRAZY / BLIND MAN** Geffen GFSTD 80	**23**	4

AFRICAN BUSINESS
Italy, male vocal / instrumental group   1 wk

17 Nov 90	**IN ZAIRE** Urban URB 64	**73**	1

AFTER 7 US, male vocal group   3 wks

3 Nov 90	**CAN'T STOP** Virgin America VUS 31	**54**	3

AFTER THE FIRE
UK, male vocal / instrumental group   12 wks

9 Jun 79	**ONE RULE FOR YOU** CBS 7025	**40**	6
8 Sep 79	**LASER LOVE** CBS 7769	**62**	2
9 Apr 83	**DER KOMMISSAR** CBS A 2399	**47**	4

AFTERNOON BOYS – See Steve WRIGHT

AFTERSHOCK US, male vocal / instrumental duo   8 wks

21 Aug 93	**SLAVE TO THE VIBE** *Virgin America VUSCD 75*	**11**	8

AGE OF CHANCE
UK, male / female vocal / instrumental group   13 wks

17 Jan 87	**KISS** *Fon AGE 5*	**50**	6
30 May 87	**WHO'S AFRAID OF THE BIG BAD NOISE!** *Fon VS 962*	**65**	2
20 Jan 90	**HIGHER THAN HEAVEN** *Virgin VS 1228*	**53**	5

A-HA Norway, male vocal / instrumental group   131 wks

28 Sep 85	● **TAKE ON ME** *Warner Bros. W 9006*	**2**	19
28 Dec 85	★ **THE SUN ALWAYS SHINES ON TV** *Warner Bros. W 8846*	**1**	12
5 Apr 86	● **TRAIN OF THOUGHT** *Warner Bros. W 8736*	**8**	8
14 Jun 86	● **HUNTING HIGH AND LOW** *Warner Bros. W 6663*	**5**	10
4 Oct 86	● **I'VE BEEN LOSING YOU** *Warner Bros. W 8594*	**8**	7
6 Dec 86	● **CRY WOLF** *Warner Bros. W 8500*	**5**	9
28 Feb 87	**MANHATTAN SKYLINE** *Warner Bros. W 8405*	**13**	6
4 Jul 87	● **THE LIVING DAYLIGHTS** *Warner Bros. W 8305*	**5**	9
26 Mar 88	● **STAY ON THESE ROADS** *Warner Bros. W 7936*	**5**	6
18 Jun 88	**THE BLOOD THAT MOVES THE BODY** *Warner Bros. W 7840*	**25**	4
27 Aug 88	**TOUCHY!** *Warner Bros. W 7749*	**11**	7
3 Dec 88	**YOU ARE THE ONE** *Warner Bros. W 7636*	**13**	10
13 Oct 90	**CRYING IN THE RAIN** *Warner Bros. W 9547*	**13**	7
15 Dec 90	**I CALL YOUR NAME** *Warner Bros. W 9462*	**44**	5
26 Oct 91	**MOVE TO MEMPHIS** *Warner Bros. W 0070*	**47**	2
5 Jun 93	**DARK IS THE NIGHT** *Warner Bros. W 0175CD*	**19**	4
18 Sep 93	**ANGEL** *Warner Bros. W 0195CD*	**41**	3
26 Mar 94	**SHAPES THAT GO TOGETHER** *Warner Bros. W 0236CD*	**27**	3

AHMAD US, male rapper   2 wks

9 Jul 94	**BACK IN THE DAY** *Giant 74321212042*	**64**	2

AIR SUPPLY
UK / Australia, male vocal / instrumental group   17 wks

27 Sep 80	**ALL OUT OF LOVE** *Arista ARIST 362*	**11**	11
2 Oct 82	**EVEN THE NIGHTS ARE BETTER** *Arista ARIST 474*	**44**	4
20 Nov 93	**GOODBYE** *Giant 74321153462*	**66**	2

AIRHEAD UK, male vocal / instrumental group   10 wks

5 Oct 91	**FUNNY HOW** *Korova KOW 47*	**57**	3
21 Dec 91	**COUNTING SHEEP** *Korova KOW 48*	**35**	5
7 Mar 92	**RIGHT NOW** *Korova KOW 49*	**50**	2

Laurel AITKEN and the UNITONE
Jamaica / Cuba, male vocal / instrumental group   3 wks

17 May 80	**RUDI GOT MARRIED** *I-Spy SEE 6*	**60**	3

AKA UK, male vocal group   2 wks

12 Oct 96	**WARNING** *RCA 74321360662*	**43**	2

Jewel AKENS US, male / vocalist   8 wks

25 Mar 65	**THE BIRDS AND THE BEES** *London HLN 9954*	**29**	8

ALANA – *See MK*

ALARM UK, male vocal / instrumental group   64 wks

24 Sep 83	**68 GUNS** *IRS PFP 1023*	**17**	7
21 Jan 84	**WHERE WERE YOU HIDING WHEN THE STORM BROKE** *IRS IRS 101*	**22**	6
31 Mar 84	**THE DECEIVER** *IRS IRS 103*	**51**	4
3 Nov 84	**THE CHANT HAS JUST BEGUN** *IRS IRS 104*	**48**	6
2 Mar 85	**ABSOLUTE REALITY** *IRS ALARM 1*	**35**	6
28 Sep 85	**STRENGTH** *IRS IRM 104*	**40**	4
18 Jan 86	**SPIRIT OF '76** *IRS IRM 109*	**22**	5
26 Apr 86	**KNIFE EDGE** *IRS IRM 112*	**43**	3
17 Oct 87	**RAIN IN THE SUMMERTIME** *IRS IRM 144*	**18**	5
12 Dec 87	**RESCUE ME** *IRS IRM 150*	**48**	2
20 Feb 88	**PRESENCE OF LOVE (LAUGHERNE)** *IRS IRM 155*	**44**	3
16 Sep 89	**SOLD ME DOWN THE RIVER** *IRS EIRS 123*	**43**	3
4 Nov 89	**A NEW SOUTH WALES / THE ROCK** *IRS EIRS 129*	**31**	5
3 Feb 90	**LOVE DON'T COME EASY** *IRS EIRS 134*	**48**	3
27 Oct 90	**UNSAFE BUILDING 1990** *IRS ALARME 2*	**54**	2
13 Apr 91	**RAW** *IRS ALARM 3*	**51**	2

A New South Wales features Morriston Orpheus Male Voice Choir.

Morris ALBERT Brazil, male vocalist   10 wks

27 Sep 75	● **FEELINGS** *Decca F 13591*	**4**	10

ALBERTO Y LOST TRIOS PARANOIAS
UK, male vocal / instrumental group   5 wks

23 Sep 78	**HEADS DOWN NO NONSENSE MINDLESS BOOGIE** *Logo GO 323*	**47**	5

ALCATRAZ US, male instrumental / production duo   4 wks

17 Feb 96	**GIV ME LUV** *AM:PM 5814332*	**12**	4

Cali ALEMAN – *See Tito PUENTE Jr and the LATIN RHYTHM featuring Tito PUENTE, INDIA and Cali ALEMAN*

ALESSI US, male vocal duo   11 wks

11 Jun 77	● **OH LORI** *A & M AMS 7289*	**8**	11

ALEX PARTY
Italy / UK, male / female vocal / instrumental group   28 wks

18 Dec 93	**SATURDAY NIGHT PARTY** *Cleveland City Imports CCICD 17000*	**49**	6
28 May 94	**SATURDAY NIGHT PARTY (READ MY LIPS) (re-entry)** *Cleveland City Imports CCICD 17000*	**29**	4
18 Feb 95	● **DON'T GIVE ME YOUR LIFE** *Systematic SYSCD 7*	**2**	13
18 Nov 95	**WRAP ME UP** *Systematic SYSCD 22*	**17**	3
19 Oct 96	**READ MY LIPS (re-mix)** *Systematic SYSCD 30*	**28**	2

Read My Lips in 96 is a remix of the first hit with added vocals.

ALFI and HARRY
US, male vocalist, David Seville under two false names   5 wks

23 Mar 56	**THE TROUBLE WITH HARRY** *London HLU 8242*	**15**	5

See also David Seville.

John ALFORD UK, male vocalist   12 wks

17 Feb 96	**SMOKE GETS IN YOUR EYES** *Love This LUVTHISCD 7*	**13**	5
25 May 96	● **BLUE MOON / ONLY YOU** *Love This LUVTHISCD 9*	**9**	4
23 Nov 96	**IF / KEEP ON RUNNING** *Love This LUVTHISCD 15*	**24**	3

ALI and FRAZIER UK, female vocal duo — 4 wks

7 Aug 93	UPTOWN TOP RANKING Arista 74321158842	33	4

ALICE IN CHAINS US, male vocal/instrumental group — 14 wks

23 Jan 93	WOULD Columbia 6588882	19	3
20 Mar 93	THEM BONES Columbia 6590902	26	3
5 Jun 93	ANGRY CHAIR Columbia 6593652	33	2
23 Oct 93	DOWN IN A HOLE Columbia 6597512	36	2
11 Nov 95	GRIND Columbia 6626232	23	2
10 Feb 96	HEAVEN BESIDE YOU Columbia 6628935	35	2

ALISHA US, female vocalist — 2 wks

25 Jan 86	BABY TALK Total Control TOCO 6	67	2

ALISHA'S ATTIC UK, female vocal duo — 16 wks

3 Aug 96	I AM I FEEL Mercury AATCD 1	14	10
2 Nov 96	ALISHA RULES THE WORLD Mercury AATCD 2	12	6

ALL ABOUT EVE
UK, female/male vocal/instrumental group — 47 wks

31 Oct 87	IN THE CLOUDS Mercury EVEN 5	47	5
23 Jan 88	WILD HEARTED WOMAN Mercury EVEN 6	33	4
9 Apr 88	EVERY ANGEL Mercury EVEN 7	30	5
30 Jul 88	● MARTHA'S HARBOUR Mercury EVEN 8	10	8
12 Nov 88	WHAT KIND OF FOOL Mercury EVEN 9	29	4
30 Sep 89	ROAD TO YOUR SOUL Mercury EVEN 10	37	4
16 Dec 89	DECEMBER Mercury EVEN 11	34	5
28 Apr 90	SCARLET Mercury EVEN 12	34	2
15 Jun 91	FAREWELL MR SORROW Mercury EVEN 14	36	2
10 Aug 91	STRANGE WAY Vertigo EVEN 15	50	3
19 Oct 91	THE DREAMER Vertigo EVEN 16	41	2
10 Oct 92	PHASED (EP) MCA MCS 1688	38	2
28 Nov 92	SOME FINER DAY MCA MCS 1706	57	1

Tracks on Phased (EP): Phased / Mine / Infra Red / Ascent-Descent.

ALL-4-ONE US, male vocal group — 23 wks

2 Apr 94	SO MUCH IN LOVE Atlantic A 7261CD	60	1
18 Jun 94	● I SWEAR Atlantic A 7255CD	2	18
19 Nov 94	SO MUCH IN LOVE (re-mix) Atlantic A 7216CD	49	2
15 Jul 95	I CAN LOVE YOU LIKE THAT Atlantic A 8193CD	33	2

ALL STAR CHOIR – See Donna SUMMER

ALL STARS – See Louis ARMSTRONG

ALL-STARS – See Junior WALKER and the ALL-STARS

ALL SYSTEMS GO UK, male vocal/instrumental group — 2 wks

18 Jun 88	POP MUZIK Unique NIQ 03	63	2

Richard ALLAN UK, male vocalist — 1 wk

24 Mar 60	AS TIME GOES BY Parlophone R 4634	44	1

Steve ALLAN UK, male vocalist — 2 wks

27 Jan 79	TOGETHER WE ARE BEAUTIFUL Creole CR 164	67	1
10 Feb 79	TOGETHER WE ARE BEAUTIFUL (re-entry) Creole CR 164	70	1

Donna ALLEN US, female vocalist — 24 wks

18 Apr 87	● SERIOUS Portrait PRT 650744 7	8	12
3 Jun 89	● JOY AND PAIN BCM BCM 257	10	10
21 Jan 95	REAL Epic 6610992	34	2

Keith ALLEN – See BLACK GRAPE; Joe STRUMMER

ALLISONS UK, male vocal duo — 27 wks

23 Feb 61	● ARE YOU SURE Fontana H 294	2	16
18 May 61	WORDS Fontana H 304	34	5
15 Feb 62	LESSONS IN LOVE Fontana H 362	30	6

ALLNIGHT BAND UK, male instrumental group — 3 wks

3 Feb 79	THE JOKER (THE WIGAN JOKER) Casino Classics CC 6	50	3

ALMIGHTY UK, male vocal/instrumental group — 22 wks

30 Jun 90	WILD AND WONDERFUL Polydor PO 75	50	2
2 Mar 91	FREE 'N' EASY Polydor PO 127	35	2
11 May 91	DEVIL'S TOY Polydor PO 144	36	2
29 Jun 91	LITTLE LOST SOMETIMES Polydor PO 151	42	2
3 Apr 93	ADDICTION Polydor PZCD 261	38	2
29 May 93	OUT OF SEASON Polydor PZCD 266	41	2
30 Oct 93	OVER THE EDGE Polydor PZCD 298	38	2
24 Sep 94	WRENCH Chrysalis CDCHS 5014	26	2
14 Jan 95	JONESTOWN MIND Chrysalis CDCHS 5017	26	3
16 Mar 96	ALL SUSSED OUT Chrysalis CDCHS 5030	28	2
25 May 96	DO YOU UNDERSTAND Raw Power RAWX 1022	38	1

Marc ALMOND UK, male vocalist — 111 wks

2 Jun 83	BLACK HEART Some Bizzare BZS 19 [1]	49	3
2 Jun 84	THE BOY WHO CAME BACK Some Bizzare BZS 23	52	3
1 Sep 84	YOU HAVE Some Bizzare BZS 24	57	3
20 Apr 85	● I FEEL LOVE (MEDLEY) Forbidden Fruit BITE 4 [2]	3	12
24 Aug 85	STORIES OF JOHNNY Some Bizzare BONK 1	23	5
26 Oct 85	LOVE LETTER Some Bizzare BONK 2	68	3
4 Jan 86	THE HOUSE IS HAUNTED (BY THE ECHO OF YOUR LAST GOODBYE) Some Bizzare GLOW 1	55	3
7 Jun 86	A WOMAN'S STORY Some Bizzare GLOW 2 [3]	41	5
18 Oct 86	RUBY RED Some Bizzare GLOW 3	47	3
14 Feb 87	MELANCHOLY ROSE Some Bizzare GLOW 4	71	1
3 Sep 88	TEARS RUN RINGS Parlophone R 6186	26	7
5 Nov 88	BITTER SWEET Some Bizzare R 6194	40	3
14 Jan 89	★ SOMETHING'S GOTTEN HOLD OF MY HEART Parlophone R 6201 [4]	1	12
8 Apr 89	ONLY THE MOMENT Parlophone R 6210	45	2
3 Mar 90	A LOVER SPURNED Some Bizzare R 6229	29	4
19 May 90	THE DESPERATE HOURS Some Bizzare R 6252	42	2
23 Mar 91	SAY HELLO WAVE GOODBYE '91 Mercury SOFT 1 [5]	38	3
18 May 91	● TAINTED LOVE Mercury SOFT 2 [5]	5	8
28 Sep 91	JACKY Some Bizzare YZ 610	17	6
11 Jan 92	MY HAND OVER MY HEART Some Bizzare YZ 633	33	5
25 Apr 92	● THE DAYS OF PEARLY SPENCER Some Bizzare YZ 638	4	7
27 Mar 93	WHAT MAKES A MAN A MAN (LIVE) Some Bizzare YZ 720CD	60	2
13 May 95	ADORED AND EXPLORED Some Bizarre MERCD 431	25	3
29 Jul 95	THE IDOL Some Bizarre MERCD 437	44	2
30 Dec 95	CHILD STAR Some Bizarre MERCD 450	41	1
28 Dec 96	YESTERDAY HAS GONE EMI Premier CDPRESX 13 [6]	58†	1

[1] Marc and the Mambas [2] Bronski Beat and Marc Almond [3] Marc Almond and the Willing Sinners [4] Marc Almond featuring special guest star Gene Pitney [5] Soft Cell/Marc Almond [6] PJ Proby and Marc Almond

I Feel Love medley comprises I Feel Love / Love To Love You Baby / Johnny Remember Me. Say Hello Wave Goodbye '91 is a re-recording of a Soft Cell hit.

ALOOF
UK, male vocal / instrumental group   **4 wks**

19 Sep 92	**ON A MISSION** Cowboy RODEO 5	...**64**	1
18 May 96	**WISH YOU WERE HERE...** East West EW 038CD	...**61**	1
30 Nov 96	**ONE NIGHT STAND** East West EW 067CD	...**30**	2

Herb ALPERT
US, male instrumentalist – trumpet   **106 wks**

3 Jan 63	**THE LONELY BULL** Stateside SS 138 [1]	...**22**	9
9 Dec 65	● **SPANISH FLEA** Pye International 7 N 25335 [2]	...**3**	20
24 Mar 66	**TIJUANA TAXI** Pye International 7 N 25352 [2]	...**37**	4
27 Apr 67	**CASINO ROYALE** A & M AMS 700 [2]	...**27**	14
3 Jul 68	● **THIS GUY'S IN LOVE WITH YOU** A & M AMS 727	...**3**	16
26 Mar 69	**THIS GUY'S IN LOVE WITH YOU** (re-entry) A & M AMS 727	...**47**	1
9 Apr 69	**THIS GUY'S IN LOVE WITH YOU** (2nd re-entry) A & M AMS 727	...**49**	1
7 May 69	**THIS GUY'S IN LOVE WITH YOU** (3rd re-entry) A & M AMS 727	...**50**	1
18 Jun 69	**WITHOUT HER** A & M AMS 755 [2]	...**36**	5
12 Dec 70	**JERUSALEM** A & M AMS 810 [2]	...**47**	1
2 Jan 71	**JERUSALEM** (re-entry) A & M AMS 810 [2]	...**42**	2
13 Oct 79	**RISE** A & M AMS 7465	...**13**	13
19 Jan 80	**ROTATION** A & M AMS 7500	...**46**	3
21 Mar 87	**KEEP YOUR EYE ON ME** Breakout USA 602	...**19**	9
6 Jun 87	**DIAMONDS** Breakout USA 605	...**27**	7

[1] Tijuana Brass   [2] Herb Alpert and the Tijuana Brass

Alpert vocalises on This Guy's In Love With You and Without Her. Janet Jackson provides uncredited vocals on Diamonds.

ALPHABETA – See Izhar COHEN and ALPHABETA

ALPHAVILLE
Germany, male vocal / instrumental group   **13 wks**

18 Aug 84	● **BIG IN JAPAN** WEA Int. X9505	...**8**	13

Gerald ALSTON
US, male vocalist   **1 wk**

15 Apr 89	**ACTIVATED** RCA ZB 42681	...**73**	1

ALTERED IMAGES
UK, male / female vocal / instrumental group   **60 wks**

28 Mar 81	**DEAD POP STARS** Epic EPC A 1023	...**67**	2
26 Sep 81	● **HAPPY BIRTHDAY** Epic EPC A 1522	...**2**	17
12 Dec 81	● **I COULD BE HAPPY** Epic EPC A 1834	...**7**	12
27 Mar 82	**SEE THOSE EYES** Epic EPC A 2198	...**11**	7
22 May 82	**PINKY BLUE** Epic EPC A 2426	...**35**	6
19 Mar 83	● **DON'T TALK TO ME ABOUT LOVE** Epic EPC A 3083	...**7**	7
28 May 83	**BRING ME CLOSER** Epic EPC A 3398	...**29**	6
16 Jul 83	**LOVE TO STAY** Epic EPC A 3582	...**46**	3

ALTERN 8
UK, male instrumental / production duo   **34 wks**

13 Jul 91	**INFILTRATE 202** Network NWK 24	...**28**	7
16 Nov 91	● **ACTIV 8 (COME WITH ME)** Network NWK 34	...**3**	9
8 Feb 92	**FREQUENCY** Network NWKT 37	...**41**	1
11 Apr 92	● **EVAPOR 8** Network NWK 38	...**6**	6
4 Jul 92	**HYPNOTIC ST-8** Network NWK 49	...**16**	4
10 Oct 92	**SHAME** Network NWKTEN 56 [1]	...**74**	1
12 Dec 92	**BRUTAL-8-E** Network NWK 59	...**43**	5
3 Jul 93	**EVERYBODY** Network NWKCD 73	...**58**	1

[1] Altern 8 vs Evelyn King

ALTHIA and DONNA
Jamaica, female vocal duo   **11 wks**

24 Dec 77	★ **UP TOWN TOP RANKING** Lightning LIG 506	...**1**	11

ALVIN and the CHIPMUNKS – See CHIPMUNKS

ALY-US
US, male vocal / insrumental group   **2 wks**

21 Nov 92	**FOLLOW ME** Cooltempo COOL 266	...**43**	2

AMAZULU
UK, female / male vocal / instrumental group   **57 wks**

6 Jul 85	**EXCITABLE** Island IS 201	...**12**	13
23 Nov 85	**DON'T YOU JUST KNOW IT** Island IS 233	...**15**	11
15 Mar 86	**THE THINGS THE LONELY DO** Island IS 267	...**43**	6
31 May 86	● **TOO GOOD TO BE FORGOTTEN** Island IS 284	...**5**	13
13 Sep 86	**MONTEGO BAY** Island IS 293	...**16**	9
10 Oct 87	**MONY MONY** EMI EM 32	...**38**	5

AMBASSADORS OF FUNK featuring MC MARIO
UK, male DJ and rapper – Simon Harris and Einstein   **8 wks**

31 Oct 92	● **SUPERMARIOLAND** Living Beat SMASH 23	...**8**	8

AMEN CORNER
UK, male vocal / instrumental group   **67 wks**

26 Jul 67	**GIN HOUSE BLUES** Deram DM 136	...**12**	10
11 Oct 67	**WORLD OF BROKEN HEARTS** Deram DM 151	...**24**	6
17 Jan 68	● **BEND ME SHAPE ME** Deram DM 172	...**3**	12
31 Jul 68	● **HIGH IN THE SKY** Deram DM 197	...**6**	13
29 Jan 69	★ **(IF PARADISE IS) HALF AS NICE** Immediate IM 073	...**1**	11
25 Jun 69	● **HELLO SUZIE** Immediate IM 081	...**4**	10
14 Feb 76	**(IF PARADISE IS) HALF AS NICE** (re-issue) Immediate IMS 103	...**34**	5

AMERICA
US, male vocal / instrumental group   **20 wks**

18 Dec 71	**HORSE WITH NO NAME** Warner Bros. K 16128	...**49**	2
8 Jan 72	● **HORSE WITH NO NAME** (re-entry) Warner Bros. K 16128	...**3**	11
25 Nov 72	**VENTURA HIGHWAY** Warner Bros. K 16219	...**43**	4
6 Nov 82	**YOU CAN DO MAGIC** Capitol CL 264	...**59**	3

AMERICAN BREED
US, male vocal / instrumental group   **6 wks**

7 Feb 68	**BEND ME SHAPE ME** Stateside SS 2078	...**24**	6

AMERICAN MUSIC CLUB
US, male vocal / instrumental group   **4 wks**

24 Apr 93	**JOHNNY MATHIS' FEET** Virgin VSCDG 1445	...**58**	2
10 Sep 94	**WISH THE WORLD AWAY** Virgin VSCDX 1512	...**46**	2

AMES BROTHERS
US, male vocal group   **6 wks**

4 Feb 55	● **NAUGHTY LADY OF SHADY LANE** HMV B 10800	...**6**	6

AMNESIA – See Frank'o MOIRAGI featuring AMNESIA

AMOS
UK, male vocalist   **10 wks**

3 Sep 94	**ONLY SAW TODAY - INSTANT KARMA** Positiva CDTIV 16	...**48**	2

Peter Andre

Peter Andre was offered a recording contract live on air after performing a version of Bobby Brown's 'Don't Be Cruel' on an Australian talent show.

Alarm

Mike Peters (pictured here) fronted the Alarm, the Welsh quartet originally tipped to be the new U2.

Tina Arena

Melbourne-based Tina Arena was awarded the trophy for the World's Best Selling Australian Artist at the World Music Awards in 1995.

25 Mar 95	**LET LOVE SHINE** Positiva CDTIV 24	**31**	2
7 Oct 95	**CHURCH OF FREEDOM** Positiva CDTIV 38	**54**	1
12 Oct 96	**STAMP!** Positiva CDTIV 65 [1]	**11**	5

[1] Jeremy Healy and Amos

Tori AMOS *US, female vocalist* **50 wks**

23 Nov 91	**SILENT ALL THESE YEARS** East West YZ 618	**51**	3
1 Feb 92	**CHINA** East West YZ 7531	**51**	2
21 Mar 92	**WINTER** East West A 7504	**25**	4
20 Jun 92	**CRUCIFY** East West A 7479	**15**	6
22 Aug 92	**SILENT ALL THESE YEARS (re-issue)** East West A 7433	**26**	4
22 Jan 94	● **CORNFLAKE GIRL** East West A 7281CD	**4**	6
19 Mar 94	● **PRETTY GOOD YEAR** East West A 7263CD	**7**	4
28 May 94	**PAST THE MISSION** East West YZ 7257CD	**31**	3
15 Oct 94	**GOD** East West A 7251CD	**44**	2
13 Jan 96	**CAUGHT A LITE SNEEZE** East West A 5524CD	**20**	3
23 Mar 96	**TALULA** East West A 8512CD1	**22**	2
3 Aug 96	**HEY JUPITER / PROFESSIONAL WIDOW** East West A 5494CD	**20**	9
9 Nov 96	**BLUE SKIES** Perfecto PERF 130CD1 [1]	**26**	2

[1] BT featuring Tori Amos

AMPS *US, male / female vocal / instrumental group* **1 wk**

| 21 Oct 95 | **TIPP CITY** 4AD BAD 5015CD | **61** | 1 |

AMY – See A.D.A.M. featuring AMY

AND WHY NOT?
UK, male vocal / instrumental group **18 wks**

14 Oct 89	**RESTLESS DAYS (SHE CRIES OUT LOUD)** Island IS 426	**38**	7
13 Jan 90	**THE FACE** Island IS 444	**13**	8
21 Apr 90	**SOMETHING YOU GOT** Island IS 452	**39**	3

Angry ANDERSON *Australia, male vocalist* **13 wks**

| 19 Nov 88 | ● **SUDDENLY** Food For Thought YUM 113 | **3** | 13 |

John ANDERSON BIG BAND *UK, big band* **5 wks**

| 21 Dec 85 | **GLENN MILLER MEDLEY** Modern GLEN 1 | **63** | 2 |
| 11 Jan 86 | **GLENN MILLER MEDLEY (re-entry)** Modern GLEN 1 | **61** | 3 |

Glenn Miller Medley comprises the following tracks: In The Mood / American Patrol / Little Brown Jug / Pennsylvania 65000.

ANDERSON BRUFORD WAKEMAN HOWE
UK, male vocal / instrumental group **2 wks**

| 24 Jun 89 | **BROTHER OF MINE** Arista 112379 | **63** | 2 |

Carl ANDERSON *US, male vocalist* **4 wks**

| 8 Jun 85 | **BUTTERCUP** Streetwave KHAN 45 | **49** | 4 |

Carleen ANDERSON *US, female vocalist* **14 wks**

12 Feb 94	**NERVOUS BREAKDOWN** Circa YRCDG 112	**27**	4
28 May 94	**MAMA SAID** Circa YRCD 114	**26**	4
13 Aug 94	**TRUE SPIRIT** Circa YRCD 118	**24**	3
14 Jan 95	**LET IT LAST** Circa YRCD 119	**16**	3

Laurie ANDERSON
US, female vocalist / multi-instrumentalist **6 wks**

| 17 Oct 81 | ● **O SUPERMAN** Warner Bros. K 17870 | **2** | 6 |

Leroy ANDERSON and his POPS CONCERT ORCHESTRA *US, orchestra* **4 wks**

28 Jun 57	**FORGOTTEN DREAMS** Brunswick 05485	**28**	1
12 Jul 57	**FORGOTTEN DREAMS (re-entry)** Brunswick 05485	**30**	1
6 Sep 57	**FORGOTTEN DREAMS (2nd re-entry)** Brunswick 05485	**24**	2

Lynn ANDERSON *US, female vocalist* **20 wks**

| 20 Feb 71 | ● **ROSE GARDEN** CBS 5360 | **3** | 20 |

Moira ANDERSON *UK, female vocalist* **2 wks**

| 27 Dec 69 | **THE HOLY CITY** Decca F 12989 | **43** | 2 |

Peter ANDRE *UK, male vocalist* **38 wks**

10 Jun 95	**TURN IT UP** Mushroom D 1000	**64**	1
16 Sep 95	**MYSTERIOUS GIRL** Mushroom D 11921	**53**	2
16 Mar 96	**ONLY ONE** Mushroom D 1307	**16**	3
13 Apr 96	**ONLY ONE (re-entry)** Mushroom D 1307	**69**	1
1 Jun 96	● **MYSTERIOUS GIRL (re-issue)** Mushroom D 2000 [1]	**2**	18
14 Sep 96	★ **FLAVA** Mushroom D 2003	**1**	9
7 Dec 96	★ **I FEEL YOU** Mushroom D 1521	**1**	4

[1] Peter Andre featuring Bubbler Ranx

Chris ANDREWS *UK, male vocalist* **36 wks**

7 Oct 65	● **YESTERDAY MAN** Decca F 12236	**3**	15
2 Dec 65	**TO WHOM IT CONCERNS** Decca F 22285	**13**	10
14 Apr 66	**SOMETHING ON MY MIND** Decca F 22365	**45**	1
28 Apr 66	**SOMETHING ON MY MIND (re-entry)** Decca F 22365	**41**	2
2 Jun 66	**WHATCHA GONNA DO NOW** Decca F 22404	**40**	4
25 Aug 66	**STOP THAT GIRL** Decca F 22472	**36**	4

Eamonn ANDREWS *Ireland, male vocalist* **3 wks**

| 20 Jan 56 | **SHIFTING WHISPERING SANDS (PARTS 1 & 2)** Parlophone R 4106 | **18** | 3 |

Hit is 'with Ron Goodwin and his Orchestra and Chorus'.

ANEKA *UK, female vocalist* **16 wks**

| 8 Aug 81 | ★ **JAPANESE BOY** Hansa HANSA 5 | **1** | 12 |
| 7 Nov 81 | **LITTLE LADY** Hansa HANSA 8 | **50** | 4 |

Simone ANGEL *Holland, female vocalist* **1 wk**

| 13 Nov 93 | **LET THIS FEELING** A & M 5803652 | **60** | 1 |

ANGELETTES *UK, female vocal group* **5 wks**

| 13 May 72 | **DON'T LET HIM TOUCH YOU** Decca F 13284 | **35** | 5 |

ANGELHEART featuring Rochelle HARRIS
UK, female vocal / instrumental duo **1 wk**

| 6 Apr 96 | **COME BACK TO ME** Hi-Life 5776312 | **68** | 1 |

16

ANGELIC UPSTARTS
UK, male vocal / instrumental group **30 wks**

21 Apr 79	**I'M AN UPSTART** *Warner Bros. K 17354*	**31**	8
11 Aug 79	**TEENAGE WARNING** *Warner Bros. K 17426*..............	**29**	6
3 Nov 79	**NEVER 'AD NOTHIN'** *Warner Bros. K 17476*	**52**	4
9 Feb 80	**OUT OF CONTROL** *Warner Bros. K 17558*	**58**	3
22 Mar 80	**WE GOTTA GET OUT OF THIS PLACE**		
	Warner Bros. K 17576	**65**	2
2 Aug 80	**LAST NIGHT ANOTHER SOLDIER** *Angelic Upstarts Z 7*.	**51**	4
7 Feb 81	**KIDS ON THE STREET** *Angelic Upstarts Z 16*	**57**	3

Bobby ANGELO and the TUXEDOS
UK, male vocal / instrumental group **6 wks**

10 Aug 61	**BABY SITTIN'** *HMV POP 892*	**30**	6

ANGELS *US, female vocal group* **1 wk**

3 Oct 63	**MY BOYFRIEND'S BACK** *Mercury AMT 1211*	**50**	1

ANGELS OF LIGHT – *See PSYCHIC TV*

ANGELWITCH *UK, male vocal / instrumental group* **1 wk**

7 Jun 80	**SWEET DANGER** *EMI 5064*.............	**75**	1

ANIMAL *US, Puppet* **3 wks**

23 Jul 94	**WIPE OUT** *BMG Kidz 74321219532*	**38**	3

ANIMAL NIGHTLIFE
UK, male / female vocal / instrumental group **22 wks**

13 Aug 83	**NATIVE BOY (UPTOWN)** *Innervision A3584*	**60**	3
18 Aug 84	**MR. SOLITAIRE** *Island IS 193*	**25**	12
6 Jul 85	**LOVE IS JUST THE GREAT PRETENDER** *Island IS 200*	**28**	6
5 Oct 85	**PREACHER, PREACHER** *Island IS 245*	**67**	1

ANIMALS *UK, male vocal / instrumental group* **147 wks**

16 Apr 64	**BABY LET ME TAKE YOU HOME** *Columbia DB 7247*	**21**	8
25 Jun 64	★ **HOUSE OF THE RISING SUN** *Columbia DB 7301*	**1**	12
17 Sep 64	● **I'M CRYING** *Columbia DB 7354*	**8**	10
4 Feb 65	● **DON'T LET ME BE MISUNDERSTOOD**		
	Columbia DB 7445	**3**	9
8 Apr 65	● **BRING IT ON HOME TO ME** *Columbia DB 7539*	**7**	11
15 Jul 65	● **WE GOTTA GET OUT OF THIS PLACE** *Columbia DB 7639*.	**2**	12
28 Oct 65	● **IT'S MY LIFE** *Columbia DB 7741*	**7**	11
17 Feb 66	**INSIDE - LOOKING OUT** *Decca F 12332*	**12**	8
2 Jun 66	● **DON'T BRING ME DOWN** *Decca F 12407*	**6**	8
27 Oct 66	**HELP ME GIRL** *Decca F 12502* [1]	**14**	10
15 Jun 67	**WHEN I WAS YOUNG** *MGM 1340* [1].............	**45**	3
6 Sep 67	**GOOD TIMES** *MGM 1344* [1].............	**20**	11
18 Oct 67	● **SAN FRANCISCAN NIGHTS** *MGM 1359* [1].............	**7**	10
14 Feb 68	**SKY PILOT** *MGM 1373* [2].............	**40**	3
15 Jan 69	**RING OF FIRE** *MGM 1461* [1].............	**35**	5
7 Oct 72	**HOUSE OF THE RISING SUN (re-issue)**		
	RAK RR 1	**25**	6
18 Sep 82	**HOUSE OF THE RISING SUN (re-entry of re-issue)**		
	RAK RR 1	**11**	10

[1] Eric Burdon and the Animals [2] Eric Burdon

ANIMOTION
US / UK, male / female vocal / instrumental group **12 wks**

11 May 85	● **OBSESSION** *Mercury PH 34*	**5**	12

Paul ANKA *Canada, male vocalist* **132 wks**

9 Aug 57	★ **DIANA** *Columbia DB 3980*	**1**	25
8 Nov 57	● **I LOVE YOU BABY** *Columbia DB 4022*	**3**	15
8 Nov 57	**TELL ME THAT YOU LOVE ME** *Columbia DB 4022*	**25**	2
31 Jan 58	● **YOU ARE MY DESTINY** *Columbia DB 4063*	**6**	13
30 May 58	**CRAZY LOVE** *Columbia DB 4110*	**26**	1
26 Sep 58	**MIDNIGHT** *Columbia DB 4172*	**26**	1
30 Jan 59	● **(ALL OF A SUDDEN) MY HEART SINGS**		
	Columbia DB 4241	**10**	13
10 Jul 59	● **LONELY BOY** *Columbia DB 4324*	**3**	17
30 Oct 59	● **PUT YOUR HEAD ON MY SHOULDER**		
	Columbia DB 4355	**7**	12
26 Feb 60	**IT'S TIME TO CRY** *Columbia DB 4390*	**28**	1
31 Mar 60	**PUPPY LOVE** *Columbia DB 4434*	**33**	4
14 Apr 60	**IT'S TIME TO CRY (re-entry)** *Columbia DB 4390*	**47**	1
5 May 60	**PUPPY LOVE (re-entry)** *Columbia DB 4434*	**37**	3
15 Sep 60	**HELLO YOUNG LOVERS** *Columbia DB 4504*.............	**44**	1
15 Mar 62	**LOVE ME WARM AND TENDER** *RCA 1276*	**19**	11
26 Jul 62	**A STEEL GUITAR AND A GLASS OF WINE** *RCA 1292* ...	**41**	4
28 Sep 74	● **(YOU'RE) HAVING MY BABY** *United Artists UP 35713* [1] .	**6**	10

[1] Paul Anka featuring Odia Coates

ANNETTE – *See VARIOUS ARTISTS (EPs & LPs) - Further Adventures Of North EP*

ANOUCHKA – *See Terry HALL*

Adam ANT *UK, male vocalist* **199 wks**

2 Aug 80	**KINGS OF THE WILD FRONTIER** *CBS 8877* [1]	**48**	5
11 Oct 80	● **DOG EAT DOG** *CBS 9039* [1]	**4**	16
6 Dec 80	● **ANTMUSIC** *CBS 9352* [1]	**2**	18
27 Dec 80	● **YOUNG PARISIANS** *Decca F13803* [1]	**9**	13
24 Jan 81	**CARTROUBLE** *Do It DUN 10* [1]	**33**	9
24 Jan 81	**ZEROX** *Do It DUN 8* [1]	**45**	9
21 Feb 81	● **KINGS OF THE WILD FRONTIER (re-entry)** *CBS 8877* [1] ...2	**2**	13
9 May 81	★ **STAND AND DELIVER** *CBS A 1065* [1]	**1**	15
12 Sep 81	★ **PRINCE CHARMING** *CBS A 1408* [1]	**1**	15
12 Dec 81	● **ANT RAP** *CBS A 1738* [1]	**3**	10
27 Feb 82	**DEUTSCHER GIRLS** *Ego 5* [1]	**13**	6
13 Mar 82	**THE ANTMUSIC EP (THE B-SIDES)** *Do It DUN 20* [1]	**46**	4
22 May 82	★ **GOODY TWO SHOES** *CBS A 2367*	**1**	11
18 Sep 82	● **FRIEND OR FOE** *CBS A 2736*	**9**	8
27 Nov 82	**DESPERATE BUT NOT SERIOUS** *CBS A 2892*	**33**	7
29 Oct 83	● **PUSS 'N BOOTS** *CBS A 3614*	**5**	11
10 Dec 83	**STRIP** *CBS A 3589*	**41**	6
22 Sep 84	**APOLLO 9** *CBS A 4719*	**13**	8
13 Jul 85	**VIVE LE ROCK** *CBS A 6367*	**50**	4
17 Feb 90	**ROOM AT THE TOP** *MCA MCA 1387*	**13**	7
28 Apr 90	**CAN'T SET RULES ABOUT LOVE** *MCA MCA 1404*.............	**47**	2
11 Feb 95	**WONDERFUL** *EMI CDEMS 366*	**32**	3
3 Jun 95	**GOTTA BE A SIN** *EMI CDEMS 379*	**48**	2

[1] Adam and the Ants

Tracks on The Antmusic EP (The B-Sides): *Friends / Kick / Physical.*

ANT and DEC – *See PJ and DUNCAN*

Mark ANTHONI – *See FIRE ISLAND*

Billie ANTHONY *UK, female vocalist* **16 wks**

15 Oct 54	● **THIS OLE HOUSE** *Columbia DB 3519*.............	**4**	16

Marc ANTHONY – *See Louie VEGA and Marc ANTHONY*

Miki ANTHONY *UK, male vocalist* **7 wks**

3 Feb 73	**IF IT WASN'T FOR THE REASON THAT I LOVE YOU**		
	Bell 1275.............	**27**	7

Ray ANTHONY US, orchestra — 2 wks

| 4 Dec 53 | ● DRAGNET Capitol CL 13983 | 7 | 1 |
| 8 Jan 54 | DRAGNET (re-entry) Capitol CL 13983 | 11 | 1 |

Richard ANTHONY France, male vocalist — 15 wks

12 Dec 63	WALKING ALONE Columbia DB 7133	37	5
2 Apr 64	IF I LOVED YOU Columbia DB 7235	48	1
23 Apr 64	IF I LOVED YOU (re-entry) Columbia DB 7235	18	9

ANTHRAX US, male vocal / instrumental group — 37 wks

28 Feb 87	I AM THE LAW Island IS LAW 1	32	5
27 Jun 87	INDIANS Island IS 325	44	4
5 Dec 87	I'M THE MAN Island IS 338	20	6
10 Sep 88	MAKE ME LAUGH Island IS 379	26	3
18 Mar 89	ANTI-SOCIAL Island IS 409	44	3
1 Sep 90	IN MY WORLD Island IS 470	29	2
5 Jan 91	GOT THE TIME Island IS 476	16	4
6 Jul 91	BRING THE NOISE Island IS 490 [1]	14	5
8 May 93	ONLY Elektra EKR 166CD	36	3
11 Sep 93	BLACK LODGE Elektra EKR 171CD	53	2

[1] Anthrax featuring Chuck D

ANTI-NOWHERE LEAGUE
UK, male vocal / instrumental group — 10 wks

23 Jan 82	STREETS OF LONDON WXYZ ABCD 1	48	5
20 Mar 82	I HATE... PEOPLE WXYZ ABCD 2	46	3
3 Jul 82	WOMAN WXYZ ABCD 4	72	2

ANTI-PASTI – See EXPLOITED

ANTICAPPELLA
Italy / UK, male / female vocal / instrumental group — 12 wks

16 Nov 91	2 231 PWL Continental PWL 205	24	4
18 Apr 92	EVERY DAY PWL Continental PWL 220	45	2
25 Jun 94	MOVE YOUR BODY Media MCSTD 1980 [1]	21	3
1 Apr 95	EXPRESS YOUR FREEDOM Media MCSTD 2048	31	2
25 May 96	2 231 (re-mix) / MOVE YOUR BODY (re-issue) Media MCSTD 40037	54	1

[1] Anticappella featuring MC Fixx It

ANTONIA – See BOMB THE BASS

ANTS – See Adam ANT

ANUNA – See Bill WHELAN featuring ANUNA and the RTE CONCERT ORCHESTRA

APACHE INDIAN UK, male vocalist — 31 wks

28 Nov 92	FE' REAL Ten TEN 416 [1]	33	3
2 Jan 93	ARRANGED MARRIAGE Island CID 544	16	6
27 Mar 93	CHOK THERE Island CID 555	30	4
14 Aug 93	● NUFF VIBES EP Island CID 560	5	10
22 Oct 93	MOVIN' ON Island CID 580	48	2
7 May 94	WRECKX SHOP MCA MCS 1725 [2]	26	2
11 Feb 95	MAKE WAY FOR THE INDIAN Island CID 586 [3]	29	2
22 Apr 95	RAGGAMUFFIN GIRL Island CID 606 [4]	31	2

[1] Maxi Priest featuring Apache Indian [2] Wreckx-N-Effect featuring Apache Indian [3] Apache Indian and Tim Dog [4] Apache Indian with Frankie Paul

The listed flip side of Fe' Real was Just Wanna Know by Maxi Priest. Tracks on Nuff Vibes EP: Boom Shack A Lak / Fun / Caste System / Warning.

APHEX TWIN UK, male producer – Richard James — 7 wks

9 May 92	DIGERIDOO R&S RSUK 12	55	2
27 Nov 93	ON Warp WAP 39CD	32	3
8 Apr 95	VENTOLIN Warp WAP 60CD	49	1
26 Oct 96	GIRL / BOY EP Warp WAP 78CD	64	1

Tracks on Girl / Boy EP: Girl / Boy Song / Milkman / Inkey $ / Beatles Under My Carpet. The EP was incorrectly listed in the chart and, because of its length, should have been considered an album. See also Polygon Window.

APHRODITE'S CHILD
Greece, male vocal / instrumental group — 7 wks

| 6 Nov 68 | RAIN AND TEARS Mercury MF 1039 | 29 | 7 |

APOLLO – See HOUSE OF VIRGINISM

APOLLO 440 UK, male instrumental / production group — 14 wks

22 Jan 94	ASTRAL AMERICA Stealth Sonic SSXCD 2	36	2
5 Nov 94	LIQUID COOL Stealth Sonic SSXCD 3	35	2
25 Mar 95	(DON'T FEAR) THE REAPER Stealth Sonic SSXCD 4	35	2
27 Jul 96	KRUPA Stealth Sonic SSXCD 5 [1]	23	4
28 Sep 96	KRUPA (re-entry) Stealth Sonic SSXCD 5 [1]	24	4

[1] Apollo Four Forty

Kim APPLEBY UK, female vocalist — 31 wks

3 Nov 90	● DON'T WORRY Parlophone R 6272	2	10
9 Feb 91	● G.L.A.D. Parlophone R 6281	10	6
29 Jun 91	MAMA Parlophone R 6291	19	8
19 Oct 91	IF YOU CARED Parlophone R 6297	44	3
31 Jul 93	LIGHT OF THE WORLD Parlophone CDR 6352	41	2
13 Nov 93	BREAKAWAY Parlophone CDR 6362	56	1
12 Nov 94	FREE SPIRIT Parlophone CDR 6397	51	1

See also Mel and Kim.

APPLEJACKS
UK, male / female vocal / instrumental group — 29 wks

5 Mar 64	● TELL ME WHEN Decca F 11833	7	13
11 Jun 64	LIKE DREAMERS DO Decca F 11916	20	11
15 Oct 64	THREE LITTLE WORDS Decca F 11981	23	5

APPLES UK, male vocal / instrumental group — 1 wk

| 23 Mar 91 | EYE WONDER Epic 6566717 | 75 | 1 |

Charlie APPLEWHITE US, male vocalist — 1 wk

| 23 Sep 55 | BLUE STAR (THE MEDIC THEME) Brunswick 05416 | 20 | 1 |

Helen APRIL – See John DUMMER and Helen APRIL

APRIL WINE Canada, male vocal / instrumental group — 9 wks

| 15 Mar 80 | I LIKE TO ROCK Capitol CL 16121 | 41 | 5 |
| 11 Apr 81 | JUST BETWEEN YOU AND ME Capitol CL 16184 | 52 | 4 |

AQUARIAN DREAM
US, male / female vocal / instrumental group — 1 wk

| 24 Feb 79 | YOU'RE A STAR Elektra LV 7 | 67 | 1 |

ARCADIA UK, male vocal / instrumental group   13 wks

26 Oct 85	● ELECTION DAY Odeon NSR 1	7	7
25 Jan 86	THE PROMISE Odeon NSR 2	37	4
26 Jul 86	THE FLAME Odeon NSR 3	58	2

Tasmin ARCHER UK, female vocalist   37 wks

12 Sep 92	★ SLEEPING SATELLITE EMI EM 233	1	15
2 Jan 93	SLEEPING SATELLITE (re-entry) EMI EM 233	67	2
20 Feb 93	IN YOUR CARE EMI CDEMS 260	16	6
29 May 93	LORDS OF THE NEW CHURCH EMI CDEM 266	26	4
21 Aug 93	ARIENNE EMI CDEM 275	30	4
8 Jan 94	SHIPBUILDING EMI CDEM 302	40	4
23 Mar 96	ONE MORE GOOD NIGHT WITH THE BOYS EMI CDEM 401	45	2

ARCHIES US, male / female vocal group   26 wks

11 Oct 69	★ SUGAR SUGAR RCA 1872	1	26

Jann ARDEN Canada, female vocalist   2 wks

13 Jul 96	INSENSITIVE A & M 5812652	40	2

Tina ARENA Australia, female vocalist   23 wks

15 Apr 95	● CHAINS Columbia 6611255	6	11
12 Aug 95	HEAVEN HELP MY HEART Columbia 6620975	25	5
2 Dec 95	SHOW ME HEAVEN Columbia 6626975	29	3
3 Aug 96	SORRENTO MOON (I REMEMBER) Columbia 6635435	22	4

ARGENT UK, male vocal / instrumental group   27 wks

4 Mar 72	● HOLD YOUR HEAD UP Epic EPC 7786	5	12
10 Jun 72	TRAGEDY Epic EPC 8115	34	7
24 Mar 73	GOD GAVE ROCK AND ROLL TO YOU Epic EPC 1243	18	8

ARIEL UK, male / female vocal / instrumental group   2 wks

27 Mar 93	LET IT SLIDE Deconstruction 74321134512	57	2

ARIZONA – See Zeitia MASSIAH

Ship's Company and Royal Marine Band of H.M.S. ARK ROYAL UK, Male choir and Marine band   6 wks

23 Dec 78	THE LAST FAREWELL BBC RESL 61	46	6

Joan ARMATRADING UK, female vocalist   53 wks

16 Oct 76	● LOVE AND AFFECTION A & M AMS 7249	10	9
23 Feb 80	ROSIE A & M AMS 7506	49	5
14 Jun 80	ME MYSELF I A & M AMS 7527	21	11
6 Sep 80	ALL THE WAY FROM AMERICA A & M AMS 7552	54	3
12 Sep 81	I'M LUCKY A & M AMS 8163	46	5
16 Jan 82	NO LOVE A & M AMS 8179	50	5
19 Feb 83	DROP THE PILOT A & M AMS 8306	11	10
16 Mar 85	TEMPTATION A & M AM 238	65	2
26 May 90	MORE THAN ONE KIND OF LOVE A & M AM 561	75	1
23 May 92	WRAPPED AROUND HER A & M AM 877	56	2

ARMOURY SHOW UK, male vocal / instrumental group   6 wks

25 Aug 84	CASTLES IN SPAIN Parlophone R 6079	69	2

26 Jan 85	WE CAN BE BRAVE AGAIN Parlophone R 6087	66	1
17 Jan 87	LOVE IN ANGER Parlophone R 6149	63	3

Louis ARMSTRONG
US, male jazz band leader, vocalist / instrumentalist – trumpet   93 wks

19 Dec 52	● TAKES TWO TO TANGO Brunswick 04995	6	10
13 Apr 56	● THEME FROM THE THREEPENNY OPERA Philips PB 574 [1]	8	11
15 Jun 56	TAKE IT SATCH EP Philips BBE 12035 [1]	29	1
13 Jul 56	THE FAITHFUL HUSSAR Philips PB 604 [1]	27	2
6 Nov 59	MACK THE KNIFE Philips PB 967 [1]	24	1
4 Jun 64	● HELLO DOLLY London HLR 9878	4	14
7 Feb 68	★ WHAT A WONDERFUL WORLD / CABARET HMV POP 1615	1	29
26 Jun 68	SUNSHINE OF LOVE Stateside SS 2116	41	7
16 Apr 88	WHAT A WONDERFUL WORLD (re-issue) A & M AM 435	53	5
19 Nov 94	● WE HAVE ALL THE TIME IN THE WORLD EMI CDEM 357	3	11
18 Mar 95	WE HAVE ALL THE TIME IN THE WORLD (re-entry) EMI CDEM 357	66	2

[1] Louis Armstrong with his All-Stars

Take It Satch *tracks: Tiger Rag / Mack The Knife / The Faithful Hussar / Back O'Town Blues.*
Mack The Knife *is a re-issue of Theme From Threepenny Opera under a different title.*
Cabaret *was not listed with What A Wonderful World until 14 Feb 68.*

ARMY OF LOVERS
Sweden / France, male / female vocal / group   12 wks

17 Aug 91	CRUCIFIED Ton Son Ton WOK 2007	47	5
28 Dec 91	OBSESSION Ton Son Ton WOK 2009	67	1
15 Feb 92	CRUCIFIED (re-issue) Ton Son Ton WOK 2017	31	5
18 Apr 92	RIDE THE BULLET Ton Son Ton WOK 2018	67	1

ARNEE and the TERMINATERS
UK, male vocal / instrumental group   7 wks

24 Aug 91	● I'LL BE BACK Epic 6574177	5	7

ARNIE'S LOVE
US, male / female vocal / instrumental group   3 wks

26 Nov 83	I'M OUT OF YOUR LIFE Streetwave WAVE 9	67	3

David ARNOLD – See BJORK

Eddy ARNOLD US, male vocalist   21 wks

17 Feb 66	● MAKE THE WORLD GO AWAY RCA 1496	8	17
26 May 66	I WANT TO GO WITH YOU RCA 1519	49	1
9 Jun 66	I WANT TO GO WITH YOU (re-entry) RCA 1519	46	2
28 Jul 66	IF YOU WERE MINE MARY RCA 1529	49	1

PP ARNOLD US, female vocalist   37 wks

4 May 67	FIRST CUT IS THE DEEPEST Immediate IM 047	18	10
2 Aug 67	THE TIME HAS COME Immediate IM 055	47	2
24 Jan 68	(IF YOU THINK) YOU'RE GROOVY Immediate IM 061	41	4
10 Jul 68	ANGEL OF THE MORNING Immediate IM 067	29	11
24 Sep 88	BURN IT UP Rhythm King LEFT 27 [1]	14	10

[1] Beatmasters with PP Arnold

ARPEGGIO US, male / female vocal group   3 wks

31 Mar 79	LOVE AND DESIRE (PART 1) Polydor POSP 40	63	3

ARRESTED DEVELOPMENT
US, male / female vocal / instrumental group   **39 wks**

16 May 92	**TENNESSEE** Cooltempo COOL 253	**46** 4
11 Jul 92	**TENNESSEE (re-entry)** Cooltempo COOL 253	**54** 3
24 Oct 92	● **PEOPLE EVERYDAY** Cooltempo COOL 265	**2** 14
9 Jan 93	● **MR. WENDAL / REVOLUTION** Cooltempo CDCOOL 268	**4** 9
3 Apr 93	**TENNESSEE (re-issue)** Cooltempo CDCOOL 270	**18** 6
28 May 94	**EASE MY MIND** Cooltempo CDCOOL 293	**33** 3

Steve ARRINGTON *US, male vocalist*   **19 wks**

27 Apr 85	● **FEEL SO REAL** Atlantic A 9576	**5** 10
6 Jul 85	**DANCIN' IN THE KEY OF LIFE** Atlantic A 9534	**21** 8
7 Sep 85	**DANCIN' IN THE KEY OF LIFE (re-entry)** Atlantic A 9534	**75** 1

ARRIVAL *UK, male / female vocal / instrumental group*   **20 wks**

| 10 Jan 70 | ● **FRIENDS** Decca F 12986 | **8** 9 |
| 6 Jun 70 | **I WILL SURVIVE** Decca F 13026 | **16** 11 |

ARROW *Montserrat, male vocalist*   **15 wks**

28 Jul 84	**HOT HOT HOT** Cooltempo ARROW 1	**59** 5
13 Jul 85	**LONG TIME** London LON 70	**30** 7
3 Sep 94	**HOT HOT HOT (re-mix)** The Hit Label HLC 7	**38** 3

ARROWS *US / UK, male vocal / instrumental group*   **16 wks**

| 25 May 74 | ● **A TOUCH TOO MUCH** RAK 171 | **8** 9 |
| 1 Feb 75 | **MY LAST NIGHT WITH YOU** RAK 189 | **25** 7 |

ARSENAL F.C. FIRST TEAM SQUAD
UK, male football team vocalists   **10 wks**

| 8 May 71 | **GOOD OLD ARSENAL** Pye 7N 45067 | **16** 7 |
| 15 May 93 | **SHOUTING FOR THE GUNNERS** London LONCD 342 [1] | **34** 3 |

[1] Arsenal FA Cup Squad featuring Tippa Irie and Peter Hunnigale

ART COMPANY
Holland, male vocal / instrumental group   **11 wks**

| 26 May 84 | **SUSANNA** Epic A 4174 | **12** 11 |

ART OF NOISE
UK, male / female instrumental / production group   **64 wks**

24 Nov 84	● **CLOSE (TO THE EDIT)** ZTT ZTPS 01	**8** 19
13 Apr 85	**MOMENTS IN LOVE / BEAT BOX** ZTT ZTPS 02	**51** 4
9 Nov 85	**LEGS** China WOK 5	**69** 1
22 Mar 86	● **PETER GUNN** China WOK 6 [1]	**8** 9
21 Jun 86	**PARANOIMIA** China WOK 9 [2]	**12** 9
18 Jul 87	**DRAGNET** China WOK 14	**60** 4
29 Oct 88	● **KISS** China CHINA 11 [3]	**5** 7
12 Aug 89	**YEBO** China CHINA 18 [4]	**63** 3
16 Jun 90	**ART OF LOVE** China CHINA 23	**67** 1
11 Jan 92	**INSTRUMENTS OF DARKNESS (ALL OF US ARE ONE PEOPLE)** China WOK 2012	**45** 5
29 Feb 92	**SHADES OF PARANOIMIA** China WOK 2014	**53** 2

[1] Art Of Noise featuring Duane Eddy [2] Art Of Noise featuring Max Headroom [3] Art Of Noise featuring Tom Jones [4] Art Of Noise featuring Mahlathini and the Mahotella Queens

ARTEMESIA *Holland, male producer – Patrick Prinz*   **3 wks**

| 15 Apr 95 | **BITS + PIECES** Hooj Choons HOOJ 31CD | **46** 2 |
| 23 Sep 95 | **BITS + PIECES (re-entry)** Hooj Choons HOOJ 31CD | **75** 1 |

See also Ethics; Movin' Melodies; Subliminal Cuts.

Neil ARTHUR *UK, male vocalist*   **2 wks**

| 5 Feb 94 | **I LOVE I HATE** Chrysalis CDCHSS 5005 | **50** 2 |

ARTIST – *See* PRINCE

ARTISTS UNITED AGAINST APARTHEID
Multi-national, male / female vocal / instrumental charity assembly   **8 wks**

| 23 Nov 85 | **SUN CITY** Manhattan MT 7 | **21** 8 |

ASAP *UK, male vocal / instrumental group*   **4 wks**

| 14 Oct 89 | **SILVER AND GOLD** EMI EM 107 | **60** 2 |
| 3 Feb 90 | **DOWN THE WIRE** EMI EM 131 | **67** 2 |

ASH *UK, male vocal / instrumental group*   **23 wks**

1 Apr 95	**KUNG FU** Infectious INFECT 21CD	**57** 1
12 Aug 95	**GIRL FROM MARS** Infectious INFECT 24CD	**11** 5
21 Oct 95	**ANGEL INTERCEPTOR** Infectious INFECT 27CD	**14** 4
27 Apr 96	● **GOLDFINGER** Infectious INFECT 39CD	**5** 5
6 Jul 96	● **OH YEAH** Infectious INFECT 41CD	**6** 7
28 Sep 96	**OH YEAH (re-entry)** Infectious INFECT 41CD	**69** 1

ASH – *See* QUENTIN and ASH

ASHA *Italy, female vocalist*   **2 wks**

| 8 Jul 95 | **JJ TRIBUTE** Ffrreedom TABCD 228 | **38** 2 |

ASHAYE *UK, male vocalist*   **3 wks**

| 15 Oct 83 | **MICHAEL JACKSON MEDLEY** Record Shack SOHO 10 | **45** 3 |

Tracks on medley: Don't Stop Til You Get Enough / Wanna Be Startin' Something / Shake Your Body Down To The Ground / Blame It On The Boogie.

John ASHER *UK, male vocalist*   **6 wks**

| 15 Nov 75 | **LET'S TWIST AGAIN** Creole CR 112 | **14** 6 |

ASHFORD and SIMPSON
US, male / female vocal duo   **22 wks**

18 Nov 78	**IT SEEMS TO HANG ON** Warner Bros. K 17237	**48** 4
5 Jan 85	● **SOLID** Capitol CL 345	**3** 15
20 Apr 85	**BABIES** Capitol CL 355	**56** 3

ASHTON, GARDNER AND DYKE
UK, male vocal / instrumental group   **14 wks**

| 16 Jan 71 | ● **THE RESURRECTION SHUFFLE** Capitol CL 15665 | **3** 14 |

ASIA *UK, male vocal / instrumental group*   **13 wks**

| 3 Jul 82 | **HEAT OF THE MOMENT** Geffen GEF A2494 | **46** 5 |

Auteurs

The track 'Former Fan' which appeared on the Auteurs' 'Back With The Killer EP', was written about Mark Chapman, the man who shot John Lennon.

Joan Armatrading

Joan had her sights set on a career as a lawyer before she set the charts alight with 'Love And Affection'.

Ash

All Ash's hits to date have been produced by Owen Morris, the man responsible for the production of the Oasis album *(What's The Story) Morning Glory.*

| 18 Sep 82 | | ONLY TIME WILL TELL Geffen GEF A2228 | 54 | 3 |
| 13 Aug 83 | | DON'T CRY Geffen A 3580 | 33 | 5 |

ASIA BLUE UK, female vocal group — 2 wks

| 27 Jun 92 | | ESCAPING Atomic WNR 882 | 50 | 2 |

ASSEMBLY UK, male vocal / instrumental group — 10 wks

| 12 Nov 83 | ● | NEVER NEVER Mute TINY 1 | 4 | 10 |

ASSOCIATES UK, male vocal / instrumental group — 47 wks

20 Feb 82	●	PARTY FEARS TWO Associates ASC 1	9	10
8 May 82		CLUB COUNTRY Associates ASC 2	13	10
7 Aug 82		LOVE HANGOVER / 18 CARAT LOVE AFFAIR Associates ASC 3	21	8
16 Jun 84		THOSE FIRST IMPRESSIONS WEA YZ 6	43	6
1 Sep 84		WAITING FOR THE LOVEBOAT WEA YZ 16	53	4
19 Jan 85		BREAKFAST WEA YZ 28	49	6
17 Sep 88		HEART OF GLASS WEA YZ 310	56	3

18 Carat Love Affair listed until 28 Aug only. Act was duo on 1982 hits.

ASSOCIATION US, male vocal / instrumental group — 8 wks

| 22 May 68 | | TIME FOR LIVING Warner Bros. WB 7195 | 23 | 8 |

Rick ASTLEY UK, male vocalist — 91 wks

8 Aug 87	★	NEVER GONNA GIVE YOU UP RCA PB 41447	1	18
31 Oct 87	●	WHENEVER YOU NEED SOMEBODY RCA PB 41567	3	12
12 Dec 87	●	WHEN I FALL IN LOVE / MY ARMS KEEP MISSING YOU RCA PB 41683	2	10
27 Feb 88	●	TOGETHER FOREVER RCA PB 41817	2	9
24 Sep 88	●	SHE WANTS TO DANCE WITH ME RCA PB 42189	6	10
26 Nov 88	●	TAKE ME TO YOUR HEART RCA PB 42573	8	10
11 Feb 89	●	HOLD ME IN YOUR ARMS RCA PB 42615	10	8
26 Jan 91		CRY FOR HELP RCA PB 44247	7	7
30 Mar 91		MOVE RIGHT OUT RCA PB 44407	58	2
29 Jun 91		NEVER KNEW LOVE RCA PB 44737	70	1
4 Sep 93		THE ONES YOU LOVE RCA 74321160142	48	2
13 Nov 93		HOPELESSLY RCA 74321175642	33	2

Before 9 Jan 88 When I Fall In Love was listed by itself. After that date My Arms Keep Missing You was the side listed.

ASWAD UK, male vocal / instrumental group — 80 wks

3 Mar 84		CHASING FOR THE BREEZE Island IS 160	51	3
6 Oct 84		54-46 (WAS MY NUMBER) Island IS 170	70	3
27 Feb 88	★	DON'T TURN AROUND Mango IS 341	1	12
21 May 88		GIVE A LITTLE LOVE Mango IS 358	11	8
24 Sep 88		SET THEM FREE Mango IS 383	70	2
1 Apr 89		BEAUTY'S ONLY SKIN DEEP Mango MNG 105	31	6
22 Jul 89		ON AND ON Mango MNG 708	25	8
18 Aug 90		NEXT TO YOU Mango MNG 753	24	6
17 Nov 90		SMILE Mango MNG 767 [1]	53	2
30 Mar 91		TOO WICKED EP Mango MNG 771	61	2
31 Jul 93		HOW LONG Polydor PZCD 252 [2]	31	5
9 Oct 93		DANCE HALL MOOD Bubblin' CDBUBB 1	48	2
18 Jun 94	●	SHINE Bubblin' CDBUBB 3	5	14
17 Sep 94		WARRIORS Bubblin' CDBUBB 4	33	3
18 Feb 95		YOU'RE NO GOOD Bubblin' CDBUBB 5	35	3
5 Aug 95		IF I WAS Bubblin' CDBUBB 6	58	1

[1] Aswad featuring Sweetie Irie [2] Yazz and Aswad

Tracks on Too Wicked EP: Best of My Love / Warrior Re-Charge / Fire / I Shot The Sheriff.

Gali ATARI – See MILK AND HONEY featuring Gali ATARI

Chet ATKINS US, male instrumentalist – guitar — 2 wks

| 17 Mar 60 | | TEENSVILLE RCA 1174 | 46 | 1 |
| 5 May 60 | | TEENSVILLE (re-entry) RCA 1174 | 49 | 1 |

ATLANTA RHYTHM SECTION
US, male vocal / instrumental group — 4 wks

| 27 Oct 79 | | SPOOKY Polydor POSP 74 | 48 | 4 |

ATLANTIC OCEAN Holland, male instrumental duo — 14 wks

19 Feb 94		WATERFALL Eastern Bloc BLOCCD 001	22	6
2 Jul 94		BODY IN MOTION Eastern Bloc BLOCCD 009	15	4
26 Nov 94		MUSIC IS A PASSION Eastern Bloc BLOCCDX 017	59	1
30 Nov 96		WATERFALL (re-mix) Eastern Bloc BLOC 104CD	21	3

ATLANTIC STARR
US, male / female vocal / instrumental group — 48 wks

9 Sep 78		GIMME YOUR LOVIN' A & M AMS 7380	66	3
29 Jun 85		SILVER SHADOW A & M AM 260	41	6
7 Sep 85		ONE LOVE A & M AM 273	58	4
15 Mar 86	●	SECRET LOVERS A & M AM 307	10	12
24 May 86		IF YOUR HEART ISN'T IN IT A & M AM 319	48	4
13 Jun 87	●	ALWAYS Warner Bros. W 8455	3	14
12 Sep 87		ONE LOVER AT A TIME Warner Bros. W 8327	57	3
27 Aug 94		EVERYBODY'S GOT SUMMER Arista 74321228072	36	2

ATMOSFEAR UK, male vocal / instrumental group — 7 wks

| 17 Nov 79 | | DANCING IN OUTER SPACE MCA 543 | 46 | 7 |

ATOMIC ROOSTER
UK, male vocal / instrumental group — 25 wks

| 6 Feb 71 | | TOMORROW NIGHT B & C CB 131 | 11 | 12 |
| 10 Jul 71 | ● | THE DEVIL'S ANSWER B & C CB 157 | 4 | 13 |

ATTRACTIONS – See Elvis COSTELLO and the ATTRACTIONS

Winifred ATWELL UK, female instrumentalist – piano — 117 wks

12 Dec 52		BRITANNIA RAG Decca F 10015	11	1
9 Jan 53	●	BRITANNIA RAG (re-entry) Decca F 10015	5	5
15 May 53		CORONATION RAG Decca F 10110	12	1
29 May 53	●	CORONATION RAG (re-entry) Decca F 10110	5	5
25 Sep 53		FLIRTATION WALTZ Decca F 10161	12	1
9 Oct 53	●	FLIRTATION WALTZ (re-entry) Decca F 10161	10	1
6 Nov 53		FLIRTATION WALTZ (2nd re-entry) Decca F10161	12	1
4 Dec 53	●	LET'S HAVE A PARTY Philips PB 213	2	9
23 Jul 54	●	RACHMANINOFF'S 18TH VARIATION ON A THEME BY PAGANINI (THE STORY OF THREE LOVES) Philips PB 234	9	7
1 Oct 54		RACHMANINOFF'S 18TH VARIATION ON A THEME BY PAGANINI (THE STORY OF THREE LOVES) (re-entry)Philips PB 234	19	2
26 Nov 54	★	LET'S HAVE ANOTHER PARTY Philips PB 268	1	8
26 Nov 54		LET'S HAVE A PARTY (re-entry) Philips PB 213	14	6
4 Nov 55	●	LET'S HAVE A DING DONG Decca F 10634	3	10
16 Mar 56	★	POOR PEOPLE OF PARIS Decca F 10681	1	16
18 May 56		PORT AU PRINCE Decca F 10727 [1]	18	6
20 Jul 56		LEFT BANK Decca F 10762	14	7
26 Oct 56	●	MAKE IT A PARTY Decca F 10796	7	12
22 Feb 57		LET'S ROCK 'N ROLL Decca F 10852	28	2
15 Mar 57		LET'S ROCK 'N ROLL (re-entry) Decca F 10852	24	2
6 Dec 57	●	LET'S HAVE A BALL Decca F 10956	4	6

7 Aug 59	SUMMER OF THE SEVENTEENTH DOLL		
	Decca F 11143	24	2
27 Nov 59	● PIANO PARTY Decca F 11183	10	7

[1] Winifred Atwell and Frank Chacksfield

Various hits listed above were medleys as follows: Let's Have a Party: Boomps A Daisy / Daisy Bell / If You Knew Suzie / Knees Up Mother Brown / The More We Are Together / She Was One Of The Early Birds / That's My Weakness Now / Three O'Clock In The Morning. Let's Have Another Party: Another Little Drink / Broken Doll / Bye Bye Blackbird / Honeysuckle And The Bee / I Wonder Where My Baby Is Tonight / Nellie Dean / Sheik of Araby / Somebody Stole My Gal / When The Red Red Robin. Let's Have a Ding Dong: Happy Days Are Here Again / Oh Johnny Oh Johnny Oh / Oh You Beautiful Doll / Ain't She Sweet / Yes We Have No Bananas / I'm Forever Blowing Bubbles / I'll Be Your Sweetheart / If These Lips Could Only Speak / Who's Taking You Home Tonight. Make It a Party: Who Were You With Last Night / Hello Hello Who's Your Lady Friend / Yes Sir That's My Baby / Don't Dilly Dally On The Way / Beer Barrel Polka / After The Ball / Peggy O'Neil / Meet Me Tonight In Dreamland / I Belong To Glasgow / Down At The Old Bull And Bush. Let's Rock 'n' Roll: Singin' The Blues / Green Door / See You Later Alligator / Shake Rattle And Roll / Rock Around The Clock / Razzle Dazzle. Let's Have a Ball: Music Music Music / This Ole House / Heartbreaker / Woody Woodpecker / Last Train To San Fernando / Bring A Little Water Sylvie / Puttin' On The Style / Don't You Rock Me Daddy-O. Piano Party: Baby Face / Comin' Thru' The Rye / Annie Laurie / Little Brown Jug / Let Him Go Let Him Tarry / Put Your Arms Around Me Honey / I'll Be With You In Apple Blossom Time / Shine On Harvest Moon / Blue Skies / I'll Never Say 'Never Again' Again / I'll See You In My Dreams. See also Various Artists (EPs & LPs) - All Star Hit Parade.

AUDIOWEB UK, male vocal / instrumental group   5 wks

14 Oct 95	SLEEPER Mother MUMCD 69	74	1
9 Mar 96	YEAH Mother MUMCD 72	73	1
15 Jun 96	INTO MY WORLD Mother MUMCD 76	42	1
19 Oct 96	SLEEPER (re-mix) Mother MUMCD 78	50	2

Brian AUGER – See Julie DRISCOLL, Brian AUGER and the TRINITY

AURRA US, male / female vocal duo   18 wks

4 May 85	LIKE I LIKE IT 10 TEN 45	51	5
19 Apr 86	YOU AND ME TONIGHT 10 TEN 71	12	8
21 Jun 86	LIKE I LIKE IT (re-issue) 10 TEN 126	43	5

David AUSTIN UK, male vocalist   3 wks

21 Jul 84	TURN TO GOLD Parlophone R 6068	68	3

Patti AUSTIN US, female vocalist   20 wks

20 Jun 81	RAZZAMATAZZ A & M AMS 8140 [1]	11	9
12 Feb 83	BABY COME TO ME Qwest K 15005 [2]	11	10
5 Sep 92	I'LL KEEP YOUR DREAMS ALIVE Ammi AMM 101 [3]	68	1

[1] Quincy Jones featuring Patti Austin [2] Patti Austin and James Ingram
[3] George Benson and Patti Austin

AUTECHRE UK, male instrumental duo   1 wk

7 May 94	BASSCAD Warp WAP 44CD	56	1

AUTEURS UK, male / female vocal / instrumental group   8 wks

27 Nov 93	LENNY VALENTINO Hut HUTCD 36	41	2
23 Apr 94	CHINESE BAKERY Hut HUTDX 41	42	2
6 Jan 96	BACK WITH THE KILLER AGAIN Hut HUTCD 65	45	3
24 Feb 96	LIGHT AIRCRAFT ON FIRE Hut HUTCD 66	58	1

AUTUMN UK, male vocal / instrumental group   6 wks

16 Oct 71	MY LITTLE GIRL Pye 7N 45090	37	6

Peter AUTY and the SINFONIA OF LONDON UK, male vocalist with UK orchestra   9 wks

14 Dec 85	WALKING IN THE AIR Stiff LAD 1	42	5
19 Dec 87	WALKING IN THE AIR (re-issue) CBS GA 3950	37	4

Label credits the Snowman featuring Peter Auty. See also Digital Dream Baby.

AVALON BOYS – See LAUREL and HARDY with the AVALON BOYS

Frankie AVALON US, male vocalist   15 wks

10 Oct 58	GINGERBREAD HMV POP 517	30	1
24 Apr 59	VENUS HMV POP 603	16	6
22 Jan 60	WHY HMV POP 688	20	4
28 Apr 60	DON'T THROW AWAY ALL THOSE TEARDROPS HMV POP 727	37	4

AVERAGE WHITE BAND UK, male vocal / instrumental vocal group   47 wks

22 Feb 75	● PICK UP THE PIECES Atlantic K 10489	6	9
26 Apr 75	CUT THE CAKE Atlantic K 10605	31	4
9 Oct 76	QUEEN OF MY SOUL Atlantic K 10825	23	7
28 Apr 79	WALK ON BY RCA XC 1087	46	5
25 Aug 79	WHEN WILL YOU BE MINE RCA XB 1096	49	5
26 Apr 80	LET'S GO ROUND AGAIN PT. 1 RCA AWB 1	12	11
26 Jul 80	FOR YOU FOR LOVE RCA AWB 2	46	4
26 Mar 94	LET'S GO ROUND AGAIN (re-mix) The Hit Label HLC 5	56	2

AVONS UK, male / female vocal group   22 wks

13 Nov 59	● SEVEN LITTLE GIRLS SITTING IN THE BACK SEAT Columbia DB 4363	3	13
7 Jul 60	WE'RE ONLY YOUNG ONCE Columbia DB 4461	49	1
21 Jul 60	WE'RE ONLY YOUNG ONCE (re-entry) Columbia DB 4461	45	1
27 Oct 60	FOUR LITTLE HEELS Columbia DB 4522	45	2
1 Dec 60	FOUR LITTLE HEELS (re-entry) Columbia DB 4522	49	1
26 Jan 61	RUBBER BALL Columbia DB 4569	30	4

AWESOME 3 UK, male / female vocal / instrumental group   8 wks

8 Sep 90	HARD UP A & M AM 591	55	3
3 Oct 92	DON'T GO Citybeat CBE 1271	75	1
4 Jun 94	DON'T GO (re-mix) Citybeat CBX 771CD	45	2
26 Oct 96	DON'T GO (2nd re-mix) XL XLS 78CD [1]	27	2

[1] Awesome 3 featuring Julie McDermott

Hoyt AXTON US, male vocalist   4 wks

7 Jun 80	DELLA AND THE DEALER Young Blood YB 82	48	4

Roy AYERS US, male vocalist / instrumentalist – vibraphone   12 wks

21 Oct 78	GET ON UP, GET ON DOWN Polydor AYERS 7	41	4
13 Jan 79	HEAT OF THE BEAT Polydor POSP 16 [1]	43	5
2 Feb 80	DON'T STOP THE FEELING Polydor STEP 6	56	3

[1] Roy Ayers and Wayne Henderson

AZ US, male rapper – Anthony Cruz   1 wk

30 Mar 96	SUGARHILL Cooltempo CDCOOL 315	67	1

Charles AZNAVOUR *France, male vocalist*　29 wks

22 Sep 73	**THE OLD FASHIONED WAY** *Barclay BAR 20*	**50**	1
20 Oct 73	**THE OLD FASHIONED WAY (re-entry)** *Barclay BAR 20*	**38**	12
22 Jun 74	★ **SHE** *Barclay BAR 26*	**1**	14
27 Jul 74	**THE OLD FASHIONED WAY (2nd re-entry)** *Barclay BAR 20*	**47**	2

AZTEC CAMERA *UK, male vocal / instrumental group*　74 wks

19 Feb 83	**OBLIVIOUS** *Rough Trade RT 122*	**47**	6
4 Jun 83	**WALK OUT TO WINTER** *Rough Trade RT 132*	**64**	4
5 Nov 83	**OBLIVIOUS (re-issue)** *WEA AZTEC 1*	**18**	11
1 Sep 84	**ALL I NEED IS EVERYTHING / JUMP** *WEA AC 1*	**34**	6
13 Feb 88	**HOW MEN ARE** *WEA YZ 168*	**25**	9
23 Apr 88	● **SOMEWHERE IN MY HEART** *WEA YZ 181*	**3**	14
6 Aug 88	**WORKING IN A GOLDMINE** *WEA YZ 199*	**31**	5
8 Oct 88	**DEEP AND WIDE AND TALL** *WEA YZ 154*	**55**	3
7 Jul 90	**THE CRYING SCENE** *WEA YZ 492*	**70**	3
6 Oct 90	**GOOD MORNING BRITAIN** *WEA YZ 521* [1]	**19**	8
18 Jul 92	**SPANISH HORSES** *WEA YZ 688*	**52**	3
1 May 93	**DREAM SWEET DREAMS** *WEA YZ 740CD1*	**67**	2

[1] Aztec Camera and Mick Jones

Jump *was listed with* All I Need Is Everything *from 22 Sep to the end of the disc's run.*

AZYMUTH *Brazil, male instrumental group*　8 wks

12 Jan 80	**JAZZ CARNIVAL** *Milestone MRC 101*	**19**	8

B

Bob AZZAM *Egypt, singing orchestra*　14 wks

26 May 60	**MUSTAPHA** *Decca F 21235*	**23**	14

Derek B *UK, male rapper*　15 wks

27 Feb 88	**GOODGROOVE** *Music Of Life 7NOTE 12*	**16**	6
7 May 88	**BAD YOUNG BROTHER** *Tuff Audio DRKB 1*	**16**	6
2 Jul 88	**WE'VE GOT THE JUICE** *Tuff Audio DRKB 2*	**56**	3

Eric B and RAKIM *US, male vocal / instrumental duo*　26 wks

7 Nov 87	**PAID IN FULL** *Fourth & Broadway BRW 78*	**15**	6
20 Feb 88	**MOVE THE CROWD** *Fourth & Broadway BRW 88*	**53**	2
12 Mar 88	**I KNOW YOU GOT SOUL** *Cooltempo COOL 146*	**13**	6
2 Jul 88	**FOLLOW THE LEADER** *MCA MCA 1256*	**21**	5
19 Nov 88	**THE MICROPHONE FIEND** *MCA MCA 1300*	**74**	1
12 Aug 89	**FRIENDS** *MCA MCA 1352* [1]	**21**	6

[1] Jody Watley with Eric B and Rakim

JAZZIE B – *See Maxi PRIEST; SOUL II SOUL*

Lisa B *US, female vocalist*　9 wks

12 Jun 93	**GLAM** *ffrr FCD 210*	**49**	2

25 Sep 93	**FASCINATED** *ffrr FCD 218*	**35**	3
8 Jan 94	**YOU AND ME** *ffrr FCD 226*	**39**	4

Lorna B – *See DJ SCOTT featuring Lorna B*

Sandy B *US, female vocalist*　2 wks

20 Feb 93	**FEEL LIKE SINGIN'** *Nervous SANCD 1*	**60**	1
18 May 96	**MAKE THE WORLD GO ROUND** *Champion CHAMPCD 322*	**73**	1

Stevie B *US, male vocalist*　9 wks

23 Feb 91	● **BECAUSE I LOVE YOU (THE POSTMAN SONG)** *Polydor PO 126*	**6**	9

Tairrie B *US, female rapper*　2 wks

1 Dec 90	**MURDER SHE WROTE** *MCA MCA 1455*	**71**	2

B-MOVIE *UK, male vocal / instrumental group*　7 wks

18 Apr 81	**REMEMBRANCE DAY** *Deram DM 437*	**61**	3
27 Mar 82	**NOWHERE GIRL** *Some Bizzare BZZ 8*	**67**	4

B-TRIBE *Spain, male / female vocal / instrumental group*　4 wks

25 Sep 93	**¡FIESTA FATAL!** *East West YZ 770CD*	**64**	4

Alice BABS *Sweden, female vocalist*　1 wk

15 Aug 63	**AFTER YOU'VE GONE** *Fontana TF 409*	**43**	1

BABY D *UK, male / female vocal / instrumental group*　40 wks

18 Dec 93	**DESTINY** *Production House PNC 057*	**69**	1
23 Jul 94	**CASANOVA** *Production House PNC 065*	**67**	1
19 Nov 94	★ **LET ME BE YOUR FANTASY** *Systematic SYSCD 4*	**1**	14
3 Jun 95	● **(EVERYBODY'S GOT TO LEARN SOMETIME) I NEED YOUR LOVING** *Systematic SYSCD 11*	**3**	12
13 Jan 96	● **SO PURE** *Systematic SYSCD 21*	**3**	7
6 Apr 96	**TAKE ME TO HEAVEN** *Systematic SYSCD 26*	**15**	5

BABY JUNE *UK, male vocalist – Tim Hegarty*　1 wk

15 Aug 92	**HEY! WHAT'S YOUR NAME** *Arista 115271*	**75**	1

BABY O *US, male / female vocal / instrumental group*　5 wks

26 Jul 80	**IN THE FOREST** *Calibre CAB 505*	**46**	5

BABY ROOTS *UK, male vocalist*　1 wk

1 Aug 92	**ROCK ME BABY** *ZYX ZYX 68027*	**71**	1

BABYBIRD *UK, male vocal / instrumental group*　14 wks

10 Aug 96	**GOODNIGHT** *Echo ECSCD 24*	**28**	2
12 Oct 96	● **YOU'RE GORGEOUS** *Echo ECSD 26*	**3†**	12

BABYFACE *US, male vocalist*　12 wks

9 Jul 94	**ROCK BOTTOM** *Epic 6601832*	**50**	4
1 Oct 94	**WHEN CAN I SEE YOU** *Epic 6606592*	**35**	3
9 Nov 96	**THIS IS FOR THE LOVER IN YOU** *Epic 6639352*	**12**	5

BABYLON ZOO
UK, male vocalist / multi-instrumentalist – Jas Mann **19 wks**

27 Jan 96	★ SPACEMAN *EMI CDEM 416*	**1**	14
27 Apr 96	ANIMAL ARMY *EMI CDEM 425*	**17**	3
5 Oct 96	THE BOY WITH THE X-RAY EYES *EMI CDEMS 440*	**32**	2

BABYS
US / UK, male vocal / instrumental group **3 wks**

| 21 Jan 78 | ISN'T IT TIME *Chrysalis CHS 2173* .... | **45** | 3 |

BACCARA
Spain, female vocal duo **25 wks**

| 17 Sep 77 | ★ YES SIR I CAN BOOGIE *RCA PB 5526* .... | **1** | 16 |
| 14 Jan 78 | ● SORRY I'M A LADY *RCA PB 5555* .... | **8** | 9 |

Burt BACHARACH
US, orchestra and chorus **11 wks**

| 20 May 65 | ● TRAINS AND BOATS AND PLANES *London HL 9968* .... | **4** | 11 |

BACHELORS
Ireland, male vocal group **187 wks**

24 Jan 63	● CHARMAINE *Decca F 11559*	**6**	19
4 Jul 63	FARAWAY PLACES *Decca F 11666*	**36**	3
29 Aug 63	WHISPERING *Decca F 11712*	**18**	10
23 Jan 64	★ DIANE *Decca F 11799*	**1**	19
19 Mar 64	● I BELIEVE *Decca F 11857*	**2**	17
4 Jun 64	● RAMONA *Decca F 11910*	**4**	13
13 Aug 64	● I WOULDN'T TRADE YOU FOR THE WORLD *Decca F 11949*	**4**	16
3 Dec 64	● NO ARMS CAN EVER HOLD YOU *Decca F 12034*	**7**	12
1 Apr 65	TRUE LOVE FOR EVER MORE *Decca F 12108*	**34**	6
20 May 65	● MARIE *Decca F 12156*	**9**	12
28 Oct 65	IN THE CHAPEL IN THE MOONLIGHT *Decca F 12256*	**27**	10
6 Jan 66	HELLO DOLLY *Decca F 12309*	**38**	4
17 Mar 66	● THE SOUND OF SILENCE *Decca F 12351*	**3**	13
7 Jul 66	CAN I TRUST YOU *Decca F 12417*	**26**	7
1 Dec 66	WALK WITH FAITH IN YOUR HEART *Decca F 22523*	**22**	9
6 Apr 67	OH HOW I MISS YOU *Decca F 22592*	**30**	8
5 Jul 67	MARTA *Decca F 22634*	**20**	9

BACHMAN-TURNER OVERDRIVE
Canada, male vocal / instrumental group **18 wks**

| 16 Nov 74 | ● YOU AIN'T SEEN NOTHING YET *Mercury 6167 025* .... | **2** | 12 |
| 1 Feb 75 | ROLL ON DOWN THE HIGHWAY *Mercury 6167 071* .... | **22** | 6 |

BACK TO THE PLANET
UK, male / female vocal / instrumental group **2 wks**

| 10 Apr 93 | TEENAGE TURTLES *Parallel LLLCD 3* .... | **52** | 1 |
| 4 Sep 93 | DAYDREAM *Parallel LLLCD 8* .... | **52** | 1 |

BACKBEAT BAND
US, male vocal / instrumental group **5 wks**

26 Mar 94	MONEY *Virgin VSCDX 1489*	**48**	3
23 Apr 94	MONEY (re-entry) *Virgin VSCDX 1489*	**73**	1
14 May 94	PLEASE MR. POSTMAN *Virgin VSCDX 1502*	**69**	1

BACKBEAT DISCIPLES – *See Arthur BAKER*

BACKROOM BOYS – *See Frank IFIELD*

BACKSTREET BOYS
US, male vocal group **26 wks**

| 28 Oct 95 | WE'VE GOT IT GOIN' ON *Jive JIVECD 386* .... | **54** | 1 |
| 16 Dec 95 | I'LL NEVER BREAK YOUR HEART *Jive JIVECD 389* .... | **42** | 3 |

1 Jun 96	GET DOWN (YOU'RE THE ONE FOR ME) *Jive JIVECD 394* ..**14**	8
24 Aug 96	● WE'VE GOT IT GOIN' ON (re-issue) *Jive JIVECD 400* **3**	7
16 Nov 96	● I'LL NEVER BREAK YOUR HEART (re-issue) *Jive JIVECD 406* ....**8†**	7

BAD ANGEL – *See BOOTH and the BAD ANGEL*

BAD BOYS INC.
UK, male vocal group **31 wks**

14 Aug 93	DON'T TALK ABOUT LOVE *A & M 5803412*	**19**	5
2 Oct 93	WHENEVER YOU NEED SOMEONE *A & M 5804032*	**26**	3
11 Dec 93	WALKING ON AIR *A & M 5804692*	**24**	6
21 May 94	● MORE TO THIS WORLD *A & M 5806072*	**8**	7
23 Jul 94	TAKE ME AWAY (I'LL FOLLOW YOU) *A & M 5806912*	**15**	6
17 Sep 94	LOVE HERE I COME *A & M 5807752*	**26**	4

BAD COMPANY
UK, male vocal / instrumental group **23 wks**

1 Jun 74	CAN'T GET ENOUGH *Island WIP 6191*	**15**	8
22 Mar 75	GOOD LOVIN' GONE BAD *Island WIP 6223*	**31**	6
30 Aug 75	FEEL LIKE MAKIN' LOVE *Island WIP 6242*	**20**	9

BAD ENGLISH
UK / US, male vocal / instrumental group **3 wks**

| 25 Nov 89 | WHEN I SEE YOU SMILE *Epic 655347 1* .... | **61** | 3 |

BAD MANNERS
UK, male vocal / instrumental group **111 wks**

1 Mar 80	NE-NE NA-NA NA-NA NU-NU *Magnet MAG 164*	**28**	14
14 Jun 80	LIP UP FATTY *Magnet MAG 175*	**15**	14
27 Sep 80	● SPECIAL BREW *Magnet MAG 180*	**3**	13
6 Dec 80	LORRAINE *Magnet MAG 181*	**21**	12
28 Mar 81	JUST A FEELING *Magnet MAG 187*	**13**	6
27 Jun 81	● CAN CAN *Magnet MAG 190*	**3**	13
26 Sep 81	● WALKING IN THE SUNSHINE *Magnet MAG 197*	**10**	9
21 Nov 81	BUONA SERA *Magnet MAG 211*	**34**	9
1 May 82	GOT NO BRAINS *Magnet MAG 216*	**44**	5
31 Jul 82	● MY GIRL LOLLIPOP (MY BOY LOLLIPOP) *Magnet MAG 232*	**9**	7
30 Oct 82	SAMSON AND DELILAH *Magnet MAG 236*	**58**	3
14 May 83	THAT'LL DO NICELY *Magnet MAG 243*	**49**	3

BAD NEWS
UK, male vocal group **5 wks**

| 12 Sep 87 | BOHEMIAN RHAPSODY *EMI EM 24* .... | **44** | 5 |

BAD RELIGION
US, male vocal / instrumental group **2 wks**

| 11 Feb 95 | 21ST CENTURY (DIGITAL BOY) *Columbia 6611435* .... | **41** | 2 |

BAD SEEDS – *See Nick CAVE*

BAD YARD CLUB – *See David MORALES and the BAD YARD CLUB*

Wally BADAROU
France, male instrumentalist – keyboards **6 wks**

| 19 Oct 85 | CHIEF INSPECTOR *Fourth & Broadway BRW 37* .... | **46** | 6 |

BADDIEL – *See LIGHTNING SEEDS*

BADFINGER
UK, male vocal / instrumental group **34 wks**

10 Jan 70	● COME AND GET IT *Apple 20*	**4**	11
9 Jan 71	● NO MATTER WHAT *Apple 31*	**5**	12
29 Jan 72	● DAY AFTER DAY *Apple 40*	**10**	11

See also Various Artists (EPs & LPs) - The Apple EP.

Beatles

The Beatles are pictured here at London Airport leaving for Nassau in the Bahamas to film their second movie *Help!*

Babylon Zoo

In its first week of release Babylon Zoo's 'Spaceman' sold a massive 420,000 copies, the highest one week sale for a debut single ever. In that week, one in every three singles sold was 'Spaceman'.

Babybird

Between 1988 and 1996 Stephen Jones, the lead singer of Babybird (pictured centre), wrote and recorded 400 songs, two of which appear in this book.

BADMAN UK, male producer – Julian Brettle   3 wks

2 Feb 91	MAGIC STYLE Citybeat CBE 759	61	3

Joan BAEZ US, female vocalist   47 wks

6 May 65	WE SHALL OVERCOME Fontana TF 564	26	10
8 Jul 65	● THERE BUT FOR FORTUNE Fontana TF 587	8	12
2 Sep 65	IT'S ALL OVER NOW BABY BLUE Fontana TF 604	22	8
23 Dec 65	FAREWELL ANGELINA Fontana TF 639	35	3
20 Jan 66	FAREWELL ANGELINA (re-entry) Fontana TF 639	49	1
28 Jul 66	PACK UP YOUR SORROWS Fontana TF 727	50	1
9 Oct 71	● THE NIGHT THEY DROVE OLD DIXIE DOWN Vanguard VS 35138	6	12

Carol BAILEY UK, female vocalist   2 wks

25 Feb 95	FEEL IT Multiply CDMULTY 3	41	2

Philip BAILEY US, male vocalist   20 wks

9 Mar 85	★ EASY LOVER CBS A 4915 [1]	1	12
18 May 85	WALKING ON THE CHINESE WALL CBS A 6202	34	8

[1] Philip Bailey (duet with Phil Collins)

Merril BAINBRIDGE Australia, female vocalist   1 wk

7 Dec 96	MOUTH Gotham 74321431012	51	1

Adrian BAKER UK, male vocalist   8 wks

19 Jul 75	● SHERRY Magnet MAG 34	10	8

See also Gidea Park.

Anita BAKER US, female vocalist   22 wks

15 Nov 86	SWEET LOVE Elektra EKR 44	13	10
31 Jan 87	CAUGHT UP IN THE RAPTURE Elektra EKR 49	51	5
8 Oct 88	GIVING YOU THE BEST THAT I GOT Elektra EKR 79	55	3
30 Jun 90	TALK TO ME Elektra EKR 111	68	2
17 Sep 94	BODY & SOUL Elektra EKR 190CD	48	2

Arthur BAKER
US, male producer / multi-instrumentalist   7 wks

20 May 89	IT'S YOUR TIME Breakout USA 654 [1]	64	2
21 Oct 89	THE MESSAGE IS LOVE Breakout USA 668 [2]	38	5

[1] Arthur Baker featuring Shirley Lewis [2] Arthur Baker and the Backbeat Disciples featuring Al Green.

See also Wally Jump Jr. and the Criminal Element.

Hylda BAKER and Arthur MULLARD
UK, female / male vocal duo   6 wks

9 Sep 78	YOU'RE THE ONE THAT I WANT Pye 7N 46121	22	6

George BAKER SELECTION
Holland, male / female vocal / instrumental group   10 wks

6 Sep 75	● PALOMA BLANCA Warner Bros. K 16541	10	10

BALAAM AND THE ANGEL
UK, male vocal / instrumental group   2 wks

29 Mar 86	SHE KNOWS Virgin VS 842	70	2

Long John BALDRY UK, male vocalist   36 wks

8 Nov 67	★ LET THE HEARTACHES BEGIN Pye 7N 17385	1	13
28 Aug 68	WHEN THE SUN COMES SHININ' THRU Pye 7N 17593	29	7
23 Oct 68	MEXICO Pye 7N 17563	15	8
29 Jan 69	IT'S TOO LATE NOW Pye 7N 17664	21	8

Edward BALL UK, male vocalist   1 wk

20 Jul 96	THE MILL HILL SELF HATE CLUB Creation CRESCD 233	57	1

Kenny BALL and his JAZZMEN
UK, male jazz band, Kenny Ball vocals and trumpet   136 wks

23 Feb 61	SAMANTHA Pye Jazz Today 7NJ 2040	13	15
11 May 61	I STILL LOVE YOU ALL Pye Jazz 7NJ 2042	24	6
31 Aug 61	SOMEDAY (YOU'LL BE SORRY) Pye Jazz 7NJ 2047	28	6
9 Nov 61	● MIDNIGHT IN MOSCOW Pye Jazz 7NJ 2049	2	21
15 Feb 62	MARCH OF THE SIAMESE CHILDREN Pye Jazz 7NJ 2051	4	13
17 May 62	THE GREEN LEAVES OF SUMMER Pye Jazz 7NJ 2054	7	14
23 Aug 62	SO DO I Pye Jazz 7NJ 2056	14	8
18 Oct 62	THE PAY OFF Pye Jazz 7NJ 2061	23	6
17 Jan 63	● SUKIYAKI Pye Jazz 7NJ 2062	10	13
25 Apr 63	CASABLANCA Pye Jazz 7NJ 2064	21	11
13 Jun 63	RONDO Pye Jazz 7NJ 2065	24	8
22 Aug 63	ACAPULCO 1922 Pye Jazz 7NJ 2067	27	6
11 Jun 64	HELLO DOLLY Pye Jazz 7NJ 2071	30	7
19 Jul 67	WHEN I'M SIXTY FOUR Pye 7N 17348	43	2

Michael BALL UK, male vocalist   39 wks

28 Jan 89	● LOVE CHANGES EVERYTHING Really Useful RUR 3	2	14
28 Oct 89	THE FIRST MAN YOU REMEMBER Really Useful RUR 6 [1]	68	2
10 Aug 91	IT'S STILL YOU Polydor PO 160	58	2
25 Apr 92	ONE STEP OUT OF TIME Polydor PO 206	20	7
12 Dec 92	IF I CAN DREAM (EP) Polydor PO 248	51	1
26 Dec 92	IF I CAN DREAM (EP) (re-entry) Polydor PO 248	68	1
11 Sep 93	SUNSET BOULEVARD Polydor PZCD 293	72	1
30 Jul 94	FROM HERE TO ETERNITY Columbia 6606905	36	3
17 Sep 94	THE LOVERS WE WERE Columbia 6607972	63	2
9 Dec 95	THE ROSE Columbia 6614535	42	4
17 Feb 96	(SOMETHING INSIDE) SO STRONG Columbia 6629005	40	2

[1] Michael Ball and Diana Morrison

Tracks on If I Can Dream EP: If I Can Dream / You Don't Have To Say You Love Me / Always On My Mind / Tell Me There's A Heaven.

BALTIMORA Ireland, male vocalist   12 wks

10 Aug 85	● TARZAN BOY Columbia DB 9102	3	12

BAM BAM US, male vocalist / multi-instrumentalist   2 wks

19 Mar 88	GIVE IT TO ME Serious 7OUS 10	65	2

Afrika BAMBAATAA US, male vocalist   23 wks

28 Aug 82	PLANET ROCK Polydor POSP 497 [1]	53	3
10 Mar 84	RENEGADES OF FUNK Tommy Boy AFR 1 [1]	30	4
1 Sep 84	UNITY (PART 1 – THE THIRD COMING) Tommy Boy AFR 2 [2]	49	5

27 Feb 88	**RECKLESS** *EMI EM 41* [3]	**17**	8
12 Oct 91	**JUST GET UP AND DANCE** *EMI USA MT 100*	**45**	3

[1] Afrika Bambaataa and the Soul Sonic Force [2] Afrika Bambaataa and James Brown [3] Afrika Bambaataa and Family featuring UB40

BANANARAMA *UK, female vocal group* — **202 wks**

13 Feb 82	● **IT AIN'T WHAT YOU DO IT'S THE WAY THAT YOU DO IT**		
	Chrysalis CHS 2570 [1]	**4**	10
10 Apr 82	● **REALLY SAYING SOMETHING** *Deram NANA 1* [2]	**5**	10
3 Jul 82	● **SHY BOY** *London NANA 2*	**4**	11
4 Dec 82	**CHEERS THEN** *London NANA 3*	**45**	7
26 Feb 83	● **NA NA HEY HEY KISS HIM GOODBYE**		
	London NANA 4	**5**	10
9 Jul 83	● **CRUEL SUMMER** *London NANA 5*	**8**	10
3 Mar 84	● **ROBERT DE NIRO'S WAITING** *London NANA 6*	**3**	11
26 May 84	**ROUGH JUSTICE** *London NANA 7*	**23**	7
24 Nov 84	**HOTLINE TO HEAVEN** *London NANA 8*	**58**	2
24 Aug 85	**DO NOT DISTURB** *London NANA 9*	**31**	6
31 May 86	● **VENUS** *London NANA 10*	**8**	13
16 Aug 86	**MORE THAN PHYSICAL** *London NANA 11*	**41**	5
14 Feb 87	**TRICK OF THE NIGHT** *London NANA 12*	**32**	5
11 Jul 87	**I HEARD A RUMOUR** *London NANA 13*	**14**	9
10 Oct 87	● **LOVE IN THE FIRST DEGREE** *London NANA 14*	**3**	12
9 Jan 88	**I CAN'T HELP IT** *London NANA 15*	**20**	6
9 Apr 88	● **I WANT YOU BACK** *London NANA 16*	**5**	10
24 Sep 88	**LOVE, TRUTH AND HONESTY** *London NANA 17*	**23**	8
19 Nov 88	**NATHAN JONES** *London NANA 18*	**15**	9
25 Feb 89	● **HELP** *London LON 222* [3]	**3**	9
10 Jun 89	**CRUEL SUMMER (re-mix)** *London NANA 19*	**19**	6
28 Jul 90	**ONLY YOUR LOVE** *London NANA 21*	**27**	4
5 Jan 91	**PREACHER MAN** *London NANA 23*	**20**	6
20 Apr 91	**LONG TRAIN RUNNING** *London NANA 24*	**30**	5
29 Aug 92	**MOVIN' ON** *London NANA 25*	**24**	5
28 Nov 92	**LAST THING ON MY MIND** *London NANA 26*	**71**	2
20 Mar 93	**MORE MORE MORE** *London NACPD 27*	**24**	4

[1] Funboy Three and Bananarama [2] Bananarama with Funboy Three
[3] Bananarama / La Na Nee Nee Noo Noo

The listed flip side of Love In The First Degree was Mr Sleaze by Stock Aitken Waterman. Act were a duo for last two hits.

BAND *Canada / US, male vocal / instrumental group* — **18 wks**

18 Sep 68	**THE WEIGHT** *Capitol CL 15559*	**21**	9
4 Apr 70	**RAG MAMA RAG** *Capitol CL 15629*	**16**	9

BAND AID
International, male / female vocal / instrumental group — **26 wks**

15 Dec 84	★ **DO THEY KNOW IT'S CHRISTMAS?** *Mercury FEED 1*	**1**	13
7 Dec 85	● **DO THEY KNOW IT'S CHRISTMAS? (re-entry)**		
	Mercury FEED 1	**3**	7
23 Dec 89	★ **DO THEY KNOW IT'S CHRISTMAS?**		
	PWL/Polydor FEED 2 [1]	**1**	6

[1] Band Aid II

BAND AKA *US, male vocal / instrumental group* — **12 wks**

15 May 82	**GRACE** *Epic EPC A 2376*	**41**	5
5 Mar 83	**JOY** *Epic EPC A 3145*	**24**	7

BAND OF GOLD
Holland, male / female vocal / instrumental group — **11 wks**

14 Jul 84	**LOVE SONGS ARE BACK AGAIN (MEDLEY)** *RCA 428*	**24**	11

BAND OF THIEVES – *See Luke GOSS and the BAND OF THIEVES*

BANDERAS *UK, female vocal / instrumental duo* — **16 wks**

23 Feb 91	**THIS IS YOUR LIFE** *London LON 290*	**16**	10
15 Jun 91	**SHE SELLS** *London LON 298*	**41**	6

BANDWAGON – *See Johnny JOHNSON and the BANDWAGON*

Honey BANE *UK, female vocalist* — **8 wks**

24 Jan 81	**TURN ME ON TURN ME OFF** *Zonophone Z 15*	**37**	5
18 Apr 81	**BABY LOVE** *Zonophone Z 19*	**58**	3

BANG *UK, male vocal duo* — **2 wks**

6 May 89	**YOU'RE THE ONE** *RCA PB 42715*	**74**	2

BANGLES *US, female vocal / instrumental group* — **94 wks**

15 Feb 86	● **MANIC MONDAY** *CBS A 6796*	**2**	12
26 Apr 86	**IF SHE KNEW WHAT SHE WANTS** *CBS A 7062*	**31**	7
5 Jul 86	**GOING DOWN TO LIVERPOOL** *CBS A 7255*	**56**	3
13 Sep 86	● **WALK LIKE AN EGYPTIAN** *CBS 650071 7*	**3**	19
10 Jan 87	**WALKING DOWN YOUR STREET** *CBS BANGS 1*	**16**	6
18 Apr 87	**FOLLOWING** *CBS BANGS 2*	**55**	3
6 Feb 88	**HAZY SHADE OF WINTER** *Def Jam BANGS 3*	**11**	10
5 Nov 88	**IN YOUR ROOM** *CBS BANGS 4*	**35**	6
18 Feb 89	★ **ETERNAL FLAME** *CBS BANGS 5*	**1**	18
10 Jun 89	**BE WITH YOU** *CBS BANGS 6*	**23**	8
14 Oct 89	**I'LL SET YOU FREE** *CBS BANGS 7*	**74**	1
9 Jun 90	**WALK LIKE AN EGYPTIAN (re-issue)** *CBS BANGS 8*	**73**	1

Tony BANKS – *See FISH*

BANNED *UK, male vocal / instrumental group* — **6 wks**

17 Dec 77	**LITTLE GIRL** *Harvest HAR 5145*	**36**	6

BANSHEES – *See SIOUXSIE and the BANSHEES*

Buju BANTON *Jamaica, male vocalist* — **1 wk**

7 Aug 93	**MAKE MY DAY** *Mercury BUJCD 2*	**72**	1

Pato BANTON *UK, male vocalist* — **31 wks**

1 Oct 94	★ **BABY COME BACK** *Virgin VSCDT 1522*	**1**	18
8 Apr 95	**BUBBLING HOT** *Virgin VSCDT 1530* [1]	**15**	7
20 Jan 96	**SPIRITS IN THE MATERIAL WORLD**		
	MCA MCSTD 2113 [2]	**36**	2
27 Jul 96	**GROOVIN'** *IRS CDEIRS 195* [3]	**14**	4

[1] Pato Banton with Ranking Roger [2] Pato Banton with Sting
[3] Pato Banton and the Reggae Revolution

The sleeve of Baby Come Back credits Ali and Robin Campbell. See also Sting.

BAR CODES featuring Alison BROWN
UK, male / female vocal group — **1 wk**

17 Dec 94	**SUPERMARKET SWEEP** *Blanca Casa BC 101CD*	**72**	1

BAR-KAYS *US, male vocal / instrumental group* — **15 wks**

23 Aug 67	**SOUL FINGER** *Stax 601 014*	**33**	7
22 Jan 77	**SHAKE YOUR RUMP TO THE FUNK**		
	Mercury 6167 417	**41**	4
12 Jan 85	**SEXOMATIC** *Club JAB 10*	**51**	4

Chris BARBER'S JAZZ BAND
UK, male jazz band, Chris Barber – trombone　　**30 wks**

13 Feb 59	● PETITE FLEUR *Pye Nixa NJ 2026*	**3**	22
31 Jul 59	PETITE FLEUR (re-entry) *Pye Nixa NJ 2026*	**22**	2
9 Oct 59	LONESOME (SI TU VOIS MA MERE)		
	Columbia DB 4333 [1]	**27**	2
4 Jan 62	REVIVAL *Columbia SCD 2166*	**50**	2
1 Feb 62	REVIVAL (re-entry) *Columbia SCD 2166*	**43**	2

[1] Chris Barber featuring Monty Sunshine

BARBRA and NEIL – *See Barbra STREISAND; Neil DIAMOND*

BARCLAY JAMES HARVEST
UK, male vocal / instrumental group　　**9 wks**

2 Apr 77	LIVE EP *Polydor 2229 198*	**49**	1
16 Apr 77	LIVE EP (re-entry) *Polydor 2229 198*	**49**	1
26 Jan 80	LOVE ON THE LINE *Polydor POSP 97*	**63**	2
22 Nov 80	LIFE IS FOR LIVING *Polydor POSP 195*	**61**	3
21 May 83	JUST A DAY AWAY *Polydor POSP 585*	**68**	2

Tracks on Live EP: *Rock 'n' Roll Star / Medicine Man (Parts 1 & 2).*

BARDO
UK, male / female vocal duo　　**8 wks**

10 Apr 82	● ONE STEP FURTHER *Epic EPC A2265*	**2**	8

Gary BARLOW *UK, male vocalist*　　**16 wks**

20 Jul 96	★ FOREVER LOVE *RCA 74321397922*	**1**	16

Gary BARNACLE – *See BIG FUN; SONIA*

BARNBRACK *UK, male vocal / instrumental group*　　**7 wks**

16 Mar 85	BELFAST *Homespun HS 092*	**45**	7

Jimmy BARNES – *See INXS*

Richard BARNES *UK, male vocalist*　　**10 wks**

23 May 70	TAKE TO THE MOUNTAINS *Philips BF 1840*	**35**	6
24 Oct 70	GO NORTH *Philips 6006 039*	**49**	1
7 Nov 70	GO NORTH (re-entry) *Philips 6006 039*	**38**	3

BARRACUDAS
UK / US, male vocal / instrumental group　　**6 wks**

16 Aug 80	SUMMER FUN *EMI-Wipe Out Z 5*	**37**	6

Wild Willy BARRETT – *See John OTWAY and Wild Willy BARRETT*

Amanda BARRIE and Johnny BRIGGS
UK, female / male vocal duo　　**3 wks**

16 Dec 95	SOMETHING STUPID *EMI Premier CDEMS 411*	**35**	3

The listed flip side of Something Stupid was Always Look On The Bright Side Of Life *by the Coronation Street Cast.*

J.J. BARRIE *Canada, male vocalist*　　**11 wks**

24 Apr 76	★ NO CHARGE *Power Exchange PX 209*	**1**	11

Featured vocalist is Vicki Brown.

Ken BARRIE *UK, male vocalist*　　**15 wks**

10 Jul 82	POSTMAN PAT *Post Music PP 001*	**44**	8
25 Dec 82	POSTMAN PAT (re-entry) *Post Music PP 001*	**54**	3
24 Dec 83	POSTMAN PAT (2nd re-entry) *Post Music PP 001* ...	**59**	4

BARRON KNIGHTS
UK, male vocal / instrumental group　　**94 wks**

9 Jul 64	● CALL UP THE GROUPS *Columbia DB 7317*	**3**	13
22 Oct 64	COME TO THE DANCE *Columbia DB 7375*	**42**	2
25 Mar 65	● POP GO THE WORKERS *Columbia DB 7525*	**5**	13
16 Dec 65	● MERRY GENTLE POPS *Columbia DB 7780*	**9**	7
1 Dec 66	UNDER NEW MANAGEMENT *Columbia DB 8071* ...	**15**	9
23 Oct 68	AN OLYMPIC RECORD *Columbia DB 8485*	**35**	4
29 Oct 77	● LIVE IN TROUBLE *Epic EPC 5752*	**7**	10
2 Dec 78	● A TASTE OF AGGRO *Epic EPC 6829*	**3**	10
8 Dec 79	FOOD FOR THOUGHT *Epic EPC 8011*	**46**	6
4 Oct 80	THE SIT SONG *Epic EPC 8994*	**44**	4
6 Dec 80	NEVER MIND THE PRESENTS *Epic EPC 9070*	**17**	8
5 Dec 81	BLACKBOARD JUMBLE *CBS A 1795*	**52**	5
19 Mar 83	BUFFALO BILL'S LAST SCRATCH *Epic EPC A 3208* ...	**49**	3

Joe BARRY *US, male vocalist*　　**1 wk**

24 Aug 61	I'M A FOOL TO CARE *Mercury AMT 1149*	**49**	1

John BARRY ORCHESTRA
UK, male instrumental group / orchestra　　**78 wks**

10 Mar 60	● HIT AND MISS *Columbia DB 4414* [1]	**10**	12
28 Apr 60	BEAT FOR BEATNIKS *Columbia DB 4446*	**40**	2
9 Jun 60	HIT AND MISS (re-entry) *Columbia DB 4414* [1]	**45**	1
14 Jul 60	NEVER LET GO *Columbia DB 4480*	**49**	1
18 Aug 60	BLUEBERRY HILL *Columbia DB 4480*	**34**	3
8 Sep 60	WALK DON'T RUN *Columbia DB 4505* [1]	**49**	1
22 Sep 60	WALK DON'T RUN (re-entry)		
	Columbia DB 4505 [1]	**11**	13
8 Dec 60	BLACK STOCKINGS *Columbia DB 4554* [1]	**27**	9
2 Mar 61	THE MAGNIFICENT SEVEN *Columbia DB 4598* [1] ...	**48**	1
16 Mar 61	THE MAGNIFICENT SEVEN (re-entry)		
	Columbia DB 4598 [1]	**45**	2
6 Apr 61	THE MAGNIFICENT SEVEN (2nd re-entry)		
	Columbia DB 4598 [1]	**50**	1
8 Jun 61	THE MAGNIFICENT SEVEN (3rd re-entry)		
	Columbia DB 4598 [1]	**47**	1
26 Apr 62	CUTTY SARK *Columbia DB 4806* [1]	**35**	2
1 Nov 62	JAMES BOND THEME *Columbia DB 4898*	**13**	11
21 Nov 63	FROM RUSSIA WITH LOVE *Ember S 181*	**44**	1
19 Dec 63	FROM RUSSIA WITH LOVE (re-entry) *Ember S 181*	**39**	2
11 Dec 71	THEME FROM 'THE PERSUADERS' *CBS 7469*	**13**	15

[1] John Barry Seven

Len BARRY *US, male vocalist*　　**24 wks**

4 Nov 65	● 1-2-3 *Brunswick 05942*	**3**	14
13 Jan 66	● LIKE A BABY *Brunswick 05949*	**10**	10

Michael BARRYMORE *UK, male vocalist*　　**4 wks**

16 Dec 95	TOO MUCH FOR ONE HEART *EMI CDEM 412*	**25**	4

Lionel BART *UK, male vocalist*　　**3 wks**

25 Nov 89	HAPPY ENDINGS (GIVE YOURSELF A PINCH)		
	EMI EM 121	**68**	1
23 Dec 89	HAPPY ENDINGS (GIVE YOURSELF A PINCH)		
	(re-entry) *EMI EM 121*	**71**	2

BAS NOIR US, female vocal duo — 1 wk

11 Feb 89	**MY LOVE IS MAGIC** 10 TEN 257	**73**	1

Rob BASE and DJ E-Z ROCK US, male vocal duo — 19 wks

16 Apr 88	**IT TAKES TWO** Citybeat CBE 724	**24**	6
14 Jan 89	**GET ON THE DANCE FLOOR** Supreme SUPE 139	**14**	7
4 Mar 89	**IT TAKES TWO (re-entry)** Citybeat CBE 724	**49**	3
22 Apr 89	**JOY AND PAIN** Supreme SUPE 143	**47**	3

BASEMENT BOYS – See Ultra NATÉ

BASIA Poland, female vocalist — 9 wks

23 Jan 88	**PROMISES** Epic BASH 4	**48**	4
28 May 88	**TIME AND TIDE** Epic BASH 5	**61**	3
14 Jan 95	**DRUNK ON LOVE** Epic 6611582	**41**	2

Count BASIE – See Frank SINATRA

Toni BASIL US, female vocalist — 16 wks

6 Feb 82	● **MICKEY** Radialchoice TIC 4.......................	**2**	12
1 May 82	**NOBODY** Radialchoice TIC 2	**52**	4

Alfie BASS – See Michael MEDWIN, Bernard BRESSLAW, Alfie BASS and Leslie FYSON

BASS BOYZ UK, male producer – James Salmon — 1 wk

28 Sep 96	**GUNZ AND PIANOZ** Polydor 5753432	**74**	1

See also Pianoman.

BASS BUMPERS
Germany / UK, male / female vocal / instrumental group — 4 wks

25 Sep 93	**RUNNIN'** Vertigo VERCD 78	**68**	1
5 Feb 94	**THE MUSIC'S GOT ME** Vertigo VERCD 84	**25**	3

Fontella BASS US, female vocalist — 15 wks

2 Dec 65	**RESCUE ME** Chess CRS 8023	**11**	10
20 Jan 66	**RECOVERY** Chess CRS 8027	**32**	5

BASS-O-MATIC UK, male multi-instrumentalist — 19 wks

12 May 90	**IN THE REALM OF THE SENSES** Virgin VS 1265	**66**	3
1 Sep 90	● **FASCINATING RHYTHM** Virgin VS 1274	**9**	11
22 Dec 90	**EASE ON BY** Virgin VS 1295	**61**	4
3 Aug 91	**FUNKY LOVE VIBRATIONS** Virgin VS 1355	**71**	1

Shirley BASSEY UK, female vocalist — 316 wks

15 Feb 57	● **BANANA BOAT SONG** Philips PB 668	**8**	10
23 Aug 57	**FIRE DOWN BELOW** Philips PB 723	**30**	1
6 Sep 57	**YOU YOU ROMEO** Philips PB 723	**29**	2
19 Dec 58	**AS I LOVE YOU** Philips PB 845	**27**	2
26 Dec 58	● **KISS ME HONEY HONEY KISS ME** Philips PB 860	**3**	17
9 Jan 59	★ **AS I LOVE YOU (re-entry)** Philips PB 845	**1**	17
31 Mar 60	**WITH THESE HANDS** Columbia DB 4421	**38**	2
21 Apr 60	**WITH THESE HANDS (re-entry)** Columbia DB 4421	**31**	2
12 May 60	**WITH THESE HANDS (2nd re-entry)** Columbia DB 4421..	**41**	2
4 Aug 60	● **AS LONG AS HE NEEDS ME** Columbia DB 4490	**2**	30
11 May 61	● **YOU'LL NEVER KNOW** Columbia DB 4643	**6**	17
27 Jul 61	★ **REACH FOR THE STARS / CLIMB EV'RY MOUNTAIN** Columbia DB 4685	**1**	16
23 Nov 61	● **I'LL GET BY** Columbia DB 4737	**10**	8
23 Nov 61	**REACH FOR THE STARS / CLIMB EV'RY MOUNTAIN (re-entry)** Columbia DB 4685	**40**	2
15 Feb 62	**TONIGHT** Columbia DB 4777	**21**	8
26 Apr 62	**AVE MARIA** Columbia DB 4816	**31**	4
31 May 62	**FAR AWAY** Columbia DB 4836	**24**	13
30 Aug 62	● **WHAT NOW MY LOVE** Columbia DB 4882	**5**	17
28 Feb 63	**WHAT KIND OF FOOL AM I?** Columbia DB 4974	**47**	2
26 Sep 63	● **I (WHO HAVE NOTHING)** Columbia DB 7113	**6**	20
23 Jan 64	**MY SPECIAL DREAM** Columbia DB 7185	**32**	7
9 Apr 64	**GONE** Columbia DB 7248	**36**	5
15 Oct 64	**GOLDFINGER** Columbia DB 7360	**21**	9
20 May 65	**NO REGRETS** Columbia DB 7535	**39**	4
11 Oct 67	**BIG SPENDER** United Artists UP 1192	**21**	15
20 Jun 70	● **SOMETHING** United Artists UP 35125	**4**	21
2 Jan 71	**THE FOOL ON THE HILL** United Artists UP 35156	**48**	1
23 Jan 71	**SOMETHING (re-entry)** United Artists UP 35125	**50**	1
27 Mar 71	**(WHERE DO I BEGIN) LOVE STORY** United Artists UP 35194	**34**	9
7 Aug 71	**FOR ALL WE KNOW** United Artists UP 35267	**46**	1
21 Aug 71	● **FOR ALL WE KNOW (re-entry)** United Artists UP 35267	**6**	23
15 Jan 72	**DIAMONDS ARE FOREVER** United Artists UP 35293	**38**	6
3 Mar 73	● **NEVER NEVER NEVER** United Artists UP 35490	**8**	18
14 Jul 73	**NEVER NEVER NEVER (re-entry)** United Artists UP 35490	**48**	1
22 Aug 87	**THE RHYTHM DIVINE** Mercury MER 253 [1]	**54**	2
16 Nov 96	**'DISCO' LA PASSIONE** East West EW 072CD [2]	**41**	1

[1] Yello featuring Shirley Bassey   [2] Chris Rea and Shirley Bassey

BASSHEADS
UK, male / female vocal / instrumental group — 19 wks

16 Nov 91	● **IS THERE ANYBODY OUT THERE** Deconstruction R 6303	**5**	8
30 May 92	**BACK TO THE OLD SCHOOL** Deconstruction R 6310	**12**	4
28 Nov 92	**WHO CAN MAKE ME FEEL GOOD** Deconstruction R 6326 ..	**38**	2
28 Aug 93	**START A BRAND NEW LIFE (SAVE ME)** Deconstruction CDR 6353	**49**	2
15 Jul 95	**IS THERE ANYBODY OUT THERE (re-mix)** Deconstruction 74321293882	**24**	3

BATES Germany, male vocal / instrumental group — 1 wk

3 Feb 96	**BILLIE JEAN** Virgin Internationsl DINSD 151	**67**	1

Mike BATT with the NEW EDITION
UK, male vocalist with male / female vocal group — 8 wks

16 Aug 75	● **SUMMERTIME CITY** Epic EPC 3460	**4**	8

BAUHAUS UK, male vocal / instrumental group — 35 wks

18 Apr 81	**KICK IN THE EYE** Beggars Banquet BEG 54	**59**	3
4 Jul 81	**THE PASSIONS OF LOVERS** Beggars Banquet BEG 59	**56**	2
6 Mar 82	**KICK IN THE EYE EP** Beggars Banquet BEG 74	**45**	4
19 Jun 82	**SPIRIT** Beggars Banquet BEG 79....................	**42**	5
9 Oct 82	**ZIGGY STARDUST** Beggars Banquet BEG 83	**15**	7
22 Jan 83	**LAGARTIJA NICK** Beggars Banquet BEG 88	**44**	4
9 Apr 83	**SHE'S IN PARTIES** Beggars Banquet BEG 91	**26**	6
29 Oct 83	**THE SINGLES 1981-83** Beggars Banquet BEG 100E......	**52**	4

Tracks on Kick In The Eye EP: Kick In The Eye (Searching For Satori) / Harry / Earwax.

Les BAXTER US, orchestra and chorus — 9 wks

13 May 55	● **UNCHAINED MELODY** Capitol CL 14257	**10**	9

BAY CITY ROLLERS
UK, male vocal / instrumental group   **116 wks**

18 Sep 71 ●	**KEEP ON DANCING** *Bell 1164*	**9** 13
9 Feb 74 ●	**REMEMBER (SHA-LA-LA)** *Bell 1338*	**6** 12
27 Apr 74 ●	**SHANG-A-LANG** *Bell 1355*	**2** 10
27 Jul 74 ●	**SUMMERLOVE SENSATION** *Bell 1369*	**3** 10
12 Oct 74 ●	**ALL OF ME LOVES ALL OF YOU** *Bell 1382*	**4** 10
8 Mar 75 ★	**BYE BYE BABY** *Bell 1409*	**1** 16
12 Jul 75 ★	**GIVE A LITTLE LOVE** *Bell 1425*	**1** 9
22 Nov 75 ●	**MONEY HONEY** *Bell 1461*	**3** 9
10 Apr 76 ●	**LOVE ME LIKE I LOVE YOU** *Bell 1477*	**4** 9
11 Sep 76 ●	**I ONLY WANNA BE WITH YOU** *Bell 1493*	**4** 9
7 May 77	**IT'S A GAME** *Arista 108*	**16** 6
30 Jul 77	**YOU MADE ME BELIEVE IN MAGIC** *Arista 127*	**34** 3

B B and Q BAND   *US, male vocal / instrumental group*   **15 wks**

18 Jul 81	**ON THE BEAT** *Capitol CL 202*	**41** 5
6 Jul 85	**GENIE** *Cooltempo COOL 110* [1]	**40** 4
20 Sep 86	**(I'M A) DREAMER** *Cooltempo COOL 132*	**35** 5
17 Oct 87	**RICOCHET** *Cooltempo COOL 154*	**71** 1

[1] Brooklyn Bronx and Queens

BBC CONCERT ORCHESTRA, BBC SYMPHONY CHORUS cond. Stephen JACKSON
UK, orchestra, chorus and conductor   **3 wks**

22 Jun 96	**ODE TO JOY (FROM BEETHOVEN'S SYMPHONY NO. 9)** *Virgin VSCDT 1591*	**36** 3

BBE   *France / Italy, male instrumental group*   **9 wks**

28 Sep 96 ●	**SEVEN DAYS AND ONE WEEK** *Positiva CDTIV 67*	**3** 9

BBG   *UK, male vocal / instrumental group*   **9 wks**

28 Apr 90	**SNAPPINESS** *Urban URB 54* [1]	**28** 5
11 Aug 90	**SOME KIND OF HEAVEN** *Urban URB 59*	**65** 2
23 Mar 96	**LET THE MUSIC PLAY** *MCA MCSTD 40029* [2]	**46** 1
18 May 96	**SNAPPINESS (re-mix)** *Hi-Life 5762972*	**50** 1

[1] BBG featuring Dina Taylor [2] BBG featuring Erin

BBM   *UK, male vocal / instrumental group*   **2 wks**

6 Aug 94	**WHERE IN THE WORLD** *Virgin VSCD 1495*	**57** 2

BC-52s – *See B-52s*

BE BOP DELUXE   *UK, male vocal / instrumental group*   **13 wks**

21 Feb 76	**SHIPS IN THE NIGHT** *Harvest HAR 5104*	**23** 8
13 Nov 76	**HOT VALVES EP** *Harvest HAR 5117*	**36** 5

Tracks on Hot Valves EP: Maid In Heaven / Blazing Apostles / Jet Silver And The Dolls Of Venus / Bring Back The Spark.

BEACH BOYS   *US, male vocal / instrumental group*   **281 wks**

1 Aug 63	**SURFIN' USA** *Capitol CL 15305*	**34** 7
9 Jul 64 ●	**I GET AROUND** *Capitol CL 15350*	**7** 13
29 Oct 64	**WHEN I GROW UP (TO BE A MAN)** *Capitol CL 15361*	**44** 2
19 Nov 64	**WHEN I GROW UP (TO BE A MAN) (re-entry)** *Capitol CL 15361*	**27** 5
21 Jan 65	**DANCE DANCE DANCE** *Capitol CL 15370*	**24** 6
3 Jun 65	**HELP ME RHONDA** *Capitol CL 15392*	**27** 10
2 Sep 65	**CALIFORNIA GIRLS** *Capitol CL 15409*	**26** 8
17 Feb 66 ●	**BARBARA ANN** *Capitol CL 15432*	**3** 10
21 Apr 66 ●	**SLOOP JOHN B** *Capitol CL 15441*	**2** 15
28 Jul 66 ●	**GOD ONLY KNOWS** *Capitol CL 15459*	**2** 14
3 Nov 66 ★	**GOOD VIBRATIONS** *Capitol CL 15475*	**1** 13
4 May 67 ●	**THEN I KISSED HER** *Capitol CL 15502*	**4** 11
23 Aug 67 ●	**HEROES AND VILLAINS** *Capitol CL 15510*	**8** 9
22 Nov 67	**WILD HONEY** *Capitol CL 15521*	**29** 6
17 Jan 68	**DARLIN'** *Capitol CL 15527*	**11** 14
8 May 68	**FRIENDS** *Capitol CL 15545*	**25** 7
24 Jul 68 ★	**DO IT AGAIN** *Capitol CL 15554*	**1** 14
25 Dec 68	**BLUEBIRDS OVER THE MOUNTAIN** *Capitol CL 15572*	**33** 5
26 Feb 69 ●	**I CAN HEAR MUSIC** *Capitol CL 15584*	**10** 13
11 Jun 69 ●	**BREAK AWAY** *Capitol CL 15598*	**6** 11
16 May 70 ●	**COTTONFIELDS** *Capitol CL 15640*	**5** 17
3 Mar 73	**CALIFORNIA SAGA - CALIFORNIA** *Reprise K 14232*	**37** 5
3 Jul 76	**GOOD VIBRATIONS (re-issue)** *Capitol CL 15875*	**18** 7
10 Jul 76	**ROCK AND ROLL MUSIC** *Reprise K 14440*	**36** 4
31 Mar 79	**HERE COMES THE NIGHT** *Caribou CRB 7204*	**37** 8
16 Jun 79 ●	**LADY LYNDA** *Caribou CRB 7427*	**6** 11
29 Sep 79	**SUMAHAMA** *Caribou CRB 7846*	**45** 4
29 Aug 81	**BEACH BOYS MEDLEY** *Capitol CL 213*	**47** 4
22 Aug 87 ★	**WIPEOUT** *Urban URB 5* [1]	**2** 12
19 Nov 88	**KOKOMO** *Elektra EKR 85*	**25** 9
2 Jun 90	**WOULDN'T IT BE NICE** *Capitol CL 579*	**58** 1
29 Jun 91	**DO IT AGAIN (re-issue)** *Capitol EMCT 1*	**61** 2
2 Mar 96	**FUN FUN FUN** *PolyGram TV 5762972* [2]	**24** 4

[1] Fat Boys and the Beach Boys [2] Status Quo with the Beach Boys

Walter BEASLEY   *US, male vocalist*   **3 wks**

23 Jan 88	**I'M SO HAPPY** *Urban URB 14*	**70** 3

BEASTIE BOYS   *US, male rap group*   **40 wks**

28 Feb 87	**(YOU GOTTA) FIGHT FOR YOUR RIGHT (TO PARTY)** *Def Jam 650418 7*	**11** 11
30 May 87	**NO SLEEP TILL BROOKLYN** *Def Jam BEAST 1*	**14** 7
18 Jul 87 ●	**SHE'S ON IT** *Def Jam BEAST 2*	**10** 8
3 Oct 87	**GIRLS / SHE'S CRAFTY** *Def Jam BEAST 3*	**34** 4
11 Apr 92	**PASS THE MIC** *Capitol 12CL 653*	**47** 2
4 Jul 92	**FROZEN METAL HEAD EP** *Capitol 12CL 665*	**55** 1
9 Jul 94	**GET IT TOGETHER / SABOTAGE** *Capitol CDCL 716*	**19** 4
26 Nov 94	**SURE SHOT** *Capitol CDCLS 726*	**27** 3

Tracks on Frozen Metal Head EP: Jimmy James / Jimmy James (Original) / Drinkin' Wine / The Blue Nun.

BEAT   *UK, male vocal / instrumental group*   **92 wks**

8 Dec 79 ●	**TEARS OF A CLOWN / RANKING FULL STOP** *2 Tone CHSTT 6*	**6** 11
23 Feb 80 ●	**HANDS OFF – SHE'S MINE** *Go Feet FEET 1*	**9** 9
3 May 80 ●	**MIRROR IN THE BATHROOM** *Go Feet FEET 2*	**4** 9
16 Aug 80	**BEST FRIEND / STAND DOWN MARGARET (DUB)** *Go Feet FEET 3*	**22** 9
13 Dec 80 ●	**TOO NICE TO TALK TO** *Go Feet FEET 4*	**7** 11
18 Apr 81	**DROWNING / ALL OUT TO GET YOU** *Go Feet FEET 6*	**22** 8
20 Jun 81	**DOORS OF YOUR HEART** *Go Feet FEET 9*	**33** 6
5 Dec 81	**HIT IT** *Go Feet FEET 11*	**70** 2
17 Apr 82	**SAVE IT FOR LATER** *Go Feet FEET 333*	**47** 4
18 Sep 82	**JEANETTE** *Go Feet FEET 15*	**45** 3
4 Dec 82	**I CONFESS** *Go Feet FEET 16*	**54** 3
30 Apr 83 ●	**CAN'T GET USED TO LOSING YOU** *Go Feet FEET 17*	**3** 11
2 Jul 83	**ACKEE 1-2-3** *Go Feet FEET 18*	**54** 4
27 Jan 96	**MIRROR IN THE BATHROOM (re-mix)** *Go Feet 74321232062*	**44** 2

See also Various Artists (EPs & LPs) - The Two Tone EP.

BEAT SYSTEM UK, male vocal / instrumental group   **3 wks**

3 Mar 90	**WALK ON THE WILD SIDE** *Fourth & Broadway BRW 163* ..**63**	2
18 Sep 93	**TO A BRIGHTER DAY (O' HAPPY DAY)** *ffrr FCD 217* **70**	1

BEATLES UK, male vocal / instrumental group   **456 wks**

11 Oct 62	**LOVE ME DO** *Parlophone R 4949* **17**	18
17 Jan 63	● **PLEASE PLEASE ME** *Parlophone R 4983* ..**2**	18
18 Apr 63	★ **FROM ME TO YOU** *Parlophone R 5015* **1**	21
6 Jun 63	**MY BONNIE** *Polydor NH 66833* 1 ....**48**	1
29 Aug 63	★ **SHE LOVES YOU** *Parlophone R 5055* **1**	31
5 Dec 63	★ **I WANT TO HOLD YOUR HAND** *Parlophone R 5084* **1**	24
26 Mar 64	★ **CAN'T BUY ME LOVE** *Parlophone R 5114* **1**	14
9 Apr 64	**SHE LOVES YOU** (re-entry) *Parlophone R 5055* ..**42**	2
14 May 64	**I WANT TO HOLD YOUR HAND** (re-entry) *Parlophone R 5084* **48**	1
11 Jun 64	**AIN'T SHE SWEET** *Polydor 52 317* **29**	6
9 Jul 64	**CAN'T BUY ME LOVE** (re-entry) *Parlophone R 5114* **47**	1
16 Jul 64	★ **A HARD DAY'S NIGHT** *Parlophone R 5160* **1**	13
3 Dec 64	★ **I FEEL FINE** *Parlophone R 5200* **1**	13
15 Apr 65	★ **TICKET TO RIDE** *Parlophone R 5265* **1**	14
29 Jul 65	★ **HELP!** *Parlophone R 5305* **1**	14
9 Dec 65	★ **DAY TRIPPER / WE CAN WORK IT OUT** *Parlophone R 5389* **1**	12
16 Jun 66	★ **PAPERBACK WRITER** *Parlophone R 5452* **1**	11
11 Aug 66	★ **YELLOW SUBMARINE / ELEANOR RIGBY** *Parlophone R 5493* **1**	13
23 Feb 67	● **PENNY LANE / STRAWBERRY FIELDS FOREVER** *Parlophone R 5570* **2**	11
12 Jul 67	★ **ALL YOU NEED IS LOVE** *Parlophone R 5620* **1**	13
29 Nov 67	★ **HELLO GOODBYE** *Parlophone R 5655* **1**	12
13 Dec 67	● **MAGICAL MYSTERY TOUR (DOUBLE EP)** *Parlophone SMMT/MMT 1* **2**	12
20 Mar 68	★ **LADY MADONNA** *Parlophone R 5675* **1**	8
4 Sep 68	★ **HEY JUDE** *Apple R 5722* **1**	16
23 Apr 69	★ **GET BACK** *Apple R 5777* 2 ....**1**	17
4 Jun 69	★ **BALLAD OF JOHN AND YOKO** *Apple R 5786* **1**	14
8 Nov 69	● **SOMETHING / COME TOGETHER** *Apple R 5814*..........**4**	12
14 Mar 70	● **LET IT BE** *Apple R 5833* **2**	9
24 Oct 70	**LET IT BE** (re-entry) *Apple R 5833* **43**	1
13 Mar 76	● **YESTERDAY** *Apple R 6013* **8**	7
27 Mar 76	**HEY JUDE** (re-entry) *Apple R 5722* **12**	7
27 Mar 76	**PAPERBACK WRITER** (re-entry) *Parlophone R 5452* **23**	5
3 Apr 76	**GET BACK** (re-entry) *Apple R 5777* 2 ......**28**	5
3 Apr 76	**STRAWBERRY FIELDS FOREVER** (re-entry) *Parlophone R 5570* **32**	3
10 Apr 76	**HELP!** (re-entry) *Parlophone R 5305* **37**	3
10 Jul 76	**BACK IN THE U.S.S.R.** *Parlophone R 6016* **19**	6
7 Oct 78	**SGT. PEPPER'S LONELY HEARTS CLUB BAND – WITH A LITTLE HELP FROM MY FRIENDS** *Parlophone R 6022* **63**	3
5 Jun 82	● **BEATLES MOVIE MEDLEY** *Parlophone R 6055* **10**	9
16 Oct 82	● **LOVE ME DO** (re-entry) *Parlophone R 4949* **4**	7
22 Jan 83	**PLEASE PLEASE ME** (re-entry) *Parlophone R 4983* **29**	4
23 Apr 83	**FROM ME TO YOU** (re-entry) *Parlophone R 5015* **40**	4
3 Sep 83	**SHE LOVES YOU** (2nd re-entry) *Parlophone R 5055* **45**	3
26 Nov 83	**I WANT TO HOLD YOUR HAND** (2nd re-entry) *Parlophone R 5084* **62**	2
31 Mar 84	**CAN'T BUY ME LOVE** (2nd re-entry) *Parlophone R 5114*..**53**	2
21 Jul 84	**A HARD DAY'S NIGHT** (re-entry) *Parlophone R 5160* **52**	2
8 Dec 84	**I FEEL FINE** (re-entry) *Parlophone R 5200* **65**	1
20 Apr 85	**TICKET TO RIDE** (re-entry) *Parlophone R 5265*..............**70**	2
30 Aug 86	**ELEANOR RIGBY / YELLOW SUBMARINE** (re-entry) *Parlophone R 5493* **63**	1
28 Feb 87	**PENNY LANE / STRAWBERRY FIELDS FOREVER** (2nd re-entry) *Parlophone R 5570* **65**	2
18 Jul 87	**ALL YOU NEED IS LOVE** (re-entry) *Parlophone R 5620* ..**47**	2
5 Dec 87	**HELLO GOODBYE** (re-entry) *Parlophone R 5655* **63**	1
26 Mar 88	**LADY MADONNA** (re-entry) *Parlophone R 5675* **67**	1
10 Sep 88	**HEY JUDE** (2nd re-entry) *Apple 5722* **52**	2
22 Apr 89	**GET BACK** (2nd re-entry) *Apple R 5777* 2 ......**74**	1
17 Oct 92	**LOVE ME DO** (2nd re-entry) *Parlophone R 4949* **53**	1
1 Apr 95	● **BABY IT'S YOU** *Apple CDR 6406* **7**	6

8 Jul 95	**BABY IT'S YOU** (re-entry) *Apple CDR 6406* **71**	1
16 Dec 95	● **FREE AS A BIRD** *Apple CDR 6422* **2**	8
16 Mar 96	● **REAL LOVE** *Apple CDR 6425* **4**	7

1 Tony Sheridan and the Beatles 2 Beatles with Billy Preston

Tracks on Magical Mystery Tour (EP): Magical Mystery Tour / Your Mother Should Know / I Am The Walrus / Fool On The Hill / Flying / Blue Jay Way.

BEATMASTERS UK, male / female instrumental group   **47 wks**

9 Jan 88	● **ROK DA HOUSE** *Rhythm King LEFT 11* 1 ....**5**	11
24 Sep 88	**BURN IT UP** *Rhythm King LEFT 27* 2 ....**14**	10
22 Apr 89	● **WHO'S IN THE HOUSE** *Rhythm King LEFT 31* 3 ....**8**	9
12 Aug 89	**HEY DJ I CAN'T DANCE TO THAT MUSIC YOU'RE PLAYING / SKA TRAIN** *Rhythm King LEFT 34* 4 ....**7**	11
2 Dec 89	**WARM LOVE** *Rhythm King LEFT 37* 5 ....**51**	2
21 Sep 91	**BOULEVARD OF BROKEN DREAMS** *Rhythm King 6573617* **62**	1
16 May 92	**DUNNO WHAT IT IS (ABOUT YOU)** *Rhythm King 6580017* 6 ....**43**	3

1 Beatmasters featuring the Cookie Crew 2 Beatmasters with P.P. Arnold
3 Beatmasters featuring Merlin 4 Beatmasters featuring Betty Boo
5 Beatmasters featuring Claudia Fontaine 6 Beatmasters featuring Elaine Vassell

BEATS INTERNATIONAL
UK, male / female vocal / instrumental group   **30 wks**

10 Feb 90	★ **DUB BE GOOD TO ME** *Go.Beat GOD 39* 1 ....**1**	13
12 May 90	● **WON'T TALK ABOUT IT** *Go.Beat GOD 43* **9**	7
15 Sep 90	**BURUNDI BLUES** *Go.Beat GOD 45* **51**	3
2 Mar 91	**ECHO CHAMBER** *Go.Beat GOD 51* **60**	2
21 Sep 91	**THE SUN DOESN'T SHINE** *Go.Beat GOD 59* **66**	2
23 Nov 91	**IN THE GHETTO** *Go.Beat GOD 64* **44**	3

1 Beats International featuring Lindy Layton

BEAUTIFUL PEOPLE
UK, male instrumental / sampling group   **1 wk**

28 May 94	**IF 60S WERE 90S** *Essential ESSX 2037* **74**	1

BEAUTIFUL SOUTH
UK, male / female vocal / instrumental group   **102 wks**

3 Jun 89	● **SONG FOR WHOEVER** *Go! Discs GOD 32* **2**	11
23 Sep 89	● **YOU KEEP IT ALL IN** *Go! Discs GOD 35* **8**	8
2 Dec 89	**I'LL SAIL THIS SHIP ALONE** *Go! Discs GOD 38* **31**	8
6 Oct 90	★ **A LITTLE TIME** *Go! Discs GOD 47* **1**	14
8 Dec 90	**MY BOOK** *Go! Discs GOD 48* **43**	6
16 Mar 91	**LET LOVE SPEAK UP ITSELF** *Go! Discs GOD 53* **51**	2
11 Jan 92	**OLD RED EYES IS BACK** *Go! Discs GOD 66* **22**	6
14 Mar 92	**WE ARE EACH OTHER** *Go! Discs GOD 71* **30**	3
13 Jun 92	**BELL BOTTOMED TEAR** *Go! Discs GOD 78* **16**	5
26 Sep 92	**36D** *Go! Discs GOD 88* **46**	2
12 Mar 94	**GOOD AS GOLD** *Go! Discs GODCD 110* **23**	5
4 Jun 94	**EVERYBODY'S TALKIN'** *Go! Discs GODCD 113* **12**	8
3 Sep 94	**PRETTIEST EYES** *Go! Discs GODCD 119* **37**	3
12 Nov 94	**ONE LAST LOVE SONG** *Go! Discs GODCD 122*..................**14**	5
18 Nov 95	**PRETENDERS TO THE THRONE** *Go! Discs GODCD 134* **18**	4
12 Oct 96	● **ROTTERDAM** *Go! Discs GODCD 155* **5**	9
14 Dec 96	● **DON'T MARRY HER** *Go! Discs GODCD 158* ....**8†**	3

BEAVIS and BUTT-HEAD – *See CHER*

Gilbert BECAUD France, male vocalist   **12 wks**

29 Mar 75	● **A LITTLE LOVE AND UNDERSTANDING** *Decca F 13537*..**10**	12

BECK US, male vocalist — 10 wks

5 Mar 94	LOSER Geffen GFSTD 67	15	6
29 Jun 96	WHERE IT'S AT Geffen GFSTD 22156	35	2
16 Nov 96	DEVIL'S HAIRCUT Geffen GFSTD 22183	22	2

Jeff BECK UK, male vocalist / instrumentalist – guitar — 57 wks

23 Mar 67	HI-HO SILVER LINING Columbia DB 8151	14	14
2 Aug 67	TALLYMAN Columbia DB 8227	30	3
28 Feb 68	LOVE IS BLUE Columbia DB 8359	23	7
9 Jul 69	GOO GOO BARABAJAGAL (LOVE IS HOT) Pye 7N 17778 [1]	12	9
4 Nov 72	HI-HO SILVER LINING (re-issue) RAK RR 3	17	11
5 May 73	I'VE BEEN DRINKING RAK RR 4 [2]	27	6
9 Oct 82	HI-HO SILVER LINING (re-entry of re-issue) RAK RR 3	62	4
7 Mar 92	PEOPLE GET READY Epic 6577567 [2]	49	3

[1] Donovan with the Jeff Beck Group [2] Jeff Beck and Rod Stewart

Robin BECK US, female vocalist — 13 wks

22 Oct 88	★ FIRST TIME Mercury MER 270	1	13

Peter BECKETT – See Barry GRAY ORCHESTRA

Shelton BECTON – See Frankie KNUCKLES

BEDAZZLED UK, male vocal / instrumental group — 1 wk

4 Jul 92	SUMMER SONG Columbia 6581627	73	1

BEDROCK featuring KYO
UK, male / female vocal / instrumental group — 3 wks

1 Jun 96	FOR WHAT YOU DREAM OF Stress CDSTR 23	25	3

BEDROCKS UK, male vocal / instrumental group — 7 wks

18 Dec 68	OB-LA-DI OB-LA-DA Columbia DB 8516	20	7

Celi BEE and the BUZZY BUNCH
US, male / female vocal / instrumental group — 1 wk

17 Jun 78	HOLD YOUR HORSES BABE TK TKR 6032	72	1

BEE GEES UK, male vocal / instrumental group — 322 wks

27 Apr 67	NEW YORK MINING DISASTER 1941 Polydor 56 161	12	10
12 Jul 67	TO LOVE SOMEBODY Polydor 56 178	50	1
26 Jul 67	TO LOVE SOMEBODY (re-entry) Polydor 56 178	41	4
20 Sep 67	★ MASSACHUSETTS Polydor 56 192	1	17
22 Nov 67	● WORLD Polydor 56 220	9	16
31 Jan 68	● WORDS Polydor 56 229	8	10
27 Mar 68	JUMBO/THE SINGER SANG HIS SONG Polydor 56 242	25	7
7 Aug 68	★ I'VE GOTTA GET A MESSAGE TO YOU Polydor 56 273	1	15
19 Feb 69	FIRST OF MAY Polydor 56 304	6	11
4 Jun 69	TOMORROW TOMORROW Polydor 56 331	23	8
16 Aug 69	● DON'T FORGET TO REMEMBER Polydor 56 343	2	15
28 Mar 70	I.O.I.O. Polydor 56 377	49	1
5 Dec 70	LONELY DAYS Polydor 2001 104	33	9
29 Jan 72	MY WORLD Polydor 2058 185	16	9
22 Jul 72	● RUN TO ME Polydor 2058 255	9	10
28 Jun 75	● JIVE TALKIN' RSO 2090 160	5	11
31 Jul 76	● YOU SHOULD BE DANCING RSO 2090 195	5	10
13 Nov 76	LOVE SO RIGHT RSO 2090 207	41	4
29 Oct 77	● HOW DEEP IS YOUR LOVE RSO 2090 259	3	15
4 Feb 78	● STAYIN' ALIVE RSO 2090 267	4	12
15 Apr 78	★ NIGHT FEVER RSO 002	1	20
13 May 78	STAYIN' ALIVE (re-entry) RSO 2090 267	63	6
25 Nov 78	● TOO MUCH HEAVEN RSO 25	3	13
17 Feb 79	★ TRAGEDY RSO 27	1	10
14 Apr 79	LOVE YOU INSIDE OUT RSO 31	13	9
5 Jan 80	SPIRITS (HAVING FLOWN) RSO 52	16	7
17 Sep 83	SOMEONE BELONGING TO SOMEONE RSO 96	49	4
26 Sep 87	★ YOU WIN AGAIN Warner Bros. W 8351	1	15
12 Dec 87	E.S.P. Warner Bros. W 8139	51	5
15 Apr 89	ORDINARY LIVES Warner Bros. W 7523	54	3
24 Jun 89	ONE Warner Bros. W 2916	71	1
2 Mar 91	● SECRET LOVE Warner Bros. W 0014	5	11
21 Aug 93	PAYING THE PRICE OF LOVE Polydor PZCD 284	23	5
27 Nov 93	● FOR WHOM THE BELL TOLLS Polydor PZCD 299	4	14
16 Apr 94	HOW TO FALL IN LOVE PART 1 Polydor PZDD 311	30	4

Act was UK / Australia up to and including Tomorrow Tomorrow.

B.E.F. – See Lalah HATHAWAY

BEGGAR and CO UK, male vocal / instrumental group — 15 wks

7 Feb 81	(SOMEBODY) HELP ME OUT Ensign ENY 201	15	10
12 Sep 81	MULE (CHANT NO. 2) RCA 130	37	5

BEGINNING OF THE END
US, male vocal / instrumental group — 6 wks

23 Feb 74	FUNKY NASSAU Atlantic K 10021	31	6

BEIJING SPRING UK, female vocal duo — 5 wks

23 Jan 93	I WANNA BE IN LOVE AGAIN MCA MCSTD 1709	43	3
8 May 93	SUMMERLANDS MCA MCSTD 1761	53	2

BEL CANTO UK, male vocal / instrumental group — 1 wk

14 Oct 95	WE'VE GOT TO WORK IT OUT Good Groove CDGG 2	65	1

Harry BELAFONTE US, male vocalist — 87 wks

1 Mar 57	● BANANA BOAT SONG HMV POP 308	2	18
14 Jun 57	● ISLAND IN THE SUN RCA 1007	3	25
6 Sep 57	SCARLET RIBBONS HMV POP 360	18	6
1 Nov 57	★ MARY'S BOY CHILD RCA 1022	1	12
22 Aug 58	LITTLE BERNADETTE RCA 1072	16	7
28 Nov 58	● MARY'S BOY CHILD (re-entry) RCA 1022	10	6
12 Dec 58	SON OF MARY RCA 1084	18	4
11 Dec 59	MARY'S BOY CHILD (2nd re-entry) RCA 1022	30	1
21 Sep 61	HOLE IN THE BUCKET RCA 1247 [1]	32	2
12 Oct 61	HOLE IN THE BUCKET (re-entry) RCA 1247 [1]	34	6

[1] Harry Belafonte and Odetta

Archie BELL and the DRELLS
US, male vocal / instrumental group — 33 wks

7 Oct 72	HERE I GO AGAIN Atlantic K 10210	11	10
27 Jan 73	THERE'S GONNA BE A SHOWDOWN Atlantic K 10263	36	5
8 May 76	SOUL CITY WALK Philadelphia International PIR 4250	13	10
11 Jun 77	EVERYBODY HAVE A GOOD TIME Philadelphia International PIR 5179	43	4
28 Jun 86	DON'T LET LOVE GET YOU DOWN Portrait A 7254	49	4

Freddie BELL and the BELLBOYS
US, male vocal / instrumental group — 10 wks

28 Sep 56	● GIDDY-UP-A-DING-DONG Mercury MT 122	4	10

Maggie BELL *UK, female vocalist* — 12 wks

15 Apr 78	HAZELL *Swansong SSK 19412*	37	3
13 May 78	HAZELL (re-entry) *Swansong SSK 19412*	74	1
17 Oct 81	HOLD ME *Swansong BAM 1* [1]	11	8

[1] B.A. Robertson and Maggie Bell

William BELL *US, male vocalist* — 22 wks

29 May 68	TRIBUTE TO A KING *Stax 601 038*	31	7
20 Nov 68	● PRIVATE NUMBER *Stax 101* [1]	8	14
26 Apr 86	HEADLINE NEWS *Absolute LUTE 1*	70	1

[1] Judy Clay and William Bell

BELL BIV DEVOE *US, male vocal group* — 29 wks

30 Jun 90	POISON *MCA MCA 1414*	19	11
22 Sep 90	DO ME *MCA MCA 1440*	56	3
15 Aug 92	● THE BEST THINGS IN LIFE ARE FREE *Perspective PERSS 7400* [1]	2	13
9 Oct 93	SOMETHING IN YOUR EYES *MCA MCSTD 1934*	60	2

[1] Luther Vandross and Janet Jackson with special guests BBD and Ralph Tresvant

BELL and JAMES *US, male vocal duo* — 3 wks

| 31 Mar 79 | LIVIN' IT UP (FRIDAY NIGHT) *A & M AMS 7424* | 68 | 1 |
| 14 Apr 79 | LIVIN' IT UP (FRIDAY NIGHT) (re-entry) *A & M AMS 7424* | 59 | 2 |

BELLAMY BROTHERS *US, male vocal duo* — 29 wks

17 Apr 76	● LET YOUR LOVE FLOW *Warner Bros. K 16690*	7	12
21 Aug 76	SATIN SHEETS *Warner Bros. K 16775*	43	3
11 Aug 79	● IF I SAID YOU HAVE A BEAUTIFUL BODY WOULD YOU HOLD IT AGAINST ME *Warner Bros. K 17405*	3	14

BELLBOYS – See Freddie BELL and the BELLBOYS

Regina BELLE *US, female vocalist* — 13 wks

| 21 Oct 89 | GOOD LOVIN' *CBS 655230* | 73 | 1 |
| 11 Dec 93 | A WHOLE NEW WORLD (ALADDIN'S THEME) *Columbia 6599002* [1] | 12 | 12 |

[1] Regina Belle and Peabo Bryson

BELLE and the DEVOTIONS
UK, female vocal group — 8 wks

| 21 Apr 84 | LOVE GAMES *CBS A 4332* | 11 | 8 |

La BELLE EPOQUE *France, female vocal duo* — 14 wks

| 27 Aug 77 | BLACK IS BLACK *Harvest HAR 5133* | 48 | 1 |
| 10 Sep 77 | ● BLACK IS BLACK (re-entry) *Harvest HAR 5133* | 2 | 13 |

BELLE STARS *UK, female vocal / instrumental group* — 42 wks

5 Jun 82	IKO IKO *Stiff BUY 150*	35	6
17 Jul 82	THE CLAPPING SONG *Stiff BUY 155*	11	9
16 Oct 82	MOCKINGBIRD *Stiff BUY 159*	51	3
15 Jan 83	● SIGN OF THE TIMES *Stiff BUY 167*	3	11
16 Apr 83	SWEET MEMORY *Stiff BUY 174*	22	9

| 13 Aug 83 | INDIAN SUMMER *Stiff BUY 185* | 52 | 3 |
| 14 Jul 84 | 80'S ROMANCE *Stiff BUY 200* | 71 | 1 |

BELLY *US, male / female vocal / instrumental group* — 9 wks

23 Jan 93	FEED THE TREE *4AD BAD 3001CD*	32	5
10 Apr 93	GEPETTO *4AD BAD 2018CD*	49	2
4 Feb 95	NOW THEY'LL SLEEP *4AD BAD 5003CD*	28	2
22 Jul 95	SEAL MY FATE *4AD BAD 5007CD*	35	2

BELMONTS – See DION

BELOVED *UK, male / female vocal / instrumental duo* — 45 wks

21 Oct 89	THE SUN RISING *WEA YZ 414*	26	7
27 Jan 90	HELLO *WEA YZ 426*	19	7
24 Mar 90	YOUR LOVE TAKES ME HIGHER *East West YZ 463*	39	3
9 Jun 90	TIME AFTER TIME *East West YZ 482*	46	4
10 Nov 90	IT'S ALRIGHT NOW *East West YZ 541*	48	3
23 Jan 93	● SWEET HARMONY *East West YZ 709CD*	8	10
10 Apr 93	YOU'VE GOT ME THINKING *East West YZ 738CD*	23	4
14 Aug 93	OUTERSPACE GIRL *East West YZ 726CD*	38	2
30 Mar 96	SATELLITE *East West EW 034CD*	19	3
10 Aug 96	EASE THE PRESSURE *East West EW 058CD*	43	2

Act were male only before '93.

BELTRAM *US, male producer – Joey Beltram* — 4 wks

| 28 Sep 91 | ENERGY FLASH (EP) *R&S RSUK 3* | 52 | 2 |
| 7 Dec 91 | THE OMEN *R&S RSUK 7* [1] | 53 | 2 |

[1] Program 2 Beltram

Tracks on Energy Flash (EP): Energy Flash / Psycho Bass / My Sound / Sub-Base Experience.

Pat BENATAR *US, female vocalist* — 53 wks

21 Jan 84	LOVE IS A BATTLEFIELD *Chrysalis CHS 2747*	49	5
12 Jan 85	WE BELONG *Chrysalis CHS 2821*	22	9
23 Mar 85	LOVE IS A BATTLEFIELD (re-issue) *Chrysalis PAT 1*	17	10
15 Jun 85	SHADOWS OF THE NIGHT *Chrysalis PAT 2*	50	4
19 Oct 85	INVINCIBLE (THEME FROM 'THE LEGEND OF BILLIE JEAN') *Chrysalis PAT 3*	53	3
15 Feb 86	SEX AS A WEAPON *Chrysalis PAT 4*	67	3
2 Jul 88	ALL FIRED UP *Chrysalis PAT 5*	19	10
1 Oct 88	DON'T WALK AWAY *Chrysalis PAT 6*	42	5
14 Jan 89	ONE LOVE *Chrysalis PAT 7*	59	3
30 Oct 93	SOMEBODY'S BABY *Chrysalis CDCHS 5001*	48	1

David BENDETH
Canada, male vocalist and multi-instrumentalist — 5 wks

| 8 Sep 79 | FEEL THE REAL *Sidewalk SID 113* | 44 | 5 |

BENELUX and Nancy DEE
Belgium / Holland / Luxembourg, female vocal group — 4 wks

| 25 Aug 79 | SWITCH *Scope SC 4* | 52 | 4 |

Nigel BENN – See PACK featuring Nigel BENN

Boyd BENNETT and his Rockets
US, male vocalist and male vocal / instrumental group — 2 wks

| 23 Dec 55 | SEVENTEEN *Parlophone R 4063* | 16 | 2 |

Chris BENNETT – See MUNICH MACHINE

34

Cliff BENNETT and the REBEL ROUSERS
UK, male vocal / instrumental group **23 wks**

1 Oct 64	● ONE WAY LOVE *Parlophone R 5173*	**9**	9
4 Feb 65	I'LL TAKE YOU HOME *Parlophone R 5229*	**42**	3
11 Aug 66	● GOT TO GET YOU INTO MY LIFE *Parlophone R 5489*	**6**	11

Peter E. BENNETT with the CO-OPERATION CHOIR *UK, male vocalist and choir* **1 wk**

7 Nov 70	THE SEAGULL'S NAME WAS NELSON *RCA 1991*	**45**	1

Tony BENNETT *US, male vocalist* **61 wks**

15 Apr 55	★ STRANGER IN PARADISE *Philips PB 420*	**1**	16
16 Sep 55	CLOSE YOUR EYES *Philips PB 445*	**18**	1
13 Apr 56	COME NEXT SPRING *Philips PB 537*	**29**	1
5 Jan 61	TILL *Philips PB 1079*	**35**	2
18 Jul 63	THE GOOD LIFE *CBS AAG 153*	**27**	13
6 May 65	IF I RULED THE WORLD *CBS 201735*	**40**	5
27 May 65	I LEFT MY HEART IN SAN FRANCISCO *CBS 201730*	**46**	2
30 Sep 65	I LEFT MY HEART IN SAN FRANCISCO (re-entry) *CBS 201730*	**40**	5
9 Dec 65	I LEFT MY HEART IN SAN FRANCISCO (2nd re-entry) *CBS 201730*	**25**	7
23 Dec 65	THE VERY THOUGHT OF YOU *CBS 202021*	**21**	9

Gary BENSON *UK, male vocalist* **8 wks**

9 Aug 75	DON'T THROW IT ALL AWAY *State STAT 10*	**20**	8

George BENSON
US, male vocalist / instrumentalist – guitar **140 wks**

25 Oct 75	SUPERSHIP *CTI CTSP 002* [1]	**30**	6
4 Jun 77	NATURE BOY *Warner Bros. K 16921*	**26**	6
24 Sep 77	THE GREATEST LOVE OF ALL *Arista 133*	**27**	7
31 Mar 79	LOVE BALLAD *Warner Bros. K 17333*	**29**	9
26 Jul 80	● GIVE ME THE NIGHT *Warner Bros. K 17673*	**7**	10
4 Oct 80	LOVE X LOVE *Warner Bros. K 17699*	**10**	8
7 Feb 81	WHAT'S ON YOUR MIND *Warner Bros. K 17748*	**45**	5
19 Sep 81	LOVE ALL THE HURT AWAY *Arista ARIST 428* [2]	**49**	3
14 Nov 81	TURN YOUR LOVE AROUND *Warner Bros. K 17877*	**29**	11
23 Jan 82	NEVER GIVE UP ON A GOOD THING *Warner Bros. K 17902*	**14**	10
21 May 83	LADY LOVE ME (ONE MORE TIME) *Warner Bros. W 9614*	**11**	10
16 Jul 83	FEEL LIKE MAKIN' LOVE *Warner Bros. W 9551*	**28**	7
24 Sep 83	● IN YOUR EYES *Warner Bros. W 9487*	**7**	10
17 Dec 83	INSIDE LOVE (SO PERSONAL) *WEA Int. W 9427*	**57**	5
19 Jan 85	20 / 20 *Warner Bros. W 9120*	**29**	9
20 Apr 85	BEYOND THE SEA (LA MER) *Warner Bros. W 9014*	**60**	3
16 Aug 86	KISSES IN THE MOONLIGHT *Warner Bros. W 8640*	**60**	4
29 Nov 86	SHIVER *Warner Bros. W 8523*	**19**	9
14 Feb 87	TEASER *Warner Bros. W 8437*	**45**	4
27 Aug 88	LET'S DO IT AGAIN *Warner Bros. W 7780*	**56**	3
5 Sep 92	I'LL KEEP YOUR DREAMS ALIVE *Ammi AMMI 101* [3]	**68**	1

[1] George 'Bad' Benson [2] Aretha Franklin and George Benson
[3] George Benson and Patti Austin

Brook BENTON *US, male vocalist* **18 wks**

10 Jul 59	ENDLESSLY *Mercury AMT 1043*	**28**	2
6 Oct 60	KIDDIO *Mercury AMT 1109*	**42**	3
3 Nov 60	KIDDIO (re-entry) *Mercury AMT 1109*	**41**	3

16 Feb 61	FOOLS RUSH IN *Mercury AMT 1121*	**50**	1
13 Jul 61	BOLL WEEVIL SONG *Mercury AMT 1148*	**30**	9

BENZ *UK, male rap / vocal group* **7 wks**

16 Dec 95	BOOM ROCK SOUL *Hacktown 74321329652*	**62**	2
16 Mar 96	URBAN CITY GIRL *Hacktown 74321348732*	**31**	3
25 May 96	MISS PARKER *Hacktown 74321377292*	**35**	2

Ingrid BERGMAN – *See Dooley WILSON*

BERLIN *US, male / female vocal / instrumental group* **39 wks**

25 Oct 86	★ TAKE MY BREATH AWAY (LOVE THEME FROM 'TOP GUN') *CBS A 7320*	**1**	15
17 Jan 87	YOU DON'T KNOW *Mercury MER 237*	**39**	6
14 Mar 87	LIKE FLAMES *Mercury MER 240*	**47**	3
20 Feb 88	TAKE MY BREATH AWAY (LOVE THEME FROM 'TOP GUN') (re-entry) *CBS A 7320*	**52**	3
13 Oct 90	● TAKE MY BREATH AWAY (re-issue) *CBS 656361 7*	**3**	12

Elmer BERNSTEIN *US, orchestra* **11 wks**

18 Dec 59	● STACCATO'S THEME *Capitol CL 15101*	**4**	10
10 Mar 60	STACCATO'S THEME (re-entry) *Capitol CL 15101*	**40**	1

Leonard BERNSTEIN, ORCHESTRA and CHORUS *US, male conductor, orchestra and chorus* **4 wks**

2 Jul 94	AMERICA – WORLD CUP THEME 1994 *Deutsche Grammophon USACD 1*	**44**	4

BERRI *UK, female vocalist* **22 wks**

26 Nov 94	THE SUNSHINE AFTER THE RAIN *Ffrreedom TABCD 223* [1]	**26**	6
2 Sep 95	● THE SUNSHINE AFTER THE RAIN (re-mix) *Ffrreedom TABCD 232*	**4**	11
2 Dec 95	SHINE LIKE A STAR *Ffrreedom TABCD 239*	**20**	5

[1] New Atlantic / U4EA featuring Berri

Chuck BERRY *US, male vocalist / instrumentalist – guitar* **91 wks**

21 Jun 57	SCHOOL DAY *Columbia DB 3951*	**24**	2
12 Jul 57	SCHOOL DAY (re-entry) *Columbia DB 3951*	**24**	2
25 Apr 58	SWEET LITTLE SIXTEEN *London HLM 8585*	**16**	5
11 Jul 63	GO GO GO *Pye International 7N 25209*	**38**	6
10 Oct 63	● LET IT ROCK / MEMPHIS TENNESSEE *Pye International 7N 25218*	**6**	13
19 Dec 63	RUN RUDOLPH RUN *Pye International 7N 25228*	**36**	6
13 Feb 64	NADINE (IS IT YOU) *Pye International 7N 25236*	**27**	6
2 Apr 64	NADINE (IS IT YOU) (re-entry) *Pye International 7N 25236*	**43**	1
7 May 64	● NO PARTICULAR PLACE TO GO *Pye International 7N 25242*	**3**	12
20 Aug 64	YOU NEVER CAN TELL *Pye International 7N 25257*	**23**	8
14 Jan 65	PROMISED LAND *Pye International 7N 25285*	**26**	6
28 Oct 72	★ MY DING-A-LING *Chess 6145 019*	**1**	17
3 Feb 73	REELIN' AND ROCKIN' *Chess 6145 020*	**18**	7

Dave BERRY *UK, male vocalist* **76 wks**

19 Sep 63	MEMPHIS TENNESSEE *Decca F 11734* [1]	**19**	13
9 Jan 64	MY BABY LEFT ME *Decca F 11803* [1]	**41**	1
23 Jan 64	MY BABY LEFT ME (re-entry) *Decca F 11803* [1]	**37**	8
30 Apr 64	BABY IT'S YOU *Decca F 11876*	**24**	6
6 Aug 64	● THE CRYING GAME *Decca F 11937*	**5**	12

26 Nov 64		ONE HEART BETWEEN TWO Decca F 12020	41	2
25 Mar 65	●	LITTLE THINGS Decca F 12103	5	12
22 Jul 65		THIS STRANGE EFFECT Decca F 12188	37	6
30 Jun 66	●	MAMA Decca F 12435	5	16

1 Dave Berry and the Cruisers

Mike BERRY UK, male vocalist — 51 wks

12 Oct 61		TRIBUTE TO BUDDY HOLLY HMV POP 912 1	24	6
3 Jan 63	●	DON'T YOU THINK IT'S TIME HMV POP 1105 1	6	12
11 Apr 63		MY LITTLE BABY HMV POP 1142 1	34	7
2 Aug 80	●	THE SUNSHINE OF YOUR SMILE Polydor 2059 261	9	12
29 Nov 80		IF I COULD ONLY MAKE YOU CARE Polydor POSP 202	37	9
5 Sep 81		MEMORIES Polydor POSP 287	55	5

1 Mike Berry with the Outlaws

Nick BERRY UK, male vocalist — 24 wks

4 Oct 86	★	EVERY LOSER WINS BBC RESL 204	1	11
27 Dec 86		EVERY LOSER WINS (re-entry) BBC RESL 204	72	2
13 Jun 92	●	HEARTBEAT Columbia 6581517	2	8
31 Oct 92		LONG LIVE LOVE Columbia 6587597	47	3

Adele BERTEI – See JELLYBEAN

BEST COMPANY UK, male vocal duo — 1 wk

| 27 Mar 93 | | DON'T YOU FORGET ABOUT ME ZYX ZYX 69468 | 65 | 1 |

BEST SHOT UK, male rap group — 2 wks

| 5 Feb 94 | | UNITED COLOURS East West YZ 795CD | 64 | 2 |

BEVERLEY SISTERS UK, female vocal group — 34 wks

27 Nov 53		I SAW MOMMY KISSING SANTA CLAUS Philips PB 188	11	1
11 Dec 53	●	I SAW MOMMY KISSING SANTA CLAUS (re-entry) Philips PB 188	6	4
13 Apr 56		WILLIE CAN Decca F 10705	23	4
1 Feb 57		I DREAMED Decca F 10832	24	2
13 Feb 59	●	LITTLE DRUMMER BOY Decca F 11107	6	13
20 Nov 59		LITTLE DONKEY Decca F 11172	14	7
23 Jun 60		GREEN FIELDS Columbia DB 4444	48	1
7 Jul 60		GREEN FIELDS (re-entry) Columbia DB 4444	29	2

See also Various Artists (EPs and LPs) - All Star Hit Parade No.2.

Frankie BEVERLY – See MAZE featuring Frankie BEVERLY

BEYOND UK, male vocal / instrumental group — 1 wk

| 21 Sep 91 | | RAGING EP Harvest HARS 530 | 68 | 1 |

Tracks on Raging EP: Great Indifference / Nail / Eve Of My Release.

B-52s US, male / female vocal / instrumental group — 60 wks

11 Aug 79		ROCK LOBSTER Island WIP 6506	37	5
9 Aug 80		GIVE ME BACK MY MAN Island WIP 6579	61	3
7 May 83		(SONG FOR A) FUTURE GENERATION Island IS 107	63	2
10 May 86		ROCK LOBSTER / PLANET CLAIRE (re-issue) Island BFT 1	12	7
3 Mar 90	●	LOVE SHACK Reprise W 9917	2	13
19 May 90		ROAM Reprise W 9827	17	7
18 Aug 90		CHANNEL Z Reprise W 9737	61	2
20 Jun 92		GOOD STUFF Reprise W 0109	21	6

| 12 Sep 92 | | TELL IT LIKE IT T-I-IS Reprise W 0130 | 61 | 3 |
| 9 Jul 94 | ● | (MEET) THE FLINTSTONES MCA MCSTD 1986 1 | 3 | 12 |

1 BC-52s

Planet Claire only listed from 17 May 86.

BG THE PRINCE OF RAP Germany, male rapper — 2 wks

| 18 Jan 92 | | TAKE CONTROL OF THE PARTY Columbia 6576330 | 71 | 2 |

BIBLE UK, male vocal / instrumental group — 8 wks

| 20 May 89 | | GRACELAND Chrysalis BIB 4 | 51 | 4 |
| 26 Aug 89 | | HONEY BE GOOD Ensign BIB 5 | 54 | 4 |

BIBLE OF DREAMS – See Johnny PANIC and the BIBLE OF DREAMS

BIDDU UK, orchestra — 13 wks

2 Aug 75		SUMMER OF '42 Epic EPC 3318	14	8
17 Apr 76		RAIN FOREST Epic EPC 4084	39	4
11 Feb 78		JOURNEY TO THE MOON Epic EPC 5910	41	1

BIG APPLE BAND – See Walter MURPHY and the BIG APPLE BAND

BIG AUDIO DYNAMITE UK / US, male vocal / instrumental group — 27 wks

22 Mar 86		E=MC² CBS A 6963	11	9
7 Jun 86		MEDICINE SHOW CBS A 7181	29	5
18 Oct 86		C'MON EVERY BEATBOX CBS 650147	51	5
21 Feb 87		V THIRTEEN CBS BAAD 2	49	5
28 May 88		JUST PLAY MUSIC CBS BAAD 4	51	3
12 Nov 94		LOOKING FOR A SONG Columbia 6610182 1	68	2

1 Big Audio

BIG BAD HORNS – See LITTLE ANGELS

BIG BAM BOO UK / Canada, male vocal / instrumental duo — 2 wks

| 28 Jan 89 | | SHOOTING FROM MY HEART MCA MCA 1281 | 61 | 2 |

BIG BEN BANJO BAND UK, instrumental group — 6 wks

10 Dec 54	●	LET'S GET TOGETHER NO. 1 Columbia DB 3549	6	4
9 Dec 55		LET'S GET TOGETHER AGAIN Columbia DB 3676	19	1
30 Dec 55		LET'S GET TOGETHER AGAIN (re-entry) Columbia DB 3676	18	1

These hits were both medleys as follows: Let's Get Together No.1: I'm Just Wild About Harry / April Showers / Rock-a-Bye Your Baby / Swanee / Darktown Strutters Ball / For Me And My Gal / Oh You Beautiful Doll / Yes Sir That's My Baby. Let's Get Together Again: I'm Looking Over A Four-Leafed Clover / By The Light Of The Silvery Moon / Oh Susannah / Baby Face / I'm Sitting On Top Of The World / My Mammy / Dixie's Land / Margie.

BIG BOPPER US, male vocalist — 8 wks

| 26 Dec 58 | | CHANTILLY LACE Mercury AMT 1002 | 30 | 1 |
| 9 Jan 59 | | CHANTILLY LACE (re-entry) Mercury AMT 1002 | 12 | 7 |

BIG COUNTRY UK, male vocal / instrumental group — 102 wks

| 26 Feb 83 | ● | FIELDS OF FIRE (400 MILES) Mercury COUNT 2 | 10 | 12 |
| 28 May 83 | | IN A BIG COUNTRY Mercury COUNT 3 | 17 | 7 |

3 Sep 83	●	**CHANCE** *Mercury COUNT 4*	**9**	9
21 Jan 84	●	**WONDERLAND** *Mercury COUNT 5*	**8**	8
29 Sep 84		**EAST OF EDEN** *Mercury MER 175*	**17**	6
1 Dec 84		**WHERE THE ROSE IS SOWN** *Mercury MER 185*	**29**	7
19 Jan 85		**JUST A SHADOW** *Mercury BCO 8*	**26**	4
12 Apr 86	●	**LOOK AWAY** *Mercury BIGC 1*	**7**	8
21 Jun 86		**THE TEACHER** *Mercury BIGC 2*	**28**	4
20 Sep 86		**ONE GREAT THING** *Mercury BIGC 3*	**19**	6
29 Nov 86		**HOLD THE HEART** *Mercury BIGC 4*	**55**	2
20 Aug 88		**KING OF EMOTION** *Mercury BIGC 5*	**16**	5
1 Oct 88		**KING OF EMOTION (re-entry)** *Mercury BIGC 5*	**74**	1
5 Nov 88		**BROKEN HEART (THIRTEEN VALLEYS)** *Mercury BIGC 6*	**47**	4
4 Feb 89		**PEACE IN OUR TIME** *Mercury BIGC 7*	**39**	3
12 May 90		**SAVE ME** *Mercury BIGC 8*	**41**	3
21 Jul 90		**HEART OF THE WORLD** *Mercury BIGC 9*	**50**	2
31 Aug 91		**REPUBLICAN PARTY REPTILE (EP)** *Vertigo BIC 1*	**37**	2
19 Oct 91		**BEAUTIFUL PEOPLE** *Vertigo BIC 2*	**72**	1
13 Mar 93		**ALONE** *Compulsion CDPULSS 4*	**24**	3
1 May 93		**SHIPS (WHERE WERE YOU)** *Compulsion CDPULSS 6*	**29**	3
10 Jun 95		**I'M NOT ASHAMED** *Transatlantic TRAX 1009*	**69**	1
9 Sep 95		**YOU DREAMER** *Transatlantic TRAD 1012*	**68**	1

Tracks on Republican Party Reptile (EP): Republican Party Reptile / Comes A Time / You And Me And The Truth.

BIG DADDY *US, male vocal / instrumental group*   **8 wks**

9 Mar 85	**DANCING IN THE DARK** *Making Waves SURF 1033*	**21**	8

BIG DADDY KANE *US, male vocalist*   **6 wks**

13 May 89	**RAP SUMMARY / WRATH OF KANE** *Cold Chillin' W 2973*	**52**	2
26 Aug 89	**SMOOTH OPERATOR** *Cold Chillin' W 2804*	**65**	1
13 Jan 90	**AIN'T NO STOPPIN' US NOW** *Cold Chillin' W 2635*	**44**	3

BIG DISH *UK, male vocal / instrumental group*   **5 wks**

12 Jan 91	**MISS AMERICA** *East West YZ 529*	**37**	5

BIG FAMILY – *See JT and the BIG FAMILY*

BIG FUN *UK, male vocal group*   **33 wks**

12 Aug 89	●	**BLAME IT ON THE BOOGIE** *Jive JIVE 217*	**4**	11
25 Nov 89	●	**CAN'T SHAKE THE FEELING** *Jive JIVE 234*	**8**	9
17 Mar 90		**HANDFUL OF PROMISES** *Jive JIVE 243*	**21**	6
23 Jun 90		**YOU'VE GOT A FRIEND** *Jive CHILD 90* [1]	**14**	6
4 Aug 90		**HEY THERE LONELY GIRL** *Jive JIVE 251*	**62**	1

[1] Big Fun and Sonia featuring Gary Barnacle

BIG MOUNTAIN
US, male / female vocal / instrumental group   **15 wks**

4 Jun 94	●	**BABY I LOVE YOUR WAY** *RCA 74321198062*	**2**	14
24 Sep 94		**SWEET SENSUAL LOVE** *Giant 74321234642*	**51**	1

BIG ROLL BAND – *See Zoot MONEY and the BIG ROLL BAND*

BIG SOUND – *See Simon DUPREE and the BIG SOUND*

BIG SOUND AUTHORITY
UK, male / female vocal / instrumental group   **12 wks**

19 Jan 85	**THIS HOUSE (IS WHERE YOUR LOVE STANDS)** *Source BSA 1*	**21**	9
8 Jun 85	**A BAD TOWN** *Source BSA 2*	**54**	3

BIG SUPREME *UK, male vocal group*   **5 wks**

20 Sep 86	**DON'T WALK** *Polydor POSP 809*	**58**	3
14 Mar 87	**PLEASE YOURSELF** *Polydor POSP 840*	**64**	2

BIG THREE *UK, vocal / instrumental group*   **17 wks**

11 Apr 63	**SOME OTHER GUY** *Decca F 11614*	**37**	7
11 Jul 63	**BY THE WAY** *Decca F 11689*	**22**	10

Barry BIGGS *Jamaica, male vocalist*   **46 wks**

28 Aug 76		**WORK ALL DAY** *Dynamic DYN 101*	**38**	5
4 Dec 76	●	**SIDESHOW** *Dynamic DYN 118*	**3**	16
23 Apr 77		**YOU'RE MY LIFE** *Dynamic DYN 127*	**36**	4
9 Jul 77		**THREE RING CIRCUS** *Dynamic DYN 128*	**22**	8
15 Dec 79		**WHAT'S YOUR SIGN GIRL** *Dynamic DYN 150*	**55**	7
20 Dec 81		**WIDE AWAKE IN A DREAM** *Dynamic DYN 10*	**44**	6

Ronald BIGGS – *See SEX PISTOLS*

Ivor BIGGUN *UK, male vocalist*   **15 wks**

2 Sep 78	**WINKER'S SONG (MISPRINT)** *Beggars Banquet BOP 1* [1]	**22**	12
12 Sep 81	**BRAS ON 45 (FAMILY VERSION)** *Dead Badger BOP 6* [2]	**50**	3

[1] Ivor Biggun and the Red Nosed Burglars [2] Ivor Biggun and the D Cups

BILBO *UK, male vocal / instrumental group*   **7 wks**

26 Aug 78	**SHE'S GONNA WIN** *Lightning LIG 548*	**42**	7

Mr. Acker BILK and his PARAMOUNT JAZZ BAND *UK, male jazz band leader, vocalist / instrumentalist – clarinet*   **171 wks**

22 Jan 60	●	**SUMMER SET** *Columbia DB 4382*	**5**	19
9 Jun 60		**GOODNIGHT SWEET PRINCE** *Melodisc MEL 1547*	**50**	1
18 Aug 60		**WHITE CLIFFS OF DOVER** *Columbia DB 4492*	**30**	9
8 Dec 60	●	**BUONA SERA** *Columbia DB 4544*	**7**	18
13 Jul 61		**THAT'S MY HOME** *Columbia DB 4673*	**7**	17
2 Nov 61		**STARS AND STRIPES FOREVER / CREOLE JAZZ** *Columbia SCD 2155*	**22**	10
30 Nov 61	●	**STRANGER ON THE SHORE** *Columbia DB 4750*	**2**	55
15 Mar 62		**FRANKIE AND JOHNNY** *Columbia DB 4795*	**42**	2
26 Jul 62		**GOTTA SEE BABY TONIGHT** *Columbia SCD 2176*	**24**	9
27 Sep 62		**LONELY** *Columbia DB 4897* [1]	**14**	11
24 Jan 63		**A TASTE OF HONEY** *Columbia DB 4949* [1]	**16**	9
21 Aug 76	●	**ARIA** *Pye 7N 45607* [2]	**5**	11

[1] Mr. Acker Bilk with the Leon Young String Chorale [2] Acker Bilk, his Clarinet and Strings

BILL *UK, male vocalist*   **1 wk**

23 Oct 93	**CAR BOOT SALE** *Mercury MINCD 1*	**73**	1

BILLIE – *See H20 featuring BILLIE*

BILLY – *See S EXPRESS*

BIMBO JET
France, male / female vocal / instrumental group   **10 wks**

26 Jul 75	**EL BIMBO** *EMI 2317*	**12**	10

Umberto BINDI *Italy, male vocalist*   **1 wk**

10 Nov 60	**IL NOSTRO CONCERTO** *Oriole CB 1577*	**47**	1

BIOHAZARD *US, male vocal / instrumental group*   **4 wks**

9 Jul 94	**TALES FROM THE HARD SIDE** *Warner Bros. W 0254CD*	**47**	2
20 Aug 94	**HOW IT IS** *Warner Bros. W 0259CD*	**62**	2

La BIONDA *Italy, male / female vocal group*   **4 wks**

7 Oct 78	**ONE FOR YOU ONE FOR ME** *Philips 6198 227*	**54**	4

BIOSPHERE
Norway, male instrumentalist – Ger Jenssen, keyboards   **2 wks**

29 Apr 95	**NOVELTY WAVES** *Apollo APOLLO 20CDX*	**51**	2

BIRDLAND *UK, male vocal / instrumental group*   **7 wks**

1 Apr 89	**HOLLOW HEART** *Lazy LAZY 13*	**70**	1
8 Jul 89	**PARADISE** *Lazy LAZY 14*	**70**	1
3 Feb 90	**SLEEP WITH ME** *Lazy LAZY 17*	**32**	3
22 Sep 90	**ROCK 'N' ROLL NIGGER** *Lazy LAZY 20*	**47**	1
2 Feb 91	**EVERYBODY NEEDS SOMEBODY** *Lazy LAZY 24*	**44**	1

BIRDS *UK, male vocal / instrumental group*   **1 wk**

27 May 65	**LEAVING HERE** *Decca F 12140*	**45**	1

Jane BIRKIN and Serge GAINSBOURG
UK / France, female / male vocal duo   **34 wks**

30 Jul 69	● **JE T'AIME... MOI NON PLUS** *Fontana TF 1042*	**2**	11
4 Oct 69	★ **JE T'AIME... MOI NON PLUS** (re-issue) *Major Minor MM 645*	**1**	14
7 Dec 74	**JE T'AIME... MOI NON PLUS** (2nd re-issue) *Antic K 11511*	**31**	9

BIS *UK, male / female vocal / instrumental group*   **4 wks**

30 Mar 96	**THE SECRET VAMPIRE SOUNDTRACK EP** *Chemikal Underground CHEM 003CD*	**25**	2
22 Jun 96	**BIS VS THE DIY CORPS EP** *Teen-C SKETCH 001CD*	**45**	1
9 Nov 96	**ATOM POWERED ACTION EP** *Wiiija WIJ 55CD*	**54**	1

Tracks on The Secret Vampire Soundtrack EP: Kandy Pop / Secret Vampires / Teen-C Power / Diska. Tracks on Bis vs The DIY Corps EP: This Is Fake DIY / Burn The Suit / Dance To The Disco Beat. Tracks on Atom Powered Action EP: Starbright Boy / Wee Love / Team Theme / Cliquesuck.

Elvin BISHOP *US, male instrumentalist – guitar*   **4 wks**

15 May 76	**FOOLED AROUND AND FELL IN LOVE** *Capricorn 2089 024*	**34**	4

Hit has vocal (uncredited) by Mickey Thomas.

BITI – See DEGREES OF MOTION featuring BITI

BIZARRE INC
UK, male / female vocal / instrumental group   **47 wks**

16 Mar 91	**PLAYING WITH KNIVES** *Vinyl Solution STORM 25R*	**43**	5
14 Sep 91	**SUCH A FEELING** *Vinyl Solution STORM 32S*	**13**	9

23 Nov 91	● **PLAYING WITH KNIVES** (re-issue) *Vinyl Solution STORM 38S*	**4**	8
3 Oct 92	● **I'M GONNA GET YOU** *Vinyl Solution STORM 46S* [1]	**3**	12
2 Jan 93	**I'M GONNA GET YOU** (re-entry) *Vinyl Solution STORM 46S* [1]	**72**	1
27 Feb 93	**TOOK MY LOVE** *Vinyl Solution STORM 60CD* [1]	**19**	5
23 Mar 96	**KEEP THE MUSIC STRONG** *Some Bizarre MERCD 451*	**33**	2
6 Jul 96	**SURPRISE** *Some Bizarre MERCD 462*	**21**	3
14 Sep 96	**GET UP SUNSHINE STREET** *Some Bizarre MERCD 471*	**45**	2

[1] Bizarre Inc featuring Angie Brown

BIZZ NIZZ
US / Belgium, male / female vocal / instrumental group   **11 wks**

31 Mar 90	● **DON'T MISS THE PARTYLINE** *Cooltempo COOL 203*	**7**	11

BJORK *Iceland, female vocalist*   **57 wks**

27 Apr 91	**OOOPS** *ZTT ZANG 19* [1]	**42**	3
19 Jun 93	**HUMAN BEHAVIOUR** *One Little Indian 112 TP7CD*	**36**	2
4 Sep 93	**VENUS AS A BOY** *One Little Indian 122 TP7CD*	**29**	4
23 Oct 93	**PLAY DEAD** *Island CID 573* [2]	**12**	6
4 Dec 93	**BIG TIME SENSUALITY** *One Little Indian 132 TP7CD*	**17**	8
19 Mar 94	**VIOLENTLY HAPPY** *One Little Indian 142 TP7CD*	**13**	4
6 May 95	● **ARMY OF ME** *One Little Indian 162 TP7CD*	**10**	5
26 Aug 95	**ISOBEL** *One Little Indian 172 TP7CD*	**23**	3
25 Nov 95	● **IT'S OH SO QUIET** *One Little Indian 182 TP7CD*	**4**	15
24 Feb 96	● **HYPERBALLAD** *One Little Indian 192 TP7CD*	**8**	4
9 Nov 96	**POSSIBLY MAYBE** *One Little Indian 193 TP7CD*	**13**	3

[1] 808 State featuring Bjork   [2] Bjork and David Arnold

BJORN AGAIN
Australia, male / female vocal / instrumental group   **8 wks**

24 Oct 92	**ERASURE-ISH (A LITTLE RESPECT / STOP!)** *M & G MAGS 32*	**25**	3
12 Dec 92	**SANTA CLAUS IS COMING TO TOWN** *M & G MAGS 35*	**55**	4
27 Nov 93	**FLASHDANCE... WHAT A FEELING** *M & G MAGCD 50*	**65**	1

BLACK *UK, male vocalist – Colin Vearncombe*   **35 wks**

27 Sep 86	**WONDERFUL LIFE** *Ugly Man JACK 71*	**72**	1
27 Jun 87	● **SWEETEST SMILE** *A & M AM 394*	**8**	10
22 Aug 87	● **WONDERFUL LIFE** *A & M AM 402*	**8**	9
16 Jan 88	**PARADISE** *A & M AM 422*	**38**	3
24 Sep 88	**THE BIG ONE** *A & M AM 468*	**54**	4
21 Jan 89	**NOW YOU'RE GONE** *A & M AM 491*	**66**	2
4 May 91	**FEEL LIKE CHANGE** *A & M AM 780*	**56**	2
15 Jun 91	**HERE IT COMES AGAIN** *A & M AM 753*	**70**	1
5 Mar 94	**WONDERFUL LIFE** (re-issue) *PolyGram TV 5805552*	**42**	3

Wonderful Life on A & M is a re-recording. It was re-issued on PolyGram TV in '94.

Cilla BLACK *UK, female vocalist*   **194 wks**

17 Oct 63	**LOVE OF THE LOVED** *Parlophone R 5065*	**35**	6
6 Feb 64	★ **ANYONE WHO HAD A HEART** *Parlophone R 5101*	**1**	17
7 May 64	★ **YOU'RE MY WORLD** *Parlophone R 5133*	**1**	17
6 Aug 64	● **IT'S FOR YOU** *Parlophone R 5162*	**7**	10
14 Jan 65	● **YOU'VE LOST THAT LOVIN' FEELIN'** *Parlophone R 5225*	**2**	9
22 Apr 65	**I'VE BEEN WRONG BEFORE** *Parlophone R 5269*	**17**	8
13 Jan 66	● **LOVE'S JUST A BROKEN HEART** *Parlophone R 5395*	**5**	11
31 Mar 66	● **ALFIE** *Parlophone R 5427*	**9**	12
9 Jun 66	● **DON'T ANSWER ME** *Parlophone R 5463*	**6**	10
20 Oct 66	● **A FOOL AM I** *Parlophone R 5515*	**13**	9

8 Jun 67	WHAT GOOD AM I *Parlophone R 5608*	24	7
29 Nov 67	I ONLY LIVE TO LOVE YOU *Parlophone R 5652*	26	11
13 Mar 68 ●	STEP INSIDE LOVE *Parlophone R 5674*	8	9
12 Jun 68	WHERE IS TOMORROW *Parlophone R 5706*	39	3
12 Feb 69 ●	SURROUND YOURSELF WITH SORROW *Parlophone R 5759*	3	12
9 Jul 69 ●	CONVERSATIONS *Parlophone R 5785*	7	12
13 Dec 69	IF I THOUGHT YOU'D EVER CHANGE YOUR MIND *Parlophone R 5820*	20	9
20 Nov 71 ●	SOMETHING TELLS ME (SOMETHING IS GONNA HAPPEN TONIGHT) *Parlophone R 5924*	3	14
2 Feb 74	BABY WE CAN'T GO WRONG *EMI 2107*	36	6
18 Sep 93	THROUGH THE YEARS *Columbia 6596982*	54	1
30 Oct 93	HEART AND SOUL *Columbia 6598562* 1	75	1

1 Cilla Black with Dusty Springfield

Frank BLACK *US, male vocalist*   4 wks

21 May 94	HEADACHE *4AD BAD 4007CD*	53	1
20 Jan 96	MEN IN BLACK *Dragnet 6627862*	37	2
27 Jul 96	I DON'T WANT TO HURT YOU (EVERY SINGLE TIME) *Dragnet 6634635*	63	1

Jeanne BLACK *US, female vocalist*   4 wks

23 Jun 60	HE'LL HAVE TO STAY *Capitol CL 15131*	41	4

BLACK BOX
Italy, male / female vocal / instrumental group   73 wks

12 Aug 89 ★	RIDE ON TIME *Deconstruction PB 43055*	1	22
17 Feb 90 ●	I DON'T KNOW ANYBODY ELSE *Deconstruction PB 43479*	4	8
2 Jun 90	EVERYBODY EVERYBODY *Deconstruction PB 43715*	16	5
3 Nov 90 ●	FANTASY *Deconstruction PB 43895*	5	11
15 Dec 90	THE TOTAL MIX *Deconstruction PB 44235*	12	8
6 Apr 91	STRIKE IT UP / RIDE ON TIME (re-mix) *Deconstruction PB 44459*	16	8
14 Dec 91	OPEN YOUR EYES *Deconstruction PB 45053*	48	4
14 Aug 93	ROCKIN' TO THE MUSIC *Deconstruction 74321158122*	39	2
24 Jun 95	NOT ANYONE *Mercury MERCD 434*	31	2
20 Apr 96	I GOT THE VIBRATION / A POSITIVE VIBRATION *Manifesto MERCD 459* 1	21	3

1 Blackbox

BLACK CROWES *US, male vocal / instrumental group*   27 wks

1 Sep 90	HARD TO HANDLE *Def American DEFA 6*	45	5
12 Jan 91	TWICE AS HARD *Def American DEFA 7*	47	3
22 Jun 91	JEALOUS AGAIN / SHE TALKS TO ANGELS *Def American DEFA 8*	70	1
24 Aug 91	HARD TO HANDLE (re-issue) *Def American DEFA 10*	39	4
26 Oct 91	SEEING THINGS *Def American DEFA 13*	72	1
2 May 92	REMEDY *Def American DEFA 16*	24	3
26 Sep 92	STING ME *Def American DEFA 21*	42	2
28 Nov 92	HOTEL ILLNESS *Def American DEFA 23*	47	3
11 Feb 95	HIGH HEAD BLUES / A CONSPIRACY *American 74321258492*	25	2
22 Jul 95	WISER TIME *American 74321298272*	34	2
27 Jul 96	ONE MIRROR TOO MANY *American 74321398572*	51	1

BLACK DIAMOND *US, male vocalist*   1 wk

17 Sep 94	LET ME BE *Systematic SYSCD 1*	56	1

BLACK DUCK *UK, male rapper*   5 wks

17 Dec 94	WHIGGLE IN LINE *Flying South CDDUCK 1*	33	5

BLACK GORILLA
UK, male / female vocal / instrumental group   6 wks

27 Aug 77	GIMME DAT BANANA *Response SR 502*	29	6

BLACK GRAPE *UK, male vocal / instrumental group*   21 wks

10 Jun 95 ●	REVEREND BLACK GRAPE *Radioactive RAXTD 16*	9	5
5 Aug 95 ●	IN THE NAME OF THE FATHER *Radioactive RAXTD 19*	8	4
2 Dec 95 ●	KELLY'S HEROES *Radioactive RAXTD 22*	17	5
25 May 96 ●	FAT NECK *Radioactive RAXTD 24*	10	3
29 Jun 96 ●	ENGLAND'S IRIE *Radioactive RAXTD 25* 1	6	4

1 Black Grape featuring Joe Strummer and Keith Allen

BLACK LACE *UK, male vocal / instrumental group*   82 wks

31 Mar 79	MARY ANN *EMI 2919*	42	4
24 Sep 83 ●	SUPERMAN (GIOCA JOUER) *Flair FLA 105*	9	18
30 Jun 84 ●	AGADOO *Flair FLA 107*	2	30
24 Nov 84 ●	DO THE CONGA *Flair FLA 108*	10	9
1 Jun 85	EL VINO COLLAPSO *Flair LACE 1*	42	5
7 Sep 85	I SPEAKA DA LINGO *Flair LACE 2*	49	4
7 Dec 85	HOKEY COKEY *Flair LACE 3*	31	6
20 Sep 86	WIG WAM BAM *Flair LACE 5*	63	3
26 Aug 89	I AM THE MUSIC MAN *Flair LACE 10*	52	3

BLACK MACHINE
France / Nigeria, male vocal / instrumental duo   5 wks

9 Apr 94	HOW GEE *London LONCD 348*	17	5

BLACK MAGIC *US, male producer – Lil' Louis*   2 wks

1 Jun 96	FREEDOM (MAKE IT FUNKY) *Positiva CDTIV 51*	41	2

See also Lil' Louis.

BLACK RIOT *US, male producer*   3 wks

3 Dec 88	WARLOCK / A DAY IN THE LIFE *Champion CHAMP 75*	68	3

A Day In The Life only listed from 17 Dec 88.

BLACK SABBATH
UK / US, male vocal / instrumental group   70 wks

29 Aug 70 ●	PARANOID *Vertigo 6059 010*	4	18
3 Jun 78	NEVER SAY DIE *Vertigo SAB 001*	21	8
14 Oct 78	HARD ROAD *Vertigo SAB 002*	33	4
5 Jul 80	NEON KNIGHTS *Vertigo SAB 3*	22	9
16 Aug 80	PARANOID (re-issue) *Nems BSS 101*	14	12
6 Dec 80	DIE YOUNG *Vertigo SAB 4*	41	7
7 Nov 81	MOB RULES *Vertigo SAB 5*	46	4
13 Feb 82	TURN UP THE NIGHT *Vertigo SAB 6*	37	5
15 Apr 89	HEADLESS CROSS *IRS EIRS 107*	62	1
13 Jun 92	TV CRIMES *IRS EIRSP 178*	33	2

Group UK only for first three hits and re-issue of Paranoid.

BLACK SHEEP *US, male rap duo*   1 wk

19 Nov 94	WITHOUT A DOUBT *Mercury MERCD 417*	60	1

BLACK SLATE
UK / Jamaica, male vocal / instrumental group **15 wks**

20 Sep 80	● **AMIGO** *Ensign ENY 42*	**9**	9
6 Dec 80	**BOOM BOOM** *Ensign ENY 47*	**51**	6

BLACK UHURU
Jamaica, male vocal / instrumental group **9 wks**

8 Sep 84	**WHAT IS LIFE?** *Island IS 150*	**56**	6
31 May 86	**THE GREAT TRAIN ROBBERY** *Real Authentic Sound RAS 7018*	**62**	3

Band of the BLACK WATCH *UK, military band* **22 wks**

30 Aug 75	● **SCOTCH ON THE ROCKS** *Spark SRL 1128*	**8**	14
13 Dec 75	**DANCE OF THE CUCKOOS (THE LAUREL AND HARDY THEME)** *Spark SRL 1135*	**37**	8

Bill BLACK'S COMBO
US, male instrumentalist – bass **8 wks**

8 Sep 60	**WHITE SILVER SANDS** *London HLU 9090*	**50**	1
3 Nov 60	**DON'T BE CRUEL** *London HLU 9212*	**32**	7

Tony BLACKBURN *UK, male vocalist* **7 wks**

24 Jan 68	**SO MUCH LOVE** *MGM 1375*	**31**	4
26 Mar 69	**IT'S ONLY LOVE** *MGM 1467*	**42**	3

BLACKBYRDS *US, male vocal / instrumental group* **6 wks**

31 May 75	**WALKING IN RHYTHM** *Fantasy FTC 114*	**23**	6

BLACKFOOT *US, male vocal / instrumental group* **5 wks**

6 Mar 82	**DRY COUNTY** *Atco K 11686*	**43**	4
18 Jun 83	**SEND ME AN ANGEL** *Atco B 9880*	**66**	1

J. BLACKFOOT *US, male vocalist* **4 wks**

17 Mar 84	**TAXI** *Allegiance ALES 2*	**48**	4

BLACKFOOT SUE *UK, male vocal / instrumental group* **15 wks**

12 Aug 72	● **STANDING IN THE ROAD** *Jam 13*	**4**	10
16 Dec 72	**SING DON'T SPEAK** *Jam 29*	**36**	5

BLACKGIRL *US, female vocal group* **3 wks**

16 Jul 94	**90S GIRL** *RCA 74321217882*	**23**	3

BLACKHEARTS – See Joan JETT and the BLACKHEARTS

Honor BLACKMAN – See Patrick MACNEE and Honor BLACKMAN

BLACKSTREET *US, male vocal group* **15 wks**

19 Jun 93	**BABY BE MINE** *MCA MCSTD 1772* [1]	**37**	3
13 Aug 94	**BOOTI CALL** *Interscope A 8250CD*	**56**	1
11 Feb 95	**U BLOW MY MIND** *Interscope A 8222CD*	**39**	2
27 May 95	**JOY** *Interscope A 8195CD*	**56**	2
19 Oct 96	● **NO DIGGITY** *Interscope IND 95003* [2]	**9**	7

[1] Blackstreet featuring Teddy Riley [2] Blackstreet featuring Dr. Dre

BLACKWELLS *US, male vocal group* **2 wks**

18 May 61	**LOVE OR MONEY** *London HLW 9334*	**46**	2

BLAGGERS I.T.A. *UK, male vocal / instrumental group* **7 wks**

12 Jun 93	**STRESSS** *Parlophone CDITA 1*	**56**	2
9 Oct 93	**OXYGEN** *Parlophone CDITA 2*	**51**	2
8 Jan 94	**ABANDON SHIP** *Parlophone CDITA 3*	**48**	3

BLAHZAY BLAHZAY *US, male rap duo* **1 wk**

2 Mar 96	**DANGER** *Mercury Black Vinyl MBVCD 2*	**56**	1

Vivian BLAINE *US, female vocalist* **1 wk**

10 Jul 53	**BUSHEL AND A PECK** *Brunswick 05100*	**12**	1

BLAIR – See Terry HALL

BLAIR *UK, male vocalist* **5 wks**

2 Sep 95	**HAVE FUN GO MAD** *Mercury MERCD 443*	**37**	3
6 Jan 96	**LIFE** *Mercury MERCD 447*	**44**	2

Peter BLAKE *UK, male vocalist* **4 wks**

8 Oct 77	**LIPSMACKIN' ROCK 'N' ROLLIN'** *Pepper UP 36295*	**40**	4

BLAME *UK, male instrumental / production duo* **2 wks**

11 Apr 92	**MUSIC TAKES YOU** *Moving Shadow SHADOW 11*	**48**	2

BLAMELESS *UK, male vocal / instrumental group* **5 wks**

4 Nov 95	**TOWN CLOWNS** *China WOKCD 2046*	**56**	1
23 Mar 96	**BREATHE (A LITTLE DEEPER)** *China WOKCD 2070*	**27**	3
1 Jun 96	**SIGNS...** *China WOKCD 2077*	**49**	1

BLANCMANGE *UK, male vocal / instrumental group* **71 wks**

17 Apr 82	**GOD'S KITCHEN / I'VE SEEN THE WORD** *London BLANC 1*	**65**	2
31 Jul 82	**FEEL ME** *London BLANC 2*	**46**	5
30 Oct 82	● **LIVING ON THE CEILING** *London BLANC 3*	**7**	14
19 Feb 83	**WAVES** *London BLANC 4*	**19**	9
7 May 83	● **BLIND VISION** *London BLANC 5*	**10**	8
26 Nov 83	**THAT'S LOVE, THAT IT IS** *London BLANC 6*	**33**	8
14 Apr 84	● **DON'T TELL ME** *London BLANC 7*	**8**	10
21 Jul 84	**THE DAY BEFORE YOU CAME** *London BLANC 8*	**22**	8
7 Sep 85	**WHAT'S YOUR PROBLEM?** *London BLANC 9*	**40**	5
10 May 86	**I CAN SEE IT** *London BLANC 11*	**71**	2

Billy BLAND *US, male vocalist* **10 wks**

19 May 60	**LET THE LITTLE GIRL DANCE** *London HL 9096*	**15**	10

BLAST featuring VDC
Italy, male / female vocal / instrumental group **5 wks**

18 Jun 94	**CRAYZY MAN** *UMM MCSTD 1982*	**22**	3
12 Nov 94	**PRINCES OF THE NIGHT** *UMM MCSTD 2011*	**40**	2

BLESSID UNION OF SOULS
US, male vocal / instrumental group **6 wks**

27 May 95	I BELIEVE *EMI CDEM 374*	**29**	5
23 Mar 96	LET ME BE THE ONE *EMI CDEM 387*	**74**	1

BLESSING *UK, male vocal / instrumental group* **13 wks**

11 May 91	HIGHWAY 5 *MCA MCS 1509*	**42**	6
18 Jan 92	HIGHWAY 5 (re-mix) *MCA MCS 1603*	**30**	6
19 Feb 94	SOUL LOVE *MCA MCSTD 1940*	**73**	1

Mary J BLIGE *US, female vocalist* **40 wks**

28 Nov 92	REAL LOVE *Uptown MCS 1721*	**68**	2
27 Feb 93	REMINISCE *Uptown MCSTD 1731*	**31**	4
12 Jun 93	YOU REMIND ME *Uptown MCSTD 1770*	**48**	3
28 Aug 93	REAL LOVE (re-mix) *Uptown MCSTD 1922*	**26**	4
4 Dec 93	YOU DON'T HAVE TO WORRY *Uptown MCSTD 1948*	**36**	2
14 May 94	MY LOVE *Uptown MCSTD 1972*	**29**	4
10 Dec 94	BE HAPPY *Uptown MCSTD 2033*	**30**	4
15 Apr 95	I'M GOIN' DOWN *Uptown MCSTD 2053*	**12**	4
29 Jul 95	● I'LL BE THERE FOR YOU-YOU'RE ALL I NEED TO GET BY *Def Jam DEFDX 11* [1]	**10**	5
30 Sep 95	MARY JANE (ALL NIGHT LONG) *Uptown MCSTD 2088*	**17**	4
16 Dec 95	(YOU MAKE ME FEEL LIKE A) NATURAL WOMAN *Uptown MCSTD 2108*	**23**	3
30 Mar 96	NOT GON' CRY *Arista 74321358252*	**39**	2

[1] Method Man featuring Mary J Blige

BLIND MELON *US, male vocal / instrumental group* **13 wks**

12 Jun 93	TONES OF HOME *Capitol CDCL 687*	**62**	2
11 Dec 93	NO RAIN *Capitol CDCL 699*	**17**	6
9 Jul 94	CHANGE *Capitol CDCL 717*	**35**	3
5 Aug 95	GALAXIE *Capitol CDCLS 755*	**37**	2

BLINK *Ireland, male vocal / instrumental group* **1 wk**

16 Jul 94	HAPPY DAY *Lime CDR 6385*	**57**	1

BLOCKHEADS – *See Ian DURY and the BLOCKHEADS*

BLONDIE
US / UK, female / male vocal / instrumental group **154 wks**

18 Feb 78	● DENIS *Chrysalis CHS 2204*	**2**	14
6 May 78	● (I'M ALWAYS TOUCHED BY YOUR) PRESENCE DEAR *Chrysalis CHS 2217*	**10**	9
26 Aug 78	PICTURE THIS *Chrysalis CHS 2242*	**12**	11
11 Nov 78	● HANGING ON THE TELEPHONE *Chrysalis CHS 2266*	**5**	12
27 Jan 79	★ HEART OF GLASS *Chrysalis CHS 2275*	**1**	12
19 May 79	★ SUNDAY GIRL *Chrysalis CHS 2320*	**1**	13
29 Sep 79	● DREAMING *Chrysalis CHS 2350*	**2**	8
24 Nov 79	UNION CITY BLUE *Chrysalis CHS 2400*	**13**	10
23 Feb 80	★ ATOMIC *Chrysalis CHS 2410*	**1**	9
12 Apr 80	★ CALL ME *Chrysalis CHS 2414*	**1**	9
8 Nov 80	★ THE TIDE IS HIGH *Chrysalis CHS 2465*	**1**	12
24 Jan 81	● RAPTURE *Chrysalis CHS 2485*	**5**	8
8 May 82	ISLAND OF LOST SOULS *Chrysalis CHS 2608*	**11**	9
24 Jul 82	WAR CHILD *Chrysalis CHS 2624*	**39**	4
3 Dec 88	DENIS (re-mix) *Chrysalis CHS 3328*	**50**	3
11 Feb 89	CALL ME (re-mix) *Chrysalis CHS 3342*	**61**	2
10 Sep 94	ATOMIC (re-mix) *Chrysalis CDCHS 5013*	**19**	4
8 Jul 95	HEART OF GLASS (re-mix) *Chrysalis CSCHS 5023*	**15**	3
28 Oct 95	UNION CITY BLUE (re-mix) *Chrysalis CDCHS 5027*	**31**	2

BLOOD SWEAT AND TEARS
US / Canada, male vocal / instrumental group **6 wks**

30 Apr 69	YOU'VE MADE ME SO VERY HAPPY *CBS 4116*	**35**	6

BLOODSTONE *US, male vocal / instrumental group* **4 wks**

18 Aug 73	NATURAL HIGH *Decca F 13382*	**40**	4

Bobby BLOOM *US, male vocalist* **24 wks**

29 Aug 70	● MONTEGO BAY *Polydor 2058 051*	**3**	14
12 Dec 70	MONTEGO BAY (re-entry) *Polydor 2058 051*	**42**	3
9 Jan 71	HEAVY MAKES YOU HAPPY *Polydor 2001 122*	**31**	5
9 Jan 71	MONTEGO BAY (2nd re-entry) *Polydor 2058 051*	**47**	2

BLOOMSBURY SET *UK, male vocal / instrumental group* **3 wks**

25 Jun 83	HANGING AROUND WITH THE BIG BOYS *Stiletto STL 13*	**56**	3

Tanya BLOUNT *US, female vocalist* **1 wk**

11 Jun 94	I'M GONNA MAKE YOU MINE *Polydor PZCD 315*	**69**	1

Kurtis BLOW *US, male vocalist* **23 wks**

15 Dec 79	CHRISTMAS RAPPIN' *Mercury BLOW 7*	**30**	6
11 Oct 80	THE BREAKS *Mercury BLOW 8*	**47**	4
16 Mar 85	PARTY TIME (THE GO-GO EDIT) *Club JAB 12*	**67**	1
15 Jun 85	SAVE YOUR LOVE (FOR NUMBER 1) *Club JAB 14* [1]	**66**	2
18 Jan 86	IF I RULED THE WORLD *Club JAB 26*	**24**	8
8 Nov 86	I'M CHILLIN' *Club JAB 42*	**64**	2

[1] René and Angela featuring Kurtis Blow

BLOW MONKEYS *UK, male vocal / instrumental group* **46 wks**

1 Mar 86	DIGGING YOUR SCENE *RCA PB 40599*	**12**	10
17 May 86	WICKED WAYS *RCA MONK 2*	**60**	2
31 Jan 87	● IT DOESN'T HAVE TO BE THIS WAY *RCA MONK 4*	**5**	8
28 Mar 87	OUT WITH HER *RCA MONK 5*	**30**	6
30 May 87	(CELEBRATE) THE DAY AFTER YOU *RCA MONK 6* [1]	**52**	2
15 Aug 87	SOME KIND OF WONDERFUL *RCA MONK 7*	**67**	1
6 Aug 88	THIS IS YOUR LIFE *RCA PB 42149*	**70**	2
8 Apr 89	THIS IS YOUR LIFE (re-mix) *RCA PB 42695*	**32**	5
15 Jul 89	CHOICE? *RCA PB 42885* [2]	**22**	6
14 Oct 89	SLAVES NO MORE *RCA PB 43201* [2]	**73**	2
26 May 90	SPRINGTIME FOR THE WORLD *RCA PB 43623*	**69**	2

[1] Blow Monkeys with Curtis Mayfield [2] Blow Monkeys featuring Sylvia Tella

BLUE *UK, male vocal / instrumental group* **8 wks**

30 Apr 77	GONNA CAPTURE YOUR HEART *Rocket ROKN 522*	**18**	8

Babbity BLUE *UK, female vocalist* **2 wks**

11 Feb 65	DON'T MAKE ME (FALL IN LOVE WITH YOU) *Decca F 12053*	**48**	2

Barry BLUE *UK, male vocalist* **48 wks**

28 Jul 73	● (DANCING) ON A SATURDAY NIGHT *Bell 1295*	**2**	15
3 Nov 73	● DO YOU WANNA DANCE *Bell 1336*	**7**	12

2 Mar 74	**SCHOOL LOVE** Bell 1345.................................**11** 9
3 Aug 74	**MISS HIT AND RUN** Bell 1364 ....**26** 7
26 Oct 74	**HOT SHOT** Bell 1379 ....**23** 5

See also Cry Sisco!

BLUE AEROPLANES
UK, male / female vocal / instrumental group **3 wks**

| 17 Feb 90 | **JACKET HANGS** Ensign ENY 628 ....**72** 1 |
| 26 May 90 | **...AND STONES** Ensign ENY 632 ....**63** 2 |

BLUE BAMBOO
Belgium, male producer – Johan Gielen **4 wks**

| 3 Dec 94 | **ABC AND D...** Escapade CDJAPE 6 ....**23** 4 |

BLUE FEATHER
Holland, male vocal / instrumental group **4 wks**

| 3 Jul 82 | **LET'S FUNK TONIGHT** Mercury MER 109 ....**50** 4 |

BLUE FLAMES – *See Georgie FAME*

BLUE GRASS BOYS – *See Johnny DUNCAN and the BLUE GRASS BOYS*

BLUE HAZE *UK, male vocal / instrumental group* **6 wks**

| 18 Mar 72 | **SMOKE GETS IN YOUR EYES** A & M AMS 891 ....**32** 6 |

BLUE JEANS – *See Bob B. SOXX and the BLUE JEANS*

BLUE MELONS
UK, male / female vocal / instrumental group **1 wk**

| 8 Jun 96 | **DO WAH DIDDY DIDDY** Fundamental FUNDCD 1 ....**70** 1 |

BLUE MERCEDES *UK, male vocal / instrumental duo* **18 wks**

10 Oct 87	**I WANT TO BE YOUR PROPERTY** MCA BONA 1 ....**23** 11
13 Feb 88	**SEE WANT MUST HAVE** MCA BONA 2 ....**57** 2
23 Jul 88	**LOVE IS THE GUN** MCA BONA 3 ....**46** 5

BLUE MINK
UK / US, male / female vocal / instrumental group **83 wks**

15 Nov 69	● **MELTING POT** Philips BF 1818 ....**3** 15
28 Mar 70	● **GOOD MORNING FREEDOM** Philips BF 1838 ....**10** 10
19 Sep 70	**OUR WORLD** Philips 6006 042 ....**17** 9
29 May 71	● **BANNER MAN** Regal Zonophone RZ 3034 ....**3** 14
11 Nov 72	**STAY WITH ME** Regal Zonophone RZ 3064...............**11** 13
17 Feb 73	**STAY WITH ME (re-entry)** Regal Zonophone RZ 3064 ....**43** 2
3 Mar 73	**BY THE DEVIL (I WAS TEMPTED)** EMI 2007 ....**26** 9
23 Jun 73	● **RANDY** EMI 2028 ....**9** 11

BLUE NILE *UK, male vocal / instrumental group* **4 wks**

30 Sep 89	**THE DOWNTOWN LIGHTS** Linn LKS 3...............**67** 1
29 Sep 90	**HEADLIGHTS ON THE PARADE** Linn LKS 4 ....**72** 1
19 Jan 91	**SATURDAY NIGHT** Linn LKS 5 ....**50** 2

BLUE OYSTER CULT
US, male vocal / instrumental group **14 wks**

| 20 May 78 | **(DON'T FEAR) THE REAPER** CBS 6333 ....**16** 14 |

BLUE PEARL
UK / US, male / female vocal / instrumental group **27 wks**

7 Jul 90	● **NAKED IN THE RAIN** Big Life BLR 23 ....**4** 13
3 Nov 90	**LITTLE BROTHER** Big Life BLR 32 ....**31** 5
11 Jan 92	**(CAN YOU) FEEL THE PASSION** Big Life BLR 67 ....**14** 6
25 Jul 92	**MOTHER DAWN** Big Life BLR 73 ....**50** 2
27 Nov 93	**FIRE OF LOVE** Logic 74321170292 [1] **71** 1

[1] Jungle High with Blue Pearl

See also Various Artists (EPs & LPs) - Gimme Shelter (EP).

BLUE RONDO A LA TURK
UK, male vocal / instrumental group **9 wks**

| 14 Nov 81 | **ME AND MR SANCHEZ** Virgin VS 463 ....**40** 4 |
| 13 Mar 82 | **KLACTOVEESEDSTEIN** Diable Noir VS 476...............**50** 5 |

BLUE ZOO *UK, male vocal / instrumental group* **17 wks**

12 Jun 82	**I'M YOUR MAN** Magnet MAG 224 ....**55** 3
16 Oct 82	**CRY BOY CRY** Magnet MAG 234 ....**13** 10
28 May 83	**I JUST CAN'T (FORGIVE AND FORGET)** Magnet MAG 241 ....**60** 4

BLUEBELLS *UK, male vocal / instrumental group* **49 wks**

12 Mar 83	**CATH** London LON 20 ....**62** 2
9 Jul 83	**SUGAR BRIDGE (IT WILL STAND)** London LON 27...............**72** 1
24 Mar 84	**I'M FALLING** London LON 45 ....**11** 12
23 Jun 84	● **YOUNG AT HEART** London LON 49 ....**8** 12
1 Sep 84	**CATH (re-issue)** London LON 54 ....**38** 7
9 Feb 85	**ALL I AM (IS LOVING YOU)** London LON 58 ....**58** 3
27 Mar 93	★ **YOUNG AT HEART (re-issue)** London LONCD 338 ....**1** 12

BLUENOTES – *See Harold MELVIN and the BLUENOTES*

BLUES BAND *UK, male vocal / instrumental group* **2 wks**

| 12 Jul 80 | **BLUES BAND EP** Arista BOOT 2...............**68** 2 |

Tracks on Blues Band EP: Maggie's Farm / Ain't it Tuff / Diddy Wah Diddy / Back Door Man.

BLUES BROTHERS *US, male vocal duo* **8 wks**

| 7 Apr 90 | **EVERYBODY NEEDS SOMEBODY TO LOVE** East West A7591 ....**12** 8 |

For the first two weeks, the flip side of Everybody Needs Somebody To Love *Think by Aretha Franklin, was listed.*

BLUETONES *UK, male vocal / instrumental group* **25 wks**

17 Jun 95	**ARE YOU BLUE OR ARE YOU BLIND** Superior Quality BLUE 001CD **31** 2
14 Oct 95	**BLUETONIC** Superior Quality BLUE 002CD **19** 3
3 Feb 96	● **SLIGHT RETURN** Superior Quality BLUE 003CD **2** 8
11 May 96	● **CUT SOME RUG / CASTLE ROCK** Superior Quality BLUE 005CD **7** 5
20 Jul 96	**CUT SOME RUG / CASTLE ROCK (re-entry)** Superior Quality BLUE 005CD **73** 1
28 Sep 96	● **MARBLEHEAD JOHNSON** Superior Quality BLUE 006CD ..**7** 6

Colin BLUNSTONE *UK, male vocalist* **29 wks**

| 12 Feb 72 | **SAY YOU DON'T MIND** Epic EPC 7765 ....**15** 9 |
| 11 Nov 72 | **I DON'T BELIEVE IN MIRACLES** Epic EPC 8434...............**31** 6 |

42

Bone Thugs-N-Harmony

Bizzy Bone, Wish Bone, Krayzie Bone, Flesh 'N' Bone and Layzie Bone were discovered by former NWA rapper, the late Eazy E.

Blur

In the much publicised head to head with Oasis in August 1995, Blur's 'Country House' outsold Oasis' 'Roll With It' by some 60,000 copies.

Boo Radleys

The Boo Radleys took their name from the elusive character in the novel *To Kill A Mockingbird* by Harper Lee.

17 Feb 73	**HOW COULD WE DARE TO BE WRONG**		
	Epic EPC 1197	**45**	2
14 Mar 81	**WHAT BECOMES OF THE BROKEN HEARTED**		
	Stiff BROKEN 1 [1]	**13**	10
29 May 82	**TRACKS OF MY TEARS** *PRT 7P 236*	**60**	2

[1] Dave Stewart – guest vocals: Colin Blunstone

See also Neil MacArthur.

BLUR *UK, male vocal / instrumental group*   **82 wks**

27 Oct 90	**SHE'S SO HIGH** *Food FOOD 26*	**48**	3
27 Apr 91 ●	**THERE'S NO OTHER WAY** *Food FOOD 29*	**8**	8
10 Aug 91	**BANG** *Food FOOD 31*	**24**	4
11 Apr 92	**POPSCENE** *Food FOOD 37*	**32**	2
1 May 93	**FOR TOMORROW** *Food CDFOODS 40*	**28**	4
10 Jul 93	**CHEMICAL WORLD** *Food CDFOODS 45*	**28**	4
16 Oct 93	**SUNDAY SUNDAY** *Food CDFOOD 46*	**26**	3
19 Mar 94 ●	**GIRLS AND BOYS** *Food CDFOODS 47*	**5**	7
11 Jun 94	**TO THE END** *Food CDFOODS 50*	**16**	5
3 Sep 94 ●	**PARKLIFE** *Food CDFOOD 53*	**10**	7
19 Nov 94	**END OF A CENTURY** *Food CDFOOD 56*	**19**	3
26 Aug 95 ★	**COUNTRY HOUSE** *Food CDFOODS 63*	**1**	11
9 Sep 95	**COUNTRY HOUSE** *Food FOODS 63*	**57**	1
25 Nov 95 ●	**THE UNIVERSAL** *Food CDFOODS 69*	**5**	9
24 Feb 96 ●	**STEREOTYPES** *Food CDFOOD 73*	**7**	5
11 May 96 ●	**CHARMLESS MAN** *Food CDFOOD 77*	**5**	6

Chart rules allow for a maximum of three formats; the seven inch of Country House, already available on 2 CDs and cassette, was therefore listed separately.

BMU *US / UK, male vocal group*   **2 wks**

18 Feb 95	**U WILL KNOW** *Mercury MERCD 420*	**23**	2

BOB and EARL *US, male vocal duo*   **13 wks**

12 Mar 69 ●	**HARLEM SHUFFLE** *Island WIP 6053*	**7**	13

BOB and MARCIA
Jamaica, male / female vocal duo   **25 wks**

14 Mar 70 ●	**YOUNG GIFTED AND BLACK**		
	Harry J HJ 6605	**5**	12
5 Jun 71	**PIED PIPER** *Trojan TR 7818*	**11**	13

BOBBYSOCKS *Norway / Sweden, female vocal duo*   **4 wks**

25 May 85	**LET IT SWING** *RCA PB 40127*	**44**	4

Karen BODDINGTON and Mark WILLIAMS
Australia, female / male vocal duo   **1 wk**

2 Sep 89	**HOME AND AWAY** *First Night SCORE 19*	**73**	1

BODY COUNT *US, male vocal / instrumental group*   **4 wks**

8 Oct 94	**BORN DEAD** *Rhyme Syndicate SYNDG 4*	**28**	2
17 Dec 94	**NECESSARY EVIL** *Virgin VSCDX 1529*	**45**	2

BODYSNATCHERS
UK, female vocal / instrumental group   **12 wks**

15 Mar 80	**LET'S DO ROCK STEADY** *2 Tone CHSTT 9*	**22**	9
19 Jul 80	**EASY LIFE** *2 Tone CHSTT 12*	**50**	3

Humphrey BOGART – *See Dooley WILSON*

Hamilton BOHANNON
US, male vocalist / instrumentalist – drums   **38 wks**

15 Feb 75	**SOUTH AFRICAN MAN** *Brunswick BR 16*	**22**	8
24 May 75 ●	**DISCO STOMP** *Brunswick BR 19*	**6**	12
5 Jul 75	**FOOT STOMPIN' MUSIC** *Brunswick BR 21*	**23**	6
6 Sep 75	**HAPPY FEELING** *Brunswick BR 24*	**49**	3
26 Aug 78	**LET'S START THE DANCE** *Mercury 6167 700*	**56**	4
13 Feb 82	**LET'S START TO DANCE AGAIN** *London HL 10582*	**49**	5

BOILING POINT *US, male vocal / instrumental group*   **6 wks**

27 May 78	**LET'S GET FUNKTIFIED** *Bang BANG 1312*	**41**	6

Marc BOLAN – *See T. REX*

CJ BOLLAND *UK, male producer*   **5 wks**

5 Oct 96	**SUGAR IS SWEETER** *Internal LIECD 35*	**11**	5

See also Ravesignal III.

Michael BOLTON *US, male vocalist*   **109 wks**

17 Feb 90 ●	**HOW AM I SUPPOSED TO LIVE WITHOUT YOU**		
	CBS 655397 7	**3**	10
28 Apr 90 ●	**HOW CAN WE BE LOVERS** *CBS 655918 7*	**10**	10
21 Jul 90	**WHEN I'M BACK ON MY FEET AGAIN**		
	CBS 656077 7	**44**	5
20 Apr 91	**LOVE IS A WONDERFUL THING** *Columbia 6567717*	**23**	8
27 Jul 91	**TIME LOVE AND TENDERNESS** *Columbia 6569897*	**28**	7
9 Nov 91 ●	**WHEN A MAN LOVES A WOMAN**		
	Columbia 6574887	**8**	9
8 Feb 92	**STEEL BARS** *Columbia 6577257*	**17**	6
9 May 92	**MISSING YOU NOW** *Columbia 6579917* [1]	**28**	4
31 Oct 92	**TO LOVE SOMEBODY** *Columbia 6584557*	**16**	6
26 Dec 92	**DRIFT AWAY** *Columbia 6588657*	**18**	5
13 Mar 93	**REACH OUT I'LL BE THERE** *Columbia 6588972*	**37**	4
13 Nov 93	**SAID I LOVED YOU BUT I LIED** *Columbia 6598762*	**15**	8
26 Feb 94	**SOUL OF MY SOUL** *Columbia 6601772*	**32**	3
14 May 94	**LEAN ON ME** *Columbia 6604132*	**14**	7
9 Sep 95 ●	**CAN I TOUCH YOU... THERE** *Columbia 6624385*	**6**	6
2 Dec 95	**A LOVE SO BEAUTIFUL** *Columbia 6627092*	**27**	5
16 Mar 96	**SOUL PROVIDER** *Columbia 6629812*	**35**	3

[1] Michael Bolton featuring Kenny G

BOMB THE BASS *UK, male producer – Tim Simenon*   **50 wks**

20 Feb 88 ●	**BEAT DIS** *Mister-ron DOOD 1*	**2**	9
27 Aug 88 ●	**MEGABLAST / DON'T MAKE ME WAIT**		
	Mister-ron DOOD 2 [1]	**6**	9
26 Nov 88 ●	**SAY A LITTLE PRAYER** *Rhythm King DOOD 3* [2]	**10**	10
27 Jul 91 ●	**WINTER IN JULY** *Rhythm King 6572757*	**7**	9
9 Nov 91	**THE AIR YOU BREATHE** *Rhythm King 6575387*	**52**	3
2 May 92	**KEEP GIVING ME LOVE** *Rhythm King 6579887*	**62**	2
1 Oct 94	**BUG POWDER DUST** *Stoned Heights BRCD 300* [3]	**24**	3
17 Dec 94	**DARKHEART** *Stoned Heights BRCD 305* [4]	**35**	3
1 Apr 95	**1 TO 1 RELIGION** *Stoned Heights BRCD 313* [5]	**53**	1
16 Sep 95	**SANDCASTLES** *Fourth & Broadway BRCD 324* [6]	**54**	1

[1] Bomb The Bass featuring Merlin and Antonia/Bomb The Bass featuring Lorraine [2] Bomb The Bass featuring Maureen [3] Bomb The Bass featuring Justin Warfield [4] Bomb The Bass featuring Spikey Tee [5] Bomb The Bass featuring Carlton [6] Bomb The Bass featuring Bernard Fowler

BOMBALURINA *UK, male / female vocal group*   **20 wks**

28 Jul 90 ★	**ITSY BITSY TEENY WEENY YELLOW POLKA DOT BIKINI**		
	Carpet CRPT 1	**1**	13

24 Nov 90	SEVEN LITTLE GIRLS SITTING IN THE BACKSEAT		
	Carpet CRPT 2 [1] 18		7

[1] Bombalurina featuring Timmy Mallett

BOMBERS
Canada, male / female vocal / instrumental group   **10 wks**

5 May 79	(EVERYBODY) GET DANCIN' *Flamingo FM 1* **37**	7
18 Aug 79	LET'S DANCE *Flamingo FM 4* **58**	3

BON JOVI *US, male vocal / instrumental group*   **177 wks**

31 Aug 85	HARDEST PART IS THE NIGHT *Vertigo VER 22* **68**	1
9 Aug 86	YOU GIVE LOVE A BAD NAME	
	Vertigo VER 26 ....**14**	10
25 Oct 86	● LIVIN' ON A PRAYER *Vertigo VER 28* **4**	15
11 Apr 87	WANTED DEAD OR ALIVE *Vertigo JOV 1* **13**	5
15 Aug 87	NEVER SAY GOODBYE *Vertigo JOV 2* **21**	5
24 Sep 88	BAD MEDICINE *Vertigo JOV 3* **17**	7
10 Dec 88	BORN TO BE MY BABY *Vertigo JOV 4* **22**	7
29 Apr 89	I'LL BE THERE FOR YOU *Vertigo JOV 5* **18**	7
26 Aug 89	LAY YOUR HANDS ON ME *Vertigo JOV 6* **18**	6
9 Dec 89	LIVING IN SIN *Vertigo JOV 7* **35**	6
24 Oct 92	● KEEP THE FAITH *Jambco JOV 8* **5**	6
23 Jan 93	BED OF ROSES *Jambco JOVCD 9* **13**	6
15 May 93	● IN THESE ARMS *Jambco JOVCD 10* **9**	7
7 Aug 93	I'LL SLEEP WHEN I'M DEAD *Jambco JOVCD 11* **17**	5
2 Oct 93	I BELIEVE *Jambco JOVCD 12* **11**	6
26 Mar 94	● DRY COUNTY *Jambco JOVCD 13* **9**	6
24 Sep 94	● ALWAYS *Jambco JOVCD 14* **2**	18
17 Dec 94	● PLEASE COME HOME FOR CHRISTMAS	
	Jambco JOVCD 16 ....**7**	6
25 Feb 95	● SOMEDAY I'LL BE SATURDAY NIGHT	
	Jambco JOVDD 15 ....**7**	7
4 Mar 95	PLEASE COME HOME FOR CHRISTMAS (re-entry)	
	Jambco JOVCD 16 ....**46**	4
10 Jun 95	● THIS AIN'T A LOVE SONG *Mercury JOVCD 17* **6**	9
30 Sep 95	● SOMETHING FOR THE PAIN *Mercury JOVCD 18* **8**	7
25 Nov 95	LIE TO ME *Mercury JOVCD 19* **10**	8
9 Mar 96	● THESE DAYS *Mercury JOVCD 20* **7**	6
6 Jul 96	HEY GOD *Mercury JOVCD 21* **13**	5

See also Jon Bon Jovi.

Jon BON JOVI *US, male vocalist*   **13 wks**

4 Aug 90	BLAZE OF GLORY *Vertigo JBJ 1* **13**	8
10 Nov 90	MIRACLE *Vertigo JBVJ 2* **29**	5

See also Bon Jovi.

Ronnie BOND *UK, male vocalist*   **5 wks**

31 May 80	IT'S WRITTEN ON YOUR BODY *Mercury MER 13* **52**	5

Gary 'U.S.' BONDS *US, male vocalist*   **39 wks**

19 Jan 61	NEW ORLEANS *Top Rank JAR 527* [1] **16**	11
20 Jul 61	● QUARTER TO THREE *Top Rank JAR 575* [1] **7**	13
30 May 81	THIS LITTLE GIRL *EMI America EA 122* **43**	6
22 Aug 81	JOLE BLON *EMI America EA 127* **51**	4
31 Oct 81	IT'S ONLY LOVE *EMI America EA 128* **43**	3
17 Jul 82	SOUL DEEP *EMI America EA 140* **59**	3

[1] U.S. Bonds

BONE *UK, male vocal / instrumental duo*   **1 wk**

2 Apr 94	WINGS OF LOVE *Deconstruction 74321176282* **55**	1

BONE THUGS-N-HARMONY *US, male rap group*   **17 wks**

4 Nov 95	1ST OF THA MONTH *Epic 6625172* **32**	2
10 Aug 96	● THA CROSSROADS *Epic 6635502* **8**	11
9 Nov 96	1ST OF THA MONTH (re-issue) *Epic 6638505* **15**	4

Elbow BONES and the RACKETEERS
US, male group leader and female backing group   **9 wks**

14 Jan 84	A NIGHT IN NEW YORK *EMI America EA 165* **33**	9

BONEY M
Jamaica / Antilles / Montserrat, male / female vocal group   **167 wks**

18 Dec 76	● DADDY COOL *Atlantic K 10827* **6**	13
12 Mar 77	● SUNNY *Atlantic K 10892* **3**	10
25 Jun 77	● MA BAKER *Atlantic K 10965* **2**	13
29 Oct 77	● BELFAST *Atlantic K 11020* **8**	13
29 Apr 78	★ RIVERS OF BABYLON / BROWN GIRL IN THE RING	
	Atlantic/Hansa K 11120 ....**1**	40
7 Oct 78	● RASPUTIN *Atlantic/Hansa K 11192* **2**	10
2 Dec 78	★ MARY'S BOY CHILD – OH MY LORD	
	Atlantic/Hansa K 11221 ....**1**	8
3 Mar 79	● PAINTER MAN *Atlantic/Hansa K 11255* **10**	6
28 Apr 79	● HOORAY HOORAY IT'S A HOLI-HOLIDAY	
	Atlantic/Hansa K 11279 ....**3**	9
11 Aug 79	GOTTA GO HOME / EL LUTE	
	Atlantic/Hansa K 11351 ....**12**	11
15 Dec 79	I'M BORN AGAIN *Atlantic/Hansa K 11410* **35**	7
26 Apr 80	MY FRIEND JACK *Atlantic/Hansa K 11463* **57**	5
14 Feb 81	CHILDREN OF PARADISE *Atlantic/Hansa K 11637* **66**	2
21 Nov 81	WE KILL THE WORLD (DON'T KILL THE WORLD)	
	Atlantic/Hansa K 11689 ....**39**	5
24 Dec 88	MEGAMIX / MARY'S BOY CHILD (re-mix)	
	Ariola 111947 ....**52**	3
5 Dec 92	● BONEY M MEGAMIX *Arista 74321125127* **7**	9
17 Apr 93	BROWN GIRL IN THE RING (re-mix)	
	Arista 74321137052 ....**38**	3

Brown Girl In The Ring only listed with Rivers of Babylon from 5 Aug 78, peaking at position 2. El Lute only listed with Gotta Go Home from 29 Sep 79. The megamixes are different.

Graham BONNET *UK, male vocalist*   **15 wks**

21 Mar 81	● NIGHT GAMES *Vertigo VER 1* **6**	11
13 Jun 81	LIAR *Vertigo VER 2* **51**	4

Graham BONNEY *UK, male vocalist*   **8 wks**

24 Mar 66	SUPERGIRL *Columbia DB 7843* **19**	8

BONO *Ireland, male vocalist*   **23 wks**

25 Jan 86	IN A LIFETIME *RCA PB 40535* [1] **20**	5
10 Jun 89	IN A LIFETIME (re-issue) *RCA PB 42873* [1] **17**	7
4 Dec 93	● I'VE GOT YOU UNDER MY SKIN *Island CID 578* [2] **4**	9
9 Apr 94	IN THE NAME OF THE FATHER *Island CID 593* [3] **46**	2

[1] Clannad featuring Bono [2] Frank Sinatra with Bono [3] Bono and Gavin Friday

I've Got You Under My Skin was the listed B-side of Stay (Faraway So Close) by U2 was listed. See also U2.

BONZO DOG DOO-DAH BAND
UK, male vocal / instrumental group   **14 wks**

6 Nov 68	● I'M THE URBAN SPACEMAN *Liberty LBF 15144* **5**	14

Betty BOO UK, female rapper | 55 wks

12 Aug 89	● HEY DJ I CAN'T DANCE TO THAT MUSIC YOU'RE PLAYING *Rhythm King LEFT 34* [1]	7	11
19 May 90	● DOIN' THE DO *Rhythm King LEFT 39*	7	12
11 Aug 90	● WHERE ARE YOU BABY *Rhythm King LEFT 43*	3	10
1 Dec 90	24 HOURS *Rhythm King LEFT 45*	25	8
8 Aug 92	LET ME TAKE YOU THERE *WEA YZ 677*	12	8
3 Oct 92	I'M ON MY WAY *WEA YZ 693*	44	3
10 Apr 93	HANGOVER *WEA YZ 719CD*	50	3

[1] Beatmasters featuring Betty Boo

BOO RADLEYS UK, male vocal / instrumental group | 25 wks

20 Jun 92	DOES THIS HURT / BOO! FOREVER *Creation CRE 128*	67	1
23 Oct 93	WISH I WAS SKINNY *Creation CRESCD 169*	75	1
12 Feb 94	BARNEY (...& ME) *Creation CRESCD 178*	48	2
11 Jun 94	LAZARUS *Creation CRESCD 187*	50	2
11 Mar 95	● WAKE UP BOO! *Creation CRESCD 191*	9	8
13 May 95	FIND THE ANSWER WITHIN *Creation CRESCD 202*	37	3
29 Jul 95	IT'S LULU *Creation CRESCD 211*	25	2
7 Oct 95	FROM THE BENCH AT BELVIDERE *Creation CRESCD 214*	24	2
17 Aug 96	WHAT'S IN THE BOX (SEE WATCHA GOT) *Creation CRESCD 220*	25	2
19 Oct 96	C'MON KIDS *Creation CRESCD 236*	18	2

BOO-YAA T.R.I.B.E. US, male rap group | 6 wks

| 30 Jun 90 | PSYKO FUNK *Fourth & Broadway BRW 179* | 43 | 3 |
| 6 Nov 93 | ANOTHER BODY MURDERED *Epic 6597942* [1] | 26 | 3 |

[1] Faith No More & Boo-Yaa T.R.I.B.E.

BOOGIE BOX HIGH UK, male vocal / instrumental duo | 11 wks

| 4 Jul 87 | ● JIVE TALKIN' *Hardback 7BOSS 4* | 7 | 11 |

BOOGIE DOWN PRODUCTIONS
US, male rap / scratch duo | 2 wks

| 4 Jun 88 | MY PHILOSOPHY / STOP THE VIOLENCE *Jive JIVEX 170* | 69 | 2 |

BOOKER T. and the M.G.'s
US, male instrumental group | 43 wks

11 Dec 68	SOUL LIMBO *Stax 102*	30	9
7 May 69	● TIME IS TIGHT *Stax 119*	4	18
30 Aug 69	SOUL CLAP '69 *Stax 127*	35	4
15 Dec 79	● GREEN ONIONS *Atlantic K 10109*	7	12

BOOM BOOM ROOM
UK, male vocal / instrumental group | 1 wk

| 8 Mar 86 | HERE COMES THE MAN *Fun After All FUN 101* | 74 | 1 |

BOOMTOWN RATS
Ireland, male vocal / instrumental group | 123 wks

27 Aug 77	LOOKING AFTER NO. 1 *Ensign ENY 4*	11	9
19 Nov 77	MARY OF THE 4TH FORM *Ensign ENY 9*	15	9
15 Apr 78	SHE'S SO MODERN *Ensign ENY 13*	12	11
17 Jun 78	● LIKE CLOCKWORK *Ensign ENY 14*	6	13
14 Oct 78	★ RAT TRAP *Ensign ENY 16*	1	15
21 Jul 79	★ I DON'T LIKE MONDAYS *Ensign ENY 30*	1	12
17 Nov 79	DIAMOND SMILES *Ensign ENY 33*	13	6
26 Jan 80	● SOMEONE'S LOOKING AT YOU *Ensign ENY 34*	4	9

22 Nov 80	● BANANA REPUBLIC *Ensign BONGO 1*	3	11
31 Jan 81	THE ELEPHANT'S GRAVEYARD (GUILTY) *Mercury BONGO 2*	26	6
12 Dec 81	NEVER IN A MILLION YEARS *Mercury MER 87*	62	4
20 Mar 82	HOUSE ON FIRE *Mercury MER 91*	24	8
18 Feb 84	TONIGHT *Mercury MER 154*	73	1
19 May 84	DRAG ME DOWN *Mercury MER 163*	50	3
2 Jul 94	I DON'T LIKE MONDAYS (re-issue) *Vertigo VERCD 87*	38	2

Daniel BOONE UK, male vocalist | 25 wks

14 Aug 71	DADDY DON'T YOU WALK SO FAST *Penny Farthing PEN 764*	17	15
1 Apr 72	BEAUTIFUL SUNDAY *Penny Farthing PEN 781*	48	1
15 Apr 72	BEAUTIFUL SUNDAY (re-entry) *Penny Farthing PEN 781*	21	9

Debby BOONE US, female vocalist | 2 wks

| 24 Dec 77 | YOU LIGHT UP MY LIFE *Warner Bros. K 17043* | 48 | 2 |

Pat BOONE US, male vocalist | 296 wks

18 Nov 55	● AIN'T THAT A SHAME *London HLD 8173*	7	9
27 Apr 56	★ I'LL BE HOME *London HLD 8253*	1	22
27 Jul 56	LONG TALL SALLY *London HLD 8291*	27	3
17 Aug 56	I ALMOST LOST MY MIND *London HLD 8303*	14	7
24 Aug 56	LONG TALL SALLY (re-entry) *London HLD 8291*	18	4
7 Dec 56	● FRIENDLY PERSUASION *London HLD 8346*	3	21
11 Jan 57	AIN'T THAT A SHAME (re-entry) *London HLD 8173*	22	2
11 Jan 57	I'LL BE HOME (re-entry) *London HLD 8253*	19	2
1 Feb 57	● DON'T FORBID ME *London HLD 8370*	2	16
26 Apr 57	WHY BABY WHY *London HLD 8404*	17	7
5 Jul 57	● LOVE LETTERS IN THE SAND *London HLD 8445*	2	21
27 Sep 57	● REMEMBER YOU'RE MINE / THERE'S A GOLDMINE IN THE SKY *London HLD 8479*	5	18
6 Dec 57	● APRIL LOVE *London HLD 8512*	7	23
13 Dec 57	WHITE CHRISTMAS *London HLD 8520*	29	1
4 Apr 58	● A WONDERFUL TIME UP THERE *London HLD 8574*	2	17
11 Apr 58	● IT'S TOO SOON TO KNOW *London HLD 8574*	7	12
27 Jun 58	● SUGAR MOON *London HLD 8640*	6	12
29 Aug 58	IF DREAMS CAME TRUE *London HLD 8675*	16	11
5 Dec 58	GEE BUT IT'S LONELY *London HLD 8739*	30	1
16 Jan 59	I'LL REMEMBER TONIGHT *London HLD 8775*	28	1
6 Feb 59	I'LL REMEMBER TONIGHT (re-entry) *London HLD 8775*	21	1
20 Feb 59	I'LL REMEMBER TONIGHT (2nd re-entry) *London HLD 8775*	18	7
10 Apr 59	WITH THE WIND AND THE RAIN IN YOUR HAIR *London HLD 8824*	21	3
22 May 59	FOR A PENNY *London HLD 8855*	28	3
26 Jun 59	FOR A PENNY (re-entry) *London HLD 8855*	19	6
31 Jul 59	'TWIXT TWELVE AND TWENTY *London HLD 8910*	18	6
18 Sep 59	'TWIXT TWELVE AND TWENTY (re-entry) *London HLD 8910*	26	2
23 Jun 60	WALKING THE FLOOR OVER YOU *London HLD 9138*	40	2
14 Jul 60	WALKING THE FLOOR OVER YOU (re-entry) *London HLD 9138*	46	2
4 Aug 60	WALKING THE FLOOR OVER YOU (2nd re-entry) *London HLD 9138*	39	2
6 Jul 61	MOODY RIVER *London HLD 9350*	18	10
7 Dec 61	● JOHNNY WILL *London HLD 9461*	4	13
15 Feb 62	I'LL SEE YOU IN MY DREAMS *London HLD 9504*	27	9
24 May 62	QUANDO QUANDO QUANDO *London HLD 9543*	41	4
12 Jul 62	● SPEEDY GONZALES *London HLD 9573*	2	19
15 Nov 62	THE MAIN ATTRACTION *London HLD 9620*	12	11

There's A Goldmine In The Sky was only listed for the week of 27 Sep 57. It peaked at position 23.

BOOOM – See Boris DLUGOSCH presents BOOOM

BOOT ROOM BOYZ – See LIVERPOOL FC

Duke BOOTEE – See GRANDMASTER FLASH, Melle MEL and the FURIOUS FIVE

BOOTH and the BAD ANGEL
UK / US, malevocal / instrumental duo   **3 wks**

22 Jun 96   **I BELIEVE** *Fontana BBCD 1* **25** 3

Ken BOOTHE *Jamaica, male vocalist*   **22 wks**

21 Sep 74 ★ **EVERYTHING I OWN** *Trojan TR 7920* **1** 12
14 Dec 74   **CRYING OVER YOU** *Trojan TR 7944* **11** 10

BOOTHILL FOOT-TAPPERS
UK, male / female vocal / instrumental group   **3 wks**

14 Jul 84   **GET YOUR FEET OUT OF MY SHOES**
             Go! Discs TAP 1 ....**64** 3

BOOTSY'S RUBBER BAND
US, male vocal / instrumental group   **3 wks**

8 Jul 78   **BOOTZILLA** *Warner Bros. K 17196* **43** 3

BOOTZILLA ORCHESTRA – *See Malcolm McLAREN*

BOSS *US, male producer – David Morales*   **1 wk**

27 Aug 94   **CONGO** *Cooltempo CDCOOL 296*....................**54** 1

See also David Morales and the Bad Yard Club.

BOSTON *US, male vocal / instrumental group*   **13 wks**

29 Jan 77   **MORE THAN A FEELING** *Epic EPC 4658* **22** 8
7 Oct 78   **DON'T LOOK BACK** *Epic EPC 6653* **43** 5

Eve BOSWELL *Hungary, female vocalist*   **13 wks**

30 Dec 55 ● **PICKIN' A CHICKEN** *Parlophone R 4082* **9** 7
2 Mar 56   **PICKIN' A CHICKEN (re-entry)** *Parlophone R 4082* **16** 3
6 Apr 56   **PICKIN' A CHICKEN (2nd re-entry)**
             Parlophone R 4082 ....**20** 3

La BOUCHE *US, male / female rap / vocal duo*   **12 wks**

24 Sep 94   **SWEET DREAMS** *Bell 74321223912*...................**63** 1
15 Jul 95   **BE MY LOVER** *Arista 74321265402* **27** 4
30 Sep 95   **FALLING IN LOVE** *Arista 74321305102* **43** 2
2 Mar 96   **BE MY LOVER (re-mix)** *Arista 74321339822* **25** 4
7 Sep 96   **SWEET DREAMS (re-issue)**
             Arista 74321398542 ....**44** 1

Judy BOUCHER *UK, female vocalist*   **23 wks**

4 Apr 87   ● **CAN'T BE WITH YOU TONIGHT** *Orbitone OR 721* **2** 14
4 Jul 87   **YOU CAUGHT MY EYE** *Orbitone OR 722* **18** 9

Peter BOUNCER – *See SHUT UP AND DANCE*

BOUNCING CZECKS
UK, male vocal / instrumental group   **1 wk**

29 Dec 84   **I'M A LITTLE CHRISTMAS CRACKER** *RCA 463* **72** 1

BOURGEOIS TAGG *US, male vocal / instrumental duo*   **6 wks**

6 Feb 88   **I DON'T MIND AT ALL** *Island IS 353* **35** 6

BOURGIE BOURGIE
UK, male vocal / instrumental group   **4 wks**

3 Mar 84   **BREAKING POINT** *MCA BOU 1* **48** 4

BOW WOW WOW
UK, female / male vocal / instrumental group   **54 wks**

26 Jul 80   **C30, C60, C90, GO** *EMI 5088* **34** 7
6 Dec 80   **YOUR CASSETTE PET** *EMI WOW 1* **58** 6
28 Mar 81   **W.O.R.K. (N.O. NAH NO NO MY DADDY DON'T)**
             EMI 5153 ....**62** 3
15 Aug 81   **PRINCE OF DARKNESS** *RCA 100* **58** 4
7 Nov 81   **CHIHUAHUA** *RCA 144* **51** 4
30 Jan 82 ● **GO WILD IN THE COUNTRY** *RCA 175* **7** 13
1 May 82   **SEE JUNGLE (JUNGLE BOY) / TV SAVAGE** *RCA 220*.......**45** 3
5 Jun 82   ● **I WANT CANDY** *RCA 238* **9** 8
31 Jul 82   **LOUIS QUATORZE** *RCA 263* **66** 2
12 Mar 83   **DO YOU WANNA HOLD ME** *RCA 314* **47** 4

*Your Cassette Pet listed as Louis Quatorze on 6 Dec 80 only. Tracks on Your Cassette Pet
(available only as a cassette) are: Louis Quatorze / Gold He Said / Umo-Sex-Al Apache /
I Want My Baby On Mars / Sexy Eiffel Towers / Giant Sized Baby Thing / Fools Rush In /
Radio G.String. RCA 263 is disc version of track on EMI WOW 1 Cassette.*

BOWA featuring MALA
US, male / female vocal / instrumental duo   **1 wk**

7 Dec 91   **DIFFERENT STORY** *Dead Dead Good GOOD 8*................**64**   1

David BOWIE *UK, male vocalist*   **426 wks**

6 Sep 69   **SPACE ODDITY** *Philips BF 1801* **48** 1
20 Sep 69 ● **SPACE ODDITY (re-entry)** *Philips BF 1801* **5** 13
24 Jun 72 ● **STARMAN** *RCA 2199* **10** 11
16 Sep 72   **JOHN I'M ONLY DANCING** *RCA 2263* **12** 10
9 Dec 72   ● **THE JEAN GENIE** *RCA 2302* **2** 13
14 Apr 73 ● **DRIVE-IN SATURDAY** *RCA 2352* **3** 10
30 Jun 73 ● **LIFE ON MARS** *RCA 2316* **3** 13
15 Sep 73 ● **THE LAUGHING GNOME** *Deram DM 123* **6** 12
20 Oct 73 ● **SORROW** *RCA 2424* **3** 15
23 Feb 74 ● **REBEL REBEL** *RCA LPBO 5009* **5** 7
20 Apr 74   **ROCK 'N' ROLL SUICIDE** *RCA LPBO 5021* **22** 7
22 Jun 74   **DIAMOND DOGS** *RCA APBO 0293* **21** 6
28 Sep 74 ● **KNOCK ON WOOD** *RCA 2466* **10** 6
1 Mar 75   **YOUNG AMERICANS** *RCA 2523* **18** 7
2 Aug 75   **FAME** *RCA 2579* **17** 8
11 Oct 75 ★ **SPACE ODDITY (re-issue)** *RCA 2593* **1** 10
29 Nov 75 ● **GOLDEN YEARS** *RCA 2640* **8** 10
22 May 76   **TVC 15** *RCA 2682* **33** 4
19 Feb 77 ● **SOUND AND VISION** *RCA PB 0905* **3** 11
15 Oct 77   **HEROES** *RCA PB 1121* **24** 8
21 Jan 78   **BEAUTY AND THE BEAST** *RCA PB 1190* **39** 3
2 Dec 78   **BREAKING GLASS (EP)** *RCA BOW 1* **54** 7
5 May 79   ● **BOYS KEEP SWINGING** *RCA BOW 2* **7** 10
21 Jul 79   **DJ** *RCA BOW 3*....................................**29** 5
15 Dec 79   **JOHN I'M ONLY DANCING (AGAIN) (1975) / JOHN
             I'M ONLY DANCING (1972)** *RCA BOW 4* **12** 8
1 Mar 80   **ALABAMA SONG** *RCA BOW 5*..........................**23** 5
16 Aug 80 ★ **ASHES TO ASHES** *RCA BOW 6*.........................**1** 10
1 Nov 80   ● **FASHION** *RCA BOW 7* **5** 12
10 Jan 81   **SCARY MONSTERS (AND SUPER CREEPS)** *RCA BOW 8* **20** 6
28 Mar 81   **UP THE HILL BACKWARDS** *RCA BOW 9* **32** 6
14 Nov 81 ★ **UNDER PRESSURE** *EMI 5250* [1] **1** 11
28 Nov 81   **WILD IS THE WIND** *RCA BOW 10* **24** 10
6 Mar 82   **BAAL'S HYMN (EP)** *RCA BOW 11* **29** 5
10 Apr 82   **CAT PEOPLE (PUTTING OUT FIRE)** *MCA 770* **26** 6
27 Nov 82 ● **PEACE ON EARTH – LITTLE DRUMMER BOY**
             RCA BOW 12 [2] **3** 8
26 Mar 83 ★ **LET'S DANCE** *EMI America EA 152* **1** 14
11 Jun 83 ● **CHINA GIRL** *EMI America EA 157* **2** 8
24 Sep 83 ● **MODERN LOVE** *EMI America EA 158* **2** 8

5 Nov 83		WHITE LIGHT, WHITE HEAT RCA 372	46	3
22 Sep 84	●	BLUE JEAN EMI America EA 181	6	8
8 Dec 84		TONIGHT EMI America EA 187	53	4
9 Feb 85		THIS IS NOT AMERICA (THE THEME FROM 'THE FALCON AND THE SNOWMAN') EMI America EA 190 [3]	14	7
8 Jun 85		LOVING THE ALIEN EMI America EA 195	19	6
27 Jul 85		LOVING THE ALIEN (re-entry) EMI America EA 195	67	1
7 Sep 85	★	DANCING IN THE STREET EMI America EA 204 [4]	1	12
15 Mar 86	●	ABSOLUTE BEGINNERS Virgin VS 838	2	9
21 Jun 86		UNDERGROUND EMI America EA 216	21	6
8 Nov 86		WHEN THE WIND BLOWS Virgin VS 906	44	6
4 Apr 87		DAY-IN DAY-OUT EMI America EA 230	17	6
27 Jun 87		TIME WILL CRAWL EMI America EA 237	33	4
29 Aug 87		NEVER LET ME DOWN EMI America EA 239	34	6
7 Apr 90		FAME (re-mix) EMI-USA FAME 90	28	6
22 Aug 92		REAL COOL WORLD Warner Bros. W 0127	53	1
27 Mar 93	●	JUMP THEY SAY Arista 74321139422	9	6
12 Jun 93		BLACK TIE WHITE NOISE Arista 74321148682 [5]	36	2
23 Oct 93		MIRACLE GOODNIGHT Arista 74321162262	40	2
4 Dec 93		BUDDHA OF SUBURBIA Arista 74321177052 [6]	35	3
23 Sep 95		THE HEART'S FILTHY LESSON RCA 74321307032	35	2
2 Dec 95		STRANGERS WHEN WE MEET / THE MAN WHO SOLD THE WORLD (LIVE) RCA 74321329402	39	2
2 Mar 96		HALLO SPACEBOY RCA 74321353842	12	4

[1] Queen and David Bowie [2] David Bowie and Bing Crosby [3] David Bowie and the Pat Metheny Group [4] David Bowie and Mick Jagger [5] David Bowie featuring Al B. Sure! [6] David Bowie featuring Lenny Kravitz

Tracks on Breaking Glass (EP): Breaking Glass / Art Decade / Ziggy Stardust. All three versions of John I'm Only Dancing are different. Tracks on Baal's Hymn (EP): Baal's Hymn / The Drowned Girl / Remembering Marie / The Dirty Song / Ballad of The Adventurers. Although uncredited, the Pet Shop Boys are featured on Hallo Spaceboy.

BOX TOPS US, male vocal / instrumental group — 33 wks

13 Sep 67	●	THE LETTER Stateside SS 2044	5	12
20 Mar 68		CRY LIKE A BABY Bell 1001	15	12
23 Aug 69		SOUL DEEP Bell 1068	22	9

BOY GEORGE UK, male vocalist — 46 wks

7 Mar 87	★	EVERYTHING I OWN Virgin BOY 100	1	9
6 Jun 87		KEEP ME IN MIND Virgin BOY 101	29	4
18 Jul 87		SOLD Virgin BOY 102	24	5
21 Nov 87		TO BE REBORN Virgin BOY 103	13	7
5 Mar 88		LIVE MY LIFE Virgin BOY 105	62	2
18 Jun 88		NO CLAUSE 28 Virgin BOY 106	57	3
8 Oct 88		DON'T CRY Virgin BOY 107	60	2
4 Mar 89		DON'T TAKE MY MIND ON A TRIP Virgin BOY 108	68	2
19 Sep 92		THE CRYING GAME Spaghetti CIAO 6	22	4
12 Jun 93		MORE THAN LIKELY Gee Street GESCD 49 [1]	40	3
1 Apr 95		FUNTIME VSCDG 1538	45	2
1 Jul 95		IL ADORE Virgin VSCDX 1543	50	2
21 Oct 95		SAME THING IN REVERSE Virgin VSCDT 1561	56	1

[1] PM Dawn featuring Boy George

BOY MEETS GIRL US, male / female vocal duo — 13 wks

3 Dec 88	●	WAITING FOR A STAR TO FALL RCA PB 49519	9	13

Jimmy BOYD US, male vocalist — 22 wks

8 May 53	●	TELL ME A STORY Philips PB 126 [1]	5	15
11 Sep 53		TELL ME A STORY (re-entry) Philips PB 126 [1]	12	1
27 Nov 53	●	I SAW MOMMY KISSING SANTA CLAUS Columbia DB 3365	3	6

[1] Frankie Laine and Jimmy Boyd

Jacqueline BOYER France, female vocalist — 2 wks

28 Apr 60		TOM PILLIBI Columbia DB 4452	33	2

BOYS US, male vocal group — 5 wks

12 Nov 88		DIAL MY HEART Motown ZB 42245	61	2
29 Sep 90		CRAZY Motown ZB 44037	57	3

BOYS NEXT DOOR – See June HUTTON and Axel STORDAHL with the BOYS NEXT DOOR

BOYSTOWN GANG US, male / female vocal group — 20 wks

22 Aug 81		AIN'T NO MOUNTAIN HIGH ENOUGH – REMEMBER ME (MEDLEY) WEA DICK 1	46	6
31 Jul 82	●	CAN'T TAKE MY EYES OFF YOU ERC 101	4	11
9 Oct 82		SIGNED SEALED DELIVERED (I'M YOURS) ERC 102	50	3

BOYZ – See HEAVY D. and the BOYZ

BOYZ II MEN US, male vocal group — 70 wks

5 Sep 92	★	END OF THE ROAD Motown TMG 1411	1	21
19 Dec 92		MOTOWNPHILLY Motown TMG 1402	23	6
27 Feb 93		IN THE STILL OF THE NITE (I'LL REMEMBER) Motown TMGCD 1415	27	4
3 Sep 94	●	I'LL MAKE LOVE TO YOU Motown TMGCD 1431	5	12
26 Nov 94		ON BENDED KNEE Motown TMGCD 1433	20	6
24 Dec 94		I'LL MAKE LOVE TO YOU (re-entry) Motown TMGCD 1431	57	3
22 Apr 95		THANK YOU Motown TMGCD 1438	26	3
8 Jul 95		WATER RUNS DRY Motown TMGCD 1443	24	3
9 Dec 95	●	ONE SWEET DAY Columbia 6626035 [1]	6	11
20 Jan 96		HEY LOVER Def Jam DEFCD 14 [2]	17	4

[1] Mariah Carey and Boyz II Men [2] LL Cool J featuring Boyz II Men

BOYZONE Ireland, male vocal group — 66 wks

10 Dec 94	●	LOVE ME FOR A REASON Polydor 8512802	2	13
29 Apr 95	●	KEY TO MY LIFE Polydor PZCD 342	3	8
12 Aug 95	●	SO GOOD Polydor 5797732	3	6
25 Nov 95	●	FATHER AND SON Polydor 5775762	2	16
9 Mar 96	●	COMING HOME NOW Polydor 5775702	4	9
19 Oct 96	★	WORDS Polydor 5755372	1†	11
14 Dec 96	★	A DIFFERENT BEAT Polydor 5732052	1†	3

BRAD US, male vocal / instrumental group — 1 wk

26 Jun 93		20TH CENTURY Epic 6592482	64	1

Scott BRADLEY UK, male vocalist — 1 wk

15 Oct 94		ZOOM Hidden Agenda HIDDCD 1	61	1

Paul BRADY UK, male vocalist — 1 wk

13 Jan 96		THE WORLD IS WHAT YOU MAKE IT Mercury PBCD 5	67	1

Billy BRAGG UK, male vocalist — 50 wks

16 Mar 85		BETWEEN THE WARS (EP) Go! Discs AGOEP 1	15	6
28 Dec 85		DAYS LIKE THESE Go! Discs GOD 8	43	5
28 Jun 86		LEVI STUBBS TEARS Go! Discs GOD 12	29	6
15 Nov 86		GREETINGS TO THE NEW BRUNETTE Go! Discs GOD 15 [1]	58	2

14 May 88 ★	**SHE'S LEAVING HOME** *Childline CHILD 1* [2] **1**	11
10 Sep 88	**WAITING FOR THE GREAT LEAP FORWARDS**	
	Go! Discs GOD 23 ....**52**	3
8 Jul 89	**WON'T TALK ABOUT IT** *Go.Beat GOD 33* [3] **29**	6
6 Jul 91	**SEXUALITY** *Go! Discs GOD 56* **27**	5
7 Sep 91	**YOU WOKE UP MY NEIGHBOURHOOD**	
	Go! Discs GOD 60 ....**54**	2
29 Feb 92	**ACCIDENT WAITING TO HAPPEN (EP)**	
	Go! Discs GOD 67 ....**33**	3
31 Aug 96	**UPFIELD** *Cooking Vinyl FRYCD 051* **46**	1

[1] Billy Bragg with Johnny Marr and Kirsty MacColl [2] Billy Bragg with Cara Tivey [3] Norman Cook featuring Billy Bragg

Tracks on Between The Wars (EP): *Between The Wars / Which Side Are You On / World Turned Upside Down / It Says Here. Tracks on* Accident Waiting To Happen (EP): *Accident Waiting To Happen / Revolution / Sulk / The Warmest Room.* She's Leaving Home *was listed with the flip side.* With A Little Help From My Friends *by Wet Wet Wet.* Won't Talk About It *was listed with the flip side.* Blame It On The Bassline *by Norman Cook featuring MC Wildski.*

BRAIDS *US, female vocal duo* **3 wks**

2 Nov 96	**BOHEMIAN RHAPSODY** *Atlantic A 5640CD* **21**	3

Wilfrid BRAMBELL and Harry H. CORBETT
UK, male vocal duo **12 wks**

28 Nov 63	**AT THE PALACE (PARTS 1 & 2)** *Pye 7N 15588* **25**	12

Bekka BRAMLETT – *See Joe* COCKER

BRAND NEW HEAVIES
UK / US, male / female vocal / instrumental group **43 wks**

5 Oct 91	**NEVER STOP** *ffrr F 165* **43**	3
15 Feb 92	**DREAM COME TRUE** *ffrr F 180* **24**	4
18 Apr 92	**ULTIMATE TRUNK FUNK EP** *ffrr F 185* **19**	6
1 Aug 92	**DON'T LET IT GO TO YOUR HEAD** *ffrr BNH 1* **24**	4
19 Dec 92	**STAY THIS WAY** *ffrr BNH 2* **40**	5
26 Mar 94	**DREAM ON DREAMER** *ffrr BNHCD 3* **15**	4
11 Jun 94	**BACK TO LOVE** *ffrr BNHCD 4* **23**	4
13 Aug 94	**MIDNIGHT AT THE OASIS** *ffrr BNHCD 5* **13**	6
5 Nov 94	**SPEND SOME TIME** *ffrr BNHCD 6* **26**	4
11 Mar 95	**CLOSE TO YOU** *ffrr BNHCD 7* **38**	3

All the above hits are credited 'featuring N'Dea Davenport' on either the sleeve or the label. Tracks on Ultimate Trunk Funk EP: *Never Stop / Stay This Way / Mr Tanaka / Never Stop (re-mix). BNH 2 is a re-mixed version of the track on the Ultimate Trunk Funk EP.*

Johnny BRANDON *UK, male vocalist* **12 wks**

11 Mar 55 ●	**TOMORROW** *Polygon P 1131* [1] **8**	6
29 Apr 55	**TOMORROW (re-entry)** *Polygon P 1131* [1] **16**	2
1 Jul 55	**DON'T WORRY** *Polygon P 1163* **18**	4

[1] Johnny Brandon and the Phantoms

BRANDY *US, female vocalist* **10 wks**

10 Dec 94	**I WANNA BE DOWN** *Atlantic A7217CD* **44**	3
3 Jun 95	**I WANNA BE DOWN (re-mix)**	
	Atlantic A 7186CD **36**	3
3 Feb 96	**SITTIN' UP IN MY ROOM** *Arista 74321344012* **30**	4

Laura BRANIGAN *US, female vocalist* **33 wks**

18 Dec 82 ●	**GLORIA** *Atlantic K 11759* **6**	13
7 Jul 84 ●	**SELF CONTROL** *Atlantic A 9676* **5**	17
6 Oct 84	**THE LUCKY ONE** *Atlantic A 9636* **56**	3

BRASS CONSTRUCTION
US, male vocal / instrumental group **35 wks**

3 Apr 76	**MOVIN'** *United Artists UP 36090* **23**	6
5 Feb 77	**HA CHA CHA (FUNKTION)** *United Artists UP 36205* **37**	5
26 Jan 80	**MUSIC MAKES YOU FEEL LIKE DANCING**	
	United Artists UP 615 ....**39**	6
28 May 83	**WALKIN' THE LINE** *Capitol CL 292* **47**	3
16 Jul 83	**WE CAN WORK IT OUT** *Capitol CL 299* **70**	2
7 Jul 84	**PARTYLINE** *Capitol CL 335* **56**	4
27 Oct 84	**INTERNATIONAL** *Capitol CL 341* **70**	2
9 Nov 85	**GIVE AND TAKE** *Capitol CL 377* **62**	3
28 May 88	**MOVIN' 1988 (re-mix)** *Syncopate SY 11* **24**	4

BRAT *UK, male vocalist – Roger Kitter* **8 wks**

10 Jul 82	**CHALK DUST – THE UMPIRE STRIKES BACK**	
	Hansa SMASH 1 ....**19**	8

BRAVADO *UK, male / female vocal / instrumental group* **3 wks**

18 Jun 94	**HARMONICA MAN** *Peach PEACHCD 5* **37**	3

Dhar BRAXTON *US, female vocalist* **8 wks**

31 May 86	**JUMP BACK (SET ME FREE)**	
	Fourth & Broadway BRW 47 ....**32**	8

Toni BRAXTON *US, female vocalist* **50 wks**

18 Sep 93	**ANOTHER SAD LOVE SONG** *LaFace 74321163502* **51**	2
15 Jan 94 ●	**BREATHE AGAIN** *LaFace 74321185442* **2**	12
2 Apr 94	**ANOTHER SAD LOVE SONG (re-issue)**	
	LaFace 74321196682 ....**15**	8
9 Jul 94	**YOU MEAN THE WORLD TO ME**	
	LaFace 74321214702 ....**30**	5
3 Dec 94	**LOVE SHOULDA BROUGHT YOU HOME**	
	LaFace 74321249412 ....**33**	3
13 Jul 96 ●	**YOU'RE MAKIN' ME HIGH** *LaFace 74321395402* **7**	11
2 Nov 96 ●	**UN-BREAK MY HEART** *LaFace 74321410632* ....**2†**	9

BREAD *US, male vocal / instrumental group* **46 wks**

1 Aug 70 ●	**MAKE IT WITH YOU** *Elektra 2101 010* **5**	14
15 Jan 72	**BABY I'M A WANT YOU** *Elektra K 12033* **14**	10
29 Apr 72	**EVERYTHING I OWN** *Elektra K 12041* **32**	6
30 Sep 72	**THE GUITAR MAN** *Elektra K 12066* **16**	9
25 Dec 76	**LOST WITHOUT YOUR LOVE** *Elektra K 12241* **27**	7

BREAK MACHINE *US, male vocal / dance group* **32 wks**

4 Feb 84 ●	**STREET DANCE** *Record Shack SOHO 13* **3**	14
12 May 84 ●	**BREAKDANCE PARTY** *Record Shack SOHO 20* **9**	8
14 Jul 84	**BREAKDANCE PARTY (re-entry)**	
	Record Shack SOHO 20 ....**65**	2
11 Aug 84	**ARE YOU READY?** *Record Shack SOHO 24* **27**	8

BREAKFAST CLUB *US, male vocal / instrumental group* **3 wks**

27 Jun 87	**RIGHT ON TRACK** *MCA MCA 1146* **54**	3

BREATHE *UK, male vocal / instrumental group* **27 wks**

30 Jul 88 ●	**HANDS TO HEAVEN** *Siren SRN 68* **4**	12
22 Oct 88	**JONAH** *Siren SRN 95* **60**	3
3 Dec 88	**HOW CAN I FALL** *Siren SRN 102* **48**	7
11 Mar 89	**DON'T TELL ME LIES** *Siren SRN 109* **45**	5

Freddy BRECK *Germany, male vocalist*   **4 wks**

| 13 Apr 74 | SO IN LOVE WITH YOU *Decca F 13481* ....**44** 4 |

BRECKER BROTHERS
US, male vocal / instrumental group   **5 wks**

| 4 Nov 78 | EAST RIVER *Arista ARIST 211*.................**34** 5 |

BREEDERS
US / UK, female / male vocal / instrumental group   **6 wks**

18 Apr 92	SAFARI (EP) *4AD BAD 2003* **69** 1
21 Aug 93	CANNONBALL (EP) *4AD BAD 3011CD* **40** 3
6 Nov 93	DIVINE HAMMER *4AD BAD 3017CD*.................**59** 1
23 Jul 94	HEAD TO TOE (EP) *4AD BADD 4012* **68** 1

Tracks on Safari (EP): Do You Love Me Now / Don't Call Home / Safari / So Sad About Us.
Tracks on Cannonball (EP): Cannonball / Cro-Aloha / Lord Of The Thighs / 900. Tracks on
Head To Toe (EP): Head To Toe / Shocker In.Gloom Town / Freed Pig.

BREEKOUT KREW *US, male vocal duo*   **3 wks**

| 24 Nov 84 | MATT'S MOOD *London LON 59*.................**51** 3 |

Ann BREEN *Ireland, female vocalist*   **2 wks**

| 19 Mar 83 | PAL OF MY CRADLE DAYS *Homespun HS 052* ....**69** 1 |
| 7 Jan 84 | PAL OF MY CRADLE DAYS (re-entry) *Homespun HS 052* ....**74** 1 |

BRENDON *UK, male vocalist*   **9 wks**

| 19 Mar 77 | GIMME SOME *Magnet MAG 80* ....**14** 9 |

Maire BRENNAN *Ireland, female vocalist*   **2 wks**

| 16 May 92 | AGAINST THE WIND *RCA PB 45399* ....**64** 2 |

Rose BRENNAN *Ireland, female vocalist*   **9 wks**

| 7 Dec 61 | TALL DARK STRANGER *Philips PB 1193* ....**31** 9 |

Walter BRENNAN *US, male vocalist*   **3 wks**

| 28 Jun 62 | OLD RIVERS *Liberty LIB 55436* ....**38** 3 |

Tony BRENT *UK, male vocalist*   **52 wks**

19 Dec 52	● WALKIN' TO MISSOURI *Columbia DB 3147* **9** 2
2 Jan 53	● MAKE IT SOON *Columbia DB 3187* **9** 4
9 Jan 53	● WALKIN' TO MISSOURI (re-entry) *Columbia DB 3147* **7** 5
23 Jan 53	GOT YOU ON MY MIND *Columbia DB 3226* **12** 1
13 Mar 53	● MAKE IT SOON (re-entry) *Columbia DB 3187* **9** 3
30 Nov 56	CINDY OH CINDY *Columbia DB 3844* **16** 6
8 Feb 57	CINDY OH CINDY (re-entry) *Columbia DB 3844* **30** 1
28 Jun 57	DARK MOON *Columbia DB 3950* **17** 14
28 Feb 58	THE CLOUDS WILL SOON ROLL BY *Columbia DB 4066* **24** 3
9 May 58	THE CLOUDS WILL SOON ROLL BY (re-entry) *Columbia DB 4066* **20** 2
5 Sep 58	GIRL OF MY DREAMS *Columbia DB 4177* **16** 7
24 Jul 59	WHY SHOULD I BE LONELY *Columbia DB 4304* **24** 4

Bernard BRESSLAW *UK, male vocalist*   **11 wks**

| 5 Sep 58 | ● MAD PASSIONATE LOVE *HMV POP 522* ....**6** 11 |

See also Michael Medwin, Bernard Bresslaw, Alfie Bass and Leslie Fyson.

Teresa BREWER *US, female vocalist*   **53 wks**

11 Feb 55	● LET ME GO LOVER *Vogue/Coral Q 72043* **9** 10
13 Apr 56	● A TEAR FELL *Vogue/Coral Q 72146* **2** 15
13 Jul 56	● SWEET OLD-FASHIONED GIRL *Vogue/Coral Q 72172* **3** 15
10 May 57	NORA MALONE *Vogue/Coral Q 72224* **26** 2
23 Jun 60	HOW DO YOU KNOW IT'S LOVE *Coral Q 72396* **21** 11

BRIAN and MICHAEL *UK, male vocal duo*   **19 wks**

| 25 Feb 78 | ★ MATCHSTALK MEN AND MATCHSTALK CATS AND DOGS *Pye 7N 46035* ....**1** 19 |

BRICK *US, male vocal / instrumental group*   **4 wks**

| 5 Feb 77 | DAZZ *Bang 004* ....**36** 4 |

Edie BRICKELL and the NEW BOHEMIANS
US, female / male vocal / instrumental group   **10 wks**

4 Feb 89	WHAT I AM *Geffen GEF 49* **31** 7
27 May 89	CIRCLE *Geffen GEF 51* **74** 1
1 Oct 94	GOOD TIMES *Geffen GFSTD 78* [1] **40** 2

[1] Edie Brickell

Alicia BRIDGES *US, female vocalist*   **11 wks**

| 11 Nov 78 | I LOVE THE NIGHT LIFE (DISCO ROUND) *Polydor 2066 936* ....**32** 10 |
| 8 Oct 94 | I LOVE THE NIGHTLIFE (DISCO ROUND) (re-mix) *Mother MUMCD 57* ....**61** 1 |

Johnny BRIGGS – *See Amanda BARRIE and Johnny BRIGGS*

BRIGHOUSE AND RASTRICK BRASS BAND
UK, male brass band   **13 wks**

| 12 Nov 77 | ● THE FLORAL DANCE *Transatlantic BIG 548* ....**2** 13 |

Bette BRIGHT *UK, female vocalist*   **5 wks**

| 8 Mar 80 | HELLO I AM YOUR HEART *Korova KOW 3* ....**50** 5 |

Sarah BRIGHTMAN *UK, female vocalist*   **79 wks**

11 Nov 78	● I LOST MY HEART TO A STARSHIP TROOPER *Ariola / Hansa AHA 527* [1] **6** 14
7 Apr 79	THE ADVENTURES OF THE LOVE CRUSADER *Ariola / Hansa AHA 538* [2] **53** 5
30 Jul 83	HIM *Polydor POSP 625* [3] **55** 4
23 Mar 85	PIE JESU *HMV WEBBER 1* [4] **3** 8
11 Jan 86	● THE PHANTOM OF THE OPERA *Polydor POSP 800* [5] **7** 10
4 Oct 86	● ALL I ASK OF YOU *Polydor POSP 802* [6] **3** 16
10 Jan 87	● WISHING YOU WERE SOMEHOW HERE AGAIN *Polydor POSP 803* **7** 11
11 Jul 92	AMIGOS PARA SIEMPRE (FRIENDS FOR LIFE) *Really Useful RUR 10* [7] **11** 11

[1] Sarah Brightman and Hot Gossip [2] Sarah Brightman and the Starship Troopers [3] Sarah Brightman and the Royal Philharmonic Orchestra

Boyzone

After five Top 5 hits Boyzone topped the chart with a cover of the Bee Gees' 1968 smash, 'Words', six months after boy band rivals Take That had signed off with another Gibb Brothers classic.

Boyz II Men

Three of the four longest running American number one hits are by Boyz II Men: 'End Of The Road' - 13 weeks at number one, 'I'll Make Love To You' - 14 weeks and their duet with Mariah Carey, 'One Sweet Day' - 16 weeks.

Bucks Fizz

The last winner for the UK in the Eurovision Song Contest was 'Making Your Mind Up' in 1981.

[4] Sarah Brightman and Paul Miles-Kingston [5] Sarah Brightman and Steve Harley [6] Cliff Richard and Sarah Brightman [7] José Carreras and Sarah Brightman

The listed flip side of Wishing You Were Somehow Here Again *was The Music Of The Night by Michael Crawford.*

BRIGHTON AND HOVE ALBION F.C.
UK, male football team vocalists　　　　　　　　**2 wks**

28 May 83	THE BOYS IN THE OLD BRIGHTON BLUE *Energy NRG 2*..**65**	2

BRILLIANT *UK, male / female vocal / instrumental group*　**13 wks**

19 Oct 85	IT'S A MAN'S MAN'S MAN'S WORLD *Food FOOD 5* **58**	5
22 Mar 86	LOVE IS WAR *Food FOOD 6*.................................**64**	4
2 Aug 86	SOMEBODY *Food FOOD 7* **67**	4

Danielle BRISEBOIS *US, female vocalist*　　　**1 wk**

9 Sep 95	GIMME LITTLE SIGN *Epic 6610782* **75**	1

Johnny BRISTOL *US, male vocalist*　　　　　**16 wks**

24 Aug 74	● HANG ON IN THERE BABY *MGM 2006 443* **3**	11
19 Jul 80	MY GUY – MY GIRL (MEDLEY)	
	Atlantic/Hansa K 11550 [1] **39**	5

[1] Amii Stewart and Johnny Bristol

BRITS – See VARIOUS ARTISTS (MONTAGES)

BROKEN ENGLISH
UK, male vocal / instrumental group　　　　　**13 wks**

30 May 87	COMIN' ON STRONG *EMI EM 5* **18**	10
3 Oct 87	LOVE ON THE SIDE *EMI EM 55* **69**	3

BRONSKI BEAT *UK, male vocal / instrumental group*　**78 wks**

2 Jun 84	● SMALLTOWN BOY *Forbidden Fruit BITE 1* **3**	13
22 Sep 84	● WHY? *Forbidden Fruit BITE 2* **6**	10
1 Dec 84	IT AIN'T NECESSARILY SO *Forbidden Fruit BITE 3* **16**	11
20 Apr 85	● I FEEL LOVE (MEDLEY) *Forbidden Fruit BITE 4* [1] **3**	12
30 Nov 85	● HIT THAT PERFECT BEAT *Forbidden Fruit BITE 6* **3**	14
29 Mar 86	COME ON, COME ON *Forbidden Fruit BITE 7* **20**	7
1 Jul 89	CHA CHA HEELS *Arista 112331* [2] **32**	7
2 Feb 91	SMALLTOWN BOY (re-mix)*London LON 287* [3] **32**	4

[1] Bronski Beat and Marc Almond [2] Eartha Kitt and Bronski Beat [3] Jimmy Somerville with Bronski Beat

Tracks on medley: I Feel Love / Love To Love You Baby / Johnny Remember Me.

Jet BRONX and the FORBIDDEN
UK, male vocal / instrumental group　　　　　**1 wk**

17 Dec 77	AIN'T DOIN' NOTHIN' *Lightning LIG 50* **49**	1

BROOK BROTHERS *UK, male vocal duo*　　**35 wks**

30 Mar 61	● WARPAINT *Pye 7N 15333* **5**	14
24 Aug 61	AIN'T GONNA WASH FOR A WEEK *Pye 7N 15369* ...**13**	10
25 Jan 62	HE'S OLD ENOUGH TO KNOW BETTER *Pye 7N 15409* ...**37**	1
16 Aug 62	WELCOME HOME BABY *Pye 7N 15453* **33**	6
21 Feb 63	TROUBLE IS MY MIDDLE NAME *Pye 7N 15498* **38**	4

Bruno BROOKES – See Liz KERSHAW and Bruno BROOKES

BROOKLYN, BRONX and QUEENS – See BB and Q Band

Elkie BROOKS *UK, female vocalist*　　　　　**91 wks**

2 Apr 77	● PEARL'S A SINGER *A & M AMS 7275* **8**	9
20 Aug 77	● SUNSHINE AFTER THE RAIN *A & M AMS 7306* **10**	9
25 Feb 78	LILAC WINE *A & M AMS 7333* **16**	7
3 Jun 78	ONLY LOVE CAN BREAK YOUR HEART	
	A & M AMS 7353 ....**43**	5
11 Nov 78	DON'T CRY OUT LOUD *A & M AMS 7395*.............**12**	11
5 May 79	THE RUNAWAY *A & M AMS 7428* **50**	5
16 Jan 82	FOOL IF YOU THINK IT'S OVER *A & M AMS 8187* ...**17**	10
1 May 82	OUR LOVE *A & M AMS 8214* **43**	5
17 Jul 82	NIGHTS IN WHITE SATIN *A & M AMS 8235* **33**	5
22 Jan 83	GASOLINE ALLEY *A & M AMS 8305* **52**	5
22 Nov 86	● NO MORE THE FOOL *Legend LM 4* **5**	16
4 Apr 87	BREAK THE CHAIN *Legend LM 8* **55**	3
11 Jul 87	WE'VE GOT TONIGHT *Legend LM 9* **69**	1

Garth BROOKS *US, male vocalist*　　　　　**14 wks**

1 Feb 92	SHAMELESS *Capitol CL 646* **71**	1
22 Jan 94	THE RED STROKES / AIN'T GOING DOWN	
	Liberty CDCLS 704 ....**13**	5
16 Apr 94	STANDING OUTSIDE THE FIRE *Liberty CDCL 712* **28**	4
18 Feb 95	THE DANCE / FRIENDS IN LOW PLACES	
	Capitol CDCL 735 ....**36**	3
17 Feb 96	SHE'S EVERY WOMAN *Capitol CDCL 767* **55**	1

Mel BROOKS *US, male vocalist*　　　　　　**10 wks**

18 Feb 84	TO BE OR NOT TO BE (THE HITLER RAP)	
	Island IS 158 ....**12**	10

Norman BROOKS *US, male vocalist*　　　**1 wk**

12 Nov 54	A SKY BLUE SHIRT AND A RAINBOW TIE	
	London L 1228 ....**17**	1

BROS *UK, male vocal / instrumental group*　　**84 wks**

5 Dec 87	WHEN WILL I BE FAMOUS *CBS ATOM 2* **62**	2
9 Jan 88	● WHEN WILL I BE FAMOUS (re-entry) *CBS ATOM 2* **2**	13
19 Mar 88	● DROP THE BOY *CBS ATOM 3* **2**	11
18 Jun 88	★ I OWE YOU NOTHING *CBS ATOM 4* **1**	11
17 Sep 88	● I QUIT *CBS ATOM 5* **4**	8
3 Dec 88	● CAT AMONG THE PIGEONS/SILENT NIGHT	
	CBS ATOM 6 ....**2**	8
29 Jul 89	● TOO MUCH *CBS ATOM 7* **2**	7
7 Oct 89	● CHOCOLATE BOX *CBS ATOM 8* **9**	6
16 Dec 89	● SISTER *CBS ATOM 9* **10**	6
10 Mar 90	MADLY IN LOVE *CBS ATOM 10* **14**	4
13 Jul 91	ARE YOU MINE *Columbia 6569707* **12**	5
21 Sep 91	TRY *Columbia 6574047* **27**	4

Act were duo for last six hits.

BROTHER BEYOND
UK, male vocal / instrumental group　　　　　**58 wks**

4 Apr 87	HOW MANY TIMES *EMI EMI 5591* **62**	3
8 Aug 87	CHAIN-GANG SMILE *Parlophone R 6160* **57**	3
23 Jan 88	CAN YOU KEEP A SECRET *Parlophone R 6174* **56**	4
30 Jul 88	● THE HARDER I TRY *Parlophone R 6193* **2**	14
5 Nov 88	● HE AIN'T NO COMPETITION *Parlophone R 6193* **6**	10
21 Jan 89	BE MY TWIN *Parlophone R 6195* **14**	6
1 Apr 89	CAN YOU KEEP A SECRET (re-mix)	
	Parlophone R 6197 ....**22**	5
28 Oct 89	DRIVE ON *Parlophone R 6233* **39**	4
9 Dec 89	WHEN WILL I SEE YOU AGAIN *Parlophone R 6239* **43**	5

10 Apr 90	**TRUST** Parlophone R 6245	**53**	2
19 Jan 91	**THE GIRL I USED TO KNOW** Parlophone R 6265	**48**	2

BROTHER LOVE – See PRATT and McCLAIN with BROTHER LOVE

BROTHERHOOD UK, male rap group   1 wk

27 Jan 96	**ONE SHOT/NOTHING IN PARTICULAR** Bite It BHOODD 3	**55**	1

BROTHERHOOD OF MAN
UK, male / female vocal group   97 wks

14 Feb 70	● **UNITED WE STAND** Deram DM 284	**10**	9
4 Jul 70	**WHERE ARE YOU GOING TO MY LOVE** Deram DM 298	**22**	10
13 Mar 76	★ **SAVE YOUR KISSES FOR ME** Pye 7N 45569	**1**	16
19 Jun 76	**MY SWEET ROSALIE** Pye 7N 45602	**30**	7
26 Feb 77	● **OH BOY (THE MOOD I'M IN)** Pye 7N 45656	**8**	12
9 Jul 77	★ **ANGELO** Pye 7N 45699	**1**	12
14 Jan 78	★ **FIGARO** Pye 7N 46037	**1**	11
27 May 78	**BEAUTIFUL LOVER** Pye 7N 46071	**15**	12
30 Sep 78	**MIDDLE OF THE NIGHT** Pye 7N 46117	**41**	6
3 Jul 82	**LIGHTNING FLASH** EMI 5309	**67**	2

BROTHERS UK, male vocal group   9 wks

29 Jan 77	● **SING ME** Bus Stop Bus 1054	**8**	9

BROTHERS FOUR US, male vocal group   2 wks

23 Jun 60	**GREENFIELDS** Philips PB 1009	**49**	1
7 Jul 60	**GREENFIELDS (re-entry)** Philips PB 1009	**40**	1

BROTHERS GRIMM – See JAZZ and the BROTHERS GRIMM

BROTHERS IN RHYTHM
UK, male instrumental / production duo   12 wks

16 Mar 91	**SUCH A GOOD FEELING** Fourth & Broadway BRW 228	**64**	2
14 Sep 91	**SUCH A GOOD FEELING (re-issue)** Fourth & Broadway BRW 228 210	**14**	8
30 Apr 94	**FOREVER AND A DAY** Stress CDSTR 36 [1]	**51**	2

BROTHERS JOHNSON
US, male vocal / instrumental duo   34 wks

9 Jul 77	**STRAWBERRY LETTER 23** A & M AMS 7297	**35**	5
2 Sep 78	**AIN'T WE FUNKIN' NOW** A & M AMS 7379	**43**	6
4 Nov 78	**RIDE-O-ROCKET** A & M AMS 7400	**50**	4
23 Feb 80	● **STOMP** A & M AMS 7509	**6**	12
31 May 80	**LIGHT UP THE NIGHT** A & M AMS 7526	**47**	4
25 Jul 81	**THE REAL THING** A & M AMS 8149	**50**	3

BROTHERS LIKE OUTLAW featuring
Alison EVELYN UK, male / female vocal group   1 wk

23 Jan 93	**GOOD VIBRATIONS** Gee Street GESCD 44	**74**	1

Edgar BROUGHTON BAND
UK, male vocal / instrumental group   10 wks

18 Apr 70	**OUT DEMONS OUT** Harvest HAR 5015	**39**	5
23 Jan 71	**APACHE DROPOUT** Harvest HAR 5032	**49**	1
6 Feb 71	**APACHE DROPOUT (re-entry)** Harvest HAR 5032	**35**	2
13 Mar 71	**APACHE DROPOUT (2nd re-entry)** Harvest HAR 5032	**35**	1
27 Mar 71	**APACHE DROPOUT (3rd re-entry)** Harvest HAR 5032	**33**	1

Crazy World of Arthur BROWN
UK, male vocal / instrumental group   14 wks

26 Jun 68	★ **FIRE** Track 604 022	**1**	14

Alison BROWN – See BAR-CODES featuring Alison BROWN

Angie BROWN – See BIZARRE INC; MOTIV 8

Bobby BROWN US, male vocalist   122 wks

6 Aug 88	**DON'T BE CRUEL** MCA MCA 1268	**42**	7
17 Dec 88	● **MY PREROGATIVE** MCA MCA 1299	**6**	17
25 Mar 89	**DON'T BE CRUEL (re-issue)** MCA MCA 1310	**13**	8
20 May 89	● **EVERY LITTLE STEP** MCA MCA 1338	**6**	9
15 Jul 89	● **ON OUR OWN (FROM GHOSTBUSTERS II)** MCA MCA 1350	**4**	9
23 Sep 89	**ROCK WIT'CHA** MCA MCA 1367	**33**	6
25 Nov 89	**RONI** MCA MCA 1384	**21**	7
9 Jun 90	**THE FREE STYLE MEGA-MIX** MCA MCA 1421	**14**	7
30 Jun 90	**SHE AIN'T WORTH IT** London LON 265 [1]	**12**	9
22 Aug 92	**HUMPIN' AROUND** MCA MCS 1680	**19**	6
17 Oct 92	**GOOD ENOUGH** MCA MCS 1704	**41**	4
19 Jun 93	**THAT'S THE WAY LOVE IS** MCA MCSTD 1783	**56**	2
22 Jan 94	**SOMETHING IN COMMON** MCA MCSTD 1957 [2]	**16**	5
25 Jun 94	**TWO CAN PLAY THAT GAME** MCA MCSTD 1973	**38**	3
1 Apr 95	● **TWO CAN PLAY THAT GAME (re-entry)** MCA MCSTD 1973	**3**	12
8 Jul 95	● **HUMPIN' AROUND (re-mix)** MCA MCSTD 2073	**8**	6
14 Oct 95	**MY PREROGATIVE (re-mix)** MCA MCSTD 2094	**17**	3
3 Feb 96	**EVERY LITTLE STEP (re-mix)** MCA MCSTD 48004	**25**	2

[1] Glenn Medeiros featuring Bobby Brown [2] Bobby Brown and Whitney Houston

Carl BROWN – See DOUBLE TROUBLE

Dennis BROWN Jamaica, male vocalist   18 wks

3 Mar 79	**MONEY IN MY POCKET** Lightning LV 5	**14**	9
3 Jul 82	**LOVE HAS FOUND ITS WAY** A & M AMS 8226	**47**	6
11 Sep 82	**HALFWAY UP HALFWAY DOWN** A & M AMS 8250	**56**	3

Diana BROWN and Barrie K. SHARPE
UK, female / male vocal duo   11 wks

2 Jun 90	**THE MASTERPLAN** ffrr F 133	**39**	6
1 Sep 90	**SUN WORSHIPPERS (POSITIVE THINKING)** ffrr F 144	**61**	2
23 Mar 91	**LOVE OR NOTHING** ffrr F 152	**71**	1
27 Jun 92	**EATING ME ALIVE** ffrr F 190	**53**	2

Errol BROWN UK, male vocalist   10 wks

4 Jul 87	**PERSONAL TOUCH** WEA YZ 130	**25**	8
28 Nov 87	**BODY ROCKIN'** WEA YZ 162	**51**	2

Foxxy BROWN – See CASE featuring Foxxy BROWN

Gloria D. BROWN US, female vocalist   3 wks

8 Jun 85	**THE MORE THEY KNOCK, THE MORE I LOVE YOU** 10 TEN 52	**57**	3

Horace BROWN US, male vocalist   7 wks

25 Feb 95	**TASTE YOUR LOVE** Uptown MCSTD 2026	**58**	1
18 May 96	**ONE FOR THE MONEY** Motown 8605232	**12**	4
12 Oct 96	**THINGS WE DO FOR LOVE** Motown 8605712	**27**	2

James BROWN US, male vocalist — 101 wks

Date	Title	Pos	Wks
23 Sep 65	**PAPA'S GOT A BRAND NEW BAG** London HL 9990 [1]	25	7
24 Feb 66	**I GOT YOU** Pye International 7N 25350 [1]	29	6
16 Jun 66	**IT'S A MAN'S MAN'S MAN'S WORLD** Pye International 7N 25371 [1]	13	9
10 Oct 70	**GET UP I FEEL LIKE BEING A SEX MACHINE** Polydor 2001 071	32	7
27 Nov 71	**HEY AMERICA** Mojo 2093 006	47	3
18 Sep 76	**GET UP OFFA THAT THING** Polydor 2066 687	22	6
29 Jan 77	**BODY HEAT** Polydor 2066 763	36	4
10 Jan 81	**RAPP PAYBACK (WHERE IZ MOSES?)** RCA 28	39	5
2 Jul 83	**BRING IT ON... BRING IT ON** Sonet SON 2258	45	4
1 Sep 84	**UNITY (PART 1 – THE THIRD COMING)** Tommy Boy AFR 2 [2]	49	5
27 Apr 85	**FROGGY MIX** Boiling Point FROG 1	50	3
1 Jun 85	**GET UP I FEEL LIKE BEING A SEX MACHINE (re-issue)** Boiling Point POSP 751	47	5
25 Jan 86	● **LIVING IN AMERICA** Scotti Brothers A 6701	5	10
1 Mar 86	**GET UP I FEEL LIKE BEING A SEX MACHINE (re-entry of re-issue)** Boiling Point POSP 751	46	4
18 Oct 86	**GRAVITY** Scotti Brothers 650059 7	65	2
30 Jan 88	**SHE'S THE ONE** Urban URB 13	45	3
23 Apr 88	**THE PAYBACK MIX** Urban URB 17	12	6
4 Jun 88	**I'M REAL** Scotti Brothers JSB 1 [3]	31	4
23 Jul 88	**I GOT YOU (I FEEL GOOD) (re-issue)** A & M AM 444	52	3
16 Nov 91	**GET UP (I FEEL LIKE BEING) A SEX MACHINE (2nd re-issue)** Polydor PO 185	69	2
24 Oct 92	**I GOT YOU (I FEEL GOOD) (re-mix)** FBI FBI 9 [4]	72	1
17 Apr 93	**CAN'T GET ANY HARDER** Polydor PZCD 262	59	2

[1] James Brown and The Famous Flames [2] Afrika Bambaataa and James Brown [3] James Brown featuring Full Force [4] James Brown v Dakeyne

Froggy Mix is a medley of twelve James Brown songs. The listed flip side of I Got You (I Feel Good) was Nowhere To Run by Martha Reeves and the Vandellas.

Joanne BROWN – See Tony OSBORNE

Jocelyn BROWN US, female vocalist — 53 wks

Date	Title	Pos	Wks
21 Apr 84	**SOMEBODY ELSE'S GUY** Fourth & Broadway BRW 5	13	9
22 Sep 84	**I WISH YOU WOULD** Fourth & Broadway BRW 14	51	3
15 Mar 86	**LOVE'S GONNA GET YOU** Warner Bros. W 8889	70	1
29 Jun 91	● **ALWAYS THERE** Talkin Loud TLK 10 [1]	6	9
14 Sep 91	**SHE GOT SOUL** A & M AM 819 [2]	57	3
7 Dec 91	● **DON'T TALK JUST KISS** Tug SNOG 2 [3]	3	11
20 Mar 93	**TAKE ME UP** A & M AMCD 210 [4]	61	1
11 Jun 94	**NO MORE TEARS (ENOUGH IS ENOUGH)** Ding Dong 74321209032 [5]	13	7
8 Oct 94	**GIMME ALL YOUR LOVIN'** Ding Dong 74321231322 [5]	22	3
13 Jul 96	● **KEEP ON JUMPIN'** Manifesto FESCD 11 [6]	8	6

[1] Incognito featuring Jocelyn Brown [2] Jamestown featuring Jocelyn Brown [3] Right Said Fred. Guest vocals: Jocelyn Brown [4] Sonic Surfers featuring Jocelyn Brown [5] Jocelyn Brown and Kym Mazelle [6] Todd Terry featuring Martha Wash and Jocelyn Brown

Joe BROWN and the BRUVVERS
UK, male vocal / instrumental group — 92 wks

Date	Title	Pos	Wks
17 Mar 60	**DARKTOWN STRUTTERS BALL** Decca F 11207	34	6
26 Jan 61	**SHINE** Pye 7N 15322 [1]	33	6
11 Jan 62	**WHAT A CRAZY WORLD WE'RE LIVING IN** Piccadilly 7N 35024	37	2
17 May 62	● **A PICTURE OF YOU** Piccadilly 7N 35047	2	19
13 Sep 62	**YOUR TENDER LOOK** Piccadilly 7N 35058	31	6
15 Nov 62	**IT ONLY TOOK A MINUTE** Piccadilly 7N 35082	6	13
7 Feb 63	● **THAT'S WHAT LOVE WILL DO** Piccadilly 7N 35106	3	14
21 Feb 63	**IT ONLY TOOK A MINUTE (re-entry)** Piccadilly 7N 35082	50	1
27 Jun 63	**NATURE'S TIME FOR LOVE** Piccadilly 7N 35129	26	6
26 Sep 63	**SALLY ANN** Piccadilly 7N 35138	28	9

Date	Title	Pos	Wks
29 Jun 67	**WITH A LITTLE HELP FROM MY FRIENDS** Pye 7N 17339 [1]	32	4
14 Apr 73	**HEY MAMA** Ammo AMO 101 [1]	33	6

[1] Joe Brown

Kathy BROWN – See PRAXIS featuring Kathy BROWN

Miquel BROWN US, female vocalist — 7 wks

Date	Title	Pos	Wks
18 Feb 84	**HE'S A SAINT, HE'S A SINNER** Record Shack SOHO 15	68	4
24 Aug 85	**CLOSE TO PERFECTION** Record Shack SOHO 48	63	3

Peter BROWN US, male vocalist — 9 wks

Date	Title	Pos	Wks
11 Feb 78	**DO YA WANNA GET FUNKY WITH ME** TK TKR 6009	43	4
17 Jun 78	**DANCE WITH ME** TK TKR 6027	57	5

Polly BROWN UK, female vocalist — 5 wks

Date	Title	Pos	Wks
14 Sep 74	**UP IN A PUFF OF SMOKE** GTO GT 2	43	5

Roy 'Chubby' BROWN UK, male comedian — 21 wks

Date	Title	Pos	Wks
13 May 95	**LIVING NEXT DOOR TO ALICE (WHO THE F**K IS ALICE)** N.O.W. CDWAG 245 [1]	64	2
26 Aug 95	● **LIVING NEXT DOOR TO ALICE (WHO THE F**K IS ALICE) (re-entry)** N.O.W. CDWAG 245 [1]	3	17
21 Dec 96	**ROCKIN' GOOD CHRISTMAS** PolyStar 5732612	51	2

[1] Smokie featuring Roy 'Chubby' Brown

Sam BROWN UK, female vocalist — 35 wks

Date	Title	Pos	Wks
11 Jun 88	**STOP** A & M AM 440	52	3
4 Feb 89	● **STOP (re-entry)** A & M AM 440	4	12
13 May 89	**CAN I GET A WITNESS** A & M AM 509	15	7
3 Mar 90	**WITH A LITTLE LOVE** A & M AM 539	44	4
5 May 90	**KISSING GATE** A & M AM 549	23	8
26 Aug 95	**JUST GOOD FRIENDS** Dick Bros. DDICK 014CD1 [1]	63	1

[1] Fish and Sam Brown

Sharon BROWN US, female vocalist — 11 wks

Date	Title	Pos	Wks
17 Apr 82	**I SPECIALIZE IN LOVE** Virgin VS 494	38	9
26 Feb 94	**I SPECIALIZE IN LOVE (re-mix)** Deep Distraxion OILYCD 025	62	2

BROWN SAUCE UK, male / female vocal group — 12 wks

Date	Title	Pos	Wks
12 Dec 81	**I WANNA BE A WINNER** BBC RESL 101	15	12

BROWN SUGAR – See SEX CLUB featuring BROWN SUGAR

Duncan BROWNE UK, male vocalist — 8 wks

Date	Title	Pos	Wks
19 Aug 72	**JOURNEY** RAK 135	23	6
22 Dec 84	**THEME FROM 'THE TRAVELLING MAN'** Towerbell TOW 64	68	2

Jackson BROWNE US, male vocalist — 14 wks

Date	Title	Pos	Wks
1 Jul 78	**STAY** Asylum K 13128	12	11
18 Oct 86	**IN THE SHAPE OF A HEART** Elektra EKR 42	66	2
25 Jun 94	**EVERYWHERE I GO** Elektra EKR 184CD1	67	1

Ronnie BROWNE – See SCOTTISH RUGBY TEAM with Ronnie BROWNE

Tom BROWNE US, male vocalist — 24 wks

19 Jul 80	● FUNKIN' FOR JAMAICA (N.Y.) Arista ARIST 357	10	11
25 Oct 80	THIGHS HIGH (GRIP YOUR HIPS AND MOVE)		
	Arista ARIST 367	45	5
30 Jan 82	FUNGI MAMA (BEBOPAFUNKADISCOLYPSO)		
	Arista ARIST 450	58	4
11 Jan 92	FUNKIN' FOR JAMAICA (re-mix)		
	Arista 114998	45	4

BROWNS US, male / female vocal group — 13 wks

18 Sep 59	● THE THREE BELLS RCA 1140	6	13

BROWNSTONE US, female vocal group — 18 wks

1 Apr 95	● IF YOU LOVE ME MJJ 6614135	8	12
15 Jul 95	GRAPEVYNE MJJ 6620942	16	4
23 Sep 95	I CAN'T TELL YOU WHY MJJ 6623775	27	2

BROWNSVILLE STATION
US, male vocal / instrumental group — 6 wks

2 Mar 74	SMOKIN' IN THE BOYS' ROOM Philips 6073 834	27	6

Dave BRUBECK QUARTET
US, male instrumental group — 30 wks

26 Oct 61	● TAKE FIVE Fontana H 339	6	15
8 Feb 62	IT'S A RAGGY WALTZ Fontana H 352	36	3
17 May 62	UNSQUARE DANCE CBS AAG 102	14	12

Tommy BRUCE and the BRUISERS
UK, male vocal / instrumental group — 21 wks

26 May 60	● AIN'T MISBEHAVIN' Columbia DB 4453	3	16
8 Sep 60	BROKEN DOLL Columbia DB 4498	36	4
22 Feb 62	BABETTE Columbia DB 4776 [1]	50	1

[1] Tommy Bruce

Claudia BRUCKEN Germany, female vocalist — 2 wks

11 Aug 90	ABSOLUT(E) Island IS 471	71	1
16 Feb 91	KISS LIKE ETHER Island IS 479	63	1

BRUISERS UK, male instrumental group — 7 wks

8 Aug 63	BLUE GIRL Parlophone R 5042	31	6
26 Sep 63	BLUE GIRL (re-entry) Parlophone R 5042	47	1

See also Tommy Bruce.

Frank BRUNO UK, male vocalist — 4 wks

23 Dec 95	EYE OF THE TIGER RCA 74321336282	28	4

BRUNO and LIZ – See Liz KERSHAW and Bruno BROOKES

Tyrone BRUNSON US, male instrumentalist – bass — 5 wks

25 Dec 82	THE SMURF Epic EPC A 3024	52	5

BRUVVERS – See Joe BROWN and the BRUVVERS

Dora BRYAN UK, female vocalist — 6 wks

5 Dec 63	ALL I WANT FOR CHRISTMAS IS A BEATLE		
	Fontana TF 427	20	6

Anita BRYANT US, female vocalist — 6 wks

26 May 60	PAPER ROSES London HLL 9144	49	1
30 Jun 60	PAPER ROSES (re-entry) London HLL 9144	45	1
14 Jul 60	PAPER ROSES (2nd re-entry) London HLL 9144	24	2
6 Oct 60	MY LITTLE CORNER OF THE WORLD London HLL 9171	48	2

Peabo BRYSON US, male vocalist — 35 wks

20 Aug 83	● TONIGHT I CELEBRATE MY LOVE Capitol CL 302 [1]	2	13
16 May 92	BEAUTY AND THE BEAST Epic 6576607 [2]	9	7
17 Jul 93	BY THE TIME THIS NIGHT IS OVER		
	Arista 74321157142 [3]	56	3
11 Dec 93	A WHOLE NEW WORLD (ALADDIN'S THEME)		
	Columbia 6599002 [4]	12	12

[1] Peabo Bryson and Roberta Flack [2] Celine Dion and Peabo Bryson
[3] Kenny G with Peabo Bryson [4] Peabo Bryson and Regina Belle

BT US, male producer – Brian Transeau — 9 wks

18 Mar 95	EMBRACING THE SUNSHINE East West YZ 895CD	34	2
16 Sep 95	LOVING YOU MORE Perfecto PERF 110CD	28	2
10 Feb 96	LOVING YOU MORE (re-mix) Perfecto PERF 117CD [1]	14	3
9 Nov 96	BLUE SKIES Perfecto PERF 130CD1 [2]	26	2

[1] BT featuring Vincent Covello [2] BT featuring Tori Amos

BT EXPRESS US, male instrumental / vocal group — 11 wks

29 Mar 75	EXPRESS Pye International 7N 25674	34	6
26 Jul 80	DOES IT FEEL GOOD / GIVE UP THE FUNK		
	(LET'S DANCE) Calibre CAB 503	52	4
23 Apr 94	EXPRESS (re-mix) PWL International PWCD 285	67	1

BUBBLEROCK – See Jonathan KING

Catherine BUCHANAN – See JELLYBEAN

Roy BUCHANAN US, male instrumentalist – guitar — 3 wks

31 Mar 73	SWEET DREAMS Polydor 2066 307	40	3

BUCKETHEADS US, male producer – Kenny Gonzales — 16 wks

4 Mar 95	● THE BOMB! (THESE SOUNDS FALL INTO MY MIND)		
	Positiva CDTIV 33	5	13
20 Jan 96	GOT MYSELF TOGETHER Positiva CDTIV 48	12	3

Lindsey BUCKINGHAM US, male vocalist — 7 wks

16 Jan 82	TROUBLE Mercury MER 85	31	7

Jeff BUCKLEY US, male vocalist — 2 wks

27 May 95	LAST GOODBYE Columbia 6620422	54	2

BUCKS FIZZ UK, male / female vocal group — 150 wks

28 Mar 81	★ MAKING YOUR MIND UP RCA 56	1	12
6 Jun 81	PIECE OF THE ACTION RCA 88	12	9

15 Aug 81	ONE OF THOSE NIGHTS RCA 114	**20**	10
28 Nov 81	★ THE LAND OF MAKE BELIEVE RCA 163	**1**	16
27 Mar 82	● MY CAMERA NEVER LIES RCA 202	**1**	8
19 Jun 82	● NOW THOSE DAYS ARE GONE RCA 241	**8**	9
27 Nov 82	● IF YOU CAN'T STAND THE HEAT RCA 300	**10**	11
12 Mar 83	RUN FOR YOUR LIFE RCA FIZ 1	**14**	7
18 Jun 83	● WHEN WE WERE YOUNG RCA 342	**10**	8
1 Oct 83	LONDON TOWN RCA 363	**34**	6
17 Dec 83	RULES OF THE GAME RCA 380	**57**	6
25 Aug 84	TALKING IN YOUR SLEEP RCA FIZ 2	**15**	9
27 Oct 84	GOLDEN DAYS RCA FIZ 3	**42**	4
29 Dec 84	I HEAR TALK RCA FIZ 4	**34**	8
22 Jun 85	YOU AND YOUR HEART SO BLUE RCA PB 40233	**43**	4
14 Sep 85	MAGICAL RCA PB 40367	**57**	3
7 Jun 86	● NEW BEGINNING (MAMBA SEYRA)		
	Polydor POSP 794	**8**	10
30 Aug 86	LOVE THE ONE YOU'RE WITH		
	Polydor POSP 813	**47**	3
15 Nov 86	KEEP EACH OTHER WARM Polydor POSP 835	**45**	4
5 Nov 88	HEART OF STONE RCA PB 42035	**50**	3

BUDGIE UK, male vocal / instrumental group   2 wks

3 Oct 81	KEEPING A RENDEZVOUS RCA BUDGIE 3	**71**	2

BUG KANN and the PLASTIC JAM
UK, male / female vocal / instrumental group   2 wks

31 Aug 91	MADE IN TWO MINUTES		
	Optimum Dance BKPJ 1S [1]	**70**	1
26 Feb 94	MADE IN 2 MINUTES (re-mix)		
	PWL International PWCD 286	**64**	1

[1] Bug Kann and Plastic Jam featuring Patti Low and Doogie

BUGGLES UK, male vocal / instrumental duo   28 wks

22 Sep 79	★ VIDEO KILLED THE RADIO STAR		
	Island WIP 6524	**1**	11
26 Jan 80	THE PLASTIC AGE Island WIP 6540	**16**	8
5 Apr 80	CLEAN CLEAN Island WIP 6584	**38**	5
8 Nov 80	ELSTREE Island WIP 6624	**55**	4

B. BUMBLE and the STINGERS
US, male instrumental group   26 wks

19 Apr 62	★ NUT ROCKER Top Rank JAR 611	**1**	15
3 Jun 72	NUT ROCKER (re-issue) Stateside SS 2203	**19**	11

BUMP UK, male instrumental / production duo   5 wks

4 Jul 92	I'M RUSHING Good Boy EDGE7 1	**40**	4
11 Nov 95	I'M RUSHING (re-mix)		
	Deconstruction 74321320692	**45**	1

BUNKER KRU – See HARLEQUIN 4's/BUNKER KRU

BUNNYMEN – See ECHO and the BUNNYMEN

Eric BURDON – See ANIMALS

Geoffrey BURGON UK, orchestra   4 wks

26 Dec 81	BRIDESHEAD THEME Chrysalis CHS 2562	**48**	4

Keni BURKE US, male vocalist   4 wks

27 Jun 81	LET SOMEBODY LOVE YOU RCA 93	**59**	3
18 Apr 92	RISIN' TO THE TOP RCA PB 49103	**70**	1

Hank C. BURNETTE
Sweden, male multi-instrumentalist   8 wks

30 Oct 76	SPINNING ROCK BOOGIE Sonet SON 2094	**21**	8

Johnny BURNETTE US, male vocalist   48 wks

29 Sep 60	● DREAMIN' London HLG 9172	**5**	16
12 Jan 61	● YOU'RE SIXTEEN London HLG 9254	**3**	12
13 Apr 61	LITTLE BOY SAD London HLG 9315	**12**	12
10 Aug 61	GIRLS London HLG 9388	**37**	5
17 May 62	CLOWN SHOES Liberty LIB 55416	**35**	3

Rocky BURNETTE US, male vocalist   7 wks

17 Nov 79	TIRED OF TOEIN' THE LINE EMI 2992	**58**	7

Jerry BURNS UK, female vocalist   1 wk

25 Apr 92	PALE RED Columbia 6579467	**64**	1

Ray BURNS UK, male vocalist   19 wks

11 Feb 55	● MOBILE Columbia DB 3563	**4**	13
26 Aug 55	THAT'S HOW A LOVE SONG WAS BORN		
	Columbia DB 3640 [1]	**14**	6

[1] Ray Burns with the Coronets

Malandra BURROWS UK, female vocalist   8 wks

1 Dec 90	JUST THIS SIDE OF LOVE Yorkshire Television DALE 1	**11**	8

Jenny BURTON US, female vocalist   2 wks

30 Mar 85	BAD HABITS Atlantic A 9583	**68**	2

BURUNDI STEIPHENSON BLACK
Burundi / France, male / female, vocal / instrumental group   14 wks

13 Nov 71	BURUNDI BLACK Barclay BAR 3	**31**	14

Lou BUSCH US, orchestra and chorus   17 wks

27 Jan 56	● ZAMBESI Capitol CL 14504	**2**	17

See also Joe 'Fingers' Carr.

BUSH UK, male vocal / instrumental group   2 wks

8 Jun 96	MACHINEHEAD Interscope IND 95505	**48**	2

Kate BUSH UK, female vocalist   168 wks

11 Feb 78	★ WUTHERING HEIGHTS EMI 2719	**1**	12
13 May 78	WUTHERING HEIGHTS (re-entry) EMI 2719	**75**	1
10 Jun 78	● MAN WITH THE CHILD IN HIS EYES EMI 2806	**6**	11
11 Nov 78	HAMMER HORROR EMI 2887	**44**	6
17 Mar 79	WOW EMI 2911	**14**	10
15 Sep 79	● KATE BUSH ON STAGE EP EMI MIEP 2991	**10**	9
26 Apr 80	BREATHING EMI 5058	**16**	7
5 Jul 80	● BABOOSHKA EMI 5085	**5**	10
4 Oct 80	ARMY DREAMERS EMI 5106	**16**	9
6 Dec 80	DECEMBER WILL BE MAGIC AGAIN EMI 5121	**29**	7
11 Jul 81	SAT IN YOUR LAP EMI 5201	**11**	7

7 Aug 82	THE DREAMING *EMI 5296*	**48**	3
17 Aug 85	● RUNNING UP THAT HILL *EMI KB 1*	**3**	11
26 Oct 85	CLOUDBUSTING *EMI KB 2*	**20**	6
1 Mar 86	HOUNDS OF LOVE *EMI KB 3*	**18**	5
10 May 86	THE BIG SKY *EMI KB 4*	**37**	3
1 Nov 86	● DON'T GIVE UP *Virgin PGS 2* [1]	**9**	11
8 Nov 86	EXPERIMENT IV *EMI KB 5*	**23**	4
30 Sep 89	THE SENSUAL WORLD *EMI EM 102*	**12**	5
2 Dec 89	THIS WOMAN'S WORK *EMI EM 119*	**25**	5
10 Mar 90	LOVE AND ANGER *EMI EM 134*	**38**	3
7 Dec 91	ROCKET MAN (I THINK IT'S GOING TO BE A LONG LONG TIME) *Mercury TRIBO 2*	**12**	8
18 Sep 93	RUBBERBAND GIRL *EMI CDEM 280*	**12**	5
27 Nov 93	MOMENTS OF PLEASURE *EMI CDEM 297*	**26**	3
16 Apr 94	THE RED SHOES *EMI CDEMS 316*	**21**	3
30 Jul 94	THE MAN I LOVE *Mercury MERCD 408* [2]	**27**	2
19 Nov 94	AND SO IS LOVE *EMI CDEMS 355*	**26**	2

[1] Peter Gabriel and Kate Bush [2] Kate Bush and Larry Adler

Tracks on On Stage EP: Them Heavy People / Don't Push Your Foot on the Heartbrake / James and the Cold Gun / L'Amour Looks Something Like You.

BUSTER *UK, male vocal / instrumental group*   **1 wk**

19 Jun 76	SUNDAY *RCA 2678*	**49**	1

Bernard BUTLER – *See David McALMONT*

Jonathan BUTLER
South Africa, male vocalist / instrumentalist – guitar   **18 wks**

25 Jan 86	IF YOU'RE READY (COME GO WITH ME) *Jive JIVE109* [1]	**30**	7
8 Aug 87	LIES *Jive JIVE 141*	**18**	11

[1] Ruby Turner featuring Jonathan Butler

BUTTERSCOTCH *UK, male vocal group*   **11 wks**

2 May 70	DON'T YOU KNOW *RCA 1937*	**17**	11

BUTTHOLE SURFERS
US, male vocal / instrumental group   **1 wk**

5 Oct 96	PEPPER *Capitol CDCL 778*	**59**	1

BUZZCOCKS *UK, male vocal / instrumental group*   **53 wks**

18 Feb 78	WHAT DO I GET *United Artists UP 36348*	**37**	3
13 May 78	I DON'T MIND *United Artists UP 36386*	**55**	2
15 Jul 78	LOVE YOU MORE *United Artists UP 36433*	**34**	6
23 Sep 78	EVER FALLEN IN LOVE (WITH SOMEONE YOU SHOULDN'T'VE) *United Artists UP 36455*	**12**	11
25 Nov 78	PROMISES *United Artists UP 36471*	**20**	10
10 Mar 79	EVERYBODY'S HAPPY NOWADAYS *United Artists UP 36499*	**29**	6
21 Jul 79	HARMONY IN MY HEAD *United Artists UP 36541*	**32**	6
25 Aug 79	SPIRAL SCRATCH EP *New Hormones ORG 1*	**31**	6
6 Sep 80	ARE EVERYTHING / WHY SHE'S A GIRL FROM THE CHAINSTORE *United Artists BP 365*	**61**	3

Tracks on Spiral Scratch EP: Breakdown / Time's Up / Boredom / Friends Of Mine. Sleeve of EP (not the label) credits 'Buzzcocks with Howard Devoto'. Why She's A Girl From The Chainstore listed from 13 Sep 80.

BUZZY BUNCH – *See Celi BEE and the BUZZY BUNCH*

BVSMP *US, male vocal group*   **12 wks**

23 Jul 88	● I NEED YOU *Debut DEBT 3044*	**3**	12

BY ALL MEANS *US, male vocal group*   **2 wks**

18 Jun 88	I SURRENDER TO YOUR LOVE *Fourth & Broadway BRW 102*	**65**	2

Max BYGRAVES *UK, male vocalist*   **131 wks**

14 Nov 52	COWPUNCHER'S CANTATA *HMV B 10250*	**11**	1
2 Jan 53	● COWPUNCHER'S CANTATA (re-entry) *HMV B 10250*	**8**	1
23 Jan 53	● COWPUNCHER'S CANTATA (2nd re-entry) *HMV B 10250*	**6**	5
6 Mar 53	● COWPUNCHER'S CANTATA (3rd re-entry) *HMV B 10250*	**10**	1
14 May 54	● HEART OF MY HEART *HMV B 10654*	**7**	8
10 Sep 54	● GILLY GILLY OSSENFEFFER KATZENELLEN BOGEN BY THE SEA *HMV B 10734*	**7**	7
5 Nov 54	GILLY GILLY OSSENFEFFER KATZENELLEN BOGEN BY THE SEA (re-entry) *HMV B 10734*	**20**	1
21 Jan 55	MR. SANDMAN *HMV B 10801*	**16**	1
18 Nov 55	● MEET ME ON THE CORNER *HMV POP 116*	**2**	11
17 Feb 56	BALLAD OF DAVY CROCKETT *HMV POP 153*	**20**	1
25 May 56	OUT OF TOWN *HMV POP 164*	**18**	7
5 Apr 57	HEART *Decca F 10862*	**14**	8
2 May 58	● YOU NEED HANDS / TULIPS FROM AMSTERDAM *Decca F 11004*	**3**	25
22 Aug 58	LITTLE TRAIN / GOTTA HAVE RAIN *Decca F 11046*	**28**	2
2 Jan 59	MY UKELELE *Decca F 11077*	**19**	4
18 Dec 59	● JINGLE BELL ROCK *Decca F 11176*	**7**	4
10 Mar 60	● FINGS AIN'T WOT THEY USED T'BE *Decca F 11214*	**5**	15
28 Jul 60	CONSIDER YOURSELF *Decca F 11251*	**50**	1
1 Jun 61	BELLS OF AVIGNON *Decca F 11350*	**36**	5
19 Feb 69	YOU'RE MY EVERYTHING *Pye 7N 17705*	**50**	1
5 Mar 69	YOU'RE MY EVERYTHING (re-entry) *Pye 7N 17705*	**34**	3
6 Oct 73	DECK OF CARDS *Pye 7N 45276*	**13**	15
9 Dec 89	WHITE CHRISTMAS *Parkfield PMS 5012*	**71**	4

See also Various Artists (EPs & LPs) - All Star Hit Parade No. 2. Cowpuncher's Cantata is a medley with the following songs: Cry Of The Wild Goose / Riders In The Sky / Mule Train / Jezebel. You Need Hands was listed by itself on 2 May 58. Tulips From Amsterdam was listed beginning 9 May 58.

BYKER GROOOVE! *UK, female vocal group*   **3 wks**

24 Dec 94	LOVE YOUR SEXY... !! *Groove GROVD 01*	**48**	3

Charlie BYRD – *See Stan GETZ*

Debra BYRD – *See Barry MANILOW*

Donald BYRD
US, male vocalist / instrumentalist – trumpet   **6 wks**

26 Sep 81	LOVING YOU / LOVE HAS COME AROUND *Elektra K 12559*	**41**	6

Gary BYRD and the GB EXPERIENCE
US, male vocalist and male / female instrumental group   **9 wks**

23 Jul 83	● THE CROWN *Motown TMGT 1312*	**6**	9

BYRDS *US, male vocal / instrumental group*   **52 wks**

17 Jun 65	★ MR. TAMBOURINE MAN *CBS 201765*	**1**	14
12 Aug 65	● ALL I REALLY WANT TO DO *CBS 201796*	**4**	10
11 Nov 65	TURN! TURN! TURN! *CBS 202008*	**26**	8
5 May 66	EIGHT MILES HIGH *CBS 202067*	**24**	9
5 Jun 68	YOU AIN'T GOIN' NOWHERE *CBS 3411*	**45**	3
13 Feb 71	CHESTNUT MARE *CBS 5322*	**19**	8

Edward BYRNES – *See Connie STEVENS*

Buzzcocks

Punk pioneers the Buzzcocks
signed to EMI's United Artists label
on 16 August 1977, the day
Elvis Presley died.

Chi-Lites

'Oh Girl' by the Chi-Lites topped
the US chart in 1972, dethroning
Roberta Flack's 'The First Time Ever
I Saw Your Face'.

Chemical Brothers

Known as the Dust Brothers until a
US duo claimed the right to the
name, the Chemical Brothers were
the first unrelated brothers to top
the charts since the Righteous
Brothers in 1990.

58

BYSTANDERS UK, male vocal / instrumental group 1 wk

9 Feb 67	**98.6** Piccadilly 7N 35363	**45**	1

Roy C US, male vocalist 24 wks

21 Apr 66	● **SHOTGUN WEDDING** Island WI 273	**6**	11
25 Nov 72	● **SHOTGUN WEDDING (re-issue)** UK 19	**8**	13

C & C MUSIC FACTORY/CLIVILLES & COLE
US, male / female vocal / instrumental group 53 wks

15 Dec 90	● **GONNA MAKE YOU SWEAT (EVERYBODY DANCE NOW)** CBS 6564540 [1]	**3**	12
30 Mar 91	**HERE WE GO** Columbia 6567557 [1]	**20**	7
6 Jul 91	● **THINGS THAT MAKE YOU GO HMMM...** Columbia 6566907 [1]	**4**	11
23 Nov 91	**JUST A TOUCH OF LOVE EVERYDAY** Columbia 6575247 [2]	**31**	3
18 Jan 92	**PRIDE (IN THE NAME OF LOVE)** Columbia 6577017 [3]	**15**	5
14 Mar 92	**A DEEPER LOVE** Columbia 6578497 [3]	**15**	5
3 Oct 92	**KEEP IT COMIN' (DANCE TILL YOU CAN'T DANCE NO MORE)** Columbia 6584307 [4]	**34**	3
27 Aug 94	**DO YOU WANNA GET FUNKY** Columbia 6607622 [5]	**27**	3
18 Feb 95	**I FOUND LOVE / TAKE A TOKE** Columbia 6612112 [6]	**26**	2
11 Nov 95	**I'LL ALWAYS BE AROUND** MCA MCSTD 40001 [5]	**42**	2

[1] C & C Music Factory (featuring Freedom Williams) [2] C & C Music Factory featuring Zelma Davis [3] Clivilles and Cole [4] C & C Music Factory featuring Q Unique and Deborah Cooper [5] C & C Music Factory [6] C & C Music Factory featuring Zelma Davis/C & C Music Factory featuring Martha Wash

ÇA VA ÇA VA UK, male vocal / instrumental group 8 wks

18 Sep 82	**WHERE'S ROMEO** Regard RG 103	**49**	5
19 Feb 83	**BROTHER BRIGHT** Regard RG 105	**65**	3

Montserrat CABALLE – See Freddie MERCURY

CABANA Brazil, male / female vocal / instrumental duo 1 wk

15 Jul 95	**BAILANDO CON LOBOS** Hi-Life 5792512	**65**	1

CABARET VOLTAIRE
UK, male vocal / instrumental group 8 wks

18 Jul 87	**DON'T ARGUE** Parlophone R 6157	**69**	2
4 Nov 89	**HYPNOTISED** Parlophone R 6227	**66**	2
12 May 90	**KEEP ON** Parlophone R 6250	**55**	2
18 Aug 90	**EASY LIFE** Parlophone R 6261	**61**	2

CACIQUE UK, male / female vocal / instrumental group 1 wk

1 Jun 85	**DEVOTED TO YOU** Diamond Duel DISC 1	**69**	1

CACTUS WORLD NEWS
Ireland, male vocal / instrumental group 7 wks

8 Feb 86	**YEARS LATER** MCA MCA 1024	**59**	3
26 Apr 86	**WORLDS APART** MCA MCA 1040	**58**	3
20 Sep 86	**THE BRIDGE** MCA MCA 1080	**74**	1

CADETS with Eileen READ
Ireland, male / female vocal group 1 wk

3 Jun 65	**JEALOUS HEART** Pye 7N 15852	**42**	1

Susan CADOGAN UK, female vocalist 19 wks

5 Apr 75	● **HURT SO GOOD** Magnet MAG 23	**4**	12
19 Jul 75	**LOVE ME BABY** Magnet MAG 36	**22**	7

Al CAIOLA US, orchestra 6 wks

15 Jun 61	**THE MAGNIFICENT SEVEN** HMV POP 889	**34**	6

CALIBRE CUTS – See VARIOUS ARTISTS (MONTAGES)

CALL US, male vocal / instrumental group 6 wks

30 Sep 89	**LET THE DAY BEGIN** MCA MCA 1362	**42**	6

Eddie CALVERT UK, male instrumentalist – trumpet 80 wks

18 Dec 53	★ **OH MEIN PAPA** Columbia DB 3337	**1**	21
8 Apr 55	★ **CHERRY PINK AND APPLE BLOSSOM WHITE** Columbia DB 3581	**1**	21
13 May 55	**STRANGER IN PARADISE** Columbia DB 3594	**14**	4
29 Jul 55	● **JOHN AND JULIE** Columbia DB 3624	**6**	11
9 Mar 56	**ZAMBESI** Columbia DB 3747	**18**	1
23 Mar 56	**ZAMBESI (re-entry)** Columbia DB 3747	**13**	6
7 Feb 58	● **MANDY** Columbia DB 3956	**9**	14
20 Jun 58	**LITTLE SERENADE** Columbia DB 4105	**28**	2

Donnie CALVIN – See ROCKER'S REVENGE

CAMEO US, male vocal / instrumental group 66 wks

31 Mar 84	**SHE'S STRANGE** Club JAB 2	**37**	8
13 Jul 85	**ATTACK ME WITH YOUR LOVE** Club JAB 16	**65**	2
14 Sep 85	**SINGLE LIFE** Club JAB 21	**15**	10
7 Dec 85	**SHE'S STRANGE (re-issue)** Club JAB 25	**22**	8
22 Mar 86	**A GOODBYE** Club JAB 28	**65**	2
30 Aug 86	● **WORD UP** Club JAB 38	**3**	13
29 Nov 86	**CANDY** Club JAB 43	**27**	9
25 Apr 87	**BACK AND FORTH** Club JAB 49	**11**	9
17 Oct 87	**SHE'S MINE** Club JAB 57	**35**	4
29 Oct 88	**YOU MAKE ME WORK** Club JAB 70	**74**	1

Andy CAMERON UK, male vocalist 8 wks

4 Mar 78	● **ALLY'S TARTAN ARMY** Klub 03	**6**	8

Tony CAMILLO'S BAZUKA
US, male instrumental / vocal group 5 wks

31 May 75	**DYNOMITE (PART 1)** A & M AMS 7168	**28**	5

CAMOUFLAGE featuring MYSTI
UK, male / female vocal / instrumental group 3 wks

24 Sep 77	**BEE STING** State STAT 58	**48**	3

Ali CAMPBELL UK, male vocalist 18 wks

20 May 95	● **THAT LOOK IN YOUR EYE** Kuff KUFFDG 1	**5**	10

| 26 Aug 95 | LET YOUR YEAH BE YEAH Kuff KUFFD 2 | 25 | 4 |
| 9 Dec 95 | SOMETHIN' STUPID Kuff KUFFDG 5 [1] | 30 | 4 |

[1] Ali and Kibibi Campbell

See also Pato Banton.

Ali and Robin CAMPBELL – See Pato BANTON

Danny CAMPBELL – See SASHA

Don CAMPBELL – See GENERAL SAINT

Ethna CAMPBELL UK, female vocalist   11 wks

| 27 Dec 75 | THE OLD RUGGED CROSS Philips 6006 475 | 33 | 11 |

Ian CAMPBELL FOLK GROUP
UK, male vocal / instrumental group   5 wks

11 Mar 65	THE TIMES THEY ARE A-CHANGIN' Transatlantic SP 5	42	2
1 Apr 65	THE TIMES THEY ARE A-CHANGIN' (re-entry) Transatlantic SP 5	47	1
15 Apr 65	THE TIMES THEY ARE A-CHANGIN' (2nd re-entry) Transatlantic SP 5	46	2

Glen CAMPBELL US, male vocalist   98 wks

29 Jan 69	● WICHITA LINEMAN Ember EMBS 261	7	13
7 May 69	GALVESTON Ember EMBS 263	14	10
6 Dec 69	● ALL I HAVE TO DO IS DREAM Capitol CL 15619 [1]	3	14
7 Feb 70	TRY A LITTLE KINDNESS Capitol CL 15622	45	2
9 May 70	● HONEY COME BACK Capitol CL 15638	4	19
26 Sep 70	EVERYTHING A MAN COULD EVER NEED Capitol CL 15653	32	5
21 Nov 70	● IT'S ONLY MAKE BELIEVE Capitol CL 15663	4	14
27 Mar 71	DREAM BABY Capitol CL 15674	39	3
4 Oct 75	● RHINESTONE COWBOY Capitol CL 15824	4	12
26 Mar 77	SOUTHERN NIGHTS Capitol CL 15907	28	6

[1] Bobbie Gentry and Glen Campbell

Jo Ann CAMPBELL US, female vocalist   3 wks

| 8 Jun 61 | MOTORCYCLE MICHAEL HMV POP 873 | 41 | 3 |

Junior CAMPBELL UK, male vocalist   18 wks

| 14 Oct 72 | ● HALLELUJAH FREEDOM Deram DM 364 | 10 | 9 |
| 2 Jun 73 | SWEET ILLUSION Deram DM 387 | 15 | 9 |

Kibibi CAMPBELL – See Ali CAMPBELL

Naomi CAMPBELL UK, female vocalist   3 wks

| 24 Sep 94 | LOVE AND TEARS Epic 6608352 | 40 | 3 |

Pat CAMPBELL Ireland, male vocalist   5 wks

| 15 Nov 69 | THE DEAL Major Minor MM 648 | 31 | 5 |

Stan CAMPBELL UK, male vocalist   3 wks

| 6 Jun 87 | YEARS GO BY WEA YZ 127 | 65 | 3 |

Tevin CAMPBELL US, male vocalist   2 wks

| 18 Apr 92 | TELL ME WHAT YOU WANT ME TO DO Qwest W 0102 | 63 | 2 |

CAN Germany, male vocal / instrumental group   10 wks

| 28 Aug 76 | I WANT MORE Virgin VS 153 | 26 | 10 |

CANDIDO US, male multi-instrumentalist   3 wks

| 18 Jul 81 | JINGO Excalibur EXC 102 | 55 | 3 |

CANDLEWICK GREEN
UK, male vocal / instrumental duo   8 wks

| 23 Feb 74 | WHO DO YOU THINK YOU ARE Decca F 13480 | 21 | 8 |

CANDY FLIP UK, male vocal / instrumental duo   14 wks

| 17 Mar 90 | ● STRAWBERRY FIELDS FOREVER Debut DEBT 3092 | 3 | 10 |
| 14 Jul 90 | THIS CAN BE REAL Debut DEBT 3099 | 60 | 4 |

CANDY GIRLS
UK, male / female instrumental / production duo   10 wks

30 Sep 95	FEE FI FO FUM VC VCRD 1 [1]	23	4
24 Feb 96	WHAM BAM VC VCRD 6 [1]	20	4
7 Dec 96	I WANT CANDY Feverpitch CDFVR 1013 [2]	30	2

[1] Candy Girls featuring Sweet Pussy Pauline [2] Candy Girls featuring Valerie Malcolm

CANDYLAND UK, male vocal / instrumental group   1 wk

| 9 Mar 91 | FOUNTAIN O' YOUTH Non Fiction YES 4 | 72 | 1 |

CANDYSKINS UK, male vocal / instrumental group   1 wk

| 19 Oct 96 | MRS HOOVER Ultimate TOPP 051CD | 65 | 1 |

CANNED HEAT US, male vocal / instrumental group   41 wks

24 Jul 68	● ON THE ROAD AGAIN Liberty LBS 15090	8	15
1 Jan 69	GOING UP THE COUNTRY Liberty LBF 15169	19	10
17 Jan 70	● LET'S WORK TOGETHER Liberty LBF 15302	2	15
11 Jul 70	SUGAR BEE Liberty LBF 15350	49	1

Freddy CANNON US, male vocalist   51 wks

14 Aug 59	TALLAHASSEE LASSIE Top Rank JAR 135	17	8
1 Jan 60	● WAY DOWN YONDER IN NEW ORLEANS Top Rank JAR 247	3	16
10 Mar 60	CALIFORNIA HERE I COME Top Rank JAR 309	33	1
17 Mar 60	INDIANA Top Rank JAR 309	42	1
24 Mar 60	CALIFORNIA HERE I COME (re-entry) Top Rank JAR 309	46	1
19 May 60	THE URGE Top Rank JAR 369	18	10
20 Apr 61	MUSKRAT RAMBLE Top Rank JAR 548	32	5
28 Jun 62	PALISADES PARK Stateside SS 101	20	9

Jim CAPALDI UK, male vocalist   17 wks

| 27 Jul 74 | IT'S ALL UP TO YOU Island WIP 6198 | 27 | 6 |
| 25 Oct 75 | ● LOVE HURTS Island WIP 6246 | 4 | 11 |

CAPERCAILLIE
UK, male / female vocal / instrumental group   3 wks

| 23 May 92 | A PRINCE AMONG ISLANDS EP Survival ZB 45393 | 39 | 2 |

| 17 Jun 95 | | **DARK ALAN (AILEIN DUINN)** *Survival SURCD 55* | **65** | 1 |

Tracks on A Prince Among Islands EP: Coisich A Ruin (Walk My Beloved) / Fagail Bhearnaraid (Leaving Bernaray) / The Lorn Theme / Gun Teann Mi Ris Na Ruinn Tha Seo (Remembrance).

CAPPELLA *Italy, male producer – Gianfranco Bortolotti*   **67 wks**

9 Apr 88		**PUSH THE BEAT / BAUHAUS** *Fast Globe FGL 1*	**60**	2
6 May 89		**HELYOM HALIB** *Music Man MMPS 7004*	**11**	9
23 Sep 89		**HOUSE ENERGY REVENGE** *Music Man MMPS 7009*	**73**	1
27 Apr 91		**EVERYBODY** *ffrr F158*	**66**	1
18 Jan 92		**TAKE ME AWAY** *PWL Continental PWL 210* [1]	**25**	5
3 Apr 93	●	**U GOT 2 KNOW** *Internal Dance IDC 1*	**6**	11
14 Aug 93		**U GOT 2 KNOW REVISITED (re-mix)** *Internal Dance IDCR 2*	**43**	3
23 Oct 93	●	**U GOT 2 LET THE MUSIC** *Internal Dance IDC 3*	**2**	12
19 Feb 94	●	**MOVE ON BABY** *Internal Dance IDC 4*	**7**	7
18 Jun 94	●	**U & ME** *Internal Dance IDC 6*	**10**	7
15 Oct 94		**MOVE IT UP / BIG BEAT** *Internal Dance IDC 7*	**16**	6
16 Sep 95		**TELL ME THE WAY** *Systematic SYSCD 17*	**17**	3

[1] Cappella featuring Loleatta Holloway

Act was fronted by a UK, male / female vocal duo from U Got 2 Let The Music. See also 49ers.

Tony CAPSTICK and the CARLTON MAIN / FRICKLEY COLLIERY BAND
UK, male vocalist and male instrumental band   **8 wks**

21 Mar 81	●	**THE SHEFFIELD GRINDER / CAPSTICK COMES HOME** *Dingles SID 27*	**3**	8

CAPTAIN BEAKY – *See Keith MICHELL*

CAPTAIN HOLLYWOOD PROJECT
US / Germany, male / female vocal / instrumental group   **31 wks**

22 Sep 90	●	**I CAN'T STAND IT** *BCM BCMR 395* [1]	**7**	10
24 Nov 90		**ARE YOU DREAMING** *BCM BCM 07504* [1]	**17**	10
27 Mar 93		**ONLY WITH YOU** *Pulse 8 CDLOSE 40*	**67**	1
6 Nov 93		**MORE AND MORE** *Pulse 8 CDLOSE 50*	**23**	5
5 Feb 94		**IMPOSSIBLE** *Pulse 8 CDLOSE 54*	**29**	3
11 Jun 94		**ONLY WITH YOU (re-issue)** *Pulse 8 CDLOSE 62*	**61**	1
1 Apr 95		**FLYING HIGH** *Pulse 8 CDLOSE 82*	**58**	1

[1] Twenty 4 Seven featuring Captain Hollywood

CAPTAIN SENSIBLE *UK, male vocalist*   **31 wks**

26 Jun 82	★	**HAPPY TALK** *A & M CAP 1*	**1**	8
14 Aug 82		**WOT** *A & M CAP 2*	**26**	7
24 Mar 84	●	**GLAD IT'S ALL OVER / DAMNED ON 45** *A & M CAP 6*	**6**	10
28 Jul 84		**THERE ARE MORE SNAKES THAN LADDERS** *A & M CAP 7*	**57**	5
10 Dec 94		**THE HOKEY COKEY** *Have A Nice Day CDHOKEY 1*	**71**	1

CAPTAIN and TENNILLE
US, male instrumentalist – keyboards and female vocalist   **24 wks**

2 Aug 75		**LOVE WILL KEEP US TOGETHER** *A & M AMS 7165*	**32**	5
24 Jan 76		**THE WAY I WANT TO TOUCH YOU** *A & M AMS 7203*	**28**	6
4 Nov 78		**YOU NEVER DONE IT LIKE THAT** *A & M AMS 7384*	**63**	3
16 Feb 80	●	**DO THAT TO ME ONE MORE TIME** *Casablanca CAN 175*	**7**	10

Irene CARA *US, female vocalist*   **33 wks**

3 Jul 82	★	**FAME** *RSO 90*	**1**	16
4 Sep 82		**OUT HERE ON MY OWN** *RSO 66*	**58**	3

---

4 Jun 83	●	**FLASHDANCE... WHAT A FEELING** *Casablanca CAN 1016*	**2**	14

CARAMBA *Sweden, male vocalist / multi-instrumentalist dog impersonator – Michael Tretow*   **6 wks**

12 Nov 83		**FEDORA (I'LL BE YOUR DAWG)** *Billco BILL 101*	**56**	6

CARAVELLES *UK, female vocal duo*   **13 wks**

8 Aug 63	●	**YOU DON'T HAVE TO BE A BABY TO CRY** *Decca F 11697*	**6**	13

CARDIGANS
Sweden, male / female vocal / instrumental group   **13 wks**

17 Jun 95		**CARNIVAL** *Trampolene PZCD 345*	**72**	1
30 Sep 95		**SICK AND TIRED** *Stockholm 5773112*	**34**	3
2 Dec 95		**CARNIVAL (re-entry)** *Trampolene PZCD 345*	**35**	2
17 Feb 96		**RISE AND SHINE** *Trampolene 5778252*	**29**	2
21 Sep 96		**LOVEFOOL** *Stockholm 5752952*	**21**	4
7 Dec 96		**BEEN IT** *Stockholm 5759672*	**56**	1

CARE *UK, male vocal / instrumental duo*   **4 wks**

12 Nov 83		**FLAMING SWORD** *Arista KBIRD 2*	**48**	4

Mariah CAREY *US, female vocalist*   **169 wks**

4 Aug 90	●	**VISION OF LOVE** *CBS 6559320*	**9**	12
10 Nov 90		**LOVE TAKES TIME** *CBS 6563647*	**37**	8
26 Jan 91		**SOMEDAY** *Columbia 6565837*	**38**	5
1 Jun 91		**THERE'S GOT TO BE A WAY** *Columbia 6569317*	**54**	3
5 Oct 91		**EMOTIONS** *Columbia 6574037*	**17**	9
11 Jan 92		**CAN'T LET GO** *Columbia 6576627*	**20**	7
18 Apr 92		**MAKE IT HAPPEN** *Columbia 6579417*	**17**	5
27 Jun 92	●	**I'LL BE THERE** *Columbia 6581377*	**2**	9
21 Aug 93	●	**DREAMLOVER** *Columbia 6594445*	**9**	10
6 Nov 93	●	**HERO** *Columbia 6598122*	**7**	15
19 Feb 94	★	**WITHOUT YOU** *Columbia 6599192*	**1**	14
18 Jun 94	●	**ANYTIME YOU NEED A FRIEND** *Columbia 6603542*	**8**	10
17 Sep 94	●	**ENDLESS LOVE** *Epic 6608062* [1]	**3**	10
10 Dec 94	●	**ALL I WANT FOR CHRISTMAS IS YOU** *Columbia 6610702*	**2**	7
7 Jan 95		**ENDLESS LOVE (re-entry)** *Epic 6608062* [1]	**70**	2
4 Feb 95		**ENDLESS LOVE (2nd re-entry)** *Epic 6608062* [1]	**55**	4
11 Mar 95		**ALL I WANT FOR CHRISTMAS IS YOU (re-entry)** *Columbia 6610702*	**59**	1
23 Sep 95	●	**FANTASY** *Columbia 6624952*	**4**	11
9 Dec 95	●	**ONE SWEET DAY** *Columbia 6626035* [2]	**6**	11
17 Feb 96	●	**OPEN ARMS** *Columbia 6629772*	**4**	6
22 Jun 96	●	**ALWAYS BE MY BABY** *Columbia 6633345*	**3**	10

[1] Luther Vandross and Mariah Carey   [2] Mariah Carey and Boyz II Men

Although he is uncredited, I'll Be There is a duet with Trey Lorenz.

CARL – *See CLUBHOUSE*

Belinda CARLISLE *US, female vocalist*   **142 wks**

12 Dec 87	★	**HEAVEN IS A PLACE ON EARTH** *Virgin VS 1036*	**1**	14
27 Feb 88	●	**I GET WEAK** *Virgin VS 1046*	**10**	9
7 May 88	●	**CIRCLE IN THE SAND** *Virgin VS 1074*	**4**	11
6 Aug 88		**MAD ABOUT YOU** *IRS IRM 118*	**67**	3
10 Sep 88		**WORLD WITHOUT YOU** *Virgin VS 1114*	**34**	6
10 Dec 88		**LOVE NEVER DIES . . .** *Virgin VS 1150*	**54**	5
7 Oct 89	●	**LEAVE A LIGHT ON** *Virgin VS 1210*	**4**	10
9 Dec 89		**LA LUNA** *Virgin VS 1230*	**38**	6
24 Feb 90		**RUNAWAY HORSES** *Virgin VS 1244*	**40**	5

26 May 90	VISION OF YOU Virgin VS 1264	41	4
13 Oct 90	● (WE WANT) THE SAME THING Virgin VS 1219	6	10
22 Dec 90	SUMMER RAIN Virgin VS 1323	23	10
20 Apr 91	VISION OF YOU (re-entry) Virgin VS 1264	71	1
28 Sep 91	LIVE YOUR LIFE BE FREE Virgin VS 1370	12	7
16 Nov 91	DO YOU FEEL LIKE I FEEL Virgin VS 1383	29	4
11 Jan 92	HALF THE WORLD Virgin VS 1388	35	4
29 Aug 92	LITTLE BLACK BOOK Virgin VS 1428	28	5
25 Sep 93	BIG SCARY ANIMAL Virgin VSCDT 1472	12	6
27 Nov 93	LAY DOWN YOUR ARMS Virgin VSCDG 1476	27	6
13 Jul 96	● IN TOO DEEP Chrysalis CDCHS 5033	6	7
21 Sep 96	● ALWAYS BREAKING MY HEART Chrysalis CDCHS 5037	8	6
30 Nov 96	LOVE IN THE KEY OF C Chrysalis CDCHS 5044	20	3

Sara CARLSON – See MANIC MC's featuring Sara CARLSON

CARLTON UK, male vocalist   3 wks

16 Feb 91	LOVE AND PAIN Smith & Mighty SNM 4	56	2
1 Apr 95	1 TO 1 RELIGION Stoned Heights BRCDX 313 [1]	53	1

[1] Bomb The Bass featuring Carlton

Carl CARLTON US, male vocalist   8 wks

18 Jul 81	SHE'S A BAD MAMA JAMA (SHE'S BUILT, SHE'S STACKED) 20th Century TC 2488	34	8

Larry CARLTON – See Mike POST

CARLTON MAIN/FRICKLEY COLLIERY BAND – See Tony CAPSTICK and the
CARLTON MAIN/FRICKLEY COLLIERY BAND

CARMEL UK, female / male vocal / instrumental group   19 wks

6 Aug 83	BAD DAY London LON 29	15	9
11 Feb 84	MORE, MORE, MORE London LON 44	23	7
14 Jun 86	SALLY London LON 90	60	3

Eric CARMEN US, male vocalist   7 wks

10 Apr 76	ALL BY MYSELF Arista 42	12	7

Jean CARN – See Bobby M featuring Jean CARN

Kim CARNEGIE UK, female vocalist   1 wk

19 Jan 91	JAZZ RAP Best ZB 44085	73	1

Kim CARNES US, female vocalist   15 wks

9 May 81	● BETTE DAVIS EYES EMI America EA 121	10	9
8 Aug 81	DRAW OF THE CARDS EMI America EA 125	49	4
9 Oct 82	VOYEUR EMI America EA 143	68	2

Renato CAROSONE and his SEXTET
Italy, male vocalist and instrumental backing group   1 wk

4 Jul 58	TORERO – CHA CHA CHA Parlophone R 4433	25	1

Mary-Chapin CARPENTER US, female vocalist   6 wks

20 Nov 93	HE THINKS HE'LL KEEP HER Columbia 6598632	71	1
7 Jan 95	ONE COOL REMOVE Columbia 6611342 [1]	40	3
3 Jun 95	SHUT UP AND KISS ME Columbia 6613675	35	2

[1] Shawn Colvin with Mary Chapin Carpenter

CARPENTERS
US, male / female vocal / instrumental duo   173 wks

5 Sep 70	● (THEY LONG TO BE) CLOSE TO YOU A & M AMS 800	6	18
9 Jan 71	WE'VE ONLY JUST BEGUN A & M AMS 813	28	7
18 Sep 71	SUPERSTAR / FOR ALL WE KNOW A & M AMS 864	18	13
1 Jan 72	MERRY CHRISTMAS DARLING A & M AME 601	45	1
23 Sep 72	● I WON'T LAST A DAY WITHOUT YOU / GOODBYE TO LOVE A & M AMS 7023	9	16
7 Jul 73	● YESTERDAY ONCE MORE A & M AMS 7073	2	17
20 Oct 73	● TOP OF THE WORLD A & M AMS 7086	5	18
2 Mar 74	JAMBALAYA (ON THE BAYOU) / MR. GUDER A & M AMS 7098	12	11
8 Jun 74	I WON'T LAST A DAY WITHOUT YOU (re-issue) A & M AMS 7111	32	5
18 Jan 75	● PLEASE MR. POSTMAN A & M AMS 7141	2	12
19 Apr 75	● ONLY YESTERDAY A & M AMS 7159	7	10
30 Aug 75	SOLITAIRE A & M AMS 7187	32	4
20 Dec 75	SANTA CLAUS IS COMIN' TO TOWN A & M AMS 7144 ..	37	4
27 Mar 76	THERE'S A KIND OF HUSH (ALL OVER THE WORLD) A & M AMS 7219	22	6
3 Jul 76	I NEED TO BE IN LOVE A & M AMS 7238	36	5
8 Oct 77	● CALLING OCCUPANTS OF INTERPLANETARY CRAFT (THE RECOGNISED ANTHEM OF WORLD CONTACT DAY) A & M AMS 7318	9	9
11 Feb 78	SWEET SWEET SMILE A & M AMS 7327	40	4
22 Oct 83	MAKE BELIEVE IT'S YOUR FIRST TIME A & M AM 147	60	3
8 Dec 90	MERRY CHRISTMAS DARLING / (THEY LONG TO BE) CLOSE TO YOU (re-issue) A & M AM 716	25	5
13 Feb 93	RAINY DAYS AND MONDAYS A & M AMCD 0180	63	2
24 Dec 94	TRYIN' TO GET THE FEELING AGAIN A & M 5807612	44	2

I Won't Last A Day Without You AMS 703 listed by itself 23 Sep 72 at position 49.
Goodbye To Love, the other side, listed by itself from 30 Sep 72 until the end of the
record's chart run. Mr Guder listed with Jambalaya from 16 Mar 74 until the end of the
record's chart run.

Joe 'Fingers' CARR
US, male instrumentalist – piano, Lou Busch under a false name   5 wks

29 Jun 56	PORTUGUESE WASHERWOMAN Capitol CL 14587	20	5

See also Lou Busch.

Linda CARR US, female vocalist   12 wks

12 Jul 75	HIGHWIRE Chelsea 2005 025 [1]	15	8
5 Jun 76	SOLD MY ROCK 'N' ROLL (GAVE IT FOR FUNKY SOUL) Spark SRL 1139 [2]	36	4

[1] Linda Carr and the Love Squad [2] Linda and the Funky Boys

Pearl CARR and Teddy JOHNSON
UK, female / male vocal duo   19 wks

20 Mar 59	SING LITTLE BIRDIE Columbia DB 4275	12	8
6 Apr 61	HOW WONDERFUL TO KNOW Columbia DB 4603	23	11

Suzi CARR US, female vocalist   1 wk

8 Oct 94	ALL OVER ME Cowboy RODEO 947CD	45	1

Valerie CARR US, female vocalist   2 wks

4 Jul 58	WHEN THE BOYS TALK ABOUT THE GIRLS Columbia DB 4131	29	1
18 Jul 58	WHEN THE BOYS TALK ABOUT THE GIRLS (re-entry) Columbia DB 4131	30	1

Vikki CARR US, female vocalist — 26 wks

1 Jun 67	● IT MUST BE HIM (SEUL SUR SON ETOILE) Liberty LIB 55917	2	20
30 Aug 67	THERE I GO Liberty LBF 15022	50	1
12 Mar 69	WITH PEN IN HAND Liberty LBF 15166	43	1
26 Mar 69	WITH PEN IN HAND (re-entry) Liberty LBF 15166	39	2
30 Apr 69	WITH PEN IN HAND (2nd re-entry) Liberty LBF 15166	40	2

Raffaella CARRA Italy, female vocalist — 12 wks

15 Apr 78	● DO IT DO IT AGAIN Epic EPC 6094	9	12

Paul CARRACK UK, male vocalist — 18 wks

16 May 87	WHEN YOU WALK IN THE ROOM Chrysalis CHS 3109	48	5
18 Mar 89	DON'T SHED A TEAR Chrysalis CHS 3164	60	3
6 Jan 96	EYES OF BLUE IRS CDEIRS 192	40	4
6 Apr 96	HOW LONG IRS CDEIRS 193	32	5
24 Aug 96	EYES OF BLUE (re-mix) IRS CDEIRS 194	45	1

José CARRERAS Spain, male vocalist — 15 wks

11 Jul 92	AMIGOS PARA SIEMPRE (FRIENDS FOR LIFE) Really Useful RUR 10 [1]	11	11
30 Jul 94	LIBIAMO / LA DONNA E MOBILE Teldec YZ 843CD [2]	21	4

[1] José Carreras and Sarah Brightman [2] José Carreras, Placido Domingo and Luciano Pavarotti

Tia CARRERE US, female vocalist — 6 wks

30 May 92	BALLROOM BLITZ Reprise W 0105	26	6

Jim CARREY US, male vocalist — 3 wks

21 Jan 95	CUBAN PETE Columbia 6606625	31	3

Dina CARROLL UK, female vocalist — 84 wks

2 Feb 91	● IT'S TOO LATE Mercury ITM 3 [1]	8	14
15 Jun 91	NAKED LOVE (JUST SAY YOU WANT ME) Mercury ITM 4 [2]	39	3
11 Jul 92	AIN'T NO MAN A & M AM 0001	16	8
10 Oct 92	SPECIAL KIND OF LOVE A & M AM 0088	16	5
5 Dec 92	SO CLOSE A & M AM 0101	20	8
27 Feb 93	THIS TIME A & M AMCD 0184	23	6
15 May 93	EXPRESS A & M 5802632	12	6
16 Oct 93	● DON'T BE A STRANGER A & M 5803892	3	13
11 Dec 93	● THE PERFECT YEAR A & M 5804812	5	11
28 Sep 96	● ESCAPING Mercury DCCD 1	3	8
21 Dec 96	ONLY HUMAN Mercury DCCD 2	33†	2

[1] Quartz introducing Dina Carroll [2] Quartz and Dina Carroll

Ronnie CARROLL UK, male vocalist — 50 wks

27 Jul 56	WALK HAND IN HAND Philips PB 605	13	8
29 Mar 57	THE WISDOM OF A FOOL Philips PB 667	20	2
31 Mar 60	FOOTSTEPS Philips PB 1004	36	3
22 Feb 62	RING A DING GIRL Philips PB 1222	46	3
2 Aug 62	● ROSES ARE RED Philips 326532 BF	3	16
15 Nov 62	IF ONLY TOMORROW Philips 326550 BF	33	4
7 Mar 63	● SAY WONDERFUL THINGS Philips 326574 BF	6	14

Jasper CARROTT UK, male vocalist — 15 wks

16 Aug 75	● FUNKY MOPED / MAGIC ROUNDABOUT DJM DJS 388	5	15

CARS US, male vocal / instrumental group — 51 wks

11 Nov 78	● MY BEST FRIEND'S GIRL Elektra K 12301	3	10
17 Feb 79	JUST WHAT I NEEDED Elektra K 12312	17	10
28 Jul 79	LET'S GO Elektra K 12371	51	1
5 Jun 82	SINCE YOU'RE GONE Elektra K 13177	37	4
29 Sep 84	● DRIVE Elektra E 9706	5	11
3 Aug 85	● DRIVE (re-entry) Elektra E 9706	4	12

CARTER – THE UNSTOPPABLE SEX MACHINE UK, male vocal / instrumental duo — 46 wks

26 Jan 91	BLOODSPORTS FOR ALL Rough Trade R 20112687	48	2
22 Jun 91	SHERIFF FATMAN Big Cat USM 1	23	7
26 Oct 91	AFTER THE WATERSHED Big Cat USM 2	11	5
11 Jan 92	RUBBISH Big Cat USM 3	14	5
25 Apr 92	● THE ONLY LIVING BOY IN NEW CROSS Big Cat USM 4	7	5
4 Jul 92	DO RE ME SO FAR SO GOOD Chrysalis USM 5	22	3
28 Nov 92	THE IMPOSSIBLE DREAM Chrysalis USM 6	21	3
4 Sep 93	LEAN ON ME I WON'T FALL OVER Chrysalis CDUSM 7	16	3
16 Oct 93	LENNY AND TERENCE Chrysalis CDUSM 8	40	2
12 Mar 94	GLAM ROCK COPS Chrysalis CDUSMS 10	24	3
19 Nov 94	LET'S GET TATTOOS Chrysalis CDUSMS 30	30	3
4 Feb 95	THE YOUNG OFFENDER'S MUM Chrysalis CDUSMS 12	34	3
30 Sep 95	BORN ON THE 5TH OF NOVEMBER Chrysalis CDUSM 13	35	2

Clarence CARTER US, male vocalist — 13 wks

10 Oct 70	● PATCHES Atlantic 2091 030	2	13

Sam CARTWRIGHT – See VOLCANO

CARVELLS UK, male vocalist / instrumentalist – Alan Carvell — 4 wks

26 Nov 77	THE L.A. RUN Creole CR 143	31	4

CASCADES US, male vocal group — 16 wks

28 Feb 63	● RHYTHM OF THE RAIN Warner Bros. WB 88	5	16

CASE featuring Foxxy BROWN
US, male instrumentalist and female vocalist — 3 wks

21 Sep 96	TOUCH ME TEASE ME Def Jam DEFCD 18	26	3

Natalie CASEY UK, female vocalist — 1 wk

7 Jan 84	CHICK CHICK CHICKEN Polydor CHICK 1	72	1

Johnny CASH US, male vocalist — 59 wks

3 Jun 65	IT AIN'T ME BABE CBS 201760	28	8
6 Sep 69	● A BOY NAMED SUE CBS 4460	4	19
23 May 70	WHAT IS TRUTH CBS 4934	21	11
15 Apr 72	● A THING CALLED LOVE CBS 7797 [1]	4	13
22 Jul 72	A THING CALLED LOVE (re-entry) CBS 7797 [1]	48	1
3 Jul 76	ONE PIECE AT A TIME CBS 4287 [2]	32	7

[1] Johnny Cash with the Evangel Temple Choir [2] Johnny Cash with the Tennessee Three

Pat CASH – See John McENROE and Pat CASH with the FULL METAL RACKETS

CASHFLOW US, male vocal / instrumental group — 8 wks

24 May 86	**MINE ALL MINE / PARTY FREAK** Club JAB 30	**15**	8

CASHMERE US, male vocal / instrumental group — 11 wks

19 Jan 85	**CAN I** Fourth & Broadway BRW 19	**29**	8
23 Mar 85	**WE NEED LOVE** Fourth & Broadway BRW 22	**52**	3

CASINOS US, male vocal group — 7 wks

23 Feb 67	**THEN YOU CAN TELL ME GOODBYE** President PT 123	**28**	7

David CASSIDY US, male vocalist — 109 wks

8 Apr 72	● **COULD IT BE FOREVER / CHERISH** Bell 1224	**2**	17
16 Sep 72	★ **HOW CAN I BE SURE** Bell 1258	**1**	11
25 Nov 72	**ROCK ME BABY** Bell 1268	**11**	9
24 Mar 73	● **I'M A CLOWN / SOME KIND OF A SUMMER** Bell MABEL 4	**3**	12
13 Oct 73	★ **DAYDREAMER / THE PUPPY SONG** Bell 1334	**1**	15
11 May 74	● **IF I DIDN'T CARE** Bell 1350	**9**	8
27 Jul 74	**PLEASE PLEASE ME** Bell 1371	**16**	6
5 Jul 75	**I WRITE THE SONGS / GET IT UP FOR LOVE** RCA 2571	**11**	8
25 Oct 75	**DARLIN'** RCA 2622	**16**	8
23 Feb 85	● **THE LAST KISS** Arista ARIST 589	**6**	9
11 May 85	**ROMANCE (LET YOUR HEART GO)** Arista ARIST 620	**54**	6

See also Partridge Family starring Shirley Jones featuring David Cassidy.

CAST UK, male vocal / instrumental group — 25 wks

15 Jul 95	**FINETIME** Polydor 5795072	**17**	4
30 Sep 95	**ALRIGHT** Polydor 5799272	**13**	4
20 Jan 96	● **SANDSTORM** Polydor 5778732	**8**	5
30 Mar 96	● **WALKAWAY** Polydor 5762852	**9**	7
26 Oct 96	● **FLYING** Polydor 5754772	**4**	5

Roy CASTLE UK, male vocalist — 3 wks

22 Dec 60	**LITTLE WHITE BERRY** Philips PB 1087	**40**	3

CASUALS UK, male vocal / instrumental group — 26 wks

14 Aug 68	● **JESAMINE** Decca F 22784	**2**	18
4 Dec 68	**TOY** Decca F 22852	**30**	8

CAT UK, male vocalist — 4 wks

23 Oct 93	**TONGUE TIED** EMI CDEM 286	**17**	4

CATATONIA UK, male / female vocal / instrumental group — 5 wks

3 Feb 96	**SWEET CATATONIA** Blanco Y Negro NEG 85CD	**61**	1
4 May 96	**LOST CAT** Blanco Y Negro NEG 88CD1	**41**	1
7 Sep 96	**YOU'VE GOT A LOT TO ANSWER FOR** Blanco Y Negro NEG 93CD1	**35**	2
30 Nov 96	**BLEED** Blanco Y Negro NEG 97CD1	**46**	1

CATCH UK, male vocal / instrumental group — 1 wk

17 Nov 90	**FREE (C'MON)** ffrr F 147	**70**	1

CATHERINE WHEEL UK, male vocal / instrumental group — 9 wks

23 Nov 91	**BLACK METALLIC (EP)** Fontana CW 1	**68**	1
8 Feb 92	**BALLOON** Fontana CW 2	**59**	1
18 Apr 92	**I WANT TO TOUCH YOU** Fontana CW 3	**35**	2
9 Jan 93	**30 CENTURY MAN** Fontana CWCD 4	**47**	2
10 Jul 93	**CRANK** Fontana CWCD 5	**66**	1
16 Oct 93	**SHOW ME MARY** Fontana CWCDA 6	**62**	1
5 Aug 95	**WAYDOWN** Fontana CWCD 7	**67**	1

Tracks on Black Metallic (EP): Black Metallic / Crawling Over Me / Let Me Down Again / Saccharine.

Lorraine CATO UK, female vocalist — 3 wks

6 Feb 93	**HOW CAN YOU TELL ME IT'S OVER** Columbia 6587662	**46**	2
3 Aug 96	**I WAS MADE TO LOVE YOU** MCA MCSTD 40055	**41**	1

CATS UK, male instrumental group — 2 wks

9 Apr 69	**SWAN LAKE** BAF 1	**48**	1
21 May 69	**SWAN LAKE (re-entry)** BAF 1	**50**	1

CATS UK UK, female vocal group — 8 wks

6 Oct 79	**LUTON AIRPORT** WEA K 18075	**22**	8

Nick CAVE and the BAD SEEDS Australia / Germany, male vocal / instrumental group — 8 wks

11 Apr 92	**STRAIGHT TO YOU / JACK THE RIPPER** Mute MUTE 140	**68**	1
12 Dec 92	**WHAT A WONDERFUL WORLD** Mute MUTE 151 [1]	**72**	1
9 Apr 94	**DO YOU LOVE ME** Mute MUTE 160	**68**	1
14 Oct 95	**WHERE THE WILD ROSES GROW** Mute CDMUTE 185 [2]	**11**	4
9 Mar 96	**HENRY LEE** Mute CDMUTE 189 [3]	**36**	1

[1] Nick Cave and Shane McGowan [2] Nick Cave and Kylie Minogue
[3] Nick Cave and the Bad Seeds and PJ Harvey

CAVEMAN UK, male rap group — 2 wks

9 Mar 91	**I'M READY** Profile PROF 330	**65**	2

CCS UK, male vocal / instrumental group — 55 wks

31 Oct 70	**WHOLE LOTTA LOVE** RAK 104	**13**	13
27 Feb 71	● **WALKIN'** RAK 109	**7**	16
4 Sep 71	● **TAP TURNS ON THE WATER** RAK 119	**5**	13
4 Mar 72	**BROTHER** RAK 126	**25**	8
4 Aug 73	**BAND PLAYED THE BOOGIE** RAK 154	**36**	5

CENTORY US, male rapper — 1 wk

17 Dec 94	**POINT OF NO RETURN** EMI CDEM 354	**67**	1

CENTRAL LINE UK, male vocal / instrumental group — 30 wks

31 Jan 81	**(YOU KNOW) YOU CAN DO IT** Mercury LINE 7	**67**	3
15 Aug 81	**WALKING INTO SUNSHINE** Mercury MER 78	**42**	10
30 Jan 82	**DON'T TELL ME** Mercury MER 90	**55**	3
20 Nov 82	**YOU'VE SAID ENOUGH** Mercury MER 117	**58**	3
22 Jan 83	**NATURE BOY** Mercury MER 131	**21**	8
11 Jun 83	**SURPRISE SURPRISE** Mercury MER 133	**48**	3

CERRONE *France, male producer / multi-instrumentalist* **21 wks**

5 Mar 77		**LOVE IN C MINOR** *Atlantic K 10895*	**31**	4
29 Jul 78	●	**SUPERNATURE** *Atlantic K 11089*	**8**	12
13 Jan 79		**JE SUIS MUSIC** *CBS 6918*	**39**	4
10 Aug 96		**SUPERNATURE (re-mix)** *Encore CDCOR 013*	**66**	1

A CERTAIN RATIO
UK, male vocal / instrumental group **3 wks**

16 Jun 90	**WON'T STOP LOVING YOU** *A & M ACR 540*	**55**	3

Peter CETERA *US, male vocalist* **13 wks**

2 Aug 86	●	**GLORY OF LOVE** *Full Moon W 8662*	**3**	13

Frank CHACKSFIELD *UK, orchestra* **41 wks**

3 Apr 53	●	**LITTLE RED MONKEY** *Parlophone R 3658* [1]	**10**	3
22 May 53	●	**TERRY'S THEME FROM 'LIMELIGHT'** *Decca F 10106*	**2**	24
12 Feb 54		**EBB TIDE** *Decca F 10122*	**9**	2
24 Feb 56		**IN OLD LISBON** *Decca F 10689*	**15**	4
18 May 56		**PORT AU PRINCE** *Decca F 10727* [2]	**18**	6
31 Aug 56		**DONKEY CART** *Decca F 10743*	**26**	2

[1] Frank Chacksfield's Tunesmiths, featuring Jack Jordan – clavioline
[2] Winifred Atwell and Frank Chacksfield

CHAIRMEN OF THE BOARD *US, male vocal group* **77 wks**

22 Aug 70	●	**GIVE ME JUST A LITTLE MORE TIME** *Invictus INV 501*	**3**	13
14 Nov 70	●	**YOU'VE GOT ME DANGLING ON A STRING** *Invictus INV 504*	**5**	13
20 Feb 71		**EVERYTHING'S TUESDAY** *Invictus INV 507*	**12**	9
15 May 71		**PAY TO THE PIPER** *Invictus INV 511*	**34**	7
4 Sep 71		**CHAIRMAN OF THE BOARD** *Invictus INV 516*	**48**	2
15 Jul 72		**WORKING ON A BUILDING OF LOVE** *Invictus INV 519*	**20**	8
7 Oct 72		**ELMO JAMES** *Invictus INV 524*	**21**	7
16 Dec 72		**I'M ON MY WAY TO A BETTER PLACE** *Invictus INV 527*	**38**	1
6 Jan 73		**I'M ON MY WAY TO A BETTER PLACE (re-entry)** *Invictus INV 527*	**30**	5
23 Jun 73		**FINDERS KEEPERS** *Invictus INV 530*	**21**	9
13 Sep 86		**LOVERBOY** *EMI EMI 5585* [1]	**56**	3

[1] Chairmen Of The Board featuring General Johnson

CHAKACHAS
Belgium, male / female vocal / instrumental group **8 wks**

11 Jan 62	**TWIST TWIST** *RCA 1264*	**48**	1
27 May 72	**JUNGLE FEVER** *Polydor 2121 064*	**29**	7

George CHAKIRIS *US, male vocalist* **1 wk**

2 Jun 60	**HEART OF A TEENAGE GIRL** *Triumph RGM 1010*	**49**	1

CHAKKA BOOM BANG
Holland, male instrumental / production group **1 wk**

20 Jan 96	**TOSSING AND TURNING** *Hooj Choons HOOJCD 39*	**57**	1

Sue CHALONER *UK, female vocalist* **1 wk**

22 May 93	**MOVE ON UP** *Pulse 8 CDLOSE 41*	**64**	1

Richard CHAMBERLAIN *US, male vocalist* **36 wks**

7 Jun 62	**THEME FROM 'DR. KILDARE' (THREE STARS WILL SHINE TONIGHT)** *MGM 1160*	**12**	10
1 Nov 62	**LOVE ME TENDER** *MGM 1173*	**15**	11
21 Feb 63	**HI-LILI HI-LO** *MGM 1189*	**20**	9
18 Jul 63	**TRUE LOVE** *MGM 1205*	**30**	6

CHAMELEON *UK, male vocal / instrumental group* **2 wks**

18 May 96	**THE WAY IT IS** *Stress CDSTR 65*	**34**	2

CHAMELEONS – *See LORI and the CHAMELEONS*

CHAMPAIGN
US, male / female vocal / instrumental group **13 wks**

9 May 81	●	**HOW 'BOUT US** *CBS A 1046*	**5**	13

CHAMPION LEGEND – *See RAZE*

CHAMPS *US, male instrumental group* **10 wks**

4 Apr 58	●	**TEQUILA** *London HLU 8580*	**5**	9
17 Mar 60		**TOO MUCH TEQUILA** *London HLH 9052*	**49**	1

CHAMPS BOYS *France, male instrumental group* **6 wks**

19 Jun 76	**TUBULAR BELLS** *Philips 6006 519*	**41**	6

Gene CHANDLER *US, male vocalist* **29 wks**

5 Jun 68	**NOTHING CAN STOP ME** *Soul City SC 102*	**41**	4
3 Feb 79	**GET DOWN** *20th Century BTC 1040*	**11**	11
1 Sep 79	**WHEN YOU'RE NUMBER 1** *20th Century TC 2411*	**43**	5
28 Jun 80	**DOES SHE HAVE A FRIEND** *20th Century TC 2451*	**28**	9

CHANELLE *US, female vocalist* **9 wks**

11 Mar 89	**ONE MAN** *Cooltempo COOL 183*	**16**	8
10 Dec 94	**ONE MAN (re-mix)** *Deep Distraxion OILYCD 031*	**50**	1

CHANGE *US, male / female vocal / instrumental group* **43 wks**

28 Jun 80	**A LOVER'S HOLIDAY / GLOW OF LOVE** *WEA K 79141*	**14**	8
6 Sep 80	**SEARCHING** *WEA K 79156*	**11**	10
2 Jun 84	**CHANGE OF HEART** *WEA YZ 7*	**17**	10
11 Aug 84	**YOU ARE MY MELODY** *WEA YZ 14*	**48**	4
16 Mar 85	**LET'S GO TOGETHER** *Cooltempo COOL 107*	**37**	7
25 May 85	**OH WHAT A FEELING** *Cooltempo COOL 109*	**56**	2
13 Jul 85	**MUTUAL ATTRACTION** *Cooltempo COOL 111*	**60**	2

CHANGING FACES *US, female vocal duo* **3 wks**

24 Sep 94	**STROKE YOU UP** *Big Beat A 8251CD*	**43**	3

Bruce CHANNEL *US, male vocalist* **28 wks**

22 Mar 62	●	**HEY! BABY** *Mercury AMT 1171*	**2**	12
26 Jun 68		**KEEP ON** *Bell 1010*	**12**	16

CHANNEL X
Belgium, male / female vocal / instrumental group **1 wk**

14 Dec 91	**GROOVE TO MOVE** *PWL Continental PWL 209*	**67**	1

CHANSON US, male / female vocal group — 7 wks

13 Jan 79	DON'T HOLD BACK Ariola ARO 140	33	7

CHANTAYS US, male instrumental group — 14 wks

18 Apr 63	PIPELINE London HLD 9696	16	14

CHANTER SISTERS UK, female vocal group — 5 wks

17 Jul 76	SIDE SHOW Polydor 2058 735	43	5

CHAOS UK, male vocal group — 2 wks

3 Oct 92	FAREWELL MY SUMMER LOVE Arista 74321116397	55	2

Harry CHAPIN US, male vocalist — 5 wks

11 May 74	W.O.L.D. Elektra K 12133	34	5

Simone CHAPMAN – See ILLEGAL NATION featuring Simone CHAPMAN

Tracy CHAPMAN US, female vocalist — 15 wks

11 Jun 88	● FAST CAR Elektra EKR 73	5	12
30 Sep 89	CROSSROADS Elektra EKR 95	61	3

CHAPTERHOUSE UK, male vocal / instrumental group — 3 wks

30 Mar 91	PEARL Dedicated STONE 003	67	1
12 Oct 91	MESMERISE Dedicated HOUSE 001	60	2

CHAQUITO UK, male arranger / conductor – Johnny Gregory — 1 wk

27 Oct 60	NEVER ON SUNDAY Fontana H 265	50	1

CHARLATANS UK, male vocal / instrumental group — 49 wks

2 Jun 90	● THE ONLY ONE I KNOW Situation Two SIT 70T	9	9
22 Sep 90	THEN Situation Two SIT 74T	12	5
9 Mar 91	OVER RISING Situation Two SIT 76	15	5
17 Aug 91	INDIAN ROPE Dead Dead Good GOOD 1T	57	1
9 Nov 91	ME. IN TIME Situation Two SIT 84	28	3
7 Mar 92	WEIRDO Situation Two SIT 88	19	4
18 Jul 92	TREMELO SONG (EP) Situation Two SIT 97T	44	2
5 Feb 94	CAN'T GET OUT OF BED Beggars Banquet BBQ 27CD	24	3
19 Mar 94	I NEVER WANT AN EASY LIFE IF ME AND HE WERE EVER TO GET THERE Beggars Banquet BBQ 31CD	38	1
2 Jul 94	JESUS HAIRDO Beggars Banquet BBQ 32CD1	48	2
7 Jan 95	CRASHIN' IN Beggars Banquet BBQ 44CD	31	2
27 May 95	JUST LOOKIN' / BULLET COMES Beggars Banquet BBQ 55CD	32	3
26 Aug 95	JUST WHEN YOU'RE THINKIN' THINGS OVER Beggars Banquet BBQ 60CD	12	3
7 Sep 96	● ONE TO ANOTHER Beggars Banquet BBQ 301CD	3	6

Tracks on Tremelo Song (EP): Tremelo Song / Happen To Die / Normality Swing.

CHARLENE US, female vocalist — 12 wks

15 May 82	★ I'VE NEVER BEEN TO ME Motown TMG 1260	1	12

Don CHARLES UK, male vocalist — 5 wks

22 Feb 62	WALK WITH ME MY ANGEL Decca F 11424	39	5

Ray CHARLES
US, male vocalist / instrumentalist – piano — 130 wks

1 Dec 60	GEORGIA ON MY MIND HMV POP 792	47	1
15 Dec 60	GEORGIA ON MY MIND (re-entry) HMV POP 792	24	7
19 Oct 61	● HIT THE ROAD JACK HMV POP 935	6	12
14 Jun 62	★ I CAN'T STOP LOVING YOU HMV POP 1034	1	17
13 Sep 62	● YOU DON'T KNOW ME HMV POP 1064	9	13
13 Dec 62	YOUR CHEATING HEART HMV POP 1099	13	8
28 Mar 63	DON'T SET ME FREE HMV POP 1133	37	3
16 May 63	● TAKE THESE CHAINS FROM MY HEART HMV POP 1161	5	20
12 Sep 63	NO ONE HMV POP 1202	35	7
31 Oct 63	BUSTED HMV POP 1221	21	10
24 Sep 64	NO ONE TO CRY TO HMV POP 1333	38	3
21 Jan 65	MAKIN' WHOOPEE HMV POP 1383	42	4
10 Feb 66	CRYIN' TIME HMV POP 1502	50	1
21 Apr 66	TOGETHER AGAIN HMV POP 1519	48	1
5 Jul 67	HERE WE GO AGAIN HMV POP 1595	38	1
19 Jul 67	HERE WE GO AGAIN (re-entry) HMV POP 1595	45	2
20 Dec 67	YESTERDAY Stateside SS 2071	44	4
31 Jul 68	ELEANOR RIGBY Stateside SS 2120	36	9
13 Jan 90	I'LL BE GOOD TO YOU Qwest W 9992 [1]	21	7

[1] Quincy Jones featuring Ray Charles and Chaka Khan

See also INXS.

Suzette CHARLES US, female vocalist — 2 wks

21 Aug 93	FREE TO LOVE AGAIN RCA 74321158372	58	2

Tina CHARLES UK, female vocalist — 63 wks

7 Feb 76	★ I LOVE TO LOVE (BUT MY BABY LOVES TO DANCE) CBS 3937	1	12
1 May 76	LOVE ME LIKE A LOVER CBS 4237	31	7
21 Aug 76	● DANCE LITTLE LADY DANCE CBS 4480	6	13
4 Dec 76	DR. LOVE CBS 4779	4	10
14 May 77	RENDEZVOUS CBS 5174	27	6
29 Oct 77	LOVE BUG – SWEETS FOR MY SWEET (MEDLEY) CBS 5680	26	4
11 Mar 78	I'LL GO WHERE YOUR MUSIC TAKES ME CBS 6062	27	8
30 Aug 86	I LOVE TO LOVE (re-mix) DMC DECK 1	67	3

CHARLES and EDDIE US, male vocal duo — 30 wks

31 Oct 92	★ WOULD I LIE TO YOU Capitol CL 673	1	17
20 Feb 93	N.Y.C. (CAN YOU BELIEVE THIS CITY) Capitol CDCL 681	33	5
22 May 93	HOUSE IS NOT A HOME Capitol CDCLS 688	29	4
13 May 95	24-7-365 Capitol CDCLS 747	38	4

Dick CHARLESWORTH and his CITY GENTS
UK, male jazz band group, Dick Charlesworth clarinet — 1 wk

4 May 61	BILLY BOY Top Rank JAR 558	43	1

CHARLOTTE UK, female vocalist — 1 wk

12 Mar 94	QUEEN OF HEARTS Big Life BLRD 106	54	1

CHARME US, male / female vocal group — 2 wks

17 Nov 84	GEORGY PORGY RCA 464	68	2

CHARO and the SALSOUL ORCHESTRA
US, female vocalist and orchestra — 4 wks

29 Apr 78	DANCE A LITTLE BIT CLOSER Salsoul SSOL 101	44	4

CHAS and DAVE UK, male vocal / instrumental duo — 66 wks

11 Nov 78	**STRUMMIN'** *EMI 2874* [1]	**52**	3
26 May 79	**GERTCHA** *EMI 2947*	**20**	8
1 Sep 79	**THE SIDEBOARD SONG (GOT MY BEER IN THE SIDEBOARD HERE)** *EMI 2986*	**55**	3
29 Nov 80 ●	**RABBIT** *Rockney 9*	**8**	11
12 Dec 81	**STARS OVER 45** *Rockney KOR 12*	**21**	8
13 Mar 82 ●	**AIN'T NO PLEASING YOU** *Rockney KOR 14*	**2**	11
17 Jul 82	**MARGATE** *Rockney KOR 15*	**46**	4
19 Mar 83	**LONDON GIRLS** *Rockney KOR 17*	**63**	3
3 Dec 83	**MY MELANCHOLY BABY** *Rockney KOR 21*	**51**	6
3 May 86 ●	**SNOOKER LOOPY** *Rockney POT 147* [2]	**6**	9

[1] Chas and Dave with Rockney [2] Matchroom Mob with Chas and Dave

See also Tottenham Hotspur FA Cup Final Squad.

CHEAP TRICK US, male vocal / instrumental group — 14 wks

5 May 79	**I WANT YOU TO WANT ME** *Epic EPC 7258*	**29**	9
2 Feb 80	**WAY OF THE WORLD** *Epic EPC 8114*	**73**	2
31 Jul 82	**IF YOU WANT MY LOVE** *Epic EPC A 2406*	**57**	3

Oliver CHEATHAM US, male vocalist — 5 wks

2 Jul 83	**GET DOWN SATURDAY NIGHT** *MCA 828*	**38**	5

CHECK 1-2 – *See* Craig McLACHLAN

Chubby CHECKER US, male vocalist — 112 wks

22 Sep 60	**THE TWIST** *Columbia DB 4503*	**49**	1
6 Oct 60	**THE TWIST (re-entry)** *Columbia DB 4503*	**44**	1
30 Mar 61	**PONY TIME** *Columbia DB 4591*	**27**	6
17 Aug 61	**LET'S TWIST AGAIN** *Columbia DB 4691*	**37**	3
28 Dec 61 ●	**LET'S TWIST AGAIN (re-entry)** *Columbia DB 4691*	**2**	27
11 Jan 62	**THE TWIST (2nd re-entry)** *Columbia DB 4503*	**14**	10
5 Apr 62	**SLOW TWISTIN'** *Columbia DB 4808*	**23**	8
19 Apr 62	**TEACH ME TO TWIST** *Columbia DB 4802* [1]	**45**	1
9 Aug 62	**DANCIN' PARTY** *Columbia DB 4876*	**19**	13
23 Aug 62	**LET'S TWIST AGAIN (2nd re-entry)** *Columbia DB 4691*	**46**	1
13 Sep 62	**LET'S TWIST AGAIN (3rd re-entry)** *Columbia DB 4691*	**49**	3
1 Nov 62	**LIMBO ROCK** *Cameo Parkway P 849*	**32**	10
20 Dec 62	**JINGLE BELL ROCK** *Cameo Parkway C 205* [1]	**40**	3
31 Oct 63	**WHAT DO YA SAY** *Cameo Parkway P 806*	**37**	4
29 Nov 75 ●	**LET'S TWIST AGAIN / THE TWIST (re-issue)** *London HL 10512*	**5**	10
18 Jun 88 ●	**THE TWIST (YO, TWIST)** *Urban URB 20* [2]	**2**	11

[1] Chubby Checker and Bobby Rydell [2] Fat Boys and Chubby Checker

CHECKMATES – *See* Emile FORD and the CHECKMATES

CHECKMATES LTD. US, male vocal / instrumental group — 8 wks

15 Nov 69	**PROUD MARY** *A & M AMS 769*	**30**	8

Judy CHEEKS US, female vocalist — 15 wks

13 Nov 93	**SO IN LOVE (THE REAL DEAL)** *Positiva CDTIV 6*	**27**	3
7 May 94	**REACH** *Positiva CDTIV 12*	**17**	4
4 Mar 95	**THIS TIME / RESPECT** *Positiva CDTIV 28*	**23**	2
17 Jun 95	**YOU'RE THE STORY OF MY LIFE / AS LONG AS YOU'RE GOOD TO ME** *Positiva CDTIV 34*	**30**	3
13 Jan 96	**REACH (re-mix)** *Positiva CDTIV 42*	**22**	3

CHEETAHS UK, male vocal / instrumental group — 6 wks

1 Oct 64	**MECCA** *Philips BF 1362*	**36**	3
21 Jan 65	**SOLDIER BOY** *Philips BF 1383*	**39**	3

CHELSEA F.C. UK, male football team vocalists — 15 wks

26 Feb 72 ●	**BLUE IS THE COLOUR** *Penny Farthing PEN 782*	**5**	12
14 May 94	**NO ONE CAN STOP US NOW** *RCA 74321210452*	**23**	3

CHEMICAL BROTHERS
UK, male instrumental / production duo — 15 wks

17 Jun 95	**LEAVE HOME** *Junior Boy's Own CHEMSD 1*	**17**	4
9 Sep 95	**LIFE IS SWEET** *Junior Boy's Own CHEMSD 2*	**25**	3
27 Jan 96	**LOOPS OF FURY (EP)** *Junior Boy's Own CHEMSD 3*	**13**	1
12 Oct 96 ★	**SETTING SUN** *Junior Boy's Own CHEMSD 4*	**1**	7

Tracks on Loops Of Fury (EP): *Loops Of Fury / (The Best Part Of) Breaking Up / Get On Up Like This / Chemical Beats.*

CHEQUERS UK, male vocal / instrumental group — 10 wks

18 Oct 75	**ROCK ON BROTHER** *Creole CR 111*	**21**	5
28 Feb 76	**HEY MISS PAYNE** *Creole CR 116*	**32**	5

CHER US, female vocalist — 171 wks

19 Aug 65 ●	**ALL I REALLY WANT TO DO** *Liberty LIB 66114*	**9**	10
31 Mar 66 ●	**BANG BANG (MY BABY SHOT ME DOWN)** *Liberty LIB 66160*	**3**	12
4 Aug 66	**I FEEL SOMETHING IN THE AIR** *Liberty LIB 12034*	**43**	2
22 Sep 66	**SUNNY** *Liberty LIB 12083*	**32**	5
6 Nov 71 ●	**GYPSIES TRAMPS AND THIEVES** *MCA MU 1142*	**4**	13
16 Feb 74	**DARK LADY** *MCA 101*	**36**	3
16 Mar 74	**DARK LADY (re-entry)** *MCA 101*	**45**	1
19 Dec 87 ●	**I FOUND SOMEONE** *Geffen GEF 31*	**5**	10
2 Apr 88	**WE ALL SLEEP ALONE** *Geffen GEF 35*	**47**	5
2 Sep 89 ●	**IF I COULD TURN BACK TIME** *Geffen GEF 59*	**6**	14
13 Jan 90	**JUST LIKE JESSE JAMES** *Geffen GEF 69*	**11**	11
7 Apr 90	**HEART OF STONE** *Geffen GEF 75*	**43**	5
11 Aug 90	**YOU WOULDN'T KNOW LOVE** *Geffen GEF 77*	**55**	3
13 Apr 91 ★	**THE SHOOP SHOOP SONG (IT'S IN HIS KISS)** *Epic 6566737*	**1**	15
13 Jul 91	**LOVE AND UNDERSTANDING** *Geffen GFS 5*	**10**	8
12 Oct 91	**SAVE UP ALL YOUR TEARS** *Geffen GFS 11*	**37**	5
7 Dec 91	**LOVE HURTS** *Geffen GFS 16*	**43**	5
18 Apr 92	**COULD'VE BEEN YOU** *Geffen GFS 19*	**31**	4
14 Nov 92	**OH NO NOT MY BABY** *Geffen GFS 29*	**33**	4
16 Jan 93	**MANY RIVERS TO CROSS** *Geffen GFSTD 31*	**37**	3
6 Mar 93	**WHENEVER YOU'RE NEAR** *Geffen GFSTD 32*	**72**	1
15 Jan 94	**I GOT YOU BABE** *Geffen GFSTD 64* [1]	**35**	3
18 Mar 95 ●	**LOVE CAN BUILD A BRIDGE** *London COCD 1* [2]	**1**	8
28 Oct 95	**WALKING IN MEMPHIS** *WEA WEA 021CD1*	**11**	7
20 Jan 96 ●	**ONE BY ONE** *WEA WEA 032CD*	**7**	9
27 Apr 96	**NOT ENOUGH LOVE IN THE WORLD** *WEA WEA 052CD*	**31**	2
17 Aug 96	**THE SUN AIN'T GONNA SHINE ANYMORE** *WEA WEA 071CD*	**26**	3

[1] Cher with Beavis and Butt-Head [2] Cher, Chrissie Hynde and Neneh Cherry with Eric Clapton

See also Sonny and Cher; Meat Loaf.

CHERELLE US, female vocalist — 25 wks

28 Dec 85 ●	**SATURDAY LOVE** *Tabu A 6829* [1]	**6**	11
1 Mar 86	**WILL YOU SATISFY?** *Tabu A 6927*	**57**	3
6 Feb 88	**NEVER KNEW LOVE LIKE THIS** *Tabu 6513827* [2]	**26**	7

China Crisis

Gary Daly (pictured right) and Eddie London of China Crisis enlisted the help of Steely Dan's Walter Becker for production duties on their 1985 hit 'Black Man Ray'.

Chubby Checker

Ernest Evans changed his name to Chubby Checker after it was suggested that he resembled a young Fats Domino.

Chicago

Chicago are shown receiving the trophy for Best Pop/Rock Band at the American Music Awards in 1986, nine years after they first triumphed in that category.

| 6 May 89 | | **AFFAIR** Tabu 654673 7 ....**67** | 2 |
| 24 Mar 90 | | **SATURDAY LOVE (re-mix)** Tabu 6558007 [1] ....**55** | 2 |

[1] Cherelle with Alexander O'Neal [2] Alexander O'Neal featuring Cherelle

CHERI *Canada, female vocal duo*   **9 wks**

| 19 Jun 82 | | **MURPHY'S LAW** Polydor POSP 459 ....**13** | 9 |

CHEROKEES *UK, male vocal / instrumental group*   **5 wks**

| 3 Sep 64 | | **SEVEN DAFFODILS** Columbia DB 7341 ....**33** | 5 |

Don CHERRY *US, male vocalist*   **11 wks**

| 10 Feb 56 | ● | **BAND OF GOLD** Philips PB 549 ....**6** | 11 |

Neneh CHERRY *US, female vocalist*   **90 wks**

10 Dec 88	●	**BUFFALO STANCE** Circa YR 21 ....**3**	13
20 May 89	●	**MANCHILD** Circa YR 30 ....**5**	10
12 Aug 89		**KISSES ON THE WIND** Circa YR 33 ....**20**	6
23 Dec 89		**INNA CITY MAMMA** Circa YR 42 ....**31**	7
29 Sep 90		**I'VE GOT YOU UNDER MY SKIN** Circa YR 53 ....**25**	5
3 Oct 92		**MONEY LOVE** Circa YR 83 ....**23**	4
16 Jun 93		**BUDDY X** Circa YRCD 98.................**35**	3
25 Jun 94	●	**7 SECONDS** Columbia 6605082 [1] **3**	21
24 Dec 94		**7 SECONDS (re-entry)** Columbia 6605082 [1] **54**	4
18 Mar 95	★	**LOVE CAN BUILD A BRIDGE** London COCD 1 [2] **1**	8
3 Aug 96	●	**WOMAN** Hut HUTCD 70 ....**9**	7
14 Dec 96		**KOOTCHI** Hut HUTDG 75 ....**38**	2

[1] Youssou N'Dour (featuring Neneh Cherry) [2] Cher, Chrissie Hynde and Neneh Cherry with Eric Clapton

CHI-LITES *US, male vocal group*   **89 wks**

28 Aug 71		**(FOR GOD'S SAKE) GIVE MORE POWER TO THE PEOPLE** MCA MU 1138 ....**32**	6
15 Jan 72	●	**HAVE YOU SEEN HER** MCA MU 1146 ....**3**	12
27 May 72		**OH GIRL** MCA MU 1156 ....**14**	9
23 Mar 74	●	**HOMELY GIRL** Brunswick BR 9 ....**5**	13
20 Jul 74		**I FOUND SUNSHINE** Brunswick BR 12 ....**35**	5
2 Nov 74	●	**TOO GOOD TO BE FORGOTTEN** Brunswick BR 13 ....**10**	11
21 Jun 75	●	**HAVE YOU SEEN HER / OH GIRL (re-issue)** Brunswick BR 20 ....**5**	9
13 Sep 75	●	**IT'S TIME FOR LOVE** Brunswick BR 25 ....**5**	10
31 Jul 76	●	**YOU DON'T HAVE TO GO** Brunswick BR 34 ....**3**	11
13 Aug 83		**CHANGING FOR YOU** R & B RBS 215 ....**61**	3

CHIC *US, male / female vocal / instrumental group*   **90 wks**

26 Nov 77	●	**DANCE DANCE DANCE (YOWSAH YOWSAH YOWSAH)** Atlantic K 11038 ....**6**	12
1 Apr 78	●	**EVERYBODY DANCE** Atlantic K 11097 ....**9**	11
18 Nov 78	●	**LE FREAK** Atlantic K 11209 ....**7**	16
24 Feb 79	●	**I WANT YOUR LOVE** Atlantic LV 16 ....**4**	11
30 Jun 79	●	**GOOD TIMES** Atlantic K 11310 ....**5**	11
13 Oct 79		**MY FORBIDDEN LOVER** Atlantic K 11385 ....**15**	8
8 Dec 79		**MY FEET KEEP DANCING** Atlantic K 11415 ....**21**	9
12 Mar 83		**HANGIN'** Atlantic A 9898 ....**64**	1
19 Sep 87		**JACK LE FREAK** Atlantic A 9198 ....**19**	6
14 Jul 90		**MEGACHIC – CHIC MEDLEY** East West A 7949 .....**58**	3
15 Feb 92		**CHIC MYSTIQUE** Warner Bros. W 0083 ....**48**	3

CHICAGO *US, male vocal / instrumental group*   **81 wks**

10 Jan 70	●	**I'M A MAN** CBS 4715 ....**8**	11
18 Jul 70	●	**25 OR 6 TO 4** CBS 5076 ....**7**	13
9 Oct 76	★	**IF YOU LEAVE ME NOW** CBS 4603 ....**1**	16
5 Nov 77		**BABY WHAT A BIG SURPRISE** CBS 5672 ....**41**	3
21 Aug 82	●	**HARD TO SAY I'M SORRY** Full Moon K 79301 ....**4**	15
27 Oct 84	●	**HARD HABIT TO BREAK** Full Moon W 9214 ....**8**	13
26 Jan 85		**YOU'RE THE INSPIRATION** Warner Bros. W 9126 ....**14**	10

CHICANE *UK, male instrumental duo*   **2 wks**

| 21 Dec 96 | | **OFFSHORE** Extravaganza 0091005.............**14†** | 2 |

Chicane are Disco Citizens under another name. See also Disco Citizens.

CHICKEN SHACK
UK, male / female vocal / instrumental group   **19 wks**

| 7 May 69 | | **I'D RATHER GO BLIND** Blue Horizon 57-3153 ....**14** | 13 |
| 6 Sep 69 | | **TEARS IN THE WIND** Blue Horizon 57-3160.........**29** | 6 |

CHICORY TIP *UK, male vocal / instrumental group*   **34 wks**

29 Jan 72	★	**SON OF MY FATHER** CBS 7737 ....**1**	13
20 May 72		**WHAT'S YOUR NAME** CBS 8021 ....**13**	8
31 Mar 73		**GOOD GRIEF CHRISTINA** CBS 1258 ....**17**	13

CHIEFTANS – See Van MORRISON

CHIFFONS *US, female vocal group*   **40 wks**

11 Apr 63		**HE'S SO FINE** Stateside SS 172 ....**16**	12
18 Jul 63		**ONE FINE DAY** Stateside SS 202 ....**29**	6
26 May 66		**SWEET TALKIN' GUY** Stateside SS 512 ....**31**	8
18 Mar 72	●	**SWEET TALKIN' GUY (re-issue)** London HL 10271 ....**4**	14

CHILD *UK, male vocal / instrumental group*   **22 wks**

29 Apr 78		**WHEN YOU WALK IN THE ROOM** Ariola Hansa AHA 511 ....**38**	5
22 Jul 78	●	**IT'S ONLY MAKE BELIEVE** Ariola Hansa AHA 522 ....**10**	12
28 Apr 79		**ONLY YOU (AND YOU ALONE)** Ariola Hansa AHA 536 ....**33**	5

Jane CHILD *Canada, female vocalist*   **8 wks**

| 12 May 90 | | **DON'T WANNA FALL IN LOVE** Warner Bros. W 9817.................**22** | 8 |

CHILDLINERS *UK / Australia, male / female vocal group*   **6 wks**

| 16 Dec 95 | ● | **THE GIFT OF CHRISTMAS** London LONCD 376 ....**9** | 6 |

CHILDREN FOR RWANDA
UK, male / female choir   **2 wks**

| 10 Sep 94 | | **LOVE CAN BUILD A BRIDGE** East West YZ 849CD ....**57** | 2 |

CHILDREN OF THE NIGHT
UK, male vocalist / producer   **2 wks**

| 26 Nov 88 | | **IT'S A TRIP (TUNE IN, TURN ON, DROP OUT)** Jive JIVE 189 ....**52** | 2 |

CHILDREN OF THE REVOLUTION – See KLF

Toni CHILDS *US, female vocalist*   **4 wks**

| 25 Mar 89 | | **DON'T WALK AWAY** A & M AM 462 ....**53** | 4 |

CHILL FAC-TORR US, male vocal / instrumental group · 8 wks

2 Apr 83	TWIST (ROUND 'N' ROUND)		
	Phillyworld PWS 109	37	8

CHIMES UK, male / female vocal / instrumental group · 28 wks

19 Aug 89	1-2-3 CBS 655166 7	60	3
2 Dec 89	HEAVEN CBS 655432 7	66	2
6 Jan 90	HEAVEN (re-entry) CBS 655432 7	69	3
19 May 90	● I STILL HAVEN'T FOUND WHAT I'M LOOKING FOR		
	CBS CHIM 1	6	9
28 Jul 90	TRUE LOVE CBS CHIM 2	48	3
29 Sep 90	HEAVEN (re-issue) CBS CHIM 3	24	6
1 Dec 90	LOVE COMES TO MIND CBS CHIM 4	49	2

CHINA BLACK UK, male vocal / instrumental duo · 35 wks

16 Jul 94	● SEARCHING Wild Card CARDD 7	4	16
29 Oct 94	STARS Wild Card CARDD 9	19	7
17 Dec 94	SEARCHING (re-entry) Wild Card CARDD 7	54	4
11 Feb 95	ALMOST SEE YOU (SOMEWHERE)		
	Wild Card CARDW 15	31	2
3 Jun 95	SWING LOW SWEET CHARIOT		
	PolyGram TV SWLOW 2 [1]	15	6

[1] Ladysmith Black Mambazo featuring China Black

CHINA CRISIS UK, male vocal / instrumental group · 66 wks

7 Aug 82	AFRICAN AND WHITE Inevitable INEV 011	45	5
22 Jan 83	CHRISTIAN Virgin VS 562	12	9
21 May 83	TRAGEDY AND MYSTERY Virgin VS 587	46	6
15 Oct 83	WORKING WITH FIRE AND STEEL Virgin VS 620	48	5
14 Jan 84	● WISHFUL THINKING Virgin VS 647	9	8
10 Mar 84	HANNA HANNA Virgin VS 665	44	3
30 Mar 85	BLACK MAN RAY Virgin VS 752	14	9
1 Jun 85	KING IN A CATHOLIC STYLE (WAKE UP)		
	Virgin VS 765	19	9
7 Sep 85	YOU DID CUT ME Virgin VS 799	54	4
8 Nov 86	ARIZONA SKY Virgin VS 898	47	4
24 Jan 87	BEST KEPT SECRET Virgin VS 926	36	5

CHINA DRUM UK, male vocal / instrumental group · 2 wks

2 Mar 96	CAN'T STOP THESE THINGS Mantra MNT 8CD	65	1
20 Apr 96	LAST CHANCE Mantra MNT 10CD	60	1

Jonny CHINGAS US, male vocalist · 6 wks

19 Feb 83	PHONE HOME CBS A 3121	43	6

CHIPMUNKS US, chipmunk vocal trio · 12 wks

24 Jul 59	RAGTIME COWBOY JOE		
	London HLU 8916 [1]	11	8
19 Dec 92	ACHY BREAKY HEART Epic 6588837 [2]	53	3
14 Dec 96	MACARENA Sony Wonder 6639981 [3]	65	1

[1] David Seville and the Chipmunks [2] Alvin and the Chipmunks featuring Billy Ray Cyrus [3] Los Del Chipmunks

The Chipmunk characters were created by David Seville, who died in 1972. His son, Ross Bagdasarian Jr., resurrected the act in 1980. See also David Seville.

CHIPPENDALES UK / US, male vocal group · 4 wks

31 Oct 92	GIVE ME YOUR BODY XSrhythm XSR 3	28	4

CHOPS-EMC + EXTENSIVE UK, male instrumental group and rapper · 1 wk

8 Aug 92	ME' ISRAELITES Faze 2 FAZE 6	60	1

CHORDETTES US, female vocal group · 25 wks

17 Dec 54	MR. SANDMAN Columbia DB 3553	11	8
31 Aug 56	● BORN TO BE WITH YOU		
	London HLA 8302	8	9
18 Apr 58	● LOLLIPOP London HLD 8584	6	8

CHORDS UK, male vocal / instrumental group · 17 wks

6 Oct 79	NOW IT'S GONE Polydor 2059 141	63	2
2 Feb 80	MAYBE TOMORROW Polydor POSP 101	40	5
26 Apr 80	SOMETHING'S MISSING Polydor POSP 146	55	3
12 Jul 80	THE BRITISH WAY OF LIFE Polydor 2059 258	54	3
18 Oct 80	IN MY STREET Polydor POSP 185	50	4

CHRIS and JAMES UK, male instrumental / production duo · 2 wks

17 Sep 94	CALM DOWN (BASS KEEPS PUMPIN')		
	Stress 12STR 38	74	1
4 Nov 95	FOX FORCE FIVE Stress CDSTR 61	71	1

Neil CHRISTIAN UK, male vocalist · 10 wks

7 Apr 66	THAT'S NICE Strike JH 301	14	10

Roger CHRISTIAN UK, male vocalist · 3 wks

30 Sep 89	TAKE IT FROM ME Island IS 427	63	3

CHRISTIANS UK, male vocal / instrumental group · 84 wks

31 Jan 87	FORGOTTEN TOWN Island IS 291	22	11
13 Jun 87	HOOVERVILLE (THEY PROMISED US THE WORLD)		
	Island IS 326	21	10
26 Sep 87	WHEN THE FINGERS POINT Island IS 335	34	7
5 Dec 87	IDEAL WORLD Island IS 347	14	13
23 Apr 88	BORN AGAIN Island IS 365	25	7
15 Oct 88	● HARVEST FOR THE WORLD Island IS 395	8	7
20 May 89	★ FERRY 'CROSS THE MERSEY PWL PWL 41 [1]	1	7
23 Dec 89	WORDS Island IS 450	18	8
7 Apr 90	I FOUND OUT Island IS 453	56	2
15 Sep 90	GREENBANK DRIVE Island IS 466	63	2
5 Sep 92	WHAT'S IN A WORD Island IS 536	33	5
14 Nov 92	FATHER Island IS 543	55	2
6 Mar 93	THE BOTTLE Island CID 549	39	3

[1] Christians, Holly Johnson, Paul McCartney, Gerry Marsden and Stock Aitken Waterman

CHRISTIE UK, male vocal / instrumental group · 37 wks

2 May 70	★ YELLOW RIVER CBS 4911	1	22
10 Oct 70	SAN BERNARDINO CBS 5169	49	1
24 Oct 70	● SAN BERNADINO (re-entry) CBS 5169	7	13
25 Mar 72	IRON HORSE CBS 7747	47	1

David CHRISTIE France, male vocalist · 12 wks

14 Aug 82	● SADDLE UP KR KR 9	9	12

John CHRISTIE Australia, male vocalist · 6 wks

25 Dec 76	HERE'S TO LOVE (AULD LANG SYNE) EMI 2554	24	6

Lou CHRISTIE US, male vocalist   35 wks

24 Feb 66	LIGHTNIN' STRIKES MGM 1297	**11**	8
28 Apr 66	RHAPSODY IN THE RAIN MGM 1308	**37**	2
13 Sep 69	● I'M GONNA MAKE YOU MINE		
	Buddah 201 057	**2**	17
27 Dec 69	SHE SOLD ME MAGIC Buddah 201 073	**25**	8

Tony CHRISTIE UK, male vocalist   47 wks

9 Jan 71	LAS VEGAS MCA MK 5058	**21**	9
8 May 71	● I DID WHAT I DID FOR MARIA MCA MK 5064	**2**	17
20 Nov 71	IS THIS THE WAY TO AMARILLO MCA MKS 5073	**18**	13
10 Feb 73	AVENUES AND ALLEYWAYS MCA MKS 5101	**37**	4
17 Jan 76	DRIVE SAFELY DARLIN' MCA 219	**35**	4

Shawn CHRISTOPHER US, female vocalist   10 wks

4 May 91	ANOTHER SLEEPLESS NIGHT		
	Arista 114186	**50**	4
21 Mar 92	DON'T LOSE THE MAGIC Arista 115097	**30**	5
2 Jul 94	MAKE MY LOVE BTB BTBCD 502	**57**	1

CHUBBY CHUNKS VOLUME II
UK, male instrumental duo   **1 wk**

4 Jun 94	TESTAMENT 4 Cleveland City CLECD 13017	**52**	1

CHUCKS UK, male / female vocal group   7 wks

24 Jan 63	LOO-BE-LOO Decca F 11569	**22**	7

CHUMBAWAMBA
UK, male / female vocal / instrumental group   **3 wks**

18 Sep 93	ENOUGH IS ENOUGH		
	One Little Indian 79 TP7CD 1	**56**	2
4 Dec 93	TIMEBOMB One Little Indian 89 TP7CD	**59**	1

1 Chumbawamba and Credit To The Nation

CHUPITO Spain, male vocalist   2 wks

23 Sep 95	AMERICAN PIE Eternal WEA 018CD	**54**	2

CHYNA – *See INCOGNITO*

CICERO UK, male vocalist   12 wks

18 Jan 92	LOVE IS EVERYWHERE Spaghetti CIAO 3	**19**	8
18 Apr 92	THAT LOVING FEELING Spaghetti CIAO 4	**46**	3
1 Aug 92	HEAVEN MUST HAVE SENT YOU BACK		
	Spaghetti CIAO 5	**70**	1

CINDERELLA US, male vocal / instrumental group   7 wks

6 Aug 88	GYPSY ROAD Vertigo VER 40	**54**	2
4 Mar 89	DON'T KNOW WHAT YOU GOT		
	Vertigo VER 43	**54**	2
17 Nov 90	SHELTER ME Vertigo VER 51	**55**	2
27 Apr 91	HEARTBREAK STATION Vertigo VER 53	**63**	1

CINDY and the SAFFRONS
UK, female vocal group   **3 wks**

15 Jan 83	PAST, PRESENT AND FUTURE Stilletto STL 9	**56**	3

Gigliola CINQUETTI Italy, female vocalist   27 wks

23 Apr 64	NON HO L'ETA PER AMARTI Decca F 21882	**17**	17
4 May 74	● GO (BEFORE YOU BREAK MY HEART) CBS 2294	**8**	10

CIRCUIT UK, male / female vocal / instrumental group   3 wks

20 Jul 91	SHELTER ME Cooltempo COOL 237	**44**	2
1 Apr 95	SHELTER ME (re-issue) Pukka CDPUKA 2	**50**	1

CIRRUS UK, male vocal group   1 wk

30 Sep 78	ROLLIN' ON Jet 123	**62**	1

CITY BOY UK, male vocal / instrumental group   20 wks

8 Jul 78	● 5-7-0-5 Vertigo 6059 207	**8**	12
28 Oct 78	WHAT A NIGHT Vertigo 6059 211	**39**	5
15 Sep 79	THE DAY THE EARTH CAUGHT FIRE Vertigo 6059 238 ..	**67**	3

CITY GENTS – *See Dick CHARLESWORTH and his CITY GENTS*

CJ & CO. US, male vocal / instrumental group   2 wks

30 Jul 77	DEVIL'S GUN Atlantic K 10956	**43**	2

Gary CLAIL ON-U SOUND SYSTEM
UK, male vocal / instrumental group   **19 wks**

14 Jul 90	BEEF RCA PB 49265 1	**64**	2
30 Mar 91	● HUMAN NATURE Perfecto PB 44401	**10**	9
8 Jun 91	ESCAPE Perfecto PB 44563	**44**	3
14 Nov 92	WHO PAYS THE PIPER Perfecto 74321117017	**31**	3
22 May 93	THESE THINGS ARE WORTH FIGHTING FOR Perfecto		
	74321147222	**45**	2

1 Gary Clail

See also Various Artists (EPs & LPs) - Gimme Shelter (EP); Primal Scream.

CLAIRE and FRIENDS
UK, female vocalist and young male / female friends   **11 wks**

7 Jun 86	IT'S 'ORRIBLE BEING IN LOVE (WHEN YOU'RE 8 ½)		
	BBC RESL 189	**13**	11

CLANNAD Ireland, male / female vocal group   29 wks

6 Nov 82	● THEME FROM HARRY'S GAME RCA 292	**5**	10
2 Jul 83	NEW GRANGE RCA 340	**65**	1
12 May 84	ROBIN (THE HOODED MAN) RCA HOOD 1	**42**	5
25 Jan 86	IN A LIFETIME RCA PB 40535 1	**20**	5
10 Jun 89	IN A LIFETIME (re-issue) RCA PB 42873 1	**17**	7
10 Aug 91	BOTH SIDES NOW MCA MCS 1546 2	**74**	1

1 Clannad featuring Bono 2 Clannad and Paul Young

Jimmy CLANTON US, male vocalist   1 wk

21 Jul 60	ANOTHER SLEEPLESS NIGHT Top Rank JAR 382	**50**	1

Eric CLAPTON
UK, male vocalist / instrumentalist – guitar   **144 wks**

20 Dec 69	COMIN' HOME Atlantic 584 308 1	**16**	9
12 Aug 72	● LAYLA Polydor 2058 130 2	**7**	11

27 Jul 74	● I SHOT THE SHERIFF RSO 2090 132	9	9
10 May 75	SWING LOW SWEET CHARIOT RSO 2090 158	19	9
16 Aug 75	KNOCKIN' ON HEAVEN'S DOOR RSO 2090 166	38	4
24 Dec 77	LAY DOWN SALLY RSO 2090 264	39	6
21 Oct 78	PROMISES RSO 21	37	7
6 Mar 82	● LAYLA (re-issue) RSO 87 [2]	4	10
5 Jun 82	I SHOT THE SHERIFF (re-issue) RSO 88	64	2
23 Apr 83	THE SHAPE YOU'RE IN Duck W 9701	75	1
16 Mar 85	FOREVER MAN Warner Bros. W 9069	51	4
4 Jan 86	EDGE OF DARKNESS BBC RESL 178 [3]	65	3
17 Jan 87	BEHIND THE MASK Duck W 8461	15	11
20 Jun 87	TEARING US APART Duck W 8299 [4]	56	3
27 Jan 90	BAD LOVE Duck W 2644	25	7
14 Apr 90	NO ALIBIS Duck W 9981	53	3
16 Nov 91	WONDERFUL TONIGHT (LIVE) Duck W 0069	30	7
8 Feb 92	TEARS IN HEAVEN Reprise W 0081	50	1
7 Mar 92	● TEARS IN HEAVEN (re-entry) Reprise W 0081	5	9
1 Aug 92	RUNAWAY TRAIN Rocket EJS 29 [5]	31	4
29 Aug 92	IT'S PROBABLY ME A & M AM 883 [6]	30	5
3 Oct 92	LAYLA (ACOUSTIC) Duck W 0134	45	3
15 Oct 94	MOTHERLESS CHILD Duck W 0271CD	63	1
18 Mar 95	★ LOVE CAN BUILD A BRIDGE London COCD 1 [7]	1	8
20 Jul 96	CHANGE THE WORLD Reprise W 0358CD	18	5

[1] Delaney and Bonnie and Friends featuring Eric Clapton [2] Derek and the Dominoes [3] Eric Clapton featuring Michael Kamen [4] Eric Clapton and Tina Turner [5] Elton John and Eric Clapton [6] Sting with Eric Clapton [7] Cher, Chrissie Hynde and Neneh Cherry with Eric Clapton

Layla (Acoustic) is, as its title suggests, a re-recording of Layla.

Dee CLARK US, male vocalist   9 wks

2 Oct 59	JUST KEEP IT UP London HL 8915	26	1
11 Oct 75	RIDE A WILD HORSE Chelsea 2005 037	16	8

Gary CLARK UK, male vocalist   8 wks

30 Jan 93	WE SAIL ON THE STORMY WATERS Circa YRCDX 93	34	4
3 Apr 93	FREEFLOATING Circa YRCDX 94	50	3
19 Jun 93	MAKE A FAMILY Circa YRCDX 105	70	1

Loni CLARK US, female vocalist   6 wks

5 Jun 93	RUSHING A & M 5802862	37	2
22 Jan 94	U A & M 5804752	28	3
17 Dec 94	LOVE'S GOT ME ON A TRIP SO HIGH A & M 5808872	59	1

Petula CLARK UK, female vocalist   247 wks

11 Jun 54	THE LITTLE SHOEMAKER Polygon P 1117	12	1
25 Jun 54	● THE LITTLE SHOEMAKER (re-entry) Polygon P 1117	7	9
18 Feb 55	MAJORCA Polygon P 1146	12	4
25 Mar 55	MAJORCA (re-entry) Polygon P 1146	18	1
25 Nov 55	● SUDDENLY THERE'S A VALLEY Pye Nixa N 15013	7	10
26 Jul 57	● WITH ALL MY HEART Pye Nixa N 15096	4	18
15 Nov 57	● ALONE Pye Nixa N 15112	8	12
28 Feb 58	BABY LOVER Pye Nixa N 15126	12	7
26 Jan 61	★ SAILOR Pye 7N 15324	1	15
13 Apr 61	SOMETHING MISSING Pye 7N 15337	44	1
13 Jul 61	● ROMEO Pye 7N 15361	3	15
16 Nov 61	● MY FRIEND THE SEA Pye 7N 15389	7	13
8 Feb 62	I'M COUNTING ON YOU Pye 7N 15407	41	2
28 Jun 62	YA YA TWIST Pye 7N 15448	14	11
20 Sep 62	YA YA TWIST (re-entry) Pye 7N 15448	45	2
2 May 63	CASANOVA / CHARIOT Pye 7N 15522	39	7
12 Nov 64	● DOWNTOWN Pye 7N 15722	2	15
11 Mar 65	I KNOW A PLACE Pye 7N 15772	17	8
12 Aug 65	YOU BETTER COME HOME Pye 7N 15864	44	1
14 Oct 65	ROUND EVERY CORNER Pye 7N 15945	43	3
4 Nov 65	YOU'RE THE ONE Pye 7N 15991	23	9
10 Feb 66	● MY LOVE Pye 7N 17038	4	9

21 Apr 66	A SIGN OF THE TIMES Pye 7N 17071	49	1
30 Jun 66	● I COULDN'T LIVE WITHOUT YOUR LOVE Pye 7N 17133	6	11
2 Feb 67	★ THIS IS MY SONG Pye 7N 17258	1	14
25 May 67	DON'T SLEEP IN THE SUBWAY Pye 7N 17325	12	11
13 Dec 67	THE OTHER MAN'S GRASS Pye 7N 17416	20	9
6 Mar 68	KISS ME GOODBYE Pye 7N 17466	50	1
30 Jan 71	THE SONG OF MY LIFE Pye 7N 45026	41	1
13 Feb 71	THE SONG OF MY LIFE (re-entry) Pye 7N 45026	32	11
15 Jan 72	I DON'T KNOW HOW TO LOVE HIM Pye 7N 45112	47	1
29 Jan 72	I DON'T KNOW HOW TO LOVE HIM (re-entry) Pye 7N 45112	49	1
19 Nov 88	● DOWNTOWN (re-mix) PRT PYS 19	10	11

Dave CLARK FIVE
UK, male vocal / instrumental group   174 wks

3 Oct 63	DO YOU LOVE ME Columbia DB 7112	30	6
21 Nov 63	★ GLAD ALL OVER Columbia DB 7154	1	19
20 Feb 64	● BITS AND PIECES Columbia DB 7210	2	11
28 May 64	● CAN'T YOU SEE THAT SHE'S MINE Columbia DB 7291	10	11
13 Aug 64	THINKING OF YOU BABY Columbia DB 7335	26	4
22 Oct 64	ANYWAY YOU WANT IT Columbia DB 7377	25	5
14 Jan 65	EVERYBODY KNOWS Columbia DB 7453	37	4
11 Mar 65	REELIN' AND ROCKIN' Columbia DB 7503	24	8
27 May 65	COME HOME Columbia DB 7580	16	8
15 Jul 65	● CATCH US IF YOU CAN Columbia DB 7625	5	11
11 Nov 65	OVER AND OVER Columbia DB 7744	45	4
19 May 66	LOOK BEFORE YOU LEAP Columbia DB 7909	50	1
16 Mar 67	YOU GOT WHAT IT TAKES Columbia DB 8152	28	8
1 Nov 67	● EVERYBODY KNOWS Columbia DB 8286	2	14
28 Feb 68	NO ONE CAN BREAK A HEART LIKE YOU Columbia DB 8342	28	7
18 Sep 68	● RED BALLOON Columbia DB 8465	7	11
27 Nov 68	LIVE IN THE SKY Columbia DB 8505	39	6
25 Oct 69	PUT A LITTLE LOVE IN YOUR HEART Columbia DB 8624	31	4
6 Dec 69	● GOOD OLD ROCK 'N ROLL Columbia DB 8638	7	12
7 Mar 70	● EVERYBODY GET TOGETHER Columbia DB 8660	8	8
4 Jul 70	HERE COMES SUMMER Columbia DB 8689	44	3
7 Nov 70	MORE GOOD OLD ROCK 'N ROLL Columbia DB 8724	34	6
1 May 93	GLAD ALL OVER (re-issue) EMI CDEMCT 8	37	3

Everybody Knows on DB 7453 and Everybody Knows on DB 8286 are two different songs.
The two Rock 'N Roll titles are medleys as follows: Good Old Rock 'N Roll / Sweet Little Sixteen / Long Tall Sally / Whole Lotta Shakin' Goin' On / Blue Suede Shoes / Lucille / Reelin' And Rockin' / Memphis Tennessee. More Good Old Rock And Roll: Rock And Roll Music / Blueberry Hill / Good Golly Miss Molly / My Blue Heaven / Keep A Knockin' / Loving You / One Night / Lawdy Miss Clawdy.

Dave CLARKE UK, male producer   6 wks

30 Sep 95	RED THREE: THUNDER / STORM Deconstruction 74321306992	45	2
3 Feb 96	SOUTHSIDE Bush 74321335382	34	2
15 Jun 96	NO ONE'S DRIVING Bush 74321380162	37	2

John Cooper CLARKE UK, male vocalist   3 wks

10 Mar 79	GIMMIX! PLAY LOUD Epic EPC 7009	39	3

Rick CLARKE UK, male vocalist   2 wks

30 Apr 88	I'LL SEE YOU ALONG THE WAY WA WA 1	63	2

Sharon Dee CLARKE – See FPI PROJECT; SERIOUS ROPE

Julian CLARY – See JOAN COLLINS FAN CLUB

CLASH UK, male vocal / instrumental group   135 wks

2 Apr 77	WHITE RIOT CBS 5058	38	3

Date	Title	Pos	Wks
8 Oct 77	**COMPLETE CONTROL** *CBS 5664*	**28**	2
4 Mar 78	**CLASH CITY ROCKERS** *CBS 5834*	**35**	4
24 Jun 78	**(WHITE MAN) IN HAMMERSMITH PALAIS** *CBS 6383*	**32**	7
2 Dec 78	**TOMMY GUN** *CBS 6788*	**19**	10
3 Mar 79	**ENGLISH CIVIL WAR (JOHNNY COMES MARCHING HOME)** *CBS 7082*	**25**	6
19 May 79	**THE COST OF LIVING EP** *CBS 7324*	**22**	8
15 Dec 79	**LONDON CALLING** *CBS 8087*	**11**	10
9 Aug 80	**BANKROBBER** *CBS 8323*	**12**	10
6 Dec 80	**THE CALL UP** *CBS 9339*	**40**	6
24 Jan 81	**HITSVILLE UK** *CBS 9480*	**56**	4
25 Apr 81	**THE MAGNIFICENT SEVEN** *CBS 1133*	**34**	5
28 Nov 81	**THIS IS RADIO CLASH** *CBS A 1797*	**47**	5
1 May 82	**KNOW YOUR RIGHTS** *CBS A 2309*	**43**	3
26 Jun 82	**ROCK THE CASBAH** *CBS A 2429*	**30**	10
25 Sep 82	**SHOULD I STAY OR SHOULD I GO / STRAIGHT TO HELL** *CBS A 2646*	**17**	9
12 Oct 85	**THIS IS ENGLAND** *CBS A 6122*	**24**	5
12 Mar 88	**I FOUGHT THE LAW** *CBS CLASH 1*	**29**	5
7 May 88	**LONDON CALLING (re-issue)** *CBS CLASH 2*	**46**	3
21 Jul 90	**RETURN TO BRIXTON** *CBS 656072 7*	**57**	2
2 Mar 91	★ **SHOULD I STAY OR SHOULD I GO (re-issue)** *Columbia 6566677*	**1**	9
13 Apr 91	**ROCK THE CASBAH (re-issue)** *Columbia 6568147*	**15**	6
8 Jun 91	**LONDON CALLING (re-issue)** *Columbia 6569467*	**64**	2

Tracks on The Cost Of Living EP: *I Fought The Law / Groovy Times / Gates Of The West / Capital Radio. CBS CLASH 1 is a re-issue of a track from The Cost of Living EP.*

CLASS ACTION featuring Chris WILTSHIRE
US, female vocal group **3 wks**

Date	Title	Pos	Wks
7 May 83	**WEEKEND** *Jive JIVE 35*	**49**	3

CLASSICS IV *US, male vocal / instrumental group* **1 wk**

Date	Title	Pos	Wks
28 Feb 68	**SPOOKY** *Liberty LBS 15051*	**46**	1

CLASSIX NOUVEAUX
UK, male vocal / instrumental group **34 wks**

Date	Title	Pos	Wks
28 Feb 81	**GUILTY** *Liberty BP 388*	**43**	7
16 May 81	**TOKYO** *Liberty BP 397*	**67**	3
8 Aug 81	**INSIDE OUTSIDE** *Liberty BP 403*	**45**	5
7 Nov 81	**NEVER AGAIN (THE DAYS TIME ERASED)** *Liberty BP 406*	**44**	4
13 Mar 82	**IS IT A DREAM** *Liberty BP 409*	**11**	9
29 May 82	**BECAUSE YOU'RE YOUNG** *Liberty BP 411*	**43**	4
30 Oct 82	**THE END... OR THE BEGINNING** *Liberty BP 414*	**60**	2

CLAWFINGER
Norway / Sweden, male vocal / instrumental group **1 wk**

Date	Title	Pos	Wks
19 Mar 94	**WARFAIR** *East West YZ 804CD1*	**54**	1

Judy CLAY – *See William BELL*

Adam CLAYTON and Larry MULLEN
Ireland, male instrumental duo **12 wks**

Date	Title	Pos	Wks
15 Jun 96	● **THEME FROM 'MISSION: IMPOSSIBLE'** *Mother MUMCD 75*	**7**	12

Merry CLAYTON *US, female vocalist* **1 wk**

Date	Title	Pos	Wks
21 May 88	**YES** *RCA PB 49563*	**70**	1

CLAYTOWN TROUPE
UK, male vocal / instrumental group **3 wks**

Date	Title	Pos	Wks
16 Jun 90	**WAYS OF LOVE** *Island IS 464*	**57**	2
14 Mar 92	**WANTED IT ALL** *EMI USA MT 102*	**74**	1

Johnny CLEGG and SAVUKA
UK / South Africa, male vocal / instrumental group **1 wk**

Date	Title	Pos	Wks
16 May 87	**SCATTERLINGS OF AFRICA** *EMI EMI 5605*	**75**	1

CLICK *US, male rap group* **1 wk**

Date	Title	Pos	Wks
29 Jun 96	**SCANDALOUS** *Jive JIVECD 393*	**54**	1

Jimmy CLIFF *Jamaica, male vocalist* **33 wks**

Date	Title	Pos	Wks
25 Oct 69	● **WONDERFUL WORLD BEAUTIFUL PEOPLE** *Trojan TR 690*	**6**	13
14 Feb 70	**VIETNAM** *Trojan TR 7722*	**47**	1
28 Feb 70	**VIETNAM (re-entry)** *Trojan TR 7722*	**46**	2
8 Aug 70	● **WILD WORLD** *Island WIP 6087*	**8**	12
19 Mar 94	**I CAN SEE CLEARLY NOW** *Columbia 6601982*	**23**	5

Buzz CLIFFORD *US, male vocalist* **13 wks**

Date	Title	Pos	Wks
2 Mar 61	**BABY SITTIN' BOOGIE** *Fontana H 297*	**17**	13

Linda CLIFFORD *US, female vocalist* **12 wks**

Date	Title	Pos	Wks
10 Jun 78	**IF MY FRIENDS COULD SEE ME NOW** *Curtom K 17163*	**50**	5
5 May 79	**BRIDGE OVER TROUBLED WATER** *RSO 30*	**28**	7

CLIMAX BLUES BAND
UK, male vocal / instrumental group **9 wks**

Date	Title	Pos	Wks
9 Oct 76	● **COULDN'T GET IT RIGHT** *BTM SBT 105*	**10**	9

Simon CLIMIE *UK, male vocalist* **2 wks**

Date	Title	Pos	Wks
19 Sep 92	**SOUL INSPIRATION** *Epic 6582837*	**60**	2

CLIMIE FISHER *UK, male vocal / instrumental duo* **44 wks**

Date	Title	Pos	Wks
5 Sep 87	**LOVE CHANGES (EVERYTHING)** *EMI EM 15*	**67**	2
12 Dec 87	● **RISE TO THE OCCASION** *EMI EM 33*	**10**	11
12 Mar 88	● **LOVE CHANGES (EVERYTHING) (re-mix)** *EMI EM 47*	**2**	12
21 May 88	**THIS IS ME** *EMI EM 58*	**22**	5
20 Aug 88	**I WON'T BLEED FOR YOU** *EMI EM 66*	**35**	4
24 Dec 88	**LOVE LIKE A RIVER** *EMI EM 81*	**22**	7
23 Sep 89	**FACTS OF LOVE** *EMI EM 103*	**50**	3

Patsy CLINE *US, female vocalist* **17 wks**

Date	Title	Pos	Wks
26 Apr 62	**SHE'S GOT YOU** *Brunswick 05866*	**43**	1
29 Nov 62	**HEARTACHES** *Brunswick 05878*	**31**	5
8 Dec 90	**CRAZY** *MCA MCA 1465*	**14**	11

George CLINTON *US, male vocalist* **10 wks**

Date	Title	Pos	Wks
4 Dec 82	**LOOPZILLA** *Capitol CL 271*	**57**	5
26 Apr 86	**DO FRIES GO WITH THAT SHAKE** *Capitol CL 402*	**57**	2
27 Aug 94	**BOP GUN (ONE NATION)** *Fourth & Broadway BRCD 308* [1]	**22**	3

[1] Ice Cube featuring George Clinton

CLOCK *UK, male / female vocal / instrumental group*　**44 wks**

30 Oct 93	HOLDING ON *Media MRLCD 007*	**66**	1
21 May 94	THE RHYTHM *Media MCSTD 1971*	**28**	2
10 Sep 94	KEEP THE FIRES BURNING *Media MCSTD 1998*	**36**	3
4 Mar 95	● AXEL F / KEEP PUSHIN' *Media MCSTD 2041*	**7**	9
1 Jul 95	WHOOMPH! (THERE IT IS) *Media MCSTD 2059*	**4**	5
26 Aug 95	● EVERYBODY *Media MCSTD 2077*	**6**	5
18 Nov 95	IN THE HOUSE *Media MCSTD 40005*	**23**	3
24 Feb 96	HOLDING ON 4 U (re-mix) *Media MCSTD 40019*	**27**	2
7 Sep 96	OH WHAT A NIGHT *Power Station MCSTD 40057*	**13**	10

Rosemary CLOONEY *US, female vocalist*　**81 wks**

14 Nov 52	● HALF AS MUCH *Columbia DB 3129*	**3**	9
5 Feb 54	● MAN *Philips PB 220*	**7**	5
8 Oct 54	★ THIS OLE HOUSE *Philips PB 336*	**1**	18
17 Dec 54	● MAMBO ITALIANO *Philips PB 382*	**1**	16
20 May 55	● WHERE WILL THE BABY'S DIMPLE BE *Philips PB 428*	**6**	13
30 Sep 55	● HEY THERE *Philips PB 494*	**4**	11
29 Mar 57	MANGOS *Philips PB 671*	**25**	2
26 Apr 57	MANGOS (re-entry) *Philips PB 671*	**17**	7

From 19 Feb 54 other side of Man, Woman by José Ferrer, was also credited.

CLOUD *UK, male instrumental group*　**1 wk**

| 31 Jan 81 | ALL NIGHT LONG / TAKE IT TO THE TOP *UK Champagne FUNK 1* | **72** | 1 |

CLOUT *South Africa, female vocal / instrumental group*　**15 wks**

| 17 Jun 78 | ● SUBSTITUTE *Carrere EMI 2788* | **2** | 15 |

CLUB NOUVEAU
US, male / female vocal / instrumental group　**12 wks**

| 21 Mar 87 | ● LEAN ON ME *King Jay W 8430* | **3** | 12 |

CLUB 69 *Austria / US, male / female vocal / instrumental duo*　**5 wks**

| 5 Dec 92 | LET ME BE YOUR UNDERWEAR *ffrr F 204* | **33** | 5 |

CLUBHOUSE *Italy, male vocal / instrumental group*　**40 wks**

23 Jul 83	DO IT AGAIN – BILLIE JEAN *Island IS 132*	**11**	6
3 Dec 83	SUPERSTITION – GOOD TIMES *Island IS 147*	**59**	3
1 Jul 89	I'M A MAN – YE KE YE KE *Music Man MMPS 7003*	**69**	3
20 Apr 91	DEEP IN MY HEART *ffrr F 157*	**59**	2
22 Jun 91	DEEP IN MY HEART (re-entry) *ffrr F 157*	**55**	2
4 Sep 93	LIGHT MY FIRE *PWL Continental PWCD 272*	**59**	1
13 Nov 93	LIGHT MY FIRE (re-entry) *PWL Continental PWCD 272*	**45**	5
25 Dec 93	LIGHT MY FIRE (2nd re-entry) *PWL Continental PWCD 272*	**53**	6
30 Apr 94	● LIGHT MY FIRE (re-mix) *PWL Continental PWCD 288*	**7**	8
23 Jul 94	LIVING IN THE SUNSHINE *PWL Continental PWCD 309* [1]	**21**	3
11 Mar 95	NOWHERE LAND *PWL International PWCD 318* [1]	**56**	1

[1] Clubhouse featuring Carl

CLUBZONE *UK / Germany, male vocal / instrumental group*　**1 wk**

| 19 Nov 94 | HANDS UP *Logic 74321236982* | **50** | 1 |

Jeremy CLYDE – See Chad STUART and Jeremy CLYDE

CLYDE VALLEY STOMPERS
UK, male instrumental group　**8 wks**

| 9 Aug 62 | PETER AND THE WOLF *Parlophone R 4928* | **25** | 8 |

CO-CO *UK, male / female vocal / instrumental group*　**7 wks**

| 22 Apr 78 | BAD OLD DAYS *Ariola Hansa AHA 513* | **13** | 7 |

CO-OPERATION CHOIR – See Peter E. BENNETT with the CO-OPERATION CHOIR

COAST TO COAST *UK, male vocal / instrumental group*　**22 wks**

| 31 Jan 81 | ● (DO) THE HUCKLEBUCK *Polydor POSP 214* | **5** | 15 |
| 23 May 81 | LET'S JUMP THE BROOMSTICK *Polydor POSP 249* | **28** | 7 |

COASTERS *US, male vocal group*　**32 wks**

27 Sep 57	SEARCHIN' *London HLE 8450*	**30**	1
15 Aug 58	YAKETY YAK *London HLE 8665*	**12**	8
27 Mar 59	● CHARLIE BROWN *London HLE 8819*	**6**	12
30 Oct 59	POISON IVY *London HLE 8938*	**15**	7
9 Apr 94	SORRY BUT I'M GONNA HAVE TO PASS *Rhino A 4519CD*	**41**	4

Odia COATES – See Paul ANKA

Luis COBOS – See Placido DOMINGO

Eddie COCHRAN *US, male vocalist*　**90 wks**

7 Nov 58	SUMMERTIME BLUES *London HLU 8702*	**18**	6
13 Mar 59	● C'MON EVERYBODY *London HLU 8792*	**6**	13
16 Oct 59	SOMETHIN' ELSE *London HLU 8944*	**22**	3
22 Jan 60	HALLELUJAH I LOVE HER SO *London HLW 9022*	**28**	1
5 Feb 60	HALLELUJAH I LOVE HER SO (re-entry) *London HLW 9022*	**22**	3
12 May 60	★ THREE STEPS TO HEAVEN *London HLG 9115*	**1**	15
6 Oct 60	SWEETIE PIE *London HLG 9196*	**38**	3
3 Nov 60	LONELY *London HLG 9196*	**41**	1
15 Jun 61	WEEKEND *London HLG 9362*	**15**	16
30 Nov 61	JEANNIE, JEANNIE, JEANNIE *London HLG 9460*	**31**	4
25 Apr 63	MY WAY *Liberty LIB 10088*	**23**	10
24 Apr 68	SUMMERTIME BLUES (re-issue) *Liberty LBF 15071*	**34**	4
13 Feb 88	C'MON EVERYBODY (re-issue) *Liberty EDDIE 501*	**14**	7

Tom COCHRANE *Canada, male vocalist*　**2 wks**

| 27 Jun 92 | LIFE IS A HIGHWAY *Capitol CL 660* | **62** | 2 |

COCK ROBIN
US, male / female vocal / instrumental group　**12 wks**

| 31 May 86 | THE PROMISE YOU MADE *CBS A 6764* | **28** | 12 |

Joe COCKER *UK, male vocalist*　**89 wks**

22 May 68	MARJORINE *Regal-Zonophone RZ 3006*	**48**	1
2 Oct 68	★ WITH A LITTLE HELP FROM MY FRIENDS *Regal-Zonophone RZ 3013*	**1**	13
27 Sep 69	● DELTA LADY *Regal-Zonophone RZ 3024*	**10**	11
4 Jul 70	THE LETTER *Regal-Zonophone RZ 3027*	**39**	6
26 Sep 81	I'M SO GLAD I'M STANDING HERE TODAY *MCA 741* [1]	**61**	3
15 Jan 83	● UP WHERE WE BELONG *Island WIP 6830* [2]	**7**	13
14 Nov 87	UNCHAIN MY HEART *Capitol CL 465*	**46**	4
13 Jan 90	WHEN THE NIGHT COMES *Capitol CL 535*	**65**	2
7 Mar 92	(ALL I KNOW) FEELS LIKE FOREVER *Capitol CL 645*	**25**	5

9 May 92	NOW THAT THE MAGIC HAS GONE *Capitol CL 657* **28**	6
4 Jul 92	UNCHAIN MY HEART (re-issue) *Capitol CL 664* **17**	6
21 Nov 92	WHEN THE NIGHT COMES (re-issue) *Capitol CL 674*..**61**	3
13 Aug 94	THE SIMPLE THINGS *Capitol CDCLS 722* **17**	5
22 Oct 94	TAKE ME HOME *Capitol CDCLS 729* [3] **41**	3
17 Dec 94	LET THE HEALING BEGIN *Capitol CDCLS 727* **32**	5
23 Sep 95	HAVE A LITTLE FAITH *Capitol CDCLS 744* **67**	2
12 Oct 96	DON'T LET ME BE MISUNDERSTOOD *Parlophone CDCLS 779* **53**	1

[1] Crusaders, featured vocalist Joe Cocker [2] Joe Cocker and Jennifer Warnes [3] Joe Cocker featuring Bekka Bramlett

COCKEREL CHORUS *UK, male vocal group*   **12 wks**

| 24 Feb 73 | NICE ONE CYRIL *Youngblood YB 1017* ....**14** | 12 |

COCKNEY REBEL – See Steve HARLEY

COCKNEY REJECTS
UK, male vocal / instrumental group   **22 wks**

1 Dec 79	I'M NOT A FOOL *EMI 5008* **65**	2
16 Feb 80	BADMAN *EMI 5035* **65**	3
26 Apr 80	THE GREATEST COCKNEY RIPOFF *EMI Z 2* **21**	7
17 May 80	I'M FOREVER BLOWING BUBBLES *EMI Z 4* **35**	4
12 Jul 80	WE CAN DO ANYTHING *EMI Z 6* **65**	2
25 Oct 80	WE ARE THE FIRM *EMI Z 10* **54**	3

El COCO *US, male vocal / instrumental group*   **4 wks**

| 14 Jan 78 | COCOMOTION *Pye International 7N 25761* ....**31** | 4 |

COCONUTS *US, female vocal group*   **3 wks**

| 11 Jun 83 | DID YOU HAVE TO LOVE ME LIKE YOU DID *EMI America EA 156* ....**60** | 3 |

See also Kid Creole and the Coconuts.

COCTEAU TWINS
UK, male / female vocal / instrumental group   **25 wks**

28 Apr 84	PEARLY-DEWDROPS' DROPS *4AD 405* **29**	5
30 Mar 85	AIKEA-GUINEA *4AD AD 501* **41**	3
23 Nov 85	TINY DYNAMINE EP *4AD BAD 510* **52**	2
7 Dec 85	ECHOES IN A SHALLOW BAY EP *4AD BAD 511* **65**	1
25 Oct 86	LOVE'S EASY TEARS *4AD AD 610* **53**	1
8 Sep 90	ICEBLINK LUCK *4AD AD 0011* **38**	3
2 Oct 93	EVANGELINE *Fontana CTCD 1* **34**	2
18 Dec 93	WINTER WONDERLAND / FROSTY THE SNOWMAN *Fontana COCCD 1* **58**	1
26 Feb 94	BLUEBEARD *Fontana CTCD 2* **33**	2
7 Oct 95	TWINLIGHTS EP *Fontana CTCD 3* **59**	1
4 Nov 95	OTHERNESS EP *Fontana CTCD 4* **59**	1
30 Mar 96	TISHBITE *Fontana CTCD 5* **34**	2
20 Jul 96	VIOLAINE *Fontana CTCD 6* **56**	1

Tracks on Tiny Dynamine EP: Pink Orange Red / Ribbed and Veined / Plain Tiger / Sultitan Itan. Tracks on Echoes In A Shallow Bay EP: Great Spangled Fritillary / Melonella / Pale Clouded White / Eggs and Their Shells. Tracks on Twinlights EP: Golden-Vein / Half-Gifts / Pink Orange Red / Rilkean Heart. Tracks on Otherness EP: Cherry Coloured Funk / Feet Like Fins / Seekers Who Are Lovers / Violane.

C.O.D *US, male vocal / instrumental group*   **2 wks**

| 14 May 83 | IN THE BOTTLE *Streetwave WAVE 2* ....**54** | 2 |

CODE RED *UK, male vocal group*   **2 wks**

| 6 Jul 96 | I GAVE YOU EVERYTHING *Polydor 5763992* ....**50** | 1 |
| 16 Nov 96 | THIS IS OUR SONG *Polydor 5756332* ....**59** | 1 |

COFFEE *US, female vocal group*   **13 wks**

| 27 Sep 80 | CASANOVA *De-Lite MER 38* ....**13** | 10 |
| 6 Dec 80 | SLIP AND DIP / I WANNA BE WITH YOU *De-Lite DE 1* ..**57** | 3 |

Alma COGAN *UK, female vocalist*   **110 wks**

19 Mar 54	● BELL BOTTOM BLUES *HMV B 10653* **4**	9
27 Aug 54	LITTLE THINGS MEAN A LOT *HMV B 10717* **11**	2
8 Oct 54	LITTLE THINGS MEAN A LOT (re-entry) *HMV B 10717*..**19**	1
22 Oct 54	LITTLE THINGS MEAN A LOT (2nd re-entry) *HMV B 10717* **18**	2
3 Dec 54	● I CAN'T TELL A WALTZ FROM A TANGO *HMV B 10786* ..**6**	11
27 May 55	★ DREAMBOAT *HMV B 10872* **1**	16
23 Sep 55	BANJO'S BACK IN TOWN *HMV B 10917* **17**	1
14 Oct 55	GO ON BY *HMV B 10917* **16**	4
16 Dec 55	TWENTY TINY FINGERS *HMV POP 129* **17**	1
23 Dec 55	● NEVER DO A TANGO WITH AN ESKIMO *HMV POP 129* ..**6**	5
30 Mar 56	WILLIE CAN *HMV POP 187* [1] **13**	8
13 Jul 56	THE BIRDS AND THE BEES *HMV POP 223* **25**	4
10 Aug 56	WHY DO FOOLS FALL IN LOVE *HMV POP 223* **22**	3
2 Nov 56	IN THE MIDDLE OF THE HOUSE *HMV POP 261* **26**	1
23 Nov 56	IN THE MIDDLE OF THE HOUSE (re-entry) *HMV POP 261* **20**	3
18 Jan 57	YOU ME AND US *HMV POP 284* **18**	6
29 Mar 57	WHATEVER LOLA WANTS *HMV POP 317* **26**	2
31 Jan 58	THE STORY OF MY LIFE *HMV POP 433* **25**	2
14 Feb 58	SUGARTIME *HMV POP 450* **16**	10
2 May 58	SUGARTIME (re-entry) *HMV POP 450* **30**	1
23 Jan 59	LAST NIGHT ON THE BACK PORCH *HMV POP 573* **27**	2
18 Dec 59	WE GOT LOVE *HMV POP 670* **26**	4
12 May 60	DREAM TALK *HMV POP 728* **48**	1
11 Aug 60	TRAIN OF LOVE *HMV POP 760* **27**	5
20 Apr 61	COWBOY JIMMY JOE *Columbia DB 4607* **37**	6

[1] Alma Cogan with Desmond Lane – penny whistle

Shaye COGAN *US, female vocalist*   **1 wk**

| 24 Mar 60 | MEAN TO ME *MGM 1063* ....**40** | 1 |

Izhar COHEN and ALPHABETA
Israel, male / female vocal group   **7 wks**

| 13 May 78 | A BA NI BI *Polydor 2001 781* ....**20** | 7 |

Marc COHN *US, male vocalist*   **15 wks**

25 May 91	WALKING IN MEMPHIS *Atlantic A 7747* **66**	4
10 Aug 91	SILVER THUNDERBIRD *Atlantic A 7657* **54**	3
12 Oct 91	WALKING IN MEMPHIS (re-issue) *Atlantic A 7585* **22**	5
29 May 93	WALK THROUGH THE WORLD *Atlantic A 7340CD* **37**	3

COLA BOY *UK, male / female vocal / instrumental duo*   **7 wks**

| 6 Jul 91 | ● 7 WAYS TO LOVE *Arista 114526* ....**8** | 7 |

COLD JAM featuring GRACE
US, male / female vocal / instrumental group   **2 wks**

| 28 Jul 90 | LAST NIGHT A DJ SAVED MY LIFE *Big Wave BWR 39*....**64** | 2 |

COLDCUT *UK, male production duo*   **36 wks**

| 20 Feb 88 | ● DOCTORIN' THE HOUSE *Ahead Of Our Time CCUT 27* [1] ....**6** | 9 |
| 10 Sep 88 | STOP THIS CRAZY THING *Ahead Of Our Time CCUT 4* [2] ....**21** | 7 |

25 Mar 89	PEOPLE HOLD ON *Ahead Of Our Time* CCUT 5 [3] **11**	9
3 Jun 89	MY TELEPHONE *Ahead Of Our Time* CCUT 6 ....**52**	2
16 Dec 89	COLDCUT'S CHRISTMAS BREAK	
	Ahead Of Our Time CCUT 7 ....**67**	3
26 May 90	FIND A WAY *Ahead Of Our Time* CCUT 8 [4] **52**	2
4 Sep 93	DREAMER *Arista* 74321156642 ....**54**	2
22 Jan 94	AUTUMN LEAVES *Arista* 74321171052 ....**50**	2

[1] Coldcut featuring Yazz and the Plastic Population [2] Coldcut featuring Junior Reid and the Ahead Of Our Time Orchestra [3] Coldcut featuring Lisa Stansfield [4] Coldcut featuring Queen Latifah

Cozy COLE *US, male instrumentalist – drums* **1 wk**

5 Dec 58	TOPSY (PARTS 1 AND 2) *London* HL 8750 ....**29**	1

George COLE – *See Dennis WATERMAN*

Lloyd COLE *UK, male vocalist* **62 wks**

26 May 84	PERFECT SKIN *Polydor* COLE 1 [1] **71**	1
9 Jun 84	PERFECT SKIN (re-entry) *Polydor* COLE 1 [1] **26**	8
25 Aug 84	FOREST FIRE *Polydor* COLE 2 [1] **41**	6
17 Nov 84	RATTLESNAKES *Poldor* COLE 3 [1] **65**	2
14 Sep 85	BRAND NEW FRIEND *Polydor* COLE 4 [1] **19**	8
9 Nov 85	LOST WEEKEND *Polydor* COLE 5 [1] **17**	7
18 Jan 86	CUT ME DOWN *Polydor* COLE 6 [1] **38**	4
3 Oct 87	MY BAG *Polydor* COLE 7 [1] **46**	4
9 Jan 88	JENNIFER SHE SAID *Polydor* COLE 8 [1] **31**	5
23 Apr 88	FROM THE HIP EP *Polydor* COLE 9 [1] **59**	4
3 Feb 90	NO BLUE SKIES *Polydor* COLE 11 ....**42**	4
7 Apr 90	DON'T LOOK BACK *Polydor* COLE 12 ....**59**	3
31 Aug 91	SHE'S A GIRL AND I'M A MAN *Polydor* COLE 14 ....**55**	2
25 Sep 93	SO YOU'D LIKE TO SAVE THE WORLD	
	Fontana VIBE D1 ....**72**	2
16 Sep 95	LIKE LOVERS DO *Fontana* LCDD 1 ....**24**	3
2 Dec 95	SENTIMENTAL FOOL *Fontana* LCDD 2 ....**73**	1

[1] Lloyd Cole and the Commotions

Tracks on From The Hip EP: From The Hip / Please / Lonely Mile / Love Your Wife.

Nat 'King' COLE *US, male vocalist* **237 wks**

14 Nov 52	● SOMEWHERE ALONG THE WAY *Capitol* CL 13774 ....**3**	7
19 Dec 52	● BECAUSE YOU'RE MINE *Capitol* CL 13811 ....**6**	2
2 Jan 53	FAITH CAN MOVE MOUNTAINS *Capitol* CL 13811 ....**11**	1
16 Jan 53	FAITH CAN MOVE MOUNTAINS (re-entry)	
	Capitol CL 13811 ....**12**	2
23 Jan 53	● BECAUSE YOU'RE MINE (re-entry) *Capitol* CL 13811 ....**10**	1
6 Feb 53	● FAITH CAN MOVE MOUNTAINS (2nd re-entry)	
	Capitol CL 13811 ....**10**	1
13 Feb 53	BECAUSE YOU'RE MINE (2nd re-entry)	
	Capitol CL 13811 ....**11**	1
24 Apr 53	● PRETEND *Capitol* CL 13878 ....**2**	18
14 Aug 53	● CAN'T I? *Capitol* CL 13937 ....**9**	3
18 Sep 53	● CAN'T I? (re-entry) *Capitol* CL 13937 ....**6**	4
18 Sep 53	● MOTHER NATURE AND FATHER TIME	
	Capitol CL 13912 ....**7**	7
30 Oct 53	● CAN'T I? (2nd re-entry) *Capitol* CL 13937 ....**10**	1
16 Apr 54	● TENDERLY *Capitol* CL 14061 ....**10**	1
10 Sep 54	● SMILE *Capitol* CL 14149 ....**2**	14
8 Oct 54	MAKE HER MINE *Capitol* CL 14149 ....**11**	2
25 Feb 55	● A BLOSSOM FELL *Capitol* CL 14235 ....**3**	10
26 Aug 55	MY ONE SIN *Capitol* CL 14327 ....**18**	1
16 Sep 55	MY ONE SIN (re-entry) *Capitol* CL 14327 ....**17**	1
27 Jan 56	● DREAMS CAN TELL A LIE *Capitol* CL 14513 .....**10**	9
11 May 56	● TOO YOUNG TO GO STEADY *Capitol* CL 14573 ....**8**	14
14 Sep 56	LOVE ME AS THOUGH THERE WERE NO TOMORROW	
	Capitol CL 14621 ....**24**	2
5 Oct 56	LOVE ME AS THOUGH THERE WERE NO TOMORROW	
	(re-entry) *Capitol* CL 14621 ....**11**	13
19 Apr 57	● WHEN I FALL IN LOVE *Capitol* CL 14709 ....**2**	20

5 Jul 57	WHEN ROCK 'N ROLL CAME TO TRINIDAD	
	Capitol CL 14733 ....**28**	1
18 Oct 57	MY PERSONAL POSSESSION *Capitol* CL 14765 ....**21**	2
25 Oct 57	STARDUST *Capitol* CL 14787 ....**24**	2
29 May 59	YOU MADE ME LOVE YOU *Capitol* CL 15017 ......**22**	3
4 Sep 59	MIDNIGHT FLYER *Capitol* CL 15056 ....**27**	1
18 Sep 59	MIDNIGHT FLYER (re-entry) *Capitol* CL 15056 .....**23**	3
12 Feb 60	TIME AND THE RIVER *Capitol* CL 15111 ....**29**	1
26 Feb 60	TIME AND THE RIVER (re-entry) *Capitol* CL 15111 ....**23**	2
31 Mar 60	TIME AND THE RIVER (2nd re-entry)	
	Capitol CL 15111 ....**47**	1
26 May 60	● THAT'S YOU *Capitol* CL 15129 ....**10**	8
10 Nov 60	JUST AS MUCH AS EVER *Capitol* CL 15163 ....**18**	10
2 Feb 61	THE WORLD IN MY ARMS *Capitol* CL 15178 ....**36**	10
16 Nov 61	LET TRUE LOVE BEGIN *Capitol* CL 15224 ....**29**	10
22 Mar 62	BRAZILIAN LOVE SONG *Capitol* CL 15241 ....**34**	4
31 May 62	THE RIGHT THING TO SAY *Capitol* CL 15250 ......**42**	4
19 Jul 62	● LET THERE BE LOVE *Capitol* CL 15257 [1] **11**	14
27 Sep 62	● RAMBLIN' ROSE *Capitol* CL 15270 ....**5**	14
20 Dec 62	DEAR LONELY HEARTS *Capitol* CL 15280 ....**37**	3
12 Dec 87	● WHEN I FALL IN LOVE (re-issue) *Capitol* CL 15975 .....**4**	7
14 Dec 91	THE CHRISTMAS SONG *Capitol* CL 641 ....**69**	2
19 Mar 94	LET'S FACE THE MUSIC AND DANCE *EMI* CDEM 312 ....**30**	3

[1] Nat 'King' Cole with George Shearing

See also Natalie Cole.

Natalie COLE *US, female vocalist* **87 wks**

11 Oct 75	THIS WILL BE *Capitol* CL 15834 ....**32**	5
8 Aug 87	JUMP START *Manhattan* MT 22 ....**44**	8
26 Mar 88	● PINK CADILLAC *Manhattan* MT 35 ....**5**	12
25 Jun 88	EVERLASTING *Manhattan* MT 46 ....**28**	6
20 Aug 88	JUMP START (re-issue) *Manhattan* MT 50 ....**36**	5
26 Nov 88	I LIVE FOR YOUR LOVE *Manhattan* MT 57 ....**23**	14
15 Apr 89	● MISS YOU LIKE CRAZY *EMI-USA* MT 63 ....**2**	15
22 Jul 89	REST OF THE NIGHT *EMI-USA* MT 69 ....**56**	2
16 Dec 89	STARTING OVER AGAIN *EMI-USA* MT 77 ....**56**	4
21 Apr 90	WILD WOMEN DO *EMI-USA* MT 81 ....**16**	7
22 Jun 91	UNFORGETTABLE *Elektra* EKR 128 ....**19**	8
16 May 92	THE VERY THOUGHT OF YOU *Elektra* EKR 147 ....**71**	1

Unforgettable features the uncredited vocals of Nat 'King' Cole.

COLETTE – *See SISTER BLISS with COLETTE*

John Ford COLEY – *See ENGLAND DAN and John Ford COLEY*

COLLAGE *US / Canada / Philippines, male vocal / instrumental group* **5 wks**

21 Sep 85	ROMEO WHERE'S JULIET? *MCA* MCA 1006 ....**46**	5

COLLAPSED LUNG *UK, male vocal / instrumental group* **3 wks**

22 Jun 96	LONDON TONIGHT / EAT MY GOAL	
	Deceptive BLUFF 029CD **31**	3

Dave and Ansil COLLINS *Jamaica, male vocal / instrumental duo* **27 wks**

27 Mar 71	★ DOUBLE BARREL *Technique* TE 901 ....**1**	15
26 Jun 71	● MONKEY SPANNER *Technique* TE 914 ....**7**	12

Edwyn COLLINS *UK, male vocalist* **21 wks**

11 Aug 84	PALE BLUE EYES *Swamplands* SWP 1 [1] **72**	2
12 Nov 94	A GIRL LIKE YOU *Setanta* ZOP 001CD1 ....**42**	3
17 Jun 95	● A GIRL LIKE YOU (re-issue) *Setanta* ZOP 003CD **4**	14

Alice Cooper

A good friend of Groucho Marx, Alice Cooper bought the 'O' from the Hollywood sign and dedicated it to Marx after his death.

Clash

The Clash's hit 'Rock The Casbah' was the first record to be broadcast on the Armed Forces radio during the Gulf War in 1990.

Cranberries

With more than 20 million records sold in just four years, the Cranberries are the most successful Irish act of the 90s so far.

Edwin Collins

Orange Juice's final hit proved to be prophetic. It was to be more than ten years before lead singer Edwin Collins would return to the upper reaches of the chart with 'A Girl Like You'.

77

	2 Mar 96	KEEP ON BURNING *Setanta ZOP 004CD1*	45	2

[1] Paul Quinn and Edwyn Collins

A Girl Like You in '94 was the only track available on all formats of the Expressly EP.

Felicia COLLINS – See LUKK featuring Felicia COLLINS

Jeff COLLINS UK, male vocalist — 8 wks

18 Nov 72	ONLY YOU *Polydor 2058 287*	40	8

Judy COLLINS US, female vocalist — 86 wks

17 Jan 70	BOTH SIDES NOW *Elektra EKSN 45043*	14	11
5 Dec 70	● AMAZING GRACE *Elektra 2101 020*	5	32
24 Jul 71	AMAZING GRACE (re-entry) *Elektra 2101 020*	48	1
4 Sep 71	AMAZING GRACE (2nd re-entry) *Elektra 2101 020*	40	7
20 Nov 71	AMAZING GRACE (3rd re-entry) *Elektra 2101 020*	50	1
18 Dec 71	AMAZING GRACE (4th re-entry) *Elektra 2101 020*	48	1
22 Apr 72	AMAZING GRACE (5th re-entry) *Elektra 2101 020*	20	19
9 Sep 72	AMAZING GRACE (6th re-entry) *Elektra 2101 020*	46	2
23 Dec 72	AMAZING GRACE (7th re-entry) *Elektra 2101 020*	49	3
17 May 75	● SEND IN THE CLOWNS *Elektra K 12177*	6	8

Phil COLLINS UK, male vocalist — 213 wks

17 Jan 81	● IN THE AIR TONIGHT *Virgin VSK 102*	2	10
7 Mar 81	I MISSED AGAIN *Virgin VS 402*	14	8
30 May 81	IF LEAVING ME IS EASY *Virgin VS 423*	17	8
23 Oct 82	THRU' THESE WALLS *Virgin VS 524*	56	2
4 Dec 82	★ YOU CAN'T HURRY LOVE *Virgin VS 531*	1	16
19 Mar 83	DON'T LET HIM STEAL YOUR HEART AWAY *Virgin VS 572*	45	5
7 Apr 84	● AGAINST ALL ODDS (TAKE A LOOK AT ME NOW) *Virgin VS 674*	2	14
26 Jan 85	SUSSUDIO *Virgin VS 736*	12	9
9 Mar 85	★ EASY LOVER *CBS A 4915* [1]	1	12
13 Apr 85	● ONE MORE NIGHT *Virgin VS 755*	4	9
27 Jul 85	TAKE ME HOME *Virgin VS 777*	19	9
23 Nov 85	● SEPARATE LIVES *Virgin VS 818* [2]	4	13
18 Jun 88	● IN THE AIR TONIGHT (re-mix) *Virgin VS 102*	4	9
3 Sep 88	★ A GROOVY KIND OF LOVE *Virgin VS 1117*	1	13
26 Nov 88	● TWO HEARTS *Virgin VS 1141*	6	11
4 Nov 89	● ANOTHER DAY IN PARADISE *Virgin VS 1234*	2	11
27 Jan 90	● I WISH IT WOULD RAIN DOWN *Virgin VS 1240*	7	9
28 Apr 90	SOMETHING HAPPENED ON THE WAY TO HEAVEN *Virgin VS 1251*	15	7
28 Jul 90	THAT'S JUST THE WAY IT IS *Virgin VS 1277*	26	5
6 Oct 90	HANG IN LONG ENOUGH *Virgin VS 1300*	34	3
8 Dec 90	DO YOU REMEMBER (LIVE) *Virgin VS 1305*	57	3
15 May 93	HERO *Atlantic A 7360* [3]	56	3
30 Oct 93	● BOTH SIDES OF THE STORY *Virgin VSCDT 1500*	7	5
1 Jan 94	BOTH SIDES OF THE STORY (re-entry) *Virgin VSCDT 1500*	61	1
15 Jan 94	EVERYDAY *Virgin VSCDT 1505*	15	5
7 Mar 94	WE WAIT AND WE WONDER *Virgin VSCD 1510*	45	2
5 Oct 96	● DANCE INTO THE LIGHT *Face Value EW 066CD*	9	6
14 Dec 96	IT'S IN YOUR EYES *Face Value EW 076CD1*	30	3

[1] Philip Bailey (duet with Phil Collins) [2] Phil Collins and Marilyn Martin
[3] David Crosby featuring Phil Collins

Rodger COLLINS US, male vocalist — 6 wks

3 Apr 76	YOU SEXY SUGAR PLUM (BUT I LIKE IT) *Fantasy FTC 132*	22	6

Willie COLLINS US, male vocalist — 4 wks

28 Jun 86	WHERE YOU GONNA BE TONIGHT? *Capitol CL 410*	46	4

Willie COLON US, male vocalist — 7 wks

28 Jun 86	SET FIRE TO ME *A & M AM 330*	41	7

COLOR ME BADD US, male vocal group — 31 wks

18 May 91	★ I WANNA SEX YOU UP *Giant W 0036*	1	14
3 Aug 91	● ALL 4 LOVE *Giant W 0053*	5	10
12 Oct 91	I ADORE MI AMOR *Giant W 0067*	44	2
9 Nov 91	I ADORE MI AMOR (re-issue) *Giant W 0076*	59	2
22 Feb 92	HEARTBREAKER *Giant W 0078*	58	1
20 Nov 93	TIME AND CHANCE *Giant 74321168992*	62	1
16 Apr 94	CHOOSE *Giant 74321199432*	65	1

COLORADO UK, female vocal group — 3 wks

21 Oct 78	CALIFORNIA DREAMIN' *Pinnacle PIN 67*	45	3

COLOUR FIELD UK, male vocal / instrumental group — 18 wks

21 Jan 84	THE COLOUR FIELD *Chrysalis COLF 1*	43	4
28 Jul 84	TAKE *Chrysalis COLF 2*	70	1
26 Jan 85	THINKING OF YOU *Chrysalis COLF 3*	12	10
13 Apr 85	CASTLES IN THE AIR *Chrysalis COLF 4*	51	3

Shawn COLVIN US, female vocalist — 7 wks

27 Nov 93	I DON'T KNOW WHY *Columbia 6598272*	62	1
12 Feb 94	ROUND OF BLUES *Columbia 6594282*	73	1
3 Sep 94	EVERY LITTLE THING HE DOES IS MAGIC *Columbia 6607742*	65	1
7 Jan 95	ONE COOL REMOVE *Columbia 6611342* [1]	40	3
12 Aug 95	I DON'T KNOW WHY (re-issue) *Columbia 6622725*	52	1

[1] Shawn Colvin with Mary Chapin Carpenter

COMETS – See Bill HALEY and his COMETS

COMING OUT CREW US, male / female vocal duo — 1 wk

18 Mar 95	FREE, GAY AND HAPPY *Out On Vinyl CDOOV 002*	50	1

COMMENTATORS
UK, male impressionist – Rory Bremner — 7 wks

22 Jun 85	N-N-NINETEEN NOT OUT *Oval 100*	13	7

COMMITMENTS
Ireland, male / female vocal / instrumental group — 1 wk

30 Nov 91	MUSTANG SALLY *MCA MCS 1598*	63	1

COMMODORES US, male vocal / instrumental group — 121 wks

24 Aug 74	MACHINE GUN *Tamla Motown TMG 902*	20	11
23 Nov 74	THE ZOO (THE HUMAN ZOO) *Tamla Motown TMG 924*	44	2
2 Jul 77	● EASY *Motown TMG 1073*	9	10
8 Oct 77	SWEET LOVE / BRICK HOUSE *Motown TMG 1086*	32	6
11 Mar 78	TOO HOT TO TROT / ZOOM *Motown TMG 1096*	38	4
24 Jun 78	FLYING HIGH *Motown TMG 1111*	37	7
5 Aug 78	★ THREE TIMES A LADY *Motown TMG 1113*	1	14
25 Nov 78	JUST TO BE CLOSE TO YOU *Motown TMG 1127*	62	4
25 Aug 79	● SAIL ON *Motown TMG 1155*	8	10
3 Nov 79	● STILL *Motown TMG 1166*	4	11
19 Jan 80	WONDERLAND *Motown TMG 1172*	40	4
1 Aug 81	LADY (YOU BRING ME UP) *Motown TMG 1238*	56	5

21 Nov 81	**OH NO** Motown TMG 1245	**44**	3
26 Jan 85	● **NIGHTSHIFT** Motown TMG 1371	**3**	14
11 May 85	**ANIMAL INSTINCT** Motown ZB 40097	**74**	1
25 Oct 86	**GOIN' TO THE BANK** Polydor POSPA 826	**43**	4
13 Aug 88	**EASY (re-issue)** Motown ZB 41793	**15**	11

Group were US/UK for 1985 and 1986 hits

COMMOTIONS – *See Lloyd COLE*

COMMUNARDS *UK, male vocal / instrumental duo* **76 wks**

12 Oct 85	**YOU ARE MY WORLD** London LON 77	**30**	8
24 May 86	**DISENCHANTED** London LON 89	**29**	5
23 Aug 86	★ **DON'T LEAVE ME THIS WAY** London LON 103 1	**1**	14
29 Nov 86	● **SO COLD THE NIGHT** London LON 110	**8**	10
21 Feb 87	**YOU ARE MY WORLD ('87) (re-mix)** London LON 123	**21**	6
12 Sep 87	**TOMORROW** London LON 143	**23**	7
7 Nov 87	● **NEVER CAN SAY GOODBYE** London LON 158	**4**	11
20 Feb 88	**FOR A FRIEND** London LON 166	**28**	7
11 Jun 88	**THERE'S MORE TO LOVE** London LON 173	**20**	8

1 Communards with Sarah Jane Morris

Perry COMO *US, male vocalist* **294 wks**

16 Jan 53	★ **DON'T LET THE STARS GET IN YOUR EYES** HMV B 10400	**1**	15
4 Jun 54	● **WANTED** HMV B 10691	**4**	14
25 Jun 54	● **IDLE GOSSIP** HMV B 10667	**3**	15
1 Oct 54	**WANTED (re-entry)** HMV B 10691	**18**	1
10 Dec 54	**PAPA LOVES MAMBO** HMV B 10776	**16**	1
30 Dec 55	**TINA MARIE** HMV POP 103	**24**	1
27 Apr 56	**JUKE BOX BABY** HMV POP 191	**22**	6
25 May 56	● **HOT DIGGITY (DOG ZIGGITY BOOM)** HMV POP 221	**4**	13
21 Sep 56	● **MORE** HMV POP 240	**10**	11
28 Sep 56	**GLENDORA** HMV POP 240	**18**	6
14 Dec 56	**MORE (re-entry)** HMV POP 240	**29**	1
7 Feb 58	★ **MAGIC MOMENTS** RCA 1036	**1**	17
7 Mar 58	● **CATCH A FALLING STAR** RCA 1036	**9**	10
9 May 58	● **KEWPIE DOLL** RCA 1055	**9**	7
30 May 58	**I MAY NEVER PASS THIS WAY AGAIN** RCA 1062	**15**	8
5 Sep 58	**MOON TALK** RCA 1071	**17**	1
7 Nov 58	● **LOVE MAKES THE WORLD GO ROUND** RCA 1086	**6**	14
21 Nov 58	**MANDOLINS IN THE MOONLIGHT** RCA 1086	**13**	12
27 Feb 59	● **TOMBOY** RCA 1111	**10**	12
10 Jul 59	**I KNOW** RCA 1126	**13**	16
26 Feb 60	● **DELAWARE** RCA 1170	**3**	13
10 May 62	**CATERINA** RCA 1283	**37**	4
14 Jun 62	**CATERINA (re-entry)** RCA 1283	**45**	2
30 Jan 71	● **IT'S IMPOSSIBLE** RCA 2043	**4**	23
15 May 71	**I THINK OF YOU** RCA 2075	**14**	11
21 Apr 73	● **AND I LOVE YOU SO** RCA 2346	**3**	31
25 Aug 73	● **FOR THE GOOD TIMES** RCA 2402	**7**	27
8 Dec 73	**WALK RIGHT BACK** RCA 2432	**33**	10
12 Jan 74	**AND I LOVE YOU SO (re-entry)** RCA 2346	**40**	4
25 May 74	**I WANT TO GIVE** RCA LPBO 7518	**31**	6

COMPAGNONS DE LA CHANSON
France, male vocal group **3 wks**

9 Oct 59	**THE THREE BELLS (THE JIMMY BROWN SONG)** Columbia DB 4358	**27**	1
23 Oct 59	**THE THREE BELLS (THE JIMMY BROWN SONG) (re-entry)** Columbia DB 4358	**21**	2

COMSAT ANGELS
UK, male vocal / instrumental group **2 wks**

21 Jan 84	**INDEPENDENCE DAY** Jive JIVE 54	**75**	1
4 Feb 84	**INDEPENDENCE DAY (re-entry)** Jive JIVE 54	**71**	1

CON FUNK SHUN *US, male vocal / instrumental group* **2 wks**

19 Jul 86	**BURNIN' LOVE** Club JAB 32	**68**	2

CONCEPT *US, male vocalist / instrumentalist – keyboards* **6 wks**

14 Dec 85	**MR. DJ** Fourth & Broadway BRW 40	**27**	6

CONFEDERATES – *See Elvis COSTELLO*

CONGREGATION *UK, male / female choir* **14 wks**

27 Nov 71	● **SOFTLY WHISPERING I LOVE YOU** Columbia DB 8830	**4**	14

CONGRESS *UK, male / female vocal / instrumental group* **4 wks**

26 Oct 91	**40 MILES** Inner Rhythm 7HEART 01	**26**	4

Arthur CONLEY *US, male vocalist* **15 wks**

27 Apr 67	● **SWEET SOUL MUSIC** Atlantic 584 083	**7**	14
10 Apr 68	**FUNKY STREET** Atlantic 583 175	**46**	1

CONNELLS *US, male vocal / instrumental group* **11 wks**

12 Aug 95	**'74-'75** TVT LONCD 369	**14**	8
16 Mar 96	**'74-'75 (re-entry)** TVT LONCD 413	**21**	3

Harry CONNICK Jr. *US, male vocalist* **11 wks**

25 May 91	**RECIPE FOR LOVE / IT HAD TO BE YOU** Columbia 6568907	**32**	6
3 Aug 91	**WE ARE IN LOVE** Columbia 6572847	**62**	2
23 Nov 91	**BLUE LIGHT RED LIGHT (SOMEONE'S THERE)** Columbia 6575367	**54**	3

Billy CONNOLLY *UK, male vocalist* **31 wks**

1 Nov 75	★ **D.I.V.O.R.C.E.** Polydor 2058 652	**1**	10
17 Jul 76	**NO CHANCE (NO CHARGE)** Polydor 2058 748	**24**	5
25 Aug 79	**IN THE BROWNIES** Polydor 2059 160	**38**	7
9 Mar 85	**SUPER GRAN** Stiff BUY 218	**32**	9

CONQUERING LION *UK, male vocal group* **1 wk**

8 Oct 94	**CODE RED** Mango CIDM 821	**53**	1

Leena CONQUEST and HIP HOP FINGER
US, female vocalist **1 wk**

18 Jun 94	**BOUNDARIES** Naturalresponse 74321208522	**67**	1

Jess CONRAD *UK, male vocalist* **13 wks**

30 Jun 60	**CHERRY PIE** Decca F 11236	**39**	1
26 Jan 61	**MYSTERY GIRL** Decca F 11315	**44**	1
9 Feb 61	**MYSTERY GIRL (re-entry)** Decca F 11315	**18**	9
11 Oct 62	**PRETTY JENNY** Decca F 11511	**50**	2

CONSORTIUM *UK, male vocal group* **9 wks**

12 Feb 69	**ALL THE LOVE IN THE WORLD** Pye 7N 17635	**22**	9

Ann CONSUELO – *See SUBTERRANIA featuring Ann CONSUELO*

CONTOURS US, male vocal group   **6 wks**

| 24 Jan 70 | JUST A LITTLE MISUNDERSTANDING Tamla Motown TMG 723 | **31** | 6 |

CONTRABAND
Germany / US, male / female vocal / instrumental group   **2 wks**

| 20 Jul 91 | ALL THE WAY FROM MEMPHIS Impact American EM 195 | **65** | 2 |

CONTROL UK, male / female vocal / instrumental group   **5 wks**

| 2 Nov 91 | DANCE WITH ME All Around The World GLOBE 105 | **17** | 5 |

CONVERT Belgium, male instrumental / production duo   **6 wks**

| 11 Jan 92 | NIGHTBIRD A & M AM 845 | **39** | 4 |
| 29 May 93 | ROCKIN' TO THE RHYTHM A & M 5802532 | **42** | 2 |

CONWAY BROTHERS US, male vocal group   **10 wks**

| 22 Jun 85 | TURN IT UP 10 TEN 57 | **11** | 10 |

Russ CONWAY UK, male instrumentalist – piano   **178 wks**

29 Nov 57	PARTY POPS Columbia DB 4031	**24**	5
29 Aug 58	GOT A MATCH Columbia DB 4166	**30**	1
28 Nov 58	● MORE PARTY POPS Columbia DB 4204	**10**	7
23 Jan 59	THE WORLD OUTSIDE Columbia DB 4234	**24**	4
20 Feb 59	★ SIDE SADDLE Columbia DB 4256	**1**	30
6 Mar 59	THE WORLD OUTSIDE (re-entry) Columbia DB 4234	**24**	3
15 May 59	★ ROULETTE Columbia DB 4298	**1**	19
21 Aug 59	● CHINA TEA Columbia DB 4337	**5**	13
13 Nov 59	● SNOW COACH Columbia DB 4368	**7**	7
20 Nov 59	● MORE AND MORE PARTY POPS Columbia DB 4373	**5**	8
10 Mar 60	ROYAL EVENT Columbia DB 4418	**15**	7
21 Apr 60	FINGS AIN'T WOT THEY USED T'BE Columbia DB 4422	**47**	1
19 May 60	LUCKY FIVE Columbia DB 4457	**14**	9
29 Sep 60	PASSING BREEZE Columbia DB 4508	**16**	10
24 Nov 60	EVEN MORE PARTY POPS Columbia DB 4535	**27**	9
19 Jan 61	PEPE Columbia DB 4564	**19**	9
25 May 61	PABLO Columbia DB 4649	**45**	2
24 Aug 61	SAY IT WITH FLOWERS Columbia DB 4665 [1]	**23**	10
30 Nov 61	● TOY BALLOONS Columbia DB 4738	**7**	11
22 Feb 62	LESSON ONE Columbia DB 4784	**21**	7
29 Nov 62	ALWAYS YOU AND ME Columbia DB 4934	**33**	4
3 Jan 63	ALWAYS YOU AND ME (re-entry) Columbia DB 4934	**35**	3

[1] Dorothy Squires and Russ Conway

Always You And Me featured Russ Conway talking as well as playing piano. Several of the discs were medleys as follows: Party Pops: When You're Smiling / I'm Looking Over a Four-Leafed Clover / When You Wore a Tulip / Row Row Row / For Me And My Girl / Shine On Harvest Moon / By The Light Of The Silvery Moon / Side By Side. More Party Pops: Music Music Music / If You Were The Only Girl In The World / Nobody's Sweetheart / Yes Sir That's My Baby / Some Of These Days / Honeysuckle And The Bee / Hello Hello Who's Your Lady Friend / Shanty In Old Shanty Town. More And More Party Pops: Sheik of Araby / Who Were You With Last Night / Any Old Iron / Tiptoe Through The Tulips / If You Were The Only Girl In The World / When I Leave The World Behind. Even More Party Pops: Ain't She Sweet / I Can't Give You Anything But Love / Yes We Have No Bananas / I May Be Wrong / Happy Days and Lonely Nights / Glad Rag Doll. He really did feature If You Were The Only Girl In The World on two different hits.

Martin COOK – See Richard DENTON and Martin COOK

Norman COOK
UK, male producer / multi-instrumentalist   **10 wks**

| 8 Jul 89 | WON'T TALK ABOUT IT / BLAME IT ON THE BASSLINE Go.Beat GOD 33 [1] | **29** | 6 |
| 21 Oct 89 | FOR SPACIOUS LIES Go.Beat GOD 37 [2] | **48** | 4 |

[1] Norman Cook featuring Billy Bragg/Norman Cook featuring MC Wildski
[2] Norman Cook featuring Lester

See also Mighty Dub Katz.

Peter COOK UK, male vocalist   **15 wks**

| 17 Jun 65 | GOODBYE-EE Decca F 12158 [1] | **18** | 10 |
| 15 Jul 65 | THE BALLAD OF SPOTTY MULDOON Decca F 12182 | **34** | 5 |

[1] Peter Cook and Dudley Moore

Brandon COOKE – See Roxanne SHANTE

Sam COOKE US, male vocalist   **82 wks**

17 Jan 58	YOU SEND ME London HLU 8506	**29**	1
14 Aug 59	ONLY SIXTEEN HMV POP 642	**23**	4
7 Jul 60	WONDERFUL WORLD HMV POP 754	**27**	8
29 Sep 60	● CHAIN GANG RCA 1202	**9**	11
27 Jul 61	● CUPID RCA 1242	**7**	14
8 Mar 62	● TWISTIN' THE NIGHT AWAY RCA 1277	**6**	14
16 May 63	ANOTHER SATURDAY NIGHT RCA 1341	**23**	12
5 Sep 63	FRANKIE AND JOHNNY RCA 1361	**30**	6
22 Mar 86	● WONDERFUL WORLD (re-issue) RCA PB 49871	**2**	11
10 May 86	ANOTHER SATURDAY NIGHT (re-issue) RCA PB 49849	**75**	1

COOKIE CREW UK, female vocal group   **31 wks**

9 Jan 88	● ROK DA HOUSE Rhythm King LEFT 11 [1]	**5**	11
7 Jan 89	BORN THIS WAY (LET'S DANCE) ffrr FFR 19	**23**	5
1 Apr 89	GOT TO KEEP ON ffrr FFR 25	**17**	9
15 Jul 89	COME AND GET SOME ffrr F 110	**42**	3
27 Jul 91	SECRETS (OF SUCCESS) ffrr F159 [2]	**53**	3

[1] Beatmasters featuring the Cookie Crew [2] Cookie Crew featuring Danny D

COOKIES US, female vocal group   **1 wk**

| 10 Jan 63 | CHAINS London HLU 9634 | **50** | 1 |

COOL DOWN ZONE
UK, male / female vocal / instrumental group   **4 wks**

| 30 Jun 90 | HEAVEN KNOWS 10 TEN 309 | **52** | 4 |

COOL JACK Italy, male instrumental / production duo   **1 wk**

| 9 Nov 96 | JUS' COME AM:PM 5819892 | **44** | 1 |

Rita COOLIDGE US, female vocalist   **24 wks**

25 Jun 77	● WE'RE ALL ALONE A & M AMS 7295	**6**	13
15 Oct 77	(YOUR LOVE HAS LIFTED ME) HIGHER AND HIGHER A & M AMS 7315	**49**	1
29 Oct 77	(YOUR LOVE HAS LIFTED ME) HIGHER AND HIGHER (re-entry) A & M AMS 7315	**48**	1
4 Feb 78	WORDS A & M AMS 7330	**25**	8
25 Jun 83	ALL TIME HIGH A & M AM 007	**75**	1

COOLIO US, male rapper   **38 wks**

| 23 Jul 94 | FANTASTIC VOYAGE Tommy Boy TB 0617CD | **41** | 2 |
| 15 Oct 94 | I REMEMBER Tommy Boy TBXCD 635 | **73** | 1 |

28 Oct 95	★ **GANGSTA'S PARADISE** Tommy Boy MCSTD 2104 [1]	.....**1**	20
20 Jan 96	● **TOO HOT** Tommy Boy TBCD 718	....**9**	6
6 Apr 96	**1234 (SUMPIN' NEW)** Tommy Boy TBCD 7721	.....**13**	7
17 Aug 96	**IT'S ALL THE WAY LIVE (NOW)**		
	Tommy Boy TBCD 7731	.....**34**	2

[1] Coolio featuring LV

COOLNOTES
UK, male / female vocal / instrumental group **28 wks**

18 Aug 84	**YOU'RE NEVER TOO YOUNG** Abstract Dance AD 1	....**42**	5
17 Nov 84	**I FORGOT** Abstract Dance AD 2	....**63**	2
23 Mar 85	**SPEND THE NIGHT** Abstract Dance AD 3	....**11**	9
13 Jul 85	**IN YOUR CAR** Abstract Dance AD 4	....**13**	9
19 Oct 85	**HAVE A GOOD FOREVER** Abstract Dance AD 5	....**73**	1
17 May 86	**INTO THE MOTION** Abstract Dance AD 8	....**66**	2

Alice COOPER *US, male vocalist* **104 wks**

15 Jul 72	★ **SCHOOL'S OUT** Warner Bros. K 16188	.....**1**	12
7 Oct 72	● **ELECTED** Warner Bros. K 16214	....**4**	10
10 Feb 73	● **HELLO HURRAY** Warner Bros. K 16248	....**6**	12
21 Apr 73	● **NO MORE MR. NICE GUY** Warner Bros. K 16262	....**10**	10
19 Jan 74	**TEENAGE LAMENT '74** Warner Bros. K 16345	....**12**	7
21 May 77	**(NO MORE) LOVE AT YOUR CONVENIENCE**		
	Warner Bros. K 16935	....**44**	2
23 Dec 78	**HOW YOU GONNA SEE ME NOW**		
	Warner Bros. K 17270	....**61**	6
6 Mar 82	**SEVEN AND SEVEN IS** (LIVE VERSION)		
	Warner Bros. K 17924	....**62**	3
8 May 82	**FOR BRITAIN ONLY / UNDER MY WHEELS**		
	Warner Bros. K 17940	....**66**	2
18 Oct 86	**HE'S BACK (THE MAN BEHIND THE MASK)**		
	MCA MCA 1090	....**61**	2
9 Apr 88	**FREEDOM** MCA MCA 1241	....**50**	3
29 Jul 89	● **POISON** Epic 655061 7	....**2**	11
7 Oct 89	**BED OF NAILS** Epic ALICE 3	....**38**	5
2 Dec 89	**HOUSE OF FIRE** Epic ALICE 4	....**65**	2
22 Jun 91	**HEY STOOPID** Epic 6569837	....**21**	6
5 Oct 91	**LOVE'S A LOADED GUN** Epic 6574387	....**38**	3
6 Jun 92	**FEED MY FRANKENSTEIN** Epic 6580927	....**27**	3
28 May 94	**LOST IN AMERICA** Epic 6603472	....**22**	3
23 Jul 94	**IT'S ME** Epic 6605632	....**34**	2

For the first five hits, 'Alice Cooper' was the name of the entire group, not just the lead vocalist.

Deborah COOPER – See C & C MUSIC FACTORY/CLIVILLES & COLE

Tommy COOPER *UK, male vocalist* **3 wks**

29 Jun 61	**DON'T JUMP OFF THE ROOF DAD** Palette PG 9019	....**40**	2
20 Jul 61	**DON'T JUMP OFF THE ROOF DAD** (re-entry)		
	Palette PG 9019	....**50**	1

Julian COPE *UK, male vocalist* **59 wks**

19 Nov 83	**SUNSHINE PLAYROOM** Mercury COPE 1	....**64**	1
31 Mar 84	**THE GREATNESS AND PERFECTION OF LOVE**		
	Mercury MER 155	....**52**	5
27 Sep 86	**WORLD SHUT YOUR MOUTH** Island IS 290	....**19**	8
17 Jan 87	**TRAMPOLENE** Island IS 305	....**31**	6
11 Apr 87	**EVE'S VOLCANO (COVERED IN SIN)** Island IS 318	....**41**	5
24 Sep 88	**CHARLOTTE ANNE** Island IS 380	....**35**	6
21 Jan 89	**5 O'CLOCK WORLD** Island IS 399	....**42**	4
24 Jun 89	**CHINA DOLL** Island IS 406	....**53**	2
9 Feb 91	**BEAUTIFUL LOVE** Island IS 483	....**32**	6
20 Apr 91	**EAST EASY RIDER** Island IS 492	....**51**	3
3 Aug 91	**HEAD** Island IS 497	....**57**	2
8 Aug 92	**WORLD SHUT YOUR MOUTH** (re-issue)		
	Island IS 534	....**44**	3

17 Oct 92	**FEAR LOVES THIS PLACE** Island IS 545	....**42**	2
12 Aug 95	**TRY TRY TRY** Echo ECSCD 11	....**24**	3
27 Jul 96	**I COME FROM ANOTHER PLANET BABY**		
	Echo ECSCD 22	....**34**	2
5 Oct 96	**PLANETARY SIT-IN (EVERY GIRL HAS YOUR NAME)**		
	Echo ECSCD 25	....**34**	1

Harry H. CORBETT – See Wilfrid BRAMBELL and Harry H. CORBETT

Frank CORDELL *UK, orchestra* **4 wks**

24 Aug 56	**SADIE'S SHAWL** HMV POP 229	....**29**	2
16 Feb 61	**BLACK BEAR** HMV POP 824	....**44**	2

Louise CORDET *France, female vocalist* **13 wks**

5 Jul 62	**I'M JUST A BABY** Decca F 11476	....**13**	13

Don CORNELL *US, male vocalist* **23 wks**

3 Sep 54	★ **HOLD MY HAND** Vogue Q 2013	....**1**	21
22 Apr 55	**STRANGER IN PARADISE** Vogue Q 72073	....**19**	2

Lynn CORNELL *UK, female vocalist* **9 wks**

20 Oct 60	**NEVER ON SUNDAY** Decca F 11277	....**30**	9

Charlotte CORNWELL – See Julie COVINGTON, Rula LENSKA, Charlotte CORNWELL and Sue JONES-DAVIES

Hugh CORNWELL
UK, male vocalist / instrumentalist – guitar **3 wks**

24 Jan 87	**FACTS + FIGURES** Virgin VS 922	....**61**	2
7 May 88	**ANOTHER KIND OF LOVE** Virgin VS 945	....**71**	1

CORO featuring TARLISA
Germany, male / female vocal / production group **1 wk**

12 Dec 92	**BECAUSE THE NIGHT** ZYX ZYX 68227	....**61**	1

CORONA *Brazil, female vocalist* **42 wks**

10 Sep 94	● **THE RHYTHM OF THE NIGHT** WEA YZ 837CD1	....**2**	14
31 Dec 94	**THE RHYTHM OF THE NIGHT** (re-entry)		
	WEA YZ 837CD1	....**55**	4
8 Apr 95	● **BABY BABY** Eternal YZ 919CD	....**5**	8
22 Jul 95	● **TRY ME OUT** Eternal YZ 955CD	....**6**	10
23 Dec 95	**I DON'T WANNA BE A STAR**		
	Eternal WEA 029CD	....**22**	6

CORONATION STREET CAST featuring
Bill WADDINGTON *UK, male / female vocal group* **3 wks**

16 Dec 95	**ALWAYS LOOK ON THE BRIGHT SIDE OF LIFE**		
	EMI Premier CDEMS 411	....**35**	3

The listed flip side of Always Look On The Bright Side Of Life was Something Stupid by Amanda Barrie and Johnny Briggs.

CORONETS *UK, male / female vocal group* **7 wks**

26 Aug 55	**THAT'S HOW A LOVE SONG WAS BORN**		
	Columbia DB 3640 [1]	....**14**	6
25 Nov 55	**TWENTY TINY FINGERS** Columbia DB 3671	....**20**	1

[1] Ray Burns with the Coronets

Briana CORRIGAN UK, female vocalist — 2 wks

11 May 96	**LOVE ME NOW** East West EW 041CD1	**48**	2

CORRS Ireland, female / male vocal / instrumental group — 3 wks

17 Feb 96	**RUNAWAY** Atlantic A 5727CD	**49**	2
7 Dec 96	**RUNAWAY (re-entry)** Atlantic A 5727CD	**60**	1

Vladimir COSMA Hungary, orchestra — 1 wk

14 Jul 79	**DAVID'S SONG (MAIN THEME FROM 'KIDNAPPED')** Decca FR 13841	**64**	1

COSMIC BABY Germany, male producer — 1 wk

26 Feb 94	**LOOPS OF INFINITY** Logic 74321191432	**70**	1

Don COSTA US, orchestra — 10 wks

13 Oct 60	**NEVER ON SUNDAY** London HLT 9195	**27**	9
22 Dec 60	**NEVER ON SUNDAY (re-entry)** London HLT 9195	**41**	1

Elvis COSTELLO UK, male vocalist — 168 wks

5 Nov 77	**WATCHING THE DETECTIVES** Stiff BUY 20	**15**	11
11 Mar 78	**(I DON'T WANNA GO TO) CHELSEA** Radar ADA 3 [1]	**16**	10
13 May 78	**PUMP IT UP** Radar ADA 10 [1]	**24**	10
28 Oct 78	**RADIO RADIO** Radar ADA 24 [1]	**29**	7
10 Feb 79	● **OLIVER'S ARMY** Radar ADA 31 [1]	**2**	12
12 May 79	**ACCIDENTS WILL HAPPEN** Radar ADA 35 [1]	**28**	8
16 Feb 80	● **I CAN'T STAND UP FOR FALLING DOWN** F. Beat XX 1 [1]	**4**	9
12 Apr 80	**HI FIDELITY** F. Beat XX 3	**30**	5
7 Jun 80	**NEW AMSTERDAM** F. Beat XX 5	**36**	6
20 Dec 80	**CLUBLAND** F. Beat XX 12 [1]	**60**	4
3 Oct 81	● **A GOOD YEAR FOR THE ROSES** F. Beat XX 17	**6**	11
12 Dec 81	**SWEET DREAMS** F. Beat XX 19	**42**	8
10 Apr 82	**I'M YOUR TOY** F. Beat XX 21 [2]	**51**	3
19 Jun 82	**YOU LITTLE FOOL** F. Beat XX 26	**52**	3
31 Jul 82	**MAN OUT OF TIME** F. Beat XX 28	**58**	2
25 Sep 82	**FROM HEAD TO TOE** F. Beat XX 30	**43**	4
11 Dec 82	**PARTY PARTY** A & M AMS 8267 [3]	**48**	6
11 Jun 83	**PILLS AND SOAP** Imp IMP 001 [4]	**16**	4
9 Jul 83	**EVERYDAY I WRITE THE BOOK** F. Beat XX 32	**28**	8
17 Sep 83	**LET THEM ALL TALK** F. Beat XX 33	**59**	2
28 Apr 84	**PEACE IN OUR TIME** Imposter TRUCE 1 [4]	**48**	3
16 Jun 84	**I WANNA BE LOVED / TURNING THE TOWN RED** F. Beat XX 35	**25**	6
25 Aug 84	**THE ONLY FLAME IN TOWN** F. Beat XX 37	**71**	2
4 May 85	**GREEN SHIRT** F. Beat ZB 40085	**71**	1
18 May 85	**GREEN SHIRT (re-entry)** F. Beat ZB 40085	**68**	1
1 Feb 86	**DON'T LET ME BE MISUNDERSTOOD** F. Beat ZB 40555 [5]	**33**	4
30 Aug 86	**TOKYO STORM WARNING** Imp IMP 007	**73**	1
4 Mar 89	**VERONICA** Warner Bros. W 7558	**31**	6
20 May 89	**BABY PLAYS AROUND (EP)** Warner Bros. W 2949	**65**	1
4 May 91	**THE OTHER SIDE OF SUMMER** Warner Bros. W 0025	**43**	4
5 Mar 94	**SULKY GIRL** Warner Bros. W 0234CD [1]	**22**	3
30 Apr 94	**13 STEPS LEAD DOWN** Warner Bros. W 0245CD [1]	**59**	1
26 Nov 94	**LONDON'S BRILLIANT PARADE** Warner Bros. W 0270CD1 [1]	**48**	2
11 May 96	**IT'S TIME** Warner Bros. W 0348CD [1]	**58**	1

[1] Elvis Costello and the Attractions [2] Elvis Costello and the Attractions with the Royal Philharmonic Orchestra [3] Elvis Costello and the Attractions with the Royal Horn Guards [4] Imposter [5] Costello Show featuring the Confederates

Tracks on Baby Plays Around (EP): Baby Plays Around / Poisoned Rose / Almost Blue / My Funny Valentine.

COTTAGERS – *See Tony REES and the COTTAGERS*

Billy COTTON and his BAND
UK, male bandleader, vocalist, with band and chorus — 25 wks

1 May 53	● **IN A GOLDEN COACH** Decca F 10058 [1]	**3**	10
18 Dec 53	**I SAW MOMMY KISSING SANTA CLAUS** Decca F 10206 [2]	**11**	3
30 Apr 54	**FRIENDS AND NEIGHBOURS** Decca F 10299 [3]	**12**	1
14 May 54	● **FRIENDS AND NEIGHBOURS (re-entry)** Decca F 10299 [3]	**3**	11

[1] Billy Cotton and his Band, vocals by Doreen Stephens [2] Billy Cotton and his Band, vocals by the Mill Girls and the Bandits [3] Billy Cotton and his Band, vocals by the Bandits

See also Various Artists (EPs & LPs) - All Star Hit Parade No. 2.

Mike COTTON'S JAZZMEN
UK, male instrumental band, Mike Cotton trumpet — 4 wks

20 Jun 63	**SWING THAT HAMMER** Columbia DB 7029	**36**	4

John COUGAR – *See John Cougar MELLENCAMP*

COUGARS UK, male instrumental group — 8 wks

28 Feb 63	**SATURDAY NITE AT THE DUCK-POND** Parlophone R 4989	**33**	8

COUNCIL COLLECTIVE
UK / US, male / female vocal / instrumental group — 6 wks

22 Dec 84	**SOUL DEEP (PART 1)** Polydor MINE 1	**24**	6

COUNT INDIGO UK, male vocalist — 1 wk

9 Mar 96	**MY UNKNOWN LOVE** Cowboy RODEO 952CD	**59**	1

COUNTING CROWS
US, male vocal / instrumental group — 8 wks

30 Apr 94	**MR. JONES** Geffen GFSTD 69	**28**	2
9 Jul 94	**ROUND HERE** Geffen GFSTD 74	**70**	1
15 Oct 94	**RAIN KING** Geffen GFSTD 82	**49**	3
19 Oct 96	**ANGELS OF THE SILENCES** Geffen GFSTD 22182	**41**	1
14 Dec 96	**A LONG DECEMBER** Geffen GFSTD 22190	**62**	1

COUNTRYMEN UK, male vocal group — 2 wks

3 May 62	**I KNOW WHERE I'M GOING** Piccadilly 7N 35029	**45**	2

Don COVAY US, male vocalist — 6 wks

7 Sep 74	**IT'S BETTER TO HAVE (AND DON'T NEED)** Mercury 6052 634	**29**	6

Vincent COVELLO – *See BT*

COVENTRY CITY CUP FINAL SQUAD
UK, male football team vocalists — 2 wks

23 May 87	**GO FOR IT!** Sky Blue SKB 1	**61**	2

COVER GIRLS US, female vocal group — 4 wks

1 Aug 92	**WISHING ON A STAR** Epic 6581437	**38**	4

COVERDALE PAGE UK, male vocal / instrumental duo 3 wks

3 Jul 93	**TAKE ME FOR A LITTLE WHILE** EMI CDEM 270	**29**	2
23 Oct 93	**TAKE A LOOK AT YOURSELF** EMI CDEM 279	**43**	1

Julie COVINGTON UK, female vocalist 29 wks

25 Dec 76	★ **DON'T CRY FOR ME ARGENTINA** MCA 260	**1**	15
3 Dec 77	**ONLY WOMEN BLEED** Virgin VS 196	**12**	11
15 Jul 78	**DON'T CRY FOR ME ARGENTINA (re-entry)** MCA 260	**63**	3

See also Julie Covington, Rula Lenska, Charlotte Cornwell and Sue Jones-Davies.

Warren COVINGTON – See Tommy DORSEY ORCHESTRA starring Warren COVINGTON

Julie COVINGTON, Rula LENSKA, Charlotte CORNWELL and Sue JONES-DAVIES
UK, female vocal group 6 wks

21 May 77	● **O.K?** Polydor 2001 714	**10**	6

See also Julie Covington.

Patrick COWLEY – See SYLVESTER

Carl COX UK, male producer 16 wks

28 Sep 91	**I WANT YOU (FOREVER)** Perfecto PB 44885 [1]	**23**	7
8 Aug 92	**DOES IT FEEL GOOD TO YOU** Perfecto PB 74321102877 [1]	**35**	3
6 Nov 93	**THE PLANET OF LOVE** Perfecto 74321161772	**44**	2
9 Mar 96	**TWO PAINTINGS AND A DRUM EP** Edel 0090715COX	**24**	2
8 Jun 96	**SENSUAL SOPHIS-TI-CAT / THE PLAYER** Ultimatum 0090875COX	**25**	2

[1] DJ Carl Cox

Tracks on Two Paintings And A Drum EP: Phoebus Apollu / Yum Yum / Siberian Snow Storm.

Deborah COX US, female vocalist 6 wks

11 Nov 95	**SENTIMENTAL** Arista 74321324962	**34**	3
24 Feb 96	**WHO DO U LOVE** Arista 74321337942	**31**	3

Michael COX UK, male vocalist 15 wks

9 Jun 60	● **ANGELA JONES** Triumph RGM 1011	**7**	13
20 Oct 60	**ALONG CAME CAROLINE** HMV POP 789	**41**	2

CRACKER US, male vocal / instrumental group 9 wks

28 May 94	**LOW** Virgin America VUSDG 80	**43**	4
23 Jul 94	**GET OFF THIS** Virgin America VUSCD 83	**41**	3
3 Dec 94	**LOW (re-entry)** Virgin America VUSDG 80	**54**	2

Sarah CRACKNELL UK, female vocalist 1 wk

14 Sep 96	**ANYMORE** Gut CDGUT 3	**39**	1

Floyd CRAMER US, male instrumentalist – piano 24 wks

13 Apr 61	★ **ON THE REBOUND** RCA 1231	**1**	14
20 Jul 61	**SAN ANTONIO ROSE** RCA 1241	**36**	8
23 Aug 62	**HOT PEPPER** RCA 1301	**46**	2

CRAMPS US, male / female vocal / instrumental group 4 wks

9 Nov 85	**CAN YOUR PUSSY DO THE DOG?** Big Beat NS 110	**68**	1
10 Feb 90	**BIKINI GIRLS WITH MACHINE GUNS** Enigma ENV 17	**35**	3

CRANBERRIES
Ireland, male / female vocal / instrumental group 45 wks

27 Feb 93	**LINGER** Island CID 556	**74**	1
12 Feb 94	**LINGER (re-issue)** Island CID 559	**14**	11
7 May 94	**DREAMS** Island CIDX 594	**27**	5
1 Oct 94	**ZOMBIE** Island CID 600	**14**	6
3 Dec 94	**ODE TO MY FAMILY** Island CIDX 601	**38**	6
11 Mar 95	**I CAN'T BE WITH YOU** Island CID 605	**23**	5
12 Aug 95	**RIDICULOUS THOUGHTS** Island CID 616	**20**	3
20 Apr 96	**SALVATION** Island CID 633	**13**	5
13 Jul 96	**FREE TO DECIDE** Island CID 637	**33**	3

Les CRANE US, male vocalist 14 wks

19 Feb 72	● **DESIDERATA** Warner Bros. K 16119	**7**	14

Whitfield CRANE – See ICE-T; MOTORHEAD

CRANES UK, male / female vocal / instrumental group 2 wks

25 Sep 93	**JEWEL** Dedicated CRANE 007CD	**29**	1
3 Sep 94	**SHINING ROAD** Dedicated CRANE 8CD1	**57**	1

CRASH TEST DUMMIES
Canada, male / female vocal / instrumental group 20 wks

23 Apr 94	● **MMM MMM MMM MMM** RCA 74321201512	**2**	11
16 Jul 94	**AFTERNOONS & COFFEESPOONS** RCA 74321219622	**23**	5
15 Apr 95	**THE BALLAD OF PETER PUMPKINHEAD** RCA 74321276772 [1]	**30**	4

[1] Crash Test Dummies featuring Ellen Reid

Beverley CRAVEN UK, female vocalist 33 wks

20 Apr 91	● **PROMISE ME** Epic 6559437	**3**	13
20 Jul 91	**HOLDING ON** Epic 6565507	**32**	7
5 Oct 91	**WOMAN TO WOMAN** Epic 6574647	**40**	5
7 Dec 91	**MEMORIES** Epic 6576617	**68**	2
25 Sep 93	**LOVE SCENES** Epic 6595952	**34**	4
20 Nov 93	**MOLLIE'S SONG** Epic 6598132	**61**	2

Jimmy CRAWFORD UK, male vocalist 11 wks

8 Jun 61	**LOVE OR MONEY** Columbia DB 4633	**49**	1
16 Nov 61	**I LOVE HOW YOU LOVE ME** Columbia DB 4717	**18**	10

Michael CRAWFORD UK, male vocalist 14 wks

10 Jan 87	● **THE MUSIC OF THE NIGHT** Polydor POSP 803	**7**	11
15 Jan 94	**THE MUSIC OF THE NIGHT** Columbia 6597382 [1]	**54**	3

[1] Barbra Streisand (duet with Michael Crawford)

The flip side of The Music Of The Night, Wishing You Were Somehow Here Again by Sarah Brightman was also listed.

Randy CRAWFORD US, female vocalist 74 wks

21 Jun 80	**LAST NIGHT AT DANCELAND** Warner Bros. K 17631	**61**	2
30 Aug 80	● **ONE DAY I'LL FLY AWAY** Warner Bros. K 17680	**2**	11

30 May 81		YOU MIGHT NEED SOMEBODY *Warner Bros. K 17803* ..**11**	13
8 Aug 81		RAINY NIGHT IN GEORGIA *Warner Bros. K 17840* **18**	9
31 Oct 81		SECRET COMBINATION *Warner Bros. K 17872* **48**	3
30 Jan 82		IMAGINE *Warner Bros. K 17906* **60**	1
13 Feb 82		IMAGINE (re-entry) *Warner Bros. K 17906* **75**	1
5 Jun 82		ONE HELLO *Warner Bros. K 17948* **48**	4
19 Feb 83		HE REMINDS ME *Warner Bros. K 17970* **65**	2
8 Oct 83		NIGHT LINE *Warner Bros. W 9530* **51**	4
29 Nov 86	●	ALMAZ *Warner Bros. W 8583*.....................................**4**	17
18 Jan 92		DIAMANTE *London LON 313* [1] **44**	7

[1] Zucchero with Randy Crawford

See also Crusaders.

Robert CRAY BAND
US, male vocal / instrumental group   **5 wks**

| 20 Jun 87 | | RIGHT NEXT DOOR (BECAUSE OF ME) *Mercury CRAY 3*..**50** | 4 |
| 20 Apr 96 | | BABY LEE *Silvertone ORECD 81* [1] ....**65** | 1 |

[1] John Lee Hooker with Robert Cray

CRAZY ELEPHANT *US, male vocal group*   **13 wks**

| 21 May 69 | | GIMME GIMME GOOD LOVIN' *Major Minor MM 609* ....**12** | 13 |

CRAZYHEAD *UK, male vocal / instrumental group*   **4 wks**

| 16 Jul 88 | | TIME HAS TAKEN ITS TOLL ON YOU *Food FOOD 12* ......**65** | 2 |
| 25 Feb 89 | | HAVE LOVE, WILL TRAVEL EP *Food SGE 2025* ....**68** | 2 |

Tracks on Have Love, Will Travel (EP): Have Love Will Travel / Out On A Limb (Live) / Baby Turpentine (Live) / Snake Eyes (Live). See also Various Artists (EPs & LPs) – The Food Christmas EP.

CREAM *UK, male vocal / instrumental group*   **59 wks**

20 Oct 66		WRAPPING PAPER *Reaction 591 007* **34**	6
15 Dec 66		I FEEL FREE *Reaction 591 011* **11**	12
8 Jun 67		STRANGE BREW *Reaction 591 015* **17**	9
5 Jun 68		ANYONE FOR TENNIS (THE SAVAGE SEVEN THEME) *Polydor 56 258* **40**	3
9 Oct 68		SUNSHINE OF YOUR LOVE *Polydor 56 286* **25**	7
15 Jan 69		WHITE ROOM *Polydor 56 300* **28**	8
9 Apr 69		BADGE *Polydor 56 315* **18**	10
28 Oct 72		BADGE (re-issue) *Polydor 2058 285* **42**	4

CREATION *UK, male vocal / instrumental group*   **3 wks**

| 7 Jul 66 | | MAKING TIME *Planet PLF 116* ....**49** | 1 |
| 3 Nov 66 | | PAINTER MAN *Planet PLF 119* ....**36** | 2 |

CREATURES *UK, male / female vocal / instrumental group*   **26 wks**

3 Oct 81		MAD EYED SCREAMER *Polydor POSPD 354* **24**	7
23 Apr 83		MISS THE GIRL *Wonderland SHE 1* **21**	7
16 Jul 83		RIGHT NOW *Wonderland SHE 2*...............................**14**	10
14 Oct 89		STANDING THERE *Wonderland SHE 17* **53**	2

CREDIT TO THE NATION *UK, male rap group*   **10 wks**

22 May 93		CALL IT WHAT YOU WANT *One Little Indian 94 TP7CD*..**57**	3
18 Sep 93		ENOUGH IS ENOUGH *One Little Indian 79 TP7CD* [1] **56**	2
12 Mar 94		TEENAGE SENSATION *One Little Indian 124 TP7DC* **24**	3
14 May 94		SOWING THE SEEDS OF HATRED *One Little Indian 134 TP7CD*...**72**	1
22 Jul 95		LIAR LIAR *One Little Indian 144 TP7CD* **60**	1

[1] Chumbawamba and Credit To The Nation

CREEDENCE CLEARWATER REVIVAL
US, male vocal / instrumental group   **94 wks**

28 May 69	●	PROUD MARY *Liberty LBF 15223*................................**8**	13
16 Aug 69	★	BAD MOON RISING *Liberty LBF 15230* **1**	15
15 Nov 69		GREEN RIVER *Liberty LBF 15250* **19**	11
14 Feb 70		DOWN ON THE CORNER *Liberty LBF 15283*..............**31**	6
4 Apr 70	●	TRAVELLIN' BAND *Liberty LBF 15310* **8**	12
20 Jun 70	●	UP AROUND THE BEND *Liberty LBF 15354* **3**	12
4 Jul 70		TRAVELLIN' BAND (re-entry) *Liberty LBF 15310* **46**	1
5 Sep 70		LONG AS I CAN SEE THE LIGHT *Liberty LBF 15384* **20**	9
20 Mar 71		HAVE YOU EVER SEEN THE RAIN *Liberty LBF 15440*....**36**	6
24 Jul 71		SWEET HITCH-HIKER *United Artists UP 35261* **36**	8
2 May 92		BAD MOON RISING (re-issue) *Epic 6580047* **71**	1

Kid CREOLE and the COCONUTS
US, male vocalist and female vocal group   **58 wks**

13 Jun 81		ME NO POP I *Ze WIP 6711* [1] **32**	7
15 May 82	●	I'M A WONDERFUL THING, BABY *Ze WIP 6756* **4**	11
24 Jul 82	●	STOOL PIGEON *Ze WIP 6793* **7**	9
9 Oct 82	●	ANNIE I'M NOT YOUR DADDY *Ze WIP 6801* **2**	8
11 Dec 82		DEAR ADDY *Ze WIP 6840* **29**	7
10 Sep 83		THERE'S SOMETHING WRONG IN PARADISE *Island IS 130* **35**	5
19 Nov 83		THE LIFEBOAT PARTY *Island IS 142*..........................**49**	4
14 Apr 90		THE SEX OF IT *CBS 655698 7* **29**	5
10 Apr 93		I'M A WONDERFUL THING BABY (re-mix) *Island CID 551* **60**	2

[1] Kid Creole and the Coconuts present Coati Mundi

See also Coconuts.

CRESCENDO
UK / US, male / female vocal / instrumental duo   **5 wks**

| 23 Dec 95 | | ARE YOU OUT THERE *ffrr FCD 270* ....**20** | 5 |

CREW CUTS *Canada, male vocal group*   **29 wks**

| 1 Oct 54 | | SH-BOOM *Mercury MB 3140* ....**12** | 9 |
| 15 Apr 55 | ● | EARTH ANGEL *Mercury MB 3202* ....**4** | 20 |

Bernard CRIBBINS *UK, male vocalist*   **29 wks**

15 Feb 62	●	HOLE IN THE GROUND *Parlophone R 4869* **9**	13
5 Jul 62	●	RIGHT SAID FRED *Parlophone R 4923* **10**	10
13 Dec 62		GOSSIP CALYPSO *Parlophone R 4961* **25**	6

CRICKETS *US, male vocal / instrumental group*   **97 wks**

27 Sep 57	★	THAT'LL BE THE DAY *Vogue Coral Q 72279*.................**1**	14
27 Dec 57	●	OH BOY *Coral Q 72298* **3**	15
10 Jan 58		THAT'LL BE THE DAY (re-entry) *Vogue Coral Q 72279* ..**29**	1
14 Mar 58	●	MAYBE BABY *Coral Q 72307* **4**	10
25 Jul 58		THINK IT OVER *Coral Q 72329*.................................**11**	7
24 Apr 59		LOVE'S MADE A FOOL OF YOU *Coral Q 72365* **26**	1
8 May 59		LOVE'S MADE A FOOL OF YOU (re-entry) *Coral Q 72365* **30**	1
15 Jan 60		WHEN YOU ASK ABOUT LOVE *Coral Q 72382* **27**	1
12 May 60		MORE THAN I CAN SAY *Coral Q 72395*.....................**42**	1
26 May 60		BABY MY HEART *Coral Q 72395* **33**	4
21 Jun 62	●	DON'T EVER CHANGE *Coral Q 55441* **5**	13
24 Jan 63		MY LITTLE GIRL *Liberty LIB 10067* **17**	9
6 Jun 63		DON'T TRY TO CHANGE ME *Liberty LIB 10092* **37**	4
14 May 64		YOU'VE GOT LOVE *Coral Q 72472* [1] **40**	6
2 Jul 64		(THEY CALL HER) LA BAMBA *Liberty LIB 55696* **21**	10

[1] Buddy Holly and the Crickets

Although not credited on the records, Buddy Holly was featured on the first four hits.

84

CRIMINAL ELEMENT ORCHESTRA – See Wally JUMP Jr. and the CRIMINAL ELEMENT

CRISPY AND COMPANY
US, male vocal / instrumental group   **11 wks**

16 Aug 75	**BRAZIL** *Creole CR 109*	**26**	5
27 Dec 75	**GET IT TOGETHER** *Creole CR 114*	**21**	6

CRITTERS *US, male vocal / instrumental group*   **5 wks**

30 Jun 66	**YOUNGER GIRL** *London HL 10047*	**38**	5

Tony CROMBIE and his ROCKETS
UK, male vocal / instrumental group, Tony Crombie-drums   **2 wks**

19 Oct 56	**TEACH YOU TO ROCK / SHORT'NIN' BREAD** *Columbia DB 3822*	**25**	2

Bing CROSBY *US, male vocalist*   **93 wks**

14 Nov 52	● **ISLE OF INNISFREE** *Brunswick 04900*	**3**	12
5 Dec 52	● **ZING A LITTLE ZONG** *Brunswick 04981* [1]	**10**	2
19 Dec 52	● **SILENT NIGHT** *Brunswick 03929*	**8**	2
19 Mar 54	● **CHANGING PARTNERS** *Brunswick 05244*	**10**	1
2 Apr 54	● **CHANGING PARTNERS (re-entry)** *Brunswick 05244*	**9**	1
23 Apr 54	**CHANGING PARTNERS (2nd re-entry)** *Brunswick 05244*	**11**	1
7 Jan 55	**COUNT YOUR BLESSINGS** *Brunswick 05339*	**18**	1
21 Jan 55	**COUNT YOUR BLESSINGS (re-entry)** *Brunswick 05339*	**11**	2
29 Apr 55	**STRANGER IN PARADISE** *Brunswick 05410*	**17**	2
27 Apr 56	**IN A LITTLE SPANISH TOWN** *Brunswick 05543*	**22**	3
23 Nov 56	● **TRUE LOVE** *Capitol CL 14645* [2]	**4**	27
24 May 57	● **AROUND THE WORLD** *Brunswick 05674*	**5**	15
9 Aug 75	**THAT'S WHAT LIFE IS ALL ABOUT** *United Artists UP 35852*	**41**	4
3 Dec 77	● **WHITE CHRISTMAS** *MCA 111*	**5**	7
27 Nov 82	● **PEACE ON EARTH – LITTLE DRUMMER BOY** *RCA BOW 12* [3]	**3**	8
17 Dec 83	**TRUE LOVE (re-issue)** *Capitol CL 315* [2]	**70**	3
21 Dec 85	**WHITE CHRISTMAS (re-issue)** *MCA BING 1*	**69**	2

[1] Bing Crosby and Jane Wyman [2] Bing Crosby and Grace Kelly
[3] David Bowie and Bing Crosby

David CROSBY – See CROSBY, STILLS, NASH and YOUNG; Phil COLLINS

CROSBY, STILLS, NASH and YOUNG
US / UK / Canada, male vocal / instrumental group   **12 wks**

16 Aug 69	**MARRAKESH EXPRESS** *Atlantic 584 283* [1]	**17**	9
21 Jan 89	**AMERICAN DREAM** *Atlantic A 9003*	**55**	3

[1] Crosby, Stills and Nash

See also Stephen Stills; Neil Young.

CROSS *UK / US, male vocal / instrumental group*   **1 wk**

17 Oct 87	**COWBOYS AND INDIANS** *Virgin VS 1007*	**74**	1

Christopher CROSS *US, male vocalist*   **27 wks**

19 Apr 80	**RIDE LIKE THE WIND** *Warner Bros. K 17582*	**69**	1
14 Feb 81	**SAILING** *Warner Bros. K 17695*	**48**	6
17 Oct 81	**ARTHUR'S THEME (BEST THAT YOU CAN DO)** *Warner Bros. K 17847*	**56**	4
9 Jan 82	● **ARTHUR'S THEME (BEST THAT YOU CAN DO) (re-entry)** *Warner Bros. K 17847*	**7**	11
5 Feb 83	**ALL RIGHT** *Warner Bros. W 9843*	**51**	5

Sheryl CROW *US, female vocalist*   **37 wks**

18 Jun 94	**LEAVING LAS VEGAS** *A & M 5806472*	**66**	1
5 Nov 94	● **ALL I WANNA DO** *A & M 5808452*	**4**	13
11 Feb 95	**STRONG ENOUGH** *A & M 5809212*	**33**	4
27 May 95	**CAN'T CRY ANYMORE** *A & M 5810552*	**33**	3
29 Jul 95	**RUN BABY RUN** *A & M 5811492*	**24**	4
11 Nov 95	**WHAT I CAN DO FOR YOU** *A & M 5812292*	**43**	1
21 Sep 96	● **IF IT MAKES YOU HAPPY** *A & M 5819032*	**9**	6
30 Nov 96	**EVERYDAY IS A WINDING ROAD** *A & M 5820232*	**12†**	5

CROWD
Multi-national, male / female vocal / instrumental charity assembly   **11 wks**

1 Jun 85	★ **YOU'LL NEVER WALK ALONE** *Spartan BRAD 1*	**1**	11

CROWDED HOUSE
Australia / New Zealand, male vocal / instrumental group   **64 wks**

6 Jun 87	**DON'T DREAM IT'S OVER** *Capitol CL 438*	**27**	8
22 Jun 91	**CHOCOLATE CAKE** *Capitol CL 618*	**69**	2
2 Nov 91	**FALL AT YOUR FEET** *Capitol CL 626*	**17**	7
29 Feb 92	● **WEATHER WITH YOU** *Capitol CL 643*	**7**	9
20 Jun 92	**FOUR SEASONS IN ONE DAY** *Capitol CL 655*	**26**	5
26 Sep 92	**IT'S ONLY NATURAL** *Capitol CL 661*	**24**	4
2 Oct 93	**DISTANT SUN** *Capitol CDCLS 697*	**19**	6
20 Nov 93	**NAILS IN MY FEET** *Capitol CDCLS 701*	**22**	4
19 Feb 94	**LOCKED OUT** *Capitol CDCLS 707*	**12**	4
11 Jun 94	**FINGERS OF LOVE** *Capitol CDCL 715*	**25**	3
24 Sep 94	**PINEAPPLE HEAD** *Capitol CDCL 723*	**27**	3
22 Jun 96	**INSTINCT** *Capitol CDCLS 774*	**12**	4
17 Aug 96	**NOT THE GIRL YOU THINK YOU ARE** *Capitol CDCLS 776*	**20**	3
9 Nov 96	**DON'T DREAM IT'S OVER (re-issue)** *Capitol CDCL 780*	**25**	2

Act were Australia/New Zealand only for first six hits and the re-issue of Don't Dream It's Over.

CROWN HEIGHTS AFFAIR
US, male vocal / instrumental group   **34 wks**

19 Aug 78	**GALAXY OF LOVE** *Mercury 6168 801*	**24**	10
11 Nov 78	**I'M GONNA LOVE YOU FOREVER** *Mercury 6168 803*	**47**	4
14 Apr 79	**DANCE LADY DANCE** *Mercury 6168 804*	**44**	4
3 May 80	● **YOU GAVE ME LOVE** *De-Lite MER 9*	**10**	12
9 Aug 80	**YOU'VE BEEN GONE** *De-Lite MER 28*	**44**	4

Julee CRUISE *US, female vocalist*   **13 wks**

10 Nov 90	● **FALLING** *Warner Bros. W 9544*	**7**	11
2 Mar 91	**ROCKIN' BACK INSIDE MY HEART** *Warner Bros. W 0004*	**66**	2

CRUISERS – See Dave BERRY

CRUSADERS *US, male vocal / instrumental group*   **16 wks**

18 Aug 79	● **STREET LIFE** *MCA 513*	**5**	11
26 Sep 81	**I'M SO GLAD I'M STANDING HERE TODAY** *MCA 741* [1]	**61**	3
7 Apr 84	**NIGHT LADIES** *MCA MCA 853*	**55**	2

[1] Crusaders, featured vocalist Joe Cocker

Vocalist on Street Life was Randy Crawford, though uncredited.

CRUSH *UK, female vocal duo*   **3 wks**

24 Feb 96	**JELLYHEAD** *Telstar CDSTAS 2809*	**50**	2
3 Aug 96	**LUV'D UP** *Telstar CDSTAS 2833*	**45**	1

Crosby, Stills, Nash and Young

CSN & Y became instant stars after playing two sets at the legendary Woodstock Festival, one acoustic the other electric.

Creedence Clearwater Revival

'Proud Mary', Creedence Clearwater Revival's tale of a Mississippi steamboat, was a million selling US hit for Ike and Tina Turner in 1971. The song is still a fixture in Tina's live shows.

Sheryl Crow

Sheryl Crow's vignette on Los Angeles life, 'All I Wanna Do', earned her two Grammy Awards in 1995, for Record Of The Year and Best Female Vocal Performance.

Bobby CRUSH *UK, male instrumentalist – piano* **4 wks**

| 4 Nov 72 | **BORSALINO** *Philips 6006 248* | **37** | 4 |

CRY BEFORE DAWN
Ireland, male vocal / instrumental group **2 wks**

| 17 Jun 89 | **WITNESS FOR THE WORLD** *Epic GONE 3* | **67** | 2 |

CRY OF LOVE
US, male / female vocal / instrumental group **1 wk**

| 15 Jan 94 | **BAD THING** *Columbia 6600462* | **60** | 1 |

CRY SISCO! *UK, male producer – Barry Blue* **9 wks**

| 2 Sep 89 | **AFRO DIZZI ACT** *Escape AWOL 1* | **42** | 8 |
| 20 Jan 90 | **AFRO DIZZI ACT (re-entry)** *Escape AWOL 1* | **70** | 1 |

CRYIN' SHAMES *UK, male vocal / instrumental group* **7 wks**

| 31 Mar 66 | **PLEASE STAY** *Decca F 12340* | **26** | 7 |

CRYPT-KICKERS – See Bobby 'Boris' PICKETT and the CRYPT-KICKERS

CRYSTAL PALACE *UK, male football team vocalists* **2 wks**

| 12 May 90 | **GLAD ALL OVER / WHERE EAGLES FLY** *Parkfield PMS 5019* | **50** | 2 |

CRYSTALS *US, female vocal group* **54 wks**

22 Nov 62		**HE'S A REBEL** *London HLU 9611*	**19**	13
20 Jun 63	●	**DA DOO RON RON** *London HLU 9732*	**5**	16
19 Sep 63	●	**THEN HE KISSED ME** *London HLU 9773*	**2**	14
5 Mar 64		**I WONDER** *London HLU 9852*	**36**	3
19 Oct 74		**DA DOO RON RON (re-issue)** *Warner Spector K 19010*	**15**	8

CSILLA *Hungary, female vocalist* **1 wk**

| 13 Jul 96 | **MAN IN THE MOON** *Worx WORXCD 001* | **69** | 1 |

CUBIC 22 *Belgium, male instrumental / production duo* **7 wks**

| 22 Jun 91 | **NIGHT IN MOTION** *XL XLS 20* | **15** | 7 |

CUD *UK, male vocal / instrumental group* **16 wks**

19 Oct 91	**OH NO WON'T DO (EP)** *A & M AMB 829*	**49**	2
28 Mar 92	**THROUGH THE ROOF** *A & M AM 857*	**44**	2
30 May 92	**RICH AND STRANGE** *A & M AM 871*	**24**	3
15 Aug 92	**PURPLE LOVE BALLOON** *A & M AM 0024*	**27**	3
10 Oct 92	**ONCE AGAIN** *A & M AM 0081*	**45**	1
12 Feb 94	**NEUROTICA** *A & M 5805172*	**37**	2
2 Apr 94	**STICKS AND STONES** *A & M 5805472*	**68**	1
3 Sep 94	**ONE GIANT LOVE** *A & M 5807292*	**52**	2

Tracks on Oh No Won't Do (EP): Oh No Won't Do / Profession / Ariel / Price Of Love. See also Various Artists (EPs & LPs) – Gimme Shelter EP.

CUFFLINKS *US, male vocal group* **30 wks**

| 29 Nov 69 | ● | **TRACY** *MCA MU 1101* | **4** | 16 |
| 14 Mar 70 | ● | **WHEN JULIE COMES AROUND** *MCA MU 1112* | **10** | 14 |

CULT *UK, male vocal / instrumental group* **80 wks**

22 Dec 84	**RESURRECTION JOE** *Beggars Banquet BEG 122*	**74**	2
25 May 85	**SHE SELLS SANCTUARY** *Beggars Banquet BEG 135*	**15**	17
28 Sep 85	**SHE SELLS SANCTUARY (re-entry)** *Beggars Banquet BEG 135*	**61**	2
5 Oct 85	**RAIN** *Beggars Banquet BEG 147*	**17**	8
30 Nov 85	**REVOLUTION** *Beggars Banquet BEG 152*	**30**	7
28 Feb 87	**LOVE REMOVAL MACHINE** *Beggars Banquet BEG 182*	**18**	7
2 May 87	**LIL' DEVIL** *Beggars Banquet BEG 188*	**11**	7
22 Aug 87	**WILD FLOWER (DOUBLE SINGLE)** *Beggars Banquet BEG 195D*	**24**	2
29 Aug 87	**WILD FLOWER** *Beggars Banquet BEG 195*	**30**	4
1 Apr 89	**FIRE WOMAN** *Beggars Banquet BEG 228*	**15**	4
8 Jul 89	**EDIE (CIAO BABY)** *Beggars Banquet BEG 230*	**32**	5
18 Nov 89	**SUN KING / EDIE (CIAO BABY) (re-issue)** *Beggars Banquet BEG 235*	**39**	2
10 Mar 90	**SWEET SOUL SISTER** *Beggars Banquet BEG 241*	**42**	4
14 Sep 91	**WILD HEARTED SON** *Beggars Banquet BEG 255*	**40**	2
29 Feb 92	**HEART OF SOUL** *Beggars Banquet BEG 260*	**51**	1
30 Jan 93	**SHE SELLS SANCTUARY (re-mix)** *Beggars Banquet BEG 253CD*	**15**	4
8 Oct 94	**COMING DOWN** *Beggars Banquet BBQ 40CD*	**50**	1
7 Jan 95	**STAR** *Beggars Banquet BBQ 45CD*	**65**	1

Tracks on double single: Wild Flower / Love Trooper / Outlaw / Horse Nation.

CULT JAM – See LISA LISA and CULT JAM

CULTURE BEAT
UK / US / Germany, male / female vocal / instrumental group **46 wks**

3 Feb 90		**CHERRY LIPS (DER ERDBEERMUND)** *Epic 655637*	**55**	3
7 Aug 93	★	**MR. VAIN** *Epic 6594682*	**1**	15
6 Nov 93	●	**GOT TO GET IT** *Epic 6597212*	**4**	11
15 Jan 94	●	**ANYTHING** *Epic 6600252*	**5**	8
2 Apr 94		**WORLD IN YOUR HANDS** *Epic 6602292*	**20**	4
27 Jan 96		**INSIDE OUT** *Epic 6626562*	**32**	2
15 Jun 96		**CRYING IN THE RAIN** *Epic 6633582*	**29**	2
28 Sep 96		**TAKE ME AWAY** *Epic 6637552*	**52**	1

CULTURE CLUB
UK, male vocal / instrumental group **103 wks**

18 Sep 82	★	**DO YOU REALLY WANT TO HURT ME** *Virgin VS 518*	**1**	18
27 Nov 82	●	**TIME (CLOCK OF THE HEART)** *Virgin VS 558*	**3**	12
9 Apr 83	●	**CHURCH OF THE POISON MIND** *Virgin VS 571*	**2**	9
17 Sep 83	★	**KARMA CHAMELEON** *Virgin VS 612*	**1**	20
10 Dec 83	●	**VICTIMS** *Virgin VS 641*	**3**	10
24 Mar 84	●	**IT'S A MIRACLE** *Virgin VS 662*	**4**	9
6 Oct 84	●	**THE WAR SONG** *Virgin VS 694*	**2**	8
1 Dec 84		**THE MEDAL SONG** *Virgin VS 730*	**32**	4
5 Jan 85		**THE MEDAL SONG (re-entry)** *Virgin VS 730*	**74**	1
15 Mar 86	●	**MOVE AWAY** *Virgin VS 845*	**7**	7
31 May 86		**GOD THANK YOU WOMAN** *Virgin VS 861*	**31**	5

Smiley CULTURE *UK, male vocalist* **13 wks**

15 Dec 84	**POLICE OFFICER** *Fashion FAD 7012*	**12**	10
6 Apr 85	**COCKNEY TRANSLATION** *Fashion FAD 7028*	**71**	1
13 Sep 86	**SCHOOLTIME CHRONICLE** *Polydor POSP 815*	**59**	2

LARRY CUNNINGHAM AND THE MIGHTY AVONS
Ireland, male vocal / instrumental group **11 wks**

| 10 Dec 64 | **TRIBUTE TO JIM REEVES** *King KG 1016* | **40** | 8 |

| 25 Feb 65 | | TRIBUTE TO JIM REEVES (re-entry) | | |
| | | King KG 1016 | 46 | 3 |

CUPID'S INSPIRATION
UK, male vocal / instrumental group   **19 wks**

| 19 Jun 68 | ● | YESTERDAY HAS GONE *Nems 56 3500* | 4 | 11 |
| 2 Oct 68 | | MY WORLD *Nems 56 3702* | 33 | 8 |

CURE *UK, male vocal / instrumental group*   **143 wks**

12 Apr 80		A FOREST *Fiction FICS 10*	31	8
4 Apr 81		PRIMARY *Fiction FICS 12*	43	6
17 Oct 81		CHARLOTTE SOMETIMES *Fiction FICS 14*	44	4
24 Jul 82		HANGING GARDEN *Fiction FICS 15*	34	4
27 Nov 82		LET'S GO TO BED *Fiction FICS 17*	44	4
8 Jan 83		LET'S GO TO BED (re-entry) *Fiction FICS 17*	75	1
9 Jul 83		THE WALK *Fiction FICS 18*	12	8
29 Oct 83	●	THE LOVE CATS *Fiction FICS 19*	7	11
7 Apr 84		THE CATERPILLAR *Fiction FICS 20*	14	7
27 Jul 85		IN BETWEEN DAYS *Fiction FICS 22*	15	10
21 Sep 85		CLOSE TO ME *Fiction FICS 23*	24	8
3 May 86		BOYS DON'T CRY *Fiction FICS 24*	22	6
18 Apr 87		WHY CAN'T I BE YOU *Fiction FICS 25*	21	5
4 Jul 87		CATCH *Fiction FICS 26*	27	4
17 Oct 87		JUST LIKE HEAVEN *Fiction FICS 27*	29	5
20 Feb 88		HOT HOT HOT!!! *Fiction FICSX 28*	45	3
22 Apr 89	●	LULLABY *Fiction FICS 29*	5	6
2 Sep 89		LOVESONG *Fiction FICS 30*	18	7
31 Mar 90		PICTURES OF YOU *Fiction FICS 34*	24	6
29 Sep 90		NEVER ENOUGH *Fiction FICS 35*	13	5
3 Nov 90		CLOSE TO ME (re-mix) *Fiction FICS 36*	13	5
28 Mar 92	●	HIGH *Fiction FICS 39*	8	3
11 Apr 92		HIGH (re-mix) *Fiction FICXS 41*	44	1
23 May 92	●	FRIDAY I'M IN LOVE *Fiction FICS 42*	6	7
17 Oct 92		A LETTER TO ELISE *Fiction FICS 46*	28	2
4 May 96		THE 13TH *Fiction 5764692*	15	2
29 Jun 96		MINT CAR *Fiction FISCD 52*	31	2
14 Dec 96		GONE *Fiction FICD 53*	60	1

CURIOSITY *UK, male vocal / instrumental group*   **58 wks**

13 Dec 86	●	DOWN TO EARTH *Mercury CAT 2* [1]	3	18
4 Apr 87		ORDINARY DAY *Mercury CAT 3* [1]	11	7
20 Jun 87	●	MISFIT *Mercury CAT 4* [1]	7	9
19 Sep 87		FREE *Mercury CAT 5* [1]	56	2
16 Sep 89		NAME AND NUMBER *Mercury CAT 6*	14	9
25 Apr 92	●	HANG ON IN THERE BABY *RCA PB 45377*	3	10
29 Aug 92		I NEED YOUR LOVIN' *RCA 74321111377*	47	2
30 Oct 93		GIMME THE SUNSHINE *RCA 74321168602*	73	1

[1] Curiosity Killed The Cat

CURLS – *See Paul EVANS and the CURLS*

Chantal CURTIS *France, female vocalist*   **3 wks**

| 14 Jul 79 | | GET ANOTHER LOVE *Pye 7P 5003* | 51 | 3 |

TC CURTIS *Jamaica, male vocalist / instrumentalist*   **4 wks**

| 23 Feb 85 | | YOU SHOULD HAVE KNOWN BETTER | | |
| | | *Hot Melt VS 754* | 50 | 4 |

CURVE *UK, male / female vocal / instrumental duo*   **13 wks**

16 Mar 91		THE BLINDFOLD (EP) *Anxious ANX 27*	68	1
25 May 91		COAST IS CLEAR *Anxious ANX 30*	34	3
9 Nov 91		CLIPPED *Anxious ANX 35*	36	2
7 Mar 92		FAIT ACCOMPLI *Anxious ANXT 36*	22	3

18 Jul 92		HORROR HEAD (EP) *Anxious ANXT 38*	31	2
4 Sep 93		BLACKERTHREETRACKER EP		
		Anxious ANXCD 42	39	2

Tracks on The Blindfold EP: *Ten Little Girls / I Speak Your Every Word / Blindfold / No Escape From Heaven.* Tracks on Horror Head (EP): *Horror Head / Falling Free / Mission From God / Today Is Not The Day.* Only track available on all formats of Blackerthreetracker EP: *Missing Link.*

CURVED AIR
UK, male / female vocal / instrumental group   **12 wks**

| 7 Aug 71 | ● | BACK STREET LUV *Warner Bros. K 16092* | 4 | 12 |

CUT 'N' MOVE
Denmark, male / female vocal / instrumental group   **4 wks**

| 2 Oct 93 | | GIVE IT UP *EMI CDEM 273* | 61 | 2 |
| 9 Sep 95 | | I'M ALIVE *EMI CDEM 375* | 49 | 2 |

Adge CUTLER – *See WURZELS*

CUTTING CREW
UK / Canada, male vocal / instrumental group   **37 wks**

16 Aug 86	●	(I JUST) DIED IN YOUR ARMS *Siren SIREN 21*	4	12
25 Oct 86		I'VE BEEN IN LOVE BEFORE *Siren SIREN 29*	31	9
10 Jan 87		I'VE BEEN IN LOVE BEFORE (re-entry)		
		Siren SIREN 29	70	1
7 Mar 87		ONE FOR THE MOCKINGBIRD *Siren SIREN 40*	52	5
21 Nov 87		I'VE BEEN IN LOVE BEFORE (re-mix)		
		Siren SRN 29	24	8
22 Jul 89		(BETWEEN A) ROCK AND A HARD PLACE		
		Siren SRN 108	66	2

CYBERSONIK *US, male sampling group*   **1 wk**

| 10 Nov 90 | | TECHNARCHY *Champion CHAMP 264* | 73 | 1 |

Johnny CYMBAL *UK, male vocalist*   **10 wks**

| 14 Mar 63 | | MR. BASS MAN *London HLR 9682* | 24 | 10 |

CYPRESS HILL *US, male rap group*   **27 wks**

31 Jul 93		INSANE IN THE BRAIN *Ruff House 6595332*	32	4
2 Oct 93		WHEN THE SH.. GOES DOWN		
		Ruff House 6596702	19	4
11 Dec 93		I AIN'T GOIN' OUT LIKE THAT		
		Ruff House 6596902	15	7
26 Feb 94		INSANE IN THE BRAIN (re-issue)		
		Ruff House 6601762	21	4
7 May 94		LICK A SHOT *Ruff House 6603192*	20	3
7 Oct 95		THROW YOUR SET IN THE AIR		
		Ruff House 6623542	15	3
17 Feb 96		ILLUSIONS *Columbia 6629052*	23	2

Billy Ray CYRUS *US, male vocalist*   **18 wks**

25 Jul 92	●	ACHY BREAKY HEART *Mercury MER 373*	3	10
10 Oct 92		COULD'VE BEEN ME *Mercury MER 378*	24	4
28 Nov 92		THESE BOOTS ARE MADE FOR WALKIN'		
		Mercury MER 384	63	1
19 Dec 92		ACHY BREAKY HEART *Epic 6588837* [1]	53	3

[1] Alvin and the Chipmunks featuring Billy Ray Cyrus

D BO GENERAL – *See URBAN SHAKEDOWN*

Chuck D
US, male rapper — **6 wks**

6 Jul 91	**BRING THE NOISE** Island IS 490 [1]	.....	**14**	5
26 Oct 96	**NO** Mercury MERCD 476	.....	**55**	1

[1] Anthrax featuring Chuck D

Dimples D
US, female rapper — **10 wks**

17 Nov 90	**SUCKER DJ** FBI FBI 11	.....	**17**	10

Longsy D
UK, male vocalist — **7 wks**

4 Mar 89	**THIS IS SKA** Big One BIG 13	.....	**56**	7

Nikki D
US, female rapper — **6 wks**

6 May 89	**MY LOVE IS SO RAW** Def Jam 6548987 [1]	.....	**34**	5
30 Mar 91	**DADDY'S LITTLE GIRL** Def Jam 6567347	.....	**75**	1

[1] Alyson Williams featuring Nikki D

Vicky D
US, female vocalist — **6 wks**

13 Mar 82	**THIS BEAT IS MINE** Virgin VS 486	.....	**42**	6

D'BORA
US, female vocalist — **4 wks**

14 Sep 91	**DREAM ABOUT YOU** Polydor PO 161	.....	**75**	1
1 Jul 95	**GOING ROUND** Vibe MCSTD 2055	.....	**40**	2
30 Mar 96	**GOOD LOVE REAL LOVE** Music Plant MCSTD 40023	.....	**58**	1

D-INFLUENCE
UK, male / female vocal / instrumental group — **4 wks**

20 Jun 92	**GOOD LOVER** East West A 8573	.....	**46**	2
27 Mar 93	**GOOD LOVER (re-mix)** East West America A 8439CD	.....	**61**	1
24 Jun 95	**MIDNITE** East West A 4418CD	.....	**58**	1

D'LUX
UK, male / female vocal / instrumental group — **1 wk**

22 Jun 96	**LOVE RESURRECTION** Logic 74321371012	.....	**58**	1

D MOB
UK, male producer – Danny D. — **48 wks**

15 Oct 88	● **WE CALL IT ACIEED** ffrr FFR 13 [1]	.....	**3**	12
3 Jun 89	● **IT IS TIME TO GET FUNKY** ffrr F 107 [2]	.....	**9**	10
21 Oct 89	**C'MON AND GET MY LOVE** ffrr F 117 [3]	.....	**15**	10
6 Jan 90	● **PUT YOUR HANDS TOGETHER** ffrr F 124 [4]	.....	**7**	8
7 Apr 90	**THAT'S THE WAY OF THE WORLD** ffrr F 132 [3]	.....	**48**	3
12 Feb 94	**WHY** ffrr FCD 227 [3]	.....	**23**	3
3 Sep 94	**ONE DAY** ffrr FCDP 239	.....	**41**	2

[1] D Mob featuring Gary Haisman [2] D Mob featuring LRS [3] D Mob with Cathy Dennis [4] D Mob featuring Nuff Juice

D:REAM
UK, male vocal / instrumental duo — **71 wks**

4 Jul 92	**U R THE BEST THING** FXU FXU 3	.....	**72**	1
30 Jan 93	**THINGS CAN ONLY GET BETTER** Magnet MAG 1010CD	..	**24**	5
24 Apr 93	**U R THE BEST THING (re-mix)** Magnet MAG 1011CD	....	**19**	8
31 Jul 93	**UNFORGIVEN** Magnet MAG 1016CD	.....	**29**	3
2 Oct 93	**STAR / I LIKE IT** Magnet MAG 1019CD	.....	**26**	4
8 Jan 94	★ **THINGS CAN ONLY GET BETTER (re-mix)** Magnet MAG 1020CD	.....	**1**	16
26 Mar 94	● **U R THE BEST THING (2nd re-mix)** Magnet MAG 1021CD	.....	**4**	10
18 Jun 94	**TAKE ME AWAY** Magnet MAG 1025CD	.....	**18**	5
10 Sep 94	**BLAME IT ON ME** Magnet MAG 1027CD	.....	**25**	5
8 Jul 95	● **SHOOT ME WITH YOUR LOVE** Magnet MAG 1034CD	.....	**7**	7
9 Sep 95	**PARTY UP THE WORLD** Magnet MAG 1037CD	.....	**20**	6
11 Nov 95	**THE POWER (OF ALL THE LOVE IN THE WORLD)** Magnet MAG 1039CD	.....	**40**	1

D-SHAKE
Holland, male instrumental / production duo — **8 wks**

2 Jun 90	**YAAAH / TECHNO TRANCE** Cooltempo COOL 213	.....	**20**	6
2 Feb 91	**MY HEART THE BEAT** Cooltempo COOL 228	.....	**42**	2

D-TEK
UK, male instrumental / production group — **1 wk**

6 Nov 93	**DROP THE ROCK (EP)** Positiva 12TIV 5	.....	**70**	1

Tracks on Drop The Rock (EP): Drop The Rock / Chunkafunk / Drop The Rock (re-mix) / Don't Breathe.

D TRAIN
US, male vocal / instrumental duo — **36 wks**

6 Feb 82	**YOU'RE THE ONE FOR ME** Epic EPC A 2016	.....	**30**	8
8 May 82	**WALK ON BY** Epic EPC A 2298	.....	**44**	6
7 May 83	**MUSIC PART 1** Prelude A 3332	.....	**23**	7
16 Jul 83	**KEEP GIVING ME LOVE** Prelude A 3497	.....	**65**	2
27 Jul 85	**YOU'RE THE ONE FOR ME (re-mix)** Prelude ZB 40302	..	**15**	11
12 Oct 85	**MUSIC** Prelude ZB 40431	.....	**62**	2

DA BRAT
US, female rapper — **1 wk**

22 Oct 94	**FUNKDAFIED** Columbia 6609212	.....	**65**	1

Ricardo DA FORCE
UK, male rapper — **10 wks**

18 Mar 95	**PUMP UP THE VOLUME** Stress CDSTR 49 [1]	.....	**51**	2
16 Sep 95	● **STAYIN' ALIVE** All Around The World CDGLOBE 131 [2]	....	**2**	7
31 Aug 96	**WHY** ffrr FCD 280	.....	**58**	1

[1] Greed featuring Ricardo Da Force [2] N-Trance featuring Ricardo Da Force

DA LENCH MOB
US, male rap group — **2 wks**

20 Mar 93	**FREEDOM GOT AN A.K.** East West America A 8431CD	..	**51**	2

Paul DA VINCI
UK, male vocalist — **8 wks**

20 Jul 74	**YOUR BABY AIN'T YOUR BABY ANYMORE** Penny Farthing PEN 843	.....	**20**	8

Terry DACTYL and the DINOSAURS
UK, male vocal / instrumental group — **16 wks**

15 Jul 72	● **SEASIDE SHUFFLE** UK 5	.....	**2**	12
13 Jan 73	**ON A SATURDAY NIGHT** UK 21	.....	**45**	4

Terry Dactyl is Jona Lewie.

DADA
US, male vocal / instrumental group   **1 wk**

| 4 Dec 93 | **DOG** IRS CDEIRSS 185 .... | **71** | 1 |

DADDY FREDDY – See Simon HARRIS

DAFFY DUCK featuring the GROOVE GANG
Germany, male instrumental / production group   **3 wks**

| 6 Jul 91 | **PARTY ZONE** East West YZ 592 .... | **58** | 3 |

Etienne DAHO – See SAINT ETIENNE

DAINTEES – See Martin STEPHENSON and the DAINTEES

DAISY CHAINSAW
UK, male / female vocal / instrumental group   **6 wks**

| 18 Jan 92 | **LOVE YOUR MONEY** Deva DEVA 001 .... | **26** | 5 |
| 28 Mar 92 | **PINK FLOWER / ROOM ELEVEN** Deva 82 TP7 .... | **65** | 1 |

DAKEYNE – See James BROWN; TINMAN

DAKOTAS
UK, male instrumental group   **13 wks**

| 11 Jul 63 | **THE CRUEL SEA** Parlophone R 5044 .... | **18** | 13 |

See also Billy J. Kramer and the Dakotas.

DALE and GRACE
US, male / female vocal duo   **2 wks**

| 9 Jan 64 | **I'M LEAVING IT UP TO YOU** London HL 9807 .... | **42** | 2 |

Jim DALE
UK, male vocalist   **22 wks**

11 Oct 57	● **BE MY GIRL** Parlophone R 4343	**2**	16
10 Jan 58	**JUST BORN** Parlophone R 4376	**27**	1
17 Jan 58	**CRAZY DREAM** Parlophone R 4376	**24**	2
7 Mar 58	**SUGARTIME** Parlophone R 4402	**25**	3

DALE SISTERS
US, female vocal group   **6 wks**

| 23 Nov 61 | **MY SUNDAY BABY** Ember S 140 .... | **36** | 6 |

DALI'S CAR
UK, male vocal / instrumental duo   **2 wks**

| 3 Nov 84 | **THE JUDGEMENT IS THE MIRROR** Paradox DOX 1 .... | **66** | 2 |

Roger DALTREY
UK, male vocalist   **46 wks**

14 Apr 73	● **GIVING IT ALL AWAY** Track 2094 110	**5**	11
4 Aug 73	**I'M FREE** Ode ODS 66302	**13**	10
14 May 77	**WRITTEN ON THE WIND** Polydor 2121 319	**46**	2
2 Aug 80	**FREE ME** Polydor 2001 980	**39**	6
11 Oct 80	**WITHOUT YOUR LOVE** Polydor POSP 181	**55**	4
3 Mar 84	**WALKING IN MY SLEEP** WEA U 9686	**56**	3
5 Oct 85	**AFTER THE FIRE** 10 TEN 69	**50**	5
8 Mar 86	**UNDER A RAGING MOON** 10 TEN 81	**43**	5

DAMAGE
UK, male vocal group   **10 wks**

20 Jul 96	**ANYTHING** Big Life BLRD 129	**68**	1
12 Oct 96	**LOVE II LOVE** Big Life BLRD 131	**12**	6
14 Dec 96	● **FOREVER** Big Life BLRD 132	**6†**	3

Carolina DAMAS – See SUENO LATINO featuring Carolina DAMAS

DAMIAN
UK, male vocalist   **26 wks**

26 Dec 87	**THE TIME WARP 2** Jive JIVE 160	**51**	6
27 Aug 88	**THE TIME WARP 2 (re-issue)** Jive JIVE 182	**64**	3
19 Aug 89	● **THE TIME WARP (re-mix)** Jive JIVE 209	**7**	13
16 Dec 89	**WIG WAM BAM** Jive JIVE 236	**49**	4

The Time Warp *is a re-mix of The Time Warp 2.*

DAMNED
UK, male vocal / instrumental group   **77 wks**

5 May 79	**LOVE SONG** Chiswick CHIS 112	**20**	8
20 Oct 79	**SMASH IT UP** Chiswick CHIS 116	**35**	5
1 Dec 79	**I JUST CAN'T BE HAPPY TODAY** Chiswick CHIS 120 ...	**46**	5
4 Oct 80	**HISTORY OF THE WORLD (PART 1)** Chiswick CHIS 135	**51**	4
28 Nov 81	**FRIDAY 13TH EP** Stale One TRY 1	**50**	4
10 Jul 82	**LOVELY MONEY** Bronze BRO 149	**42**	4
9 Jun 84	**THANKS FOR THE NIGHT** Damned DAMNED 1	**43**	4
30 Mar 85	**GRIMLY FIENDISH** MCA GRIM 1	**21**	7
22 Jun 85	**THE SHADOW OF LOVE** MCA GRIM 2	**25**	8
21 Sep 85	**IS IT A DREAM** MCA GRIM 3	**34**	4
8 Feb 86	● **ELOISE** MCA GRIM 4	**3**	9
19 Apr 86	**ELOISE (re-entry)** MCA GRIM 4	**72**	1
22 Nov 86	**ANYTHING** MCA GRIM 5	**32**	4
7 Feb 87	**GIGOLO** MCA GRIM 6	**29**	3
25 Apr 87	**ALONE AGAIN OR** MCA GRIM 7	**27**	6
28 Nov 87	**IN DULCE DECORUM** MCA GRIM 8	**72**	1

Tracks on Friday 13th EP: Disco Man / Limit Club / Billy Bad Breaks / Citadel.

Kenny DAMON
US, male vocalist   **1 wk**

| 19 May 66 | **WHILE I LIVE** Mercury MF 907 .... | **48** | 1 |

Vic DAMONE
US, male vocalist   **22 wks**

6 Dec 57	**AN AFFAIR TO REMEMBER** Philips PB 745	**29**	1
31 Jan 58	**AN AFFAIR TO REMEMBER (re-entry)** Philips PB 745 ...	**30**	1
9 May 58	★ **ON THE STREET WHERE YOU LIVE** Philips PB 819	**1**	17
1 Aug 58	**THE ONLY MAN ON THE ISLAND** Philips PB 837	**24**	3

DAN-I
UK, male vocalist   **9 wks**

| 10 Nov 79 | **MONKEY CHOP** Island WIP 6520 .... | **30** | 9 |

DANA
UK, female vocalist   **75 wks**

4 Apr 70	★ **ALL KINDS OF EVERYTHING** Rex R 11054	**1**	15
25 Jul 70	**ALL KINDS OF EVERYTHING (re-entry)** Rex R 11054 ...	**47**	1
13 Feb 71	**WHO PUT THE LIGHTS OUT** Rex R 11062	**14**	11
25 Jan 75	● **PLEASE TELL HIM THAT I SAID HELLO** GTO GT 6	**8**	14
13 Dec 75	● **IT'S GONNA BE A COLD COLD CHRISTMAS** GTO GT 45	**4**	6
6 Mar 76	**NEVER GONNA FALL IN LOVE AGAIN** GTO GT 55	**31**	4
16 Oct 76	**FAIRYTALE** GTO GT 66	**13**	16
31 Mar 79	**SOMETHING'S COOKIN' IN THE KITCHEN** GTO GT 243	**44**	5
15 May 82	**I FEEL LOVE COMIN' ON** Creole CR 32	**66**	3

DANCE CONSPIRACY
UK, male instrumental / production duo   **1 wk**

| 3 Oct 92 | **DUB WAR** XL XLT 34 .... | **72** | 1 |

DANCE FLOOR VIRUS
Italy, male vocal / instrumental group   **2 wks**

| 21 Oct 95 | **MESSAGE IN A BOTTLE** Epic 6623742 .... | **49** | 2 |

DANCE 2 TRANCE
Germany, male instrumental / production duo　　　**8 wks**

24 Apr 93	P.OWER OF A.MERICAN N.ATIVES *Logic 74321139582* ..**25**	4
24 Jul 93	TAKE A FREE FALL *Logic 74321153602* **36**	3
4 Feb 95	WARRIOR *Logic 74321257722* **56**	1

Evan DANDO – *See Kirsty MacCOLL*

D'ANGELO *US, male vocalist*　　　**9 wks**

28 Oct 95	BROWN SUGAR *Cooltempo CDCOOL 307* **24**	3
2 Mar 96	CRUISIN' *Cooltempo CDCOOL 316* **31**	2
2 Mar 96	COLD WORLD *Geffen GFSTD 22114* [1] **40**	2
15 Jun 96	LADY *Cooltempo CDCOOLS 323* **21**	2

[1] Genius/GZA featuring D'Angelo

DANGER DANGER *US, male vocal / instrumental group*　**5 wks**

8 Feb 92	MONKEY BUSINESS *Epic 6577517* **42**	2
28 Mar 92	I STILL THINK ABOUT YOU *Epic 6578387* **46**	2
13 Jun 92	COMIN' HOME *Epic 6581337* **75**	1

Charlie DANIELS BAND
US, male vocal / instrumental group　　　**10 wks**

22 Sep 79	THE DEVIL WENT DOWN TO GEORGIA		
	Epic EPC 7737 ....**14**	10

Johnny DANKWORTH
UK, male orchestral / group leader / instrumentalist – alto sax　**33 wks**

22 Jun 56	● EXPERIMENTS WITH MICE *Parlophone R 4185* **7**	12
23 Feb 61	● AFRICAN WALTZ *Columbia DB 4590* **9**	21

DANNY and the JUNIORS *US, male vocal group*　**19 wks**

17 Jan 58	● AT THE HOP *HMV POP 436* **3**	14
10 Jul 76	AT THE HOP (re-issue) *ABC 4123* **39**	5

DANNY WILSON
UK, male vocal / instrumental group　　　**28 wks**

22 Aug 87	MARY'S PRAYER *Virgin VS 934* **42**	7
2 Apr 88	● MARY'S PRAYER (re-entry) *Virgin VS 934* **3**	11
17 Jun 89	THE SECOND SUMMER OF LOVE *Virgin VS 1186* **23**	9
16 Sep 89	NEVER GONNA BE THE SAME *Virgin VS 1203* **69**	1

DANSE SOCIETY *UK, male vocal / instrumental group*　**5 wks**

27 Aug 83	WAKE UP *Society SOC 5* **61**	3
5 Nov 83	HEAVEN IS WAITING *Society SOC 6* **60**	2

Steven DANTE *UK, male vocalist*　　　**16 wks**

26 Sep 87	THE REAL THING *Chrysalis CHS 3167* [1] **13**	10
9 Jul 88	I'M TOO SCARED *Cooltempo DANTE 1* **34**	6

[1] Jellybean featuring Steven Dante

Tonja DANTZLER *US, female vocalist*　　　**1 wk**

17 Dec 94	IN AND OUT OF MY LIFE *ffrr FCD 246* **66**	1

DANY – *See DOUBLE DEE featuring DANY*

DANZIG *US, male vocal / instrumental group*　　　**1 wk**

14 May 94	MOTHER *American MOMDD 1* **62**	1

DAPHNE *US, female vocalist*　　　**1 wk**

9 Dec 95	CHANGE *Stress CDSTR 54* **71**	1

Terence Trent D'ARBY *US, male vocalist*　**77 wks**

14 Mar 87	● IF YOU LET ME STAY *CBS TRENT 1* **7**	13
20 Jun 87	● WISHING WELL *CBS TRENT 2* **4**	11
10 Oct 87	DANCE LITTLE SISTER (PART ONE) *CBS TRENT 3* **20**	7
9 Jan 88	● SIGN YOUR NAME *CBS TRENT 4* **2**	10
20 Jan 90	TO KNOW SOMEONE DEEPLY IS TO KNOW		
	SOMEONE SOFTLY *CBS TRENT 6* **55**	3
17 Apr 93	DO YOU LOVE ME LIKE YOU SAY *Columbia 6590732* **14**	6
19 Jun 93	DELICATE *Columbia 6593312* [1] **14**	6
28 Aug 93	SHE KISSED ME *Columbia 6595922* **16**	7
20 Nov 93	LET HER DOWN EASY *Columbia 6598642* **18**	7
8 Apr 95	HOLDING ON TO YOU *Columbia 6614235* **20**	6
5 Aug 95	VIBRATOR *Columbia 6622585* **57**	1

[1] Terence Trent D'Arby featuring Des'ree

Richard DARBYSHIRE *US, male vocalist*　**7 wks**

20 Aug 88	COMING BACK FOR MORE *Chrysalis JEL 4* [1] **41**	3
24 Jul 93	THIS I SWEAR *Dome CDDOME 1003* **50**	3
12 Feb 94	WHEN ONLY LOVE WILL DO *Dome CDDOME 1008* **54**	1

[1] Jellybean featuring Richard Darbyshire

DARE *UK, male vocal / instrumental group*　**7 wks**

29 Apr 89	THE RAINDANCE *A & M AM 483* **62**	2
29 Jul 89	ABANDON *A & M AM 519* **71**	2
10 Aug 91	WE DON'T NEED A REASON *A & M AM 755* **52**	2
5 Oct 91	REAL LOVE *A & M AM 824* **67**	1

Bobby DARIN *US, male vocalist*　**161 wks**

1 Aug 58	SPLISH SPLASH *London HLE 8666* **28**	1
15 Aug 58	SPLISH SPLASH (re-entry) *London HLE 8666* **18**	6
9 Jan 59	QUEEN OF THE HOP *London HLE 8737* **24**	2
29 May 59	★ DREAM LOVER *London HLE 8867* **1**	19
25 Sep 59	★ MACK THE KNIFE *London HLK 8939* **1**	16
22 Jan 60	MACK THE KNIFE (re-entry) *London HLK 8939* **30**	1
29 Jan 60	● LA MER (BEYOND THE SEA) *London HLK 9034* **8**	10
10 Mar 60	MACK THE KNIFE (2nd re-entry) *London HLE 8939* **50**	1
31 Mar 60	● CLEMENTINE *London HLK 9086* **8**	12
21 Apr 60	LA MER (BEYOND THE SEA) (re-entry)		
	London HLE 9034 ....**40**	2
30 Jun 60	BILL BAILEY *London HLK 9142* **36**	1
14 Jul 60	BILL BAILEY (re-entry) *London HLK 9142* **34**	1
16 Mar 61	● LAZY RIVER *London HLK 9303* **2**	13
6 Jul 61	NATURE BOY *London HLK 9375* **24**	7
12 Oct 61	● YOU MUST HAVE BEEN A BEAUTIFUL BABY		
	London HLK 9429 ....**10**	11
26 Oct 61	COME SEPTEMBER *London HLK 9407* [1] **50**	1
21 Dec 61	● MULTIPLICATION *London HLK 9474* **5**	13
19 Jul 62	● THINGS *London HLK 9575* **2**	17
4 Oct 62	IF A MAN ANSWERS *Capitol CL 15272* **24**	6
29 Nov 62	BABY FACE *London HLK 9624* **40**	4
25 Jul 63	EIGHTEEN YELLOW ROSES *Capitol CL 15306* **37**	4
13 Oct 66	● IF I WERE A CARPENTER *Atlantic 584 051* **9**	12
14 Apr 79	DREAM LOVER (re-issue) / MACK THE KNIFE		
	(re-issue) *Lightning LIG 9017* **64**	1

[1] Bobby Darin Orchestra

DARKMAN *UK, male rapper* — **7 wks**

14 May 94	YABBA DABBA DOO *Wild Card CARDD 6*	**49**	2
20 Aug 94	WHO'S THE DARKMAN *Wild Card CARDD 8*	**46**	2
3 Dec 94	YABBA DABBA DOO (re-issue) *Wild Card CARDD 11*	**37**	2
21 Oct 95	BRAND NEW DAY *Wild Card 5771892*	**74**	1

DARLING BUDS
UK, male / female vocal / instrumental group — **20 wks**

8 Oct 88	BURST *Epic BLOND 1*	**50**	5
7 Jan 89	HIT THE GROUND *CBS BLOND 2*	**27**	5
25 Mar 89	LET'S GO ROUND THERE *CBS BLOND 3*	**49**	4
22 Jul 89	YOU'VE GOT TO CHOOSE *CBS BLOND 4*	**45**	3
2 Jun 90	TINY MACHINE *CBS BLOND 5*	**60**	2
12 Sep 92	SURE THING *Epic 6582157*	**71**	1

Guy DARRELL *UK, male vocalist* — **13 wks**

18 Aug 73	I'VE BEEN HURT *Santa Ponsa PNS 4*	**12**	13

James DARREN *US, male vocalist* — **25 wks**

11 Aug 60	BECAUSE THEY'RE YOUNG *Pye International 7N 25059*	**29**	7
14 Dec 61	GOODBYE CRUEL WORLD *Pye International 7N 25116*	**28**	9
29 Mar 62	HER ROYAL MAJESTY *Pye International 7N 25125*	**36**	3
21 Jun 62	CONSCIENCE *Pye International 7N 25138*	**30**	6

DARTS *UK, male / female vocal / instrumental group* — **117 wks**

5 Nov 77	● DADDY COOL / THE GIRL CAN'T HELP IT *Magnet MAG 100*	**6**	13
28 Jan 78	● COME BACK MY LOVE *Magnet MAG 110*	**2**	12
6 May 78	● BOY FROM NEW YORK CITY *Magnet MAG 116*	**2**	13
5 Aug 78	● IT'S RAINING *Magnet MAG 126*	**2**	11
11 Nov 78	DON'T LET IT FADE AWAY *Magnet MAG 134*	**18**	11
10 Feb 79	● GET IT *Magnet MAG 140*	**10**	9
21 Jul 79	● DUKE OF EARL *Magnet MAG 147*	**6**	11
20 Oct 79	CAN'T GET ENOUGH OF YOUR LOVE *Magnet MAG 156*	**43**	6
1 Dec 79	REET PETITE *Magnet MAG 160*	**51**	7
31 May 80	LET'S HANG ON *Magnet MAG 174*	**11**	14
6 Sep 80	PEACHES *Magnet MAG 179*	**66**	3
29 Nov 80	WHITE CHRISTMAS / SH-BOOM (LIFE COULD BE A DREAM) *Magnet MAG 184*	**48**	7

DAS E.F.X. – See ICE CUBE

N'Dea DAVENPORT – See BRAND NEW HEAVIES; GURU

Anne-Marie DAVID *France, female vocalist* — **9 wks**

28 Apr 73	WONDERFUL DREAM *Epic EPC 1446*	**13**	9

F.R. DAVID *France, male vocalist* — **13 wks**

2 Apr 83	● WORDS *Carrere CAR 248*	**2**	12
18 Jun 83	MUSIC *Carrere CAR 282*	**71**	1

DAVID and JONATHAN *UK, male vocal duo* — **22 wks**

13 Jan 66	MICHELLE *Columbia DB 7800*	**11**	6
7 Jul 66	● LOVERS OF THE WORLD UNITE *Columbia DB 7950*	**7**	16

Jim DAVIDSON *UK, male vocalist* — **4 wks**

27 Dec 80	WHITE CHRISTMAS / TOO RISKY *Scratch SCR 001*	**52**	4

Paul DAVIDSON *Jamaica, male vocalist* — **10 wks**

27 Dec 75	● MIDNIGHT RIDER *Tropical ALO 56*	**10**	10

Dave DAVIES *UK, male vocalist* — **17 wks**

19 Jul 67	● DEATH OF A CLOWN *Pye 7N 17356*	**3**	10
6 Dec 67	SUSANNAH'S STILL ALIVE *Pye 7N 17429*	**20**	7

Windsor DAVIES and Don ESTELLE
UK, male vocal duo — **16 wks**

17 May 75	★ WHISPERING GRASS *EMI 2290*	**1**	12
25 Oct 75	PAPER DOLL *EMI 2361*	**41**	4

Billie DAVIS *UK, female vocalist* — **33 wks**

30 Aug 62	WILL I WHAT *Parlophone R 4932* [1]	**18**	10
7 Feb 63	● TELL HIM *Decca F 11572*	**10**	12
30 May 63	HE'S THE ONE *Decca F 11658*	**40**	3
9 Oct 68	I WANT YOU TO BE MY BABY *Decca F 12823*	**33**	8

[1] Mike Sarne with Billie Davis

Billy DAVIS Jr. – See Marilyn McCOO and Billy DAVIS Jr.

Darlene DAVIS *US, female vocalist* — **5 wks**

7 Feb 87	I FOUND LOVE *Serious 7OUS 1*	**55**	5

John DAVIS and the MONSTER ORCHESTRA
US, male vocal / instrumental group — **2 wks**

10 Feb 79	AIN'T THAT ENOUGH FOR YOU *Miracle M 2*	**70**	2

Mac DAVIS *US, male vocalist* — **22 wks**

4 Nov 72	BABY DON'T GET HOOKED ON ME *CBS 8250*	**29**	6
15 Nov 80	IT'S HARD TO BE HUMBLE *Casablanca CAN 210*	**27**	16

Richie DAVIS – See SHUT UP AND DANCE

Ruth DAVIS – See Bo KIRKLAND and Ruth DAVIS

Sammy DAVIS Jr. *US, male vocalist* — **35 wks**

29 Jul 55	SOMETHING'S GOTTA GIVE *Brunswick 05428*	**19**	2
19 Aug 55	SOMETHING'S GOTTA GIVE (re-entry) *Brunswick 05428*	**11**	5
9 Sep 55	● LOVE ME OR LEAVE ME *Brunswick 05428*	**8**	6
30 Sep 55	THAT OLD BLACK MAGIC *Brunswick 05450*	**16**	1
7 Oct 55	HEY THERE *Brunswick 05469*	**19**	1
4 Nov 55	LOVE ME OR LEAVE ME (re-entry) *Brunswick 05428*	**18**	2
20 Apr 56	IN A PERSIAN MARKET *Brunswick 05518*	**28**	1
28 Dec 56	ALL OF YOU *Brunswick 05629*	**28**	1
16 Jun 60	HAPPY TO MAKE YOUR ACQUAINTANCE *Brunswick 05830* [1]	**46**	1
22 Mar 62	WHAT KIND OF FOOL AM I? / GONNA BUILD A MOUNTAIN *Reprise R 20048*	**26**	8
13 Dec 62	ME AND MY SHADOW *Reprise R 20128* [2]	**20**	7
7 Feb 63	ME AND MY SHADOW (re-entry) *Reprise R 20128* [2]	**47**	2

[1] Sammy Davis Jr. and Carmen McRae [2] Frank Sinatra and Sammy Davis Jr.

Skeeter DAVIS *US, female vocalist* — **13 wks**

14 Mar 63	END OF THE WORLD *RCA 1328*	**18**	13

TJ DAVIS – See FULL MONTY ALLSTARS featuring TJ DAVIS

Zelma DAVIS – See C & C MUSIC FACTORY/CLIVILLES & COLE

DAVIS PINCKNEY PROJECT – See GO GO LORENZO and the DAVIS PINCKNEY PROJECT

Spencer DAVIS GROUP
UK, male vocal / instrumental group   **71 wks**

5 Nov 64	I CAN'T STAND IT *Fontana TF 499*	47	3
25 Feb 65	EVERY LITTLE BIT HURTS *Fontana TF 530*	43	2
18 Mar 65	EVERY LITTLE BIT HURTS (re-entry) *Fontana TF 530*.....	41	1
10 Jun 65	STRONG LOVE *Fontana TF 571*	50	1
24 Jun 65	STRONG LOVE (re-entry) *Fontana TF 571*	44	3
2 Dec 65	★ KEEP ON RUNNING *Fontana TF 632*	1	14
24 Mar 66	★ SOMEBODY HELP ME *Fontana TF 679*	1	10
1 Sep 66	WHEN I COME HOME *Fontana TF 739*	12	9
3 Nov 66	● GIMME SOME LOVING *Fontana TF 762*	2	12
26 Jan 67	● I'M A MAN *Fontana TF 785*	9	7
9 Aug 67	TIME SELLER *Fontana TF 854*	30	5
10 Jan 68	MR. SECOND CLASS *United Artists UP 1203*	35	4

DAWN
US, male / female vocal group   **109 wks**

16 Jan 71	● CANDIDA *Bell 1118* 9	9	11
10 Apr 71	★ KNOCK THREE TIMES *Bell 1146*	1	27
31 Jul 71	● WHAT ARE YOU DOING SUNDAY *Bell 1169* [1]	3	12
10 Mar 73	★ TIE A YELLOW RIBBON ROUND THE OLD OAK TREE		
	Bell 1287 [1]	1	39
4 Aug 73	SAY, HAS ANYBODY SEEN MY SWEET GYPSY ROSE		
	Bell 1322 [1]	12	15
5 Jan 74	TIE A YELLOW RIBBON ROUND THE OLD OAK TREE		
	(re-entry) *Bell 1287* [1]	41	1
9 Mar 74	WHO'S IN THE STRAWBERRY PATCH WITH SALLY		
	Bell 1343 [2]	37	4

[1] Dawn featuring Tony Orlando [2] Tony Orlando and Dawn

Julie DAWN – See Cyril STAPLETON

Liz DAWN – See Joe LONGTHORNE

Dana DAWSON *US, female vocalist*   **14 wks**

15 Jul 95	● 3 IS FAMILY *EMI CDEM 378*	9	8
28 Oct 95	GOT TO GIVE ME LOVE *EMI CDEM 392*	27	2
4 May 96	SHOW ME *EMI CDEMS 423*	28	3
20 Jul 96	HOW I WANNA BE LOVED *EMI CDEMS 432*	42	1

Bobby DAY *US, male vocalist*   **2 wks**

7 Nov 58	ROCKIN' ROBIN *London HL 8726*	29	2

Darren DAY *UK, male vocalist*   **6 wks**

8 Oct 94	YOUNG GIRL *Bell 74321231082*	42	2
8 Jun 96	SUMMER HOLIDAY MEDLEY *RCA 74321384472*........	17	4

Doris DAY *US, female vocalist*   **146 wks**

14 Nov 52	● SUGARBUSH *Columbia DB 3123* [1]	8	2
21 Nov 52	● MY LOVE AND DEVOTION *Columbia DB 3157*	10	2
5 Dec 52	● SUGARBUSH (re-entry) *Columbia DB 3123* [1]	8	6
3 Apr 53	MA SAYS PA SAYS *Columbia DB 3242* [2]	12	1
17 Apr 53	FULL TIME JOB *Columbia DB 3242* [2]	11	1
24 Jul 53	● LET'S WALK THATA-WAY *Philips PB 157* [2]	4	14
2 Apr 54	★ SECRET LOVE *Philips PB 230*	1	29
27 Aug 54	● BLACK HILLS OF DAKOTA *Philips PB 287*	7	8
1 Oct 54	● IF I GIVE MY HEART TO YOU *Philips PB 325*	4	11
8 Apr 55	● READY WILLING AND ABLE *Philips PB 402*	7	9
9 Sep 55	LOVE ME OR LEAVE ME *Philips PB 479*	20	1
21 Oct 55	I'LL NEVER STOP LOVING YOU *Philips PB 497*	17	2
25 Nov 55	I'LL NEVER STOP LOVING YOU (re-entry)		
	Philips PB 497	19	1
29 Jun 56	★ WHATEVER WILL BE WILL BE *Philips PB 586*......	1	22
13 Jun 58	A VERY PRECIOUS LOVE *Philips PB 799*	16	11
15 Aug 58	EVERYBODY LOVES A LOVER *Philips PB 843*	25	3
26 Sep 58	EVERYBODY LOVES A LOVER (re-entry)		
	Philips PB 843	27	1
12 Mar 64	● MOVE OVER DARLING *CBS AAG 183*	8	16
18 Apr 87	● MOVE OVER DARLING (re-issue) *CBS LEGS 1*	45	6

[1] Doris Day and Frankie Laine [2] Doris Day and Johnnie Ray

Patti DAY *US, female vocalist*   **1 wk**

9 Dec 89	RIGHT BEFORE MY EYES *Debut DEBT 3080*	69	1

Taylor DAYNE *US, female vocalist*   **54 wks**

23 Jan 88	● TELL IT TO MY HEART *Arista 109616*	3	13
19 Mar 88	● PROVE YOUR LOVE *Arista 109830*	8	10
11 Jun 88	I'LL ALWAYS LOVE YOU *Arista 111536*	41	7
18 Nov 89	WITH EVERY BEAT OF MY HEART *Arista 112760*	53	2
14 Apr 90	I'LL BE YOUR SHELTER *Arista 112996*	43	5
4 Aug 90	LOVE WILL LEAD YOU BACK *Arista 113277*	69	1
3 Jul 93	CAN'T GET ENOUGH OF YOUR LOVE		
	Arista 74321147852	14	8
16 Apr 94	I'LL WAIT *Arista 74321203472*	29	3
4 Feb 95	ORIGINAL SIN (THEME FROM THE SHADOW)		
	Arista 74321223462	63	1
18 Nov 95	SAY A PRAYER *Arista 74321324292*	58	1
13 Jan 96	TELL IT TO MY HEART (re-mix)		
	Arista 74321335962	23	3

DAYTON *US, male vocalist*   **1 wk**

10 Dec 83	THE SOUND OF MUSIC *Capitol CL 318*...................	75	1

DAZZ BAND *US, male vocal / instrumental group*   **12 wks**

3 Nov 84	LET IT ALL BLOW *Motown TMG 1361*	12	12

DBM *Germany, male / female vocal / instrumental group*   **3 wks**

12 Nov 77	DISCO BEATLEMANIA *Atlantic K 11027*....................	45	3

D, B, M and T *UK, male vocal / instrumental group*   **8 wks**

1 Aug 70	MR. PRESIDENT *Fontana 6007 022*	33	8

See also Dave Dee, Dozy, Beaky, Mick and Tich.

Nino DE ANGELO *Germany, male vocalist*   **5 wks**

21 Jul 84	GUARDIAN ANGEL *Carrere CAR 335*	57	5

Chris DE BURGH *Ireland, male vocalist*   **66 wks**

23 Oct 82	DON'T PAY THE FERRYMAN *A & M AMS 8256*............	48	5
12 May 84	HIGH ON EMOTION *A & M AM 190*	44	5
12 Jul 86	★ THE LADY IN RED *A & M AM 331*	1	14
20 Sep 86	FATAL HESITATION *A & M AM 346*	44	4
13 Dec 86	A SPACEMAN CAME TRAVELLING / THE BALLROOM		
	OF ROMANCE *A & M AM 365*	40	5
21 Feb 87	THE LADY IN RED (re-entry) *A & M AM 331*	74	1
12 Dec 87	THE SIMPLE TRUTH (A CHILD IS BORN)		
	A & M AM 427	69	2

2 Jan 88	THE SIMPLE TRUTH (A CHILD IS BORN) (re-entry)		
	A & M AM 427 ....**55**	1
29 Oct 88	● MISSING YOU *A & M AM 474* **3**	12
7 Jan 89	TENDER HANDS *A & M AM 486* **43**	6
14 Oct 89	THIS WAITING HEART *A & M AM 528* **59**	3
25 May 91	THE SIMPLE TRUTH (A CHILD IS BORN) (re-issue)		
	A & M RELF 1 ....**36**	2
11 Apr 92	SEPARATE TABLES *A & M AM 863* **30**	4
21 May 94	BLONDE HAIR BLUE JEANS *A & M 5805932* ...**51**	1
9 Dec 95	THE SNOWS OF NEW YORK *A & M 5813132*....**60**	1

DE CASTRO SISTERS US, female vocal group   1 wk

| 11 Feb 55 | TEACH ME TONIGHT *London HL 8104* ....**20** | 1 |

DE-CODE featuring Beverli SKEETE
UK, male/female vocal/instrumental group   1 wk

| 18 May 96 | WONDERWALL / SOME MIGHT SAY *Neoteric NRCD 2*....**69** | 1 |

DE LA SOUL US, male rap/sampling group   56 wks

8 Apr 89	ME MYSELF AND I *Big Life BLR 7* **22**	8
8 Jul 89	SAY NO GO *Big Life BLR 10* **18**	7
21 Oct 89	EYE KNOW *Big Life BLR 13* **14**	7
23 Dec 89	THE MAGIC NUMBER / BUDDY *Big Life BLR 14* **7**	8
24 Mar 90	MAMA GAVE BIRTH TO THE SOUL CHILDREN		
	Gee Street GEE 26 [1] **14**	7
27 Apr 91	● RING RING RING (HA HA HEY) *Big Life BLR 42* **10**	7
3 Aug 91	A ROLLER SKATING JAM NAMED 'SATURDAYS'		
	Big Life BLR 55 ....**22**	5
23 Nov 91	KEEPIN' THE FAITH *Big Life BLR 64* **50**	2
18 Sep 93	BREAKADAWN *Big Life BLRD 103*.................**39**	3
2 Apr 94	FALLIN' *Epic 6602622* [2] **59**	1
29 Jun 96	STAKES IS HIGH *Tommy Boy TBCD 7730* **55**	1

[1] Queen Latifah + De La Soul [2] Teenage Fanclub and De La Soul

Buddy only listed for first three weeks, peaking at position 8. See also Jungle Brothers.

Donna DE LORY US, female vocalist   1 wk

| 24 Jul 93 | JUST A DREAM *MCA MCSTD 1750* ....**71** | 1 |

Lynsey DE PAUL UK, female vocalist   54 wks

19 Aug 72	● SUGAR ME *MAM 81* **5**	11
2 Dec 72	GETTING A DRAG *MAM 88* **18**	8
27 Oct 73	WON'T SOMEBODY DANCE WITH ME *MAM 109* **14**	7
8 Jun 74	OOH I DO *Warner Bros. K 16401* **25**	6
2 Nov 74	● NO HONESTLY *Jet 747* **7**	11
22 Mar 75	MY MAN AND ME *Jet 750* **40**	4
26 Mar 77	ROCK BOTTOM *Polydor 2058 859* [1] **19**	7

[1] Lynsey De Paul and Mike Moran

Tullio DE PISCOPO Italy, male vocalist   4 wks

| 28 Feb 87 | STOP BAJON... PRIMAVERA *Greyhound GREY 9* ....**58** | 4 |

Rebecca DE RUVO Sweden, female vocalist   1 wk

| 1 Oct 94 | I CAUGHT YOU OUT *Arista 74321230782* ....**72** | 1 |

Teri DE SARIO US, female vocalist   5 wks

| 2 Sep 78 | AIN'T NOTHIN' (GONNA KEEP ME FROM YOU) | | |
| | *Casablanca CAN 128* ....**52** | 5 |

Stephanie DE SYKES UK, female vocalist   17 wks

20 Jul 74	● BORN WITH A SMILE ON MY FACE		
	Bradley's BRAD 7409 [1] **2**	10
19 Apr 75	WE'LL FIND OUR DAY *Bradley's BRAD 7509* **17**	7

[1] Stephanie De Sykes with Rain

DE VANTE – *See VARIOUS ARTISTS (EPs and LPs) – The Dangerous Minds EP*

William DE VAUGHN US, male vocalist   10 wks

6 Jul 74	BE THANKFUL FOR WHAT YOU'VE GOT		
	Chelsea 2005 002 ....**31**	5
20 Sep 80	BE THANKFUL FOR WHAT YOU'VE GOT *EMI 5101* **44**	5

EMI version of hit is a new recording.

Tony DE VIT UK, male producer   9 wks

4 Mar 95	BURNING UP *Icon ICONCD 001* **25**	3
12 Aug 95	HOOKED *Labello Dance LAD 18CD* [1] **28**	2
9 Sep 95	TO THE LIMIT *X:Plode BANG 1CD* **44**	2
30 May 96	I'LL BE THERE *Labello Dance LAD 25CD1* [1] **37**	2

[1] 99th Floor Elevators featuring Tony De Vit

DE'LACY US, male/female vocal/instrumental group   14 wks

| 2 Sep 95 | ● HIDEAWAY *Slip 'N' Slide 74321310472* ....**9** | 10 |
| 31 Aug 96 | THAT LOOK *Slip 'N' Slide 74321398322* ....**19** | 4 |

DEACON BLUE
UK, male/female vocal/instrumental group   111 wks

23 Jan 88	DIGNITY *CBS DEAC 4* **31**	8
9 Apr 88	WHEN WILL YOU MAKE MY TELEPHONE RING		
	CBS DEAC 5 ....**34**	7
16 Jul 88	CHOCOLATE GIRL *CBS DEAC 6* **43**	7
15 Oct 88	● REAL GONE KID *CBS DEAC 7*....................**8**	13
4 Mar 89	WAGES DAY *CBS DEAC 8* **18**	6
20 May 89	FERGUS SINGS THE BLUES *CBS DEAC 9* **14**	6
16 Sep 89	LOVE AND REGRET *CBS DEAC 10* **28**	5
6 Jan 90	QUEEN OF THE NEW YEAR *CBS DEAC 11* **21**	5
25 Aug 90	● FOUR BACHARACH AND DAVID SONGS EP		
	CBS DEAC 12 ....**2**	9
25 May 91	YOUR SWAYING ARMS *Columbia 6568937* **23**	4
27 Jul 91	● TWIST AND SHOUT *Columbia 6573027* **10**	9
12 Oct 91	CLOSING TIME *Columbia 6575027* **42**	3
14 Dec 91	COVER FROM THE SKY *Columbia 6576737* **31**	4
28 Nov 92	YOUR TOWN *Columbia 6587867* **14**	8
13 Feb 93	WILL WE BE LOVERS *Columbia 6589732* **31**	4
24 Apr 93	ONLY TENDER LOVE *Columbia 6591842* **22**	4
17 Jul 93	HANG YOUR HEAD *Columbia 6594602* **21**	3
2 Apr 94	I WAS RIGHT AND YOU WERE WRONG		
	Columbia 6602222 ....**32**	3
28 May 94	DIGNITY *Columbia 6604485* **20**	3

Tracks on Four Bacharach and David Songs EP: I'll Never Fall In Love Again / The Look Of Love / Message To Michael / Are You There (With Another Girl). Dignity in '94 was the original recording of the song first issued in '87 but never before a hit.

DEAD DRED UK, male instrumental/production duo   2 wks

| 5 Nov 94 | DRED BASS *Moving Shadow SHADOW 50CD* ....**60** | 2 |

DEAD END KIDS UK, male vocal/instrumental group   10 wks

| 26 Mar 77 | ● HAVE I THE RIGHT *CBS 4972* ....**6** | 10 |

DEAD KENNEDYS
US, male vocal / instrumental group   **9 wks**

1 Nov 80	**KILL THE POOR** Cherry Red CHERRY 16	**49**	3
30 May 81	**TOO DRUNK TO FUCK** Cherry Red CHERRY 24	**36**	6

DEAD OR ALIVE UK, male vocal / instrumental group   **70 wks**

24 Mar 84	**THAT'S THE WAY (I LIKE IT)** Epic A 4271	**22**	9
9 Mar 85	★ **YOU SPIN ME ROUND (LIKE A RECORD)** Epic A 4861	**1**	23
20 Apr 85	**LOVER COME BACK TO ME** Epic A 6086	**11**	8
29 Jun 85	**IN TOO DEEP** Epic A 6360	**14**	8
21 Sep 85	**MY HEART GOES BANG (GET ME TO THE DOCTOR)** Epic A 6571	**23**	6
20 Sep 86	**BRAND NEW LOVER** Epic A 650075 7	**31**	4
10 Jan 87	**SOMETHING IN MY HOUSE** Epic BURNS 1	**12**	7
4 Apr 87	**HOOKED ON LOVE** Epic BURNS 2	**69**	2
3 Sep 88	**TURN ROUND AND COUNT 2 TEN** Epic BURNS 4	**70**	1
22 Jul 89	**COME HOME WITH ME BABY** Epic BURNS 5	**62**	2

DEADLY SINS UK / Italy, male vocal / instrumental duo   **2 wks**

30 Apr 94	**WE ARE GOING ON DOWN** Ffrreedom TABCD 220	**45**	2

Hazell DEAN UK, female vocalist   **71 wks**

18 Feb 84	**EVERGREEN / JEALOUS LOVE** Proto ENA 114	**63**	3
21 Apr 84	● **SEARCHIN' (I GOTTA FIND A MAN)** Proto ENA 109	**6**	15
28 Jul 84	● **WHATEVER I DO (WHEREVER I GO)** Proto ENA 119	**4**	11
3 Nov 84	**BACK IN MY ARMS (ONCE AGAIN)** Proto ENA 122	**41**	4
2 Mar 85	**NO FOOL (FOR LOVE)** Proto ENA 123	**41**	5
12 Oct 85	**THEY SAY IT'S GONNA RAIN** Parlophone R 6107	**58**	4
2 Apr 88	● **WHO'S LEAVING WHO** EMI EM 45	**4**	11
25 Jun 88	**MAYBE (WE SHOULD CALL IT A DAY)** EMI EM 62	**15**	6
24 Sep 88	**TURN IT INTO LOVE** EMI EM 71	**21**	7
26 Aug 89	**LOVE PAINS** Lisson DOLE 12	**48**	4
23 Mar 91	**BETTER OFF WITHOUT YOU** Lisson DOLE 19	**72**	1

Jimmy DEAN US, male vocalist   **17 wks**

26 Oct 61	● **BIG BAD JOHN** Philips PB 1187	**2**	13
8 Nov 62	**LITTLE BLACK BOOK** CBS AAG 122	**33**	4

Letitia DEAN and Paul MEDFORD
UK, female / male vocal duo   **7 wks**

25 Oct 86	**SOMETHING OUTA NOTHING** BBC RESL 203	**12**	7

DEAR JON UK, female / male vocal / instrumental group   **1 wk**

22 Apr 95	**ONE GIFT OF LOVE** MDMC DEVCS 2	**68**	1

DeBARGE US, male / female vocal group   **17 wks**

6 Apr 85	● **RHYTHM OF THE NIGHT** Gordy TMG 1376	**4**	14
21 Sep 85	**YOU WEAR IT WELL** Gordy ZB 40345 [1]	**54**	3

[1] El DeBarge with DeBarge

El DeBARGE US, male vocalist   **3 wks**

28 Jun 86	**WHO'S JOHNNY ('SHORT CIRCUIT' THEME)** Gordy ELD 1	**60**	2
31 Mar 90	**SECRET GARDEN** Qwest W 9992 [1]	**67**	1

[1] Quincy Jones featuring Al B. Sure!, James Ingram, El DeBarge and Barry White

Diana DECKER US, female vocalist   **10 wks**

23 Oct 53	● **POPPA PICCOLINO** Columbia DB 3325	**2**	8
8 Jan 54	● **POPPA PICCOLINO (re-entry)** Columbia DB 3325	**5**	2

Dave DEE UK, male vocalist   **4 wks**

14 Mar 70	**MY WOMAN'S MAN** Fontana TF 1074	**42**	4

See also Dave Dee, Dozy, Beaky, Mick and Tich.

Dave DEE, DOZY, BEAKY, MICK and TICH
UK, male vocal / instrumental group   **141 wks**

23 Dec 65	**YOU MAKE IT MOVE** Fontana TF 630	**26**	8
3 Mar 66	● **HOLD TIGHT** Fontana TF 671	**4**	17
9 Jun 66	● **HIDEAWAY** Fontana TF 711	**10**	11
15 Sep 66	● **BEND IT** Fontana TF 746	**2**	12
8 Dec 66	● **SAVE ME** Fontana TF 775	**3**	10
9 Mar 67	**TOUCH ME TOUCH ME** Fontana TF 798	**13**	9
18 May 67	● **OKAY!** Fontana TF 830	**4**	11
11 Oct 67	● **ZABADAK!** Fontana TF 873	**3**	14
14 Feb 68	★ **LEGEND OF XANADU** Fontana TF 903	**1**	12
3 Jul 68	● **LAST NIGHT IN SOHO** Fontana TF 953	**8**	11
2 Oct 68	**WRECK OF THE ANTOINETTE** Fontana TF 971	**14**	9
5 Mar 69	**DON JUAN** Fontana TF 1000	**23**	9
14 May 69	**SNAKE IN THE GRASS** Fontana TF 1020	**23**	8

See also Dave Dee; D, B, M and T.

Jazzy DEE US, male vocalist   **5 wks**

5 Mar 83	**GET ON UP** Laurie LRS 101	**53**	5

Joey DEE and the STARLITERS
US, male vocal / instrumental group   **8 wks**

8 Feb 62	**PEPPERMINT TWIST** Columbia DB 4758	**33**	8

Kiki DEE UK, female vocalist   **79 wks**

10 Nov 73	**AMOUREUSE** Rocket PIG 4	**13**	13
7 Sep 74	**I GOT THE MUSIC IN ME** Rocket PIG 12 [1]	**19**	8
12 Apr 75	**(YOU DONT KNOW) HOW GLAD I AM** Rocket PIG 16 [1]	**33**	4
3 Jul 76	★ **DON'T GO BREAKING MY HEART** Rocket ROKN 512 [2]	**1**	14
11 Sep 76	**LOVING AND FREE / AMOUREUSE (re-issue)** Rocket ROKN 515	**13**	8
19 Feb 77	**FIRST THING IN THE MORNING** Rocket ROKN 520	**32**	5
11 Jun 77	**CHICAGO** Rocket ROKN 526	**28**	4
21 Feb 81	**STAR** Ariola ARO 251	**13**	10
23 May 81	**PERFECT TIMING** Ariola ARO 257	**66**	3
20 Nov 93	● **TRUE LOVE** Rocket EJSCX 32 [2]	**2**	10

[1] Kiki Dee Band [2] Elton John and Kiki Dee

On 18 Sep, 25 Sep and 2 Oct 1976, Loving And Free was listed by itself. Chicago was one side of a double-sided chart entry, the other being Bite Your Lip (Get Up And Dance) by Elton John.

Nancy DEE – See BENELUX and Nancy DEE

DEEE-LITE
US / Russia / Japan, male / female vocal / instrumental group   **30 wks**

18 Aug 90	● **GROOVE IS IN THE HEART / WHAT IS LOVE** Elektra EKR 114	**2**	13
24 Nov 90	**POWER OF LOVE / DEEE-LITE THEME** Elektra EKR 117 ..	**25**	7

23 Feb 91	**HOW DO YOU SAY... LOVE / GROOVE IS IN THE HEART (re-mix)** *Elektra EKR 118*..........**52**	2
27 Apr 91	**GOOD BEAT / RIDING ON THROUGH** *Elektra EKR 122* **53**	3
13 Jun 92	**RUNAWAY** *Elektra EKR 148* **45**	3
30 Jul 94	**PICNIC IN THE SUMMERTIME** *Elektra EKR 186CD1* **43**	2

What Is Love only listed from 25 Aug 90.

Carol DEENE *UK, female vocalist*   **25 wks**

26 Oct 61	**SAD MOVIES** *HMV POP 922* **44**	3
25 Jan 62	**NORMAN** *HMV POP 973* **24**	8
5 Jul 62	**JOHNNY GET ANGRY** *HMV POP 1027* **32**	4
23 Aug 62	**SOME PEOPLE** *HMV POP 1058* **25**	10

DEEP BLUE *UK, male producer – Sean O'Keefe*   **2 wks**

| 16 Apr 94 | **HELICOPTER TUNE** *Moving Shadow SHADOW 41CD* ......**68** | 2 |

DEEP BLUE SOMETHING
US, male vocal / instrumental group   **17 wks**

6 Jul 96	**BREAKFAST AT TIFFANY'S** *Interscope IND 80032* **55**	2
21 Sep 96	★ **BREAKFAST AT TIFFANY'S (re-entry)** *Interscope IND 80032* **1**	12
7 Dec 96	**JOSEY** *Interscope IND 95518* **27**	3

DEEP C *UK, male / female vocal / instrumental group*   **3 wks**

| 19 Jan 91 | **AFRICAN REIGN** *M & G MAGS 4* ....**75** | 1 |
| 8 Jun 91 | **CHILL TO THE PANIC** *M & G MAGS 10* ....**73** | 2 |

DEEP CREED '94
US, male producer – Armand van Helden   **1 wk**

| 7 May 94 | **CAN U FEEL IT** *Eastern Bloc BLOCCD 005* ....**59** | 1 |

DEEP DISH *US, male instrumental / production duo*   **1 wk**

| 26 Oct 96 | **STAY GOLD** *Deconstruction 74321418222* ....**41** | 1 |

DEEP FEELING *UK, male vocal / instrumental group*   **5 wks**

| 25 Apr 70 | **DO YOU LOVE ME** *Page One POF 165* ....**45** | 1 |
| 9 May 70 | **DO YOU LOVE ME (re-entry)** *Page One POF 165*..........**34** | 4 |

DEEP FOREST *France, male instrumental duo*   **14 wks**

5 Feb 94	● **SWEET LULLABY** *Columbia 6599242*..........**10**	6
21 May 94	**DEEP FOREST** *Columbia 6604115* **20**	4
23 Jul 94	**SAVANNA DANCE** *Columbia 6606355* **28**	2
24 Jun 95	**MARTA'S SONG** *Columbia 6621402* **26**	2

DEEP PURPLE *UK, male vocal / instrumental group*   **85 wks**

15 Aug 70	● **BLACK NIGHT** *Harvest HAR 5020*..........**2**	21
27 Feb 71	● **STRANGE KIND OF WOMAN** *Harvest HAR 5033*..........**8**	12
13 Nov 71	**FIREBALL** *Harvest HAR 5045* **15**	13
1 Apr 72	**NEVER BEFORE** *Purple PUR 102* **35**	6
16 Apr 77	**SMOKE ON THE WATER** *Purple PUR 132* **21**	7
15 Oct 77	**NEW LIVE AND RARE EP** *Purple PUR 135* **31**	4
7 Oct 78	**NEW LIVE AND RARE II EP** *Purple PUR 137* **45**	3
2 Aug 80	**BLACK NIGHT (re-issue)** *Harvest HAR 5210* **43**	6
1 Nov 80	**NEW LIVE AND RARE VOLUME 3 EP** *Harvest SHEP 101* **48**	3
26 Jan 85	**PERFECT STRANGERS** *Polydor POSP 719* **48**	3
15 Jun 85	**KNOCKING AT YOUR BACK DOOR / PERFECT**	

18 Jun 88	**STRANGERS** *Polydor POSP 749* **68**	1
18 Jun 88	**HUSH** *Polydor PO 4* **62**	2
20 Oct 90	**KING OF DREAMS** *RCA PB 49247* **70**	1
2 Mar 91	**LOVE CONQUERS ALL** *RCA PB 49225* **57**	2
24 Jun 95	**BLACK NIGHT (re-mix)** *EMI CDEM 382* **66**	1

Tracks on New Live And Rare EP: Black Night (Live) / Painted Horse / When A Blind Man Cries. New Live And Rare II EP: Burn (Edited Version) / Coronarias Redig / Mistreated (Live) / Interpolating Rock Me Baby. New Live And Rare Volume 3 EP: Smoke On The Water / Bird Has Flown / Grabsplatter.

DEEP RIVER BOYS *US, male vocal group*   **1 wk**

| 7 Dec 56 | **THAT'S RIGHT** *HMV POP 263* ....**29** | 1 |

Rick DEES and his CAST OF IDIOTS
US, male vocalist with male / female vocal / instrumental group   **9 wks**

| 18 Sep 76 | ● **DISCO DUCK (PART ONE)** *RSO 2090 204* ....**6** | 9 |

DEF LEPPARD *UK, male vocal / instrumental group*   **110 wks**

17 Nov 79	**WASTED** *Vertigo 6059 247* **61**	3
23 Feb 80	**HELLO AMERICA** *Vertigo LEPP 1* **45**	4
5 Feb 83	**PHOTOGRAPH** *Vertigo VER 5* **66**	3
27 Aug 83	**ROCK OF AGES** *Vertigo VER 6* **41**	4
1 Aug 87	● **ANIMAL** *Bludgeon Riffola LEP 1* **6**	9
19 Sep 87	**POUR SOME SUGAR ON ME** *Bludgeon Riffola LEP 2* **18**	6
28 Nov 87	**HYSTERIA** *Bludgeon Riffola LEP 3* **26**	5
9 Jan 88	**HYSTERIA (re-entry)** *Bludgeon Riffola LEP 3* **74**	1
9 Apr 88	**ARMAGEDDON IT** *Bludgeon Riffola LEP 4* **20**	5
16 Jul 88	**LOVE BITES** *Bludgeon Riffola LEP 5* **11**	8
11 Feb 89	**ROCKET** *Bludgeon Riffola LEP 6* **15**	7
28 Mar 92	● **LET'S GET ROCKED** *Bludgeon Riffola DEF 7* **2**	7
27 Jun 92	**MAKE LOVE LIKE A MAN** *Bludgeon Riffola LEP 7* **12**	5
12 Sep 92	**HAVE YOU EVER NEEDED SOMEONE SO BAD** *Bludgeon Riffola LEP 8* **16**	5
30 Jan 93	**HEAVEN IS** *Bludgeon Riffola LEPCD 9* **13**	5
1 May 93	**TONIGHT** *Bludgeon Riffola LEPCD 10* **34**	3
18 Sep 93	**TWO STEPS BEHIND** *Bludgeon Riffola LEPCD 12* **32**	5
15 Jan 94	**ACTION** *Bludgeon Riffola LEPCD 13* **14**	5
14 Oct 95	● **WHEN LOVE AND HATE COLLIDE** *Bludgeon Riffola LEPCD 14* **2**	10
4 May 96	**SLANG** *Bludgeon Riffola LEPCD 15* **17**	5
13 Jul 96	**WORK IT OUT** *Bludgeon Riffola LEPCD 16* **22**	3
28 Sep 96	**ALL I WANT IS EVERYTHING** *Bludgeon Riffola LEPCD 17* **38**	2
30 Nov 96	**BREATHE A SIGH** *Bludgeon Riffola LEPCD 18* **43**	1

DEFINITION OF SOUND *UK, male rap duo*   **25 wks**

9 Mar 91	**WEAR YOUR LOVE LIKE HEAVEN** *Circa YR 61* **17**	9
1 Jun 91	**NOW IS TOMORROW** *Circa YR 66* **46**	4
8 Feb 92	**MOIRA JANE'S CAFE** *Circa YR 80* **34**	4
19 Sep 92	**WHAT ARE YOU UNDER** *Circa YR 95* **68**	1
14 Nov 92	**CAN I GET OVER** *Circa YR 97* **61**	2
20 May 95	**BOOM BOOM** *Fontana DOSCD 1* **59**	1
2 Dec 95	**PASS THE VIBES** *Fontana DOSCD 2* **23**	3
24 Feb 96	**CHILD** *Fontana DOSCD 3* **48**	1

DEGREES OF MOTION featuring BITI
US, female vocal group   **21 wks**

25 Apr 92	**DO YOU WANT IT RIGHT NOW** *ffrr F 184* **31**	5
18 Jul 92	**SHINE ON** *ffrr F 192* [1] **43**	3
7 Nov 92	**SOUL FREEDOM – FREE YOUR SOUL** *ffrr FX 201* **64**	1
19 Mar 94	● **SHINE ON (re-mix)** *ffrr FCD 229* **8**	8
25 Jun 94	**DO YOU WANT IT RIGHT NOW (re-mix)** *ffrr FCD 236* **26**	4

[1] Degrees Of Motion featuring Biti with Kit West

Divine Comedy

The Divine Comedy's Neil Hannon was inspired to write 'Something For The Weekend' by actress Kate Beckinsale.

Celine Dion

At the age of 20 Canadian-born Celine Dion won the 1988 Eurovision Song Contest, representing Switzerland. She pipped the UK entry, 'Go' by Scot Fitzgerald, to the title by a single point.

Dead Or Alive

Dead Or Alive's 'You Spin Me Round (Like A Record)' was the first number one for producers Stock, Atiken and Waterman, it was also their longest chart visitor, spending 23 weeks in the Top 75.

Dexy's Midnight Runners

'Come On Eileen', the best selling single of 1982, also won the award for Best British Single at the following year's Brit Awards.

DEJA US, male / female vocal duo — 1 wk

29 Aug 87	**SERIOUS** 10 TEN 132	**75**	1

DEJA VU UK, male vocal / instrumental duo — 1 wk

5 Feb 94	**WHY WHY WHY** Cowboy RODEO 941CD	**57**	1

Desmond DEKKER and the ACES
Jamaica, male vocal / instrumental group — 71 wks

12 Jul 67	**007** Pyramid PYR 6004	**14**	11
19 Mar 69	★ **ISRAELITES** Pyramid PYR 6058	**1**	14
25 Jun 69	● **IT MIEK** Pyramid PYR 6068	**7**	11
2 Jul 69	**ISRAELITES (re-entry)** Pyramid PYR 6058	**45**	1
10 Jan 70	**PICKNEY GAL** Pyramid PYR 6078	**42**	3
22 Aug 70	● **YOU CAN GET IT IF YOU REALLY WANT** Trojan TR 7777 [1]	**2**	15
10 May 75	● **ISRAELITES (re-issue)** Cactus CT 57 [1]	**10**	9
30 Aug 75	**SING A LITTLE SONG** Cactus CT 73 [1]	**16**	7

[1] Desmond Dekker

DEL AMITRI UK, male vocal / instrumental group — 59 wks

19 Aug 89	**KISS THIS THING GOODBYE** A & M AM 515	**59**	2
13 Jan 90	**NOTHING EVER HAPPENS** A & M AM 536	**11**	9
24 Mar 90	**KISS THIS THING GOODBYE (re-issue)** A & M AM 551	**43**	4
16 Jun 90	**MOVE AWAY JIMMY BLUE** A & M AM 555	**36**	6
3 Nov 90	**SPIT IN THE RAIN** A & M AM 589	**21**	6
9 May 92	**ALWAYS THE LAST TO KNOW** A & M AM 870	**13**	7
11 Jul 92	**BE MY DOWNFALL** A & M AM 884	**30**	4
12 Sep 92	**JUST LIKE A MAN** A & M AM 0057	**25**	4
23 Jan 93	**WHEN YOU WERE YOUNG** A & M AMCD 0132	**20**	3
18 Feb 95	**HERE AND NOW** A & M 5809692	**21**	4
29 Apr 95	**DRIVING WITH THE BRAKES ON** A & M 5810072	**18**	4
8 Jul 95	**ROLL TO ME** A & M 5811312	**22**	4
28 Oct 95	**TELL HER THIS** A & M 5812172	**32**	2

DELAGE UK, female vocal group — 2 wks

15 Dec 90	**ROCK THE BOAT** PWL/Polydor PO 113	**63**	2

DELANEY and BONNIE and FRIENDS featuring Eric CLAPTON – *See Eric CLAPTON*

DELEGATION
UK, male vocal / instrumental group — 7 wks

23 Apr 77	**WHERE IS THE LOVE (WE USED TO KNOW)** State STAT 40	**22**	6
20 Aug 77	**YOU'VE BEEN DOING ME WRONG** State STAT 55	**49**	1

DELFONICS US, male vocal group — 23 wks

10 Apr 71	**DIDN'T I (BLOW YOUR MIND THIS TIME)** Bell 1099	**43**	1
24 Apr 71	**DIDN'T I (BLOW YOUR MIND THIS TIME) (re-entry)** Bell 1099	**22**	8
10 Jul 71	**LA-LA MEANS I LOVE YOU** Bell 1165	**19**	10
16 Oct 71	**READY OR NOT HERE I COME** Bell 1175	**41**	4

'DELIVERANCE' SOUNDTRACK
US, male instrumental duo, Eric Weissberg – banjo and Steve Mandell – guitar — 7 wks

31 Mar 73	**DUELLING BANJOS** Warner Bros. K 16223	**17**	7

DELLS US, male vocal group — 9 wks

16 Jul 69	**I CAN SING A RAINBOW – LOVE IS BLUE (MEDLEY)** Chess CRS 8099	**15**	9

DELRONS – *See REPARATA and the DELRONS*

DELTA – *See David MORALES; Crystal WATERS*

DELUXE US, female vocalist — 1 wk

18 Mar 89	**JUST A LITTLE MORE** Unyque UNQ 5	**74**	1

DEMOLITION MAN – *See PRIZNA featuring DEMOLITION MAN*

Chaka DEMUS and PLIERS
Jamaica, male vocal duo — 54 wks

12 Jun 93	● **TEASE ME** Mango CIDM 806	**3**	15
18 Sep 93	● **SHE DON'T LET NOBODY** Mango CIDM 810	**4**	10
18 Dec 93	★ **TWIST AND SHOUT** Mango CIDM 814 [1]	**1**	13
12 Mar 94	**MURDER SHE WROTE** Mango CIDM 812	**27**	4
18 Jun 94	**I WANNA BE YOUR MAN** Mango CIDM 817	**19**	6
27 Aug 94	**GAL WINE** Mango CIDM 818	**20**	4
1 Apr 95	**TWIST AND SHOUT (re-entry)** Mango CIDM 814 [1]	**67**	1
31 Aug 96	**EVERY KINDA PEOPLE** Island Jamaica IJCD 2005	**47**	1

[1] Chaka Demus and Pliers featuring Jack Radics and Taxi Gang

Terry DENE UK, male vocalist — 20 wks

7 Jun 57	**A WHITE SPORT COAT** Decca F 10895	**18**	6
19 Jul 57	**START MOVIN'** Decca F 10914	**15**	8
26 Jul 57	**A WHITE SPORT COAT (re-entry)** Decca F 10895	**30**	1
16 May 58	**STAIRWAY OF LOVE** Decca F 11016	**16**	5

Cathy DENNIS UK, female vocalist — 62 wks

21 Oct 89	**C'MON AND GET MY LOVE** ffrr F 117 [1]	**15**	10
7 Apr 90	**THAT'S THE WAY OF THE WORLD** ffrr F 132 [1]	**48**	3
4 May 91	● **TOUCH ME (ALL NIGHT LONG)** Polydor CATH 3	**5**	10
20 Jul 91	**JUST ANOTHER DREAM** Polydor CATH 2	**13**	7
5 Oct 91	**TOO MANY WALLS** Polydor CATH 4	**17**	7
7 Dec 91	**EVERYBODY MOVE** Polydor CATH 5	**25**	8
29 Aug 92	**YOU LIED TO ME** Polydor CATH 6	**34**	4
21 Nov 92	**IRRESISTIBLE** Polydor CATH 7	**24**	6
6 Feb 93	**FALLING** Polydor CATHD 8	**32**	2
12 Feb 94	**WHY** ffrr FCD 227 [1]	**23**	3
10 Aug 96	**WEST END PAD** Polydor 5752812	**25**	2

[1] D Mob with Cathy Dennis

Jackie DENNIS UK, male vocalist — 10 wks

14 Mar 58	● **LA DEE DAH** Decca F 10992	**4**	9
27 Jun 58	**PURPLE PEOPLE EATER** Decca F 11033	**29**	1

Stefan DENNIS Australia, male vocalist — 8 wks

6 May 89	**DON'T IT MAKE YOU FEEL GOOD** Sublime LIME 105	**16**	7
7 Oct 89	**THIS LOVE AFFAIR** Sublime LIME 113	**67**	1

DENNISONS UK, male vocal / instrumental group — 13 wks

15 Aug 63	**BE MY GIRL** Decca F 11691	**46**	6
7 May 64	**WALKIN' THE DOG** Decca F 11880	**36**	7

Richard DENTON and Martin COOK
UK, male orchestra leaders/instrumental duo, guitar and keyboards **7 wks**

| 15 Apr 78 | THEME FROM 'THE HONG KONG BEAT' BBC RESL 52 | **25** | 7 |

John DENVER *US, male vocalist* **22 wks**

| 17 Aug 74 | ★ ANNIE'S SONG RCA APBO 0295 | **1** | 13 |
| 12 Dec 81 | PERHAPS LOVE CBS A 1905 [1] | **46** | 9 |

[1] Placido Domingo with John Denver

Karl DENVER *UK, male vocalist* **127 wks**

22 Jun 61	● MARCHETA Decca F 11360	**8**	20
19 Oct 61	● MEXICALI ROSE Decca F 11395	**8**	11
25 Jan 62	● WIMOWEH Decca F 11420	**4**	17
22 Feb 62	● NEVER GOODBYE Decca F 11431	**9**	18
7 Jun 62	A LITTLE LOVE A LITTLE KISS Decca F 11470	**19**	10
20 Sep 62	BLUE WEEKEND Decca F 11505	**33**	5
21 Mar 63	CAN YOU FORGIVE ME Decca F 11608	**32**	8
13 Jun 63	INDIAN LOVE CALL Decca F 11674	**32**	8
22 Aug 63	STILL Decca F 11720	**13**	15
5 Mar 64	MY WORLD OF BLUE Decca F 11828	**29**	6
4 Jun 64	LOVE ME WITH ALL YOUR HEART Decca F 11905	**37**	6
9 Jun 90	LAZYITIS – ONE ARMED BOXER Factory FAC 2227 [1]	**46**	3

[1] Happy Mondays and Karl Denver

DEODATO *US, male multi-instrumentalist* **9 wks**

| 5 May 73 | ● ALSO SPRACH ZARATHUSTRA (2001) Creed Taylor CTI 4000 | **7** | 9 |

DEPARTMENT S *UK, male vocal/instrumental group* **13 wks**

| 4 Apr 81 | IS VIC THERE? Demon D 1003 | **22** | 10 |
| 11 Jul 81 | GOING LEFT RIGHT Stiff BUY 118 | **55** | 3 |

DEPECHE MODE *UK, male vocal/instrumental group* **208 wks**

4 Apr 81	DREAMING OF ME Mute MUTE 013	**57**	4
13 Jun 81	NEW LIFE Mute MUTE 014	**11**	15
19 Sep 81	● JUST CAN'T GET ENOUGH Mute MUTE 016	**8**	10
13 Feb 82	● SEE YOU Mute MUTE 018	**6**	10
8 May 82	THE MEANING OF LOVE Mute MUTE 022	**12**	8
28 Aug 82	LEAVE IN SILENCE Mute BONG 1	**18**	10
12 Feb 83	GET THE BALANCE RIGHT Mute 7BONG 2	**13**	8
23 Jul 83	● EVERYTHING COUNTS Mute 7BONG 3	**6**	11
1 Oct 83	LOVE IN ITSELF.2 Mute 7BONG 4	**21**	7
24 Mar 84	● PEOPLE ARE PEOPLE Mute 7BONG 5	**4**	10
1 Sep 84	● MASTER AND SERVANT Mute 7BONG 6	**9**	9
10 Nov 84	SOMEBODY / BLASPHEMOUS RUMOURS Mute 7BONG 7	**16**	6
11 May 85	SHAKE THE DISEASE Mute BONG 8	**18**	9
28 Sep 85	IT'S CALLED A HEART Mute BONG 9	**18**	4
22 Feb 86	STRIPPED Mute BONG 10	**15**	5
26 Apr 86	A QUESTION OF LUST Mute BONG 11	**28**	5
23 Aug 86	A QUESTION OF TIME Mute BONG 12	**17**	6
9 May 87	STRANGELOVE Mute BONG 13	**16**	5
5 Sep 87	NEVER LET ME DOWN AGAIN Mute BONG 14	**22**	4
9 Jan 88	BEHIND THE WHEEL Mute BONG 15	**21**	5
28 May 88	LITTLE 15 (IMPORT) Mute LITTLE 15	**60**	2
25 Feb 89	EVERYTHING COUNTS Mute BONG 16	**22**	7
9 Sep 89	PERSONAL JESUS Mute BONG 17	**13**	8
17 Feb 90	● ENJOY THE SILENCE Mute BONG 18	**6**	9
19 May 90	POLICY OF TRUTH Mute BONG 19	**16**	6
29 Sep 90	WORLD IN MY EYES Mute BONG 20	**17**	6
27 Feb 93	● I FEEL YOU Mute CDBONG 21	**8**	7
8 May 93	WALKING IN MY SHOES Mute CDBONG 22	**14**	4
25 Sep 93	● CONDEMNATION Mute CDBONG 23	**9**	4
22 Jan 94	● IN YOUR ROOM Mute CDBONG 24	**8**	4

BONG 16 *is a live version of* BONG 3.

DEPTH CHARGE *UK, male producer – Jonathan Kane* **1 wk**

| 29 Jul 95 | LEGEND OF THE GOLDEN SNAKE DC DC 01CD | **75** | 1 |

DEREK and the DOMINOES – *See Eric CLAPTON*

DESIRELESS *France, female vocalist* **19 wks**

| 31 Oct 87 | VOYAGE VOYAGE CBS DESI 1 | **53** | 6 |
| 14 May 88 | ● VOYAGE VOYAGE (re-mix) CBS DESI 2 | **5** | 13 |

DESIYA featuring Melissa YIANNAKOU
UK, male/female vocal/instrumental duo **1 wk**

| 1 Feb 92 | COMIN' ON STRONG Black Market 12MKT 2 | **74** | 1 |

Kevin DESIMONS – *See Barry MANILOW*

DESKEE *UK, male instrumentalist* **3 wks**

| 3 Feb 90 | LET THERE BE HOUSE Big One VBIG 19 | **52** | 2 |
| 8 Sep 90 | DANCE, DANCE Big One VBIG 22 | **74** | 1 |

DES'REE *UK, female vocalist* **43 wks**

31 Aug 91	FEEL SO HIGH Dusted Sound 6573667	**51**	5
11 Jan 92	FEEL SO HIGH (re-issue) Dusted Sound 6576897	**13**	7
21 Mar 92	MIND ADVENTURES Dusted Sound 6578637	**43**	3
27 Jun 92	WHY SHOULD I LOVE YOU Dusted Sound 6580917	**44**	3
19 Jun 93	DELICATE Columbia 6593312 [1]	**14**	6
9 Apr 94	YOU GOTTA BE Dusted Sound 6601342	**20**	7
18 Jun 94	I AIN'T MOVIN' Dusted Sound 6604672	**44**	3
3 Sep 94	LITTLE CHILD Dusted Sound 6604515	**69**	1
11 Mar 95	YOU GOTTA BE (re-mix) Dusted Sound 6613215	**14**	8

[1] Terence Trent D'Arby featuring Des'ree

DESTRY – *See ZOO EXPERIENCE featuring DESTRY*

Marcella DETROIT *US, female vocalist* **16 wks**

12 Mar 94	I BELIEVE London LONCD 347	**11**	8
14 May 94	AIN'T NOTHING LIKE THE REAL THING London LONCD 350 [1]	**24**	4
16 Jul 94	I'M NO ANGEL London LOCDP 351	**33**	4

[1] Marcella Detroit and Elton John

DETROIT EMERALDS *US, male vocal group* **44 wks**

10 Feb 73	● FEEL THE NEED IN ME Janus 6146 020	**4**	15
5 May 73	YOU WANT IT YOU GOT IT Westbound 6146 103	**12**	9
11 Aug 73	I THINK OF YOU Westbound 6146 104	**27**	9
18 Jun 77	FEEL THE NEED Atlantic K 10945	**12**	11

The second Feel The Need was a re-recording of Feel The Need In Me.

DETROIT SPINNERS *US, male vocal group* **93 wks**

14 Nov 70	IT'S A SHAME Tamla Motown TMG 755 [1]	**20**	11
21 Apr 73	COULD IT BE I'M FALLING IN LOVE Atlantic K 10283	**11**	11
29 Sep 73	● GHETTO CHILD Atlantic K 10359	**7**	10
19 Oct 74	THEN CAME YOU Atlantic K 10495 [2]	**29**	6

11 Sep 76	THE RUBBERBAND MAN *Atlantic K 10807*	**16** 11
29 Jan 77	WAKE UP SUSAN *Atlantic K 10799*	**29** 6
7 May 77	COULD IT BE I'M FALLING IN LOVE EP *Atlantic K 10935*	**32** 3
23 Feb 80	★ WORKING MY WAY BACK TO YOU – FORGIVE ME GIRL *Atlantic K 11432*	**1** 14
10 May 80	BODY LANGUAGE *Atlantic K 11392*	**40** 7
28 Jun 80	● CUPID – I'VE LOVED YOU FOR A LONG TIME *Atlantic K 11498*	**4** 10
24 Jun 95	I'LL BE AROUND *Cooltempo CDCOOL 306* ③	**30** 4

① Motown Spinners ② Dionne Warwicke and the Detroit Spinners ③ Rappin' 4-Tay featuring the Spinners

Group was known simply as the Spinners in the US. Tracks on Could It Be I'm Falling In Love EP: Could It Be I'm Falling In Love / You're Throwing A Good Love Away / Games People Play / Lazy Susan.

DETROIT WHEELS – *See Mitch RYDER and the DETROIT WHEELS*

DEUCE *UK, male / female vocal group*   **23 wks**

21 Jan 95	CALL IT LOVE *London LONCD 355*	**11** 10
22 Apr 95	● I NEED YOU *London LONCD 365*	**10** 5
19 Aug 95	ON THE BIBLE *London LONCD 368*	**13** 6
29 Jun 96	NO SURRENDER *Love This LUVTHISCD 10*	**29** 2

dEUS *Belgium, male vocal / instrumental group*   **4 wks**

11 Feb 95	HOTEL LOUNGE (BE THE DEATH OF ME) *Island CID 603*	**55** 1
13 Jul 96	THEME FROM TURNPIKE (EP) *Island CID 630*	**68** 1
19 Oct 96	LITTLE ARITHMETICS *Island CID 643*	**44** 2

Tracks on Theme From Turnpike (EP): Theme From Turnpike / Worried About Satan / Overflow / My Little Contessa.

Sidney DEVINE *UK, male vocalist*   **1 wk**

1 Apr 78	SCOTLAND FOREVER *Philips SCOT 1*	**48** 1

DEVO *US, male vocal / instrumental group*   **23 wks**

22 Apr 78	(I CAN'T ME GET NO) SATISFACTION *Stiff BOY 1*	**41** 8
13 May 78	JOCKO HOMO *Stiff DEV 1*	**62** 3
12 Aug 78	BE STIFF *Stiff BOY 2*	**71** 1
2 Sep 78	COME BACK JONEE *Virgin VS 223*	**60** 4
22 Nov 80	WHIP IT *Virgin VS 383*	**51** 7

Sheila B. DEVOTION *France, female vocalist*   **33 wks**

11 Mar 78	SINGIN' IN THE RAIN PART 1 *Carrere EMI 2751*	**11** 13
22 Jul 78	YOU LIGHT MY FIRE *Carrere EMI 2828*	**44** 6
24 Nov 79	SPACER *Carrere CAR 128*	**18** 14

DEVOTIONS – *See BELLE and the DEVOTIONS*

Howard DEVOTO – *See BUZZCOCKS*

DEXY'S MIDNIGHT RUNNERS
UK, male vocal / instrumental group   **93 wks**

19 Jan 80	DANCE STANCE *Oddball Productions R 6028*	**40** 6
22 Mar 80	★ GENO *Late Night Feelings R 6033*	**1** 14
12 Jul 80	● THERE THERE MY DEAR *Late Night Feelings R 6038*	**7** 9
21 Mar 81	PLAN B *Parlophone R 6046*	**58** 2
11 Jul 81	SHOW ME *Mercury DEXYS 6*	**16** 9
20 Mar 82	THE CELTIC SOUL BROTHERS *Mercury DEXYS 8* ①	**45** 4
3 Jul 82	★ COME ON EILEEN *Mercury DEXYS 9* ①	**1** 17
2 Oct 82	● JACKIE WILSON SAID (I'M IN HEAVEN WHEN YOU SMILE) *Mercury DEXYS 10* ②	**5** 7
4 Dec 82	LET'S GET THIS STRAIGHT (FROM THE START) / OLD *Mercury DEXYS 11* ②	**17** 9
2 Apr 83	THE CELTIC SOUL BROTHERS (MORE PLEASE, THANK YOU) *Mercury DEXYS 12* ②	**20** 6
22 Nov 86	BECAUSE OF YOU *Mercury BRUSH 1*	**13** 10

① Dexy's Midnight Runners with the Emerald Express ② Kevin Rowland and Dexy's Midnight Runners

DEXYS 12 is a different version from DEXYS 8.

Tony DI BART *UK, male vocalist*   **18 wks**

9 Apr 94	★ THE REAL THING *Cleveland City Blues CCBCD 15001*	**1** 12
20 Aug 94	DO IT *Cleveland City Blues CCBCD 15003*	**21** 4
20 May 95	WHY DID YA *Cleveland City Blues CCBCD 15004*	**46** 1
2 Mar 96	TURN YOUR LOVE AROUND *Cleveland City Blues CCBCD 15006*	**66** 1

Jim DIAMOND *UK, male vocalist*   **30 wks**

3 Nov 84	★ I SHOULD HAVE KNOWN BETTER *A & M AM 220*	**1** 13
2 Feb 85	I SLEEP ALONE AT NIGHT *A & M AM 229*	**72** 1
18 May 85	REMEMBER I LOVE YOU *A & M AM 247*	**42** 5
22 Feb 86	● HI HO SILVER *A & M AM 296*	**5** 11

Neil DIAMOND *US, male vocalist*   **121 wks**

7 Nov 70	● CRACKLIN' ROSIE *Uni UN 529*	**3** 17
20 Feb 71	● SWEET CAROLINE *Uni UN 531*	**8** 11
8 May 71	● I AM... I SAID *Uni UN 532*	**4** 12
13 May 72	SONG SUNG BLUE *Uni UN 538*	**14** 13
14 Aug 76	IF YOU KNOW WHAT I MEAN *CBS 4398*	**35** 4
23 Oct 76	BEAUTIFUL NOISE *CBS 4601*	**13** 9
24 Dec 77	DESIREE *CBS 5869*	**39** 6
25 Nov 78	● YOU DON'T BRING ME FLOWERS *CBS 6803* ①	**5** 12
3 Mar 79	FOREVER IN BLUE JEANS *CBS 7047*	**16** 12
15 Nov 80	LOVE ON THE ROCKS *Capitol CL 16173*	**17** 12
14 Feb 81	HELLO AGAIN *Capitol CL 16176*	**51** 4
20 Nov 82	HEARTLIGHT *CBS A 2814*	**47** 7
21 Nov 92	MORNING HAS BROKEN *Columbia 6588267*	**36** 2

① Barbra and Neil

Barbra was Barbra Streisand.

Gregg DIAMOND BIONIC BOOGIE
US, male / female vocal group   **3 wks**

20 Jan 79	CREAM (ALWAYS RISES TO THE TOP) *Polydor POSP 18*	**61** 3

DIAMOND HEAD *UK, male vocal / instrumental group*   **2 wks**

11 Sep 82	IN THE HEAT OF THE NIGHT *MCA DHM 102*	**67** 2

DIAMONDS *Canada, male vocal group*   **17 wks**

31 May 57	● LITTLE DARLIN' *Mercury MT 148*	**3** 17

DIANA – *See Diana ROSS*

DICK and DEEDEE *US, male / female vocal duo*   **3 wks**

26 Oct 61	THE MOUNTAIN'S HIGH *London HLG 9408*	**37** 3

Charles DICKENS *UK, male vocalist*   **8 wks**

1 Jul 65	THAT'S THE WAY LOVE GOES *Pye 7N 15887*	**37** 8

Gwen DICKEY US, female vocalist   6 wks

27 Jan 90	**CAR WASH** Swanyard SYR 7..................................	**72**	2
2 Jul 94	**AIN'T NOBODY (LOVES ME BETTER)**		
	X-clusive XCLU 010CD [1]	**21**	4

[1] KWS and Gwen Dickey

Neville DICKIE UK, male instrumentalist – piano   10 wks

| 25 Oct 69 | **ROBIN'S RETURN** Major Minor MM 644.......................... | **33** | 7 |
| 20 Dec 69 | **ROBIN'S RETURN (re-entry)** Major Minor MM 644 .... | **43** | 3 |

DICKIES US, male vocal / instrumental group   28 wks

16 Dec 78	**SILENT NIGHT** A & M AMS 7403	**47**	4
21 Apr 79	● **BANANA SPLITS (TRA LA LA SONG)**		
	A & M AMS 7431	**7**	8
21 Jul 79	**PARANOID** A & M AMS 7368	**45**	6
15 Sep 79	**NIGHTS IN WHITE SATIN** A & M AMS 7469	**39**	5
16 Feb 80	**FAN MAIL** A & M AMS 7504	**57**	3
19 Jul 80	**GIGANTOR** A & M AMS 7544	**72**	2

Bruce DICKINSON UK, male vocalist   22 wks

28 Apr 90	**TATTOOED MILLIONAIRE** EMI EM 138	**18**	5
23 Jun 90	**ALL THE YOUNG DUDES** EMI EM·142	**23**	5
25 Aug 90	**DIVE! DIVE! DIVE!** EMI EM 151	**45**	5
4 Apr 92	● **(I WANT TO BE) ELECTED** London LON 319 [1]	**9**	5
28 May 94	**TEARS OF THE DRAGON** EMI CDEM 322	**28**	2
8 Oct 94	**SHOOT ALL THE CLOWNS** EMI CDEMS 341	**37**	2
13 Apr 96	**BACK FROM THE EDGE** Raw Power RAWX 1012	**68**	1

[1] Mr Bean and Smear Campaign featuring Bruce Dickinson

Barbara DICKSON UK, female vocalist   49 wks

17 Jan 76	● **ANSWER ME** RSO 2090 174	**9**	7
26 Feb 77	**ANOTHER SUITCASE IN ANOTHER HALL** MCA 266	**18**	7
19 Jan 80	**CARAVAN SONG** Epic EPC 8103	**41**	7
15 Mar 80	**JANUARY FEBRUARY** Epic EPC 8115	**11**	10
14 Jun 80	**IN THE NIGHT** Epic EPC 8593	**48**	2
5 Jan 85	★ **I KNOW HIM SO WELL** RCA CHESS 3 [1] **1**	16

[1] Elaine Paige and Barbara Dickson

DICTATORS US, male vocal / instrumental group   2 wks

| 17 Sep 77 | **SEARCH AND DESTROY** Asylum K 13091 .... | **49** | 1 |
| 1 Oct 77 | **SEARCH AND DESTROY (re-entry)** Asylum K 13091 ..... | **50** | 1 |

Bo DIDDLEY US, male vocalist / instrumentalist – guitar   10 wks

| 10 Oct 63 | **PRETTY THING** Pye International 7N 25217 .... | **34** | 6 |
| 18 Mar 65 | **HEY GOOD LOOKIN'** Chess 8000 .... | **39** | 4 |

DIDDY US, male producer   1 wk

| 19 Feb 94 | **GIVE ME LOVE** Positiva CDTIV 8 .... | **52** | 1 |

DIESEL PARK WEST
UK, male vocal / instrumental group   15 wks

4 Feb 89	**ALL THE MYTHS ON SUNDAY** Food FOOD 17	**66**	2
1 Apr 89	**LIKE PRINCES DO** Food FOOD 19	**58**	3
5 Aug 89	**WHEN THE HOODOO COMES** Food FOOD 20	**62**	2
18 Jan 92	**FALL TO LOVE** Food FOOD 35	**48**	3

| 21 Mar 92 | **BOY ON TOP OF THE NEWS** Food FOOD 36 .... | **58** | 2 |
| 5 Sep 92 | **GOD ONLY KNOWS** Food FOOD 39 .... | **57** | 3 |

See also Various Artists (EPs and LPs) - The Food Christmas EP.

DIFFORD and TILBROOK
UK, male vocal / instrumental duo   2 wks

| 30 Jun 84 | **LOVE'S CRASHING WAVES** A & M AM 193................... | **57** | 2 |

DIGABLE PLANETS
US, male / female vocal / instrumental group   2 wks

| 13 Feb 93 | **REBIRTH OF SLICK (COOL LIKE DAT)** | | |
| | Pendulum EKR 159CD .... | **67** | 2 |

DIGITAL DREAM BABY
UK, male vocalist – Peter Auty   4 wks

| 14 Dec 91 | **WALKING IN THE AIR** Columbia 6576067 .... | **49** | 4 |

Hit is a dance re-mix of Walking In The Air by Peter Auty.

DIGITAL EXCITATION
Belgium, male producer – Frank De Wulf   2 wks

| 29 Feb 92 | **PURE PLEASURE** R&S RSUK 10 .... | **37** | 2 |

DIGITAL ORGASM
Belgium, male / female vocal / instrumental group   14 wks

7 Dec 91	**RUNNING OUT OF TIME** Dead Dead Good GOOD 009	**16**	9
18 Apr 92	**STARTOUCHERS** DDG International GOOD 13	**31**	3
25 Jul 92	**MOOG ERUPTION** DDG International GOOD 17	**62**	2

DIGITAL UNDERGROUND US, male vocal group   4 wks

| 16 Mar 91 | **SAME SONG** Big Life BLR 40 .... | **52** | 4 |

DILEMMA Italy, male instrumental / production group   1 wk

| 6 Apr 96 | **IN SPIRIT** ffrr FCD 274.................................. | **42** | 1 |

Ricky DILLARD – See Farley 'Jackmaster' Funk

Paolo DINI – See FPI PROJECT

Mark DINNING US, male vocalist   4 wks

| 10 Mar 60 | **TEEN ANGEL** MGM 1053 .... | **37** | 3 |
| 7 Apr 60 | **TEEN ANGEL (re-entry)** MGM 1053 .... | **42** | 1 |

DINOSAUR Jr. US, male vocal / instrumental group   12 wks

2 Feb 91	**THE WAGON** Blanco Y Negro NEG 48	**49**	2
14 Nov 92	**GET ME** Blanco Y Negro NEG 60	**44**	1
30 Jan 93	**START CHOPPIN** Blanco Y Negro NEG 61CD....................	**20**	3
12 Jun 93	**OUT THERE** Blanco Y Negro NEG 63CD	**44**	3
27 Aug 94	**FEEL THE PAIN** Blanco Y Negro NEG 74CD....................	**25**	3
11 Feb 95	**I DON'T THINK SO** Blanco Y Negro NEG 77CD	**67**	1

DINOSAURS – See Terry DACTYL and the DINOSAURS

DIO UK / US, male vocal / instrumental group   22 wks

| 20 Aug 83 | **HOLY DIVER** Vertigo DIO 1 .... | **72** | 2 |

29 Oct 83	**RAINBOW IN THE DARK** Vertigo DIO 2	**46**	3
11 Aug 84	**WE ROCK** Vertigo DIO 3	**42**	4
29 Sep 84	**MYSTERY** Vertigo DIO 4	**34**	4
10 Aug 85	**ROCK 'N' ROLL CHILDREN** Vertigo DIO 5	**26**	6
2 Nov 85	**HUNGRY FOR HEAVEN** Vertigo DIO 6	**72**	1
17 May 86	**HUNGRY FOR HEAVEN (re-issue)** Vertigo DIO 7	**56**	2
1 Aug 87	**I COULD HAVE BEEN A DREAMER** Vertigo DIO 8	**69**	1

DION US, male vocalist   35 wks

26 Jun 59	**A TEENAGER IN LOVE** London HLU 8874 [1]	**28**	2
19 Jan 61	**LONELY TEENAGER** Top Rank JAR 521	**47**	1
2 Nov 61	**RUNAROUND SUE** Top Rank JAR 586	**11**	9
15 Feb 62	● **THE WANDERER** HMV POP 971	**10**	12
22 May 76	**THE WANDERER (re-issue)** Philips 6146 700	**16**	9
19 Aug 89	**KING OF THE NEW YORK STREET** Arista 112556	**74**	2

[1] Dion and the Belmonts

Celine DION Canada, female vocalist   123 wks

16 May 92	● **BEAUTY AND THE BEAST** Epic 6576607 [1]	**9**	7
4 Jul 92	**IF YOU ASKED ME TO** Epic 6581927	**60**	2
14 Nov 92	**LOVE CAN MOVE MOUNTAINS** Epic 6587787	**46**	2
26 Dec 92	**IF YOU ASKED ME TO (re-entry)** Epic 6581927	**57**	3
3 Apr 93	**WHERE DOES MY HEART BEAT NOW** Epic 6563265	**72**	1
29 Jan 94	● **THE POWER OF LOVE** Epic 6597992	**4**	10
23 Apr 94	**MISLED** Epic 6602922	**40**	3
22 Oct 94	★ **THINK TWICE** Epic 6606422	**1**	31
20 May 95	● **ONLY ONE ROAD** Epic 6613535	**8**	8
9 Sep 95	● **TU M'AIMES ENCORE (TO LOVE ME AGAIN)** Epic 6624255	**7**	9
2 Dec 95	**MISLED (re-issue)** Epic 6626495	**15**	6
2 Mar 96	● **FALLING INTO YOU** Epic 6629795	**10**	10
1 Jun 96	● **BECAUSE YOU LOVED ME (THEME FROM 'UP CLOSE AND PERSONAL')** Epic 6632382	**5**	16
5 Oct 96	● **IT'S ALL COMING BACK TO ME NOW** Epic 6637112	**3†**	13
21 Dec 96	● **ALL BY MYSELF** Epic 6640622	**6†**	2

[1] Celine Dion and Peabo Bryson

DIONNE Canada, female vocalist   2 wks

23 Sep 89	**COME GET MY LOVIN'** Citybeat CBC 745	**69**	2

Wasis DIOP – See Lena FIAGBE

DIRE STRAITS UK, male vocal / instrumental group   119 wks

10 Mar 79	● **SULTANS OF SWING** Vertigo 6059 206	**8**	11
28 Jul 79	**LADY WRITER** Vertigo 6059 230	**51**	6
17 Jan 81	● **ROMEO AND JULIET** Vertigo MOVIE 1	**8**	11
4 Apr 81	**SKATEAWAY** Vertigo MOVIE 2	**37**	5
10 Oct 81	**TUNNEL OF LOVE** Vertigo MUSIC 3	**54**	3
4 Sep 82	● **PRIVATE INVESTIGATIONS** Vertigo DSTR 1	**2**	8
22 Jan 83	**TWISTING BY THE POOL** Vertigo DSTR 2	**14**	7
18 Feb 84	**LOVE OVER GOLD (LIVE) / SOLID ROCK (LIVE)** Vertigo DSTR 6	**50**	3
20 Apr 85	**SO FAR AWAY** Vertigo DSTR 9	**20**	6
6 Jul 85	● **MONEY FOR NOTHING** Vertigo DSTR 10	**4**	16
26 Oct 85	**BROTHERS IN ARMS** Vertigo DSTR 11	**16**	13
11 Jan 86	● **WALK OF LIFE** Vertigo DSTR 12	**2**	11
3 May 86	**YOUR LATEST TRICK** Vertigo DSTR 13	**26**	6
5 Nov 88	**SULTANS OF SWING (re-issue)** Vertigo DSTR 15	**62**	1
31 Aug 91	**CALLING ELVIS** Vertigo DSTR 16	**21**	4
2 Nov 91	**HEAVY FUEL** Vertigo DSTR 17	**55**	2
29 Feb 92	**ON EVERY STREET** Vertigo DSTR 18	**42**	2
27 Jun 92	**THE BUG** Vertigo DSTR 19	**67**	1
22 May 93	**ENCORES EP** Vertigo DSCD 20	**31**	3

Tracks on Encores EP: Your Latest Trick / The Bug / Solid Rock / Local Hero-Wild Theme.

DIRECKT UK, male instrumental / production duo   2 wks

13 Aug 94	**TWO FATT GUITARS (REVISITED)** UFG UFG 7CD	**36**	2

DIRECT DRIVE
UK, male / female vocal / instrumental group   3 wks

26 Jan 85	**ANYTHING** Polydor POSP 728	**67**	2
4 May 85	**A.B.C. (FALLING IN LOVE'S NOT EASY)** Boiling Point POSP 742	**75**	1

DISCHARGE UK, male vocal / instrumental group   3 wks

24 Oct 81	**NEVER AGAIN** Clay CLAY 6	**64**	3

DISCO ANTHEM
Holland, male producer – Lex van Coeverden   2 wks

18 Jun 94	**SCREAM** Sweat MCSTD 1977	**47**	2

DISCO CITIZENS UK, male instrumental / production duo   2 wks

22 Jul 95	**RIGHT HERE RIGHT NOW** Deconstruction 74321293872	**40**	2

See also Chicane.

DISCO EVANGELISTS
UK, male instrumental / production group   2 wks

8 May 93	**DE NIRO** Positiva CDTIV 2	**59**	2

DISCO TEX and the SEX-O-LETTES
US, male vocalist / female vocal group   22 wks

23 Nov 74	● **GET DANCING** Chelsea 2005 013	**8**	12
26 Apr 75	● **I WANNA DANCE WIT CHOO (DOO DAT DANCE)** Chelsea 2005 024 [1]	**6**	10

[1] Disco Tex and the Sex-O-Lettes featuring Sir Monti Rock III

DISPOSABLE HEROES OF HIPHOPRISY
US, male vocal / instrumental duo   7 wks

4 Apr 92	**TELEVISION THE DRUG OF THE NATION** Fourth & Broadway BRW 241	**57**	2
30 May 92	**LANGUAGE OF VIOLENCE** Fourth & Broadway 12BRW 248	**68**	1
19 Dec 92	**TELEVISION THE DRUG OF THE NATION (re-entry)** Fourth & Broadway BRW 241	**44**	4

Sacha DISTEL France, male vocalist   27 wks

10 Jan 70	**RAINDROPS KEEP FALLING ON MY HEAD** Warner Bros. WB 7345	**50**	1
24 Jan 70	● **RAINDROPS KEEP FALLING ON MY HEAD (re-entry)** Warner Bros. WB 7345	**10**	20
27 Jun 70	**RAINDROPS KEEP FALLING ON MY HEAD (2nd re-entry)** Warner Bros. WB 7345	**43**	4
1 Aug 70	**RAINDROPS KEEP FALLING ON MY HEAD (3rd re-entry)** Warner Bros. WB 7345	**47**	1
15 Aug 70	**RAINDROPS KEEP FALLING ON MY HEAD (4th re-entry)** Warner Bros. WB 7345	**44**	1

DIVA Norway, female vocal duo   2 wks

7 Oct 95	**THE SUN ALWAYS SHINES ON TV** East West YZ 947CD	**53**	1
20 Jul 96	**EVERYBODY (MOVE YOUR BODY)** East West EW 035CD	**44**	1

DIVERSIONS
UK, male / female vocal / instrumental group   **3 wks**

20 Sep 75	**FATTIE BUM BUM** Gull GULS 18	**34**	3

DIVINE
US, male vocalist   **24 wks**

15 Oct 83	**LOVE REACTION** Design Communication DES 4	**65**	2
14 Jul 84	**YOU THINK YOU'RE A MAN** Proto ENA 118	**16**	10
20 Oct 84	**I'M SO BEAUTIFUL** Proto ENA 121	**52**	2
27 Apr 85	**WALK LIKE A MAN** Proto ENA 125	**23**	7
20 Jul 85	**TWISTIN' THE NIGHT AWAY** Proto ENA 127	**47**	3

DIVINE COMEDY
UK, male vocalist / multi-instrumentalist – Neil Hannon   **9 wks**

29 Jun 96	**SOMETHING FOR THE WEEKEND** Setanta SETCD 26	**14**	5
24 Aug 96	**BECOMING MORE LIKE ALFIE** Setanta SETCD 27	**27**	2
16 Nov 96	**THE FROG PRINCESS** Setanta SETCD 32	**15**	2

DIVINYLS
Australia, male / female vocal / instrumental duo   **12 wks**

18 May 91	● **I TOUCH MYSELF** Virgin America VUS 36	**10**	12

DIXIE CUPS
US, female vocal group   **16 wks**

18 Jun 64	**CHAPEL OF LOVE** Pye International 7N 25245	**22**	8
13 May 65	**IKO IKO** Red Bird RB 10024	**23**	8

DIZZY HEIGHTS
UK, male vocal / instrumental group   **4 wks**

18 Dec 82	**CHRISTMAS RAPPING** Polydor WRAP 1	**49**	4

DJ BOBO
Switzerland, male vocalist – René Baumann   **4 wks**

24 Sep 94	**EVERYBODY** PWL Continental PWCD 312	**47**	2
17 Jun 95	**LOVE IS ALL AROUND** Avex UK AXEXCD 7	**49**	2

DJ DADO
Italy, male producer   **6 wks**

6 Apr 96	● **X-FILES** ZYX ZYX 8065R8	**8**	6

DJ DISCIPLE
US, male vocalist   **1 wk**

12 Nov 94	**ON THE DANCEFLOOR** Mother MUMCD 55	**67**	1

DJ DUKE
US, male producer   **7 wks**

8 Jan 94	**BLOW YOUR WHISTLE** ffrr FCD 228	**15**	5
16 Jul 94	**TURN IT UP (SAY YEAH)** ffrr FCD 235	**31**	2

DJ E-Z ROCK – See Rob BASE and DJ E-Z ROCK

DJ 'FAST' EDDIE
US, male producer   **15 wks**

11 Apr 87	**CAN U DANCE** Champion CHAMP 41 [1]	**71**	2
14 Nov 87	**CAN U DANCE (re-entry)** Champion CHAMP 41 [1]	**67**	2
21 Jan 89	**HIP HOUSE / I CAN DANCE** DJ International DJIN 5	**47**	4
11 Mar 89	**YO YO GET FUNKY** DJ International DJIN 7	**54**	3
28 Oct 89	**GIT ON UP** DJ International 655366 7 [2]	**49**	4

[1] Kenny 'Jammin'' Jason and 'Fast' Eddie Smith [2] DJ 'Fast' Eddie featuring Sundance

DJ HYPE
UK, male producer   **1 wk**

20 Mar 93	**SHOT IN THE DARK** Suburban Base SUBBASE 20CD	**63**	1

See also Various Artists (EPs & LPs) – Subplates Volume 1

DJ JAZZY JEFF and the FRESH PRINCE – See JAZZY JEFF and the FRESH PRINCE

DJ KRUSH
Japan, male producer   **2 wks**

16 Mar 96	**MEISO** Mo Wax MW 042CD	**52**	1
12 Oct 96	**ONLY THE STRONG SURVIVE** Mo Wax MW 060CD	**71**	1

DJ MIKO
Italy, male producer   **10 wks**

13 Aug 94	● **WHAT'S UP** Systematic SYSCD 2	**6**	10

DJ MISJAH and DJ TIM
Holland, male instrumental / production duo   **3 wks**

23 Mar 96	**ACCESS** Ffrreedom TABCD 240	**16**	3

DJ POWER
Italy, male producer – Steve Gambaroli   **2 wks**

7 Mar 92	**EVERYBODY PUMP** Cooltempo COOL 252	**46**	2

DJ PROFESSOR
Italy, male producer   **5 wks**

10 Aug 91	**WE GOTTA DO IT** Fourth & Broadway BRW 225 [1]	**57**	2
28 Mar 92	**ROCK ME STEADY** PWL Continental PWL 219	**49**	2
8 Oct 94	**ROCKIN' ME** Citra CITRA 1CD [2]	**56**	1

[1] DJ Professor featuring Francesco Zappala [2] Professor

DJ SCOTT featuring Lorna B
UK, male / female vocal / instrumental duo   **5 wks**

28 Jan 95	**DO YOU WANNA PARTY** Steppin' Out SPONCD 2	**36**	3
1 Apr 95	**SWEET DREAMS** Steppin' Out SPONCD 3	**37**	2

DJ Doc SCOTT
UK, male producer   **2 wks**

1 Feb 92	**NHS EP** Absolute 2 ABS 001DJ	**64**	2

Tracks on NHS EP: Surgery / Night Nurse.

DJ SEDUCTION
UK, male producer – John Kallum   **8 wks**

22 Feb 92	**HARDCORE HEAVEN / YOU AND ME** Ffrreedom TAB 103	**26**	5
11 Jul 92	**COME ON** Ffrreedom TAB 111	**37**	3

DJ SHADOW
UK, male producer   **3 wks**

25 Mar 95	**WHAT DOES YOUR SOUL LOOK LIKE** Mo Wax MW 027CD	**59**	1
14 Sep 96	**MIDNIGHT IN A PERFECT WORLD** Mo Wax MW 057CD	**54**	1
9 Nov 96	**STEM** Mo Wax MW 058CD	**74**	1

DJ SUPREME
UK, male producer – Nick Destri   **2 wks**

5 Oct 96	**THA WILDSTYLE** Distinctive DISNCD 19	**39**	2

DJ TIM – See DJ MISJAH and DJ TIM

DJAIMIN Switzerland, male producer — **2 wks**

19 Sep 92	**GIVE YOU** Cooltempo COOL 262	**45**	2

DJH featuring STEFY
Italy, male instrumental / production group — **14 wks**

16 Feb 91	**THINK ABOUT...** RCA PB 44385	**22**	6
13 Jul 91	**I LIKE IT** RCA PB 44741	**16**	7
19 Oct 91	**MOVE YOUR LOVE** RCA PB 44965	**73**	1

DJPC Belgium, male producer — **5 wks**

26 Oct 91	**INSSOMNIAK** Hype 7PUM 005	**62**	4
29 Feb 92	**INSSOMNIAK (re-issue)** Hype PUMR 005	**64**	1

DJs RULE Canada, male instrumental / production duo — **1 wk**

2 Mar 96	**GET INTO THE MUSIC** Distinctive DISNCD 9	**72**	1

DJUM DJUM – See LEFTFIELD

Boris DLUGOSCH presents BOOOM
Germany / US, male / female instrumental / vocal duo — **2 wks**

7 Dec 96	**KEEP PUSHIN'** Manifesto FESCD 17	**41**	2

DNA UK, male production duo — **29 wks**

28 Jul 90	● **TOM'S DINER** A & M AM 592 [1]	**2**	10
18 Aug 90	**LA SERENISSIMA** Raw Bass RBASS 006	**34**	8
3 Aug 91	**REBEL WOMAN** DNA 7DNA 001 [2]	**42**	4
1 Feb 92	**CAN YOU HANDLE IT** EMI EM 219 [3]	**17**	5
9 May 92	**BLUE LOVE (CALL MY NAME)** EMI EM 226 [4]	**66**	2

[1] DNA featuring Suzanne Vega [2] DNA, rap performed by Jazzi P.
[3] DNA featuring Sharon Redd [4] DNA featuring Joe Nye

Carl DOBKINS Jr. US, male vocalist — **1 wk**

31 Mar 60	**LUCKY DEVIL** Brunswick 05817	**44**	1

Anita DOBSON UK, female vocalist — **13 wks**

9 Aug 86	● **ANYONE CAN FALL IN LOVE** BBC RESL 191 [1]	**4**	9
18 Jul 87	**TALKING OF LOVE** Parlophone R 6159	**43**	4

[1] Anita Dobson featuring the Simon May Orchestra

DOCTOR and the MEDICS
UK, male / female vocal / instrumental group — **25 wks**

10 May 86	★ **SPIRIT IN THE SKY** IRS IRM 113	**1**	15
9 Aug 86	**BURN** IRS IRM 119	**29**	6
22 Nov 86	**WATERLOO** IRS IRM 125 [1]	**45**	4

[1] Doctor and the Medics featuring Roy Wood

DR. ALBAN Nigeria, male producer — **28 wks**

5 Sep 92	● **IT'S MY LIFE** Logic 7432115330	**2**	12
14 Nov 92	**ONE LOVE** Logic 74321108727	**45**	2
10 Apr 93	**SING HALLELUJAH!** Logic 74321136202	**16**	8
26 Mar 94	**LOOK WHO'S TALKING** Logic 74321195342	**55**	3
13 Aug 94	**AWAY FROM HOME** Logic 74321222682	**42**	2
29 Apr 95	**SWEET DREAMS** Logic 74321251552 [1]	**59**	1

[1] Swing featuring Dr. Alban

DR. DRE US, male rapper — **26 wks**

22 Jan 94	**NUTHIN' BUT A 'G' THANG / LET ME RIDE** Death Row A 8328CD	**31**	3
3 Sep 94	**DRE DAY** Death Row A 8292CD	**59**	2
15 Apr 95	**NATURAL BORN KILLAZ** Death Row A 8197CD [1]	**45**	2
10 Jun 95	**KEEP THEIR HEADS RINGIN'** Priority PTYCD 103	**25**	4
13 Apr 96	● **CALIFORNIA LOVE** Death Row DRWCD 3 [2]	**6**	8
19 Oct 96	● **NO DIGGITY** Interscope IND 95003 [3]	**9**	7

[1] Dr. Dre and Ice Cube [2] 2Pac featuring Dr. Dre [3] Blackstreet featuring Dr. Dre

DR. FEELGOOD UK, male vocal / instrumental group — **29 wks**

11 Jun 77	**SNEAKIN' SUSPICION** United Artists UP 36255	**47**	3
24 Sep 77	**SHE'S A WIND UP** United Artists UP 36304	**34**	5
30 Sep 78	**DOWN AT THE DOCTOR'S** United Artists UP 36444	**48**	5
20 Jan 79	● **MILK AND ALCOHOL** United Artists UP 36468	**9**	9
5 May 79	**AS LONG AS THE PRICE IS RIGHT** United Artists YUP 36506	**40**	6
8 Dec 79	**PUT HIM OUT OF YOUR MIND** United Artists BP 306	**73**	1

DR. HOOK US, male vocal / instrumental group — **104 wks**

24 Jun 72	● **SYLVIA'S MOTHER** CBS 7929 [1]	**2**	13
26 Jun 76	● **A LITTLE BIT MORE** Capitol CL 15871	**2**	14
30 Oct 76	● **IF NOT YOU** Capitol CL 15885	**5**	10
25 Mar 78	**MORE LIKE THE MOVIES** Capitol CL 15967	**14**	10
22 Sep 79	★ **WHEN YOU'RE IN LOVE WITH A BEAUTIFUL WOMAN** Capitol CL 16039	**1**	17
5 Jan 80	● **BETTER LOVE NEXT TIME** Capitol CL 16112	**8**	8
29 Mar 80	● **SEXY EYES** Capitol CL 16127	**4**	9
23 Aug 80	**YEARS FROM NOW** Capitol CL 16154	**47**	6
8 Nov 80	**SHARING THE NIGHT TOGETHER** Capitol CL 16171	**43**	4
22 Nov 80	**GIRLS CAN GET IT** Mercury MER 51	**40**	5
1 Feb 92	**WHEN YOU'RE IN LOVE WITH A BEAUTIFUL WOMAN (re-issue)** Capitol EMCT 4	**44**	4
6 Jun 92	**A LITTLE BIT MORE (re-issue)** EMI EMCT 6	**47**	4

[1] Dr. Hook and The Medicine Show

DR. OCTAGON US, male producer – Keith Thornton — **1 wk**

7 Sep 96	**BLUE FLOWERS** Mo Wax MW 055CD	**66**	1

DOCTOR SPIN UK, male instrumental / production duo — **8 wks**

3 Oct 92	● **TETRIS** Carpet CRPT 4	**6**	8

Ken DODD UK, male vocalist — **233 wks**

7 Jul 60	● **LOVE IS LIKE A VIOLIN** Decca F 11248	**8**	18
15 Jun 61	**ONCE IN EVERY LIFETIME** Decca F 11355	**28**	7
10 Aug 61	**ONCE IN EVERY LIFETIME (re-entry)** Decca F 11355	**47**	1
24 Aug 61	**ONCE IN EVERY LIFETIME (2nd re-entry)** Decca F 11355	**31**	10
1 Feb 62	**PIANISSIMO** Decca F 11422	**21**	15
29 Aug 63	**STILL** Columbia DB 7094	**35**	10
6 Feb 64	**EIGHT BY TEN** Columbia DB 7191	**22**	11
23 Jul 64	**HAPPINESS** Columbia DB 7325	**31**	13
26 Nov 64	**SO DEEP IS THE NIGHT** Columbia DB 7398	**31**	7
2 Sep 65	★ **TEARS** Columbia DB 7659	**1**	24
18 Nov 65	● **THE RIVER (LE COLLINE SONO IN FIORO)** Columbia DB 7750	**3**	14
12 May 66	● **PROMISES** Columbia DB 7914	**6**	14
4 Aug 66	**MORE THAN LOVE** Columbia DB 7976	**14**	11
27 Oct 66	**IT'S LOVE** Columbia DB 8031	**36**	7

19 Jan 67	**LET ME CRY ON YOUR SHOULDER**	
	Columbia DB 8101	**11** 10
30 Jul 69	**TEARS WON'T WASH AWAY THESE HEARTACHES**	
	Columbia DB 8600	**22** 11
5 Dec 70	**BROKEN HEARTED** Columbia DB 8725	**15** 9
13 Feb 71	**BROKEN HEARTED (re-entry)** Columbia DB 8725	**38** 1
10 Jul 71	**WHEN LOVE COMES ROUND AGAIN (L'ARCA DI NOE)** Columbia DB 8796	**19** 16
18 Nov 72	**JUST OUT OF REACH (OF MY TWO EMPTY ARMS)** Columbia DB 8947	**29** 11
29 Nov 75	**(THINK OF ME) WHEREVER YOU ARE** EMI 2342	**21** 8
26 Dec 81	**HOLD MY HAND** Images IMGS 0002	**44** 5

Rory DODD – See Jim STEINMAN

DODGY UK, male vocal / instrumental group   36 wks

8 May 93	**LOVEBIRDS** A & M AMCD 0177	**65** 2
3 Jul 93	**I NEED ANOTHER (EP)** A & M 5803172	**67** 2
6 Aug 94	**THE MELOD-EP** Bostin 5806772	**53** 1
1 Oct 94	**STAYING OUT FOR THE SUMMER** Bostin 5807972	**38** 2
7 Jan 95	**SO LET ME GO FAR** Bostin 5809032	**30** 3
11 Mar 95	**MAKING THE MOST OF** Bostin 5809892 [1]	**22** 3
10 Jun 95	**STAYING OUT FOR THE SUMMER (re-mix)** Bostin 5810952	**19** 5
8 Jun 96	**IN A ROOM** A & M 5816252	**12** 6
10 Aug 96	● **GOOD ENOUGH** A & M 5818152	**4** 4
16 Nov 96	**IF YOU'RE THINKING OF ME** A & M 5819992	**11** 4

[1] Dodgy with the Kick Horns

Tracks on I Need Another (EP): *I Need Another / If I Fall / Hendre DDU.* Tracks on The Melod-EP: *Melodies Haunt You / The Snake / Don't Go / Summer Fayre.*

DOG EAT DOG US, male vocal / instrumental group   7 wks

19 Aug 95	**NO FRONTS** Roadrunner RR 23312	**64** 1
3 Feb 96	● **NO FRONTS (re-entry)** Roadrunner RR 23312	**9** 5
13 Jul 96	**ISMS** Roadrunner RR 23083	**43** 1

Tim DOG US, male rapper   3 wks

29 Oct 94	**BITCH WITH A PERM** Dis-stress DISCD 1	**49** 1
11 Feb 95	**MAKE WAY FOR THE INDIAN** Island CID 586 [1]	**29** 2

[1] Apache Indian and Tim Dog

Nate DOGG – See Warren G

DOGS D'AMOUR UK, male vocal / instrumental group   15 wks

4 Feb 89	**HOW COME IT NEVER RAINS** China CHINA 13	**44** 3
5 Aug 89	**SATELLITE KID** China CHINA 17	**26** 3
14 Oct 89	**TRAIL OF TEARS** China CHINA 20	**47** 3
23 Jun 90	**VICTIMS OF SUCCESS** China CHINA 24	**36** 3
15 Sep 90	**EMPTY WORLD** China CHINA 27	**61** 2
19 Jun 93	**ALL OR NOTHING** China WOKCD 2033	**53** 1

Ken DOH UK, male producer – Michael Devlin   7 wks

30 Mar 96	● **I NEED A LOVER TONIGHT** ffrr FCD 272	**7** 7

Joe DOLAN Ireland, male vocalist   40 wks

25 Jun 69	● **MAKE ME AN ISLAND** Pye 7N 17738	**3** 18
1 Nov 69	**TERESA** Pye 7N 17833	**20** 7
8 Nov 69	**MAKE ME AN ISLAND (re-entry)** Pye 7N 17738	**48** 1
28 Feb 70	**YOU'RE SUCH A GOOD LOOKING WOMAN** Pye 7N 17891	**17** 13
17 Sep 77	**I NEED YOU** Pye 7N 45702	**43** 1

Thomas DOLBY UK, male vocalist/multi-instrumentalist   51 wks

3 Oct 81	**EUROPA AND THE PIRATE TWINS** Parlophone R 6051	**48** 3
14 Aug 82	**WINDPOWER** Venice In Peril VIPS 103	**31** 8
6 Nov 82	**SHE BLINDED ME WITH SCIENCE** Venice In Peril VIPS 104	**49** 4
16 Jul 83	**SHE BLINDED ME WITH SCIENCE (re-issue)** Venice In Peril VIP 105	**56** 4
21 Jan 84	**HYPERACTIVE!** Parlophone Odeon R 6065	**17** 9
31 Mar 84	**I SCARE MYSELF** Parlophone Odeon R 6067	**46** 5
16 Apr 88	**AIRHEAD** Manhattan MT 38	**53** 3
9 May 92	**CLOSE BUT NO CIGAR** Virgin VS 1410	**22** 5
11 Jul 92	**I LOVE YOU GOODBYE** Virgin VS 1417	**36** 4
26 Sep 92	**SILK PYJAMAS** Virgin VS 1430	**62** 2
22 Jan 94	**HYPERACTIVE! (re-mix)** Parlophone CDEMCTS 10	**23** 4

Joe DOLCE MUSIC THEATRE US, male vocalist   10 wks

7 Feb 81	★ **SHADDAP YOU FACE** Epic EPC 9518	**1** 10

DOLL UK, male / female vocal / instrumental group   8 wks

13 Jan 79	**DESIRE ME** Beggars Banquet BEG 11	**28** 8

DOLLAR UK, male / female vocal duo   128 wks

11 Nov 78	**SHOOTING STAR** Carrere 2871	**14** 12
19 May 79	**WHO WERE YOU WITH IN THE MOONLIGHT** Carrere CAR 110	**14** 12
18 Aug 79	● **LOVE'S GOTTA HOLD ON ME** Carrere CAR 122	**4** 13
24 Nov 79	**I WANNA HOLD YOUR HAND** Carrere CAR 131	**9** 14
25 Oct 80	**TAKIN' A CHANCE ON YOU** WEA K 18353	**62** 3
15 Aug 81	**HAND HELD IN BLACK AND WHITE** WEA BUCK 1	**19** 12
14 Nov 81	● **MIRROR MIRROR (MON AMOUR)** WEA BUCK 2	**4** 17
20 Mar 82	**RING RING** Carrere CAR 225	**61** 2
27 Mar 82	● **GIVE ME BACK MY HEART** WEA BUCK 3	**4** 9
19 Jun 82	**VIDEOTHEQUE** WEA BUCK 4	**17** 10
18 Sep 82	**GIVE ME SOME KINDA MAGIC** WEA BUCK 5	**34** 6
16 Aug 86	**WE WALKED IN LOVE** Arista DIME 1	**61** 4
26 Dec 87	● **O L'AMOUR** London LON 146	**7** 11
16 Jul 88	**IT'S NATURE'S WAY (NO PROBLEM)** London LON 179	**58** 3

Placido DOMINGO Spain, male vocalist   24 wks

12 Dec 81	**PERHAPS LOVE** CBS A 1905 [1]	**46** 9
27 May 89	**TILL I LOVED YOU** CBS 654843 7 [2]	**24** 9
16 Jun 90	**NESSUN DORMA FROM 'TURANDOT'** Epic 656005 7 [3]	**59** 2
30 Jul 94	**LIBIAMO / LA DONNA E MOBILE** Teldec YZ 843CD [4]	**21** 4

[1] Placido Domingo with John Denver [2] Placido Domingo and Jennifer Rush [3] Luis Cobos featuring Placido Domingo [4] José Carreras, Placido Domingo and Luciano Pavarotti

---

DOMINO US, male vocal / instrumental group   6 wks

22 Jan 94	**GETTO JAM** Chaos 6600402	**33** 4
14 May 94	**SWEET POTATO PIE** Chaos 6603292	**42** 2

Fats DOMINO
US, male vocalist/instrumentalist – piano   109 wks

27 Jul 56	**I'M IN LOVE AGAIN** London HLU 8280	**28** 1
17 Aug 56	**I'M IN LOVE AGAIN (re-entry)** London HLU 8280	**12** 13
30 Nov 56	**BLUEBERRY HILL** London HLU 8330	**26** 1
21 Dec 56	● **BLUEBERRY HILL (re-entry)** London HLU 8330	**6** 14
25 Jan 57	**AIN'T THAT A SHAME** London HLU 8173	**23** 2

Doors

The Doors were inducted into the Rock And Roll Hall of Fame in 1993, two years after the release of the biopic starring Val Kilmer as Jim Morrison.

Donovan

There was a gap of nearly 22 years between 'Goo Goo Barabajagal', Donovan's duet with Jeff Beck, and his next chart entry Jennifer Juniper with the Singing Corner, aka Trevor and Simon from BBC TV's *Going Live*.

Dodgy

Lead singer Nigel Clark (pictured far right) headed a band called Three Cheers For Tokyo before he met drummer Matthew Priest (far left) and formed Dodgy in 1988.

Dollar

Thereze Bazar and David Van Day were a breakaway duo from Guys and Dolls. Van Day additionally scored a minor hit in 1983 with 'Young Americans Talking'.

1 Feb 57		HONEY CHILE London HLU 8356	29	1
29 Mar 57		BLUE MONDAY London HLP 8377	23	1
19 Apr 57		BLUE MONDAY (re-entry) London HLP 8377	30	1
19 Apr 57		I'M WALKIN' London HLP 8407	19	7
19 Jul 57		VALLEY OF TEARS London HLP 8449	25	1
28 Mar 58		THE BIG BEAT London HLP 8575	20	4
4 Jul 58		SICK AND TIRED London HLP 8628	26	1
22 May 59		MARGIE London HLP 8865	18	5
16 Oct 59		I WANT TO WALK YOU HOME London HLP 8942	14	5
18 Dec 59		BE MY GUEST London HLP 9005	11	8
19 Feb 60		BE MY GUEST (re-entry) London HLP 9005	19	3
17 Mar 60		COUNTRY BOY London HLP 9073	19	11
21 Jul 60		WALKING TO NEW ORLEANS London HLP 9163	19	10
10 Nov 60		THREE NIGHTS A WEEK London HLP 9198	45	2
5 Jan 61		MY GIRL JOSEPHINE London HLP 9244	32	4
27 Jul 61		IT KEEPS RAININ' London HLP 9374	49	1
30 Nov 61		WHAT A PARTY London HLP 9456	43	1
29 Mar 62		JAMBALAYA London HLP 9520	41	1
31 Oct 63		RED SAILS IN THE SUNSET HMV POP 1219	34	6
24 Apr 76		BLUEBERRY HILL (re-issue) United Artists UP 35797	41	5

DON PABLO'S ANIMALS
Italy, male instrumental group **10 wks**

| 19 May 90 | ● | VENUS Rumour RUMA 18 | 4 | 10 |

DON-E *UK, male vocalist* **7 wks**

| 9 May 92 | | LOVE MAKES THE WORLD GO ROUND Fourth & Broadway BRW 242 | 18 | 6 |
| 25 Jul 92 | | PEACE IN THE WORLD Fourth & Broadway BRW 256 | 41 | 1 |

Lonnie DONEGAN *UK, male vocalist* **321 wks**

6 Jan 56	●	ROCK ISLAND LINE Decca F 10647	8	13
13 Apr 56		ROCK ISLAND LINE (re-entry) Decca F 10647	16	3
20 Apr 56		STEWBALL Pye Nixa N 15036	27	1
27 Apr 56	●	LOST JOHN / STEWBALL Pye Nixa N 15036	2	17
11 May 56		ROCK ISLAND LINE (2nd re-entry) Decca F 10647	19	6
6 Jul 56		SKIFFLE SESSION EP Pye Nixa NJE 1017	20	2
7 Sep 56	●	BRING A LITTLE WATER SYLVIE / DEAD OR ALIVE Pye Nixa N 15071	7	12
21 Dec 56		LONNIE DONEGAN SHOWCASE LP Pye Nixa NPT 19012	26	3
11 Jan 57		BRING A LITTLE WATER SYLVIE / DEAD OR ALIVE (re-entry) Pye Nixa N 15071	30	1
18 Jan 57	●	DON'T YOU ROCK ME DADDY-O Pye Nixa N 15080	4	17
5 Apr 57	★	CUMBERLAND GAP Pye Nixa N 15087	1	12
7 Jun 57	★	GAMBLIN' MAN / PUTTING ON THE STYLE Pye Nixa N 15093	1	19
11 Oct 57	●	MY DIXIE DARLING Pye Nixa N 15108	10	15
20 Dec 57		JACK O' DIAMONDS Pye Nixa 7N 15116	14	7
11 Apr 58	●	GRAND COOLIE DAM Pye Nixa 7N 15129	6	15
11 Jul 58		SALLY DON'T YOU GRIEVE / BETTY BETTY BETTY Pye Nixa 7N 15148	11	7
26 Sep 58		LONESOME TRAVELLER Pye Nixa 7N 15158	28	1
14 Nov 58		LONNIE'S SKIFFLE PARTY Pye Nixa 7N 15165	23	5
21 Nov 58	●	TOM DOOLEY Pye Nixa 7N 15172	3	14
6 Feb 59	●	DOES YOUR CHEWING GUM LOSE ITS FLAVOUR Pye Nixa 7N 15181	3	12
8 May 59		FORT WORTH JAIL Pye Nixa 7N 15198	14	5
26 Jun 59	●	BATTLE OF NEW ORLEANS Pye Nixa 7N 15206	2	16
11 Sep 59		SAL'S GOT A SUGAR LIP Pye Nixa 7N 15223	13	4
4 Dec 59		SAN MIGUEL Pye Nixa 7N 15237	19	4
24 Mar 60	★	MY OLD MAN'S A DUSTMAN Pye Nixa 7N 15256	1	13
26 May 60	●	I WANNA GO HOME Pye Nixa 7N 15267	5	17
25 Aug 60	●	LORELEI Pye Nixa 7N 15275	10	8
24 Nov 60		LIVELY Pye Nixa 7N 15312	13	9
8 Dec 60		VIRGIN MARY Pye Nixa 7N 15315	27	5
11 May 61	●	HAVE A DRINK ON ME Pye Nixa 7N 15354	8	15
31 Aug 61	●	MICHAEL ROW THE BOAT / LUMBERED Pye Nixa 7N 15371	6	11

18 Jan 62		THE COMANCHEROS Pye 7N 15410	14	10
5 Apr 62	●	THE PARTY'S OVER Pye 7N 15424	9	12
16 Aug 62		PICK A BALE OF COTTON Pye 7N 15455	11	10

Stewball had one week on the chart by itself on 20 Apr 56. Lost John, the other side, replaced it on 27 Apr 56 but Stewball was given co-billing with Lost John for the weeks of 11, 18 and 25 May 56, peaking at position 7. Dead Or Alive was not listed with Bring A Little Water Sylvie for the week 7 Sep 56. Putting On The Style was not listed with Gamblin' Man for the weeks of 7 and 14 Jun 56. Tracks on Skiffle Session EP: Railroad Bill / Stockalee / Ballad of Jesse James / Ol' Riley. Tracks on Lonnie Donegan Showcase (LP): Wabash Cannonball / How Long / How Long Blues / Nobody's Child / I Shall Not Be Moved / I'm Alabammy Bound / I'm A Rambling Man / Wreck Of The Old '97 / Frankie And Johnny.

Ral DONNER *US, male vocalist* **10 wks**

| 21 Sep 61 | | YOU DON'T KNOW WHAT YOU'VE GOT (UNTIL YOU LOSE IT) Parlophone R 4820 | 25 | 10 |

DONOVAN *UK, male vocalist* **100 wks**

25 Mar 65	●	CATCH THE WIND Pye 7N 15801	4	13
3 Jun 65	●	COLOURS Pye 7N 15866	4	12
11 Nov 65		TURQUOISE Pye 7N 15984	30	6
8 Dec 66	●	SUNSHINE SUPERMAN Pye 7N 17241	2	11
9 Feb 67	●	MELLOW YELLOW Pye 7N 17267	8	8
25 Oct 67	●	THERE IS A MOUNTAIN Pye 7N 17403	8	11
21 Feb 68	●	JENNIFER JUNIPER Pye 7N 17457	5	11
29 May 68	●	HURDY GURDY MAN Pye 7N 17537	4	10
4 Dec 68		ATLANTIS Pye 7N 17660	23	8
9 Jul 69		GOO GOO BARABAJAGAL (LOVE IS HOT) Pye 7N 17778 [1]	12	9
1 Dec 90		JENNIFER JUNIPER Fontana SYP 1 [2]	68	1

[1] Donovan with the Jeff Beck Group [2] Singing Corner meets Donovan

Jason DONOVAN *Australia, male vocalist* **137 wks**

10 Sep 88	●	NOTHING CAN DIVIDE US PWL PWL 17	5	12
10 Dec 88	★	ESPECIALLY FOR YOU PWL PWL 24 [1]	1	14
4 Mar 89	★	TOO MANY BROKEN HEARTS PWL PWL 32	1	13
10 Jun 89	●	SEALED WITH A KISS PWL PWL 39	1	10
9 Sep 89	●	EVERY DAY (I LOVE YOU MORE) PWL PWL 43	2	9
9 Dec 89	●	WHEN YOU COME BACK TO ME PWL PWL 46	2	11
7 Apr 90	●	HANG ON TO YOUR LOVE PWL PWL 51	8	7
30 Jun 90		ANOTHER NIGHT PWL PWL 55	18	5
1 Sep 90		RHYTHM OF THE RAIN PWL PWL 60	9	6
27 Oct 90		I'M DOING FINE PWL PWL 69	22	6
18 May 91		RSVP PWL PWL 80	17	5
22 Jun 91	★	ANY DREAM WILL DO Really Useful RUR 7	1	12
24 Aug 91		HAPPY TOGETHER PWL PWL 203	10	6
7 Dec 91		JOSEPH MEGA REMIX Really Useful RUR 9 [2]	13	8
18 Jul 92		MISSION OF LOVE Polydor PO 222	26	4
28 Nov 92		AS TIME GOES BY Polydor PO 245	26	6
7 Aug 93		ALL AROUND THE WORLD Polydor PZCD 278	41	3

[1] Kylie Minogue and Jason Donovan [2] Jason Donovan and Original London Cast featuring Linzi Hately, David Easter and Johnny Amobi

DOOBIE BROTHERS
US, male vocal / instrumental group **45 wks**

9 Mar 74		LISTEN TO THE MUSIC Warner Bros. K 16208	29	7
7 Jun 75		TAKE ME IN YOUR ARMS (ROCK ME A LITTLE WHILE) Warner Bros. K 16559	29	5
17 Feb 79		WHAT A FOOL BELIEVES Warner Bros. K 17314	31	10
5 May 79		WHAT A FOOL BELIEVES (re-entry) Warner Bros. K 17314	72	1
14 Jul 79		MINUTE BY MINUTE Warner Bros. K 17411	47	4
24 Jan 87		WHAT A FOOL BELIEVES (re-issue) Warner Bros. W 8451 [1]	57	3
29 Jul 89		THE DOCTOR Capitol CL 536	73	2
27 Nov 93	●	LONG TRAIN RUNNIN' Warner Bros. W 0217CD	7	10

14 May 94	LISTEN TO THE MUSIC (re-mix)		
	Warner Bros. W 0228CD	37	3

[1] Doobie Brothers featuring Michael McDonald

DOOGIE – See BUG KANN and PLASTIC JAM featuring Patti LOW and DOOGIE

DOOLEYS *UK, male / female vocal / instrumental group*　**83 wks**

13 Aug 77	THINK I'M GONNA FALL IN LOVE WITH YOU		
	GTO GT 95	13	10
12 Nov 77	● LOVE OF MY LIFE GTO GT 110	9	11
13 May 78	DON'T TAKE IT LYIN' DOWN GTO GT 220	60	3
2 Sep 78	A ROSE HAS TO DIE GTO GT 229	11	11
10 Feb 79	HONEY I'M LOST GTO GT 242	24	9
16 Jun 79	● WANTED GTO GT 249	3	14
22 Sep 79	● THE CHOSEN FEW GTO GT 258	7	11
8 Mar 80	LOVE PATROL GTO GT 260	29	7
6 Sep 80	BODY LANGUAGE GTO GT 276	46	4
10 Oct 81	AND I WISH GTO GT 300	52	3

Val DOONICAN *Ireland, male vocalist*　**143 wks**

15 Oct 64	● WALK TALL Decca F 11982	3	21
21 Jan 65	● THE SPECIAL YEARS Decca F 12049	7	12
8 Apr 65	I'M GONNA GET THERE SOMEHOW Decca F 12118	25	5
22 Apr 65	THE SPECIAL YEARS (re-entry) Decca F 12049	49	1
17 Mar 66	● ELUSIVE BUTTERFLY Decca F 12358	5	12
3 Nov 66	● WHAT WOULD I BE Decca F 12505	2	17
23 Feb 67	MEMORIES ARE MADE OF THIS Decca F 12566	11	12
25 May 67	TWO STREETS Decca F 12608	39	4
18 Oct 67	● IF THE WHOLE WORLD STOPPED LOVING		
	Pye 7N 17396	3	19
21 Feb 68	YOU'RE THE ONLY ONE Pye 7N 17465	37	4
12 Jun 68	NOW Pye 7N 17534	43	2
23 Oct 68	IF I KNEW THEN WHAT I KNOW NOW Pye 7N 17616	14	13
23 Apr 69	RING OF BRIGHT WATER Pye 7N 17713	48	1
4 Dec 71	MORNING Philips 6006 177	12	13
10 Mar 73	HEAVEN IS MY WOMAN'S LOVE Philips 6028 031	34	6
28 Apr 73	HEAVEN IS MY WOMAN'S LOVE (re-entry)		
	Philips 6028 031	47	1

DOOP *Holland, male instrumental duo*　**12 wks**

12 Mar 94	★ DOOP Citybeat CBE 774CD	1	12

DOORS *US, male vocal / instrumental group*　**42 wks**

16 Aug 67	LIGHT MY FIRE Elektra EKSN 45014	49	1
28 Aug 68	HELLO I LOVE YOU Elektra EKSN 45037	15	12
16 Oct 71	RIDERS ON THE STORM Elektra K 12021	50	1
30 Oct 71	RIDERS ON THE STORM (re-entry) Elektra K 12021	22	10
20 Mar 76	RIDERS ON THE STORM (re-issue) Elektra K 12203	33	5
3 Feb 79	HELLO I LOVE YOU (re-issue) Elektra K 12215	71	2
27 Apr 91	BREAK ON THROUGH Elektra EKR 121	64	2
1 Jun 91	● LIGHT MY FIRE (re-issue) Elektra EKR 125	7	8
10 Aug 91	RIDERS ON THE STORM (re-issue) Elektra EKR 131	68	1

D.O.P. *UK, male instrumental / production duo*　**2 wks**

3 Feb 96	STOP STARTING TO START STOPPING EP		
	Hi-Life 5779472	58	1
13 Jul 96	GROOVY BEAT Hi-Life 5750652	54	1

Tracks on Stop Starting To Stop Stopping EP: Gusta / Dance To The House / Can You Feel It / How Do Y'All Feel.

Charlie DORE *UK, female vocalist*　**2 wks**

17 Nov 79	PILOT OF THE AIRWAVES Island WIP 6526	66	2

DOROTHY *UK, male instrumental duo*　**5 wks**

9 Dec 95	WHAT'S THAT TUNE (DOO DOO DOO DOO DOO-		
	DOO-DOO-DOO-DOO-DOO) RCA 74321330912	31	5

Lee DORSEY *US, male vocalist*　**36 wks**

3 Feb 66	GET OUT OF MY LIFE WOMAN Stateside SS 485	22	7
5 May 66	CONFUSION Stateside SS 506	38	6
11 Aug 66	● WORKING IN THE COALMINE Stateside SS 528	8	11
27 Oct 66	● HOLY COW Stateside SS 552	6	12

Tommy DORSEY ORCHESTRA starring Warren COVINGTON *US, orchestra;*
Warren Covington, male instrumentalist – trombone　**19 wks**

17 Oct 58	● TEA FOR TWO CHA CHA Brunswick 05757	3	19

D.O.S.E. – See Mark E SMITH

DOUBLE *Switzerland, male vocal / instrumental duo*　**10 wks**

25 Jan 86	● THE CAPTAIN OF HER HEART Polydor POSP 779	8	9
5 Dec 87	DEVIL'S BALL Polydor POSP 888	71	1

DOUBLE DEE featuring DANY
Italy, male vocal / instrumental duo　**4 wks**

1 Dec 90	FOUND LOVE Epic 6563766	63	2
25 Nov 95	FOUND LOVE (re-mix) Sony S3 DANUCD 1	33	2

DOUBLE TROUBLE
UK, male instrumental / production duo　**35 wks**

27 May 89	JUST KEEP ROCKIN' Desire WANT 9 [1]	11	12
7 Oct 89	● STREET TUFF Desire WANT 18 [1]	3	14
12 May 90	TALK BACK Desire WANT 27 [2]	71	1
30 Jun 90	LOVE DON'T LIVE HERE ANYMORE		
	Desire WANT 32 [3]	21	6
15 Jun 91	RUB-A-DUB Desire WANT 41	66	2

[1] Double Trouble and the Rebel MC [2] Double Trouble featuring Janette Sewell [3] Double Trouble featuring Janette Sewell and Carl Brown

DOUBLE YOU? *Italy, male vocalist – Willie Morales*　**3 wks**

2 May 92	PLEASE DON'T GO ZYX ZYX 67487	41	3

Carl DOUGLAS *Jamaica, male vocalist*　**28 wks**

17 Aug 74	★ KUNG FU FIGHTING Pye 7N 45377	1	13
30 Nov 74	DANCE THE KUNG FU Pye 7N 45418	35	5
3 Dec 77	RUN BACK Pye 7N 46018	25	10

Carol DOUGLAS *US, female vocalist*　**4 wks**

22 Jul 78	NIGHT FEVER Gull GULS 61	66	4

Craig DOUGLAS *UK, male vocalist*　**112 wks**

12 Jun 59	A TEENAGER IN LOVE Top Rank JAR 133	13	11
7 Aug 59	★ ONLY SIXTEEN Top Rank JAR 159	1	15
22 Jan 60	● PRETTY BLUE EYES Top Rank JAR 268	4	14
28 Apr 60	● THE HEART OF A TEENAGE GIRL Top Rank JAR 340	10	9
11 Aug 60	OH! WHAT A DAY Top Rank JAR 406	43	1
20 Apr 61	● A HUNDRED POUNDS OF CLAY Top Rank JAR 555	9	9

29 Jun 61	● **TIME** *Top Rank JAR 569*..	**9**	14
22 Mar 62	● **WHEN MY LITTLE GIRL IS SMILING** *Top Rank JAR 610*	**9**	13
28 Jun 62	● **OUR FAVOURITE MELODIES** *Columbia DB 4854*	**9**	10
18 Oct 62	**OH LONESOME ME** *Decca F 11523*	**15**	12
28 Feb 63	**TOWN CRIER** *Decca F 11575*	**36**	4

DOWLANDS *UK, male vocal duo*   **7 wks**

9 Jan 64	**ALL MY LOVING** *Oriole CB 1897*....................................	**33**	7

Robert DOWNEY Jr. *US, male vocalist*   **1 wk**

30 Jan 93	**SMILE** *Epic 6589052*	**68**	1

Don DOWNING *US, male vocalist*   **10 wks**

10 Nov 73	**LONELY DAYS, LONELY NIGHTS** *People PEO 102*............	**32**	10

Will DOWNING *US, male vocalist*   **35 wks**

2 Apr 88	**A LOVE SUPREME** *Fourth & Broadway BRW 90*	**14**	10
25 Jun 88	**IN MY DREAMS** *Fourth & Broadway BRW 104*	**34**	6
1 Oct 88	**FREE** *Fourth & Broadway BRW 112*	**58**	5
21 Jan 89	**WHERE IS THE LOVE** *Fourth & Broadway BRW 122* [1]	**19**	7
28 Oct 89	**TEST OF TIME** *Fourth & Broadway BRW 146*	**67**	2
24 Feb 90	**COME TOGETHER AS ONE** *Fourth & Broadway BRW 159*	**48**	4
18 Sep 93	**THERE'S NO LIVING WITHOUT YOU** *Fourth & Broadway BRCD 278*	**67**	1

[1] Mica Paris and Will Downing

Lamont DOZIER – See HOLLAND-DOZIER featuring Lamont DOZIER

Charlie DRAKE *UK, male vocalist*   **37 wks**

8 Aug 58	● **SPLISH SPLASH** *Parlophone R 4461*	**7**	11
24 Oct 58	**VOLARE** *Parlophone R 4478*	**28**	2
27 Oct 60	**MR. CUSTER** *Parlophone R 4701*	**12**	12
5 Oct 61	**MY BOOMERANG WON'T COME BACK** *Parlophone R 4824*	**14**	11
1 Jan 72	**PUCKWUDGIE** *Columbia DB 8829*	**47**	1

DRAMATIS *UK, male vocal / instrumental group*   **8 wks**

5 Dec 81	**LOVE NEEDS NO DISGUISE** *Beggars Banquet BEG 68* [1]	**33**	7
13 Nov 82	**I CAN SEE HER NOW** *Rocket XPRES 83*	**57**	1

[1] Gary Numan and Dramatis

Rusty DRAPER *US, male vocalist*   **4 wks**

11 Aug 60	**MULE SKINNER BLUES** *Mercury AMT 1101*	**39**	4

DREAD ZEPPELIN *US, male vocal / instrumental group*   **3 wks**

1 Dec 90	**YOUR TIME IS GONNA COME** *IRS DREAD 1*	**59**	1
13 Jul 91	**STAIRWAY TO HEAVEN** *IRS DREAD 2*	**62**	2

DREADZONE *UK, male instrumental group*   **13 wks**

6 May 95	**ZION YOUTH** *Virgin VSCDG 1537*	**49**	2
29 Jul 95	**CAPTAIN DREAD** *Virgin VSCDG 1541*	**49**	2
23 Sep 95	**MAXIMUM (EP)** *Virgin VSCDT 1555*	**56**	2
6 Jan 96	**LITTLE BRITAIN** *Virgin VSCDG 1565*	**20**	6

30 Mar 96	**LIFE LOVE AND UNITY** *Virgin VSCDT 1583*	**56**	1

Tracks on Maximum (EP): Maximum / Fight The Power 95 / One Way.

DREAM ACADEMY
UK, male / female vocal / instrumental group   **10 wks**

30 Mar 85	**LIFE IN A NORTHERN TOWN** *Blanco Y Negro NEG 10*	**15**	8
14 Sep 85	**THE LOVE PARADE** *Blanco Y Negro NEG 16*	**68**	2

DREAM FREQUENCY *UK, male producer – Ian Bland*   **12 wks**

12 Jan 91	**LOVE PEACE AND HARMONY** *Citybeat CBE 756*	**71**	2
25 Jan 92	**FEEL SO REAL** *Citybeat CBE 763* [1]	**23**	5
25 Apr 92	**TAKE ME** *Citybeat CBE 768*	**39**	3
21 May 94	**GOOD TIMES / THE DREAM** *Citybeat CBE 773CD*	**67**	1
10 Sep 94	**YOU MAKE ME FEEL MIGHTY REAL** *Citybeat CBE 775CD*	**65**	1

[1] Dream Frequency featuring Debbie Sharp

DREAM WARRIORS *Canada, male rap group*   **19 wks**

14 Jul 90	**WASH YOUR FACE IN MY SINK** *Fourth & Broadway BRW 183*	**16**	8
24 Nov 90	**MY DEFINITION OF A BOOMBASTIC JAZZ STYLE** *Fourth & Broadway BRW 197*	**13**	8
25 Apr 92	**LUDI** *Fourth & Broadway BRW 206*	**39**	3

DREAMERS – See FREDDIE and the DREAMERS

DREAMHOUSE *UK, male vocal / instrumental group*   **2 wks**

3 Jun 95	**STAY** *Chase CDPALACE 1*..	**62**	2

DREAMWEAVERS *US, male / female vocal group*   **18 wks**

10 Feb 56	★ **IT'S ALMOST TOMORROW** *Brunswick 05515*	**1**	18

DRELLS – See Archie BELL and the DRELLS

Eddie DRENNON and B.B.S. UNLIMITED
US, male vocal / instrumental group   **6 wks**

28 Feb 76	**LET'S DO THE LATIN HUSTLE** *Pye International 7N 25702*................................	**20**	6

Alan DREW *UK, male vocalist*   **2 wks**

26 Sep 63	**ALWAYS THE LONELY ONE** *Columbia DB 7090*..............	**48**	2

DRIFTERS *US, male vocal group*   **176 wks**

8 Jan 60	**DANCE WITH ME** *London HLE 8988*	**17**	4
10 Mar 60	**DANCE WITH ME (re-entry)** *London HLE 8988*..............	**35**	1
3 Nov 60	● **SAVE THE LAST DANCE FOR ME** *London HLK 9201*	**2**	18
16 Mar 61	**I COUNT THE TEARS** *London HLK 9287*	**28**	6
5 Apr 62	**WHEN MY LITTLE GIRL IS SMILING** *London HLK 9522* ..	**31**	3
10 Oct 63	**I'LL TAKE YOU HOME** *London HLK 9785*	**37**	5
24 Sep 64	**UNDER THE BOARDWALK** *Atlantic AT 4001*	**45**	4
8 Apr 65	**AT THE CLUB** *Atlantic AT 4019*......................................	**35**	7
29 Apr 65	**COME ON OVER TO MY PLACE** *Atlantic AT 4023*..........	**40**	5
2 Feb 67	**BABY WHAT I MEAN** *Atlantic 584 065*............................	**49**	1
25 Mar 72	**AT THE CLUB (re-issue)** *Atlantic K 10148*	**39**	1
8 Apr 72	● **AT THE CLUB / SATURDAY NIGHT AT THE MOVIES** **(re-entry of re-issue)** *Atlantic K 10148*	**3**	19
26 Aug 72	● **COME ON OVER TO MY PLACE (re-issue)** *Atlantic K 10216*	**9**	11

4 Aug 73 ●	LIKE SISTER AND BROTHER *Bell 1313*	**7** 12
15 Jun 74 ●	KISSIN' IN THE BACK ROW OF THE MOVIES *Bell 1358*	**2** 13
12 Oct 74 ●	DOWN ON THE BEACH TONIGHT *Bell 1381*	**7** 9
8 Feb 75	LOVE GAMES *Bell 1396*	**33** 6
6 Sep 75 ●	THERE GOES MY FIRST LOVE *Bell 1433*	**3** 12
29 Nov 75 ●	CAN I TAKE YOU HOME LITTLE GIRL *Bell 1462*	**10** 10
13 Mar 76	HELLO HAPPINESS *Bell 1469*	**12** 8
11 Sep 76	EVERY NITE'S A SATURDAY NIGHT WITH YOU *Bell 1491*	**29** 7
18 Dec 76 ●	YOU'RE MORE THAN A NUMBER IN MY LITTLE RED BOOK *Arista 78*	**5** 12
14 Apr 79	SAVE THE LAST DANCE FOR ME / WHEN MY LITTLE GIRL IS SMILING (re-issue) *Lightning LIG 9014*	**69** 2

Saturday Night at the Movies only received chart credit with At The Club after the re-issue's return to the chart on 8 Apr 72.

Julie DRISCOLL, Brian AUGER and the TRINITY *UK, female vocalist / male instrumental group*   **16 wks**

17 Apr 68 ●	THIS WHEEL'S ON FIRE *Marmalade 598 006*	**5** 16

DRIVER 67 *UK, male vocalist – Paul Phillips*   **12 wks**

23 Dec 78 ●	CAR 67 *Logo GO 336*	**7** 12

DRIZABONE *UK, male instrumental / production duo*   **18 wks**

22 Jun 91	REAL LOVE *Fourth & Broadway BRW 223*	**16** 8
26 Oct 91	CATCH THE FIRE *Fourth & Broadway BRW 232*	**54** 2
23 Apr 94	PRESSURE *Fourth & Broadway BRCD 264*	**33** 2
4 Mar 95	REAL LOVE *Fourth & Broadway BRCD 311*	**24** 4
15 Oct 96	BRIGHTEST STAR *Fourth & Broadway BRCD 293*	**45** 2

Real Love in '95 is a re-recording.

Frank D'RONE *US, male vocalist*   **6 wks**

22 Dec 60	STRAWBERRY BLONDE *Mercury AMT 1123*	**24** 6

DRUGSTORE *UK / US / Brazil, male / female vocal / instrumental group*   **1 wk**

10 Jun 95	FADER *Honey HONCD 7*	**72** 1

DRUM CLUB *UK, male instrumental / production duo*   **1 wk**

6 Nov 93	SOUND SYSTEM *Butterfly BFLD 10*	**62** 1

DRUM THEATRE *UK, male vocal / instrumental group*   **8 wks**

15 Feb 86	LIVING IN THE PAST *Epic A 6798*	**67** 2
17 Jan 87	ELDORADO *Epic EMU 1*	**44** 6

DRUPI *Italy, male vocalist*   **12 wks**

1 Dec 73	VADO VIA *A & M AMS 7083*	**17** 12

DSK *UK, male instrumental / production group*   **3 wks**

31 Aug 91	WHAT WOULD WE DO / READ MY LIPS *Boy's Own BOI 6*	**46** 3

DSM *US, male rap group*   **4 wks**

7 Dec 85	WARRIOR GROOVE *10 DAZZ 45-7*	**68** 4

DTI *US, male vocal / instrumental group*   **1 wk**

16 Apr 88	KEEP THIS FREQUENCY CLEAR / KEEP IT CLEAR *Premiere UK ERE 501*	**73** 1

DTOX *UK, male / female vocal / instrumental group*   **1 wk**

21 Nov 92	SHATTERED GLASS *Vitality VITal 1*	**75** 1

John DU CANN *UK, male vocalist*   **6 wks**

22 Sep 79	DON'T BE A DUMMY *Vertigo 6059 241*	**33** 6

John DU PREZ – *See MODERN ROMANCE*

DUB WAR *UK, male vocal / instrumental group*   **4 wks**

3 Jun 95	STRIKE IT *Earache MOSH 138CD*	**70** 1
27 Jan 96	ENEMY MAKER *Earache MOSH 147CD*	**41** 2
24 Aug 96	CRY DIGNITY *Earache MOSH 163CDD*	**59** 1

DUBLINERS *Ireland, male vocal / instrumental group*   **45 wks**

30 Mar 67 ●	SEVEN DRUNKEN NIGHTS *Major Minor MM 506*	**7** 17
30 Aug 67	BLACK VELVET BAND *Major Minor MM 530*	**15** 15
20 Dec 67	MAIDS WHEN YOU'RE YOUNG NEVER WED AN OLD MAN *Major Minor MM 551*	**43** 3
28 Mar 87 ●	THE IRISH ROVER *Stiff BUY 258* [1]	**8** 8
16 Jun 90	JACK'S HEROES / WHISKEY IN THE JAR *Pogue Mahone YZ 500* [1]	**63** 2

[1] Pogues and the Dubliners

DUBSTAR *UK, male / female vocal / instrumental group*   **19 wks**

8 Jul 95	STARS *Food CDFOOD 61*	**40** 3
30 Sep 95	ANYWHERE *Food CDFOOD 67*	**37** 3
6 Jan 96	NOT SO MANIC NOW *Food CDFOODS 71*	**18** 5
30 Mar 96	STARS (re-issue) *Food CDFOODS 75*	**15** 6
3 Aug 96	ELEVATOR SONG *Food CDFOOD 80*	**25** 2

Mary DUFF – *See Daniel O'DONNELL*

DUFFO *Australia, male vocalist*   **2 wks**

24 Mar 79	GIVE ME BACK ME BRAIN *Beggars Banquet BEG 15*	**60** 2

Stephen 'Tin Tin' DUFFY *UK, male vocalist*   **24 wks**

9 Jul 83	HOLD IT *Curve X 9763* [1]	**55** 4
2 Mar 85 ●	KISS ME *10 TIN 2*	**4** 11
18 May 85	ICING ON THE CAKE *10 TIN 3*	**14** 9

[1] Tin Tin

DUKE *UK, male vocalist*   **5 wks**

25 May 96	SO IN LOVE WITH YOU *Encore CDCOR 009*	**66** 1
26 Oct 96	SO IN LOVE WITH YOU (re-issue) *Pukka CDPUKKA 11*	**22** 4

George DUKE *US, male vocalist / instrumentalist*   **6 wks**

12 Jul 80	BRAZILIAN LOVE AFFAIR *Epic EPC 8751*	**36** 6

Dubstar

Newcastle-based pop trio Dubstar are fronted by singer Sarah Blackwood.

Dreadzone

Greg Roberts (pictured left) and Leo Willitams, the rhythm section of Big Audio Dynamite, formed the basis of Dreadzone. They are predominantly an instrumental act but were joined by rapper Earl Sixteen for the radio version of 'Little Britain'.

Ian Dury And The Blockheads

Ian Dury's 'Profoundly In Love With Pandora' was the theme to the TV adaptation of Sue Townshend's novel, *The Secret Diary Of Adrian Mole, Aged 13³/₄*.

DUKE BAYSEE UK, male vocalist — 6 wks

3 Sep 94	SUGAR SUGAR Bell 74321228702	30	4
21 Jan 95	DO YOU LOVE ME Double Dekker CDDEK 1	46	2

DUKES UK, male vocal duo — 13 wks

17 Oct 81	MYSTERY GIRL WEA K 18867	47	7
1 May 82	THANK YOU FOR THE PARTY WEA K 19136	53	6

Candy DULFER
Holland, female instrumentalist – saxophone — 14 wks

24 Feb 90	● LILY WAS HERE RCA ZB 43045 [1]	6	12
4 Aug 90	SAXUALITY RCA PB 43769	60	2

[1] David A. Stewart featuring Candy Dulfer

Thuli DUMAKUDE South Africa, male vocalist — 1 wk

2 Jan 88	THE FUNERAL (SEPTEMBER 25, 1977) MCA MCA 1228	75	1

The listed flip side of The Funeral was Cry Freedom by George Fenton and Jonas Gwangwa.

John DUMMER and Helen APRIL
UK, male / female vocal duo — 3 wks

28 Aug 82	BLUE SKIES Speed SPEED 8	54	3

DUNBLANE UK, male / female vocal / instrumental group — 2 wks

21 Dec 96	★ KNOCKIN' ON HEAVEN'S DOOR – THROW THESE GUNS AWAY BMG 74321442182	1†	2

Johnny DUNCAN and the BLUE GRASS BOYS US, male vocal / instrumental group — 20 wks

26 Jul 57	● LAST TRAIN TO SAN FERNANDO Columbia DB 3959	2	17
25 Oct 57	BLUE BLUE HEARTACHES Columbia DB 3996	27	1
29 Nov 57	FOOTPRINTS IN THE SNOW Columbia DB 4029	27	1
3 Jan 58	FOOTPRINTS IN THE SNOW (re-entry) Columbia DB 4029	28	1

David DUNDAS UK, male vocalist — 14 wks

24 Jul 76	● JEANS ON Air CHS 2094	3	9
9 Apr 77	ANOTHER FUNNY HONEYMOON Air CHS 2136	29	5

Erroll DUNKLEY Jamaica, male vocalist — 14 wks

22 Sep 79	O.K. FRED Scope SC 6	11	11
2 Feb 80	SIT DOWN AND CRY Scope SC 11	52	3

Clive DUNN UK, male vocalist — 28 wks

28 Nov 70	★ GRANDAD Columbia DB 8726	1	27
26 Jun 71	GRANDAD (re-entry) Columbia D8 8726	50	1

Simon DUPREE and the BIG SOUND
UK, male vocal / instrumental group — 16 wks

22 Nov 67	● KITES Parlophone R 5646	9	13
3 Apr 68	FOR WHOM THE BELL TOLLS Parlophone R 5670	43	3

DURAN DURAN UK, male vocal / instrumental group — 216 wks

21 Feb 81	PLANET EARTH EMI 5137	12	11
9 May 81	CARELESS MEMORIES EMI 5168	37	7
25 Jul 81	● GIRLS ON FILM EMI 5206	5	11
28 Nov 81	MY OWN WAY EMI 5254	14	11
15 May 82	● HUNGRY LIKE THE WOLF EMI 5295	5	12
21 Aug 82	● SAVE A PRAYER EMI 5327	2	9
13 Nov 82	● RIO EMI 5346	9	11
26 Mar 83	★ IS THERE SOMETHING I SHOULD KNOW EMI 5371	1	9
29 Oct 83	● UNION OF THE SNAKE EMI 5429	3	7
24 Dec 83	UNION OF THE SNAKE (re-entry) EMI 5429	66	4
4 Feb 84	● NEW MOON ON MONDAY EMI DURAN 1	9	7
28 Apr 84	★ THE REFLEX EMI DURAN 2	1	14
3 Nov 84	● WILD BOYS Parlophone DURAN 3	2	14
18 May 85	● A VIEW TO A KILL Parlophone DURAN 007	2	16
1 Nov 86	● NOTORIOUS EMI DDN 45	7	6
3 Jan 87	NOTORIOUS (re-entry) EMI DDN 45	73	1
21 Feb 87	SKIN TRADE EMI TRADE 1	22	6
25 Apr 87	MEET EL PRESIDENTE EMI TOUR 1	24	5
1 Oct 88	I DON'T WANT YOUR LOVE EMI YOUR 1	14	5
7 Jan 89	● ALL SHE WANTS IS EMI DD 11	9	5
22 Apr 89	DO YOU BELIEVE IN SHAME EMI DD 12	30	4
16 Dec 89	BURNING THE GROUND EMI DD 13	31	5
4 Aug 90	VIOLENCE OF SUMMER (LOVE'S TAKING OVER) Parlophone DD 14	20	4
17 Nov 90	SERIOUS Parlophone DD 15	48	3
30 Jan 93	● ORDINARY WORLD Parlophone CDDDS 16	6	9
10 Apr 93	COME UNDONE Parlophone CDDDS 17	13	8
4 Sep 93	TOO MUCH INFORMATION Parlophone CDDDS 18	35	3
25 Mar 95	PERFECT DAY Parlophone CDDDS 20	28	4
17 Jun 95	WHITE LINES (DON'T DO IT) Parlophone CDDD 19	17	5

Group were UK / US from Burning The Ground.

Jimmy DURANTE US, male vocalist — 1 wk

14 Dec 96	MAKE SOMEONE HAPPY Warner Bros. W 0385CD	69	1

Judith DURHAM Australia, female vocalist — 5 wks

15 Jun 67	OLIVE TREE Columbia DB 8207	33	5

Ian DURY and the BLOCKHEADS
UK, male vocal / instrumental group — 55 wks

29 Apr 78	● WHAT A WASTE Stiff BUY 27	9	12
9 Dec 78	★ HIT ME WITH YOUR RHYTHM STICK Stiff BUY 38 [1]	1	15
4 Aug 79	● REASONS TO BE CHEERFUL (PT. 3) Stiff BUY 50	3	8
30 Aug 80	I WANT TO BE STRAIGHT Stiff BUY 90	22	7
15 Nov 80	SUEPERMAN'S BIG SISTER Stiff BUY 100	51	3
25 May 85	HIT ME WITH YOUR RHYTHM STICK (re-mix) Stiff BUY 214	55	4
26 Oct 85	PROFOUNDLY IN LOVE WITH PANDORA EMI EMI 5534 [2]	45	5
27 Jul 91	HIT ME WITH YOUR RHYTHM STICK (2nd re-mix) Flying FLYR 1	73	1

[1] Ian and the Blockheads [2] Ian Dury

Slim DUSTY Australia, male vocalist — 15 wks

30 Jan 59	● A PUB WITH NO BEER Columbia DB 4212	3	15

Ondrea DUVERN – See HUSTLERS CONVENTION featuring Dave LAUDAT and Ondrea DUVERN

Bob DYLAN US, male vocalist — 135 wks

25 Mar 65	● TIMES THEY ARE A-CHANGIN' CBS 201751	9	11
29 Apr 65	● SUBTERRANEAN HOMESICK BLUES CBS 201753	9	9

EARTH WIND AND FIRE
US, male vocal / instrumental group   **125 wks**

12 Feb 77		SATURDAY NITE *CBS 4835*	**17**	9
11 Feb 78		FANTASY *CBS 6056*	**14**	10
13 May 78		JUPITER *CBS 6267*	**41**	5
29 Jul 78		MAGIC MIND *CBS 6490*	**75**	1
12 Aug 78		MAGIC MIND (re-entry) *CBS 6490*	**54**	4
7 Oct 78		GOT TO GET YOU INTO MY LIFE *CBS 6553*	**33**	7
9 Dec 78	●	SEPTEMBER *CBS 6922*	**3**	13
12 May 79	●	BOOGIE WONDERLAND *CBS 7292* [1]	**4**	13
28 Jul 79	●	AFTER THE LOVE HAS GONE *CBS 7721*	**4**	10
6 Oct 79		STAR *CBS 7902*	**16**	8
15 Dec 79		CAN'T LET GO *CBS 8077*	**46**	4
8 Mar 80		IN THE STONE *CBS 8252*	**53**	3
11 Oct 80		LET ME TALK *CBS 8982*	**29**	5
20 Dec 80		BACK ON THE ROAD *CBS 9377*	**63**	4
7 Nov 81	●	LET'S GROOVE *CBS A 1679*	**3**	13
6 Feb 82		I'VE HAD ENOUGH *CBS A 1959*	**29**	6
5 Feb 83		FALL IN LOVE WITH ME *CBS A 2927*	**47**	4
7 Nov 87		SYSTEM OF SURVIVAL *CBS EWF 1*	**54**	3

[1] Earth Wind and Fire with the Emotions

EARTHLING
UK, male vocal / instrumental duo   **2 wks**

14 Oct 95	ECHO ON MY MIND PART II *Cooltempo CDCOOL 312*	**61**	1
1 Jun 96	BLOOD MUSIC EP *Cooltempo CDCOOL 319*	**69**	1

Tracks on Blood Music EP: First Transmission/Because The Night/Soup Or No Soup/Infinite M.

EAST OF EDEN
UK, male instrumental group   **12 wks**

17 Apr 71	●	JIG A JIG *Deram DM 297*	**7**	12

EAST 17
UK, male vocal group   **144 wks**

29 Aug 92	●	HOUSE OF LOVE *London LON 325*	**10**	9
14 Nov 92		GOLD *London LON 331*	**28**	4
19 Dec 92		GOLD (re-entry) *London LON 331*	**64**	4
30 Jan 93	●	DEEP *London LOCDP 334*	**5**	10
10 Apr 93		SLOW IT DOWN *London LONCD 339*	**13**	7
26 Jun 93		WEST END GIRLS *London LONCD 344*	**11**	7
4 Dec 93	●	IT'S ALRIGHT *London LONCD 345*	**3**	14
14 May 94	●	AROUND THE WORLD *London LONCD 349*	**3**	13
1 Oct 94	●	STEAM *London LONCD 353*	**7**	8
3 Dec 94	★	STAY ANOTHER DAY *London LONCD 354*	**1**	15
25 Mar 95	●	LET IT RAIN *London LONCD 363*	**10**	7
6 May 95		STAY ANOTHER DAY (re-entry) *London LONCD 354*	**64**	1
17 Jun 95		HOLD MY BODY TIGHT *London LONCD 367*	**12**	7
4 Nov 95	●	THUNDER *London LONCD 373*	**4**	14
10 Feb 96	●	DO U STILL *London LONCD 379*	**7**	7
10 Aug 96		SOMEONE TO LOVE *London LONCD 385*	**16**	8
2 Nov 96	●	IF YOU EVER *London LONCD 388* [1]	**2†**	9

[1] East 17 featuring Gabrielle

EAST SIDE BEAT
Italy, male vocal / instrumental duo   **18 wks**

30 Nov 91	●	RIDE LIKE THE WIND *ffrr F 176*	**3**	11
19 Dec 92		ALIVE AND KICKING *ffrr F 206*	**26**	6
29 May 93		YOU'RE MY EVERYTHING *ffrr FCD 207*	**65**	1

Sheena EASTON
UK, female vocalist   **103 wks**

5 Apr 80		MODERN GIRL *EMI 5042*	**56**	3
19 Jul 80	●	9 TO 5 *EMI 5066*	**3**	15
9 Aug 80	●	MODERN GIRL (re-entry) *EMI 5042*	**8**	12
25 Oct 80		ONE MAN WOMAN *EMI 5114*	**14**	6
14 Feb 81		TAKE MY TIME *EMI 5135*	**44**	5

2 May 81		WHEN HE SHINES *EMI 5166*	**12**	8
27 Jun 81	●	FOR YOUR EYES ONLY *EMI 5195*	**8**	13
12 Sep 81		JUST ANOTHER BROKEN HEART *EMI 5232*	**33**	8
5 Dec 81		YOU COULD HAVE BEEN WITH ME *EMI 5252*	**54**	3
31 Jul 82		MACHINERY *EMI 5326*	**38**	5
12 Feb 83		WE'VE GOT TONIGHT *Liberty UP 658* [1]	**28**	7
21 Jan 89		THE LOVER IN ME *MCA MCA 1289*	**15**	8
18 Mar 89		DAYS LIKE THIS *MCA MCA 1325*	**43**	3
15 Jul 89		101 *MCA MCA 1348*	**54**	2
18 Nov 89		THE ARMS OF ORION *Warner Bros. W 2757* [2]	**27**	5

[1] Kenny Rogers and Sheena Easton   [2] Prince with Sheena Easton

See also Prince.

EASTSIDE CONNECTION
US, disco aggregation   **3 wks**

8 Apr 78	YOU'RE SO RIGHT FOR ME *Creole CR 149*	**44**	3

Clint EASTWOOD
US, male vocalist   **2 wks**

7 Feb 70	I TALK TO THE TREES *Paramount PARA 3004*	**18**	2

This is the flip of Wand'rin' Star by Lee Marvin and was listed with Marvin's A-side for two weeks only.

Clint EASTWOOD – *See GENERAL SAINT*

EASYBEATS
Australia, male vocal / instrumental group   **24 wks**

27 Oct 66	●	FRIDAY ON MY MIND *United Artists UP 1157*	**6**	15
10 Apr 68		HELLO HOW ARE YOU *United Artists UP 2209*	**20**	9

EAT
UK / US, male / female vocal / instrumental group   **1 wk**

12 Jun 93	BLEED ME WHITE *Fiction FICCD 48*	**73**	1

Cleveland EATON
US, male instrumentalist – keyboards   **6 wks**

23 Sep 78	BAMA BOOGIE WOOGIE *Gull GULS 63*	**35**	6

EAV
Austria, male vocal / instrumental group   **4 wks**

27 Sep 86	BA-BA-BANKROBBERY (ENGLISH VERSION??) *Columbia DB 9139*	**63**	4

EAV is short for Erste Allgemeine Verunsicherung.

EAZY-E
US, male rapper   **3 wks**

6 Jan 96	JUST TAH LET YOU KNOW *Epic 6628162*	**30**	3

ECHO AND THE BUNNYMEN
UK, male vocal / instrumental group   **73 wks**

17 May 80		RESCUE *Korova KOW 1*	**62**	1
18 Apr 81		CROCODILES *Korova ECHO 1*	**37**	4
18 Jul 81		A PROMISE *Korova KOW 15*	**49**	4
29 May 82		THE BACK OF LOVE *Korova KOW 24*	**19**	7
22 Jan 83	●	THE CUTTER *Korova KOW 26*	**8**	8
16 Jul 83		NEVER STOP *Korova KOW 28*	**15**	7
28 Jan 84	●	THE KILLING MOON *Korova KOW 32*	**9**	6
21 Apr 84		SILVER *Korova KOW 34*	**30**	5
14 Jul 84		SEVEN SEAS *Korova KOW 35*	**16**	7
19 Oct 85		BRING ON THE DANCING HORSES *Korova KOW 43*	**21**	7
13 Jun 87		THE GAME *WEA YZ 134*	**28**	4
1 Aug 87		LIPS LIKE SUGAR *WEA YZ 144*	**36**	4

Enya

Enya's 'Orinoco Flow' was sampled for the dance hit 'We've Got To Live Together' by RAF. Similarly 'Boadicea' was plundered from her *Celts* album by the Fugees for their hit 'Ready Or Not'.

Earth Wind And Fire

This elemental troupe are synonymous with the disco heydays of the 70s, but they had their biggest hit with 'Let's Groove' in 1981.

East 17

East 17 were denied a second number one single with 'If You Ever' by the Spice Girls' 'Say You'll Be There'.

20 Feb 88	**PEOPLE ARE STRANGE** *WEA YZ 175*	**29**	5
2 Mar 91	**PEOPLE ARE STRANGE (re-issue)** *East West YZ 567*	**34**	4

ECHOBELLY
UK / Sweden, male / female vocal / instrumental group　　**13 wks**

2 Apr 94	**INSOMNIAC** *Fauve FAUV 1CD*	**47**	1
2 Jul 94	**I CAN'T IMAGINE THE WORLD WITHOUT ME** *Fauve FAUV 2CD*	**39**	2
5 Nov 94	**CLOSE... BUT** *Fauve FAUV 4CD*	**59**	1
2 Sep 95	**GREAT THINGS** *Fauve FAUV 5CD*	**13**	3
4 Nov 95	**KING OF THE KERB** *Fauve FAUV 7CD*	**25**	3
2 Mar 96	**DARK THERAPY** *Fauve FAUV 8CD*	**20**	3

Billy ECKSTINE *US, male vocalist*　　**48 wks**

12 Nov 54	● **NO ONE BUT YOU** *MGM 763*	**3**	17
27 Sep 57	**PASSING STRANGERS** *Mercury MT 164* [1]	**22**	2
13 Feb 59	● **GIGI** *Mercury AMT 1018*	**8**	14
12 Mar 69	**PASSING STRANGERS (re-issue)** *Mercury MF 1082* [1]	**20**	15

[1] Billy Eckstine and Sarah Vaughan

EDDIE and the HOTRODS
UK, male vocal / instrumental group　　**26 wks**

11 Sep 76	**LIVE AT THE MARQUEE EP** *Island IEP 2*	**43**	5
13 Nov 76	**TEENAGE DEPRESSION** *Island WIP 6354*	**35**	4
23 Apr 77	**I MIGHT BE LYING** *Island WIP 6388*	**44**	3
13 Aug 77	● **DO ANYTHING YOU WANNA DO** *Island WIP 6401* [1]	**9**	10
21 Jan 78	**QUIT THIS TOWN** *Island WIP 6411*	**36**	4

[1] Rods

Tracks on Live At The Marquee EP: 96 Tears/Get Out Of Denver/Medley: Gloria/Satisfaction.

EDDY *UK, female vocalist*　　**2 wks**

9 Jul 94	**SOMEDAY** *Positiva CDTIV 14*	**49**	2

Duane EDDY and the REBELS *US, male instrumentalist – guitar and male instrumental group*　　**196 wks**

5 Sep 58	**REBEL ROUSER** *London HL 8669*	**19**	10
2 Jan 59	**CANNONBALL** *London HL 8764*	**22**	4
19 Jun 59	● **PETER GUNN THEME** *London HLW 8879*	**6**	10
24 Jul 59	**YEP** *London HLW 8879*	**17**	5
4 Sep 59	**FORTY MILES OF BAD ROAD** *London HLW 8929*	**11**	9
11 Sep 59	**PETER GUNN THEME (re-entry)** *London HLW 8879*	**27**	1
18 Dec 59	**SOME KINDA EARTHQUAKE** *London HLW 9007*	**12**	5
19 Feb 60	**BONNIE CAME BACK** *London HLW 9050*	**13**	10
28 Apr 60	● **SHAZAM!** *London HLW 9104*	**4**	13
21 Jul 60	● **BECAUSE THEY'RE YOUNG** *London HLW 9162*	**2**	18
10 Nov 60	**KOMMOTION** *London HLW 9225*	**13**	10
12 Jan 61	● **PEPE** *London HLW 9257*	**2**	14
20 Apr 61	**THEME FROM DIXIE** *London HLW 9324*	**7**	10
22 Jun 61	**RING OF FIRE** *London HLW 9370*	**17**	10
14 Sep 61	**DRIVIN' HOME** *London HLW 9406*	**30**	4
5 Oct 61	**CARAVAN** *Parlophone R 4826* [1]	**42**	3
24 May 62	**DEEP IN THE HEART OF TEXAS** *RCA 1288* [1]	**19**	8
23 Aug 62	**BALLAD OF PALADIN** *RCA 1300* [1]	**10**	10
8 Nov 62	● **DANCE WITH THE GUITAR MAN** *RCA 1316* [2]	**4**	16
14 Feb 63	**BOSS GUITAR** *RCA 1329* [2]	**27**	8
30 May 63	**LONELY BOY LONELY GUITAR** *RCA 1344* [2]	**35**	4
29 Aug 63	**YOUR BABY'S GONE SURFIN'** *RCA 1357* [2]	**49**	1
8 Mar 75	● **PLAY ME LIKE YOU PLAY YOUR GUITAR** *GTO GT 11* [2]	**9**	9
22 Mar 86	● **PETER GUNN** *China WOK 6* [3]	**8**	9

[1] Duane Eddy [2] Duane Eddy and the Rebelettes [3] Art Of Noise featuring Duane Eddy

EDDY and the SOUL BAND
US, male vocal / instrumental group　　**7 wks**

23 Feb 85	**THE THEME FROM 'SHAFT'** *Club JAB 11*	**13**	7

Randy EDELMAN *US, male vocalist*　　**18 wks**

6 Mar 76	**CONCRETE AND CLAY** *20th Century BTC 2261*	**11**	7
18 Sep 76	**UPTOWN UPTEMPO WOMAN** *20th Century BTC 2225*	**25**	7
15 Jan 77	**YOU** *20th Century BTC 2253*	**49**	2
17 Jul 82	**NOBODY MADE ME** *Rocket XPRES 81*	**60**	2

EDELWEISS
Austria, male / female vocal / instrumental group　　**10 wks**

29 Apr 89	● **BRING ME EDELWEISS** *WEA YZ 353*	**5**	10

EDEN
UK / Australia, male / female vocal / instrumental group　　**2 wks**

6 Mar 93	**DO U FEEL 4 ME** *Logic 74321135422*	**51**	2

EDISON LIGHTHOUSE
UK, male vocal / instrumental group　　**13 wks**

24 Jan 70	★ **LOVE GROWS (WHERE MY ROSEMARY GOES)** *Bell 1091*	**1**	12
30 Jan 71	**IT'S UP TO YOU PETULA** *Bell 1136*	**49**	1

Dave EDMUNDS
UK, male vocalist / multi-instrumentalist　　**93 wks**

21 Nov 70	★ **I HEAR YOU KNOCKING** *MAM 1*	**1**	14
20 Jan 73	● **BABY I LOVE YOU** *Rockfield ROC 1*	**8**	13
9 Jun 73	● **BORN TO BE WITH YOU** *Rockfield ROC 2*	**5**	12
2 Jul 77	**I KNEW THE BRIDE** *Swansong SSK 19411*	**26**	8
30 Jun 79	● **GIRLS TALK** *Swansong SSK 19418*	**4**	11
22 Sep 79	**QUEEN OF HEARTS** *Swansong SSK 19419*	**11**	9
24 Nov 79	**CRAWLING FROM THE WRECKAGE** *Swansong SSK 19420*	**59**	4
9 Feb 80	**SINGING THE BLUES** *Swansong SSK 19422*	**28**	8
28 Mar 81	**ALMOST SATURDAY NIGHT** *Swansong SSK 19424*	**58**	3
20 Jun 81	**THE RACE IS ON** *Swansong SSK 19425* [1]	**34**	6
26 Mar 83	**SLIPPING AWAY** *Arista ARIST 522*	**60**	4
7 Apr 90	**KING OF LOVE** *Capitol CL 568*	**68**	1

[1] Dave Edmunds and the Stray Cats

Alton EDWARDS *South Africa, male vocalist*　　**9 wks**

9 Jan 82	**I JUST WANNA (SPEND SOME TIME WITH YOU)** *Streetwave STRA 1897*	**20**	9

Dennis EDWARDS featuring Siedah GARRETT *US, male / female vocal duo*　　**10 wks**

24 Mar 84	**DON'T LOOK ANY FURTHER** *Gordy TMG 1334*	**45**	5
20 Jun 87	**DON'T LOOK ANY FURTHER (re-entry)** *Gordy TMG 1334*	**55**	5

See also Michael Jackson.

Rupie EDWARDS *Jamaica, male vocalist*　　**16 wks**

23 Nov 74	● **IRE FEELINGS (SKANGA)** *Cactus CT 38*	**9**	10
8 Feb 75	**LEGO SKANGA** *Cactus CT 51*	**32**	6

Tommy EDWARDS *US, male vocalist* **18 wks**

3 Oct 58	★ IT'S ALL IN THE GAME *MGM 989*	**1** 17
7 Aug 59	MY MELANCHOLY BABY *MGM 1020*	**29** 1

EFUA *UK, female vocalist* **5 wks**

3 Jul 93	SOMEWHERE *Virgin VSCDT 1463*	**42** 5

EGGS ON LEGS *UK, male vocalist* **1 wk**

23 Sep 95	COCK A DOODLE DO IT *Avex UK AVEXCD 18*	**42** 1

EGYPTIAN EMPIRE *UK, male producer – Tim Taylor* **2 wks**

24 Oct 92	THE HORN TRACK *Ffrreedom TAB 115*	**61** 2

EIGHTH WONDER
UK, male / female vocal / instrumental group **25 wks**

2 Nov 85	STAY WITH ME *CBS A 6594*	**65** 2
20 Feb 88	● I'M NOT SCARED *CBS SCARE 1*	**7** 13
25 Jun 88	CROSS MY HEART *CBS 651552 7*	**13** 8
1 Oct 88	BABY BABY *CBS BABE 1*	**65** 2

808 STATE *UK, male instrumental group* **64 wks**

18 Nov 89	● PACIFIC STATE *ZTT ZANG 1*	**10** 9
31 Mar 90	THE EXTENDED PLEASURE OF DANCE EP *ZTT 2T*	**56** 1
2 Jun 90	● THE ONLY RHYME THAT BITES *ZTT ZANG 3* [1]	**10** 10
15 Sep 90	TUNES SPLITS THE ATOM *ZTT ZANG 6* [1]	**18** 7
10 Nov 90	● CUBIK / OLYMPIC *ZTT ZANG 5*	**10** 10
16 Feb 91	● IN YER FACE *ZTT ZANG 14*	**9** 6
27 Apr 91	OOOPS *ZTT ZANG 19* [2]	**42** 3
17 Aug 91	LIFT / OPEN YOUR MIND *ZTT ZANG 20*	**38** 4
29 Aug 92	TIME BOMB / NIMBUS *ZTT ZANG 33*	**59** 1
12 Dec 92	ONE IN TEN *ZTT ZANG 39* [3]	**17** 8
30 Jan 93	PLAN 9 *ZTT ZANG 38CD*	**50** 2
26 Jun 93	10 X 10 *ZTT ZANG 42CD*	**67** 1
13 Aug 94	BOMBADIN *ZTT ZANG 54CD*	**67** 1
29 Jun 96	BOND *ZTT ZANG 80CD*	**57** 1

[1] MC Tunes versus 808 State [2] 808 State featuring Bjork
[3] 808 State vs UB40

Tracks on The Extended Pleasure Of Dance EP: Ancodia / Cubik / Cuba Bora. Cubik is a re-issue of one of the tracks from The Extended Pleasure Of Dance EP. See also Various Artists (EPs & LPs) - Gimme Shelter (EP).

88.3 – See Lisa MAY

EINSTEIN *UK, male rapper* **6 wks**

18 Nov 89	ANOTHER MONSTERJAM *ffrr F 116* [1]	**65** 1
15 Dec 90	TURN IT UP *Swanyard SYD 9* [2]	**42** 4
24 Aug 96	THE POWER *Arista 74321398672* [3]	**42** 1

[1] Simon Harris featuring Einstein [2] Technotronic featuring Melissa and Einstein [3] Snap featuring Einstein

See also Ambassadors Of Funk featuring MC Mario.

EL MARIACHI *US, male producer – Roger Sanchez* **2 wks**

9 Nov 96	CUBA *ffrr FCD 286*	**38** 2

ELASTICA *UK, female / male vocal / instrumental group* **11 wks**

12 Feb 94	LINE UP *Deceptive BLUFF 004CD*	**20** 3

22 Oct 94	CONNECTION *Deceptive BLUFF 010CD*	**17** 4
25 Feb 95	WAKING UP *Deceptive BLUFF 011CD*	**13** 4

Donnie ELBERT *US, male vocalist* **29 wks**

8 Jan 72	● WHERE DID OUR LOVE GO? *London HL 10352*	**8** 10
26 Feb 72	I CAN'T HELP MYSELF *Avco 6105 009*	**11** 10
29 Apr 72	LITTLE PIECE OF LEATHER *London HL 10370*	**27** 9

ELECTRA *UK, male vocal / instrumental group* **7 wks**

6 Aug 88	JIBARO *ffrr FFR 9*	**54** 3
30 Dec 89	IT'S YOUR DESTINY / AUTUMN LOVE *London F 121*	**51** 4

ELECTRAFIXION *UK, male vocal / instrumental group* **6 wks**

19 Nov 94	ZEPHYR *WEA YZ 865CD*	**47** 2
9 Sep 95	LOWDOWN *WEA YZ 977CD*	**54** 2
4 Nov 95	NEVER *Spacejunk WEA 022CD*	**58** 1
16 Mar 96	SISTER PAIN *Spacejunk WEA 037CD1*	**27** 1

ELECTRIBE 101
UK / Germany, male / female vocal / instrumental group **13 wks**

28 Oct 89	TELL ME WHEN THE FEVER ENDED *Mercury MER 310*	**32** 5
24 Feb 90	TALKING WITH MYSELF *Mercury MER 316*	**23** 5
22 Sep 90	YOU'RE WALKING *Mercury MER 328*	**50** 3

ELECTRIC LIGHT ORCHESTRA
UK, male vocal / instrumental group **255 wks**

29 Jul 72	● 10538 OVERTURE *Harvest HAR 5053*	**9** 8
27 Jan 73	● ROLL OVER BEETHOVEN *Harvest HAR 5063*	**6** 10
6 Oct 73	SHOWDOWN *Harvest HAR 5077*	**12** 10
9 Mar 74	MA-MA-MA-BELLE *Warner Bros. K 16349*	**22** 8
10 Jan 76	● EVIL WOMAN *Jet 764*	**10** 8
3 Jul 76	STRANGE MAGIC *Jet 779*	**38** 3
13 Nov 76	● LIVIN' THING *Jet UP 36184*	**4** 12
19 Feb 77	● ROCKARIA! *Jet UP 36209*	**9** 9
21 May 77	● TELEPHONE LINE *Jet UP 36254*	**8** 9
29 Oct 77	TURN TO STONE *Jet UP 36313*	**18** 12
28 Jan 78	● MR. BLUE SKY *Jet UP 36342*	**6** 11
10 Jun 78	● WILD WEST HERO *Jet JET 109*	**6** 14
7 Oct 78	● SWEET TALKIN' WOMAN *Jet 121*	**6** 9
9 Dec 78	ELO EP *Jet ELO 1*	**34** 8
19 May 79	● SHINE A LITTLE LOVE *Jet 144*	**6** 10
21 Jul 79	● THE DIARY OF HORACE WIMP *Jet 150*	**8** 9
1 Sep 79	● DON'T BRING ME DOWN *Jet 153*	**3** 9
17 Nov 79	● CONFUSION / LAST TRAIN TO LONDON *Jet 166*	**8** 10
24 May 80	I'M ALIVE *Jet 179*	**20** 9
21 Jun 80	★ XANADU *Jet 185* [1]	**1** 11
2 Aug 80	ALL OVER THE WORLD *Jet 195*	**11** 8
22 Nov 80	DON'T WALK AWAY *Jet 7004*	**21** 10
1 Aug 81	● HOLD ON TIGHT *Jet 7011*	**4** 12
24 Oct 81	TWILIGHT *Jet 7015*	**30** 7
9 Jan 82	TICKET TO THE MOON / HERE IS THE NEWS *Jet 7018*	**24** 8
18 Jun 83	ROCK 'N' ROLL IS KING *Jet A 3500*	**13** 9
3 Sep 83	SECRET MESSAGES *Jet A 3720*	**48** 3
1 Mar 86	CALLING AMERICA *Epic A 6844*	**28** 7
11 May 91	HONEST MEN *Telstar ELO 100* [2]	**60** 1

[1] Olivia Newton-John and Electric Light Orchestra [2] Electric Light Orchestra Part 2

Here Is The News listed from 16 Jan 82. Tracks on ELO EP: Out of My Head / Strange Magic / Ma-Ma-Ma-Belle / Evil Woman.

ELECTRIC PRUNES *US, male vocal / instrumental group* **5 wks**

9 Feb 67	I HAD TOO MUCH TO DREAM LAST NIGHT *Reprise RS 20532*	**49** 1

11 May 67		GET ME TO THE WORLD ON TIME *Reprise RS 20564*	42	4

ELECTRONIC *UK, male vocal / instrumental group*   **31 wks**

16 Dec 89		GETTING AWAY WITH IT *Factory FAC 2577*	12	9
27 Apr 91	●	GET THE MESSAGE *Factory FAC 2877*	8	7
21 Sep 91		FEEL EVERY BEAT *Factory FAC 3287*	39	4
4 Jul 92	●	DISAPPOINTED *Parlophone R 6311*	6	5
6 Jul 96		FORBIDDEN CITY *Parlophone CDR 6436*	14	4
28 Sep 96		FOR YOU *Parlophone CDR 6445*	16	2

ELECTRONICAS *Holland, male instrumental group*   **8 wks**

19 Sep 81		ORIGINAL BIRD DANCE *Polydor POSP 360*	22	8

ELECTROSET *UK, male instrumental production group*   **4 wks**

21 Nov 92		HOW DOES IT FEEL *ffrr F 203*	27	3
15 Jul 95		SENSATION *Ffrreedom TABCD 231*	69	1

ELEGANTS *US, male vocal group*   **2 wks**

26 Sep 58		LITTLE STAR *HMV POP 520*	25	2

ELEVATION *UK, male instrumental / production duo*   **1 wk**

23 May 92		CAN YOU FEEL IT *Nova Mute 12NOMU 3*	62	1

ELEVATORMAN
UK, male instrumental / production group   **4 wks**

14 Jan 95		FUNK AND DRIVE *Wired WIRED 211*	37	3
1 Jul 95		FIRED UP *Wired WIRED 216*	44	1

ELGINS *US, male / female vocal group*   **20 wks**

1 May 71	●	HEAVEN MUST HAVE SENT YOU *Tamla Motown TMG 771*	3	13
9 Oct 71		PUT YOURSELF IN MY PLACE *Tamla Motown TMG 787*	28	7

ELIAS and his ZIGZAG JIVE FLUTES
South Africa, male instrumental group   **14 wks**

25 Apr 58	●	TOM HARK *Columbia DB 4109*	2	14

Yvonne ELLIMAN *US, female vocalist*   **44 wks**

29 Jan 72		I DON'T KNOW HOW TO LOVE HIM *MCA MMKS 5077*	47	1
6 Nov 76	●	LOVE ME *RSO 2090 205*	6	13
7 May 77		HELLO STRANGER *RSO 2090 236*	26	5
13 Aug 77		I CAN'T GET YOU OUT OF MY MIND *RSO 2090 251*	17	13
6 May 78	●	IF I CAN'T HAVE YOU *RSO 2090 266*	4	12

I Don't Know How To Love Him was one of four tracks on a Maxi-Single, two of which were credited during the disc's one week on the chart. The other track credited was Superstar by Murray Head.

Duke ELLINGTON *US, orchestra*   **4 wks**

5 Mar 54	●	SKIN DEEP *Philips PB 243*	7	4

Lance ELLINGTON *UK, male vocalist*   **1 wk**

21 Aug 93		LONELY (HAVE WE LOST OUR LOVE) *RCA 74321158332*	57	1

Ray ELLINGTON *UK, orchestra*   **4 wks**

15 Nov 62		THE MADISON *Ember S 102*	41	2
20 Dec 62		THE MADISON (re-entry) *Ember S 102*	36	2

Bern ELLIOTT and the FENMEN
UK, male vocal / instrumental group   **22 wks**

21 Nov 63		MONEY *Decca F 11770*	14	13
19 Mar 64		NEW ORLEANS *Decca F 11852*	24	9

Joe ELLIOTT – *See Mick RONSON with Joe ELLIOTT*

Greg ELLIS – *See Reva RICE and Greg ELLIS*

Joey B ELLIS *US, male vocalist*   **10 wks**

16 Feb 91		GO FOR IT (HEART AND FIRE) *Capitol CL 601* [1]	20	8
18 May 91		THOUGHT U WERE THE ONE FOR ME *Capitol CL 614*	58	2

[1] Rocky V featuring Joey B. Ellis and Tynetta Hare

Shirley ELLIS *US, female vocalist*   **17 wks**

6 May 65	●	THE CLAPPING SONG *London HLR 9961*	6	13
8 Jul 78		THE CLAPPING SONG (EP) *MCA MCEP 1*	59	4

Tracks on The Clapping Song (EP): The Clapping Song / Ever See a Diver Kiss His Wife While The Bubbles Bounce Above The Water / The Name Game / The Nitty Gritty. The Clapping Song itself qualifies as a re-issue.

ELLIS, BEGGS AND HOWARD
UK, male vocal / instrumental group   **8 wks**

2 Jul 88		BIG BUBBLES, NO TROUBLES *RCA PB 42089*	59	3
11 Mar 89		BIG BUBBLES, NO TROUBLES (re-entry) *RCA PB 42089*	41	5

Keith EMERSON *UK, male instrumentalist – piano*   **5 wks**

10 Apr 76		HONKY TONK TRAIN BLUES *Manticore K 13513*	21	5

See also Emerson, Lake and Palmer.

EMERSON, LAKE AND PALMER
UK, male instrumental group   **13 wks**

4 Jun 77	●	FANFARE FOR THE COMMON MAN *Atlantic K 10946*	2	13

See also Keith Emerson; Greg Lake.

Dick EMERY *UK, male vocalist*   **8 wks**

26 Feb 69		IF YOU LOVE HER *Pye 7N 17644*	32	4
13 Jan 73		YOU ARE AWFUL *Pye 7N 45202*	43	4

EMF *UK, male vocal / instrumental group*   **50 wks**

3 Nov 90	●	UNBELIEVABLE *Parlophone R 6273*	3	13
2 Feb 91	●	I BELIEVE *Parlophone R 6279*	6	7
27 Apr 91		CHILDREN *Parlophone R 6288*	19	5
31 Aug 91		LIES *Parlophone R 6295*	28	3
2 May 92		UNEXPLAINED EP *Parlophone SGE 2026*	18	4
19 Sep 92		THEY'RE HERE *Parlophone R 6321*	29	3
21 Nov 92		IT'S YOU *Parlophone R 6327*	23	3
25 Feb 95		PERFECT DAY *Parlophone CDRS 6401*	27	3

| 8 Jul 95 | ● | **I'M A BELIEVER** *Parlophone CDR 6412* [1] .... | **3** | 8 |
| 28 Oct 95 | | **AFRO KING** *Parlophone CDRS 6416* .... | **51** | 1 |

[1] EMF and Reeves and Mortimer

Tracks on Unexplained EP: Getting Through / Far From Me / The Same / Search And Destroy

EMMA *UK, female vocalist* — **6 wks**

| 28 Apr 90 | | **GIVE A LITTLE LOVE BACK TO THE WORLD** *Big Wave BWR 33* .... | **33** | 6 |

An EMOTIONAL FISH
UK, male vocal / instrumental group — **5 wks**

| 23 Jun 90 | | **CELEBRATE** *East West YZ 489* .... | **46** | 5 |

EMOTIONS *US, female vocal group* — **28 wks**

10 Sep 77	●	**BEST OF MY LOVE** *CBS 5555*	**4**	10
24 Dec 77		**I DON'T WANNA LOSE YOUR LOVE** *CBS 5819*	**40**	5
12 May 79	●	**BOOGIE WONDERLAND** *CBS 7292* [1]	**4**	13

[1] Earth Wind and Fire with the Emotions

EMPIRION *UK, male instrumental / production group* — **1 wk**

| 6 Jul 96 | | **NARCOTIC INFLUENCE** *XL XLS 72CD* .... | **64** | 1 |

EN VOGUE *US, female vocal / instrumental group* — **56 wks**

5 May 90	●	**HOLD ON** *East West America 7908*	**5**	11
21 Jul 90		**LIES** *East West America 7893*	**44**	4
4 Apr 92		**MY LOVIN'** *East West America A 8578*	**69**	3
9 May 92	●	**MY LOVIN' (re-entry)** *East West America A 8578*	**4**	9
15 Aug 92		**GIVING HIM SOMETHING HE CAN FEEL** *East West America A 8524*	**44**	3
7 Nov 92		**GIVING HIM SOMETHING HE CAN FEEL (re-issue) / FREE YOUR MIND** *East West America A 8524*	**16**	8
16 Jan 93		**GIVE IT UP TURN IT LOOSE** *East West America A 8445CD*	**22**	4
10 Apr 93		**LOVE DON'T LOVE YOU** *East West America A 8424CD*	**64**	1
9 Oct 93		**RUNAWAY LOVE** *East West America A 8359CD*	**36**	3
19 Mar 94	●	**WHATTA MAN** *ffrr FCD 222* [1]	**7**	10

[1] Salt-N-Pepa with En Vogue

ENERGISE *UK, male vocal / instrumental group* — **1 wk**

| 16 Feb 91 | | **REPORT TO THE DANCEFLOOR** *Network NWKT 16* ..... | **69** | 1 |

ENERGY ORCHARD
Ireland, male vocal / instrumental group — **6 wks**

| 27 Jan 90 | | **BELFAST** *MCA MCA 1392* .... | **52** | 4 |
| 7 Apr 90 | | **SAILORTOWN** *MCA MCA 1402* .... | **73** | 2 |

Harry ENFIELD *UK, male vocalist* — **7 wks**

| 7 May 88 | ● | **LOADSAMONEY (DOIN' UP THE HOUSE)** *Mercury DOSH 1* .... | **4** | 7 |

ENGLAND DAN and John Ford COLEY
US, male vocal duo — **12 wks**

| 25 Sep 76 | | **I'D REALLY LOVE TO SEE YOU TONIGHT** *Atlantic K 10810* .... | **26** | 7 |
| 23 Jun 79 | | **LOVE IS THE ANSWER** *Big Tree K 11296* ..... | **45** | 5 |

ENGLAND SISTERS *UK, female vocal group* — **1 wk**

| 17 Mar 60 | | **HEARTBEAT** *HMV POP 710* .... | **33** | 1 |

ENGLAND WORLD CUP SQUAD
UK, male football team vocalists — **46 wks**

18 Apr 70	★	**BACK HOME** *Pye 7N 17920*	**1**	16
15 Aug 70		**BACK HOME (re-entry)** *Pye 7N 17920*	**46**	1
10 Apr 82	●	**THIS TIME (WE'LL GET IT RIGHT) / ENGLAND WE'LL FLY THE FLAG** *England ER 1*	**2**	13
19 Apr 86		**WE'VE GOT THE WHOLE WORLD AT OUR FEET / WHEN WE ARE FAR FROM HOME** *Columbia DB 9128*	**66**	2
21 May 88		**ALL THE WAY** *MCA GOAL 1* [1]	**64**	2
2 Jun 90	★	**WORLD IN MOTION...** *Factory/MCA FAC 2937* [2]	**1**	12

[1] England Football Team and the 'sound' of Stock, Aitken and Waterman
[2] Englandneworder

ENGLAND RUGBY WORLD CUP SQUAD – *See* UNION *featuring the* ENGLAND WORLD CUP SQUAD

Kim ENGLISH *US, female vocalist* — **6 wks**

23 Jul 94		**NITE LIFE** *Hi-Life PZCD 323*	**35**	2
4 Mar 95		**TIME FOR LOVE** *Hi-Life HICD 8*	**48**	1
9 Sep 95		**I KNOW A PLACE** *Hi-Life 5798072*	**52**	1
30 Nov 96		**NITE LIFE (re-mix)** *Hi-Life 5755332*	**35**	2

Scott ENGLISH *US, male vocalist* — **10 wks**

| 9 Oct 71 | | **BRANDY** *Horse HOSS 7* .... | **12** | 10 |

ENIGMA *UK, male vocal / instrumental group* — **15 wks**

| 23 May 81 | | **AIN'T NO STOPPING** *Creole CR 9* .... | **11** | 8 |
| 8 Aug 81 | | **I LOVE MUSIC** *Creole CR 14* .... | **25** | 7 |

ENIGMA
Germany / Romania, male / female vocal / instrumental duo — **42 wks**

15 Dec 90	★	**SADNESS PART 1** *Virgin International DINS 101*	**1**	12
30 Mar 91		**MEA CULPA PART II** *Virgin International DINS 104*	**55**	3
10 Aug 91		**PRINCIPLES OF LUST** *Virgin International DINS 110*	**59**	2
11 Jan 92		**THE RIVERS OF BELIEF** *Virgin International DINS 112*	**68**	2
29 Jan 94	●	**RETURN TO INNOCENCE** *Virgin International DINSD 123*	**3**	14
14 May 94		**THE EYES OF TRUTH** *Virgin International DINSD 126*	**21**	4
20 Aug 94		**AGE OF LONELINESS** *Virgin International DINSD 135*	**21**	5

ENYA *Ireland, female vocalist* — **57 wks**

15 Oct 88	★	**ORINOCO FLOW** *WEA YZ 312*	**1**	13
24 Dec 88		**EVENING FALLS...** *WEA YZ 356*	**20**	4
10 Jun 89		**STORMS IN AFRICA (PART I)** *WEA YZ 368*	**41**	4
19 Oct 91		**CARIBBEAN BLUE** *WEA YZ 604*	**13**	7
7 Dec 91		**HOW CAN I KEEP FROM SINGING** *WEA YZ 365*	**32**	5
1 Aug 92	●	**BOOK OF DAYS** *WEA YZ 640*	**10**	6
14 Nov 92		**THE CELTS** *WEA YZ 705*	**29**	4
18 Nov 95	●	**ANYWHERE IS** *WEA WEA 023CD*	**7**	12
7 Dec 96		**ON MY WAY HOME** *WEA WEA 047CD*	**26**	2

EON *UK, male producer – Ian Bela* — **1 wk**

| 17 Aug 91 | | **FEAR: THE MINDKILLER** *Vinyl Solution STORM 33* ..... | **63** | 1 |

EQUALS UK / Guyana, male vocal / instrumental group **69 wks**

21 Feb 68	I GET SO EXCITED *President PT 180*	44	4
1 May 68	BABY COME BACK *President PT 135*	50	1
15 May 68	★ BABY COME BACK (re-entry) *President PT 135*	1	17
21 Aug 68	LAUREL AND HARDY *President PT 200*	35	5
27 Nov 68	SOFTLY SOFTLY *President PT 222*	48	3
2 Apr 69	MICHAEL AND THE SLIPPER TREE *President PT 240*	24	7
30 Jul 69	● VIVA BOBBY JOE *President PT 260*	6	14
27 Dec 69	RUB A DUB DUB *President PT 275*	34	7
19 Dec 70	● BLACK SKIN BLUE EYED BOYS *President PT 325*	9	11

ERASURE UK, male vocal / instrumental duo **195 wks**

5 Oct 85	WHO NEEDS LOVE LIKE THAT *Mute MUTE 40*	55	2
25 Oct 86	● SOMETIMES *Mute MUTE 51*	2	17
28 Feb 87	IT DOESN'T HAVE TO BE *Mute MUTE 56*	12	9
30 May 87	● VICTIM OF LOVE *Mute MUTE 61*	7	9
3 Oct 87	● THE CIRCUS *Mute MUTE 66*	6	10
5 Mar 88	● SHIP OF FOOLS *Mute MUTE 74*	6	8
11 Jun 88	CHAINS OF LOVE *Mute MUTE 83*	11	7
1 Oct 88	● A LITTLE RESPECT *Mute MUTE 85*	4	10
10 Dec 88	● CRACKERS INTERNATIONAL EP *Mute MUTE 93*	2	13
30 Sep 89	● DRAMA! *Mute MUTE 89*	4	8
9 Dec 89	YOU SURROUND ME *Mute MUTE 99*	15	9
10 Mar 90	● BLUE SAVANNAH *Mute MUTE 109*	3	10
2 Jun 90	STAR *Mute MUTE 111*	11	7
29 Jun 91	● CHORUS *Mute MUTE 125*	3	9
21 Sep 91	● LOVE TO HATE YOU *Mute MUTE 131*	4	9
7 Dec 91	AM I RIGHT (EP) *Mute MUTE 134*	15	6
11 Jan 92	AM I RIGHT (EP) (re-mix) *Mute L12MUTE 134*	22	3
28 Mar 92	● BREATH OF LIFE *Mute MUTE 142*	8	6
13 Jun 92	★ ABBA-ESQUE EP *Mute MUTE 144*	1	12
7 Nov 92	● WHO NEEDS LOVE (LIKE THAT) (re-mix) *Mute MUTE 150*	10	4
23 Apr 94	● ALWAYS *Mute CDMUTE 152*	4	9
30 Jul 94	● RUN TO THE SUN *Mute CDMUTE 153*	6	5
3 Dec 94	I LOVE SATURDAY *Mute CDMUTE 166*	20	6
23 Sep 95	STAY WITH ME *Mute CDMUTE 174*	15	4
9 Dec 95	FINGERS AND THUMBS (COLD SUMMER'S DAY) *Mute CDMUTE 178*	20	3

Tracks on Crackers International EP: Stop / The Hardest Part / Knocking On Your Door / She Won't Be Home. Tracks on Am I Right EP: Am I Right / Carry On Clangers / Let It Flow / Waiting For Sex. Tracks on Am I Right (Re-mix EP): Am I Right / Chorus / Love To Hate You / Perfect Stranger. Tracks on Abba-esque EP: Lay All Your Love On Me / SOS / Take A Chance On Me / Voulez-Vous. Take A Chance on Me credits MC Kinky, see also Kinky.

ERIC and the GOOD GOOD FEELING
UK, male / female vocal / instrumental group **1 wk**

3 Jun 89	GOOD GOOD FEELING *Equinox EQN 1*	73	1

ERIK UK, female vocalist **5 wks**

10 Apr 93	LOOKS LIKE I'M IN LOVE AGAIN *PWL Sanctuary PWCD 252* [1]	46	2
29 Jan 94	GOT TO BE REAL *PWL International PWCD 278*	42	2
1 Oct 94	WE GOT THE LOVE *WL International PWCD 305*	55	1

[1] Key West featuring Erik

ERIN – See SHUT UP AND DANCE; BBG

EROTIC DRUM BAND
Canada, male / female vocal / instrumental group **3 wks**

9 Jun 79	LOVE DISCO STYLE *Scope SC 1*	47	3

ERUPTION US, male / female vocal / instrumental group **21 wks**

18 Feb 78	● I CAN'T STAND THE RAIN *Atlantic K 11068* [1]	5	11
21 Apr 79	● ONE WAY TICKET *Atlantic/Hansa K 11266*	9	10

[1] Eruption featuring Precious Wilson

ESCORTS UK, male vocal / instrumental group **2 wks**

2 Jul 64	THE ONE TO CRY *Fontana TF 474*	49	2

ESCRIMA UK, male producer – Paul Newman **4 wks**

11 Feb 95	TRAIN OF THOUGHT *Ffrreedom TABCD 225*	36	2
7 Oct 95	DEEPER *Hooj Choons TABCD 236*	27	2

ESKIMOS & EGYPT
UK, male vocal / instrumental group **4 wks**

13 Feb 93	FALL FROM GRACE *One Little Indian EEF 96CD*	51	2
29 May 93	UK-USA *One Little Indian 99 TP7CD*	52	2

ESPIRITU
UK / France, male / female vocal / instrumental duo **10 wks**

6 Mar 93	CONQUISTADOR *Heavenly HVN 28CD*	47	2
7 Aug 93	LOS AMERICANOS *Heavenly HVN 33CD*	45	2
20 Aug 94	BONITA MANANA *Columbia 6606925*	50	1
25 Mar 95	ALWAYS SOMETHING THERE TO REMIND ME *WEA YZ 911CD* [1]	14	5

[1] Tin Tin Out featuring Espiritu

ESSEX US, male / female vocal group **5 wks**

8 Aug 63	EASIER SAID THAN DONE *Columbia DB 7077*	41	5

David ESSEX UK, male vocalist **199 wks**

18 Aug 73	● ROCK ON *CBS 1693*	3	11
10 Nov 73	● LAMPLIGHT *CBS 1902*	7	15
11 May 74	AMERICA *CBS 2176*	32	5
12 Oct 74	★ GONNA MAKE YOU A STAR *CBS 2492*	1	17
14 Dec 74	● STARDUST *CBS 2828*	7	10
5 Jul 75	● ROLLING STONE *CBS 3425*	5	7
13 Sep 75	★ HOLD ME CLOSE *CBS 3572*	1	10
6 Dec 75	IF I COULD *CBS 3776*	13	8
20 Mar 76	CITY LIGHTS *CBS 4050*	24	4
16 Oct 76	COMING HOME *CBS 4486*	24	6
17 Sep 77	COOL OUT TONIGHT *CBS 5495*	23	6
11 Mar 78	STAY WITH ME BABY *CBS 6063*	45	5
19 Aug 78	● OH WHAT A CIRCUS *Mercury 6007 185*	3	11
21 Oct 78	BRAVE NEW WORLD *CBS 6705*	55	3
3 Mar 79	IMPERIAL WIZARD *Mercury 6007 202*	32	8
5 Apr 80	SILVER DREAM MACHINE (PART 1) *Mercury BIKE 1*	4	11
14 Jun 80	HOT LOVE *Mercury HOT 11*	57	4
26 Jun 82	ME AND MY GIRL (NIGHT-CLUBBING) *Mercury MER 107*	13	10
11 Dec 82	A WINTER'S TALE *Mercury MER 127*	2	10
4 Jun 83	THE SMILE *Mercury ESSEX 1*	52	4
27 Aug 83	● TAHITI (FROM 'MUTINY ON THE BOUNTY') *Mercury BOUNT 1*	8	11
26 Nov 83	YOU'RE IN MY HEART *Mercury ESSEX 2*	67	2
17 Dec 83	YOU'RE IN MY HEART (re-entry) *Mercury ESSEX 2*	59	4
23 Feb 85	FALLING ANGELS RIDING (MUTINY) *Mercury ESSEX 5*	29	7
18 Apr 87	MYFANWY *Arista RIS 11*	41	7
26 Nov 94	TRUE LOVE WAYS *PolyGram TV TLWCD 2* [1]	38	3

[1] David Essex and Catherine Zeta Jones

Gloria ESTEFAN *US, female vocalist* — 196 wks

Date	Title	Pos	Wks
11 Aug 84	● DR BEAT *Epic A 4614* [1]	6	14
17 May 86	BAD BOY *Epic A 6537* [1]	16	11
16 Jul 88	● ANYTHING FOR YOU *Epic 651673 7* [2]	10	14
22 Oct 88	● 1-2-3 *Epic 652958 7* [2]	9	9
17 Dec 88	RHYTHM IS GONNA GET YOU *Epic 654514 7* [2]	16	9
31 Dec 88	1-2-3 (re-entry) *Epic 652958 7* [2]	72	1
11 Feb 89	● CAN'T STAY AWAY FROM YOU *Epic 651444 7* [2]	7	12
15 Jul 89	● DON'T WANNA LOSE YOU *Epic 655054 0*	6	10
16 Sep 89	OYE MI CANTO (HEAR MY VOICE) *Epic 655287 7*	16	8
25 Nov 89	GET ON YOUR FEET *Epic 655450 7*	23	7
3 Mar 90	HERE WE ARE *Epic 655473 9*	23	6
26 May 90	CUTS BOTH WAYS *Epic 655982 7*	49	5
26 Jan 91	COMING OUT OF THE DARK *Epic 6565747*	25	5
6 Apr 91	SEAL OUR FATE *Epic 6567737*	24	7
8 Jun 91	REMEMBER ME WITH LOVE *Epic 6569687*	22	6
21 Sep 91	LIVE FOR LOVING YOU *Epic 6573827*	33	5
24 Oct 92	ALWAYS TOMORROW *Epic 6583977*	24	4
12 Dec 92	● MIAMI HIT MIX / CHRISTMAS THROUGH YOUR EYES *Epic 6588377*	8	9
13 Feb 93	I SEE YOUR SMILE *Epic 6589612*	48	2
3 Apr 93	GO AWAY *Epic 6590952*	13	6
3 Jul 93	MI TIERRA *Epic 6593512*	36	3
14 Aug 93	IF WE WERE LOVERS / CON LOS ANOS QUE ME QUEDIN *Epic 6595702*	40	3
18 Dec 93	MONTUNO *Epic 6599972*	55	2
15 Oct 94	TURN THE BEAT AROUND *Epic 6606822*	21	6
3 Dec 94	HOLD ME THRILL ME KISS ME *Epic 6610802*	11	10
18 Feb 95	EVERLASTING LOVE *Epic 6611595*	19	5
18 Mar 95	HOLD ME THRILL ME KISS ME (re-entry) *Epic 6610802*	68	1
25 May 96	REACH *Epic 6632642*	15	6
3 Aug 96	REACH (re-entry) *Epic 6632642*	68	1
17 Aug 96	REACH (2nd re-entry) *Epic 6632642*	55	1
24 Aug 96	YOU'LL BE MINE (PARTY TIME) *Epic 6636505*	18	3
14 Dec 96	I'M NOT GIVING YOU UP *Epic 6640222*	28†	3

[1] Miami Sound Machine [2] Gloria Estefan and Miami Sound Machine

Christmas Through Your Eyes *only listed from 19 Dec '92.*

Don ESTELLE – *See Windsor DAVIES and Don ESTELLE*

Deon ESTUS *US, male vocalist / instrumentalist – bass* — 7 wks

Date	Title	Pos	Wks
25 Jan 86	MY GUY – MY GIRL *Sedition EDIT 3310* [1]	63	3
29 Apr 89	HEAVEN HELP ME *Mika MIKA 2*	41	4

[1] Amii Stewart and Deon Estus

ETERNAL *UK, female vocal group* — 92 wks

Date	Title	Pos	Wks
2 Oct 93	● STAY *EMI CDEM 283*	4	9
15 Jan 94	● SAVE OUR LOVE *EMI CDEM 296*	8	7
30 Apr 94	● JUST A STEP FROM HEAVEN *EMI CDEM 311*	8	10
20 Aug 94	● SO GOOD *EMI CDEM 339*	13	7
5 Nov 94	● OH BABY I... *EMI CDEM 353*	4	13
24 Dec 94	CRAZY *EMI CDEMX 364*	15	7
21 Oct 95	● POWER OF A WOMAN *EMI CDEM 396*	5	8
9 Dec 95	● I AM BLESSED *EMI CDEMS 408*	7	12
9 Mar 96	● GOOD THING *EMI CDEM 419*	8	6
17 Aug 96	● SOMEDAY *EMI CDEMS 439*	4	9
7 Dec 96	● SECRETS *EMI CDEM 459*	9†	4

ETHICS *Holland, male producer – Patrick Prinz* — 5 wks

Date	Title	Pos	Wks
25 Nov 95	TO THE BEAT OF THE DRUM (LA LUNA) *VC VCRD 5*	13	5

See also Artemesia; Movin' Melodies; Subliminal Cuts.

ETHIOPIANS *Jamaica, male vocal / instrumental group* — 6 wks

Date	Title	Pos	Wks
13 Sep 67	TRAIN TO SKAVILLE *Rio RIO 130*	40	6

Tony ETORIA *UK, male vocalist* — 8 wks

Date	Title	Pos	Wks
4 Jun 77	I CAN PROVE IT *GTO GT 89*	21	8

E.U. – *See SALT-N-PEPA*

EUROGROOVE *UK, male / female vocal group* — 7 wks

Date	Title	Pos	Wks
20 May 95	MOVE YOUR BODY *Avex UK AVEXCD 4*	29	2
5 Aug 95	DIVE TO PARADISE *Avex UK AVEXCD 10*	31	2
21 Oct 95	IT'S ON YOU (SCAN ME) *Avex UK AVEXCD 17*	25	2
3 Feb 96	MOVE YOUR BODY (re-mix) *Avex UK AVEXCD 22*	44	1

EUROPE *Sweden, male vocal / instrumental group* — 46 wks

Date	Title	Pos	Wks
1 Nov 86	★ THE FINAL COUNTDOWN *Epic A 7127*	1	15
31 Jan 87	ROCK THE NIGHT *Epic EUR 1*	12	9
18 Apr 87	CARRIE *Epic EUR 2*	22	8
20 Aug 88	SUPERSTITIOUS *Epic EUR 3*	34	5
1 Feb 92	I'LL CRY FOR YOU *Epic 6576977*	28	5
21 Mar 92	HALFWAY TO HEAVEN *Epic 6578517*	42	4

EURYTHMICS
UK, female / male vocal / instrumental duo — 198 wks

Date	Title	Pos	Wks
4 Jul 81	NEVER GONNA CRY AGAIN *RCA 68*	63	3
20 Nov 82	LOVE IS A STRANGER *RCA DA 1*	54	5
12 Feb 83	● SWEET DREAMS (ARE MADE OF THIS) *RCA DA 2*	2	14
9 Apr 83	● LOVE IS A STRANGER (re-entry) *RCA DA 1*	6	8
9 Jul 83	● WHO'S THAT GIRL? *RCA DA 3*	3	10
5 Nov 83	● RIGHT BY YOUR SIDE *RCA DA 4*	10	11
21 Jan 84	● HERE COMES THE RAIN AGAIN *RCA DA 5*	8	8
3 Nov 84	● SEXCRIME (NINETEEN EIGHTY FOUR) *Virgin VS 728*	4	13
19 Jan 85	JULIA *Virgin VS 734*	44	4
20 Apr 85	WOULD I LIE TO YOU? *RCA PB 40101*	17	8
6 Jul 85	★ THERE MUST BE AN ANGEL (PLAYING WITH MY HEART) *RCA PB 40247*	1	13
2 Nov 85	● SISTERS ARE DOIN' IT FOR THEMSELVES *RCA PB 40339* [1]	9	11
11 Jan 86	IT'S ALRIGHT (BABY'S COMING BACK) *RCA PB 40375*	12	8
14 Jun 86	WHEN TOMORROW COMES *RCA DA 7*	30	6
6 Sep 86	● THORN IN MY SIDE *RCA DA 8*	5	11
29 Nov 86	THE MIRACLE OF LOVE *RCA DA 9*	23	9
28 Feb 87	MISSIONARY MAN *RCA DA 10*	31	4
24 Oct 87	BEETHOVEN (I LOVE TO LISTEN TO) *RCA DA 11*	25	5
26 Dec 87	SHAME *RCA DA 14*	41	6
9 Apr 88	I NEED A MAN *RCA DA 15*	26	5
11 Jun 88	YOU HAVE PLACED A CHILL IN MY HEART *RCA DA 16*	16	8
26 Aug 89	REVIVAL *RCA DA 17*	26	6
4 Nov 89	DON'T ASK ME WHY *RCA DA 19*	25	6
3 Feb 90	THE KING AND QUEEN OF AMERICA *RCA DA 20*	29	5
12 May 90	ANGEL *RCA DA 21*	23	6
9 Mar 91	LOVE IS A STRANGER (re-issue) *RCA PB 44265*	46	3
16 Nov 91	SWEET DREAMS (ARE MADE OF THIS) (re-mix) *RCA PB 45031*	48	2

[1] Eurythmics and Aretha Franklin

EUSEBE *UK, male / female vocal group* — 3 wks

Date	Title	Pos	Wks
26 Aug 95	SUMMERTIME HEALING *Mama's Yard CDMAMA 4*	32	3

EVANGEL TEMPLE CHOIR – *See Johnny CASH*

Everything But The Girl

Everything But The Girl's hit 'Missing' was the first record to spend a whole year on the American singles chart.

Eternal

Eternal are the only female group to string together five consecutive Top 10 hits.

David Essex

David Essex played Che Guevara in the original stage production of the Tim Rice and Andrew Lloyd-Webber musical *Evita*. The part was played by Antonio Banderas in the recent Alan Parker film version.

Faith EVANS US, female vocalist | 4 wks

| 14 Oct 95 | YOU USED TO LOVE ME Puff Daddy 74321299812 | 42 | 2 |
| 23 Nov 96 | STRESSED OUT Jive JIVECD 404 [1] | 33 | 2 |

[1] A Tribe Called Quest featuring Faith Evans and Raphael Saadiq

Maureen EVANS UK, female vocalist | 37 wks

22 Jan 60	THE BIG HURT Oriole CB 1533	26	2
17 Mar 60	LOVE KISSES AND HEARTACHES Oriole CB 1540	44	1
2 Jun 60	PAPER ROSES Oriole CB 1550	40	5
29 Nov 62	● LIKE I DO Oriole CB 1760	3	18
27 Feb 64	I LOVE HOW YOU LOVE ME Oriole CB 1906	34	10
14 May 64	I LOVE HOW YOU LOVE ME (re-entry) Oriole CB 1906	50	1

Paul EVANS US, male vocalist | 14 wks

27 Nov 59	SEVEN LITTLE GIRLS SITTING IN THE BACK SEAT London HLL 8968 [1]	25	1
31 Mar 60	MIDNITE SPECIAL London HLL 9045	41	1
16 Dec 78	● HELLO THIS IS JOANIE (THE TELEPHONE ANSWERING MACHINE SONG) Spring 2066 932	6	12

[1] Paul Evans and the Curls

EVASIONS UK, male / female vocal / instrumental group | 8 wks

| 13 Jun 81 | WIKKA WRAP Groove GP 107 | 20 | 8 |

E.V.E. UK / US, female vocal group | 5 wks

| 1 Oct 94 | GROOVE OF LOVE Gasoline Alley MCSTD 2007 | 30 | 3 |
| 28 Jan 95 | GOOD LIFE Gasoline Alley MCSTD 2038 | 39 | 2 |

Alison EVELYN – See BROTHERS LIKE OUTLAW featuring Alison EVELYN

EVERCLEAR US, male vocal / instrumental group | 4 wks

| 1 Jun 96 | HEARTSPARK DOLLARSIGN Capitol CDCLS 773 | 48 | 2 |
| 31 Aug 96 | SANTA MONICA (WATCH THE WORLD DIE) Capitol CDCL 775 | 40 | 2 |

Betty EVERETT US, female vocalist | 14 wks

| 14 Jan 65 | GETTING MIGHTY CROWDED Fontana TF 520 | 29 | 7 |
| 30 Oct 68 | IT'S IN HIS KISS President PT 215 | 34 | 7 |

Kenny EVERETT UK, male vocalist | 12 wks

| 12 Nov 77 | CAPTAIN KREMMEN (RETRIBUTION) DJM DJS 10810 [1] | 32 | 4 |
| 26 Mar 83 | ● SNOT RAP RCA KEN 1 | 9 | 8 |

[1] Kenny Everett and Mike Vickers

Phil EVERLY US, male vocalist | 24 wks

6 Nov 82	LOUISE Capitol CL 266	47	6
19 Feb 83	● SHE MEANS NOTHING TO ME Capitol CL 276 [1]	9	9
10 Dec 94	ALL I HAVE TO DO IS DREAM EMI CDEMS 359 [2]	14	6
25 Feb 95	ALL I HAVE TO DO IS DREAM (re-entry) EMI CDEMS 359 [2]	58	3

[1] Phil Everly and Cliff Richard [2] Cliff Richard and Phil Everly

All I Have To Do Is Dream was listed with its flip side Miss You Nights by Cliff Richard. See also Everly Brothers

EVERLY BROTHERS US, male vocal duo | 337 wks

12 Jul 57	● BYE BYE LOVE London HLA 8440	6	16
8 Nov 57	● WAKE UP LITTLE SUSIE London HLA 8498	2	13
23 May 58	★ ALL I HAVE TO DO IS DREAM / CLAUDETTE London HLA 8618	1	21
12 Sep 58	● BIRD DOG London HLA 8685	2	16
23 Jan 59	● PROBLEMS London HLA 8781	6	12
22 May 59	TAKE A MESSAGE TO MARY London HLA 8863	29	1
29 May 59	POOR JENNY London HLA 8863	14	11
19 Jun 59	TAKE A MESSAGE TO MARY (re-entry) London HLA 8863	27	1
3 Jul 59	TAKE A MESSAGE TO MARY (2nd re-entry) London HLA 8863	20	8
11 Sep 59	● ('TIL) I KISSED YOU London HLA 8934	2	15
12 Feb 60	LET IT BE ME London HLA 9039	13	5
31 Mar 60	LET IT BE ME (re-entry) London HLA 9039	26	4
14 Apr 60	★ CATHY'S CLOWN Warner Bros. WB 1	1	18
14 Jul 60	● WHEN WILL I BE LOVED London HLA 9157	4	16
22 Sep 60	● LUCILLE / SO SAD (TO WATCH GOOD LOVE GO BAD) Warner Bros. WB 19	4	15
15 Dec 60	LIKE STRANGERS London HLA 9250	11	10
9 Feb 61	★ WALK RIGHT BACK / EBONY EYES Warner Bros. WB 33	1	16
15 Jun 61	★ TEMPTATION Warner Bros. WB 42	1	15
5 Oct 61	MUSKRAT / DON'T BLAME ME Warner Bros. WB 50	20	6
18 Jan 62	● CRYIN' IN THE RAIN Warner Bros. WB 56	6	15
17 May 62	HOW CAN I MEET HER Warner Bros. WB 67	12	10
25 Oct 62	NO ONE CAN MAKE MY SUNSHINE SMILE Warner Bros. WB 79	11	11
21 Mar 63	SO IT WILL ALWAYS BE Warner Bros. WB 94	23	11
13 Jun 63	IT'S BEEN NICE Warner Bros. WB 99	26	5
17 Oct 63	THE GIRL SANG THE BLUES Warner Bros. WB 109	25	9
16 Jul 64	FERRIS WHEEL Warner Bros. WB 135	22	10
3 Dec 64	GONE GONE GONE Warner Bros. WB 146	36	7
6 May 65	THAT'LL BE THE DAY Warner Bros. WB 158	30	4
20 May 65	● THE PRICE OF LOVE Warner Bros. WB 161	2	14
26 Aug 65	I'LL NEVER GET OVER YOU Warner Bros. WB 5639	35	5
21 Oct 65	LOVE IS STRANGE Warner Bros. WB 5649	11	9
8 May 68	IT'S MY TIME Warner Bros. WB 7192	39	6
22 Sep 84	ON THE WINGS OF A NIGHTINGALE Mercury MER 170	41	9

All I Have To Do Is Dream was listed without Claudette for its first week on the chart, but from 30 May 58 both sides were charted for 20 more weeks. See also Phil Everly.

EVERTON FOOTBALL CLUB UK, male football team vocalists | 8 wks

| 11 May 85 | HERE WE GO Columbia DB 9106 [1] | 14 | 5 |
| 20 May 95 | ALL TOGETHER NOW MDMC DEVCS 3 | 24 | 3 |

[1] Everton 1985

EVERYTHING BUT THE GIRL UK, male / female vocal / instrumental duo | 86 wks

12 May 84	EACH AND EVERYONE Blanco Y Negro NEG 1	28	7
21 Jul 84	MINE Blanco Y Negro NEG 3	58	2
6 Oct 84	NATIVE LAND Blanco Y Negro NEG 6	73	2
2 Aug 86	COME ON HOME Blanco Y Negro NEG 21	44	7
11 Oct 86	DON'T LEAVE ME BEHIND Blanco Y Negro NEG 23	72	2
13 Feb 88	THESE EARLY DAYS Blanco Y Negro NEG 30	75	1
9 Jul 88	●● I DON'T WANT TO TALK ABOUT IT Blanco Y Negro NEG 34	3	9
27 Jan 90	DRIVING Blanco Y Negro NEG 40	54	2
22 Feb 92	COVERS EP Blanco Y Negro NEG 54	13	6
24 Apr 93	THE ONLY LIVING BOY IN NEW YORK (EP) Blanco Y Negro NEG 62CD	42	5
19 Jun 93	I DIDN'T KNOW I WAS LOOKING FOR LOVE (EP) Blanco Y Negro NEG 64CD	72	1
4 Jun 94	ROLLERCOASTER (EP) Blanco Y Negro NEG 69CD	65	1
20 Aug 94	MISSING Blanco Y Negro NEG 71CD1	69	1
28 Oct 95	● MISSING (re-mix) Blanco Y Negro NEG 84CD	3	22
20 Apr 96	● WALKING WOUNDED Virgin VSCDT 1577	6	6

F

FACES *UK, male vocal / instrumental group*   **46 wks**

18 Dec 71	●	STAY WITH ME *Warner Bros. K 16136*	**6** 14
17 Feb 73	●	CINDY INCIDENTALLY *Warner Bros. K 16247*	**2** 9
8 Dec 73	●	POOL HALL RICHARD / I WISH IT WOULD RAIN *Warner Bros. K 16341*	**8** 11
7 Dec 74		YOU CAN MAKE ME DANCE SING OR ANYTHING *Warner Bros. K 16494* [1]	**12** 9
4 Jun 77		THE FACES EP *Riva 8*	**41** 3

[1] Rod Stewart and the Faces

You Can Make Me Dance Sing Or Anything *was subtitled 'Even Take The Dog For A Walk, Mend A Fuse, Fold Away The Ironing Board or Any Other Domestic Short Comings'. Tracks on The Faces EP: Memphis / You Can Make Me Dance Sing Or Anything / Stay With Me / Cindy Incidentally.*

FACTORY OF UNLIMITED RHYTHM
Jamaica, male / female vocal / instrumental group   **1 wk**

1 Jun 96	THE SWEETEST SURRENDER *Kuff KUFFD 6*	**59** 1

Donald FAGEN *US, male vocalist*   **2 wks**

3 Jul 93	TOMORROW'S GIRLS *Reprise W 0180CDX*	**46** 2

Joe FAGIN *UK, male vocalist*   **20 wks**

7 Jan 84	●	THAT'S LIVIN' ALRIGHT *Towerbell TOW 46*	**3** 11
5 Apr 86		BACK WITH THE BOYS AGAIN / GET IT RIGHT *Towerbell TOW 84*	**53** 9

Yvonne FAIR *US, female vocalist*   **11 wks**

24 Jan 76	●	IT SHOULD HAVE BEEN ME *Tamla Motown TMG 1013*	**5** 11

FAIR WEATHER *UK, male vocal / instrumental group*   **12 wks**

18 Jul 70	●	NATURAL SINNER *RCA 1977*	**6** 12

Fair Weather is led by Andy Fairweather-Low

FAIRGROUND ATTRACTION
UK, female / male vocal / instrumental group   **27 wks**

16 Apr 88	★	PERFECT *RCA PB 41845*	**1** 13
30 Jul 88	●	FIND MY LOVE *RCA PB 42079*	**7** 10
19 Nov 88		A SMILE IN A WHISPER *RCA PB 42249*	**75** 1
28 Jan 89		CLARE *RCA PB 42607*	**49** 3

FAIRPORT CONVENTION
UK, male / female vocal / instrumental group   **9 wks**

23 Jul 69	SI TU DOIS PARTIR *Island WIP 6064*	**21** 8
27 Sep 69	SI TU DOIS PARTIR (re-entry) *Island WIP 6064*	**49** 1

Andy FAIRWEATHER-LOW *UK, male vocalist*   **18 wks**

21 Sep 74	●	REGGAE TUNE *A & M AMS 7129*	**10** 8
6 Dec 75	●	WIDE EYED AND LEGLESS *A & M AMS 7202*	**6** 10

Adam FAITH *UK, male vocalist*   **251 wks**

20 Nov 59	★	WHAT DO YOU WANT *Parlophone R 4591*	**1** 19
22 Jan 60	★	POOR ME *Parlophone R 4623*	**1** 17
14 Apr 60	●	SOMEONE ELSE'S BABY *Parlophone R 4643*	**2** 13
30 Jun 60	●	WHEN JOHNNY COMES MARCHING HOME / MADE YOU *Parlophone R 4665*	**5** 13
15 Sep 60	●	HOW ABOUT THAT *Parlophone R 4689*	**4** 14
17 Nov 60	●	LONELY PUP (IN A CHRISTMAS SHOP) *Parlophone R 4708*	**4** 11
9 Feb 61	●	WHO AM I / THIS IS IT! *Parlophone R 4735*	**5** 14
27 Apr 61		EASY GOING ME *Parlophone R 4766*	**12** 10
20 Jul 61		DON'T YOU KNOW IT *Parlophone R 4807*	**12** 10
26 Oct 61	●	THE TIME HAS COME *Parlophone R 4837*	**4** 14
18 Jan 62		LONESOME *Parlophone R 4864*	**12** 9
3 May 62	●	AS YOU LIKE IT *Parlophone R 4896*	**5** 15
30 Aug 62	●	DON'T THAT BEAT ALL *Parlophone R 4930*	**8** 11
13 Dec 62		BABY TAKE A BOW *Parlophone R 4964*	**22** 6
31 Jan 63		WHAT NOW *Parlophone R 4990* [1]	**31** 5
11 Jul 63		WALKIN' TALL *Parlophone R 5039*	**23** 6
19 Sep 63	●	THE FIRST TIME *Parlophone R 5061* [2]	**5** 13
12 Dec 63		WE ARE IN LOVE *Parlophone R 5091* [2]	**11** 12
12 Mar 64		IF HE TELLS YOU *Parlophone R 5109* [2]	**25** 9
28 May 64		I LOVE BEING IN LOVE WITH YOU *Parlophone R 5138* [1]	**33** 6
26 Nov 64		MESSAGE TO MARTHA (KENTUCKY BLUEBIRD) *Parlophone R 5201*	**12** 11
11 Feb 65		STOP FEELING SORRY FOR YOURSELF *Parlophone R 5235*	**23** 6
17 Jun 65		SOMEONE'S TAKEN MARIA AWAY *Parlophone R 5289*	**34** 5
20 Oct 66		CHERYL'S GOIN' HOME *Parlophone R 5516*	**46** 2

[1] Adam Faith with Johnny Keating and his Orchestra [2] Adam Faith and the Roulettes

Horace FAITH *Jamaica, male vocalist*   **10 wks**

12 Sep 70	BLACK PEARL *Trojan TR 7790*	**13** 10

Percy FAITH *Canada, orchestra*   **30 wks**

10 Mar 60	●	THE THEME FROM 'A SUMMER PLACE' *Philips PB 989*	**2** 30

FAITH BROTHERS *UK, male vocal / instrumental group*   **6 wks**

13 Apr 85	THE COUNTRY OF THE BLIND *Siren SIREN 2*	**63** 3
6 Jul 85	A STRANGER ON HOME GROUND *Siren SIREN 4*	**69** 3

FAITH, HOPE and CHARITY
US, male / female vocal group   **4 wks**

31 Jan 76	JUST ONE LOOK *RCA 2632*	**38** 4

FAITH, HOPE and CHARITY
UK, female vocal group   **3 wks**

23 Jun 90	BATTLE OF THE SEXES *WEA YZ 480*	**53** 3

FAITH NO MORE *US, male vocal / instrumental group*   **55 wks**

6 Feb 88		WE CARE A LOT *Slash LASH 17*	**53** 3
10 Feb 90		EPIC *Slash LASH 21*	**37** 4
14 Apr 90		FROM OUT OF NOWHERE *Slash LASH 24*	**23** 6
14 Jul 90		FALLING TO PIECES *Slash LASH 25*	**41** 3
8 Sep 90		EPIC (re-issue) *Slash LASH 26*	**25** 5
6 Jun 92	●	MIDLIFE CRISIS *Slash LASH 37*	**10** 5
15 Aug 92		A SMALL VICTORY *Slash LASH 39*	**29** 5
12 Sep 92		A SMALL VICTORY (re-mix) *Slash LASHX 40*	**55** 1
21 Nov 92		EVERYTHING'S RUINED *Slash LASH 43*	**28** 3
16 Jan 93	●	I'M EASY / BE AGGRESSIVE *Slash LACDP 44*	**3** 7
13 Mar 93		I'M EASY / BE AGGRESSIVE (re-entry) *Slash LACDP 44*	**75** 1
6 Nov 93		ANOTHER BODY MURDERED *Epic 6597942* [1]	**26** 3
11 Mar 95		DIGGING THE GRAVE *Slash LASCD 51*	**16** 4

| 27 May 95 | **RICOCHET** Slash LASCD 53 | **27** | 2 |
| 29 Jul 95 | **EVIDENCE** Slash LASCD 54 | **32** | 3 |

[1] Faith No More & Boo-Yaa T.R.I.B.E.

Marianne FAITHFULL *UK, female vocalist* — 59 wks

13 Aug 64	● **AS TEARS GO BY** Decca F 11923	**9**	13
18 Feb 65	● **COME AND STAY WITH ME** Decca F 12075	**4**	13
6 May 65	● **THIS LITTLE BIRD** Decca F 12162	**6**	11
22 Jul 65	● **SUMMER NIGHTS** Decca F 12193	**10**	10
4 Nov 65	**YESTERDAY** Decca F 12268	**36**	4
9 Mar 67	**IS THIS WHAT I GET FOR LOVING YOU** Decca F 22524	**43**	2
24 Nov 79	**THE BALLAD OF LUCY JORDAN** Island WIP 6491	**48**	6

FAITHLESS *UK, male / female vocal / instrumental group* — 18 wks

5 Aug 95	**SALVA MEA (SAVE ME)** Cheeky CHEKCD 008	**30**	2
9 Dec 95	**INSOMNIA** Cheeky CHEKCD 010	**27**	2
23 Mar 96	**DON'T LEAVE** Cheeky CHEKCD 012	**34**	2
26 Oct 96	● **INSOMNIA (re-mix)** Cheeky CHEKCD 017	**3†**	10
21 Dec 96	● **SALVA MEA (re-issue)** Cheeky CHEKCD 018	**9†**	2

FALCO *Austria, male vocalist* — 26 wks

22 Mar 86	★ **ROCK ME AMADEUS** A & M AM 278	**1**	15
31 May 86	● **VIENNA CALLING** A & M AM 318	**10**	8
2 Aug 86	**JEANNY** A & M AM 333	**68**	1
27 Sep 86	**THE SOUND OF MUSIK** WEA U 8591	**61**	2

FALL *UK, male vocalist / multi-instrumentalist – Mark E. Smith* — 24 wks

13 Sep 86	**MR. PHARMACIST** Beggars Banquet BEG 168	**75**	1
20 Dec 86	**HEY! LUCIANI** Beggars Banquet BEG 176	**59**	1
9 May 87	**THERE'S A GHOST IN MY HOUSE** Beggars Banquet BEG 187	**30**	4
31 Oct 87	**HIT THE NORTH** Beggars Banquet BEG 200	**57**	5
30 Jan 88	**VICTORIA** Beggars Banquet BEG 206	**35**	3
26 Nov 88	**BIG NEW PRINZ / JERUSALEM (DOUBLE SINGLE)** Beggars Banquet FALL 2/3	**59**	2
27 Jan 90	**TELEPHONE THING** Cog Sinister SIN 4	**58**	1
8 Sep 90	**WHITE LIGHTNING** Cog Sinister SIN 6	**56**	2
14 Mar 92	**FREE RANGE** Cog Sinister SINS 8	**40**	1
17 Apr 93	**WHY ARE PEOPLE GRUDGEFUL** Permanent CDSPERM 9	**43**	1
25 Dec 93	**BEHIND THE COUNTER** Permanent CDSPERM 13	**75**	1
30 Apr 94	**15 WAYS** Permanent CDSPERM 14	**65**	1
17 Feb 96	**THE CHISELERS** Jet JETSCD 500	**60**	1

Tracks on Big New Prinz / Jerusalem double single: Big New Prinz / Wrong Place Right Time Number Two / Jerusalem / Acid Priest 2088.

Harold FALTERMEYER *Germany, male instrumentalist – keyboards* — 23 wks

23 Mar 85	**AXEL F** MCA MCA 949	**62**	4
1 Jun 85	● **AXEL F (re-entry)** MCA MCA 949	**2**	18
24 Aug 85	**FLETCH THEME** MCA MCA 991	**74**	1

Agnetha FALTSKOG *Sweden, female vocalist* — 12 wks

28 May 83	**THE HEAT IS ON** Epic A 3436	**35**	6
13 Aug 83	**WRAP YOUR ARMS AROUND ME** Epic A 3622	**44**	5
22 Oct 83	**CAN'T SHAKE LOOSE** Epic A 3812	**63**	1

Georgie FAME *UK, male vocalist* — 115 wks

17 Dec 64	★ **YEH YEH** Columbia DB 7428 [1]	**1**	12
4 Mar 65	**IN THE MEANTIME** Columbia DB 7494 [1]	**22**	8
29 Jul 65	**LIKE WE USED TO BE** Columbia DB 7633 [1]	**33**	7
28 Oct 65	**SOMETHING** Columbia DB 7727 [1]	**23**	7
23 Jun 66	★ **GET AWAY** Columbia DB 7946 [1]	**1**	11
22 Sep 66	**SUNNY** Columbia DB 8015	**13**	8
22 Dec 66	**SITTING IN THE PARK** Columbia DB 8096 [1]	**12**	10
22 Mar 67	**BECAUSE I LOVE YOU** CBS 202587	**15**	8
13 Sep 67	**TRY MY WORLD** CBS 2945	**37**	5
13 Dec 67	★ **BALLAD OF BONNIE AND CLYDE** CBS 3124	**1**	13
9 Jul 69	**PEACEFUL** CBS 4295	**16**	9
13 Dec 69	**SEVENTH SON** CBS 4659	**25**	7
10 Apr 71	**ROSETTA** CBS 7108 [2]	**11**	10

[1] Georgie Fame and the Blue Flames [2] Fame and Price Together

FAMILY *UK, male vocal / instrumental group* — 44 wks

1 Nov 69	**NO MULE'S FOOL** Reprise RS 27001	**29**	7
22 Aug 70	**STRANGE BAND** Reprise RS 27009	**11**	12
17 Jul 71	● **IN MY OWN TIME** Reprise K 14090	**4**	13
23 Sep 72	**BURLESQUE** Reprise K 14196	**13**	12

FAMILY CAT *UK, male vocal / instrumental group* — 4 wks

28 Aug 93	**AIRPLANE GARDENS / ATMOSPHERIC ROAD** Dedicated FCUK 003CD	**69**	1
21 May 94	**WONDERFUL EXCUSE** Dedicated 74321208432	**48**	1
30 Jul 94	**GOLDENBOOK** Dedicated 74321220072	**42**	2

FAMILY COOKIN' – See LIMMIE and the FAMILY COOKIN'

FAMILY DOGG *UK, male / female vocal group* — 14 wks

| 28 May 69 | ● **WAY OF LIFE** Bell 1055 | **6** | 14 |

FAMILY FOUNDATION
UK, male / female vocal / instrumental group — 4 wks

| 13 Jun 92 | **XPRESS YOURSELF** 380 PEW 1 | **42** | 4 |

FAMILY STAND
US, male / female vocal / instrumental group — 11 wks

| 31 Mar 90 | ● **GHETTO HEAVEN** East West A 7997 | **10** | 11 |

FAMILY STONE – See SLY and the FAMILY STONE

FAMOUS FLAMES - See James BROWN

FANTASTIC FOUR *US, male vocal group* — 4 wks

| 24 Feb 79 | **B.Y.O.F. (BRING YOUR OWN FUNK)** Atlantic LV 14 | **62** | 4 |

FANTASTICS *US, male vocal group* — 12 wks

| 27 Mar 71 | ● **SOMETHING OLD, SOMETHING NEW** Bell 1141 | **9** | 12 |

FANTASY UFO *UK, male instrumental group* — 6 wks

| 29 Sep 90 | **FANTASY** XL XLT 15 | **56** | 3 |
| 10 Aug 91 | **MIND BODY SOUL** Strictly Underground YZ 591 [1] | **50** | 3 |

[1] Fantasy UFO featuring Jay Groove

FAR CORPORATION
UK / US / Germany / Switzerland, male vocal / instrumental group — 11 wks

| 26 Oct 85 | ● **STAIRWAY TO HEAVEN** Arista ARIST 639 | **8** | 11 |

Don FARDON UK, male vocalist — 22 wks

18 Apr 70	BELFAST BOY *Young Blood YB 1010*	32	5
10 Oct 70	● INDIAN RESERVATION *Young Blood YB 1015*	3	17

FARGETTA Italy / UK, male / female vocal / instrumental duo — 3 wks

23 Jan 93	MUSIC *Synthetic CDR 6334* [1]	34	2
10 Aug 96	THE MUSIC IS MOVING *Arista 74321381572*	74	1

[1] Fargetta and Anne-Marie Smith

Chris FARLOWE UK, male vocalist — 36 wks

27 Jan 66	THINK *Immediate IM 023*	49	1
10 Feb 66	THINK (re-entry) *Immediate IM 023*	37	2
23 Jun 66	★ OUT OF TIME *Immediate IM 035*	1	13
27 Oct 66	RIDE ON BABY *Immediate IM 038*	31	7
16 Feb 67	MY WAY OF GIVING IN *Immediate IM 041*	48	1
29 Jun 67	MOANIN' *Immediate IM 056*	46	2
13 Dec 67	HANDBAGS AND GLADRAGS *Immediate IM 065*	33	6
27 Sep 75	OUT OF TIME (re-issue) *Immediate IMS 101*	44	4

FARM UK, male vocal / instrumental group — 54 wks

5 May 90	STEPPING STONE / FAMILY OF MAN *Produce MILK 101*	58	4
1 Sep 90	● GROOVY TRAIN *Produce MILK 102*	6	10
8 Dec 90	● ALL TOGETHER NOW *Produce MILK 103*	4	12
13 Apr 91	SINFUL! *Siren SRN 138* [1]	28	5
4 May 91	DON'T LET ME DOWN *Produce MILK 104*	36	3
24 Aug 91	MIND *Produce MILK 105*	31	4
14 Dec 91	LOVE SEE NO COLOUR *Produce MILK 106*	58	4
4 Jul 92	RISING SUN *End Product 6581737*	48	3
17 Oct 92	DON'T YOU WANT ME *End Product 6584687*	18	5
2 Jan 93	LOVE SEE NO COLOUR (re-issue) *End Product 6588682*	35	4

[1] Pete Wylie with the Farm

FARMERS BOYS UK, male vocal / instrumental group — 17 wks

9 Apr 83	MUCK IT OUT *EMI 5380*	48	6
30 Jul 83	FOR YOU *EMI 5401*	66	3
4 Aug 84	IN THE COUNTRY *EMI FAB 2*	44	5
3 Nov 84	PHEW WOW *EMI FAB 3*	59	3

John FARNHAM Australia, male vocalist — 17 wks

25 Apr 87	● YOU'RE THE VOICE *Wheatley PB 41093*	6	17

Joanne FARRELL US, female vocalist — 2 wks

24 Jun 95	ALL I WANNA DO *Big Beat A 8194CD*	40	2

Joe FARRELL US, male instrumentalist – saxophone — 4 wks

16 Dec 78	NIGHT DANCING *Warner Bros. LV 2*	57	4

Dionne FARRIS US, female vocalist — 5 wks

18 Mar 95	I KNOW *Columbia 6613542*	47	2
27 May 95	I KNOW (re-entry) *Columbia 6613542*	41	3

Gene FARROW and G.F. BAND
UK, male vocal / instrumental group — 8 wks

1 Apr 78	MOVE YOUR BODY *Magnet MAG 109*	33	5

13 May 78	MOVE YOUR BODY (re-entry) *Magnet MAG 109*	67	1
5 Aug 78	DON'T STOP NOW *Magnet MAG 125*	71	1
19 Aug 78	DON'T STOP NOW (re-entry) *Magnet MAG 125*	74	1

FASCINATIONS US, female vocal group — 6 wks

3 Jul 71	GIRLS ARE OUT TO GET YOU *Mojo 2092 004*	32	6

FASHION UK, male vocal / instrumental group — 12 wks

3 Apr 82	STREETPLAYER (MECHANIK) *Arista ARIST 456*	46	5
21 Aug 82	LOVE SHADOW *Arista ARIST 483*	51	5
18 Feb 84	EYE TALK *De Stijl A 4106*	69	2

Susan FASSBENDER UK, female vocalist — 8 wks

17 Jan 81	TWILIGHT CAFE *CBS 9468*	21	8

FASTWAY UK, male vocal / instrumental group — 1 wk

2 Apr 83	EASY LIVIN' *CBS A 3196*	74	1

FAT BOYS US, male vocal rap group — 29 wks

4 May 85	JAIL HOUSE RAP *Sultra U 9123*	63	2
22 Aug 87	WIPEOUT *Urban URB 5* [1]	2	12
18 Jun 88	THE TWIST (YO, TWIST) *Urban URB 20* [2]	2	11
5 Nov 88	LOUIE LOUIE *Urban URB 26*	46	4

[1] Fat Boys and the Beach Boys [2] Fat Boys and Chubby Checker

FAT LADY SINGS
Ireland, male vocal / instrumental group — 2 wks

17 Jul 93	DRUNKARD LOGIC *East West YZ 756CD*	56	2

FAT LARRY'S BAND
US, male vocal / instrumental group — 26 wks

2 Jul 77	CENTER CITY *Atlantic K 10951*	31	5
10 Mar 79	BOOGIE TOWN *Fantasy FTC 168* [1]	46	4
18 Aug 79	LOOKING FOR LOVE TONIGHT *Fantasy FTC 179*	46	6
18 Sep 82	● ZOOM *Virgin VS 546*	2	11

[1] F.L.B.

FATBACK BAND
US, male vocal / instrumental group — 67 wks

6 Sep 75	YUM YUM (GIMME SOME) *Polydor 2066 590*	40	6
6 Dec 75	(ARE YOU READY) DO THE BUS STOP *Polydor 2066 637*	18	10
21 Feb 76	● (DO THE) SPANISH HUSTLE *Polydor 2066 656*	10	7
29 May 76	PARTY TIME *Polydor 2066 682*	41	4
14 Aug 76	NIGHT FEVER *Spring 2066 706*	38	4
12 Mar 77	DOUBLE DUTCH *Spring 2066 777*	31	4
9 Aug 80	BACKSTROKIN' *Spring POSP 149* [1]	41	9
23 Jun 84	I FOUND LOVIN' *Master Mix CHE 8401*	49	4
4 May 85	GIRLS ON MY MIND *Atlantic/Cotillion FBACK 1* [1]	69	2
6 Sep 86	I FOUND LOVIN' (re-mix) *Important TAN 10*	55	5
5 Sep 87	● I FOUND LOVIN' (re-entry) *Master Mix CHE 8401*	7	12

[1] Fatback

FATHER ABRAHAM - *See SMURFS*

FATHER ABRAPHART and the SMURPS - *See Jonathan KING*

FATIMA MANSIONS
Ireland, male vocal / instrumental group   **11 wks**

23 May 92	**EVIL MAN** *Radioactive SKX 56*	**59**	1
1 Aug 92	**1000%** *Radioactive SKX 59*	**61**	3
19 Sep 92	● **(EVERYTHING I DO) I DO IT FOR YOU**		
	Columbia 6583827	**7**	6
6 Aug 94	**THE LOYALISER** *Kitchenware SKCD 67*	**58**	1

(Everything I Do) I Do It For You *was listed with* Theme From M.A.S.H. (Suicide Is Painless) *by Manic Street Preachers.*

FBI - *See REDHEAD KINGPIN and the FBI*

Phil FEARON *UK, male vocalist*   **63 wks**

23 Apr 83	● **DANCING TIGHT** *Ensign ENY 501* 1	**4**	11
30 Jul 83	**WAIT UNTIL TONIGHT (MY LOVE)**		
	Ensign ENY 503 1	**20**	8
22 Oct 83	**FANTASY REAL** *Ensign ENY 507* 2	**41**	6
10 Mar 84	● **WHAT DO I DO** *Ensign ENY 510* 2	**5**	10
14 Jul 84	● **EVERYBODY'S LAUGHING** *Ensign ENY 514* 2	**10**	10
15 Jun 85	**YOU DON'T NEED A REASON** *Ensign ENY 517* 2	**42**	4
27 Jul 85	**THIS KIND OF LOVE** *Ensign ENY 521* 3	**70**	3
2 Aug 86	● **I CAN PROVE IT** *Ensign PF 1*	**8**	9
15 Nov 86	**AIN'T NOTHING BUT A HOUSEPARTY** *Ensign PF 2*	**60**	2

1 Galaxy featuring Phil Fearon 2 Phil Fearon and Galaxy 3 Phil Fearon and Galaxy featuring Dee Galdes

Wilton FELDER
US, male instrumentalist – tenor sax   **7 wks**

1 Nov 80	**INHERIT THE WIND** *MCA 646*	**39**	5
16 Feb 85	**(NO MATTER HOW HIGH I GET) I'LL STILL BE**		
	LOOKIN' UP TO YOU *MCA MCA 919*	**63**	2

Bobby Womack is the uncredited lead vocalist on both hits. Alltrinna Grayson co-vocalises on MCA 919.

José FELICIANO
US, male vocalist / instrumentalist – guitar   **23 wks**

| 18 Sep 68 | ● **LIGHT MY FIRE** *RCA 1715* | **6** | 16 |
| 18 Oct 69 | **AND THE SUN WILL SHINE** *RCA 1871* | **25** | 7 |

FELIX *UK, male producer*   **29 wks**

8 Aug 92	● **DON'T YOU WANT ME** *Deconstruction 74321110507*	**6**	11
24 Oct 92	**IT WILL MAKE ME CRAZY**		
	Deconstruction 74321118137	**11**	6
22 May 93	**STARS** *Deconstruction 74321147102*	**29**	3
12 Aug 95	● **DON'T YOU WANT ME (re-mix)**		
	Deconstruction 74321293972	**10**	5
19 Oct 96	**DON'T YOU WANT ME (2nd re-mix)**		
	Deconstruction 74321418142	**17**	4

Julie FELIX *US, female vocalist*   **19 wks**

| 18 Apr 70 | **IF I COULD (EL CONDOR PASA)** *RAK 101* | **19** | 11 |
| 17 Oct 70 | **HEAVEN IS HERE** *RAK 105* | **22** | 8 |

FELLY – *See TECHNOTRONIC*

FEMME FATALE
US, male / female vocal / instrumental group   **2 wks**

| 11 Feb 89 | **FALLING IN AND OUT OF LOVE** | | |
| | *MCA MCA 1309* | **69** | 2 |

FENDERMEN *US, male vocal / instrumental duo – guitars*   **9 wks**

18 Aug 60	**MULE SKINNER BLUES** *Top Rank JAR 395*	**50**	1
1 Sep 60	**MULE SKINNER BLUES (re-entry)**		
	Top Rank JAR 395	**37**	2
29 Sep 60	**MULE SKINNER BLUES (2nd re-entry)**		
	Top Rank JAR 395	**32**	6

FENMEN – *See Bern ELLIOTT and the FENMEN*

George FENTON and Jonas GWANGWA
UK / South Africa, male instrumental production duo   **1 wk**

| 2 Jan 88 | **CRY FREEDOM** *MCA MCA 1228* | **75** | 1 |

The listed flip side of Cry Freedom was The Funeral by Thuli Dumakude.

Peter FENTON *UK, male vocalist*   **3 wks**

| 10 Nov 66 | **MARBLE BREAKS IRON BENDS** *Fontana TF 748* | **46** | 3 |

Shane FENTON and the FENTONES
UK, male vocal / instrumental group   **28 wks**

26 Oct 61	**I'M A MOODY GUY** *Parlophone R 4827*	**22**	8
1 Feb 62	**WALK AWAY** *Parlophone R 4866*	**38**	5
5 Apr 62	**IT'S ALL OVER NOW** *Parlophone R 4883*	**29**	7
12 Jul 62	**CINDY'S BIRTHDAY** *Parlophone R 4921*	**19**	8

Fenton later became Alvin Stardust.

FENTONES *UK, male instrumental group*   **4 wks**

| 19 Apr 62 | **THE MEXICAN** *Parlophone R 4899* | **41** | 3 |
| 27 Sep 62 | **THE BREEZE AND I** *Parlophone R 4937* | **48** | 1 |

Sheila FERGUSON *US, female vocalist*   **1 wk**

| 5 Feb 94 | **WHEN WILL I SEE YOU AGAIN** | | |
| | *XSrhythm CDSTAS 2711* | **60** | 1 |

FERKO STRING BAND
US, male vocal / instrumental group   **2 wks**

| 12 Aug 55 | **ALABAMA JUBILEE** *London HL 8140* | **20** | 2 |

Luisa FERNANDEZ *Spain, female vocalist*   **8 wks**

| 11 Nov 78 | **LAY LOVE ON YOU** *Warner Bros. K 17061* | **31** | 8 |

Pamela FERNANDEZ *US, female vocalist*   **3 wks**

17 Sep 94	**KICKIN' IN THE BEAT** *Ore AG 5CD*	**43**	2
3 Jun 95	**LET'S START OVER / KICKIN' IN THE BEAT (re-mix)**		
	Ore AG 9CD	**59**	1

FERRANTE and TEICHER
US, male instrumental duo – pianos   **18 wks**

18 Aug 60	**THEME FROM 'THE APARTMENT'**		
	London HLT 9164	**44**	1
9 Mar 61	● **EXODUS (THEME FROM 'EXODUS')**		
	London HLT 9298 and HMV POP 881	**6**	17

Theme From 'Exodus' available first on London, then on HMV when the American label, United Artists, changed its UK outlet.

José FERRER | US, male vocalist | 3 wks

19 Feb 54	● WOMAN Philips PB 220	7	3

Woman coupled with Man by Rosemary Clooney.

Tony FERRINO | UK, male vocalist, comedian Steve Coogan | 2 wks

23 Nov 96	HELP YOURSELF / BIGAMY AT CHRISTMAS RCA 74321430302	42	2

FERRY AID | International, male / female charity ensemble | 7 wks

4 Apr 87	★ LET IT BE The Sun AID 1	1	7

Bryan FERRY | UK, male vocalist | 133 wks

29 Sep 73	● A HARD RAIN'S GONNA FALL Island WIP 6170	10	9
25 May 74	THE IN CROWD Island WIP 6196	13	6
31 Aug 74	SMOKE GETS IN YOUR EYES Island WIP 6205	17	8
5 Jul 75	YOU GO TO MY HEAD Island WIP 6234	33	3
12 Jun 76	● LET'S STICK TOGETHER (LET'S WORK TOGETHER) Island WIP 6307	4	10
7 Aug 76	● EXTENDED PLAY EP Island IEP 1	7	9
5 Feb 77	● THIS IS TOMORROW Polydor 2001 704	9	9
14 May 77	TOKYO JOE Polydor 2001 711	15	7
13 May 78	WHAT GOES ON Polydor POSP 3	67	2
5 Aug 78	SIGN OF THE TIMES Polydor 2001 798	37	8
11 May 85	● SLAVE TO LOVE EG FERRY 1	10	9
31 Aug 85	DON'T STOP THE DANCE EG FERRY 2	21	7
7 Dec 85	WINDSWEPT EG FERRY 3	46	3
29 Mar 86	IS YOUR LOVE STRONG ENOUGH? EG FERRY 4	22	7
10 Oct 87	THE RIGHT STUFF Virgin VS 940	37	6
13 Feb 88	KISS AND TELL Virgin VS 1034	41	5
29 Oct 88	LET'S STICK TOGETHER (re-mix) EG EGO 44	12	7
11 Feb 89	THE PRICE OF LOVE (re-mix) EG EGO 46	49	3
22 Apr 89	HE'LL HAVE TO GO EG EGO 48	63	1
6 Mar 93	I PUT A SPELL ON YOU Virgin VSCDG 1400	18	5
29 May 93	WILL YOU LOVE ME TOMORROW Virgin VSCDG 1455	23	5
4 Sep 93	GIRL OF MY BEST FRIEND Virgin VSCDG 1488	57	2
29 Oct 94	YOUR PAINTED SMILE Virgin VSCDG 1508	52	1
11 Feb 95	MAMOUNA Virgin VSCDG 1528	57	1

Tracks on Extended Play EP: Price Of Love / Shame Shame Shame / Heart On My Sleeve / It's Only Love.

FEVER – See Tippa IRIE

Lena FIAGBE | UK, female vocalist | 13 wks

24 Jul 93	YOU COME FROM EARTH Mother MUMCD 42 [1]	69	1
23 Oct 93	GOTTA GET IT RIGHT Mother MUMCD 44	20	5
16 Apr 94	WHAT'S IT LIKE TO BE BEAUTIFUL Mother MUMCD 49	52	3
25 Jun 94	VISIONS Mother MUMCD 53	48	2
10 Feb 96	AFRICAN DREAM Mercury MERCD 453 [2]	44	2

[1] Lena [2] Wasis Diop featuring Lena Fiagbe

Karel FIALKA | UK, male vocalist / multi-instrumentalist | 12 wks

17 May 80	THE EYES HAVE IT Blueprint BLU 2005	52	4
5 Sep 87	● HEY MATTHEW IRS IRM 140	9	8

FIAT LUX | UK, male vocal / instrumental group | 4 wks

28 Jan 84	SECRETS Polydor FIAT 2	65	3
17 Mar 84	BLUE EMOTION Polydor FIAT 3	59	1

FICTION FACTORY | UK, male vocal / instrumental group | 11 wks

14 Jan 84	● (FEELS LIKE) HEAVEN CBS A 3996	6	9
17 Mar 84	GHOST OF LOVE CBS A 3819	64	2

FIDDLER'S DRAM | UK, male / female vocal / instrumental group | 9 wks

15 Dec 79	● DAY TRIP TO BANGOR (DIDN'T WE HAVE A LOVELY TIME) Dingles SID 211	3	9

FIDELFATTI featuring RONNETTE | Italy, male producer and female vocalist | 1 wk

27 Jan 90	JUST WANNA TOUCH ME Urban URB 46	65	1

Billy FIELD | Australia, male vocalist | 3 wks

12 Jun 82	YOU WEREN'T IN LOVE WITH ME CBS A 2344	67	3

Ernie FIELDS | US, orchestra | 8 wks

25 Dec 59	IN THE MOOD London HL 8985	13	8

Gracie FIELDS | UK, female vocalist | 15 wks

31 May 57	● AROUND THE WORLD Columbia DB 3953	8	8
2 Aug 57	AROUND THE WORLD (re-entry) Columbia DB 3953	24	1
6 Nov 59	LITTLE DONKEY Columbia DB 4360	30	1
20 Nov 59	LITTLE DONKEY (re-entry) Columbia DB 4360	20	5

Richard 'Dimples' FIELDS | US, male vocalist | 4 wks

20 Feb 82	I'VE GOT TO LEARN TO SAY NO Epic EPC A 1918	56	4

FIELDS OF THE NEPHILIM | UK, male vocal / instrumental group | 9 wks

24 Oct 87	BLUE WATER Situation Two SIT 48	75	1
4 Jun 88	MOONCHILD Situation Two SIT 52	28	3
27 May 89	PSYCHONAUT Situation Two ST 57	35	3
4 Aug 90	FOR HER LIGHT Beggars Banquet BEG 244T	54	1
24 Nov 90	SUMERLAND (DREAMED) Beggars Banquet BEG 250	37	1

FIFTH DIMENSION | US, male / female vocal group | 21 wks

16 Apr 69	AQUARIUS / LET THE SUNSHINE IN (MEDLEY) Liberty LBF 15193	11	12
17 Jan 70	WEDDING BELL BLUES Liberty LBF 15288	16	9

52ND STREET | UK, male / female vocal / instrumental group | 13 wks

2 Nov 85	TELL ME (HOW IT FEELS) 10 TEN 74	54	5
11 Jan 86	YOU'RE MY LAST CHANCE 10 TEN 89	49	4
8 Mar 86	I CAN'T LET YOU GO 10 TEN 114	57	4

53RD AND THIRD – See Jonathan KING

FINAL CUT – See TRUE FAITH with FINAL CUT

FINE YOUNG CANNIBALS | UK, male vocal / instrumental group | 79 wks

8 Jun 85	● JOHNNY COME HOME London LON 68	8	13

9 Nov 85	BLUE *London LON 79*	**41**	6
11 Jan 86	● SUSPICIOUS MINDS *London LON 82*	**8**	9
12 Apr 86	FUNNY HOW LOVE IS *London LON 88*	**58**	4
21 Mar 87	● EVER FALLEN IN LOVE *London LON 121*	**9**	10
7 Jan 89	● SHE DRIVES ME CRAZY *London LON 199*	**5**	11
15 Apr 89	● GOOD THING *London LON 218*	**7**	8
19 Aug 89	DON'T LOOK BACK *London LON 220*	**34**	4
18 Nov 89	I'M NOT THE MAN I USED TO BE *London LON 244*	**20**	8
24 Feb 90	I'M NOT SATISFIED *London LON 252*	**46**	3
16 Nov 96	THE FLAME *ffrr LONCD 389*	**17**	3

FINITRIBE *UK, male instrumental / production group*   **2 wks**

11 Jul 92	FOREVERGREEN *One Little Indian 74 TP12F*	**51**	1
19 Nov 94	BRAND NEW *ffr FCD 247*	**69**	1

FINK BROTHERS *UK, male vocal / instrumental duo*   **4 wks**

9 Feb 85	MUTANTS IN MEGA CITY ONE *Zarjazz JAZZ 2*	**50**	4

FINN *New Zealand, male vocal / instrumental duo*   **5 wks**

14 Oct 95	SUFFER NEVER *Parlophone CDRS 6417*	**29**	3
9 Dec 95	ANGEL'S HEAP *Parlophone CDRS 6421*	**41**	2

Micky FINN – *See URBAN SHAKEDOWN featuring Micky FINN*

Tim FINN *New Zealand, male vocalist*   **6 wks**

26 Jun 93	PERSUASION *Capitol 6592482*	**43**	3
18 Sep 93	HIT THE GROUND RUNNING *Capitol CDCLS 694*	**50**	3

See also Finn.

Elisa FIORILLO *US, female vocalist*   **14 wks**

28 Nov 87	● WHO FOUND WHO *Chrysalis CHS JEL 1* [1]	**10**	10
13 Feb 88	HOW CAN I FORGET YOU *Chrysalis ELISA 1*	**50**	4

[1] Jellybean featuring Elisa Fiorillo

FIRE INC. – *See Jim STEINMAN*

FIRE ISLAND *UK, male instrumental / production group*   **5 wks**

8 Aug 92	IN YOUR BONES / FIRE ISLAND		
	Boy's Own BOIX 11	**66**	1
12 Mar 94	THERE BUT FOR THE GRACE OF GOD		
	Junior Boy's Own JBO 18CD [1]	**32**	3
4 Mar 95	IF YOU SHOULD NEED A FRIEND		
	Junior Boy's Own JBO 26CDS [2]	**51**	1

[1] Fire Island featuring Love Nelson [2] Fire Island featuring Mark Anthoni

See also Heller and Farley Project.

FIREBALLS *US, male instrumental group*   **17 wks**

27 Jul 61	QUITE A PARTY *Pye International 7N 25092*	**29**	9
14 Nov 63	SUGAR SHACK *London HLD 9789* [1]	**45**	4
19 Dec 63	SUGAR SHACK (re-entry) *London HLD 9789* [1]	**46**	4

[1] Jimmy Gilmer and the Fireballs

FIREHOUSE *US, male vocal / instrumental group*   **2 wks**

13 Jul 91	DON'T TREAT ME BAD *Epic 6567807*	**71**	1
19 Dec 92	WHEN I LOOK INTO YOUR EYES *Epic 6588347*	**65**	1

FIRM *UK, male vocal / instrumental group*   **21 wks**

17 Jul 82	ARTHUR DALEY ('E'S ALRIGHT) *Bark HID 1*	**14**	9
6 Jun 87	★ STAR TREKKIN' *Bark TREK 1*	**1**	12

FIRST CHOICE *US, female vocal group*   **21 wks**

19 May 73	ARMED AND EXTREMELY DANGEROUS *Bell 1297*	**16**	10
4 Aug 73	● SMARTY PANTS *Bell 1324*	**9**	11

FIRST CLASS *UK, male vocal group*   **10 wks**

15 Jun 74	BEACH BABY *UK 66*	**13**	10

FIRST EDITION – *See Kenny ROGERS*

FIRST LIGHT *UK, male vocal / instrumental duo*   **5 wks**

21 May 83	EXPLAIN THE REASONS *London LON 26*	**65**	3
28 Jan 84	WISH YOU WERE HERE *London LON 43*	**71**	2

FISCHER-Z *UK, male vocal / instrumental group*   **7 wks**

26 May 79	THE WORKER *United Artists UP 36509*	**53**	5
3 May 80	SO LONG *United Artists BP 342*	**72**	2

FISH *UK, male vocalist*   **20 wks**

18 Oct 86	SHORT CUT TO SOMEWHERE *Charisma CB 426* [1]	**75**	1
28 Oct 89	STATE OF MIND *EMI EM 109*	**32**	3
6 Jan 90	BIG WEDGE *EMI EM 125*	**25**	4
17 Mar 90	A GENTLEMAN'S EXCUSE ME *EMI EM 135*	**30**	3
28 Sep 91	INTERNAL EXILE *Polydor FISHY 1*	**37**	2
11 Jan 92	CREDO *Polydor FISHY 2*	**38**	2
4 Jul 92	SOMETHING IN THE AIR *Polydor FISHY 3*	**51**	2
16 Apr 94	LADY LET IT LIE *Dick Bros. DDICK 3CD1*	**46**	1
1 Oct 94	FORTUNES OF WAR *Dick Bros. DDICK 008CD1*	**67**	1
26 Aug 95	JUST GOOD FRIENDS *Dick Bros. DDICK 014CD1* [2]	**63**	1

[1] Fish and Tony Banks [2] Fish and Sam Brown

FISHBONE *US, male vocal / instrumental group*   **3 wks**

1 Aug 92	EVERYDAY SUNSHINE / FIGHT THE YOUTH		
	Columbia 6581937	**60**	2
28 Aug 93	SWIM *Columbia 6596252*	**54**	1

Eddie FISHER *US, male vocalist*   **105 wks**

2 Jan 53	★ OUTSIDE OF HEAVEN *HMV B 10362*	**1**	16
23 Jan 53	EVERYTHING I HAVE IS YOURS *HMV B 10398*	**12**	1
6 Feb 53	● EVERYTHING I HAVE IS YOURS (re-entry) *HMV B 10398*	**8**	4
1 May 53	● DOWNHEARTED *HMV B 10450*	**3**	15
1 May 53	OUTSIDE OF HEAVEN (re-entry) *HMV B 10362*	**12**	1
22 May 53	★ I'M WALKING BEHIND YOU *HMV B 10489* [1]	**1**	18
6 Nov 53	● WISH YOU WERE HERE *HMV B 10564*	**8**	9
22 Jan 54	● OH MY PAPA *HMV B 10614*	**9**	1
5 Feb 54	OH MY PAPA (re-entry) *HMV B 10614*	**11**	1
26 Feb 54	● OH MY PAPA (2nd re-entry) *HMV B 10614*	**10**	1
12 Mar 54	OH MY PAPA (3rd re-entry) *HMV B 10614*	**11**	1
29 Oct 54	I NEED YOU NOW *HMV B 10755*	**16**	2
19 Nov 54	I NEED YOU NOW (re-entry) *HMV B 10755*	**13**	7
21 Jan 55	I NEED YOU NOW (2nd re-entry) *HMV B 10755*	**19**	1
18 Mar 55	● (I'M ALWAYS HEARING) WEDDING BELLS		
	HMV B 10839	**5**	11
23 Nov 56	● CINDY OH CINDY *HMV POP 273*	**5**	16

[1] Eddie Fisher with Sally Sweetland (soprano)

Eddie Fisher

Eddie Fisher's ex-wives have clocked up 37 weeks on chart: 17 for Debbie Reynolds (also pictured) and 20 for Connie Stevens. Elizabeth Taylor has yet to score.

Joe Fagin

Joe Fagin's biggest hit, 'That's Living Alright', was the theme to the TV comedy/drama *Auf Wiedersehen Pet*, which starred fellow chart star Jimmy Nail.

Falco

Falco is the only Austrian to top the UK chart. He did so with a tribute to his fellow countryman, Wolfgang Amedeus Mozart.

Mike Flowers Pops

When Oasis and Mike Flowers Pops simultaneously held down Top 10 positions with 'Wonderwall' in 1995, it was the first time that two versions of the same song were in the Top 10 since 'When I Fall In Love' by Rick Astley and Nat 'King' Cole in December 1987.

Mark FISHER featuring Dotty GREEN
UK, male instrumentalist – keyboards and female vocalist **2 wks**

29 Jun 85	**LOVE SITUATION** *Total Control TOCO 3*	59	2

Toni FISHER
US, female vocalist **1 wk**

12 Feb 60	**THE BIG HURT** *Top Rank JAR 261*	30	1

FITS OF GLOOM
UK / Italy, male vocal duo **4 wks**

4 Jun 94	**HEAVEN** *Media MCSTD 1981*	47	2
5 Nov 94	**THE POWER OF LOVE** *Media MCSTD 2016* [1]	49	2

[1] Fits Of Gloom featuring Lizzy Mack

Ella FITZGERALD
US, female vocalist **29 wks**

23 May 58	**SWINGIN' SHEPHERD BLUES** *HMV POP 486*	15	5
16 Oct 59	**BUT NOT FOR ME** *HMV POP 657*	25	2
25 Dec 59	**BUT NOT FOR ME (re-entry)** *HMV POP 657*	29	1
21 Apr 60	**MACK THE KNIFE** *HMV POP 736*	19	9
6 Oct 60	**HOW HIGH THE MOON** *HMV POP 782*	46	1
22 Nov 62	**DESAFINADO** *Verve VS 502*	38	4
27 Dec 62	**DESAFINADO (re-entry)** *Verve VS 502*	41	2
30 Apr 64	**CAN'T BUY ME LOVE** *Verve VS 519*	34	5

Scott FITZGERALD
UK, male vocalist **12 wks**

14 Jan 78	● **IF I HAD WORDS** *Pepper UP 36333* [1]	3	10
7 May 88	**GO** *PRT PYS 10*	52	2

[1] Scott Fitzgerald and Yvonne Keeley and the St Thomas More School Choir

FIVE SMITH BROTHERS
UK, male vocal group **1 wk**

22 Jul 55	**I'M IN FAVOUR OF FRIENDSHIP** *Decca F 10527*	20	1

FIVE STAR
UK, male / female vocal group **140 wks**

4 May 85	**ALL FALL DOWN** *Tent PB 40039*	15	12
20 Jul 85	**LET ME BE THE ONE** *Tent PB 40193*	18	9
14 Sep 85	**LOVE TAKE OVER** *Tent PB 40353*	25	9
16 Nov 85	**R.S.V.P.** *Tent PB 40445*	45	5
11 Jan 86	● **SYSTEM ADDICT** *Tent PB 40515*	3	11
12 Apr 86	● **CAN'T WAIT ANOTHER MINUTE** *Tent PB 40697*	7	10
26 Jul 86	● **FIND THE TIME** *Tent PB 40799*	7	10
13 Sep 86	● **RAIN OR SHINE** *Tent PB 40901*	2	11
22 Nov 86	**IF I SAY YES** *Tent PB 41047*	15	9
7 Feb 87	● **STAY OUT OF MY LIFE** *Tent PB 41131*	9	8
18 Apr 87	● **THE SLIGHTEST TOUCH** *Tent PB 41265*	4	9
22 Aug 87	**WHENEVER YOU'RE READY** *Tent PB 41477*	11	6
10 Oct 87	**STRONG AS STEEL** *Tent PB 41565*	16	7
5 Dec 87	**SOMEWHERE SOMEBODY** *Tent PB 41661*	23	6
4 Jun 88	**ANOTHER WEEKEND** *Tent PB 42081*	18	4
6 Aug 88	**ROCK MY WORLD** *Tent PB 42145*	28	4
17 Sep 88	**THERE'S A BRAND NEW WORLD** *Tent PB 42235*	61	2
19 Nov 88	**LET ME BE YOURS** *Tent PB 42343*	51	2
8 Apr 89	**WITH EVERY HEARTBEAT** *Tent PB 42693*	49	2
10 Mar 90	**TREAT ME LIKE A LADY** *Tent FIVE 1*	54	2
7 Jul 90	**HOT LOVE** *Tent FIVE 2*	68	1

FIVE THIRTY
UK, male vocal / instrumental group **4 wks**

4 Aug 90	**ABSTAIN** *East West YZ 530*	75	1
25 May 91	**13TH DISCIPLE** *East West YZ 577*	67	1
3 Aug 91	**SUPERNOVA** *East West YZ 594*	75	1
2 Nov 91	**YOU (EP)** *East West YZ 624*	72	1

Tracks on You (EP): You / Cuddly Drug / Slow Train Into The Ocean.

5000 VOLTS
UK, male / female vocal / instrumental group **18 wks**

6 Sep 75	● **I'M ON FIRE** *Philips 6006 464*	4	9
24 Jul 76	● **DR. KISS KISS** *Philips 6006 533*	8	9

FIXX
UK, male vocal / instrumental group **8 wks**

24 Apr 82	**STAND OR FALL** *MCA FIXX 2*	54	4
17 Jul 82	**RED SKIES** *MCA FIXX 3*	57	4

FKW
UK, male vocal / instrumental group **8 wks**

2 Oct 93	**NEVER GONNA (GIVE YOU UP)** *PWL International PWCD 273*	48	2
11 Dec 93	**SEIZE THE DAY** *PWL International PWCD 279*	45	2
5 Mar 94	**JINGO** *PWL International PWCD 283*	30	3
4 Jun 94	**THIS IS THE WAY** *PWL International PWCD 307*	63	1

Roberta FLACK
US, female vocalist **79 wks**

27 May 72	**THE FIRST TIME EVER I SAW YOUR FACE** *Atlantic K 10161*	14	14
5 Aug 72	**WHERE IS THE LOVE** *Atlantic K 10202* [1]	29	7
17 Feb 73	● **KILLING ME SOFTLY WITH HIS SONG** *Atlantic K 10282*	6	14
24 Aug 74	**FEEL LIKE MAKING LOVE** *Atlantic K 10467*	34	7
6 May 78	**THE CLOSER I GET TO YOU** *Atlantic K 11099* [1]	42	4
17 May 80	● **BACK TOGETHER AGAIN** *Atlantic K 11481* [1]	3	11
30 Aug 80	**DON'T MAKE ME WAIT TOO LONG** *Atlantic K 11555*	44	7
20 Aug 83	● **TONIGHT I CELEBRATE MY LOVE** *Capitol CL 302* [2]	2	13
29 Jul 89	**UH-UH OOH OOH LOOK OUT (HERE IT COMES)** *Atlantic A 8941*	72	2

[1] Roberta Flack and Donny Hathaway [2] Peabo Bryson and Roberta Flack

FLAJ – *See GETO BOYS featuring FLAJ*

FLAMING LIPS
US, male vocal / instrumental group **1 wk**

9 Mar 96	**THIS HERE GIRAFFE** *Warner Bros. W 0335CD*	72	1

FLAMINGOS
US, male vocal group **5 wks**

4 Jun 69	**BOOGALOO PARTY** *Philips BF 1786*	26	5

Michael FLANDERS
UK, male vocalist **3 wks**

27 Feb 59	**LITTLE DRUMMER BOY** *Parlophone R 4528*	20	2
17 Apr 59	**LITTLE DRUMMER BOY (re-entry)** *Parlophone R 4528*	24	1

FLASH AND THE PAN
Australia, male vocal / instrumental group **15 wks**

23 Sep 78	**AND THE BAND PLAYED ON (DOWN AMONG THE DEAD MEN)** *Ensign ENY 15*	54	4
21 May 83	● **WAITING FOR A TRAIN** *Easybeat EASY 1*	7	11

Lester FLATT and Earl SCRUGGS
US, male instrumental duo – banjos **6 wks**

15 Nov 67	**FOGGY MOUNTAIN BREAKDOWN** *CBS 3038 and Mercury MF 1007*	39	6

The versions on the two labels were not the same cuts; CBS had a 1965 recording, Mercury a 1949. The chart did not differentiate and listed both together.

Fogwell FLAX and the ANKLEBITERS from FREEHOLD JUNIOR SCHOOL
UK, male vocalist and school choir **2 wks**

26 Dec 81	ONE NINE FOR SANTA *EMI 5255*	**68** 2

F L B – *See* FAT LARRY'S BAND

FLEE-REKKERS *UK, male instrumental group* **13 wks**

19 May 60	GREEN JEANS *Triumph RGM 1008*	**23** 13

FLEETWOOD MAC
UK / US, male / female vocal / instrumental group **223 wks**

10 Apr 68	BLACK MAGIC WOMAN *Blue Horizon 57 3138*	**37** 7
17 Jul 68	NEED YOUR LOVE SO BAD *Blue Horizon 57 3139*	**31** 13
4 Dec 68	★ ALBATROSS *Blue Horizon 57 3145*	**1** 20
16 Apr 69	● MAN OF THE WORLD *Immediate IM 080*	**2** 14
23 Jul 69	NEED YOUR LOVE SO BAD (re-issue) *Blue Horizon 57 3157*	**32** 6
13 Sep 69	NEED YOUR LOVE SO BAD (re-entry of re-issue) *Blue Horizon 57 3157*	**42** 3
4 Oct 69	● OH WELL *Reprise RS 27000*	**2** 16
23 May 70	● THE GREEN MANALISHI (WITH THE TWO-PRONG CROWN) *Reprise RS 27007*	**10** 12
12 May 73	● ALBATROSS (re-issue) *CBS 8306*	**2** 15
13 Nov 76	SAY YOU LOVE ME *Reprise K 14447*	**40** 4
19 Feb 77	GO YOUR OWN WAY *Warner Bros. K 16872*	**38** 4
30 Apr 77	DON'T STOP *Warner Bros. K 16930*	**32** 5
9 Jul 77	DREAMS *Warner Bros. K 16969*	**24** 9
22 Oct 77	YOU MAKE LOVING FUN *Warner Bros. K 17013*	**45** 2
11 Mar 78	RHIANNON *Reprise K 14430*	**46** 3
6 Oct 79	● TUSK *Warner Bros. K 17468*	**6** 10
22 Dec 79	SARA *Warner Bros. K 17533*	**37** 8
25 Sep 82	GYPSY *Warner Bros. K 17997*	**46** 3
18 Dec 82	● OH DIANE *Warner Bros. FLEET 1*	**9** 15
4 Apr 87	● BIG LOVE *Warner Bros. W 8398*	**9** 12
11 Jul 87	SEVEN WONDERS *Warner Bros. W 8317*	**56** 4
26 Sep 87	● LITTLE LIES *Warner Bros. W 8291*	**5** 12
26 Dec 87	FAMILY MAN *Warner Bros. W 8114*	**54** 4
2 Apr 88	● EVERYWHERE *Warner Bros. W 8143*	**4** 10
18 Jun 88	ISN'T IT MIDNIGHT *Warner Bros. W 7860*	**60** 2
17 Dec 88	AS LONG AS YOU FOLLOW *Warner Bros. W 7644*	**66** 3
5 May 90	SAVE ME *Warner Bros. W 9866*	**53** 3
25 Aug 90	IN THE BACK OF MY MIND *Warner Bros. W 9739*	**58** 3

Group were UK and male only up to and including the re-issue of Albatross.

FLEETWOODS *US, male / female vocal group* **8 wks**

24 Apr 59	● COME SOFTLY TO ME *London HLU 8841*	**6** 8

Rochelle FLEMING – *See* FIRST CHOICE featuring Rochelle FLEMING

La FLEUR
Holland, male / female vocal / instrumental group **4 wks**

30 Jul 83	BOOGIE NIGHTS *Proto ENA 111*	**51** 4

KC FLIGHTT *US, male rapper* **4 wks**

1 Apr 89	PLANET E *RCA PT 49404*	**48** 4

Dread FLIMSTONE and the NEW TONE AGE FAMILY *US, male vocal / instrumental group* **1 wk**

30 Nov 91	FROM THE GHETTO *Urban URB 87*	**66** 1

Berni FLINT *UK, male vocalist* **11 wks**

19 Mar 77	● I DON'T WANT TO PUT A HOLD ON YOU *EMI 2599*	**3** 10
23 Jul 77	SOUTHERN COMFORT *EMI 2621*	**48** 1

FLINTLOCK *UK, male vocal / instrumental group* **5 wks**

29 May 76	DAWN *Pinnacle P 8419*	**30** 5

F.L.O. – *See* Rahni HARRIS and F.L.O.

FLOATERS *US, male vocal / instrumental group* **11 wks**

23 Jul 77	★ FLOAT ON *ABC 4187*	**1** 11

A FLOCK OF SEAGULLS
UK, male vocal / instrumental group **46 wks**

27 Mar 82	I RAN *Jive JIVE 14*	**43** 6
12 Jun 82	SPACE AGE LOVE SONG *Jive JIVE 17*	**34** 6
6 Nov 82	● WISHING (IF I HAD A PHOTOGRAPH OF YOU) *Jive JIVE 25*	**10** 12
23 Apr 83	NIGHTMARES *Jive JIVE 33*	**53** 3
25 Jun 83	TRANSFER AFFECTION *Jive JIVE 41*	**38** 5
14 Jul 84	THE MORE YOU LIVE, THE MORE YOU LOVE *Jive JIVE 62*	**26** 11
19 Oct 85	WHO'S THAT GIRL (SHE'S GOT IT) *Jive JIVE 106*	**66** 3

FLOORPLAY *UK, male instrumental / production duo* **1 wk**

27 Jan 96	AUTOMATIC *Perfecto PERF 115CD*	**50** 1

FLOWERED UP *UK, male vocal / instrumental group* **17 wks**

28 Jul 90	IT'S ON *Heavenly HVN 3*	**54** 4
24 Nov 90	PHOBIA *Heavenly HVN 7*	**75** 1
11 May 91	TAKE IT *London FUP 1*	**34** 4
17 Aug 91	IT'S ON / EGG RUSH (re-issue) *London FUP 2*	**38** 3
2 May 92	WEEKENDER *Heavenly HVN 16*	**20** 5

See also Various Artists (EPs & LPs): The Fred EP.

FLOWERPOT MEN *UK, male vocal group* **12 wks**

23 Aug 67	● LET'S GO TO SAN FRANCISCO *Deram DM 142*	**4** 12

Mike FLOWERS POPS
UK, male / female vocal / instrumental group **12 wks**

30 Dec 95	● WONDERWALL *London LONCD 378*	**2** 7
13 Apr 96	WONDERWALL (re-entry) *London LONCD 378*	**52** 2
8 Jun 96	LIGHT MY FIRE / PLEASE RELEASE ME *London LONCD 384*	**39** 2
28 Dec 96	DON'T CRY FOR ME ARGENTINA *Love This LUVTHIS 16*	**30†** 1

Eddie FLOYD *US, male vocalist* **29 wks**

2 Feb 67	KNOCK ON WOOD *Atlantic 584 041*	**50** 1
2 Mar 67	KNOCK ON WOOD (re-entry) *Atlantic 584 041*	**19** 17
16 Mar 67	RAISE YOUR HAND *Stax 601 001*	**42** 3
9 Aug 67	THINGS GET BETTER *Stax 601 016*	**31** 8

FLUFFY *UK, female vocal / instrumental group* **2 wks**

17 Feb 96	HUSBAND *Parkway PARK 006CD*	**58** 1
5 Oct 96	NOTHING *Virgin VSCDT 1614*	**52** 1

FLUKE *UK, male instrumental / production group*   **17 wks**

20 Mar 93	SLID *Circa YRCD 103*	59	1
19 Jun 93	ELECTRIC GUITAR *Circa YRCD 104*	58	2
11 Sep 93	GROOVY FEELING *Circa YRCD 106*	45	3
23 Apr 94	BUBBLE *Circa YRCD 110*	37	2
29 Jul 95	BULLET *Circa YRCD 121*	23	3
16 Dec 95	TOSH *Circa YRCD 122*	32	3
16 Nov 96	ATOM BOMB *Circa YRCD 125*	20	3

See also Lucky Monkeys.

FLYING LIZARDS
UK, male / female vocal / instrumental group   **16 wks**

| 4 Aug 79 | ● MONEY *Virgin VS 276* | 5 | 10 |
| 9 Feb 80 | T.V. *Virgin VS 325* | 43 | 6 |

FLYING PICKETS *UK, male vocal group*   **20 wks**

26 Nov 83	★ ONLY YOU *10 TEN 14*	1	11
21 Apr 84	● WHEN YOU'RE YOUNG AND IN LOVE *10 TEN 20*	7	8
8 Dec 84	WHO'S THAT GIRL *10 GIRL 1*	71	1

Jerome FLYNN – *See Robson GREEN and Jerome FLYNN*

FM *UK, male vocal / instrumental group*   **11 wks**

31 Jan 87	FROZEN HEART *Portrait DIDGE 1*	64	2
20 Jun 87	LET LOVE BE THE LEADER *Portrait MERV 1*	71	2
5 Aug 89	BAD LUCK *Epic 655031 7*	54	4
7 Oct 89	SOMEDAY (YOU'LL COME RUNNING) *CBS DINK 1*	64	2
10 Feb 90	EVERYTIME I THINK OF YOU *Epic DINK 2*	73	1

FOCUS *Holland, male instrumental group*   **21 wks**

| 20 Jan 73 | HOCUS POCUS *Polydor 2001 211* | 20 | 10 |
| 27 Jan 73 | ● SYLVIA *Polydor 2001 422* | 4 | 11 |

FOG *US, male / female vocal / instrumental group*   **2 wks**

| 19 Feb 94 | BEEN A LONG TIME *Columbia 6601212* | 44 | 2 |

Dan FOGELBERG *US, male vocalist*   **4 wks**

| 15 Mar 80 | LONGER *Epic EPC 8230* | 59 | 4 |

Ben FOLDS FIVE *US, male vocal / instrumental group*   **2 wks**

| 14 Sep 96 | UNDERGROUND *Caroline CDCAR 008* | 37 | 2 |

FOLK IMPLOSION *US, male vocal / instrumental duo*   **1 wk**

| 15 Jun 96 | NATURAL ONE *London LONCD 382* | 45 | 1 |

Claudia FONTAINE – *See BEATMASTERS*

Wayne FONTANA *UK, male vocalist*   **31 wks**

9 Dec 65	IT WAS EASIER TO HURT HER *Fontana TF 642*	36	6
21 Apr 66	COME ON HOME *Fontana TF 684*	16	12
25 Aug 66	GOODBYE BLUEBIRD *Fontana TF 737*	49	1
8 Dec 66	PAMELA PAMELA *Fontana TF 770*	11	12

See also Wayne Fontana and the Mindbenders.

Wayne FONTANA and the MINDBENDERS
UK, male vocalist, male vocal / instrumental backing group   **45 wks**

11 Jul 63	HELLO JOSEPHINE *Fontana TF 404*	46	2
28 May 64	STOP LOOK AND LISTEN *Fontana TF 451*	37	4
8 Oct 64	● UM UM UM UM UM UM *Fontana TF 497*	5	15
4 Feb 65	● GAME OF LOVE *Fontana TF 535*	2	11
17 Jun 65	JUST A LITTLE BIT TOO LATE *Fontana TF 579*	20	7
30 Sep 65	SHE NEEDS LOVE *Fontana TF 611*	32	6

See also Wayne Fontana; Mindbenders.

FOO FIGHTERS *US, male vocal / instrumental group*   **12 wks**

1 Jul 95	● THIS IS A CALL *Roswell CDCL 753*	5	4
16 Sep 95	I'LL STICK AROUND *Roswell CDCL 757*	18	3
2 Dec 95	FOR ALL THE COWS *Roswell CDCL 762*	28	2
6 Apr 96	BIG ME *Roswell CDCL 768*	19	3

FOOL'S GARDEN
Germany, male vocal / instrumental group   **4 wks**

| 25 May 96 | LEMON TREE *Encore CDCOR 014* | 61 | 1 |
| 3 Aug 96 | LEMON TREE (re-issue) *Encore CDCOR 018* | 26 | 3 |

FOR REAL *US, female vocal group*   **1 wk**

| 1 Jul 95 | YOU DON'T KNOW NOTHIN' *A & M 5811232* | 54 | 1 |

Bill FORBES *UK, male vocalist*   **1 wk**

| 15 Jan 60 | TOO YOUNG *Columbia DB 4386* | 29 | 1 |

FORBIDDEN – *See Jet BRONX and the FORBIDDEN*

FORCE MDs *US, male vocal group*   **9 wks**

| 12 Apr 86 | TENDER LOVE *Tommy Boy IS 269* | 23 | 9 |

Baby FORD *UK, male instrumentalist – keyboards*   **16 wks**

10 Sep 88	OOCHY KOOCHY *Rhythm King 7BFORD 1*	58	6
24 Dec 88	CHIKKI CHIKKI AHH AHH *Rhythm King 7BFORD 2*	75	1
7 Jan 89	CHIKKI CHIKKI AHH AHH (re-entry) *Rhythm King 7BFORD 2*	54	3
17 Jun 89	CHILDREN OF THE REVOLUTION *Rhythm King 7BFORD 4*	53	4
17 Feb 90	BEACH BUMP *Rhythm King 7BFORD 6*	68	2

Clinton FORD *UK, male vocalist*   **25 wks**

23 Oct 59	OLD SHEP *Oriole CB 1500*	27	1
17 Aug 61	TOO MANY BEAUTIFUL GIRLS *Oriole CB 1623*	48	1
8 Mar 62	FANLIGHT FANNY *Oriole CB 1706*	22	10
5 Jan 67	RUN TO THE DOOR *Piccadilly 7N 35361*	25	13

Emile FORD and the CHECKMATES
UK, male vocal / instrumental group   **87 wks**

30 Oct 59	★ WHAT DO YOU WANT TO MAKE THOSE EYES AT ME FOR *Pye 7N 15225*	1	25
5 Feb 60	● ON A SLOW BOAT TO CHINA *Pye 7N 15245*	3	14
26 May 60	YOU'LL NEVER KNOW WHAT YOU'RE MISSING ('TIL YOU TRY) *Pye 7N 15268*	12	9
1 Sep 60	THEM THERE EYES *Pye 7N 15282* 1	18	16
8 Dec 60	● COUNTING TEARDROPS *Pye 7N 15314*	4	12
2 Mar 61	WHAT AM I GONNA DO *Pye 7N 15331*	33	6

18 May 61	**HALF OF MY HEART** Piccadilly 7N 35003 [1]		**50**	1
22 Jun 61	**HALF OF MY HEART (re-entry)** Piccadilly 7N 35003 [1]		**42**	3
8 Mar 62	**I WONDER WHO'S KISSING HER NOW** Piccadilly 7N 35033		**43**	1

[1] Emile Ford

Lita FORD *US, female vocalist*   7 wks

17 Dec 88	**KISS ME DEADLY** RCA PB 49575		**75**	1
20 May 89	**CLOSE MY EYES FOREVER** Dreamland PB 49409 [1]		**47**	3
11 Jan 92	**SHOT OF POISON** RCA PB 49145		**63**	3

[1] Lita Ford duet with Ozzy Osbourne

Martyn FORD *UK, orchestra*   3 wks

14 May 77	**LET YOUR BODY GO DOWNTOWN** Mountain TOP 26		**38**	3

Mary FORD – See Les PAUL and Mary FORD

Penny FORD *US, female vocalist*   7 wks

4 May 85	**DANGEROUS** Total Experience FB 49975 [1]		**43**	5
29 May 93	**DAYDREAMING** Columbia 6590592		**43**	2

[1] Pennye Ford

Tennessee Ernie FORD *US, male vocalist*   42 wks

21 Jan 55	★ **GIVE ME YOUR WORD** Capitol CL 14005		**1**	24
6 Jan 56	★ **SIXTEEN TONS** Capitol CL 14500		**1**	11
13 Jan 56	● **THE BALLAD OF DAVY CROCKETT** Capitol CL 14506		**3**	7

Julia FORDHAM *UK, female vocalist*   32 wks

2 Jul 88	**HAPPY EVER AFTER** Circa YR 15		**27**	9
25 Feb 89	**WHERE DOES THE TIME GO** Circa YR 23		**41**	5
31 Aug 91	**I THOUGHT IT WAS YOU** Circa YR 69		**64**	2
18 Jan 92	**LOVE MOVES (IN MYSTERIOUS WAYS)** Circa YR 73		**19**	9
30 May 92	**I THOUGHT IT WAS YOU (re-mix)** Circa YR 90		**45**	3
30 Apr 94	**DIFFERENT TIME DIFFERENT PLACE** Circa YRCD 111		**41**	3
23 Jul 94	**I CAN'T HELP MYSELF** Circa YRCD 116		**62**	1

FOREIGNER *UK / US, male vocal / instrumental group*   78 wks

6 May 78	**FEELS LIKE THE FIRST TIME** Atlantic K 11086		**39**	6
15 Jul 78	**COLD AS ICE** Atlantic K 10986		**24**	10
28 Oct 78	**HOT BLOODED** Atlantic K 11167		**42**	3
24 Feb 79	**BLUE MORNING BLUE DAY** Atlantic K 11236		**45**	4
29 Aug 81	**URGENT** Atlantic K 11665		**54**	4
10 Oct 81	**JUKE BOX HERO** Atlantic K 11678		**48**	4
12 Dec 81	● **WAITING FOR A GIRL LIKE YOU** Atlantic K 11696		**8**	13
8 May 82	**URGENT (re-issue)** Atlantic K 11728		**45**	5
8 Dec 84	★ **I WANT TO KNOW WHAT LOVE IS** Atlantic A 9596		**1**	16
6 Apr 85	**THAT WAS YESTERDAY** Atlantic A 9571		**28**	6
22 Jun 85	**COLD AS ICE (re-mix)** Atlantic A 9539		**64**	2
19 Dec 87	**SAY YOU WILL** Atlantic A 9169		**71**	4
22 Oct 94	**WHITE LIE** Arista 74321232862		**58**	1

FORMATIONS *US, male vocal group*   11 wks

31 Jul 71	**AT THE TOP OF THE STAIRS** Mojo 2027 001		**50**	1
14 Aug 71	**AT THE TOP OF THE STAIRS (re-entry)** Mojo 2027 001		**28**	10

George FORMBY
UK, male vocalist / instrumentalist – ukelele   3 wks

21 Jul 60	**HAPPY GO LUCKY ME / BANJO BOY** Pye 7N 15269		**40**	3

See also 2 In A Tent.

FORREST *US, male vocalist*   20 wks

26 Feb 83	● **ROCK THE BOAT** CBS A 3121		**4**	10
14 May 83	**FEEL THE NEED IN ME** CBS A 3411		**17**	8
17 Sep 83	**ONE LOVER (DON'T STOP THE SHOW)** CBS A 3734		**67**	2

Sharon FORRESTER *Jamaica, female vocalist*   1 wk

11 Feb 95	**LOVE INSIDE** ffrr FCD 253		**50**	1

Lance FORTUNE *UK, male vocalist*   17 wks

19 Feb 60	● **BE MINE** Pye 7N 15240		**4**	12
5 May 60	**THIS LOVE I HAVE FOR YOU** Pye 7N 15260		**26**	5

FORTUNES *UK, male vocal / instrumental group*   65 wks

8 Jul 65	● **YOU'VE GOT YOUR TROUBLES** Decca F 12173		**2**	14
7 Oct 65	● **HERE IT COMES AGAIN** Decca F 12243		**4**	14
3 Feb 66	**THIS GOLDEN RING** Decca F 12321		**15**	9
11 Sep 71	● **FREEDOM COME FREEDOM GO** Capitol CL 15693		**6**	17
29 Jan 72	● **STORM IN A TEACUP** Capitol CL 15707		**7**	11

---

45 KING *US, male producer – Mark King*   6 wks

28 Oct 89	**THE KING IS HERE / THE 900 NUMBER** Dance Trax DRX 9		**60**	5
11 Aug 90	**THE KING IS HERE / THE 900 NUMBER (re-entry)** Dance Trax DRX 9		**73**	1

49ERS *Italy, male producer – Gianfranco Bortolotti*   27 wks

16 Dec 89	● **TOUCH ME** Fourth & Broadway BRW 157		**3**	13
17 Mar 90	**DON'T YOU LOVE ME** Fourth & Broadway BRW 167		**12**	6
9 Jun 90	**GIRL TO GIRL** Fourth & Broadway BRW 174		**31**	3
6 Jun 92	**GOT TO BE FREE** Fourth & Broadway BRW 255		**46**	2
29 Aug 92	**THE MESSAGE** Fourth & Broadway BRW 257		**68**	1
18 Mar 95	**ROCKIN' MY BODY** Media MCSTD 2021 [1]		**31**	2

[1] 49ers featuring Ann-Marie Smith

See also Cappella.

FOSTER and ALLEN *Ireland, male vocal duo*   47 wks

27 Feb 82	**A BUNCH OF THYME** Ritz RITZ 5		**18**	11
30 Oct 82	**OLD FLAMES** Ritz RITZ 028		**51**	8
19 Feb 83	**MAGGIE** Ritz RITZ 025		**27**	9
29 Oct 83	**I WILL LOVE YOU ALL MY LIFE** Ritz RITZ 056		**49**	6
30 Jun 84	**JUST FOR OLD TIME'S SAKE** Ritz RITZ 066		**47**	6
29 Mar 86	**AFTER ALL THESE YEARS** Ritz RITZ 106		**43**	7

Itsy FOSTER – See EXOTICA featuring Itsy FOSTER

FOUNDATIONS *UK, male vocal / instrumental group*   56 wks

27 Sep 67	★ **BABY NOW THAT I'VE FOUND YOU** Pye 7N 17366		**1**	16
24 Jan 68	**BACK ON MY FEET AGAIN** Pye 7N 17417		**18**	10
1 May 68	**ANY OLD TIME** Pye 7N 17503		**48**	1
15 May 68	**ANY OLD TIME (re-entry)** Pye 7N 17503		**50**	1

20 Nov 68	● BUILD ME UP BUTTERCUP *Pye 7N 17636* **2**	15
12 Mar 69	● IN THE BAD BAD OLD DAYS *Pye 7N 17702* **8**	10
13 Sep 69	BORN TO LIVE AND BORN TO DIE *Pye 7N 17809* **46**	3

FOUR ACES *US, male vocal group*   **40 wks**

30 Jul 54	● THREE COINS IN THE FOUNTAIN *Brunswick 05308* [1] **5**	5
22 Oct 54	THREE COINS IN THE FOUNTAIN (re-entry)	
	Brunswick 05308 [1] **17**	1
7 Jan 55	● MR. SANDMAN *Brunswick 05355* [1] **9**	5
20 May 55	STRANGER IN PARADISE *Brunswick 05418* **6**	6
18 Nov 55	● LOVE IS A MANY SPLENDOURED THING	
	Brunswick 05480 [1] **2**	13
19 Oct 56	WOMAN IN LOVE *Brunswick 05589* [1] **19**	3
4 Jan 57	FRIENDLY PERSUASION *Brunswick 05623* [1] **29**	1
23 Jan 59	THE WORLD OUTSIDE *Brunswick 05773* **18**	6

[1] Four Aces featuring Al Roberts

FOUR BUCKETEERS *UK, male / female vocal group*   **6 wks**

3 May 80	THE BUCKET OF WATER SONG *CBS 8393* **26**	6

FOUR ESQUIRES *US, male vocal group*   **2 wks**

31 Jan 58	LOVE ME FOREVER *London HLO 8533* **23**	2

4 HERO *UK, male instrumental group*   **4 wks**

24 Nov 90	MR. KIRK'S NIGHTMARE *Reinforced RIVET 1203* **73**	2
9 May 92	COOKIN' UP YAH BRAIN *Reinforced RIVET 1216* **59**	2

400 BLOWS *UK, male vocal / instrumental duo*   **4 wks**

29 Jun 85	MOVIN' *Illuminated ILL 61* **54**	4

FOUR KNIGHTS *US, male vocal group*   **11 wks**

4 Jun 54	● I GET SO LONELY *Capitol CL 14076*............................**5**	7
30 Jul 54	● I GET SO LONELY (re-entry) *Capitol CL 14076* **10**	4

FOUR LADS *Canada, male vocal group*   **23 wks**

19 Dec 52	● FAITH CAN MOVE MOUNTAINS *Columbia DB 3154* [1] **7**	2
9 Jan 53	● FAITH CAN MOVE MOUNTAINS (re-entry)	
	Columbia DB 3154 [1] **9**	1
22 Oct 54	● RAIN RAIN RAIN *Philips PB 311* [2] **8**	16
28 Apr 60	STANDING ON THE CORNER *Philips PB 1000* **34**	4

[1] Johnnie Ray and the Four Lads   [2] Frankie Laine and the Four Lads

4 NON BLONDES
US, female / male vocal / instrumental group   **19 wks**

19 Jun 93	● WHAT'S UP *Interscope A 8412CD* **2**	17
16 Oct 93	SPACEMAN *Interscope A 8349CD* **53**	2

4 OF US *Ireland, male vocal / instrumental group*   **6 wks**

27 Feb 93	SHE HITS ME *Columbia 6589192* **35**	4
1 May 93	I MISS YOU *Columbia 6591722* **62**	2

FOUR PENNIES *UK, male vocal / instrumental group*   **56 wks**

16 Jan 64	DO YOU WANT ME TO *Philips BF 1296* **47**	1
6 Feb 64	DO YOU WANT ME TO (re-entry) *Philips BF 1296* **49**	1

2 Apr 64	★ JULIET *Philips BF 1322* **1**	15
16 Jul 64	I FOUND OUT THE HARD WAY *Philips BF 1349* **14**	11
29 Oct 64	BLACK GIRL *Philips BF 1366* **20**	12
7 Oct 65	UNTIL IT'S TIME FOR YOU TO GO *Philips BF 1435* **19**	11
17 Feb 66	TROUBLE IS MY MIDDLE NAME *Philips BF 1469* **32**	5

FOUR PREPS *US, male vocal group*   **23 wks**

13 Jun 58	● BIG MAN *Capitol CL 14873* **2**	13
19 Sep 58	BIG MAN (re-entry) *Capitol CL 14873* **22**	1
26 May 60	GOT A GIRL *Capitol CL 15128* **28**	6
14 Jul 60	GOT A GIRL (re-entry) *Capitol CL 15128* **47**	1
2 Nov 61	MORE MONEY FOR YOU AND ME (MEDLEY)	
	Capitol CL 15217 ....**39**	2

Tracks on medley: Mr. Blue / Alley Oop / Smoke Gets In Your Eyes / In This Whole Wide World / A Worried Man / Tom Dooley / A Teenager In Love, all with new lyrics.

FOUR SEASONS *US, male vocal group*   **151 wks**

4 Oct 62	● SHERRY *Stateside SS 122* **8**	16
17 Jan 63	BIG GIRLS DON'T CRY *Stateside SS 145* **13**	10
28 Mar 63	WALK LIKE A MAN *Stateside SS 169* **12**	12
27 Jun 63	AIN'T THAT A SHAME *Stateside SS 194* **38**	3
27 Aug 64	● RAG DOLL *Philips BF 1347* [1] **2**	13
18 Nov 65	● LET'S HANG ON *Philips BF 1439* [1] **4**	16
31 Mar 66	WORKIN' MY WAY BACK TO YOU *Philips BF 1474* [2] **50**	3
2 Jun 66	OPUS 17 (DON'T YOU WORRY 'BOUT ME)	
	Philips BF 1493 [2] **20**	9
29 Sep 66	I'VE GOT YOU UNDER MY SKIN *Philips BF 1511* [2] **12**	11
12 Jan 67	TELL IT TO THE RAIN *Philips BF 1538* [2] **37**	5
19 Apr 75	● NIGHT *Mowest MW 3024* [3] **7**	9
20 Sep 75	● WHO LOVES YOU *Warner Bros. K 16602* **6**	9
31 Jan 76	★ DECEMBER 1963 (OH WHAT A NIGHT)	
	Warner Bros. K 16688 ....**1**	10
24 Apr 76	● SILVER STAR *Warner Bros. K 16742* **3**	9
27 Nov 76	WE CAN WORK IT OUT *Warner Bros. K 16845* **34**	4
18 Jun 77	RHAPSODY *Warner Bros. K 16932* **37**	3
20 Aug 77	DOWN THE HALL *Warner Bros. K 16982* **34**	5
29 Oct 88	DECEMBER '63 (OH WHAT A NIGHT) (re-mix)	
	BR 45277 [3] **49**	4

[1] Four Seasons with the Sound of Frankie Valli   [2] Four Seasons with Frankie Valli   [3] Frankie Valli and the Four Seasons

FOUR SHEPHERD BOYS – See Michael HOLLIDAY

FOUR TOPS *US, male vocal group*   **318 wks**

1 Jul 65	I CAN'T HELP MYSELF *Tamla Motown TMG 515* **23**	9
2 Sep 65	IT'S THE SAME OLD SONG *Tamla Motown TMG 528*......**34**	8
21 Jul 66	LOVING YOU IS SWEETER THAN EVER	
	Tamla Motown TMG 568...............................**21**	12
13 Oct 66	★ REACH OUT (I'LL BE THERE) *Tamla Motown TMG 579* **1**	16
12 Jan 67	● STANDING IN THE SHADOWS OF LOVE	
	Tamla Motown TMG 589 ....**6**	8
30 Mar 67	● BERNADETTE *Tamla Motown TMG 601* **8**	10
15 Jun 67	SEVEN ROOMS OF GLOOM *Tamla Motown TMG 612* **12**	9
11 Oct 67	YOU KEEP RUNNING AWAY *Tamla Motown TMG 623* ...**26**	7
13 Dec 67	● WALK AWAY RENEE *Tamla Motown TMG 634* **3**	11
13 Mar 68	IF I WERE A CARPENTER *Tamla Motown TMG 647* **7**	11
21 Aug 68	YESTERDAY'S DREAMS *Tamla Motown TMG 665* **23**	15
13 Nov 68	I'M IN A DIFFERENT WORLD *Tamla Motown TMG 675*...**27**	13
28 May 69	WHAT IS A MAN *Tamla Motown TMG 698* **16**	11
27 Sep 69	DO WHAT YOU GOTTA DO *Tamla Motown TMG 710*......**11**	11
21 Mar 70	● I CAN'T HELP MYSELF (re-issue)	
	Tamla Motown TMG 732 ....**10**	11
30 May 70	● IT'S ALL IN THE GAME *Tamla Motown TMG 736* **5**	14
12 Sep 70	IT'S ALL IN THE GAME (re-entry)	
	Tamla Motown TMG 736................................**48**	2
3 Oct 70	● STILL WATER (LOVE) *Tamla Motown TMG 752* **10**	10
19 Dec 70	STILL WATER (LOVE) (re-entry)	
	Tamla Motown TMG 752................................**44**	2

1 May 71	**JUST SEVEN NUMBERS (CAN STRAIGHTEN OUT MY LIFE)** Tamla Motown TMG 770 ......**36** 5	
26 Jun 71	**RIVER DEEP MOUNTAIN HIGH** Tamla Motown TMG 777 [1] **11** 10	
25 Sep 71 ●	**SIMPLE GAME** Tamla Motown TMG 785 ......**3** 11	
20 Nov 71	**YOU GOTTA HAVE LOVE IN YOUR HEART** Tamla Motown TMG 793 [1] **25** 10	
11 Mar 72	**BERNADETTE (re-issue)** Tamla Motown TMG 803 ......**23** 7	
5 Aug 72	**WALK WITH ME TALK WITH ME DARLING** Tamla Motown TMG 823 ......**32** 6	
18 Nov 72	**KEEPER OF THE CASTLE** Probe PRO 575 ......**18** 9	
10 Nov 73	**SWEET UNDERSTANDING LOVE** Probe PRO 604 ......**29** 10	
17 Oct 81 ●	**WHEN SHE WAS MY GIRL** Casablanca CAN 1005 ......**3** 10	
19 Dec 81	**DON'T WALK AWAY** Casablanca CAN 1006 ......**16** 11	
6 Mar 82	**TONIGHT I'M GONNA LOVE YOU ALL OVER** Casablanca CAN 1008 ......**43** 4	
26 Jun 82	**BACK TO SCHOOL AGAIN** RSO 89 ......**62** 2	
23 Jul 88	**REACH OUT I'LL BE THERE (re-mix)** Motown ZB 41943 ......**11** 9	
17 Sep 88	**INDESTRUCTIBLE** Arista 111717 ......**55** 4	
3 Dec 88 ●	**LOCO IN ACAPULCO** Arista 111850 ......**7** 13	
25 Feb 89	**INDESTRUCTIBLE** Arista 112074 [2] **30** 7	

[1] Supremes and the Four Tops [2] Four Tops featuring Smokey Robinson

The original US recording of Indestructible was not issued until after the chart run of the UK-only mix.

4MANDU UK, male vocal group   6 wks

29 Jul 95	**THIS IS IT** Final Vinyl 74321291222 ......**45** 3	
17 Feb 96	**DO IT FOR LOVE** Arista 74321343902 ......**45** 2	
15 Jun 96	**BABY DON'T GO** Arista 74321375914 ......**47** 1	

FOURMOST UK, male vocal/instrumental group   64 wks

12 Sep 63 ●	**HELLO LITTLE GIRL** Parlophone R 5056 ......**9** 17	
26 Dec 63	**I'M IN LOVE** Parlophone R 5078 ......**17** 12	
23 Apr 64	**A LITTLE LOVING** Parlophone R 5128 ......**6** 13	
13 Aug 64	**HOW CAN I TELL HER** Parlophone R 5157 ......**33** 4	
26 Nov 64	**BABY I NEED YOUR LOVIN'** Parlophone R 5194 ......**24** 12	
9 Dec 65	**GIRLS GIRLS GIRLS** Parlophone R 5379 ......**33** 6	

14-18 UK, male vocalist – Peter Waterman   4 wks

1 Nov 75	**GOODBYE-EE** Magnet MAG 48 ......**33** 4	

FOX UK/US, male/female vocal/instrumental group   29 wks

15 Feb 75 ●	**ONLY YOU CAN** GTO GT 8 ......**3** 11	
10 May 75	**IMAGINE ME IMAGINE YOU** GTO GT 21 ......**15** 8	
10 Apr 76	**S-S-S-SINGLE BED** GTO GT 57 ......**4** 10	

Noosha FOX UK, female vocalist   6 wks

12 Nov 77	**GEORGINA BAILEY** GTO GT 106 ......**31** 6	

Samantha FOX UK, female vocalist   71 wks

22 Mar 86 ●	**TOUCH ME (I WANT YOUR BODY)** Jive FOXY 1 ......**3** 10	
28 Jun 86 ●	**DO YA DO YA (WANNA PLEASE ME)** Jive FOXY 2 ......**10** 7	
6 Sep 86	**HOLD ON TIGHT** Jive FOXY 3 ......**26** 5	
13 Dec 86	**I'M ALL YOU NEED** Jive FOXY 4 ......**41** 6	
30 May 87 ●	**NOTHING'S GONNA STOP ME NOW** Jive FOXY 5 ......**8** 9	
25 Jul 87	**I SURRENDER (TO THE SPIRIT OF THE NIGHT)** Jive FOXY 6 ......**25** 7	
17 Oct 87	**I PROMISE YOU (GET READY)** Jive FOXY 7 ......**58** 3	
19 Dec 87	**TRUE DEVOTION** Jive FOXY 8 ......**62** 3	
21 May 88	**NAUGHTY GIRLS** Jive FOXY 9 [1] **31** 5	
19 Nov 88	**LOVE HOUSE** Jive FOXY 10 ......**32** 6	

28 Jan 89	**I ONLY WANNA BE WITH YOU** Jive FOXY 11 ......**16** 8	
17 Jun 89	**I WANNA HAVE SOME FUN** Jive FOXY 12 ......**63** 2	

[1] Samantha Fox featuring Full Force

Bruce FOXTON UK, male vocalist   9 wks

30 Jul 83	**FREAK** Arista BFOX 1 ......**23** 5	
29 Oct 83	**THIS IS THE WAY** Arista BFOX 2 ......**56** 3	
21 Apr 84	**IT MAKES ME WONDER** Arista BFOX 3 ......**74** 1	

Inez FOXX US, female vocalist   8 wks

23 Jul 64	**HURT BY LOVE** Sue WI 323 ......**40** 3	
19 Feb 69	**MOCKINGBIRD** United Artists UP 2269 [1] **36** 2	
19 Mar 69	**MOCKINGBIRD (re-entry)** United Artists UP 2269 [1] **33** 3	

[1] Inez and Charlie Foxx

John FOXX UK, male vocalist   31 wks

26 Jan 80	**UNDERPASS** Virgin VS 318 ......**31** 8	
29 Mar 80	**NO-ONE DRIVING (DOUBLE SINGLE)** Virgin VS 338 ......**32** 4	
19 Jul 80	**BURNING CAR** Virgin VS 360 ......**35** 7	
8 Nov 80	**MILES AWAY** Virgin VS 382 ......**51** 3	
29 Aug 81	**EUROPE (AFTER THE RAIN)** Virgin VS 393 ......**40** 5	
2 Jul 83	**ENDLESSLY** Virgin VS 543 ......**66** 3	
17 Sep 83	**YOUR DRESS** Virgin VS 615 ......**61** 1	

Tracks on double single: No-one Driving / Glimmer / Mr. No / This City.

FPI PROJECT
Italy, male instrumental / production group   16 wks

9 Dec 89 ●	**GOING BACK TO MY ROOTS / RICH IN PARADISE** Rumour RUMAT 9 ......**9** 12	
9 Mar 91	**EVERYBODY (ALL OVER THE WORLD)** Rumour RUMA 29 ......**65** 3	
7 Aug 93	**COME ON (AND DO IT)** Synthetic SYNTH 006CD **59** 1	

Going Back To My Roots was a vocal track available in two formats and featured either Paolo Dini or Sharon D. Clarke.

FRAGGLES UK/US, puppets   8 wks

18 Feb 84	**'FRAGGLE ROCK' THEME** RCA 389 ......**33** 8	

Peter FRAMPTON UK, male vocalist   24 wks

1 May 76 ●	**SHOW ME THE WAY** A & M AMS 7218 ......**10** 12	
11 Sep 76	**BABY I LOVE YOUR WAY** A & M AMS 7246 ......**43** 5	
6 Nov 76	**DO YOU FEEL LIKE WE DO** A & M AMS 7260 ......**39** 4	
23 Jul 77	**I'M IN YOU** A & M AMS 7298 ......**41** 3	

Connie FRANCIS US, female vocalist   241 wks

4 Apr 58 ★	**WHO'S SORRY NOW** MGM 975 ......**1** 25	
27 Jun 58	**I'M SORRY I MADE YOU CRY** MGM 982 ......**11** 10	
22 Aug 58 ★	**CAROLINA MOON / STUPID CUPID** MGM 985 ......**1** 19	
31 Oct 58	**I'LL GET BY** MGM 993 ......**19** 6	
21 Nov 58	**FALLIN'** MGM 993 ......**20** 5	
26 Dec 58	**YOU ALWAYS HURT THE ONE YOU LOVE** MGM 998 ......**13** 7	
13 Feb 59 ●	**MY HAPPINESS** MGM 1001 ......**4** 14	
29 May 59	**MY HAPPINESS (re-entry)** MGM 1001 ......**30** 1	
3 Jul 59 ●	**LIPSTICK ON YOUR COLLAR** MGM 1018 ......**3** 16	
11 Sep 59	**PLENTY GOOD LOVIN'** MGM 1036 ......**18** 6	
4 Dec 59	**AMONG MY SOUVENIRS** MGM 1046 ......**11** 10	
17 Mar 60	**VALENTINO** MGM 1060 ......**27** 8	

Fugees

The Fugees' hit 'Killing Me Softly' was originally recorded by Lori Lieberman in 1972. The song was inspired by a Don McLean live performance in Los Angeles.

Billy Fury

The young Ronald Wycherley was discovered by pop impresario Larry Parnes, who rechristened him Billy Fury.

Fun Boy Three

Written by Terry Hall and Belinda Carlisle, 'Our Lips Are Sealed' was the final hit for the Fun Boy Three and also the Go-Gos' US debut.

Foreigner

'Waiting For A Girl Like You' spent a record 10 frustrating weeks at number two without making the top spot in the American charts.

19 May 60	● MAMA / ROBOT MAN *MGM 1076*............................**2** 19

19 May 60	● **MAMA / ROBOT MAN** *MGM 1076*............................**2** 19
18 Aug 60	● **EVERYBODY'S SOMEBODY'S FOOL** *MGM 1086*....**5** 13
3 Nov 60	● **MY HEART HAS A MIND OF ITS OWN** *MGM 1100*..**3** 15
12 Jan 61	**MANY TEARS AGO** *MGM 1111*....................**12** 9
16 Mar 61	● **WHERE THE BOYS ARE / BABY ROO** *MGM 1121*.........**5** 14
15 Jun 61	**BREAKIN' IN A BRAND NEW BROKEN HEART** *MGM 1136*..**12** 11
14 Sep 61	● **TOGETHER** *MGM 1138*..............................**6** 11
14 Dec 61	**BABY'S FIRST CHRISTMAS** *MGM 1145*..........**30** 4
26 Apr 62	**DON'T BREAK THE HEART THAT LOVES YOU** *MGM 1157*..**39** 3
2 Aug 62	● **VACATION** *MGM 1165*..............................**10** 9
20 Dec 62	**I'M GONNA BE WARM THIS WINTER** *MGM 1185*.........**48** 1
10 Jun 65	**MY CHILD** *MGM 1271*..............................**26** 6
20 Jan 66	**JEALOUS HEART** *MGM 1293*......................**44** 2

Baby Roo *listed with* Where The Boys Are *for first eight weeks only.*

Jill FRANCIS *UK, female vocalist* **1 wk**

3 Jul 93	**MAKE LOVE TO ME** *Glady Wax GW 003CD*......**70** 1

Claude FRANCOIS *France, male vocalist* **4 wks**

10 Jan 76	**TEARS ON THE TELEPHONE** *Bradley's BRAD 7528*.........**35** 4

Joe FRANK – *See HAMILTON, Joe FRANK and REYNOLDS*

FRANK AND WALTERS
Ireland, male vocal / instrumental group **13 wks**

21 Mar 92	**HAPPY BUSMAN** *Setanta HOO 2* **49** 2
12 Sep 92	**THIS IS NOT A SONG** *Setanta HOO 3* **46** 3
9 Jan 93	**AFTER ALL** *Setanta HOCD 4* **11** 5
17 Apr 93	**FASHION CRISIS HITS NEW YORK** *Setanta HOOCD 5* **42** 3

FRANKË *UK, male vocalist – Frankë Pharoah* **3 wks**

7 Nov 92	**UNDERSTAND THIS GROOVE** *China WOK 2028* **60** 2
21 May 94	**LOVE COME HOME** *Triangle BLUESCD 001* [1] **73** 1

[1] Our Tribe with Frankë Pharoah and Kristine W

FRANKIE GOES TO HOLLYWOOD
UK, male vocal / instrumental group **137 wks**

26 Nov 83	★ **RELAX** *ZTT ZTAS 1* **1** 48
16 Jun 84	★ **TWO TRIBES** *ZTT ZTAS 3* **1** 20
10 Nov 84	**TWO TRIBES (re-entry)** *ZTT ZTAS 3* **73** 1
1 Dec 84	★ **THE POWER OF LOVE** *ZTT ZTAS 5* **1** 11
16 Feb 85	**RELAX (re-entry)** *ZTT ZTAS 1* **58** 4
23 Feb 85	**THE POWER OF LOVE (re-entry)** *ZTT ZTAS 5* **64** 1
30 Mar 85	● **WELCOME TO THE PLEASURE DOME** *ZTT ZTAS 7* **2** 11
6 Sep 86	● **RAGE HARD** *ZTT ZTAS 22* **4** 7
22 Nov 86	**WARRIORS (OF THE WASTELAND)** *ZTT ZTAS 25* **19** 8
7 Mar 87	**WATCHING THE WILDLIFE** *ZTT ZTAS 26*..........**28** 6
2 Oct 93	● **RELAX (re-issue)** *ZTT FGTH 1CD* **5** 7
20 Nov 93	**WELCOME TO THE PLEASURE DOME (re-mix)** *ZTT FGTH 2CD* **18** 3
18 Dec 93	● **THE POWER OF LOVE (re-issue)** *ZTT FGTH 3CD* **10** 7
26 Feb 94	**TWO TRIBES (re-mix)** *ZTT FGTH 4CD* **16** 3

Aretha FRANKLIN *US, female vocalist* **177 wks**

8 Jun 67	● **RESPECT** *Atlantic 584 115* **10** 14
23 Aug 67	**BABY I LOVE YOU** *Atlantic 584 127* **39** 4
20 Dec 67	**CHAIN OF FOOLS / SATISFACTION** *Atlantic 584 157*....................................**43** 2

10 Jan 68	**SATISFACTION (re-entry)** *Atlantic 584 157* **37** 5
13 Mar 68	**SINCE YOU'VE BEEN GONE** *Atlantic 584 172* **47** 1
22 May 68	**THINK** *Atlantic 584 186* **26** 9
7 Aug 68	● **I SAY A LITTLE PRAYER** *Atlantic 584 206* **4** 14
22 Aug 70	**DON'T PLAY THAT SONG** *Atlantic 2091 027* **13** 11
2 Oct 71	**SPANISH HARLEM** *Atlantic 2091 138* **14** 9
8 Sep 73	**ANGEL** *Atlantic K 10346* **37** 5
16 Feb 74	**UNTIL YOU COME BACK TO ME (THAT'S WHAT I'M GONNA DO)** *Atlantic K 10399* **26** 8
6 Dec 80	**WHAT A FOOL BELIEVES** *Arista ARIST 377* **46** 7
19 Sep 81	**LOVE ALL THE HURT AWAY** *Arista ARIST 428* [1] **49** 3
4 Sep 82	**JUMP TO IT** *Arista ARIST 479* **42** 5
23 Jul 83	**GET IT RIGHT** *Arista ARIST 537* **74** 2
13 Jul 85	**FREEWAY OF LOVE** *Arista ARIST 624* **68** 3
2 Nov 85	● **SISTERS ARE DOIN' IT FOR THEMSELVES** *RCA PB 40339* [2] **9** 11
23 Nov 85	**WHO'S ZOOMIN' WHO** *Arista ARIST 633* **11** 14
22 Feb 86	**ANOTHER NIGHT** *Arista ARIST 657* **54** 6
10 May 86	**FREEWAY OF LOVE (re-entry)** *Arista ARIST 624* **51** 3
25 Oct 86	**JUMPIN' JACK FLASH** *Arista ARIST 678* **58** 3
31 Jan 87	★ **I KNEW YOU WERE WAITING (FOR ME)** *Epic DUET 1* [3] **1** 9
14 Mar 87	**JIMMY LEE** *Arista RIS 6* **46** 4
6 May 89	**THROUGH THE STORM** *Arista 112185* [4] **41** 3
9 Sep 89	**IT ISN'T, IT WASN'T, IT AIN'T NEVER GONNA BE** *Arista 112545* [5] **29** 5
7 Apr 90	**THINK** *East West A 7951* **31** 2
27 Jul 91	**EVERYDAY PEOPLE** *Arista 114420* **69** 1
12 Feb 94	● **A DEEPER LOVE** *Arista 74321187022* **5** 7
25 Jun 94	**WILLING TO FORGIVE** *Arista 74321213342* **17** 7

[1] Aretha Franklin and George Benson [2] Eurythmics and Aretha Franklin [3] Aretha Franklin and George Michael [4] Aretha Franklin and Elton John [5] Aretha Franklin and Whitney Houston

Think *on* East West *is a re-recording. It was the flip side of* Everybody Needs Somebody To Love *by* Blues Brothers *and was listed for the first two weeks of that record's run.*

Erma FRANKLIN *US, female vocalist* **10 wks**

10 Oct 92	● **(TAKE A LITTLE) PIECE OF MY HEART** *Epic 6583847*..**9** 10

Rodney FRANKLIN *US, male instrumentalist – piano* **9 wks**

19 Apr 80	● **THE GROOVE** *CBS 8529*..........................**7** 9

FRANTIC FIVE – *See Don LANG*

FRANTIQUE *US, female vocal group* **12 wks**

11 Aug 79	● **STRUT YOUR FUNKY STUFF** *Philadelphia International PIR 7728* **10** 12

Elizabeth FRASER – *See Ian McCULLOCH*

Wendy FRASER – *See Patrick SWAYZE featuring Wendy FRASER*

FRASH *UK, male vocal / instrumental group* **1 wk**

18 Feb 95	**HERE I GO AGAIN** *PWL International FLIPCD 1* **69** 1

FRAZIER CHORUS
UK, male / female vocal / instrumental group **14 wks**

4 Feb 89	**DREAM KITCHEN** *Virgin VS 1145* **57** 3
15 Apr 89	**TYPICAL!** *Virgin VS 1174* **53** 2
15 Jul 89	**SLOPPY HEART** *Virgin VS 1192* **73** 1
9 Jun 90	**CLOUD 8** *Virgin VS 1252* **52** 3
25 Aug 90	**NOTHING** *Virgin VS 1284* **51** 3
16 Feb 91	**WALKING ON AIR** *Virgin VS 1330* **60** 2

FREAK POWER
UK / Canada, male vocal / instrumental group   **17 wks**

16 Oct 93	**TURN ON TUNE IN COP OUT** *Fourth & Broadway BRCD 284*	**29**	5
26 Feb 94	**RUSH** *Fourth & Broadway BRCD 291*	**62**	2
18 Mar 95	● **TURN ON TUNE IN COP OUT (re-issue)** *Fourth & Broadway BRCD 317*	**3**	9
8 Jun 96	**NEW DIRECTION** *Fourth & Broadway BRCD 331*	**60**	1

FREAKY REALISTIC
UK / Japan, male / female vocal / instrumental group   **3 wks**

3 Apr 93	**KOOCHIE RYDER** *Frealism FRECD 2*	**52**	2
3 Jul 93	**LEONARD NIMOY** *Frealism FRECD 3*	**71**	1

Stan FREBERG *US, male vocalist*   **5 wks**

19 Nov 54	**SH-BOOM** *Capitol CL 14187* 1	**15**	2
27 Jul 56	**ROCK ISLAND LINE / HEARTBREAK HOTEL** *Capitol CL 14608*	**24**	1
10 Aug 56	**ROCK ISLAND LINE / HEARTBREAK HOTEL (re-entry)** *Capitol CL 14608*	**29**	1
12 May 60	**THE OLD PAYOLA ROLL BLUES** *Capitol CL 15122*	**40**	1

1 Stan Freberg with the Toads

John FRED and the PLAYBOY BAND
US, male vocal / instrumental group   **12 wks**

3 Jan 68	● **JUDY IN DISGUISE (WITH GLASSES)** *Pye International 7N 25442*	**3**	12

FREDDIE and the DREAMERS
UK, male vocal / instrumental group   **85 wks**

9 May 63	● **IF YOU GOTTA MAKE A FOOL OF SOMEBODY** *Columbia DB 7032*	**3**	14
8 Aug 63	● **I'M TELLING YOU NOW** *Columbia DB 7086*	**2**	11
7 Nov 63	● **YOU WERE MADE FOR ME** *Columbia DB 7147*	**3**	15
20 Feb 64	**OVER YOU** *Columbia DB 7214*	**13**	11
14 May 64	**I LOVE YOU BABY** *Columbia DB 7286*	**16**	8
16 Jul 64	**JUST FOR YOU** *Columbia DB 7322*	**41**	3
5 Nov 64	● **I UNDERSTAND** *Columbia DB 7381*	**5**	15
22 Apr 65	**A LITTLE YOU** *Columbia DB 7526*	**26**	5
4 Nov 65	**THOU SHALT NOT STEAL** *Columbia DB 7720*	**44**	3

FREDERICK – *See NINA and FREDERICK*

Dee FREDRIX *UK, female vocalist*   **5 wks**

27 Feb 93	**AND SO I WILL WAIT FOR YOU** *East West YZ 725CD*	**56**	4
3 Jul 93	**DIRTY MONEY** *East West YZ 750CD*	**74**	1

FREE *UK, male vocal / instrumental group*   **75 wks**

6 Jun 70	● **ALL RIGHT NOW** *Island WIP 6082*	**2**	16
1 May 71	● **MY BROTHER JAKE** *Island WIP 6100*	**4**	11
27 May 72	**LITTLE BIT OF LOVE** *Island WIP 6129*	**13**	10
13 Jan 73	● **WISHING WELL** *Island WIP 6146*	**7**	10
21 Jul 73	**ALL RIGHT NOW (re-entry)** *Island WIP 6082*	**15**	9
18 Feb 78	**FREE EP** *Island IEP 6*	**11**	7
23 Oct 82	**FREE EP (re-entry)** *Island IEP 6*	**57**	3
9 Feb 91	● **ALL RIGHT NOW (re-mix)** *Island IS 486*	**8**	9

Tracks on Free EP: All Right Now / My Brother Jake / Wishing Well.

FREE SPIRIT *UK, male / female vocal duo*   **1 wk**

13 May 95	**NO MORE RAINY DAYS** *Columbia 6612822*	**68**	1

FREEEZ *UK, male vocal / instrumental group*   **48 wks**

7 Jun 80	**KEEP IN TOUCH** *Calibre CAB 103*	**49**	3
7 Feb 81	● **SOUTHERN FREEEZ** *Beggars Banquet BEG 51*	**8**	11
18 Apr 81	**FLYING HIGH** *Beggars Banquet BEG 55*	**35**	5
18 Jun 83	● **I.O.U.** *Beggars Banquet BEG 96*	**2**	15
1 Oct 83	**POP GOES MY LOVE** *Beggars Banquet BEG 98*	**26**	6
17 Jan 87	**I.O.U. (re-mix)** *Citybeat CBE 709* 1	**23**	6
30 May 87	**SOUTHERN FREEEZ (re-mix)** *Total Control TOCO 14*	**63**	2

1 Freeez featuring John Rocca

FREEFALL featuring PSYCHOTROPIC
UK / US, male instrumental / production group   **1 wk**

27 Jul 91	**FEEL SURREAL** *ffrr FX 160*	**63**	1

FREEHOLD JUNIOR SCHOOL – *See Fogwell FLAX and the ANKLEBITERS from FREEHOLD JUNIOR SCHOOL*

FREIHEIT *Germany, male vocal / instrumental group*   **9 wks**

17 Dec 88	**KEEPING THE DREAM ALIVE** *CBS 652989 7*	**14**	9

Deborah FRENCH – *See E-LUSTRIOUS featuring Deborah FRENCH*

Nicki FRENCH *UK, female vocalist*   **16 wks**

15 Oct 94	**TOTAL ECLIPSE OF THE HEART** *Bags Of Fun BAGSCD 1*	**54**	1
14 Jan 95	● **TOTAL ECLIPSE OF THE HEART (re-entry)** *Bags Of Fun BAGSCD 1*	**5**	12
22 Apr 95	**FOR ALL WE KNOW** *Bags Of Fun BAGSCD 4*	**42**	2
15 Jul 95	**DID YOU EVER REALLY LOVE ME** *Love This LUVTHISCD 2*	**55**	1

FREQUENCY 9 – *See VARIOUS ARTISTS (EPs & LPs) - The Further Adventures Of North EP*

FRESH 4 featuring Lizz E
UK, male scratch group and female vocal group   **9 wks**

7 Oct 89	● **WISHING ON A STAR** *10 TEN 287*	**10**	9

Doug E. FRESH and the GET FRESH CREW
US, male vocalist and rap / scratch group   **11 wks**

9 Nov 85	● **THE SHOW** *Cooltempo COOL 116*	**7**	11

FRESH PRINCE – *See JAZZY JEFF and FRESH PRINCE*

FRESHIES *UK, male vocal / instrumental group*   **3 wks**

14 Feb 81	**I'M IN LOVE WITH THE GIRL ON A CERTAIN MANCHESTER MEGASTORE CHECKOUT DESK** *MCA 670*	**54**	3

Matt FRETTON *UK, male vocalist*   **5 wks**

11 Jun 83	**IT'S SO HIGH** *Chrysalis MATT 1*	**50**	5

FREUR *UK, male vocal / instrumental group*   **4 wks**

23 Apr 83	**DOOT DOOT** *CBS A 3141*	**59**	4

Glenn FREY *US, male vocalist*   **20 wks**

2 Mar 85	**THE HEAT IS ON** *MCA MCA 941*	**12**	12
22 Jun 85	**SMUGGLER'S BLUES** *BBC RESL 170*	**22**	8

FRIDA *Norway, female vocalist*   12 wks

| 21 Aug 82 | I KNOW THERE'S SOMETHING GOING ON Epic EPC A2603 | 43 | 7 |
| 17 Dec 83 | TIME Epic A 3983 [1] | 45 | 5 |

[1] Frida and B.A. Robertson

Gavin FRIDAY – *See BONO*

Dean FRIEDMAN *US, male vocalist*   22 wks

3 Jun 78	WOMAN OF MINE *Lifesong LS 401*	52	5
23 Sep 78	● LUCKY STARS *Lifesong LS 402*	3	10
18 Nov 78	LYDIA *Lifesong LS 403*	31	7

FRIENDS AGAIN
UK, male vocal / instrumental group   3 wks

| 4 Aug 84 | THE FRIENDS AGAIN EP *Mercury FA 1* | 59 | 3 |

Tracks on The Friends Again EP: Lullaby On Board / Wand You Wave / Thank You For Being An Angel.

FRIJID PINK *US, male vocal / instrumental group*   16 wks

| 28 Mar 70 | ● HOUSE OF THE RISING SUN *Deram DM 288* | 4 | 16 |

Robert FRIPP – *See David SYLVIAN*

Jane FROMAN *US, female vocalist*   4 wks

| 17 Jun 55 | I WONDER *Capitol CL 14254* | 14 | 4 |

FRONT 242
Belgium / US, male vocal / instrumental group   1 wk

| 1 May 93 | RELIGION *RRE RRE 106CD* | 46 | 1 |

Bernard FROST – *See BOMB THE BASS*

FUGEES (REFUGEE CAMP)
US, male / female vocal / instrumental group   42 wks

6 Apr 96	FU-GEE-LA *Columbia 6630662*	21	5
8 Jun 96	★ KILLING ME SOFTLY *Columbia 6633435*	1	20
14 Sep 96	★ READY OR NOT *Columbia 6637215*	1	12
30 Nov 96	● NO WOMAN NO CRY *Columbia 6639925*	2†	5

FULL CIRCLE *US, male vocal group*   5 wks

| 7 Mar 87 | WORKIN' UP A SWEAT *EMI America EA 229* | 41 | 5 |

FULL FORCE *US, male vocal / instrumental group*   37 wks

4 May 85	I WONDER IF I TAKE YOU HOME CBS A 6057 [1]	53	6
3 Aug 85	I WONDER IF I TAKE YOU HOME (re-entry) CBS A 6057 [1]	12	11
21 Dec 85	● ALICE I WANT YOU JUST FOR ME CBS A 6640	9	11
21 May 88	NAUGHTY GIRLS *Jive FOXY 9* [2]	31	5
4 Jun 88	I'M REAL *Scotti Brothers JSB 1* [3]	31	4

[1] Lisa Lisa and Cult Jam with Full Force [2] Samantha Fox featuring Full Force [3] James Brown featuring Full Force

FULL INTENTION
UK, male instrumental / production duo   3 wks

| 6 Apr 96 | AMERICA (I LOVE AMERICA) *Stress CDSTR 56* | 32 | 2 |
| 10 Aug 96 | UPTOWN DOWNTOWN *Stress CDSTR 67* | 61 | 1 |

FULL METAL RACKETS – *See John McENROE and Pat CASH with the FULL METAL RACKETS*

FULL MONTY ALLSTARS featuring TJ DAVIS
UK, male vocal / instrumental group   1 wk

| 27 Jul 96 | BRILLIANT FEELING *Arista 74321380902* | 72 | 1 |

Bobby FULLER FOUR
US, male vocal / instrumental group   4 wks

| 14 Apr 66 | I FOUGHT THE LAW *London HL 10030* | 33 | 4 |

FUN BOY THREE *UK, male vocal / instrumental group*   70 wks

7 Nov 81	THE LUNATICS (HAVE TAKEN OVER THE ASYLUM) *Chrysalis CHS 2563*	20	12
13 Feb 82	● IT AIN'T WHAT YOU DO IT'S THE WAY THAT YOU DO IT *Chrysalis CHS 2570* [1]	4	10
10 Apr 82	● REALLY SAYING SOMETHING *Deram NANA 1* [2]	5	10
8 May 82	THE TELEPHONE ALWAYS RINGS *Chrysalis CHS 2609*	17	9
31 Jul 82	SUMMERTIME *Chrysalis CHS 2629*	18	8
15 Jan 83	THE MORE I SEE (THE LESS I BELIEVE) *Chrysalis CHS 2664*	68	1
5 Feb 83	● TUNNEL OF LOVE *Chrysalis CHS 2678*	10	10
30 Apr 83	● OUR LIPS ARE SEALED *Chrysalis FUNB 1*	7	10

[1] Fun Boy Three and Bananarama [2] Bananarama with the Fun Boy Three

FUN LOVIN' CRIMINALS
US, male vocal / instrumental group   7 wks

8 Jun 96	THE GRAVE AND THE CONSTANT *Chrysalis CDCHS 5031*	72	1
17 Aug 96	SCOOBY SNACKS *Chrysalis CDCHS 5034*	22	3
16 Nov 96	THE FUN LOVIN' CRIMINAL *Chrysalis CDCHS 5040*	28	3

Farley 'Jackmaster' FUNK *US, male producer*   16 wks

23 Aug 86	● LOVE CAN'T TURN AROUND *DJ International LON 105*	10	12
11 Feb 89	AS ALWAYS *Champion CHAMP 90* [1]	49	2
14 Dec 96	LOVE CAN'T TURN AROUND (re-mix) *4 Liberty LIBTCD 27* [2]	40	2

[1] Farley 'Jackmaster' Funk featuring Ricky Dillard [2] Farley 'Jackmaster' Funk with Darryl Pandy

Love Can't Turn Around in 96 is a re-recording.

FUNK MASTERS
UK, male / female vocal / instrumental group   12 wks

| 18 Jun 83 | ● IT'S OVER *Master Funk Records 7MP 004* | 8 | 12 |

FUNKADELIC *US, male vocal / instrumental group*   12 wks

| 9 Dec 78 | ● ONE NATION UNDER A GROOVE (PART 1) *Warner Bros. K 17246* | 9 | 12 |

FUNKAPOLITAN *UK, male vocal / instrumental group*   7 wks

| 22 Aug 81 | AS TIME GOES BY *London LON 001* | 41 | 7 |

FUNKDOOBIEST US, male rap group — 6 wks

11 Dec 93	**WOPBABALUBOP** Immortal 6597112	**37**	4
5 Mar 94	**BOW WOW WOW** Immortal 6594052	**34**	2

FUNKY BOYS – See Linda CARR

FUNKY BUNCH – See MARKY MARK and the FUNKY BUNCH

FUNKY POETS US, male vocal group — 1 wk

7 May 94	**BORN IN THE GHETTO** Epic 6603522	**72**	1

FUNKY WORM UK, male / female vocal / instrumental group — 14 wks

30 Jul 88	**HUSTLE! (TO THE MUSIC...)** Fon FON 15	**13**	8
26 Nov 88	**THE SPELL!** Fon FON 16	**61**	3
20 May 89	**U + ME = LOVE** Fon FON 19	**46**	3

FUREYS Ireland, male vocal group — 14 wks

10 Oct 81	**WHEN YOU WERE SWEET SIXTEEN** Ritz RITZ 003 [1]	**14**	11
3 Apr 82	**I WILL LOVE YOU (EV'RY TIME WHEN WE ARE GONE)** Ritz RITZ 012	**54**	3

[1] Fureys with Davey Arthur

FURIOUS FIVE – See GRANDMASTER FLASH, Melle MEL and the FURIOUS FIVE

FURNITURE UK, male / female vocal / instrumental group — 10 wks

14 Jun 86	**BRILLIANT MIND** Stiff BUY 251	**21**	10

Billy FURY UK, male vocalist — 281 wks

27 Feb 59	**MAYBE TOMORROW** Decca F 11102	**22**	3
27 Mar 59	**MAYBE TOMORROW (re-entry)** Decca F 11102	**18**	6
26 Jun 59	**MARGO** Decca F 11128	**28**	1
10 Mar 60 ●	**COLETTE** Decca F 11200	**9**	10
26 May 60	**THAT'S LOVE** Decca F 11237	**19**	11
22 Sep 60	**WONDROUS PLACE** Decca F 11267	**25**	9
19 Jan 61	**A THOUSAND STARS** Decca F 11311	**14**	10
27 Apr 61	**DON'T WORRY** Decca F 11334	**40**	2
11 May 61 ●	**HALFWAY TO PARADISE** Decca F 11349	**3**	23
7 Sep 61 ●	**JEALOUSY** Decca F 11384	**2**	12
14 Dec 61 ●	**I'D NEVER FIND ANOTHER YOU** Decca F 11409	**5**	15
15 Mar 62	**LETTER FULL OF TEARS** Decca F 11437	**32**	6
3 May 62 ●	**LAST NIGHT WAS MADE FOR LOVE** Decca F 11458	**4**	16
19 Jul 62 ●	**ONCE UPON A DREAM** Decca F 11485	**7**	13
25 Oct 62	**BECAUSE OF LOVE** Decca F 11508	**18**	14
14 Feb 63 ●	**LIKE I'VE NEVER BEEN GONE** Decca F11582	**3**	15
16 May 63 ●	**WHEN WILL YOU SAY I LOVE YOU** Decca F 11655	**3**	12
25 Jul 63 ●	**IN SUMMER** Decca F 11701	**5**	11
3 Oct 63	**SOMEBODY ELSE'S GIRL** Decca F 11744	**18**	7
2 Jan 64	**DO YOU REALLY LOVE ME TOO** Decca F 11792	**13**	10
30 Apr 64	**I WILL** Decca F 11888	**14**	12
23 Jul 64 ●	**IT'S ONLY MAKE BELIEVE** Decca F 11939	**10**	10
14 Jan 65	**I'M LOST WITHOUT YOU** Decca F 12048	**16**	10
22 Jul 65 ●	**IN THOUGHTS OF YOU** Decca F 12178	**9**	11
16 Sep 65	**RUN TO MY LOVIN' ARMS** Decca F 12230	**25**	7
10 Feb 66	**I'LL NEVER QUITE GET OVER YOU** Decca F 12325	**35**	5
4 Aug 66	**GIVE ME YOUR WORD** Decca F 12459	**27**	7
4 Sep 82	**LOVE OR MONEY** Polydor POSP 488	**57**	5
13 Nov 82	**DEVIL OR ANGEL** Polydor POSP 528	**58**	4
4 Jun 83	**FORGET HIM** Polydor POSP 558	**59**	4

FUTURE FORCE UK / US, male / female vocal / instrumental duo — 1 wk

17 Aug 96	**WHAT YOU WANT** AM:PM 5816592	**47**	1

FUTURE SOUND OF LONDON UK, male instrumental / production duo — 19 wks

23 May 92	**PAPUA NEW GUINEA** Jumpin' & Pumpin' TOT 17	**22**	6
6 Nov 93	**CASCADE** Virgin VSCDT 1478	**27**	3
30 Jul 94	**EXPANDER** Jumpin' & Pumpin' CDSTOT 37	**72**	1
13 Aug 94	**LIFEFORMS** Virgin VSCD 1484	**14**	3
27 May 95	**FAR-OUT SON OF LUNG AND THE RAMBLINGS OF A MADMAN** Virgin VSCDT 1540	**22**	3
26 Oct 96	**MY KINGDOM** Virgin VSCDT 1605	**13**	3

FUZZBOX – See WE'VE GOT A FUZZBOX AND WE'RE GONNA USE IT

Leslie FYSON – See Michael MEDWIN, Bernard BRESSLAW, Alfie BASS and Leslie FYSON

G

Bobby G UK, male vocalist — 12 wks

1 Dec 84	**BIG DEAL** BBC RESL 151	**75**	1
15 Dec 84	**BIG DEAL (re-entry)** BBC RESL 151	**65**	5
19 Oct 85	**BIG DEAL (2nd re-entry)** BBC RESL 151	**46**	6

Gina G Australia, female vocalist — 33 wks

6 Apr 96 ★	**OOH AAH... JUST A LITTLE BIT** Eternal WEA 041CD	**1**	23
21 Sep 96	**OOH AAH...JUST A LITTLE BIT (re-entry)** Eternal WEA 041CD	**62**	1
5 Oct 96	**OOH AAH...JUST A LITTLE BIT (2nd re-entry)** Eternal WEA 041CD	**64**	1
9 Nov 96 ●	**I BELONG TO YOU** Eternal WEA 081CD	**6†**	8

Kenny G US, male instrumentalist – saxophone — 22 wks

21 Apr 84	**HI! HOW YA DOIN'?** Arista ARIST 561	**70**	3
30 Aug 86	**WHAT DOES IT TAKE (TO WIN YOUR LOVE)** Arista ARIST 672	**64**	2
4 Jul 87	**SONGBIRD** Arista RIS 18	**22**	7
9 May 92	**MISSING YOU NOW** Columbia 6579917 [1]	**28**	4
24 Apr 93	**FOREVER IN LOVE** Arista 74321145552	**47**	3
17 Jul 93	**BY THE TIME THIS NIGHT IS OVER** Arista 74321157142 [2]	**56**	3

[1] Michael Bolton featuring Kenny G [2] Kenny G with Peabo Bryson

Warren G US, male rapper — 29 wks

23 Jul 94 ●	**REGULATE** Death Row A 8290CD [1]	**5**	14
12 Nov 94	**THIS DJ** RAL RALCD 1	**12**	5
31 Dec 94	**THIS DJ (re-entry)** RAL RALCD 1	**68**	2
25 Mar 95	**DO YOU SEE** RAL RALCD 3	**29**	2
23 Nov 96 ●	**WHAT'S LOVE GOT TO DO WITH IT** Interscope IND 97008 [2]	**2†**	6

[1] Warren G and Nate Dogg [2] Warren G featuring Adina Howard

Eric GABLE *US, male vocalist*   **1 wk**

19 Mar 94	**PROCESS OF ELIMINATION** *Epic 6602282* **63**	1	

Peter GABRIEL *UK, male vocalist*   **112 wks**

9 Apr 77	**SOLSBURY HILL** *Charisma CB 301* **13**	9
9 Feb 80	● **GAMES WITHOUT FRONTIERS** *Charisma CB 354*..........**4**	11
10 May 80	**NO SELF CONTROL** *Charisma CB 360* **33**	6
23 Aug 80	**BIKO** *Charisma CB 370* **38**	3
25 Sep 82	**SHOCK THE MONKEY** *Charisma SHOCK 1* **58**	5
9 Jul 83	**I DON'T REMEMBER** *Charisma GAB 1* **62**	3
2 Jun 84	**WALK THROUGH THE FIRE** *Virgin VS 689* **69**	3
26 Apr 86	● **SLEDGEHAMMER** *Virgin PGS 1* **4**	16
1 Nov 86	● **DON'T GIVE UP** *Virgin PGS 2* [1] **9**	11
28 Mar 87	**BIG TIME** *Charisma PGS 3* **13**	7
11 Jul 87	**RED RAIN** *Charisma PGS 4* **46**	3
21 Nov 87	**BIKO (LIVE)** *Charisma PGS 6* **49**	6
3 Jun 89	**SHAKING THE TREE** *Virgin VS 1167* [2] **61**	3
22 Dec 90	**SOLSBURY HILL / SHAKING THE TREE (re-issue)** *Virgin VS 1322* [3] **57**	4
19 Sep 92	**DIGGING IN THE DIRT** *Realworld PGS 7* **24**	4
16 Jan 93	● **STEAM** *Realworld PGSDG 8* **10**	7
3 Apr 93	**BLOOD OF EDEN** *Realworld PGSDG 9* **43**	4
25 Sep 93	**KISS THAT FROG** *Realworld PGSDG 10* **46**	3
25 Jun 94	**LOVETOWN** *Epic 6604802* **49**	2
3 Sep 94	**SW LIVE EP** *Realworld PGSCD 11* **39**	2

[1] Peter Gabriel and Kate Bush   [2] Youssou N'Dour and Peter Gabriel
[3] Peter Gabriel/Youssou N'Dour and Peter Gabriel

Tracks available on all formats of SW Live EP: Red Rain / San Jacinto. Red Rain is a live version of his '87 hit.

GABRIELLE *UK, female vocalist*   **69 wks**

19 Jun 93	★ **DREAMS** *Go.Beat GODCD 99* **1**	15
2 Oct 93	● **GOING NOWHERE** *Go.Beat GODCD 106* **9**	7
11 Dec 93	**I WISH** *Go.Beat GODCD 108* **26**	5
26 Feb 94	**BECAUSE OF YOU** *Go.Beat GODCD 109* **24**	5
24 Feb 96	● **GIVE ME A LITTLE MORE TIME** *Go.Beat GODCD 139* **5**	18
22 Jun 96	**FORGET ABOUT THE WORLD** *Go.Beat GODCD 146* **23**	5
5 Oct 96	**IF YOU REALLY CARED** *Go.Beat GODCD 153* **15**	5
2 Nov 96	● **IF YOU EVER** *London LONCD 388* [1] ....**2†**	9

[1] East 17 featuring Gabrielle

Yvonne GAGE *US, female vocalist*   **4 wks**

16 Jun 84	**DOIN' IT IN A HAUNTED HOUSE** *Epic A 4519*..................**45**	4

Danni'elle GAHA *Australia, female vocalist*   **7 wks**

1 Aug 92	**STUCK IN THE MIDDLE** *Epic 6581247*................**68**	2
27 Feb 93	**DO IT FOR LOVE** *Epic 6584612* **52**	2
12 Jun 93	**SECRET LOVE** *Epic 6592212* **41**	3

Rosie GAINES *US, female vocalist*   **1 wk**

11 Nov 95	**I WANT U** *Motown 8604852*..........................**70**	1

Serge GAINSBOURG – *See Jane BIRKIN and Serge GAINSBOURG*

GALAXY – *See Phil FEARON*

Dee GALDES – *See Phil FEARON*

Eve GALLAGHER *UK, female vocalist*   **8 wks**

1 Dec 90	**LOVE COME DOWN** *More Protein PROT 6*..................**61**	3

29 Dec 90	**LOVE COME DOWN (re-entry)** *More Protein PROT 6* **68**	1
15 Apr 95	**YOU CAN HAVE IT ALL** *Cleveland City CLECD 13023* **43**	2
28 Oct 95	**LOVE COME DOWN** *Cleveland City CLECD 13028* **57**	1
6 Jul 96	**HEARTBREAK** *React CDREACT 78* [1] **44**	1

[1] Mrs Wood featuring Eve Gallagher

Love Come Down in 95 is a re-recording.

GALLAGHER and LYLE
UK, male vocal / instrumental duo   **27 wks**

28 Feb 76	● **I WANNA STAY WITH YOU** *A & M AMS 7211* **6**	9
22 May 76	● **HEART ON MY SLEEVE** *A & M AMS 7227* **6**	10
11 Sep 76	**BREAKAWAY** *A & M AMS 7245* **35**	4
29 Jan 77	**EVERY LITTLE TEARDROP** *A & M AMS 7274* **32**	4

Patsy GALLANT *Canada, female vocalist*   **9 wks**

10 Sep 77	● **FROM NEW YORK TO L.A.** *EMI 2620* **6**	9

GALLIANO *UK, male / female vocal / instrumental group*   **14 wks**

30 May 92	**SKUNK FUNK** *Talkin Loud TLK 23* **41**	2
1 Aug 92	**PRINCE OF PEACE** *Talkin Loud TLK 24* **47**	3
10 Oct 92	**JUS' REACH (RECYCLED)** *Talkin Loud TLK 29* **66**	2
28 May 94	**LONG TIME GONE** *Talkin Loud TLKCD 48* **15**	3
30 Jul 94	**TWYFORD DOWN** *Talkin Loud TLKCD 49* **37**	2
27 Jul 96	**EASE YOUR MIND** *Talkin Loud TLCD 10* **45**	2

James GALWAY *UK, male instrumentalist – flute*   **13 wks**

27 May 78	● **ANNIE'S SONG** *RCA Red Seal RB 5085* **3**	13

GANG OF FOUR *UK, male vocal / instrumental group*   **5 wks**

16 Jun 79	**AT HOME HE'S A TOURIST** *EMI 2956* **58**	3
22 May 82	**I LOVE A MAN IN UNIFORM** *EMI 5299* **65**	2

GANG STARR *US, male rap group*   **8 wks**

13 Oct 90	**JAZZ THING** *CBS 356377 7* **66**	2
23 Feb 91	**TAKE A REST** *Cooltempo COOL 230* **63**	1
25 May 91	**LOVESICK** *Cooltempo COOL 234* **50**	3
13 Jun 92	**2 DEEP** *Cooltempo COOL 256* **67**	2

GAP BAND *US, male vocal / instrumental group*   **82 wks**

12 Jul 80	● **OOPS UP SIDE YOUR HEAD** *Mercury MER 22* **6**	14
27 Sep 80	**PARTY LIGHTS** *Mercury MER 37* **30**	8
27 Dec 80	**BURN RUBBER ON ME (WHY YOU WANNA HURT ME)** *Mercury MER 52* **22**	11
11 Apr 81	**HUMPIN'** *Mercury MER 63* **36**	6
27 Jun 81	**YEARNING FOR YOUR LOVE** *Mercury MER 73* **47**	4
5 Jun 82	**EARLY IN THE MORNING** *Mercury MER 97* **55**	3
19 Feb 83	**OUTSTANDING** *Total Experience TE 001* **68**	2
31 Mar 84	**SOMEDAY** *Total Experience TE 5* **17**	8
23 Jun 84	**JAMMIN' IN AMERICA** *Total Experience TE 6* **64**	2
13 Dec 86	● **BIG FUN** *Total Experience FB 49779* **4**	12
14 Mar 87	**HOW MUSIC CAME ABOUT (BOP B DA B DA DA)** *Total Experience FB 49755* **61**	2
11 Jul 87	**OOPS UPSIDE YOUR HEAD (re-mix)** *Club JAB 54* **20**	8
18 Feb 89	**I'M GONNA GIT YOU SUCKA** *Arista 112016* **63**	2

GARBAGE
US / UK, male / female vocal / instrumental group   **21 wks**

19 Aug 95	**SUBHUMAN** *Mushroom D 1138*..........................**50**	1

30 Sep 95	ONLY HAPPY WHEN IT RAINS *Mushroom D 1199*	29	3
2 Dec 95	QUEER *Mushroom D 1237*	13	4
23 Mar 96 ●	STUPID GIRL *Mushroom D 1271*	4	7
23 Nov 96 ●	MILK *Mushroom D 1494* [1]	10†	6

[1] Garbage featuring Tricky

Boris GARDINER
Jamaica, male vocalist / instrumentalist   **38 wks**

17 Jan 70	ELIZABETHAN REGGAE *Duke DU 39*	48	1
31 Jan 70	ELIZABETHAN REGGAE (re-entry) *Duke DU 39*	14	13
26 Jul 86 ★	I WANT TO WAKE UP WITH YOU *Revue REV 733*	1	15
4 Oct 86	YOU'RE EVERYTHING TO ME *Revue REV 735*	11	8
27 Dec 86	THE MEANING OF CHRISTMAS *Revue REV 740*	69	1

The first copies of Elizabethan Reggae, an instrumental, were printed with the label incorrectly crediting Byron Lee as the performer. The charts for the first entry, and the first four weeks of the re-entry, all reprinted this error. All charts and discs printed after 28 Feb 1970 gave Boris Gardiner the credit he deserved.

Paul GARDINER *UK, male instrumentalist – bass*   **4 wks**

| 25 Jul 81 | STORMTROOPER IN DRAG *Beggars Banquet BEG 61* | 49 | 4 |

Uncredited vocalist is Gary Numan.

Art GARFUNKEL *US, male vocalist*   **37 wks**

13 Sep 75 ★	I ONLY HAVE EYES FOR YOU *CBS 3575*	1	11
3 Mar 79 ★	BRIGHT EYES *CBS 6947*	1	19
7 Jul 79	SINCE I DON'T HAVE YOU *CBS 7371*	38	7

Judy GARLAND *US, female vocalist*   **2 wks**

| 10 Jun 55 | THE MAN THAT GOT AWAY *Philips PB 366* | 18 | 2 |

Lee GARRETT *US, male vocalist*   **7 wks**

| 29 May 76 | YOU'RE MY EVERYTHING *Chrysalis CHS 2087* | 15 | 7 |

Leif GARRETT *US, male vocalist*   **14 wks**

| 20 Jan 79 ● | I WAS MADE FOR DANCIN' *Scotti Brothers K 11202* | 4 | 10 |
| 21 Apr 79 | FEEL THE NEED *Scotti Brothers K 11274* | 38 | 4 |

Lesley GARRETT and Amanda THOMPSON
UK, female vocal / instrumental duo   **10 wks**

| 6 Nov 93 | AVE MARIA *Internal Affairs KGBD 012* | 16 | 10 |

Siedah GARRETT – See Dennis EDWARDS; Michael JACKSON

David GARRICK *UK, male vocalist*   **16 wks**

| 9 Jun 66 | LADY JANE *Piccadilly 7N 35317* | 28 | 7 |
| 22 Sep 66 | DEAR MRS. APPLEBEE *Piccadilly 7N 35335* | 22 | 9 |

GARY'S GANG *US, male vocal / instrumental group*   **18 wks**

24 Feb 79 ●	KEEP ON DANCIN' *CBS 7109*	8	10
2 Jun 79	LET'S LOVE DANCE TONIGHT *CBS 7328*	49	4
6 Nov 82	KNOCK ME OUT *Arista ARIST 499*	45	4

Barbara GASKIN – See Dave STEWART

GAT DECOR
UK, male instrumental / production group   **10 wks**

| 16 May 92 | PASSION *Effective EFFS 1* | 29 | 4 |
| 9 Mar 96 ● | PASSION (re-mix) *Way Of Life WAYDA 1* | 6 | 6 |

David GATES *US, male vocalist*   **2 wks**

| 22 Jul 78 | TOOK THE LAST TRAIN *Elektra K 12307* | 50 | 2 |

GAY GORDON and the MINCE PIES
UK, male / female vocal / instrumental group   **5 wks**

| 6 Dec 86 | THE ESSENTIAL WALLY PARTY MEDLEY *Lifestyle XY 2* | 60 | 5 |

GAYE BYKERS ON ACID
UK, male vocal / instrumental group   **2 wks**

| 31 Oct 87 | GIT DOWN (SHAKE YOUR THANG) *Purple Fluid VS 1008* | 54 | 2 |

Marvin GAYE *US, male vocalist*   **200 wks**

30 Jul 64	ONCE UPON A TIME *Stateside SS 316* [1]	50	1
10 Dec 64	HOW SWEET IT IS (TO BE LOVED BY YOU) *Stateside SS 360*	49	1
29 Sep 66	LITTLE DARLIN' *Tamla Motown TMG 574*	50	1
26 Jan 67	IT TAKES TWO *Tamla Motown TMG 590* [2]	16	11
17 Jan 68	IF I COULD BUILD MY WHOLE WORLD AROUND YOU *Tamla Motown TMG 635* [3]	41	7
12 Jun 68	AIN'T NOTHIN' LIKE THE REAL THING *Tamla Motown TMG 655* [3]	34	7
2 Oct 68	YOU'RE ALL I NEED TO GET BY *Tamla Motown TMG 668* [3]	19	19
22 Jan 69	YOU AIN'T LIVIN' 'TILL YOU'RE LOVIN' *Tamla Motown TMG 681* [3]	21	8
12 Feb 69 ★	I HEARD IT THROUGH THE GRAPEVINE *Tamla Motown TMG 686*	1	15
4 Jun 69	GOOD LOVIN' AIN'T EASY TO COME BY *Tamla Motown TMG 697* [3]	26	7
23 Jul 69 ●	TOO BUSY THINKING 'BOUT MY BABY *Tamla Motown TMG 705*	5	16
30 Jul 69	GOOD LOVIN' AIN'T EASY TO COME BY (re-entry) *Tamla Motown TMG 697* [3]	48	1
15 Nov 69 ●	ONION SONG *Tamla Motown TMG 715* [3]	9	12
9 May 70 ●	ABRAHAM MARTIN AND JOHN *Tamla Motown TMG 734*	9	14
11 Dec 71	SAVE THE CHILDREN *Tamla Motown TMG 796*	41	6
22 Sep 73	LET'S GET IT ON *Tamla Motown TMG 868*	31	7
23 Mar 74 ●	YOU ARE EVERYTHING *Tamla Motown TMG 890* [4]	5	12
20 Jul 74	STOP LOOK LISTEN (TO YOUR HEART) *Tamla Motown TMG 906* [4]	25	8
7 May 77 ●	GOT TO GIVE IT UP *Motown TMG 1069*	7	10
24 Feb 79	POPS WE LOVE YOU *Motown TMG 1136* [5]	66	5
30 Oct 82 ●	(SEXUAL) HEALING *CBS A 2855*	4	14
8 Jan 83	MY LOVE IS WAITING *CBS A 3048*	34	5
18 May 85	SANCTIFIED LADY *CBS A 4894*	51	4
26 Apr 86 ●	I HEARD IT THRU THE GRAPEVINE (re-issue) *Tamla Motown ZB 40701*	8	8
14 May 94	LUCKY LUCKY ME *Motown TMGCD 1426*	67	1

[1] Marvin Gaye and Mary Wells [2] Marvin Gaye and Kim Weston [3] Marvin Gaye and Tammi Terrell [4] Diana Ross and Marvin Gaye [5] Diana Ross, Marvin Gaye, Smokey Robinson and Stevie Wonder

GAYLE & GILLIAN *Australia, female vocal duo*   **2 wks**

| 3 Jul 93 | MAD IF YA DON'T *Mushroom CDMUSH 1* | 75 | 1 |
| 19 Mar 94 | WANNA BE YOUR LOVER *Mushroom D 11598* | 62 | 1 |

Gabrielle

There was a two year hiatus between the release of 'Because Of You' and 'Give Me A Little More Time', during which time Gabrielle gave birth to her son Jordan.

Gina G

Before Gina G's 'Ohh Ahh...Just A Little Bit', only four other UK Eurovision entries had topped the chart: 'Puppet On A String' by Sandie Shaw, 'Congratulations' by Cliff Richard, 'Save Your Kisses For Me' by Brotherhood Of Man and 'Making Your Mind Up' by Bucks Fizz.

Marvin Gaye

Marvin Gaye's only number one 'I Heard It Through The Grapevine' was originally recorded by Gladys Knight and the Pips in 1967.

Crystal GAYLE *US, female vocalist*　　**28 wks**

| 12 Nov 77 | ● | DON'T IT MAKE MY BROWN EYES BLUE *United Artists UP 36307* | **5** | 14 |
| 26 Aug 78 | | TALKING IN YOUR SLEEP *United Artists UP 36422* | **11** | 14 |

Michelle GAYLE *UK, female vocalist*　　**42 wks**

7 Aug 93		LOOKING UP *RCA 74321154532*	**11**	6
24 Sep 94	●	SWEETNESS *RCA 74321230192*	**4**	16
17 Dec 94		I'LL FIND YOU *RCA 74321247762*	**26**	7
27 May 95		FREEDOM *RCA 74321284692*	**16**	6
26 Aug 95		HAPPY JUST TO BE WITH YOU *RCA 74321302692*	**11**	7

Roy GAYLE – *See MIRAGE*

Gloria GAYNOR *US, female vocalist*　　**72 wks**

7 Dec 74	●	NEVER CAN SAY GOODBYE *MGM 2006 463*	**2**	13
8 Mar 75		REACH OUT (I'LL BE THERE) *MGM 2006 499*	**14**	8
9 Aug 75		ALL I NEED IS YOUR SWEET LOVIN' *MGM 2006 531*	**44**	4
17 Jan 76		HOW HIGH THE MOON *MGM 2006 558*	**33**	4
3 Feb 79	★	I WILL SURVIVE *Polydor 2095 017*	**1**	15
6 Oct 79		LET ME KNOW (I HAVE A RIGHT) *Polydor STEP 5*	**32**	7
24 Dec 83		I AM WHAT I AM (FROM 'LA CAGE AUX FOLLES) *Chrysalis CHS 2765*	**13**	12
26 Jun 93	●	I WILL SURVIVE (re-mix) *Polydor PZCD 270*	**5**	10

GAZ *US, male vocal / instrumental group*　　**4 wks**

| 24 Feb 79 | | SING SING *Salsoul SSOL 116* | **60** | 4 |

GAZZA *UK, male vocalist – Paul Gascoigne*　　**14 wks**

| 10 Nov 90 | ● | FOG ON THE TYNE (REVISITED) *Best ZB 44083* [1] | **2** | 9 |
| 22 Dec 90 | | GEORDIE BOYS (GAZZA RAP) *Best ZB 44229* | **31** | 5 |

[1] Gazza and Lindisfarne

GBH *UK, male vocal / instrumental group*　　**5 wks**

| 6 Feb 82 | | NO SURVIVORS *Clay CLAY 8* | **63** | 2 |
| 20 Nov 82 | | GIVE ME FIRE *Clay CLAY 16* | **69** | 3 |

G-CLEFS *US, male vocal group*　　**12 wks**

| 30 Nov 61 | | I UNDERSTAND *London HLU 9433* | **17** | 12 |

J. GEILS BAND *US, male vocal / instrumental group*　　**20 wks**

9 Jun 79		ONE LAST KISS *EMI America AM 507*	**74**	1
13 Feb 82	●	CENTERFOLD *EMI America EA 135*	**3**	9
10 Apr 82		FREEZE-FRAME *EMI America EA 134*	**27**	7
26 Jun 82		ANGEL IN BLUE *EMI America EA 138*	**55**	3

Bob GELDOF *Ireland, male vocalist*　　**15 wks**

1 Nov 86		THIS IS THE WORLD CALLING *Mercury BOB 101*	**25**	5
21 Feb 87		LOVE LIKE A ROCKET *Mercury BOB 102*	**61**	3
23 Jun 90		THE GREAT SONG OF INDIFFERENCE *Mercury BOB 104*	**15**	6
7 May 94		CRAZY *Vertigo VERCX 85*	**65**	1

GEM – *See ONE TRIBE featuring GEM*

GEMINI *UK, male vocal duo*　　**7 wks**

| 30 Sep 95 | | EVEN THOUGH YOU BROKE MY HEART *EMI CDEMS 391* | **40** | 3 |

| 10 Feb 96 | | STEAL YOUR LOVE AWAY *EMI CDEMS 407* | **37** | 2 |
| 29 Jun 96 | | COULD IT BE FOREVER *EMI CDEMS 426* | **38** | 2 |

GEMS FOR JEM
UK, male instrumental / production duo　　**2 wks**

| 6 May 95 | | LIFTING ME HIGHER *Box 21 CDSBOKS 3* | **28** | 2 |

GENE *UK, male vocal / instrumental group*　　**12 wks**

13 Aug 94		BE MY LIGHT BE MY GUIDE *Costermonger COST 002CD*	**54**	1
12 Nov 94		SLEEP WELL TONIGHT *Costermonger COST 003CD*	**36**	2
4 Mar 95		HAUNTED BY YOU *Costermonger COST 004CD*	**32**	2
22 Jul 95		OLYMPIAN *Costermonger COST 005CD*	**18**	2
13 Jan 96		FOR THE DEAD *Costermonger COST 006CD*	**14**	3
2 Nov 96		FIGHTING FIT *Costermonger COST 9CD*	**22**	2

GENE AND JIM ARE INTO SHAKES
UK, male vocal / instrumental duo　　**2 wks**

| 19 Mar 88 | | SHAKE! (HOW ABOUT A SAMPLING GENE) *Rough Trade RT 216* | **68** | 2 |

GENE LOVES JEZEBEL
UK, male vocal / instrumental group　　**7 wks**

29 Mar 86		SWEETEST THING *Beggars Banquet BEG 156*	**75**	1
14 Jun 86		HEARTACHE *Beggars Banquet BEG 161*	**71**	2
5 Sep 87		THE MOTION OF LOVE *Beggars Banquet BEG 192*	**56**	3
5 Dec 87		GORGEOUS *Beggars Banquet BEG 202*	**68**	1

GENERAL LEVY *UK, male vocalist*　　**13 wks**

4 Sep 93		MONKEY MAN *ffrr FCD 214*	**75**	1
18 Jun 94		INCREDIBLE *Renk RENKT 42CD* [1]	**39**	3
10 Sep 94	●	INCREDIBLE (re-mix) *Renk CDRENK 45* [1]	**8**	9

[1] M-Beat featuring General Levy

GENERAL PUBLIC *UK, male vocal / instrumental group*　　**4 wks**

| 10 Mar 84 | | GENERAL PUBLIC *Virgin VS 659* | **60** | 3 |
| 2 Jul 94 | | I'LL TAKE YOU THERE *Epic 6605532* | **73** | 1 |

GENERAL SAINT *UK, male vocalist*　　**9 wks**

29 Sep 84		LAST PLANE (ONE WAY TICKET) *MCA MCA 910* [1]	**51**	3
2 Apr 94		OH CAROL! *Copasetic COPCD 0009* [2]	**54**	5
6 Aug 94		SAVE THE LAST DANCE FOR ME *Copasetic COPCD 12* [2]	**75**	1

[1] Clint Eastwood and General Saint [2] General Saint featuring Don Campbell

GENERATION X *UK, male vocal / instrumental group*　　**31 wks**

17 Sep 77		YOUR GENERATION *Chrysalis CHS 2165*	**36**	4
11 Mar 78		READY STEADY GO *Chrysalis CHS 2207*	**47**	3
20 Jan 79		KING ROCKER *Chrysalis CHS 2261*	**11**	9
7 Apr 79		VALLEY OF THE DOLLS *Chrysalis CHS 2310*	**23**	7
30 Jun 79		FRIDAY'S ANGELS *Chrysalis CHS 2330*	**62**	2
18 Oct 80		DANCING WITH MYSELF *Chrysalis CHS 2444* [1]	**62**	2
24 Jan 81		DANCING WITH MYSELF (EP) *Chrysalis CHS 2488* [1]	**60**	4

[1] Gen X

Tracks on Dancing With Myself (EP): *Dancing With Myself / Untouchables / Rock On / King Rocker.*

146

GENESIS UK, male vocal / instrumental group   183 wks

6 Apr 74	I KNOW WHAT I LIKE (IN YOUR WARDROBE) Charisma CB 224	21	7
26 Feb 77	YOUR OWN SPECIAL WAY Charisma CB 300	43	7
28 May 77	SPOT THE PIGEON EP Charisma GEN 001	14	7
11 Mar 78 ●	FOLLOW YOU FOLLOW ME Charisma CB 309	7	13
8 Jul 78	MANY TOO MANY Charisma CB 315	43	5
15 Mar 80	TURN IT ON AGAIN Charisma CB 356	8	10
17 May 80	DUCHESS Charisma CB 363	46	5
13 Sep 80	MISUNDERSTANDING Charisma CB 369	42	5
22 Aug 81 ●	ABACAB Charisma CB 388	9	8
31 Oct 81	KEEP IT DARK Charisma CB 391	33	4
13 Mar 82	MAN ON THE CORNER Charisma CB 393	41	5
22 May 82 ●	3 X 3 EP Charisma GEN 1	10	8
3 Sep 83 ●	MAMA Virgin/Charisma MAMA 1	4	10
12 Nov 83	THAT'S ALL Charisma/Virgin TATA 1	16	11
11 Feb 84	ILLEGAL ALIEN Charisma/Virgin AL1	46	3
10 Mar 84	ILLEGAL ALIEN (re-entry) Charisma/Virgin AL1	70	1
31 May 86	INVISIBLE TOUCH Virgin GENS 1	15	8
30 Aug 86	IN TOO DEEP Virgin GENS 2	19	9
22 Nov 86	LAND OF CONFUSION Virgin GENS 3	14	12
14 Mar 87	TONIGHT TONIGHT TONIGHT Virgin GENS 4	18	6
20 Jun 87	THROWING IT ALL AWAY Virgin GENS 5	22	8
2 Nov 91 ●	NO SON OF MINE Virgin GENS 6	6	6
4 Jan 92	NO SON OF MINE (re-entry) Virgin GENS 6	70	1
11 Jan 92	I CAN'T DANCE Virgin GENS 7	7	9
18 Apr 92	HOLD ON MY HEART Virgin GENS 8	16	5
25 Jul 92	JESUS HE KNOWS ME Virgin GENS 9	20	7
21 Nov 92 ●	INVISIBLE TOUCH (LIVE) Virgin GENS 10	7	4
20 Feb 93	TELL ME WHY Virgin GENDG 11	40	3

Tracks on Spot The Pigeon EP: Match Of The Day / Pigeons / Inside and Out. Tracks on 3 X 3 EP: Paperlate / You Might Recall / Me And Virgil

GENEVA UK, male vocal / instrumental group   2 wks

26 Oct 96	NO ONE SPEAKS Nude NUD 22CD	32	2

GENEVIEVE France, female vocalist   1 wk

5 May 66	ONCE CBS 202061	43	1

GENIUS/GZA – See D'ANGELO

Bobbie GENTRY US, female vocalist   48 wks

13 Sep 67	ODE TO BILLY JOE Capitol CL 15511	13	11
30 Aug 69 ★	I'LL NEVER FALL IN LOVE AGAIN Capitol CL 15606	1	19
6 Dec 69 ●	ALL I HAVE TO DO IS DREAM Capitol CL 15619 [1]	3	14
21 Feb 70	RAINDROPS KEEP FALLIN' ON MY HEAD Capitol CL 15626	40	4

[1] Bobbie Gentry and Glen Campbell

GEORDIE UK, male vocal / instrumental group   35 wks

2 Dec 72	DON'T DO THAT Regal Zonophone RZ 3067	32	7
17 Mar 73 ●	ALL BECAUSE OF YOU EMI 2008	6	13
16 Jun 73	CAN YOU DO IT EMI 2031	13	9
25 Aug 73	ELECTRIC LADY EMI 2048	32	6

Robin GEORGE
UK, male vocalist / instrumentalist – guitar   2 wks

27 Apr 85	HEARTLINE Bronze BRO 191	68	2

Sophia GEORGE Jamaica, female vocalist   11 wks

7 Dec 85 ●	GIRLIE GIRLIE Winner WIN 01	7	11

GEORGIA SATELLITES
US, male vocal / instrumental group   8 wks

7 Feb 87	KEEP YOUR HANDS TO YOURSELF Elektra EKR 50	69	1
16 May 87	BATTLESHIP CHAINS Elektra EKR 58	44	4
21 Jan 89	HIPPY HIPPY SHAKE Elektra EKR 86	63	3

GEORGIE PORGIE US, male producer   2 wks

12 Aug 95	EVERYBODY MUST PARTY Vibe MCSTD 2068	61	1
4 May 96	TAKE ME HIGHER Music Plant MCSTD 40031	61	1

GEORGIO US, male vocalist   3 wks

20 Feb 88	LOVER'S LANE Motown ZB 41611	54	3

Danyel GERARD France, male vocalist   12 wks

18 Sep 71	BUTTERFLY CBS 7454	11	12

GERIDEAU – See PROJECT featuring GERIDEAU

GERRY and the PACEMAKERS
UK, male vocal / instrumental group   114 wks

14 Mar 63 ★	HOW DO YOU DO IT? Columbia DB 4987	1	18
30 May 63 ★	I LIKE IT Columbia DB 7041	1	15
10 Oct 63 ★	YOU'LL NEVER WALK ALONE Columbia DB 7126	1	19
16 Jan 64 ●	I'M THE ONE Columbia DB 7189	2	15
16 Apr 64 ●	DON'T LET THE SUN CATCH YOU CRYING Columbia DB 7268	6	11
3 Sep 64	IT'S GONNA BE ALL RIGHT Columbia DB 7353	24	7
17 Dec 64 ●	FERRY ACROSS THE MERSEY Columbia DB 7437	8	13
25 Mar 65	I'LL BE THERE Columbia DB 7504	15	9
18 Nov 65	WALK HAND IN HAND Columbia DB 7738	29	7

GET FRESH CREW – See Doug E. FRESH and the GET FRESH CREW

GET READY UK, male vocal group   1 wk

3 Jun 95	WILD WILD WEST Mega GACXCD 2698	65	1

GETO BOYS featuring FLAJ US, male rap group   1 wk

11 May 96	THE WORLD IS A GHETTO Virgin America VUSCD 104	49	1

Stan GETZ US, male instrumentalist – tenor sax   29 wks

8 Nov 62	DESAFINADO HMV POP 1061 [1]	11	13
23 Jul 64	THE GIRL FROM IPANEMA (GAROTA DE IPANEMA) Verve VS 520 [2]	29	10
25 Aug 84	THE GIRL FROM IPANEMA (re-issue) Verve IPA 1 [3]	55	6

[1] Stan Getz and Charlie Byrd [2] Stan Getz and Joao Gilberto [3] Astrud Gilberto

The re-issue of The Girl From Ipanema was credited only to Astrud Gilberto, the vocalist, even though it was exactly the same recording as the original hit.

GHOST DANCE UK, male vocal / instrumental group   2 wks

17 Jun 89	DOWN TO THE WIRE Chrysalis CHS 3376	66	2

Andy GIBB UK, male vocalist   30 wks

25 Jun 77	I JUST WANNA BE YOUR EVERYTHING RSO 2090 237	26	7
13 May 78	SHADOW DANCING RSO 001	42	6

12 Aug 78	● AN EVERLASTING LOVE *RSO 015*.............................**10**	10
27 Jan 79	(OUR LOVE) DON'T THROW IT ALL AWAY *RSO 26* **32**	7

Barry GIBB – *See Barbra STREISAND*

Robin GIBB *UK, male vocalist*   **21 wks**

9 Jul 69	● SAVED BY THE BELL *Polydor 56-337* **2**	16
15 Nov 69	SAVED BY THE BELL (re-entry) *Polydor 56-337*...........**49**	1
7 Feb 70	AUGUST OCTOBER *Polydor 56-371* **45**	3
11 Feb 84	ANOTHER LONELY NIGHT IN NEW YORK	
	Polydor POSP 668..........................**71**	1

Steve GIBBONS BAND
UK, male vocal / instrumental group   **14 wks**

6 Aug 77	TULANE *Polydor 2058 889* **12**	10
13 May 78	EDDY VORTEX *Polydor 2059 017* **56**	4

Georgia GIBBS *US, female vocalist*   **2 wks**

22 Apr 55	TWEEDLE DEE *Mercury MB 3196* **20**	1
13 Jul 56	KISS ME ANOTHER *Mercury MT 110* **24**	1

Debbie GIBSON *US, female vocalist*   **70 wks**

26 Sep 87	ONLY IN MY DREAMS *Atlantic A 9322* **54**	5
23 Jan 88	● SHAKE YOUR LOVE *Atlantic A 9187* **7**	8
19 Mar 88	ONLY IN MY DREAMS (re-entry) *Atlantic A 9322*...........**11**	7
7 May 88	OUT OF THE BLUE *Atlantic A 9091* **19**	7
9 Jul 88	● FOOLISH BEAT *Atlantic A 9059* **9**	9
15 Oct 88	STAYING TOGETHER *Atlantic A 9020* **53**	2
28 Jan 89	LOST IN YOUR EYES *Atlantic A 8970* **34**	7
29 Apr 89	ELECTRIC YOUTH *Atlantic A 8919* **14**	8
19 Aug 89	WE COULD BE TOGETHER *Atlantic A 8896* **22**	8
9 Mar 91	ANYTHING IS POSSIBLE *Atlantic A 7735* **51**	2
3 Apr 93	SHOCK YOUR MAMA *Atlantic A 7386CD* **74**	1
24 Jul 93	YOU'RE THE ONE THAT I WANT *Epic 6595222* 1 ....**13**	6

1 Craig McLachlan and Debbie Gibson

Don GIBSON *US, male vocalist*   **16 wks**

31 Aug 61	SEA OF HEARTBREAK *RCA 1243*..................................**14**	13
1 Feb 62	LONESOME NUMBER ONE *RCA 1272*.............................**47**	3

Wayne GIBSON *UK, male vocalist*   **13 wks**

3 Sep 64	KELLY *Pye 7N 15680* **48**	2
23 Nov 74	UNDER MY THUMB *Pye Disco Demand DDS 2001*...........**17**	11

GIBSON BROTHERS
Martinique, male vocal / instrumental group   **54 wks**

10 Mar 79	CUBA *Island WIP 6483*...**41**	9
21 Jul 79	● OOH! WHAT A LIFE *Island WIP 6503* **10**	12
17 Nov 79	● QUE SERA MI VIDA (IF YOU SHOULD GO)	
	Island WIP 6525 ....**5**	11
23 Feb 80	CUBA/BETTER DO IT SALSA (re-issue) *Island WIP 6561* **12**	9
12 Jul 80	MARIANA *Island WIP 6617* **11**	10
9 Jul 83	MY HEART'S BEATING WILD (TIC TAC TIC TAC)	
	Stiff BUY 184 ....**56**	3

GIDEA PARK
UK, male vocal / instrumentalist – Adrian Baker   **19 wks**

4 Jul 81	BEACHBOY GOLD *Stone SON 2162* **11**	13
12 Sep 81	SEASONS OF GOLD *Polo POLO 14* **28**	6

GIGOLO AUNTS *US, male vocal / instrumental group*   **4 wks**

23 Apr 94	MRS. WASHINGTON *Fire BLAZE 68CD* **74**	1
13 May 95	WHERE I FIND MY HEAVEN *Fire BLAZE 87CD*................**29**	3

Astrud GILBERTO – *See Stan GETZ*

Joao GILBERTO – *See Stan GETZ*

Donna GILES *US, male vocalist*   **4 wks**

13 Aug 94	AND I'M TELLING YOU I'M NOT GOING *Ore AG 4CD* ..**43**	2
10 Feb 96	AND I'M TELLING YOU I'M NOT GOING (re-mix)	
	Ore AGR 4CD **27**	2

Johnny GILL *US, male vocalist*   **12 wks**

23 Feb 91	WRAP MY BODY TIGHT *Motown ZB 44271*.....................**57**	2
28 Nov 92	SLOW AND SEXY *Epic 6587727* 1 ....**17**	7
17 Jul 93	THE FLOOR *Motown TMGCD 1416* **53**	1
29 Jan 94	A CUTE SWEET LOVE ADDICTION	
	Motown TMGCD 1420 ....**46**	2

1 Shabba Ranks featuring Johnny Gill

Vince GILL – *See Amy GRANT*

GILLAN *UK, male vocal / instrumental group*   **46 wks**

14 Jun 80	SLEEPIN' ON THE JOB *Virgin VS 355* **55**	3
4 Oct 80	TROUBLE *Virgin VS 377*..**14**	6
14 Feb 81	MUTUALLY ASSURED DESTRUCTION *Virgin VS 103* **32**	5
21 Mar 81	NEW ORLEANS *Virgin VS 406* **17**	10
20 Jun 81	NO LAUGHING IN HEAVEN *Virgin VS 425* **31**	6
10 Oct 81	NIGHTMARE *Virgin VS 441* **36**	6
23 Jan 82	RESTLESS *Virgin VS 465* **25**	7
4 Sep 82	LIVING FOR THE CITY *Virgin VS 519*.............................**50**	3

GILLETTE – *See 20 FINGERS*

Stuart GILLIES *UK, male vocalist*   **10 wks**

31 Mar 73	AMANDA *Philips 6006 293*..**13**	10

Jimmy GILMER – *See FIREBALLS*

James GILREATH *US, male vocalist*   **10 wks**

2 May 63	LITTLE BAND OF GOLD *Pye International 7N 25190*........**29**	10

Jim GILSTRAP *US, male vocalist*   **11 wks**

15 Mar 75	● SWING YOUR DADDY *Chelsea 2005 021* **4**	11

Gordon GILTRAP *UK, male instrumentalist – guitar*   **10 wks**

14 Jan 78	HEARTSONG *Electric WOT 19* **21**	7
28 Apr 79	FEAR OF THE DARK *Electric WOT 29* 1 ....**58**	3

1 Gordon Giltrap Band

GIN BLOSSOMS *US, male vocal / instrumental group*   **12 wks**

5 Feb 94	HEY JEALOUSY *Fontana GINCD 3* **24**	5
16 Apr 94	FOUND OUT ABOUT YOU *Fontana GINCD 4* **40**	3
10 Feb 96	TIL I HEAR IT FROM YOU *A & M 5812272* **39**	2
27 Apr 96	FOLLOW YOU DOWN *A & M 5815512* **30**	2

GINGERBREADS – See GOLDIE and the GINGERBREADS

GIPSY KINGS *France, male vocal / instrumental group* — **2 wks**

3 Sep 94	**HITS MEDLEY** *Columbia 6606022*	**53**	2

Martine GIRAULT *US, female vocalist* — **6 wks**

29 Aug 92	**REVIVAL** *ffrr FX 195*	**53**	2
30 Jan 93	**REVIVAL (re-issue)** *ffrr FCD 205*	**37**	3
28 Oct 95	**BEEN THINKING ABOUT YOU** *RCA 74321316142*	**63**	1

GIRL *UK, male vocal / instrumental group* — **3 wks**

12 Apr 80	**HOLLYWOOD TEASE** *Jet 176*	**50**	3

GIRLFRIEND *Australia, female vocal group* — **6 wks**

30 Jan 93	**TAKE IT FROM ME** *Arista 74321114252*	**47**	4
15 May 93	**GIRL'S LIFE** *Arista 74321138452*	**68**	2

GIRLSCHOOL *UK, female vocal / instrumental group* — **25 wks**

2 Aug 80	**RACE WITH THE DEVIL** *Bronze BRO 100*	**49**	6
21 Feb 81 ●	**ST. VALENTINE'S DAY MASSACRE EP** *Bronze BRO 116* 1	**5**	8
11 Apr 81	**HIT AND RUN** *Bronze BRO 118*	**32**	6
11 Jul 81	**C'MON LET'S GO** *Bronze BRO 126*	**42**	3
3 Apr 82	**WILDLIFE (EP)** *Bronze BRO 144*	**58**	2

1 Motorhead and Girlschool (also known as Headgirl)

Tracks on St. Valentine's Day Massacre EP: *Please Don't Touch / Emergency / Bomber.*
Tracks on Wildlife (EP): *Don't Call It Love / Wildlife / Don't Stop.*

Junior GISCOMBE – See JUNIOR

GLADIATORS – See NERO and the GLADIATORS

GLADIATORS *UK, male / female vocal group* — **1 wk**

30 Nov 96	**THE BOYS ARE BACK IN TOWN** *RCA 74321417002*	**70**	1

GLAM *Italy, male instrumental / production group* — **2 wks**

1 May 93	**HELL'S PARTY** *Six6 SIXCD 001*	**42**	2

GLAM METAL DETECTIVES
UK, male / female vocal group — **2 wks**

11 Mar 95	**EVERYBODY UP!** *ZTT ZANG 62CD*	**29**	2

GLASS TIGER *Canada, male vocal / instrumental group* — **18 wks**

18 Oct 86	**DON'T FORGET ME (WHEN I'M GONE)** *Manhattan MT 13*	**29**	9
31 Jan 87	**SOMEDAY** *Manhattan MT 17*	**66**	2
26 Oct 91	**MY TOWN** *EMI EM 212*	**33**	7

My Town features the uncredited vocals of Rod Stewart.

Mayson GLEN ORCHESTRA – See Paul HENRY and the Mayson GLEN ORCHESTRA

GLENN and CHRIS *UK, male vocal duo* — **8 wks**

18 Apr 87	**DIAMOND LIGHTS** *Record Shack KICK 1*	**12**	8

Gary GLITTER *UK, male vocalist* — **170 wks**

10 Jun 72 ●	**ROCK AND ROLL (PARTS 1 & 2)** *Bell 1216*	**2**	15
23 Sep 72 ●	**I DIDN'T KNOW I LOVED YOU (TILL I SAW YOU ROCK 'N' ROLL)** *Bell 1259*	**4**	11
20 Jan 73 ●	**DO YOU WANNA TOUCH ME? (OH YEAH)** *Bell 1280*	**2**	11
7 Apr 73 ●	**HELLO HELLO I'M BACK AGAIN** *Bell 1299*	**2**	14
21 Jul 73 ★	**I'M THE LEADER OF THE GANG (I AM)** *Bell 1321*	**1**	12
17 Nov 73 ★	**I LOVE YOU LOVE ME LOVE** *Bell 1337*	**1**	14
30 Mar 74 ●	**REMEMBER ME THIS WAY** *Bell 1349*	**3**	8
15 Jun 74 ★	**ALWAYS YOURS** *Bell 1359*	**1**	9
23 Nov 74 ●	**OH YES! YOU'RE BEAUTIFUL** *Bell 1391*	**2**	10
3 May 75 ●	**LOVE LIKE YOU AND ME** *Bell 1423*	**10**	6
21 Jun 75 ●	**DOING ALRIGHT WITH THE BOYS** *Bell 1429*	**6**	7
8 Nov 75	**PAPA OOM MOW MOW** *Bell 1451*	**38**	5
13 Mar 76	**YOU BELONG TO ME** *Bell 1473*	**40**	5
22 Jan 77	**IT TAKES ALL NIGHT LONG** *Arista 85*	**25**	6
16 Jul 77	**A LITTLE BOOGIE WOOGIE IN THE BACK OF MY MIND** *Arista 112*	**31**	5
20 Sep 80	**GARY GLITTER EP** *GTO GT 282*	**57**	3
10 Oct 81	**AND THEN SHE KISSED ME** *Bell BELL 1497*	**39**	5
5 Dec 81	**ALL THAT GLITTERS** *Bell BELL 1498*	**48**	5
23 Jun 84	**DANCE ME UP** *Arista ARIST 570*	**25**	5
1 Dec 84 ●	**ANOTHER ROCK AND ROLL CHRISTMAS** *Arista ARIST 592*	**7**	7
10 Oct 92	**AND THE LEADER ROCKS ON** *EMI EM 252*	**58**	2
21 Nov 92	**THROUGH THE YEARS** *EMI EM 256*	**49**	3
16 Dec 95	**HELLO HELLO I'M BACK AGAIN (AGAIN!)** *Carlton Sounds 3036000192*	**50**	2

Rock And Roll Part 1 not listed with Part 2 for weeks of 10 and 17 Jun 72. Tracks on Gary Glitter EP: I'm The Leader Of The Gang (I Am) / Rock And Roll (Part 2) / Hello Hello I'm Back Again / Do You Wanna Touch Me? (Oh Yeah). All were re-issues. Hello Hello I'm Back Again in 95 is a re-recording.

GLITTER BAND *UK, male vocal / instrumental group* — **60 wks**

23 Mar 74 ●	**ANGEL FACE** *Bell 1348*	**4**	10
3 Aug 74 ●	**JUST FOR YOU** *Bell 1368*	**10**	8
19 Oct 74 ●	**LET'S GET TOGETHER AGAIN** *Bell 1383*	**8**	8
18 Jan 75 ●	**GOODBYE MY LOVE** *Bell 1395*	**2**	9
12 Apr 75 ●	**THE TEARS I CRIED** *Bell 1416*	**8**	8
9 Aug 75	**LOVE IN THE SUN** *Bell 1437*	**15**	8
28 Feb 76 ●	**PEOPLE LIKE YOU AND PEOPLE LIKE ME** *Bell 1471*	**5**	9

GLOVE *UK, male vocal / instrumental group* — **3 wks**

20 Aug 83	**LIKE AN ANIMAL** *Wonderland SHE 3*	**52**	3

GLOWORM *UK / US, male vocal / instrumental group* — **17 wks**

6 Feb 93	**I LIFT MY CUP** *Pulse 8 CDLOSE 37*	**20**	4
14 May 94 ●	**CARRY ME HOME** *Go.Beat GODCD 112*	**9**	11
6 Aug 94	**I LIFT MY CUP (re-issue)** *Pulse 8 CDLOSE 67*	**46**	2

GO GO LORENZO and the DAVIS PINCKNEY PROJECT *US, male vocal / instrumental group* — **8 wks**

6 Dec 86	**YOU CAN DANCE (IF YOU WANT TO)** *Boiling Point POSP 836*	**46**	8

GO-GOs *US, female vocal / instrumental group* — **10 wks**

15 May 82	**OUR LIPS ARE SEALED** *IRS GDN 102*	**47**	6
26 Jan 91	**COOL JERK** *IRS AM 712*	**60**	1
18 Feb 95	**THE WHOLE WORLD LOST ITS HEAD** *IRS CDEIRS 190*	**29**	3

GO WEST *UK, male vocal / instrumental duo* — **85 wks**

23 Feb 85 ●	**WE CLOSE OUR EYES** *Chrysalis CHS 2850*	**5**	14

11 May 85	**CALL ME** Chrysalis GOW 1	**12**	10
3 Aug 85	**GOODBYE GIRL** Chrysalis GOW 2	**25**	7
23 Nov 85	**DON'T LOOK DOWN – THE SEQUEL** Chrysalis GOW 3	**13**	10
29 Nov 86	**TRUE COLOURS** Chrysalis GOW 4	**48**	7
9 May 87	**I WANT TO HEAR IT FROM YOU** Chrysalis GOW 5	**43**	3
12 Sep 87	**THE KING IS DEAD** Chrysalis GOW 6	**67**	2
28 Jul 90	**THE KING OF WISHFUL THINKING** Chrysalis GOW 8	**18**	10
17 Oct 92	**FAITHFUL** Chrysalis GOW 9	**13**	6
16 Jan 93	**WHAT YOU WON'T DO FOR LOVE** Chrysalis CDGOWS 10	**15**	5
27 Mar 93	**STILL IN LOVE** Chrysalis CDGOWS 11	**43**	3
2 Oct 93	**TRACKS OF MY TEARS** Chrysalis CDGOWS 12	**16**	5
4 Dec 93	**WE CLOSE OUR EYES (re-mix)** Chrysalis CDGOWS 13	**40**	3

GOATS US, male rap group — **2 wks**

29 May 93	**AAAH D YAAA / TYPICAL AMERICAN** Ruff House 6593032	**53**	2

Typical American only listed from 5 Jun, peaking at position 65.

GOD MACHINE US, male vocal / instrumental group — **2 wks**

30 Jan 93	**HOME** Fiction FICCD 47	**65**	2

GODIEGO Japan / US, male vocal / instrumental group — **11 wks**

15 Oct 77	**THE WATER MARGIN** BBC RESL 50	**37**	4
16 Feb 80	**GANDHARA** BBC RESL 66	**56**	7

The Water Margin is the English version of the song, which shared chart credit with the Japanese language version by Pete Mac Jr.

GODLEY and CREME
UK, male vocal / instrumental duo — **36 wks**

12 Sep 81	● **UNDER YOUR THUMB** Polydor POSP 322	**3**	11
21 Nov 81	● **WEDDING BELLS** Polydor POSP 369	**7**	11
30 Mar 85	**CRY** Polydor POSP 732	**19**	11
16 Aug 86	**CRY (re-entry)** Polydor POSP 732	**66**	3

Andrew GOLD
US, male vocalist / instrumentalist – piano — **36 wks**

2 Apr 77	**LONELY BOY** Asylum K 13076	**11**	9
25 Mar 78	● **NEVER LET HER SLIP AWAY** Asylum K 13112	**5**	13
24 Jun 78	**HOW CAN THIS BE LOVE** Asylum K 13126	**19**	10
14 Oct 78	**THANK YOU FOR BEING A FRIEND** Asylum K 13135	**42**	4

Brian and Tony GOLD – See RED DRAGON with Brian and Tony GOLD

GOLDBUG UK, male / female vocal / instrumental group — **5 wks**

27 Jan 96	● **WHOLE LOTTA LOVE** Acid Jazz JAZID 125CD	**3**	5

GOLDEN EARRING
Holland, male vocal / instrumental group — **16 wks**

8 Dec 73	● **RADAR LOVE** Track 2094 116	**7**	13
8 Oct 77	**RADAR LOVE** Polydor 2121 335	**44**	3

These are two different recordings of the same song.

GOLDIE UK, male vocal / instrumental group — **11 wks**

27 May 78	● **MAKING UP AGAIN** Bronze BRO 50	**7**	11

GOLDIE and the GINGERBREADS
US, female vocal / instrumental group — **5 wks**

25 Feb 65	**CAN'T YOU HEAR MY HEART BEAT?** Decca F 12070	**25**	5

GOLDIE UK, male producer — **7 wks**

3 Dec 94	**INNER CITY LIFE** ffrr FCD 251 [1]	**49**	2
9 Sep 95	**ANGEL** ffrr FCD 266	**41**	3
11 Nov 95	**INNER CITY LIFE (re-mix)** ffrr FCD 267	**39**	2

[1] Goldie presents Metalheads

Bobby GOLDSBORO US, male vocalist — **47 wks**

17 Apr 68	● **HONEY** United Artists UP2215	**2**	15
4 Aug 73	● **SUMMER (THE FIRST TIME)** United Artists UP35558	**9**	10
3 Aug 74	**HELLO SUMMERTIME** United Artists UP35705	**14**	10
29 Mar 75	● **HONEY (re-issue)** United Artists UP35633	**2**	12

Glen GOLDSMITH US, male vocalist — **24 wks**

7 Nov 87	**I WON'T CRY** Reproduction PB 41493	**34**	7
12 Mar 88	**DREAMING** Reproduction PB 41711	**12**	11
11 Jun 88	**WHAT YOU SEE IS WHAT YOU GET** Reproduction PB 42075	**33**	5
3 Sep 88	**SAVE A LITTLE BIT** Reproduction PB 42147	**73**	1

Leroy GOMEZ – See SANTA ESMERALDA and Leroy GOMEZ

GOMPIE Holland, male vocal / instrumental group — **12 wks**

20 May 95	**ALICE (WHO THE X IS ALICE) (LIVING NEXT DOOR TO ALICE)** Habana HABSCD 5	**34**	5
2 Sep 95	**ALICE (WHO THE X IS ALICE) (LIVING NEXT DOOR TO ALICE) (re-entry)** Habana HABSCD 5	**17**	7

GONZALEZ UK / US, male vocal / instrumental group — **11 wks**

31 Mar 79	**HAVEN'T STOPPED DANCING YET** Sidewalk SID 102	**15**	11

GOOD GIRLS US, female vocal group — **1 wk**

24 Jul 93	**JUST CALL ME** Motown TMGCD 1417	**75**	1

GOODBYE MR. MACKENZIE
UK, male / female vocal / instrumental group — **13 wks**

20 Aug 88	**GOODBYE MR MACKENZIE** Capitol CL 501	**62**	2
11 Mar 89	**THE RATTLER** Capitol CL 522	**37**	6
29 Jul 89	**GOODWILL CITY / I'M SICK OF YOU** Capitol CL 538	**49**	2
21 Apr 90	**LOVE CHILD** Parlophone R 6247	**52**	2
23 Jun 90	**BLACKER THAN BLACK** Parlophone R 6257	**61**	1

GOODIES UK, male vocal group — **38 wks**

7 Dec 74	● **THE IN BETWEENIES / FATHER CHRISTMAS DO NOT TOUCH ME** Bradley's BRAD 7421	**7**	9
15 Mar 75	● **FUNKY GIBBON / SICK MAN BLUES** Bradley's BRAD 7504	**4**	10
21 Jun 75	**BLACK PUDDING BERTHA (THE QUEEN OF NORTHERN SOUL)** Bradley's BRAD 7517	**19**	7
27 Sep 75	**NAPPY LOVE / WILD THING** Bradley's BRAD 7524	**21**	6
13 Dec 75	**MAKE A DAFT NOISE FOR CHRISTMAS** Bradley's BRAD 7533	**20**	6

Go West

Go West returned to the chart in 1990 after a break of three years with 'The King Of Wishful Thinking', from the *Pretty Woman* film soundtrack.

Debbie Gibson

When 'Foolish Beat' topped the American chart in 1988, 17-year-old Debbie Gibson became the youngest artist ever to write, perform and produce a US number one.

Daryl Hall and John Oates

Daryl Hall and John Oates covered Mike Oldfield's 'Family Man' and took the song 30 places higher than the original.

151

Cuba GOODING US, male vocalist   2 wks

19 Nov 83	**HAPPINESS IS JUST AROUND THE BEND** *London LON 41*	**72**	2

GOODMEN Holland, male instrumental / production duo   19 wks

7 Aug 93	**GIVE IT UP** *Fresh Fruit TABCD 118*	**23**	5
9 Oct 93	● **GIVE IT UP (re-entry)** *Fresh Fruit TABCD 118*	**5**	14

Ron GOODWIN UK, orchestra   24 wks

15 May 53	● **TERRY'S THEME FROM 'LIMELIGHT'** *Parlophone R 3686*	**3**	23
28 Oct 55	**BLUE STAR (THE MEDIC THEME)** *Parlophone R 4074*	**20**	1

See also Eamonn Andrews.

GOODY GOODY US, female vocal duo   5 wks

2 Dec 78	**NUMBER ONE DEE JAY** *Atlantic LV 3*	**55**	5

GOOMBAY DANCE BAND
Germany / Montserrat, male / female vocal / instrumental group   16 wks

27 Feb 82	★ **SEVEN TEARS** *Epic EPC A 1242*	**1**	12
15 May 82	**SUN OF JAMAICA** *Epic EPC A 2345*	**50**	4

GOONS UK, male vocal group   30 wks

29 Jun 56	● **I'M WALKING BACKWARDS FOR CHRISTMAS /** **BLUEBOTTLE BLUES** *Decca F 10756*	**4**	10
14 Sep 56	● **BLOODNOK'S ROCK 'N' ROLL CALL /** **YING TONG SONG** *Decca E 10780*	**3**	10
21 Jul 73	● **YING TONG SONG (re-issue)** *Decca F 13414*	**9**	10

Bluebottle Blues only listed from 13 Jul 56. It peaked at position 5.

Lonnie GORDON US, female vocalist   23 wks

24 Jun 89	**(I'VE GOT YOUR) PLEASURE CONTROL** *ffrr F 106* [1]	**60**	3
27 Jan 90	● **HAPPENIN' ALL OVER AGAIN** *Supreme SUPE 159*	**4**	10
11 Aug 90	**BEYOND YOUR WILDEST DREAMS** *Supreme SUPE 167*	**48**	2
17 Nov 90	**IF I HAVE TO STAND ALONE** *Supreme SUPE 181*	**68**	1
4 May 91	**GONNA CATCH YOU** *Supreme SUPE 185*	**32**	5
7 Oct 95	**LOVE EVICTION** *X:Plode BANG 2CD* [2]	**32**	2

[1] Simon Harris featuring Lonnie Gordon [2] Quartz Lock featuring
Lonnie Gordon

Lesley GORE US, female vocalist   20 wks

20 Jun 63	● **IT'S MY PARTY** *Mercury AMT 1205*	**9**	12
24 Sep 64	**MAYBE I KNOW** *Mercury MF 829*	**20**	8

GORKY'S ZYGOTIC MYNCI
UK, male / female vocal / instrumental group   1 wk

9 Nov 96	**PATIO SONG** *Fontana GZMCD 1*	**41**	1

Eydie GORMÉ US, female vocalist   33 wks

24 Jan 58	**LOVE ME FOREVER** *HMV POP 432*	**21**	5
21 Jun 62	● **YES MY DARLING DAUGHTER** *CBS AAG 105*	**10**	9
31 Jan 63	**BLAME IT ON THE BOSSA NOVA** *CBS AAG 131*	**32**	6
22 Aug 63	● **I WANT TO STAY HERE** *CBS AAG 163* [1]	**3**	13

[1] Steve and Eydie

G.O.S.H. UK, male / female charity ensemble   11 wks

28 Nov 87	**THE WISHING WELL** *MBS GOSH 1*	**22**	11

Luke GOSS and the BAND OF THIEVES
UK, male vocal / instrumental group   3 wks

12 Jun 93	**SWEETER THAN THE MIDNIGHT RAIN** *Sabre CDSAB 1*	**52**	2
21 Aug 93	**GIVE ME ONE MORE CHANCE** *Sabre CDSAB 2*	**68**	1

Matt GOSS UK, male vocalist   5 wks

26 Aug 95	**THE KEY** *Atlas 5811532*	**40**	2
27 Apr 96	**IF YOU WERE HERE TONIGHT** *Atlas 5762932*	**23**	3

Nigel GOULDING – *See Abigail MEAD and Nigel GOULDING*

Graham GOULDMAN UK, male vocalist   4 wks

23 Jun 79	**SUNBURN** *Mercury SUNNY 1*	**52**	4

GQ US, male vocal / instrumental group   6 wks

10 Mar 79	**DISCO NIGHTS (ROCK FREAK)** *Arista ARIST 245*	**42**	6

GRACE UK, female vocalist   17 wks

8 Apr 95	● **NOT OVER YET** *Perfecto PERF 104CD*	**6**	8
23 Sep 95	**I WANT TO LIVE** *Perfecto PERF 109CD*	**30**	2
24 Feb 96	**SKIN ON SKIN** *Perfecto PERF 116CD*	**21**	3
1 Jun 96	**DOWN TO EARTH** *Perfecto PERF 120CD*	**20**	2
28 Sep 96	**IF I COULD FLY** *Perfecto PERF 127CD*	**29**	2

GRACE BROTHERS UK, male instrumental duo   1 wk

20 Apr 96	**ARE YOU BEING SERVED** *EMI Premier PRESCD 1*	**51**	1

Charlie GRACIE US, male vocalist   39 wks

19 Apr 57	**BUTTERFLY** *Parlophone R 4290*	**12**	8
14 Jun 57	● **FABULOUS** *Parlophone R 4313*	**8**	16
23 Aug 57	**I LOVE YOU SO MUCH IT HURTS / WANDERIN' EYES** *London HLU 8467*	**14**	2
6 Sep 57	● **WANDERIN' EYES** *London HLU 8467*	**6**	12
6 Sep 57	**I LOVE YOU SO MUCH IT HURTS** *London HLU 8467*	**20**	2
10 Jan 58	**COOL BABY** *London HLU 8521*	**26**	1

I Love You So Much It Hurts and Wanderin' Eyes were listed together for two weeks, then listed separately for a further two and 12 weeks respectively.

Eve GRAHAM – *See NEW SEEKERS*

Jaki GRAHAM UK, female vocalist   75 wks

23 Mar 85	● **COULD IT BE I'M FALLING IN LOVE** *Chrysalis GRAN 6* [1]	**5**	11
29 Jun 85	● **ROUND AND ROUND** *EMI JAKI 4*	**9**	11
31 Aug 85	**HEAVEN KNOWS** *EMI JAKI 5*	**59**	3
16 Nov 85	**MATED** *EMI JAKI 6* [1]	**20**	10
3 May 86	● **SET ME FREE** *EMI JAKI 7*	**7**	12
9 Aug 86	**BREAKING AWAY** *EMI JAKI 8*	**16**	8
15 Nov 86	**STEP RIGHT UP** *EMI JAKI 9*	**15**	12
9 Jul 88	**NO MORE TEARS** *EMI JAKI 12*	**60**	2
24 Jun 89	**FROM NOW ON** *EMI JAKI 15*	**73**	2
16 Jul 94	**AIN'T NOBODY** *Pulse 8 CDLOSE 64*	**44**	2
4 Feb 95	**YOU CAN COUNT ON ME** *Avex UK AVEXCD 1*	**62**	1
8 Jul 95	**ABSOLUTE E-SENSUAL** *Avex UK AVEXCD 5*	**69**	1

[1] David Grant and Jaki Graham

Larry GRAHAM US, male vocalist — 4 wks

3 Jul 82	SOONER OR LATER Warner Bros. K 17925	54	4

Ron GRAINER ORCHESTRA UK, orchestra — 7 wks

9 Dec 78	A TOUCH OF VELVET A STING OF BRASS Casino Classics CC 5	60	7

GRAND FUNK RAILROAD
US, male vocal / instrumental group — 1 wk

6 Feb 71	INSIDE LOOKING OUT Capitol CL 15668	40	1

GRAND PLAZ
UK, male instrumental / production group — 4 wks

8 Sep 90	WOW WOW – NA NA Urban URB 6 0	41	4

GRAND PRIX UK, male vocal / instrumental group — 1 wk

27 Feb 82	KEEP ON BELIEVING RCA 162	75	1

GRAND PUBA US, male rapper — 6 wks

13 Jan 96	WHY YOU TREAT ME SO BAD Virgin VSCDT 1566 [1]	11	5
30 Mar 96	WILL YOU BE MY BABY GHQ 74321339092 [2]	53	1

[1] Shaggy featuring Grand Puba [2] Infiniti featuring Grand Puba

GRANDMASTER FLASH, Melle MEL and the FURIOUS FIVE
US, male vocal duo and male vocal group — 87 wks

28 Aug 82	● THE MESSAGE Sugarhill SHL 117 [1]	8	9
22 Jan 83	MESSAGE II (SURVIVAL) Sugarhill SH 119 [2]	74	2
19 Nov 83	WHITE LINES (DON'T DON'T DO IT) Sugarhill SH 130 [3]	60	3
11 Feb 84	● WHITE LINES (DON'T DON'T DO IT) (re-entry) Sugarhill SH 130 [3]	7	38
30 Jun 84	BEAT STREET BREAKDOWN Atlantic A9659 [4]	42	7
22 Sep 84	WE DON'T WORK FOR FREE Sugarhill SH 136 [4]	45	4
24 Nov 84	WHITE LINES (DON'T DON'T DO IT) (2nd re-entry) Sugarhill SH 130 [3]	75	1
15 Dec 84	● STEP OFF (PART 1) Sugarhill SH 139 [4]	8	12
5 Jan 85	WHITE LINES (DON'T DON'T DO IT) (3rd re-entry) Sugarhill SH 130 [3]	73	1
16 Feb 85	SIGN OF THE TIMES Elektra E 9677 [5]	72	1
16 Mar 85	PUMP ME UP Sugarhill SH 141 [4]	45	6
8 Jan 94	WHITE LINES (DON'T DO IT) (re-mix) WGAF WGAFCD 103 [3]	59	3

[1] Grandmaster Flash and the Furious Five [2] Melle Mel and Duke Bootee [3] Grandmaster and Melle Mel [4] Grandmaster Melle Mel and the Furious Five [5] Grandmaster Flash

GRANDMIXER US, male 'scratch' DJ — 3 wks

24 Dec 83	CRAZY CUTS Island IS 146	73	2
14 Jan 84	CRAZY CUTS (re-entry) Island IS 146	71	1

GRANGE HILL CAST
UK, male / female vocal charity assembly — 6 wks

19 Apr 86	● JUST SAY NO BBC RESL 183	5	6

Gerri GRANGER US, female vocalist — 3 wks

30 Sep 78	I GO TO PIECES (EVERYTIME) Casino Classics CC3	50	3

Amy GRANT US, female vocalist — 39 wks

11 May 91	● BABY BABY A & M AM 727	2	13
3 Aug 91	EVERY HEARTBEAT A & M AM 783	25	7
2 Nov 91	THAT'S WHAT LOVE IS FOR A & M AM 666	60	3
15 Feb 92	GOOD FOR ME A & M AM 810	60	1
13 Aug 94	LUCKY ONE A & M 5807322	60	1
22 Oct 94	SAY YOU'LL BE MINE A & M 5808292	41	2
24 Jun 95	BIG YELLOW TAXI A & M 5809972	20	10
14 Oct 95	HOUSE OF LOVE A & M 5812332 [1]	46	2

[1] Amy Grant with Vince Gill

Boysie GRANT – See Ezz RECO and the LAUNCHERS with Boysie GRANT

David GRANT UK, male vocalist — 59 wks

30 Apr 83	STOP AND GO Chrysalis GRAN 1	19	9
16 Jul 83	● WATCHING YOU WATCHING ME Chrysalis GRAN 2	10	13
8 Oct 83	LOVE WILL FIND A WAY Chrysalis GRAN 3	24	6
26 Nov 83	ROCK THE MIDNIGHT Chrysalis GRAN 4	46	4
23 Mar 85	● COULD IT BE I'M FALLING IN LOVE Chrysalis GRAN 6 [1]	5	11
16 Nov 85	MATED EMI JAKI 6 [1]	20	10
1 Aug 87	CHANGE Polydor POSP 871	55	4
12 May 90	KEEP IT TOGETHER Fourth & Broadway BRW 169	56	2

[1] David Grant and Jaki Graham

Eddy GRANT
Guyana, male vocalist / multi-instrumentalist — 94 wks

2 Jun 79	LIVING ON THE FRONT LINE Ensign ENY 26	11	11
15 Nov 80	● DO YOU FEEL MY LOVE Ensign ENY 45	8	11
4 Apr 81	CAN'T GET ENOUGH OF YOU Ensign ENY 207	13	10
25 Jul 81	I LOVE YOU, YES I LOVE YOU Ensign ENY 216	37	6
16 Oct 82	★ I DON'T WANNA DANCE Ice ICE 56	1	15
15 Jan 83	● ELECTRIC AVENUE Ice ICE 57	2	9
19 Mar 83	LIVING ON THE FRONT LINE / DO YOU FEEL MY LOVE (re-issue) Mercury MER 135	47	4
23 Apr 83	WAR PARTY Ice ICE 58	42	4
29 Oct 83	TILL I CAN'T TAKE LOVE NO MORE Ice ICE 60	42	7
19 May 84	ROMANCING THE STONE Ice ICE 61	52	3
23 Jan 88	● GIMME HOPE JO'ANNA Ice ICE 78701	7	12
27 May 89	WALKING ON SUNSHINE Blue Wave R 6217	63	2

Gogi GRANT US, female vocalist — 11 wks

29 Jun 56	● WAYWARD WIND London HLB 8282	9	11

Julie GRANT UK, female vocalist — 17 wks

3 Jan 63	UP ON THE ROOF Pye 7N 15483	33	3
28 Mar 63	COUNT ON ME Pye 7N 15508	24	9
24 Sep 64	COME TO ME Pye 7N 15684	31	5

Rudy GRANT Guyana, male vocalist — 3 wks

14 Feb 81	LATELY Ensign ENY 202	58	3

GRAPEFRUIT UK, male vocal / instrumental group — 19 wks

14 Feb 68	DEAR DELILAH RCA 1656	21	9
14 Aug 68	C'MON MARIANNE RCA 1716	31	10

GRAVEDIGGAZ US, male rap group   4 wks

11 Mar 95	SIX FEET DEEP EP Gee Street GESCD 62	64	1
5 Aug 95	THE HELL EP Fourth & Broadway BRCD 326 [1]	12	3

[1] Tricky vs the Gravediggaz

Tracks on Six Feet Deep EP: Bang Your Head / Mommy / Suicide. Tracks on The Hell EP: Hell Is Round The Corner / Hell Is Round The Corner (remix) / Psychosis / Tonite Is A Special Nite.

Dobie GRAY US, male vocalist   11 wks

25 Feb 65	THE IN CROWD London HL 9953	25	7
27 Sep 75	OUT ON THE FLOOR Black Magic BM 107	42	4

Dorian GRAY UK, male vocalist   7 wks

27 Mar 68	I'VE GOT YOU ON MY MIND Parlophone R 5667	36	7

Les GRAY UK, male vocalist   5 wks

26 Feb 77	A GROOVY KIND OF LOVE Warner Bros. K 16883	32	5

Barry GRAY ORCHESTRA UK, orchestra   8 wks

11 Jul 81	THUNDERBIRDS PRT 7P 216	61	2
14 Jun 86	JOE 90 / 'CAPTAIN SCARLET' THEME PRT 7PX 345 [1]	53	6

[1] Barry Gray Orchestra with Peter Beckett – keyboards

Alltrinna GRAYSON – See Wilton FELDER

GREAT WHITE US, male vocal / instrumental group   5 wks

24 Feb 90	HOUSE OF BROKEN LOVE Capitol CL 562	44	2
16 Feb 91	CONGO SQUARE Capitol CL 605	62	1
7 Sep 91	CALL IT ROCK 'N' ROLL Capitol CL 625	67	2

Buddy GRECO US, male vocalist   8 wks

7 Jul 60	LADY IS A TRAMP Fontana H 225	26	8

GREED – See Ricardo DA FORCE

GREEDIES
Ireland / UK / US, male vocal / instrumental group   5 wks

15 Dec 79	A MERRY JINGLE Vertigo GREED 1	28	5

Al GREEN US, male vocalist   68 wks

9 Oct 71	● TIRED OF BEING ALONE London HL 10337	4	13
8 Jan 72	● LET'S STAY TOGETHER London HL 10348	7	12
20 May 72	LOOK WHAT YOU DONE FOR ME London HL 10369	44	4
19 Aug 72	I'M STILL IN LOVE WITH YOU London HL 10382	35	5
16 Nov 74	SHA-LA-LA (MAKE ME HAPPY) London HL 10470	20	11
15 Mar 75	L.O.V.E. London HL 10482	24	8
3 Dec 88	PUT A LITTLE LOVE IN YOUR HEART A & M AM 484 [1]	28	8
21 Oct 89	THE MESSAGE IS LOVE Breakout USA 668 [2]	38	5
2 Oct 93	LOVE IS A BEAUTIFUL THING Arista 74321162692	56	2

[1] Annie Lennox and Al Green [2] Arthur Baker and the Backbeat Disciples featuring Al Green

Dotty GREEN – See Mark FISHER featuring Dotty GREEN

Jesse GREEN US, male vocalist   26 wks

7 Aug 76	NICE AND SLOW EMI 2492	17	12
18 Dec 76	FLIP EMI 2564	26	8
11 Jun 77	COME WITH ME EMI 2615	29	6

Robson GREEN and Jerome FLYNN – See ROBSON and JEROME

GREEN DAY US, male vocal / instrumental group   25 wks

20 Aug 94	BASKET CASE Reprise W 0257CD	55	2
29 Oct 94	WELCOME TO PARADISE Reprise W 0269CDX	20	3
28 Jan 95	● BASKET CASE (re-issue) Reprise W 0279CD	7	6
18 Mar 95	LONGVIEW Reprise W 0278CD	30	3
20 May 95	WHEN I COME AROUND Reprise W 0294CD	27	3
7 Oct 95	GEEK STINK BREATH Reprise W 0320CD	16	3
6 Jan 96	STUCK WITH ME Reprise W 0327CD	24	3
6 Jul 96	BRAIN STEW / JADED Reprise W 0339CD	28	2

GREEN JELLY US, male vocal / instrumental group   15 wks

5 Jun 93	● THREE LITTLE PIGS Zoo 74321151422	5	8
14 Aug 93	ANARCHY IN THE UK Zoo 74321159052	27	3
25 Dec 93	I'M THE LEADER OF THE GANG Arista 74321174892 [1]	25	4

[1] Hulk Hogan with Green Jelly

Norman GREENBAUM US, male vocalist   20 wks

21 Mar 70	★ SPIRIT IN THE SKY Reprise RS 20885	1	20

Lorne GREENE Canada, male vocalist   8 wks

17 Dec 64	RINGO RCA 1428	22	8

Lee GREENWOOD US, male vocalist   6 wks

19 May 84	THE WIND BENEATH MY WINGS MCA 877	49	6

Iain GREGORY UK, male vocalist   2 wks

4 Jan 62	CAN'T YOU HEAR THE BEAT OF A BROKEN HEART Pye 7N 15397	39	2

Johnny GREGORY – See CHAQUITO

Band of the GRENADIER GUARDS – See ST. JOHN'S COLLEGE SCHOOL CHOIR and the Band of the GRENADIER GUARDS

GREYHOUND
Jamaica, male vocal / instrumental group   33 wks

26 Jun 71	● BLACK AND WHITE Trojan TR 7820	6	13
8 Jan 72	MOON RIVER Trojan TR 7848	12	11
25 Mar 72	I AM WHAT I AM Trojan TR 7853	20	9

GRID UK, male instrumental / production duo   47 wks

7 Jul 90	FLOATATION East West YZ 475	60	2
29 Sep 90	A BEAT CALLED LOVE East West YZ 498	64	4
25 Jul 92	FIGURE OF 8 Virgin VSTG 1421	50	3
3 Oct 92	HEARTBEAT Virgin VST 1427	72	1
13 Mar 93	CRYSTAL CLEAR Virgin VSCDT 1442	27	4
30 Oct 93	TEXAS COWBOYS Deconstruction 74321167762	21	3
4 Jun 94	● SWAMP THING Deconstruction 74321205842	3	17
17 Sep 94	ROLLERCOASTER Deconstruction 74321230772	19	4

3 Dec 94	TEXAS COWBOYS (re-issue)		
	Deconstruction 74321244032	17	6
23 Sep 95	DIABLO Deconstruction 74321308402	32	2

Zaine GRIFF New Zealand, male vocalist — 6 wks

16 Feb 80	TONIGHT Automatic K 17547	54	3
31 May 80	ASHES AND DIAMONDS Automatic K 17610	68	3

Billy GRIFFIN US, male vocalist — 12 wks

8 Jan 83	HOLD ME TIGHTER IN THE RAIN CBS A 2935	17	9
14 Jan 84	SERIOUS CBS A 4053	64	3

Clive GRIFFIN UK, male vocalist — 5 wks

24 Jun 89	HEAD ABOVE WATER Mercury STEP 4	60	2
11 May 91	I'LL BE WAITING Mercury STEP 6	56	3

Ronnie GRIFFITH US, female vocalist — 4 wks

30 Jun 84	(THE BEST PART OF) BREAKING UP		
	Making Waves SURF 101	63	4

GRIMETHORPE COLLIERY BAND – See Peter SKELLERN

GROOVE CORPORATION
UK / Italy, male / female vocal / instrumental group — 1 wk

16 Apr 94	RAIN Six6 SIXCD 109	71	1

GROOVE GANG – See DAFFY DUCK featuring the GROOVE GANG

Jay GROOVE – See FANTASY UFO

GROOVE THEORY UK, male vocal / instrumental duo — 3 wks

18 Nov 95	TELL ME Epic 6623882	31	3

Henry GROSS US, male vocalist — 4 wks

28 Aug 76	SHANNON Life Song ELS 45002	32	4

GROUND LEVEL
Australia, male instrumental / production group — 2 wks

30 Jan 93	DREAMS OF HEAVEN Faze 2 CDFAZE 14	54	2

GROUP THERAPY US, male rap group — 1 wk

30 Nov 96	EAST COAST / WEST COAST KILLAS		
	Interscope IND 95516	51	1

Boring Bob GROVER – See PIRANHAS

GSP UK, male instrumental / production duo — 3 wks

3 Oct 92	THE BANANA SONG Yoyo YOYO 1	37	3

GTO UK, male / female instrumental / production duo — 7 wks

4 Aug 90	PURE Cooltempo COOL 218	57	3
7 Sep 91	LISTEN TO THE RHYTHM FLOW / BULLFROG		
	React REACT 7001	72	2
2 May 92	ELEVATION React REACT 4	59	2

See also Tricky Disco; Technohead – they are the same act.

GUESS WHO Canada, male vocal / instrumental group — 14 wks

16 Feb 67	HIS GIRL King KG 1044	45	1
9 May 70	AMERICAN WOMAN RCA 1943	45	2
30 May 70	AMERICAN WOMAN (re-entry) RCA 1943	19	11

GUN UK, male vocal / instrumental group — 11 wks

20 Nov 68	● RACE WITH THE DEVIL CBS 3734	8	11

GUN UK, male vocal / instrumental group — 43 wks

1 Jul 89	BETTER DAYS A & M AM 505	33	9
16 Sep 89	MONEY (EVERYBODY LOVES HER)		
	A & M AM 520	73	2
11 Nov 89	INSIDE OUT A & M AM 531	57	2
10 Feb 90	TAKING ON THE WORLD A & M AM 541	50	3
14 Jul 90	SHAME ON YOU A & M AM 573	33	4
14 Mar 92	STEAL YOUR FIRE A & M AM 851	24	4
2 May 92	HIGHER GROUND A & M AM 869	48	2
4 Jul 92	WELCOME TO THE REAL WORLD		
	A & M AM 885	43	2
9 Jul 94	● WORD UP A & M 5806672	8	7
24 Sep 94	DON'T SAY IT'S OVER A & M 5807572	19	3
25 Feb 95	THE ONLY ONE A & M 5809552	29	3
15 Apr 95	SOMETHING WORTHWHILE A & M 5810452	39	2

GUNS N' ROSES US, male vocal / instrumental group — 107 wks

3 Oct 87	WELCOME TO THE JUNGLE Geffen GEF 30	67	2
20 Aug 88	SWEET CHILD O' MINE Geffen GEF 43	24	8
29 Oct 88	WELCOME TO THE JUNGLE (re-issue) / NIGHTRAIN		
	Geffen GEF 47	24	5
18 Mar 89	● PARADISE CITY Geffen GEF 50	6	9
3 Jun 89	● SWEET CHILD O' MINE (re-mix) Geffen GEF 55	6	9
1 Jul 89	● PATIENCE Geffen GEF 56	10	7
2 Sep 89	● NIGHTRAIN (re-issue) Geffen GEF 60	17	5
13 Jul 91	● YOU COULD BE MINE Geffen GFS 6	3	10
21 Sep 91	● DON'T CRY Geffen GFS 9	8	4
21 Dec 91	● LIVE AND LET DIE Geffen GFS 17	5	7
7 Mar 92	● NOVEMBER RAIN Geffen GFS 18	4	5
23 May 92	● KNOCKIN' ON HEAVEN'S DOOR Geffen GFS 21	2	9
21 Nov 92	● YESTERDAYS / NOVEMBER RAIN (re-issue)		
	Geffen GFS 27	8	9
29 May 93	● THE CIVIL WAR EP Geffen GEFSTD 43	11	3
20 Nov 93	● AIN'T IT FUN Geffen GFSTD 62	9	3
4 Jun 94	● SINCE I DON'T HAVE YOU Geffen GFSTD 70	10	6
14 Jan 95	● SYMPATHY FOR THE DEVIL Geffen GFSTD 86	9	6

The re-issue of November Rain only listed from 28 Nov 92. Tracks on The Civil War EP:
Civil War / Garden Of Eden / Dead Horse / Interview.

GURU US, male instrumentalist — 11 wks

11 Sep 93	TRUST ME Cooltempo CDCOOL 278 [1]	34	2
13 Nov 93	NO TIME TO PLAY Cooltempo CDCOOL 282 [2]	25	3
19 Aug 95	WATCH WHAT YOU SAY		
	Cooltempo CDCOOL 308 [3]	28	3
18 Nov 95	FEEL THE MUSIC Cooltempo CDCOOLS 313	34	2
13 Jul 96	LIVIN' IN THIS WORLD / LIFESAVER		
	Cooltempo CDCOOL 320	61	1

[1] Guru featuring N'Dea Davenport [2] Guru featuring DC Lee [3] Guru featuring Chaka Khan

GURU JOSH UK, male vocal / instrumental group — 14 wks

24 Feb 90	● INFINITY Deconstruction PB 43475	5	10
16 Jun 90	WHOSE LAW (IS IT ANYWAY)		
	Deconstruction PB 43647	26	4

Adrian GURVITZ UK, male vocalist — 16 wks

| 30 Jan 82 | ● CLASSIC RAK 339 | 8 | 13 |
| 12 Jun 82 | YOUR DREAM RAK 343 | 61 | 3 |

GUSTO US, male producer – Edward Green — 8 wks

| 2 Mar 96 | ● DISCO'S REVENGE Manifesto FESCD 6 | 9 | 5 |
| 7 Sep 96 | LET'S ALL CHANT Manifesto FESCD 13 | 21 | 3 |

Gwen GUTHRIE US, female vocalist — 25 wks

19 Jul 86	● AIN'T NOTHING GOIN' ON BUT THE RENT Boiling Point POSP 807	5	12
11 Oct 86	(THEY LONG TO BE) CLOSE TO YOU Boiling Point POSP 822	25	7
14 Feb 87	GOOD TO GO LOVER / OUTSIDE IN THE RAIN Boiling Point POSP 841	37	4
4 Sep 93	AIN'T NOTHIN' GOIN' ON BUT THE RENT (re-mix) Polydor PZCD 276	42	2

GUY US, male vocal group — 4 wks

| 4 May 91 | HER MCA MCS 1575 | 58 | 4 |

See also Various Artists (EPs and LPs) – The New York Undercover EP.

A GUY CALLED GERALD
UK, male producer – Gerald Simpson — 23 wks

8 Apr 89	VOODOO RAY Rham! RS 804	55	8
24 Jun 89	VOODOO RAY (re-entry) Rham! RS 804	12	10
16 Dec 89	FX / EYES OF SORROW Subscape AGCG 1	52	5

GUYS and DOLLS UK, male / female vocal group — 33 wks

1 Mar 75	● THERE'S A WHOLE LOT OF LOVING Magnet MAG 20	2	11
17 May 75	HERE I GO AGAIN Magnet MAG 30	33	5
21 Feb 76	● YOU DON'T HAVE TO SAY YOU LOVE ME Magnet MAG 50	5	8
6 Nov 76	STONEY GROUND Magnet MAG 76	38	4
13 May 78	ONLY LOVIN' DOES IT Magnet MAG 115	42	5

Jonas GWANGWA – See George FENTON and Jonas GWANGWA

GYRES UK, male vocal / instrumental group — 2 wks

| 13 Apr 96 | POP COP Sugar SUGA 9CD | 71 | 1 |
| 6 Jul 96 | ARE YOU READY Sugar SUGA 11CD | 71 | 1 |

HABIT UK, male vocal / instrumental group — 2 wks

| 30 Apr 88 | LUCY Virgin VS 1063 | 56 | 2 |

Steve HACKETT
UK, male vocalist / instrumentalist – guitar — 2 wks

| 2 Apr 83 | CELL 151 Charisma CELL 1 | 66 | 2 |

HADDAWAY Trinidad & Tobago, male vocalist — 52 wks

5 Jun 93	● WHAT IS LOVE Logic 74321148502	2	15
25 Sep 93	● LIFE Logic 74321164212	6	9
18 Dec 93	● I MISS YOU Logic 74321181522	9	14
2 Apr 94	● ROCK MY HEART Logic 74321194122	9	9
24 Jun 95	FLY AWAY Logic 74321286942	20	3
23 Sep 95	CATCH A FIRE Logic 74321306652	39	2

Tony HADLEY UK, male vocalist — 7 wks

7 Mar 92	LOST IN YOUR LOVE EMI EM 222	42	4
29 Aug 92	FOR YOUR BLUE EYES ONLY EMI EM 234	67	2
16 Jan 93	GAME OF LOVE EMI CDEM 254	72	1

Sammy HAGAR
US, male vocalist / instrumentalist – guitar — 15 wks

15 Dec 79	THIS PLANET'S ON FIRE / SPACE STATION NO. 5 Capitol CL 16114	52	5
16 Feb 80	I'VE DONE EVERYTHING FOR YOU Capitol CL 16120	36	5
24 May 80	HEARTBEAT / LOVE OR MONEY Capitol RED 1	67	2
16 Jan 82	PIECE OF MY HEART Geffen GEFA 1884	67	1
30 Jan 82	PIECE OF MY HEART (re-entry) Geffen GEFA 1884	67	2

Paul HAIG UK, male vocalist — 3 wks

| 28 May 83 | HEAVEN SENT Island IS 111 | 74 | 3 |

HAIRCUT 100 UK, male vocal / instrumental group — 47 wks

24 Oct 81	● FAVOURITE SHIRTS (BOY MEETS GIRL) Arista CLIP 1	4	14
30 Jan 82	● LOVE PLUS ONE Arista CLIP 2	3	12
10 Apr 82	● FANTASTIC DAY Arista CLIP 3	9	9
21 Aug 82	● NOBODY'S FOOL Arista CLIP 4	9	7
6 Aug 83	PRIME TIME Polydor HC 1	46	5

Curtis HAIRSTON US, male vocalist — 16 wks

15 Oct 83	I WANT YOU (ALL TONIGHT) RCA 368	44	5
27 Apr 85	I WANT YOUR LOVIN' (JUST A LITTLE BIT) London LON 66	13	7
6 Dec 86	CHILLIN' OUT Atlantic A 9335	57	4

Gary HAISMAN – See D MOB

HALE and PACE and the STONKERS
UK, male comedy duo and backing group — 7 wks

| 9 Mar 91 | ★ THE STONK London LON 296 | 1 | 7 |

Bill HALEY and his COMETS
US, male vocal / instrumental group — 199 wks

17 Dec 54	● SHAKE RATTLE AND ROLL Brunswick 05338	4	14
7 Jan 55	ROCK AROUND THE CLOCK Brunswick 05317	17	2
15 Apr 55	MAMBO ROCK Brunswick 05405	14	2
14 Oct 55	★ ROCK AROUND THE CLOCK (re-entry) Brunswick 05317	1	17
30 Dec 55	● ROCK-A-BEATIN' BOOGIE Brunswick 05509	4	9
9 Mar 56	● SEE YOU LATER ALLIGATOR Brunswick 05530	7	13
25 May 56	● THE SAINTS ROCK 'N ROLL Brunswick 05565	5	24
17 Aug 56	● ROCKIN' THROUGH THE RYE Brunswick 05582	3	18
14 Sep 56	RAZZLE DAZZLE Brunswick 05453	13	8
21 Sep 56	● ROCK AROUND THE CLOCK (2nd re-entry) Brunswick 05317	5	11
21 Sep 56	SEE YOU LATER ALLIGATOR (re-entry) Brunswick 05530	12	8
9 Nov 56	● RIP IT UP Brunswick 05615	4	18

9 Nov 56	**ROCK 'N ROLL STAGE SHOW (LP)**			
	Brunswick LAT 8139		**30**	1
23 Nov 56	**RUDY'S ROCK** Brunswick 05616		**30**	1
14 Dec 56	**ROCK AROUND THE CLOCK (3rd re-entry)**			
	Brunswick 05317		**24**	2
14 Dec 56	**RUDY'S ROCK (re-entry)** Brunswick 05616		**26**	4
4 Jan 57	**ROCK AROUND THE CLOCK (4th re-entry)**			
	Brunswick 05317		**25**	2
4 Jan 57	**ROCKIN' THROUGH THE RYE (re-entry)**			
	Brunswick 05582		**19**	5
25 Jan 57	**ROCK AROUND THE CLOCK (5th re-entry)**			
	Brunswick 05317		**22**	2
1 Feb 57	**ROCK THE JOINT** London HLF 8371		**20**	4
8 Feb 57	● **DON'T KNOCK THE ROCK** Brunswick 05640		**7**	8
3 Apr 68	**ROCK AROUND THE CLOCK (re-issue)** MCA MU 1013		**20**	11
16 Mar 74	**ROCK AROUND THE CLOCK (2nd re-issue)** MCA 128		**12**	10
25 Apr 81	**HALEY'S GOLDEN MEDLEY** MCA 694		**50**	5

Tracks on Rock 'N Roll Stage Show LP: Calling All Comets / Rockin' Through The Rye / A Rockin' Little Tune / Hide And Seek / Hey There Now / Goofin' Around / Hook Line and Sinker / Rudy's Rock / Choo Choo Ch'Boogie / Blue Comets Rock / Hot Dog Buddy Buddy / Tonight's The Night. Occasionally, some of the Rock Around The Clock labels billed the song as (We're Gonna) Rock Around The Clock.

Aaron HALL *US, male vocalist*   **3 wks**

13 Jun 92	**DON'T BE AFRAID** MCA MCS 1632		**56**	2
23 Oct 93	**GET A LITTLE FREAKY WITH ME**			
	MCA MCSTD 1936		**66**	1

See also Various Artists (EPs and LPs) – The Dangerous Minds EP.

Audrey HALL *Jamaica, female vocalist*   **20 wks**

25 Jan 86	**ONE DANCE WON'T DO** Germain DG7-1985		**20**	11
5 Jul 86	**SMILE** Germain DG 15		**14**	9

Daryl HALL *US, male vocalist*   **26 wks**

2 Aug 86	**DREAMTIME** RCA HALL 1		**28**	8
25 Sep 93	**I'M IN A PHILLY MOOD** Epic 6595555		**59**	2
8 Jan 94	**STOP LOVING ME STOP LOVING YOU**			
	Epic 6599982		**30**	6
26 Mar 94	**I'M IN A PHILLY MOOD (re-entry)** Epic 6595555		**52**	2
14 May 94	**HELP ME FIND A WAY TO YOUR HEART**			
	Epic 6604102		**70**	1
2 Jul 94	**GLORYLAND** Mercury MERCD 404 [1]		**36**	4
10 Jun 95	**WHEREVER WOULD I BE** Columbia 6620592 [2]		**44**	3

[1] Daryl Hall and the Sounds Of Blackness [2] Dusty Springfield and Daryl Hall

See also Daryl Hall and John Oates.

Daryl HALL and John OATES
US, male vocal / instrumental duo   **84 wks**

16 Oct 76	**SHE'S GONE** Atlantic K 10828		**42**	4
14 Jun 80	**RUNNING FROM PARADISE** RCA RUN 1		**41**	6
20 Sep 80	**YOU'VE LOST THAT LOVIN' FEELIN'** RCA 1		**55**	3
15 Nov 80	**KISS ON MY LIST** RCA 15		**33**	8
23 Jan 82	● **I CAN'T GO FOR THAT (NO CAN DO)** RCA 172		**8**	8
10 Apr 82	**PRIVATE EYES** RCA 134		**32**	7
30 Oct 82	● **MANEATER** RCA 290		**6**	11
22 Jan 83	**ONE ON ONE** RCA 305		**63**	3
30 Apr 83	**FAMILY MAN** RCA 323		**15**	7
12 Nov 83	**SAY IT ISN'T SO** RCA 375		**69**	3
10 Mar 84	**ADULT EDUCATION** RCA 396		**63**	2
20 Oct 84	**OUT OF TOUCH** RCA RCA 449		**48**	5
9 Feb 85	**METHOD OF MODERN LOVE** RCA 472		**21**	8
22 Jun 85	**OUT OF TOUCH (re-mix)** RCA PB 4 9967		**62**	3
21 Sep 85	**A NIGHT AT THE APOLLO LIVE!** RCA PB 49935 [1]		**58**	2
29 Sep 90	**SO CLOSE** Arista 113600 [2]		**69**	1

26 Jan 91	**EVERYWHERE I LOOK** Arista 113980		**74**	1

[1] Daryl Hall and John Oates featuring David Ruffin and Eddie Kendricks
[2] Hall and Oates

A Night At The Apollo Live! is a medley of The Way You Do The Things You Do / My Girl. See also Daryl Hall.

Pam HALL *Jamaica, female vocalist*   **4 wks**

16 Aug 86	**DEAR BOOPSIE** Bluemountain BM 027		**54**	4

Terry HALL *UK, male vocalist*   **5 wks**

11 Nov 89	**MISSING** Chrysalis CHS 3381		**75**	1
27 Aug 94	**FOREVER J** Anxious ANX 1024CDX		**67**	1
12 Nov 94	**SENSE** Anxious ANX 1027CD		**54**	2
28 Oct 95	**CHASING A RAINBOW** Anxious ANX 1033CD1		**62**	1

The sleeve, not the label, of Missing credits Terry, Blair and Anouchka.

Toni HALLIDAY – *See LEFTFIELD*

HALO JAMES *UK, male vocal / instrumental group*   **24 wks**

7 Oct 89	**WANTED** Epic HALO 1		**45**	5
23 Dec 89	● **COULD HAVE TOLD YOU SO** Epic HALO 2		**6**	12
17 Mar 90	**BABY** Epic HALO 3		**43**	4
19 May 90	**MAGIC HOUR** Epic HALO 4		**59**	3

George HAMILTON IV *US, male vocalist*   **13 wks**

7 Mar 58	**WHY DON'T THEY UNDERSTAND** HMV POP 429		**22**	9
18 Jul 58	**I KNOW WHERE I'M GOING** HMV POP 505		**29**	1
8 Aug 58	**I KNOW WHERE I'M GOING (re-entry)** HMV POP 505		**23**	3

Lynne HAMILTON *Australia, female vocalist*   **11 wks**

29 Apr 89	● **ON THE INSIDE (THEME FROM 'PRISONER CELL BLOCK H')** A1 A1 311		**3**	11

Mike 'Tone' HAMILTON – *Ian McNABB*

Russ HAMILTON *UK, male vocalist*   **26 wks**

24 May 57	● **WE WILL MAKE LOVE** Oriole CB 1359		**2**	20
27 Sep 57	**WEDDING RING** Oriole CB 1388		**20**	6

HAMILTON, Joe FRANK and REYNOLDS
US, male vocal group   **6 wks**

13 Sep 75	**FALLIN' IN LOVE** Pye International 7N 25690		**33**	6

Marvin HAMLISCH *US, male instrumentalist – piano*   **13 wks**

30 Mar 74	**THE ENTERTAINER** MCA 121		**25**	13

HAMMER *US, male rapper*   **68 wks**

9 Jun 90	● **U CAN'T TOUCH THIS** Capitol CL 578 [1]		**3**	16
6 Oct 90	● **HAVE YOU SEEN HER** Capitol CL 590 [1]		**8**	7
8 Dec 90	● **PRAY** Capitol CL 599 [1]		**8**	10
23 Feb 91	**HERE COMES THE HAMMER** Capitol CL 610 [1]		**15**	5
1 Jun 91	**YO!! SWEETNESS** Capitol CL 616 [1]		**16**	5
20 Jul 91	**(HAMMER HAMMER) THEY PUT ME IN THE MIX**			
	Capitol CL 607 [1]		**20**	4
26 Oct 91	**2 LEGIT 2 QUIT** Capitol CL 636		**60**	2

George Harrison

George Harrison was the first
Beatle to have a solo number one,
and, despite a low musical profile,
he is also the highest charting
Beatle in the last ten years.

PJ Harvey

PJ Harvey first graced the chart in
1992 with 'Sheela-Na-Gig'. A
Sheela-Na-Gig is an Irish pagan
fertility symbol.

Rolf Harris

'Two Little Boys', a number one for
Rolf Harris in 1969, was actually
written in 1903 by Edward Madden
and Theodore Morse.

21 Dec 91	● **ADDAMS GROOVE** Capitol CL 642	**4**	9
21 Mar 92	**DO NOT PASS ME BY** Capitol CL 650 `2` ..	**14**	6
12 Mar 94	**IT'S ALL GOOD** RCA 74321188612	**52**	1
13 Aug 94	**DON'T STOP** RCA 74321220012	**72**	1
3 Jun 95	**STRAIGHT TO MY FEET** Priority PTYCD 102 `3`	**57**	1

`1` MC Hammer `2` Hammer featuring Tramaine Hawkins, introducing Trina Johnson and the Voices `3` Hammer featuring Deion Saunders

Jan HAMMER
Czechoslovakia, male instrumentalist – keyboards **26 wks**

12 Oct 85	● **'MIAMI VICE' THEME** MCA MCA 1000	**5**	8
19 Sep 87	● **'CROCKETT'S' THEME** MCA MCA 1193	**2**	12
1 Jun 91	**'CROCKETT'S' THEME (re-issue)** MCA MCS 1541	**47**	6

Albert HAMMOND *UK, male vocalist* **11 wks**

30 Jun 73	**FREE ELECTRIC BAND** Mums 1494	**19**	11

Beres HAMMOND – See Maxi PRIEST

Herbie HANCOCK
US, male vocalist / instrumentalist – keyboards **41 wks**

26 Aug 78	**I THOUGHT IT WAS YOU** CBS 6530	**15**	9
3 Feb 79	**YOU BET YOUR LOVE** CBS 7010	**18**	10
30 Jul 83	● **ROCKIT** CBS A 3577	**8**	12
8 Oct 83	**AUTO DRIVE** CBS A 3802	**33**	4
21 Jan 84	**FUTURE SHOCK** CBS A 4075	**54**	3
4 Aug 84	**HARDROCK** CBS A 4616	**65**	3

HANDBAGGERS
UK, male / female vocal / instrumental group **1 wk**

15 Jun 96	**U FOUND OUT** Tidy Trax TIDY 104CD	**55**	1

HANDLEY FAMILY *UK, male / female vocal group* **7 wks**

7 Apr 73	**WAM BAM** GL 100	**30**	7

Jayn HANNA *UK, female vocalist* **1 wk**

13 Apr 96	**LOVELIGHT (RIDE ON A LOVE TRAIN)** VC VCRD 10	**42**	1

HANNAH and her SISTERS – See Hannah JONES

HANNAH – See MAN WITH NO NAME

HANOI ROCKS
Finland / UK, male vocal / instrumental group **2 wks**

7 Jul 84	**UP AROUND THE BEND** CBS A 4513	**61**	2

HAPPENINGS *US, male vocal group* **14 wks**

18 May 67	**I GOT RHYTHM** Stateside SS 2013	**28**	9
16 Aug 67	**MY MAMMY** Pye International 7N 25501 and B.T. Puppy BTS 45530 ..	**34**	5

Pye gave the American B.T. Puppy label its own identification halfway through the success of My Mammy.

HAPPY CLAPPERS
UK, male / female vocal / instrumental group **17 wks**

3 Jun 95	**I BELIEVE** Shindig SHIN 4CD	**21**	3

26 Aug 95	**HOLD ON** Shindig SHIN 7CD	**27**	2
18 Nov 95	● **I BELIEVE (re-issue)** Shindig SHIN 9CD	**7**	8
15 Jun 96	**CAN'T HELP IT** Coliseum TOGA 004CD	**18**	3
21 Dec 96	**NEVER AGAIN** Coliseum TOGA 012CD	**49**	1

HAPPY MONDAYS
UK, male vocal / instrumental group **51 wks**

30 Sep 89	**WFL** Factory FAC 2327	**68**	2
25 Nov 89	**MADCHESTER RAVE ON EP** Factory FAC 2427	**19**	14
7 Apr 90	● **STEP ON** Factory FAC 2727	**5**	11
9 Jun 90	**LAZYITIS – ONE ARMED BOXER** Factory FAC 2227 `1` ..	**46**	3
20 Oct 90	● **KINKY AFRO** Factory FAC 3027	**5**	7
9 Mar 91	**LOOSE FIT** Factory FAC 3127	**17**	7
30 Nov 91	**JUDGE FUDGE** Factory FAC 3327	**24**	3
19 Sep 92	**STINKIN THINKIN** Factory FAC 3627	**31**	3
21 Nov 92	**SUNSHINE AND LOVE** Factory FAC 3727	**62**	1

`1` Happy Mondays and Karl Denver

Tracks on Madchester Rave On EP: Hallelujah / Holy Ghost / Clap Your Hands / Rave On.

Paul HARDCASTLE *UK, male producer* **66 wks**

7 Apr 84	**YOU'RE THE ONE FOR ME – DAYBREAK – A.M.** Total Control TOCO 1	**41**	4
28 Jul 84	**GUILTY** Total Control TOCO 2	**55**	3
22 Sep 84	**RAIN FOREST** Bluebird BR 8	**41**	5
17 Nov 84	**EAT YOUR HEART OUT** Cooltempo COOL 102	**59**	4
4 May 85	★ **NINETEEN** Chrysalis CHS 2860	**1**	16
15 Jun 85	**RAIN FOREST (re-issue)** Bluebird 10 BR 15	**53**	4
9 Nov 85	**JUST FOR MONEY** Chrysalis CASH 1	**19**	5
1 Feb 86	● **DON'T WASTE MY TIME** Chrysalis PAUL 1 `1`	**8**	11
21 Jun 86	**FOOLIN' YOURSELF** Chrysalis PAUL 2	**51**	3
11 Oct 86	**THE WIZARD** Chrysalis PAUL 3	**15**	6
9 Apr 88	**WALK IN THE NIGHT** Chrysalis PAUL 4	**54**	3
4 Jun 88	**40 YEARS** Chrysalis PAUL 5	**53**	2

`1` Paul Hardcastle featuring Carol Kenyon

Just for Money features the voices of Laurence Olivier, Bob Hoskins, Ed O'Ross and Alan Talbot, who are credited on the sleeve only. See also Silent Underdog.

HARDCORE RHYTHM TEAM
UK, male vocal / production group **1 wk**

14 Mar 92	**HARDCORE – THE FINAL CONFLICT** Furious FRUT 001 ..	**69**	1

HARDFLOOR
Germany, male instrumental / production group **5 wks**

26 Dec 92	**HARDTRANCE ACPERIENCE** Harthouse UK HARTUK 1 ..	**56**	4
10 Apr 93	**TRANCESCRIPT** Harthouse UK HARTUK 5CD	**72**	1

Tim HARDIN *US, male vocalist* **1 wk**

5 Jan 67	**HANG ON TO A DREAM** Verve VS 1504	**50**	1

Mike HARDING *UK, male vocalist* **8 wks**

2 Aug 75	**ROCHDALE COWBOY** Rubber ADUB 3	**22**	8

Françoise HARDY *France, female vocalist* **26 wks**

25 Jun 64	**TOUS LES GARCONS ET LES FILLES** Pye 7N 15653	**36**	7
7 Jan 65	**ET MEME** Pye 7N 15740	**31**	4
25 Mar 65	**ALL OVER THE WORLD** Pye 7N 15802	**16**	15

Tynetta HARE – See Joey B ELLIS

Niki HARIS – *See SNAP*

Morten HARKET *Norway, male vocalist* **1 wk**

| 19 Aug 95 | A KIND OF CHRISTMAS CARD Warner Bros. W 0304CD | 53 | 1 |

HARLEM COMMUNITY CHOIR – *See John LENNON*

HARLEQUIN 4's / BUNKER KRU
US, male vocal / instrumental group with UK, male production duo **4 wks**

| 19 Mar 88 | SET IT OFF *Champion CHAMP 64* | 55 | 4 |

HARLEY QUINNE *UK, male vocal group* **8 wks**

| 14 Oct 72 | NEW ORLEANS *Bell 1255* | 19 | 8 |

Steve HARLEY and COCKNEY REBEL
UK, male vocalist and male vocal / instrumental backing group **69 wks**

11 May 74	● JUDY TEEN *EMI 2128* [1]	5	11
10 Aug 74	● MR. SOFT *EMI 2191* [1]	8	9
8 Feb 75	★ MAKE ME SMILE (COME UP AND SEE ME) *EMI 2263*	1	9
7 Jun 75	MR. RAFFLES (MAN IT WAS MEAN) *EMI 2299*	13	6
31 Jul 76	● HERE COMES THE SUN *EMI 2505* [2]	10	7
6 Nov 76	LOVE'S A PRIMA DONNA *EMI 2539* [2]	41	4
20 Oct 79	FREEDOM'S PRISONER *EMI 2994* [2]	58	3
13 Aug 83	BALLERINA (PRIMA DONNA) *Stilleto STL 14* [2]	51	5
11 Jan 86	● THE PHANTOM OF THE OPERA *Polydor POSP 800* [3]	7	10
25 Apr 92	MAKE ME SMILE (COME UP AND SEE ME) (re-issue) *EMI EMCT 5* [2]	46	2
30 Dec 95	MAKE ME SMILE (COME UP AND SEE ME) (2nd re-issue) *EMI CDHARLEY 1*	33	3

[1] Cockney Rebel [2] Steve Harley [3] Sarah Brightman and Steve Harley

HARMONIX *UK, male producer – Hamish Brown* **2 wks**

| 30 Mar 96 | LANDSLIDE *Deconstruction 74321330762* | 28 | 2 |

HARMONY GRASS *UK, male vocal/instrumental group* **7 wks**

| 29 Jan 69 | MOVE IN A LITTLE CLOSER *RCA 1772* | 24 | 7 |

Charlie HARPER *UK, male vocalist* **1 wk**

| 19 Jul 80 | BARMY LONDON ARMY *Gem GEMS 35* | 68 | 1 |

HARPERS BIZARRE *US, male vocal group* **13 wks**

| 30 Mar 67 | 59TH STREET BRIDGE SONG (FEELING GROOVY) *Warner Bros. WB 5890* | 34 | 7 |
| 4 Oct 67 | ANYTHING GOES *Warner Bros. WB 7063* | 33 | 6 |

HARPO *Sweden, male vocalist* **6 wks**

| 17 Apr 76 | MOVIE STAR *DJM DJS 400* | 24 | 6 |

T. HARRINGTON – *See Rahni HARRIS and F.L.O.*

Anita HARRIS *UK, female vocalist* **50 wks**

29 Jun 67	● JUST LOVING YOU *CBS 2724*	6	30
11 Oct 67	PLAYGROUND *CBS 2991*	46	3
24 Jan 68	ANNIVERSARY WALTZ *CBS 3211*	21	9
14 Aug 68	DREAM A LITTLE DREAM OF ME *CBS 3637*	33	8

Emmylou HARRIS *US, female vocalist* **6 wks**

| 6 Mar 76 | HERE THERE AND EVERYWHERE *Reprise K 14415* | 30 | 6 |

Jet HARRIS *UK, male instrumentalist – bass* **18 wks**

| 24 May 62 | BESAME MUCHO *Decca F 11466* | 22 | 7 |
| 16 Aug 62 | MAIN TITLE THEME FROM 'MAN WITH THE GOLDEN ARM' *Decca F 11488* | 12 | 11 |

See also Jet Harris and Tony Meehan.

Jet HARRIS and Tony MEEHAN
UK, male instrumental duo – bass and drums **39 wks**

10 Jan 63	★ DIAMONDS *Decca F 11563*	1	13
25 Apr 63	● SCARLETT O'HARA *Decca F 11644*	2	13
5 Sep 63	● APPLEJACK *Decca F 11710*	4	13

See also Jet Harris; Tony Meehan.

Keith HARRIS and ORVILLE
UK, male ventriloquist vocalist with feathered dummy **20 wks**

18 Dec 82	● ORVILLE'S SONG *BBC RESL 124*	4	11
24 Dec 83	COME TO MY PARTY *BBC RESL 138* [1]	44	4
14 Dec 85	WHITE CHRISTMAS *Columbia DB 9121*	40	5

[1] Keith Harris and Orville with Dippy

Major HARRIS *US, male vocalist* **9 wks**

| 9 Aug 75 | LOVE WON'T LET ME WAIT *Atlantic K 10585* | 37 | 7 |
| 5 Nov 83 | ALL MY LIFE *London LON 37* | 61 | 2 |

Max HARRIS *UK, orchestra* **10 wks**

| 1 Dec 60 | GURNEY SLADE *Fontana H 282* | 11 | 10 |

Rahni HARRIS and F.L.O.
US, male instrumental group **7 wks**

| 16 Dec 78 | SIX MILLION STEPS (WEST RUNS SOUTH) *Mercury 6007 198* | 43 | 7 |

Hit has credit 'vocals by T. Harrington and O. Rasbury'.

Richard HARRIS *Ireland, male vocalist* **18 wks**

| 26 Jun 68 | ● MACARTHUR PARK *RCA 1699* | 4 | 12 |
| 8 Jul 72 | MACARTHUR PARK (re-issue) *Probe GFF 101* | 38 | 6 |

Rochelle HARRIS – *See ANGELHEART featuring Rochelle HARRIS*

Rolf HARRIS *Australia, male vocalist* **71 wks**

21 Jul 60	● TIE ME KANGAROO DOWN SPORT *Columbia DB 4483*	9	13
25 Oct 62	● SUN ARISE *Columbia DB 4888*	3	16
28 Feb 63	JOHNNY DAY *Columbia DB 4979*	44	2
16 Apr 69	BLUER THAN BLUE *Columbia DB 8553*	30	8
22 Nov 69	★ TWO LITTLE BOYS *Columbia DB 8630*	1	24
20 Jun 70	TWO LITTLE BOYS (re-entry) *Columbia DB 8630*	50	1
13 Feb 93	● STAIRWAY TO HEAVEN *Vertigo VERCD 73*	7	6
1 Jun 96	● BOHEMIAN RHAPSODY *Living Beat LBECD 41*	50	1

Ronnie HARRIS UK, male vocalist — 3 wks

24 Sep 54	STORY OF TINA Columbia DB 3499	12	3

Sam HARRIS US, male vocalist — 2 wks

9 Feb 85	HEARTS ON FIRE / OVER THE RAINBOW Motown TMG 1370	67	2

Simon HARRIS UK, male producer — 17 wks

19 Mar 88	BASS (HOW LOW CAN YOU GO) ffrr FFR 4	12	6
29 Oct 88	HERE COMES THAT SOUND ffrr FFR 12	38	4
24 Jun 89	(I'VE GOT YOUR) PLEASURE CONTROL ffrr F 106 [1]	60	3
18 Nov 89	ANOTHER MONSTERJAM ffrr F 116 [2]	65	1
10 Mar 90	RAGGA HOUSE (ALL NIGHT LONG) Living Beat 7SMASH 9 [3]	56	3

[1] Simon Harris featuring Lonnie Gordon [2] Simon Harris featuring Einstein
[3] Simon Harris featuring Daddy Freddy

George HARRISON UK, male vocalist — 82 wks

23 Jan 71	★ MY SWEET LORD Apple R 5884	1	17
14 Aug 71	● BANGLA DESH Apple R 5912	10	9
2 Jun 73	● GIVE ME LOVE (GIVE ME PEACE ON EARTH) Apple R 5988	8	10
21 Dec 74	DING DONG Apple R 6002	38	5
11 Oct 75	YOU Apple R 6007	38	5
10 Mar 79	BLOW AWAY Dark Horse K 17327	51	5
23 May 81	ALL THOSE YEARS AGO Dark Horse 3 K 17807	13	7
24 Oct 87	● GOT MY MIND SET ON YOU Dark Horse W 8178	2	14
6 Feb 88	WHEN WE WAS FAB Dark Horse W 8131	25	7
25 Jun 88	THIS IS LOVE Dark Horse W 7913	55	3

Noel HARRISON UK, male vocalist — 14 wks

26 Feb 69	● WINDMILLS OF YOUR MIND Reprise RS 20758	8	14

Deborah HARRY US, female vocalist — 52 wks

1 Aug 81	BACKFIRED Chrysalis CHS 2526 [1]	32	6
15 Nov 86	● FRENCH KISSIN' IN THE USA Chrysalis CHS 3066 [1]	8	7
28 Feb 87	FREE TO FALL Chrysalis CHS 3093 [1]	46	4
9 May 87	IN LOVE WITH LOVE Chrysalis CHS 3128 [1]	45	5
7 Oct 89	I WANT THAT MAN Chrysalis CHS 3369	13	10
2 Dec 89	BRITE SIDE Chrysalis CHS 3452	59	4
31 Mar 90	SWEET AND LOW Chrysalis CHS 3491	57	3
5 Jan 91	WELL DID YOU EVAH! Chrysalis CHS 3646 [2]	42	4
3 Jul 93	I CAN SEE CLEARLY NOW Chrysalis CDCHSS 4900	23	4
18 Sep 93	STRIKE ME PINK Chrysalis CDCHSS 5000	46	2

[1] Debbie Harry [2] Deborah Harry and Iggy Pop

HARRY J. ALL STARS
Jamaica, male instrumental group — 25 wks

25 Oct 69	● LIQUIDATOR Trojan TR 675	9	20
29 Mar 80	LIQUIDATOR (re-issue) Trojan TRO 9063	42	5

Re-issue of Liquidator coupled with re-issue of Long Shot Kick De Bucket by the Pioneers.

Richard HARTLEY/Michael REED ORCHESTRA
UK, male instrumentalist – synthesizer, orchestra — 10 wks

25 Feb 84	● THE MUSIC OF TORVILL AND DEAN EP Safari SKATE 1	9	10

Tracks on EP: Bolero / Capriccio Espagnole Opus. 34 (Nos.4 and 5) by Richard Hartley; Barnum On Ice / Discoskate by the Michael Reed Orchestra.

Dan HARTMAN US, male vocalist — 34 wks

21 Oct 78	● INSTANT REPLAY Sky 6706	8	15
13 Jan 79	THIS IS IT Blue Sky SKY 6999	17	8
18 May 85	SECOND NATURE MCA MCA 957	66	2
24 Aug 85	I CAN DREAM ABOUT YOU MCA MCA 988	12	8
1 Apr 95	KEEP THE FIRE BURNIN' Columbia 6611552 [1]	49	1

[1] Dan Hartman starring Loleatta Holloway

PJ HARVEY UK, female vocalist — 13 wks

29 Feb 92	SHEELA-NA-GIG Too Pure PURE 008	69	1
1 May 93	50 FT QUEENIE Island CID 538	27	2
17 Jul 93	MAN-SIZE Island CID 569	42	2
18 Feb 95	DOWN BY THE WATER Island CID 607	38	2
22 Jul 95	C'MON BILLY Island CID 614	29	2
28 Oct 95	SEND HIS LOVE TO ME Island CID 610	34	2
9 Mar 96	HENRY LEE Mute CDMUTE 189 [1]	36	1
23 Nov 96	THAT WAS MY VEIL Island CID 648 [2]	75	1

[1] Nick Cave and the Bad Seeds and PJ Harvey [2] John Parish + Polly Jean Harvey

For the first three hits PJ Harvey was the name of the entire group, not just the lead singer.

Steve HARVEY UK, male vocalist — 6 wks

28 May 83	SOMETHING SPECIAL London LON 25	46	4
29 Oct 83	TONIGHT London LON 36	63	2

Sensational Alex HARVEY BAND
UK, male vocal / instrumental group — 25 wks

26 Jul 75	● DELILAH Vertigo ALEX 001	7	7
22 Nov 75	GAMBLIN' BAR ROOM BLUES Vertigo ALEX 002	38	8
19 Jun 76	THE BOSTON TEA PARTY Mountain TOP 12	13	10

David HASSELHOFF US, male vocalist — 2 wks

13 Nov 93	IF I COULD ONLY SAY GOODBYE Arista 74321172262	35	2

Tony HATCH UK, orchestra — 1 wk

4 Oct 62	OUT OF THIS WORLD Pye 7N 15460	50	1

Juliana HATFIELD US, female vocalist — 2 wks

11 Sep 93	MY SISTER Mammoth YZ 767CD [1]	71	1
18 Mar 95	UNIVERSAL HEART-BEAT East West YZ 916CD	65	1

[1] Juliana Hatfield Three

Donny HATHAWAY – See Roberta FLACK

Lalah HATHAWAY US, female vocalist — 10 wks

1 Sep 90	HEAVEN KNOWS Virgin America VUS 28	66	2
2 Feb 91	BABY DON'T CRY Virgin America VUS 35	54	3
27 Jul 91	FAMILY AFFAIR Ten TEN 369 [1]	37	5

[1] BEF featuring Lalah Hathaway

HAVANA UK, male instrumental / production group — 1 wk

6 Mar 93	ETHNIC PRAYER Limbo LIMBO 007CD	71	1

Nic HAVERSON UK, male vocalist　　　　3 wks

| 30 Jan 93 | HEAD OVER HEELS Telstar CDHOH 1 | 48 | 3 |

Chesney HAWKES UK, male vocalist　　　　25 wks

23 Feb 91	★ THE ONE AND ONLY Chrysalis CHS 3627	1	16
22 Jun 91	I'M A MAN NOT A BOY Chrysalis CHS 3708	27	5
28 Sep 91	SECRETS OF THE HEART Chrysalis CHS 3681	57	3
29 May 93	WHAT'S WRONG WITH THIS PICTURE Chrysalis CDCHS 3969	63	1

Screamin' Jay HAWKINS US, male vocalist　　　　3 wks

| 3 Apr 93 | HEART ATTACK AND VINE Columbia 6591092 | 42 | 3 |

Sophie B. HAWKINS US, female vocalist　　　　37 wks

4 Jul 92	DAMN I WISH I WAS YOUR LOVER Columbia 6581077	14	9
12 Sep 92	CALIFORNIA HERE I COME Columbia 6583177	53	3
6 Feb 93	I WANT YOU Columbia 6587772	49	2
13 Aug 94	RIGHT BESIDE YOU Columbia 6606915	13	12
26 Nov 94	DON'T DON'T TELL ME NO Columbia 6610152	36	5
11 Mar 95	AS I LAY ME DOWN Columbia 6612125	24	6

Edwin HAWKINS SINGERS featuring Dorothy Combs MORRISON
US, male / female vocal group　　　　13 wks

| 21 May 69 | ● OH HAPPY DAY Buddah 201 048 | 2 | 12 |
| 23 Aug 69 | OH HAPPY DAY (re-entry) Buddah 201 048 | 43 | 1 |

HAWKWIND
UK, male vocal / instrumental group with female dancer　　　　28 wks

1 Jul 72	● SILVER MACHINE United Artists UP 35381	3	15
11 Aug 73	URBAN GUERRILLA United Artists UP 35566	39	3
21 Oct 78	SILVER MACHINE (re-entry) United Artists UP 35381	34	5
19 Jul 80	SHOT DOWN IN THE NIGHT Bronze BRO 98	59	3
15 Jan 83	SILVER MACHINE (2nd re-entry) United Artists UP 35381	67	2

See also Various Artists (EPs & LPs) – Gimme Shelter (EP).

Bill HAYES US, male vocalist　　　　9 wks

| 6 Jan 56 | ● BALLAD OF DAVY CROCKETT London HLA 8220 | 2 | 9 |

Isaac HAYES US, male vocalist / multi-instrumentalist　　　　21 wks

| 4 Dec 71 | ● THEME FROM 'SHAFT' Stax 2025 069 | 4 | 12 |
| 3 Apr 76 | ● DISCO CONNECTION ABC 4100 [1] | 10 | 9 |

[1] Isaac Hayes Movement

HAYSI FANTAYZEE UK, male / female vocal duo　　　　25 wks

24 Jul 82	JOHN WAYNE IS BIG LEGGY Regard RG 100	11	10
13 Nov 82	HOLY JOE Regard RG 104	51	3
22 Jan 83	SHINY SHINY Regard RG 106	16	10
25 Jun 83	SISTER FRICTION Regard RG 108	62	2

Justin HAYWARD UK, male vocalist　　　　20 wks

| 25 Oct 75 | ● BLUE GUITAR Threshold TH 21 [1] | 8 | 7 |
| 8 Jul 78 | ● FOREVER AUTUMN CBS 6368 | 5 | 13 |

[1] Justin Hayward and John Lodge

Leon HAYWOOD US, male vocalist　　　　11 wks

| 15 Mar 80 | DON'T PUSH IT, DON'T FORCE IT 20th Century Fox TC 2443 | 12 | 11 |

HAYWOODE UK, female vocalist　　　　31 wks

17 Sep 83	A TIME LIKE THIS CBS A 3651	48	7
29 Sep 84	I CAN'T LET YOU GO CBS A 4664	63	4
13 Apr 85	ROSES CBS A 6069	65	3
5 Oct 85	GETTING CLOSER CBS A 6582	67	2
21 Jun 86	ROSES (re-issue) CBS A 7224	11	11
13 Sep 86	I CAN'T LET YOU GO (re-issue) CBS 650076 7	50	4

Ofra HAZA Israel, female vocalist　　　　8 wks

| 30 Apr 88 | IM NIN'ALU WEA YZ 190 | 15 | 8 |

Lee HAZLEWOOD – See Nancy SINATRA

Murray HEAD UK, male vocalist　　　　15 wks

29 Jan 72	SUPERSTAR MCA MMKS 5077	47	1
10 Nov 84	ONE NIGHT IN BANGKOK RCA CHESS 1	12	13
16 Feb 85	ONE NIGHT IN BANGKOK (re-entry) RCA CHESS 1	74	1

Superstar was one of four tracks on a maxi single, two of which were credited during the disc's one week on the chart. The other track credited was I Don't Know How To Love Him by Yvonne Elliman.

Roy HEAD US, male vocalist　　　　5 wks

| 4 Nov 65 | TREAT HER RIGHT Vocalion V-P 9248 | 30 | 5 |

HEADBANGERS UK, male vocal / instrumental group　　　　3 wks

| 10 Oct 81 | STATUS ROCK Magnet MAG 206 | 60 | 3 |

HEADBOYS UK, male vocal / instrumental group　　　　8 wks

| 22 Sep 79 | THE SHAPE OF THINGS TO COME RSO 40 | 45 | 8 |

HEADGIRL – See MOTORHEAD; GIRLSCHOOL

Max HEADROOM – See ART OF NOISE

HEADS UK, male instrumental group　　　　4 wks

| 21 Jun 86 | AZTEC LIGHTNING (THEME FROM BBC 'WORLD CUP GRANDSTAND') BBC RESL 184 | 45 | 4 |

HEADS with Shaun RYDER
US / UK, male / female vocal / instrumental group　　　　1 wk

| 9 Nov 96 | DON'T TAKE MY KINDNESS FOR WEAKNESS Radioactive MCSTD 48024 | 60 | 1 |

Heads are Talking Heads minus lead singer David Byrne. See also Talking Heads.

HEADSWIM UK, male vocal / instrumental group　　　　1 wk

| 25 Feb 95 | CRAWL Epic 6612252 | 64 | 1 |

HEAR 'N AID International, male / female vocal / instrumental charity assembly — 6 wks

19 Apr 86	STARS Vertigo HEAR 1	26	6

HEART US, female / male vocal / instrumental group — 76 wks

29 Mar 86	THESE DREAMS Capitol CL 394	62	4
13 Jun 87	● ALONE Capitol CL 448	3	16
19 Sep 87	WHO WILL YOU RUN TO Capitol CL 457	30	7
12 Dec 87	THERE'S THE GIRL Capitol CL 473	34	7
5 Mar 88	● NEVER / THESE DREAMS (re-issue) Capitol CL 482	8	9
14 May 88	WHAT ABOUT LOVE Capitol CL 487	14	6
22 Oct 88	NOTHIN' AT ALL Capitol CL 507	38	3
24 Mar 90	● ALL I WANNA DO IS MAKE LOVE TO YOU Capitol CL 569	8	13
28 Jul 90	I DIDN'T WANT TO NEED YOU Capitol CL 580	47	3
17 Nov 90	STRANDED Capitol CL 595	60	2
14 Sep 91	YOU'RE THE VOICE Capitol CLS 624	56	2
20 Nov 93	WILL YOU BE THERE (IN THE MORNING) Capitol CDCLS 700	19	4

HEARTBEAT UK, male / female vocal / instrumental group — 5 wks

24 Oct 87	TEARS FROM HEAVEN Priority P 17	32	4
23 Apr 88	THE WINNER Priority P 19	70	1

HEARTBEAT COUNTRY
UK, male vocalist – Bill Maynard — 1 wk

31 Dec 94	HEARTBEAT MMM MMM 01CD	75†	1

HEARTBREAKERS – See Tom PETTY and the HEARTBREAKERS; Stevie NICKS

Ted HEATH UK, orchestra — 56 wks

16 Jan 53	VANESSA Decca F 9983	11	1
3 Jul 53	● HOT TODDY Decca F 10093	6	11
23 Oct 53	DRAGNET Decca F 10176	12	1
27 Nov 53	● DRAGNET (re-entry) Decca F 10176	9	1
11 Dec 53	DRAGNET (2nd re-entry) Decca F 10176	11	1
15 Jan 54	DRAGNET (3rd re-entry) Decca F 10176	11	1
5 Feb 54	DRAGNET (4th re-entry) Decca F 10176	12	1
12 Feb 54	SKIN DEEP Decca F 10246	9	3
6 Jul 56	THE FAITHFUL HUSSAR Decca F 10746	18	9
14 Mar 58	● SWINGIN' SHEPHERD BLUES Decca F 11000	3	14
11 Apr 58	TEQUILA Decca F 11003	21	6
4 Jul 58	TOM HARK Decca F 11025	24	2
5 Oct 61	SUCU SUCU (THEME FROM 'TOP SECRET') Decca F 11392	36	4
9 Nov 61	SUCU SUCU (THEME FROM 'TOP SECRET') (re-entry) Decca F 11392	47	1

HEATWAVE UK / US, male vocal / instrumental group — 80 wks

22 Jan 77	● BOOGIE NIGHTS GTO GT 77	2	14
7 May 77	TOO HOT TO HANDLE / SLIP YOUR DISC TO THIS GTO GT 91	15	11
14 Jan 78	THE GROOVE LINE GTO GT 115	12	8
3 Jun 78	MIND BLOWING DECISIONS GTO GT 226	12	11
4 Nov 78	● ALWAYS AND FOREVER / MIND BLOWING DECISIONS (re-mix) GTO GT 236	9	14
26 May 79	RAZZLE DAZZLE GTO GT 248	43	5
17 Jan 81	GANGSTERS OF THE GROOVE GTO GT 285	19	8
21 Mar 81	JITTERBUGGIN' GTO GT 290	34	7
1 Sep 90	MIND BLOWING DECISIONS (re-mix) Brothers Organisation HW 1	65	2

Mind Blowing Decisions on GT 236 is an extended remixed version of GT 226

HEAVEN 17 UK, male vocal / instrumental group — 87 wks

21 Mar 81	(WE DON'T NEED THIS) FASCIST GROOVE THANG Virgin VS 400	45	5
5 Sep 81	PLAY TO WIN Virgin VS 433	46	7
14 Nov 81	PENTHOUSE AND PAVEMENT Virgin VS 455	57	3
30 Oct 82	LET ME GO Virgin VS 532	41	6
16 Apr 83	● TEMPTATION Virgin VS 570	2	13
25 Jun 83	● COME LIVE WITH ME Virgin VS 607	5	11
10 Sep 83	CRUSHED BY THE WHEELS OF INDUSTRY Virgin VS 628	17	7
1 Sep 84	SUNSET NOW Virgin VS 708	24	6
27 Oct 84	THIS IS MINE Virgin VS 722	23	7
19 Jan 85	...(AND THAT'S NO LIE) Virgin VS 740	52	5
17 Jan 87	TROUBLE Virgin VS 920	51	3
21 Nov 92	● TEMPTATION (re-mix) Virgin VS 1446	4	11
27 Feb 93	(WE DON'T NEED THIS) FASCIST GROOVE THANG Virgin VSCDT 1451	40	2
10 Apr 93	PENTHOUSE AND PAVEMENT (re-mix) Virgin VSCDT 1457	54	1

Carol Kenyon is the uncredited vocalist on Temptation. Fascist Groove Thang in '93 is a re-recording. See also Various Artists (EPs & LPs) - Gimme Shelter (EP).

HEAVY D. and the BOYZ
Jamaica / US, male vocal / instrumental group — 28 wks

6 Dec 86	MR. BIG STUFF MCA MCA 1106	61	8
15 Jul 89	WE GOT OUR OWN THANG MCA MCA 23942	69	2
6 Jul 91	● NOW THAT WE FOUND LOVE MCA MCS 1550	2	12
28 Sep 91	IS IT GOOD TO YOU MCA MCS 1564	46	3
8 Oct 94	THIS IS YOUR NIGHT MCA MCSTD 2010	30	3

HEAVY PETTIN' UK, male vocal / instrumental group — 2 wks

17 Mar 84	LOVE TIMES LOVE Polydor HEP 3	69	2

HEAVY STEREO UK, male vocal / instrumental group — 4 wks

22 Jul 95	SLEEP FREAK Creation CRESCD 203	46	1
28 Oct 95	SMILER Creation CRESCD 213	46	1
10 Feb 96	CHINESE BURN Creation CRESCD 218	45	1
24 Aug 96	MOUSE IN A HOLE Creation CRESCD 230	53	1

HEAVY WEATHER US, male vocalist – Peter Lee — 1 wk

29 Jun 96	LOVE CAN'T TURN AROUND Pukka CDPUKKA 6	56	1

Bobby HEBB US, male vocalist — 15 wks

8 Sep 66	SUNNY Philips BF 1503	12	9
19 Aug 72	LOVE LOVE LOVE Philips 6051 023	32	6

HED BOYS UK, male instrumental / production duo — 6 wks

6 Aug 94	GIRLS + BOYS Deconstruction 74321223322	21	4
4 Nov 95	GIRLS + BOYS (re-mix) Deconstruction 74321322032	36	2

HEDGEHOPPERS ANONYMOUS
UK, male vocal / instrumental group — 12 wks

30 Sep 65	● IT'S GOOD NEWS WEEK Decca F 12241	5	12

Neal HEFTI US, male orchestra — 4 wks

9 Apr 88	'BATMAN' THEME RCA PB 49571	55	4

Den HEGARTY UK, male vocalist   2 wks

31 Mar 79	**VOODOO VOODOO** Magnet MAG 143	**73**	2

Anita HEGERLAND – See Mike OLDFIELD

HEINZ UK, male vocalist   35 wks

8 Aug 63 ●	**JUST LIKE EDDIE** Decca F 11693	**5**	15
28 Nov 63	**COUNTRY BOY** Decca F 11768	**26**	9
27 Feb 64	**YOU WERE THERE** Decca F 11831	**26**	8
15 Oct 64	**QUESTIONS I CAN'T ANSWER** Columbia DB 7374	**39**	2
18 Mar 65	**DIGGIN' MY POTATOES** Columbia DB 7482 [1]	**49**	1

[1] Heinz and the Wild Boys

HELICOPTER UK, male instrumental / production duo   4 wks

27 Aug 94	**ON YA WAY** Helicopter TIG 007CD	**32**	2
22 Jun 96	**ON YA WAY (re-mix)** Systematic SYSCD 27	**37**	2

HELIOCENTRIC WORLD
UK, male / female vocal / instrumental group   2 wks

14 Jan 95	**WHERE'S YOUR LOVE BEEN** Talkin Loud TLKCD 51	**71**	2

HELLER and FARLEY PROJECT
UK, male instrumental / production duo   4 wks

24 Feb 96	**ULTRA FLAVA** AM:PM 5814372	**22**	3
28 Dec 96	**ULTRA FLAVA (re-mix)** AM:PM 5820552	**32†**	1

Duo also known as Fire Island. See also Fire Island.

HELLO UK, male vocal / instrumental group   21 wks

9 Nov 74 ●	**TELL HIM** Bell 1377	**6**	12
18 Oct 75 ●	**NEW YORK GROOVE** Bell 1438	**9**	9

HELLOWEEN US, male vocal / instrumental group   7 wks

27 Aug 88	**DR STEIN** Noise International 7HELLO 1	**57**	3
12 Nov 88	**I WANT OUT** Noise International 7HELLO 2	**69**	2
2 Mar 91	**KIDS OF THE CENTURY** EMI EM 178	**56**	2

Bobby HELMS US, male vocalist   7 wks

29 Nov 57	**MY SPECIAL ANGEL** Brunswick 05721	**22**	3
21 Feb 58	**NO OTHER BABY** Brunswick 05730	**30**	1
1 Aug 58	**JACQUELINE** Brunswick 05748	**20**	3

Jimmy HELMS UK, male vocalist   10 wks

24 Feb 73 ●	**GONNA MAKE YOU AN OFFER YOU CAN'T REFUSE** Cube BUG 27	**8**	10

HELTAH SKELTAH and ORIGINOO GUNN CLAPPAZ as the FABULOUS FIVE
US, male vocal / instrumental duo   1 wk

1 Jun 96	**BLAH** Priority PTYCD 117	**60**	1

Eddie HENDERSON
US, male vocalist / instrumentalist – trumpet   6 wks

28 Oct 78	**PRANCE ON** Capitol CL 16015	**44**	6

Joe 'Mr. Piano' HENDERSON
UK, male instrumentalist – piano   23 wks

3 Jun 55	**SING IT WITH JOE** Polygon P 1167	**14**	4
2 Sep 55	**SING IT AGAIN WITH JOE** Polygon P 1184	**18**	3
25 Jul 58	**TRUDIE** Pye Nixa N 15147	**14**	12
24 Oct 58	**TRUDIE (re-entry)** Pye Nixa N 15147	**23**	2
23 Oct 59	**TREBLE CHANCE** Pye 7N 15224	**28**	1
24 Mar 60	**OOH LA LA** Pye 7N 15257	**46**	1

First two hits are medleys as follows: Sing It With Joe: Margie / I'm Nobody's Sweetheart / Somebody Stole My Gal / Moonlight Bay / By The Light Of The Silvery Moon / Cuddle Up A Little Closer. Sing It Again With Joe: Put Your Arms Around Me Honey / Ain't She Sweet / When You're Smiling / Shine On Harvest Moon / My Blue Heaven / Show Me The Way To Go Home.

Wayne HENDERSON – See Roy AYERS

Jimi HENDRIX EXPERIENCE US / UK, male vocal /
instrumental group, Jimi Hendrix – vocals and guitar   87 wks

5 Jan 67 ●	**HEY JOE** Polydor 56 139	**6**	10
23 Mar 67 ●	**PURPLE HAZE** Track 604 001	**3**	14
11 May 67 ●	**THE WIND CRIES MARY** Track 604 004	**6**	11
30 Aug 67	**BURNING OF THE MIDNIGHT LAMP** Track 604 007	**18**	9
23 Oct 68 ●	**ALL ALONG THE WATCHTOWER** Track 604 025	**5**	11
16 Apr 69	**CROSSTOWN TRAFFIC** Track 604 029	**37**	3
7 Nov 70 ★	**VOODOO CHILE** Track 2095 001	**1**	13
30 Oct 71	**GYPSY EYES / REMEMBER** Track 2094 010	**35**	5
12 Feb 72	**JOHNNY B. GOODE** Polydor 2001 277 [1]	**35**	5
21 Apr 90	**CROSSTOWN TRAFFIC (re-issue)** Polydor PO 71 [1]	**61**	3
20 Oct 90	**ALL ALONG THE WATCHTOWER (EP)** Polydor PO 100 [1]	**52**	3

[1] Jimi Hendrix

Tracks on All Along The Watchtower (EP): All Along The Watchtower / Voodoo Chile / Hey Joe.

Nona HENDRYX US, female vocalist   2 wks

16 May 87	**WHY SHOULD I CRY** EMI America EA 234	**60**	2

Don HENLEY US, male vocalist   24 wks

12 Feb 83	**DIRTY LAUNDRY** Asylum E 9894	**59**	3
9 Feb 85	**THE BOYS OF SUMMER** Geffen A 4945	**12**	10
29 Jul 89	**THE END OF THE INNOCENCE** Geffen GEF 57	**48**	5
3 Oct 92	**SOMETIMES LOVE JUST AIN'T ENOUGH** MCA MCS 1692 [1]	**22**	6

[1] Patty Smyth with Don Henley

Clarence 'Frogman' HENRY US, male vocalist   35 wks

4 May 61 ●	**BUT I DO** Pye International 7N 25078	**3**	19
13 Jul 61 ●	**YOU ALWAYS HURT THE ONE YOU LOVE** Pye International 7N 25089	**6**	12
21 Sep 61	**LONELY STREET / WHY CAN'T YOU** Pye International 7N 25108	**42**	2
17 Jul 93	**(I DON'T KNOW WHY) BUT I DO (re-issue)** MCA MCSTD 1797	**65**	2

Kevin HENRY – See L.A. MIX

Paul HENRY and the Mayson GLEN
ORCHESTRA UK, male vocalist / orchestra   2 wks

14 Jan 78	**BENNY'S THEME** Pye 7N 46027	**39**	2

Pauline HENRY *UK, female vocalist* — **21 wks**

18 Sep 93	**TOO MANY PEOPLE** Sony S2 6595942	**38**	2
6 Nov 93	**FEEL LIKE MAKING LOVE** Sony S2 6597972	**12**	7
29 Jan 94	**CAN'T TAKE YOUR LOVE** Sony S2 6599902	**30**	3
21 May 94	**WATCH THE MIRACLE START** Sony S2 6602772	**54**	1
30 Sep 95	**SUGAR FREE** Sony S2 6624362	**57**	2
23 Dec 95	**LOVE HANGOVER** Sony S2 6626132	**37**	3
24 Feb 96	**NEVER KNEW LOVE LIKE THIS** Sony S2 6629382 ☐**1**	**40**	2
1 Jun 96	**HAPPY** Sony S2 6630692	**46**	1

1 Pauline Henry featuring Wayne Marshall

HERD *UK, male vocal / instrumental group* — **35 wks**

13 Sep 67	● **FROM THE UNDERWORLD** Fontana TF 856	**6**	13
20 Dec 67	**PARADISE LOST** Fontana TF 887	**15**	9
10 Apr 68	● **I DON'T WANT OUR LOVING TO DIE** Fontana TF 925	**5**	13

HERMAN'S HERMITS
UK, male vocal / instrumental group — **211 wks**

20 Aug 64	★ **I'M INTO SOMETHING GOOD** Columbia DB 7338	**1**	15
19 Nov 64	**SHOW ME GIRL** Columbia DB 7408	**19**	9
18 Feb 65	**SILHOUETTES** Columbia DB 7475	**3**	12
29 Apr 65	● **WONDERFUL WORLD** Columbia DB 7546	**7**	9
2 Sep 65	**JUST A LITTLE BIT BETTER** Columbia DB 7670	**15**	9
23 Dec 65	● **A MUST TO AVOID** Columbia DB 7791	**6**	11
24 Mar 66	**YOU WON'T BE LEAVING** Columbia DB 7861	**20**	7
23 Jun 66	**THIS DOOR SWINGS BOTH WAYS** Columbia DB 7947	**18**	7
6 Oct 66	● **NO MILK TODAY** Columbia DB 8012	**7**	11
1 Dec 66	**EAST WEST** Columbia DB 8076	**37**	7
9 Feb 67	● **THERE'S A KIND OF HUSH** Columbia DB 8123	**7**	11
17 Jan 68	**I CAN TAKE OR LEAVE YOUR LOVING** Columbia DB 8327	**11**	9
1 May 68	**SLEEPY JOE** Columbia DB 8404	**12**	10
17 Jul 68	● **SUNSHINE GIRL** Columbia DB 8446	**8**	14
18 Dec 68	● **SOMETHING'S HAPPENING** Columbia DB 8504	**6**	15
23 Apr 69	● **MY SENTIMENTAL FRIEND** Columbia DB 8563	**2**	12
8 Nov 69	**HERE COMES THE STAR** Columbia DB 8626	**33**	9
7 Feb 70	● **YEARS MAY COME, YEARS MAY GO** Columbia DB 8656	**7**	11
2 May 70	**YEARS MAY COME, YEARS MAY GO** (re-entry) Columbia DB 8656	**45**	1
23 May 70	**BET YER LIFE I DO** RAK 102	**22**	10
14 Nov 70	**LADY BARBARA** RAK 106 ☐**1**	**13**	12

1 Peter Noone and Herman's Hermits

See also Peter Noone.

HERNANDEZ *UK, male vocalist* — **3 wks**

15 Apr 89	**ALL MY LOVE** Epic HER 1	**58**	3

Patrick HERNANDEZ *Guadeloupe, male vocalist* — **14 wks**

16 Jun 79	● **BORN TO BE ALIVE** Gem GEM 4	**10**	14

HERREYS *Sweden, male vocal group* — **3 wks**

26 May 84	**DIGGI LOO-DIGGI LEY** Panther PAN 5	**46**	3

Kristin HERSH *US, female vocalist* — **3 wks**

22 Jan 94	**YOUR GHOST** 4AD BAD 4001CD	**45**	2
16 Apr 94	**STRINGS** 4AD BAD 4006CD	**60**	1

Nick HEYWARD *UK, male vocalist* — **65 wks**

19 Mar 83	**WHISTLE DOWN THE WIND** Arista HEY 1	**13**	8
4 Jun 83	**TAKE THAT SITUATION** Arista HEY 2	**11**	10
24 Sep 83	**BLUE HAT FOR A BLUE DAY** Arista HEY 3	**14**	8
3 Dec 83	**ON A SUNDAY** Arista HEY 4	**52**	5
2 Jun 84	**LOVE ALL DAY** Arista HEY 5	**31**	6
3 Nov 84	**WARNING SIGN** Arista HEY 6	**25**	8
5 Jan 85	**WARNING SIGN** (re-entry) Arista HEY 6	**72**	1
8 Jun 85	**LAURA** Arista HEY 8	**45**	4
10 May 86	**OVER THE WEEKEND** Arista HEY 9	**43**	5
10 Sep 88	**YOU'RE MY WORLD** Warner Bros. W 7758	**67**	2
21 Aug 93	**KITE** Epic 6594882	**44**	2
16 Oct 93	**HE DOESN'T LOVE YOU LIKE I DO** Epic 6597282	**58**	2
30 Sep 95	**THE WORLD** Epic 6623845	**47**	2
13 Jan 96	**ROLLERBLADE** Epic 6627912	**37**	2

HI-FIVE *US, male vocal group* — **8 wks**

1 Jun 91	**I LIKE THE WAY (THE KISSING GAME)** Jive JIVE 271	**43**	6
24 Oct 92	**SHE'S PLAYING HARD TO GET** Jive JIVE 316	**55**	2

HI GLOSS *US, disco aggregation* — **13 wks**

8 Aug 81	**YOU'LL NEVER KNOW** Epic EPC A 1387	**12**	13

HI-LUX *UK, male instrumental / production duo* — **3 wks**

18 Feb 95	**FEEL IT** Cheeky CHEKCD 006	**41**	2
2 Sep 95	**NEVER FELT THIS WAY / FEEL IT** Champion CHAMPCD 319	**58**	1

HI POWER *Germany, male rap group* — **1 wk**

1 Sep 90	**CULT OF SNAP / SIMBA GROOVE** Rumour RUMAT 24	**73**	1

HI-TEK 3 featuring YA KID K
Belgium, male / female vocal / instrumental group — **10 wks**

3 Feb 90	**SPIN THAT WHEEL** Brothers Organisation BORG 1	**69**	3
29 Sep 90	**SPIN THAT WHEEL (TURTLES GET REAL)** (re-issue) Brothers Organisation BORG 16	**15**	7

See also Technotronic.

HI TENSION *UK, male vocal / instrumental group* — **23 wks**

6 May 78	**HI TENSION** Island WIP 6422	**13**	12
12 Aug 78	● **BRITISH HUSTLE / PEACE ON EARTH** Island WIP 6446	**8**	11

Peace On Earth *credited with British Hustle from 2 Sep 78 to end of record's chart run.*

Al HIBBLER *US, male vocalist* — **17 wks**

13 May 55	● **UNCHAINED MELODY** Brunswick 05420	**2**	17

Bertie HIGGINS *US, male vocalist* — **4 wks**

5 Jun 82	**KEY LARGO** Epic EPC A 2168	**60**	4

HIGH *UK, male vocal group* — **11 wks**

25 Aug 90	**UP AND DOWN** London LON 272	**53**	4
27 Oct 90	**TAKE YOUR TIME** London LON 280	**56**	2
12 Jan 91	**BOX SET GO** London LONG 286	**28**	3
6 Apr 91	**MORE...** London LON 297	**67**	2

HIGH NUMBERS UK, male vocal / instrumental group 4 wks

| 5 Apr 80 | I'M THE FACE Back Door DOOR 4 | 49 | 4 |

The High Numbers were an early version of the Who. See also the Who.

HIGH SOCIETY UK, male vocal / instrumental group 4 wks

| 15 Nov 80 | I NEVER GO OUT IN THE RAIN Eagle ERS 002 | 53 | 4 |

HIGHLY LIKELY UK, male vocal / instrumental group 4 wks

| 21 Apr 73 | WHATEVER HAPPENED TO YOU ('LIKELY LADS' THEME) BBC RESL 10 | 35 | 4 |

HIGHWAYMEN US, male vocal group 18 wks

7 Sep 61	★ MICHAEL HMV POP 910	1	14
7 Dec 61	GYPSY ROVER HMV POP 948	41	3
11 Jan 62	GYPSY ROVER (re-entry) HMV POP 948	43	1

HIJACK UK, male producer 3 wks

| 6 Jan 90 | THE BADMAN IS ROBBIN' Rhyme Syndicate 655517 7 | 56 | 3 |

Benny HILL UK, male vocalist 43 wks

16 Feb 61	GATHER IN THE MUSHROOMS Pye 7N 15327	12	8
1 Jun 61	TRANSISTOR RADIO Pye 7N 15359	24	6
16 May 63	HARVEST OF LOVE Pye 7N 15520	20	8
13 Nov 71	★ ERNIE (THE FASTEST MILKMAN IN THE WEST) Columbia DB 8833	1	17
30 May 92	ERNIE (THE FASTEST MILKMAN IN THE WEST) (re-issue) EMI ERN 1	29	4

Chris HILL UK, male vocalist / producer 14 wks

| 6 Dec 75 | ● RENTA SANTA Philips 6006 491 | 10 | 7 |
| 4 Dec 76 | ● BIONIC SANTA Philips 6006 551 | 10 | 7 |

Dan HILL Canada, male vocalist 13 wks

| 18 Feb 78 | SOMETIMES WHEN WE TOUCH 20th Century BTC 2355 | 46 | 1 |
| 4 Mar 78 | SOMETIMES WHEN WE TOUCH (re-entry) 20th Century BTC 2355 | 13 | 12 |

Lonnie HILL US, male vocalist 4 wks

| 22 Mar 86 | GALVESTON BAY 10 TEN 111 | 51 | 4 |

Roni HILL US, female vocalist 4 wks

| 7 May 77 | YOU KEEP ME HANGIN' ON – STOP IN THE NAME OF LOVE (MEDLEY) Creole CR 138 | 36 | 4 |

Vince HILL UK, male vocalist 91 wks

7 Jun 62	THE RIVER'S RUN DRY Piccadilly 7N 35043	49	1
28 Jun 62	THE RIVER'S RUN DRY (re-entry) Piccadilly 7N 35043	41	1
6 Jan 66	TAKE ME TO YOUR HEART AGAIN Columbia DB 7781	13	11
17 Mar 66	HEARTACHES Columbia DB 7852	28	5
2 Jun 66	MERCI CHERI Columbia DB 7924	36	6
9 Feb 67	● EDELWEISS Columbia DB 8127	2	17
11 May 67	ROSES OF PICARDY Columbia DB 8185	13	11
27 Sep 67	LOVE LETTERS IN THE SAND Columbia DB 8268	23	9

26 Jun 68	IMPORTANCE OF YOUR LOVE Columbia DB 8414	32	12
12 Feb 69	DOESN'T ANYBODY KNOW MY NAME? Columbia DB 8515	50	1
25 Oct 69	LITTLE BLUE BIRD Columbia DB 8616	42	1
25 Sep 71	LOOK AROUND Columbia DB 8804	12	16

HILLTOPPERS US, male vocal group 30 wks

27 Jan 56	● ONLY YOU London HLD 8221	3	22
10 Aug 56	ONLY YOU (re-entry) London HLD 8221	24	1
14 Sep 56	TRYIN' London HLD 8298	30	1
5 Apr 57	MARIANNE London HLD 8381	20	2
26 Apr 57	MARIANNE (re-entry) London HLD 8381	23	4

Ronnie HILTON UK, male vocalist 128 wks

26 Nov 54	● I STILL BELIEVE HMV B 10785	3	14
10 Dec 54	VENI VIDI VICI HMV B 10785	12	8
11 Mar 55	● A BLOSSOM FELL HMV B 10808	10	5
26 Aug 55	STARS SHINE IN YOUR EYES HMV B 10901	13	7
11 Nov 55	YELLOW ROSE OF TEXAS HMV B 10924	15	2
10 Feb 56	YOUNG AND FOOLISH HMV POP 154	17	1
24 Feb 56	YOUNG AND FOOLISH (re-entry) HMV POP 154	20	1
9 Mar 56	YOUNG AND FOOLISH (2nd re-entry) HMV POP 154	19	1
20 Apr 56	★ NO OTHER LOVE HMV POP 198	1	14
29 Jun 56	● WHO ARE WE HMV POP 221	6	12
21 Sep 56	WOMAN IN LOVE HMV POP 248	30	1
9 Nov 56	TWO DIFFERENT WORLDS HMV POP 274	13	13
24 May 57	● AROUND THE WORLD HMV POP 338	4	18
2 Aug 57	WONDERFUL WONDERFUL HMV POP 364	27	2
21 Feb 58	MAGIC MOMENTS HMV POP 446	22	2
18 Apr 58	I MAY NEVER PASS THIS WAY AGAIN HMV POP 468 [1]	30	1
2 May 58	I MAY NEVER PASS THIS WAY AGAIN (re-entry) HMV POP 468 [1]	30	1
6 Jun 58	I MAY NEVER PASS THIS WAY AGAIN (2nd re-entry) HMV POP 468 [1]	27	1
9 Jan 59	THE WORLD OUTSIDE HMV POP 559 [1]	18	6
21 Aug 59	THE WONDER OF YOU HMV POP 638	22	3
21 May 64	DON'T LET THE RAIN COME DOWN HMV POP 1291	21	10
11 Feb 65	A WINDMILL IN OLD AMSTERDAM HMV POP 1378	23	13

[1] Ronnie Hilton with the Michael Sammes Singers

HINDSIGHT UK, male vocal / instrumental group 3 wks

| 5 Sep 87 | LOWDOWN Circa YR 5 | 62 | 3 |

Gregory HINES – *See Luther VANDROSS*

HIPSWAY UK, male vocal / instrumental group 21 wks

13 Jul 85	THE BROKEN YEARS Mercury MER 193	72	3
14 Sep 85	ASK THE LORD Mercury MER 195	72	1
22 Feb 86	THE HONEYTHIEF Mercury MER 212	17	9
10 May 86	ASK THE LORD Mercury LORD 1	50	5
20 Sep 86	LONG WHITE CAR Mercury MER 230	55	2
1 Apr 89	YOUR LOVE Mercury MER 279	66	1

LORD 1 was a re-recording of MER 195.

HISTORY – *See Q-TEE*

Carol HITCHCOCK Australia, female vocalist 5 wks

| 30 May 87 | GET READY A & M AM 391 | 56 | 5 |

HITHOUSE Holland, male producer – Peter Slaghuis 13 wks

| 5 Nov 88 | JACK TO THE SOUND OF THE UNDERGROUND Supreme SUPE 137 | 14 | 12 |

Jimi Hendrix

Arguably the most influential guitar player of all time, Hendrix is credited with inventing the heavy metal sound.

Hue And Cry

Hue and Cry's 'Looking For Linda' was the true story of a woman who disappeared after going out to buy a packet of cigarettes.

Hootie And The Blowfish

South Carolina four-piece Hootie And The Blowfish utilised the vocal talents of David Crosby on their debut hit, 'Hold My Hand'.

19 Aug 89 **MOVE YOUR FEET TO THE RHYTHM OF THE BEAT**
Supreme SUPE 149 ....**69** 1

HITMAN HOWIE TEE – *See REAL ROXANNE*

Edmund HOCKRIDGE *Canada, male vocalist* **18 wks**

17 Feb 56	● **YOUNG AND FOOLISH** *Nixa N 15039* **10**		7
13 Apr 56	**YOUNG AND FOOLISH (re-entry)** *Nixa N 15039* **28**		1
4 May 56	**YOUNG AND FOOLISH (2nd re-entry)** *Nixa N 15039* **26**		1
11 May 56	**NO OTHER LOVE** *Nixa N 15048* **24**		2
1 Jun 56	**NO OTHER LOVE (re-entry)** *Nixa N 15048* **29**		1
15 Jun 56	**NO OTHER LOVE (2nd re-entry)** *Nixa N 15048*..**30**		1
31 Aug 56	**BY THE FOUNTAINS OF ROME** *Pye Nixa N 15063* **17**		5

Eddie HODGES *US, male vocalist* **10 wks**

28 Sep 61	**I'M GONNA KNOCK ON YOUR DOOR** *London HLA 9369* **37**	6
9 Aug 62	**MADE TO LOVE (GIRLS GIRLS GIRLS)** *London HLA 9576* **37**	4

Roger HODGSON – *See SUPERTRAMP*

Susanna HOFFS *US, female vocalist* **8 wks**

2 Mar 91	**MY SIDE OF THE BED** *Columbia 6565547* **44**	4
11 May 91	**UNCONDITIONAL LOVE** *Columbia 6567827*..........**65**	2
19 Oct 96	**ALL I WANT** *London LONCD 387* **32**	2

Hulk HOGAN – *See GREEN JELLY*

HOLE *US, female / male vocal / instrumental group* **7 wks**

17 Apr 93	**BEAUTIFUL SON** *City Slang EFA 0491603* **54**	1
9 Apr 94	**MISS WORLD** *City Slang EFA 049362* **64**	1
15 Apr 95	**DOLL PARTS** *Geffen GFSTD 91* **16**	3
29 Jul 95	**VIOLET** *Geffen GFSTD 94* **17**	2

HOLLAND-DOZIER featuring Lamont DOZIER *US, male vocal duo* **5 wks**

28 Oct 72	**WHY CAN'T WE BE LOVERS** *Invictus INV 525* **29**	5

Jennifer HOLLIDAY *US, female vocalist* **6 wks**

4 Sep 82	**AND I'M TELLING YOU I'M NOT GOING** *Geffen GEF A 2644* **32**	6

Michael HOLLIDAY *UK, male vocalist* **63 wks**

30 Mar 56	**NOTHIN' TO DO** *Columbia DB 3746* **20**		1
27 Apr 56	**NOTHIN' TO DO (re-entry)** *Columbia DB 3746* **23**		2
15 Jun 56	**GAL WITH THE YALLER SHOES** *Columbia DB 3783* [1] **13**		3
22 Jun 56	**HOT DIGGITY (DOG ZIGGITY BOOM)** *Columbia DB 3783* [1] **14**		5
3 Aug 56	**HOT DIGGITY (DOG ZIGGITY BOOM) / GAL WITH THE YALLER SHOES (re-entry)** *Columbia DB 3783* [1] **17**		3
5 Oct 56	**TEN THOUSAND MILES** *Columbia DB 3813* **24**		3
17 Jan 58	★ **THE STORY OF MY LIFE** *Columbia DB 4058* **1**		15
14 Mar 58	**IN LOVE** *Columbia DB 4087* **26**		3
16 May 58	● **STAIRWAY OF LOVE** *Columbia DB 4121* **3**		13
11 Jul 58	**I'LL ALWAYS BE IN LOVE WITH YOU** *Columbia DB 4155* **27**		1
1 Jan 60	★ **STARRY EYED** *Columbia DB 4378* **1**		12
14 Apr 60	**SKYLARK** *Columbia DB 4437* **39**		3

1 Sep 60 **LITTLE BOY LOST** *Columbia DB 4475* **50** 1

[1] Michael Holliday with the Norrie Paramor Orchestra and the Four Shepherd Boys

When Hot Diggity (Dog Ziggity Boom) / Gal With The Yaller Shoes re-entered the chart on 3 Aug 56 Hot Diggity (Dog Ziggity Boom) was listed by itself on 3 Aug and 10 Aug. Both sides were listed on 17 Aug, Gal With The Yaller Shoes peaking at position 25.

HOLLIES *UK, male vocal / instrumental group* **318 wks**

30 May 63	**(AIN'T THAT) JUST LIKE ME** *Parlophone R 5030* **25**		10
29 Aug 63	**SEARCHIN'** *Parlophone R 5052* **12**		14
21 Nov 63	● **STAY** *Parlophone R 5077* **8**		16
27 Feb 64	● **JUST ONE LOOK** *Parlophone R 5104* **2**		13
21 May 64	● **HERE I GO AGAIN** *Parlophone R 5137* **4**		12
17 Sep 64	● **WE'RE THROUGH** *Parlophone R 5178* **7**		11
28 Jan 65	● **YES I WILL** *Parlophone R 5232* **9**		13
27 May 65	★ **I'M ALIVE** *Parlophone R 5287* **1**		14
2 Sep 65	● **LOOK THROUGH ANY WINDOW** *Parlophone R 5322* **4**		11
9 Dec 65	**IF I NEEDED SOMEONE** *Parlophone R 5392* **20**		9
24 Feb 66	● **I CAN'T LET GO** *Parlophone R 5409* **2**		10
23 Jun 66	● **BUS STOP** *Parlophone R 5469* **5**		9
13 Oct 66	● **STOP STOP STOP** *Parlophone R 5508* **2**		12
16 Feb 67	● **ON A CAROUSEL** *Parlophone R 5562* **4**		11
1 Jun 67	● **CARRIE-ANNE** *Parlophone R 5602* **3**		11
27 Sep 67	**KING MIDAS IN REVERSE** *Parlophone R 5637* **18**		8
27 Mar 68	● **JENNIFER ECCLES** *Parlophone R 5680* **7**		11
2 Oct 68	**LISTEN TO ME** *Parlophone R 5733* **11**		11
5 Mar 69	● **SORRY SUZANNE** *Parlophone R 5765* **3**		12
4 Oct 69	● **HE AIN'T HEAVY, HE'S MY BROTHER** *Parlophone R 5806* **3**		15
18 Apr 70	● **I CAN'T TELL THE BOTTOM FROM THE TOP** *Parlophone R 5837* **7**		10
3 Oct 70	**GASOLINE ALLEY BRED** *Parlophone R 5862* **14**		7
22 May 71	**HEY WILLY** *Parlophone R 5905* **22**		7
26 Feb 72	**THE BABY** *Polydor 2058 199* **26**		6
2 Sep 72	**LONG COOL WOMAN (IN A BLACK DRESS)** *Parlophone R 5939* **32**		8
13 Oct 73	**THE DAY THAT CURLY BILLY SHOT DOWN CRAZY SAM MCGHEE** *Polydor 2058 403* **24**		6
9 Feb 74	● **THE AIR THAT I BREATHE** *Polydor 2058 435* **2**		13
14 Jun 80	**SOLDIER'S SONG** *Polydor 2059 246* **58**		3
29 Aug 81	**HOLLIEDAZE (MEDLEY)** *EMI 5229* **28**		7
3 Sep 88	★ **HE AIN'T HEAVY, HE'S MY BROTHER (re-issue)** *EMI EM 74* **1**		11
3 Dec 88	**THE AIR THAT I BREATHE (re-issue)** *EMI EM 80* **60**		5
20 Mar 93	**THE WOMAN I LOVE** *EMI CDEM 264* **42**		2

Loleatta HOLLOWAY *US, female vocalist* **14 wks**

31 Aug 91	**GOOD VIBRATIONS** *Interscope A 8764* [1] **14**		7
18 Jan 92	**TAKE ME AWAY** *PWL Continental PWL 210* [2] **25**		5
26 Mar 94	**STAND UP** *Six6 SIXCD 111* **68**		1
1 Apr 95	**KEEP THE FIRE BURNIN'** *Columbia 6611552* [3] **49**		1

[1] Marky Mark and the Funky Bunch featuring Loleatta Holloway
[2] Cappella featuring Loleatta Holloway [3] Dan Hartman starring Loleatta Holloway

Buddy HOLLY *US, male vocalist* **190 wks**

6 Dec 57	● **PEGGY SUE** *Coral Q 72293* **6**		17
14 Mar 58	**LISTEN TO ME** *Coral Q 72288* **16**		2
20 Jun 58	● **RAVE ON** *Coral Q 72325* **5**		14
29 Aug 58	**EARLY IN THE MORNING** *Coral Q 72333* **17**		4
16 Jan 59	**HEARTBEAT** *Coral Q 72346* **30**		1
27 Feb 59	★ **IT DOESN'T MATTER ANYMORE** *Coral Q 72360* **1**		21
31 Jul 59	**MIDNIGHT SHIFT** *Brunswick 05800* **26**		3
11 Sep 59	**PEGGY SUE GOT MARRIED** *Coral Q 72376* **13**		10
28 Apr 60	**HEARTBEAT (re-issue)** *Coral Q 72392* **30**		3
26 May 60	**TRUE LOVE WAYS** *Coral Q 72397* **25**		7
20 Oct 60	**LEARNIN' THE GAME** *Coral Q 72411* **36**		3

26 Jan 61	**WHAT TO DO** *Coral Q 72419*	**34**	6
6 Jul 61	**BABY I DON'T CARE / VALLEY OF TEARS** *Coral Q 72432*..**12**		14
15 Mar 62	**LISTEN TO ME** (re-issue) *Coral Q 72449*	**48**	1
13 Sep 62	**REMINISCING** *Coral Q 72455*	**17**	11
14 Mar 63	● **BROWN-EYED HANDSOME MAN** *Coral Q 72459*	**3**	17
6 Jun 63	● **BO DIDDLEY** *Coral Q 72463*	**4**	12
5 Sep 63	● **WISHING** *Coral Q 72466*	**10**	11
19 Dec 63	**WHAT TO DO** *Coral Q 72469*	**27**	8
14 May 64	**YOU'VE GOT LOVE** *Coral Q 72472* [1]	**40**	6
10 Sep 64	**LOVE'S MADE A FOOL OF YOU** *Coral Q 72475*	**39**	6
3 Apr 68	**PEGGY SUE / RAVE ON** (re-issue) *MCA MU 1012*	**32**	9
10 Dec 88	**TRUE LOVE WAYS** (re-issue) *MCA MCA 1302*	**65**	4

[1] Buddy Holly and the Crickets

Buddy Holly's version of Love's Made A Fool Of You is not the same version as the Crickets' hit of 1959, on which Holly did not appear. Valley Of Tears was not listed together with Baby I Don't Care until 13 Jul 61. What To Do on Q 72469 was a re-recording.

HOLLY and the IVYS
UK, male / female vocal / instrumental group **4 wks**

19 Dec 81	**CHRISTMAS ON 45** *Decca SANTA 1*	**40**	4

HOLLYWOOD ARGYLES *US, male vocal group* **10 wks**

21 Jul 60	**ALLEY OOP** *London HLU 9146*	**24**	10

HOLLYWOOD BEYOND *UK, male vocalist* **14 wks**

12 Jul 86	● **WHAT'S THE COLOUR OF MONEY?** *WEA YZ 76*	**7**	10
20 Sep 86	**NO MORE TEARS** *WEA YZ 81*	**47**	4

Eddie HOLMAN *US, male vocalist* **13 wks**

19 Oct 74	● **(HEY THERE) LONELY GIRL** *ABC 4012*	**4**	13

David HOLMES *UK, male producer* **1 wk**

6 Apr 96	**GONE** *Go! Discs GODCD 140*	**75**	1

Rupert HOLMES *US, male vocalist* **14 wks**

12 Jan 80	**ESCAPE (THE PINA COLADA SONG)** *Infinity INF 120*	**23**	7
22 Mar 80	**HIM** *MCA 565*	**31**	7

John HOLT *Jamaica, male vocalist* **14 wks**

14 Dec 74	● **HELP ME MAKE IT THROUGH THE NIGHT** *Trojan TR 7909* ..**6**		14

A HOMEBOY, A HIPPIE and A FUNKI DREDD
UK, male vocal / instrumental group **9 wks**

13 Oct 90	**TOTAL CONFUSION** *Tam Tam 7TTT 031*	**56**	3
29 Dec 90	**FREEDOM** *Tam Tam 7TTT 039*	**68**	4
8 Jan 94	**HERE WE GO AGAIN** *Polydor PZCD 302*	**57**	2

HONEYBUS *UK, male vocal / instrumental group* **12 wks**

20 Mar 68	● **I CAN'T LET MAGGIE GO** *Deram DM 182*	**8**	12

HONEYCOMBS
UK, male / female vocal / instrumental group **39 wks**

23 Jul 64	★ **HAVE I THE RIGHT** *Pye 7N 15664*	**1**	15
22 Oct 64	**IS IT BECAUSE** *Pye 7N 15705*	**38**	6

29 Apr 65	**SOMETHING BETTER BEGINNING** *Pye 7N 15827*	**39**	4
5 Aug 65	**THAT'S THE WAY** *Pye 7N 15890*	**12**	14

HONEYCRACK *UK, male vocal / instrumental group* **9 wks**

4 Nov 95	**SITTING AT HOME** *Epic 6625382*	**42**	2
24 Feb 96	**GO AWAY** *Epic 6628642*	**41**	2
11 May 96	**KING OF MISERY** *Epic 6631472*	**32**	2
20 Jul 96	**SITTING AT HOME** (re-issue) *Epic 6635032*	**32**	2
16 Nov 96	**ANYWAY** *EG EGO 52A*	**67**	1

HONEYDRIPPERS
UK / US, male vocal / instrumental group **3 wks**

2 Feb 85	**SEA OF LOVE** *Es Paranza YZ 33*	**56**	3

HONKY *UK, male vocal / instrumental group* **5 wks**

28 May 77	**JOIN THE PARTY** *Creole CR 137*	**28**	5

HONKY *UK, male vocal / instrumental group* **5 wks**

30 Oct 93	**THE HONKY DOODLE DAY EP** *ZTT ZANG 45CD*	**61**	1
19 Feb 94	**THE WHISTLER** *ZTT ZANG 48CD*	**41**	2
20 Apr 96	**HIP HOP DON'T YA DROP** *Higher Ground HIGHS 1CD*	**70**	1
10 Aug 96	**WHAT'S GOIN DOWN** *Higher Ground HIGHS 2CD*	**49**	1

Tracks on The Honky Doodle Day EP: KKK (Boom Boom Tra La La La) / Honky Doodle Dub / Chains.

Frank HOOKER and POSITIVE PEOPLE
US, male vocal / instrumental group **4 wks**

5 Jul 80	**THIS FEELIN'** *DJM DJS 10947*	**48**	4

John Lee HOOKER *US, male vocalist* **23 wks**

11 Jun 64	**DIMPLES** *Stateside SS 297*	**23**	10
24 Oct 92	**BOOM BOOM** *Pointblank POB 3*	**16**	5
16 Jan 93	**BOOGIE AT RUSSIAN HILL** *Pointblank POBDX 4*	**53**	2
15 May 93	**GLORIA** *Exile VANCD 11* [1]	**31**	3
11 Feb 95	**CHILL OUT (THINGS GONNA CHANGE)** *Pointblank POBD 10*	**45**	2
20 Apr 96	**BABY LEE** *Silvertone ORECD 81* [2]	**65**	1

[1] Van Morrison and John Lee Hooker [2] John Lee Hooker with Robert Cray

HOOTERS *US, male vocal / instrumental group* **9 wks**

21 Nov 87	**SATELLITE** *CBS 651168 7*	**22**	9

HOOTIE AND THE BLOWFISH
US, male vocal / instrumental group **5 wks**

25 Feb 95	**HOLD MY HAND** *Atlantic A 7230CD*	**50**	3
27 May 95	**LET HER CRY** *Atlantic A 7188CD*	**75**	1
4 May 96	**OLD MAN AND ME (WHEN I GET TO HEAVEN)** *Atlantic A 5513CD*	**57**	1

HOPE A.D. *UK, male producer – David Hope* **1 wk**

4 Jun 94	**TREE FROG** *Sun-Up SUN 003CD*	**73**	1

See also Mind Of Kane.

Mary HOPKIN *UK, female vocalist* **74 wks**

4 Sep 68	★ **THOSE WERE THE DAYS** *Apple 2*	**1**	21

2 Apr 69	● GOODBYE Apple 10	2 14
31 Jan 70	● TEMMA HARBOUR Apple 22	6 11
28 Mar 70	● KNOCK KNOCK WHO'S THERE Apple 26	2 14
31 Oct 70	THINK ABOUT YOUR CHILDREN Apple 30	19 7
2 Jan 71	THINK ABOUT YOUR CHILDREN (re-entry) Apple 30	46 2
31 Jul 71	LET MY NAME BE SORROW Apple 34	46 1
20 Mar 76	IF YOU LOVE ME Good Earth GD 2	32 4

See also Various Artists (EPs & LPs) – The Apple EP.

Anthony HOPKINS UK, male vocalist   1 wk

27 Dec 86	DISTANT STAR Juice AA 5	75 1

Bruce HORNSBY and the RANGE
US, male vocal / instrumental group   15 wks

2 Aug 86	THE WAY IT IS RCA PB 49805	15 10
25 Apr 87	MANDOLIN RAIN RCA PB 49769	70 1
28 May 88	THE VALLEY ROAD RCA PB 49561	44 4

HORSE UK, female / male vocal / instrumental group   8 wks

24 Nov 90	CAREFUL Capitol CL 587	52 3
21 Aug 93	SHAKE THIS MOUNTAIN Oxygen GASPD 7	52 2
23 Oct 93	GOD'S HOME MOVIE Oxygen GASXD 10	56 1
15 Jan 94	CELEBRATE Oxygen GASPD 11	49 2

Johnny HORTON US, male vocalist   15 wks

26 Jun 59	BATTLE OF NEW ORLEANS Philips PB 932	16 4
19 Jan 61	NORTH TO ALASKA Philips PB 1062	23 11

HOT BLOOD France, male instrumental group   5 wks

9 Oct 76	SOUL DRACULA Creole CR 132	32 5

HOT BUTTER US, male instrumental group   19 wks

22 Jul 72	● POPCORN Pye International 7N 25583	5 16
23 Dec 72	POPCORN (re-entry) Pye International 7N 25583	50 3

HOT CHOCOLATE UK, male vocal / instrumental group   272 wks

15 Aug 70	● LOVE IS LIFE RAK 103	6 12
6 Mar 71	YOU COULD HAVE BEEN A LADY RAK 110	22 9
28 Aug 71	● I BELIEVE (IN LOVE) RAK 118	8 11
28 Oct 72	YOU'LL ALWAYS BE A FRIEND RAK 139	23 8
14 Apr 73	● BROTHER LOUIE RAK 149	7 10
18 Aug 73	RUMOURS RAK 157	44 3
16 Mar 74	● EMMA RAK 168	3 10
30 Nov 74	CHERI BABE RAK 188	31 9
24 May 75	DISCO QUEEN RAK 202	11 7
9 Aug 75	● A CHILD'S PRAYER RAK 212	7 10
8 Nov 75	● YOU SEXY THING RAK 221	2 12
20 Mar 76	DON'T STOP IT NOW RAK 230	11 8
26 Jun 76	MAN TO MAN RAK 238	14 8
21 Aug 76	HEAVEN IS IN THE BACK SEAT OF MY CADILLAC RAK 240	25 8
18 Jun 77	★ SO YOU WIN AGAIN RAK 259	1 11
26 Nov 77	● PUT YOUR LOVE IN ME RAK 266	10 9
4 Mar 78	EVERY 1'S A WINNER RAK 270	12 11
2 Dec 78	I'LL PUT YOU TOGETHER AGAIN RAK 286	13 11
19 May 79	MINDLESS BOOGIE RAK 292	46 5
28 Jul 79	GOING THROUGH THE MOTIONS RAK 296	53 4
3 May 80	● NO DOUBT ABOUT IT RAK 310	2 11
19 Jul 80	ARE YOU GETTING ENOUGH OF WHAT MAKES YOU HAPPY RAK 318	17 7
13 Dec 80	LOVE ME TO SLEEP RAK 324	50 5

30 May 81	YOU'LL NEVER BE SO WRONG RAK 331	52 4
17 Apr 82	● GIRL CRAZY RAK 341	7 11
10 Jul 82	● IT STARTED WITH A KISS RAK 344	5 12
25 Sep 82	CHANCES RAK 350	32 5
7 May 83	● WHAT KINDA BOY YOU LOOKING FOR (GIRL) RAK 357	10 9
17 Sep 83	TEARS ON THE TELEPHONE RAK 363	37 5
4 Feb 84	I GAVE YOU MY HEART (DIDN'T I) RAK 369	13 10
17 Jan 87	● YOU SEXY THING (re-mix) EMI 5592	10 10
4 Apr 87	EVERY 1'S A WINNER (re-mix) EMI 5607	69 2
6 Mar 93	IT STARTED WITH A KISS (re-issue) EMI CDEMCTS 7	31 5

HOT GOSSIP – See Sarah BRIGHTMAN

HOT HOUSE UK, male / female vocal / instrumental group   3 wks

14 Feb 87	DON'T COME TO STAY Deconstruction CHEZ 1	74 1
24 Sep 88	DON'T COME TO STAY (re-issue) Deconstruction PB 42233	70 2

HOT STREAK US, male vocal / instrumental group   8 wks

10 Sep 83	BODY WORK Polydor POSP 642	19 8

HOTHOUSE FLOWERS
Ireland, male vocal / instrumental group   35 wks

14 May 88	DON'T GO London LON 174	11 8
23 Jul 88	I'M SORRY London LON 187	53 3
12 May 90	GIVE IT UP London LON 258	30 5
28 Jul 90	I CAN SEE CLEARLY NOW London LON 269	23 7
20 Oct 90	MOVIES London LON 276	68 2
13 Feb 93	EMOTIONAL TIME London LONCD 335	38 4
8 May 93	ONE TONGUE London LOCDP 340	45 3
19 Jun 93	ISN'T IT AMAZING London LOCDP 343	46 2
27 Nov 93	THIS IS IT (YOUR SOUL) London LONCD 346	67 1

HOTLEGS UK, male vocal / instrumental group   14 wks

4 Jul 70	● NEANDERTHAL MAN Fontana 6007 019	2 14

HOTRODS – See EDDIE and the HOTRODS

HOTSHOTS UK, male vocal group   15 wks

2 Jun 73	● SNOOPY VS. THE RED BARON Mooncrest MOON 5	4 15

A HOUSE Ireland, male vocal / instrumental group   8 wks

13 Jun 92	ENDLESS ART Setanta AHOU 1	46 3
8 Aug 92	TAKE IT EASY ON ME Setanta AHOU 2	55 2
25 Jun 94	WHY ME Setanta CDAHOU 4	52 1
1 Oct 94	HERE COME THE GOOD TIMES Setanta CDAHOUS 5	37 2

HOUSE ENGINEERS UK, male vocal / instrumental duo   2 wks

5 Dec 87	GHOST HOUSE Syncopate SY 8	69 2

HOUSE OF LOVE UK, male vocal / instrumental group   21 wks

22 Apr 89	NEVER Fontana HOL 1	41 2
18 Nov 89	I DON'T KNOW WHY I LOVE YOU Fontana HOL 2	41 3
3 Feb 90	SHINE ON Fontana HOL 3	20 4
7 Apr 90	BEATLES AND THE STONES Fontana HOL 4	36 4
26 Oct 91	THE GIRL WITH THE LONELIEST EYES Fontana HOL 5	58 1
2 May 92	FEEL Fontana HOL 6	45 3
27 Jun 92	YOU DON'T UNDERSTAND Fontana HOL 7	46 3
5 Dec 92	CRUSH ME Fontana HOL 810	67 1

HOUSE OF PAIN US, male rap group   **24 wks**

10 Oct 92	**JUMP AROUND** *Ruffness XLS 32* **32**	4
22 May 93	● **JUMP AROUND (re-issue) / TOP O' THE MORNING** **TO YA** *Ruffness XL 43CD* **8**	7
23 Oct 93	**SHAMROCKS AND SHENANIGANS / WHO'S THE** **MAN** *Ruffness XLS 46CD* **23**	4
16 Jul 94	**ON POINT** *Ruffness XLS 52CD* **19**	3
12 Nov 94	**IT AIN'T A CRIME** *Ruffness XLS 55CD1* **37**	2
1 Jul 95	**OVER THERE (I DON'T CARE)** *Ruffness XLS 61CD1* **20**	3
5 Oct 96	**FED UP** *Tommy Boy TBCD 7744* **68**	1

HOUSE OF VIRGINISM
Sweden, male vocal / instrumental group   **6 wks**

20 Nov 93	**I'LL BE THERE FOR YOU (DOYA DODODO DOYA)** *ffrr FCD 221* **29**	3
30 Jul 94	**REACHIN** *ffrr FCD 238* **35**	2
17 Feb 96	**EXCLUSIVE** *Logic 74321324102* [1] **67**	1

[1] Apollo presents House Of Virginism

HOUSE OF ZEKKARIYAS – See WOMACK and WOMACK

HOUSEMARTINS *UK, male vocal / instrumental group*   **59 wks**

8 Mar 86	**SHEEP** *Go! Discs GOD 9* **54**	3
5 Apr 86	**SHEEP (re-entry)** *Go! Discs GOD 9* **71**	1
7 Jun 86	● **HAPPY HOUR** *Go! Discs GOD 11* **3**	13
4 Oct 86	**THINK FOR A MINUTE** *Go! Discs GOD 13* **18**	8
6 Dec 86	★ **CARAVAN OF LOVE** *Go! Discs GOD 16* **1**	11
23 May 87	**FIVE GET OVER EXCITED** *Go! Discs GOD 18* **11**	6
5 Sep 87	**ME AND THE FARMER** *Go! Discs GOD 19* **15**	5
21 Nov 87	**BUILD** *Go! Discs GOD 21* **15**	8
23 Apr 88	**THERE IS ALWAYS SOMETHING THERE TO REMIND** **ME** *Go! Discs GOD 22* **35**	4

HOUSEMASTER BOYZ and the RUDE BOY OF HOUSE *US, male vocal / instrumental group*   **14 wks**

9 May 87	**HOUSE NATION** *Magnetic Dance MAGD 1* **48**	6
12 Sep 87	● **HOUSE NATION (re-entry)** *Magnetic Dance MAGD 1* **8**	8

Thelma HOUSTON *US, female vocalist*   **22 wks**

5 Feb 77	**DON'T LEAVE ME THIS WAY** *Motown TMG 1060* **13**	8
27 Jun 81	**IF YOU FEEL IT** *RCA 77* **48**	4
1 Dec 84	**YOU USED TO HOLD ME SO TIGHT** *MCA MCA 932* **49**	8
21 Jan 95	**DON'T LEAVE ME THIS WAY** *Dynamo DYND 001* **35**	2

Don't Leave Me This Way *in 95 is a re-recording.*

Whitney HOUSTON *US, female vocalist*   **221 wks**

16 Nov 85	★ **SAVING ALL MY LOVE FOR YOU** *Arista ARIST 640* **1**	16
25 Jan 86	● **HOW WILL I KNOW** *Arista ARIST 656* **5**	12
25 Jan 86	**HOLD ME** *Asylum EKR 32* [1] **44**	5
12 Apr 86	● **GREATEST LOVE OF ALL** *Arista ARIST 658* **8**	11
23 May 87	★ **I WANNA DANCE WITH SOMEBODY** **(WHO LOVES ME)** *Arista RIS 1* **1**	16
22 Aug 87	**DIDN'T WE ALMOST HAVE IT ALL** *Arista RIS 31* **14**	8
14 Nov 87	● **SO EMOTIONAL** *Arista RIS 43* **5**	11
12 Mar 88	**WHERE DO BROKEN HEARTS GO** *Arista 109793* **14**	8
28 May 88	● **LOVE WILL SAVE THE DAY** *Arista 111516* **10**	7
24 Sep 88	★ **ONE MOMENT IN TIME** *Arista 111613* **1**	12
9 Sep 89	**IT ISN'T, IT WASN'T, IT AIN'T NEVER GONNA BE** *Arista 112545* [2] **29**	5
20 Oct 90	● **I'M YOUR BABY TONIGHT** *Arista 113594* **5**	9
22 Dec 90	**ALL THE MAN THAT I NEED** *Arista 114000* **13**	10
29 Dec 90	**I'M YOUR BABY TONIGHT (re-entry)** *Arista 113594* **69**	1
6 Jul 91	**MY NAME IS NOT SUSAN** *Arista 114510* **29**	5
28 Sep 91	**I BELONG TO YOU** *Arista 114727* **54**	2
14 Nov 92	★ **I WILL ALWAYS LOVE YOU** *Arista 74321120657* **1**	23
20 Feb 93	● **I'M EVERY WOMAN** *Arista 74321131502* **4**	11
24 Apr 93	● **I HAVE NOTHING** *Arista 74321146142* **3**	10
31 Jul 93	**RUN TO YOU** *Arista 74321153332* **15**	6
6 Nov 93	**QUEEN OF THE NIGHT** *Arista 74321169302* **14**	5
18 Dec 93	**I WILL ALWAYS LOVE YOU (re-entry)** *Arista 74321120652* **25**	6
22 Jan 94	**SOMETHING IN COMMON** *MCA MCSTD 1957* [3] **16**	5
18 Nov 95	**EXHALE (SHOOP SHOOP)** *Arista 74321332472* **11**	9
24 Feb 96	**COUNT ON ME** *Arista 74321345842* [4] **12**	6
21 Dec 96	**STEP BY STEP** *Arista 74321449332* ....**17†**	2

[1] Teddy Pendergrass with Whitney Houston [2] Aretha Franklin and Whitney Houston [3] Bobby Brown and Whitney Houston [4] Whitney Houston and Ce Ce Winans

Adina HOWARD *US, female vocalist*   **10 wks**

4 Mar 95	**FREAK LIKE ME** *East West A 4473CD* **67**	1
6 May 95	**FREAK LIKE ME (re-entry)** *East West A 4473CD* **33**	3
23 Nov 96	● **WHAT'S LOVE GOT TO DO WITH IT** *Interscope IND 97008* [1] **2**	6

[1] Warren G featuring Adina Howard

Billy HOWARD *UK, male vocalist*   **12 wks**

13 Dec 75	● **KING OF THE COPS** *Penny Farthing PEN 892* **6**	12

Miki HOWARD *US, female vocalist*   **2 wks**

26 May 90	**UNTIL YOU COME BACK (THAT'S WHAT I'M** **GONNA DO)** *East West 7935* **67**	2

Nick HOWARD *Australia, male vocalist*   **1 wk**

21 Jan 95	**EVERYBODY NEEDS SOMEBODY** *Bell 74321220942* **64**	1

Robert HOWARD – See Kym MAZELLE

HOWLIN' WOLF *US, male vocalist*   **5 wks**

4 Jun 64	**SMOKESTACK LIGHTNIN'** *Pye International 7N 25244* **42**	5

H$_2$0 featuring BILLIE
US / Switzerland, male / female vocal / instrumental group   **3 wks**

14 Sep 96	**NOBODY'S BUSINESS** *AM:PM 5818832* **19**	3

H$_2$O *UK, male vocal / instrumental group*   **16 wks**

21 May 83	**DREAM TO SLEEP** *RCA 330* **17**	10
13 Aug 83	**JUST OUTSIDE OF HEAVEN** *RCA 349* **38**	6

Al HUDSON *US, male vocalist*   **22 wks**

9 Sep 78	**DANCE, GET DOWN (FEEL THE GROOVE) / HOW DO** **YOU DO** *ABC 4229* **57**	4
15 Sep 79	**YOU CAN DO IT** *MCA 511* [1] **15**	10
8 Dec 79	**MUSIC** *MCA 542* [2] **56**	6
29 Jun 85	**LET'S TALK** *MCA 972* [2] **64**	2

[1] Al Hudson and the Partners [2] One Way featuring Al Hudson

Lavine HUDSON *UK, female vocalist*   **3 wks**

21 May 88	INTERVENTION *Virgin VS 1067*	**57**	3

HUDSON-FORD *UK, male vocal / instrumental duo*   **20 wks**

18 Aug 73	● PICK UP THE PIECES *A & M AMS 7078*	**8**	9
16 Feb 74	BURN BABY BURN *A & M AMS 7096*	**15**	9
29 Jun 74	FLOATING IN THE WIND *A & M AMS 7116*	**35**	2

See also Monks.

HUE AND CRY *UK, male vocal / instrumental duo*   **59 wks**

13 Jun 87	● LABOUR OF LOVE *Circa YR 4*	**6**	16
19 Sep 87	STRENGTH TO STRENGTH *Circa YR 6*	**46**	5
30 Jan 88	I REFUSE *Circa YR 8*	**47**	3
22 Oct 88	ORDINARY ANGEL *Circa YR 18*	**42**	6
28 Jan 89	LOOKING FOR LINDA *Circa YR 24*	**15**	9
6 May 89	VIOLENTLY (EP) *Circa YR 29*	**21**	6
30 Sep 89	SWEET INVISIBILITY *Circa YR 37*	**55**	3
25 May 91	MY SALT HEART *Circa YR 64*	**47**	3
3 Aug 91	LONG TERM LOVERS OF PAIN (EP) *Circa YR 71*	**48**	3
11 Jul 92	PROFOUNDLY YOURS *Fidelity FIDEL 1*	**74**	1
13 Mar 93	LABOUR OF LOVE (re-mix) *Circa HUESCD 1*	**25**	4

Tracks on Violently (EP): Violently / The Man With The Child In His Eyes / Calamity John.
Tracks on Long Term Lovers Of Pain (EP): Long Term Lovers Of Pain / Heart Of Saturday Night / Remember And Gold / Stars Crash Down.

HUES CORPORATION *US, male / female vocal group*   **16 wks**

27 Jul 74	● ROCK THE BOAT *RCA APBO 0232*	**6**	10
19 Oct 74	ROCKIN' SOUL *RCA PB 10066*	**24**	6

HUFF and PUFF *UK, male instrumental / production duo*   **2 wks**

2 Nov 96	HELP ME MAKE IT *Skyway SKYWCD 4*	**31**	2

David HUGHES *UK, male vocalist*   **1 wk**

21 Sep 56	BY THE FOUNTAINS OF ROME *Philips PB 606*	**27**	1

HUGO and LUIGI *US, male vocal duo*   **2 wks**

24 Jul 59	LA PLUME DE MA TANTE *RCA 1127*	**29**	2

HUMAN LEAGUE
UK, male / female vocal / instrumental group   **155 wks**

3 May 80	HOLIDAY 80 (DOUBLE SINGLE) *Virgin SV 105*	**56**	5
21 Jun 80	EMPIRE STATE HUMAN *Virgin VS 351*	**62**	2
28 Feb 81	BOYS AND GIRLS *Virgin VS 395*	**48**	4
2 May 81	THE SOUND OF THE CROWD *Virgin VS 416*	**12**	10
8 Aug 81	● LOVE ACTION (I BELIEVE IN LOVE) *Virgin VS 435*	**3**	13
10 Oct 81	● OPEN YOUR HEART *Virgin VS 453*	**6**	9
5 Dec 81	★ DON'T YOU WANT ME *Virgin VS 466*	**1**	13
9 Jan 82	BEING BOILED *EMI FAST 4*	**6**	9
6 Feb 82	HOLIDAY 80 (DOUBLE SINGLE) (re-entry) *Virgin SV 105*	**46**	5
20 Nov 82	● MIRROR MAN *Virgin VS 522*	**2**	10
23 Apr 83	● (KEEP FEELING) FASCINATION *Virgin VS 569*	**2**	9
5 May 84	THE LEBANON *Virgin VS 672*	**11**	6
23 Jun 84	THE LEBANON (re-entry) *Virgin VS 672*	**75**	1
30 Jun 84	LIFE ON YOUR OWN *Virgin VS 688*	**16**	6
17 Nov 84	LOUISE *Virgin VS 723*	**13**	10
23 Aug 86	● HUMAN *Virgin VS 880*	**8**	8
22 Nov 86	I NEED YOUR LOVING *Virgin VS 900*	**72**	1

---

15 Oct 88	LOVE IS ALL THAT MATTERS *Virgin VS 1025*	**41**	5
18 Aug 90	HEART LIKE A WHEEL *Virgin VS 1262*	**29**	5
7 Jan 95	● TELL ME WHEN *East West YZ 882CD1*	**6**	9
18 Mar 95	ONE MAN IN MY HEART *East West YZ 904CD1*	**13**	8
17 Jun 95	FILLING UP WITH HEAVEN *East West YZ 944CD1*	**36**	2
28 Oct 95	DON'T YOU WANT ME (re-mix) *Virgin VSCDT 1557*	**16**	3
20 Jan 96	STAY WITH ME TONIGHT *East West EW 020CD*	**40**	2

Tracks on double single: Being Boiled / Marianne / Rock And Roll – Nightclubbing / Dancevision.

HUMAN RESOURCE
Holland, male instrumental / production group   **14 wks**

14 Sep 91	DOMINATOR *R&S RSUK 4*	**36**	7
21 Dec 91	THE COMPLETE DOMINATOR (re-mix) *R&S RSUK 4X*	**18**	7

HUMANOID *UK, male producer*   **13 wks**

26 Nov 88	STAKKER HUMANOID *Westside WSR 12*	**17**	8
22 Apr 89	SLAM *Westside WSR 14*	**54**	2
8 Aug 92	STAKKER HUMANOID (re-issue) *Jumpin' + Pumpin' TOT 27*	**40**	3

HUMBLE PIE *UK, male vocal / instrumental group*   **10 wks**

23 Aug 69	● NATURAL BORN BUGIE *Immediate IM 082*	**4**	10

Engelbert HUMPERDINCK *UK, male vocalist*   **235 wks**

26 Jan 67	★ RELEASE ME *Decca F 12541*	**1**	56
25 May 67	● THERE GOES MY EVERYTHING *Decca F 12610*	**2**	29
23 Aug 67	★ THE LAST WALTZ *Decca F 12655*	**1**	27
10 Jan 68	● AM I THAT EASY TO FORGET *Decca F 12722*	**3**	13
24 Apr 68	● A MAN WITHOUT LOVE *Decca F 12770*	**2**	15
25 Sep 68	● LES BICYCLETTES DE BELSIZE *Decca F 12834*	**5**	15
5 Feb 69	● THE WAY IT USED TO BE *Decca F 12879*	**3**	14
9 Aug 69	I'M A BETTER MAN (FOR HAVING LOVED YOU) *Decca F 12957*	**15**	13
15 Nov 69	● WINTER WORLD OF LOVE *Decca F 12980*	**7**	13
30 May 70	MY MARIE *Decca F 13032*	**31**	7
12 Sep 70	SWEETHEART *Decca F 13068*	**22**	6
31 Oct 70	SWEETHEART (re-entry) *Decca F 13068*	**50**	1
11 Sep 71	ANOTHER TIME ANOTHER PLACE *Decca F 13212*	**13**	12
4 Mar 72	TOO BEAUTIFUL TO LAST *Decca F 13281*	**14**	10
20 Oct 73	LOVE IS ALL *Decca F 13443*	**44**	3
17 Nov 73	LOVE IS ALL (re-entry) *Decca F 13443*	**45**	1

Peter HUNNIGALE – *See ARSENAL F.C. First Team Squad*

Geraldine HUNT *Canada, female vocalist*   **5 wks**

25 Oct 80	CAN'T FAKE THE FEELING *Champagne FIZZ 501*	**44**	5

Lisa HUNT – *See LOVESTATION*

Marsha HUNT *US, female vocalist*   **3 wks**

21 May 69	WALK ON GILDED SPLINTERS *Track 604 030*	**46**	2
2 May 70	KEEP THE CUSTOMER SATISFIED *Track 604 037*	**41**	1

Tommy HUNT *US, male vocalist*   **17 wks**

11 Oct 75	CRACKIN' UP *Spark SRL 1132*	**39**	5
21 Aug 76	LOVING ON THE LOSING SIDE *Spark SRL 1146*	**28**	9
4 Dec 76	ONE FINE MORNING *Spark SRL 1148*	**44**	3

HUNTER – *See Ruby TURNER*

Ian HUNTER *UK, male vocalist* — **10 wks**

3 May 75	**ONCE BITTEN TWICE SHY** *CBS 3194*	**14**	10

Tab HUNTER *US, male vocalist* — **30 wks**

8 Feb 57	★ **YOUNG LOVE** *London HLD 8380*	**1**	18
12 Apr 57	● **99 WAYS** *London HLD 8410*	**5**	11
5 Jul 57	**99 WAYS (re-entry)** *London HLD 8410*	**29**	1

Steve 'Silk' HURLEY *US, male vocalist* — **9 wks**

10 Jan 87	★ **JACK YOUR BODY** *DJ International LON 117*	**1**	9

HURRICANES – See JOHNNY and the HURRICANES

Phil HURTT *US, male vocalist* — **5 wks**

11 Nov 78	**GIVING IT BACK** *Fantasy FTC 161*	**36**	5

HUSTLERS CONVENTION featuring Dave LAUDAT and Ondrea DUVERNEY
UK, male instrumental/production duo — **1 wks**

20 May 95	**DANCE TO THE MUSIC** *Stress CDSTR 53*	**71**	1

Willie HUTCH *US, male vocalist* — **8 wks**

4 Dec 82	**IN AND OUT** *Motown TMG 1285*	**51**	7
6 Jul 85	**KEEP ON JAMMIN'** *Motown ZB 40173*	**73**	1

June HUTTON and Axel STORDAHL with the BOYS NEXT DOOR
US, female vocalist and male orchestra with male vocal group — **7 wks**

7 Aug 53	● **SAY YOU'RE MINE AGAIN** *Capitol CL 13918*	**10**	3
4 Sep 53	● **SAY YOU'RE MINE AGAIN (re-entry)** *Capitol CL 13918*	**6**	4

HWA featuring SONIC THE HEDGEHOG
UK, male producer – Jeremy Healey — **6 wks**

5 Dec 92	**SUPERSONIC** *Internal Affairs KGB 008*	**33**	6

Brian HYLAND *US, male vocalist* — **72 wks**

7 Jul 60	● **ITSY BITSY TEENY WEENY YELLOW POLKA DOT BIKINI** *London HLR 9161*	**8**	13
20 Oct 60	**FOUR LITTLE HEELS** *London HLR 9203*	**29**	6
10 May 62	● **GINNY COME LATELY** *HMV POP 1013*	**5**	15
2 Aug 62	● **SEALED WITH A KISS** *HMV POP 1051*	**3**	15
8 Nov 62	**WARMED OVER KISSES** *HMV POP 1079*	**28**	6
27 Mar 71	**GYPSY WOMAN** *Uni UN 530*	**45**	1
10 Apr 71	**GYPSY WOMAN (re-entry)** *Uni UN 530*	**42**	5
28 Jun 75	● **SEALED WITH A KISS (re-issue)** *ABC 4059*	**7**	11

Sheila HYLTON *Jamaica, female vocalist* — **12 wks**

15 Sep 79	**BREAKFAST IN BED** *United Artists BP 304*	**57**	5
17 Jan 81	**THE BED'S TOO BIG WITHOUT YOU** *Island WIP 6671*	**35**	7

Phyllis HYMAN *US, female vocalist* — **9 wks**

16 Feb 80	**YOU KNOW HOW TO LOVE ME** *Arista ARIST 323*	**47**	6
12 Sep 81	**YOU SURE LOOK GOOD TO ME** *Arista ARIST 424*	**56**	3

Dick HYMAN TRIO
US, male instrumentalist, Dick Hyman, keyboards — **10 wks**

16 Mar 56	● **THEME FROM 'THE THREEPENNY OPERA'** *MGM 890*	**9**	10

Chrissie HYNDE – See PRETENDERS/Chrissie HYNDE

HYPER GO GO *UK, male instrumental/production duo* — **14 wks**

22 Aug 92	**HIGH** *Deconstruction 74321110497*	**30**	5
31 Jul 93	**NEVER LET GO** *Positiva CDTIV 3*	**45**	3
5 Feb 94	**RAISE** *Positiva CDTIV 9*	**36**	2
26 Nov 94	**IT'S ALRIGHT** *Positiva CDTIV 20*	**49**	1
6 Apr 96	**DO WATCHA DO** *Avex UK AVEXCD 24* [1]	**54**	1
12 Oct 96	**HIGH (re-mix)** *Distinctive DISNCD 24*	**32**	2

[1] Hyper Go Go and Adeva

HYPERLOGIC *UK, male instrumental/production duo* — **2 wks**

29 Jul 95	**ONLY ME** *Systematic SYSCD 15*	**35**	2

HYPERSTATE *UK, male/female vocal/instrumental duo* — **1 wk**

6 Feb 93	**TIME AFTER TIME** *M & G MAGCD 34*	**71**	1

HYPNOTIST *UK, male producer – Caspar Pound* — **5 wks**

28 Sep 91	**THE HOUSE IS MINE** *Rising High RSN 4*	**65**	2
21 Dec 91	**THE HARDCORE EP** *Rising High RSN 13*	**68**	3

Tracks on The Hardcore EP: Hardcore U Know The Score / The Ride / Night Of The Livin' E Heads / God Of The Universe.

HYSTERIC EGO *UK, male producer – Rob White* — **4 wks**

31 Aug 96	**WANT LOVE** *WEA WEA 070CD*	**28**	4

HYSTERICS *UK, male vocal/instrumental group* — **5 wks**

12 Dec 81	**JINGLE BELLS LAUGHING ALL THE WAY** *Record Delivery KA 5*	**44**	5

HYSTERIX *UK, male/female vocal/instrumental group* — **4 wks**

7 May 94	**MUST BE THE MUSIC** *Deconstruction 74321207362*	**40**	3
18 Feb 95	**EVERYTHING** *Deconstruction 74321236882*	**65**	1

Janis IAN *US, female vocalist* — **10 wks**

17 Nov 79	**FLY TOO HIGH** *CBS 7936*	**44**	7
28 Jun 80	**THE OTHER SIDE OF THE SUN** *CBS 8611*	**44**	3

ICE CUBE *US, male rapper* — **22 wks**

27 Mar 93	**IT WAS A GOOD DAY** *Fourth & Broadway BRCD 270*	**27**	4

7 Aug 93	**CHECK YO SELF**		
	Fourth & Broadway BRCD 283 [1]	....**36**	4
11 Sep 93	**WICKED** Fourth & Broadway BRCD 282	....**62**	1
18 Dec 93	**REALLY DOE** Fourth & Broadway BRCD 302	....**66**	1
26 Mar 94	**YOU KNOW HOW WE DO IT**		
	Fourth & Broadway BRCD 303	....**41**	3
27 Aug 94	**BOP GUN (ONE NATION)**		
	Fourth & Broadway BRCD 308 [2]	....**22**	3
24 Dec 94	**YOU KNOW HOW WE DO IT (re-entry)**		
	Fourth & Broadway BRCD 303	....**46**	2
11 Mar 95	**HAND OF THE DEAD BODY**		
	Virgin America VUSCD 88 [3]	....**41**	2
15 Apr 95	**NATURAL BORN KILLAZ** Death Row A 8197CD [4]	....**45**	2

[1] Ice Cube featuring Das EFX [2] Ice Cube featuring George Clinton
[3] Scarface featuring Ice Cube [4] Dr. Dre and Ice Cube

ICE MC UK, male rapper   5 wks

6 Aug 94	**THINK ABOUT THE WAY (BOM DIGI DIGI BOM...)**		
	WEA YZ 829CD	....**42**	2
8 Apr 95	**IT'S A RAINY DAY** Eternal YZ 902CD	....**73**	1
14 Sep 96	**BOM DIGI BOM (THINK ABOUT THE WAY)**		
	(re-issue) Eternal WEA 073CD	....**38**	2

ICE-T US, male rapper   28 wks

18 Mar 89	**HIGH ROLLERS** Sire W 7574	....**63**	2
17 Feb 90	**YOU PLAYED YOURSELF** Sire W 9994	....**64**	2
29 Sep 90	**SUPERFLY 1990** Capitol CL 586 [1]	....**48**	3
8 May 93	**I AIN'T NEW TA THIS** Rhyme Syndicate SYNDD 1	....**62**	2
18 Dec 93	**THAT'S HOW I'M LIVIN'**		
	Rhyme Syndicate SYNDD 2	....**21**	6
9 Apr 94	**GOTTA LOTTA LOVE** Rhyme Syndicate SYNDD 3	....**24**	4
10 Dec 94	**BORN TO RAISE HELL** Fox 74321230152 [2]	....**47**	2
1 Jun 96	**I MUST STAND** Rhyme Syndicate SYNDD 5	....**23**	3
7 Dec 96	**THE LANE** Rhyme Syndicate SYNDD 6	....**18†**	4

[1] Curtis Mayfield and Ice-T [2] Motorhead / Ice-T / Whitfield Crane

ICEHOUSE
New Zealand, male vocal / instrumental group   28 wks

5 Feb 83	**HEY LITTLE GIRL** Chrysalis CHS 2670	....**17**	10
23 Apr 83	**STREET CAFE** Chrysalis COOL 1	....**62**	4
3 May 86	**NO PROMISES** Chrysalis CHS 2978	....**72**	1
29 Aug 87	**CRAZY** Chrysalis CHS 3156	....**74**	1
13 Feb 88	**CRAZY (re-entry)** Chrysalis CHS 3156	....**38**	8
14 May 88	**ELECTRIC BLUE** Chrysalis CHS 3239	....**53**	4

ICICLE WORKS UK, male vocal / instrumental group   28 wks

24 Dec 83	**LOVE IS A WONDERFUL COLOUR**		
	Beggars Banquet BEG 99	....**15**	8
10 Mar 84	**BIRDS FLY (WHISPER TO A SCREAM) / IN THE**		
	CAULDRON OF LOVE Beggars Banquet BEG 108	....**53**	4
26 Jul 86	**UNDERSTANDING JANE** Beggars Banquet BEG 160	....**52**	3
4 Oct 86	**WHO DO YOU WANT FOR YOUR LOVE**		
	Beggars Banquet BEG 172	....**54**	4
14 Feb 87	**EVANGELINE** Beggars Banquet BEG 181	....**53**	4
30 Apr 88	**LITTLE GIRL LOST** Beggars Banquet BEG 215	....**59**	4
17 Mar 90	**MOTORCYCLE RIDER** Epic WORKS 100	....**73**	1

ICON UK, male / female vocal / instrumental duo   1 wk

15 Jun 96	**TAINTED LOVE** Eternal WEA 057CD	....**51**	1

IDEAL LIFE UK, male producer – Jon Da Silva   2 wks

6 Aug 94	**HOT** Cleveland City CLECD 13019	....**49**	2

IDES OF MARCH US, male vocal / instrumental group   9 wks

6 Jun 70	**VEHICLE** Warner Bros. WB 7378	....**31**	9

Eric IDLE featuring Richard WILSON
UK, male vocal duo   3 wks

17 Dec 94	**ONE FOOT IN THE GRAVE** Victa CDVICTA 1	....**50**	3

Billy IDOL UK, male vocalist   106 wks

11 Sep 82	**HOT IN THE CITY** Chrysalis CHS 2625	....**58**	4
24 Mar 84	**REBEL YELL** Chrysalis IDOL 2	....**62**	2
30 Jun 84	**EYES WITHOUT A FACE** Chrysalis IDOL 3	....**18**	11
29 Sep 84	**FLESH FOR FANTASY** Chrysalis IDOL 4	....**54**	3
13 Jul 85	● **WHITE WEDDING** Chrysalis IDOL 5	....**6**	15
14 Sep 85	● **REBEL YELL (re-issue)** Chrysalis IDOL 6	....**6**	12
4 Oct 86	**TO BE A LOVER** Chrysalis IDOL 8	....**22**	8
7 Mar 87	**DON'T NEED A GUN** Chrysalis IDOL 9	....**26**	5
13 Jun 87	**SWEET SIXTEEN** Chrysalis IDOL 10	....**17**	9
3 Oct 87	● **MONY MONY** Chrysalis IDOL 11	....**7**	10
16 Jan 88	**HOT IN THE CITY (re-mix)** Chrysalis IDOL 12	....**13**	9
13 Aug 88	**CATCH MY FALL** Chrysalis IDOL 13	....**63**	3
28 Apr 90	**CRADLE OF LOVE** Chrysalis IDOL 14	....**34**	4
11 Aug 90	**L.A. WOMAN** Chrysalis IDOL 15	....**70**	2
22 Dec 90	**PRODIGAL BLUES** Chrysalis IDOL 16	....**47**	4
26 Jun 93	**SHOCK TO THE SYSTEM** Chrysalis CDCHS 3994	....**30**	3
10 Sep 94	**SPEED** Fox 74321223472	....**47**	2

Frank IFIELD UK, male vocalist   162 wks

19 Feb 60	**LUCKY DEVIL** Columbia DB 4399	....**22**	5
7 Apr 60	**LUCKY DEVIL (re-entry)** Columbia DB 4399	....**33**	2
29 Sep 60	**GOTTA GET A DATE** Columbia DB 4496	....**49**	1
5 Jul 62	★ **I REMEMBER YOU** Columbia DB 4856	....**1**	28
25 Oct 62	★ **LOVESICK BLUES** Columbia DB 4913	....**1**	17
24 Jan 63	★ **WAYWARD WIND** Columbia DB 4960	....**1**	13
11 Apr 63	● **NOBODY'S DARLIN' BUT MINE** Columbia DB 7007	....**4**	16
27 Jun 63	★ **CONFESSIN'** Columbia DB 7062	....**1**	16
17 Oct 63	**MULE TRAIN** Columbia DB 7131	....**22**	6
9 Jan 64	● **DON'T BLAME ME** Columbia DB 7184	....**8**	13
23 Apr 64	**ANGRY AT THE BIG OAK TREE** Columbia DB 7263	....**25**	8
23 Jul 64	**I SHOULD CARE** Columbia DB 7319	....**33**	3
1 Oct 64	**SUMMER IS OVER** Columbia DB 7355	....**25**	6
19 Aug 65	**PARADISE** Columbia DB 7655	....**26**	9
23 Jun 66	**NO ONE WILL EVER KNOW** Columbia DB 7940	....**25**	4
8 Dec 66	**CALL HER YOUR SWEETHEART** Columbia DB 8078	....**24**	11
7 Dec 91	**THE YODELLING SONG** EMI 7YODEL 1 [1]	....**40**	4

[1] Frank Ifield featuring the Backroom Boys

Julio IGLESIAS Spain, male vocalist   75 wks

24 Oct 81	★ **BEGIN THE BEGUINE (VOLVER A EMPEZAR)** CBS A 1612	..**1**	14
6 Mar 82	● **QUIEREME MUCHO (YOURS)** CBS A 1939	....**3**	9
9 Oct 82	**AMOR** CBS A 2801	....**32**	7
9 Apr 83	**HEY!** CBS JULIO 1	....**31**	7
7 Apr 84	**TO ALL THE GIRLS I'VE LOVED BEFORE** CBS A 4252 [1]	....**17**	10
7 Jul 84	**ALL OF YOU** CBS A 4522 [2]	....**43**	8
6 Aug 88	● **MY LOVE** CBS JULIO 2 [3]	....**5**	11
4 Jun 94	**CRAZY** Columbia 6603695	....**43**	3
27 Aug 94	**CRAZY (re-entry)** Columbia 6603695	....**50**	2
26 Nov 94	**FRAGILE** Columbia 6610192	....**53**	2
31 Dec 94	**FRAGILE (re-entry)** Columbia 6610192	....**66**	2

[1] Julio Iglesias and Willie Nelson [2] Julio Iglesias and Diana Ross
[3] Julio Iglesias featuring Stevie Wonder

IGNORANTS UK, male vocal duo   3 wks

25 Dec 93	**PHAT GIRLS** Spaghetti CIOCD 8	....**59**	3

I-LEVEL *UK, male vocal / instrumental group*   **9 wks**

16 Apr 83	**MINEFIELD** *Virgin VS 563*	**52**	6
18 Jun 83	**TEACHER** *Virgin VS 595*	**56**	3

ILLEGAL MOTION featuring Simone CHAPMAN *UK, male / female vocal / instrumental duo*   **1 wk**

9 Oct 93	**SATURDAY LOVE** *Arista 74321163032*	**67**	1

IMAGINATION *UK, male vocal / instrumental group*   **105 wks**

16 May 81	● **BODY TALK** *R & B RBS 201*	**4**	18
5 Sep 81	**IN AND OUT OF LOVE** *R & B RBS 202*	**16**	9
14 Nov 81	**FLASHBACK** *R & B RBS 206*	**16**	13
6 Mar 82	● **JUST AN ILLUSION** *R & B RBS 208*	**2**	11
26 Jun 82	● **MUSIC AND LIGHTS** *R & B RBS 210*	**5**	9
25 Sep 82	**IN THE HEAT OF THE NIGHT** *R & B RBS 211*	**22**	8
11 Dec 82	**CHANGES** *R & B RBS 213*	**31**	8
4 Jun 83	**LOOKING AT MIDNIGHT** *R & B RBS 214*	**29**	7
5 Nov 83	**NEW DIMENSIONS** *R & B RBS 216*	**56**	3
26 May 84	**STATE OF LOVE** *R & B RBS 218*	**67**	2
24 Nov 84	**THANK YOU MY LOVE** *R & B RBS 219*	**22**	15
16 Jan 88	**INSTINCTUAL** *RCA PB 41697*	**62**	2

IMMACULATE FOOLS *UK, male vocal / instrumental group*   **4 wks**

26 Jan 85	**IMMACULATE FOOLS** *A & M AM 227*	**51**	4

IMMATURE – See SMOOTH

IMPALAS *US, male vocal group*   **1 wk**

21 Aug 59	**SORRY (I RAN ALL THE WAY HOME)** *MGM 1015*	**28**	1

IMPEDANCE *UK, male producer – Daniel Haydon*   **4 wks**

11 Nov 89	**TAINTED LOVE** *Jumpin' & Pumpin' TOT 4*	**54**	4

IMPERIAL DRAG *UK, male vocal / instrumental group*   **1 wk**

12 Oct 96	**BOY OR A GIRL** *Columbia 6632992*	**54**	1

IMPERIAL TEEN *US, male / female vocal / instrumental group*   **1 wk**

7 Sep 96	**YOU'RE ONE** *Slash LASCD 57*	**69**	1

IMPERIALS – See LITTLE ANTHONY and the IMPERIALS

IMPOSTER – See Elvis COSTELLO

IMPRESSIONS *US, male vocal group*   **10 wks**

22 Nov 75	**FIRST IMPRESSIONS** *Curtom K 16638*	**16**	10

IN CROWD *UK, male vocal / instrumental group*   **1 wk**

20 May 65	**THAT'S HOW STRONG MY LOVE IS** *Parlophone R 5276*	**48**	1

IN TUA NUA *Ireland, male / female vocal / instrumental group*   **2 wks**

14 May 88	**ALL I WANTED** *Virgin VS 1072*	**69**	2

INAURA *UK, male vocal / instrumental group*   **1 wk**

18 May 96	**COMA AROMA** *EMI CDEM 421*	**57**	1

INCANTATION *UK, male instrumental group*   **12 wks**

4 Dec 82	**CACHARPAYA (ANDES PUMPSA DAESI)** *Beggars Banquet BEG 84*	**12**	12

INCOGNITO *UK, male / female vocal / instrumental group*   **37 wks**

15 Nov 80	**PARISIENNE GIRL** *Ensign ENY 44*	**73**	2
29 Jun 91	● **ALWAYS THERE** *Talkin Loud TLK 10* [1]	**6**	9
14 Sep 91	**CRAZY FOR YOU** *Talkin Loud TLK 14* [2]	**59**	2
6 Jun 92	**DON'T YOU WORRY 'BOUT A THING** *Talkin Loud TLK 21*	**19**	6
15 Aug 92	**CHANGE** *Talkin Loud TLK 26*	**52**	2
21 Aug 93	**STILL A FRIEND OF MINE** *Talkin Loud TLKCD 42*	**47**	2
20 Nov 93	**GIVIN' IT UP** *Talkin Loud TLKCD 44*	**43**	2
12 Mar 94	**PIECES OF A DREAM** *Talkin Loud TLKCD 46*	**35**	2
27 May 95	**EVERYDAY** *Talkin Loud TLKCD 55*	**23**	3
5 Aug 95	**I HEAR YOUR NAME** *Talkin Loud TLKCD 56*	**42**	3
11 May 96	**JUMP TO MY LOVE / ALWAYS THERE** *Talkin Loud TLCD 7*	**29**	3
26 Oct 96	**OUT OF THE STORM** *Talkin Loud TLCD 14*	**57**	1

[1] Incognito featuring Jocelyn Brown [2] Incognito featuring Chyna

Always There *in 96 is a re-recording.*

INDEEP *US, male / female vocal duo*   **11 wks**

22 Jan 83	**LAST NIGHT A DJ SAVED MY LIFE** *Sound Of New York SNY 1*	**13**	9
14 May 83	**WHEN BOYS TALK** *Sound Of New York SNY 3*	**67**	2

INDIA *US, female vocalist*   **6 wks**

26 Feb 94	**LOVE AND HAPPINESS (YEMAYA Y OCHUN)** *Cooltempo CDCOOL 287* [1]	**50**	2
5 Aug 95	**I CAN'T GET NO SLEEP** *A & M 5811412* [2]	**44**	2
16 Mar 96	**OYE COMO VA** *Media MCSTD 40013* [3]	**36**	2

[1] River Ocean featuring India [2] Masters At Work present India
[3] Tito Puente Jr and the Latin Rhythm featuring Tito Puente, India and Cali Aleman

INDIAN VIBES *UK, male vocal / instrumental group*   **1 wk**

24 Sep 94	**MATHAR** *Virgin International DINSD 136*	**68**	1

Los INDIOS TABAJARAS *Brazil, male instrumental duo – guitars*   **17 wks**

31 Oct 63	● **MARIA ELENA** *RCA 1365*	**5**	17

INFINITI – See GRAND PUBA

INGRAM *US, male vocal / instrumental group*   **2 wks**

11 Jun 83	**SMOOTHIN' GROOVIN'** *Streetwave WAVE 3*	**56**	2

James INGRAM *US, male vocalist*   **42 wks**

12 Feb 83	**BABY COME TO ME** *Qwest K 15005* [1]	**11**	10
18 Feb 84	**YAH MO B THERE** *Qwest W 9394* [2]	**44**	5
7 Apr 84	**YAH MO B THERE (re-entry)** *Qwest W 9394* [2]	**69**	3
12 Jan 85	**YAH MO B THERE (re-mix)** *Qwest W 9394* [2]	**12**	8
11 Jul 87	● **SOMEWHERE OUT THERE** *MCA MCA 1132* [3]	**8**	13

| 31 Mar 90 | **SECRET GARDEN** Qwest W 9992 [4] ....**67** | 1 |
| 16 Apr 94 | **THE DAY I FALL IN LOVE** Columbia 6600282 [5] ....**64** | 2 |

[1] Patti Austin and James Ingram [2] James Ingram with Michael McDonald [3] Linda Ronstadt and James Ingram [4] Quincy Jones featuring Al B. Sure!, James Ingram, El DeBarge and Barry White [5] Dolly Parton and James Ingram

INK SPOTS *US, male vocal group*   **4 wks**

| 29 Apr 55 | ● **MELODY OF LOVE** Parlophone R 3977 ....**10** | 4 |

John INMAN *UK, male vocalist*   **6 wks**

| 25 Oct 75 | **ARE YOU BEING SERVED SIR** DJM DJS 602 ....**39** | 6 |

INMATES *UK, male vocal / instrumental group*   **9 wks**

| 8 Dec 79 | **THE WALK** Radar ADA 47 ....**36** | 9 |

INNER CIRCLE
Jamaica, male vocal / instrumental group   **35 wks**

24 Feb 79	**EVERYTHING IS GREAT** Island WIP 6472 ....**37**	8
12 May 79	**STOP BREAKING MY HEART** Island WIP 6488 ......**50**	3
31 Oct 92	**SWEAT (A LA LA LA LA LONG)** Magnet 9031776802 ...**43**	5
1 May 93	● **SWEAT (A LA LA LA LA LONG) (re-entry)** Magnet 9031776802 ....**3**	14
31 Jul 93	**BAD BOYS** Magnet MAG 1017CD **52**	3
10 Sep 94	**GAMES PEOPLE PLAY** Magnet MAG 1026CD **67**	2

INNER CITY *US, male / female vocal / instrumental duo*   **74 wks**

3 Sep 88	● **BIG FUN** 10 TEN 240 [1] **8**	14
10 Dec 88	● **GOOD LIFE** 10 TEN 249 ....**4**	12
22 Apr 89	**AIN'T NOBODY BETTER** 10 TEN 252 ....**10**	7
29 Jul 89	**DO YOU LOVE WHAT YOU FEEL** 10 TEN 273 ....**16**	7
18 Nov 89	**WATCHA GONNA DO WITH MY LOVIN'** 10 TEN 290 ....**12**	9
13 Oct 90	**THAT MAN (HE'S ALL MINE)** 10 TEN 334 ....**42**	4
23 Feb 91	**TILL WE MEET AGAIN** Ten TEN 337 ....**47**	2
7 Dec 91	**LET IT REIGN** Ten TEN 392 ....**51**	2
4 Apr 92	**HALLELUJAH '92** Ten TEN 398 ....**22**	4
13 Jun 92	**PENNIES FROM HEAVEN** Ten TEN 405 ....**24**	4
12 Sep 92	**PRAISE** Ten TENX 408 ....**59**	2
27 Feb 93	**TILL WE MEET AGAIN (re-mix)** Ten TENCD 414 ....**55**	1
5 Feb 94	**DO YA** Six6 SIXCD 107 ....**44**	2
9 Jul 94	**SHARE MY LIFE** Six6 SIXCD 114 ....**62**	1
10 Feb 96	**YOUR LOVE** Six6 SIXCD 127 ....**28**	2
5 Oct 96	**DO ME RIGHT** Six6 SIXXCD 2 ....**47**	1

[1] Inner City featuring Kevin Saunderson

INNERZONE ORCHESTRA
US, male producer – Carl Craig   **1 wk**

| 28 Sep 96 | **BUG IN THE BASSBIN** Mo Wax MW 049CD ....**68** | 1 |

INNOCENCE
UK, male / female vocal / instrumental group   **33 wks**

3 Mar 90	**NATURAL THING** Cooltempo COOL 201 ....**16**	7
21 Jul 90	**SILENT VOICE** Cooltempo COOL 212 ....**37**	5
13 Oct 90	**LET'S PUSH IT** Cooltempo COOL 220 ....**25**	6
8 Dec 90	**A MATTER OF FACT** Cooltempo COOL 223 ....**37**	7
30 Mar 91	**REMEMBER THE DAY** Cooltempo COOL 226 ....**56**	2
20 Jun 92	**I'LL BE THERE** Cooltempo COOL 255 ....**26**	3
3 Oct 92	**ONE LOVE IN MY LIFETIME** Cooltempo COOL 263 ...**40**	2
21 Nov 92	**BUILD** Cooltempo COOL 267 ....**72**	1

INSPIRAL CARPETS
UK, male vocal / instrumental group   **50 wks**

18 Nov 89	**MOVE** Cow DUNG 6 ....**49**	2
17 Mar 90	**THIS IS HOW IT FEELS** Cow DUNG 7 ....**14**	8
30 Jun 90	**SHE COMES IN THE FALL** Cow DUNG 10 ....**27**	6
17 Nov 90	**ISLAND HEAD EP** Cow DUNG 11 ....**21**	4
30 Mar 91	**CARAVAN** Cow DUNG 13 ....**30**	5
22 Jun 91	**PLEASE BE CRUEL** Cow DUNG 15 ....**50**	2
29 Feb 92	**DRAGGING ME DOWN** Cow DUNG 16 ....**12**	5
30 May 92	**TWO WORLDS COLLIDE** Cow DUNG 17 ....**32**	2
19 Sep 92	**GENERATIONS** Cow DUNG 18T **28**	3
14 Nov 92	**BITCHES BREW** Cow DUNG 20T **36**	2
5 Jun 93	**HOW IT SHOULD BE** Cow DUNG 22CD **49**	1
22 Jan 94	**SATURN 5** Cow DUNG 23CD **20**	4
5 Mar 94	**I WANT YOU** Cow DUNG 24CD [1] **18**	3
7 May 94	**UNIFORM** Cow DUNG 26CD **51**	1
16 Sep 95	**JOE** Cow DUNG 27CD **37**	2

[1] Inspiral Carpets featuring Mark E. Smith

Tracks on Island Head EP: Biggest Mountain / Gold Top / Weakness / I'll Keep It In Mind.

INSPIRATIONAL CHOIR *US, male / female choir*   **11 wks**

| 22 Dec 84 | **ABIDE WITH ME** Epic A 4997 ....**44** | 5 |
| 14 Dec 85 | **ABIDE WITH ME (re-issue)** Portrait A 4997 ......**36** | 6 |

Label credits the Royal Choral Society.

INSTANT FUNK *US, male vocal / instrumental group*   **5 wks**

| 20 Jan 79 | **GOT MY MIND MADE UP** Salsoul SSOL 114 ....**46** | 5 |

INTASTELLA *UK, male / female vocal / instrumental group* **6 wks**

25 May 91	**DREAM SOME PARADISE** MCA MCS 1520 ....**69**	1
24 Aug 91	**PEOPLE** MCA MCS 1559 ....**74**	2
16 Nov 91	**CENTURY** MCA MCS 1585 ....**70**	2
23 Sep 95	**THE NIGHT** Planet 3 GXY 2005CD **60**	1

INTELLIGENT HOODLUM *US, male rap group*   **3 wks**

| 6 Oct 90 | **BACK TO REALITY** A & M AM 598 ....**55** | 3 |

INTERACTIVE
Germany, male instrumental / production group   **4 wks**

| 13 Apr 96 | **FOREVER YOUNG** Ffrreedom TABCD 235 ....**28** | 4 |

INTRUDERS *US, male vocal group*   **21 wks**

13 Apr 74	**I'LL ALWAYS LOVE MY MAMA** Philadelphia International PIR 2159 ....**32**	7
6 Jul 74	**(WIN PLACE OR SHOW) SHE'S A WINNER** Philadelphia International PIR 2212 ....**14**	9
22 Dec 84	**WHO DO YOU LOVE?** Streetwave KHAN 34 ....**65**	5

INVADERS OF THE HEART – See Jah WOBBLE'S INVADERS OF THE HEART

INVISIBLE GIRLS – See Pauline MURRAY and the INVISIBLE GIRLS

INXS *Australia, male vocal / instrumental group*   **116 wks**

19 Apr 86	**WHAT YOU NEED** Mercury INXS 5 ....**51**	6
28 Jun 86	**LISTEN LIKE THIEVES** Mercury INXS 6 ....**46**	7
30 Aug 86	**KISS THE DIRT (FALLING DOWN THE MOUNTAIN)** Mercury INXS 7 ....**54**	3

24 Oct 87	**NEED YOU TONIGHT** *Mercury INXS 8*	**58** 3
9 Jan 88	**NEW SENSATION** *Mercury INXS 9*	**25** 6
12 Mar 88	**DEVIL INSIDE** *Mercury INXS 10*	**47** 5
25 Jun 88	**NEVER TEAR US APART** *Mecury INXS 11*	**24** 7
12 Nov 88 ●	**NEED YOU TONIGHT (re-issue)** *Mercury INXS 12*	**2** 11
8 Apr 89	**MYSTIFY** *Mercury INXS 13*	**14** 7
15 Sep 90	**SUICIDE BLONDE** *Mercury INXS 14*	**11** 6
8 Dec 90	**DISAPPEAR** *Mercury INXS 15*	**21** 8
26 Jan 91	**GOOD TIMES** *Atlantic A 7751* [1]	**18** 8
30 Mar 91	**BY MY SIDE** *Mercury INXS 16*	**42** 4
13 Jul 91	**BITTER TEARS** *Mercury INXS 17*	**30** 3
2 Nov 91	**SHINING STAR (EP)** *Mercury INXS 18*	**27** 3
18 Jul 92	**HEAVEN SENT** *Mercury INXS 19*	**31** 3
5 Sep 92	**BABY DON'T CRY** *Mercury INXS 20*	**20** 5
14 Nov 92	**TASTE IT** *Mercury INXS 23*	**21** 4
13 Feb 93	**BEAUTIFUL GIRL** *Mercury INXCD 24*	**23** 5
23 Oct 93	**THE GIFT** *Mercury INXCD 25*	**11** 4
11 Dec 93	**PLEASE (YOU GOT THAT...)** *Mercury INXCD 26*	**50** 3
22 Oct 94	**THE STRANGEST PARTY (THESE ARE THE TIMES)** *Mercury INXCD 27*	**15** 5

[1] Jimmy Barnes and INXS

Tracks on Shining Star (EP): *Shining Star / Send A Message (Live) / Faith In Each Other (Live) / Bitter Tears (Live)*. Although uncredited Please (You Got That...) *is a duet with Ray Charles.*

Sweetie IRIE – *See ASWAD; SCRITTI POLITTI*

Tippa IRIE *UK, male vocalist*   **14 wks**

22 Mar 86	**HELLO DARLING** *Greensleeves/UK Bubb TIPPA 4*	**22** 7
19 Jul 86	**HEARTBEAT** *Greensleeves/UK Bubb TIPPA 5*	**59** 3
15 May 93	**SHOUTING FOR THE GUNNERS** *London LONCD 342* [1]	**34** 3
8 Jul 95	**STAYING ALIVE 95** *Telstar CDSTAS 2776* [2]	**48** 1

[1] Arsenal FA Cup Squad featuring Tippa Irie and Peter Hunnigale
[2] Fever featuring Tippa Irie

IRON MAIDEN *UK, male vocal / instrumental group*   **144 wks**

23 Feb 80	**RUNNING FREE** *EMI 5032*	**34** 5
7 Jun 80	**SANCTUARY** *EMI 5065*	**29** 5
8 Nov 80	**WOMEN IN UNIFORM** *EMI 5105*	**35** 4
14 Mar 81	**TWILIGHT ZONE / WRATH CHILD** *EMI 5145*	**31** 5
27 Jun 81	**PURGATORY** *EMI 5184*	**52** 3
26 Sep 81	**MAIDEN JAPAN** *EMI 5219*	**43** 4
20 Feb 82 ●	**RUN TO THE HILLS** *EMI 5263*	**7** 10
15 May 82	**THE NUMBER OF THE BEAST** *EMI 5287*	**18** 8
23 Apr 83	**FLIGHT OF ICARUS** *EMI 5378*	**11** 6
2 Jul 83	**THE TROOPER** *EMI 5397*	**12** 7
18 Aug 84	**2 MINUTES TO MIDNIGHT** *EMI 5849*	**11** 6
3 Nov 84	**ACES HIGH** *EMI 5502*	**20** 5
5 Oct 85	**RUNNING FREE (LIVE)** *EMI EMI 5532*	**19** 5
14 Dec 85	**RUN TO THE HILLS (LIVE)** *EMI 5542*	**26** 6
6 Sep 86	**WASTED YEARS** *EMI EMI 5583*	**18** 4
22 Nov 86	**STRANGER IN A STRANGE LAND** *EMI EMI 5589*	**22** 4
27 Dec 86	**STRANGER IN A STRANGE LAND (re-entry)** *EMI EMI 5589*	**71** 2
26 Mar 88 ●	**CAN I PLAY WITH MADNESS** *EMI EM 49*	**3** 6
13 Aug 88 ●	**THE EVIL THAT MEN DO** *EMI EM 64*	**5** 6
19 Nov 88 ●	**THE CLAIRVOYANT** *EMI EM 79*	**6** 8
18 Nov 89 ●	**INFINITE DREAMS** *EMI EM 117*	**6** 5
30 Dec 89	**INFINITE DREAMS (re-entry)** *EMI EM 117*	**74** 1
22 Sep 90 ●	**HOLY SMOKE** *EMI EM 153*	**3** 4
5 Jan 91 ★	**BRING YOUR DAUGHTER... TO THE SLAUGHTER** *EMI EMPD 171*	**1** 5
25 Apr 92 ●	**BE QUICK OR BE DEAD** *EMI EM 229*	**2** 4
11 Jul 92	**FROM HERE TO ETERNITY** *EMI EMS 240*	**21** 4
13 Mar 93 ●	**FEAR OF THE DARK (LIVE)** *EMI CDEMS 263*	**8** 3
16 Oct 93 ●	**HALLOWED BE THY NAME (LIVE)** *EMI CDEM 288*	**9** 3
7 Oct 95 ●	**MAN ON THE EDGE** *EMI CDEMS 398*	**10** 3
21 Sep 96	**VIRUS** *EMI CDEM 443*	**16** 3

IRONHORSE *Canada, male vocal / instrumental group*   **3 wks**

5 May 79	**SWEET LUI-LOUISE** *Scotti Brothers K 11271*	**60** 3

Big Dee IRWIN *US, male vocalist*   **17 wks**

21 Nov 63 ●	**SWINGING ON A STAR** *Colpix PX 11010*	**7** 17

This hit was in fact a vocal duet by Big Dee Irwin and Little Eva, though she was not credited.

Chris ISAAK *US, male vocalist*   **21 wks**

24 Nov 90 ●	**WICKED GAME** *London LON 279*	**10** 10
2 Feb 91	**BLUE HOTEL** *Reprise W 0005*	**17** 7
3 Apr 93	**CAN'T DO A THING (TO STOP ME)** *Reprise W 0161CD*	**36** 3
10 Jul 93	**SAN FRANCISCO DAYS** *Reprise W 0182CD*	**62** 1

ISHA-D *UK, male / female vocal / instrumental duo*   **3 wks**

22 Jul 95	**STAY (TONIGHT)** *Cleveland City Blues CCBCD 15005*	**28** 3

Ronald ISLEY – *See Rod STEWART; R. KELLY*

ISLEY BROTHERS *US, male vocal / instrumental group*   **108 wks**

25 Jul 63	**TWIST AND SHOUT** *Stateside SS 112*	**42** 1
28 Apr 66	**THIS OLD HEART OF MINE (IS WEAK FOR YOU)** *Tamla Motown TMG 555*	**47** 1
1 Sep 66	**I GUESS I'LL ALWAYS LOVE YOU** *Tamla Motown TMG 572*	**45** 2
23 Oct 68 ●	**THIS OLD HEART OF MINE (IS WEAK FOR YOU) (re-entry)** *Tamla Motown TMG 555*	**3** 16
15 Jan 69	**I GUESS I'LL ALWAYS LOVE YOU (re-issue)** *Tamla Motown TMG 683*	**11** 9
16 Apr 69 ●	**BEHIND A PAINTED SMILE** *Tamla Motown TMG 693*	**5** 12
25 Jun 69	**IT'S YOUR THING** *Major Minor MM 621*	**30** 5
30 Aug 69	**PUT YOURSELF IN MY PLACE** *Tamla Motown TMG 708*	**13** 11
22 Sep 73	**THAT LADY** *Epic EPC 1704*	**14** 9
19 Jan 74	**HIGHWAY OF MY LIFE** *Epic EPC 1980*	**25** 8
25 May 74	**SUMMER BREEZE** *Epic EPC 2244*	**16** 8
10 Jul 76 ●	**HARVEST FOR THE WORLD** *Epic EPC 4369*	**10** 8
13 May 78	**TAKE ME TO THE NEXT PHASE** *Epic EPC 6292*	**50** 4
3 Nov 79	**IT'S A DISCO NIGHT (ROCK DON'T STOP)** *Epic EPC 7911*	**14** 11
16 Jul 83	**BETWEEN THE SHEETS** *Epic A 3513*	**52** 3

ISLEY JASPER ISLEY
US, male vocal / instrumental group   **5 wks**

23 Nov 85	**CARAVAN OF LOVE** *Epic A 6612*	**52** 5

ISOTONIK *UK, male producer – Chris Paul*   **9 wks**

11 Jan 92	**DIFFERENT STROKES** *Ffrreedom TAB 101*	**12** 5
2 May 92	**EVERYWHERE I GO / LET'S GET DOWN** *Ffrreedom TAB 108*	**25** 4

Let's Get Down only listed from 9 May 92.

IT BITES *UK, male vocal / instrumental group*   **21 wks**

12 Jul 86 ●	**CALLING ALL THE HEROES** *Virgin VS 872*	**6** 12
18 Oct 86	**WHOLE NEW WORLD** *Virgin VS 896*	**54** 3
23 May 87	**THE OLD MAN AND THE ANGEL** *Virgin VS 941*	**72** 1
13 May 89	**STILL TOO YOUNG TO REMEMBER** *Virgin VS 1184*	**66** 3
24 Feb 90	**STILL TOO YOUNG TO REMEMBER (re-issue)** *Virgin VS 1238*	**60** 2

Jamiroquai

The Top 10 success of 'Stillness In Time' was due in no small part to the inclusion of the David Morales mix of 'Space Cowboy' as the B-side.

Jam

In 1983 the Jam enjoyed 14 chart entries including nine that entered in the week ending 22 January, a record that was to be equalled by Oasis in November 1996.

INXS

Despite their massive stadium success INXS have only enjoyed one Top 10 hit, the re-issue of 'Need You Tonight' in 1988.

IT'S IMMATERIAL
UK, male vocal / instrumental group   **10 wks**

| 12 Apr 86 | DRIVING AWAY FROM HOME (JIM'S TUNE) *Siren SIREN 15* | **18** | 7 |
| 2 Aug 86 | ED'S FUNKY DINER (FRIDAY NIGHT, SATURDAY MORNING) *Siren SIREN 24* | **65** | 3 |

ITTY BITTY BOOZY WOOZY
Holland, male instrumental / production duo   **2 wks**

| 25 Nov 95 | TEMPO FIESTA (PARTY TIME) *Systematic SYSCD 23* | **34** | 2 |

Duo also known as Klubbheads. See also Klubbheads.

Burl IVES *US, male vocalist*   **25 wks**

| 25 Jan 62 | ● A LITTLE BITTY TEAR *Brunswick 05863* | **9** | 15 |
| 17 May 62 | FUNNY WAY OF LAUGHIN' *Brunswick 05868* | **29** | 10 |

IVY LEAGUE *UK, male vocal group*   **31 wks**

4 Feb 65	● FUNNY HOW LOVE CAN BE *Piccadilly 7N 35222*	**8**	9
6 May 65	THAT'S WHY I'M CRYING *Piccadilly 7N 35228*	**22**	8
24 Jun 65	● TOSSING AND TURNING *Piccadilly 7N 35251*	**3**	13
14 Jul 66	WILLOW TREE *Piccadilly 7N 35326*	**50**	1

IZIT *UK, male / female vocal / instrumental group*   **3 wks**

| 2 Dec 89 | STORIES *ffrr F 122* | **52** | 3 |

J PAC *UK, male vocal / instrumental duo*   **2 wks**

| 22 Jul 95 | ROCK 'N' ROLL (DOLE) *East West YZ 953CD* | **51** | 2 |

JACK 'N' CHILL *UK, male instrumental group*   **21 wks**

6 Jun 87	THE JACK THAT HOUSE BUILT *Oval TEN 174*	**48**	5
9 Jan 88	● THE JACK THAT HOUSE BUILT (re-entry) *Oval TEN 174*	**6**	11
9 Jul 88	BEATIN' THE HEAT *10 TEN 234*	**42**	5

Terry JACKS *Canada, male vocalist*   **21 wks**

| 23 Mar 74 | ★ SEASONS IN THE SUN *Bell 1344* | **1** | 12 |
| 29 Jun 74 | ● IF YOU GO AWAY *Bell 1362* | **8** | 9 |

Chad JACKSON *UK, male producer*   **10 wks**

| 2 Jun 90 | ● HEAR THE DRUMMER (GET WICKED) *Big Wave BWR 36* | **3** | 10 |

Dee D JACKSON *UK, female vocalist*   **14 wks**

| 22 Apr 78 | ● AUTOMATIC LOVER *Mercury 6007 171* | **4** | 9 |
| 2 Sep 78 | METEOR MAN *Mercury 6007 182* | **48** | 5 |

Freddie JACKSON *US, male vocalist*   **31 wks**

23 Nov 85	YOU ARE MY LADY *Capitol CL 379*	**49**	4
22 Feb 86	ROCK ME TONIGHT (FOR OLD TIME'S SAKE) *Capitol CL 358*	**18**	9
11 Oct 86	TASTY LOVE *Capitol CL 428*	**73**	1
7 Feb 87	HAVE YOU EVER LOVED SOMEBODY *Capitol CL 437*	**33**	6
9 Jul 88	NICE 'N' SLOW *Capitol CL 502*	**56**	2
15 Oct 88	CRAZY (FOR ME) *Capitol CL 510*	**41**	3
5 Sep 92	ME AND MRS JONES *Capitol CL 668*	**32**	5
15 Jan 94	MAKE LOVE EASY *RCA 74321179162*	**70**	1

Janet JACKSON *US, female vocalist*   **190 wks**

22 Mar 86	● WHAT HAVE YOU DONE FOR ME LATELY *A & M AM 308*	**3**	14
31 May 86	NASTY *A & M AM 316*	**19**	9
9 Aug 86	● WHEN I THINK OF YOU *A & M AM 337*	**10**	10
1 Nov 86	CONTROL *A & M AM 359*	**42**	5
21 Mar 87	● LET'S WAIT AWHILE *Breakout USA 601*	**3**	10
13 Jun 87	PLEASURE PRINCIPLE *Breakout USA 604*	**24**	5
14 Nov 87	FUNNY HOW TIME FLIES (WHEN YOU'RE HAVING FUN) *Breakout USA 613*	**59**	2
2 Sep 89	MISS YOU MUCH *Breakout USA 663*	**22**	7
4 Nov 89	RHYTHM NATION *Breakout USA 673*	**23**	5
27 Jan 90	COME BACK TO ME *Breakout USA 681*	**20**	7
31 Mar 90	ESCAPADE *Breakout USA 684*	**17**	7
7 Jul 90	ALRIGHT *A & M USA 693*	**20**	5
8 Sep 90	BLACK CAT *A & M EM 587*	**15**	6
27 Oct 90	LOVE WILL NEVER DO (WITHOUT YOU) *A & M EM 700*	**34**	4
15 Aug 92	● THE BEST THINGS IN LIFE ARE FREE *Perspective PERSS 7400* [1]	**2**	13
8 May 93	● THAT'S THE WAY LOVE GOES *Virgin VSCDG 1460*	**2**	10
31 Jul 93	IF *Virgin VSCDT 1474 (?)*	**14**	7
20 Nov 93	● AGAIN *Virgin VSCDG 1481*	**6**	11
12 Mar 94	BECAUSE OF LOVE *Virgin VSCDG 1488*	**19**	4
18 Jun 94	ANY TIME ANY PLACE *Virgin VSCDT 1501*	**13**	5
26 Nov 94	YOU WANT THIS *Virgin VSCDT 1519*	**14**	3
18 Mar 95	● WHOOPS NOW / WHAT'LL I DO *Virgin VSCDT 1533*	**9**	8
10 Jun 95	● SCREAM *Epic 6620222* [2]	**3**	12
24 Jun 95	SCREAM (re-mix) *Epic 6621277* [2]	**43**	2
23 Sep 95	● RUNAWAY *A & M 5811972*	**6**	7
2 Dec 95	SCREAM (re-entry) *Epic 6620222* [2]	**72**	1
16 Dec 95	● THE BEST THINGS IN LIFE ARE FREE (re-mix) *A & M 5813092* [3]	**7**	7
6 Apr 96	TWENTY FOREPLAY *A & M 5815112*	**22**	4

[1] Luther Vandross and Janet Jackson with special guests BBD and Ralph Tresvant [2] Michael Jackson and Janet Jackson [3] Luther Vandross and Janet Jackson

See also Herb Alpert.

Jermaine JACKSON *US, male vocalist*   **43 wks**

10 May 80	● LET'S GET SERIOUS *Motown TMG 1183*	**8**	11
26 Jul 80	BURNIN' HOT *Motown TMG 1194*	**32**	6
30 May 81	YOU LIKE ME DON'T YOU *Motown TMG 1222*	**41**	5
12 May 84	SWEETEST SWEETEST *Arista JJK 1*	**52**	4
27 Oct 84	WHEN THE RAIN BEGINS TO FALL *Arista ARIST 584* [1]	**68**	2
16 Feb 85	● DO WHAT YOU DO *Arista ARIST 609*	**6**	13
21 Oct 89	DON'T TAKE IT PERSONAL *Arista 112634*	**69**	2

[1] Jermaine Jackson and Pia Zadora

Joe JACKSON *UK, male vocalist*   **49 wks**

4 Aug 79	IS SHE REALLY GOING OUT WITH HIM? *A & M AMS 7459*	**13**	9
12 Jan 80	● IT'S DIFFERENT FOR GIRLS *A & M AMS 7493*	**5**	9
4 Jul 81	JUMPIN' JIVE *A & M AMS 8145* [1]	**43**	5
8 Jan 83	● STEPPIN' OUT *A & M AMS 8262*	**6**	8
12 Mar 83	BREAKING US IN TWO *A & M AM 101*	**59**	4

179

28 Apr 84		**HAPPY ENDING** *A & M AM 186*	**58**	3
7 Jul 84		**BE MY NUMBER TWO** *A & M AM 200*	**70**	2
7 Jun 86		**LEFT OF CENTER** *A & M AM 320* [2]	**32**	9

[1] Joe Jackson's Jumpin' Jive [2] Suzanne Vega featuring Joe Jackson

Michael JACKSON *US, male vocalist*   **459 wks**

12 Feb 72	●	**GOT TO BE THERE** *Tamla Motown TMG 797*	**5**	11
20 May 72	●	**ROCKIN' ROBIN** *Tamla Motown TMG 816*	**3**	14
19 Aug 72	●	**AIN'T NO SUNSHINE** *Tamla Motown TMG 826*	**8**	11
25 Nov 72	●	**BEN** *Tamla Motown TMG 834*	**7**	14
18 Nov 78		**EASE ON DOWN THE ROAD** *MCA 396* [1]	**45**	4
15 Sep 79	●	**DON'T STOP TILL YOU GET ENOUGH** *Epic EPC 7763*	**3**	12
24 Nov 79	●	**OFF THE WALL** *Epic EPC 8045*	**7**	10
9 Feb 80	●	**ROCK WITH YOU** *Epic EPC 8206*	**7**	9
3 May 80	●	**SHE'S OUT OF MY LIFE** *Epic EPC 8384*	**3**	9
26 Jul 80		**GIRLFRIEND** *Epic EPC 8782*	**41**	5
23 May 81	★	**ONE DAY IN YOUR LIFE** *Motown TMG 976*	**1**	14
1 Aug 81		**WE'RE ALMOST THERE** *Motown TMG 977*	**46**	4
6 Nov 82	●	**THE GIRL IS MINE** *Epic EPC A 2729* [2]	**8**	9
15 Jan 83		**THE GIRL IS MINE (re-entry)** *Epic EPC A 2729* [2]	**75**	1
29 Jan 83	★	**BILLIE JEAN** *Epic EPC A 3084*	**1**	15
9 Apr 83	●	**BEAT IT** *Epic EPC A 3258*	**3**	12
11 Jun 83	●	**WANNA BE STARTIN' SOMETHING** *Epic A 3427*	**8**	9
23 Jul 83		**HAPPY (LOVE THEME FROM 'LADY SINGS THE BLUES')** *Tamla Motown TMG 986*	**52**	3
15 Oct 83	●	**SAY SAY SAY** *Parlophone R 6062* [3]	**2**	15
19 Nov 83	●	**THRILLER** *Epic A 3643*	**10**	18
31 Mar 84	●	**P.Y.T. (PRETTY YOUNG THING)** *Epic A 4136*	**11**	8
2 Jun 84	●	**FAREWELL MY SUMMER LOVE** *Motown TMG 1342*	**7**	12
11 Aug 84		**GIRL YOU'RE SO TOGETHER** *Motown TMG 1355*	**33**	8
8 Aug 87	★	**I JUST CAN'T STOP LOVING YOU** *Epic 650202 7*	**1**	9
26 Sep 87	●	**BAD** *Epic 651155 7*	**3**	11
5 Dec 87	●	**THE WAY YOU MAKE ME FEEL** *Epic 651275 7*	**3**	10
20 Feb 88		**MAN IN THE MIRROR** *Epic 651388 7*	**21**	5
28 May 88		**GET IT** *Motown ZB 41883* [4]	**37**	4
16 Jul 88	●	**DIRTY DIANA** *Epic 651546 7*	**4**	8
10 Sep 88		**ANOTHER PART OF ME** *Epic 652844 7*	**15**	6
26 Nov 88	●	**SMOOTH CRIMINAL** *Epic 653026 7*	**8**	10
25 Feb 89	●	**LEAVE ME ALONE** *Epic 654672 7*	**2**	9
15 Jul 89		**LIBERIAN GIRL** *Epic 654947 0*	**13**	6
23 Nov 91	★	**BLACK OR WHITE** *Epic 6575987*	**1**	10
18 Jan 92		**BLACK OR WHITE (re-mix)** *Epic 6577316*	**14**	6
15 Feb 92	●	**REMEMBER THE TIME / COME TOGETHER** *Epic 6577747* ...3		8
2 May 92	●	**IN THE CLOSET** *Epic 6580187*	**8**	6
25 Jul 92	●	**WHO IS IT** *Epic 6581797*	**10**	7
12 Sep 92		**JAM** *Epic 6583607*	**13**	5
5 Dec 92	●	**HEAL THE WORLD** *Epic 6584887*	**2**	15
27 Feb 93	●	**GIVE IN TO ME** *Epic 6590692*	**2**	9
10 Jul 93	●	**WILL YOU BE THERE** *Epic 6592222*	**9**	8
18 Dec 93	●	**GONE TOO SOON** *Epic 6599762*	**33**	5
10 Jun 95	●	**SCREAM** *Epic 6620222*	**3**	12
24 Jun 95		**SCREAM (re-mix)** *Epic 6621277* [5]	**43**	2
1 Sep 95	★	**YOU ARE NOT ALONE (re-entry)** *Epic 6623102*	**1**	15
2 Dec 95		**SCREAM (re-entry)** *Epic 6620222* [5]	**72**	1
9 Dec 95	★	**EARTH SONG** *Epic 6626955*	**1**	17
20 Apr 96	●	**THEY DON'T CARE ABOUT US** *Epic 6629502*	**4**	12
3 Aug 96		**THEY DON'T CARE ABOUT US (re-entry)** *Epic 6629502* 66		1
17 Aug 96		**THEY DON'T CARE ABOUT US (2nd re-entry)** *Epic 6629502*	**66**	1
24 Aug 96	●	**WHY** *Epic 6629502* [6]	**2**	9
16 Nov 96	●	**STRANGER IN MOSCOW** *Epic 6637872*	**4†**	7

[1] Diana Ross and Michael Jackson [2] Michael Jackson and Paul McCartney
[3] Paul McCartney and Michael Jackson [4] Stevie Wonder and Michael Jackson [5] Michael Jackson and Janet Jackson [6] 3T featuring Michael Jackson

The sleeve of I Just Can't Stop Loving You *credits Siedah Garrett but the label does not.*
Come Together *was only listed from 7 Mar 92. It peaked at position 10.*

Mick JACKSON *UK, male vocalist*   **16 wks**

30 Sep 78		**BLAME IT ON THE BOOGIE** *Atlantic K 11102*	**15**	8
3 Feb 79		**WEEKEND** *Atlantic K 11224*	**38**	8

Millie JACKSON *US, female vocalist*   **8 wks**

18 Nov 72		**MY MAN A SWEET MAN** *Mojo 2093 022*	**50**	1
10 Mar 84		**I FEEL LIKE WALKIN' IN THE RAIN** *Sire W 9348*	**55**	2
15 Jun 85		**ACT OF WAR** *Rocket EJS 8* [1]	**32**	5

[1] Elton John and Millie Jackson

Stonewall JACKSON *US, male vocalist*   **2 wks**

17 Jul 59		**WATERLOO** *Philips PB 941*	**24**	2

Tony JACKSON – *See Q*

Tony JACKSON and the VIBRATIONS
UK, male vocal / instrumental group   **3 wks**

8 Oct 64		**BYE BYE BABY** *Pye 7N 15685*	**38**	3

Wanda JACKSON *US, female vocalist*   **11 wks**

1 Sep 60		**LET'S HAVE A PARTY** *Capitol CL 15147*	**32**	8
26 Jan 61		**MEAN MEAN MAN** *Capitol CL 15176*	**46**	1
9 Feb 61		**MEAN MEAN MAN (re-entry)** *Capitol CL 15176*	**40**	2

JACKSON SISTERS *US, female vocal group*   **2 wks**

20 Jun 87		**I BELIEVE IN MIRACLES** *Urban URB 4*	**72**	2

JACKSONS *US, male vocal group*   **235 wks**

31 Jan 70	●	**I WANT YOU BACK** *Tamla Motown TMG 724* [1]	**2**	13
16 May 70	●	**ABC** *Tamla Motown TMG 738* [1]	**8**	11
1 Aug 70	●	**THE LOVE YOU SAVE** *Tamla Motown TMG 746* [1]	**7**	9
21 Nov 70	●	**I'LL BE THERE** *Tamla Motown TMG 758* [1]	**4**	16
10 Apr 71		**MAMA'S PEARL** *Tamla Motown TMG 769* [1]	**25**	7
17 Jul 71		**NEVER CAN SAY GOODBYE** *Tamla Motown TMG 778* [1]	**33**	7
11 Nov 72	●	**LOOKIN' THROUGH THE WINDOWS** *Tamla Motown TMG 833* [1]	**9**	11
23 Dec 72		**SANTA CLAUS IS COMING TO TOWN** *Tamla Motown TMG 837* [1]	**43**	3
17 Feb 73	●	**DOCTOR MY EYES** *Tamla Motown TMG 842* [1]	**9**	10
9 Jun 73		**HALLELUJAH DAY** *Tamla Motown TMG 856* [1]	**20**	9
8 Sep 73		**SKYWRITER** *Tamla Motown TMG 865* [1]	**25**	8
9 Apr 77		**ENJOY YOURSELF** *Epic EPC 5063*	**42**	4
4 Jun 77	★	**SHOW YOU THE WAY TO GO** *Epic EPC 5266*	**1**	10
13 Aug 77		**DREAMER** *Epic EPC 5458*	**22**	9
5 Nov 77		**GOIN' PLACES** *Epic EPC 5732*	**26**	7
11 Feb 78		**EVEN THOUGH YOU'VE GONE** *Epic EPC 5919*	**31**	4
23 Sep 78	●	**BLAME IT ON THE BOOGIE** *Epic EPC 6683*	**8**	12
3 Feb 79		**DESTINY** *Epic EPC 6983*	**39**	6
24 Mar 79	●	**SHAKE YOUR BODY (DOWN TO THE GROUND)** *Epic EPC 7181*	**4**	12
25 Oct 80		**LOVELY ONE** *Epic EPC 9302*	**29**	6
13 Dec 80		**HEARTBREAK HOTEL** *Epic EPC 9391*	**44**	6
28 Feb 81	●	**CAN YOU FEEL IT** *Epic EPC 9554*	**6**	15
4 Jul 81	●	**WALK RIGHT NOW** *Epic EPC A 1294*	**7**	11
7 Jul 84		**STATE OF SHOCK** *Epic EPC A 4431* [2]	**14**	8
8 Sep 84		**TORTURE** *Epic A 4675*	**26**	6
16 Apr 88	●	**I WANT YOU BACK (re-mix)** *Motown ZB 41913* [3]	**8**	9
13 May 89		**NOTHIN' (THAT COMPARES 2 U)** *Epic 654808 7*	**33**	6

[1] Jackson Five [2] Jacksons, lead vocals Mick Jagger and Michael Jackson
[3] Michael Jackson with the Jackson Five

JACKY – *See Jackie LEE*

JACQUELINE – *See MACK VIBE featuring JACQUELINE*

180

JADE US, female vocal group — 28 wks

Date	Title	Pos	Wks
20 Mar 93	● DON'T WALK AWAY Giant W 0160CD	7	8
3 Jul 93	I WANNA LOVE YOU Giant 74321151662	13	7
18 Sep 93	ONE WOMAN Giant 74321165122	22	5
5 Feb 94	ALL THRU THE NITE Giant 74321187552 [1]	32	3
11 Feb 95	EVERY DAY OF THE WEEK Giant 74321260242	19	5

[1] P.O.V. featuring Jade

JADE 4 U – See Praga KHAN

JAGGED EDGE UK, male vocal / instrumental group — 2 wks

Date	Title	Pos	Wks
15 Sep 90	YOU DON'T LOVE ME Polydor PO 97	66	2

Mick JAGGER UK, male vocalist — 42 wks

Date	Title	Pos	Wks
14 Nov 70	MEMO FROM TURNER Decca F 13067	32	5
7 Jul 84	STATE OF SHOCK Epic A 4431 [1]	14	8
16 Feb 85	JUST ANOTHER NIGHT CBS A 4722	32	6
7 Sep 85	★ DANCING IN THE STREET EMI America EA 204 [2]	1	12
12 Sep 87	LET'S WORK CBS 651028 7	31	7
6 Feb 93	SWEET THING Atlantic A 7410CD	24	4

[1] Jacksons, lead vocals Mick Jagger and Michael Jackson [2] David Bowie and Mick Jagger

JAGS UK, male vocal / instrumental group — 11 wks

Date	Title	Pos	Wks
8 Sep 79	BACK OF MY HAND Island WIP 6501	17	10
2 Feb 80	WOMAN'S WORLD Island WIP 6531	75	1

JALN BAND
UK / Jamaica, male vocal / instrumental group — 17 wks

Date	Title	Pos	Wks
11 Sep 76	DISCO MUSIC / I LIKE IT Magnet MAG 73	21	9
27 Aug 77	I GOT TO SING Magnet MAG 97	40	4
1 Jul 78	GET UP Magnet MAG 118	53	4

JAM UK, male vocal / instrumental group — 203 wks

Date	Title	Pos	Wks
7 May 77	IN THE CITY Polydor 2058 866	40	6
23 Jul 77	ALL AROUND THE WORLD Polydor 2058 903	13	8
5 Nov 77	THE MODERN WORLD Polydor 2058 945	36	4
11 Mar 78	NEWS OF THE WORLD Polydor 2058 995	27	5
26 Aug 78	DAVID WATTS / 'A' BOMB IN WARDOUR STREET Polydor 2059 054	25	8
21 Oct 78	DOWN IN THE TUBE STATION AT MIDNIGHT Polydor POSP 8	15	7
17 Mar 79	STRANGE TOWN Polydor POSP 34	15	9
25 Aug 79	WHEN YOU'RE YOUNG Polydor POSP 69	17	7
3 Nov 79	● THE ETON RIFLES Polydor POSP 83	3	12
22 Mar 80	★ GOING UNDERGROUND / DREAMS OF CHILDREN Polydor POSP 113	1	9
26 Apr 80	ALL AROUND THE WORLD (re-entry) Polydor 2058 903	43	3
26 Apr 80	DAVID WATTS / 'A' BOMB IN WARDOUR STREET (re-entry) Polydor 2059 054	54	3
26 Apr 80	IN THE CITY (re-entry) Polydor 2058 866	40	4
26 Apr 80	NEWS OF THE WORLD (re-entry) Polydor 2058 995	53	3
26 Apr 80	STRANGE TOWN (re-entry) Polydor POSP 34	44	4
26 Apr 80	THE MODERN WORLD (re-entry) Polydor 2058 945	52	3
23 Aug 80	★ START Polydor 2059 266	1	8
7 Feb 81	THAT'S ENTERTAINMENT (IMPORT) Metronome 0030 364	21	7
6 Jun 81	● FUNERAL PYRE Polydor POSP 257	4	6
24 Oct 81	● ABSOLUTE BEGINNERS Polydor POSP 350	4	6
13 Feb 82	★ TOWN CALLED MALICE / PRECIOUS Polydor POSP 400	1	8
3 Jul 82	● JUST WHO IS THE FIVE O'CLOCK HERO Polydor 2059 504	8	5
18 Sep 82	● THE BITTEREST PILL (I EVER HAD TO SWALLOW) Polydor POSP 505	2	7
4 Dec 82	★ BEAT SURRENDER Polydor POSP 540	1	9
22 Jan 83	ALL AROUND THE WORLD (2nd re-entry) Polydor 2058 903	38	4
22 Jan 83	DAVID WATTS / 'A' BOMB IN WARDOUR STREET (2nd re-entry) Polydor 2059 054	50	4
22 Jan 83	DOWN IN THE TUBE STATION AT MIDNIGHT (re-entry) Polydor POSP 8	30	6
22 Jan 83	GOING UNDERGROUND / DREAMS OF CHILDREN (re-entry) Polydor POSP 113	21	6
22 Jan 83	IN THE CITY (2nd re-entry) Polydor 2058 866	47	4
22 Jan 83	NEWS OF THE WORLD (2nd re-entry) Polydor 2058 995	39	4
22 Jan 83	STRANGE TOWN (2nd re-entry) Polydor POSP 34	42	5
22 Jan 83	THE MODERN WORLD (2nd re-entry) Polydor 2058 945	51	4
22 Jan 83	WHEN YOU'RE YOUNG (re-entry) Polydor POSP 69	53	4
29 Jan 83	THAT'S ENTERTAINMENT (re-issue) Polydor POSP 482	60	3
5 Feb 83	START (re-entry) Polydor 2059 266	62	2
5 Feb 83	THE ETON RIFLES (re-entry) Polydor POSP 83	54	3
5 Feb 83	TOWN CALLED MALICE / PRECIOUS (re-entry) Polydor POSP 400	73	1
29 Jun 91	THAT'S ENTERTAINMENT (2nd re-issue) Polydor PO 155	57	2

JAM and SPOON featuring PLAVKA
Germany, male / female vocal / instrumental group — 23 wks

Date	Title	Pos	Wks
2 May 92	TALES FROM A DANCEOGRAPHIC OCEAN EP R&S RSUK 14 [1]	49	1
6 Jun 92	THE COMPLETE STELLA (re-mix) R&S RSUK 14X [1]	66	2
26 Feb 94	RIGHT IN THE NIGHT (FALL IN LOVE WITH MUSIC) Epic 6600822	31	4
24 Sep 94	FIND ME (ODYSSEY TO ANYOONA) Epic 6608082	37	3
10 Jun 95	● RIGHT IN THE NIGHT (FALL IN LOVE WITH MUSIC) (re-issue) Epic 6620182	10	8
16 Sep 95	FIND ME (ODYSSEY TO ANYOONA) (re-issue) Epic 6623242	22	3
25 Nov 95	ANGEL (LADADI O-HEYO) Epic 6626382	26	2

[1] Jam and Spoon

Tracks on Tales From A Danceographic Ocean EP: Stella / Keep On Movin' / My First Fantastic FF. The Complete Stella is a re-mix of a track from the EP. See also Tokyo Ghetto Pussy.

JAM MACHINE Italy / US, male vocal / instrumental group — 1 wk

Date	Title	Pos	Wks
23 Dec 89	EVERYDAY Deconstruction PB 43299	68	1

JAM ON THE MUTHA
UK, male vocal / instrumental group — 2 wks

Date	Title	Pos	Wks
11 Aug 90	HOTEL CALIFORNIA M & G MAGS 3	62	2

JAM TRONIK
Germany, male / female vocal / instrumental group — 7 wks

Date	Title	Pos	Wks
24 Mar 90	ANOTHER DAY IN PARADISE Debut DEBT 3093	19	7

JAMES UK, male vocal / instrumental group — 51 wks

Date	Title	Pos	Wks
12 May 90	HOW WAS IT FOR YOU Fontana JIM 5	32	3
7 Jul 90	COME HOME Fontana JIM 6	32	4
8 Dec 90	LOSE CONTROL Fontana JIM 7	38	5
30 Mar 91	● SIT DOWN Fontana JIM 8	2	10
30 Nov 91	● SOUND Fontana JIM 9	9	7
1 Feb 92	BORN OF FRUSTRATION Fontana JIM 10	13	6
4 Apr 92	RING THE BELLS Fontana JIM 11	37	2
18 Jul 92	SEVEN (EP) Fontana JIM 12	46	2
11 Sep 93	SOMETIMES Fontana JIMCD 13	18	4
13 Nov 93	LAID Fontana JIMCD 14	25	4
2 Apr 94	JAM J / SAY SOMETHING Fontana JIMCD 152	24	4

Tracks on Seven (EP): Seven / Goalie's Ball / William Burroughs / Still Alive. Say Something only listed with Jam J for first two weeks of record's run.

JAMES – *See CHRIS and JAMES*

Dick JAMES *UK, male vocalist*   **13 wks**

20 Jan 56	**ROBIN HOOD** *Parlophone R 4117* **14**		8
18 May 56	**ROBIN HOOD / BALLAD OF DAVY CROCKETT**		
	(re-entry) *Parlophone R 4117* **29**		1
11 Jan 57	**GARDEN OF EDEN** *Parlophone R 4255*.............**18**		4

Robin Hood is with Stephen James and his Chums.

Etta JAMES *US, female vocalist*   **7 wks**

10 Feb 96	● **I JUST WANT TO MAKE LOVE TO YOU**		
	MCA MCSTD 48003 ....**5**		7

Freddie JAMES *Canada, male vocalist*   **3 wks**

24 Nov 79	**GET UP AND BOOGIE** *Warner Bros. K 17478* **54**		3

Jimmy JAMES and the VAGABONDS
UK, male vocal / instrumental group   **25 wks**

11 Sep 68	**RED RED WINE** *Pye 7N 17579* **36**		8
24 Apr 76	**I'LL GO WHERE YOUR MUSIC TAKES ME** *Pye 7N 45585*..**23**		8
17 Jul 76	● **NOW IS THE TIME** *Pye 7N 45606* **5**		9

Joni JAMES *US, female vocalist*   **2 wks**

6 Mar 53	**WHY DON'T YOU BELIEVE ME** *MGM 582* **11**		1
30 Jan 59	**THERE MUST BE A WAY** *MGM 1002* **24**		1

Rick JAMES *US, male vocalist*   **30 wks**

8 Jul 78	**YOU AND I** *Motown TMG 1110*........................**46**		7
7 Jul 79	**I'M A SUCKER FOR YOUR LOVE** *Motown TMG 1146* [1]..**43**		8
6 Sep 80	**BIG TIME** *Motown TMG 1198* **41**		6
4 Jul 81	**GIVE IT TO ME BABY** *Motown TMG 1229* **47**		3
12 Jun 82	**STANDING ON THE TOP (PART 1)**		
	Motown TMG 1263 [2] **53**		3
3 Jul 82	**DANCE WIT' ME** *Motown TMG 1266* **53**		3

[1] Teena Marie, co-lead vocals Rick James [2] Temptations featuring Rick James

Sonny JAMES *US, male vocalist*   **8 wks**

30 Nov 56	**THE CAT CAME BACK** *Capitol CL 14635*...........**30**		1
8 Feb 57	**YOUNG LOVE** *Capitol CL 14683*.......................**11**		7

Tommy JAMES and the SHONDELLS
US, male vocal / instrumental group   **25 wks**

21 Jul 66	**HANKY PANKY** *Roulette RK 7000* **38**		7
5 Jun 68	★ **MONY MONY** *Major Minor MM 567*.....................**1**		18

Wendy JAMES *UK, female vocalist*   **4 wks**

20 Feb 93	**THE NAMELESS ONE** *MCA MCSTD 1732* **34**		3
17 Apr 93	**LONDON'S BRILLIANT** *MCA MCSTD 1763* **62**		1

JAMES BOYS *UK, male vocal duo*   **6 wks**

19 May 73	**OVER AND OVER** *Penny Farthing PEN 806* **39**		6

JAMESTOWN – *See Jocelyn BROWN*

JAMIROQUAI *UK, male vocal / instrumental group*   **60 wks**

31 Oct 92	**WHEN YOU GONNA LEARN** *Acid Jazz JAZID 46T* **52**		2
20 Feb 93	**WHEN YOU GONNA LEARN (re-entry)**		
	Acid Jazz JAZID 46 ....**69**		1
13 Mar 93	● **TOO YOUNG TO DIE** *Sony S2 6590112* **10**		7
5 Jun 93	**BLOW YOUR MIND** *Sony S2 6592972* **12**		6
14 Aug 93	**EMERGENCY ON PLANET EARTH** *Sony S2 6595782* ...**32**		3
25 Sep 93	**WHEN YOU GONNA LEARN (re-issue)**		
	Sony S2 6596952 ....**28**		3
8 Oct 94	**SPACE COWBOY** *Sony S2 6608512* **17**		5
19 Nov 94	**HALF THE MAN** *Sony S2 6610032* **15**		8
1 Jul 95	● **STILLNESS IN TIME** *Sony S2 6620255* **9**		5
1 Jun 96	**DO U KNOW WHERE YOU'RE COMING FROM**		
	Renk CDRENK 63 [1] **12**		5
31 Aug 96	● **VIRTUAL INSANITY** *Sony S2 6636132* **3**		11
7 Dec 96	● **COSMIC GIRL** *Sony S2 6638292* ....**6†**		4

[1] M-Beat featuring Jamiroquai

JAMMERS *US, male vocal / instrumental group*   **2 wks**

29 Jan 83	**BE MINE TONIGHT** *Salsoul Sal 101* **65**		2

JAN and DEAN *US, male vocal duo*   **18 wks**

24 Aug 61	**HEART AND SOUL** *London HLH 9395* **24**		8
15 Aug 63	**SURF CITY** *Liberty LIB 55580* **26**		10

JAN and KJELD *Denmark, male vocal duo*   **4 wks**

21 Jul 60	**BANJO BOY** *Ember S 101* **36**		4

JANE'S ADDICTION
US, male vocal / instrumental group   **4 wks**

23 Mar 91	**BEEN CAUGHT STEALING** *Warner Bros. W 0011*...........**34**		3
1 Jun 91	**CLASSIC GIRL** *Warner Bros. W 0031* **60**		1

Horst JANKOWSKI
Germany, male instrumentalist – piano   **18 wks**

29 Jul 65	● **A WALK IN THE BLACK FOREST** *Mercury MF 861* **3**		18

Samantha JANUS *UK, female vocalist*   **3 wks**

11 May 91	**A MESSAGE TO YOUR HEART** *Hollywood HWD 104* **30**		3

Philip JAP *UK, male vocalist*   **8 wks**

31 Jul 82	**SAVE US** *A & M AMS 8217* **53**		4
25 Sep 82	**TOTAL ERASURE** *A & M JAP 1* **41**		4

JAPAN *UK, male vocal / instrumental group*   **81 wks**

18 Oct 80	**GENTLEMEN TAKE POLAROIDS** *Virgin VS 379* **60**		2
9 May 81	**THE ART OF PARTIES** *Virgin VS 409* **48**		5
19 Sep 81	**QUIET LIFE** *Hansa HANSA 6* **19**		9
7 Nov 81	**VISIONS OF CHINA** *Virgin VS 436* **32**		12
23 Jan 82	**EUROPEAN SON** *Hansa HANSA 10* **31**		6
20 Mar 82	● **GHOSTS** *Virgin VS 472* **5**		8
22 May 82	**CANTONESE BOY** *Virgin VS 502* **24**		6
3 Jul 82	● **I SECOND THAT EMOTION** *Hansa HANSA 12*............**9**		11
9 Oct 82	**LIFE IN TOKYO** *Hansa HANSA 17* **28**		6
20 Nov 82	**NIGHT PORTER** *Virgin VS 554* **29**		9

12 Mar 83	ALL TOMORROW'S PARTIES *Hansa HANSA 18*	38	4
21 May 83	CANTON (LIVE) *Virgin VS 581*	42	3

See also Rain Tree Crow.

Jean-Michel JARRE
France, male instrumentalist / producer　　　　　　**28 wks**

27 Aug 77	● OXYGENE PART IV *Polydor 2001 721*	4	9
20 Jan 79	EQUINOXE PART 5 *Polydor POSP 20*	45	5
23 Aug 86	FOURTH RENDEZ-VOUS *Polydor POSP 788*	65	4
5 Nov 88	REVOLUTIONS *Polydor PO 25*	52	2
7 Jan 89	LONDON KID *Polydor PO 32* [1]	52	3
7 Oct 89	OXYGENE PART IV (re-mix) *Polydor PO 55*	65	2
26 Jun 93	CHRONOLOGIE PART 4 *Polydor POCS 274*	55	2
30 Oct 93	CHRONOLOGIE PART 4 (re-mix) *Polydor POCS 274*	56	1

[1] Jean-Michel Jarre featuring Hank Marvin

Al JARREAU *US, male vocalist*　　　　　　**30 wks**

26 Sep 81	WE'RE IN THIS LOVE TOGETHER *Warner Bros. K 17849*	55	4
14 May 83	MORNIN' *WEA U9929*	28	6
16 Jul 83	TROUBLE IN PARADISE *WEA Int. U9871*	36	5
24 Sep 83	BOOGIE DOWN *WEA U9814*	63	3
16 Nov 85	DAY BY DAY *Polydor POSP 770* [1]	53	3
5 Apr 86	THE MUSIC OF GOODBYE (LOVE THEME FROM 'OUT OF AFRICA') *MCA MCA 1038* [2]	75	1
7 Mar 87	● 'MOONLIGHTING' THEME *WEA U8407*	8	8

[1] Shakatak featuring Al Jarreau [2] Melissa Manchester and Al Jarreau

Kenny 'Jammin'' JASON – *See DJ 'FAST' EDDIE*

JAVELLS featuring Nosmo KING
UK, male / female vocal group　　　　　　**8 wks**

9 Nov 74	GOODBYE NOTHING TO SAY *Pye Disco Demand DDS 2003*	26	8

Peter JAY and the JAYWALKERS
UK, male instrumental group, Peter Jay – drums　　**11 wks**

8 Nov 62	CAN CAN 62 *Decca F 11531*	31	11

JAYHAWKS *US, male / female vocal / instrumental group*　**1 wk**

15 Jul 95	BAD TIME *American 74321291632*	70	1

JAZZ and the BROTHERS GRIMM
UK, male vocal / instrumental group　　　　　　**2 wks**

9 Jul 88	(LET'S ALL GO BACK) DISCO NIGHTS *Ensign ENY 616*	57	2

JAZZY JEFF and the FRESH PRINCE
US, male vocal / instrumental rap duo　　　　　**47 wks**

4 Oct 86	GIRLS AIN'T NOTHING BUT TROUBLE *Champion CHAMP 18* [1]	21	8
3 Aug 91	● SUMMERTIME *Jive JIVE 279* [1]	8	8
9 Nov 91	RING MY BELL *Jive JIVE 288* [1]	53	2
11 Sep 93	★ BOOM! SHAKE THE ROOM *Jive JIVECD 335*	1	13
20 Nov 93	I'M LOOKING FOR THE ONE (TO BE WITH ME) *Jive JIVECD 345*	24	4
19 Feb 94	CAN'T WAIT TO BE WITH YOU *Jive JIVECD 348*	29	4
4 Jun 94	TWINKLE TWINKLE (I'M NOT A STAR) *Jive JIVECD 354*	62	2
6 Aug 94	SUMMERTIME (re-entry) *Jive JIVECD 279*	29	4

2 Dec 95	BOOM! SHAKE THE ROOM (re-mix) *Jive JIVECD 387*	40	2

[1] DJ Jazzy Jeff and the Fresh Prince

JB's ALL STARS
UK, male / female vocal / instrumental group　　**4 wks**

11 Feb 84	BACKFIELD IN MOTION *RCA Victor RCA 384*	48	4

JC 001 *UK, male rapper*　　　　　　**4 wks**

24 Apr 93	NEVER AGAIN *Anxious ANX 1012CD*	67	2
26 Jun 93	CUPID *Anxious ANX 1014CD*	56	2

JEFFERSON *UK, male vocalist*　　　　　　**8 wks**

9 Apr 69	COLOUR OF MY LOVE *Pye 7N 17706*	22	8

JEFFERSON STARSHIP – See STARSHIP

Garland JEFFREYS *US, male vocalist*　　　**1 wk**

8 Feb 92	HAIL HAIL ROCK 'N' ROLL *RCA PB 49171*	72	1

JELLYBEAN *US, male producer*　　　　　　**47 wks**

1 Feb 86	SIDEWALK TALK *EMI America EA 210* [1]	47	4
26 Sep 87	THE REAL THING *Chrysalis CHS 3167* [2]	13	10
28 Nov 87	● WHO FOUND WHO *Chrysalis CHS JEL 1* [3]	10	10
12 Dec 87	JINGO *Chrysalis JEL 2*	12	10
12 Mar 88	JUST A MIRAGE *Chrysalis JEL 3* [4]	13	10
20 Aug 88	COMING BACK FOR MORE *Chrysalis JEL 4* [5]	41	3

[1] Jellybean featuring Catherine Buchanan [2] Jellybean featuring Steven Dante [3] Jellybean featuring Elisa Fiorillo [4] Jellybean featuring Adele Bertei [5] Jellybean featuring Richard Darbyshire

JELLYFISH *US, male vocal / instrumental group*　　**20 wks**

26 Jan 91	THE KING IS HALF UNDRESSED *Charisma CUSS 1*	39	6
27 Apr 91	BABY'S COMING BACK *Charisma CUSS 2*	51	4
3 Aug 91	THE SCARY-GO-ROUND EP *Charisma CUSS 3*	49	3
26 Oct 91	I WANNA STAY HOME *Charisma CUSS 4*	59	2
1 May 93	THE GHOST AT NUMBER ONE *Charisma CUSDG 10*	43	3
17 Jul 93	NEW MISTAKE *Charisma CUSDG 11*	55	2

Tracks on The Scary-Go-Round EP: Now She Knows She's Wrong / Bedspring Kiss / She Still Loves Him (Live) / Baby's Coming Back (Live).

JERU THE DAMAJA *US, male rapper*　　　**1 wk**

7 Dec 96	YA PLAYIN YASELF *ffrr FCD 289*	67	1

JESUS AND MARY CHAIN
UK, male vocal / instrumental group　　　　　**56 wks**

2 Mar 85	NEVER UNDERSTAND *Blanco Y Negro NEG 8*	47	4
8 Jun 85	YOU TRIP ME UP *Blanco Y Negro NEG 13*	55	3
12 Oct 85	JUST LIKE HONEY *Blanco Y Negro NEG 17*	45	3
26 Jul 86	SOME CANDY TALKING *Blanco Y Negro NEG 19*	13	5
2 May 87	● APRIL SKIES *Blanco Y Negro NEG 24*	8	6
15 Aug 87	HAPPY WHEN IT RAINS *Blanco Y Negro NEG 25*	25	5
7 Nov 87	DARKLANDS *Blanco Y Negro NEG 29*	33	4
9 Apr 88	SIDEWALKING *Blanco Y Negro NEG 32*	30	3
23 Sep 89	BLUES FROM A GUN *Blanco Y Negro NEG 41*	32	2
18 Nov 89	HEAD ON *Blanco Y Negro NEG 42*	57	2
8 Sep 90	ROLLERCOASTER (EP) *blanco y negro NEG 45*	46	2
15 Feb 92	● REVERENCE *Blanco Y Negro NEG 55*	10	4

14 Mar 92	**FAR GONE AND OUT** Blanco Y Negro NEG 56	**23**	3
4 Jul 92	**ALMOST GOLD** Blanco Y Negro NEG 57	**41**	2
10 Jul 93	**SOUND OF SPEED (EP)** Blanco Y Negro NEG 66CD	**30**	2
30 Jul 94	**SOMETIMES ALWAYS** Blanco Y Negro NEG 70CD	**22**	3
22 Oct 94	**COME ON** Blanco Y Negro NEG 73CD1	**52**	2
17 Jun 95	**I HATE ROCK 'N' ROLL** Blanco Y Negro NEG 81CD	**61**	1

Tracks on Rollercoaster (EP): Rollercoaster / Silverblade / Lowlife / Tower Of Song. Tracks on Sound Of Speed EP: Snakedriver / Something I Can't Have / Write Record Release Blues / Little Red Rooster.

JESUS JONES UK, male vocal / instrumental group · 50 wks

25 Feb 89	**INFO-FREAKO** Food FOOD 18	**42**	3
8 Jul 89	**NEVER ENOUGH** Food FOOD 21	**42**	3
23 Sep 89	**BRING IT ON DOWN** Food FOOD 22	**46**	3
7 Apr 90	**REAL REAL REAL** Food FOOD 24	**19**	8
6 Oct 90	**RIGHT HERE RIGHT NOW** Food FOOD 25	**31**	4
12 Jan 91	● **INTERNATIONAL BRIGHT YOUNG THING** Food FOOD 27	**7**	7
2 Mar 91	**WHO WHERE WHY** Food FOOD 28	**21**	7
20 Jul 91	**RIGHT HERE RIGHT NOW (re-issue)** Food FOOD 30	**31**	4
9 Jan 93	● **THE DEVIL YOU KNOW** Food CDPERV 1	**10**	5
10 Apr 93	**THE RIGHT DECISION** Food CDPERV 2	**36**	3
10 Jul 93	**ZEROES & ONES** Food CDFOODS 44	**30**	3

See also Various Artists (EPs & LPs) – The Food Christmas EP.

JESUS LIZARD US, male vocal / instrumental group · 2 wks

| 6 Mar 93 | **PUSS** Touch And Go TG 83CD | **12** | 2 |

The listed flip side of Puss was Oh, The Guilt by Nirvana.

JESUS LOVES YOU UK, male vocalist – Boy George · 18 wks

11 Nov 89	**AFTER THE LOVE** More Protein PROT 2	**68**	1
23 Feb 91	**BOW DOWN MISTER** More Protein PROT 8	**27**	8
8 Jun 91	**GENERATIONS OF LOVE** More Protein PROT 10	**35**	8
12 Dec 92	**SWEET TOXIC LOVE** Virgin VS 1449	**65**	1

JETHRO TULL UK, male vocal / instrumental group · 68 wks

1 Jan 69	**LOVE STORY** Island WIP 6048	**29**	8
14 May 69	● **LIVING IN THE PAST** Island WIP 6056	**3**	14
1 Nov 69	● **SWEET DREAM** Chrysalis WIP 6070	**7**	11
24 Jan 70	● **TEACHER / THE WITCH'S PROMISE** Chrysalis WIP 6077	**4**	9
18 Sep 71	**LIFE IS A LONG SONG / UP THE POOL** Chrysalis WIP 6106	**11**	8
11 Dec 76	**RING OUT SOLSTICE BELLS (EP)** Chrysalis CXP 2	**28**	6
15 Sep 84	**LAP OF LUXURY** Chrysalis TULL 1	**70**	2
16 Jan 88	**SAID SHE WAS A DANCER** Chrysalis TULL 4	**55**	4
21 Mar 92	**ROCKS ON THE ROAD** Chrysalis TULLX 7	**47**	3
22 May 93	**LIVING IN THE (SLIGHTLY MORE RECENT) PAST** Chrysalis CDCHSS 3970	**32**	3

Tracks on Ring Out Solstice Bells EP: Ring Out Solstice Bells / March the Mad Scientist / The Christmas Song / Pan Dance. Living In The (Slightly More Recent) Past is a live version of the original.

JETS UK, male vocal / instrumental group · 38 wks

22 Aug 81	**SUGAR DOLL** EMI 5211	**55**	3
31 Oct 81	**YES TONIGHT JOSEPHINE** EMI 5247	**25**	11
6 Feb 82	**LOVE MAKES THE WORLD GO ROUND** EMI 5262	**21**	9
24 Apr 82	**THE HONEYDRIPPER** EMI 5289	**58**	3
9 Oct 82	**SOMEBODY TO LOVE** EMI 5342	**56**	3
6 Aug 83	**BLUE SKIES** EMI 5405	**53**	3
17 Dec 83	**ROCKIN' AROUND THE CHRISTMAS TREE** PRT 7P 297	**62**	4
13 Oct 84	**PARTY DOLL** PRT JETS 2	**72**	2

JETS US, male / female vocal / instrumental group · 19 wks

31 Jan 87	● **CRUSH ON YOU** MCA MCA 1048	**5**	13
25 Apr 87	**CURIOSITY** MCA MCA 1119	**41**	4
28 May 88	**ROCKET 2 U** MCA MCA 1226	**69**	2

Joan JETT and the BLACKHEARTS
US, female vocalist with male vocal / instrumental group · 21 wks

24 Apr 82	● **I LOVE ROCK 'N' ROLL** Epic EPC A 2087	**4**	10
10 Jul 82	**CRIMSON AND CLOVER** Epic EPC A 2485	**60**	3
20 Aug 88	**I HATE MYSELF FOR LOVING YOU** London LON 195	**46**	6
31 Mar 90	**DIRTY DEEDS** Chrysalis CHS 3518 [1]	**69**	1
19 Feb 94	**I LOVE ROCK & ROLL (re-issue)** Reprise W 0232CD	**75**	1

[1] Joan Jett

JHELISA US, female vocalist · 1 wk

| 1 Jul 95 | **FRIENDLY PRESSURE** Dorado DOR 040CD | **75** | 1 |

JIGSAW UK, male vocal / instrumental group · 16 wks

| 1 Nov 75 | ● **SKY HIGH** Splash CPI 1 | **9** | 11 |
| 6 Aug 77 | **IF I HAVE TO GO AWAY** Splash CP 11 | **36** | 5 |

JILTED JOHN UK, male vocalist · 12 wks

| 12 Aug 78 | ● **JILTED JOHN** EMI International INT 567 | **4** | 12 |

JIMMY THE HOOVER
UK, male / female vocal / instrumental group · 8 wks

| 25 Jun 83 | **TANTALISE (WO WO EE YEH YEH)** Innervision A 3406 | **18** | 8 |

JINGLE BELLES US / UK, female vocal group · 4 wks

| 17 Dec 83 | **CHRISTMAS SPECTRE** Passion PASH 14 | **37** | 4 |

JINNY Italy, female vocalist · 16 wks

29 Jun 91	**KEEP WARM** Virgin VS 1356	**68**	3
22 May 93	**FEEL THE RHYTHM** Logic 401633001022	**74**	1
15 Jul 95	**KEEP WARM (re-mix)** Multiply CDMULTY 5	**11**	8
16 Dec 95	**WANNA BE WITH YOU** Multiply CDMULTY 8	**30**	4

JIVE BUNNY and the MASTERMIXERS
UK, male production / mixing group · 68 wks

15 Jul 89	★ **SWING THE MOOD** Music Factory Dance MFD 001	**1**	19
14 Oct 89	★ **THAT'S WHAT I LIKE** Music Factory Dance MFD 002	**1**	12
16 Dec 89	★ **LET'S PARTY** Music Factory Dance MFD 003	**1**	6
17 Mar 90	● **THAT SOUNDS GOOD TO ME** Music Factory Dance MFD 004	**4**	6
25 Aug 90	● **CAN CAN YOU PARTY** Music Factory Dance MFD 007	**8**	6
17 Nov 90	**LET'S SWING AGAIN** Music Factory Dance MFD 009	**19**	5
22 Dec 90	**THE CRAZY PARTY MIXES** Music Factory Dance MFD 010	**13**	5
23 Mar 91	**OVER TO YOU JOHN (HERE WE GO AGAIN)** Music Factory Dance MFD 012	**28**	5
20 Jul 91	**HOT SUMMER SALSA** Music Factory Dance MFD 013	**43**	2
23 Nov 91	**ROCK 'N' ROLL DANCE PARTY** Music Factory Dance MFD 015	**48**	2

See also Liz Kershaw and Bruno Brookes.

JJ UK, male / female vocal / instumental duo   3 wks

9 Feb 91	**IF THIS IS LOVE** Columbia 6566097	**55**	3

JKD BAND UK, male vocal / instrumental group   4 wks

1 Jul 78	**DRAGON POWER** Satril SAT 132	**58**	4

JM SILK US, male vocal / instrumental duo   6 wks

25 Oct 86	**I CAN'T TURN AROUND** RCA PB 49793	**62**	3
7 Mar 87	**LET THE MUSIC TAKE CONTROL** RCA PB 49767	**47**	3

JMD – See TYREE

JO BOXERS UK, male vocal / instrumental group   33 wks

19 Feb 83	● **BOXER BEAT** RCA BOXX 1	**3**	15
21 May 83	● **JUST GOT LUCKY** RCA BOXX 2	**7**	9
13 Aug 83	**JOHNNY FRIENDLY** RCA BOXX 3	**31**	8
12 Nov 83	**JEALOUS LOVE** RCA BOXX 4	**72**	1

JO JO GUNNE US, male vocal / instrumental group   12 wks

25 Mar 72	● **RUN RUN RUN** Asylum AYM 501	**6**	12

JOAN COLLINS FAN CLUB
UK, male vocalist – Julian Clary   3 wks

18 Jun 88	**LEADER OF THE PACK** 10 TEN 227	**60**	3

John Paul JOANS UK, male vocalist   7 wks

19 Dec 70	**MAN FROM NAZARETH** RAK 107	**41**	3
16 Jan 71	**MAN FROM NAZARETH (re-entry)** RAK 107	**25**	4

JOCKMASTER B.A. – See MAD JOCKS featuring JOCKMASTER B.A.

JOCKO US, male vocalist   3 wks

23 Feb 80	**RHYTHM TALK** Philadelphia International PIR 8222	**56**	3

JODECI US, male vocal group   19 wks

16 Jan 93	**CHERISH** Uptown MCSTD 1726	**56**	2
11 Dec 93	**CRY FOR YOU** Uptown MCSTD 1951	**56**	1
16 Jul 94	**FEENIN'** Uptown MCSTD 1984	**18**	3
28 Jan 95	**CRY FOR YOU (re-issue)** Uptown MCSTD 2039	**20**	3
24 Jun 95	**FREEK 'N YOU** Uptown MCSTD 2072	**17**	5
9 Dec 95	**LOVE U 4 LIFE** Uptown MCSTD 2105	**23**	3
25 May 96	**GET ON UP** MCA MCSTD 48010	**20**	2

JODIE Australia, female vocalist   1 wk

25 Feb 95	**ANYTHING YOU WANT** Mercury MERCD 423	**47**	1

JOE US, male vocalist   10 wks

22 Jan 94	**I'M IN LUV** Mercury JOECD 1	**22**	4
25 Jun 94	**THE ONE FOR ME** Mercury JOECD 2	**34**	2
22 Oct 94	**ALL OR NOTHING** Mercury JOECD 3	**56**	1
27 Apr 96	**ALL THE THINGS (YOUR MAN WON'T DO)** Island CID 634	**34**	3

JOE PUBLIC US, male rap group   5 wks

11 Jul 92	**LIVE AND LEARN** Columbia 6575267	**43**	4
28 Nov 92	**I'VE BEEN WATCHIN'** Columbia 6587657	**75**	1

Billy JOEL US, male vocalist / instrumentalist – piano   146 wks

11 Feb 78	**JUST THE WAY YOU ARE** CBS 5872	**19**	9
24 Jun 78	**MOVIN' OUT (ANTHONY'S SONG)** CBS 6412	**35**	6
2 Dec 78	**MY LIFE** CBS 6821	**12**	15
28 Apr 79	**UNTIL THE NIGHT** CBS 7242	**50**	3
12 Apr 80	**ALL FOR LEYNA** CBS 8325	**40**	4
9 Aug 80	**IT'S STILL ROCK AND ROLL TO ME** CBS 8753	**14**	11
15 Oct 83	★ **UPTOWN GIRL** CBS A 3775	**1**	17
10 Dec 83	● **TELL HER ABOUT IT** CBS A 3655	**4**	10
18 Feb 84	● **AN INNOCENT MAN** CBS A 4142	**8**	10
28 Apr 84	**THE LONGEST TIME** CBS A 4280	**25**	8
23 Jun 84	**LEAVE A TENDER MOMENT ALONE / GOODNIGHT SAIGON** CBS A 4521	**29**	7
22 Feb 86	**SHE'S ALWAYS A WOMAN / JUST THE WAY YOU ARE (re-issue)** CBS A 6862	**53**	1
20 Sep 86	**A MATTER OF TRUST** CBS 650057 7	**52**	4
30 Sep 89	● **WE DIDN'T START THE FIRE** CBS JOEL 1	**7**	10
16 Dec 89	**LENINGRAD** CBS JOEL 3	**53**	4
10 Mar 90	**I GO TO EXTREMES** CBS JOEL 2	**70**	2
29 Aug 92	**ALL SHOOK UP** Columbia 6583437	**27**	4
31 Jul 93	● **THE RIVER OF DREAMS** Columbia 6595432	**3**	14
23 Oct 93	**ALL ABOUT SOUL** Columbia 6597362	**32**	4
26 Feb 94	**NO MAN'S LAND** Columbia 6599202	**50**	3

Goodnight Saigon *only listed from 30 Jun 84.*

JOHANN Germany, male producer – Johann Bley   1 wk

16 Mar 96	**NEW KICKS** Perfecto PERF 118CD	**54**	1

Elton JOHN UK, male vocalist / instrumentalist – piano   526 wks

23 Jan 71	● **YOUR SONG** DJM DJS 233	**7**	12
22 Apr 72	● **ROCKET MAN (I THINK IT'S GOING TO BE A LONG LONG TIME)** DJM DJX 501	**2**	13
9 Sep 72	**HONKY CAT** DJM DJS	**31**	6
4 Nov 72	● **CROCODILE ROCK** DJM DJS 271	**5**	14
20 Jan 73	● **DANIEL** DJM DJS 275	**4**	10
7 Jul 73	● **SATURDAY NIGHT'S ALRIGHT FOR FIGHTING** DJM DJX 502	**7**	9
29 Sep 73	● **GOODBYE YELLOW BRICK ROAD** DJM DJS 285	**6**	16
8 Dec 73	**STEP INTO CHRISTMAS** DJM DJS 290	**24**	7
2 Mar 74	**CANDLE IN THE WIND** DJM DJS 297	**11**	9
1 Jun 74	**DON'T LET THE SUN GO DOWN ON ME** DJM DJS 302	**16**	8
14 Sep 74	**THE BITCH IS BACK** DJM DJS 322	**15**	7
23 Nov 74	● **LUCY IN THE SKY WITH DIAMONDS** DJM DJS 340	**10**	10
8 Mar 75	**PHILADELPHIA FREEDOM** DJM DJS 354 [1]	**12**	9
28 Jun 75	**SOMEONE SAVED MY LIFE TONIGHT** DJS 385	**22**	5
4 Oct 75	**ISLAND GIRL** DJM DJS 610	**14**	8
20 Mar 76	● **PINBALL WIZARD** DJM DJS 652	**7**	7
3 Jul 76	★ **DON'T GO BREAKING MY HEART** Rocket ROKN 512 [2]	**1**	14
25 Sep 76	**BENNIE AND THE JETS** DJM DJS 10705	**37**	5
13 Nov 76	**SORRY SEEMS TO BE THE HARDEST WORD** Rocket ROKN 517	**11**	10
26 Feb 77	**CRAZY WATER** Rocket ROKN 521	**27**	6
11 Jun 77	**BITE YOUR LIP (GET UP AND DANCE)** Rocket ROKN 526	**28**	4
15 Apr 78	**EGO** Rocket ROKN 538	**34**	6
21 Oct 78	**PART TIME LOVE** Rocket XPRES 1	**15**	13
16 Dec 78	● **SONG FOR GUY** Rocket XPRES 5	**4**	10
12 May 79	**ARE YOU READY FOR LOVE** Rocket XPRES 13	**42**	6
24 May 80	**LITTLE JEANNIE** Rocket XPRES 32	**33**	7
23 Aug 80	**SARTORIAL ELOQUENCE** Rocket XPRES 41	**44**	5
21 Mar 81	**I SAW HER STANDING THERE** DJM DJS 10965 [3]	**40**	4
23 May 81	**NOBODY WINS** Rocket XPRES 54	**42**	5
27 Mar 82	● **BLUE EYES** Rocket XPRES 71	**8**	10

Jesus Jones

Jesus Jones covered labelmates Crazyhead's 'I Don't Want That Kind Of Love' for the Food Christmas EP.

Jon Of The Pleased Wimmin

A regular at the legendary Kinky Gerlinky club nights in London, Jon Of The Pleased Wimmin has progressed from club character to club DJ and chart star.

Kinks

The best selling Kinks single in the US is their 1983 hit Come Dancing. In the UK the song was the band's first major hit for 11 years, but only peaked at number 12.

12 Jun 82		EMPTY GARDEN *Rocket XPRES 77* **51**	4
30 Apr 83	●	I GUESS THAT'S WHY THEY CALL IT THE BLUES *Rocket XPRES 91* **5**	15
30 Jul 83	●	I'M STILL STANDING *Rocket EJS 1* **4**	11
15 Oct 83		KISS THE BRIDE *Rocket EJS 2* **20**	7
10 Dec 83		COLD AS CHRISTMAS *Rocket EJS 3* **33**	6
26 May 84	●	SAD SONGS (SAY SO MUCH) *Rocket PH 7* **7**	12
11 Aug 84	●	PASSENGERS *Rocket EJS 5* **5**	11
20 Oct 84		WHO WEARS THESE SHOES *Rocket EJS 6* **50**	3
2 Mar 85		BREAKING HEARTS (AIN'T WHAT IT USED TO BE) *Rocket EJS 7* **59**	3
15 Jun 85		ACT OF WAR *Rocket EJS 8* [4] **32**	5
12 Oct 85	●	NIKITA *Rocket EJS 9* **3**	13
9 Nov 85		THAT'S WHAT FRIENDS ARE FOR *Arista ARIST 638* [5] **16**	9
7 Dec 85		WRAP HER UP *Rocket EJS 10* **12**	10
1 Mar 86		CRY TO HEAVEN *Rocket EJS 11* **47**	4
4 Oct 86		HEARTACHE ALL OVER THE WORLD *Rocket EJS 12* **45**	4
29 Nov 86		SLOW RIVERS *Rocket EJS 13* [6] **44**	8
20 Jun 87		FLAMES OF PARADISE *CBS 6508657* [7] **59**	3
16 Jan 88	●	CANDLE IN THE WIND *Rocket EJS 15* **5**	11
4 Jun 88		I DON'T WANNA GO ON WITH YOU LIKE THAT *Rocket EJS 16* **30**	8
3 Sep 88		TOWN OF PLENTY *Rocket EJS 17* **74**	1
6 May 89		THROUGH THE STORM *Arista 112185* [8] **41**	3
26 Aug 89		HEALING HANDS *Rocket EJS 19* **45**	5
4 Nov 89		SACRIFICE *Rocket EJS 20* **55**	3
9 Jun 90	★	SACRIFICE / HEALING HANDS (re-issue) *Rocket EJS 22* ..**1**	15
18 Aug 90		CLUB AT THE END OF THE STREET / WHISPERS *Rocket EJS 23* **47**	3
20 Oct 90		YOU GOTTA LOVE SOMEONE *Rocket EJS 24* **33**	4
15 Dec 90		EASIER TO WALK AWAY *Rocket EJS 25* **67**	1
29 Dec 90		EASIER TO WALK AWAY (re-entry) *Rocket EJS 25* **63**	1
7 Dec 91	★	DON'T LET THE SUN GO DOWN ON ME *Epic 6576467* [9] **1**	10
6 Jun 92	●	THE ONE *Rocket EJS 28* **10**	8
1 Aug 92		RUNAWAY TRAIN *Rocket EJS 29* [10] **31**	4
7 Nov 92		THE LAST SONG *Rocket EJS 30* **21**	4
22 May 93		SIMPLE LIFE *Rocket EJSCD 31* **44**	2
20 Nov 93	●	TRUE LOVE *Rocket EJSCX 32* [2] **2**	10
26 Feb 94	●	DON'T GO BREAKING MY HEART *Rocket EJRCD 33* [11] **7**	7
14 May 94		AIN'T NOTHING LIKE THE REAL THING *London LONCD 350* [12] **24**	4
9 Jul 94		CAN YOU FEEL THE LOVE TONIGHT *Mercury EJCD 34* ..**14**	9
8 Oct 94		CIRCLE OF LIFE *Rocket EJSCD 35* **11**	12
4 Mar 95		BELIEVE *Rocket EJSCD 36* **15**	7
20 May 95		MADE IN ENGLAND *Rocket EJSCD 37* **18**	5
3 Feb 96		PLEASE *Rocket EJSCD 40* **33**	3
14 Dec 96	●	LIVE LIKE HORSES *Rocket LLHDD 1* [13] ....**9†**	3

[1] Elton John Band [2] Elton John and Kiki Dee [3] Elton John Band featuring John Lennon and the Muscle Shoals Horns [4] Elton John and Millie Jackson [5] Dionne Warwick and Friends featuring Elton John, Stevie Wonder and Gladys Knight [6] Elton John and Cliff Richard [7] Jennifer Rush and Elton John [8] Aretha Franklin and Elton John [9] George Michael and Elton John [10] Elton John and Eric Clapton [11] Elton John with RuPaul [12] Marcella Detroit and Elton John [13] Elton John and Luciano Pavarotti

Bite Your Lip (Get Up And Dance) *was one side of a double-sided chart entry, the other being* Chicago *by Kiki Dee.* Wrap Her Up *features George Michael as uncredited co-vocalist. The 1988 version of* Candle In The Wind *was a live recording.*

Robert JOHN *US, male vocalist* **13 wks**

17 Jul 68		IF YOU DON'T WANT MY LOVE *CBS 3436* **42**	5
20 Oct 79		SAD EYES *EMI American EA 101* **31**	8

JOHNNA *US, female vocalist* **3 wks**

10 Feb 96		DO WHAT YOU FEEL *PWL International PWL 323CD* **43**	2
11 May 96		IN MY DREAMS *PWL International PWL 325CD* **66**	1

JOHNNY and CHARLEY *Spain, male vocal duo* **1 wk**

14 Oct 65		LA YENKA *Pye International 7N 25326* **49**	1

JOHNNY and the HURRICANES
US, male instrumental group **88 wks**

9 Oct 59	●	RED RIVER ROCK *London HL 8948* **3**	16
25 Dec 59	●	REVEILLE ROCK *London HL 9017* **14**	5
17 Mar 60	●	BEATNIK FLY *London HLI 9072* **8**	19
16 Jun 60	●	DOWN YONDER *London HLX 9134* **8**	11
29 Sep 60	●	ROCKING GOOSE *London HLX 9190* **3**	20
2 Mar 61		JA-DA *London HLX 9289* **14**	9
6 Jul 61		OLD SMOKIE / HIGH VOLTAGE *London HLX 9378* **24**	8

JOHNNY HATES JAZZ
UK, male vocal / instrumental group **45 wks**

11 Apr 87	●	SHATTERED DREAMS *Virgin VS 948* **5**	14
29 Aug 87		I DON'T WANT TO BE A HERO *Virgin VS 1000* **11**	10
21 Nov 87		TURN BACK THE CLOCK *Virgin VS 1017* **12**	11
27 Feb 88		HEART OF GOLD *Virgin VS 1045* **19**	7
9 Jul 88		DON'T SAY IT'S LOVE *Virgin VS 1081* **48**	3

Bryan JOHNSON *UK, male vocalist* **11 wks**

10 Mar 60		LOOKING HIGH HIGH HIGH *Decca F 11213* **20**	11

Carey JOHNSON *Australia, male vocalist* **8 wks**

25 Apr 87		REAL FASHION REGGAE STYLE *Oval TEN 170* **19**	8

Denise JOHNSON *UK, female vocalist* **4 wks**

24 Aug 91		DON'T FIGHT IT FEEL IT *Creation CRE 110* [1] **41**	2
14 May 94		RAYS OF THE RISING SUN *Magnet MAG 1022CD* **45**	2

[1] Primal Scream featuring Denise Johnson

Don JOHNSON *US, male vocalist* **12 wks**

18 Oct 86		HEARTBEAT *Epic 650064 7* **46**	5
5 Nov 88		TILL I LOVED YOU (LOVE THEME FROM 'GOYA') *CBS BARB 2* [1] **16**	7

[1] Barbra Streisand and Don Johnson

General JOHNSON – *See* CHAIRMEN OF THE BOARD

Holly JOHNSON *UK, male vocalist* **36 wks**

14 Jan 89	●	LOVE TRAIN *MCA MCA 1306* **4**	11
1 Apr 89	●	AMERICANOS *MCA MCA 1323* **4**	11
20 May 89	★	FERRY 'CROSS THE MERSEY *PWL PWL 41* [1] **1**	7
24 Jun 89		ATOMIC CITY *MCA MCA 1342* **18**	4
30 Sep 89		HEAVEN'S HERE *MCA MCA 1365* **62**	2
1 Dec 90		WHERE HAS LOVE GONE *MCA MCA 1460* **73**	1

[1] Christians, Holly Johnson, Paul McCartney, Gerry Marsden and Stock Aitken Waterman

Howard JOHNSON *US, male vocalist* **6 wks**

4 Sep 82		KEEPIN' LOVE NEW / SO FINE *A & M USA 1221* **45**	6

Keepin' Love New *listed 4 Sep 82 only.*

Johnny JOHNSON and the BANDWAGON
US, male vocal group **50 wks**

16 Oct 68	●	BREAKIN' DOWN THE WALLS OF HEARTACHE *Direction 58-3670* [1] **4**	15

5 Feb 69	**YOU** *Direction 58-3923* [1]	**34**	4
28 May 69	**LET'S HANG ON** *Direction 58-4180* [1]	**36**	6
25 Jul 70	● **SWEET INSPIRATION** *Bell 1111*	**10**	12
24 Oct 70	**SWEET INSPIRATION (re-entry)** *Bell 1111*	**46**	1
28 Nov 70	● **(BLAME IT) ON THE PONY EXPRESS** *Bell 1128*	**7**	12

[1] Bandwagon

Kevin JOHNSON *Australia, male vocalist* — 6 wks

11 Jan 75	**ROCK 'N ROLL (I GAVE YOU THE BEST YEARS OF MY LIFE)** *UK UKR 84*	**23**	6

LJ JOHNSON *US, male vocalist* — 6 wks

7 Feb 76	**YOUR MAGIC PUT A SPELL ON ME** *Philips 6006 492*	**27**	6

Laurie JOHNSON *UK, orchestra* — 12 wks

28 Sep 61	● **SUCU SUCU** *Pye 7N 15383*	**9**	12

Lou JOHNSON *US, male vocalist* — 2 wks

26 Nov 64	**MESSAGE TO MARTHA** *London HL 9929*	**36**	2

Marv JOHNSON *US, male vocalist* — 39 wks

12 Feb 60	● **YOU GOT WHAT IT TAKES** *London HLT 9013*	**7**	16
5 May 60	**I LOVE THE WAY YOU LOVE** *London HLT 9109*	**35**	3
11 Aug 60	**AIN'T GONNA BE THAT WAY** *London HLT 9165*	**50**	1
22 Jan 69	● **I'LL PICK A ROSE FOR MY ROSE** *Tamla Motown TMG 680*	**10**	11
25 Oct 69	**I MISS YOU BABY** *Tamla Motown TMG 713*	**25**	8

Orlando JOHNSON – See SECCHI featuring Orlando JOHNSON

Paul JOHNSON *UK, male vocalist* — 7 wks

21 Feb 87	**WHEN LOVE COMES CALLING** *CBS PJOHN 1*	**52**	5
25 Feb 89	**NO MORE TOMORROWS** *CBS PJOHN 7*	**67**	2

Teddy JOHNSON – See Pearl CARR and Teddy JOHNSON

Bruce JOHNSTON *US, male instrumentalist – keyboards* — 4 wks

27 Aug 77	**PIPELINE** *CBS 5514*	**33**	4

Sabrina JOHNSTON *US, female vocalist* — 19 wks

7 Sep 91	● **PEACE** *East West YZ 616*	**8**	10
7 Dec 91	**FRIENDSHIP** *East West YZ 637*	**58**	4
11 Jul 92	**I WANNA SING** *East West YZ 661*	**46**	2
3 Oct 92	**PEACE (re-mix)** *Epic 6584377*	**35**	2
13 Aug 94	**SATISFY MY LOVE** *Champion CHAMPCD 311*	**62**	1

The listed flipside of Peace (re-mix) was Gypsy Woman (re-mix) by Crystal Waters.

JOHNSTON BROTHERS *UK, male vocal group* — 33 wks

3 Apr 53	● **OH HAPPY DAY** *Decca F 10071*	**4**	8
5 Nov 54	**WAIT FOR ME DARLING** *Decca F 10362* [1]	**18**	1
21 Jan 55	**HAPPY DAYS AND LONELY NIGHTS** *Decca F 10389* [2]	**14**	2
7 Oct 55	★ **HERNANDO'S HIDEAWAY** *Decca F 10608*	**1**	13
30 Dec 55	● **JOIN IN AND SING AGAIN** *Decca F 10636*	**9**	1
13 Apr 56	**NO OTHER LOVE** *Decca F 10721*	**22**	1
30 Nov 56	**IN THE MIDDLE OF THE HOUSE** *Decca F 10781*	**27**	1
7 Dec 56	**JOIN IN AND SING (NO. 3)** *Decca F 10814*	**30**	1
28 Dec 56	**JOIN IN AND SING (NO. 3) (re-entry)** *Decca F 10814*	**24**	1
8 Feb 57	**GIVE HER MY LOVE** *Decca F 10828*	**27**	1
19 Apr 57	**HEART** *Decca F 10860*	**23**	3

[1] Joan Regan and the Johnston Brothers [2] Suzi Miller and the Johnston Brothers

The following two hits were medleys: Join In And Sing Again: Sheik Of Araby / Yes Sir That's My Baby / California Here I Come / Some Of These Days / Charleston / Margie. Join In And Sing (No.3): Coal Black Morning / When You're Smiling / Alexander's Ragtime Band / Sweet Sue Just You / When You Wore A Tulip / If You Were The Only Girl In The World. See also Various Artists (EPs & LPs) – All Star Hit Parade No. 2.

James JOLIS – *Barry MANILOW*

JOJO – See 2PAC

JOLLY BROTHERS
Jamaica, male vocal / instrumental group — 7 wks

28 Jul 79	**CONSCIOUS MAN** *United Artists UP 36415*	**46**	7

JOLLY ROGER *UK, male vocalist* — 12 wks

10 Sep 88	**ACID MAN** *10 TEN 236*	**23**	12

JOMANDA *US, female vocal group* — 10 wks

22 Apr 89	**MAKE MY BODY ROCK** *RCA PB 42749*	**44**	3
29 Jun 91	**GOT A LOVE FOR YOU** *Giant W 0040*	**43**	4
11 Sep 93	**I LIKE IT** *Big Beat A 8377CD*	**67**	1
13 Nov 93	**NEVER** *Big Beat A 8347CD*	**40**	2

JON and VANGELIS
UK, male vocalist / Greece, male multi-instrumentalist — 28 wks

5 Jan 80	● **I HEAR YOU NOW** *Polydor POSP 96*	**8**	11
12 Dec 81	● **I'LL FIND MY WAY HOME** *Polydor JV 1*	**6**	13
30 Jul 83	**HE IS SAILING** *Polydor JV 4*	**61**	2
18 Aug 84	**STATE OF INDEPENDENCE** *Polydor JV 5*	**67**	2

See also Vangelis.

JON OF THE PLEASED WIMMIN *UK, male DJ* — 5 wks

18 Feb 95	**PASSION** *Perfecto YZ 884CD*	**27**	3
6 Apr 96	**GIVE ME STRENGTH** *Perfecto PERF 119CD*	**30**	2

Aled JONES *UK, male vocalist* — 24 wks

20 Jul 85	**MEMORY** *BBC RESL 175*	**42**	4
30 Nov 85	● **WALKING IN THE AIR** *HMV ALED 1*	**5**	11
14 Dec 85	**PICTURES IN THE DARK** *Virgin VS 836* [1]	**50**	6
20 Dec 86	**A WINTER STORY** *HMV ALED 2*	**51**	3

[1] Mike Oldfield featuring Aled Jones, Anita Hegerland and Barry Palmer

Barbara JONES *Jamaica, female vocalist* — 7 wks

31 Jan 81	**JUST WHEN I NEEDED YOU MOST** *Sonet SON 2221*	**31**	7

Catherine Zeta JONES *UK, female vocalist* — 9 wks

19 Sep 92	**FOR ALL TIME** *Columbia 6583547*	**36**	5
26 Nov 94	**TRUE LOVE WAYS** *PolyGram TV TLWCD 2* [1]	**38**	3
1 Apr 95	**IN THE ARMS OF LOVE** *Wow! WOWCD 7101*	**72**	1

[1] David Essex and Catherine Zeta Jones

Georgia JONES – See PLUX featuring Georgia JONES

Grace JONES US, female vocalist — 45 wks

26 Jul 80	PRIVATE LIFE Island WIP 6629		17	8
20 Jun 81	PULL UP TO THE BUMPER Island WIP 6696		53	4
30 Oct 82	THE APPLE STRETCHING / NIPPLE TO THE BOTTLE Island WIP 6779		50	4
9 Apr 83	MY JAMAICAN GUY Island IS 103		56	3
12 Oct 85	SLAVE TO THE RHYTHM ZTT IS 206		12	8
18 Jan 86	PULL UP TO THE BUMPER (re-issue) / LA VIE EN ROSE Island IS 240		12	9
1 Mar 86	LOVE IS THE DRUG Island IS 266		35	4
15 Nov 86	I'M NOT PERFECT (BUT I'M PERFECT FOR YOU) Manhattan MT 15		56	3
7 May 94	SLAVE TO THE RHYTHM (re-mix) Zance ZANG 50CD1		28	2

La Vie En Rose was only listed from 1 Feb 86.

Hannah JONES US, female vocalist — 9 wks

14 Sep 91	BRIDGE OVER TROUBLED WATER Dance Pool 6565467 [1]		21	8
30 Jan 93	KEEP IT ON TMRC CDTMRC 7		67	1

[1] PJB featuring Hannah and her Sisters

Howard JONES UK, male vocalist — 106 wks

17 Sep 83	● NEW SONG WEA HOW 1		3	12
26 Nov 83	● WHAT IS LOVE WEA HOW 2		2	15
14 Jan 84	NEW SONG (re-entry) WEA HOW 1		60	3
18 Feb 84	HIDE AND SEEK WEA HOW 3		12	9
26 May 84	● PEARL IN THE SHELL WEA HOW 4		7	10
11 Aug 84	● LIKE TO GET TO KNOW YOU WELL WEA HOW 5		4	12
9 Feb 85	● THINGS CAN ONLY GET BETTER WEA HOW 6		6	8
20 Apr 85	● LOOK MAMA WEA HOW 7		10	6
29 Jun 85	LIFE IN ONE DAY WEA HOW 8		14	7
15 Mar 86	NO ONE IS TO BLAME WEA HOW 9		16	7
4 Oct 86	ALL I WANT WEA HOW 10		35	4
29 Nov 86	YOU KNOW I LOVE YOU... DON'T YOU? WEA HOW 11		43	3
21 Mar 87	A LITTLE BIT OF SNOW WEA HOW 12		70	1
4 Mar 89	EVERLASTING LOVE WEA HOW 13		62	3
11 Apr 92	LIFT ME UP East West HOW 15		52	3

Janie JONES UK, female vocalist — 3 wks

27 Jan 66	WITCHES' BREW HMV POP 1495		46	3

Jimmy JONES US, male vocalist — 47 wks

17 Mar 60	● HANDY MAN MGM 1051		3	21
16 Jun 60	★ GOOD TIMIN' MGM 1078		1	15
18 Aug 60	HANDY MAN (re-entry) MGM 1051		32	3
8 Sep 60	I JUST GO FOR YOU MGM 1091		35	4
17 Nov 60	READY FOR LOVE MGM 1103		46	1
30 Mar 61	I TOLD YOU SO MGM 1123		33	3

Juggy JONES US, male multi-instrumentalist — 4 wks

7 Feb 76	INSIDE AMERICA Contempo CS 2080		39	4

Lavinia JONES South Africa, female vocalist — 2 wks

18 Feb 95	SING IT TO YOU (DEE-DOOB-DEE-DOO) Virgin International DINDG 142		45	2

Mick JONES – See AZTEC CAMERA

Oran 'Juice' JONES US, male vocalist — 14 wks

15 Nov 86	● THE RAIN Def Jam A 7303		4	14

Paul JONES UK, male vocalist — 34 wks

6 Oct 66	● HIGH TIME HMV POP 1554		4	15
19 Jan 67	● I'VE BEEN A BAD BAD BOY HMV POP 1576		5	9
23 Aug 67	THINKIN' AIN'T FOR ME HMV POP 1602		47	1
13 Sep 67	THINKIN' AIN'T FOR ME (re-entry) HMV POP 1602		32	7
5 Feb 69	AQUARIUS Columbia DB 8514		45	2

Quincy JONES
US, male producer / instrumentalist – keyboards — 41 wks

29 Jul 78	STUFF LIKE THAT A & M AMS 7367		34	9
11 Apr 81	AI NO CORRIDA (I-NO-KO-REE-DA) A & M AMS 8109		14	10
20 Jun 81	RAZZAMATAZZ A & M AMS 8140 [1]		11	9
5 Sep 81	BETCHA' WOULDN'T HURT ME A & M AMS 8157		52	3
13 Jan 90	I'LL BE GOOD TO YOU Qwest W 2697 [2]		21	7
31 Mar 90	SECRET GARDEN Qwest W 9992 [3]		67	1
14 Sep 96	STOMP Qwest W 0372CD		28	2

[1] Quincy Jones featuring Patti Austin [2] Quincy Jones featuring Ray Charles and Chaka Khan [3] Quincy Jones featuring Al B. Sure!, James Ingram, El DeBarge and Barry White

Uncredited vocals on Stuff Like That were by Ashford and Simpson and Chaka Khan, and on Ai No Corrida by Dune.

Rickie Lee JONES US, female vocalist — 9 wks

23 Jun 79	CHUCK E.'S IN LOVE Warner Bros. K 17390		18	9

Shirley JONES – See PARTRIDGE FAMILY starring Shirley JONES featuring David CASSIDY; VARIOUS ARTISTS (EPs & LPs) – Carousel Soundtrack

Tammy JONES UK, female vocalist — 10 wks

26 Apr 75	● LET ME TRY AGAIN Epic EPC 3211		5	10

Tom JONES UK, male vocalist — 356 wks

11 Feb 65	★ IT'S NOT UNUSUAL Decca F 12062		1	14
6 May 65	ONCE UPON A TIME Decca F 12121		32	4
8 Jul 65	WITH THESE HANDS Decca F 12191		13	11
12 Aug 65	WHAT'S NEW PUSSYCAT Decca F 12203		11	10
13 Jan 66	THUNDERBALL Decca F 12292		35	4
19 May 66	ONCE THERE WAS A TIME / NOT RESPONSIBLE Decca F 12390		18	9
18 Aug 66	THIS AND THAT Decca F 12461		44	3
10 Nov 66	★ GREEN GREEN GRASS OF HOME Decca F 22511		1	22
16 Feb 67	● DETROIT CITY Decca F 22555		8	10
13 Apr 67	● FUNNY FAMILIAR FORGOTTEN FEELINGS Decca F 12599		7	15
26 Jul 67	● I'LL NEVER FALL IN LOVE AGAIN Decca F 12639		2	25
22 Nov 67	● I'M COMING HOME Decca F 12693		2	16
28 Feb 68	● DELILAH Decca F 12747		2	17
17 Jul 68	● HELP YOURSELF Decca F 12812		5	26
27 Nov 68	A MINUTE OF YOUR TIME Decca F 12854		14	15
14 May 69	● LOVE ME TONIGHT Decca F 12924		9	12
13 Dec 69	● WITHOUT LOVE Decca F 12990		10	11
14 Mar 70	WITHOUT LOVE (re-entry) Decca F 12990		49	1
18 Apr 70	● DAUGHTER OF DARKNESS Decca F 13013		5	15
15 Aug 70	I (WHO HAVE NOTHING) Decca F 13061		16	8
17 Oct 70	I (WHO HAVE NOTHING) (re-entry) Decca F 13061		47	3
16 Jan 71	SHE'S A LADY Decca F 13113		13	9
27 Mar 71	SHE'S A LADY (re-entry) Decca F 13113		47	1
5 Jun 71	PUPPET MAN Decca F 13183		49	1
19 Jun 71	PUPPET MAN (re-entry) Decca F 13183		50	1
23 Oct 71	● TILL Decca F 13236		2	15

1 Apr 72	● **THE YOUNG NEW MEXICAN PUPPETEER** Decca F 13298	..6	12
14 Apr 73	**LETTER TO LUCILLE** Decca F 13393	**31**	8
7 Sep 74	**SOMETHING 'BOUT YOU BABY I LIKE** Decca F 13550	36	5
16 Apr 77	**SAY YOU'LL STAY UNTIL TOMORROW** EMI 2583	**40**	3
18 Apr 87	● **A BOY FROM NOWHERE** Epic OLE 1	**2**	12
30 May 87	**IT'S NOT UNUSUAL (re-issue)** Decca F 103	**17**	8
2 Jan 88	**I WAS BORN TO BE ME** Epic OLE 4	**61**	1
29 Oct 88	● **KISS** China CHINA 11 [1]	**5**	7
29 Apr 89	**MOVE CLOSER** Jive JIVE 203	**49**	3
26 Jan 91	**COULDN'T SAY GOODBYE** Dover ROJ 10	**51**	2
16 Mar 91	**CARRYING A TORCH** Dover ROJ 12	**57**	2
4 Jul 92	**DELILAH (re-issue)** The Hit Label TOM 10	**68**	2
6 Feb 93	**ALL YOU NEED IS LOVE** Childline CHILDCD 93	**19**	4
5 Nov 94	**IF I ONLY KNEW** ZTT ZANG 59CD	**11**	9

[1] Art Of Noise featuring Tom Jones

See also Various Artists (EPs & LPs) – Gimme Shelter (EP).

Sue JONES-DAVIES – *See Julie COVINGTON, Rula LENSKA, Charlotte CORNWELL and Sue JONES-DAVIES*

Alison JORDAN *UK, female vocalist* **4 wks**

9 May 92	**BOY FROM NEW YORK CITY** Arista 74321100427	**23**	4

Dick JORDAN *UK, male vocalist* **4 wks**

17 Mar 60	**HALLELUJAH I LOVE HER SO** Oriole CB 1534	**47**	1
9 Jun 60	**LITTLE CHRISTINE** Oriole CB 1548	**39**	3

Jack JORDAN – *See Frank CHACKSFIELD*

Montell JORDAN *US, male vocalist* **15 wks**

13 May 95	**THIS IS HOW WE DO IT** Def Jam DEFCD 07	**11**	8
2 Sep 95	**SOMETHIN' 4 DA HONEYZ** Def Jam DEFCD 10	**15**	4
19 Oct 96	**I LIKE** Def Jam DEFCD 19 [1]	**24**	3

[1] Montell Jordan featuring Slick Rick

Ronny JORDAN *UK, male instrumentalist – guitar* **7 wks**

1 Feb 92	**SO WHAT!** Antilles ANN 14	**32**	4
25 Sep 93	**UNDER YOUR SPELL** Island CID 565	**72**	1
15 Jan 94	**TINSEL TOWN** Island CID 566	**64**	1
28 May 94	**COME WITH ME** Island CID 584	**63**	1

David JOSEPH *UK, male vocalist* **21 wks**

26 Feb 83	**YOU CAN'T HIDE (YOUR LOVE FROM ME)** Island IS 101	..13	9
28 May 83	**LET'S LIVE IT UP (NITE PEOPLE)** Island IS 116	**26**	5
18 Feb 84	**JOYS OF LIFE** Island IS 153	**61**	2
31 May 86	**EXPANSIONS '86 (EXPAND YOUR MIND)** Fourth & Broadway BRW 48 [1]	**58**	5

[1] Chris Paul featuring David Joseph

Martyn JOSEPH *UK, male vocalist* **10 wks**

20 Jun 92	**DOLPHINS MAKE ME CRY** Epic 6581347	**34**	4
12 Sep 92	**WORKING MOTHER** Epic 6582937	**65**	1
9 Jan 93	**PLEASE SIR** Epic 6588552	**45**	3
3 Jun 95	**TALK ABOUT IT IN THE MORNING** Epic 6613342	**43**	2

JOURNEY *US, male vocal / instrumental group* **9 wks**

27 Feb 82	**DON'T STOP BELIEVIN'** CBS A 1728	**62**	4
11 Sep 82	**WHO'S CRYING NOW** CBS A 2725	**46**	5

Ruth JOY *UK, female vocalist* **3 wks**

26 Aug 89	**DON'T PUSH IT** MCA RJOY 1	**66**	2
22 Feb 92	**FEEL** MCA MCS 1574	**67**	1

JOY DIVISION *UK, male vocal / instrumental group* **24 wks**

28 Jun 80	**LOVE WILL TEAR US APART** Factory FAC 23	**13**	9
29 Oct 83	**LOVE WILL TEAR US APART (re-entry)** Factory FAC 23	**19**	7
18 Jun 88	**ATMOSPHERE** Factory FAC 2137	**34**	5
17 Jun 95	**LOVE WILL TEAR US APART (re-mix)** London YOJCD 1	**19**	3

JOY STRINGS
UK, male / female vocal / instrumental group **11 wks**

27 Feb 64	**IT'S AN OPEN SECRET** Regal-Zonophone RZ 501	**32**	7
17 Dec 64	**A STARRY NIGHT** Regal-Zonophone RZ 504	**35**	4

JOYRIDER *UK, male vocal / instrumental group* **4 wks**

27 Jul 96	**RUSH HOUR** Paradox PDOXD 012	**22**	3
28 Sep 96	**ALL GONE AWAY** A & M 5819552	**54**	1

JT and the BIG FAMILY
Italy, male / female vocal / instrumental group **8 wks**

3 Mar 90	● **MOMENTS IN SOUL** Champion CHAMP 237	**7**	8

JTQ *UK, male instrumental group* **6 wks**

3 Apr 93	**LOVE THE LIFE** Big Life BLRD 93 [1]	**34**	3
3 Jul 93	**SEE A BRIGHTER DAY** Big Life BLRDA 97 [1]	**49**	2
25 Feb 95	**LOVE WILL KEEP US TOGETHER** Acid Jazz JAZID 112CD [2]	**63**	1

[1] JTQ with Noel McKoy [2] JTQ featuring Alison Limerick

JUDAS PRIEST *UK, male vocal / instrumental group* **51 wks**

20 Jan 79	**TAKE ON THE WORLD** CBS 6915	**14**	10
12 May 79	**EVENING STAR** CBS 7312	**53**	4
29 Mar 80	**LIVING AFTER MIDNIGHT** CBS 8379	**12**	7
7 Jun 80	**BREAKING THE LAW** CBS 8644	**12**	6
23 Aug 80	**UNITED** CBS 8897	**26**	8
21 Feb 81	**DON'T GO** CBS 9520	**51**	3
25 Apr 81	**HOT ROCKIN'** CBS 1153	**60**	3
21 Aug 82	**YOU'VE GOT ANOTHER THING COMIN'** CBS A 2611	**66**	2
21 Jan 84	**FREEWHEEL BURNIN'** CBS A 4054	**42**	3
23 Apr 88	**JOHNNY B. GOODE** Atlantic A 9114	**64**	2
15 Sep 90	**PAINKILLER** CBS 656273 7	**74**	1
23 Mar 91	**A TOUCH OF EVIL** Columbia 6565897	**58**	1
24 Apr 93	**NIGHT CRAWLER** Columbia 6590972	**63**	1

JUDGE DREAD *UK, male vocalist* **95 wks**

26 Aug 72	**BIG SIX** Big Shot BI 608	**11**	27
9 Dec 72	● **BIG SEVEN** Big Shot BI 613	**8**	18
21 Apr 73	**BIG EIGHT** Big Shot BI 619	**14**	10
5 Jul 75	● **JE T'AIME (MOI NON PLUS)** Cactus CT 65	**9**	9
27 Sep 75	**BIG TEN** Cactus CT 77	**14**	7
6 Dec 75	**CHRISTMAS IN DREADLAND / COME OUTSIDE** Cactus CT 80	**14**	7
8 May 76	**THE WINKLE MAN** Cactus CT 90	**35**	4
28 Aug 76	**Y VIVA SUSPENDERS** Cactus CT 99	**27**	4
2 Apr 77	**5TH ANNIVERSARY EP** Cactus CT 98	**31**	4

14 Jan 78	**UP WITH THE COCK / BIG PUNK** *Cactus CT 110*	**49**	1
16 Dec 78	**HOKEY COKEY / JINGLE BELLS** *EMI 2881*	**59**	4

Tracks on 5th Anniversary EP: Jamaica Jerk (off) / Bring Back The Skins / End Of The World / Big Everything.

JUICY US, male / female vocal duo   5 wks

22 Feb 86	**SUGAR FREE** *Epic A 6917*	**45**	5

JUICY LUCY UK, male vocal / instrumental group   17 wks

7 Mar 70	**WHO DO YOU LOVE** *Vertigo V 1*	**14**	12
10 Oct 70	**PRETTY WOMAN** *Vertigo 6059 015*	**45**	2
31 Oct 70	**PRETTY WOMAN (re-entry)** *Vertigo 6059 015*	**44**	3

JULIA and COMPANY US, male / female vocal group   10 wks

3 Mar 84	**BREAKIN' DOWN (SUGAR SAMBA)** *London LON 46*	**15**	8
23 Feb 85	**I'M SO HAPPY** *Next Plateau LON 61*	**56**	2

JULUKA
UK / South Africa, male / female vocal / instrumental group   4 wks

12 Feb 83	**SCATTERLINGS OF AFRICA** *Safari ZULU 1*	**44**	4

Wally JUMP Jr. and the CRIMINAL ELEMENT
US, male producer – Arthur Baker   19 wks

28 Feb 87	**TURN ME LOOSE** *London LON 126*	**60**	2
5 Sep 87	**PUT THE NEEDLE TO THE RECORD** *Cooltempo COOL 150* [1]	**63**	3
12 Dec 87	**TIGHTEN UP – I JUST CAN'T STOP DANCING** *Breakout USA 621*	**24**	7
19 Mar 88	**PRIVATE PARTY** *Breakout USA 624*	**57**	3
6 Oct 90	**EVERYBODY (RAP)** *Deconstruction PB 44701* [2]	**30**	4

[1] Criminal Element Orchestra [2] Criminal Element Orchestra and Wendell Williams

JUMPING JACKS – *See Danny PEPPERMINT and the JUMPING JACKS*

Rosemary JUNE US, female vocalist   9 wks

23 Jan 59	**I'LL BE WITH YOU IN APPLE BLOSSOM TIME** *Pye International 7N 25005*	**14**	9

JUNGLE BOOK US, male / female vocal group   8 wks

8 May 93	**THE JUNGLE BOOK GROOVE** *Hollywood HWCD 128*	**14**	8

JUNGLE BROTHERS US, male rap group   17 wks

22 Oct 88	**I'LL HOUSE YOU** *Gee Street GEE 003* [1]	**22**	5
18 Mar 89	**BLACK IS BLACK / STRAIGHT OUT OF THE JUNGLE** *Gee Street GEE 15*	**72**	1
31 Mar 90	**WHAT 'U' WAITIN' '4'** *Eternal W 9865*	**35**	5
21 Jul 90	**DOIN' OUR OWN DANG** *Eternal W 9754*	**33**	6

[1] Richie Rich meets the Jungle Brothers

Doin' Our Own Dang features the uncredited De La Soul and Monie Love.

JUNGLE HIGH – *See BLUE PEARL*

JUNIOR UK, male vocalist   57 wks

24 Apr 82	● **MAMA USED TO SAY** *Mercury MER 98*	**7**	13

10 Jul 82	**TOO LATE** *Mercury MER 112*	**20**	9
25 Sep 82	**LET ME KNOW / I CAN'T HELP IT** *Mercury MER 116*	**53**	3
23 Apr 83	**COMMUNICATION BREAKDOWN** *Mercury MER 134*	**57**	3
8 Sep 84	**SOMEBODY** *London LON 50*	**64**	2
9 Feb 85	**DO YOU REALLY (WANT MY LOVE)** *London LON 60*	**47**	4
30 Nov 85	**OH LOUISE** *London LON 75*	**74**	3
4 Apr 87	● **ANOTHER STEP (CLOSER TO YOU)** *MCA KIM 5* [1]	**6**	11
25 Aug 90	**STEP OFF** *MCA MCA 1432* [2]	**63**	3
15 Aug 92	**THEN CAME YOU** *MCA MCS 1676* [2]	**32**	5
31 Oct 92	**ALL OVER THE WORLD** *MCA MCS 1691* [2]	**74**	1

[1] Kim Wilde and Junior [2] Junior Giscombe

JUNIOR M.A.F.I.A. US, male / female rap ensemble   2 wks

3 Feb 96	**I NEED YOU TONIGHT** *Big Beat A 8130CD* [1]	**66**	1
19 Oct 96	**GETTIN' MONEY** *Big Beat A 5674CD*	**63**	1

[1] Junior M.A.F.I.A. featuring Aaliyah

JUNIORS – *See DANNY and the JUNIORS*

JUST LUIS Australia, male vocalist   3 wks

14 Oct 95	**AMERICAN PIE** *Pro-Activ CDPTV 1*	**31**	2
17 Feb 96	**AMERICAN PIE (re-entry)** *Pro-Activ CDPTV 1*	**70**	1

Jimmy JUSTICE UK, male vocalist   35 wks

29 Mar 62	● **WHEN MY LITTLE GIRL IS SMILING** *Pye 7N 15421*	**9**	13
14 Jun 62	● **AIN'T THAT FUNNY** *Pye 7N 15443*	**8**	11
23 Aug 62	**SPANISH HARLEM** *Pye 7N 15457*	**20**	11

JUSTIFIED ANCIENTS OF MU MU
UK, male production duo – The KLF under an assumed name   6 wks

9 Nov 91	● **IT'S GRIM UP NORTH** *KLF Communications JAMS 028*	**10**	5
4 Jan 92	**IT'S GRIM UP NORTH (re-entry)** *KLF Communications JAMS 028*	**67**	1

Bill JUSTIS US, male instrumentalist – alto sax   8 wks

10 Jan 58	**RAUNCHY** *London HLS 8517*	**24**	2
31 Jan 58	**RAUNCHY (re-entry)** *London HLS 8517*	**11**	6

Patrick JUVET France, male vocalist   19 wks

2 Sep 78	**GOT A FEELING** *Casablanca CAN 127*	**34**	7
4 Nov 78	**I LOVE AMERICA** *Casablanca CAN 132*	**12**	12

JX UK, male producer – Jake Williams   30 wks

2 Apr 94	**SON OF A GUN** *Internal Dance IDC 5*	**13**	6
1 Apr 95	**YOU BELONG TO ME** *Ffrreedom TABCD 227*	**17**	5
19 Aug 95	● **SON OF A GUN (re-mix)** *Ffrreedom TABCD 233*	**6**	6
18 May 96	● **THERE'S NOTHING I WON'T DO** *Ffrreedom TABCD 241*	**4**	13

K

Frank K featuring Wiston OFFICE
Italy / US, male vocal / instrumental duo   1 wk

26 Jan 91	**EVERYBODY LET'S SOMEBODY LOVE** *Urban URB 66*	**61**	1

Leila K *Sweden, female vocalist* **22 wks**

25 Nov 89 ●	**GOT TO GET** Arista 112696 [1]	8	14
17 Mar 90	**ROK THE NATION** Arista 112971 [1]	41	3
23 Jan 93	**OPEN SESAME** Polydor PQCD 1	23	4
3 Jul 93	**CA PLANE POUR MOI** Polydor PQCD 3	69	1

[1] Rob 'N' Raz featuring Leila K

K CREATIVE *UK, male vocal / instrumental group* **2 wks**

7 Mar 92	**THREE TIMES A MAYBE** Talkin Loud TLK 17	58	2

The listed flipside of Three Times A Maybe *was* Feed The Feeling *by* Perception.

Ernie K-DOE *US, male vocalist* **7 wks**

11 May 61	**MOTHER-IN-LAW** London HLU 9330	29	7

K-KLASS
UK, male / female vocal / instrumental group **30 wks**

4 May 91	**RHYTHM IS A MYSTERY** Deconstruction CREED 11	61	2
9 Nov 91 ●	**RHYTHM IS A MYSTERY (re-issue)** Deconstruction R 6302	3	10
25 Apr 92	**SO RIGHT** Deconstruction R 6309	20	5
7 Nov 92	**DON'T STOP** Deconstruction R 6325	32	3
27 Nov 93	**LET ME SHOW YOU** Deconstruction CDR 6367	13	7
28 May 94	**WHAT YOU'RE MISSING** Deconstruction CDRS 6380	24	3

Joshua KADISON *US, male vocalist* **19 wks**

26 Feb 94	**JESSIE** SBK CDSBK 43	69	2
1 Oct 94	**JESSIE (re-entry)** SBK CDSBK 43	48	3
12 Nov 94	**BEAUTIFUL IN MY EYES** SBK CDSBK 50	65	1
29 Apr 95	**JESSIE (re-issue)** SBK CDSBK 53	15	10
12 Aug 95	**BEAUTIFUL IN MY EYES (re-issue)** SBK CDSBK 55	37	3

KADOC *UK / Spain, male vocal / instrumental group* **9 wks**

6 Apr 96	**THE NIGHTTRAIN** Positiva CDTIV 26	14	8
17 Aug 96	**YOU GOT TO BE THERE** Positiva CDTIV 58	45	1

Bert KAEMPFERT *Germany, orchestra* **10 wks**

23 Dec 65	**BYE BYE BLUES** Polydor BM 56 504	24	10

KAJAGOOGOO *UK, male vocal / instrumental group* **50 wks**

22 Jan 83 ★	**TOO SHY** EMI 5359	1	13
2 Apr 83 ●	**OOH TO BE AH** EMI 5383	7	8
4 Jun 83	**HANG ON NOW** EMI 5394	13	7
17 Sep 83 ●	**BIG APPLE** EMI 5423	8	8
3 Mar 84	**THE LION'S MOUTH** EMI 5449	25	7
5 May 84	**TURN YOUR BACK ON ME** EMI 5646	47	4
21 Sep 85	**SHOULDN'T DO THAT** Parlophone R 6106 [1]	63	3

[1] Kaja

KALEEF *UK, male vocal group* **7 wks**

30 Mar 96	**WALK LIKE A CHAMPION** Payday KACD 5 [1]	23	3
7 Dec 96	**GOLDEN BROWN** Unity UNITY 010CD	.........22†	4

[1] Kaliphz featuring Prince Naseem

KALIN TWINS *US, male vocal duo* **18 wks**

18 Jul 58 ★	**WHEN** Brunswick 05751	1	18

Kitty KALLEN *US, female vocalist* **23 wks**

2 Jul 54 ★	**LITTLE THINGS MEAN A LOT** Brunswick 05287	1	23

Gunter KALLMAN CHOIR
Germany, male / female vocal group **3 wks**

24 Dec 64	**ELISABETH SERENADE** Polydor NH 24678	45	3

Nick KAMEN *UK, male vocalist* **33 wks**

8 Nov 86 ●	**EACH TIME YOU BREAK MY HEART** WEA YZ 90	5	12
28 Feb 87	**LOVING YOU IS SWEETER THAN EVER** WEA YZ 106	16	9
16 May 87	**NOBODY ELSE** WEA YZ 122	47	3
28 May 88	**TELL ME** WEA YZ 184	40	5
28 Apr 90	**I PROMISED MYSELF** WEA YZ 454	50	4

Ini KAMOZE *Jamaica, male vocalist* **15 wks**

7 Jan 95 ●	**HERE COMES THE HOTSTEPPER** Columbia 6610472	4	15

KANDIDATE *UK, male vocal / instrumental group* **28 wks**

19 Aug 78	**DON'T WANNA SAY GOODNIGHT** RAK 280	47	6
17 Mar 79	**I DON'T WANNA LOSE YOU** RAK 289	11	12
4 Aug 79	**GIRLS GIRLS GIRLS** RAK 295	34	7
22 Mar 80	**LET ME ROCK YOU** RAK 306	58	3

Eden KANE *UK, male vocalist* **73 wks**

1 Jun 61 ★	**WELL I ASK YOU** Decca F 11353	1	21
14 Sep 61 ●	**GET LOST** Decca F 11381	10	11
18 Jan 62 ●	**FORGET ME NOT** Decca F 11418	3	14
10 May 62 ●	**I DON'T KNOW WHY** Decca F 11460	7	13
30 Jan 64 ●	**BOYS CRY** Fontana TF 438	8	14

KANE GANG *UK, male vocal / instrumental group* **37 wks**

19 May 84	**SMALL TOWN CREED** Kitchenware SK 11	60	2
7 Jul 84	**CLOSEST THING TO HEAVEN** Kitchenware SK 15	12	11
10 Nov 84	**RESPECT YOURSELF** Kitchenware SK 16	21	10
26 Jan 85	**RESPECT YOURSELF (re-entry)** Kitchenware SK 16	75	1
9 Mar 85	**GUN LAW** Kitchenware SK 20	53	4
27 Jun 87	**MOTORTOWN** Kitchenware SK 30	45	5
16 Apr 88	**DON'T LOOK ANY FURTHER** Kitchenware SK 33	52	4

KANSAS *US, male vocal / instrumental group* **7 wks**

1 Jul 78	**CARRY ON WAYWARD SON** Kirshner KIR 4932	51	7

Mory KANTE *Guinea, male vocalist* **14 wks**

23 Jul 88	**YEKE YEKE** London LON 171	29	9
11 Mar 95	**YEKE YEKE (re-mix)** Ffrreedom TABCD 226	25	3
30 Nov 96	**YEKE YEKE (2nd re-mix)** ffrr FCD 288	28	2

KAOMA *France, male / female vocal / instrumental group* **20 wks**

21 Oct 89 ●	**LAMBADA** CBS 655011 7	4	18
27 Jan 90	**DANCANDO LAMBADA** CBS 655235 7	62	2

KAOTIC CHEMISTRY
UK, male instrumental / production group **1 wk**

31 Oct 92	**LSD (EP)** *Moving Shadow SHADOW 20*	**68**	1

Tracks on LSD (EP): Space Cakes / LSD / Illegal Substances / Drumtrip II.

KARIN – *See UNIQUE 3*

KARIYA
US, female vocalist **9 wks**

8 Jul 89	**LET ME LOVE YOU FOR TONIGHT** *Sleeping Bag SBUK 4*	**44**	6
21 Oct 89	**LET ME LOVE YOU FOR TONIGHT (re-entry)** *Sleeping Bag SBUK 4*	**57**	3

Mick KARN
UK, male instrumentalist – saxophone **6 wks**

9 Jul 83	**AFTER A FASHION** *Musicfest FEST 1* [1]	**39**	4
17 Jan 87	**BUOY** *Virgin VS 910* [2]	**63**	2

[1] Midge Ure and Mick Karn [2] Mick Karn featuring David Sylvian

KARTOON KREW
US, male vocal / instrumental group **6 wks**

7 Dec 85	**INSPECTOR GADGET** *Champion CHAMP 6*	**58**	6

KASENETZ-KATZ SINGING ORCHESTRAL CIRCUS
US, male vocal / instrumental group **15 wks**

20 Nov 68	**QUICK JOEY SMALL (RUN JOEY RUN)** *Buddah 201 022*	**19**	15

KATRINA and the WAVES
US / UK, female / male vocal / instrumental group **22 wks**

4 May 85	● **WALKING ON SUNSHINE** *Capitol CL 354*	**8**	12
5 Jul 86	**SUN STREET** *Capitol CL 407*	**22**	9
8 Jun 96	**WALKING ON SUNSHINE (re-issue)** *EMI Premier PRESCD 2*	**53**	1

KAVANA
UK, male vocalist **5 wks**

11 May 96	**CRAZY CHANCE** *Nemesis NMSD 1*	**35**	3
24 Aug 96	**WHERE ARE YOU** *Nemesis NMSD 2*	**26**	2

Niamh KAVANAGH
Ireland, female vocalist **5 wks**

12 Jun 93	**IN YOUR EYES** *Arista 74321154152*	**24**	5

Janet KAY
UK, female vocalist **24 wks**

9 Jun 79	● **SILLY GAMES** *Scope SC 2*	**2**	14
11 Aug 90	**SILLY GAMES** *Arista 113452* [1]	**22**	7
11 Aug 90	**SILLY GAMES (re-mix)** *Music Factory Dance MFD 006*	**62**	3

[1] Lindy Layton featuring Janet Kay

Danny KAYE
US, male vocalist **10 wks**

27 Feb 53	● **WONDERFUL COPENHAGEN** *Brunswick 05023*	**5**	10

KAYE SISTERS
UK, female vocal group **45 wks**

25 May 56	**IVORY TOWER** *HMV POP 209* [1]	**20**	5
1 Nov 57	● **GOTTA HAVE SOMETHING IN THE BANK FRANK** *Philips PB 751* [2]	**8**	11
3 Jan 58	**SHAKE ME I RATTLE / ALONE** *Philips PB 752*	**27**	1
1 May 59	● **COME SOFTLY TO ME** *Philips PB 913* [2]	**9**	9
7 Jul 60	● **PAPER ROSES** *Philips PB 1024*	**7**	19

[1] Three Kayes [2] Frankie Vaughan and The Kaye Sisters

KC – *See 2PAC*

KC and the SUNSHINE BAND
US, male vocal / instrumental group **104 wks**

17 Aug 74	● **QUEEN OF CLUBS** *Jayboy BOY 88*	**7**	12
23 Nov 74	**SOUND YOUR FUNKY HORN** *Jayboy BOY 83*	**17**	9
29 Mar 75	**GET DOWN TONIGHT** *Jayboy BOY 93*	**21**	9
2 Aug 75	● **THAT'S THE WAY (I LIKE IT)** *Jayboy BOY 99*	**4**	10
22 Nov 75	**I'M SO CRAZY ('BOUT YOU)** *Jayboy BOY 101*	**34**	3
17 Jul 76	**(SHAKE SHAKE SHAKE) SHAKE YOUR BOOTY** *Jayboy BOY 110*	**22**	8
11 Dec 76	**KEEP IT COMIN' LOVE** *Jayboy BOY 112*	**31**	8
30 Apr 77	**I'M YOUR BOOGIE MAN** *TK XB 2167*	**41**	4
6 May 78	**BOOGIE SHOES** *TK TKR 6025*	**34**	5
22 Jul 78	**IT'S THE SAME OLD SONG** *TK TKR 6037*	**47**	5
8 Dec 79	● **PLEASE DON'T GO** *TK TKR 7558*	**3**	12
16 Jul 83	★ **GIVE IT UP** *Epic EPC A 3017*	**1**	14
24 Sep 83	**(YOU SAID) YOU'D GIMME SOME MORE** *Epic A 2760*	**41**	3
11 May 91	**THAT'S THE WAY I LIKE IT (re-mix)** *Music Factory Dance M7FAC 2*	**59**	2

KE
US, male vocalist **1 wk**

13 Apr 96	**STRANGE WORLD** *Venture 74321349412*	**73**	1

Johnny KEATING
UK, orchestra **14 wks**

1 Mar 62	● **THEME FROM 'Z CARS'** *Piccadilly 7N 35032*	**8**	14

Kevin KEEGAN
UK, male vocalist **6 wks**

9 Jun 79	**HEAD OVER HEELS IN LOVE** *EMI 2965*	**31**	6

Yvonne KEELEY – *See Scott FITZGERALD*

Nelson KEENE
UK, male vocalist **5 wks**

25 Aug 60	**IMAGE OF A GIRL** *HMV POP 771*	**37**	4
29 Sep 60	**IMAGE OF A GIRL (re-entry)** *HMV POP 771*	**45**	1

KEITH
US, male vocalist **8 wks**

26 Jan 67	**98.6** *Mercury MF 955*	**24**	7
16 Mar 67	**TELL ME TO MY FACE** *Mercury MF 968*	**50**	1

Jerry KELLER
US, male vocalist **14 wks**

28 Aug 59	★ **HERE COMES SUMMER** *London HLR 8890*	**1**	14

Frank KELLY
Ireland, male vocalist **5 wks**

24 Dec 83	**CHRISTMAS COUNTDOWN** *Ritz RITZ 062*	**26**	4
29 Dec 84	**CHRISTMAS COUNTDOWN (re-entry)** *Ritz RITZ 062*	**54**	1

Frankie KELLY
US, male vocalist / instrumentalist **2 wks**

2 Nov 85	**AIN'T THAT THE TRUTH** *10 TEN 87*	**65**	2

Grace KELLY – *See Bing CROSBY*

Keith KELLY *UK, male vocalist*   5 wks

5 May 60	**TEASE ME** *Parlophone R 4640*	**46** 1
19 May 60	**TEASE ME (re-entry)** *Parlophone R 4640*	**27** 3
18 Aug 60	**LISTEN LITTLE GIRL** *Parlophone R 4676*	**47** 1

R KELLY *US, male vocalist*   45 wks

9 May 92	**SHE'S GOT THAT VIBE** *Jive JIVET 292* [1]	**57** 2
20 Nov 93	**SEX ME** *Jive JIVECD 346* [1]	**75** 1
14 May 94	**YOUR BODY'S CALLIN'** *Jive JIVECD 353*	**19** 4
3 Sep 94	**SUMMER BUNNIES** *Jive JIVECD 358*	**23** 3
22 Oct 94	● **SHE'S GOT THAT VIBE (re-issue)** *Jive JIVECD 364*	**3** 13
21 Jan 95	● **BUMP N' GRIND** *Jive JIVECD 368*	**8** 9
6 May 95	**THE 4 PLAY EPS** *Jive JIVECD 376*	**23** 3
11 Nov 95	**YOU REMIND ME OF SOMETHING** *Jive JIVECD 388*	**24** 3
2 Mar 96	**DOWN LOW (NOBODY HAS TO KNOW)** *Jive JIVECD 392* [2]	**23** 3
22 Jun 96	**THANK GOD IT'S FRIDAY** *Jive JIVECD 395*	**14** 4

[1] R Kelly and Public Announcement [2] R Kelly featuring Ronald Isley

The 4 Play EPs *was available on 2 CDs, each featuring* Your Body's Callin' *and three further tracks.*

Roberta KELLY *US, female vocalist*   3 wks

| 21 Jan 78 | **ZODIACS** *Oasis/Hansa 3* | **48** 1 |
| 4 Feb 78 | **ZODIACS (re-entry)** *Oasis/Hansa 3* | **44** 2 |

KELLY FAMILY
Ireland, male/female vocal/instrumental group   1 wk

| 21 Oct 95 | **AN ANGEL** *EMI CDEM 390* | **69** 1 |

Johnny KEMP *Barbados, male vocalist*   1 wk

| 27 Aug 88 | **JUST GOT PAID** *CBS 651470 7* | **68** 1 |

Tara KEMP *US, female vocalist*   2 wks

| 20 Apr 91 | **HOLD YOU TIGHT** *Giant W 0020* | **69** 2 |

Graham KENDRICK *UK, male vocalist*   4 wks

| 9 Sep 89 | **LET THE FLAME BURN BRIGHTER** *Power P 30* | **55** 4 |

Eddie KENDRICKS *US, male vocalist*   20 wks

3 Nov 73	**KEEP ON TRUCKIN'** *Tamla Motown TMG 873*	**18** 14
16 Mar 74	**BOOGIE DOWN** *Tamla Motown TMG 888*	**39** 4
21 Sep 85	**A NIGHT AT THE APOLLO LIVE!** *RCA PB 49935* [1]	**58** 2

[1] Daryl Hall and John Oates featuring David Ruffin and Eddie Kendrick

A Night At The Apollo Live! *is a medley of* The Way You Do The Things You Do / My Girl. *Kendricks dropped the 's' from his name for last hit.*

KENECKIE
UK, female/male vocal/instrumental group   3 wks

| 14 Sep 96 | **PUNKA** *Emidisc CDDISC 001* | **43** 2 |
| 16 Nov 96 | **MILLIONAIRE SWEEPER** *Emidisc CDDISC 002* | **60** 1 |

Jane KENNAWAY and STRANGE BEHAVIOUR
UK, female vocalist, male instrumental group   3 wks

| 24 Jan 81 | **I.O.U.** *Deram DM 436* | **65** 3 |

Brian KENNEDY *UK, male vocalist*   6 wks

| 22 Jun 96 | **A BETTER MAN** *RCA 74321382642* | **28** 3 |
| 21 Sep 96 | **LIFE, LOVE AND HAPPINESS** *RCA 74321409921* | **27** 3 |

KENNY *Ireland, male vocalist*   16 wks

| 3 Mar 73 | **HEART OF STONE** *RAK 144* | **11** 13 |
| 30 Jun 73 | **GIVE IT TO ME NOW** *RAK 153* | **38** 3 |

KENNY *UK, male vocal/instrumental group*   39 wks

7 Dec 74	● **THE BUMP** *RAK 186*	**3** 15
8 Mar 75	● **FANCY PANTS** *RAK 196*	**4** 9
7 Jun 75	**BABY I LOVE YOU OK** *RAK 207*	**12** 7
16 Aug 75	● **JULIE ANN** *RAK 214*	**10** 8

Gerard KENNY *US, male vocalist*   21 wks

9 Dec 78	**NEW YORK, NEW YORK** *RCA PB 5117*	**43** 8
21 Jun 80	**FANTASY** *RCA PB 5256*	**65** 1
5 Jul 80	**FANTASY (re-entry)** *RCA PB 5256*	**34** 5
18 Feb 84	**THE OTHER WOMAN, THE OTHER MAN** *Impression IMS 3*	**69** 4
4 May 85	**NO MAN'S LAND ('WIDOWS' THEME)** *WEA YZ 38*	**56** 3

Klark KENT *US, male vocalist/multi-instrumentalist*   4 wks

| 26 Aug 78 | **DON'T CARE** *A & M AMS 7376* | **48** 4 |

Carol KENYON – *See Paul HARDCASTLE; HEAVEN 17; RAPINATION*

KERBDOG *Ireland, male vocal/instrumental group*   4 wks

12 Mar 94	**DRY RISER** *Vertigo VERCC 83*	**60** 1
6 Aug 94	**DUMMY CRUSHER** *Vertigo VERCD 86*	**37** 2
12 Oct 96	**SALLY** *Fontana KERCD 2*	**69** 1

KERRI and MICK *Australia, female/male vocal duo*   3 wks

| 28 Apr 84 | **'SONS AND DAUGHTERS' THEME** *A1 A1 286* | **68** 3 |

Liz KERSHAW and Bruno BROOKES
UK, male/female vocal duo   3 wks

| 2 Dec 89 | **IT TAKES TWO BABY** *Spartan CIN 101* [1] | **53** 2 |
| 1 Dec 90 | **LET'S DANCE** *Jive BRUNO 1* [2] | **54** 1 |

[1] Liz Kershaw, Bruno Brookes, Jive Bunny and Londonbeat [2] Bruno and Liz and the Radio 1 DJ Posse

See also *Jive Bunny and the Mastermixers; Londonbeat.*

Nik KERSHAW *UK, male vocalist*   87 wks

19 Nov 83	**I WON'T LET THE SUN GO DOWN ON ME** *MCA MCA 816*	**47** 5
28 Jan 84	● **WOULDN'T IT BE GOOD** *MCA NIK 2*	**4** 14
14 Apr 84	**DANCING GIRLS** *MCA NIK 3*	**13** 9
16 Jun 84	● **I WON'T LET THE SUN GO DOWN ON ME (re-issue)** *MCA NIK 4*	**2** 13

15 Sep 84	HUMAN RACING *MCA NIK 5*	**19**	7
17 Nov 84	● THE RIDDLE *MCA NIK 6*	**3**	11
16 Mar 85	● WIDE BOY *MCA NIK 7*	**9**	8
3 Aug 85	● DON QUIXOTE *MCA NIK 8*	**10**	7
30 Nov 85	WHEN A HEART BEATS *MCA NIK 9*	**27**	7
11 Oct 86	NOBODY KNOWS *MCA NIK 10*	**44**	3
13 Dec 86	RADIO MUSICOLA *MCA NIK 11*	**43**	2
4 Feb 89	ONE STEP AHEAD *MCA NIK 12*	**55**	1

KEVIN THE GERBIL *UK, male gerbil vocalist*   6 wks

4 Aug 84	SUMMER HOLIDAY *Magnet RAT 3*	**50**	6

KEY WEST – See ERIK

KEYNOTES – See Dave KING

Chaka KHAN *US, female vocalist*   93 wks

2 Dec 78	I'M EVERY WOMAN *Warner Bros. K 17269*	**11**	13
31 Mar 84	● AIN'T NOBODY *Warner Bros. RCK 1* [1]	**8**	12
20 Oct 84	★ I FEEL FOR YOU *Warner Bros. W 9209*	**1**	16
19 Jan 85	THIS IS MY NIGHT *Warner Bros. W 9097*	**14**	6
20 Apr 85	EYE TO EYE *Warner Bros. W 9009*	**16**	7
12 Jul 86	LOVE OF A LIFETIME *Warner Bros. W 8671*	**52**	4
21 Jan 89	IT'S MY PARTY *Warner Bros. W 7678*	**71**	2
6 May 89	● I'M EVERY WOMAN (re-mix) *Warner Bros. W 2963*	**8**	8
8 Jul 89	● AIN'T NOBODY (re-mix) *Warner Bros. W 2880* [1]	**6**	9
7 Oct 89	I FEEL FOR YOU (re-mix) *Warner Bros. W 2764*	**45**	2
13 Jan 90	I'LL BE GOOD TO YOU *Qwest W 2697* [2]	**21**	7
28 Mar 92	LOVE YOU ALL MY LIFETIME *Warner Bros. W 0087*	**49**	3
17 Jul 93	DON'T LOOK AT ME THAT WAY *Warner Bros. W 0192CD*	**73**	1
19 Aug 95	WATCH WHAT YOU SAY *Cooltempo CDCOOL 308* [3]	**28**	3

[1] Rufus and Chaka Khan [2] Quincy Jones featuring Ray Charles and Chaka Khan [3] Guru featuring Chaka Khan

See also Quincy Jones.

Praga KHAN *Belgium, male producer*   8 wks

4 Apr 92	FREE YOUR BODY / INJECTED WITH A POISON *Profile PROFT 347* [1]	**16**	6
11 Jul 92	RAVE ALERT *Profile PROF 369*	**39**	2

[1] Praga Khan featuring Jade 4 U

Mary KIANI *UK, female vocalist*   11 wks

12 Aug 95	WHEN I CALL YOUR NAME *Mercury MERCD 440*	**18**	4
23 Dec 95	I GIVE IT ALL TO YOU / I IMAGINE *Mercury MERCD 449*	**35**	4
27 Apr 96	LET THE MUSIC PLAY *Mercury MERCD 456*	**19**	3

KICK HORNS – See DODGY

KICK SQUAD
UK / Germany, male vocal / instrumental group   2 wks

10 Nov 90	SOUND CLASH (CHAMPION SOUND) *Kickin KICK 2*	**59**	2

KICKING BACK with TAXMAN
UK, male / female vocal / instrumental duo with male rapper   8 wks

17 Mar 90	DEVOTION *10 TEN 297*	**47**	4
7 Jul 90	EVERYTHING *10 TEN 307*	**54**	4

KICKS LIKE A MULE
UK, male instrumental / production duo   6 wks

1 Feb 92	● THE BOUNCER *Tribal Bass TRIBE 3S*	**7**	6

K.I.D. *Antilles, male / female vocal / instrumental group*   4 wks

28 Feb 81	DON'T STOP *EMI 5143*	**49**	4

KID 'N' PLAY *US, male vocal / instrumental duo*   7 wks

18 Jul 87	LAST NIGHT *Cooltempo COOL 148*	**71**	1
26 Mar 88	DO THIS MY WAY *Cooltempo COOL 164*	**48**	3
17 Sep 88	GITTIN' FUNKY *Cooltempo COOL 168*	**55**	3

KID UNKNOWN *UK, male producer – Paul Fitzpatrick*   1 wk

2 May 92	NIGHTMARE *Warp WAP 20CD*	**64**	1

Carol KIDD featuring Terry WAITE
UK, female / male vocal duo   3 wks

17 Oct 92	WHEN I DREAM *The Hit Label HLS 1*	**58**	3

Johnny KIDD and the PIRATES
UK, male vocal / instrumental group   62 wks

12 Jun 59	PLEASE DON'T TOUCH *HMV POP 615* [1]	**26**	3
17 Jul 59	PLEASE DON'T TOUCH (re-entry) *HMV POP 615* [1]	**25**	2
12 Feb 60	YOU GOT WHAT IT TAKES *HMV POP 698*	**25**	3
16 Jun 60	★ SHAKIN' ALL OVER *HMV POP 753*	**1**	19
6 Oct 60	RESTLESS *HMV POP 790*	**22**	7
13 Apr 61	LINDA LU *HMV POP 853*	**47**	1
10 Jan 63	SHOT OF RHYTHM AND BLUES *HMV POP 1088*	**48**	1
25 Jul 63	I'LL NEVER GET OVER YOU *HMV POP 1173*	**4**	15
28 Nov 63	HUNGRY FOR LOVE *HMV POP 1228*	**20**	10
30 Apr 64	ALWAYS AND EVER *HMV POP 1269*	**46**	1

[1] Johnny Kidd

KIDS FROM 'FAME' *US, male / female vocal group*   36 wks

14 Aug 82	● HI-FIDELITY *RCA 254* [1]	**5**	10
2 Oct 82	● STARMAKER *RCA 280*	**3**	10
11 Dec 82	MANNEQUIN *RCA 299* [2]	**50**	6
9 Apr 83	FRIDAY NIGHT (LIVE VERSION) *RCA 320*	**13**	10

[1] Kids From Fame featuring Valerie Landsberg [2] Kids From Fame featuring Gene Anthony Ray

Greg KIHN BAND *US, male vocal / instrumental group*   2 wks

23 Apr 83	JEOPARDY *Beserkley E 9847*	**63**	2

KILLING JOKE *UK, male vocal / instrumental group*   48 wks

23 May 81	FOLLOW THE LEADERS *Malicious Damage EGMDS 101*	**55**	5
20 Mar 82	EMPIRE SONG *Malicious Damage EGO 4*	**43**	4
30 Oct 82	BIRDS OF A FEATHER *EG EGO 10*	**64**	2
25 Jun 83	LET'S ALL (GO TO THE FIRE DANCES) *EG EGO 11*	**51**	3
15 Oct 83	ME OR YOU? *EG EGO 14*	**57**	1
7 Apr 84	EIGHTIES *EG EGO 16*	**60**	5
21 Jul 84	A NEW DAY *EG EGO 17*	**56**	2
2 Feb 85	LOVE LIKE BLOOD *EG EGO 20*	**16**	9
30 Mar 85	KINGS AND QUEENS *EG EGO 21*	**58**	3
16 Aug 86	ADORATIONS *EG EGO 27*	**42**	6
18 Oct 86	SANITY *EG EGO 30*	**70**	1

7 May 94	**MILLENIUM** Butterfly BFLD 12	**34**	2
16 Jul 94	**PANDEMONIUM** Butterfly BFLD 17	**28**	3
4 Feb 95	**JANA** Butterfly BFLDA 21	**54**	1
23 Mar 96	**DEMOCRACY** Butterfly BFLDA 33	**39**	1

Andy KIM Canada, male vocalist — 12 wks

24 Aug 74	● **ROCK ME GENTLY** Capitol CL 15787	**2**	12

Bianca KINANE Ireland, female vocalist — 2 wks

18 May 96	**ALL THE LOVER I NEED** Coliseum TOGA 003CD	**59**	1
21 Sep 96	**THE WOMAN IN ME** Coliseum TOGA 007CD	**73**	1

KING UK / Ireland, male vocal / instrumental group — 44 wks

12 Jan 85	● **LOVE AND PRIDE** CBS A 4988	**2**	14
23 Mar 85	**WON'T YOU HOLD MY HAND NOW** CBS A 6094	**24**	8
17 Aug 85	● **ALONE WITHOUT YOU** CBS A 6308	**8**	9
19 Oct 85	**THE TASTE OF YOUR TEARS** CBS A 6618	**11**	9
11 Jan 86	**TORTURE** CBS A 6761	**23**	4

See also Paul King.

BB KING US, male vocalist / instrumentalist – guitar — 10 wks

15 Apr 89	● **WHEN LOVE COMES TO TOWN** Island IS 411 [1]	**6**	7
18 Jul 92	**SINCE I MET YOU BABY** Virgin VS 1423 [2]	**59**	3

[1] U2 with BB King [2] Gary Moore and BB King

Ben E KING US, male vocalist — 35 wks

2 Feb 61	**FIRST TASTE OF LOVE** London HLK 9258	**27**	11
22 Jun 61	**STAND BY ME** London HLK 9358	**50**	1
6 Jul 61	**STAND BY ME (re-entry)** London HLK 9358	**27**	6
5 Oct 61	**AMOR AMOR** London HLK 9416	**38**	4
14 Feb 87	★ **STAND BY ME (re-issue)** Atlantic A 9361	**1**	11
4 Jul 87	**SAVE THE LAST DANCE FOR ME** Manhattan MT 25	**69**	2

Carole KING US, female vocalist — 29 wks

20 Sep 62	● **IT MIGHT AS WELL RAIN UNTIL SEPTEMBER** London HLU 9591	**3**	13
7 Aug 71	● **IT'S TOO LATE** A & M AMS 849	**6**	12
28 Oct 72	**IT MIGHT AS WELL RAIN UNTIL SEPTEMBER (re-issue)** London HL 10391	**43**	4

Dave KING Canada, male vocalist — 29 wks

17 Feb 56	● **MEMORIES ARE MADE OF THIS** Decca F 10684 [1]	**5**	15
13 Apr 56	**YOU CAN'T BE TRUE TO TWO** Decca F 10720 [1]	**11**	9
21 Dec 56	**CHRISTMAS AND YOU** Decca F 10791	**23**	2
24 Jan 58	**THE STORY OF MY LIFE** Decca F 10973	**20**	3

[1] Dave King featuring The Keynotes

See also Various Artists (EPs & LPs) – All Star Hit Parade.

Denis KING – See STUTZ BEARCATS and the Denis KING ORCHESTRA

Diana KING Jamaica, female vocalist — 18 wks

8 Jul 95	● **SHY GUY** Columbia 6621682	**2**	13
28 Oct 95	**AIN'T NOBODY** Columbia 6625495	**13**	5

Evelyn 'Champagne' KING US, female vocalist — 76 wks

13 May 78	**SHAME** RCA PC 1122	**39**	23
3 Feb 79	**I DON'T KNOW IF IT'S RIGHT** RCA PB 1386	**67**	2
27 Jun 81	**I'M IN LOVE** RCA 95 [1]	**27**	11
26 Sep 81	**IF YOU WANT MY LOVIN'** RCA 131 [1]	**43**	6
28 Aug 82	● **LOVE COME DOWN** RCA 249 [1]	**7**	13
20 Nov 82	**BACK TO LOVE** RCA 287 [1]	**40**	4
19 Feb 83	**GET LOOSE** RCA 315 [1]	**45**	5
9 Nov 85	**YOUR PERSONAL TOUCH** RCA PB 49915	**37**	5
29 Mar 86	**HIGH HORSE** RCA PB 49891	**55**	3
23 Jul 88	**HOLD ON TO WHAT YOU'VE GOT** Manhattan MT 49	**47**	3
10 Oct 92	**SHAME (re-mix)** Network NWKTEN 56 [2]	**74**	1

[1] Evelyn King [2] Altern 8 vs Evelyn King

Jonathan KING UK, male vocalist — 128 wks

29 Jul 65	● **EVERYONE'S GONE TO THE MOON** Decca F 12187	**4**	11
10 Jan 70	**LET IT ALL HANG OUT** Decca F 12988	**26**	7
16 Jan 71	**IT'S THE SAME OLD SONG** B & C CB 139 [1]	**19**	9
3 Apr 71	**SUGAR SUGAR** RCA 2064 [2]	**12**	14
29 May 71	**LAZY BONES** Decca F 13177	**23**	8
20 Nov 71	**HOOKED ON A FEELING** Decca F 13241	**23**	10
5 Feb 72	**FLIRT** Decca F 13276	**22**	9
14 Oct 72	● **LOOP DI LOVE** UK 7 [3]	**4**	13
26 Jan 74	**(I CAN'T GET NO) SATISFACTION** UK 53 [4]	**29**	5
6 Sep 75	● **UNA PALOMA BLANCA** UK 105	**5**	11
20 Sep 75	**CHICK-A-BOOM (DON'T YA JES LOVE IT)** UK 2012 002 [5]	**36**	4
7 Feb 76	**IN THE MOOD** UK 121 [6]	**46**	3
26 Jun 76	● **IT ONLY TAKES A MINUTE** UK 135 [7]	**9**	9
7 Oct 78	**ONE FOR YOU ONE FOR ME** GTO GT 237	**29**	6
16 Dec 78	**LICK A SMURP FOR CHRISTMAS (ALL FALL DOWN)** Petrol GAS 1 [8]	**58**	4
16 Jun 79	**YOU'RE THE GREATEST LOVER** UK International INT 586	**67**	2
3 Nov 79	**GLORIA** Ariola ARO 198	**65**	3

[1] Weathermen [2] Sakkarin [3] Shag [4] Bubblerock [5] 53rd and 3rd featuring the Sound Of Shag [6] Sound 9418 [7] One Hundred Ton And A Feather [8] Father Abraphart and the Smurps

Petrol GAS 1 transferred to Magnet MAG 139 after the first week on chart.

Nosmo KING – See JAVELLS featuring Nosmo KING

Paul KING UK, male vocalist — 3 wks

2 May 87	**I KNOW** CBS PKING 1	**59**	3

See also King.

Solomon KING US, male vocalist — 28 wks

3 Jan 68	● **SHE WEARS MY RING** Columbia DB 8325	**3**	18
1 May 68	**WHEN WE WERE YOUNG** Columbia DB 8402	**21**	10

Albert KING – See Gary MOORE

Tony KING – See Kylie MINOGUE

KING BEE UK, male rapper — 6 wks

26 Jan 91	**MUST BEE THE MUSIC** Columbia 6565827	**44**	4
23 Mar 91	**BACK BY DOPE DEMAND** First Bass 7RUFF 6X	**61**	2

KING BROTHERS UK, male vocal / instrumental group — 74 wks

31 May 57	● **A WHITE SPORT COAT** Parlophone R 4310	**6**	14
9 Aug 57	**IN THE MIDDLE OF AN ISLAND** Parlophone R 4338	**19**	13

6 Dec 57	WAKE UP LITTLE SUSIE *Parlophone R 4367*	22 3
31 Jan 58	PUT A LIGHT IN THE WINDOW *Parlophone R 4389*	29 1
14 Feb 58	PUT A LIGHT IN THE WINDOW (re-entry) *Parlophone R 4389*	28 1
28 Feb 58	PUT A LIGHT IN THE WINDOW (2nd re-entry) *Parlophone R 4389*	25 2
14 Apr 60	● STANDING ON THE CORNER *Parlophone R 4639*	4 11
28 Jul 60	MAIS OUI *Parlophone R 4672*	16 10
12 Jan 61	DOLL HOUSE *Parlophone R 4715*	21 8
2 Mar 61	76 TROMBONES *Parlophone R 4737*	19 11

KING KURT *UK, male vocal / instrumental group*   16 wks

15 Oct 83	DESTINATION ZULULAND *Stiff BUY 189*	36 6
28 Apr 84	MACK THE KNIFE *Stiff BUY 199*	55 4
4 Aug 84	BANANA BANANA *Stiff BUY 206*	54 4
15 Nov 86	AMERICA *Polydor KURT 1*	73 1
2 May 87	THE LAND OF RING DANG DO *Polydor KURT 2*	67 1

KING SUN-D'MOET *US, male rap / scratch duo*   3 wks

11 Jul 87	HEY LOVE *Flame MELT 5*	66 3

KING TRIGGER
UK, male / female vocal / instrumental group   4 wks

14 Aug 82	THE RIVER *Chrysalis CHS 2623*	57 4

KINGDOM COME *US, male vocal / instrumental group*   2 wks

16 Apr 88	GET IT ON *Polydor KCS 1*	75 1
6 May 89	DO YOU LIKE IT *Polydor KCS 3*	73 1

KINGMAKER *UK, male vocal / instrumental group*   22 wks

18 Jan 92	IDIOTS AT THE WHEEL EP *Scorch SCORCH 3*	30 3
23 May 92	EAT YOURSELF WHOLE *Scorch SCORCHG 5*	15 3
31 Oct 92	ARMCHAIR ANARCHIST *Scorch SCORCHG 6*	47 2
8 May 93	10 YEARS ASLEEP *Scorch CDSCORCHS 8*	15 4
19 Jun 93	QUEEN JANE *Scorch CDSCORS 9*	29 4
30 Oct 93	SATURDAY'S NOT WHAT IT USED TO BE *Scorch CDSCORCH 10*	63 1
15 Apr 95	YOU AND I WILL NEVER SEE THINGS EYE TO EYE *Scorch CDSCORCHS 11*	33 3
3 Jun 95	IN THE BEST POSSIBLE TASTE (PART 2) *Scorch CDSCORCHS 12*	41 2

Tracks on Idiots At The Wheel EP: *Really Scrape The Sky / Revelation / Every Teenage Suicide / Strip Away. See also Various Artists (EPs & LPs)* – Gimme Shelter *(EP).*

KINGS OF SWING ORCHESTRA
Australia, orchestra   5 wks

1 May 82	SWITCHED ON SWING *Philips Swing 1*	48 5

KINGSMEN *US, male vocal / instrumental group*   7 wks

30 Jan 64	LOUIE LOUIE *Pye International 7N 25231*	26 7

KINGSTON TRIO *US, male vocal / instrumental group*   15 wks

21 Nov 58	● TOM DOOLEY *Capitol CL 14951*	5 14
4 Dec 59	SAN MIGUEL *Capitol CL 15073*	29 1

KINKS *UK, male vocal / instrumental group*   213 wks

13 Aug 64	★ YOU REALLY GOT ME *Pye 7N 15673*	1 12
29 Oct 64	● ALL DAY AND ALL OF THE NIGHT *Pye 7N 15714*	2 14
21 Jan 65	★ TIRED OF WAITING FOR YOU *Pye 7N 15759*	1 10
25 Mar 65	EVERYBODY'S GONNA BE HAPPY *Pye 7N 15813*	17 8
27 May 65	● SET ME FREE *Pye 7N 15854*	9 11
5 Aug 65	● SEE MY FRIEND *Pye 7N 15919*	10 9
2 Dec 65	● TILL THE END OF THE DAY *Pye 7N 15981*	8 12
3 Mar 66	● DEDICATED FOLLOWER OF FASHION *Pye 7N 17064*	4 11
9 Jun 66	★ SUNNY AFTERNOON *Pye 7N 17125*	1 13
24 Nov 66	● DEAD END STREET *Pye 7N 17222*	5 11
11 May 67	● WATERLOO SUNSET *Pye 7N 17321*	2 11
18 Oct 67	● AUTUMN ALMANAC *Pye 7N 17400*	3 11
17 Apr 68	WONDERBOY *Pye 7N 17468*	36 5
17 Jul 68	DAYS *Pye 7N 17573*	12 10
16 Apr 69	PLASTIC MAN *Pye 7N 17724*	31 4
10 Jan 70	VICTORIA *Pye 7N 17865*	33 4
4 Jul 70	● LOLA *Pye 7N 17961*	2 14
12 Dec 70	● APEMAN *Pye 7N 45016*	5 14
27 May 72	SUPERSONIC ROCKET SHIP *RCA 2211*	16 8
27 Jun 81	BETTER THINGS *Arista ARIST 415*	46 5
6 Aug 83	COME DANCING *Arista ARIST 502*	12 9
15 Oct 83	DON'T FORGET TO DANCE *Arista ARIST 524*	58 3
15 Oct 83	YOU REALLY GOT ME (re-issue) *PRT KD1*	47 4

KINKY *UK, female rapper*   1 wk

24 Aug 96	EVERYBODY *Feverpitch CDFVR 1009*	26 1

See also Erasure.

KINKY MACHINE *UK, male vocal / instrumental group*   4 wks

6 Mar 93	SUPERNATURAL GIVER *Lemon LEMON 006CD*	70 1
29 May 93	SHOCKAHOLIC *Oxygen GASPD 5*	70 1
14 Aug 93	GOING OUT WITH GOD *Oxygen GASPD 9*	74 1
2 Jul 94	10 SECOND BIONIC MAN *Oxygen GASPD 14*	66 1

Fern KINNEY *US, female vocalist*   11 wks

16 Feb 80	★ TOGETHER WE ARE BEAUTIFUL *WEA K 79111*	1 11

KINSHASA BAND – *See Johnny* WAKELIN

Kathy KIRBY *UK, female vocalist*   54 wks

15 Aug 63	DANCE ON *Decca F 11682*	11 13
7 Nov 63	● SECRET LOVE *Decca F 11759*	4 18
20 Feb 64	● LET ME GO LOVER *Decca F 11832*	10 11
7 May 64	YOU'RE THE ONE *Decca F 11892*	17 9
4 Mar 65	I BELONG *Decca F 12087*	36 3

Bo KIRKLAND and Ruth DAVIS
US, male / female vocal duo   9 wks

4 Jun 77	YOU'RE GONNA GET NEXT TO ME *EMI International INT 532*	12 9

KISS *US, male vocal / instrumental group*   57 wks

30 Jun 79	I WAS MADE FOR LOVIN' YOU *Casablanca CAN 152*	50 7
20 Feb 82	A WORLD WITHOUT HEROES *Casablanca KISS 002*	55 3
30 Apr 83	CREATURES OF THE NIGHT *Casablanca KISS 4*	34 4
29 Oct 83	LICK IT UP *Vertigo KISS 5*	31 5
8 Sep 84	HEAVEN'S ON FIRE *Vertigo VER 12*	43 5
9 Nov 85	TEARS ARE FALLING *Vertigo KISS 6*	57 2
3 Oct 87	● CRAZY CRAZY NIGHTS *Vertigo KISS 7*	4 9
5 Dec 87	REASON TO LIVE *Vertigo KISS 8*	33 7
10 Sep 88	TURN ON THE NIGHT *Vertigo KISS 9*	41 5
18 Nov 89	HIDE YOUR HEART *Vertigo KISS 10*	59 2
31 Mar 90	FOREVER *Vertigo KISS 11*	65 2

11 Jan 92	● **GOD GAVE ROCK AND ROLL TO YOU II**		
	Interscope A 8696 ....**4**	8
9 May 92	**UNHOLY** *Mercury KISS 12* **26**	2

KISS AMC *UK, female vocal duo*   **5 wks**

1 Jul 89	**A BIT OF...** *Syncopate SY 29*.................**58**	2
19 Aug 89	**A BIT OF U2 (re-entry)** *Syncopate SY 29* **58**	2
3 Feb 90	**MY DOCS** *Syncopate XAMC 1* **66**	1

Before the re-entry of A Bit Of U2, copyright problems meant that the disc was unable to be given its full title.

KISSING THE PINK
UK, male / female vocal / instrumental group   **14 wks**

5 Mar 83	**LAST FILM** *Magnet KTP 3*......................**19**	14

Mac and Katie KISSOON
UK, male / female vocal duo   **33 wks**

19 Jun 71	**CHIRPY CHIRPY CHEEP CHEEP** *Young Blood YB 1026* **41**	1
18 Jan 75	● **SUGAR CANDY KISSES** *Polydor 2058 531* **3**	10
3 May 75	● **DON'T DO IT BABY** *State STAT 4*.................**9**	8
30 Aug 75	**LIKE A BUTTERFLY** *State STAT 9* **18**	9
15 May 76	**THE TWO OF US** *State STAT 21* **46**	5

Kevin KITCHEN *UK, male vocalist*   **3 wks**

20 Apr 85	**PUT MY ARMS AROUND YOU** *China WOK 1* **64**	3

Eartha KITT *US, female vocalist*   **34 wks**

1 Apr 55	● **UNDER THE BRIDGES OF PARIS** *HMV B 10647* **7**	9
10 Jun 55	**UNDER THE BRIDGES OF PARIS (re-entry)**	
	HMV B 10647 ....**20**	1
3 Dec 83	**WHERE IS MY MAN** *Record Shack SOHO 11* **36**	11
7 Jul 84	**I LOVE MEN** *Record Shack SOHO 21* **50**	3
12 Apr 86	**THIS IS MY LIFE** *Record Shack SOHO 61* **73**	1
1 Jul 89	**CHA CHA HEELS** *Arista 112331* [1] **32**	7
5 Mar 94	**IF I LOVE YA THEN I NEED YA IF I NEED YA THEN I**	
	WANT YOU AROUND *RCA 74321190342* **43**	2

[1] Eartha Kitt and Bronski Beat

KLAXONS *Belgium, male vocal / instrumental group*   **6 wks**

10 Dec 83	**THE CLAP CLAP SOUND** *PRT 7P 290*................**45**	6

KLEEER *US, male / female vocal / instrumental group*   **10 wks**

17 Mar 79	**KEEEP YOUR BODY WORKING** *Atlantic LV 21* **51**	6
14 Mar 81	**GET TOUGH** *Atlantic 11560* **49**	4

KLF *UK, male vocal / instrumental duo*   **51 wks**

11 Aug 90	● **WHAT TIME IS LOVE (LIVE AT TRANCENTRAL)**	
	KLF Communications KLF 004 [1] **5**	12
19 Jan 91	★ **3 AM ETERNAL** *KLF Communications KLF 005* [1] **1**	11
4 May 91	● **LAST TRAIN TO TRANCENTRAL**	
	KLF Communications KLF 008 ....**2**	9
7 Dec 91	● **JUSTIFIED AND ANCIENT**	
	KLF Communications KLF 099 [2] **2**	12
7 Mar 92	● **AMERICA: WHAT TIME IS LOVE**	
	KLF Communications KLFUSA 004 ....**4**	7

[1] KLF featuring the Children Of The Revolution [2] KLF Guest vocals: Tammy Wynette

See also Justified Ancients Of Mu Mu.

KLUBBHEADS
Holland, male instrumental / production duo   **6 wks**

11 May 96	● **KLUBBHOPPING** *AM:PM 5815572* **10**	6

Duo also known as Itty Bitty Boozy Woozy. See also Itty Bitty Boozy Woozy.

KNACK *US, male vocal / instrumental group*   **12 wks**

30 Jun 79	● **MY SHARONA** *Capitol CL 16087* **6**	10
13 Oct 79	**GOOD GIRLS DON'T** *Capitol CL 16097* **66**	2

Beverley KNIGHT *UK, female vocalist*   **6 wks**

8 Apr 95	**FLAVOUR OF THE OLD SCHOOL**	
	Dome CDDOME 101 ....**50**	2
2 Sep 95	**DOWN FOR THE ONE** *Dome CDDOME 102* **55**	1
21 Oct 95	**FLAVOUR OF THE OLD SCHOOL (re-mix)**	
	Dome CDDOME 105 ....**33**	2
23 Mar 96	**MOVING ON UP (ON THE RIGHT SIDE)**	
	Dome CDDOME 107 ....**42**	1

Frederick KNIGHT *US, male vocalist*   **10 wks**

10 Jun 72	**I'VE BEEN LONELY SO LONG** *Stax 2025 098* **22**	10

Gladys KNIGHT and the PIPS
US, female vocalist and male vocal backing group   **187 wks**

8 Jun 67	**TAKE ME IN YOUR ARMS AND LOVE ME**	
	Tamla Motown TMG 604...................**13**	15
27 Dec 67	**I HEARD IT THROUGH THE GRAPEVINE**	
	Tamla Motown TMG 629...................**47**	1
17 Jun 72	**JUST WALK IN MY SHOES** *Tamla Motown TMG 813* **35**	8
25 Nov 72	**HELP ME MAKE IT THROUGH THE NIGHT**	
	Tamla Motown TMG 830...................**11**	17
3 Mar 73	**LOOK OF LOVE** *Tamla Motown TMG 844*...................**21**	9
26 May 73	**NEITHER ONE OF US** *Tamla Motown TMG 855* **31**	7
5 Apr 75	● **THE WAY WE WERE – TRY TO REMEMBER**	
	Buddah BDS 428...................**4**	15
2 Aug 75	● **BEST THING THAT EVER HAPPENED TO ME**	
	Buddah BDS 432...................**7**	10
15 Nov 75	**PART TIME LOVE** *Buddah BDS 438* **30**	5
8 May 76	● **MIDNIGHT TRAIN TO GEORGIA** *Buddah BDS 444* **10**	9
21 Aug 76	**MAKE YOURS A HAPPY HOME** *Buddah BDS 447*...................**35**	4
6 Nov 76	**SO SAD THE SONG** *Buddah BDS 448* **20**	9
15 Jan 77	**NOBODY BUT YOU** *Buddah BDS 451* **34**	2
28 May 77	● **BABY DON'T CHANGE YOUR MIND** *Buddah BDS 458*.....**4**	12
24 Sep 77	**HOME IS WHERE THE HEART IS** *Buddah BDS 460* **35**	4
8 Apr 78	**THE ONE AND ONLY** *Buddah BDS 470* **32**	4
13 May 78	**THE ONE AND ONLY (re-entry)** *Buddah BDS 470* **66**	1
24 Jun 78	**COME BACK AND FINISH WHAT YOU STARTED**	
	Buddah BDS 473...................**15**	13
30 Sep 78	**IT'S A BETTER THAN GOOD TIME** *Buddah BDS 478*.......**59**	4
30 Aug 80	**TASTE OF BITTER LOVE** *CBS 8890* **35**	6
8 Nov 80	**BOURGIE BOURGIE** *CBS 9081* **32**	6
26 Dec 81	**WHEN A CHILD IS BORN** *CBS S 1758* [1] **74**	2
9 Nov 85	**THAT'S WHAT FRIENDS ARE FOR** *Arista ARIST 638* [2] **16**	9
16 Jan 88	**LOVE OVERBOARD** *MCA MCA 1223*...................**42**	4
10 Jun 89	● **LICENCE TO KILL** *MCA MCA 1339* [3] **6**	11

[1] Johnny Mathis and Gladys Knight [2] Dionne Warwick and Friends featuring Elton John, Stevie Wonder and Gladys Knight [3] Gladys Knight

Robert KNIGHT *US, male vocalist*   **26 wks**

17 Jan 68	**EVERLASTING LOVE** *Monument MON 1008* **40**	2
24 Nov 73	● **LOVE ON A MOUNTAIN TOP** *Monument MNT 1875* **10**	16
9 Mar 74	**EVERLASTING LOVE (re-issue)**	
	Monument MNT 2106 ....**19**	8

Mark KNOPFLER
UK, male vocalist / instrumentalist – guitar   **7 wks**

12 Mar 83	GOING HOME (THEME OF 'LOCAL HERO')		
	Vertigo DSTR 4	**56**	3
16 Mar 96	DARLING PRETTY *Vertigo VERCD 88*	**33**	2
25 May 96	CANNIBALS *Vertigo VERCD 89*	**42**	2

Buddy KNOX *US, male vocalist*   **5 wks**

10 May 57	PARTY DOLL *Columbia DB 3914*	**29**	3
16 Aug 62	SHE'S GONE *Liberty LIB 55473*	**45**	2

Frankie KNUCKLES *US, male producer*   **19 wks**

17 Jun 89	TEARS *ffrr F 108* [1]	**50**	3
21 Oct 89	YOUR LOVE *Trax TRAXT 3*	**59**	4
27 Jul 91	THE WHISTLE SONG *Virgin America VUS 47*	**17**	5
23 Nov 91	IT'S HARD SOMETIMES *Virgin America VUS 52* [2]	**67**	1
6 Jun 92	RAIN FALLS *Virgin America VUST 60* [3]	**48**	2
27 May 95	TOO MANY FISH *Virgin America VUSCD 89* [4]	**34**	2
18 Nov 95	WHADDA U WANT (FROM ME)		
	Virgin America VUSCD 98 [4]	**36**	2

[1] Frankie Knuckles presents Satoshi Tomiie [2] Frankie Knuckles featuring Shelton Becton [3] Frankie Knuckles featuring Lisa Michaelis [4] Frankie Knuckles featuring Adeva

Moe KOFFMAN QUARTETTE
Canada, male instrumental group, Moe Koffman – flute   **2 wks**

28 Mar 58	SWINGIN' SHEPHERD BLUES *London HLJ 8549*	**23**	2

KOKOMO *US, male instrumentalist - piano*   **7 wks**

13 Apr 61	ASIA MINOR *London HLU 9305*	**35**	7

KOKOMO *UK, male / female vocal / instrumental group*   **3 wks**

29 May 82	A LITTLE BIT FURTHER AWAY *CBS A 2064*	**45**	3

KON KAN *Canada, male vocal / instrumental duo*   **13 wks**

4 Mar 89	● I BEG YOUR PARDON *Atlantic A 8969*	**5**	13

John KONGOS
South Africa, male vocalist / multi-instrumentalist   **25 wks**

22 May 71	● HE'S GONNA STEP ON YOU AGAIN *Fly BUG 8*	**4**	14
20 Nov 71	● TOKOLOSHE MAN *Fly BUG 14*	**4**	11

KOOL AND THE GANG
US, male vocal / instrumental group   **207 wks**

27 Oct 79	● LADIES NIGHT *Mercury KOOL 7*	**9**	12
19 Jan 80	TOO HOT *Mercury KOOL 8*	**23**	8
12 Jul 80	HANGIN' OUT *De-Lite KOOL 9*	**52**	4
1 Nov 80	● CELEBRATION *De-Lite KOOL 10*	**7**	13
21 Feb 81	JONES VS JONES / SUMMER MADNESS		
	De-Lite KOOL 11	**17**	11
30 May 81	TAKE IT TO THE TOP *De-Lite DE 2*	**15**	9
31 Oct 81	STEPPIN' OUT *De-Lite DE 4*	**12**	13
19 Dec 81	● GET DOWN ON IT *De-Lite DE 5*	**3**	12
6 Mar 82	TAKE MY HEART (YOU CAN HAVE IT IF		
	YOU WANT IT) *De-Lite DE 6*	**29**	7
7 Aug 82	BIG FUN *De-Lite DE 7*	**14**	8
16 Oct 82	● OOH LA LA LA (LET'S GO DANCIN') *De-Lite DE 9*	**6**	9
4 Dec 82	HI DE HI, HI DE HO *De-Lite DE 14*	**29**	8
10 Dec 83	STRAIGHT AHEAD *De-Lite DE 15*	**15**	10
11 Feb 84	● JOANNA / TONIGHT *De-Lite DE 16*	**2**	11
14 Apr 84	● (WHEN YOU SAY YOU LOVE SOMEBODY) IN THE		
	HEART *De-Lite DE 17*	**7**	8
24 Nov 84	FRESH *De-Lite DE 18*	**11**	12
9 Feb 85	MISLED *De-Lite DE 19*	**28**	5
11 May 85	● CHERISH *De-Lite DE 20*	**4**	22
2 Nov 85	EMERGENCY *De-Lite DE 21*	**50**	3
22 Nov 86	VICTORY *Club JAB 44*	**67**	2
20 Dec 86	VICTORY (re-entry) *Club JAB 44*	**30**	10
21 Mar 87	STONE LOVE *Club JAB 47*	**45**	4
31 Dec 88	CELEBRATION (re-mix) *Club JAB 78*	**56**	5
6 Jul 91	GET DOWN ON IT (re-mix) *Mercury MER 346*	**69**	1

Funky Stuff and Hollywood Swinging only appeared on 12-inch and EP versions of Kool 11, although the chart listed all four songs.

KOOLROCK STEADY – See TYREE

KOON + STEPHENSON – See WESTBAM

KORGIS *UK, male vocal / instrumental duo*   **27 wks**

23 Jun 79	IF I HAD YOU *Rialto TREB 103*	**13**	12
24 May 80	● EVERYBODY'S GOT TO LEARN SOMETIME		
	Rialto TREB 115	**5**	12
30 Aug 80	IF IT'S ALRIGHT WITH YOU BABY *Rialto TREB 118*	**56**	3

KORN *US, male vocal / instrumental group*   **2 wks**

19 Oct 96	NO PLACE TO HIDE *Epic 6638452*	**26**	2

KRAFTWERK *Germany, male instrumental / vocal group*   **69 wks**

10 May 75	AUTOBAHN *Vertigo 6147 012*	**11**	9
28 Oct 78	NEON LIGHTS *Capitol CL 15998*	**53**	3
9 May 81	POCKET CALCULATOR *EMI 5175*	**39**	6
11 Jul 81	COMPUTER LOVE / THE MODEL *EMI 5207*	**36**	8
26 Dec 81	★ COMPUTER LOVE / THE MODEL (re-entry) *EMI 5207*	**1**	13
20 Feb 82	SHOWROOM DUMMIES *EMI 5272*	**25**	5
6 Aug 83	TOUR DE FRANCE *EMI 5413*	**22**	8
25 Aug 84	TOUR DE FRANCE (re-entry) *EMI 5413*	**24**	11
1 Jun 91	THE ROBOTS *EMI EM 192*	**20**	4
2 Nov 91	RADIOACTIVITY *EMI EM 201*	**43**	2

Billy J KRAMER and the DAKOTAS
UK, male vocalist and male instrumental backing group   **71 wks**

2 May 63	● DO YOU WANT TO KNOW A SECRET?		
	Parlophone R 5023	**2**	15
1 Aug 63	★ BAD TO ME *Parlophone R 5049*	**1**	14
7 Nov 63	● I'LL KEEP YOU SATISFIED *Parlophone R 5073*	**4**	13
27 Feb 64	★ LITTLE CHILDREN *Parlophone R 5105*	**1**	13
23 Jul 64	● FROM A WINDOW *Parlophone R 5156*	**10**	8
20 May 65	TRAINS AND BOATS AND PLANES		
	Parlophone R 5285	**12**	8

KRANKIES *UK, male / female vocal duo*   **6 wks**

7 Feb 81	FAN'DABI'DOZI *Monarch MON 21*	**71**	1
7 Mar 81	FAN'DABI'DOZI (re-entry) *Monarch MON 21*	**46**	5

Lenny KRAVITZ *US, male vocalist*   **52 wks**

2 Jun 90	MR. CABDRIVER *Virgin America VUS 20*	**58**	2
4 Aug 90	LET LOVE RULE *Virgin America VUS 26*	**39**	4
30 Mar 91	ALWAYS ON THE RUN *Virgin America VUS 34*	**41**	3
15 Jun 91	IT AIN'T OVER TIL IT'S OVER *Virgin America VUS 43*	**11**	4
14 Sep 91	STAND BY MY WOMAN *Virgin America VUS 45*	**55**	3

20 Feb 93 ●	**ARE YOU GONNA GO MY WAY** *Virgin America VUSDG 65*	**4**	11
22 May 93	**BELIEVE** *Virgin America VUSCD 72*	**30**	5
28 Aug 93	**HEAVEN HELP** *Virgin America VUSDG 73*	**20**	7
4 Dec 93	**BUDDHA OF SUBURBIA** *Arista 74321177052* 1	**35**	3
4 Dec 93	**IS THERE ANY LOVE IN YOUR HEART** *Virgin America VUSDG 76*	**52**	2
9 Sep 95	**ROCK AND ROLL IS DEAD** *Virgin America VUSCD 93*	**22**	3
23 Dec 95	**CIRCUS** *Virgin America VUSCD 96*	**54**	2
2 Mar 96	**CAN'T GET YOU OFF MY MIND** *Virgin America VUSCD 100*	**54**	2

1 David Bowie featuring Lenny Kravitz

KRAZE *US, male / female vocal / instrumental group* **6 wks**

22 Oct 88	**THE PARTY** *MCA MCA 1288*	**29**	5
17 Jun 89	**LET'S PLAY HOUSE** *MCA MCA 1337*	**71**	1

KREUZ *UK, male vocal group* **1 wk**

8 Jul 95	**PARTY ALL NIGHT** *Diesel DES 004C*	**75**	1

KREW-KATS *UK, male instrumental group* **10 wks**

9 Mar 61	**TRAMBONE** *HMV POP 840*	**33**	9
18 May 61	**TRAMBONE (re-entry)** *HMV POP 840*	**49**	1

KRIS KROSS *US, male vocal duo* **22 wks**

30 May 92 ●	**JUMP** *Ruff House 6578547*	**2**	8
25 Jul 92	**WARM IT UP** *Ruff House 6582187*	**16**	6
17 Oct 92	**I MISSED THE BUS** *Ruff House 6583927*	**57**	1
19 Dec 92	**IT'S A SHAME** *Ruff House 6588587*	**31**	5
11 Sep 93	**ALRIGHT** *Ruff House 6595652*	**47**	2

Marty KRISTIAN – See NEW SEEKERS

KROKUS
Switzerland / Argentina, male vocal / instrumental group **2 wks**

16 May 81	**INDUSTRIAL STRENGTH EP** *Ariola ARO 258*	**62**	2

Tracks on Industrial Strength EP: Bedside Radio / Easy Rocker / Celebration / Bye Bye Baby.

KRS ONE *US, male rapper* **1 wk**

18 May 96	**RAPPAZ R N DAINJA** *Jive JIVECD 396*	**47**	1

KRUSH *UK, male / female vocal / instrumental group* **16 wks**

5 Dec 87 ●	**HOUSE ARREST** *Club JAB 63*	**3**	15
14 Nov 92	**WALKING ON SUNSHINE** *Network NWK 55*	**71**	1

KRUSH PERSPECTIVE *US, female vocal group* **2 wks**

16 Jan 93	**LET'S GET TOGETHER (SO GROOVY NOW)** *Perspective PERD 7416*	**61**	2

K7 *US, male vocalist* **22 wks**

11 Dec 93 ●	**COME BABY COME** *Big Life BLRD 105*	**3**	16
2 Apr 94	**HI DE HO** *Big Life BLRD 108* 1	**17**	5
25 Jun 94	**ZUNGA ZENG** *Big Life BLRD 111* 1	**63**	1

1 K7 and the Swing Kids

K3M *Italy, male / female vocal / instrumental duo* **1 wk**

21 Mar 92	**LISTEN TO THE RHYTHM** *PWL Continental PWL 214*	**71**	1

KULA SHAKER *UK, male vocal / instrumental group* **24 wks**

4 May 96	**GRATEFUL WHEN YOU'RE DEAD – JERRY WAS THERE** *Columbia KULACD 2*	**35**	3
6 Jul 96 ●	**TATTVA** *Columbia KULACD 3*	**4**	8
7 Sep 96 ●	**HEY DUDE** *Columbia KULACD 4*	**2**	7
23 Nov 96 ●	**GOVINDA** *Columbia KULACD 5*	**7†**	6

Charlie KUNZ *US, male instrumentalist – piano* **4 wks**

17 Dec 54	**PIANO MEDLEY NO. 114** *Decca F 10419*	**20**	3
14 Jan 55	**PIANO MEDLEY NO. 114 (re-entry)** *Decca F 10419*	**16**	1

Medley titles: There Must Be A Reason / Hold My Hand / If I Give My Heart To You / Little Things Mean A Lot / Make Her Mine / My Son My Son.

KURSAAL FLYERS *UK, male vocal / instrumental group* **10 wks**

20 Nov 76	**LITTLE DOES SHE KNOW** *CBS 4689*	**14**	10

KUT KLOSE *US, female vocal group* **1 wk**

29 Apr 95	**I LIKE** *Elektra EKR 200CD*	**72**	1

Li KWAN *UK, male producer - Joey Negro* **2 wks**

17 Dec 94	**I NEED A MAN** *Deconstruction 74321252192*	**51**	2

See also Joey Negro.

KWS *UK, male vocal / instrumental group* **36 wks**

25 Apr 92 ★	**PLEASE DON'T GO / GAME BOY** *Network NWK 46*	**1**	16
22 Aug 92 ●	**ROCK YOUR BABY** *Network NWK 54*	**8**	7
12 Dec 92	**HOLD BACK THE NIGHT** *Network NWK 65* 1	**30**	5
5 Jun 93	**CAN'T GET ENOUGH OF YOUR LOVE** *Network NWKCD 72*	**71**	1
9 Apr 94	**IT SEEMS TO HANG ON** *X-clusive XCLU 006CD*	**58**	1
2 Jul 94	**AIN'T NOBODY (LOVES ME BETTER)** *X-clusive XCLU 010CD* 2	**21**	4
19 Nov 94	**THE MORE I GET THE MORE I WANT** *X-clusive XCLU 011CD* 3	**35**	2

1 KWS features guest vocal from the Trammps 2 KWS and Gwen Dickey
3 KWS featuring Teddy Pendergrass

Game Boy was only listed from 9 May 92.

KYO – See BEDROCK featuring KYO

Jonny L *UK, male vocalist* **1 wk**

28 Aug 93	**OOH I LIKE IT** *XL XLS 44CD*	**73**	1

LA GANZ *US, male vocal / instrumental group* **1 wk**

9 Nov 96	**LIKE A PLAYA** *Jive JIVECD 405*	**75**	1

L.A. GUNS US, male/female vocal/instrumental group — 4 wks

30 Nov 91	SOME LIE 4 LOVE Mercury MER 358	61 1
21 Dec 91	THE BALLAD OF JAYNE Mercury MER 361	53 3

L.A. MIX UK, male/female vocal/instrumental duo — 25 wks

10 Oct 87	DON'T STOP (JAMMIN') Breakout USA 615	47 4
21 May 88 ●	CHECK THIS OUT Breakout USA 629	6 7
8 Jul 89 ●	GET LOOSE Breakout USA 659 [1]	25 6
16 Sep 89	LOVE TOGETHER Breakout USA 662 [2]	66 2
15 Sep 90	COMING BACK FOR MORE A & M AM 579	50 3
19 Jan 91	MYSTERIES OF LOVE A & M AM 707	46 2
23 Mar 91	WE SHOULDN'T HOLD HANDS IN THE DARK A & M AM 755	69 1

[1] L.A. Mix performed by Jazzi P [2] L.A. Mix featuring Kevin Henry

LA NA NEE NEE NOO NOO – See BANANARAMA

Danny LA RUE UK, male vocalist — 9 wks

18 Dec 68	ON MOTHER KELLY'S DOORSTEP Page One POF 108	33 9

Denise LA SALLE US, female vocalist — 13 wks

15 Jun 85 ●	MY TOOT TOOT Epic A 6334	6 13

LABELLE US, female vocal group — 9 wks

22 Mar 75	LADY MARMALADE (VOULEZ-VOUS COUCHER AVEC MOI CE SOIR?) Epic EPC 2852	17 9

See also Patti Labelle.

Patti LABELLE US, female vocalist — 21 wks

3 May 86 ●	ON MY OWN MCA MCA 1045 [1]	2 13
2 Aug 86	OH, PEOPLE MCA MCA 1075	26 6
3 Sep 94	THE RIGHT KINDA LOVER MCA MCSTD 1995	50 2

[1] Patti Labelle and Michael McDonald

See also Labelle.

LADIES CHOICE UK, male vocalist — 4 wks

25 Jan 86	FUNKY SENSATION Sure Delight SD 01	41 4

LADY J – See RAZE

LADY OF RAGE US, female rapper — 1 wk

8 Oct 94	AFRO PUFFS Interscope A 8288CD	72 1

LADYSMITH BLACK MAMBAZO
South Africa, male vocal group — 11 wks

3 Jun 95	SWING LOW SWEET CHARIOT PolyGram TV SWLOW 2 [1]	15 6
3 Jun 95	WORLD IN UNION '95 PolyGram TV RUGBY 2 [2]	47 5

[1] Ladysmith Black Mambazo featuring China Black [2] Ladysmith Black Mambazo featuring PJ Powers

LAID BACK Norway, male vocal/instrumental duo — 4 wks

5 May 90	BAKERMAN Arista 112356	44 4

Cleo LAINE UK, female vocalist — 14 wks

29 Dec 60	LET'S SLIP AWAY Fontana H 269	42 1
14 Sep 61 ●	YOU'LL ANSWER TO ME Fontana H 326	5 13

Frankie LAINE US, male vocalist — 281 wks

14 Nov 52 ●	HIGH NOON Columbia DB 3113	7 7
14 Nov 52 ●	SUGARBUSH Columbia DB 3123 [1]	8 2
5 Dec 52 ●	SUGARBUSH (re-entry) Columbia DB 3123 [1]	8 6
20 Mar 53	GIRL IN THE WOOD Columbia DB 2907	11 1
3 Apr 53 ★	I BELIEVE Philips PB 117	1 36
8 May 53 ●	TELL ME A STORY Philips PB 126 [2]	5 15
4 Sep 53 ●	WHERE THE WINDS BLOW Philips PB 167	2 12
11 Sep 53	TELL ME A STORY (re-entry) Philips PB 126 [2]	12 1
16 Oct 53 ★	HEY JOE Philips PB 172	1 8
30 Oct 53 ★	ANSWER ME Philips PB 196	1 17
8 Jan 54 ●	BLOWING WILD Philips PB 207	2 12
26 Mar 54 ●	GRANADA Philips PB 242	10 1
9 Apr 54 ●	GRANADA (re-entry) Philips PB 242	9 1
16 Apr 54 ●	THE KID'S LAST FIGHT Philips PB 258	3 10
13 Aug 54 ●	MY FRIEND Philips PB 316	3 15
8 Oct 54 ●	THERE MUST BE A REASON Philips PB 306	9 9
22 Oct 54 ●	RAIN RAIN RAIN Philips PB 311 [3]	8 16
11 Mar 55	IN THE BEGINNING Philips PB 404	20 1
24 Jun 55 ●	COOL WATER Philips PB 465	2 22
15 Jul 55 ●	STRANGE LADY IN TOWN Philips PB 478	6 13
11 Nov 55	HUMMING BIRD Philips PB 498	16 1
25 Nov 55 ●	HAWKEYE Philips PB 519	7 8
20 Jan 56 ●	SIXTEEN TONS Philips PB 539	10 3
4 May 56	HELL HATH NO FURY Philips PB 585	28 1
7 Sep 56 ★	A WOMAN IN LOVE Philips PB 617	1 21
28 Dec 56	MOONLIGHT GAMBLER Philips PB 638	13 12
29 Mar 57	MOONLIGHT GAMBLER (re-entry) Philips PB 638	28 1
26 Apr 57	LOVE IS A GOLDEN RING Philips PB 676	19 5
4 Oct 57	GOOD EVENING FRIENDS / UP ABOVE MY HEAD I HEAR MUSIC IN THE AIR Philips PB 708 [4]	25 4
13 Nov 59 ●	RAWHIDE Philips PB 965	6 17
31 Mar 60	RAWHIDE (re-entry) Philips PB 965	41 1
11 May 61	GUNSLINGER Philips PB 1135	50 1

[1] Doris Day and Frankie Laine [2] Frankie Laine and Jimmy Boyd
[3] Frankie Laine and the Four Lads [4] Frankie Laine and Johnnie Ray

Greg LAKE UK, male vocalist — 12 wks

6 Dec 75 ●	I BELIEVE IN FATHER CHRISTMAS Manticore K 13511	2 7
25 Dec 82	I BELIEVE IN FATHER CHRISTMAS (re-entry) Manticore K 13511	72 3
24 Dec 83	I BELIEVE IN FATHER CHRISTMAS (2nd re-entry) Manticore K 13511	65 2

See also Emerson, Lake and Palmer.

Annabel LAMB UK, female vocalist — 7 wks

27 Aug 83	RIDERS ON THE STORM A & M AM 131	27 7

LAMBRETTAS UK, male vocal/instrumental group — 24 wks

1 Mar 80 ●	POISON IVY Rocket XPRESS 25	7 12
24 May 80	D-A-A-ANCE Rocket XPRESS 33	12 8
23 Aug 80	ANOTHER DAY (ANOTHER GIRL) ocket XPRESS 36	49 4

LANCASTRIANS
UK, male vocal/instrumental group — 2 wks

24 Dec 64	WE'LL SING IN THE SUNSHINE Pye 7N 15732	47 2

Major LANCE US, male vocalist — 2 wks

13 Feb 64	UM UM UM UM UM UM Columbia DB 7205	40	2

Valerie LANDSBERG – See KIDS FROM FAME

LANDSCAPE UK, male vocal / instrumental group — 20 wks

28 Feb 81 ●	EINSTEIN A GO-GO RCA 22	5	13
23 May 81	NORMAN BATES RCA 60	40	7

Desmond LANE – See Alma COGAN; Cyril STAPLETON

Ronnie LANE and SLIM CHANCE
UK, male vocalist and male instrumental group — 12 wks

12 Jan 74	HOW COME GM GMS 011	11	8
15 Jun 74	THE POACHER GM GMS 024	36	4

Don LANG UK, male vocalist — 18 wks

4 Nov 55	CLOUDBURST HMV POP 115 [1]	16	2
2 Dec 55	CLOUDBURST (re-entry) HMV POP 115 [1]	18	1
13 Jan 56	CLOUDBURST (2nd re-entry) HMV POP 115 [1]	20	1
5 Jul 57	SCHOOL DAY HMV POP 350 [2]	26	2
23 May 58 ●	WITCH DOCTOR HMV POP 488 [2]	5	11
10 Mar 60	SINK THE BISMARCK HMV POP 714	43	1

[1] Don Lang and the Mairants-Langhorn Big Six [2] Don Lang and his Frantic Five

kd lang Canada, female vocalist — 25 wks

16 May 92	CONSTANT CRAVING Sire W 0100	52	4
22 Aug 92	CRYING Virgin America VUS 63 [1]	13	6
27 Feb 93	CONSTANT CRAVING (re-issue) Sire W 0157CD	15	8
1 May 93	THE MIND OF LOVE Sire W 0170CD1	72	1
26 Jun 93	MISS CHATELAINE Sire W 0181CDX	68	2
11 Dec 93	JUST KEEP ME MOVING Sire W 0227CD	59	1
30 Sep 95	IF I WERE YOU Sire W 0319CD	53	1
18 May 96	YOU'RE OK Warner Bros. W 0332CD	44	2

[1] Roy Orbison (duet with kd lang)

Thomas LANG UK, male vocalist — 3 wks

30 Jan 88	THE HAPPY MAN Epic VOW 4	67	3

Mario LANZA US, male vocalist — 32 wks

14 Nov 52 ●	BECAUSE YOU'RE MINE HMV DA 2017	3	24
4 Feb 55	DRINKING SONG HMV DA 2065	13	1
18 Feb 55	I'LL WALK WITH GOD HMV DA 2062	18	1
22 Apr 55	SERENADE HMV DA 2065	19	1
6 May 55	I'LL WALK WITH GOD (re-entry) HMV DA 2062	20	1
6 May 55	SERENADE (re-entry) HMV DA 2065	15	2
14 Sep 56	SERENADE HMV DA 2085	25	1
12 Oct 56	SERENADE (re-entry) HMV DA 2085	29	1

DA 2065 and DA 2085 are two different songs.

Julius LAROSA US, male vocalist — 9 wks

4 Jul 58	TORERO RCA 1063	15	9

LA'S UK, male vocal / instrumental group — 18 wks

14 Jan 89	THERE SHE GOES Go! Discs GOLAS 2	59	4
15 Sep 90	TIMELESS MELODY Go! Discs GOLAS 4	57	2
3 Nov 90	THERE SHE GOES (re-issue) Go! Discs GOLAS 5	13	9
16 Feb 91	FEELIN' Go! Discs GOLAS 6	43	3

James LAST BAND Germany, male orchestra — 4 wks

3 May 80	THE SEDUCTION (LOVE THEME) Polydor PD 2071	48	4

LAST RHYTHM Italy, male instrumental / production group — 1 wk

14 Sep 96	LAST RHYTHM Stress CDSTR 76	62	1

LATE SHOW UK, male vocal / instrumental group — 6 wks

3 Mar 79	BRISTOL STOMP Decca F 13822	40	6

LATIN QUARTER
UK, male / female vocal / instrumental group — 10 wks

18 Jan 86	RADIO AFRICA Rockin' Horse RH 102	19	9
18 Apr 87	NOMZAMO (ONE PEOPLE ONE CAUSE) Rockin' Horse RH 113	73	1

LATIN RHYTHM – See Tito PUENTE JR and the LATIN RHYTHM featuring Tito PUENTE, INDIA and Cali ALEMAN

LATIN THING
Canada / Spain, male / female vocal / instrumental group — 1 wk

13 Jul 96	LATIN THING Faze 2 CDFAZE 33	41	1

Gino LATINO Italy, male producer — 7 wks

20 Jan 90	WELCOME ffrr F 126	17	7

LATINO RAVE – See VARIOUS ARTISTS (MONTAGES)

LATOUR US, male vocalist / producer — 7 wks

8 Jun 91	PEOPLE ARE STILL HAVING SEX Polydor PO 147	15	7

Stacy LATTISAW US, female vocalist — 14 wks

14 Jun 80 ●	JUMP TO THE BEAT Atlantic/Cotillion K 11496	3	11
30 Aug 80	DYNAMITE Atlantic K 11554	51	3

Dave LAUDAT – See HUSTLERS CONVENTION featuring Dave LAUDAT and Ondrea DUVERN

LAUNCHERS – See Ezz RECO and the LAUNCHERS with Boysie GRANT

Cyndi LAUPER US, female vocalist — 101 wks

14 Jan 84 ●	GIRLS JUST WANT TO HAVE FUN Portrait A 3943	2	12
24 Mar 84	TIME AFTER TIME Portrait A 4290	54	4
16 Jun 84	TIME AFTER TIME (re-entry) Portrait A 4290	3	13
1 Sep 84	SHE BOP Portrait A 4620	46	5
17 Nov 84	ALL THROUGH THE NIGHT Portrait A 4849	64	2
20 Sep 86	TRUE COLOURS Portrait 650026 7	12	11
27 Dec 86	CHANGE OF HEART Portrait CYNDI 1	74	1
10 Jan 87	CHANGE OF HEART (re-entry) Portrait CYNDI 1	67	1
28 Mar 87	WHAT'S GOING ON Portrait CYN 1	57	3
20 May 89 ●	I DROVE ALL NIGHT Epic CYN 4	7	12
5 Aug 89	MY FIRST NIGHT WITHOUT YOU Epic CYN 5	53	4
30 Dec 89	HEADING WEST Epic CYN 6	68	1
6 Jun 92	THE WORLD IS STONE Epic 6579707	15	7

13 Nov 93	THAT'S WHAT I THINK *Epic 6598782*	**31**	4
8 Jan 94	WHO LET IN THE RAIN *Epic 6590392*	**32**	4
17 Sep 94	● HEY NOW (GIRLS JUST WANT TO HAVE FUN) *Epic 6608072*	**4**	13
11 Feb 95	I'M GONNA BE STRONG *Epic 6611962*	**37**	2
26 Aug 95	COME ON HOME *Epic 6614255*	**39**	2

Hey Now (Girls Just Want To Have Fun) is a re-recording of her first hit.

LAUREL and HARDY
UK, male vocal / instrumental duo　　　　**2 wks**

2 Apr 83	CLUNK CLINK *CBS A 3213*	**65**	2

LAUREL and HARDY with the AVALON BOYS featuring Chill WILLS
UK / US, male vocal duo with US, male vocal group　　**10 wks**

22 Nov 75	● THE TRAIL OF THE LONESOME PINE *United Artists UP 36026*	**2**	10

Joanna LAW *UK, female vocalist*　　**8 wks**

7 Jul 90	FIRST TIME EVER *Citybeat CBE 752*	**67**	3
14 Sep 96	THE GIFT *Deconstruction 74321401912* [1]	**15**	5

[1] Way Out West featuring Miss Joanna Law

Joanna's contribution to The Gift is a sample from First Time Ever.

Joey LAWRENCE *US, male vocalist*　　**14 wks**

26 Jun 93	NOTHIN' MY LOVE CAN'T FIX *EMI CDEM 271*	**13**	7
28 Aug 93	I CAN'T HELP MYSELF *EMI CDEM 277*	**27**	4
30 Oct 93	STAY FOREVER *EMI CDEM 289*	**41**	3

Lee LAWRENCE *UK, male vocalist*　　**10 wks**

20 Nov 53	CRYING IN THE CHAPEL *Decca F 10177*	**11**	1
11 Dec 53	● CRYING IN THE CHAPEL (re-entry) *Decca F 10177*	**7**	5
2 Dec 55	SUDDENLY THERE'S A VALLEY *Columbia DB 3681*	**19**	1
16 Dec 55	SUDDENLY THERE'S A VALLEY (re-entry) *Columbia DB 3681*	**14**	3

Sophie LAWRENCE *UK, female vocalist*　　**7 wks**

3 Aug 91	LOVE'S UNKIND *IQ ZB 44821*	**21**	7

Steve LAWRENCE *US, male vocalist*　　**27 wks**

21 Apr 60	● FOOTSTEPS *HMV POP 726*	**4**	13
18 Aug 60	GIRLS GIRLS GIRLS *London HLT 9166*	**49**	1
22 Aug 63	● I WANT TO STAY HERE *CBS AAG 163* [1]	**3**	13

[1] Steve and Eydie

Lindy LAYTON *UK, female vocalist*　　**15 wks**

11 Aug 90	SILLY GAMES *Arista 113452* [1]	**22**	7
26 Jan 91	ECHO MY HEART *Arista 113845*	**42**	2
31 Aug 91	WITHOUT YOU (ONE AND ONE) *Arista 114636*	**71**	2
24 Apr 93	WE GOT THE LOVE *PWL International PWCD 250*	**38**	3
30 Oct 93	SHOW ME *PWL International PWCD 275*	**47**	1

[1] Lindy Layton featuring Janet Kay

See also Beats International.

Doug LAZY *US, male vocalist*　　**9 wks**

15 Jul 89	LET IT ROLL *Atlantic A 8866* [1]	**27**	5
4 Nov 89	LET THE RHYTHM PUMP *Atlantic A 8784*	**45**	3
26 May 90	LET THE RHYTHM PUMP (re-mix) *East West A 7919*	**63**	1

[1] Raze presents Doug Lazy

Keith LE BLANC – *See Malcolm X*

Vicky LEANDROS *Greece, female vocalist*　　**29 wks**

8 Apr 72	● COME WHAT MAY *Philips 6000 049*	**2**	16
23 Dec 72	THE LOVE IN YOUR EYES *Philips 6000 081*	**48**	3
20 Jan 73	THE LOVE IN YOUR EYES (re-entry) *Philips 6000 081*	**40**	4
7 Apr 73	THE LOVE IN YOUR EYES (2nd re-entry) *Philips 6000 081*	**46**	1
7 Jul 73	WHEN BOUZOUKIS PLAYED *Philips 6000 111*	**44**	2
28 Jul 73	WHEN BOUZOUKIS PLAYED (re-entry) *Philips 6000 111*	**45**	3

Denis LEARY *US, male vocalist*　　**2 wks**

13 Jan 96	ASSHOLE *A & M 5813352*	**58**	2

Brenda LEE *US, female vocalist*　　**210 wks**

17 Mar 60	SWEET NOTHIN'S *Brunswick 05819*	**45**	1
7 Apr 60	● SWEET NOTHIN'S (re-entry) *Brunswick 05819*	**4**	18
30 Jun 60	I'M SORRY *Brunswick 05833*	**12**	16
20 Oct 60	I WANT TO BE WANTED *Brunswick 05839*	**31**	6
19 Jan 61	LET'S JUMP THE BROOMSTICK *Brunswick 05823*	**12**	15
6 Apr 61	EMOTIONS *Brunswick 05847*	**45**	1
20 Jul 61	DUM DUM *Brunswick 05854*	**22**	8
16 Nov 61	FOOL NUMBER ONE *Brunswick 05860*	**38**	3
8 Feb 62	BREAK IT TO ME GENTLY *Brunswick 05864*	**46**	2
5 Apr 62	● SPEAK TO ME PRETTY *Brunswick 05867*	**3**	12
21 Jun 62	● HERE COMES THAT FEELING *Brunswick 05871*	**5**	12
13 Sep 62	IT STARTED ALL OVER AGAIN *Brunswick 05876*	**15**	11
29 Nov 62	● ROCKIN' AROUND THE CHRISTMAS TREE *Brunswick 05880*	**6**	7
17 Jan 63	● ALL ALONE AM I *Brunswick 05882*	**7**	17
28 Mar 63	● LOSING YOU *Brunswick 05886*	**10**	16
18 Jul 63	I WONDER *Brunswick 05891*	**14**	9
31 Oct 63	SWEET IMPOSSIBLE YOU *Brunswick 05896*	**28**	6
9 Jan 64	● AS USUAL *Brunswick 05899*	**5**	15
9 Apr 64	THINK *Brunswick 05903*	**26**	8
10 Sep 64	IS IT TRUE *Brunswick 05915*	**17**	8
10 Dec 64	CHRISTMAS WILL BE JUST ANOTHER LONELY DAY *Brunswick 05921*	**29**	5
4 Feb 65	THANKS A LOT *Brunswick 05927*	**41**	2
29 Jul 65	TOO MANY RIVERS *Brunswick 05936*	**22**	12

Byron LEE – *See Boris GARDINER*

Curtis LEE *US, male vocalist*　　**2 wks**

31 Aug 61	PRETTY LITTLE ANGEL EYES *London HLX 9397*	**47**	1
14 Sep 61	PRETTY LITTLE ANGEL EYES (re-entry) *London HLX 9397*	**48**	1

Dee C LEE *UK, female vocalist*　　**20 wks**

9 Nov 85	● SEE THE DAY *CBS A 6570*	**3**	12
8 Mar 86	COME HELL OR WATERS HIGH *CBS A 6869*	**46**	5
13 Nov 93	NO TIME TO PLAY *Cooltempo CDCOOL 282* [1]	**25**	3

[1] Guru featuring D.C. Lee

Garry LEE and SHOWDOWN
Canada, male vocal / instrumental group **3 wks**

31 Jul 93	**THE RODEO SONG** *Party Dish VCD 101*	**44**	3

Jackie LEE
UK, female vocalist **31 wks**

10 Apr 68 ●	**WHITE HORSES** *Philips BF 1674* [1]	**10**	14
2 Jan 71	**RUPERT** *Pye 7N 45003*	**14**	17

[1] Jacky

Leapy LEE
UK, male vocalist **28 wks**

21 Aug 68 ●	**LITTLE ARROWS** *MCA MU 1028*	**2**	21
20 Dec 69	**GOOD MORNING** *MCA MK 5021*	**47**	1
10 Jan 70	**GOOD MORNING (re-entry)** *MCA MK 5021*	**29**	6

Peggy LEE
US, female vocalist **29 wks**

24 May 57 ●	**MR. WONDERFUL** *Brunswick 05671*	**5**	13
15 Aug 58 ●	**FEVER** *Capitol CL 14902*	**5**	11
23 Mar 61	**TILL THERE WAS YOU** *Capitol CL 15184*	**40**	1
6 Apr 61	**TILL THERE WAS YOU (re-entry)** *Capitol CL 15184*	**30**	3
22 Aug 92	**FEVER (re-issue)** *Capitol PEG 1*	**75**	1

Toney LEE
US, male vocalist **4 wks**

29 Jan 83	**REACH UP** *TMT TMT 2*	**64**	4

LEEDS UNITED FC
UK, male football team vocalists **13 wks**

29 Apr 72 ●	**LEEDS UNITED** *Chapter One SCH 168*	**10**	10
25 Apr 92	**LEEDS LEEDS LEEDS** *Q Music LUFC 2*	**61**	1
9 May 92	**LEEDS LEEDS LEEDS (re-entry)** *Q Music LUFC 2*	**54**	2

Carol LEEMING – *See STAXX*

Raymond LEFEVRE
France, orchestra **2 wks**

15 May 68	**SOUL COAXING** *Major Minor MM 559*	**46**	2

LEFTFIELD
UK, male instrumental / production duo **15 wks**

12 Dec 92	**SONG OF LIFE** *Hard Hands HAND 002T*	**59**	1
13 Nov 93	**OPEN UP** *Hard Hands HAND 009CD* [1]	**13**	5
25 Mar 95	**ORIGINAL** *Hard Hands HAND 18CD* [2]	**18**	3
5 Aug 95	**THE AFRO-LEFT (EP)** *Hard Hands HAND 23CD* [3]	**22**	3
20 Jan 96	**RELEASE THE PRESSURE** *Hard Hands HAND 29CD*	**13**	3

[1] Leftfield Lydon [2] Leftfield Halliday [3] Leftfield featuring Djum Djum

Tracks on The Afro-Left (EP): Afro-Left / Afro Ride / Afro Central / Afro Sol.

Paul LEKAKIS
US, male vocalist **4 wks**

30 May 87	**BOOM BOOM (LET'S GO BACK TO MY ROOM)** *Champion CHAMP 43*	**60**	4

LEMON PIPERS
US, male vocal / instrumental group **16 wks**

7 Feb 68 ●	**GREEN TAMBOURINE** *Pye International 7N 25444*	**7**	11
1 May 68	**RICE IS NICE** *Pye International 7N 25454*	**41**	5

LEMON TREES
UK, male vocal / instrumental group **9 wks**

26 Sep 92	**LOVE IS IN YOUR EYES** *Oxygen GASP 1*	**75**	1

7 Nov 92	**THE WAY I FEEL** *Oxygen GASP 2*	**62**	2
13 Feb 93	**LET IT LOOSE** *Oxygen GASPD 3*	**55**	2
17 Apr 93	**CHILD OF LOVE** *Oxygen GASPD 4*	**55**	3
3 Jul 93	**I CAN'T FACE THE WORLD** *Oxygen GASPD 6*	**52**	1

LEMONHEADS
US / Australia, male vocal / instrumental group **26 wks**

17 Oct 92	**IT'S A SHAME ABOUT RAY** *Atlantic A 7423*	**70**	1
5 Dec 92	**MRS ROBINSON / BEIN' AROUND** *Atlantic A 7401*	**19**	9
6 Feb 93	**CONFETTI / MY DRUG BUDDY** *Atlantic A 7430CD*	**44**	2
10 Apr 93	**IT'S A SHAME ABOUT RAY (re-issue)** *Atlantic A 5764CD*	**31**	3
16 Oct 93	**INTO YOUR ARMS** *Atlantic A 7302CD*	**14**	4
27 Nov 93	**IT'S ABOUT TIME** *Atlantic A 7296CD*	**57**	2
14 May 94	**BIG GAY HEART** *Atlantic A 7259CD*	**55**	2
28 Sep 96	**IF I COULD TALK I'D TELL YOU** *Atlantic A 5495CD*	**39**	2
14 Dec 96	**IT'S ALL TRUE** *Atlantic A 5635CD*	**61**	1

LENA – *See Lena FIAGBE*

John LENNON
UK, male vocalist **184 wks**

9 Jul 69 ●	**GIVE PEACE A CHANCE** *Apple 13* [1]	**2**	13
1 Nov 69	**COLD TURKEY** *Apple APPLES 1001* [1]	**14**	8
21 Feb 70 ●	**INSTANT KARMA** *Apple APPLES 1003* [2]	**5**	9
20 Mar 71 ●	**POWER TO THE PEOPLE** *Apple R 5892* [3]	**7**	9
9 Dec 72 ●	**HAPPY XMAS (WAR IS OVER)** *Apple R 5970* [4]	**4**	8
24 Nov 73	**MIND GAMES** *Apple R 5994*	**26**	9
19 Oct 74	**WHATEVER GETS YOU THROUGH THE NIGHT** *Apple R 5998* [5]	**36**	4
4 Jan 75	**HAPPY XMAS (WAR IS OVER) (re-entry)** *Apple R 5970* [4]	**48**	1
8 Feb 75	**NUMBER 9 DREAM** *Apple R 6003*	**23**	8
3 May 75	**STAND BY ME** *Apple R 6005*	**30**	7
1 Nov 75 ●	**IMAGINE** *Apple R 6009*	**6**	11
8 Nov 80 ★	**(JUST LIKE) STARTING OVER** *Geffen K 79186*	**1**	15
20 Dec 80 ●	**HAPPY XMAS (WAR IS OVER) (2nd re-entry)** *Apple R 5970* [4]	**2**	9
27 Dec 80 ★	**IMAGINE (re-entry)** *Apple R 6009*	**1**	13
24 Jan 81 ★	**WOMAN** *Geffen K 79195*	**1**	11
24 Jan 81	**GIVE PEACE A CHANCE (re-entry)** *Apple 13*	**33**	5
21 Mar 81	**I SAW HER STANDING THERE** *DJM DJS 10965* [6]	**40**	4
4 Apr 81	**WATCHING THE WHEELS** *Geffen K 79207*	**30**	6
19 Dec 81	**HAPPY XMAS (WAR IS OVER) (3rd re-entry)** *Apple R 5970* [4]	**28**	5
20 Nov 82	**LOVE** *Parlophone R 6059*	**41**	7
25 Dec 82	**HAPPY XMAS (WAR IS OVER) (4th re-entry)** *Apple R 5970* [4]	**56**	3
21 Jan 84 ●	**NOBODY TOLD ME** *Ono Music/Polydor POSP 700*	**6**	6
17 Mar 84	**BORROWED TIME** *Polydor POSP 701*	**32**	6
30 Nov 85	**JEALOUS GUY** *Parlophone R 6117*	**65**	2
10 Dec 88	**IMAGINE / JEALOUS GUY / HAPPY XMAS (WAR IS OVER) (re-issue)** *Parlophone R 6199*	**45**	5

[1] Plastic Ono Band [2] Lennon, Ono and the Plastic Ono Band
[3] The Elton John Band featuring John Lennon and the Muscle Shoals Horns [4] John and Yoko and the Plastic Ono Band with the Harlem Community Choir [5] John Lennon with the Plastic Ono Nuclear Band
[6] The Elton John Band featuring John Lennon and the Muscle Shoals Horns

Julian LENNON
UK, male vocalist **46 wks**

6 Oct 84 ●	**TOO LATE FOR GOODBYES** *Charisma JL 1*	**6**	11
15 Dec 84	**VALOTTE** *Charisma JL 2*	**55**	6
9 Mar 85	**SAY YOU'RE WRONG** *Charisma JL 3*	**75**	1
7 Dec 85	**BECAUSE** *EMI 5538*	**40**	7
11 Mar 89	**NOW YOU'RE IN HEAVEN** *Virgin VS 1154*	**59**	3
24 Aug 91 ●	**SALTWATER** *Virgin VS 1361*	**6**	13
30 Nov 91	**HELP YOURSELF** *Virgin VS 1379*	**53**	2
25 Apr 92	**GET A LIFE** *Virgin VS 1398*	**56**	3

Annie LENNOX UK, female vocalist — 68 wks

3 Dec 88	PUT A LITTLE LOVE IN YOUR HEART A&M AM 484 [1]	28	8
28 Mar 92	● WHY RCA PB 45317	5	8
6 Jun 92	PRECIOUS RCA 74321100257	23	5
22 Aug 92	● WALKING ON BROKEN GLASS RCA 74321107227	8	8
31 Oct 92	COLD RCA 74321116902	26	4
13 Feb 93	● LITTLE BIRD / LOVE SONG FOR A VAMPIRE RCA 743211233832	3	12
18 Feb 95	● NO MORE 'I LOVE YOU'S RCA 74321257162	2	12
10 Jun 95	A WHITER SHADE OF PALE RCA 74321284822	16	6
30 Sep 95	WAITING IN VAIN RCA 74321316132	31	3
9 Dec 95	SOMETHING SO RIGHT RCA 74321332392 [2]	44	2

[1] Annie Lennox and Al Green [2] Annie Lennox featuring Paul Simon

Rula LENSKA – See Julie COVINGTON, Rula LENSKA, Charlotte CORNWELL and Sue JONES-DAVIES

Phillip LEO UK, male vocalist — 3 wks

| 23 Jul 94 | SECOND CHANCE EMI CDEM 327 | 57 | 2 |
| 25 Mar 95 | THINKING ABOUT YOUR LOVE EMI CDEM 358 | 64 | 1 |

LeSHAUN – See LL Cool J

LESTER – See Norman COOK

Ketty LESTER US, female vocalist — 16 wks

| 19 Apr 62 | ● LOVE LETTERS London HLN 9527 | 4 | 12 |
| 19 Jul 62 | BUT NOT FOR ME London HLN 9574 | 45 | 4 |

LET LOOSE UK, male vocal / instrumental group — 62 wks

24 Apr 93	CRAZY FOR YOU Vertigo VERCD 74	44	3
9 Apr 94	SEVENTEEN Mercury MERCD 400	44	2
25 Jun 94	● CRAZY FOR YOU (re-issue) Mercury MERCD 402	2	20
22 Oct 94	SEVENTEEN (re-mix) Mercury MERCD 406	11	6
24 Dec 94	CRAZY FOR YOU (re-entry of re-issue) Mercury MERCD 402	46	4
7 Jan 95	SEVENTEEN (re-entry of re-mix) Mercury MERCD 406	47	3
28 Jan 95	ONE NIGHT STAND Mercury MERCD 419	12	6
29 Apr 95	● BEST IN ME Mercury MERCD 428	8	5
4 Nov 95	EVERYBODY SAY EVERYBODY DO Mercury MERCD 446	29	3
13 Jan 96	EVERYBODY SAY EVERYBODY DO (re-entry) Mercury MERCD 446	71	1
22 Jun 96	● MAKE IT WITH YOU Mercury MERCD 464	7	6
7 Sep 96	TAKE IT EASY Mercury MERCD 472	25	2
16 Nov 96	DARLING BE HOME SOON Mercury MERCD 475	65	1

Gerald LETHAN – See WALL OF SOUND featuring Gerald LETHAN

LETTERMEN US, male vocal group — 3 wks

| 23 Nov 61 | THE WAY YOU LOOK TONIGHT Capitol CL 15222 | 36 | 3 |

LEVEL 42 UK, male vocal / instrumental group — 177 wks

30 Aug 80	LOVE MEETING LOVE Polydor POSP 170	61	4
18 Apr 81	LOVE GAMES Polydor POSP 234	38	6
8 Aug 81	TURN IT ON Polydor POSP 286	57	4
14 Nov 81	STARCHILD Polydor POSP 343	47	4
8 May 82	ARE YOU HEARING (WHAT I HEAR)? Polydor POSP 396	49	5
2 Oct 82	WEAVE YOUR SPELL Polydor POSP 500	43	4
15 Jan 83	THE CHINESE WAY Polydor POSP 538	24	8
16 Apr 83	OUT OF SIGHT, OUT OF MIND Polydor POSP 570	41	4
30 Jul 83	● THE SUN GOES DOWN (LIVING IT UP) Polydor POSP 622	10	12
22 Oct 83	MICRO KID Polydor POSP 643	37	5
1 Sep 84	HOT WATER Polydor POSP 697	18	9
3 Nov 84	THE CHANT HAS BEGUN Polydor POSP 710	41	5
21 Sep 85	● SOMETHING ABOUT YOU Polydor POSP 759	6	17
7 Dec 85	LEAVING ME NOW Polydor POSP 776	15	11
26 Apr 86	● LESSONS IN LOVE Polydor POSP 790	3	13
14 Feb 87	● RUNNING IN THE FAMILY Polydor POSP 842	6	10
25 Apr 87	● TO BE WITH YOU AGAIN Polydor POSP 855	10	7
12 Sep 87	● IT'S OVER Polydor POSP 900	10	8
12 Dec 87	CHILDREN SAY Polydor POSP 911	22	6
3 Sep 88	HEAVEN IN MY HANDS Polydor PO 14	12	5
29 Oct 88	TAKE A LOOK Polydor PO 24	32	4
21 Jan 89	TRACIE Polydor PO 34	25	5
28 Oct 89	TAKE CARE OF YOURSELF Polydor PO 58	39	4
17 Aug 91	GUARANTEED RCA PB 44745	17	4
19 Oct 91	OVERTIME RCA PB 44997	62	2
18 Apr 92	MY FATHER'S SHOES RCA PB 45271	55	1
26 Feb 94	FOREVER NOW RCA 74321190272	19	4
30 Apr 94	ALL OVER YOU RCA 74321205662	26	2
6 Aug 94	LOVE IN A PEACEFUL WORLD RCA 74321220332	31	3

LEVELLERS UK, male vocal / instrumental group — 38 wks

21 Sep 91	ONE WAY China WOK 2008	51	2
7 Dec 91	FAR FROM HOME China WOK 2010	71	1
23 May 92	15 YEARS (EP) China WOKX 2020	11	5
10 Jul 93	BELARUSE China WOKCD 2034	12	5
30 Jul 94	THIS GARDEN China WOKCD 2039	12	4
14 May 94	JULIE (EP) China WOKCD 2042	17	3
12 Aug 95	HOPE ST. China WOKCD 2059	12	5
14 Oct 95	FANTASY China WOKCD 2067	16	3
23 Dec 95	JUST THE ONE China WOKCD 2076 [1]	12	8
20 Jul 96	EXODUS – LIVE China WOKCD 2082	24	2

[1] Levellers, special guest Joe Strummer

Tracks on 15 Years (EP): 15 Years / Dance Before The Storm / The River Flow (Live) / Plastic Jeezus. Tracks on Julie (EP): Julie / English Civil War / Lowlands Of Holland / 100 years.

LEVERT UK, male vocal group — 10 wks

| 22 Aug 87 | ● CASANOVA Atlantic A 9217 | 9 | 10 |

Hank LEVINE US, orchestra — 4 wks

| 21 Dec 61 | IMAGE HMV POP 947 | 45 | 4 |

LEVITICUS UK, male vocalist — 1 wk

| 25 Mar 95 | BURIAL ffrr FCD 255 | 66 | 1 |

Barrington LEVY Jamaica, male vocalist — 11 wks

2 Feb 85	HERE I COME London LON 62	41	4
15 Jun 91	TRIBAL BASE Desire WANT 44 [1]	20	6
24 Sep 94	WORK MCA MCSTD 2003	65	1

[1] Rebel MC featuring Tenor Fly and Barrington Levy

Jona LEWIE UK, male vocalist — 20 wks

| 10 May 80 | YOU'LL ALWAYS FIND ME IN THE KITCHEN AT PARTIES Stiff BUY 73 | 16 | 9 |
| 29 Nov 80 | ● STOP THE CAVALRY Stiff BUY 104 | 3 | 11 |

On some copies first title was simply Kitchen At Parties. See also Terry Dactyl and the Dinosaurs.

CJ LEWIS *UK, male vocalist* — 32 wks

23 Apr 94	● SWEETS FOR MY SWEET *Black Market BMITD 017*	**3** 13
23 Jul 94	● EVERYTHING IS ALRIGHT (UPTIGHT) *Black Market BMITD 019*	**10** 7
8 Oct 94	BEST OF MY LOVE *Black Market BMITD 021*	**13** 6
17 Dec 94	DOLLARS *Black Market BMITD 023*	**34** 4
9 Sep 95	R TO THE A *Black Market BMITD 030*	**34** 2

Darlene LEWIS *US, female vocalist* — 4 wks

16 Apr 94	LET THE MUSIC (LIFT YOU UP) *KMS/Eastern Bloc KMSCD 10*	**16** 4

All formats of Let The Music (Lift You Up) featured versions by Loveland featuring Rachel McFarlane and also by Darlene Lewis.

Dee LEWIS *UK, female vocalist* — 5 wks

18 Jun 88	BEST OF MY LOVE *Mercury DEE 3*	**47** 5

Donna LEWIS *UK, female vocalist* — 14 wks

7 Sep 96	● I LOVE YOU ALWAYS FOREVER *Atlantic A 5495CD*	**5** 14

Gary LEWIS and the PLAYBOYS
US, male vocal / instrumental group — 7 wks

8 Feb 75	MY HEART'S SYMPHONY *United Artists UP 35780*	**36** 7

Huey LEWIS and the NEWS
US, male vocal / instrumental group — 66 wks

27 Oct 84	IF THIS IS IT *Chrysalis CHS 2829*	**39** 6
31 Aug 85	THE POWER OF LOVE *Chrysalis HUEY 1*	**11** 10
23 Nov 85	HEART AND SOUL (EP) *Chrysalis HUEY 2*	**61** 4
8 Feb 86	● THE POWER OF LOVE (re-issue) /DO YOU BELIEVE IN LOVE (re-issue) *Chrysalis HUEY 3*	**9** 12
10 May 86	THE HEART OF ROCK AND ROLL *Chrysalis HUEY 4*	**49** 3
23 Aug 86	STUCK WITH YOU *Chrysalis HUEY 5*	**12** 12
6 Dec 86	HIP TO BE SQUARE *Chrysalis HUEY 6*	**41** 8
21 Mar 87	SIMPLE AS THAT *Chrysalis HUEY 7*	**47** 5
16 Jul 88	PERFECT WORLD *Chrysalis HUEY 10*	**48** 6

Tracks on Heart and Soul EP: Heart and Soul / Hope You Love Me Like You Say You Do / Heart of Rock And Roll / Buzz Buzz Buzz. Do You Believe In Love only listed from 15 Feb 86.

Jerry LEWIS *US, male vocalist* — 8 wks

8 Feb 57	ROCK-A-BYE YOUR BABY (WITH A DIXIE MELODY) *Brunswick 05636*	**12** 7
5 Apr 57	ROCK-A-BYE YOUR BABY (WITH A DIXIE MELODY) (re-entry) *Brunswick 05636*	**22** 1

Jerry Lee LEWIS
US, male vocalist / instrumentalist – piano — 68 wks

27 Sep 57	● WHOLE LOTTA SHAKIN' GOIN' ON *London HLS 8457*	**8** 10
20 Dec 57	★ GREAT BALLS OF FIRE *London HLS 8529*	**1** 12
27 Dec 57	WHOLE LOTTA SHAKIN' GOIN' ON (re-entry) *London HLS 8457*	**26** 1
11 Apr 58	● BREATHLESS *London HLS 8592*	**8** 7
23 Jan 59	HIGH SCHOOL CONFIDENTIAL *London HLS 8780*	**12** 6
1 May 59	LOVIN' UP A STORM *London HLS 8840*	**28** 1
9 Jun 60	BABY BABY BYE BYE *London HLS 9131*	**47** 1
4 May 61	● WHAT'D I SAY *London HLS 9335*	**10** 12
3 Aug 61	WHAT'D I SAY (re-entry) *London HLS 9335*	**49** 2
6 Sep 62	SWEET LITTLE SIXTEEN *London HLS 9584*	**38** 5

14 Mar 63	GOOD GOLLY MISS MOLLY *London HLS 9688*	**31** 6
6 May 72	CHANTILLY LACE *Mercury 6052 141*	**33** 5

Linda LEWIS *UK, female vocalist* — 30 wks

2 Jun 73	ROCK-A-DOODLE-DOO *Raft RA 18502*	**15** 11
12 Jul 75	● IT'S IN HIS KISS *Arista 17*	**6** 8
17 Apr 76	BABY I'M YOURS *Arista 43*	**33** 6
2 Jun 79	I'D BE SURPRISINGLY GOOD FOR YOU *Ariola ARO 166*	**40** 5

Ramsey LEWIS *US, male instrumentalist – piano* — 8 wks

15 Apr 72	WADE IN THE WATER *Chess 6145 004*	**31** 8

Shirley LEWIS – *See Arthur BAKER*

John LEYTON *UK, male vocalist* — 70 wks

3 Aug 61	★ JOHNNY REMEMBER ME *Top Rank JAR 577*	**1** 15
5 Oct 61	● WILD WIND *Top Rank JAR 585*	**2** 10
28 Dec 61	SON THIS IS SHE *HMV POP 956*	**15** 10
15 Mar 62	LONE RIDER *HMV POP 992*	**40** 5
3 May 62	LONELY CITY *HMV POP 1014*	**14** 11
23 Aug 62	DOWN THE RIVER NILE *HMV POP 1054*	**42** 3
21 Feb 63	CUPBOARD LOVE *HMV POP 1122*	**22** 12
18 Jul 63	I'LL CUT YOUR TAIL OFF *HMV POP 1175*	**50** 1
8 Aug 63	I'LL CUT YOUR TAIL OFF (re-entry) *HMV POP 1175*	**36** 2
20 Feb 64	MAKE LOVE TO ME *HMV POP 1264*	**49** 1

LEYTON BUZZARDS
UK, male vocal / instrumental group — 5 wks

3 Mar 79	SATURDAY NIGHT (BENEATH THE PLASTIC PALM TREES) *Chrysalis CHS 2288*	**53** 5

LFO *UK, male instrumental group* — 15 wks

14 Jul 90	LFO *Warp WAP 5*	**12** 10
6 Jul 91	WE ARE BACK / NURTURE *Warp 7WAP 14*	**47** 3
1 Feb 92	WHAT IS HOUSE (EP) *Warp WAP 17*	**62** 2

Tracks on What Is House (EP): Tan Ta Ra / Mashed Potato / What Is House / Syndrome.

LIBERACE *US, male instrumentalist – piano* — 2 wks

17 Jun 55	UNCHAINED MELODY *Philips PB 430*	**20** 1
19 Oct 56	I DON'T CARE *Columbia DB 3834*	**28** 1

I Don't Care also featured Liberace as vocalist.

LIBERATION *UK, male instrumental / production duo* — 3 wks

24 Oct 92	LIBERATION *ZYX ZYX 68657*	**28** 3

LIBRA presents TAYLOR
UK, male vocal / instrumental group — 1 wk

26 Oct 96	ANOMALY – CALLING YOUR NAME *Platipus PLATCD 24*	**71** 1

LICK THE TINS
UK, male / female vocal / instrumental group — 8 wks

29 Mar 86	CAN'T HELP FALLING IN LOVE *Sedition EDIT 3308*	**42** 8

Lightning Seeds

'Three Lions' returned to the top of the chart in July 1996 as football fever gripped the nation in the run up to the Euro 96 semi-final clash with Germany.

Jerry Lee Lewis

Jerry Lee Lewis' debut hit, 'Whole Lotta Shakin' Goin' On' sold a reported 6 million copies worldwide.

Longpigs

The Longpigs got their name from the term cannibals use to refer to human flesh.

Ben LIEBRAND
Holland, male producer / multi-instrumentalist **2 wks**

9 Jun 90	**PULS(T)AR** *Epic LIEB 1*	**68**	2

LIEUTENANT PIGEON
UK, male / female instrumental group **29 wks**

16 Sep 72	★ **MOULDY OLD DOUGH** *Decca F 13278*	**1**	19
16 Dec 72	**DESPERATE DAN** *Decca F 13365*	**17**	10

LIGHT OF THE WORLD
UK, male vocal / instrumental group **25 wks**

14 Apr 79	**SWINGIN'** *Ensign ENY 22*	**45**	5
14 Jul 79	**MIDNIGHT GROOVIN'** *Ensign ENY 29*	**72**	1
18 Oct 80	**LONDON TOWN** *Ensign ENY 43*	**41**	5
17 Jan 81	**I SHOT THE SHERIFF** *Ensign ENY 46*	**40**	5
28 Mar 81	**I'M SO HAPPY** *Ensign MER 64*	**35**	6
21 Nov 81	**RIDE THE LOVE TRAIN** *EMI 5242*	**49**	3

LIGHTER SHADE OF BROWN *US, male vocal duo* **3 wks**

9 Jul 94	**HEY DJ** *Mercury MERCD 401*	**33**	3

Gordon LIGHTFOOT *Canada, male vocalist* **26 wks**

19 Jun 71	**IF YOU COULD READ MY MIND** *Reprise RS 20974*	**30**	9
3 Aug 74	**SUNDOWN** *Reprise K 14327*	**33**	7
15 Jan 77	**THE WRECK OF THE EDMUND FITZGERALD** *Reprise K 14451*	**40**	4
16 Sep 78	**DAYLIGHT KATY** *Warner Bros. K 17214*	**41**	6

Terry LIGHTFOOT and his NEW ORLEANS JAZZMEN *UK, male jazz band, Terry Lightfoot vocalist / instrumentalist – clarinet* **17 wks**

7 Sep 61	**TRUE LOVE** *Columbia DB 4696*	**33**	4
23 Nov 61	**KING KONG** *Columbia SCD 2165*	**29**	12
3 May 62	**TAVERN IN THE TOWN** *Columbia DB 4822*	**49**	1

LIGHTHOUSE FAMILY
UK, male vocal / instrumental duo **31 wks**

27 May 95	**LIFTED** *Wild Card CARDW 17*	**61**	2
14 Oct 95	**OCEAN DRIVE** *Wild Card 5797072*	**34**	3
10 Feb 96	● **LIFTED (re-issue)** *Wild Card 5779432*	**4**	10
1 Jun 96	**OCEAN DRIVE (re-issue)** *Wild Card 5766192*	**11**	8
21 Sep 96	**GOODBYE HEARTBREAK** *Wild Card 5753492*	**14**	6
21 Dec 96	**LOVING EVERY MINUTE** *Wild Card 5731012*	**20†**	2

LIGHTNING SEEDS
UK, male vocal / instrumental group **65 wks**

22 Jul 89	**PURE** *Ghetto GTG 4*	**16**	8
14 Mar 92	**THE LIFE OF RILEY** *Virgin VS 1402*	**28**	6
30 May 92	**SENSE** *Virgin VS 1414*	**31**	5
20 Aug 94	**LUCKY YOU** *Epic 6606282*	**43**	2
14 Jan 95	**CHANGE** *Epic 6609865*	**13**	6
15 Apr 95	**MARVELLOUS** *Epic 6614265*	**24**	5
22 Jul 95	**PERFECT** *Epic 6621792*	**18**	5
21 Oct 95	**LUCKY YOU (re-issue)** *Epic 6625182*	**15**	6
9 Mar 96	**READY OR NOT** *Epic 6629672*	**20**	4
1 Jun 96	★ **THREE LIONS (THE OFFICIAL SONG OF THE ENGLAND FOOTBALL TEAM)** *Epic 6632732* [1]	**1**	15
2 Nov 96	**WHAT IF...** *Epic 6638635*	**14**	3

[1] Baddiel and Skinner and the Lightning Seeds

LIL' LOUIS *US, male producer* **18 wks**

29 Jul 89	● **FRENCH KISS** *ffrr FX 115*	**2**	11
13 Jan 90	**I CALLED U** *ffrr F 123*	**16**	6
26 Sep 92	**SAVED MY LIFE** *ffrr FX 197* [1]	**74**	1

[1] Lil' Louis and the World

See also Black Magic; Lil Mo' Yin Yang.

LIL MO' YIN YANG
US, male instrumental / production duo **2 wks**

9 Mar 96	**REACH** *Multiply CDMULTY 9*	**28**	2

One half of Lil Mo' Yin Yang is Lil' Louis. See also Lil' Louis.

LIMAHL *UK, male vocalist* **25 wks**

5 Nov 83	**ONLY FOR LOVE** *EMI LML 1*	**16**	7
7 Jan 84	**ONLY FOR LOVE (re-entry)** *EMI LML 1*	**75**	1
2 Jun 84	**TOO MUCH TROUBLE** *EMI LML 2*	**64**	3
13 Oct 84	● **NEVER ENDING STORY** *EMI LML 3*	**4**	14

Alison LIMERICK *UK, female vocalist* **38 wks**

30 Mar 91	**WHERE LOVE LIVES** *Arista 144208*	**27**	8
12 Oct 91	**COME BACK (FOR REAL LOVE)** *Arista 114530*	**53**	2
21 Dec 91	**MAGIC'S BACK (THEME FROM THE GHOSTS OF OXFORD STREET)** *RCA PB 45223* [1]	**42**	4
29 Feb 92	**MAKE IT ON MY OWN** *Arista 114996*	**16**	6
18 Jul 92	**GETTIN' IT RIGHT** *Arista 74321102867*	**57**	2
28 Nov 92	**HEAR MY CALL** *Arista 115337*	**73**	1
8 Jan 94	**TIME OF OUR LIVES** *Arista 74321180332*	**36**	4
19 Mar 94	**LOVE COME DOWN** *Arista 74321191952*	**36**	2
25 Feb 95	**LOVE WILL KEEP US TOGETHER** *Acid Jazz JAZID 112CD* [2]	**63**	1
6 Jul 96	● **WHERE LOVE LIVES (re-mix)** *Arista 74321381592*	**9**	6
14 Sep 96	**MAKE IT ON MY OWN (re-mix)** *Arista 74321407812*	**30**	2

[1] Malcolm McLaren featuring Alison Limerick [2] JTQ featuring Alison Limerick

LIMIT *Holland, male vocal / instrumental duo* **8 wks**

5 Jan 85	**SAY YEAH** *Portrait A 4808*	**17**	8

LIMMIE and the FAMILY COOKIN'
US, male / female vocal group **28 wks**

21 Jul 73	● **YOU CAN DO MAGIC** *Avco 6105 019*	**3**	13
20 Oct 73	**DREAMBOAT** *Avco 6105 025*	**31**	5
6 Apr 74	● **A WALKIN' MIRACLE** *Avco 6105 027*	**6**	10

Bob LIND *US, male vocalist* **10 wks**

10 Mar 66	● **ELUSIVE BUTTERFLY** *Fontana TF 670*	**5**	9
26 May 66	**REMEMBER THE RAIN** *Fontana TF 702*	**46**	1

LINDA and the FUNKY BOYS – *See Linda CARR*

LINDISFARNE *UK, male vocal / instrumental group* **55 wks**

26 Feb 72	● **MEET ME ON THE CORNER** *Charisma CB 173*	**5**	11
13 May 72	● **LADY ELEANOR** *Charisma CB 153*	**3**	11
23 Sep 72	**ALL FALL DOWN** *Charisma CB 191*	**34**	5
3 Jun 78	● **RUN FOR HOME** *Mercury 6007 177*	**10**	15

7 Oct 78	**JUKE BOX GYPSY** Mercury 6007 187	**56**	4
10 Nov 90	● **FOG ON THE TYNE (REVISITED)** Best ZB 44083 [1]	**2**	9

[1] Gazza and Lindisfarne

LINER UK, male vocal / instrumental group   6 wks

10 Mar 79	**KEEP REACHING OUT FOR LOVE** Atlantic K 11235	**49**	3
26 May 79	**YOU AND ME** Atlantic K 11285	**44**	3

Laurie LINGO and the DIPSTICKS
UK, male vocal duo, disc jockeys Dave Lee Travis and Paul Burnett   **7 wks**

17 Apr 76	● **CONVOY G.B.** State STAT 23	**4**	7

LINX UK, male vocal / instrumental duo   45 wks

20 Sep 80	**YOU'RE LYING** Chrysalis CHS 2461	**15**	10
7 Mar 81	● **INTUITION** Chrysalis CHS 2500	**7**	11
13 Jun 81	**THROW AWAY THE KEY** Chrysalis CHS 2519	**21**	9
5 Sep 81	**SO THIS IS ROMANCE** Chrysalis CHS 2546	**15**	9
21 Nov 81	**CAN'T HELP MYSELF** Chrysalis CHS 2565	**55**	3
10 Jul 82	**PLAYTHING** Chrysalis CHS 2621	**48**	3

LIONROCK UK, male producer – Justin Robertson   10 wks

5 Dec 92	**LIONROCK** Deconstruction 74321124381	**63**	1
8 May 93	**PACKET OF PEACE** Deconstruction 74321144372	**32**	3
23 Oct 93	**CARNIVAL** Deconstruction 74321164862	**34**	2
27 Aug 94	**TRIPWIRE** Deconstruction 74321204702	**44**	1
6 Apr 96	**STRAIGHT AT YER HEAD** Deconstruction 74321342972	**33**	2
27 Jul 96	**FIRE UP THE SHOESAW** Deconstruction 74321382652	**43**	1

LIPPS INC. US, male / female vocal / instrumental group   13 wks

17 May 80	● **FUNKYTOWN** Casablanca CAN 194	**2**	13

LIQUID UK, male instrumental / production duo   18 wks

21 Mar 92	**SWEET HARMONY** XL XLS 28	**15**	6
5 Sep 92	**THE FUTURE MUSIC EP** XL XLT 33	**59**	2
20 Mar 93	**TIME TO GET UP** XL XLS 40CD	**46**	2
8 Jul 95	**SWEET HARMONY (re-mix) / ONE LOVE FAMILY** XL XLS 65CD	**14**	6
21 Oct 95	**CLOSER** XL XLS 66CD	**47**	2

Tracks on The Future Music EP: Liquid Is Liquid / Music / House (Is A Feeling) / The Year 3000.

LIQUID GOLD
UK, male / female vocal / instrumental group   **46 wks**

2 Dec 78	**ANYWAY YOU DO IT** Creole CR 159	**41**	7
23 Feb 80	● **DANCE YOURSELF DIZZY** Polo POLO 1	**2**	14
31 May 80	● **SUBSTITUTE** Polo POLO 4	**8**	9
1 Nov 80	**THE NIGHT THE WINE AND THE ROSES** Polo POLO 6	**32**	7
28 Mar 81	**DON'T PANIC** Polo POLO 8	**42**	5
21 Aug 82	**WHERE DID WE GO WRONG** Polo POLO 23	**56**	4

LIQUID OXYGEN US, male producer   2 wks

28 Apr 90	**THE PLANET DANCE (MOVE YA BODY)** Champion CHAMP 242	**56**	2

LISA LISA US, female vocalist   32 wks

4 May 85	**I WONDER IF I TAKE YOU HOME** CBS A 6057 [1]	**53**	6

3 Aug 85	**I WONDER IF I TAKE YOU HOME (re-entry)** CBS A 6057 [1]	**12**	11
31 Oct 87	**LOST IN EMOTION** CBS 651036 7 [2]	**58**	4
13 Jul 91	**LET THE BEAT HIT 'EM** Columbia 6572867 [2]	**17**	6
24 Aug 91	**LET THE BEAT HIT 'EM PART 2** Columbia 6573747 [2]	**49**	2
26 Mar 94	**SKIP TO MY LU** Chrysalis CDCHS 5006	**34**	3

[1] Lisa Lisa and Cult Jam with Full Force   [2] Lisa Lisa and Cult Jam

LISA MARIE – See Malcolm McLAREN

LISA MARIE EXPERIENCE
UK, male instrumental / production duo   **15 wks**

27 Apr 96	● **KEEP ON JUMPIN'** ffrr FCD 271	**7**	10
20 Jul 96	**KEEP ON JUMPIN' (re-entry)** ffrr FCD 271	**61**	3
10 Aug 96	**DO THAT TO ME** Positiva CDTIV 57	**33**	2

De Etta LITTLE and Nelson PIGFORD
US, female / male vocal duo   **5 wks**

13 Aug 77	**YOU TAKE MY HEART AWAY** United Artists UP 36257	**35**	5

LITTLE ANGELS UK, male vocal / instrumental group   41 wks

4 Mar 89	**BIG BAD EP** Polydor LTLEP 2	**74**	1
24 Feb 90	**KICKING UP DUST** Polydor LTL 5	**46**	4
12 May 90	**RADICAL YOUR LOVER** Polydor LTL 6 [1]	**34**	4
4 Aug 90	**SHE'S A LITTLE ANGEL** Polydor LTL 7	**21**	3
2 Feb 91	**BONEYARD** Polydor LTL 8	**33**	4
30 Mar 91	**PRODUCT OF THE WORKING CLASS** Polydor LTL 9	**40**	2
1 Jun 91	**YOUNG GODS** Polydor LTL 10	**34**	2
20 Jul 91	**I AIN'T GONNA CRY** Polydor LTL 11	**26**	3
7 Nov 92	**TOO MUCH TOO YOUNG** Polydor LTL 12	**22**	3
9 Jan 93	**WOMANKIND** Polydor LTLCD 13	**12**	5
24 Apr 93	**SOAPBOX** Polydor LTLCD 14	**33**	4
25 Sep 93	**SAIL AWAY** Polydor LTLCD 15	**45**	3
9 Apr 94	**TEN MILES HIGH** Polydor LTLCD 16	**18**	3

[1] Little Angels featuring the Big Bad Horns

Tracks on Big Bad EP: She's A Little Angel / Don't Waste My Time / Better Than The Rest / Sex In Cars. See also Various Artists (EPs & LPs) – Gimme Shelter (EP).

LITTLE ANTHONY and the IMPERIALS
US, male vocal group   **17 wks**

31 Jul 76	**BETTER USE YOUR HEAD** United Artists UP 36141	**42**	4
24 Dec 77	**WHO'S GONNA LOVE ME** Power Exchange PX 266 [1]	**17**	9

[1] Imperials

LITTLE BENNY and the MASTERS
US, male rapper / instrumentalist – trumpet, and male
instrumental group   **7 wks**

2 Feb 85	**WHO COMES TO BOOGIE** Bluebird 10 BR 13	**33**	7

LITTLE CAESAR UK, male vocalist   3 wks

9 Jun 90	**THE WHOLE OF THE MOON** A1 EAU 1	**68**	3

LITTLE EVA US, female vocalist   45 wks

6 Sep 62	● **THE LOCO-MOTION** London HL 9581	**2**	17
3 Jan 63	**KEEP YOUR HANDS OFF MY BABY** London HLU 9633	**30**	5
7 Mar 63	**LET'S TURKEY TROT** London HLU 9687	**13**	12
29 Jul 72	**THE LOCO-MOTION (re-entry)** London HL 9581	**11**	11

See also Big Dee Irwin.

LITTLE RICHARD
US, male vocalist / instrumentalist – piano **108 wks**

14 Dec 56	RIP IT UP *London HLO 8336*	.30	1
8 Feb 57	● LONG TALL SALLY *London HLO 8366*	.3	16
22 Feb 57	TUTTI FRUTTI *London HLO 8366*	.29	1
8 Mar 57	SHE'S GOT IT *London HLO 8382*	.15	7
15 Mar 57	● THE GIRL CAN'T HELP IT *London HLO 8382*	.9	11
24 May 57	SHE'S GOT IT (re-entry) *London HLO 8382*	.28	2
28 Jun 57	● LUCILLE *London HLO 8446*	.10	9
13 Sep 57	JENNY JENNY *London HLO 8470*	.11	5
29 Nov 57	KEEP A KNOCKIN' *London HLO 8509*	.21	7
28 Feb 58	● GOOD GOLLY MISS MOLLY *London HLU 8560*	.8	9
11 Jul 58	OOH MY SOUL *London HLO 8647*	.30	1
25 Jul 58	OOH MY SOUL (re-entry) *London HLO 8647*	.22	3
2 Jan 59	● BABY FACE *London HLU 8770*	.2	15
3 Apr 59	BY THE LIGHT OF THE SILVERY MOON *London HLU 8831*	.17	5
5 Jun 59	KANSAS CITY *London HLU 8868*	.26	5
11 Oct 62	HE GOT WHAT HE WANTED *Mercury AMT 1189*	.38	4
4 Jun 64	BAMA LAMA BAMA LOO *London HL 9896*	.20	7
2 Jul 77	GOOD GOLLY MISS MOLLY / RIP IT UP *Creole CR 140*	.37	4
14 Jun 86	GREAT GOSH A'MIGHTY (IT'S A MATTER OF TIME) *MCA MCA 1049*	.62	2
25 Oct 86	OPERATOR *WEA YZ 89*	.67	2

The versions of Good Golly Miss Molly and Rip It Up on Creole are re-recordings.

LITTLE STEVEN
US, male vocalist / instrumentalist – guitar **3 wks**

23 May 87	BITTER FRUIT *Manhattan MT 21*	.66	3

LITTLE T – See REBEL MC

LITTLE TONY *Italy, male vocalist* **3 wks**

15 Jan 60	TOO GOOD *Decca F 11190*	.19	3

LIVE *US, male vocal / instrumental group* **9 wks**

18 Feb 95	I ALONE *Radioactive RAXTD 13*	.48	4
1 Jul 95	SELLING THE DRAMA *Radioactive RAXTD 17*	.30	2
7 Oct 95	ALL OVER YOU *Radioactive RAXTD 20*	.48	1
13 Jan 96	LIGHTNING CRASHES *Radioactive RAXTD 23*	.33	2

LIVE REPORT *UK, male vocal / instrumental group* **1 wk**

20 May 89	WHY DO I ALWAYS GET IT WRONG *Brouhaha CUE 7*	.73	1

LIVERPOOL EXPRESS
UK, male vocal / instrumental group **26 wks**

26 Jun 76	YOU ARE MY LOVE *Warner Bros. K 16743*	.11	9
16 Oct 76	HOLD TIGHT *Warner Bros. K 16799*	.46	2
18 Dec 76	EVERY MAN MUST HAVE A DREAM *Warner Bros. K 16854*	.17	11
4 Jun 77	DREAMIN' *Warner Bros. K 16933*	.40	4

LIVERPOOL FC *UK, male football team vocalists* **21 wks**

28 May 77	WE CAN DO IT (EP) *State STAT 50*	.15	4
23 Apr 83	LIVERPOOL (WE'RE NEVER GONNA...) / LIVERPOOL (ANTHEM) *Mean MEAN 102*	.54	4
17 May 86	SITTING ON THE TOP OF THE WORLD *Columbia DB 9116*	.50	2
14 May 88	● ANFIELD RAP (RED MACHINE IN FULL EFFECT) *Virgin LFC 1*	.3	6

18 May 96	● PASS AND MOVE (IT'S THE LIVERPOOL GROOVE) *Telstar LFCCD 96* [1]	.4	5

[1] Liverpool FC and the Boot Room Boyz

Tracks on We Can Do It (EP): We Can Do It / Liverpool Lou / We Shall Not Be Moved / You'll Never Walk Alone.

LIVIN' JOY
US / Italy, male / female vocal / instrumental group **36 wks**

3 Sep 94	DREAMER *Undiscovered MCSTD 1993*	.18	6
13 May 95	★ DREAMER (re-mix) *Undiscovered MCSTD 2056*	.1	11
15 Jun 96	● DON'T STOP MOVIN' *Undiscovered MCSTD 40041*	.5	14
2 Nov 96	● FOLLOW THE RULES *Undiscovered MCSTD 40081*	.9	5

LIVING COLOUR *US, male vocal / instrumental group* **22 wks**

27 Oct 90	TYPE *Epic LCL 7*	.75	1
2 Feb 91	LOVE REARS ITS UGLY HEAD *Epic 6565937*	.12	11
1 Jun 91	SOLACE OF YOU *Epic 6569087*	.33	5
26 Oct 91	CULT OF PERSONALITY *Epic 6575357*	.67	2
20 Feb 93	LEAVE IT ALONE *Epic 6589762*	.34	2
17 Apr 93	AUSLANDER *Epic 6591732*	.53	1

LIVING IN A BOX
UK, male vocal / instrumental group **62 wks**

4 Apr 87	● LIVING IN A BOX *Chrysalis LIB 1*	.5	13
13 Jun 87	SCALES OF JUSTICE *Chrysalis LIB 2*	.30	6
26 Sep 87	SO THE STORY GOES *Chrysalis LIB 3* [1]	.34	8
30 Jan 88	LOVE IS THE ART *Chrysalis LIB 4*	.45	4
18 Feb 89	● BLOW THE HOUSE DOWN *Chrysalis LIB 5*	.10	9
10 Jun 89	GATECRASHING *Chrysalis LIB 6*	.36	6
23 Sep 89	● ROOM IN YOUR HEART *Chrysalis LIB 7*	.5	13
30 Dec 89	DIFFERENT AIR *Chrysalis LIB 8*	.64	1
13 Jan 90	DIFFERENT AIR (re-entry) *Chrysalis LIB 8*	.57	2

[1] Living In A Box featuring Bobby Womack

Dandy LIVINGSTONE *Jamaica, male vocalist* **19 wks**

2 Sep 72	SUZANNE BEWARE OF THE DEVIL *Horse HOSS 16*	.14	11
13 Jan 73	BIG CITY / THINK ABOUT THAT *Horse HOSS 25*	.26	8

LL COOL J *US, male rapper* **47 wks**

4 Jul 87	I'M BAD *Def Jam 650856 7*	.71	1
12 Sep 87	● I NEED LOVE *Def Jam 651101 7*	.8	10
21 Nov 87	GO CUT CREATOR GO *Def Jam LLCJ 1*	.66	2
13 Feb 88	GOING BACK TO CALI / JACK THE RIPPER *Def Jam LLCJ 2*	.37	4
10 Jun 89	I'M THAT TYPE OF GUY *Def Jam LLCJ 3*	.43	5
1 Dec 90	AROUND THE WAY GIRL / MAMA SAID KNOCK YOU OUT *Def Jam 6564470*	.41	4
9 Mar 91	AROUND THE WAY GIRL (re-issue) *Columbia 6564470*	.36	4
10 Apr 93	HOW I'M COMIN' *Def Jam 6591692*	.37	2
20 Jan 96	HEY LOVER *Def Jam DEFCD 14* [1]	.17	4
1 Jun 96	DOIN' IT *Def Jam DEFCD 15* [2]	.15	3
5 Oct 96	● LOUNGIN' *Def Jam DEFCD 30*	.7	8

[1] LL Cool J featuring Boyz II Men [2] LL Cool J, guest vocals by LeShaun

Jack The Ripper only listed from 20 Feb 88.

Kelly LLORENNA *UK, female vocalist* **6 wks**

7 May 94	SET YOU FREE *All Around The World CDGLOBE 124* [1]	.39	4

24 Feb 96   **BRIGHTER DAY** Pukka CDPUKKA 5 ....**43** 2

[1] N-Trance featuring Kelly Llorenna

See also N-Trance.

David LLOYDIE – *See SOUNDMAN and David LLOYDIE featuring Elizabeth TROY*

LNR *US, male vocal / instrumental duo*   **2 wks**

3 Jun 89   **WORK IT TO THE BONE** Kool Kat KOOL 501 ....**64** 2

LO-PRO – *See X-PRESS 2*

LOBO *US, male vocalist*   **25 wks**

19 Jun 71   ● **ME AND YOU AND A DOG NAMED BOO**
             Philips 6073 801 ....**4** 14
8 Jun 74   ● **I'D LOVE YOU TO WANT ME** UK 68 ....**5** 11

LOBO *Holland, male vocalist*   **11 wks**

25 Jul 81   ● **THE CARIBBEAN DISCO SHOW**
             Polydor POSP 302 ....**8** 11

Tone LOC *US, male rapper*   **19 wks**

11 Feb 89   **WILD THING / LOC'ED AFTER DARK**
             Fourth & Broadway BRW 121 ....**21** 8
20 May 89   **FUNKY COLD MEDINA / ON FIRE**
             Fourth & Broadway BRW 129 ....**13** 9
5 Aug 89   **I GOT IT GOIN' ON** Fourth & Broadway BRW 140 ....**55** 2

Hank LOCKLIN *US, male vocalist*   **41 wks**

11 Aug 60   ● **PLEASE HELP ME I'M FALLING** RCA 1188 ....**9** 19
15 Feb 62   **FROM HERE TO THERE TO YOU** RCA 1273 ....**44** 3
15 Nov 62   **WE'RE GONNA GO FISHIN'** RCA 1305 ....**18** 11
5 May 66   **I FEEL A CRY COMING ON** RCA 1510 ....**29** 8

LOCKSMITH *US, male vocal / instrumental group*   **6 wks**

23 Aug 80   **UNLOCK THE FUNK** Arista ARIST 364 ....**42** 6

LOCOMOTIVE *UK, male vocal / instrumental group*   **8 wks**

16 Oct 68   **RUDI'S IN LOVE** Parlophone R 5718 ....**25** 8

John LODGE – *See Justin HAYWARD*

Lisa LOEB and NINE STORIES
US, female / male vocal / instrumental group   **17 wks**

3 Sep 94   ● **STAY (I MISSED YOU)** RCA 74321212522 ....**6** 15
16 Sep 95   **DO YOU SLEEP** Geffen GFSTD 96 ....**45** 2

Nils LOFGREN
US, male vocalist / instrumentalist – guitar   **3 wks**

8 Jun 85   **SECRETS IN THE STREET** Towerbell TOW 68 ....**53** 3

Johnny LOGAN *Ireland, male vocalist*   **24 wks**

3 May 80   ★ **WHAT'S ANOTHER YEAR** Epic EPC 8572 ....**1** 8
23 May 87   ● **HOLD ME NOW** Epic LOG 1 ....**2** 11
22 Aug 87   **I'M NOT IN LOVE** Epic LOG 2 ....**51** 5

Kenny LOGGINS *US, male vocalist*   **21 wks**

28 Apr 84   ● **FOOTLOOSE** CBS A 4101 ....**6** 10
1 Nov 86   **DANGER ZONE** CBS A 7188 ....**45** 11

LOLA *US, female vocalist*   **1 wk**

28 Mar 87   **WAX THE VAN** Syncopate SY 1 ....**65** 1

Jackie LOMAX – *See VARIOUS ARTISTS (EPs & LPs) – The Apple EP*

Alain LOMBARD – *See Mady MESPLÉ and Danielle MILLET with the PARIS OPERA-COMIQUE ORCHESTRA conducted by Alain LOMBARD*

Julie LONDON *US, female vocalist*   **3 wks**

5 Apr 57   **CRY ME A RIVER** London HLU 8240 ....**22** 3

Laurie LONDON *UK, male vocalist*   **12 wks**

8 Nov 57   **HE'S GOT THE WHOLE WORLD IN HIS HANDS**
             Parlophone R 4359 ....**12** 12

LONDON BOYS *UK, male vocal duo*   **46 wks**

10 Dec 88   ● **REQUIEM** WEA YZ 345 ....**59** 6
1 Apr 89   ● **REQUIEM (re-entry)** WEA YZ 345 ....**4** 15
1 Jul 89   ● **LONDON NIGHTS** WEA YZ 393 ....**2** 9
16 Sep 89   **HARLEM DESIRE** WEA YZ 415 ....**17** 7
2 Dec 89   **MY LOVE** WEA YZ 433 ....**46** 6
16 Jun 90   **CHAPEL OF LOVE** East West YZ 458 ....**75** 1
19 Jan 91   **FREEDOM** East West YZ 554 ....**54** 2

LONDON COMMUNITY GOSPEL CHOIR – *See Sal SOLO*

LONDON PHILHARMONIC ORCHESTRA – *See Cliff RICHARD*

LONDON STRING CHORALE
UK, orchestra / choir   **13 wks**

15 Dec 73   **GALLOPING HOME** Polydor 2058 280 ....**49** 3
19 Jan 74   **GALLOPING HOME (re-entry)**
             Polydor 2058 280 ....**31** 10

LONDON SYMPHONY ORCHESTRA
UK, orchestra   **5 wks**

6 Jan 79   **THEME FROM 'SUPERMAN' (MAIN TITLE)**
             Warner Bros. K 17292 ....**32** 5

Orchestra conducted by John Williams.

LONDONBEAT *UK / US, male vocal group*   **45 wks**

26 Nov 88   **9 A.M. (THE COMFORT ZONE)**
             Anxious ANX 008 ....**19** 10
18 Feb 89   **FAILING IN LOVE AGAIN** Anxious ANX 007 ....**60** 2
1 Sep 90   ● **I'VE BEEN THINKING ABOUT YOU**
             Anxious ANX 14 ....**2** 13
24 Nov 90   **A BETTER LOVE** Anxious ANX 21 ....**52** 5
2 Mar 91   **NO WOMAN NO CRY** Anxious ANX 25 ....**64** 2
20 Jul 91   **A BETTER LOVE (re-issue)** Anxious ANX 32 ....**23** 6
27 Jun 92   **YOU BRING ON THE SUN** Anxious ANX 37 ....**32** 4
24 Oct 92   **THAT'S HOW I FEEL ABOUT YOU**
             Anxious ANX 40 ....**69** 1
8 Apr 95   **I'M JUST YOUR PUPPET ON A... (STRING)**
             Anxious 74321270982 ....**55** 1
20 May 95   **COME BACK** Anxious 74321226682 ....**69** 1

LONE JUSTICE
US, female / male vocal / instrumental group   **4 wks**

7 Mar 87	**I FOUND LOVE** Geffen GEF 18	**45**	4

Shorty LONG US, male vocalist   **7 wks**

17 Jul 68	**HERE COMES THE JUDGE** Tamla Motown TMG 663	**30**	7

LONG AND THE SHORT
UK, male vocal / instrumental group   **8 wks**

10 Sep 64	**THE LETTER** Decca F 11964	**35**	5
24 Dec 64	**CHOC ICE** Decca F 12043	**49**	3

LONG RYDERS US, male vocal / instrumental group   **4 wks**

5 Oct 85	**LOOKING FOR LEWIS AND CLARK** Island IS 237	**59**	4

LONGPIGS UK, male vocal / instrumental group   **14 wks**

22 Jul 95	**SHE SAID** Mother MUMCD 66	**67**	1
28 Sep 95	**JESUS CHRIST** Mother MUMCD 68	**61**	1
17 Feb 96	**FAR** Mother MUMCD 71	**37**	2
13 Apr 96	**ON AND ON** Mother MUMCD 74	**16**	3
22 Jun 96	**SHE SAID (re-issue)** Mother MUMCD 77	**16**	4
5 Oct 96	**LOST MYSELF** Mother MUMCD 82	**22**	3

Joe LONGTHORNE UK, male vocalist   **6 wks**

30 Apr 94	**YOUNG GIRL** EMI CDEM 310	**61**	2
10 Dec 94	**PASSING STRANGERS** EMI CDEM 362 [1]	**34†**	4

[1] Joe Longthorne and Liz Dawn

LOOK UK, male vocal / instrumental group   **15 wks**

20 Dec 80	● **I AM THE BEAT** MCA 647	**6**	12
29 Aug 81	**FEEDING TIME** MCA 736	**50**	3

LOOSE ENDS
UK, male / female vocal / instrumental group   **76 wks**

25 Feb 84	**TELL ME WHAT YOU WANT** Virgin VS 658	**74**	1
28 Apr 84	**EMERGENCY (DIAL 999)** Virgin VS 677	**41**	6
21 Jul 84	**CHOOSE ME (RESCUE ME)** Virgin VS 697	**59**	3
23 Feb 85	**HANGIN' ON A STRING (CONTEMPLATING)** Virgin VS 748	**13**	13
11 May 85	**MAGIC TOUCH** Virgin VS 761	**16**	7
27 Jul 85	**GOLDEN YEARS** Virgin VS 795	**59**	4
14 Jun 86	**STAY A LITTLE WHILE, CHILD** Virgin VS 819	**52**	5
20 Sep 86	**SLOW DOWN** Virgin VS 884	**27**	7
29 Nov 86	**NIGHTS OF PLEASURE** Virgin VS 919	**42**	7
4 Jun 88	**MR BACHELOR** Virgin VS 1080	**50**	4
25 Aug 90	**DON'T BE A FOOL** 10 TEN 312	**13**	9
17 Nov 90	**LOVE'S GOT ME** 10 TEN 330	**40**	4
20 Jun 92	**HANGIN' ON A STRING (re-mix)** Ten TEN 406	**25**	5
5 Sep 92	**MAGIC TOUCH (re-mix)** Ten TEN 409	**75**	1

Trini LOPEZ US, male vocalist   **37 wks**

12 Sep 63	● **IF I HAD A HAMMER** Reprise R 20198	**4**	17
12 Dec 63	**KANSAS CITY** Reprise R 20236	**35**	5
12 May 66	**I'M COMING HOME CINDY** Reprise R 20455	**28**	5
6 Apr 67	**GONNA GET ALONG WITHOUT YA NOW** Reprise R 20547	**41**	5
19 Dec 81	**TRINI TRAX** RCA 154	**59**	5

LORD ROCKINGHAM'S XI
UK, male instrumental group   **21 wks**

24 Oct 58	★ **HOOTS MON** Decca F 11059	**1**	17
6 Feb 59	**WEE TOM** Decca F 11104	**16**	3
25 Sep 93	**HOOTS MON (re-issue)** Decca 8820982	**60**	1

Both of the group's hits contain a little spoken Scottish.

LORD TANAMO Trinidad & Tobago, male vocalist   **2 wks**

1 Dec 90	**I'M IN THE MOOD FOR LOVE** Mooncrest MOON 1009	**58**	2

Jerry LORDAN UK, male vocalist   **15 wks**

8 Jan 60	**I'LL STAY SINGLE** Parlophone R 4588	**26**	2
26 Feb 60	**WHO COULD BE BLUER** Parlophone R 4627	**17**	9
10 Mar 60	**I'LL STAY SINGLE (re-entry)** Parlophone R 4588	**41**	1
19 May 60	**WHO COULD BE BLUER (re-entry)** Parlophone R 4627	**45**	1
2 Jun 60	**SING LIKE AN ANGEL** Parlophone R 4653	**36**	2

Traci LORDS US, female vocalist   **1 wk**

7 Oct 95	**FALLEN ANGEL** Radioactive RAXTD 18	**72**	1

Sophia LOREN – See Peter SELLERS

Trey LORENZ US, male vocalist   **5 wks**

21 Nov 92	**SOMEONE TO HOLD** Epic 6587857	**65**	2
30 Jan 93	**PHOTOGRAPH OF MARY** Epic 6589542	**38**	3

See also Mariah Carey.

LORI and the CHAMELEONS
UK, female / male vocal / instrumental group   **1 wk**

8 Dec 79	**TOUCH** Sire SIR 4025	**70**	1

LORRAINE – See BOMB THE BASS

LOS BRAVOS
Spain / Germany, male vocal / instrumental group   **24 wks**

30 Jun 66	● **BLACK IS BLACK** Decca F 22419	**2**	13
8 Sep 66	**I DON'T CARE** Decca F 22484	**16**	11

LOS DEL CHIPMUNKS – See CHIPMUNKS

LOS DEL MAR featuring Wil VELOZ
Cuba / Canada, male vocal / instrumental group   **7 wks**

8 Jun 96	**MACARENA** Pulse 8 CDLOSE 101	**66**	2
6 Jul 96	**MACARENA (re-entry)** Pulse 8 CDLOSE 101	**43**	5

LOS DEL RIO Spain, male vocal / instrumental duo   **19 wks**

1 Jun 96	**MACARENA** RCA 74321345372	**64**	1
13 Jul 96	● **MACARENA (re-entry)** RCA 74321345372	**2**	18

LOS LOBOS US, male vocal / instrumental group   **24 wks**

6 Apr 85	**DON'T WORRY BABY / WILL THE WOLF SURVIVE** London LASH 4	**57**	4
18 Jul 87	★ **LA BAMBA** Slash LASH 13	**1**	11
26 Sep 87	**COME ON LET'S GO** Slash LASH 14	**18**	9

Joe LOSS UK, orchestra — 53 wks

29 Jun 61	**WHEELS CHA CHA** HMV POP 880	**21**	21
19 Oct 61	**SUCU SUCU** HMV POP 937	**48**	1
29 Mar 62	**THE MAIGRET THEME** HMV POP 995	**20**	10
1 Nov 62	**MUST BE MADISON** HMV POP 1075	**20**	13
5 Nov 64	**MARCH OF THE MODS** HMV POP 1351	**35**	4
24 Dec 64	**MARCH OF THE MODS (re-entry)** HMV POP 1351	**31**	4

LOST UK, male / instrumental / production duo — 1 wk

22 Jun 91	**TECHNO FUNK** Perfecto PT 44560	**75**	1

LOST BOYZ US, male rap group — 1 wk

2 Nov 96	**MUSIC MAKES ME HIGH** Universal MCSTD 48015	**42**	1

See also Various Artists (EPs and LPs) – The New York Undercover EP

LOTUS EATERS UK, male vocal / instrumental duo — 16 wks

2 Jul 83	**FIRST PICTURE OF YOU** Sylvan SYL 1	**15**	12
8 Oct 83	**YOU DON'T NEED SOMEONE NEW** Sylvan SYL 2	**53**	4

Bonnie LOU US, female vocalist — 10 wks

5 Feb 54	● **TENNESSEE WIG WALK** Parlophone R 3730	**4**	10

Lippy LOU UK, female rapper — 2 wks

22 Apr 95	**LIBERATION** More Protein PROCD 105	**57**	2

Louchie LOU and Michie ONE
UK, female vocal duo — 36 wks

29 May 93	● **SHOUT** ffrr FCD 211	**7**	8
14 Aug 93	**SOMEBODY ELSE'S GUY** ffrr FCD 216	**54**	2
26 Aug 95	**GET DOWN ON IT** China WOKCD 2054	**58**	1
13 Apr 96	● **CECILIA** WEA WEA 042CD1 1	**4**	17
15 Jun 96	**GOOD SWEET LOVIN'** Indochina ID 050CD	**34**	2
24 Aug 96	**CECILIA (re-entry)** WEA WEA 042CD1 1	**65**	1
7 Sep 96	**CECILIA (2nd re-entry)** WEA WEA 042CD1 1	**59**	1
21 Sep 96	**NO MORE ALCOHOL** WEA WEA 065CD1 1	**24**	4

1 Suggs featuring Louchie Lou and Michie One

LOUD UK, male vocal / instrumental group — 2 wks

28 Mar 92	**EASY** China WOK 2016	**67**	2

John D. LOUDERMILK US, male vocalist — 10 wks

4 Jan 62	**THE LANGUAGE OF LOVE** RCA 1269	**13**	10

Louie LOUIE US, male vocalist — 5 wks

19 Dec 92	**THE THOUGHT OF IT** Hardback YZ 724	**34**	5

LOUISE UK, female vocalist — 33 wks

7 Oct 95	● **LIGHT OF MY LIFE** EMI CDEMS 397	**8**	8
16 Mar 96	**IN WALKED LOVE** EMI CDEMS 413	**17**	6
8 Jun 96	● **NAKED** EMI CDEM 431	**5**	8
31 Aug 96	● **UNDIVIDED LOVE** EMI CDEM 441	**5**	6
30 Nov 96	● **ONE KISS FROM HEAVEN** EMI CDEM 454	**9†**	5

Darlene LOVE US, female vocalist — 5 wks

19 Dec 92	**ALL ALONE ON CHRISTMAS** Arista 7432112476	**31**	4
1 Jan 94	**ALL ALONE ON CHRISTMAS (re-entry)** Arista 7432112476	**72**	1

Geoff LOVE – See MANUEL and his MUSIC OF THE MOUNTAINS

Monie LOVE UK, female rapper — 49 wks

4 Feb 89	**I CAN DO THIS** Cooltempo COOL 177	**37**	4
24 Jun 89	**GRANDPA'S PARTY** Cooltempo COOL 184	**16**	9
14 Jul 90	**MONIE IN THE MIDDLE** Cooltempo COOL 210	**46**	3
22 Sep 90	**IT'S A SHAME (MY SISTER)** Cooltempo COOL 219 1	**12**	8
1 Dec 90	**DOWN TO EARTH** Cooltempo COOL 222	**31**	6
6 Apr 91	**RING MY BELL** Cooltempo COOL 224 2	**20**	5
25 Jul 92	**FULL TERM LOVE** Cooltempo COOL 258	**34**	4
13 Mar 93	**BORN 2 B.R.E.E.D.** Cooltempo CDCOOL 269	**18**	5
12 Jun 93	**IN A WORD OR 2 / THE POWER** Cooltempo CDCOOL 273	**33**	3
21 Aug 93	**NEVER GIVE UP** Cooltempo CDCOOL 276	**41**	2

1 Monie Love featuring True Image 2 Monie Love vs Adeva

See also Jungle Brothers.

Vikki LOVE – See NUANCE featuring Vikki LOVE

LOVE AFFAIR UK, male vocal / instrumental group — 56 wks

3 Jan 68	★ **EVERLASTING LOVE** CBS 3125	**1**	12
17 Apr 68	● **RAINBOW VALLEY** CBS 3366	**5**	13
11 Sep 68	● **A DAY WITHOUT LOVE** CBS 3674	**6**	12
19 Feb 69	**ONE ROAD** CBS 3994	**16**	9
16 Jul 69	● **BRINGING ON BACK THE GOOD TIMES** CBS 4300	**9**	10

LOVE AND MONEY UK, male vocal / instrumental group — 23 wks

24 May 86	**CANDYBAR EXPRESS** Mercury MONEY 1	**56**	4
25 Apr 87	**LOVE AND MONEY** Mercury MONEY 4	**68**	4
17 Sep 88	**HALLELUJAH MAN** Fontana MONEY 5	**63**	4
14 Jan 89	**STRANGE KIND OF LOVE** Fontana MONEY 6	**45**	5
25 Mar 89	**JOCELYN SQUARE** Fontana MONEY 7	**51**	4
16 Nov 91	**WINTER** Fontana MONEY 9	**52**	2

LOVE CITY GROOVE UK, male / female vocal / instrumental group — 11 wks

8 Apr 95	● **LOVE CITY GROOVE** Planet 3 GXY 2003CD	**7**	11

LOVE DECADE UK, male / female vocal / instrumental group — 14 wks

6 Jul 91	**DREAM ON (IS THIS A DREAM)** All Around The World GLOBE 100	**52**	2
23 Nov 91	**SO REAL** All Around The World GLOBE 106	**14**	7
11 Apr 92	**I FEEL YOU** All Around The World GLOBE 107	**34**	3
6 Feb 93	**WHEN THE MORNING COMES** All Around The World CDGLOBE 114	**69**	1
17 Feb 96	**IS THIS A DREAM** All Around The World CDGLOBE 132	**39**	1

Is This A Dream in 96 is a re-recording.

LOVE DECREE UK, male vocal / instrumental group — 4 wks

16 Sep 89	**SOMETHING SO REAL (CHINHEADS THEME)** Ariola 112642	**61**	4

Sean Maguire

Sean Maguire came to the public's attention as an actor in *Grange Hill* and later *Eastenders* before embarking on a singing career.

Lush

The tragic suicide of drummer Chris Acland (pictured far right) came after the band's highest chart placings.

Manfred Mann

Manfred Mann was born Michael Lubowitz in Johannesburg, South Africa.

Louise

Louise Nurding dropped her surname on leaving Eternal and opened her solo chart career with five straight hits, four of them Top 10, from her debut album 'Naked'.

214

LOVE/HATE US, male vocal / instrumental group — 4 wks

30 Nov 91	EVIL TWIN Columbia 6575967	59	1
4 Apr 92	WASTED IN AMERICA Columbia 6578897	38	3

LOVE INC UK, male vocal / production duo — 3 wks

9 Feb 91	LOVE IS THE MESSAGE Love EVOL 1	59	3

LOVE NELSON – See FIRE ISLAND

LOVE REACTION – See Zodiac MINDWARP and the LOVE REACTION

LOVE SCULPTURE UK, instrumental group — 14 wks

27 Nov 68	● SABRE DANCE Parlophone R 5744	5	14

LOVE SQUAD – See Linda CARR

LOVE TO INFINITY
UK, male / female vocal / instrumental group — 4 wks

24 Jun 95	KEEP LOVE TOGETHER Mushroom D 00467	38	2
18 Nov 95	SOMEDAY Mushroom D 1143	75	1
3 Aug 96	PRAY FOR LOVE Mushroom D 1213	69	1

LOVE TRIBE US, male / female vocal / instrumental duo — 3 wks

29 Jun 96	STAND UP AM:PM 5816272	23	3

LOVE UNLIMITED US, female vocal group — 25 wks

17 Jun 72	WALKIN' IN THE RAIN WITH THE ONE I LOVE Uni UN 539	14	10
25 Jan 75	IT MAY BE WINTER OUTSIDE (BUT IN MY HEART IT'S SPRING) 20th Century BTC 2149	11	9

LOVE UNLIMITED ORCHESTRA US, orchestra — 10 wks

2 Feb 74	● LOVE'S THEME Pye International 7N 25635	10	10

LOVEBUG STARSKI US, male vocalist — 9 wks

31 May 86	AMITYVILLE (THE HOUSE ON THE HILL) Epic A 7182	12	9

LOVEDEEJAY AKEMI – See YOSH presents LOVEDEEJAY AKEMI

LOVEHAPPY
US / UK, male / female vocal / instrumental group — 3 wks

18 Feb 95	MESSAGE OF LOVE MCA MCSTD 2040	37	2
20 Jul 96	MESSAGE OF LOVE (re-mix) MCA MCSTD 40052	70	1

Bill LOVELADY UK, male vocalist — 10 wks

18 Aug 79	REGGAE FOR IT NOW Charisma CB 337	12	10

LOVELAND featuring the voice of Rachel McFARLANE UK, male / female vocal / instrumental group — 15 wks

16 Apr 94	LET THE MUSIC (LIFT YOU UP) KMS/Eastern Bloc KMSCD 10 [1]	16	4
5 Nov 94	(KEEP ON) SHINING / HOPE (NEVER GIVE UP) Eastern Bloc BLOCCD 016	37	2
14 Jan 95	I NEED SOMEBODY Eastern Bloc BLOCCD 019	21	3
10 Jun 95	DON'T MAKE ME WAIT Eastern Bloc BLOC 20CD	22	3
2 Sep 95	THE WONDER OF LOVE Eastern Bloc BLOC 22CD	53	1
11 Nov 95	I NEED SOMEBODY (re-mix) Eastern Bloc BLOC 23CD	38	2

[1] Loveland featuring Rachel McFarlane vs Darlene Lewis

All formats of Let the Music (Lift You Up) featured versions by Loveland featuring Rachel McFarlane and also by Darlene Lewis.

LOVER SPEAKS UK, male vocal / instrumental duo — 5 wks

16 Aug 86	NO MORE 'I LOVE YOU'S' A & M AM 326	58	5

Michael LOVESMITH US, male vocalist — 1 wk

5 Oct 85	AIN'T NOTHIN' LIKE IT Motown ZB 40369	75	1

LOVESTATION UK, male production group — 4 wks

13 Mar 93	SHINE ON ME RCA 743211337912 [1]	71	1
13 Nov 93	BEST OF MY LOVE Fresh FRSHD 1	73	1
18 Mar 95	LOVE COME RESCUE ME Fresh FRSHD 22	42	2

[1] Lovestation featuring Lisa Hunt

Lene LOVICH US, female vocalist — 38 wks

17 Feb 79	● LUCKY NUMBER Stiff BUY 42	3	11
12 May 79	SAY WHEN Stiff BUY 46	19	10
20 Oct 79	BIRD SONG Stiff BUY 53	39	7
29 Mar 80	WHAT WILL I DO WITHOUT YOU Stiff BUY 69	58	3
14 Mar 81	NEW TOY Stiff BUY 97	53	5
27 Nov 82	IT'S YOU ONLY YOU (MEIN SCHMERZ) Stiff BUY 164	68	2

LOVIN' SPOONFUL
US / Canada, male vocal / instrumental group — 33 wks

14 Apr 66	● DAYDREAM Pye International 7N 25361	2	13
14 Jul 66	● SUMMER IN THE CITY Kama Sutra KAS 200	8	11
5 Jan 67	NASHVILLE CATS Kama Sutra KAS 204	26	7
9 Mar 67	DARLING BE HOME SOON Kama Sutra KAS 207	44	2

LOVINDEER UK, male vocalist — 3 wks

27 Sep 86	MAN SHORTAGE TSOJ TS 1	69	3

Gary LOW Italy, male vocalist — 3 wks

8 Oct 83	I WANT YOU Savoir Faire FAIS 004	52	3

Patti LOW – See BUG KANN and the PLASTIC JAM

Jim LOWE US, male vocalist — 9 wks

26 Oct 56	● THE GREEN DOOR London HLD 8317	8	9

Nick LOWE UK, male vocalist — 27 wks

11 Mar 78	● I LOVE THE SOUND OF BREAKING GLASS Radar ADA	7	8
9 Jun 79	CRACKIN' UP Radar ADA 34	34	5
25 Aug 79	CRUEL TO BE KIND Radar ADA 43	12	11
26 May 84	HALF A BOY HALF A MAN F. Beat XX 34	53	3

LOWRELL US, male vocalist — 9 wks

24 Nov 79	MELLOW MELLOW RIGHT ON AVI AVIS 108	37	9

L7 US, female vocal / instrumental group — 18 wks

4 Apr 92	PRETEND WE'RE DEAD *Slash LASH 34*	21	7
30 May 92	EVERGLADE *Slash LASH 36*	27	3
12 Sep 92	MONSTER *Slash LASH 38*	33	3
28 Nov 92	PRETEND WE'RE DEAD (re-issue) *Slash LASH 42*	50	3
9 Jul 94	ANDRES *Slash LASCD 48*	34	2

L.T.D. US, male vocal / instrumental group — 3 wks

9 Sep 78	HOLDING ON (WHEN LOVE IS GONE) *A & M AMS 7378*	70	3

LUCAS US, male vocalist — 4 wks

6 Aug 94	LUCAS WITH THE LID OFF *WEA YZ 832CD*	37	4

Carrie LUCAS US, female vocalist — 6 wks

16 Jun 79	DANCE WITH YOU *Solar FB 1482*	40	6

Tammy LUCAS – See Teddy RILEY

LUCIANA UK, female vocalist — 5 wks

23 Apr 94	GET IT UP FOR LOVE *Chrysalis CDCHS 5008*	55	2
6 Aug 94	IF YOU WANT *Chrysalis CDCHS 5009*	47	2
5 Nov 94	WHAT GOES AROUND / ONE MORE RIVER *Chrysalis CDCHS 5015*	67	1

LUCKY MONKEYS UK, male instrumental group — 1 wk

9 Nov 96	BJANGO *Hi-Life 5757132*	50	1

Lucky Monkeys is a pseudonym for Fluke. See also Fluke.

Robin LUKE US, male vocalist — 6 wks

17 Oct 58	SUSIE DARLIN' *London HLD 8676*	24	3
21 Nov 58	SUSIE DARLIN' (re-entry) *London HLD 8676*	23	1
5 Dec 58	SUSIE DARLIN' (2nd re-entry) *London HLD 8676*	23	2

LUKK featuring Felicia COLLINS
US, male / female vocal / instrumental group — 1 wk

28 Sep 85	ON THE ONE *Important TAN 6*	72	1

LULU UK, female vocalist — 165 wks

14 May 64	● SHOUT *Decca F 11884* [1]	7	13
12 Nov 64	HERE COMES THE NIGHT *Decca F 12017*	50	1
17 Jun 65	● LEAVE A LITTLE LOVE *Decca F 12169*	8	11
2 Sep 65	TRY TO UNDERSTAND *Decca F 12214*	25	8
13 Apr 67	● THE BOAT THAT I ROW *Columbia DB 8169*	6	11
29 Jun 67	LET'S PRETEND *Columbia DB 8221*	11	11
8 Nov 67	LOVE LOVES TO LOVE LOVE *Columbia DB 8295*	32	6
28 Feb 68	● ME THE PEACEFUL HEART *Columbia DB 8358*	9	9
5 Jun 68	BOY *Columbia DB 8425*	15	7
6 Nov 68	● I'M A TIGER *Columbia DB 8500*	9	13
12 Mar 69	● BOOM BANG-A-BANG *Columbia DB 8550*	2	13
22 Nov 69	OH ME OH MY (I'M A FOOL FOR YOU BABY) *Atco 226008*	47	2
26 Jan 74	● THE MAN WHO SOLD THE WORLD *Polydor 2001 490*	3	9
19 Apr 75	TAKE YOUR MAMA FOR A RIDE *Chelsea 2005 022*	37	4
12 Dec 81	I COULD NEVER MISS YOU (MORE THAN I DO) *Alfa ALFA 1700*	62	4
16 Jan 82	I COULD NEVER MISS YOU (MORE THAN I DO) (re-entry) *Alfa ALFA 1700*	63	1
19 Jul 86	● SHOUT *Jive LULU1/Decca SHOUT 1*	8	10
30 Jan 93	INDEPENDENCE *Dome CDDOME 1001*	11	5
3 Apr 93	I'M BACK FOR MORE *Dome CDDOME 1002* [2]	27	5
4 Sep 93	LET ME WAKE UP IN YOUR ARMS *Dome CDDOME 1005*	51	2
9 Oct 93	★ RELIGHT MY FIRE *RCA 74321167722* [3]	1	12
27 Nov 93	HOW 'BOUT US *Dome CDDOME 1007*	46	3
27 Aug 94	GOODBYE BABY AND AMEN *Dome CDDOME 1011*	40	2
26 Nov 94	EVERY WOMAN KNOWS *Dome CDDOME 1013*	44	2

[1] Lulu and the Luvvers [2] Lulu and Bobby Womack [3] Take That featuring Lulu

The newly recorded Shout entered the chart on 19 Jul 86, and the next week the original Decca version by Lulu and the Luvvers also charted. For all subsequent weeks Gallup amalgamated both versions under one entry.

Bob LUMAN US, male vocalist — 21 wks

8 Sep 60	● LET'S THINK ABOUT LIVING *Warner Bros. WB 18*	6	18
15 Dec 60	WHY WHY BYE BYE *Warner Bros. WB 28*	46	1
4 May 61	THE GREAT SNOWMAN *Warner Bros. WB 37*	49	2

LUNIZ US, male rap duo — 16 wks

17 Feb 96	● I GOT 5 ON IT *Virgin America VUSCD 101*	3	13
11 May 96	PLAYA HATA *Virgin America VUSCD 103*	20	3

LURKERS UK, male vocal / instrumental group — 11 wks

3 Jun 78	AIN'T GOT A CLUE *Beggars Banquet BEG 6*	45	3
5 Aug 78	I DON'T NEED TO TELL HER *Beggars Banquet BEG 9*	49	4
3 Feb 79	JUST THIRTEEN *Beggars Banquet BEG 14*	66	2
9 Jun 79	OUT IN THE DARK / CYANIDE *Beggars Banquet BEG 19*	72	1
17 Nov 79	NEW GUITAR IN TOWN *Beggars Banquet BEG 28*	72	1

LUSCIOUS JACKSON
US, female vocal / instrumental group — 2 wks

18 Mar 95	DEEP SHAG / CITYSONG *Capitol CDCL 739*	69	1
21 Oct 95	HERE *Capitol CDCL 758*	59	1

LUSH UK, female / male vocal / instrumental group — 19 wks

10 Mar 90	MAD LOVE EP *4AD BAD 003*	55	1
27 Oct 90	SWEETNESS AND LIGHT *4AD BAD 0013*	47	2
19 Oct 91	NOTHING NATURAL *4AD AD 1016*	43	2
11 Jan 92	FOR LOVE (EP) *4AD BAD 2001*	35	2
11 Jun 94	HYPOCRITE *4AD BAD 4008CD*	52	2
11 Jun 94	DESIRE LINES *4AD BAD 4010CD*	60	1
20 Jan 96	SINGLE GIRL *4AD BAD 6001CD*	21	3
9 Mar 96	LADYKILLERS *4AD BAD 6002CD*	22	3
27 Jul 96	500 (SHAKE BABY SHAKE) *4AD BAD 6009CD*	21	3

Tracks on Mad Love EP: De-Luxe / Leaves Me Cold / Downer / Thoughtforms. Tracks on For Love (EP): For Love / Starlust / Outdoor Miner / Astronaut.

LUVVERS – See LULU

LV US, male vocalist — 24 wks

28 Oct 95	★ GANGSTA'S PARADISE *Tommy Boy MCSTD 2104* [1]	1	19
23 Dec 95	THROW YOUR HANDS UP / GANGSTA'S PARADISE *Tommy Boy TBCD 699*	24	4
4 May 96	I AM LV *Tommy Boy TBCD 7724*	64	1

[1] Coolio featuring LV

The version of Gangsta's Paradise coupled with Throw Your Hands Up is a re-recorded version without Coolio's vocals.

Annabella LWIN UK, female vocalist   1 wk

28 Jan 95	**DO WHAT YOU DO** Sony S2 6611235	**61**	1

LWS Italy, male instrumental group   1 wk

29 Oct 94	**GOSP** Transworld TRANNY 4CD	**65**	1

Frankie LYMON and the TEENAGERS
US, male vocal group   33 wks

29 Jun 56	★ **WHY DO FOOLS FALL IN LOVE** Columbia DB 3772 [1]	**1**	16
29 Mar 57	**I'M NOT A JUVENILE DELINQUENT** Columbia DB 3878	**12**	7
12 Apr 57	● **BABY BABY** Columbia DB 3878	**4**	12
20 Sep 57	**GOODY GOODY** Columbia DB 3983	**24**	3

[1] Teenagers featuring Frankie Lymon

Kenny LYNCH UK, male vocalist   59 wks

30 Jun 60	**MOUNTAIN OF LOVE** HMV POP 751	**33**	3
13 Sep 62	**PUFF** HMV POP 1057	**33**	5
25 Oct 62	**PUFF (re-entry)** HMV POP 1057	**46**	1
6 Dec 62	● **UP ON THE ROOF** HMV POP 1090	**10**	12
20 Jun 63	● **YOU CAN NEVER STOP ME LOVING YOU** HMV POP 1165	**10**	14
16 Apr 64	**STAND BY ME** HMV POP 1280	**39**	1
27 Aug 64	**WHAT AM I TO YOU** HMV POP 1321	**37**	4
1 Oct 64	**WHAT AM I TO YOU (re-entry)** HMV POP 1321	**44**	2
17 Jun 65	**I'LL STAY BY YOU** HMV POP 1430	**29**	7
20 Aug 83	**HALF THE DAY'S GONE AND WE HAVEN'T EARNT A PENNY** Satril SAT 510	**50**	4

Cheryl LYNN US, female vocalist   2 wks

8 Sep 84	**ENCORE** Streetwave KHAN 23	**68**	2

Patti LYNN UK, female vocalist   5 wks

10 May 62	**JOHNNY ANGEL** Fontana H 391	**37**	5

Tami LYNN US, female vocalist   20 wks

22 May 71	● **I'M GONNA RUN AWAY FROM YOU** Mojo 2092 001	**4**	14
3 May 75	**I'M GONNA RUN AWAY FROM YOU (re-issue)** Contempo Raries CS 9026	**36**	6

Vera LYNN UK, female vocalist   46 wks

14 Nov 52	● **AUF WIEDERSEHEN** Decca F 9927	**10**	1
14 Nov 52	● **FORGET ME NOT** Decca F 9985	**7**	1
14 Nov 52	● **HOMING WALTZ** Decca F 9959	**9**	3
28 Nov 52	● **FORGET ME NOT (re-entry)** Decca F 9985	**5**	5
5 Jun 53	**WINDSOR WALTZ** Decca F 10092	**11**	1
15 Oct 54	★ **MY SON MY SON** Decca F 10372 [1]	**1**	14
8 Jun 56	**WHO ARE WE** Decca F 10715	**30**	1
26 Oct 56	**A HOUSE WITH LOVE IN IT** Decca F 10799	**17**	13
15 Mar 57	**THE FAITHFUL HUSSAR (DON'T CRY MY LOVE)** Decca F 10846	**29**	2
21 Jun 57	**TRAVELLIN' HOME** Decca F 10903	**20**	5

[1] Vera Lynn with Frank Weir, his saxophone, his Orchestra and Chorus

Jeff LYNNE UK, male vocalist   4 wks

30 Jun 90	**EVERY LITTLE THING** Reprise W 9799	**59**	4

Philip LYNOTT Ireland, male vocalist   36 wks

5 Apr 80	**DEAR MISS LONELY HEARTS** Vertigo SOLO 1	**32**	6
21 Jun 80	**KING'S CALL** Vertigo SOLO 2	**35**	6
21 Mar 81	**YELLOW PEARL** Vertigo SOLO 3	**56**	3
26 Dec 81	**YELLOW PEARL (re-entry)** Vertigo SOLO 3	**14**	9
18 May 85	● **OUT IN THE FIELDS** 10 TEN 49 [1]	**5**	10
24 Jan 87	**KING'S CALL (re-mix)** Vertigo LYN 1	**68**	2

[1] Gary Moore and Phil Lynott

See also Gary Moore.

LYNYRD SKYNYRD
US, male vocal / instrumental group   21 wks

11 Sep 76	**FREE BIRD (EP)** MCA 251	**31**	4
22 Dec 79	**FREE BIRD (EP) (re-entry)** MCA 251	**43**	8
19 Jun 82	**FREE BIRD (EP) (2nd re-entry)** MCA 251	**21**	9

Tracks on Free Bird (EP): Free Bird / Sweet Home Alabama / Double Trouble.

Barbara LYON US, female vocalist   12 wks

24 Jun 55	**STOWAWAY** Columbia DB 3619	**12**	8
21 Dec 56	**LETTER TO A SOLDIER** Columbia DB 3865	**27**	4

Humphrey LYTTELTON BAND
UK, male jazz band, Humphrey Lyttelton – trumpet   6 wks

13 Jul 56	**BAD PENNY BLUES** Parlophone R 4184	**19**	6

M UK, male vocalist / multi-instrumentalist – Robin Scott   39 wks

7 Apr 79	● **POP MUZIK** MCA 413	**2**	14
8 Dec 79	**MOONLIGHT AND MUZAK** MCA 541	**33**	9
15 Mar 80	**THAT'S THE WAY THE MONEY GOES** MCA 570	**45**	5
22 Nov 80	**OFFICIAL SECRETS** MCA 650	**64**	2
10 Jun 89	**POP MUZIK (re-mix)** Freestyle FRS 1	**15**	9

Bobby M featuring Jean CARN
US, male / female vocal / instrumental duo   3 wks

29 Jan 83	**LET'S STAY TOGETHER** Gordy TMG 1288	**53**	3

M-BEAT UK, male producer   24 wks

18 Jun 94	**INCREDIBLE** Renk RENK 42CD [1]	**39**	3
10 Sep 94	● **INCREDIBLE (re-mix)** Renk CDRENK 44 [1]	**8**	9
17 Dec 94	**SWEET LOVE** Renk CDRENK 49 [2]	**18**	7
1 Jun 96	**DO U KNOW WHERE YOU'RE COMING FROM** Renk CDRENK 63 [3]	**12**	5

[1] M-Beat featuring General Levy   [2] M-Beat featuring Nazlyn
[3] M-Beat featuring Jamiroquai

M-D-EMM UK, male producer – Mark Ryder — 3 wks

| 22 Feb 92 | GET DOWN Strictly Underground 7STUR 13 | 55 | 2 |
| 30 May 92 | MOVE YOUR FEET Strictly Underground STUR 15 | 67 | 1 |

M + M Canada, male / female vocal duo — 4 wks

| 28 Jul 84 | BLACK STATIONS WHITE STATIONS RCA 426 | 46 | 4 |

See also Martha and the Muffins.

M and O BAND UK, male vocal / instrumental group — 6 wks

| 28 Feb 76 | LET'S DO THE LATIN HUSTLE Creole CR 120 | 16 | 6 |

M PEOPLE UK, male / female vocal / instrumental group — 105 wks

26 Oct 91	HOW CAN I LOVE YOU MORE Deconstruction PB 44855	29	9
7 Mar 92	COLOUR MY LIFE Deconstruction PB 45241	35	4
18 Apr 92	SOMEDAY Deconstruction PB 45369 [1]	38	3
10 Oct 92	EXCITED Deconstruction 74321116337	29	5
5 Feb 93	● HOW CAN I LOVE YOU MORE (re-mix) Deconstruction 74321130232	8	8
26 Jun 93	● ONE NIGHT IN HEAVEN Deconstruction 74321151852	6	11
25 Sep 93	● MOVING ON UP Deconstruction 74321166162	2	11
4 Dec 93	● DON'T LOOK ANY FURTHER Deconstruction 74321177112	9	10
12 Mar 94	● RENAISSANCE Deconstruction 74321194132	5	7
17 Sep 94	ELEGANTLY AMERICAN: ONE NIGHT IN HEAVEN / MOVING ON UP (re-mixes) Deconstruction 74321231882	31	2
19 Nov 94	● SIGHT FOR SORE EYES Deconstruction 74321245472	6	9
4 Feb 95	● OPEN YOUR HEART Deconstruction 74321261532	9	7
24 Jun 95	● SEARCH FOR THE HERO Deconstruction 74321287962	9	7
14 Oct 95	LOVE RENDEZVOUS Deconstruction 74321319282	32	4
25 Nov 95	ITCHYCOO PARK Deconstruction 74321330732	11	8

[1] M People with Heather Small

Pete MAC Jr. US, male vocalist — 4 wks

| 15 Oct 77 | THE WATER MARGIN BBC RESL 50 | 37 | 4 |

This is the Japanese version of the song which shared chart credit with the English language version by Godiego. See also Godiego.

MAC BAND featuring the McCAMPBELL BROTHERS US, male vocal group — 17 wks

| 18 Jun 88 | ● ROSES ARE RED MCA MCA 1264 | 8 | 13 |
| 10 Sep 88 | STALEMATE MCA MCA 1271 | 40 | 4 |

Stalemate credits the McCampbell Brothers on the sleeve only, not on the label.

Keith MAC PROJECT UK, male / female vocal / instrumental group — 1 wk

| 25 Jun 94 | DE DAH DAH (SPICE OF LIFE) Public Demand PPDCD 3 | 66 | 1 |

David McALMONT UK, male vocalist — 13 wks

27 May 95	● YES Hut HUTCD 53 [1]	8	8
4 Nov 95	YOU DO Hut HUTDG 57 [1]	17	4
27 Apr 96	HYMN Blanco Y Negro NEG 87CD [2]	65	1

[1] McAlmont and Butler [2] Ultramarine featuring David McAlmont

Neil MacARTHUR UK, male vocalist — 5 wks

| 5 Feb 69 | SHE'S NOT THERE Deram DM 225 | 34 | 5 |

Neil MacArthur is Colin Blunstone under a false name.

David MacBETH UK, male vocalist — 4 wks

| 30 Oct 59 | MR. BLUE Pye 7N 15231 | 18 | 4 |

Nicko McBRAIN UK, male vocalist / instrumentalist – drums — 1 wk

| 13 Jul 91 | RHYTHM OF THE BEAST EMI NICK 01 | 72 | 1 |

Frankie McBRIDE Ireland, male vocalist — 15 wks

| 9 Aug 67 | FIVE LITTLE FINGERS Emerald MD 1081 | 19 | 15 |

Dan McCAFFERTY UK, male vocalist — 3 wks

| 13 Sep 75 | OUT OF TIME Mountain TOP 1 | 41 | 3 |

CW McCALL US, male vocalist — 10 wks

| 14 Feb 76 | ● CONVOY MGM 2006 560 | 2 | 10 |

David McCALLUM UK, male vocalist — 4 wks

| 14 Apr 66 | COMMUNICATION Capitol CL 15439 | 32 | 4 |

McCAMPBELL BROTHERS – See MAC BAND featuring the McCAMPBELL BROTHERS

Paul McCARTNEY UK, male vocalist — 397 wks

27 Feb 71	● ANOTHER DAY Apple R 5889	2	12
28 Aug 71	BACK SEAT OF MY CAR Apple R 5914 [1]	39	5
26 Feb 72	GIVE IRELAND BACK TO THE IRISH Apple R 5936 [2]	16	9
27 May 72	● MARY HAD A LITTLE LAMB Apple R 5949 [2]	9	11
9 Dec 72	HI HI HI / C MOON Apple R 5973 [2]	5	13
7 Apr 73	● MY LOVE Apple R 5985 [3]	9	11
9 Jun 73	● LIVE AND LET DIE Apple R 5987 [2]	9	13
15 Sep 73	LIVE AND LET DIE (re-entry) Apple R 5987 [2]	49	1
3 Nov 73	HELEN WHEELS Apple R 5993 [3]	12	12
2 Mar 74	● JET Apple R 5996 [3]	7	9
6 Jul 74	● BAND ON THE RUN Apple R 5997 [3]	3	11
9 Nov 74	JUNIOR'S FARM Apple R 5999 [3]	16	10
31 May 75	● LISTEN TO WHAT THE MAN SAID Capitol R 6006 [2]	6	8
18 Oct 75	LETTING GO Capitol R 6008 [2]	41	3
15 May 76	● SILLY LOVE SONGS Parlophone R 6014 [2]	2	11
7 Aug 76	● LET 'EM IN Parlophone R 6015 [2]	2	10
19 Feb 77	MAYBE I'M AMAZED Parlophone R 6017 [2]	28	5
19 Nov 77	★ MULL OF KINTYRE / GIRLS' SCHOOL Capitol R 6018 [2]	1	17
1 Apr 78	● WITH A LITTLE LUCK Parlophone R 6019 [2]	5	9
1 Jul 78	I'VE HAD ENOUGH Parlophone R 6020 [2]	42	7
9 Sep 78	LONDON TOWN Parlophone R 6021 [2]	60	4
7 Apr 79	● GOODNIGHT TONIGHT Parlophone R 6023 [2]	5	10
16 Jun 79	OLD SIAM SIR MPL R 6026 [2]	35	6
1 Sep 79	GETTING CLOSER / BABY'S REQUEST R 6027 [2]	60	3
1 Dec 79	● WONDERFUL CHRISTMASTIME Parlophone R 6029	6	8
19 Apr 80	● COMING UP Parlophone R 6035	2	9
21 Jun 80	● WATERFALLS Parlophone R 6037	9	8
10 Apr 82	★ EBONY AND IVORY Parlophone R 6054 [4]	1	10
3 Jul 82	TAKE IT AWAY Parlophone R 6056	15	10
9 Oct 82	TUG OF WAR Parlophone R 6057	53	3
6 Nov 82	THE GIRL IS MINE Epic EPC A 2729 [5]	8	9
15 Jan 83	THE GIRL IS MINE (re-entry) Epic EPC A 2729 [5]	75	1
15 Oct 83	● SAY SAY SAY Parlophone R 6062 [6]	2	15

17 Dec 83	★ PIPES OF PEACE Parlophone R 6064	1	12
6 Oct 84	● NO MORE LONELY NIGHTS (BALLAD) Parlophone R 6080	2	15
24 Nov 84	WE ALL STAND TOGETHER Parlophone R 6086 [7]	3	13
30 Nov 85	SPIES LIKE US Parlophone R 6118	13	10
21 Dec 85	WE ALL STAND TOGETHER (re-entry) Parlophone R 6086	32	5
26 Jul 86	PRESS Parlophone R 6133	25	8
13 Dec 86	ONLY LOVE REMAINS Parlophone R 6148	34	5
28 Nov 87	● ONCE UPON A LONG AGO Parlophone R 6170	10	7
20 May 89	★ FERRY 'CROSS THE MERSEY PWL PWL 41 [8]	1	7
20 May 89	MY BRAVE FACE Parlophone R 6213	18	5
29 Jul 89	THIS ONE Parlophone R 6223	18	6
25 Nov 89	FIGURE OF EIGHT Parlophone R 6235	42	3
17 Feb 90	PUT IT THERE Parlophone R 6246	32	2
20 Oct 90	BIRTHDAY Parlophone R 6271	29	3
8 Dec 90	ALL MY TRIALS Parlophone R 6278	35	5
5 Feb 93	HOPE OF DELIVERANCE Parlophone CDR 6330	18	6
6 Mar 93	C'MON PEOPLE Parlophone CDRS 6338	41	3

[1] Paul and Linda McCartney [2] Wings [3] Paul McCartney and Wings [4] Paul McCartney with Stevie Wonder [5] Michael Jackson and Paul McCartney [6] Paul McCartney and Michael Jackson [7] Paul McCartney and the Frog Chorus [8] Christians, Holly Johnson, Paul McCartney, Gerry Marsden and Stock Aitken Waterman

R 6027 credits no label at all, although the number is a Parlophone one.

Kirsty MacCOLL UK, female vocalist 65 wks

13 Jun 81	THERE'S A GUY WORKS DOWN THE CHIPSHOP SWEARS HE'S ELVIS Polydor POSP 250	14	9
19 Jan 85	● A NEW ENGLAND Stiff BUY 216	7	10
15 Nov 86	GREETINGS TO THE NEW BRUNETTE Go! Discs GOD 12 [1]	58	2
5 Dec 87	FAIRYTALE OF NEW YORK Pogue Mahone NY 7 [2]	2	9
8 Apr 89	FREE WORLD Virgin KMA 1	43	6
1 Jul 89	DAYS Virgin KMA 2	12	9
25 May 91	WALKING DOWN MADISON Virgin VS 1348	23	7
17 Aug 91	MY AFFAIR Virgin VS 1354	56	2
14 Dec 91	FAIRYTALE OF NEW YORK PM YZ 628 [2]	36	5
4 Mar 95	CAROLINE Virgin VSCDX 1517	58	2
24 Jun 95	PERFECT DAY Virgin VSCDT 1552 [3]	75	1
29 Jul 95	DAYS (re-issue) Virgin VSCDT 1558	42	3

[1] Billy Bragg with Johnny Marr and Kirsty MacColl [2] Pogues featuring Kirsty MacColl [3] Kirsty MacColl and Evan Dando

Marilyn McCOO and Billy DAVIS Jr.
US, female / male vocal duo 9 wks

| 19 Mar 77 | ● YOU DON'T HAVE TO BE A STAR (TO BE IN MY SHOW) ABC 4147 | 7 | 9 |

Van McCOY US, orchestra 36 wks

31 May 75	● THE HUSTLE Avco 6105 038 [1]	3	12
1 Nov 75	CHANGE WITH THE TIMES Avco 6105 042	36	4
12 Feb 77	SOUL CHA CHA H & L 6105 065	34	6
9 Apr 77	● THE SHUFFLE H & L 6105 076	4	14

[1] Van McCoy with the Soul City Symphony

McCOYS US, male vocal / instrumental group 18 wks

| 2 Sep 65 | ● HANG ON SLOOPY Immediate IM 001 | 5 | 14 |
| 16 Dec 65 | FEVER Immediate IM 021 | 44 | 4 |

George McCRAE US, male vocalist 62 wks

29 Jun 74	★ ROCK YOUR BABY Jayboy BOY 85	1	14
5 Oct 74	● I CAN'T LEAVE YOU ALONE Jayboy BOY 90	9	9
14 Dec 74	YOU CAN HAVE IT ALL Jayboy BOY 92	23	9
22 Mar 75	SING A HAPPY SONG Jayboy BOY 95	38	4
19 Jul 75	● IT'S BEEN SO LONG Jayboy BOY 100	4	11
18 Oct 75	I AIN'T LYIN' Jayboy BOY 105	12	7
24 Jan 76	HONEY I Jayboy BOY 107	33	4
25 Feb 84	ONE STEP CLOSER (TO LOVE) President PT 522	57	4

Gwen McCRAE US, female vocalist 5 wks

| 30 Apr 88 | ALL THIS LOVE THAT I'M GIVING Flame MELT 7 | 63 | 2 |
| 13 Feb 93 | ALL THIS LOVE I'M GIVING KTDA CDKTDA 2 [1] | 36 | 3 |

[1] Music And Mystery featuring Gwen McCrae

All This Love I'm Giving is a re-recording of her first hit.

MacCRARYS US, male vocal / instrumental group 4 wks

| 31 Jul 82 | LOVE ON A SUMMER NIGHT Capitol CL 251 | 52 | 4 |

Ian McCULLOCH UK, male vocalist 14 wks

15 Dec 84	SEPTEMBER SONG Korova KOW 40	51	5
2 Sep 89	PROUD TO FALL WEA YZ 417	51	4
12 May 90	CANDLELAND (THE SECOND COMING) East West YZ 452 [1]	75	1
22 Feb 92	LOVER LOVER LOVER East West YZ 643	47	4

[1] Ian McCulloch featuring Elizabeth Fraser

Martine McCUTCHEON – See UNO CLIO featuring Martine McCUTCHEON

Gene McDANIELS US, male vocalist 2 wks

| 16 Nov 61 | TOWER OF STRENGTH London HLG 9448 | 49 | 1 |
| 30 Nov 61 | TOWER OF STRENGTH (re-entry) London HLG 9448 | 49 | 1 |

Julie McDERMOTT – See THIRD DIMENSION; AWESOME 3

Charles McDEVITT SKIFFLE GROUP featuring Nancy WHISKEY
UK, male / female vocal / instrumental group 20 wks

12 Apr 57	● FREIGHT TRAIN Oriole CB 1352	5	17
14 Jun 57	GREENBACK DOLLAR Oriole CB 1371	28	1
5 Jul 57	GREENBACK DOLLAR (re-entry) Oriole CB 1371	30	1
20 Sep 57	FREIGHT TRAIN (re-entry) Oriole CB 1352	27	1

Michael McDONALD US, male vocalist 45 wks

18 Feb 84	YAH MO B THERE Qwest W 9394 [1]	44	5
7 Apr 84	YAH MO B THERE (re-entry) Qwest W 9394 [1]	69	1
12 Jan 85	YAH MO B THERE (2nd re-entry) Qwest W 9394 [1]	12	8
3 May 86	● ON MY OWN MCA MCA 1045 [2]	2	13
26 Jul 86	I KEEP FORGETTIN' Warner Bros K 17992	43	6
6 Sep 86	SWEET FREEDOM MCA MCA 1073	12	10

[1] James Ingram with Michael McDonald [2] Patti Labelle and Michael McDonald

The '85 entry of Yah Mo B There is a re-mix of the original hit with the same catalogue number. See also Doobie Brothers.

Carrie McDOWELL US, female vocalist 3 wks

| 26 Sep 87 | UH UH NO NO CASUAL SEX Motown ZV 41501 | 68 | 3 |

John McENROE and Pat CASH with the FULL METAL RACKETS US/Australia, male vocal/instrumental duo with UK backing group | 1 wk

13 Jul 91	ROCK 'N' ROLL Music For Nations KUT 141	66	1

MACEO and the MACS US, male vocal/instrumental group | 5 wks

16 May 87	CROSS THE TRACK (WE BETTER GO BACK) Urban URBX 1	54	5

McFADDEN and WHITEHEAD US, male vocal duo | 10 wks

19 May 79 ●	AIN'T NO STOPPIN' US NOW Philadelphia International PIR 7365	5	10

Rachel McFARLANE – See LOVELAND featuring Rachel McFARLANE

Bobby McFERRIN US, male vocalist | 15 wks

24 Sep 88 ●	DON'T WORRY BE HAPPY Manhattan MT 56	2	11
17 Dec 88	THINKIN' ABOUT YOUR BODY Manhattan BLUE 6	46	4

Mike McGEAR UK, male vocalist | 4 wks

5 Oct 74	LEAVE IT Warner Bros. K 16446	36	4

Maureen McGOVERN US, female vocalist | 8 wks

5 Jun 76	THE CONTINENTAL 20th Century BTC 2222	16	8

Shane MacGOWAN UK, male vocalist | 9 wks

12 Dec 92	WHAT A WONDERFUL WORLD Mute MUTE 151 [1]	72	1
3 Sep 94	THE CHURCH OF THE HOLY SPOOK ZTT ZANG 57CD	74	1
15 Oct 94	THAT WOMAN'S GOT ME DRINKING ZTT ZANG 57CD [2]	34	3
29 Apr 95	HAUNTED ZTT ZANG 65CD [3]	30	2
20 Apr 96	MY WAY ZTT ZANG 79CD	29	2

[1] Nick Cave and Shane MacGowan [2] Shane MacGowan and the Popes
[3] Shane MacGowan and Sinead O'Connor

Freddie McGREGOR Jamaica, male vocalist | 16 wks

27 Jun 87 ●	JUST DON'T WANT TO BE LONELY Germain DG 24	9	11
19 Sep 87	THAT GIRL (GROOVY SITUATION) Polydor POSP 884	47	5

Mary MacGREGOR US, female vocalist | 10 wks

19 Feb 77 ●	TORN BETWEEN TWO LOVERS Ariola America AA 111	4	10

McGUINNESS FLINT UK, male vocal/instrumental group | 26 wks

21 Nov 70 ●	WHEN I'M DEAD AND GONE Capitol CL 15662	2	14
1 May 71 ●	MALT AND BARLEY BLUES Capitol CL 15682	5	12

Barry McGUIRE US, male vocalist | 13 wks

9 Sep 65 ●	EVE OF DESTRUCTION RCA 1469	3	13

McGUIRE SISTERS US, female vocal group | 24 wks

1 Apr 55	NO MORE Vogue Coral Q 72050	20	1
15 Jul 55	SINCERELY Vogue Coral Q 72050	14	4
1 Jun 56	DELILAH JONES Vogue Coral Q 72161	24	2
14 Feb 58	SUGARTIME Coral Q 72305	14	6
1 May 59	MAY YOU ALWAYS Coral Q 72356	15	10
17 Jul 59	MAY YOU ALWAYS (re-entry) Coral Q 72356	28	1

MACHEL Trinidad, male vocal | 2 wks

14 Sep 96	COME DIG IT London LONCD 386	56	2

MACHINE HEAD UK, male vocal/instrumental group | 2 wks

27 May 95	OLD Roadrunner RR 23403	43	2

Craig MACK US, male rapper | 3 wks

12 Nov 94	FLAVA IN YA EAR Bad Boy 74321242582	57	2
1 Apr 95	GET DOWN Puff Daddy 74321263402	54	1

See also Various Artists (EPs and LPs) – The Dangerous Minds EP.

Lizzy MACK UK, female vocalist | 3 wks

5 Nov 94	THE POWER OF LOVE Media MCSTD 2016 [1]	49	2
4 Nov 95	DON'T GO Power Station MCSTD 40004	52	1

[1] Fits Of Gloom featuring Lizzy Mack

Lonnie MACK US, male instrumentalist – guitar | 3 wks

14 Apr 79	MEMPHIS Lightning LIG 9011	47	3

Memphis was coupled with Let's Dance by Chris Montez as a double A-side.

MACK VIBE featuring JACQUELINE US, male/female vocal/instrumental duo | 1 wk

4 Feb 95	I CAN'T LET YOU GO MCA MCSTD 20020	53	1

Maria McKEE US, female vocalist | 23 wks

15 Sep 90 ★	SHOW ME HEAVEN Epic 656303 7	1	14
26 Jan 91	BREATHE Geffen GFS 1	59	1
1 Aug 92	SWEETEST CHILD Geffen GFS 23	45	4
22 May 93	I'M GONNA SOOTHE YOU Geffen GFSTD 39	35	3
18 Sep 93	I CAN'T MAKE IT ALONE Geffen GFSTD 53	74	1

Kenneth McKELLAR UK, male vocalist | 4 wks

10 Mar 66	A MAN WITHOUT LOVE Decca F 12341	30	4

Terence McKENNA – See SHAMEN

Gisele McKENZIE Canada, female vocalist | 6 wks

17 Jul 53	SEVEN LONELY DAYS Capitol CL 13920	12	1
31 Jul 53	SEVEN LONELY DAYS (re-entry) Capitol CL 13920	11	1
21 Aug 53 ●	SEVEN LONELY DAYS (2nd re-entry) Capitol CL 13920	6	4

Scott McKENZIE US, male vocalist — 18 wks

12 Jul 67	★ SAN FRANCISCO (BE SURE TO WEAR SOME FLOWERS IN YOUR HAIR) CBS 2816	1 17
1 Nov 67	LIKE AN OLD TIME MOVIE CBS 3009 [1]	50 1

[1] The Voice Of Scott McKenzie

Ken MACKINTOSH UK, orchestra — 9 wks

15 Jan 54	THE CREEP HMV BD 1295	12 1
29 Jan 54	● THE CREEP (re-entry) HMV BD 1295	10 1
7 Feb 58	RAUNCHY HMV POP 426	19 6
10 Mar 60	NO HIDING PLACE HMV POP 713	45 1

Vivienne McKONE UK, female vocalist — 5 wks

25 Jul 92	SING (OOH-EE-OOH) ffrr F 183	47 4
31 Oct 92	BEWARE ffrr F 202	69 1

McKOY UK, male / female vocal group — 2 wks

6 Mar 93	FIGHT Righttrack CDTUM 1	54 2

Noel McKOY – See JTQ; McKOY

Craig McLACHLAN Australia, male vocalist — 40 wks

16 Jun 90	● MONA Epic 655784 7 [1]	2 11
4 Aug 90	AMANDA Epic 656170 7 [1]	19 6
10 Nov 90	I ALMOST FELT LIKE CRYING Epic 656310 7 [1]	50 1
23 May 92	ONE REASON WHY Epic 6580677	29 6
14 Nov 92	ON MY OWN Epic 6584677	59 2
24 Jul 93	YOU'RE THE ONE THAT I WANT Epic 6595222 [2]	13 6
25 Dec 93	GREASE Epic 6600242	44 4
8 Jul 95	EVERYDAY MDMC DEVCS 6 [3]	65 2

[1] Craig McLachlan and Check 1-2 [2] Craig McLachlan and Debbie Gibson [3] Craig McLachlan and the Culprits

Tommy McLAIN US, male vocalist — 1 wk

8 Sep 66	SWEET DREAMS London HL 10065	49 1

Malcolm McLAREN UK, male vocalist — 64 wks

4 Dec 82	● BUFFALO GALS Charisma MALC 1 [1]	9 12
26 Feb 83	SOWETO Charisma MALC 2 [2]	32 5
2 Jul 83	● DOUBLE DUTCH Charisma MALC 3	3 13
17 Dec 83	DUCK FOR THE OYSTER Charisma MALC 4	54 5
1 Sep 84	MADAM BUTTERFLY (UN BEL DI VEDREMO) Charisma MALC 5	13 9
27 May 89	WALTZ DARLING Epic WALTZ 2 [3]	31 8
19 Aug 89	SOMETHING'S JUMPIN' IN YOUR SHIRT Epic WALTZ 3 [4]	29 7
25 Nov 89	HOUSE OF THE BLUE DANUBE Epic WALTZ 4 [3]	73 1
21 Dec 91	MAGIC'S BACK (THEME FROM 'THE GHOSTS OF OXFORD STREET') RCA PB 45223 [5]	42 4

[1] Malcolm McLaren and the World's Famous Supreme Team [2] Malcolm McLaren and the McLarenettes [3] Malcolm McLaren and the Bootzilla Orchestra [4] Malcolm McLaren and the Bootzilla Orchestra featuring Lisa Marie [5] Malcolm McLaren featuring Alison Limerick

Bitty McLEAN UK, male vocalist — 50 wks

31 Jul 93	● IT KEEP RAININ' (TEARS FROM MY EYES) Brilliant CDBRIL 1	2 15
30 Oct 93	PASS IT ON Brilliant CDBRIL 2	35 3
15 Jan 94	● HERE I STAND Brilliant CDBRIL 3	10 6
9 Apr 94	● DEDICATED TO THE ONE I LOVE Brilliant CDBRIL 4	6 10
6 Aug 94	WHAT GOES AROUND Brilliant CDBRIL 5	36 3
8 Apr 95	OVER THE RIVER Brilliant CDBRIL 9	27 4
17 Jun 95	WE'VE ONLY JUST BEGUN Brilliant CDBRIL 10	23 5
30 Sep 95	NOTHING CAN CHANGE THIS LOVE Brilliant CDBRIL 11	55 2
27 Jan 96	NATURAL HIGH Brilliant CDBRIL 12	63 1
5 Oct 96	SHE'S ALRIGHT Kuff KUFFD 9	53 1

Don McLEAN US, male vocalist — 68 wks

22 Jan 72	● AMERICAN PIE United Artists UP 35325	2 16
13 May 72	★ VINCENT United Artists UP 35359	1 15
14 Apr 73	EVERYDAY United Artists UP 35519	38 5
10 May 80	★ CRYING EMI 5051	1 14
17 Apr 82	CASTLES IN THE AIR EMI 5258	47 8
5 Oct 91	AMERICAN PIE (re-issue) Liberty EMCT 3	12 10

Jackie McLEAN US, male instrumentalist – alto sax — 4 wks

7 Jul 79	DR. JACKYLL AND MISTER FUNK RCA PB 1575	53 4

Phil McLEAN US, male vocalist — 4 wks

18 Jan 62	SMALL SAD SAM Top Rank JAR 597	34 4

Ian McNABB UK, male vocalist — 6 wks

23 Jan 93	IF LOVE WAS LIKE GUITARS This Way Up WAY 233	67 1
2 Jul 94	YOU MUST BE PREPARED TO DREAM This Way Up WAY 3199 [1]	54 1
17 Sep 94	GO INTO THE LIGHT This Way Up WAY 3699	66 2
27 Apr 96	DON'T PUT YOUR SPELL ON ME This Way Up WAY 5033	72 1
6 Jul 96	MERSEYBEAST This Way Up WAY 5266	74 1

[1] Ian McNabb featuring Ralph Molina and Billy Talbot of Crazyhorse with Mike 'Tone' Hamilton

Patrick MACNEE and Honor BLACKMAN UK, male / female vocal duo — 7 wks

1 Dec 90	● KINKY BOOTS Deram KINKY 1	5 7

Rita MacNEIL Canada, female vocalist — 10 wks

6 Oct 90	WORKING MAN Polydor PO 98	11 10

Clyde McPHATTER US, male vocalist — 1 wk

24 Aug 56	TREASURE OF LOVE London HLE 8293	27 1

Carmen McRAE – See Sammy DAVIS Jr

Gordon MacRAE – See VARIOUS ARTISTS (EPs & LPs) – Carousel Soundtrack

Ralph McTELL UK, male vocalist — 18 wks

7 Dec 74	● STREETS OF LONDON Reprise K 14380	2 12
20 Dec 75	DREAMS OF YOU Warner Bros. K 16648	36 6

MAD COBRA featuring Ritchie STEPHENS Jamaica / UK, male vocal duo — 2 wks

15 May 93	LEGACY Columbia 6592852	64 2

MAD JOCKS featuring JOCKMASTER B.A.
UK, male vocal / instrumental group　　　　　**9 wks**

19 Dec 87	**JOCK MIX 1** *Debut DEBT 3037*..................**46**	5
18 Dec 93	**PARTY FOUR EP** *SMP CDSSKM 24* **57**	4

Tracks on Party Four EP: No Lager / Here We Go Again / Jock Party Mix / Jock Jak Mix.

MAD STUNTMAN – *See REEL 2 REAL*

Danny MADDEN *US, male vocalist*　　　　　**2 wks**

14 Jul 90	**THE FACTS OF LIFE** *Eternal YZ 473* **72**	2

MADDER ROSE
US, male / female vocal / instrumental group　　　　　**2 wks**

26 Mar 94	**PANIC ON** *Atlantic A 8301CD* **65**	1
16 Jul 94	**CAR SONG** *Seed A 7256CD* **68**	1

MADNESS *UK, male vocal / instrumental group*　　　　　**258 wks**

1 Sep 79	**THE PRINCE** *2 Tone TT 3* **16**	11
10 Nov 79	● **ONE STEP BEYOND** *Stiff BUY 56* **7**	14
5 Jan 80	● **MY GIRL** *Stiff BUY 62* **3**	10
5 Apr 80	● **WORK REST AND PLAY EP** *Stiff BUY 71* **6**	8
13 Sep 80	● **BAGGY TROUSERS** *Stiff BUY 84* **3**	20
22 Nov 80	● **EMBARRASSMENT** *Stiff BUY 102* **4**	12
24 Jan 81	● **THE RETURN OF THE LOS PALMAS SEVEN** *Stiff BUY 108*..**7**	11
25 Apr 81	● **GREY DAY** *Stiff BUY 112* **4**	10
26 Sep 81	● **SHUT UP** *Stiff BUY 126* **7**	9
5 Dec 81	● **IT MUST BE LOVE** *Stiff BUY 134* **4**	12
20 Feb 82	● **CARDIAC ARREST** *Stiff BUY 140* **14**	10
22 May 82	★ **HOUSE OF FUN** *Stiff BUY 146* **1**	9
24 Jul 82	● **DRIVING IN MY CAR** *Stiff BUY 153* **4**	8
27 Nov 82	● **OUR HOUSE** *Stiff BUY 163* **5**	13
19 Feb 83	● **TOMORROW'S (JUST ANOTHER DAY) / MADNESS**	
	(IS ALL IN THE MIND) *Stiff BUY 169* **8**	9
20 Aug 83	● **WINGS OF A DOVE** *Stiff BUY 181* **2**	10
5 Nov 83	● **THE SUN AND THE RAIN** *Stiff BUY 192* **5**	10
11 Feb 84	**MICHAEL CAINE** *Stiff BUY 196* **11**	8
2 Jun 84	**ONE BETTER DAY** *Stiff BUY 201* **17**	7
31 Aug 85	**YESTERDAY'S MEN** *Zarjazz JAZZ 5* **18**	7
26 Oct 85	**UNCLE SAM** *Zarjazz JAZZ 7* **21**	11
1 Feb 86	**SWEETEST GIRL** *Zarjazz JAZZ 8* **35**	6
8 Nov 86	**(WAITING FOR) THE GHOST TRAIN** *Zarjazz JAZZ 9* **18**	7
3 Jan 87	**(WAITING FOR) THE GHOST TRAIN (re-entry)**	
	Zarjazz JAZZ 9 ....**74**	1
19 Mar 88	**I PRONOUNCE YOU** *Virgin VS 1054* [1] **44**	4
15 Feb 92	● **IT MUST BE LOVE (re-issue)** *Virgin VS 1405* **6**	9
25 Apr 92	**HOUSE OF FUN (re-issue)** *Virgin VS 1413* **40**	3
8 Aug 92	**MY GIRL (re-issue)** *Virgin VS 1425* **27**	4
28 Nov 92	**THE HARDER THEY COME** *Go! Discs GOD 93* **44**	3
27 Feb 93	**NIGHT BOAT TO CAIRO** *Virgin VSCDT 1447* **56**	2

[1] The Madness

Tracks on Work Rest and Play EP: Night Boat to Cairo / Deceives The Eye / The Young And The Old / Don't Quote Me On That. Night Boat To Cairo in '93 is a re-issue of a track from the Work Rest And Play EP. See also Various Artists (EPs & LPs) – The Two Tone EP.

MADONNA *US, female vocalist*　　　　　**430 wks**

14 Jan 84	● **HOLIDAY** *Sire W 9405* **6**	11
17 Mar 84	● **LUCKY STAR** *Sire W 9522* **14**	9
2 Jun 84	**BORDERLINE** *Sire W 9260* **56**	4
17 Nov 84	● **LIKE A VIRGIN** *Sire W 9210* **3**	18
2 Mar 85	● **MATERIAL GIRL** *Sire W 9083* **3**	10
8 Jun 85	● **CRAZY FOR YOU** *Geffen A 6323* **2**	15
27 Jul 85	★ **INTO THE GROOVE** *Sire W 8934* **1**	14
3 Aug 85	● **HOLIDAY (re-entry)** *Sire W 9405* **2**	10

21 Sep 85	● **ANGEL** *Sire W 8881* **5**	9
12 Oct 85	● **GAMBLER** *Geffen A 6585* **4**	11
7 Dec 85	● **DRESS YOU UP** *Sire W 8848*................**5**	11
4 Jan 86	**GAMBLER (re-entry)** *Geffen A 6585* **61**	1
25 Jan 86	● **BORDERLINE (re-entry)** *Sire W 9260* **2**	9
26 Apr 86	● **LIVE TO TELL** *Sire W 8717* **2**	12
28 Jun 86	★ **PAPA DON'T PREACH** *Sire W 8636* **1**	14
4 Oct 86	★ **TRUE BLUE** *Sire W 8550* **1**	15
13 Dec 86	● **OPEN YOUR HEART** *Sire W 8480* **4**	9
4 Apr 87	★ **LA ISLA BONITA** *Sire W 8378* **1**	11
18 Jul 87	★ **WHO'S THAT GIRL** *Sire W 8341* **1**	10
19 Sep 87	● **CAUSING A COMMOTION** *Sire W 8224* **4**	9
12 Dec 87	● **THE LOOK OF LOVE** *Sire W 8115* **9**	7
18 Mar 89	★ **LIKE A PRAYER** *Sire W 7539* **1**	12
3 Jun 89	● **EXPRESS YOURSELF** *Sire W 2948* **5**	10
16 Sep 89	● **CHERISH** *Sire W 2883* **3**	8
16 Dec 89	● **DEAR JESSIE** *Sire W 2668* **5**	9
7 Apr 90	★ **VOGUE** *Sire W 9851* **1**	14
21 Jul 90	● **HANKY PANKY** *Sire W 9789* **2**	9
8 Dec 90	● **JUSTIFY MY LOVE** *Sire W 9000* **2**	10
2 Mar 91	● **CRAZY FOR YOU (re-mix)** *Sire W 0008* **2**	8
13 Apr 91	● **RESCUE ME** *Sire W 0024* **3**	8
8 Jun 91	● **HOLIDAY (re-issue)** *Sire W 0037* **5**	7
25 Jul 92	● **THIS USED TO BE MY PLAYGROUND** *Sire W 0122*..**3**	9
17 Oct 92	● **EROTICA** *Maverick W 0138* **3**	8
12 Dec 92	● **DEEPER AND DEEPER** *Maverick W 0146* **6**	8
9 Jan 93	**EROTICA (re-entry)** *Maverick W 0138* **65**	1
6 Mar 93	**BAD GIRL** *Maverick W 0145CD* **10**	7
3 Apr 93	● **FEVER** *Maverick W 0168CD* **6**	6
31 Jul 93	**RAIN** *Maverick W 0190CD* **7**	8
2 Apr 94	● **I'LL REMEMBER** *Maverick W 0240CD* **7**	8
8 Oct 94	● **SECRET** *Maverick W 0268CD* **5**	9
17 Dec 94	**TAKE A BOW** *Maverick W 0278CD* **16**	9
25 Feb 95	● **BEDTIME STORY** *Maverick W 0285CD* **4**	8
6 May 95	**BEDTIME STORY (re-entry)** *Maverick W 0285CD* **66**	1
26 Aug 95	● **HUMAN NATURE** *Maverick W 0300CD* **8**	5
4 Nov 95	● **YOU'LL SEE** *Maverick W 0324CD* **5**	13
6 Jan 96	● **OH FATHER** *Maverick W 0326CD* **16**	6
23 Mar 96	**ONE MORE CHANCE** *Maverick W 0337CD* **11**	4
2 Nov 96	● **YOU MUST LOVE ME** *Warner Bros. W 0378CD* **10**	4
28 Dec 96	● **DON'T CRY FOR ME ARGENTINA**	
	Warner Bros. W 0384CD ....**3†**	1

MAGAZINE *UK, male vocal / instrumental group*　　　　　**7 wks**

11 Feb 78	**SHOT BY BOTH SIDES** *Virgin VS 200* **41**	4
26 Jul 80	**SWEET HEART CONTRACT** *Virgin VS 368*......**54**	3

MAGIC AFFAIR
US / Germany, male / female vocal / instrumental group　　　　　**8 wks**

4 Jun 94	**OMEN III** *EMI CDEM 317* **17**	4
27 Aug 94	**GIVE ME ALL YOUR LOVE** *EMI CDEM 340* **30**	2
5 Nov 94	**IN THE MIDDLE OF THE NIGHT** *EMI CDEM 349* **38**	2

MAGIC LADY *US, female vocal duo*　　　　　**3 wks**

14 May 88	**BETCHA CAN'T LOSE (WITH MY LOVE)**	
	Motown ZB 42003 ....**58**	3

MAGIC LANTERNS
UK, male vocal / instrumental group　　　　　**3 wks**

7 Jul 66	**EXCUSE ME BABY** *CBS 202094* **46**	1
28 Jul 66	**EXCUSE ME BABY (re-entry)** *CBS 202094*......**44**	1
11 Aug 66	**EXCUSE ME BABY (2nd re-entry)** *CBS 202094* **46**	1

MAGNUM *UK, male vocal / instrumental group*　　　　　**26 wks**

22 Mar 80	**MAGNUM (DOUBLE SINGLE)** *Jet 175* **47**	6
12 Jul 86	**LONELY NIGHT** *Polydor POSP 798* **70**	2

19 Mar 88	DAYS OF NO TRUST Polydor POSP 910	32	4
7 May 88	START TALKING LOVE Polydor POSP 920	22	4
2 Jul 88	IT MUST HAVE BEEN LOVE Polydor POSP 930	33	4
23 Jun 90	ROCKIN' CHAIR Polydor PO 88	27	4
25 Aug 90	HEARTBROKE AND BUSTED Polydor PO 94	49	2

Tracks on double single: Invasion / Kingdom of Madness / All of My Life / Great Adventure.

Sean MAGUIRE UK, male vocalist — 31 wks

20 Aug 94	SOMEONE TO LOVE Parlophone CDR 6390	14	7
5 Nov 94	TAKE THIS TIME Parlophone CDR 6395	27	4
31 Dec 94	TAKE THIS TIME (re-entry) Parlophone CDR 6395	74	1
25 Mar 95	SUDDENLY Parlophone CDR 6403	18	5
24 Jun 95	NOW I'VE FOUND YOU Parlophone CDLEEPYS 1	22	3
18 Nov 95	YOU TO ME ARE EVERYTHING Parlophone CDR 6420	16	3
25 May 96	GOOD DAY Parlophone CDR 6432	12	4
3 Aug 96	DON'T PULL YOUR LOVE Parlophone CDR 6440	14	4

Siobhan MAHER – See OCEANIC

MAHLATHINI and the MAHOTELLA QUEENS – See ART OF NOISE

MAI TAI Holland, female vocal group — 30 wks

25 May 85	● HISTORY Virgin VS 773	8	13
3 Aug 85	● BODY AND SOUL Virgin VS 801	9	13
15 Feb 86	FEMALE INTUITION Virgin VS 844	54	4

MAIN INGREDIENT US, male vocal group — 7 wks

| 29 Jun 74 | JUST DON'T WANT TO BE LONELY RCA APBO 0205 | 27 | 7 |

MAISONETTES UK, male / female vocal group — 12 wks

| 11 Dec 82 | ● HEARTACHE AVENUE Ready Steady Go! RSG 1 | 7 | 12 |

Raven MAIZE US, male vocalist — 1 wk

| 5 Aug 89 | FOREVER TOGETHER Republic LIC 014 | 67 | 1 |

MAKADOPOULOS and his GREEK SERENADERS
Greece, male vocal / instrumental group — 14 wks

| 20 Oct 60 | NEVER ON SUNDAY Palette PG 9005 | 36 | 14 |

Jack E. MAKOSSA Kenya, male producer — 5 wks

| 12 Sep 87 | THE OPERA HOUSE Champion CHAMP 50 | 48 | 5 |

MALA – See BOWA featuring MALA

MALAIKA US, female vocalist — 1 wk

| 31 Jul 93 | GOTTA KNOW (YOUR NAME) A & M 5802732 | 68 | 1 |

Carl MALCOLM Jamaica, male vocalist — 8 wks

| 13 Sep 75 | ● FATTIE BUM BUM UK 108 | 8 | 8 |

Valerie MALCOLM – See CANDY GIRLS

Timmy MALLETT – See BOMBALURINA

MAMA CASS US, female vocalist — 27 wks

| 14 Aug 68 | DREAM A LITTLE DREAM OF ME RCA 1726 | 11 | 12 |
| 16 Aug 69 | ● IT'S GETTING BETTER Stateside SS 8021 | 8 | 15 |

See also Mamas and the Papas.

MAMAS and the PAPAS
US, female / male vocal group — 64 wks

28 Apr 66	CALIFORNIA DREAMIN' RCA 1503	23	9
12 May 66	● MONDAY MONDAY RCA 1516	3	13
28 Jul 66	I SAW HER AGAIN RCA 1533	11	11
9 Feb 67	WORDS OF LOVE RCA 1564	47	3
6 Apr 67	● DEDICATED TO THE ONE I LOVE RCA 1576	2	17
26 Jul 67	● CREEQUE ALLEY RCA 1613	9	11

See also Mama Cass.

MAMBAS – See Marc ALMOND

A MAN CALLED ADAM
UK, male / female vocal / instrumental group — 4 wks

| 29 Sep 90 | BAREFOOT IN THE HEAD Big Life BLR 28 | 70 | 2 |
| 20 Oct 90 | BAREFOOT IN THE HEAD (re-entry) Big Life BLR 28 | 60 | 2 |

MAN TO MAN US, male vocal / instrumental duo — 19 wks

13 Sep 86	MALE STRIPPER Bolts BOLTS 4 [1]	64	3
3 Jan 87	MALE STRIPPER (re-entry) Bolts BOLTS 4 [1]	63	1
7 Feb 87	● MALE STRIPPER (2nd re-entry) Bolts BOLTS 4 [1]	4	12
4 Jul 87	I NEED A MAN / ENERGY IS EUROBEAT Bolts BOLTS 5	43	3

[1] Man 2 Man meet Man Parrish

MAN WITH NO NAME
UK, male producer – Martin Freeland — 4 wks

30 Sep 95	FLOOR-ESSENCE Perfecto PERF 108CD	68	1
20 Jan 96	PAINT A PICTURE Perfecto PERF 114CD [1]	42	2
12 Oct 96	TELEPORT / SUGAR RUSH Perfecto PERF 126CD	55	1

[1] Man With No Name featuring Hannah

Melissa MANCHESTER – See Al JARREAU

MANCHESTER UNITED FOOTBALL CLUB
UK, male football team vocalists — 49 wks

8 May 76	MANCHESTER UNITED Decca F 13633	50	1
21 May 83	GLORY GLORY MAN. UNITED EMI 5390	13	5
18 May 85	● WE ALL FOLLOW MAN. UNITED Columbia DB 9107	10	5
19 Jun 93	UNITED (WE LOVE YOU) Living Beat LBECD 026 [1]	37	2
30 Apr 94	★ COME ON YOU REDS PolyGram TV MANU 2	1	15
13 May 95	● WE'RE GONNA DO IT AGAIN PolyGram TV MANU 952 [2]	6	6
4 May 96	● MOVE MOVE MOVE (THE RED TRIBE) Music Collection MANUCD 1 [3]	6	11
3 Aug 96	MOVE MOVE MOVE (THE RED TRIBE) (re-entry) Music Collection MANUCD 1 [3]	50	4

[1] Manchester United and the Champions [2] Manchester United Football Squad featuring Stryker [3] 1996 Manchester United FA Cup Squad

Henry MANCINI US, orchestra / chorus — 23 wks

| 7 Dec 61 | MOON RIVER RCA 1256 | 46 | 2 |

28 Dec 61		MOON RIVER (re-entry) *RCA 1256*	**44**	1
24 Sep 64	●	HOW SOON *RCA 1414*	**10**	12
25 Mar 72		THEME FROM 'CADE'S COUNTY' *RCA 2182*	**42**	1
11 Feb 84		MAIN THEME FROM 'THE THORNBIRDS' *Warner Bros. 9677*	**23**	7

Steve MANDELL – *See 'DELIVERANCE' SOUNDTRACK*

MANFRED MANN
South Africa / UK, male vocal / instrumental group　　**217 wks**

23 Jan 64	●	5-4-3-2-1 *HMV POP 1252*	**5**	13
16 Apr 64		HUBBLE BUBBLE (TOIL AND TROUBLE) *HMV POP 1282*	**11**	8
16 Jul 64	★	DO WAH DIDDY DIDDY *HMV POP 1320*	**1**	14
15 Oct 64	●	SHA LA LA *HMV POP 1346*	**3**	12
14 Jan 65	●	COME TOMORROW *HMV POP 1381*	**4**	9
15 Apr 65		OH NO NOT MY BABY *HMV POP 1413*	**11**	10
16 Sep 65	●	IF YOU GOTTA GO GO NOW *HMV POP 1466*	**2**	12
21 Apr 66	★	PRETTY FLAMINGO *HMV POP 1523*	**1**	12
7 Jul 66		YOU GAVE ME SOMEBODY TO LOVE *HMV POP 1541*	**36**	4
4 Aug 66	●	JUST LIKE A WOMAN *Fontana TF 730*	**10**	10
27 Oct 66	●	SEMI-DETACHED SUBURBAN MR. JAMES *Fontana TF 757*	**2**	12
30 Mar 67	●	HA HA SAID THE CLOWN *Fontana TF 812*	**4**	11
25 May 67		SWEET PEA *Fontana TF 828*	**36**	4
24 Jan 68	★	MIGHTY QUINN *Fontana TF 897*	**1**	11
12 Jun 68	●	MY NAME IS JACK *Fontana TF 943*	**8**	11
18 Dec 68	●	FOX ON THE RUN *Fontana TF 985*	**5**	12
30 Apr 69	●	RAGAMUFFIN MAN *Fontana TF 1013*	**8**	11
8 Sep 73	●	JOYBRINGER *Vertigo 6059 083* [1]	**9**	10
28 Aug 76	●	BLINDED BY THE LIGHT *Bronze BRO 29* [1]	**6**	10
20 May 78	●	DAVY'S ON THE ROAD AGAIN *Bronze BRO 52* [1]	**6**	12
17 Mar 79		YOU ANGEL YOU *Bronze BRO 68* [1]	**54**	5
7 Jul 79		DON'T KILL IT CAROL *Bronze BRO 77* [1]	**45**	4

[1] Manfred Mann's Earth Band

MANHATTAN TRANSFER
US, male / female vocal group　　**72 wks**

7 Feb 76		TUXEDO JUNCTION *Atlantic K 10670*	**24**	6
5 Feb 77	★	CHANSON D'AMOUR *Atlantic K 10886*	**1**	13
28 May 77		DON'T LET GO *Atlantic K 10930*	**32**	6
18 Feb 78		WALK IN LOVE *Atlantic K 11075*	**48**	1
4 Mar 78		WALK IN LOVE (re-entry) *Atlantic K 11075*	**12**	11
20 May 78		ON A LITTLE STREET IN SINGAPORE *Atlantic K 11136*	**20**	9
16 Sep 78		WHERE DID OUR LOVE GO / JE VOULAIS TE DIRE (QUE JE T'ATTENDS) *Atlantic K 11182*	**40**	4
23 Dec 78		WHO WHAT WHEN WHERE WHY *Atlantic K 11233*	**49**	6
17 May 80		TWILIGHT ZONE – TWILIGHT TONE (MEDLEY) *Atlantic K 11476*	**25**	8
21 Jan 84		SPICE OF LIFE *Atlantic A 9728*	**19**	8

MANHATTANS *US, male vocal group*　　**31 wks**

19 Jun 76	●	KISS AND SAY GOODBYE *CBS 4317*	**4**	11
2 Oct 76	●	HURT *CBS 4562*	**4**	11
23 Apr 77		IT'S YOU *CBS 5093*	**43**	3
26 Jul 80		SHINING STAR *CBS 8624*	**45**	4
6 Aug 83		CRAZY *CBS A 3578*	**63**	2

M.A.N.I.C. *UK, male vocal / production duo*　　**1 wk**

| 18 Apr 92 | | I'M COMIN' HARDCORE *Union City UCRT 2* | **60** | 1 |

MANIC MC's featuring Sara CARLSON
UK, male production duo and female vocalist　　**5 wks**

| 12 Aug 89 | | MENTAL *RCA PB 43037* | **30** | 5 |

MANIC STREET PREACHERS
UK, male vocal / instrumental group　　**78 wks**

25 May 91		YOU LOVE US *Heavenly HVN 10*	**62**	2
10 Aug 91		STAY BEAUTIFUL *Columbia 6573377*	**40**	3
9 Nov 91		LOVE'S SWEET EXILE / REPEAT *Columbia 6575827*	**26**	3
1 Feb 92		YOU LOVE US (re-issue) *Columbia 6577247*	**16**	4
28 Mar 92		SLASH 'N' BURN *Columbia 6578737*	**20**	4
13 Jun 92		MOTORCYCLE EMPTINESS *Columbia 6580837*	**17**	6
19 Sep 92	●	THEME FROM 'M.A.S.H.' (SUICIDE IS PAINLESS) *Columbia 6583827*	**7**	6
21 Nov 92		LITTLE BABY NOTHING *Columbia 6587967*	**29**	3
12 Jun 93		FROM DESPAIR TO WHERE *Columbia 6593372*	**25**	4
31 Jul 93		LA TRISTESSE DURERA (SCREAM TO A SIGH) *Columbia 6594772*	**22**	5
2 Oct 93		ROSES IN THE HOSPITAL *Columbia 6597272*	**15**	3
12 Feb 94		LIFE BECOMING A LANDSLIDE *Columbia 6600702*	**36**	2
11 Jun 94		FASTER / PCP *Epic 6604472*	**16**	3
13 Aug 94		REVOL *Epic 6606862*	**22**	3
15 Oct 94		SHE IS SUFFERING *Epic 6608952*	**25**	3
27 Apr 96	●	A DESIGN FOR LIFE *Epic 6630705*	**2**	10
27 Jul 96		A DESIGN FOR LIFE (re-entry) *Epic 6630705*	**71**	1
3 Aug 96	●	EVERYTHING MUST GO *Epic 6634685*	**5**	6
12 Oct 96	●	KEVIN CARTER *Epic 6637752*	**9**	4
14 Dec 96	●	AUSTRALIA *Epic 6640442*	**7**	3

The listed flipside of Theme From M.A.S.H. (Suicide Is Painless) *was with* (Everything I Do) I Do It For You *by Fatima Mansions.*

Barry MANILOW *US, male vocalist*　　**136 wks**

22 Feb 75		MANDY *Arista 1*	**11**	9
6 May 78		CAN'T SMILE WITHOUT YOU *Arista 176*	**43**	7
29 Jul 78		SOMEWHERE IN THE NIGHT / COPACABANA (AT THE COPA) *Arista 196*	**42**	10
23 Dec 78		COULD IT BE MAGIC *Arista ARIST 229*	**25**	10
8 Nov 80		LONELY TOGETHER *Arista ARIST 373*	**21**	13
7 Feb 81		I MADE IT THROUGH THE RAIN *Arista ARIST 384*	**37**	6
11 Apr 81		BERMUDA TRIANGLE *Arista ARIST 406*	**15**	9
26 Sep 81		LET'S HANG ON *Arista ARIST 429*	**12**	11
12 Dec 81		THE OLD SONGS *Arista ARIST 443*	**48**	8
20 Feb 82		IF I SHOULD LOVE AGAIN *Arista ARIST 453*	**66**	2
17 Apr 82		STAY *Arista ARIST 464* [1]	**23**	8
16 Oct 82		I WANNA DO IT WITH YOU *Arista ARIST 495*	**8**	8
4 Dec 82		I'M GONNA SIT RIGHT DOWN AND WRITE MYSELF A LETTER *Arista ARIST 503*	**36**	7
25 Jun 83		SOME KIND OF FRIEND *Arista ARIST 516*	**48**	2
27 Aug 83		YOU'RE LOOKING HOT TONIGHT *Arista ARIST 542*	**47**	6
10 Dec 83		READ 'EM AND WEEP *Arista ARIST 551*	**17**	7
8 Apr 89		PLEASE DON'T BE SCARED *Arista 112186*	**35**	5
10 Apr 93		COPACABANA (AT THE COPA) (re-mix) *Arista 74321136912*	**22**	4
20 Nov 93		COULD IT BE MAGIC *Arista 74321174882*	**36**	3
6 Aug 94		LET ME BE YOUR WINGS *EMI CDEM 336* [2]	**73**	1

[1] Barry Manilow featuring Kevin DeSimone and James Jolis [2] Barry Manilow and Debra Byrd

ARIST 464 was available as both a live and studio recording. Could It Be Magic in '93 is a re-recording.

MANIX *UK, male / female vocal / instrumental group*　　**6 wks**

23 Nov 91		MANIC MINDS *Reinforced RIVET 1209*	**63**	2
7 Mar 92		OBLIVION (HEAD IN THE CLOUDS) (EP) *Reinforced RIVET 1212*	**43**	3
8 Aug 92		RAINBOW PEOPLE *Reinforced RIVET 1221*	**57**	1

Tracks on Oblivion (Head In The Clouds) (EP): Oblivion (Head In The Clouds) / Never Been To Belgium (Gotta Rush) / I Can't Stand It / You Held My Hand.

MANKEY *UK, male producer – Andy Manston*　　**1 wk**

| 16 Nov 96 | | BELIEVE IN ME *Frisky DISKY 3* | **74** | 1 |

MANKIND UK, male instrumental group — 12 wks

25 Nov 78	DR. WHO Pinnacle PIN 71	25	12

Aimee MANN US, female vocalist — 9 wks

31 Oct 87	TIME STAND STILL Vertigo RUSH 13 [1]	42	3
28 Aug 93	I SHOULD'VE KNOWN Imago 72787250432	55	2
20 Nov 93	STUPID THING Imago 72787250432	47	2
5 Mar 94	I SHOULD'VE KNOWN (re-issue) Imago 72787250602 ..	45	2

[1] Rush with Aimee Mann

Johnny MANN SINGERS
US, male / female vocal group — 13 wks

12 Jul 67	● UP, UP AND AWAY Liberty LIB 55972	6	13

MANSUN UK, male vocal / instrumental group — 11 wks

6 Apr 96	ONE EP Parlophone CDR 6430	37	2
15 Jun 96	TWO EP Parlophone CDR 6437	32	2
21 Sep 96	STRIPPER VICAR Parlophone CDR 6447	19	3
7 Dec 96	WIDE OPEN SPACE Parlophone CDR 6453	15	4

Tracks on One EP: Egg Shaped Fred / Ski Jump Nose / Lemonade Secret Drinker / Thief.
Tracks on Two EP: Take It Easy Chicken / Drastic Sturgeon / The Greatest Pain / Moronica.

MANTOVANI UK, orchestra — 52 wks

19 Dec 52	● WHITE CHRISTMAS Decca F 10017	6	3
29 May 53	★ MOULIN ROUGE Decca F 10094	1	21
23 Oct 53	● SWEDISH RHAPSODY Decca F 10168	2	17
13 Nov 53	● MOULIN ROUGE (re-entry) Decca F 10094	10	1
4 Dec 53	MOULIN ROUGE (2nd re-entry) Decca F 10094	12	1
26 Feb 54	SWEDISH RHAPSODY (re-entry) Decca F 10168	12	1
11 Feb 55	LONELY BALLERINA Decca F 10395	16	3
18 Mar 55	LONELY BALLERINA (re-entry) Decca F 10395	18	1
31 May 57	AROUND THE WORLD Decca F 10888	20	4

See also David Whitfield.

MANTRONIX US / Jamaica, male vocal / instrumental duo — 48 wks

22 Feb 86	LADIES 10 TEN 116	55	4
17 May 86	BASSLINE 10 TEN 118	34	6
7 Feb 87	WHO IS IT 10 TEN 137	40	6
4 Jul 87	SCREAM (PRIMAL SCREAM) 10 TEN 169	46	4
30 Jan 88	SING A SONG (BREAK IT DOWN) 10 TEN 206	61	2
12 Mar 88	SIMPLE SIMON (YOU GOTTA REGARD) 10 TEN 217 ..	72	2
6 Jan 90	● GOT TO HAVE YOUR LOVE Capitol CL 559 [1]	4	11
12 May 90	● TAKE YOUR TIME Capitol CL 573 [1]	10	7
2 Mar 91	DON'T GO MESSIN' WITH MY HEART Capitol CL 608 ..	22	5
22 Jun 91	STEP TO ME (DO ME) Capitol CL 613	59	1

[1] Mantronix featuring Wondress

MANUEL and his MUSIC OF THE MOUNTAINS
UK, orchestra, leader Geoff Love — 31 wks

28 Aug 59	THE HONEYMOON SONG Columbia DB 4323	29	2
25 Sep 59	THE HONEYMOON SONG (re-entry)		
	Columbia DB 4323	22	5
6 Nov 59	THE HONEYMOON SONG (2nd re-entry)		
	Columbia DB 4323	27	2
13 Oct 60	NEVER ON SUNDAY Columbia DB 4515	29	10
13 Oct 66	SOMEWHERE MY LOVE Columbia DB 7969	42	2
31 Jan 76	● RODRIGO'S GUITAR CONCERTO DE ARANJUEZ		
	(THEME FROM 2ND MOVEMENT) EMI 2383	3	10

MARATHON
Germany / UK, male vocal / instrumental group — 3 wks

25 Jan 92	MOVIN' Ten TEN 395..	36	3

MARAUDERS UK, male vocal / instrumental group — 4 wks

8 Aug 63	THAT'S WHAT I WANT Decca F 11695	48	1
22 Aug 63	THAT'S WHAT I WANT (re-entry) Decca F 11695	43	3

MARBLES UK, male vocal duo — 18 wks

25 Sep 68	● ONLY ONE WOMAN Polydor 56 272	5	12
26 Mar 69	THE WALLS FELL DOWN Polydor 56 310	28	6

MARC and the MAMBAS – See Marc ALMOND

MARCELS US, male vocal group — 17 wks

13 Apr 61	★ BLUE MOON Pye International 7N 25073	1	13
8 Jun 61	SUMMERTIME Pye International 7N 25083	46	4

Little Peggy MARCH US, female vocalist — 7 wks

12 Sep 63	HELLO HEARTACHE GOODBYE LOVE RCA 1362	29	7

MARDI GRAS UK, male vocal / instrumental group — 9 wks

5 Aug 72	TOO BUSY THINKING 'BOUT MY BABY Bell 1226	19	9

MARIA – See Maria NAYLER

Kelly MARIE UK, female vocalist — 36 wks

2 Aug 80	★ FEELS LIKE I'M IN LOVE Calibre PLUS 1	1	16
18 Oct 80	LOVING JUST FOR FUN Calibre PLUS 4	21	7
7 Feb 81	HOT LOVE Calibre PLUS 5	22	10
30 May 81	LOVE TRIAL Calibre PLUS 7	51	3

Teena MARIE US, female vocalist — 28 wks

7 Jul 79	I'M A SUCKER FOR YOUR LOVE Motown TMG 1146 [1] ..	43	8
31 May 80	● BEHIND THE GROOVE Motown TMG 1185	6	10
11 Oct 80	I NEED YOUR LOVIN' Motown TMG 1203	28	6
26 Mar 88	OO LA LA LA Epic 651423 7	74	2
10 Nov 90	SINCE DAY ONE Epic 656429 7	69	2

[1] Teena Marie, co-lead vocals Rick James

MARILLION UK, male vocal / instrumental group — 103 wks

20 Nov 82	MARKET SQUARE HEROES EMI 5351	60	2
12 Feb 83	HE KNOWS YOU KNOW EMI 5362	35	4
16 Apr 83	MARKET SQUARE HEROES (re-entry) EMI 5351	53	6
18 Jun 83	GARDEN PARTY EMI 5393	16	5
11 Feb 84	PUNCH AND JUDY EMI MARIL 1	29	4
12 May 84	ASSASSING EMI MARIL 2	22	5
18 May 85	● KAYLEIGH EMI MARIL 3	2	14
7 Sep 85	● LAVENDER EMI MARIL 4	5	9
30 Nov 85	HEART OF LOTHIAN EMI MARIL 5......................	29	6
23 May 87	● INCOMMUNICADO EMI MARIL 6	6	5
25 Jul 87	SUGAR MICE EMI MARIL 7	22	5
7 Nov 87	WARM WET CIRCLES EMI MARIL 8......................	22	4
26 Nov 88	FREAKS (LIVE) EMI MARIL 9	24	3
9 Sep 89	HOOKS IN YOU Capitol MARIL 10	30	3
9 Dec 89	UNINVITED GUEST EMI MARIL 11	53	2
14 Apr 90	EASTER EMI MARIL 12	34	2

8 Jun 91	**COVER MY EYES (PAIN AND HEAVEN)** *EMI MARIL 13* ..**34**	4
3 Aug 91	**NO ONE CAN** *EMI MARIL 14* **33**	4
5 Oct 91	**DRY LAND** *EMI MARIL 15*....................................**34**	2
23 May 92	**SYMPATHY** *EMI MARIL 16*..................................**17**	3
1 Aug 92	**NO ONE CAN (re-issue)** *EMI MARIL 17* **26**	4
26 Mar 94	**THE HOLLOW MAN** *EMI CDEMS 307*.................**30**	2
7 May 94	**ALONE AGAIN IN THE LAP OF LUXURY** *EMI CDEMS 318*..**53**	3
10 Jun 95	**BEAUTIFUL** *EMI CDMARILS 18*............................**29**	2

MARILYN UK, male vocalist　　26 wks

5 Nov 83	● **CALLING YOUR NAME** *Love MAZ 1* **4**	12
11 Feb 84	**CRY AND BE FREE** *Love MAZ 2*............................**31**	6
21 Apr 84	**YOU DON'T LOVE ME** *Love MAZ 3*.....................**40**	7
13 Apr 85	**BABY U LEFT ME (IN THE COLD)** *Love MAZ 4* **70**	1

Marino MARINI and his QUARTET
Italy, male vocalist and instrumental group　　17 wks

3 Oct 58	**VOLARE** *Durium DC 16632* **13**	7
10 Oct 58	● **COME PRIMA** *Durium DC 16632* **2**	14
20 Mar 59	**CIAO CIAO BAMBINA** *Durium DC 16636* **25**	1
3 Apr 59	**CIAO CIAO BAMBINA (re-entry)** *Durium DC 16636* **24**	1

MARION UK, male vocal / instrumental group　　8 wks

25 Feb 95	**SLEEP** *London LONCD 360* **53**	1
13 May 95	**TOYS FOR BOYS** *London LONCD 366* **57**	1
21 Oct 95	**LET'S ALL GO TOGETHER** *London LONCD 371* **37**	2
3 Feb 96	**TIME** *London LONCD 377* **29**	2
30 Mar 96	**SLEEP (re-mix)** *London LONCD 381* **17**	2

MARK 'OH Germany, male producer – Marko Albrecht　　3 wks

6 May 95	**TEARS DON'T LIE** *Systematic SYSCD 9* **24**	3

Pigmeat MARKHAM US, male vocalist　　8 wks

17 Jul 68	**HERE COMES THE JUDGE** *Chess CRS 8077*..........**19**	8

Biz MARKIE US, male rapper　　2 wks

26 May 90	**JUST A FRIEND** *Cold Chillin' W 9823* **55**	2

Yannis MARKOPOULOS Greece, orchestra　　8 wks

17 Dec 77	**WHO PAYS THE FERRYMAN** *BBC RESL 51* **11**	8

Guy MARKS Australia, male vocalist　　8 wks

13 May 78	**LOVING YOU HAS MADE ME BANANAS** *ABC 4211* **25**	8

MARKY MARK and the FUNKY BUNCH
US, male / female vocal / instrumental group　　14 wks

31 Aug 91	**GOOD VIBRATIONS** *Interscope A 8764* 1 ....**14**	7
2 Nov 91	**WILDSIDE** *Interscope A 8674* **42**	3
12 Dec 92	**YOU GOTTA BELIEVE** *Interscope A 8480* **54**	4

1 Marky Mark and the Funky Bunch featuring Loleatta Holloway

Bob MARLEY and the WAILERS
Jamaica, male vocal / instrumental group　　142 wks

27 Sep 75	**NO WOMAN NO CRY** *Island WIP 6244* **22**	7
25 Jun 77	**EXODUS** *Island WIP 6390* **14**	9

10 Sep 77	**WAITING IN VAIN** *Island WIP 6402* **27**	6
10 Dec 77	● **JAMMING / PUNKY REGGAE PARTY** *Island WIP 6410* **9**	12
25 Feb 78	● **IS THIS LOVE** *Island WIP 6420* **9**	9
10 Jun 78	**SATISFY MY SOUL** *Island WIP 6440* **21**	10
20 Oct 79	**SO MUCH TROUBLE IN THE WORLD** *Island WIP 6510* **56**	4
21 Jun 80	● **COULD YOU BE LOVED** *Island WIP 6610* **5**	12
13 Sep 80	**THREE LITTLE BIRDS** *Island WIP 6641* **17**	9
13 Jun 81	● **NO WOMAN NO CRY (re-entry)** *Island WIP 6244* **8**	11
7 May 83	● **BUFFALO SOLDIER** *Island/Tuff Gong 1S 108* **4**	12
21 Apr 84	● **ONE LOVE – PEOPLE GET READY** *Island IS 169* ...**5**	11
23 Jun 84	**WAITING IN VAIN (re-issue)** *Island IS 180* **31**	4
8 Dec 84	**COULD YOU BE LOVED (re-issue)** *Island IS 210* ..**71**	2
18 May 91	**ONE LOVE – PEOPLE GET READY (re-issue)** *Tuff Gong TGX 1* **42**	3
19 Sep 92	● **IRON LION ZION** *Tuff Gong TGX 2* **5**	9
28 Nov 92	**WHY SHOULD I / EXODUS** *Tuff Gong TGX 3* **42**	3
2 Jan 93	**WHY SHOULD I / EXODUS (re-entry)** *Tuff Gong TGX 3* **75**	1
20 May 95	**KEEP ON MOVING** *Tuff Gong TGXCD 4* **17**	4
8 Jun 96	**WHAT GOES AROUND COMES AROUND** *Anansi ANACS 002* 1 ....**42**	1

1 Bob Marley

Exodus on Tuff Gong TGX 3 only listed with Why Should I from 5 Dec 92 and is a different version from the Island hit. It peaked at position 53.

Ziggy MARLEY and the MELODY MAKERS
Jamaica, male / female vocal / instrumental group　　11 wks

11 Jun 88	**TOMORROW PEOPLE** *Virgin VS 1049* **22**	10
23 Sep 89	**LOOK WHO'S DANCING** *Virgin America VUS 5*...............**65**	1

MARMALADE UK, male vocal / instrumental group　　130 wks

22 May 68	● **LOVIN' THINGS** *CBS 3412* **6**	13
23 Oct 68	**WAIT FOR ME MARIANNE** *CBS 3708* **30**	5
4 Dec 68	★ **OB-LA-DI OB-LA-DA** *CBS 3892* **1**	20
11 Jun 69	● **BABY MAKE IT SOON** *CBS 4287* **9**	13
20 Dec 69	● **REFLECTIONS OF MY LIFE** *Decca F 12982* **3**	12
18 Jul 70	● **RAINBOW** *Decca F 13035* **3**	14
27 Mar 71	**MY LITTLE ONE** *Decca F 13135* **15**	11
4 Sep 71	● **COUSIN NORMAN** *Decca F 13214* **6**	11
27 Nov 71	**BACK ON THE ROAD** *Decca F 13251* **35**	7
22 Jan 72	**BACK ON THE ROAD (re-entry)** *Decca F 13251* **50**	1
1 Apr 72	● **RADANCER** *Decca F 13297* **6**	12
21 Feb 76	● **FALLING APART AT THE SEAMS** *Target TGT 105* **9**	11

MARMION
Spain / Holland, male instrumental / production duo　　1 wk

18 May 96	**SCHONEBERG** *Hooj Choons HOOJCD 43*...........**53**	1

Johnny MARR – See Billy BRAGG

MARRADONA UK, male / female vocal / instrumental group 3 wks

26 Feb 94	**OUT OF MY HEAD** *Peach PWCD 282*..................**38**	3

M/A/R/R/S UK, male instrumental / scratch group　　14 wks

5 Sep 87	★ **PUMP UP THE VOLUME / ANITINA (THE FIRST TIME I SEE SHE DANCE)** *4AD AD 70* **1**	14

The B-side of this record was listed on the chart at the record company's request without evidence of consumer interest.

Gerry MARSDEN – See CHRISTIANS; Holly JOHNSON; Paul McCARTNEY; STOCK AITKEN WATERMAN; GERRY and the PACEMAKERS

Manic Street Preachers

Despite the disappearance of founder member Richey Edwards, the Manics had their most successful year to date in 1996, with four Top 10 sinlges.

Metallica

Metallica's 'Hero Of The Day' was dedicated to Lemmy of Motorhead who celebrated his 50th birthday in 1996.

Marmalade

Marmalade's chart-topping cover of the Beatles' 'Ob-La-Di Ob-La-Da' twice replaced Scaffold's 'Lily The Pink' at number one.

Richard Marx

The first appearance of Richard Marx on the UK charts was as a backing singer on Lionel Richie's 1983 hit 'You Are'.

Stevie MARSH *UK, female vocalist* **4 wks**

4 Dec 59	THE ONLY BOY IN THE WORLD *Decca F 11181*	**29**	2
25 Dec 59	THE ONLY BOY IN THE WORLD (re-entry) *Decca F 11181*	**24**	2

Joy MARSHALL *UK, female vocalist* **2 wks**

23 Jun 66	THE MORE I SEE YOU *Decca F 12422*	**34**	2

Keith MARSHALL *UK, male vocalist* **10 wks**

4 Apr 81	ONLY CRYING *Arrival PIK 2*	**12**	10

Wayne MARSHALL *UK, male vocalist* **7 wks**

1 Oct 94	OOH AAH (G-SPOT) *Soultown SOULCDS 322*	**29**	3
3 Jun 95	SPIRIT *Soultown SOULCDS 00352*	**58**	1
24 Feb 96	NEVER KNEW LOVE LIKE THIS *Sony S2 6629382* [1]	**40**	2
7 Dec 96	G SPOT (re-mix) *MBA INTER 9006*	**50**	1

[1] Pauline Henry featuring Wayne Marshall

MARSHALL HAIN
UK, male / female vocal / instrumental duo **19 wks**

3 Jun 78	● DANCING IN THE CITY *Harvest HAR 5157*	**3**	15
14 Oct 78	COMING HOME *Harvest HAR 5168*	**39**	4

Lena MARTELL *UK, female vocalist* **18 wks**

29 Sep 79	★ ONE DAY AT A TIME *Pye 7N 46021*	**1**	18

MARTHA and the MUFFINS
Canada, female / male vocal / instrumental group **10 wks**

1 Mar 80	● ECHO BEACH *Dindisc DIN 9*	**10**	10

See also M + M, who are Martha and a Muffin.

MARTHA and the VANDELLAS – *See Martha REEVES and the VANDELLAS*

MARTIKA *US, female vocalist* **57 wks**

29 Jul 89	● TOY SOLDIERS *CBS 655049 7*	**5**	11
14 Oct 89	● I FEEL THE EARTH MOVE *CBS 655294 7*	**7**	14
13 Jan 90	MORE THAN YOU KNOW *CBS 655526 7*	**15**	7
17 Mar 90	WATER *CBS 655731 7*	**59**	3
17 Aug 91	● LOVE... THY WILL BE DONE *Columbia 6573137*	**9**	9
30 Nov 91	MARTIKA'S KITCHEN *Columbia 6575687*	**17**	10
22 Feb 92	COLOURED KISSES *Columbia 6577097*	**41**	3

Billie Ray MARTIN *Germany, female vocalist* **19 wks**

19 Nov 94	YOUR LOVING ARMS *Magnet MAG 1028CD*	**38**	3
20 May 95	● YOUR LOVING ARMS (re-mix) *Magnet MAG 1031CD*	**6**	9
2 Sep 95	RUNNING AROUND TOWN *Magnet MAG 1035CD*	**29**	2
6 Jan 96	IMITATION OF LIFE *Magnet MAG 1040CD*	**29**	3
6 Apr 96	SPACE OASIS *Magnet MAG 1042CD*	**66**	1

Dean MARTIN *US, male vocalist* **156 wks**

18 Sep 53	● KISS *Capitol CL 13893*	**9**	1
2 Oct 53	● KISS (re-entry) *Capitol CL 13893*	**5**	7
22 Jan 54	● THAT'S AMORE *Capitol CL 14008*	**2**	11
1 Oct 54	● SWAY *Capitol CL 14138*	**6**	7
22 Oct 54	HOW DO YOU SPEAK TO AN ANGEL *Capitol CL 14150*	**15**	2
19 Nov 54	HOW DO YOU SPEAK TO AN ANGEL (re-entry) *Capitol CL 14150*	**17**	4
28 Jan 55	● NAUGHTY LADY OF SHADY LANE *Capitol CL 14226*	**5**	10
4 Feb 55	MAMBO ITALIANO *Capitol CL 14227*	**14**	2
25 Feb 55	● LET ME GO LOVER *Capitol CL 14226*	**3**	9
1 Apr 55	● UNDER THE BRIDGES OF PARIS *Capitol CL 14255*	**6**	8
10 Feb 56	★ MEMORIES ARE MADE OF THIS *Capitol CL 14523*	**1**	16
2 Mar 56	YOUNG AND FOOLISH *Capitol CL 14519*	**20**	1
27 Apr 56	INNAMORATA *Capitol CL 14507*	**21**	3
22 Mar 57	THE MAN WHO PLAYS THE MANDOLINO *Capitol CL 14690*	**21**	2
13 Jun 58	● RETURN TO ME *Capitol CL 14844*	**2**	22
29 Aug 58	● VOLARE (NEL BLU DIPINTO DI BLU) *Capitol CL 14910*	**2**	14
27 Aug 64	EVERYBODY LOVES SOMEBODY *Reprise R 20281*	**11**	13
12 Nov 64	THE DOOR IS STILL OPEN TO MY HEART *Reprise R 20307*	**42**	4
5 Feb 69	● GENTLE ON MY MIND *Reprise RS 23343*	**2**	23
30 Aug 69	GENTLE ON MY MIND (re-entry) *Reprise RS 23343*	**49**	1
22 Jun 96	THAT'S AMORE (re-issue) *EMI Premier PRESCD 3*	**43**	2

Juan MARTIN *Spain, male instrumentalist – guitar* **7 wks**

28 Jan 84	● LOVE THEME FROM 'THE THORN BIRDS' *WEA X 9518*	**10**	7

Linda MARTIN *Ireland, female vocalist* **2 wks**

30 May 92	WHY ME *Columbia 6581317*	**59**	2

Marilyn MARTIN – *See Phil COLLINS*

Ray MARTIN *UK, orchestra* **11 wks**

14 Nov 52	● BLUE TANGO *Columbia DB 3051*	**8**	1
28 Nov 52	● BLUE TANGO (re-entry) *Columbia DB 3051*	**10**	3
4 Dec 53	● SWEDISH RHAPSODY *Columbia DB 3346*	**10**	1
18 Dec 53	● SWEDISH RHAPSODY (re-entry) *Columbia DB 3346*	**4**	3
15 Jun 56	CAROUSEL WALTZ *Columbia DB 3771*	**28**	1
3 Aug 56	CAROUSEL WALTZ (re-entry) *Columbia DB 3771*	**24**	2

Tony MARTIN *US, male vocalist* **28 wks**

22 Apr 55	● STRANGER IN PARADISE *HMV B 10849*	**6**	13
13 Jul 56	● WALK HAND IN HAND *HMV POP 222*	**2**	15

Vince MARTIN – *See TARRIERS*

Wink MARTINDALE *US, male vocalist* **41 wks**

4 Dec 59	DECK OF CARDS *London HLD 8962*	**18**	5
15 Jan 60	DECK OF CARDS (re-entry) *London HLD 8962*	**28**	2
31 Mar 60	DECK OF CARDS (2nd re-entry) *London HLD 8962*	**45**	1
18 Apr 63	● DECK OF CARDS (3rd re-entry) *London HLD 8962*	**5**	21
20 Oct 73	DECK OF CARDS (re-issue) *Dot DOT 109*	**22**	12

Al MARTINO *US, male vocalist* **87 wks**

14 Nov 52	★ HERE IN MY HEART *Capitol CL 13779*	**1**	18
21 Nov 52	● TAKE MY HEART *Capitol CL 13769*	**9**	1
30 Jan 53	● NOW *Capitol CL 13835*	**3**	12
10 Jul 53	● RACHEL *Capitol CL 13879*	**10**	4
11 Sep 53	RACHEL (re-entry) *Capitol CL 13879*	**12**	1
4 Jun 54	WANTED *Capitol CL 14128*	**12**	1
18 Jun 54	● WANTED (re-entry) *Capitol CL 14128*	**4**	14
1 Oct 54	● THE STORY OF TINA *Capitol CL 14163*	**10**	8
1 Oct 54	WANTED (2nd re-entry) *Capitol CL 14128*	**17**	1
23 Sep 55	THE MAN FROM LARAMIE *Capitol CL 14343*	**19**	2
28 Oct 55	THE MAN FROM LARAMIE (re-entry) *Capitol CL 14343*	**20**	1
31 Mar 60	SUMMERTIME *Top Rank JAR 312*	**49**	1
29 Aug 63	I LOVE YOU BECAUSE *Capitol CL 15300*	**48**	1

22 Aug 70	**SPANISH EYES** Capitol CL 15430	**49** 1
14 Jul 73	● **SPANISH EYES (re-entry)** Capitol CL 15430	**5** 21

MARVELETTES US, female vocal group   10 wks

15 Jun 67	**WHEN YOU'RE YOUNG AND IN LOVE** Tamla Motown TMG 609	**13** 10

Hank MARVIN
UK, male vocalist / instrumentalist – guitar   **36 wks**

13 Sep 69	● **THROW DOWN A LINE** Columbia DB 8615 [1]	**7** 9
21 Feb 70	**JOY OF LIVING** Columbia DB 8657 [1]	**25** 8
6 Mar 82	**DON'T TALK** Polydor POSP 420	**49** 4
22 Mar 86	★ **LIVING DOLL** WEA YZ 65 [2]	**1** 11
7 Jan 89	**LONDON KID** Polydor PO 32 [3]	**52** 3
17 Oct 92	**WE ARE THE CHAMPIONS** PolyGram TV PO 229 [4]	**66** 1

[1] Cliff and Hank [2] Cliff Richard and the Young Ones featuring Hank B. Marvin [3] Jean-Michel Jarre featuring Hank Marvin [4] Hank Marvin featuring Brian May

Lee MARVIN US, male vocalist   23 wks

7 Feb 70	★ **WAND'RIN' STAR** Paramount PARA 3004	**1** 18
20 Jun 70	**WAND'RIN' STAR (re-entry)** Paramount PARA 3004	**42** 3
15 Aug 70	**WAND'RIN' STAR (2nd re-entry)** Paramount PARA 3004	**47** 2

I Talk To The Trees by Clint Eastwood, the flip side of Wand'rin' Star was listed with Wand'rin' Star for 7 Feb 70 and 14 Feb 70 only.

MARVIN THE PARANOID ANDROID
UK, robot   **4 wks**

16 May 81	**MARVIN** Polydor POSP 261	**53** 4

Richard MARX US, male vocalist   75 wks

27 Feb 88	**SHOULD'VE KNOWN BETTER** Manhattan MT 32	**50** 5
14 May 88	**ENDLESS SUMMER NIGHTS** Manhattan MT 39	**50** 3
17 Jun 89	**SATISFIED** EMI-USA MT 64	**52** 4
2 Sep 89	● **RIGHT HERE WAITING** EMI-USA MT 72	**2** 10
11 Nov 89	**ANGELIA** EMI-USA MT 74	**45** 4
24 Mar 90	**TOO LATE TO SAY GOODBYE** EMI-USA MT 80	**38** 3
7 Jul 90	**CHILDREN OF THE NIGHT** EMI-USA MT 84	**54** 2
1 Sep 90	**ENDLESS SUMMER NIGHTS (re-issue)** EMI-USA MT 89	**60** 2
19 Oct 91	**KEEP COMING BACK** Capitol CL 634	**55** 2
9 May 92	● **HAZARD** Capitol CL 654	**3** 15
29 Aug 92	**TAKE THIS HEART** Capitol CL 667	**13** 6
28 Nov 92	**CHAINS AROUND MY HEART** Capitol CL 676	**29** 6
29 Jan 94	**NOW AND FOREVER** Capitol CDCLS 703	**13** 6
30 Apr 94	**SILENT SCREAM** Capitol CDCLS 714	**32** 4
13 Aug 94	**THE WAY SHE LOVES ME** Capitol CDCL 721	**38** 3

MARXMAN UK / Ireland, rap / instrumental group   5 wks

6 Mar 93	**ALL ABOUT EVE** Talkin Loud TLKCD 35	**28** 4
1 May 93	**SHIP AHOY** Talkin Loud TLKCD 39	**64** 1

Sinead O'Connor provides uncredited vocals on Ship Ahoy.

MARY JANE GIRLS US, female vocal group   11 wks

25 Jun 83	**ALL NIGHT LONG** Gordy TMG 1309	**13** 9
8 Oct 83	**BOYS** Gordy TMG 1315	**74** 1
18 Feb 95	**ALL NIGHT LONG (re-mix)** Motown TMGCD 1436	**51** 1

Carolyne MAS US, female vocalist   2 wks

2 Feb 80	**QUOTE GOODBYE QUOTE** Mercury 6167 873	**71** 2

MASH US, male vocal / instrumental group   12 wks

10 May 80	★ **THEME FROM 'M*A*S*H*' (SUICIDE IS PAINLESS)** CBS 8536	**1** 12

MASH! UK / US, male / female vocal group   3 wks

21 May 94	**U DON'T HAVE TO SAY U LOVE ME** React CDREACT 37	**37** 2
4 Feb 95	**LET'S SPEND THE NIGHT TOGETHER** Playa CDXPLAYA 2	**66** 1

Barbara MASON US, female vocalist   5 wks

21 Jan 84	**ANOTHER MAN** Streetwave KHAN 3	**45** 5

Glen MASON UK, male vocalist   7 wks

28 Sep 56	**GLENDORA** Parlophone R 4203	**28** 2
16 Nov 56	**GREEN DOOR** Parlophone R 4244	**24** 5

Mary MASON UK, female vocalist   6 wks

8 Oct 77	**ANGEL OF THE MORNING – ANY WAY THAT YOU WANT ME** Epic EPC 5552	**27** 6

MASQUERADE UK, male / female vocal group   10 wks

11 Jan 86	**ONE NATION** Streetwave KHAN 59	**54** 6
5 Jul 86	**(SOLUTION TO) THE PROBLEM** Streetwave KHAN 67	**65** 2
26 Jul 86	**(SOLUTION TO) THE PROBLEM (re-entry)** Streetwave KHAN 67	**64** 2

MASS ORDER US, male vocal / instrumental duo   5 wks

14 Mar 92	**LIFT EVERY VOICE (TAKE ME AWAY)** Columbia 6577487	**35** 3
23 May 92	**LET'S GET HAPPY** Columbia 6580737	**45** 2

MASS PRODUCTION
US, male vocal / instrumental group   **7 wks**

12 Mar 77	**WELCOME TO OUR WORLD (OF MERRY MUSIC)** Atlantic K 10898	**44** 3
17 May 80	**SHANTE** Atlantic K 11475	**59** 4

Zeitia MASSIAH UK, female vocalist   2 wks

12 Mar 94	**I SPECIALIZE IN LOVE** Union City UCRCD 27 [1]	**74** 1
24 Sep 94	**THIS IS THE PLACE** Virgin VSCDT 1511	**62** 1

[1] Arizona featuring Zeitia

MASSIEL Spain, female vocalist   4 wks

24 Apr 68	**LA LA LA** Philips BF 1667	**35** 4

MASSIVE ATTACK
UK, male / female vocal / instrumental group   **31 wks**

23 Feb 91	**UNFINISHED SYMPATHY** Wild Bunch WBRS 2 [1]	**13** 9
8 Jun 91	**SAFE FROM HARM** Wild Bunch WBRS 3	**25** 6

22 Feb 92	**MASSIVE ATTACK EP** *Wild Bunch WBRS 4*	**27**	4
29 Oct 94	**SLY** *Wild Bunch WBRDX 5*	**24**	4
21 Jan 95	**PROTECTION** *Wild Bunch WBRX 6* [2]	**14**	4
1 Apr 95	**KARMACOMA** *Wild Bunch WBRX 7*	**28**	4

[1] Massive [2] Massive Attack featuring Tracey Thorn

Tracks on Massive Attack EP: Hymn Of The Big Wheel / Home Of The Whale / Be Thankful / Any Love.

MASSIVO featuring TRACY
UK, male / female vocal / instrumental group **11 wks**

| 26 May 90 | **LOVING YOU** *Debut DEBT 3097* | **25** | 11 |

MASTER SINGERS *UK, male vocal group* **7 wks**

| 14 Apr 66 | **HIGHWAY CODE** *Parlophone R 5428* | **25** | 6 |
| 17 Nov 66 | **WEATHER FORECAST** *Parlophone R 5523* | **50** | 1 |

MASTERMIXERS – *See JIVE BUNNY and the MASTERMIXERS*

MASTERS AT WORK – *See INDIA*

Sammy MASTERS *US, male vocalist* **5 wks**

| 9 Jun 60 | **ROCKIN' RED WING** *Warner Bros. WB 10* | **36** | 5 |

MATCH *UK, male vocal / instrumental group* **3 wks**

| 16 Jun 79 | **BOOGIE MAN** *Flamingo FM 2* | **48** | 3 |

MATCHBOX *UK, male vocal / instrumental group* **66 wks**

3 Nov 79	**ROCKABILLY REBEL** *Magnet MAG 155*	**18**	12
19 Jan 80	**BUZZ BUZZ A DIDDLE IT** *Magnet MAG 157*	**22**	8
10 May 80	**MIDNITE DYNAMOS** *Magnet MAG 169*	**14**	12
27 Sep 80 ●	**WHEN YOU ASK ABOUT LOVE** *Magnet MAG 191*	**4**	12
29 Nov 80	**OVER THE RAINBOW – YOU BELONG TO ME (MEDLEY)** *Magnet MAG 192*	**15**	11
4 Apr 81	**BABES IN THE WOOD** *Magnet MAG 193*	**46**	6
1 Aug 81	**LOVE'S MADE A FOOL OF YOU** *Magnet MAG 194*	**63**	3
29 May 82	**ONE MORE SATURDAY NIGHT** *Magnet MAG 223*	**63**	2

MATCHROOM MOB – *See CHAS and DAVE*

Mireille MATHIEU *France, female vocalist* **7 wks**

| 13 Dec 67 | **LA DERNIERE VALSE** *Columbia DB 8323* | **26** | 7 |

Johnny MATHIS *US, male vocalist* **137 wks**

23 May 58	**TEACHER TEACHER** *Fontana H 130*	**27**	5
26 Sep 58 ●	**A CERTAIN SMILE** *Fontana H 142*	**4**	16
19 Dec 58	**WINTER WONDERLAND** *Fontana H 165*	**17**	3
7 Aug 59 ●	**SOMEONE** *Fontana H 199*	**6**	15
27 Nov 59	**THE BEST OF EVERYTHING** *Fontana H 218*	**30**	1
29 Jan 60	**MISTY** *Fontana H 219*	**12**	9
24 Mar 60	**YOU ARE BEAUTIFUL** *Fontana H 234*	**38**	8
14 Apr 60	**MISTY (re-entry)** *Fontana H 219*	**46**	2
26 May 60	**YOU ARE BEAUTIFUL (re-entry)** *Fontana H 234*	**46**	1
28 Jul 60	**STARBRIGHT** *Fontana H 254*	**47**	2
6 Oct 60 ●	**MY LOVE FOR YOU** *Fontana H 267*	**9**	18
4 Apr 63	**WHAT WILL MARY SAY** *CBS AAG 135*	**49**	1
25 Jan 75 ●	**I'M STONE IN LOVE WITH YOU** *CBS 2653*	**10**	12
13 Nov 76 ★	**WHEN A CHILD IS BORN (SOLEADO)** *CBS 4599*	**1**	12
25 Mar 78 ●	**TOO MUCH TOO LITTLE TOO LATE** *CBS 6164* [1]	**3**	14
29 Jul 78	**YOU'RE ALL I NEED TO GET BY** *CBS 6483* [1]	**45**	6
11 Aug 79	**GONE GONE GONE** *CBS 7730*	**15**	10

| 26 Dec 81 | **WHEN A CHILD IS BORN** *CBS S 1758* [2] | **74** | 2 |

[1] Johnny Mathis and Deniece Williams [2] Johnny Mathis and Gladys Knight

Ivan MATIAS *US, male vocalist* **1 wk**

| 6 Apr 96 | **SO GOOD (TO COME HOME TO) / I'VE HAD ENOUGH** *Arista 74321345072* | **69** | 1 |

MATT BIANCO *UK, male vocalist* **65 wks**

11 Feb 84	**GET OUT OF YOUR LAZY BED** *WEA BIANCO 1*	**15**	8
14 Apr 84	**SNEAKING OUT THE BACK DOOR / MATT'S MOOD** *WEA YZ 3*	**44**	7
10 Nov 84	**HALF A MINUTE** *WEA YZ 26*	**23**	10
2 Mar 85	**MORE THAN I CAN BEAR** *WEA YZ 34*	**50**	7
5 Oct 85	**YEH YEH** *WEA YZ 46*	**13**	10
1 Mar 86	**JUST CAN'T STAND IT** *WEA YZ 62*	**66**	2
14 Jun 86	**DANCING IN THE STREET** *WEA YZ 72*	**64**	3
4 Jun 88	**DON'T BLAME IT ON THAT GIRL / WAP-BAM-BOOGIE** *WEA YZ 188*	**11**	13
27 Aug 88	**GOOD TIMES** *WEA YZ 302*	**55**	3
4 Feb 89	**NERVOUS / WAP BAM BOOGIE (re-mix)** *WEA YZ 328*	**59**	4

Matt's Mood only credited from 5 May 84. Act was a UK / Poland male / female vocal / instrumental group on first five hits.

Al MATTHEWS *US, male vocalist* **8 wks**

| 23 Aug 75 | **FOOL** *CBS 3429* | **16** | 8 |

John MATTHEWS – *See UNDERCOVER*

MATTHEWS SOUTHERN COMFORT
UK, male vocal / instrumental group **18 wks**

| 26 Sep 70 ★ | **WOODSTOCK** *Uni UNS 526* | **1** | 18 |

MATUMBI *UK, male vocal / instrumental group* **7 wks**

| 29 Sep 79 | **POINT OF VIEW** *Matumbi RIC 101* | **35** | 7 |

Susan MAUGHAN *UK, female vocalist* **25 wks**

11 Oct 62 ●	**BOBBY'S GIRL** *Philips 326544 BF*	**3**	19
14 Feb 63	**HAND A HANDKERCHIEF TO HELEN** *Philips 326562 BF*	**41**	3
9 May 63	**SHE'S NEW TO YOU** *Philips 326586 BF*	**45**	3

MAUREEN *UK, female vocalist* **22 wks**

26 Nov 88 ●	**SAY A LITTLE PRAYER** *Rhythm King DOOD 3* [1]	**10**	10
16 Jun 90	**THINKING OF YOU** *Urban URB 55*	**11**	9
12 Jan 91	**WHERE HAS ALL THE LOVE GONE** *Urban URB 65*	**51**	3

[1] Bomb The Bass featuring Maureen

Some copies of Thinking Of You are credited to the fuller name of Maureen Walsh.

Paul MAURIAT *France, orchestra* **14 wks**

| 21 Feb 68 | **LOVE IS BLUE (L'AMOUR EST BLEU)** *Philips BF 1637* | **12** | 14 |

MAX Q *Australia, male vocal / instrumental duo* **3 wks**

| 17 Feb 90 | **SOMETIMES** *Mercury MXQ 2* | **53** | 3 |

MAX WEBSTER
Canada, male vocal / instrumental group　　　　**3 wks**

| 19 May 79 | **PARADISE SKIES** *Capitol CL 16079* | **43** | 3 |

MAXIMA featuring LILY
UK / Spain, male / female vocal / instrumental duo　　**2 wks**

| 14 Aug 93 | **IBIZA** *Yo! Yo! CDLILY 1* | **55** | 2 |

MAXWELL *US, male vocalist*　　　　**4 wks**

| 11 May 96 | **...'TIL THE COPS COME KNOCKIN' THE OPUS** *Columbia 6631792* | **63** | 1 |
| 24 Aug 96 | **ASCENSION NO ONE'S GONNA LOVE YOU SO DON'T EVER WONDER** *Columbia 6636265* | **39** | 3 |

MAXX
UK / Sweden / Germany, male / female vocal / instrumental group　**24 wks**

21 May 94	●	**GET-A-WAY** *Pulse 8 CDLOSE 59*	**4**	12
6 Aug 94	●	**NO MORE (I CAN'T STAND IT)** *Pulse 8 CDLOSE 66*	**8**	8
29 Oct 94		**YOU CAN GET IT** *Pulse 8 CDLOSE 75*	**21**	3
22 Jul 95		**I CAN MAKE YOU FEEL LIKE** *Pulse 8 CDLOSE 88*	**56**	1

Billy MAY *US, orchestra*　　　　**10 wks**

| 27 Apr 56 | ● | **MAIN TITLE THEME FROM 'MAN WITH THE GOLDEN ARM'** *Capitol CL 14551* | **9** | 10 |

Brian MAY *UK, male vocalist / instrumentalist – guitar*　　**31 wks**

5 Nov 83		**STAR FLEET** *EMI 5436* [1]	**65**	3
7 Dec 91	●	**DRIVEN BY YOU** *Parlophone R 6304*	**6**	9
5 Sep 92	●	**TOO MUCH LOVE WILL KILL YOU** *Parlophone R 6320*	**5**	9
17 Oct 92		**WE ARE THE CHAMPIONS** *PolyGram TV PO 229* [2]	**66**	1
21 Nov 92		**BACK TO THE LIGHT** *Parlophone R 6329*	**19**	4
19 Jun 93		**RESURRECTION** *Parlophone CDRS 6351* [3]	**23**	3
18 Dec 93		**LAST HORIZON** *Parlophone CDR 6371*	**51**	2

[1] Brian May and Friends [2] Hank Marvin featuring Brian May [3] Brian May with Cozy Powell

Lisa MAY *UK, female vocalist*　　　　**2 wks**

| 15 Jul 95 | **WISHING ON A STAR** *Urban Gorilla UG 3CD* [1] | **16** | 1 |
| 14 Sep 96 | **THE CURSE OF VOODOO RAY** *Fontana VOOCD 1* | **64** | 1 |

[1] 88.3 featuring Lisa MAY

Mary MAY *UK, female vocalist*　　　　**1 wk**

| 27 Feb 64 | **ANYONE WHO HAD A HEART** *Fontana TF 440* | **49** | 1 |

Simon MAY *UK, male vocalist*　　　　**21 wks**

9 Oct 76	●	**SUMMER OF MY LIFE** *Pye 7N 45627*	**7**	8
21 May 77		**WE'LL GATHER LILACS – ALL MY LOVING (MEDLEY)** *Pye 7N 45688*	**49**	1
4 Jun 77		**WE'LL GATHER LILACS – ALL MY LOVING (MEDLEY) (re-entry)** *Pye 7N 45688*	**50**	1
26 Oct 85		**HOWARD'S WAY** *BBC RESL 174* [1]	**21**	11

[1] Simon May Orchestra

See also Anita Dobson; Marti Webb.

Curtis MAYFIELD *US, male vocalist*　　　　**18 wks**

31 Jul 71	**MOVE ON UP** *Buddah 2011 080*	**12**	10
2 Dec 78	**NO GOODBYES** *Atlantic LV 1*	**65**	3
30 May 87	**(CELEBRATE) THE DAY AFTER YOU** *RCA MONK 6* [1]	**52**	2
29 Sep 90	**SUPERFLY 1990** *Capitol CL 586* [2]	**48**	3

[1] Blow Monkeys with Curtis Mayfield [2] Curtis Mayfield and Ice-T

MAYTALS *Jamaica, male vocal / instrumental group*　　**4 wks**

| 25 Apr 70 | **MONKEY MAN** *Trojan TR 7711* | **50** | 1 |
| 9 May 70 | **MONKEY MAN (re-entry)** *Trojan TR 7711* | **47** | 3 |

MAYTE *US, female vocalist*　　　　**1 wk**

| 18 Nov 95 | **IF EYE LOVE U 2 NIGHT** *NPG 0061635* | **67** | 1 |

MAZE featuring Frankie BEVERLY
US, male vocal / instrumental group　　　　**14 wks**

20 Jul 85	**TOO MANY GAMES** *Capitol CL 363*	**36**	7
23 Aug 86	**I WANNA BE WITH YOU** *Capitol CL 421*	**55**	3
27 May 89	**JOY AND PAIN** *Capitol CL 531* [1]	**57**	4

[1] Maze

Kym MAZELLE *US, female vocalist*　　　　**61 wks**

12 Nov 88		**USELESS (I DON'T NEED YOU NOW)** *Syncopate SY 18*	**53**	3
14 Jan 89	●	**WAIT** *RCA PB 42595* [1]	**7**	10
25 Mar 89		**GOT TO GET YOU BACK** *Syncopate SY 25*	**29**	4
7 Oct 89		**LOVE STRAIN** *Syncopate SY 30*	**52**	3
20 Jan 90		**WAS THAT ALL IT WAS** *Syncopate SY 32*	**33**	6
26 May 90		**USELESS (I DON'T NEED YOU NOW) (re-mix)** *Syncopate SY 36*	**48**	2
24 Nov 90		**MISSING YOU** *Ten TEN 345* [2]	**22**	7
25 May 91		**NO ONE CAN LOVE YOU MORE THAN ME** *Parlophone R 6287*	**62**	2
26 Dec 92		**LOVE ME THE RIGHT WAY** *Arista 74321128097* [3]	**22**	10
11 Jun 94		**NO MORE TEARS (ENOUGH IS ENOUGH)** *Ding Dong 74321209032* [4]	**13**	7
8 Oct 94		**GIMME ALL YOUR LOVIN'** *Ding Dong 74321231322* [4]	**22**	3
23 Dec 95		**SEARCHING FOR THE GOLDEN EYE** *Eternal WEA 027CD* [5]	**40**	3
28 Sep 96		**LOVE ME THE RIGHT WAY (re-mix)** *Logic 74321404442* [3]	**55**	1

[1] Robert Howard and Kym Mazelle [2] Soul II Soul featuring Kym Mazelle [3] Rapination and Kym Mazelle [4] Jocelyn Brown and Kym Mazelle [5] Motiv 8 and Kym Mazelle

MAZZY STAR *US, male / female vocal / instrumental duo*　**3 wks**

| 27 Aug 94 | **FADE INTO YOU** *Capitol CDCL 720* | **48** | 1 |
| 2 Nov 96 | **FLOWERS IN DECEMBER** *Capitol CDCL 781* | **40** | 2 |

MC DUKE *US, male rapper*　　　　**1 wk**

| 11 Mar 89 | **I'M RIFFIN (ENGLISH RASTA)** *Music Of Life 7NOTE 25* | **75** | 1 |

MC ERIC – *See TECHNOTRONIC*

MC FIX IT – *See ANTICAPPELLA*

MC Mikee FREEDOM – *See NOMAD*

MC HAMMER – *See HAMMER*

MC LETHAL UK, male producer   1 wk

14 Nov 92	**THE RAVE DIGGER** Network NWKT 60	**66**	1

MC LYTE US, female rapper   3 wks

15 Jan 94	**RUFFNECK** Atlantic A 8336CD	**67**	1
29 Jun 96	**KEEP ON KEEPIN' ON** East West A 4287CD [1]	**39**	2

[1] MC Lyte featuring Xscape

MC MARIO – See AMBASSADORS OF FUNK featuring MC MARIO

MC MIKER 'G' and Deejay SVEN
Holland, male vocal / instrumental rap duo   7 wks

6 Sep 86	● **HOLIDAY RAP** Debut DEBT 3008	**6**	7

MC SAR – See REAL McCOY

MC SKAT KAT and the STRAY MOB
US, male vocal / instrumental group   2 wks

9 Nov 91	**SKAT STRUT** Virgin America VUS 51	**64**	2

M.C. SOLAAR – See URBAN SPECIES

MC SPY-D + FRIENDS
UK, male / female vocal / instrumental group   2 wks

11 Mar 95	**THE AMAZING SPIDER-MAN** Parlophone CDR 6404	**37**	2

MC TUNES UK, male rapper   18 wks

2 Jun 90	● **THE ONLY RHYME THAT BITES** ZTT ZANG 3 [1]	**10**	10
15 Sep 90	**TUNES SPLITS THE ATOM** ZTT ZANG 6 [1]	**18**	7
1 Dec 90	**PRIMARY RHYMING** ZTT ZANG 10	**67**	1

[1] MC Tunes versus 808 State

MC WILDSKI UK, male rapper   10 wks

8 Jul 89	**BLAME IT ON THE BASSLINE** Go.Beat GOD 33 [1]	**29**	6
3 Mar 90	**WARRIOR** Arista 112956	**49**	4

[1] Norman Cook featuring MC Wildski

Blame It On The Bassline *was listed with* Won't Talk About It *by Norman Cook featuring Billy Bragg.*

ME AND YOU featuring WE THE PEOPLE BAND
Jamaica / UK, male / female vocal / instrumental group   9 wks

28 Jul 79	**YOU NEVER KNOW WHAT YOU'VE GOT** Laser LAS 8	**31**	9

ME ME ME UK, male vocal / instrumental group   4 wks

17 Aug 96	**HANGING AROUND** Indolent DUFF 005CD	**19**	4

Abigail MEAD and Nigel GOULDING
UK / US, female / male producers   10 wks

26 Sep 87	● **FULL METAL JACKET (I WANNA BE YOUR DRILL INSTRUCTOR)** Warner Bros. W 8187	**2**	10

MEAT BEAT MANIFESTO UK, male production duo   1 wk

20 Feb 93	**MINDSTREAM** Play It Again Sam BIAS 232CD	**55**	1

MEAT LOAF US, male vocalist   142 wks

20 May 78	**YOU TOOK THE WORDS RIGHT OUT OF MY MOUTH** Epic EPC 5980	**33**	8
19 Aug 78	**TWO OUT OF THREE AIN'T BAD** Epic EPC 6281	**32**	8
10 Feb 79	**BAT OUT OF HELL** Epic EPC 7018	**15**	7
26 Sep 81	**I'M GONNA LOVE HER FOR BOTH OF US** Epic EPCA 1580	**62**	3
28 Nov 81	● **DEAD RINGER FOR LOVE** Epic EPCA 1697	**5**	17
28 May 83	**IF YOU REALLY WANT TO** Epic A 3357	**59**	2
24 Sep 83	**MIDNIGHT AT THE LOST AND FOUND** Epic A 3748	**17**	8
14 Jan 84	**RAZOR'S EDGE** Epic A 4080	**41**	3
6 Oct 84	**MODERN GIRL** Arista ARIST 585	**17**	9
22 Dec 84	**NOWHERE FAST** Arista ARIST 600	**67**	4
23 Mar 85	**PIECE OF THE ACTION** Arista ARIST 603	**47**	5
30 Aug 86	**ROCK 'N' ROLL MERCENARIES** Arista ARIST 666 [1]	**31**	6
22 Jun 91	**DEAD RINGER FOR LOVE (re-issue)** Epic 6569827	**53**	2
27 Jun 92	**TWO OUT OF THREE AIN'T BAD (re-issue)** Epic 6574917	**69**	1
9 Oct 93	★ **I'D DO ANYTHING FOR LOVE (BUT I WON'T DO THAT)** Virgin VSCDT 1443	**1**	19
18 Dec 93	● **BAT OUT OF HELL (re-issue)** Epic 6600062	**8**	9
19 Feb 94	**ROCK AND ROLL DREAMS COME THROUGH** Virgin VSCDT 1479	**11**	7
7 May 94	**OBJECTS IN THE REAR VIEW MIRROR MAY APPEAR CLOSER THAN THEY ARE** Virgin VSCDT 1492	**26**	4
28 Oct 95	● **I'D LIE FOR YOU (AND THAT'S THE TRUTH)** Virgin VSCDT 1563	**2**	11
27 Jan 96	● **NOT A DRY EYE IN THE HOUSE** Virgin VSCDT 1567	**7**	6
27 Apr 96	**RUNNIN' FOR THE RED LIGHT (I GOTTA LIFE)** Virgin VSCDX 1582	**21**	3

[1] Meat Loaf featuring John Parr

Dead Ringer For Love *features Cher as uncredited co-vocalist.*

MECHANICS – See MIKE + the MECHANICS

MECO US, orchestra   9 wks

1 Oct 77	● **'STAR WARS' THEME – CANTINA BAND** RCA XB 1028	**7**	9

Glenn MEDEIROS US, male vocalist   26 wks

18 Jun 88	★ **NOTHING'S GONNA CHANGE MY LOVE FOR YOU** London LON 184	**1**	13
3 Sep 88	**LONG AND LASTING LOVE (ONCE IN A LIFETIME)** London LON 202	**42**	4
30 Jun 90	**SHE AIN'T WORTH IT** London LON 265 [1]	**12**	9

[1] Glenn Medeiros featuring Bobby Brown

Paul MEDFORD – See Letitia DEAN and Paul MEDFORD

MEDICINE HEAD UK, male vocal / instrumental duo   37 wks

26 Jun 71	**(AND THE) PICTURES IN THE SKY** Dandelion DAN 7003	**22**	8
5 May 73	● **ONE AND ONE IS ONE** Polydor 2001 432	**3**	13
4 Aug 73	**RISING SUN** Polydor 2058 389	**11**	9
9 Feb 74	**SLIP AND SLIDE** Polydor 2058 436	**22**	7

MEDICINE SHOW – See DR. HOOK

Bill MEDLEY US, male vocalist   29 wks

31 Oct 87	● **(I'VE HAD) THE TIME OF MY LIFE (LOVE THEME FROM 'DIRTY DANCING')** RCA PB 49625 [1]	**6**	12

27 Aug 88	HE AIN'T HEAVY, HE'S MY BROTHER		
	Scotti Brothers PO 10	25	6
15 Dec 90	● (I'VE HAD) THE TIME OF MY LIFE (re-entry)		
	RCA PB 49625 [1]	8	11

[1] Bill Medley and Jennifer Warnes

Michael MEDWIN, Bernard BRESSLAW, Alfie BASS and Leslie FYSON
UK, male vocal group   **9 wks**

| 30 May 58 | ● THE SIGNATURE TUNE OF 'THE ARMY GAME' | | |
| | HMV POP 490 | 5 | 9 |

See also Bernard Bresslaw.

MEECHIE US, female vocalist   **1 wk**

| 2 Sep 95 | YOU BRING ME JOY Vibe MCSTD 2069 | 74 | 1 |

Tony MEEHAN COMBO
UK, male instrumental group, Tony Meehan – drums   **4 wks**

| 16 Jan 64 | SONG OF MEXICO Decca F 11801 | 39 | 4 |

See also Jet Harris and Tony Meehan.

MEGA CITY FOUR UK, male vocal / instrumental group   **7 wks**

19 Oct 91	WORDS THAT SAY Big Life MEGA 2	66	1
8 Feb 92	STOP (EP) Big Life MEGA 3	36	2
16 May 92	SHIVERING SAND Big Life MEGA 4	35	2
1 May 93	IRON SKY Big Life MEGAD 5	48	1
17 Jul 93	WALLFLOWER Big Life MEGAD 6	69	1

Tracks on Stop (EP): Stop / Desert Song / Back To Zero / Overlap.

MEGABASS – See VARIOUS ARTISTS (MONTAGES)

MEGADETH US, male vocal / instrumental group   **32 wks**

19 Dec 87	WAKE UP DEAD Capitol CL 476	65	2
27 Feb 88	ANARCHY IN THE UK Capitol CL 480	45	3
21 May 88	MARY JANE Capitol CL 489	46	2
13 Jan 90	NO MORE MR. NICE GUY SBK SBK 4	13	6
29 Sep 90	HOLY WARS... THE PUNISHMENT DUE Capitol CLP 588	24	3
16 Mar 91	HANGAR 18 Capitol CLS 604	26	4
27 Jun 92	SYMPHONY OF DESTRUCTION Capitol CLS 662	15	3
24 Oct 92	SKIN O' MY TEETH Capitol CLP 669	13	3
29 May 93	SWEATING BULLETS Capitol CDCL 682	26	3
7 Jan 95	TRAIN OF CONSEQUENCES Capitol CDCL 730	22	3

Melle MEL – See GRANDMASTER FLASH, Melle MEL and the FURIOUS FIVE

MEL and KIM UK, female vocal duo   **51 wks**

20 Sep 86	● SHOWING OUT (GET FRESH AT THE WEEKEND)		
	Supreme SUPE 107	3	19
7 Mar 87	★ RESPECTABLE Supreme SUPE 111	1	15
11 Jul 87	● F.L.M. Supreme SUPE 113	7	10
27 Feb 88	● THAT'S THE WAY IT IS Supreme SUPE 117	10	7

MEL and KIM – See Mel SMITH; Kim WILDE

George MELACHRINO ORCHESTRA
UK, orchestra   **9 wks**

| 12 Oct 56 | AUTUMN CONCERTO HMV B 10958 | 18 | 9 |

MELANIE US, female vocalist   **35 wks**

26 Sep 70	● RUBY TUESDAY Buddah 2011 038	9	14
9 Jan 71	RUBY TUESDAY (re-entry) Buddah 2011 038	43	1
16 Jan 71	WHAT HAVE THEY DONE TO MY SONG MA		
	Buddah 2011 038	39	1
1 Jan 72	● BRAND NEW KEY Buddah 2011 105	4	12
16 Feb 74	WILL YOU LOVE ME TOMORROW		
	Neighbourhood NBH 9	37	5
24 Sep 83	EVERY BREATH OF THE WAY		
	Neighbourhood HOOD NB1	70	2

John Cougar MELLENCAMP US, male vocalist   **18 wks**

23 Oct 82	JACK AND DIANE Riva RIVA 37 [1]	25	8
1 Feb 86	SMALL TOWN Riva JCM 5	53	4
10 May 86	R.O.C.K. IN THE U.S.A. Riva JCM 6	67	3
3 Sep 94	WILD NIGHT Mercury MERCD 409 [2]	34	3

[1] John Cougar [2] John Mellencamp featuring Me'Shell NdegeoCello

MELODIANS Jamaica, male vocal / instrumental group   **1 wk**

| 10 Jan 70 | SWEET SENSATION Trojan TR 695 | 41 | 1 |

MELODY MAKERS – See Ziggy MARLEY and the MELODY MAKERS

MELTDOWN UK / US, male instrumental / production duo   **1 wk**

| 27 Apr 96 | MY LIFE IS IN YOUR HANDS Sony S3 DANU 7CD | 44 | 1 |

Harold MELVIN and the BLUENOTES
US, male vocal group   **52 wks**

13 Jan 73	● IF YOU DON'T KNOW ME BY NOW CBS 8496	9	9
12 Jan 74	THE LOVE I LOST Philadelphia International PIR 1879	21	8
13 Apr 74	SATISFACTION GUARANTEED (OR TAKE YOUR		
	LOVE BACK) Philadelphia International PIR 2187	32	6
31 May 75	GET OUT Route RT 06	35	5
28 Feb 76	WAKE UP EVERYBODY		
	Philadelphia International PIR 3866	23	7
22 Jan 77	● DON'T LEAVE ME THIS WAY		
	Philadelphia International PIR 4909 [1]	5	10
2 Apr 77	REACHING FOR THE WORLD ABC 4161	48	1
28 Apr 84	DON'T GIVE ME UP London LON 47	59	4
4 Aug 84	TODAY'S YOUR LUCKY DAY London LON 52 [2]	66	2

[1] Harold Melvin and the Bluenotes featuring Theodore Pendergrass
[2] Harold Melvin and the Bluenotes featuring Nikko

MEMBERS UK, male vocal / instrumental group   **14 wks**

| 3 Feb 79 | THE SOUND OF THE SUBURBS Virgin VS 242 | 12 | 9 |
| 7 Apr 79 | OFFSHORE BANKING BUSINESS Virgin VS 248 | 31 | 5 |

MEN AT WORK
Australia, male vocal / instrumental group   **39 wks**

30 Oct 82	WHO CAN IT BE NOW? Epic EPC A 2392	45	5
8 Jan 83	★ DOWN UNDER Epic EPC A 1980	1	12
9 Apr 83	OVERKILL Epic EPC A 3220	21	10
2 Jul 83	IT'S A MISTAKE Epic EPC A 3475	33	6
10 Sep 83	DR. HECKYLL AND MR. JIVE Epic EPC A 3668	31	6

MEN THEY COULDN'T HANG
UK, male vocal / instrumental group   **4 wks**

| 2 Apr 88 | THE COLOURS Magnet SELL 6 | 61 | 4 |

233

MEN WITHOUT HATS
Canada, male vocal / instrumental group **11 wks**

8 Oct 83	● **THE SAFETY DANCE** *Statik TAK 1*	6	11

Sergio MENDES *Brazil, male conductor* **5 wks**

9 Jul 83	**NEVER GONNA LET YOU GO** *A & M AM 118*	45	5

Uncredited vocals by Joe Pizzulo and Leza Miller.

Andrea MENDEZ *UK, female vocalist* **1 wk**

3 Aug 96	**BRING ME LOVE** *AM:PM 5817872*	44	1

MENSWEAR *UK, male vocal / instrumental group* **18 wks**

15 Apr 95	**I'LL MANAGE SOMEHOW** *Laurel LAUCD 4*	49	1
1 Jul 95	**DAYDREAMER** *Laurel LAUCD 5*	14	4
30 Sep 95	**STARDUST** *Laurel LAUCD 6*	16	3
16 Dec 95	**SLEEPING IN** *Laurel LAUCD 7*	24	3
23 Mar 96	● **BEING BRAVE** *Laurel LAUCD 8*	10	4
7 Sep 96	**WE LOVE YOU** *Laurel LAUCD 11*	22	3

MENTAL AS ANYTHING
Australia, male vocal / instrumental group **13 wks**

7 Feb 87	● **LIVE IT UP** *Epic ANY 1*	3	13

Freddie MERCURY *UK, male vocalist* **79 wks**

22 Sep 84	● **LOVE KILLS** *CBS A 4735*	10	8
20 Apr 85	**I WAS BORN TO LOVE YOU** *CBS A 6019*	11	10
13 Jul 85	**MADE IN HEAVEN** *CBS A 6413*	57	4
21 Sep 85	**LIVING ON MY OWN** *CBS A 6555*	50	3
24 May 86	**TIME** *EMI EMI 5559*	32	5
7 Mar 87	● **THE GREAT PRETENDER** *Parlophone R 6151*	4	9
7 Nov 87	● **BARCELONA** *Polydor POSP 887* [1]	8	9
8 Aug 92	● **BARCELONA (re-issue)** *Polydor PO 221* [1]	2	8
12 Dec 92	● **IN MY DEFENCE** *Parlophone R 6331*	8	7
6 Feb 93	**THE GREAT PRETENDER (re-issue)** *Parlophone CDR 6336*	29	3
31 Jul 93	★ **LIVING ON MY OWN (re-mix)** *Parlophone CDR 6355*	1	13

[1] Freddie Mercury and Montserrat Caballe

MERCY MERCY *UK, male vocal / instrumental group* **2 wks**

21 Sep 85	**WHAT ARE WE GONNA DO ABOUT IT?** *Ensign ENY 522*	59	2

Tony MERRICK *UK, male vocalist* **1 wk**

2 Jun 66	**LADY JANE** *Columbia DB 7913*	49	1

MERSEYBEATS *UK, male vocal / instrumental group* **64 wks**

12 Sep 63	**IT'S LOVE THAT REALLY COUNTS** *Fontana TF 412*	24	12
16 Jan 64	● **I THINK OF YOU** *Fontana TF 431*	5	17
16 Apr 64	**DON'T TURN AROUND** *Fontana TF 459*	13	11
9 Jul 64	**WISHIN' AND HOPIN'** *Fontana TF 482*	13	10
5 Nov 64	**LAST NIGHT** *Fontana TF 504*	40	3
14 Oct 65	**I LOVE YOU, YES I DO** *Fontana TF 607*	22	8
20 Jan 66	**I STAND ACCUSED** *Fontana TF 645*	38	3

MERSEYS *UK, male vocal duo* **13 wks**

28 Apr 66	● **SORROW** *Fontana TF 694*	4	13

MERTON PARKAS *UK, male vocal / instrumental group* **6 wks**

4 Aug 79	**YOU NEED WHEELS** *Beggars Banquet BEG 22*	40	6

Mady MESPLÉ and Danielle MILLET with the PARIS OPERA-COMIQUE ORCHESTRA conduced by Alain Lombard
France, female vocal duo and orchestra **4 wks**

6 Apr 85	**FLOWER DUET (FROM LAKME)** *EMI 5481*	47	4

MESSIAH *UK, male instrumental / production group* **13 wks**

20 Jun 92	**TEMPLE OF DREAMS** *Kickin KICK 12S*	20	5
26 Sep 92	**I FEEL LOVE** *Kickin KICK 22S* [1]	19	5
27 Nov 93	**THUNDERDOME** *WEA YZ 790CD1*	29	3

[1] Messiah featuring Precious Wilson

METAL GURUS *UK, male vocal / instrumental group* **2 wks**

8 Dec 90	**MERRY XMAS EVERYBODY** *Mercury GURU 1*	55	2

METALHEADS – *See GOLDIE*

METALLICA
US / Denmark, male vocal / instrumental group **45 wks**

22 Aug 87	**THE $5.98 EP – GARAGE DAYS REVISITED** *Vertigo METAL 112*	27	4
3 Sep 88	**HARVESTER OF SORROW** *Vertigo METAL 212*	20	3
22 Apr 89	**ONE** *Vertigo METAL 5*	13	7
10 Aug 91	● **ENTER SANDMAN** *Vertigo METAL 7*	5	4
9 Nov 91	**THE UNFORGIVEN** *Vertigo METAL 8*	15	4
2 May 92	● **NOTHING ELSE MATTERS** *Vertigo METAL 10*	6	6
31 Oct 92	**WHEREVER I MAY ROAM** *Vertigo METAL 9*	25	4
20 Feb 93	**SAD BUT TRUE** *Vertigo METCD 11*	20	3
1 Jun 96	● **UNTIL IT SLEEPS** *Vertigo UKMETCD 12*	5	4
28 Sep 96	**HERO OF THE DAY** *Vertigo METCD 13*	17	4
7 Dec 96	**MAMA SAID** *Vertigo METCD 14*	19	2

Tracks on The $5.98 EP: Garage Days Revisited / Helpless / Crash Course in Brain Surgery / The Small Hours / Last Caress / Green Hell.

METEORS *UK, male vocal / instrumental group* **2 wks**

26 Feb 83	**JOHNNY REMEMBER ME** *ID EYE 1*	66	2

Pat METHENY GROUP - *See David BOWIE*

METHOD MAN *US, male rapper* **6 wks**

29 Apr 95	**RELEASE YO' DELF** *Def Jam DEFCD 6*	46	1
29 Jul 95	● **I'LL BE THERE FOR YOU – YOU'RE ALL I NEED TO GET BY** *Def Jam DEFCD 11* [1]	10	5

[1] Method Man featuring Mary J Blige

MEZZOFORTE *Iceland, male instrumental group* **10 wks**

5 Mar 83	**GARDEN PARTY** *Steinar STE 705*	17	9
11 Jun 83	**ROCKALL** *Steinar STE 710*	75	1

MFSB *US, orchestra* **18 wks**

27 Apr 74	**TSOP (THE SOUND OF PHILADELPHIA)** *Philadelphia International PIR 2289* [1]	22	9

| 26 Jul 75 | **SEXY** *Philadelphia International PIR 3381* | **37** | 5 |
| 31 Jan 81 | **MYSTERIES OF THE WORLD** *Sound Of Philadelphia PIR 9501* | **41** | 4 |

[1] MFSB featuring the Three Degrees

M.G.'s – *See BOOKER T. and the M.G.'s*

MIAMI SOUND MACHINE – *See Gloria ESTEFAN*

George MICHAEL *UK, male vocalist* **178 wks**

4 Aug 84	★ **CARELESS WHISPER** *Epic A 4603*	**1**	17
5 Apr 86	★ **A DIFFERENT CORNER** *Epic A 7033*	**1**	10
31 Jan 87	★ **I KNEW YOU WERE WAITING (FOR ME)** *Epic DUET 2* [1]	**1**	9
13 Jun 87	● **I WANT YOUR SEX** *Epic LUST 1*	**3**	10
24 Oct 87	● **FAITH** *Epic EMU 3*	**2**	12
9 Jan 88	**FATHER FIGURE** *Epic EMU 4*	**11**	6
23 Apr 88	● **ONE MORE TRY** *Epic EMU 5*	**8**	7
16 Jul 88	**MONKEY** *Epic EMU 6*	**13**	6
3 Dec 88	**KISSING A FOOL** *Epic EMU 7*	**18**	6
25 Aug 90	● **PRAYING FOR TIME** *Epic GEO 1*	**6**	7
27 Oct 90	**WAITING FOR THAT DAY** *Epic GEO 2*	**23**	5
15 Dec 90	**FREEDOM** *Epic GEO 3*	**28**	6
16 Feb 91	**HEAL THE PAIN** *Epic 6566477*	**31**	4
30 Mar 91	**COWBOYS AND ANGELS** *Epic 6567747*	**45**	3
7 Dec 91	★ **DON'T LET THE SUN GO DOWN ON ME** *Epic 6576467* [2]	**1**	10
13 Jun 92	● **TOO FUNKY** *Epic 6580587*	**4**	9
1 May 93	● **FIVE LIVE EP** *Parlophone CDRS 6340* [3]	**1**	11
24 Jul 93	**FIVE LIVE EP (re-entry)** *Parlophone CDRS 6340* [3]	**74**	1
20 Jan 96	★ **JESUS TO A CHILD** *Virgin VSCDG 1571*	**1**	10
20 Apr 96	**JESUS TO A CHILD (re-entry)** *Virgin VSCDG 1571*	**68**	1
4 May 96	**FAST LOVE** *Virgin VSCDG 1579*	**1**	14
4 May 96	**JESUS TO A CHILD (2nd re-entry)** *Virgin VSCDG 1571*	**65**	2
31 Aug 96	● **SPINNING THE WHEEL** *Virgin VSCDG 1595*	**2**	12

[1] Aretha Franklin and George Michael [2] George Michael and Elton John
[3] George Michael and Queen with Lisa Stansfield

Tracks on Five Live EP: Somebody To Love / These Are The Days Of Our Lives / Calling You / Papa Was A Rolling Stone-Killer (medley). The first track on the EP features Queen, the second Queen and Lisa Stansfield. See also Elton John; Lisa Moorish.

MICHAELA *UK, female vocalist* **6 wks**

| 2 Sep 89 | ● **H-A-P-P-Y RADIO** *London H 1* | **62** | 4 |
| 28 Apr 90 | **TAKE GOOD CARE OF MY HEART** *London WAC 90* | **66** | 2 |

Lisa MICHAELIS – *See Frankie KNUCKLES*

Keith MICHELL *Australia, male vocalist* **25 wks**

27 Mar 71	**I'LL GIVE YOU THE EARTH (TOUS LES BATEAUX, TOUS LES OISEAUX)** *Spark SRL 1046*	**43**	1
17 Apr 71	**I'LL GIVE YOU THE EARTH (TOUS LES BATEAUX, TOUS LES OISEAUX) (re-entry)** *Spark SRL 1046*	**30**	10
26 Jan 80	● **CAPTAIN BEAKY / WILFRED THE WEASEL** *Polydor POSP 106*	**5**	10
29 Mar 80	**THE TRIAL OF HISSING SID** *Polydor HISS 1* [1]	**53**	4

[1] Keith Michell, Captain Beaky and his Band

MICHELLE *Trinidad, female vocalist* **1 wk**

| 8 Jun 96 | **STANDING HERE ALL ALONE** *Positiva CDTIV 54* | **69** | 1 |

Lloyd MICHELS – *See MISTURA featuring Lloyd MICHELS*

MICK and PAT – *See PAT and MICK*

MICROBE *UK, male vocalist* **7 wks**

| 14 May 69 | **GROOVY BABY** *CBS 4158* | **29** | 7 |

MICRODISNEY
Ireland, male vocal / instrumental group **3 wks**

| 21 Feb 87 | **TOWN TO TOWN** *Virgin VS 927* | **55** | 3 |

MIDDLE OF THE ROAD
UK, male / female vocal / instrumental group **76 wks**

5 Jun 71	★ **CHIRPY CHIRPY CHEEP CHEEP** *RCA 2047*	**1**	34
4 Sep 71	● **TWEEDLE DEE TWEEDLE DUM** *RCA 2110*	**2**	17
11 Dec 71	● **SOLEY SOLEY** *RCA 2151*	**5**	12
25 Mar 72	**SACRAMENTO (A WONDERFUL TOWN)** *RCA 2184*	**49**	1
8 Apr 72	**SACRAMENTO (A WONDERFUL TOWN) (re-entry)** *RCA 2184*	**23**	6
29 Jul 72	**SAMSON AND DELILAH** *RCA 2237*	**26**	6

MIDI XPRESS *UK, male vocal / instrumental duo* **1 wk**

| 11 May 96 | **CHASE** *Labello Dance LAD 26CD* | **73** | 1 |

Bette MIDLER *US, female vocalist* **26 wks**

17 Jun 89	● **WIND BENEATH MY WINGS** *Atlantic A 8972*	**5**	12
13 Oct 90	**FROM A DISTANCE** *Atlantic A 7820*	**45**	5
15 Jun 91	● **FROM A DISTANCE (re-entry)** *Atlantic A 7820*	**6**	9

MIDNIGHT BAND – *See Tony RALLO and the MIDNIGHT BAND*

MIDNIGHT COWBOY SOUNDTRACK
US, orchestra **4 wks**

| 8 Nov 80 | **MIDNIGHT COWBOY** *United Artists UP 634* | **47** | 4 |

MIDNIGHT OIL
Australia, male vocal / instrumental group **32 wks**

23 Apr 88	**BEDS ARE BURNING** *Sprint OIL 1*	**48**	5
2 Jul 88	**THE DEAD HEART** *Spring OIL 2*	**68**	2
25 Mar 89	● **BEDS ARE BURNING (re-issue)** *Sprint OIL 3*	**6**	13
1 Jul 89	**THE DEAD HEART (re-issue)** *Sprint OIL 4*	**62**	4
10 Feb 90	**BLUE SKY MINE** *CBS OIL 5*	**66**	2
17 Apr 93	**TRUGANINI** *Columbia 6590492*	**29**	4
3 Jul 93	**MY COUNTRY** *Columbia 6593702*	**66**	1
6 Nov 93	**IN THE VALLEY** *Columbia 6598492*	**60**	1

MIDNIGHT STAR
US, male / female vocal / instrumental group **26 wks**

23 Feb 85	**OPERATOR** *Solar MCA 942*	**66**	2
28 Jun 86	**HEADLINES** *Solar MCA 1065*	**16**	8
4 Oct 86	● **MIDAS TOUCH** *Solar MCA 1096*	**8**	10
7 Feb 87	**ENGINE NO. 9** *Solar MCA 1117*	**64**	3
2 May 87	**WET MY WHISTLE** *Solar MCA 1127*	**60**	3

MIGHTY AVENGERS
UK, male vocal / instrumental group **2 wks**

| 26 Nov 64 | **SO MUCH IN LOVE** *Decca F 11962* | **46** | 2 |

MIGHTY AVONS – *See Larry CUNNINGHAM and the MIGHTY AVONS*

MIGHTY DIAMONDS – *See VARIOUS ARTISTS* – Gimme Shelter (EP).

MIGHTY DUB KATZ UK, male producer – Norman Cook · **1 wk**

7 Dec 96	**JUST ANOTHER GROOVE** ffrr FCD 287	**43**	1

See also Norman Cook.

MIGHTY LEMON DROPS
UK, male vocal / instrumental group · **7 wks**

13 Sep 86	**THE OTHER SIDE OF YOU** Blue Guitar AZUR 1	**67**	2
18 Apr 87	**OUT OF HAND** Blue Guitar AZUR 4	**66**	3
23 Jan 88	**INSIDE OUT** Blue Guitar AZUR 6	**74**	2

MIGHTY MORPH'N POWER RANGERS
US, male / female vocal group · **13 wks**

17 Dec 94	● **POWER RANGERS** RCA 74321253022	**3**	9
25 Feb 95	**POWER RANGERS (re-entry)** RCA 74321253022	**57**	2
25 Mar 95	**POWER RANGERS (2nd re-entry)** RCA 74321253022	**65**	1
8 Apr 95	**POWER RANGERS (3rd re-entry)** RCA 74321253022	**74**	1

MIGHTY WAH – See WAH!

MIGIL FIVE UK, male vocal / instrumental group · **20 wks**

19 Mar 64	● **MOCKINGBIRD HILL** Pye 7N 15597	**10**	13
4 Jun 64	**NEAR YOU** Pye 7N 15645	**31**	7

MIG29 Italy, male instrumental / production group · **2 wks**

22 Feb 92	**MIG29** Champion CHAMP 292	**62**	2

MIKE UK, male producer – Mark Jolley · **2 wks**

19 Nov 94	**TWANGLING THREE FINGERS IN A BOX** Pukka CDMIKE 100	**40**	2

MIKE and the MECHANICS
UK, male vocal / instrumental group · **64 wks**

15 Feb 86	**SILENT RUNNING (ON DANGEROUS GROUND)** WEA U 8908	**21**	9
31 May 86	**ALL I NEED IS A MIRACLE** WEA U 8765	**53**	4
14 Jan 89	● **THE LIVING YEARS** WEA U 7717	**2**	11
16 Mar 91	**WORD OF MOUTH** Virgin VS 1345	**13**	10
15 Jun 91	**A TIME AND PLACE** Virgin VS 1351	**58**	3
8 Feb 92	**EVERYBODY GETS A SECOND CHANCE** Virgin VS 1396	**56**	4
25 Feb 95	**OVER MY SHOULDER** Virgin VSCDT 1526	**12**	9
17 Jun 95	**A BEGGAR ON A BEACH OF GOLD** Virgin VSCDT 1535	**33**	5
2 Sep 95	**ANOTHER CUP OF COFFEE** Virgin VSCDT 1554	**51**	4
17 Feb 96	**ALL I NEED IS A MIRACLE (re-mix)** Virgin VSCDT 1576	**27**	4
1 Jun 96	**SILENT RUNNING (re-issue)** Virgin VSCDT 1585	**61**	1

MIKI and GRIFF UK, female / male vocal duo · **25 wks**

2 Oct 59	**HOLD BACK TOMORROW** Pye 7N 15213	**26**	2
13 Oct 60	**ROCKIN' ALONE** Pye 7N 15296	**44**	3
1 Feb 62	**LITTLE BITTY TEAR** Pye 7N 15412	**16**	13
22 Aug 63	**I WANNA STAY HERE** Pye 7N 15555	**23**	7

John MILES UK, male vocalist / multi-instrumentalist · **30 wks**

18 Oct 75	**HIGH FLY** Decca F 13595	**17**	6
20 Mar 76	● **MUSIC** Decca F 13627	**3**	9
16 Oct 76	**REMEMBER YESTERDAY** Decca F 13667	**32**	5
18 Jun 77	● **SLOW DOWN** Decca F 13709	**10**	10

Robert MILES Italy, male instrumentalist – keyboards · **34 wks**

24 Feb 96	● **CHILDREN** Deconstruction 74321348322	**2**	18
8 Jun 96	● **FABLE** Deconstruction 74321382622	**7**	7
3 Aug 96	**FABLE (re-entry)** Deconstruction 74321382622	**71**	1
31 Aug 96	**FABLE (2nd re-entry)** Deconstruction 74321382622	**69**	1
16 Nov 96	● **ONE AND ONE** Deconstruction 74321427692 ☐1	**3†**	7

☐1 Robert Miles featuring Maria Nayler

June MILES-KINGSTON – See Jimmy SOMERVILLE

Paul MILES-KINGSTON – See Sarah BRIGHTMAN

MILK AND HONEY featuring Gali ATARI
Israel, male / female vocal / instrumental group · **8 wks**

14 Apr 79	● **HALLELUJAH** Polydor 2001 870	**5**	8

MILL GIRLS – See Billy COTTON

MILLA US, female vocalist · **1 wk**

18 Jun 94	**GENTLEMAN WHO FELL** SBK CDSBK 49	**65**	1

Frankie MILLER UK, male vocalist · **32 wks**

4 Jun 77	**BE GOOD TO YOURSELF** Chrysalis CHS 2147	**27**	6
14 Oct 78	● **DARLIN'** Chrysalis CHS 2255	**6**	15
20 Jan 79	**WHEN I'M AWAY FROM YOU** Chrysalis CHS 2276	**42**	5
21 Mar 92	**CALEDONIA** MCS MCS 2001	**45**	6

Gary MILLER UK, male vocalist · **35 wks**

21 Oct 55	**YELLOW ROSE OF TEXAS** Nixa N 15004	**13**	5
13 Jan 56	● **ROBIN HOOD** Nixa N 15020	**10**	6
11 Jan 57	**GARDEN OF EDEN** Pye Nixa N 15070	**14**	6
1 Mar 57	**GARDEN OF EDEN (re-entry)** Pye Nixa N 15070	**27**	1
19 Jul 57	**WONDERFUL WONDERFUL** Pye Nixa N 15094	**29**	1
17 Jan 58	**STORY OF MY LIFE** Pye Nixa N 15094	**14**	6
21 Dec 61	**THERE GOES THAT SONG AGAIN / THE NIGHT IS YOUNG** Pye 7N 15404	**29**	9
1 Mar 62	**THERE GOES THAT SONG AGAIN (re-entry)** Pye 7N 15404	**48**	1

The Night Is Young *only listed with* There Goes That Song Again *for weeks 21 and 28 Dec 61 and 4 Jan 62. It peaked at position 32.*

Glenn MILLER US, orchestra, Glenn Miller, trombone · **9 wks**

12 Mar 54	**MOONLIGHT SERENADE** HMV BD 5942	**12**	1
24 Jan 76	**MOONLIGHT SERENADE / LITTLE BROWN JUG / IN THE MOOD (re-issue)** RCA 2644	**13**	8

Jody MILLER US, female vocalist · **1 wk**

21 Oct 65	**HOME OF THE BRAVE** Capitol CL 15415	**49**	1

Leza MILLER – See Sergio MENDES

Mitch MILLER US, orchestra and chorus · **13 wks**

7 Oct 55	● **YELLOW ROSE OF TEXAS** Philips PB 505	**2**	13

Ned MILLER US, male vocalist · **22 wks**

14 Feb 63	● **FROM A JACK TO A KING** London HL 9658	**2**	21
18 Feb 65	**DO WHAT YOU DO DO WELL** London HL 9937	**48**	1

Roger MILLER US, male vocalist — 42 wks

18 Mar 65	★ KING OF THE ROAD *Philips BF 1397*	**1**	15
3 Jun 65	ENGINE ENGINE NO. 9 *Philips BF 1416*	**33**	5
21 Oct 65	KANSAS CITY STAR *Philips BF 1437*	**48**	1
16 Dec 65	ENGLAND SWINGS *Philips BF 1456*	**45**	1
6 Jan 66	ENGLAND SWINGS (re-entry) *Philips BF 1456*	**13**	7
27 Mar 68	LITTLE GREEN APPLES *Mercury MF 1021*	**19**	10
2 Apr 69	LITTLE GREEN APPLES (re-entry) *Mercury MF 1021*	**48**	1
7 May 69	LITTLE GREEN APPLES (2nd re-entry) *Mercury MF 1021*	**39**	2

Suzi MILLER – See JOHNSTON BROTHERS

Steve MILLER BAND
US, male vocal / instrumental group — 36 wks

23 Oct 76	ROCK 'N ME *Mercury 6078 804*	**11**	9
19 Jun 82	● ABRACADABRA *Mercury STEVE 3*	**2**	11
4 Sep 82	KEEPS ME WONDERING WHY *Mercury STEVE 4*	**52**	3
11 Aug 90	★ THE JOKER *Capitol CL 583*	**1**	13

Lisa MILLETT – See SHEER BRONZE

MILLI VANILLI France / Germany, male duo — 50 wks

1 Oct 88	● GIRL YOU KNOW IT'S TRUE *Cooltempo COOL 170*	**3**	13
17 Dec 88	BABY DON'T FORGET MY NUMBER *Cooltempo COOL 178*	**16**	11
22 Jul 89	BLAME IT ON THE RAIN *Cooltempo COOL 180*	**53**	5
30 Sep 89	● GIRL I'M GONNA MISS YOU *Cooltempo COOL 191*	**2**	15
2 Dec 89	BLAME IT ON THE RAIN (re-entry) *Cooltempo COOL 180*	**52**	5
10 Mar 90	ALL OR NOTHING *Cooltempo COOL 199*	**74**	1

MILLICAN and NESBITT UK, male vocal duo — 14 wks

1 Dec 73	VAYA CON DIOS *Pye 7N 45310*	**20**	11
18 May 74	FOR OLD TIME'S SAKE *Pye 7N 45357*	**38**	3

MILLIE Jamaica, female vocalist — 33 wks

12 Mar 64	● MY BOY LOLLIPOP *Fontana TF 449*	**2**	18
25 Jun 64	SWEET WILLIAM *Fontana TF 479*	**30**	9
11 Nov 65	BLOODSHOT EYES *Fontana TF 617*	**48**	1
25 Jul 87	MY BOY LOLLIPOP (re-issue) *Island WIP 6574*	**46**	5

MILLIONAIRE HIPPIES
UK, male producer – Danny Rampling — 4 wks

18 Dec 93	I AM THE MUSIC HEAR ME! *Deconstruction 74321175432*	**52**	3
10 Sep 94	C'MON *Deconstruction 74321229372*	**59**	1

Garry MILLS UK, male vocalist — 31 wks

7 Jul 60	● LOOK FOR A STAR *Top Rank JAR 336*	**7**	14
20 Oct 60	TOP TEEN BABY *Top Rank JAR 500*	**24**	12
22 Jun 61	I'LL STEP DOWN *Decca F 11358*	**39**	5

Hayley MILLS UK, female vocalist — 11 wks

19 Oct 61	LET'S GET TOGETHER *Decca F 21396*	**17**	11

Stephanie MILLS US, female vocalist — 33 wks

18 Oct 80	● NEVER KNEW LOVE LIKE THIS BEFORE *20th Century TC 2460*	**4**	14
23 May 81	TWO HEARTS *20th Century TC 2492* [1]	**49**	5
15 Sep 84	THE MEDICINE SONG *Club JAB 8*	**29**	9
5 Sep 87	(YOU'RE PUTTIN') A RUSH ON ME *MCA MCA 1187*	**62**	2
1 May 93	NEVER DO YOU WRONG *MCA MCSTD 1767*	**57**	2
10 Jul 93	ALL DAY ALL NIGHT *MCA MCSTD 1778*	**68**	1

[1] Stephanie Mills featuring Teddy Pendergrass

Warren MILLS Zambia, male vocalist — 1 wk

28 Sep 85	SUNSHINE *Jive JIVE 99*	**74**	1

MILLS BROTHERS US, male vocal group — 1 wk

9 Jan 53	● GLOW WORM *Brunswick 05007*	**10**	1

MILLTOWN BROTHERS
UK, male vocal / instrumental group — 16 wks

2 Feb 91	WHICH WAY SHOULD I JUMP *A & M AM 711*	**38**	5
13 Apr 91	HERE I STAND *A & M AM 758*	**41**	4
6 Jul 91	APPLE GREEN *A & M AM 787*	**43**	4
22 May 93	TURN OFF *A & M 5802692*	**55**	1
17 Jul 93	IT'S ALL OVER NOW BABY BLUE *A & M 5803332*	**48**	2

CB MILTON Holland, male vocalist — 5 wks

21 May 94	IT'S A LOVING THING *Logic 74321208062*	**49**	2
25 Mar 95	IT'S A LOVING THING (re-mix) *Logic 74321267212*	**34**	2
19 Aug 95	HOLD ON *Logic 74321292112*	**62**	1

Garnet MIMMS and TRUCKIN' CO.
US, male vocalist and male instrumental group — 1 wk

25 Jun 77	WHAT IT IS *Arista 109*	**44**	1

MIND OF KANE UK, male producer – David Hope — 1 wk

27 Jul 91	STABBED IN THE BACK *Deja Vu DJV 007*	**64**	1

See also Hope AD.

MINDBENDERS UK, male vocal / instrumental group — 34 wks

13 Jan 66	● A GROOVY KIND OF LOVE *Fontana TF 644*	**2**	14
5 May 66	CAN'T LIVE WITH YOU (CAN'T LIVE WITHOUT YOU) *Fontana TF 697*	**28**	7
25 Aug 66	ASHES TO ASHES *Fontana TF 731*	**14**	9
20 Sep 67	THE LETTER *Fontana TF 869*	**42**	4

See also Wayne Fontana and the Mindbenders.

MINDS OF MEN
UK, male / female vocal / instrumental group — 1 wk

22 Jun 96	BRAND NEW DAY *Perfecto PERF 121CD*	**41**	1

Zodiac MINDWARP and the LOVE REACTION
UK, male / female vocal / instrumental group — 11 wks

9 May 87	PRIME MOVER *Mercury ZOD 1*	**18**	6
14 Nov 87	BACKSEAT EDUCATION *Mercury ZOD 2*	**49**	3
2 Apr 88	PLANET GIRL *Mercury ZOD 3*	**63**	2

Sal MINEO US, male vocalist — 11 wks

12 Jul 57	START MOVIN' *Philips PB 707*	**16**	11

Marcello MINERBI *Italy, orchestra*   **16 wks**

22 Jul 65	● ZORBA'S DANCE *Durium DRS 54001*	6	16

MINI POPS *UK, male / female vocal group*   **2 wks**

26 Dec 87	SONGS FOR CHRISTMAS '87 EP *Bright BULB 9*	39	2

Tracks on Songs For Christmas '87 EP: Thanks For Giving Us Christmas / The Man In Red / Christmas Time Around The World / Shine On.

MINISTRY *US, male vocal / instrumental group*   **3 wks**

8 Aug 92	NWO *Sire W 0125TE*	49	1
6 Jan 96	THE FALL *Warner Bros. W 0328CD*	53	2

MINK DE VILLE *US, male vocal / instrumental group*   **9 wks**

6 Aug 77	SPANISH STROLL *Capitol CLX 103*	20	9

Liza MINNELLI *US, female vocalist*   **15 wks**

12 Aug 89	● LOSING MY MIND *Epic ZEE 1*	6	7
7 Oct 89	DON'T DROP BOMBS *Epic ZEE 2*	46	3
25 Nov 89	SO SORRY I SAID *Epic ZEE 3*	62	2
3 Mar 90	LOVE PAINS *Epic ZEE 4*	41	3

Dannii MINOGUE *Australia, female vocalist*   **52 wks**

30 Mar 91	● LOVE AND KISSES *MCA MCS 1529*	8	8
18 May 91	SUCCESS *MCA MCS 1538*	11	7
27 Jul 91	● JUMP TO THE BEAT *MCA MCS 1556*	8	6
19 Oct 91	BABY LOVE *MCA MCS 1580*	14	6
14 Dec 91	I DON'T WANNA TAKE THIS PAIN *MCA MCS 1600*	40	5
1 Aug 92	SHOW YOU THE WAY TO GO *MCA MCS 1671*	30	3
12 Dec 92	LOVE'S ON EVERY CORNER *MCA MCSR 1723*	44	4
17 Jul 93	● THIS IS IT *MCA MCSTD 1790*	10	8
2 Oct 93	THIS IS THE WAY *MCA MCSTD 1935*	27	3
11 Jun 94	GET INTO YOU *Mushroom D 11751*	36	2

Kylie MINOGUE *Australia, female vocalist*   **201 wks**

23 Jan 88	★ I SHOULD BE SO LUCKY *PWL PWL 8*	1	16
14 May 88	● GOT TO BE CERTAIN *PWL PWL 12*	2	12
6 Aug 88	● THE LOCO-MOTION *PWL PWL 14*	2	11
22 Oct 88	● JE NE SAIS PAS POURQUOI *PWL PWL 21*	2	13
10 Dec 88	★ ESPECIALLY FOR YOU *PWL PWL 24* [1]	1	14
6 May 89	★ HAND ON YOUR HEART *PWL PWL 35*	1	11
5 Aug 89	● WOULDN'T CHANGE A THING *PWL PWL 42*	2	9
4 Nov 89	● NEVER TOO LATE *PWL PWL 45*	4	8
20 Jan 90	★ TEARS ON MY PILLOW *PWL PWL 47*	1	8
12 May 90	● BETTER THE DEVIL YOU KNOW *PWL PWL 56*	2	10
3 Nov 90	● STEP BACK IN TIME *PWL PWL 64*	4	8
2 Feb 91	● WHAT DO I HAVE TO DO *PWL PWL 72*	6	8
1 Jun 91	● SHOCKED *PWL PWL 81*	6	7
7 Sep 91	WORD IS OUT *PWL PWL 204*	16	5
2 Nov 91	● IF YOU WERE WITH ME NOW *PWL PWL 208* [2]	4	7
30 Nov 91	KEEP ON PUMPIN' IT *PWL PWL 207* [3]	49	1
25 Jan 92	● GIVE ME JUST A LITTLE MORE TIME *PWL PWL 212*	2	8
25 Apr 92	FINER FEELINGS *PWL International PWL 227*	11	6
22 Aug 92	WHAT KIND OF FOOL (HEARD IT ALL BEFORE) *PWL International PWL 241*	14	5
28 Nov 92	CELEBRATION *PWL International PWL 257*	20	7
10 Sep 94	● CONFIDE IN ME *Deconstruction 74321227482*	2	9
26 Nov 94	PUT YOURSELF IN MY PLACE *Deconstruction 74321246572*	11	9
22 Jul 95	WHERE IS THE FEELING *Deconstruction 74321293612*	16	3

14 Oct 95	WHERE THE WILD ROSES GROW *Mute CDMUTE 185* [4]	11	4

[1] Kylie Minogue and Jason Donovan [2] Kylie Minogue and Keith Washington [3] Visionmasters with Tony King featuring Kylie Minogue [4] Nick Cave and Kylie Minogue

Morris MINOR and the MAJORS
UK, male vocal group   **11 wks**

19 Dec 87	● STUTTER RAP (NO SLEEP 'TIL BEDTIME) *10 TEN 203*	4	11

Sugar MINOTT *Jamaica, male vocalist*   **16 wks**

28 Mar 81	● GOOD THING GOING (WE'VE GOT A GOOD THING GOING) *RCA 58*	4	12
17 Oct 81	NEVER MY LOVE *RCA 138*	52	4

MINT JULEPS *UK, female vocal group*   **7 wks**

22 Mar 86	ONLY LOVE CAN BREAK YOUR HEART *Stiff BUY 241*	62	2
30 May 87	EVERY KINDA PEOPLE *Stiff BUY 257*	58	5

MIRACLES *US, male vocal group*   **10 wks**

10 Jan 76	● LOVE MACHINE *Tamla Motown TMG 1015*	3	10

See also Smokey Robinson and the Miracles.

MIRAGE *UK, male vocal / instrumental group*   **35 wks**

14 Jan 84	GIVE ME THE NIGHT *Passion PASH 15* [1]	49	4
22 Sep 85	● JACK MIX II / III *Debut DEBT 3022*	4	11
25 Jul 87	SERIOUS MIX *Debut DEBT 3028*	42	4
7 Nov 87	● JACK MIX IV *Debut DEBT 3035*	8	10
27 Feb 88	JACK MIX VII *Debut DEBT 3042*	50	3
2 Jul 88	PUSH THE BEAT *Debut DEBT 3050*	67	2
11 Nov 89	LATINO HOUSE *Debut DEBT 3085*	70	1

[1] Mirage featuring Roy Gayle

Jack Mix III only listed with Jack Mix II from 6 Jun 87.

Danny MIRROR *Holland, male vocalist*   **9 wks**

17 Sep 77	● I REMEMBER ELVIS PRESLEY (THE KING IS DEAD) *Sonet SON 2121*	4	9

MISSION *UK, male vocal / instrumental group*   **58 wks**

14 Jun 86	SERPENTS KISS *Chapter 22 CHAP 6*	70	3
26 Jul 86	GARDEN OF DELIGHT / LIKE A HURRICANE *Chapter 22 CHAP 7*	49	4
18 Oct 86	STAY WITH ME *Mercury MYTH 1*	30	4
17 Jan 87	WASTELAND *Mercury MYTH 2*	11	6
14 Mar 87	SEVERINA *Mercury MYTH 3*	25	5
13 Feb 88	TOWER OF STRENGTH *Mercury MYTH 4*	12	7
23 Apr 88	BEYOND THE PALE *Mercury MYTH 6*	32	4
13 Jan 90	BUTTERFLY ON A WHEEL *Mercury MYTH 8*	12	4
10 Mar 90	DELIVERANCE *Mercury MYTH 9*	27	4
2 Jun 90	INTO THE BLUE *Mercury MYTH 10*	32	3
17 Nov 90	HANDS ACROSS THE OCEAN *Mercury MYTH 11*	28	2
25 Apr 92	NEVER AGAIN *Mercury MYTH 12*	34	3
20 Jun 92	LIKE A CHILD AGAIN *Mercury MYTH 13*	30	2
17 Oct 92	SHADES OF GREEN *Vertigo MYTH 14*	49	2
8 Jan 94	TOWER OF STRENGTH (re-mix) *Vertigo MYTCD 15*	33	3
26 Mar 94	AFTERGLOW *Vertigo MYTCD 16*	53	1
4 Feb 95	SWOON *Neverland HOOKCD 002*	73	1

238

MRS. MILLS UK, female instrumentalist – piano   **5 wks**

14 Dec 61	**MRS MILLS' MEDLEY** Parlophone R 4856	**18**	5

Mrs Mills' Medley *consisted of the following tunes: I Want To Be Happy / Sheik Of Araby / Baby Face / Somebody Stole My Gal / Ma (He's Making Eyes At Me) / Swanee / Ain't She Sweet / California Here I Come.*

MRS. WOOD UK, female producer   **3 wks**

16 Sep 95	**JOANNA** React CDREACT 066	**40**	2
6 Jul 96	**HEARTBREAK** React CDREACT 78 [1]	**44**	1

[1] Mrs. Wood featuring Eve Gallagher

MISTA E UK, male producer – Damon Rochefort   **5 wks**

10 Dec 88	**DON'T BELIEVE THE HYPE** Urban URB 28	**41**	5

MR. BEAN and SMEAR CAMPAIGN featuring Bruce DICKINSON
UK, male comedians and male vocalist   **5 wks**

4 Apr 92	● **(I WANT TO BE) ELECTED** London LON 319	**9**	5

MR. BIG UK, male vocal / instrumental group   **14 wks**

12 Feb 77	● **ROMEO** EMI 2567	**4**	10
21 May 77	**FEEL LIKE CALLING HOME** EMI 2610	**35**	4

MR. BIG US, male vocal / instrumental group   **17 wks**

7 Mar 92	● **TO BE WITH YOU** Atlantic A 7514	**3**	11
23 May 92	**JUST TAKE MY HEART** Atlantic A 7490	**26**	4
8 Aug 92	**GREEN TINTED SIXTIES MIND** Atlantic A 7468	**72**	1
20 Nov 93	**WILD WORLD** Atlantic A 7310CD	**59**	1

MR. BLOBBY UK, male vocalist   **16 wks**

4 Dec 93	★ **MR. BLOBBY** Destiny Music CDDMUS 104	**1**	12
16 Dec 95	**CHRISTMAS IN BLOBBYLAND** Destiny DMUSCD 108	**36**	4

MR. BLOE UK, male instrumentalist – harmonica   **18 wks**

9 May 70	● **GROOVIN' WITH MR. BLOE** DJM DJS 216	**2**	18

MR. FINGERS US, male producer – Larry Heard   **5 wks**

17 Mar 90	**WHAT ABOUT THIS LOVE** ffrr F 131	**74**	1
7 May 92	**CLOSER** MCA MCS 1601	**50**	3
23 May 92	**ON MY WAY** MCA MCS 1630	**71**	1

MR. FOOD UK, male vocalist   **3 wks**

9 Jun 90	**...AND THAT'S BEFORE ME TEA!** Tangible TGB 005	**62**	3

MR. LEE US, male producer – Leroy Haggard   **6 wks**

6 Aug 88	**PUMP UP LONDON** Breakout USA 639	**64**	2
11 Nov 89	**GET BUSY** Jive JIVE 231	**71**	1
24 Feb 90	**GET BUSY (re-entry)** Jive JIVE 231	**41**	3

MR. MISTER US, male vocal / instrumental group   **22 wks**

21 Dec 85	● **BROKEN WINGS** RCA PB 49945	**4**	13
1 Mar 86	**KYRIE** RCA PB 49927	**11**	9

MR. ROY UK, male instrumental / production group   **6 wks**

7 May 94	**SOMETHING ABOUT YOU** Fresh FRSHD 11	**74**	1
21 Jan 95	**SAVED** Fresh FRSHD 21	**24**	4
16 Dec 95	**SOMETHING ABOUT U (CAN'T BE BEAT) (re-mix)** Fresh FRSHCD 33	**49**	1

MR. and MRS. SMITH
UK, male / female instrumental / production group   **1 wk**

12 Oct 96	**GOTTA GET LOOSE** Hooj Choons HOOJCD 46	**70**	1

MR. V UK, male producer – Rob Villiers   **2 wks**

6 Aug 94	**GIVE ME LIFE** Cheeky CHEKCD 005	**40**	2

MISTURA featuring Lloyd MICHELS
US, male instrumental group, Lloyd Michels – trumpet   **10 wks**

15 May 76	**THE FLASHER** Route RT 30	**23**	10

Cameron MITCHELL – See VARIOUS ARTISTS (EPs & LPs) – Carousel Soundtrack

Guy MITCHELL US, male vocalist   **163 wks**

14 Nov 52	● **FEET UP** Columbia DB 3151	**2**	10
13 Feb 53	★ **SHE WEARS RED FEATHERS** Columbia DB 3238	**1**	15
24 Apr 53	● **PRETTY LITTLE BLACK EYED SUSIE** Columbia DB 3255	**2**	11
12 Jun 53	**SHE WEARS RED FEATHERS (re-entry)** Columbia DB 3238	**12**	1
28 Aug 53	★ **LOOK AT THAT GIRL** Philips PB 162	**1**	14
6 Nov 53	● **CHICKA BOOM** Philips PB 178	**5**	9
18 Dec 53	● **CLOUD LUCKY SEVEN** Philips PB 210	**2**	16
15 Jan 54	● **CHICKA BOOM (re-entry)** Philips PB 178	**4**	6
19 Feb 54	● **CUFF OF MY SHIRT** Philips PB 225	**9**	1
26 Feb 54	**SIPPIN' SODA** Philips PB 210	**11**	1
19 Mar 54	**CUFF OF MY SHIRT (re-entry)** Philips PB 225	**12**	1
2 Apr 54	**CUFF OF MY SHIRT (2nd re-entry)** Philips PB 225	**11**	1
30 Apr 54	● **DIME AND A DOLLAR** Philips PB 248	**8**	1
14 May 54	● **DIME AND A DOLLAR (re-entry)** Philips PB 248	**8**	4
7 Dec 56	★ **SINGING THE BLUES** Philips PB 650	**1**	22
15 Feb 57	● **KNEE DEEP IN THE BLUES** Philips PB 669	**3**	12
26 Apr 57	★ **ROCK-A-BILLY** Philips PB 685	**1**	14
26 Jul 57	**IN THE MIDDLE OF A DARK DARK NIGHT / SWEET STUFF** Philips PB 712	**27**	2
23 Aug 57	**IN THE MIDDLE OF A DARK DARK NIGHT / SWEET STUFF (re-entry)** Philips PB 712	**25**	2
11 Oct 57	**CALL ROSIE ON THE PHONE** Philips PB 743	**17**	6
27 Nov 59	**HEARTACHES BY THE NUMBER** Philips PB 964	**26**	2
18 Dec 59	● **HEARTACHES BY THE NUMBER (re-entry)** Philips PB 964	**5**	13

Joni MITCHELL Canada, female vocalist   **15 wks**

13 Jun 70	**BIG YELLOW TAXI** Reprise RS 20906	**11**	15

Willie MITCHELL
US, male instrumentalist – guitar   **3 wks**

24 Apr 68	**SOUL SERENADE** London HLU 10186	**43**	1
11 Dec 76	**THE CHAMPION** London HL 10545	**47**	2

Mark Morrison

When Mark Morrison hit number one with 'Return Of The Mac', he was the first act from Leicester to do so since Showaddywaddy 20 years earlier.

Alanis Morissette

Alanis Morissette's album *Jagged Little Pill* is the biggest selling album by a female vocalist ever.

Kylie Minogue with Nick Cave

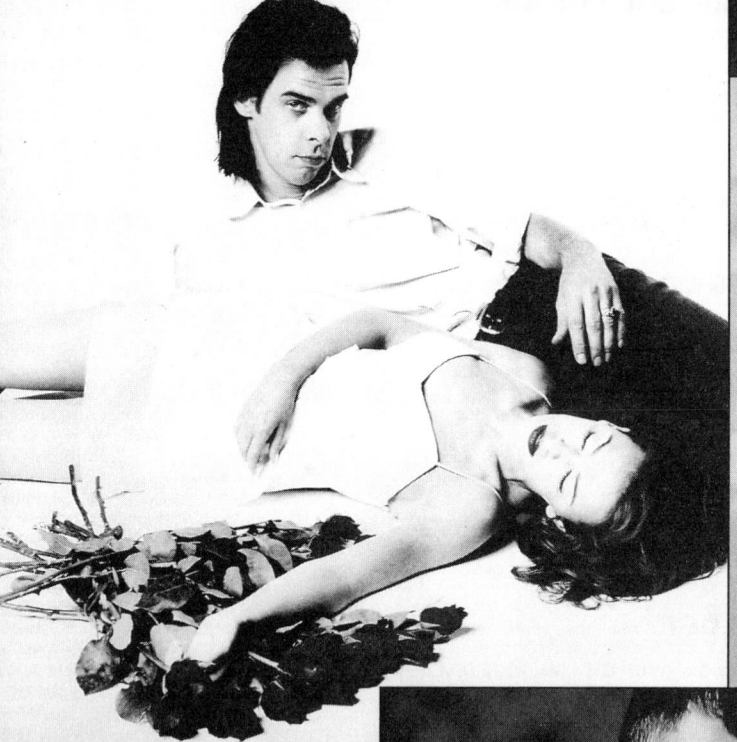

Kylie's collaboration with Nick Cave, 'Where The Wild Roses Grow', failed to achieve the Top 10 status of her previous duets with Jason Donovan and Keith Washington.

Robert Miles

Otherwise known as Roberto Milani, Robert Miles' 'Children' was the biggest selling single in Europe in 1996.

MIX FACTORY
UK, male / female vocal / instrumental group   **2 wks**

30 Jan 93	**TAKE ME AWAY (PARADISE)**		
	All Around The World CDGLOBE 120	**51**	2

MIXMASTER *Italy, male producer – Daniele Davoli*   **10 wks**

4 Nov 89	● **GRAND PIANO** *BCM BCM 344*	**9**	10

MIXTURES
Australia, male vocal / instrumental group   **21 wks**

16 Jan 71	● **THE PUSHBIKE SONG** *Polydor 2058 083*	**2**	21

Hank MIZELL *US, male vocalist*   **13 wks**

20 Mar 76	● **JUNGLE ROCK** *Charly CS 1005*	**3**	13

MK *US, male producer – Mark Kinchen*   **3 wks**

4 Feb 95	**ALWAYS** *Activ CDTV 3* 1	**69**	1
27 May 95	**BURNING** *Activ CDTVR 6*	**44**	2

1 MK featuring Alana

Alana appears on both hits, although she is only credited on the first.

MN8 *UK / Trinidad, male vocal group*   **47 wks**

4 Feb 95	● **I'VE GOT A LITTLE SOMETHING FOR YOU**		
	Columbia 6608802	**2**	13
29 Apr 95	● **IF YOU ONLY LET ME IN** *Columbia 6613252*	**6**	7
15 Jul 95	● **HAPPY** *Columbia 6622192*	**8**	7
4 Nov 95	**BABY IT'S YOU** *Columbia 6624522*	**22**	2
6 Jan 96	**BABY IT'S YOU (re-entry)** *Columbia 6624522*	**59**	1
24 Feb 96	**PATHWAY TO THE MOON** *Columbia 6629212*	**25**	2
31 Aug 96	**TUFF ACT TO FOLLOW** *Columbia 6635345*	**15**	3
26 Oct 96	**DREAMING** *Columbia 6638302*	**21**	3

MNO *Belgium, male instrumental / production group*   **2 wks**

28 Sep 91	**GOD OF ABRAHAM** *A & M AM 820*	**66**	2

MOBILES *UK, male / female vocal / instrumental group*   **14 wks**

9 Jan 82	● **DROWNING IN BERLIN** *Rialto RIA 3*	**9**	10
27 Mar 82	**AMOUR AMOUR** *Rialto RIA 5*	**45**	4

MOBY *US, male producer – Richard Hall*   **28 wks**

27 Jul 91	**GO** *Outer Rhythm FOOT 15*	**46**	3
19 Oct 91	● **GO (re-entry)** *Outer Rhythm FOOT 15*	**10**	7
3 Jul 93	**I FEEL IT** *Equinox AXISCD 001*	**38**	3
11 Sep 93	**MOVE** *Mute CDMUTE 158*	**21**	5
28 May 94	**HYMN** *Mute CDMUTE 161*	**31**	2
29 Oct 94	**FEELING SO REAL** *Mute CDMUTE 173*	**30**	2
25 Feb 95	**EVERY TIME YOU TOUCH ME** *Mute CDMUTE 176*	**28**	3
1 Jul 95	**INTO THE BLUE** *Mute CDMUTE 179A*	**34**	2
7 Sep 96	**THAT'S WHEN I REACH FOR MY REVOLVER**		
	Mute CDMUTE 184	**50**	1

MOCK TURTLES *UK, male vocal / instrumental group*   **15 wks**

9 Mar 91	**CAN YOU DIG IT** *Siren SRN 136*	**18**	11
29 Jun 91	**AND THEN SHE SMILES** *Siren SRN 139*	**44**	4

MODERN LOVERS – *See Jonathan RICHMAN and the MODERN LOVERS*

MODERN ROMANCE
UK, male vocal / instrumental group   **77 wks**

15 Aug 81	**EVERYBODY SALSA** *WEA K 18815*	**12**	10
7 Nov 81	● **AY AY AY AY MOOSEY** *WEA K 18883*	**10**	12
30 Jan 82	**QUEEN OF THE RAPPING SCENE (NOTHING EVER GOES THE WAY YOU PLAN)** *WEA K 18928*	**37**	8
14 Aug 82	**CHERRY PINK AND APPLE BLOSSOM WHITE**		
	WEA K 19245 1	**15**	8
13 Nov 82	● **BEST YEARS OF OUR LIVES** *WEA ROM 1*	**4**	13
26 Feb 83	**HIGH LIFE** *WEA ROM 2*	**8**	8
7 May 83	**DON'T STOP THAT CRAZY RHYTHM**		
	WEA ROM 3	**14**	6
6 Aug 83	● **WALKING IN THE RAIN** *WEA X 9733*	**7**	12

1 Modern Romance featuring John du Prez

MODERN TALKING
Germany, male vocal / instrumental duo   **22 wks**

15 Jun 85	**YOU'RE MY HEART, YOU'RE MY SOUL**		
	Magnet MAG 277	**69**	2
17 Aug 85	**YOU'RE MY HEART, YOU'RE MY SOUL (re-entry)**		
	Magnet MAG 277	**56**	5
12 Oct 85	**YOU CAN WIN IF YOU WANT** *Magnet MAG 282*	**70**	2
16 Aug 86	● **BROTHER LOUIE** *RCA PB 40875*	**4**	10
4 Oct 86	**ATLANTIS IS CALLING (S.O.S. FOR LOVE)**		
	RCA PB 40969	**55**	3

MODETTES *UK, female vocal / instrumental group*   **6 wks**

12 Jul 80	**PAINT IT BLACK** *Deram DET-R 1*	**42**	5
18 Jul 81	**TONIGHT** *Deram DET 3*	**68**	1

Domenico MODUGNO *Italy, male vocalist*   **13 wks**

5 Sep 58	● **VOLARE (NEL BLU DIPINTO DI BLU)** *Oriole ICB 5000*	**10**	12
27 Mar 59	**CIAO CIAO BAMBINA** *Oriole CB 1489*	**29**	1

MOHAWKS *Jamaica, male vocal / instrumental group*   **2 wks**

24 Jan 87	**THE CHAMP** *Pama PM 1*	**58**	2

Frank'o MOIRAGHI featuring AMNESIA
Italy, male / female vocal / instrumental duo   **4 wks**

1 Jun 96	**FEEL MY BODY** *Multiply CDMULTY 10*	**39**	2
26 Oct 96	**FEEL MY BODY (re-mix)** *Multiply CDMULTY 15*	**40**	2

MOIST *Canada, male vocal / instrumental group*   **10 wks**

12 Nov 94	**PUSH** *Chrysalis CDCHS 5016*	**35**	3
25 Feb 95	**SILVER** *Chrysalis CDCHS 5019*	**50**	2
29 Apr 95	**FREAKY BE BEAUTIFUL** *Chrysalis CDCHS 5022*	**47**	2
19 Aug 95	**PUSH (re-issue)** *Chrysalis CDCHS 5024*	**20**	3

MOJO *UK, male instrumental group*   **3 wks**

22 Aug 81	**DANCE ON** *Creole CR 17*	**70**	3

MOJOS *UK, male vocal / instrumental group*   **26 wks**

26 Mar 64	● **EVERYTHING'S ALRIGHT** *Decca F 11853*	**9**	11
11 Jun 64	**WHY NOT TONIGHT** *Decca F 11918*	**25**	10
10 Sep 64	**SEVEN DAFFODILS** *Decca F 11959*	**30**	5

MOKENSTEF US, female vocal group   **1 wk**

23 Sep 95   HE'S MINE *Def Jam DEFCD 13* **70** 1

MOLELLA – See OUTHERE BROTHERS

Ralph MOLINA – See Ian McNABB

Sam MOLLISON – See SASHA

MOLLY HALF HEAD UK, male vocal/instrumental group **1 wk**

3 Jun 95   SHINE *Columbia 6620732* **73** 1

MOLOKO Ireland/UK, male/female vocal/instrumental duo **3 wks**

24 Feb 96   DOMINOID *Echo ECSCD 016* **65** 1
25 May 96   FUN FOR ME *Echo ECSCD 20* **36** 2

MOMENTS US, male vocal group   **32 wks**

8 Mar 75 ● GIRLS *All Platinum 6146 302* [1] **3** 10
19 Jul 75 ● DOLLY MY LOVE *All Platinum 6146 306*...........**10** 9
25 Oct 75   LOOK AT ME (I'M IN LOVE) *All Platinum 6146 309* **42** 4
22 Jan 77 ● JACK IN THE BOX *All Platinum 6146 318* **7** 9

[1] Moments and Whatnauts

Jay MONDI and the LIVING BASS
US, male/female vocal/instrumental group   **3 wks**

24 Mar 90   ALL NIGHT LONG *10 TEN 304* **63** 3

MONDO KANE UK, male vocal/instrumental group **2 wks**

16 Aug 86   NEW YORK AFTERNOON *Lisson DOLE 2* **70** 2

MONÉ US, female vocalist   **2 wks**

12 Aug 95   WE CAN MAKE IT *A & M 5811592* **64** 1
16 Mar 96   MOVIN' *AM:PM 5814392* **48** 1

Zoot MONEY and the BIG ROLL BAND
UK, male vocal/instrumental   **8 wks**

18 Aug 66   BIG TIME OPERATOR *Columbia DB 7975* **25** 8

MONICA US, female vocalist   **8 wks**

29 Jul 95   DON'T TAKE IT PERSONAL (JUST ONE OF DEM DAYS) *Arista 74321301452* **32** 3
17 Feb 96   LIKE THIS AND LIKE THAT *Rowdy 74321344222*...........**33** 2
8 Jun 96   BEFORE YOU WALK OUT OF MY LIFE *Rowdy 74321374042* **22** 3

MONIFAH – See VARIOUS ARTISTS (EPs and LPs) – The New York Undercover EP

TS MONK US, male/female vocal/instrumental group **6 wks**

7 Mar 81   BON BON VIE *Mirage K 11653* **63** 2
25 Apr 81   CANDIDATE FOR LOVE *Mirage K 11648* **58** 4

MONKEES US/UK, male vocal/instrumental group **101 wks**

5 Jan 67 ★ I'M A BELIEVER *RCA 1560* **1** 17
26 Jan 67   LAST TRAIN TO CLARKSVILLE *RCA 1547* **23** 7

6 Apr 67 ● A LITTLE BIT ME A LITTLE BIT YOU *RCA 1580* **3** 12
22 Jun 67 ● ALTERNATE TITLE *RCA 1604* **2** 12
16 Aug 67   PLEASANT VALLEY SUNDAY *RC 1620* **11** 8
15 Nov 67 ● DAYDREAM BELIEVER *RCA 1645* **5** 17
27 Mar 68   VALLERI *RCA 1673* **12** 8
26 Jun 68   D.W. WASHBURN *RCA 1706* **17** 6
26 Mar 69   TEARDROP CITY *RCA 1802* **46** 1
25 Jun 69   SOMEDAY MAN *RCA 1824* **47** 1
15 Mar 80   THE MONKEES EP *Arista ARIST 326* **33** 9
18 Oct 86   THAT WAS THEN, THIS IS NOW *Arista ARIST 673*...........**68** 1
1 Apr 89   THE MONKEES EP *Arista 112157* **62** 2

Tracks on Arista 326 EP: I'm a Believer / Daydream Believer / Last Train to Clarksville / A Little Bit Me A Little Bit You. Tracks on Arista 112157 EP: Daydream Believer / Monkees Theme / Last Train To Clarksville.

MONKEY MAFIA – See PATRA

MONKS UK, male vocal/instrumental duo   **9 wks**

21 Apr 79   NICE LEGS SHAME ABOUT HER FACE *Carrere CAR 104* **19** 9

The Monks were Hudson-Ford under a different name.

Matt MONRO UK, male vocalist   **127 wks**

15 Dec 60 ● PORTRAIT OF MY LOVE *Parlophone R 4714* **3** 16
9 Mar 61 ● MY KIND OF GIRL *Parlophone R 4755* **5** 12
18 May 61   WHY NOT NOW/CAN THIS BE LOVE *Parlophone R 4775*..**24** 9
28 Sep 61   GONNA BUILD A MOUNTAIN *Parlophone R 4819* **44** 3
8 Feb 62 ● SOFTLY AS I LEAVE YOU *Parlophone R 4868* **10** 18
14 Jun 62   WHEN LOVE COMES ALONG *Parlophone R 4911*...........**46** 3
8 Nov 62   MY LOVE AND DEVOTION *Parlophone R 4954*...........**29** 5
14 Nov 63   FROM RUSSIA WITH LOVE *Parlophone R 5068*...........**20** 13
17 Sep 64 ● WALK AWAY *Parlophone R 5171* **4** 20
24 Dec 64   FOR MAMA *Parlophone R 5215* **36** 4
25 Mar 65   WITHOUT YOU *Parlophone R 5251* **37** 4
21 Oct 65 ● YESTERDAY *Parlophone R 5348* **8** 12
24 Nov 73   AND YOU SMILED *EMI 2091* **28** 8

Gerry MONROE UK, male vocalist   **57 wks**

23 May 70 ● SALLY *Chapter One CH 122* **4** 20
19 Sep 70   CRY *Chapter One CH 128* **38** 5
14 Nov 70 ● MY PRAYER *Chapter One CH 132* **9** 12
17 Apr 71   IT'S A SIN TO TELL A LIE *Chapter One CH 144*...........**13** 12
21 Aug 71   LITTLE DROPS OF SILVER *Chapter One CH 152*...........**37** 6
12 Feb 72   GIRL OF MY DREAMS *Chapter One CH 159* **43** 2

MONSOON UK, male/female vocal/instrumental group **12 wks**

3 Apr 82   EVER SO LONELY *Mobile Suit Corp CORP 2* **12** 9
5 Jun 82   SHAKTI (THE MEANING OF WITHIN) *Mobile Suit Corp CORP 4* **41** 3

MONSTER MAGNET
US, male vocal/instrumental group   **3 wks**

29 May 93   TWIN EARTH *A & M 5802812* **67** 1
18 Mar 95   NEGASONIC TEENAGE WARHEAD *A & M 5809812*.......**49** 1
6 May 95   DOPES TO INFINITY *A & M 5810332* **58** 1

MONTANA SEXTET
US, male/female vocal/instrumental group   **1 wk**

15 Jan 83   HEAVY VIBES *Virgin VS 560*...................**59** 1

Hugo MONTENEGRO US, orchestra   **26 wks**

11 Sep 68 ★ THE GOOD THE BAD AND THE UGLY *RCA 1727*...............**1** 24

8 Jan 69	HANG 'EM HIGH *RCA 1771*	**50** 1
19 Mar 69	THE GOOD THE BAD AND THE UGLY (re-entry) *RCA 1727*	**48** 1

Chris MONTEZ *US, male vocalist*   61 wks

4 Oct 62	● LET'S DANCE *London HLU 9596*	**2** 18
17 Jan 63	● SOME KINDA FUN *London HLU 9650*	**10** 9
30 Jun 66	● THE MORE I SEE YOU *Pye International 7N 25369*	**3** 13
22 Sep 66	THERE WILL NEVER BE ANOTHER YOU *Pye International 7N 25381*	**37** 4
14 Oct 72	● LET'S DANCE (re-issue) *London HLU 10205*	**9** 14
14 Apr 79	LET'S DANCE (2nd re-issue) *Lightning LIG 9011*	**47** 3

The second re-issue of Let's Dance on Lightning was coupled with Memphis by Lonnie Mack as a double A-side.

MONTROSE *US, male vocal / instrumental group*   2 wks

28 Jun 80	SPACE STATION NO. 5 / GOOD ROCKIN' TONIGHT *WB HM 9*	**71** 2

MONTY PYTHON *UK, male comedy group*   9 wks

5 Oct 91	● ALWAYS LOOK ON THE BRIGHT SIDE OF LIFE *Virgin PYTH 1*	**3** 9

MONYAKA *US / Jamaica, male vocal / instrumental group*   8 wks

10 Sep 83	GO DEH YAKA (GO TO THE TOP) *Polydor POSP 641*	**14** 8

MOOD *UK, male vocal / instrumental group*   10 wks

6 Feb 82	DON'T STOP *RCA 171*	**59** 4
22 May 82	PARIS IS ONE DAY AWAY *RCA 211*	**42** 5
30 Oct 82	PASSION IN DARK ROOMS *RCA 276*	**74** 1

MOODSWINGS – *See PRETENDERS/Chrissie HYNDE*

MOODY BLUES *UK, male vocal / instrumental group*   114 wks

10 Dec 64	★ GO NOW *Decca F 12022*	**1** 14
4 Mar 65	I DON'T WANT TO GO ON WITHOUT YOU *Decca F 12095*	**33** 9
10 Jun 65	FROM THE BOTTOM OF MY HEART *Decca F 12166*	**22** 9
18 Nov 65	EVERYDAY *Decca F 12266*	**44** 2
27 Dec 67	NIGHTS IN WHITE SATIN *Deram DM 161*	**19** 11
7 Aug 68	VOICES IN THE SKY *Deram DM 196*	**27** 10
4 Dec 68	RIDE MY SEE-SAW *Deram DM 213*	**42** 1
2 May 70	● QUESTION *Threshold TH 4*	**2** 12
6 May 72	ISN'T LIFE STRANGE *Threshold TH 9*	**13** 10
2 Dec 72	● NIGHTS IN WHITE SATIN (re-entry) *Deram DM 161*	**9** 11
10 Feb 73	I'M JUST A SINGER (IN A ROCK 'N' ROLL BAND) *Threshold TH 13*	**36** 4
10 Nov 79	NIGHTS IN WHITE SATIN (2nd re-entry) *Deram DM 161*	**14** 12
20 Aug 83	BLUE WORLD *Threshold TH 30*	**35** 5
25 Jun 88	I KNOW YOU'RE OUT THERE SOMEWHERE *Polydor POSP 921*	**52** 4

MOONTREKKERS *UK, male instrumental group*   1 wk

2 Nov 61	NIGHT OF THE VAMPIRE *Parlophone R 4814*	**50** 1

Chante MOORE *US, female vocalist*   4 wks

20 Mar 93	LOVE'S TAKEN OVER *MCA MCSTD 1744*	**54** 3
4 Mar 95	FREE / SAIL ON *MCA MCSTD 2042*	**69** 1

Dorothy MOORE *US, female vocalist*   24 wks

19 Jun 76	● MISTY BLUE *Contempo CS 2087*	**5** 12
16 Oct 76	FUNNY HOW TIME SLIPS AWAY *Contempo CS 2092*	**38** 3
15 Oct 77	I BELIEVE YOU *Epic EPC 5573*	**20** 9

Dudley MOORE – *See Peter COOK*

Gary MOORE
UK, male vocalist / instrumentalist – guitar   103 wks

21 Apr 79	● PARISIENNE WALKWAYS *MCA 419*	**8** 11
21 Jan 84	HOLD ON TO LOVE *10 TEN 13*	**65** 3
11 Aug 84	EMPTY ROOMS *10 TEN 25*	**51** 5
18 May 85	● OUT IN THE FIELDS *10 TEN 49* [1]	**5** 10
27 Jul 85	EMPTY ROOMS (re-issue) *10 TEN 58*	**23** 8
20 Dec 86	OVER THE HILLS AND FAR AWAY *10 TEN 134*	**20** 8
28 Feb 87	WILD FRONTIER *10 TEN 159*	**35** 5
9 May 87	FRIDAY ON MY MIND *10 TEN 164*	**26** 6
29 Aug 87	THE LONER *10 TEN 178*	**53** 5
5 Dec 87	TAKE A LITTLE TIME (DOUBLE SINGLE) *10 TEN 190*	**75** 1
14 Jan 89	AFTER THE WAR *Virgin GMS 1*	**37** 4
18 Mar 89	READY FOR LOVE *Virgin GMS 2*	**56** 2
24 Mar 90	OH PRETTY WOMAN *Virgin VS 1233* [2]	**48** 3
12 May 90	STILL GOT THE BLUES (FOR YOU) *Virgin VS 1267*	**31** 7
18 Aug 90	WALKING BY MYSELF *Virgin VS 1281*	**48** 5
15 Dec 90	TOO TIRED *Virgin VS 1306*	**71** 1
22 Feb 92	COLD DAY IN HELL *Virgin VS 1393*	**24** 5
9 May 92	STORY OF THE BLUES *Virgin VS 1412*	**40** 4
18 Jul 92	SINCE I MET YOU BABY *Virgin VS 1423* [3]	**59** 3
24 Oct 92	SEPARATE WAYS *Virgin VS 1437*	**59** 1
8 May 93	PARISIENNE WALKWAYS (re-mix) *Virgin VSCDX 1456*	**32** 4
17 Jun 95	NEED YOUR LOVE SO BAD *Virgin VSCDG 1546*	**48** 2

[1] Gary Moore and Phil Lynott   [2] Gary Moore featuring Albert King
[3] Gary Moore and BB King

Parisienne Walkways features uncredited vocals by Phil Lynott. Tracks on double single: Take A Little Time / Out In The Fields / All Messed Up / Thunder Rising.

Jackie MOORE *US, female vocalist*   5 wks

15 Sep 79	THIS TIME BABY *CBS 7722*	**49** 5

Mark MOORE – *See S EXPRESS*

Melba MOORE *US, female vocalist*   29 wks

15 May 76	● THIS IS IT *Buddah BDS 443*	**9** 8
26 May 79	PICK ME UP I'LL DANCE *Epic EPC 7234*	**48** 5
9 Oct 82	LOVE'S COMIN' AT YA *EMI America EA 146*	**15** 8
15 Jan 83	MIND UP TONIGHT *Capitol CL 272*	**22** 6
5 Mar 83	UNDERLOVE *Capitol CL 281*	**60** 2

Ray MOORE *UK, male vocalist*   9 wks

29 Nov 86	O' MY FATHER HAD A RABBIT *Play PLAY 213*	**24** 7
5 Dec 87	BOG EYED JOG *Play PLAY 224*	**61** 2

Sam MOORE – *See SAM and DAVE; Lou REED*

Lisa MOORISH *UK, female vocalist*   11 wks

7 Jan 95	JUST THE WAY IT IS *Go.Beat GODCD 123*	**42** 3
19 Aug 95	I'M YOUR MAN *Go.Beat GODCD 128*	**24** 3
3 Feb 96	MR. FRIDAY NIGHT *Go.Beat GODCD 137*	**24** 3
18 May 96	LOVE FOR LIFE *Go.Beat GODCD 145*	**37** 2

I'm Your Man features the uncredited vocals of George Michael.

Angel MORAES US, male producer — 1 wk

16 Nov 96	HEAVEN KNOWS – DEEP DEEP DOWN *ffrr FCD 282*	72	1

David MORALES and the BAD YARD CLUB
US, male producer — 6 wks

10 Jul 93	GIMME LUV (EENIE MEENIE MINY MO) *Mercury MERCD 390*	37	3
20 Nov 93	THE PROGRAM *Mercury MERCD 396*	66	1
24 Aug 96	IN DE GHETTO *Manifesto FESCD 12* [1]	35	2

[1] David Morales and the Bad Yard Club featuring Crystal Waters and Delta

See also Boss; Pulse featuring Antoinette Roberson.

Mike MORAN – See Lynsey DE PAUL

MORCHEEBA UK, male/female vocal/instrumental group — 3 wks

13 Jul 96	TAPE LOOP *Indochina ID 045CD*	42	1
5 Oct 96	TRIGGER HIPPIE *Indochina ID 052CD*	40	2

MORE UK, male vocal/instrumental group — 2 wks

14 Mar 81	WE ARE THE BAND *Atlantic K 11561*	59	2

George MOREL featuring Heather WILDMAN
US, male/female vocal/instrumental duo — 2 wks

26 Oct 96	LET'S GROOVE *Positiva CDTIV 62*	42	2

Derrick MORGAN Jamaica, male vocalist — 1 wk

17 Jan 70	MOON HOP *Crab 32*	49	1

Jamie J. MORGAN US, male vocalist — 6 wks

10 Feb 90	WALK ON THE WILD SIDE *Tabu 655596 7*	27	6

Jane MORGAN US, female vocalist — 22 wks

5 Dec 58	★ THE DAY THE RAINS CAME *London HLR 8751*	1	16
22 May 59	IF ONLY I COULD LIVE MY LIFE AGAIN *London HLR 8810*	27	1
21 Jul 60	ROMANTICA *London HLR 9120*	39	5

Meli'sa MORGAN US, female vocalist — 7 wks

9 Aug 86	FOOL'S PARADISE *Capitol CL 415*	41	5
25 Jun 88	GOOD LOVE *Capitol CL 483*	59	2

Ray MORGAN UK, male vocalist — 6 wks

25 Jul 70	THE LONG AND WINDING ROAD *B & C CB 128*	32	6

Erick 'More' MORILLO presents RAW
US, male/female vocal/instrumental duo — 1 wk

4 Feb 95	HIGHER (FEEL IT) *A & M 5809412*	74	1

Alanis MORISSETTE Canada, female vocalist — 31 wks

5 Aug 95	YOU OUGHTA KNOW *Maverick W 0307CD*	22	7
28 Oct 95	HAND IN MY POCKET *Maverick W 0312CD*	26	3
24 Feb 96	YOU LEARN *Maverick W 0334CD*	24	4
20 Apr 96	IRONIC *Maverick W 0343CD*	11	9
3 Aug 96	● HEAD OVER FEET *Maverick W 0355CD*	7	7
7 Dec 96	● ALL I REALLY WANT *Maverick W 0382CD*	59	1

Giorgio MORODER
Italy, male instrumentalist – synthesizer — 34 wks

24 Sep 77	FROM HERE TO ETERNITY *Oasis 1* [1]	16	10
17 Mar 79	CHASE *Casablanca CAN 144*	48	6
22 Sep 84	● TOGETHER IN ELECTRIC DREAMS *Virgin VS 713* [2]	3	13
29 Jun 85	GOODBYE BAD TIMES *Virgin VS 772* [2]	44	5

[1] Giorgio [2] Giorgio Moroder and Phil Oakey

Ennio MORRICONE Italy, orchestra — 12 wks

11 Apr 81	● CHI MAI (THEME FROM THE TV SERIES `THE LIFE AND TIMES OF DAVID LLOYD GEORGE') *BBC RESL 92*	2	12

Sarah Jane MORRIS – See COMMUNARDS

Diana MORRISON – See Michael BALL

Dorothy Combs MORRISON – See Edwin HAWKINS SINGERS featuring Dorothy Combs MORRISON

Mark MORRISON UK, male vocalist — 47 wks

22 Apr 95	CRAZY *WEA YZ 907CD*	19	4
16 Sep 95	LET'S GET DOWN *WEA WEA 001CD*	39	2
16 Mar 96	★ RETURN OF THE MACK *WEA WEA 040CD*	1	23
27 Jul 96	● CRAZY (re-mix) *WEA WEA 054CD1*	6	8
31 Aug 96	RETURN OF THE MACK (re-entry) *WEA WEA 040CD*	60	1
19 Oct 96	CRAZY (re-entry of re-mix) *WEA WEA 054CD1*	71	1
19 Oct 96	● TRIPPIN' *WEA WEA 079CD1*	8	6
21 Dec 96	● HORNY *WEA WEA 090CD1*	5†	2

Van MORRISON UK, male vocalist — 16 wks

20 Oct 79	BRIGHT SIDE OF THE ROAD *Mercury 6001 121*	63	3
1 Jul 89	HAVE I TOLD YOU LATELY *Polydor VANS 1*	74	1
9 Dec 89	WHENEVER GOD SHINES HIS LIGHT *Polydor VANS 2* [1]	20	6
15 May 93	GLORIA *Exile VANCD 11* [2]	31	3
18 Mar 95	HAVE I TOLD YOU LATELY THAT I LOVE YOU *RCA 74321271702* [3]	71	1
10 Jun 95	DAYS LIKE THIS *Exile VANCD 12*	65	1
2 Dec 95	NO RELIGION *Exile 5775792*	54	1

[1] Van Morrison with Cliff Richard [2] Van Morrison and John Lee Hooker [3] Chieftans with Van Morrison

Have I Told You Lately That I Love You is a re-recording of his second hit.

MORRISSEY UK, male vocalist — 68 wks

27 Feb 88	● SUEDEHEAD *HMV POP 1618*	5	6
11 Jun 88	● EVERYDAY IS LIKE SUNDAY *HMV POP 1619*	9	6
11 Feb 89	● LAST OF THE FAMOUS INTERNATIONAL PLAYBOYS *HMV POP 1620*	6	5
29 Apr 89	● INTERESTING DRUG *HMV POP 1621*	9	4
25 Nov 89	OUIJA BOARD OUIJA BOARD *HMV POP 1622*	18	4
5 May 90	NOVEMBER SPAWNED A MONSTER *HMV POP 1623*	12	4
20 Oct 90	PICCADILLY PALARE *HMV POP 1624*	18	2
23 Feb 91	OUR FRANK *HMV POP 1625*	26	3
13 Apr 91	SING YOUR LIFE *HMV POP 1626*	33	2
27 Jul 91	PREGNANT FOR THE LAST TIME *HMV POP 1627*	25	4
12 Oct 91	MY LOVE LIFE *HMV POP 1628*	29	2

9 May 92	**WE HATE IT WHEN OUR FRIENDS BECOME SUCCESSFUL** *HMV POP 1629*	**17**	3
18 Jul 92	**YOU'RE THE ONE FOR ME, FATTY** *HMV POP 1630*	**19**	3
19 Dec 92	**CERTAIN PEOPLE I KNOW** *HMV POP 1631*	**35**	4
12 Mar 94	● **THE MORE YOU IGNORE ME THE CLOSER I GET** *Parlophone CDR 6372*	**8**	3
11 Jun 94	**HOLD ON TO YOUR FRIENDS** *Parlophone CDR 6383*	**47**	2
20 Aug 94	**INTERLUDE** *Parlophone CDR 6365* [1]	**25**	2
28 Jan 95	**BOXERS** *Parlophone CDR 6400*	**23**	3
2 Sep 95	**DAGENHAM DAVE** *RCA Victor 74321299802*	**26**	2
9 Dec 95	**THE BOY RACER** *RCA Victor 74321332952*	**36**	2
23 Dec 95	**SUNNY** *Parlophone CDR 6243*	**42**	2

[1] Morrissey and Siouxsie

MORRISTON ORPHEUS MALE VOICE CHOIR – *See ALARM*

Buddy MORROW *US, orchestra*   **1 wk**

20 Mar 53	**NIGHT TRAIN** *HMV B 10347*	**12**	1

MORTIMER – *See Vic REEVES; EMF*

Mickie MOST *UK, male vocalist*   **1 wk**

25 Jul 63	**MISTER PORTER** *Decca F 11664*	**45**	1

MOTELS *US / UK, male / female vocal / instrumental group*   **7 wks**

11 Oct 80	**WHOSE PROBLEM?** *Capitol CL 16162*	**42**	4
10 Jan 81	**DAYS ARE O.K.** *Capitol CL 16149*	**41**	3

Wendy MOTEN *US, female vocalist*   **13 wks**

5 Feb 94	● **COME IN OUT OF THE RAIN** *EMI-USA CDMT 105*	**8**	9
14 May 94	**SO CLOSE TO LOVE** *EMI-USA CDMTS 106*	**35**	4

MOTHER *UK, male instrumental / production duo*   **4 wks**

12 Jun 93	**ALL FUNKED UP** *Bosting BYSNCD 101*	**34**	2
1 Oct 94	**GET BACK** *Six6 SIXT 119*	**73**	1
31 Aug 96	**ALL FUNKED UP (re-mix)** *Six6 SIXXCD 1*	**66**	1

MOTIV 8 *UK, male producer – Steve Rodway*   **10 wks**

17 Jul 93	**ROCKIN' FOR MYSELF** *Nuff Respect NUFF 002CD* [1]	**67**	1
7 May 94	**ROCKIN' FOR MYSELF (re-mix)** *WEA YZ 814CD*	**18**	4
21 Oct 95	**BREAK THE CHAIN** *Eternal WEA 010CD*	**31**	2
23 Dec 95	**SEARCHING FOR THE GOLDEN EYE** *Eternal WEA 027CD* [2]	**40**	3

[1] Motiv 8 featuring Angie Brown [2] Motiv 8 featuring Kym Mazelle

MOTLEY CRUE *US, male vocal / instrumental group*   **27 wks**

24 Aug 85	**SMOKIN' IN THE BOYS ROOM** *Elektra EKR 16*	**71**	2
8 Feb 86	**HOME SWEET HOME / SMOKIN' IN THE BOYS ROOM (re-issue)** *Elektra EKR 33*	**51**	3
1 Aug 87	**GIRLS GIRLS GIRLS** *Elektra EKR 59*	**26**	6
16 Jan 88	**YOU'RE ALL I NEED / WILD SIDE** *Elektra EKR 65*	**23**	4
4 Nov 89	**DR. FEELGOOD** *Elektra EKR 97*	**50**	3
12 May 90	**WITHOUT YOU** *Elektra EKR 109*	**39**	3
7 Sep 91	**PRIMAL SCREAM** *Elektra EKR 133*	**32**	2
11 Jan 92	**HOME SWEET HOME (re-mix)** *Elektra EKR 136*	**37**	2
5 Mar 94	**HOOLIGAN'S HOLIDAY** *Elektra EKR 180CDX*	**36**	2

Wild Side only listed with You're All I Need from 30 Jan 88. It peaked at position 26.

MOTORHEAD *UK, male vocal / instrumental group*   **81 wks**

16 Sep 78	**LOUIE LOUIE** *Bronze BRO 60*	**75**	1
30 Sep 78	**LOUIE LOUIE (re-entry)** *Bronze BRO 60*	**68**	1
10 Mar 79	**OVERKILL** *Bronze BRO 67*	**39**	4
14 Apr 79	**OVERKILL (re-entry)** *Bronze BRO 67*	**57**	3
30 Jun 79	**NO CLASS** *Bronze BRO 78*	**61**	4
1 Dec 79	**BOMBER** *Bronze BRO 85*	**34**	7
3 May 80	● **THE GOLDEN YEARS EP** *Bronze BRO 92*	**8**	7
1 Nov 80	**ACE OF SPADES** *Bronze BRO 106*	**15**	12
22 Nov 80	**BEER DRINKERS AND HELL RAISERS** *Big Beat SWT 61*	**43**	4
21 Feb 81	● **ST. VALENTINE'S DAY MASSACRE EP** *Bronze BRO 116* [1]	**5**	8
11 Jul 81	● **MOTORHEAD LIVE** *Bronze BRO 124*	**6**	7
3 Apr 82	**IRON FIST** *Bronze BRO 146*	**29**	5
21 May 83	**I GOT MINE** *Bronze BRO 165*	**46**	2
30 Jul 83	**SHINE** *Bronze BRO 167*	**59**	2
1 Sep 84	**KILLED BY DEATH** *Bronze BRO 185*	**51**	2
5 Jul 86	**DEAF FOREVER** *GWR GWR 2*	**67**	1
5 Jan 91	**THE ONE TO SING THE BLUES** *Epic 6565787*	**45**	3
14 Nov 92	**'92 TOUR EP** *Epic 6588096*	**63**	1
11 Sep 93	**ACE OF SPADES** *WGAF CDWGAF 101*	**23**	5
10 Dec 94	**BORN TO RAISE HELL** *Fox 74321230152* [2]	**47**	2

[1] Motorhead and Girlschool (also known as Headgirl) [2] Motorhead / Ice-T / Whitfield Crane

Tracks on The Golden Years EP: Dead Men Tell No Tales / Too Late Too Late / Leaving Here / Stone Dead Forever. Tracks on St. Valentine's Day Massacre EP: Please Don't Touch / Emergency / Bomber. Tracks on '92 Tour EP: Hellraiser / You Better Run / Going To Brazil / Ramones.

MOTORS *UK, male vocal / instrumental group*   **29 wks**

24 Sep 77	**DANCING THE NIGHT AWAY** *Virgin VS 186*	**42**	4
10 Jun 78	● **AIRPORT** *Virgin VS 219*	**4**	13
19 Aug 78	**FORGET ABOUT YOU** *Virgin VS 222*	**13**	9
12 Apr 80	**LOVE AND LONELINESS** *Virgin VS 263*	**58**	3

MOTOWN SPINNERS – *See DETROIT SPINNERS*

MOTT THE HOOPLE
UK, male vocal / instrumental group   **55 wks**

12 Aug 72	● **ALL THE YOUNG DUDES** *CBS 8271*	**3**	11
16 Jun 73	**HONALOOCHIE BOOGIE** *CBS 1530*	**12**	9
8 Sep 73	● **ALL THE WAY FROM MEMPHIS** *CBS 1764*	**10**	8
24 Nov 73	**ROLL AWAY THE STONE** *CBS 1895*	**8**	12
30 Mar 74	**GOLDEN AGE OF ROCK 'N' ROLL** *CBS 2177*	**16**	7
22 Jun 74	**FOXY FOXY** *CBS 2439*	**33**	5
2 Nov 74	**SATURDAY GIG** *CBS 2754*	**41**	3

Nana MOUSKOURI *Greece, female vocalist*   **11 wks**

11 Jan 86	● **ONLY LOVE** *Philips PH 38*	**2**	11

MOUTH and MACNEAL
Holland, male / female vocal duo   **10 wks**

4 May 74	● **I SEE A STAR** *Decca F 13504*	**8**	10

MOVE *UK, male vocal / instrumental group*   **110 wks**

5 Jan 67	● **NIGHT OF FEAR** *Deram DM 109*	**2**	10
6 Apr 67	● **I CAN HEAR THE GRASS GROW** *Deram DM 117*	**5**	10
6 Sep 67	● **FLOWERS IN THE RAIN** *Regal Zonophone RZ3001*	**2**	11
7 Feb 68	● **FIRE BRIGADE** *Regal Zonophone RZ3005*	**3**	11
25 Dec 68	★ **BLACKBERRY WAY** *Regal Zonophone RZ3015*	**1**	12
23 Jul 69	**CURLY** *Regal Zonophone RZ3021*	**12**	12

25 Apr 70	● BRONTOSAURUS *Regal Zonophone RZ3026*	7	10
3 Jul 71	TONIGHT *Harvest HAR 5038*	11	10
23 Oct 71	CHINATOWN *Harvest HAR 5043*	23	8
13 May 72	● CALIFORNIA MAN *Harvest HAR 5050*	7	14

MOVEMENT US, male vocal / instrumental group   2 wks

| 24 Oct 92 | JUMP! *Arista 74321116677* | 57 | 2 |

MOVEMENT 98 featuring Carroll THOMPSON
UK, male / female vocal / instrumental group   8 wks

| 19 May 90 | JOY AND HEARTBREAK *Circa YR 45* | 27 | 5 |
| 15 Sep 90 | SUNRISE *Circa YR 51* | 58 | 3 |

See also Courtney Pine.

MOVIN' MELODIES
Holland, male producer – Patrick Prinz   2 wks

| 22 Oct 94 | LA LUNA *Effective EFFS 017CD* [1] | 64 | 1 |
| 29 Jun 96 | INDICA *Hooj Choons HOOJCD 44* | 62 | 1 |

[1] Movin' Melodies Production

See also Artemesia; Ethics; Subliminal Cuts.

Alison MOYET UK, female vocalist   107 wks

23 Jun 84	● LOVE RESURRECTION *CBS A 4497*	10	11
13 Oct 84	● ALL CRIED OUT *CBS A 4757*	8	11
1 Dec 84	INVISIBLE *CBS A 4930*	21	10
16 Mar 85	● THAT OLE DEVIL CALLED LOVE *CBS A 6044*	2	10
29 Nov 86	● IS THIS LOVE? *CBS MOYET 1*	3	16
7 Mar 87	● WEAK IN THE PRESENCE OF BEAUTY *CBS MOYET 2*	6	10
30 May 87	ORDINARY GIRL *CBS MOYET 3*	43	4
28 Nov 87	● LOVE LETTERS *CBS MOYET 5*	4	10
6 Apr 91	IT WON'T BE LONG *Columbia 6567577*	50	4
1 Jun 91	WISHING YOU WERE HERE *Columbia 6569397*	72	1
12 Oct 91	THIS HOUSE *Columbia 6575157*	40	5
12 Mar 93	WHISPERING YOUR NAME *Columbia 6601622*	18	7
16 Oct 93	FALLING *Columbia 6595962*	42	3
28 May 94	GETTING INTO SOMETHING *Columbia 6603565*	51	2
22 Oct 94	ODE TO BOY *Columbia 6607952*	59	1
26 Aug 95	SOLID WOOD *Columbia 6623265*	44	2

MOZAIC UK, female vocal group   7 wks

5 Aug 95	SING IT (THE HALLELUJAH SONG) *Perfecto PERF 106CD*	14	4
10 Aug 96	RAYS OF THE RISING SUN *Perfecto PERF 123CD*	32	2
30 Nov 96	MOVING UP MOVING ON *Perfecto PERF 131CD*	62	1

MTUME US, male / female vocal / instrumental group   12 wks

| 14 May 83 | JUICY FRUIT *Epic A 3424* | 34 | 9 |
| 22 Sep 84 | PRIME TIME *Epic A 4720* | 57 | 3 |

MUD UK, male vocal / instrumental group   139 wks

10 Mar 73	CRAZY *RAK 146*	12	12
23 Jun 73	HYPNOSIS *RAK 152*	16	13
27 Oct 73	● DYNA-MITE *RAK 159*	4	12
19 Jan 74	★ TIGER FEET *RAK 166*	1	11
13 Apr 74	● THE CAT CREPT IN *RAK 170*	2	9
27 Jul 74	● ROCKET *RAK 178*	6	9
30 Nov 74	★ LONELY THIS CHRISTMAS *RAK 187*	1	10
15 Feb 75	● THE SECRETS THAT YOU KEEP *RAK 194*	3	9

26 Apr 75	★ OH BOY *RAK 201*	1	9
21 Jun 75	● MOONSHINE SALLY *RAK 208*	10	7
2 Aug 75	ONE NIGHT *RAK 213*	32	4
4 Oct 75	● L-L-LUCY *Private Stock PVT 41*	10	6
29 Nov 75	● SHOW ME YOU'RE A WOMAN *Private Stock PVT 45*	8	8
15 May 76	SHAKE IT DOWN *Private Stock PVT 65*	12	8
27 Nov 76	● LEAN ON ME *Private Stock PVT 85*	7	9
21 Dec 85	LONELY THIS CHRISTMAS (re-entry) *RAK 187*	61	3

MUDHONEY US, male vocal / instrumental group   2 wks

| 17 Aug 91 | LET IT SLIDE *Subpop SP 15154* | 60 | 1 |
| 24 Oct 92 | SUCK YOU DRY *Reprise W 0137* | 65 | 1 |

MUDLARKS UK, male / female vocal group   19 wks

2 May 58	● LOLLIPOP *Columbia DB 4099*	2	9
6 Jun 58	● BOOK OF LOVE *Columbia DB 4133*	8	9
27 Feb 59	THE LOVE GAME *Columbia DB 4250*	30	1

MUFFINS – *See* MARTHA and the MUFFINS

Idris MUHAMMAD US, male vocalist   3 wks

| 17 Sep 77 | COULD HEAVEN EVER BE LIKE THIS *Kudu 935* | 42 | 3 |

MUKKAA UK, male instrumental / production duo   1 wk

| 27 Feb 93 | BURUCHACCA *Limbo LIMBO 008* | 74 | 1 |

Maria MULDAUR US, female vocalist   8 wks

| 29 Jun 74 | MIDNIGHT AT THE OASIS *Reprise K 14331* | 21 | 8 |

Arthur MULLARD – *See* Hylda BAKER and Arthur MULLARD

Larry MULLEN – *See* Adam CLAYTON and Larry MULLEN

Coati MUNDI – *See* Kid CREOLE and the COCONUTS

MUNDY Ireland, male vocalist   2 wks

| 3 Aug 96 | TO YOU I BESTOW *Epic MUNDY 1CD* | 60 | 1 |
| 5 Oct 96 | LIFE'S A CINCH *Epic MUNDY 2CD* | 75 | 1 |

MUNGO JERRY UK, male vocal / instrumental group   87 wks

6 Jun 70	★ IN THE SUMMERTIME *Dawn DNX 2502*	1	20
6 Feb 71	BABY JUMP *Dawn DNX 2505*	32	1
20 Feb 71	★ BABY JUMP (re-entry) *Dawn DNX 2505*	1	12
29 May 71	● LADY ROSE *Dawn DNX 2510*	5	12
18 Sep 71	YOU DON'T HAVE TO BE IN THE ARMY TO FIGHT IN THE WAR *Dawn DNX 2513*	13	8
22 Apr 72	OPEN UP *Dawn DNX 2514*	21	8
7 Jul 73	● ALRIGHT ALRIGHT ALRIGHT *Dawn DNS 1037*	3	12
10 Nov 73	WILD LOVE *Dawn DNS 1051*	32	5
6 Apr 74	LONGLEGGED WOMAN DRESSED IN BLACK *Dawn DNS 1061*	13	9

MUNICH MACHINE
Germany, male instrumental group   8 wks

| 10 Dec 77 | GET ON THE FUNK TRAIN *Oasis OASIS 2* | 41 | 4 |
| 4 Nov 78 | A WHITER SHADE OF PALE *Oasis OASIS 5* [1] | 42 | 4 |

[1] Munich Machine introducing Chris Bennett

David MUNROW – *See* EARLY MUSIC CONSORT

Olivia Newton-John

A young Olivia Newton-John won a Hayley Mills lookalike contest in Australia before moving to England and landing a regular spot on Cliff Richard's television series.

Musical Youth

The Douchie in Musical Youth's 'Pass The Douchie' is a Jamaican cooking pot. The original song was 'Pass The Kouchie', which referred to a different sort of pot altogether!

Jimmy Nail

Jimmy Nail found chart success with the songs from his self-penned BBC drama series *Crocodile Shoes* and *Crocodile Shoes II*.

MUPPETS US, puppets — 15 wks

28 May 77	● HALFWAY DOWN THE STAIRS Pye 7N 45698	7	8
17 Dec 77	THE MUPPET SHOW MUSIC HALL EP Pye 7NX 8004	19	7

Halfway Down the Stairs is sung by Jerry Nelson as Kermit the Frog's nephew, Robin. Tracks on The Muppet Show Music Hall EP: Don't Dilly Dally On The Way / Waiting At The Church / The Boy In The Gallery / Wotcher (Knocked 'Em In The Old Kent Road).

Lydia MURDOCK US, female vocalist — 9 wks

24 Sep 83	SUPERSTAR Korova KOW 30	14	9

Shirley MURDOCK US, female vocalist — 2 wks

12 Apr 86	TRUTH OR DARE Elektra EKR 36	60	2

Eddie MURPHY – See Shabba RANKS

Noel MURPHY Ireland, male vocalist — 4 wks

27 Jun 87	MURPHY AND THE BRICKS Murphy's STACK 1	57	4

Walter MURPHY and the BIG APPLE BAND
US, orchestra — 9 wks

10 Jul 76	A FIFTH OF BEETHOVEN Private Stock PVT 59	28	9

Anne MURRAY Canada, female vocalist — 40 wks

24 Oct 70	SNOWBIRD Capitol CL 15654	23	17
21 Oct 72	DESTINY Capitol CL 15734	41	4
9 Dec 78	YOU NEEDED ME Capitol CL 16011	22	14
21 Apr 79	I JUST FALL IN LOVE AGAIN Capitol CL 16069	58	2
19 Apr 80	DAYDREAM BELIEVER Capitol CL 16123	61	3

Keith MURRAY US, male rapper — 1 wk

2 Nov 96	THE RHYME Jive JIVECD 407	59	1

Pauline MURRAY and the INVISIBLE GIRLS
UK, female vocalist with male vocal / instrumental group — 2 wks

2 Aug 80	DREAM SEQUENCE (ONE) Illusive IVE 1	67	2

Ruby MURRAY UK, female vocalist — 110 wks

3 Dec 54	● HEARTBEAT Columbia DB 3542	3	16
28 Jan 55	★ SOFTLY SOFTLY Columbia DB 3558	1	22
4 Feb 55	● HAPPY DAYS AND LONELY NIGHTS Columbia DB 3577	6	8
4 Mar 55	● LET ME GO LOVER Columbia DB 3577	5	7
18 Mar 55	● IF ANYONE FINDS THIS I LOVE YOU Columbia DB 3580 [1]	4	11
1 Jul 55	● EVERMORE Columbia DB 3617	3	17
8 Jul 55	SOFTLY SOFTLY (re-entry) Columbia DB 3558	20	1
14 Oct 55	● I'LL COME WHEN YOU CALL Columbia DB 3643	6	7
31 Aug 56	YOU ARE MY FIRST LOVE Columbia DB 3770	16	4
5 Oct 56	YOU ARE MY FIRST LOVE (re-entry) Columbia DB 3770	21	1
12 Dec 58	REAL LOVE Columbia DB 4192	18	6
5 Jun 59	● GOODBYE JIMMY GOODBYE Columbia DB 4305	10	13
9 Oct 59	GOODBYE JIMMY GOODBYE (re-entry) Columbia DB 4305	26	1

[1] Ruby Murray with Anne Warren

Junior MURVIN Jamaica, male vocalist — 9 wks

3 May 80	POLICE AND THIEVES Island WIP 6539	23	9

MUSIC AND MYSTERY – See Gwen McCRAE

MUSIC RELIEF '94
UK, male / female vocal / instrumental group — 1 wk

5 Nov 94	WHAT'S GOING ON Jive RWANDACD 1	70	1

MUSICAL YOUTH UK, male vocal / instrumental group — 55 wks

25 Sep 82	★ PASS THE DUTCHIE MCA YOU 1	1	12
20 Nov 82	YOUTH OF TODAY MCA YOU 2	13	9
8 Jan 83	PASS THE DUTCHIE (re-entry) MCA YOU 1	65	1
12 Feb 83	● NEVER GONNA GIVE YOU UP MCA YOU 3	6	10
16 Apr 83	HEARTBREAKER MCA YOU 4	44	3
9 Jul 83	TELL ME WHY MCA YOU 5	33	6
22 Oct 83	007 MCA YOU 6	26	6
14 Jan 84	SIXTEEN MCA YOU 7	23	8

See also Donna Summer.

MUSIQUE US, female vocal group — 12 wks

18 Nov 78	IN THE BUSH CBS 6791	16	12

MUSTAFAS – See STAIFFI and his MUSTAFAS

MXM Italy, male / female vocal / instrumental group — 1 wk

2 Jun 90	NOTHING COMPARES 2 U London LON 267	68	1

MY BLOODY VALENTINE
UK, male / female vocal / instrumental group — 5 wks

5 May 90	SOON Creation CRE 073	41	3
16 Feb 91	TO HERE KNOWS WHEN Creation CRE 085	29	2

MY LIFE STORY
UK, male / female vocal / instrumental group — 4 wks

17 Aug 96	12 REASONS WHY I LOVE HER Parlophone CDR 6442	32	2
9 Nov 96	SPARKLE Parlophone CDR 6450	34	2

Tim MYCROFT – See SOUNDS NICE

Alicia MYERS US, female vocalist — 3 wks

1 Sep 84	YOU GET THE BEST FROM ME (SAY SAY SAY) MCA MCA 914	58	3

Richard MYHILL UK, male vocalist — 9 wks

1 Apr 78	IT TAKES TWO TO TANGO Mercury 6007 167	17	9

Alannah MYLES Canada, female vocalist — 17 wks

17 Mar 90	● BLACK VELVET East West A 8742	2	15
16 Jun 90	LOVE IS East West A 8918	61	2

Marie MYRIAM France, female vocalist — 4 wks

28 May 77	L'OISEAU ET L'ENFANT Polydor 2056 634	42	4

MYSTERIANS – See ? (QUESTION MARK) and the MYSTERIANS

MYSTI – See CAMOUFLAGE featuring MYSTI

MYSTIC MERLIN
US, male vocal / instrumental and magic group   **9 wks**

| 26 Apr 80 | **JUST CAN'T GIVE YOU UP** *Capitol CL 16133* | **20** | 9 |

Youssou N'DOUR *Senegal, male vocalist*   **34 wks**

3 Jun 89	**SHAKING THE TREE** *Virgin VS 1167* [1]	**61**	3
22 Dec 90	**SHAKING THE TREE (re-issue)** *Virgin VS 1322* [1]	**57**	4
25 Jun 94	● **7 SECONDS** *Columbia 6605082* [2]	**3**	21
24 Dec 94	**7 SECONDS (re-entry)** *Columbia 6605082* [2]	**54**	4
14 Jan 95	**UNDECIDED** *Columbia 6609712*	**53**	2

[1] Youssou N'Dour and Peter Gabriel [2] Youssou N'Dour (featuring Neneh Cherry)

The re-issue of Shaking The Tree was listed with its flip side, Solsbury Hill by Peter Gabriel.

N-JOI *UK, male instrumental / production group*   **28 wks**

27 Oct 90	**ANTHEM** *Deconstruction PB 44041*	**45**	5
2 Mar 91	**ADRENALIN (EP)** *Deconstruction PT 44344*	**23**	5
6 Apr 91	● **ANTHEM (re-issue)** *Deconstruction PB 44445*	**8**	8
22 Feb 92	**LIVE IN MANCHESTER (PARTS 1 + 2)** *Deconstruction PT 45252*	**12**	5
24 Jul 93	**THE DRUMSTRUCK (EP)** *Deconstruction 74321154832*	**33**	3
17 Dec 94	**PAPILLON** *Deconstruction 74321252132*	**70**	1
8 Jul 95	**BAD THINGS** *Deconstruction 74321277292*	**57**	1

Tracks on Adrenalin (EP): Adrenalin / The Kraken / Rhythm Zone / Phoenix. Tracks on The Drumstruck (EP): The Void / Boom Bass / Drumstruck.

N-TRANCE *UK, male instrumental / production duo*   **37 wks**

7 May 94	**SET YOU FREE** *All Around The World CDGLOBE 124* [1]	**39**	4
22 Oct 94	**TURN UP THE POWER** *All Around The World CDGLOBE 125*	**23**	3
14 Jan 95	● **SET YOU FREE (re-mix)** *All Around The World CDGLOBE 126*	**2**	15
16 Sep 95	● **STAYIN' ALIVE** *All Around The World CDGLOBE 131* [2]	**2**	11
24 Feb 96	**ELECTRONIC PLEASURE** *All Around The World CDGLOBE 135*	**11**	4

[1] N-Trance featuring Kelly Llorenna [2] N-Trance featuring Ricardo Da Force

Although she is the vocalist on both versions of Set You Free, Kelly Llorenna is only credited on the former. Similarly, Ricardo da Force is the vocalist on both Stayin' Alive and Electronic Pleasure.

Jimmy NAIL *UK, male vocalist*   **71 wks**

27 Apr 85	● **LOVE DON'T LIVE HERE ANYMORE** *Virgin VS 764*	**3**	11
11 Jul 92	★ **AIN'T NO DOUBT** *East West YZ 686*	**1**	12
3 Oct 92	**LAURA** *East West YZ 702*	**58**	2
26 Nov 94	● **CROCODILE SHOES** *East West YZ 867CD*	**4**	13

11 Feb 95	**COWBOY DREAMS** *East West YZ 878CD*	**13**	7
11 Mar 95	**CROCODILE SHOES (re-entry)** *East West YZ 867CD*	**68**	3
8 Apr 95	**CROCODILE SHOES (2nd re-entry)** *East West YZ 867CD*	**56**	4
6 May 95	**CALLING OUT YOUR NAME** *East West YZ 935CD*	**65**	1
28 Oct 95	**BIG RIVER** *East West EW 008CD*	**18**	5
23 Dec 95	**LOVE** *East West EW 018CD*	**33**	4
3 Feb 96	**BIG RIVER (re-mix)** *East West EW 024CD*	**72**	2
16 Nov 96	**COUNTRY BOY** *East West EW 070CD*	**25†**	7

NAKED EYES *UK, male vocal / instrumental duo*   **3 wks**

| 23 Jul 83 | **ALWAYS SOMETHING THERE TO REMIND ME** *RCA 348* | **59** | 3 |

NAPOLEON XIV *US, male vocalist*   **10 wks**

| 4 Aug 66 | ● **THEY'RE COMING TO TAKE ME AWAY HA-HAAA!** *Warner Bros. WB 5831* | **4** | 10 |

NARADA – See Narada Michael WALDEN

NAS *US, male rapper*   **8 wks**

| 28 May 94 | **IT AIN'T HARD TO TELL** *Columbia 6604702* | **64** | 1 |
| 17 Aug 96 | **IF I RULED THE WORLD** *Columbia 6634022* | **12** | 7 |

Johnny NASH *US, male vocalist*   **106 wks**

7 Aug 68	● **HOLD ME TIGHT** *Regal Zonophone RZ 3010*	**5**	16
8 Jan 69	● **YOU GOT SOUL** *Major Minor MM 586*	**6**	12
2 Apr 69	● **CUPID** *Major Minor MM 603*	**6**	11
25 Jun 69	**CUPID (re-entry)** *Major Minor MM 603*	**50**	1
1 Apr 72	**STIR IT UP** *CBS 7800*	**13**	12
24 Jun 72	● **I CAN SEE CLEARLY NOW** *CBS 8113*	**5**	15
7 Oct 72	● **THERE ARE MORE QUESTIONS THAN ANSWERS** *CBS 8351*	**9**	9
14 Jun 75	★ **TEARS ON MY PILLOW (I CAN'T TAKE IT)** *CBS 3220*	**1**	11
11 Oct 75	**LET'S BE FRIENDS** *CBS 3597*	**42**	3
12 Jun 76	**(WHAT A) WONDERFUL WORLD** *Epic EPC 4294*	**25**	7
9 Nov 85	**ROCK ME BABY** *2000 AD FED 19*	**47**	4
15 Apr 89	**I CAN SEE CLEARLY NOW (re-mix)** *Epic JN 1*	**54**	5

NASHVILLE TEENS
UK, male vocal / instrumental group   **37 wks**

9 Jul 64	● **TOBACCO ROAD** *Decca F 11930*	**6**	13
22 Oct 64	● **GOOGLE EYE** *Decca F 12000*	**10**	11
4 Mar 65	**FIND MY WAY BACK HOME** *Decca F 12089*	**34**	6
20 May 65	**THIS LITTLE BIRD** *Decca F 12143*	**38**	4
3 Feb 66	**THE HARD WAY** *Decca F 12316*	**45**	2
24 Feb 66	**THE HARD WAY (re-entry)** *Decca F 12316*	**48**	1

NATASHA *UK, female vocalist*   **16 wks**

| 5 Jun 82 | ● **IKO IKO** *Towerbell TOW 22* | **10** | 11 |
| 4 Sep 82 | **THE BOOM BOOM ROOM** *Towerbell TOW 25* | **44** | 5 |

Ultra NATÉ *US, female vocalist*   **5 wks**

9 Dec 89	**IT'S OVER NOW** *Eternal YZ 440*	**62**	3
23 Feb 91	**IS IT LOVE** *Eternal YZ 509* [1]	**71**	1
29 Jan 94	**SHOW ME** *Warner Bros. W 0219CD*	**62**	1

[1] Basement Boys present Ultra Naté II

NATURAL BORN GROOVES
Holland, male instrumental / production duo   **1 wk**

| 2 Nov 96 | **FORERUNNER** *XL XLS 76CD* | **64** | 1 |

NATURAL LIFE
UK, male / female vocal / instrumental group **3 wks**

7 Mar 92	**NATURAL LIFE** *Tribe NLIFE 3*	**47**	3

NATURAL SELECTION
US, male vocal / instrumental duo **2 wks**

9 Nov 91	**DO ANYTHING** *East West A 8724*	**69**	2

NATURALS
UK, male vocal / instrumental group **9 wks**

20 Aug 64	**I SHOULD HAVE KNOWN BETTER** *Parlophone R 5165*	**24**	9

David NAUGHTON
US, male vocalist **6 wks**

25 Aug 79	**MAKIN' IT** *RSO 32*	**44**	6

NAUGHTY BY NATURE
US, male rap group **16 wks**

9 Nov 91	**O.P.P.** *Big Life BLR 62*	**73**	1
20 Jun 92	**O.P.P. (re-issue)** *Big Life BLR 74*	**35**	3
30 Jan 93	**HIP HOP HOORAY** *Big Life BLRD 89*	**22**	3
19 Jun 93	**IT'S ON** *Big Life BLRD 99*	**48**	2
27 Nov 93	**HIP HOP HOORAY (re-mix)** *Big Life BLRDA 104*	**20**	4
29 Apr 95	**FEEL ME FLOW** *Big Life BLRD 115*	**23**	3

Maria NAYLER
UK, female vocalist **10 wks**

9 Mar 96	**BE AS ONE** *Deconstruction 74321342962* 1	**17**	3
16 Nov 96	● **ONE AND ONE** *Deconstruction 74321427692* 2	**3**	7

1 Sasha and Maria 2 Robert Miles featuring Maria Nayler

NAZARETH
UK, male vocal / instrumental group **75 wks**

5 May 73	● **BROKEN DOWN ANGEL** *Mooncrest MOON 1*	**9**	11
21 Jul 73	● **BAD BAD BOY** *Mooncrest MOON 9*	**10**	9
13 Oct 73	**THIS FLIGHT TONIGHT** *Mooncrest MOON 14*	**11**	13
23 Mar 74	**SHANGHAI'D IN SHANGHAI** *Mooncrest MOON 22*	**41**	4
14 Jun 75	**MY WHITE BICYCLE** *Mooncrest MOON 47*	**14**	8
15 Nov 75	**HOLY ROLLER** *Mountain TOP 3*	**36**	4
24 Sep 77	**HOT TRACKS EP** *Mountain NAZ 1*	**15**	11
18 Feb 78	**GONE DEAD TRAIN** *Mountain NAZ 002*	**49**	2
13 May 78	**PLACE IN YOUR HEART** *Mountain TOP 37*	**70**	1
27 May 78	**PLACE IN YOUR HEART (re-entry)** *Mountain TOP 37*	**74**	1
27 Jan 79	**MAY THE SUN SHINE** *Mountain NAZ 003*	**22**	8
28 Jul 79	**STAR** *Mountain TOP 45*	**54**	3

Tracks on Hot Tracks EP: *Love Hurts / This Flight Tonight / Broken Down Angel / Hair of the Dog.*

NAZLYN – *See M-BEAT*

Me'Shell NDEGEOCELLO
US, female vocalist / instrumentalist – bass **4 wks**

12 Feb 94	**IF THAT'S YOUR BOYFRIEND (HE WASN'T LAST NIGHT)** *Maverick W 0223CD1*	**74**	1
3 Sep 94	**WILD NIGHT** *Mercury MERCD 409* 1	**34**	3

1 John Mellencamp featuring Me'Shell NdegeoCello

NEARLY GOD
UK, male / female vocal / instrumental group **2 wks**

20 Apr 96	**POEMS** *Durban Poison DPCD 3*	**28**	2

Terry NEASON
UK, female vocalist **1 wk**

25 Jun 94	**LIFEBOAT** *WEA YZ 830*	**72**	1

NEBULA II
UK, male instrumental / production group **3 wks**

1 Feb 92	**SEANCE / ATHEAMA** *Reinforced RIVET 1211*	**55**	2
16 May 92	**FLATLINERS** *J4M 12NEBULA 2*	**54**	1

NED'S ATOMIC DUSTBIN
UK, male vocal / instrumental group **24 wks**

14 Jul 90	**KILL YOUR TELEVISION** *Chapter 22 CHAP 48*	**53**	2
27 Oct 90	**UNTIL YOU FIND OUT** *Chapter 22 CHAP 52*	**51**	2
9 Mar 91	**HAPPY** *Columbia 6566807*	**16**	4
21 Sep 91	**TRUST** *Furtive 6574627*	**21**	4
10 Oct 92	**NOT SLEEPING AROUND** *Furtive 6583866*	**19**	3
5 Dec 92	**INTACT** *Furtive 6588166*	**36**	6
25 Mar 95	**ALL I ASK OF MYSELF IS THAT I HOLD TOGETHER** *Furtive 6613565*	**33**	2
15 Jul 95	**STUCK** *Furtive 6620562*	**64**	1

Joey NEGRO
UK, male producer – Dave Lee **10 wks**

18 Mar 89	**REACHIN'** *Republic LIC 006* 1	**70**	1
16 Nov 91	**DO WHAT YOU FEEL** *Ten TEN 391*	**36**	3
21 Dec 91	**REACHIN' (re-mix)** *Republic LIC 160* 2	**70**	1
18 Jul 92	**ENTER YOUR FANTASY EP** *Ten TEN 397*	**35**	3
25 Sep 93	**WHAT HAPPENED TO THE MUSIC** *Virgin VSCD 1466*	**51**	2

1 Phase II 2 Joey Negro presents Phase II

Tracks on Enter Your Fantasy EP: *Love Fantasy / Get Up / Enter Your Mind / Everybody.*
See also Li Kwan

neil
UK, male vocalist **10 wks**

14 Jul 84	● **HOLE IN MY SHOE** *WEA YZ 10*	**2**	10

Vince NEIL
US, male vocalist **1 wk**

3 Oct 92	**YOU'RE INVITED (BUT YOUR FRIEND CAN'T COME)** *Hollywood HWD 123*	**63**	1

NELSON
US, male vocal duo **3 wks**

27 Oct 90	**(CAN'T LIVE WITHOUT YOUR) LOVE AND AFFECTION** *DGC GEF 82*	**54**	3

Bill NELSON
UK, male vocalist / instrumentalist – guitar and synthesizer **12 wks**

24 Feb 79	**FURNITURE MUSIC** *Harvest HAR 5176* 1	**59**	3
5 May 79	**REVOLT INTO STYLE** *Harvest HAR 5183* 1	**69**	2
5 Jul 80	**DO YOU DREAM IN COLOUR?** *Cocteau COQ 1*	**52**	4
13 Jun 81	**YOUTH OF NATION ON FIRE** *Mercury WILL 2*	**73**	3

1 Bill Nelson's Red Noise

Pete NELSON – *See WHITE PLAINS*

Phyllis NELSON
US, female vocalist **24 wks**

23 Feb 85	★ **MOVE CLOSER** *Carrerre CAR 337*	**1**	21
21 May 94	**MOVE CLOSER (re-issue)** *EMI CDEMCT 9*	**34**	3

Ricky NELSON US, male vocalist — 137 wks

21 Feb 58	STOOD UP London HLP 8542	27	1
7 Mar 58	STOOD UP (re-entry) London HLP 8542	29	1
22 Aug 58	● POOR LITTLE FOOL London HLP 8670	4	13
7 Nov 58	● SOMEDAY London HLP 8732	9	13
21 Nov 58	I GOT A FEELING London HLP 8732	27	1
28 Nov 58	POOR LITTLE FOOL (re-entry) London HLP 8670	28	1
17 Apr 59	● IT'S LATE London HLP 8817	3	20
15 May 59	NEVER BE ANYONE ELSE BUT YOU London HLP 8817	19	1
5 Jun 59	NEVER BE ANYONE ELSE BUT YOU (re-entry) London HLP 8817	14	9
4 Sep 59	SWEETER THAN YOU London HLP 8927	19	3
11 Sep 59	JUST A LITTLE TOO MUCH London HLP 8927	11	8
15 Jan 60	I WANNA BE LOVED London HLP 9021	30	1
7 Jul 60	YOUNG EMOTIONS London HLP 9121	48	1
1 Jun 61	● HELLO MARY LOU/TRAVELLIN' MAN London HLP 9347	2	18
16 Nov 61	EVERLOVIN' London HLP 9440 [1]	23	5
29 Mar 62	YOUNG WORLD London HLP 9524 [1]	19	13
30 Aug 62	TEENAGE IDOL London HLP 9583 [1]	39	4
17 Jan 63	IT'S UP TO YOU London HLP 9648 [1]	22	9
17 Oct 63	FOOLS RUSH IN Brunswick 05895 [1]	12	9
30 Jan 64	FOR YOU Brunswick 05900 [1]	14	10
21 Oct 72	GARDEN PARTY MCA MU 1165 [1]	41	4
24 Aug 91	HELLO MARY LOU (GOODBYE HEART) (re-issue) Liberty EMCT 2	45	5

[1] Rick Nelson

Sandy NELSON US, male instrumentalist – drums — 42 wks

6 Nov 59	● TEEN BEAT Top Rank JAR 197	9	11
5 Feb 60	TEEN BEAT (re-entry) Top Rank JAR 197	25	1
14 Dec 61	● LET THERE BE DRUMS London HLP 9466	3	16
22 Mar 62	DRUMS ARE MY BEAT London HLP 9521	30	6
7 Jun 62	DRUMMIN' UP A STORM London HLP 9558	39	8

Shara NELSON UK, female vocalist — 22 wks

24 Jul 93	DOWN THAT ROAD Cooltempo CDCOOL 275	19	6
18 Sep 93	ONE GOODBYE IN TEN Cooltempo CDCOOL 279	21	5
12 Feb 94	UPTIGHT Cooltempo CDCOOL 286	19	5
4 Jun 94	NOBODY Cooltempo CDCOOL 290	49	1
10 Sep 94	INSIDE OUT / DOWN THAT ROAD (re-mix) Cooltempo CDCOOLX 295	34	3
16 Sep 95	ROUGH WITH THE SMOOTH Cooltempo CDCOOL 311	30	2

Willie NELSON US, male vocalist — 13 wks

31 Jul 82	ALWAYS ON MY MIND CBS A 2511	49	3
7 Apr 84	TO ALL THE GIRLS I'VE LOVED BEFORE CBS A 4252 [1]	17	10

[1] Julio Iglesias and Willie Nelson

NENA Germany, female / male vocal / instrumental group — 14 wks

4 Feb 84	★ 99 RED BALLOONS Epic A 4074	1	12
5 May 84	JUST A DREAM Epic H 3249	70	2

Frances NERO US, female vocalist — 9 wks

13 Apr 91	FOOTSTEPS FOLLOWING ME Debut DEBT 3109	17	9

NERO and the GLADIATORS
UK, male instrumental group — 6 wks

23 Mar 61	ENTRY OF THE GLADIATORS Decca F 11329	50	1
6 Apr 61	ENTRY OF THE GLADIATORS (re-entry) Decca F 11329	37	4
27 Jul 61	IN THE HALL OF THE MOUNTAIN KING Decca F 11367	48	1

Ann NESBY US, female vocalist — 2 wks

21 Dec 96	WITNESS EP AM:PM 5875612	42†	2

Tracks on Witness EP: Can I Get A Witness / (mix) / In The Spirit / I'm Still Wearing Your Name.

Michael NESMITH US, male vocalist — 6 wks

26 Mar 77	RIO Island WIP 6373	28	6

NETWORK UK, male vocal / instrumental group — 4 wks

12 Dec 92	BROKEN WINGS Chrysalis CHS 3923	46	4

NEVADA UK, male / female vocal / instrumental group — 1 wk

8 Jan 83	IN THE BLEAK MID WINTER Polydor POSP 203	71	1

Robbie NEVIL US, male vocalist — 24 wks

20 Dec 86	● C'EST LA VIE Manhattan MT 14	3	11
2 May 87	DOMINOES Manhattan MT 19	26	6
11 Jul 87	WOT'S IT TO YA Manhattan MT 24	43	7

Aaron NEVILLE – See Linda RONSTADT; NEVILLE BROTHERS

NEVILLE BROTHERS
US, male vocal / instrumental group — 7 wks

25 Nov 89	WITH GOD ON OUR SIDE A & M AM 545	47	6
7 Jul 90	BIRD ON A WIRE A & M AM 568	72	1

NEW ATLANTIC
UK, male instrumental / production duo — 15 wks

29 Feb 92	I KNOW 3 Beat 3BT 1	12	7
3 Oct 92	INTO THE FUTURE 3 Beat 3BT 2 [1]	70	1
13 Feb 93	TAKE OFF SOME TIME 3 Beat 3BTCD 14	64	1
26 Nov 94	THE SUNSHINE AFTER THE RAIN Ffrreedom TABCD 223 [2]	26	6

[1] New Atlantic featuring Linda Wright [2] New Atlantic/U4EA featuring Berri

The Sunshine After The Rain was re-issued in 95, credited simply to the vocalist Berri.

NEW BOHEMIANS – See Edie BRICKELL and the NEW BOHEMIANS

NEW EDITION US, male vocal group — 32 wks

16 Apr 83	★ CANDY GIRL London LON 21	1	13
13 Aug 83	POPCORN LOVE London LON 31	43	5
23 Feb 85	MR. TELEPHONE MAN MCA MCA 938	19	9
15 Apr 89	CRUCIAL MCA MCA 23934	70	1
10 Aug 96	HIT ME OFF MCA MCSTD 48014	20	4

NEW GENERATION UK, male vocal / instrumental group — 5 wks

26 Jun 68	SMOKEY BLUES AWAY Spark SRL 1007	38	5

NEW KIDS ON THE BLOCK US, male vocal group — 90 wks

16 Sep 89	HANGIN' TOUGH CBS BLOCK 1	52	4
11 Nov 89	★ YOU GOT IT (THE RIGHT STUFF) CBS BLOCK 2	1	13

6 Jan 90	★ **HANGIN' TOUGH (re-issue)** CBS BLOCK 3	**1**	9
17 Mar 90	● **I'LL BE LOVING YOU (FOREVER)** CBS BLOCK 4	**5**	8
12 May 90	● **COVER GIRL** CBS BLOCK 5	**4**	8
16 Jun 90	● **STEP BY STEP** CBS BLOCK 6	**2**	7
4 Aug 90	● **TONIGHT** CBS BLOCK 7	**3**	10
13 Oct 90	● **LET'S TRY AGAIN / DIDN'T I BLOW YOUR MIND** CBS BLOCK 8	**8**	5
8 Dec 90	● **THIS ONE'S FOR THE CHILDREN** CBS BLOCK 9	**9**	7
9 Feb 91	**GAMES** CBS 6566267	**14**	4
18 May 91	**CALL IT WHAT YOU WANT** Columbia 6567857	**12**	5
14 Dec 91	● **IF YOU GO AWAY** Columbia 6576667	**9**	5
19 Feb 94	**DIRTY DAWG** Columbia 6600362 [1]	**27**	3
26 Mar 94	**NEVER LET YOU GO** Columbia 6602072 [1]	**42**	2

[1] NKOTB

NEW MODEL ARMY
UK, male vocal / instrumental group **33 wks**

27 Apr 85	**NO REST** EMI NMA 1	**28**	5
3 Aug 85	**BETTER THAN THEM / NO SENSE** EMI NMA 2	**49**	2
30 Nov 85	**BRAVE NEW WORLD** EMI NMA 3	**57**	1
8 Nov 86	**FIFTY-FIRST STATE** EMI NMA 4	**71**	2
28 Feb 87	**POISON STREET** EMI NMA 5	**64**	1
26 Sep 87	**WHITE COATS EP** EMI NMA 6	**50**	3
21 Jan 89	**STUPID QUESTION** EMI NMA 7	**31**	3
11 Mar 89	**VAGABONDS** EMI NMA 8	**37**	3
10 Jun 89	**GREEN AND GREY** EMI NMA 9	**37**	3
8 Sep 90	**GET ME OUT** EMI NMA 10	**34**	3
3 Nov 90	**PURITY** EMI NMA 11	**61**	2
8 Jun 91	**SPACE** EMI NMA 12	**39**	2
20 Feb 93	**HERE COMES THE WAR** Epic 6589352	**25**	2
24 Jul 93	**LIVING IN THE ROSE (THE BALLADS EP)** Epic 6592492	**51**	1

Tracks on White Coats EP: *The Charge / Chinese Whispers / My Country. Tracks on* Living In The Rose (The Ballads EP): *Living In The Rose / Drummy B / Marry The Sea / Sleepwalking. See also Various Artists (EPs & LPs) – Gimme Shelter (EP).*

NEW MUSIK *UK, male vocal / instrumental group* **27 wks**

6 Oct 79	**STRAIGHT LINES** GTO GT 255	**53**	5
19 Jan 80	**LIVING BY NUMBERS** GTO GT 261	**13**	8
26 Apr 80	**THIS WORLD OF WATER** GTO GT 268	**31**	7
12 Jul 80	**SANCTUARY** GTO GT 275	**31**	7

NEW ORDER
UK, male / female vocal / instrumental group **179 wks**

14 Mar 81	**CEREMONY** Factory FAC 33	**34**	5
3 Oct 81	**PROCESSION / EVERYTHING'S GONE GREEN** Factory FAC 53	**38**	5
22 May 82	**TEMPTATION** Factory FAC 63	**29**	7
19 Mar 83	**BLUE MONDAY** Factory FAC 73	**12**	17
13 Aug 83	● **BLUE MONDAY (re-entry)** Factory FAC 73	**9**	17
3 Sep 83	**CONFUSION** Factory FAC 93	**12**	7
7 Jan 84	**BLUE MONDAY (2nd re-entry)** Factory FAC 73	**52**	4
28 Apr 84	**THIEVES LIKE US** Factory FAC 103	**18**	5
25 May 85	**THE PERFECT KISS** Factory FAC 123	**46**	4
9 Nov 85	**SUB-CULTURE** Factory FAC 133	**63**	4
29 Mar 86	**SHELLSHOCK** Factory FAC 143	**28**	5
27 Sep 86	**STATE OF THE NATION** Factory FAC 153	**30**	3
27 Sep 86	**THE PEEL SESSIONS (1ST JUNE 1982)** Strange Fruit SFPS 001	**54**	1
15 Nov 86	**BIZARRE LOVE TRIANGLE** Factory FAC 163	**56**	2
1 Aug 87	● **TRUE FAITH** Factory FAC 183/7	**4**	10
19 Dec 87	**TOUCHED BY THE HAND OF GOD** Factory FAC 193/7	**20**	7
7 May 88	● **BLUE MONDAY (re-mix)** Factory FAC 737	**3**	11
10 Dec 88	**FINE TIME** Factory FAC 2237	**11**	8
11 Mar 89	**ROUND AND ROUND** Factory FAC 2637	**21**	7
9 Sep 89	**RUN 2** Factory FAC 273	**49**	2
2 Jun 90	★ **WORLD IN MOTION...** Factory/MCA FAC 2937 [1]	**1**	12
17 Apr 93	● **REGRET** Centredate Co. NUOCD 1	**4**	7
3 Jul 93	**RUINED IN A DAY** Centredate Co. NUOCD 2	**22**	4

4 Sep 93	**WORLD (THE PRICE OF LOVE)** Centredate Co. NUOCD 3	**13**	5
18 Dec 93	**SPOOKY** Centredate Co. NUOCD 4	**22**	4
19 Nov 94	● **TRUE FAITH (re-mix)** Centredate Co. NUOCD 5	**9**	8
21 Jan 95	**NINETEEN63** London NUOCD 6	**21**	4
5 Aug 95	**BLUE MONDAY (2nd re-mix)** London NUOCD 7	**17**	4

[1] Englandneworder

Group male only on first hit. Blue Monday in 1988 is a re-mixed version of the original 1983 hit which was made available on 7-inch for the first time, hence the slight difference in catalogue number. Sales for the re-mix and the original were combined from 7 May 1988 onwards when calculating its chart position.

NEW ORLEANS JAZZMEN – *See Terry LIGHTFOOT and his NEW ORLEANS JAZZMEN*

NEW POWER GENERATION
US, male / female vocal / instrumental group **7 wks**

1 Apr 95	**GET WILD** NPG 0061045	**19**	4
19 Aug 95	**THE GOOD LIFE** NPG 0061515	**29**	3

See also Prince.

NEW SEEKERS
UK, male / female vocal / instrumental group **144 wks**

17 Oct 70	**WHAT HAVE THEY DONE TO MY SONG MA** Philips 6006 027	**48**	1
31 Oct 70	**WHAT HAVE THEY DONE TO MY SONG MA (re-entry)** Philips 6006 027	**44**	1
16 Jan 70	**WHAT HAVE THEY DONE TO MY SONG MA (2nd re-entry)** Philips 6006 027	**39**	1
10 Jul 71	● **NEVER ENDING SONG OF LOVE** Philips 6006 125	**2**	19
18 Dec 71	★ **I'D LIKE TO TEACH THE WORLD TO SING (IN PERFECT HARMONY)** Polydor 2058 184	**1**	21
4 Mar 72	● **BEG STEAL OR BORROW** Polydor 2058 201	**2**	13
10 Jun 72	● **CIRCLES** Polydor 2058 242	**4**	16
2 Dec 72	**COME SOFTLY TO ME** Polydor 2058 315 [1]	**20**	11
24 Feb 73	**PINBALL WIZARD – SEE ME FEEL ME (MEDLEY)** Polydor 2058 338	**16**	8
7 Apr 73	**NEVERTHELESS (I'M IN LOVE WITH YOU)** Polydor 2068 340 [2]	**34**	5
16 Jun 73	**GOODBYE IS JUST ANOTHER WORD** Polydor 2058 368	**36**	5
24 Nov 73	★ **YOU WON'T FIND ANOTHER FOOL LIKE ME** Polydor 2058 421 [3]	**1**	16
9 Mar 74	● **I GET A LITTLE SENTIMENTAL OVER YOU** Polydor 2058 439	**5**	9
14 Aug 76	**IT'S SO NICE (TO HAVE YOU HOME)** CBS 4391	**44**	4
29 Jan 77	**I WANNA GO BACK** CBS 4786	**25**	4
15 Jul 78	**ANTHEM (ONE DAY IN EVERY WEEK)** CBS 6413	**21**	10

[1] New Seekers featuring Marty Kristian [2] Eve Graham and the New Seekers [3] New Seekers featuring Lyn Paul

NEW TONE AGE FAMILY – *See Dread FLIMSTONE and the NEW TONE AGE FAMILY*

NEW VAUDEVILLE BAND
UK, male vocal / instrumental group **43 wks**

8 Sep 66	● **WINCHESTER CATHEDRAL** Fontana TF 741	**4**	19
26 Jan 67	● **PEEK-A-BOO** Fontana TF 784 [1]	**7**	11
11 May 67	**FINCHLEY CENTRAL** Fontana TF 824	**11**	9
2 Aug 67	**GREEN STREET GREEN** Fontana TF 853	**37**	4

[1] New Vaudeville Band featuring Tristram

NEW WORLD *Australia, male vocal / instrumental group* **53 wks**

27 Feb 71	**ROSE GARDEN** RAK 111	**15**	11
3 Jul 71	● **TOM TOM TURNAROUND** RAK 117	**6**	15
4 Dec 71	**KARA KARA** RAK 123	**17**	13

| 13 May 72 | ● SISTER JANE *RAK 130* .... | **9** | 13 |
| 12 May 73 | ROOF TOP SINGING *RAK 148* .... | **50** | 1 |

NEW YORK CITY *US, male vocal group*   **11 wks**

| 21 Jul 73 | I'M DOING FINE NOW *RCA 2351* .... | **20** | 11 |

NEW YORK SKYY
US, male / female vocal / instrumental group   **2 wks**

| 16 Jan 82 | LET'S CELEBRATE *Epic EPC A 1898* .... | **71** | 1 |
| 30 Jan 82 | LET'S CELEBRATE (re-entry) *Epic EPC A 1898* .... | **67** | 1 |

NEWBEATS *US, male vocal group*   **22 wks**

| 10 Sep 64 | BREAD AND BUTTER *Hickory 1269* .... | **15** | 9 |
| 23 Oct 71 | ● RUN BABY RUN *London HL 10341* .... | **10** | 13 |

Booker NEWBURY III *US, male vocalist*   **11 wks**

| 28 May 83 | ● LOVE TOWN *Polydor POSP 613* .... | **6** | 8 |
| 8 Oct 83 | TEDDY BEAR *Polydor POSP 637* .... | **44** | 3 |

Mickey NEWBURY *US, male vocalist*   **5 wks**

| 1 Jul 72 | AMERICAN TRILOGY *Elektra K 12047* .... | **42** | 5 |

NEWCLEUS *US, male vocal / instrumental group*   **6 wks**

| 3 Sep 83 | JAM ON REVENGE (THE WIKKI WIKKI SONG) *Beckett BKS 8* .... | **44** | 6 |

Anthony NEWLEY *UK, male vocalist*   **129 wks**

1 May 59	● I'VE WAITED SO LONG *Decca F 11127*	**3**	15
8 May 59	IDLE ON PARADE EP *Decca DFE 6566*	**13**	4
12 Jun 59	● PERSONALITY *Decca F 11142*	**6**	12
15 Jan 60	★ WHY *Decca F 11194*	**1**	17
24 Mar 60	★ DO YOU MIND *Decca F 11220*	**1**	15
14 Jul 60	● IF SHE SHOULD COME TO YOU *Decca F 11254*	**4**	15
24 Nov 60	● STRAWBERRY FAIR *Decca F 11295*	**3**	11
16 Mar 61	● AND THE HEAVENS CRIED *Decca F 11331*	**6**	12
15 Jun 61	POP GOES THE WEASEL / BEE BOM *Decca F 11362*	**12**	9
3 Aug 61	WHAT KIND OF FOOL AM I? *Decca F 11376*	**36**	8
25 Jan 62	D-DARLING *Decca F 11419*	**25**	6
26 Jul 62	THAT NOISE *Decca F 11486*	**34**	5

Bee Bom only listed together with Pop Goes The Weasel for weeks of 15 and 22 June 61. It peaked at position 15. Tracks on Idle On Parade EP: I've Waited So Long / Idle Rock-A-Boogie / Idle On Parade / Saturday Night Rock-A-Boogie.

Tara NEWLEY – *See E-ZEE POSSEE*

Alfred NEWMAN – *See VARIOUS ARTISTS (EPs & LPs) – Carousel Soundtrack*

Brad NEWMAN *UK, male vocalist*   **1 wk**

| 22 Feb 62 | SOMEBODY TO LOVE *Fontana H 357* .... | **47** | 1 |

Dave NEWMAN *UK, male vocalist*   **6 wks**

| 15 Apr 72 | THE LION SLEEPS TONIGHT *Pye 7N 45134* .... | **48** | 1 |
| 29 Apr 72 | THE LION SLEEPS TONIGHT (re-entry) *Pye 7N 45134* .... | **34** | 5 |

NEWS – *See Huey LEWIS and the NEWS*

NEWS *UK, male vocal / instrumental group*   **3 wks**

| 29 Aug 81 | AUDIO VIDEO *George GEORGE 1* .... | **52** | 3 |

NEWTON *UK, male vocalist*   **2 wks**

| 15 Jul 95 | SKY HIGH *Bags Of Fun BAGSCD 6* .... | **56** | 2 |

Juice NEWTON *US, female vocalist*   **6 wks**

| 2 May 81 | ANGEL OF THE MORNING *Capitol CL 16189* .... | **43** | 6 |

Olivia NEWTON-JOHN *UK, female vocalist*   **225 wks**

20 Mar 71	● IF NOT FOR YOU *Pye International 7N 25543*	**7**	11
23 Oct 71	● BANKS OF THE OHIO *Pye International 7N 25568*	**6**	17
11 Mar 72	WHAT IS LIFE *Pye International 7N 25575*	**16**	8
13 Jan 73	TAKE ME HOME COUNTRY ROADS *Pye International 7N 25599*	**15**	13
16 Mar 74	LONG LIVE LOVE *Pye International 7N 25638*	**11**	8
12 Oct 74	I HONESTLY LOVE YOU *EMI 2216*	**22**	6
11 Jun 77	● SAM *EMI 2616*	**6**	11
20 May 78	★ YOU'RE THE ONE THAT I WANT *RSO 006* [1]	**1**	26
16 Sep 78	● SUMMER NIGHTS *RSO 18* [1]	**1**	19
4 Nov 78	● HOPELESSLY DEVOTED TO YOU *RSO 17*	**2**	11
16 Dec 78	● A LITTLE MORE LOVE *EMI 2879*	**4**	12
30 Jun 79	DEEPER THAN THE NIGHT *EMI 2954*	**64**	3
21 Jun 80	★ XANADU *Jet 185* [2]	**1**	11
23 Aug 80	MAGIC *Jet 196*	**32**	7
25 Oct 80	SUDDENLY *Jet 7002* [3]	**15**	7
10 Oct 81	● PHYSICAL *EMI 5234*	**7**	16
16 Jan 82	LANDSLIDE *EMI 5257*	**18**	9
17 Apr 82	MAKE A MOVE ON ME *EMI 5291*	**43**	7
23 Oct 82	HEART ATTACK *EMI 5347*	**46**	4
15 Jan 83	I HONESTLY LOVE YOU (re-issue) *EMI 5360*	**52**	4
12 Nov 83	TWIST OF FATE *EMI 5438*	**57**	2
22 Dec 90	● THE GREASE MEGAMIX *Polydor PO 114* [1]	**3**	10
23 Mar 91	GREASE – THE DREAM MIX *PWL/Polydor PO 136* [4]	**47**	2
4 Jul 92	I NEED LOVE *Mercury MER 370*	**75**	1
9 Dec 95	HAD TO BE *EMI CDEMS 410* [5]	**22**	4

[1] John Travolta and Olivia Newton-John [2] Olivia Newton-John and Electric Light Orchestra [3] Olivia Newton-John and Cliff Richard [4] Frankie Valli, John Travolta and Olivia Newton-John [5] Cliff Richard and Olivia Newton-John

NICE *UK, male instrumental group*   **15 wks**

| 10 Jul 68 | AMERICA *Immediate IM 068* .... | **21** | 15 |

Paul NICHOLAS *UK, male vocalist*   **31 wks**

17 Apr 76	REGGAE LIKE IT USED TO BE *RSO 2090 185*	**17**	8
9 Oct 76	● DANCING WITH THE CAPTAIN *RSO 2090 206*	**8**	9
4 Dec 76	● GRANDMA'S PARTY *RSO 2090 216*	**9**	11
9 Jul 77	HEAVEN ON THE 7TH FLOOR *RSO 2090 249*	**40**	3

Sue NICHOLLS *UK, female vocalist*   **8 wks**

| 3 Jul 68 | WHERE WILL YOU BE *Pye 7N 17565* .... | **17** | 8 |

Stevie NICKS *US, female vocalist*   **30 wks**

15 Aug 81	STOP DRAGGIN' MY HEART AROUND *WEA K 79231* [1]	**50**	4
25 Jan 86	I CAN'T WAIT *Parlophone R 6110*	**54**	4
29 Mar 86	TALK TO ME *Parlophone R 6124*	**68**	2
6 May 89	ROOMS ON FIRE *EMI EM 90*	**16**	7

12 Aug 89	LONG WAY TO GO *EMI EM 97*	60	2
11 Nov 89	WHOLE LOTTA TROUBLE *EMI EM 114*	62	2
24 Aug 91	SOMETIMES IT'S A BITCH *EMI EM 203*	40	4
9 Nov 91	I CAN'T WAIT (re-issue) *EMI EM 214*	47	2
2 Jul 94	MAYBE LOVE *EMI CDEMS 328*	42	3

[1] Stevie Nicks with Tom Petty and the Heartbreakers

NICOLE *Germany, female vocalist* — 10 wks

| 8 May 82 | ★ A LITTLE PEACE *CBS A 2365* | 1 | 9 |
| 21 Aug 82 | GIVE ME MORE TIME *CBS A 2467* | 75 | 1 |

NICOLE *US, female vocalist* — 9 wks

28 Dec 85	NEW YORK EYES *Portrait A 6805* [1]	41	7
26 Dec 92	ROCK THE HOUSE *React 12REACT 12* [2]	63	1
6 Jul 96	RUNNIN' AWAY *Ore AG 18CD*	69	1

[1] Nicole with Timmy Thomas [2] Source featuring Nicole

NICOLETTE *UK, female vocalist* — 1 wk

| 23 Dec 95 | NO GOVERNMENT *Talkin Loud TLCD 1* | 67 | 1 |

NIGHTCRAWLERS featuring John REID
UK, male vocalist / multi-instrumentalist – John Reid — 35 wks

15 Oct 94	PUSH THE FEELING ON *ffrr FCD 245* [1]	22	5
4 Mar 95	● PUSH THE FEELING ON (re-mix) *ffrr FCD 257*	3	11
27 May 95	● SURRENDER YOUR LOVE *Final Vinyl 74321283982*	7	7
9 Sep 95	DON'T LET THE FEELING GO *Final Vinyl 7432129882*	13	4
20 Jan 96	LET'S PUSH IT *Final Vinyl 74321328142*	23	4
20 Apr 96	SHOULD I EVER (FALL IN LOVE) *Arista 74321358072*	34	2
27 Jul 96	KEEP ON PUSHING OUR LOVE *Arista 74321390422* [2]	30	2

[1] Nightcrawlers [2] Nightcrawlers featuring John Reid and Alysha Warren

Maxine NIGHTINGALE *UK, female vocalist* — 16 wks

| 1 Nov 75 | ● RIGHT BACK WHERE WE STARTED FROM *United Artists UP 36015* | 8 | 8 |
| 12 Mar 77 | LOVE HIT ME *United Artists UP 36215* | 11 | 8 |

NIGHTMARES ON WAX
UK, male instrumental group — 5 wks

| 27 Oct 90 | AFTERMATH / I'M FOR REAL *Warp WAP 6* | 38 | 5 |

NIGHTWRITERS *US, male vocal / instrumental duo* — 2 wks

| 23 May 92 | LET THE MUSIC USE YOU *Ffrreedom TABX 112* | 51 | 2 |

NIKKE? NICOLE! *US, female rapper* — 1 wk

| 1 Jun 91 | NIKKE DOES IT BETTER *Love EVOL 5* | 73 | 1 |

NIKKO– See Harold MELVIN and the BLUENOTES

NILSSON *US, male vocalist* — 55 wks

27 Sep 69	EVERYBODY'S TALKIN' *RCA 1876*	50	1
11 Oct 69	EVERYBODY'S TALKIN' (re-entry) *RCA 1876*	23	9
14 Mar 70	EVERYBODY'S TALKIN' (2nd re-entry) *RCA 1876*	39	5
5 Feb 72	★ WITHOUT YOU *RCA 2165*	1	20
3 Jun 72	COCONUT *RCA 2214*	42	5

16 Oct 76	WITHOUT YOU (re-issue) *RCA 2733*	22	8
20 Aug 77	ALL I THINK ABOUT IS YOU *RCA PB 9104*	43	3
19 Feb 94	WITHOUT YOU (re-issue) *RCA 74321193092*	47	4

NINA and FREDERICK
Denmark, female / male vocal duo — 29 wks

18 Dec 59	MARY'S BOY CHILD *Columbia DB 4375*	26	1
10 Mar 60	LISTEN TO THE OCEAN *Columbia DB 4332*	47	1
7 Apr 60	LISTEN TO THE OCEAN (re-entry) *Columbia DB 4332*	46	1
17 Nov 60	● LITTLE DONKEY *Columbia DB 4536*	3	10
28 Sep 61	LONGTIME BOY *Columbia DB 4703*	43	3
5 Oct 61	SUCU SUCU *Columbia DB 4632*	23	13

NINE INCH NAILS
US, male vocalist – Trent Reznor and backing musicians — 12 wks

14 Sep 91	HEAD LIKE A HOLE *TVT IS 484*	45	4
16 Nov 91	SIN *TVT IS 508*	35	2
9 Apr 94	MARCH OF THE PIGS *TVT CID 592*	45	3
18 Jun 94	CLOSER *TVT CIDX 596*	25	3

999 *UK, male vocal / instrumental group* — 13 wks

25 Nov 78	HOMICIDE *United Artists UP 36467*	40	3
27 Oct 79	FOUND OUT TOO LATE *Radar ADA 46*	69	2
16 May 81	OBSESSED *Albion ION 1011*	71	1
18 Jul 81	LIL RED RIDING HOOD *Albion ION 1017*	59	3
14 Nov 81	INDIAN RESERVATION *Albion ION 1023*	51	4

911 *UK, male vocal group* — 12 wks

11 May 96	NIGHT TO REMEMBER *Ginga CDGINGA 1*	38	2
10 Aug 96	LOVE SENSATION *Ginga CDGINGA 2*	21	4
9 Nov 96	● DON'T MAKE ME WAIT *Ginga VSCDT 1618*	10	6

9.9 *US, female / male vocal group* — 3 wks

| 6 Jul 85 | ALL OF ME FOR ALL OF YOU *RCA PB 49951* | 53 | 3 |

1910 FRUITGUM CO.
US, male vocal / instrumental group — 16 wks

| 20 Mar 68 | ● SIMON SAYS *Pye International 7N 25447* | 2 | 16 |

1927 *Australia, male vocal / instrumental group* — 6 wks

| 22 Apr 89 | THAT'S WHEN I THINK OF YOU *WEA YZ 351* | 46 | 6 |

99TH FLOOR ELEVATORS – See Tony DE VIT

NIRVANA *UK / Ireland, male vocal / instrumental duo* — 6 wks

| 15 May 68 | RAINBOW CHASER *Island WIP 6029* | 34 | 6 |

NIRVANA *US, male vocal / instrumental group* — 36 wks

30 Nov 91	● SMELLS LIKE TEEN SPIRIT *DGC DGCS 5*	7	6
14 Mar 92	● COME AS YOU ARE *DGC DGCS 7*	9	5
25 Jul 92	LITHIUM *DGC DGCS 9*	11	6
12 Dec 92	IN BLOOM *Geffen GFS 34*	28	7
6 Mar 93	OH THE GUILT *Touch And Go TG 83CD*	12	2
11 Sep 93	● HEART-SHAPED BOX *Geffen GFSTD 54*	5	5
18 Dec 93	ALL APOLOGIES / RAPE ME *Geffen GFSTD 66*	32	5

The listed flip side of Oh The Guilt was Puss by Jesus Lizard.

NITRO DELUXE
US, male multi-instrumentalist – Lee Junior   **16 wks**

14 Feb 87	**THIS BRUTAL HOUSE** Cooltempo COOL 142 ....**47**	7
13 Jun 87	**THIS BRUTAL HOUSE (re-entry)**		
	Cooltempo COOL 142 ....**62**	4
6 Feb 88	**LET'S GET BRUTAL** Cooltempo COOL 142 ....**24**	5

Let's Get Brutal is a re-mixed version of This Brutal House.

NITZER EBB *UK, male vocal / instrumental group*   **3 wks**

11 Jan 92	**GODHEAD** Mute 1MUTE 135T **56**	1
11 Apr 92	**ASCEND** Mute 110MUTE 145 ....**52**	1
4 Mar 95	**KICK IT** Mute LCDMUTE 155 ....**75**	1

NKOTB – *See NEW KIDS ON THE BLOCK*

NO DICE *UK, male vocal / instrumental group*   **2 wks**

5 May 79	**COME DANCING** EMI 2927 ....**65**	2

NO DOUBT *US, male / female vocal / instrumental group*   **2 wks**

26 Oct 96	**JUST A GIRL** Interscope IND 80034 ....**38**	2

NO SWEAT *Ireland, male vocal / instrumental group*   **5 wks**

13 Oct 90	**HEART AND SOUL** London LON 274 ....**64**	4
2 Feb 91	**TEAR DOWN THE WALLS** London LON 288 ....**61**	1

NO WAY JOSÉ *US, male instrumental group*   **6 wks**

3 Aug 85	**TEQUILA** Fourth & Broadway BRW 28 ....**47**	6

NO WAY SIS *US, male vocal / instrumental group*   **2 wks**

21 Dec 96	**I'D LIKE TO TEACH THE WORLD TO SING**		
	EMI CDEM 461 ....**27†**	2

NOLANS *Ireland, female vocal group*   **90 wks**

6 Oct 79	**SPIRIT BODY AND SOUL** Epic EPC 7796 [1] **34**	6
22 Dec 79	● **I'M IN THE MOOD FOR DANCING** Epic EPC 8068 ....**3**	15
12 Apr 80	**DON'T MAKE WAVES** Epic EPC 8349 ....**12**	11
13 Sep 80	● **GOTTA PULL MYSELF TOGETHER** Epic EPC 8878 ....**9**	13
6 Dec 80	**WHO'S GONNA ROCK YOU** Epic EPC 9325 ....**12**	11
14 Mar 81	● **ATTENTION TO ME** Epic EPC 9571 ....**9**	13
15 Aug 81	**CHEMISTRY** Epic EPC A1485.........**15**	8
20 Feb 82	**DON'T LOVE ME TOO HARD** Epic EPC A 1927.........**14**	12
1 Apr 95	**I'M IN THE MOOD FOR DANCING (re-mix)**		
	Living Beat LBECD 31.........**51**	1

[1] Nolan Sisters

NOMAD *UK, male / female vocal / instrumental duo*   **22 wks**

2 Feb 91	● **(I WANNA GIVE YOU) DEVOTION**		
	Rumour RUMA 25 [1] **2**	10
4 May 91	**JUST A GROOVE** Rumour RUMA 33 ....**16**	6
28 Sep 91	**SOMETHING SPECIAL** Rumour RUMA 35.........**73**	1
25 Apr 92	**YOUR LOVE IS LIFTING ME** Rumour RUMA 48 ....**60**	2
7 Nov 92	**24 HOURS A DAY** Rumour RUMA 60 ....**61**	1
25 Nov 95	**(I WANNA GIVE YOU) DEVOTION (re-mix)**		
	Rumour RUMACD 75 ....**42**	2

[1] Nomad featuring MC Mikee Freedom

NONCHALANT *US, female vocalist*   **1 wk**

29 Jun 96	**5 O'CLOCK** MCA MCSTD 48011 ....**44**	1

Peter NOONE *UK, male vocalist*   **9 wks**

22 May 71	**OH YOU PRETTY THING** RAK 114 ....**12**	9

See also Herman's Hermits.

NOOTROPIC *UK, male instrumental / production duo*   **1 wk**

16 Mar 96	**I SEE ONLY YOU** Hi-Life 5779832 ....**42**	1

Ken NORDENE – *See Billy VAUGHN*

Chris NORMAN – *See Suzi QUATRO*

NORTHERN UPROAR
UK, male vocal / instrumental group   **8 wks**

21 Oct 95	**ROLLERCOASTER / ROUGH BOYS**		
	Heavenly HVN 047CD.........**41**	2
3 Feb 96	**FROM A WINDOW / THIS MORNING**		
	Heavenly HVN 051CD.........**17**	3
20 Apr 96	**LIVIN' IT UP** Heavenly HVN 52CD **24**	2
22 Jun 96	**TOWN** Heavenly HVN 54CD **48**	1

NORTHSIDE
UK, male vocal / instrumental group   **12 wks**

9 Jun 90	**SHALL WE TAKE A TRIP / MOODY PLACES**		
	Factory FAC 268 ....**50**	5
3 Nov 90	**MY RISING STAR** Factory FAC 2987 ....**32**	3
1 Jun 91	**TAKE 5** Factory FAC 3087 ....**40**	4

Freddie NOTES and the RUDIES
Jamaica, male vocal / instrumental group   **2 wks**

10 Oct 70	**MONTEGO BAY** Trojan TR 7791 ....**45**	2

NOTORIOUS B.I.G. *US, male rapper*   **6 wks**

29 Oct 94	**JUICY** Bad Boy 74321240102 ....**72**	1
1 Apr 95	**BIG POPPA** Puff Daddy 74321263412 ....**63**	1
15 Jul 95	**CAN'T YOU SEE** Tommy Boy TBCD 700 [1] **43**	2
19 Aug 95	**ONE MORE CHANCE / STAY WITH ME**		
	Puff Daddy 74321300782 ....**34**	2

[1] Total featuring the Notorious B.I.G.

NOTTINGHAM FOREST F.C. – *See PAPER LACE*

Heather NOVA *Bermuda, female vocalist*   **1 wk**

25 Feb 95	**WALK THIS WORLD** Butterfly BFLD 19 ....**69**	1

Nancy NOVA *UK, female vocalist*   **2 wks**

4 Sep 82	**NO NO NO** EMI 5328.........**63**	2

NT GANG
Germany, male vocal / instrumental group   **1 wk**

2 Apr 88	**WAM BAM**		
	Cooltempo COOL 163 ....**71**	1

NU COLOURS
UK, male / female vocal / instrumental group **11 wks**

6 Jun 92	**TEARS** *Wild Card CARD 1*	**55**	2
10 Oct 92	**POWER** *Wild Card CARD 3*	**64**	1
5 Jun 93	**WHAT IN THE WORLD** *Wild Card CARDD 4*	**57**	2
27 Nov 93	**POWER (re-issue)** *Wild Card CARDD 5*	**40**	2
25 May 96	**DESIRE** *Wild Card 5763652*	**31**	2
24 Aug 96	**SPECIAL KIND OF LOVER** *Wild Card 5752012*	**38**	2

NU MATIC *UK, male instrumental / production duo* **1 wk**

8 Aug 92	**SPRING IN MY STEP** *XL XLS 31*	**58**	1

NU SHOOZ *US, male / female vocal duo* **17 wks**

24 May 86 ●	**I CAN'T WAIT** *Atlantic A 9446*	**2**	14
26 Jul 86	**POINT OF NO RETURN** *Atlantic A 9392*	**48**	3

NU SOUL featuring Kelli RICH
US, male / female vocal / instrumental duo **2 wks**

13 Jan 96	**HIDE-A-WAY** *ffrr FCD 269*	**27**	2

NUANCE featuring Vikki LOVE
US, male / female vocal / instrumental group **3 wks**

19 Jan 85	**LOVERIDE** *Fourth & Broadway BRW 20*	**59**	3

NUBIAN PRINZ – *See POWERCUT featuring NUBIAN PRINZ*

NUFF JUICE – *See D MOB*

Gary NUMAN *UK, male vocalist* **164 wks**

19 May 79	★ **ARE 'FRIENDS' ELECTRIC**		
	Beggars Banquet BEG 18 [1]	**1**	16
1 Sep 79	★ **CARS** *Beggars Banquet BEG 23*	**1**	11
24 Nov 79 ●	**COMPLEX** *Beggars Banquet BEG 29*	**6**	9
24 May 80 ●	**WE ARE GLASS** *Beggars Banquet BEG 35*	**5**	7
30 Aug 80 ●	**I DIE: YOU DIE** *Beggars Banquet BEG 46*	**6**	7
20 Dec 80	**THIS WRECKAGE** *Beggars Banquet BEG 50*	**20**	7
29 Aug 81 ●	**SHE'S GOT CLAWS** *Beggars Banquet BEG 62*	**6**	6
5 Dec 81	**LOVE NEEDS NO DISGUISE**		
	lBeggars Banquet BEG 68 [2]	**33**	7
6 Mar 82	**MUSIC FOR CHAMELEONS**		
	Beggars Banquet BEG 70	**19**	7
19 Jun 82 ●	**WE TAKE MYSTERY (TO BED)**		
	Beggars Banquet BEG 77	**9**	4
28 Aug 82	**WHITE BOYS AND HEROES**		
	Beggars Banquet BEG 81	**20**	4
3 Sep 83	**WARRIORS** *Beggars Banquet BEG 95*	**20**	5
22 Oct 83	**SISTER SURPRISE** *Beggars Banquet BEG 101*	**32**	3
3 Nov 84	**BERSERKER** *Numa NU 4*	**32**	5
22 Dec 84	**MY DYING MACHINE** *Numa NU 6*	**66**	1
9 Feb 85	**CHANGE YOUR MIND** *Polydor POSP 722* [3]	**17**	8
25 May 85	**THE LIVE EP** *Numa NUM 7*	**27**	4
10 Aug 85	**YOUR FASCINATION** *Numa NU 9*	**46**	5
21 Sep 85	**CALL OUT THE DOGS** *Numa NU 11*	**49**	2
16 Nov 85	**MIRACLES** *Numa NU 13*	**49**	3
19 Apr 86	**THIS IS LOVE** *Numa NU 16*	**28**	3
28 Jun 86	**I CAN'T STOP** *Numa NU 17*	**27**	4
4 Oct 86	**NEW THING FROM LONDON TOWN**		
	Numa NU 19 [3]	**52**	3
6 Dec 86	**I STILL REMEMBER** *Numa NU 21*	**74**	1
28 Mar 87	**RADIO HEART** *GFM GFM 109* [4]	**35**	6
13 Jun 87	**LONDON TIMES** *GFM GFM 112* [4]	**48**	2
19 Sep 87	**CARS (E REG MODEL) / ARE 'FRIENDS' ELECTRIC**		
	(re-mix) *Beggars Banquet BEG 199*	**16**	7
30 Jan 88	**NO MORE LIES** *Polydor POSP 894* [3]	**34**	3
1 Oct 88	**NEW ANGER** *Illegal ILS 1003*	**46**	2
3 Dec 88	**AMERICA** *Illegal ILS 1004*	**49**	1
3 Jun 89	**I'M ON AUTOMATIC** *Polydor PO 43* [3]	**44**	2
16 Mar 91	**HEART** *IRS NUMAN 1*	**43**	2
21 Mar 92	**THE SKIN GAME** *Numa NU 23*	**68**	1
1 Aug 92	**MACHINE + SOUL** *Numa NUM 124*	**72**	1
4 Sep 93	**CARS (2nd re-mix)** *Beggars Banquet BEG 264CD*	**53**	1
16 Mar 96	**CARS (re-issue of re-mix)**		
	PolyGram TV PRMCD 1	**17**	4

[1] Tubeway Army [2] Gary Numan and Dramatis [3] Sharpe and Numan
[4] Radio Heart featuring Gary Numan

Tracks on The Live EP: Are 'Friends' Electric / Berserker / Cars / We Are Glass. See also Paul Gardiner. Cars in 96 is a re-issue of the 87 remix.

NUMBER ONE CUP
US, male vocal / instrumental group **1 wk**

2 Mar 96	**DIVEBOMB** *Blue Rose BRRC 10032*	**61**	1

Bobby NUNN
US, male vocalist / multi-instrumentalist **3 wks**

4 Feb 84	**DON'T KNOCK IT (UNTIL YOU TRY IT)**		
	Motown TMG 1323	**65**	3

NUSH *UK, male instrumental / production duo* **7 wks**

23 Jul 94	**U GIRLS** *Blunted Vinyl BLNCDX 006*	**58**	1
22 Apr 95	**MOVE THAT BODY** *Blunted Vinyl BLNCD 012*	**46**	2
16 Sep 95	**U GIRLS (LOOK SO SEXY) (re-mix)**		
	Blunted Vinyl BLNCD 13	**15**	4

NUT *UK, female vocalist* **2 wks**

8 Jun 96	**BRAINS** *Epic NUTCD 2*	**64**	1
21 Sep 96	**CRAZY** *Epic NUTCD 5*	**56**	1

NUTTIN' NYCE *US, female vocal group* **2 wks**

10 Jun 95	**DOWN 4 WHATEVA** *Jive JIVECD 365*	**62**	1
12 Aug 95	**FROGGY STYLE** *Jive JIVECD 381*	**68**	1

NWA *US, male rap group* **15 wks**

9 Sep 89	**EXPRESS YOURSELF** *Fourth & Broadway BRW 144*	**50**	4
26 May 90	**EXPRESS YOURSELF (re-entry)**		
	Fourth & Broadway BRW 144	**26**	5
1 Sep 90	**GANGSTA, GANGSTA** *Fourth & Broadway BRW 191*	**70**	1
10 Nov 90	**100 MILES AND RUNNIN'**		
	Fourth & Broadway BRW 200	**38**	3
23 Nov 91	**ALWAYZ INTO SOMETHIN'**		
	Fourth & Broadway BRW 238	**60**	2

Joe NYE – *See DNA*

NYLON MOON *Italy, male instrumental duo* **2 wks**

13 Apr 96	**SKY PLUS** *Positiva CDTIV 50*	**43**	2

Michael NYMAN
UK, male instrumentalist – piano **2 wks**

19 Mar 94	**THE HEART ASKS PLEASURE FIRST – THE PROMISE**		
	Virgin VEND 3	**60**	2

Phil OAKEY – *See Giorgio MORODER*

OASIS *UK, male vocal / instrumental group* **220 wks**

Date	Title	Pos	Wks
23 Apr 94	SUPERSONIC *Creation CRESCD 176*.........................**31**		3
2 Jul 94	SHAKERMAKER *Creation CRESCD 182* **11**		5
20 Aug 94 ●	LIVE FOREVER *Creation CRESCD 185* **10**		5
22 Oct 94 ●	CIGARETTES AND ALCOHOL *Creation CRESCD 190* **7**		6
31 Dec 94 ●	WHATEVER *Creation CRESCD 195* **3**		10
31 Dec 94	CIGARETTES AND ALCOHOL (re-entry)		
	Creation CRESCD 190.......................**69**		1
6 May 95 ★	SOME MIGHT SAY *Creation CRESCD 204* **1**		14
13 May 95	SOME MIGHT SAY *Creation CRE 204T* **71**		1
24 Jun 95	SUPERSONIC (re-entry) *Creation CRESCD 176* **44**		3
24 Jun 95	WHATEVER (re-entry) *Creation CRESCD 195*...........**48**		3
24 Jun 95	LIVE FOREVER (re-entry) *Creation CRESCD 185* **50**		3
24 Jun 95	SHAKERMAKER (re-entry) *Creation CRESCD 182*.........**52**		3
24 Jun 95	CIGARETTES AND ALCOHOL (2nd re-entry)		
	Creation CRESCD 190.......................**53**		3
26 Aug 95 ●	ROLL WITH IT *Creation CRESCD 212*........................**2**		11
26 Aug 95	SOME MIGHT SAY (re-entry) *Creation CRESCD 204* **73**		1
11 Nov 95 ●	WONDERWALL *Creation CRESCD 215* **2**		20
25 Nov 95	WIBBLING RIVALRY (INTERVIEWS WITH NOEL AND		
	LIAM GALLAGHER) *Fierce Panda NING 12CD* [1] **52**		2
9 Dec 95	WHATEVER (2nd re-entry) *Creation CRESCD 195*...........**75**		1
30 Dec 95	CIGARETTES AND ALCOHOL (3rd re-entry)		
	Creation CRESCD 190.......................**58**		7
30 Dec 95	WHATEVER (3rd re-entry) *Creation CRESCD 195* **55**		3
30 Dec 95	SUPERSONIC (2nd re-entry) *Creation CRESCD 176* **54**		4
6 Jan 96	SHAKERMAKER (2nd re-entry) *Creation CRESCD 182* ..**61**		2
6 Jan 96	LIVE FOREVER (2nd re-entry) *Creation CRESCD 185*.....**64**		1
6 Jan 96	SOME MIGHT SAY (2nd re-entry) *Creation CRESCD 204*..**59**		3
6 Jan 96	ROLL WITH IT (re-entry) *Creation CRESCD 212*...........**65**		3
20 Jan 96	LIVE FOREVER (3rd re-entry) *Creation CRESCD 185* **71**		2
27 Jan 96	WHATEVER (4th re-entry) *Creation CRESCD 195* **61**		3
24 Feb 96	WHATEVER (5th re-entry) *Creation CRESCD 195* **55**		15
2 Mar 96 ★	DON'T LOOK BACK IN ANGER *Creation CRESCD 221* **1**		16
2 Mar 96	CIGARETTES AND ALCOHOL (4th re-entry)		
	Creation CRESCD 190.......................**62**		4
2 Mar 96	SUPERSONIC (3rd re-entry) *Creation CRESCD 176* **71**		1
2 Mar 96	SHAKERMAKER (3rd re-entry) *Creation CRESCD 182* ...**74**		1
2 Mar 96	LIVE FOREVER (4th re-entry) *Creation CRESCD 185* **74**		2
16 Mar 96	SOME MIGHT SAY (3rd re-entry) *Creation CRESCD 204*..**75**		1
13 Apr 96	CIGARETTES AND ALCOHOL (5th re-entry)		
	Creation CRESCD 190.......................**74**		2
11 May 96	CIGARETTES AND ALCOHOL (6th re-entry)		
	Creation CRESCD 190.......................**72**		3
17 Aug 96	WHATEVER (6th re-entry) *Creation CRESCD 195* **62**		4
24 Aug 96	WONDERWALL (re-entry) *Creation CRESCD 215* **60**		5
24 Aug 96	SOME MIGHT SAY (4th re-entry)		
	Creation CRESCD 204.......................**70**		1
24 Aug 96	CIGARETTES AND ALCOHOL (7th re-entry)		
	Creation CRESCD 190.......................**72**		1
21 Sep 96	WHATEVER (7th re-entry) *Creation CRESCD 195* **66**		1
16 Nov 96	WHATEVER (8th re-entry) *Creation CRESCD 195* ....**34†**		7
16 Nov 96	WONDERWALL (2nd re-entry)		
	Creation CRESCD 215 ....**36†**		7
16 Nov 96	CIGARETTES AND ALCOHOL (8th re-entry)		
	Creation CRESCD 190.......................**38**		5
16 Nov 96	SOME MIGHT SAY (5th re-entry)		
	Creation CRESCD 204.......................**40**		4
16 Nov 96	LIVE FOREVER (5th re-entry) *Creation CRESCD 185* **42**		2
16 Nov 96	SUPERSONIC (4th re-entry) *Creation CRESCD 176*.........**47**		2
16 Nov 96	SHAKERMAKER (4th re-entry) *Creation CRESCD 182* **48**		2
16 Nov 96	DON'T LOOK BACK IN ANGER (re-entry)		
	Creation CRESCD 221...................................**53**		5
16 Nov 96	ROLL WITH IT (2nd re-entry) *Creation CRESCD 212*.......**55**		2
28 Dec 96	DON'T LOOK BACK IN ANGER (2nd re-entry)		
	Creation CRESCD 221 ....**67†**		1
28 Dec 96	CIGARETTES AND ALCOHOL (9th re-entry)		
	Creation CRESCD 190 ....**71†**		1
28 Dec 96	SOME MIGHT SAY (6th re-entry)		
	Creation CRESCD 204 ....**73†**		1
28 Dec 96	LIVE FOREVER (6th re-entry) *Creation CRESCD 185* ....**75†**		1

[1] Oas*s

Chart rules allow for a maximum of three formats; the twelve inch of Some Might Say, already available on 2 CDs and cassette, was therefore listed separately.

John OATES – *See Daryl HALL and John OATES*

OBERNKIRCHEN CHILDREN'S CHOIR
Germany, children's choir **26 wks**

Date	Title	Pos	Wks
22 Jan 54 ●	HAPPY WANDERER (DER FROHLICHE WANDERER)		
	Parlophone R 3799.......................................**2**		23
9 Jul 54 ●	HAPPY WANDERER (DER FROHLICHE		
	WANDERER) (re-entry) *Parlophone R 3799* **8**		3

Dermot O'BRIEN *Ireland, male vocalist* **2 wks**

Date	Title	Pos	Wks
20 Oct 66	THE MERRY PLOUGHBOY *Envoy ENV 016* **46**		1
3 Nov 66	THE MERRY PLOUGHBOY (re-entry) *Envoy ENV 016* **50**		1

Billy OCEAN *UK, male vocalist* **153 wks**

Date	Title	Pos	Wks
21 Feb 76 ●	LOVE REALLY HURTS WITHOUT YOU *GTO GT 52* **2**		10
10 Jul 76	L.O.D. (LOVE ON DELIVERY) *GTO GT 62* **19**		8
13 Nov 76	STOP ME (IF YOU'VE HEARD IT ALL BEFORE)		
	GTO GT 72 ....**12**		11
19 Mar 77 ●	RED LIGHT SPELLS DANGER *GTO GT 85* **2**		10
1 Sep 79	AMERICAN HEARTS *GTO GT 244* **54**		5
19 Jan 80	ARE YOU READY *GTO GT 259* **42**		7
13 Oct 84 ●	CARIBBEAN QUEEN (NO MORE LOVE ON THE RUN)		
	Jive Jive 77 ....**6**		14
19 Jan 85	LOVERBOY *Jive JIVE 80* **15**		10
11 May 85 ●	SUDDENLY *Jive JIVE 90* **4**		14
17 Aug 85	MYSTERY LADY *Jive JIVE 98* **49**		4
25 Jan 86 ★	WHEN THE GOING GETS TOUGH, THE TOUGH GET		
	GOING *Jive JIVE 114* **1**		13
12 Apr 86	THERE'LL BE SAD SONGS (TO MAKE YOU CRY)		
	Jive JIVE 117 ....**12**		13
9 Aug 86	LOVE ZONE *Jive JIVE 124* **49**		3
11 Oct 86	BITTERSWEET *Jive JIVE 133* **44**		4
10 Jan 87	LOVE IS FOREVER *Jive JIVE 134* **34**		7
6 Feb 88 ●	GET OUTTA MY DREAMS GET INTO MY CAR		
	Jive BOS 1 ....**3**		11
7 May 88	CALYPSO CRAZY *Jive BOS 2* **35**		4
6 Aug 88	THE COLOUR OF LOVE *Jive BOS 3* **65**		3
6 Feb 93	PRESSURE *Jive BOSCD 6* **55**		2

OCEAN COLOUR SCENE
UK, male vocal / instrumental group **27 wks**

Date	Title	Pos	Wks
23 Mar 91	YESTERDAY TODAY *!Phfft FIT 2* **49**		1
17 Feb 96	THE RIVERBOAT SONG *MCA MCSTD 40021*..................**15**		5
6 Apr 96 ●	YOU'VE GOT IT BAD *MCA MCSTD 40036* **7**		4
15 Jun 96 ●	THE DAY WE CAUGHT THE TRAIN *MCA MCSTD 40046* **4**		11
28 Sep 96 ●	THE CIRCLE *MCA MCSTD 40077*......................**6**		6

OCEANIC *UK, male / female vocal / instrumental group* **26 wks**

Date	Title	Pos	Wks
24 Aug 91 ●	INSANITY *Dead Dead Good GOOD 4* **3**		15
30 Nov 91	WICKED LOVE *Dead Dead Good GOOD 5* **25**		3

Odyssey

The disco classic 'Use It Up And Wear It Out' hit number one in the UK, but missed the chart completely in Odyssey's homeland.

Ocean Colour Scene

Ocean Colour Scene's Steve Craddock (far right) played guitar on Paul Weller's *Wild Wood* album, Weller returned the favour, playing keyboards on 'The Riverboat Song'.

Gilbert O'Sullivan

At art college Raymond O'Sullivan was a member to two bands, the Doodles and the Prefects before changing his name to Gilbert and embarking on a solo career.

28 Dec 91	WICKED LOVE (re-entry) *Dead Dead Good GOOD 5*	**65**	2
13 Jun 92	CONTROLLING ME *Dead Dead Good GOOD 14*	**14**	5
14 Nov 92	IGNORANCE *Dead Dead Good GOOD 22* [1]	**72**	1

[1] Oceanic featuring Siobhan Maher

Des O'CONNOR *UK, male vocalist*   117 wks

1 Nov 67	● CARELESS HANDS *Columbia DB 8275*	**6**	17
8 May 68	★ I PRETEND *Columbia DB 8397*	**1**	36
20 Nov 68	● 1-2-3 O'LEARY *Columbia DB 8492*	**4**	11
7 May 69	DICK-A-DUM-DUM (KING'S ROAD) *Columbia DB 8566*	**14**	10
29 Nov 69	LONELINESS *Columbia DB 8632*	**18**	11
14 Mar 70	I'LL GO ON HOPING *Columbia DB 8661*	**30**	7
26 Sep 70	THE TIP OF MY FINGERS *Columbia DB 8713*	**15**	15
8 Nov 86	● THE SKYE BOAT SONG *Tembo TML 119* [1]	**10**	10

[1] Roger Whittaker and Des O'Connor

Hazel O'CONNOR *UK, female vocalist*   46 wks

16 Aug 80	● EIGHTH DAY *A & M AMS 7553*	**5**	11
25 Oct 80	GIVE ME AN INCH *A & M AMS 7569*	**41**	4
21 Mar 81	● D-DAYS *Albion ION 1009*	**10**	9
23 May 81	WILL YOU *A & M AMS 8131*	**8**	10
1 Aug 81	(COVER PLUS) WE'RE ALL GROWN UP *Albion ION 1018*	**41**	6
3 Oct 81	HANGING AROUND *Albion ION 1022*	**45**	3
23 Jan 82	CALLS THE TUNE *A & M AMS 8203*	**60**	3

Sinead O'CONNOR *Ireland, female vocalist*   60 wks

16 Jan 88	MANDINKA *Ensign ENY 611*	**17**	9
20 Jan 90	★ NOTHING COMPARES 2 U *Ensign ENY 630*	**1**	14
21 Jul 90	THE EMPEROR'S NEW CLOTHES *Ensign ENY 633*	**31**	5
20 Oct 90	THREE BABIES *Ensign ENY 635*	**42**	4
8 Jun 91	MY SPECIAL CHILD *Ensign ENY 646*	**42**	3
14 Dec 91	SILENT NIGHT *Ensign ENY 652*	**60**	4
12 Sep 92	SUCCESS HAS MADE A FAILURE OF OUR HOME *Ensign ENY 656*	**18**	4
12 Dec 92	DON'T CRY FOR ME ARGENTINA *Ensign ENY 657*	**53**	4
19 Feb 94	YOU MADE ME THE THIEF OF YOUR HEART *Island CID 588*	**42**	3
26 Nov 94	THANK YOU FOR HEARING ME *Ensign CDENYS 662*	**13**	7
29 Apr 95	HAUNTED *ZTT ZANG 65CD* [1]	**30**	4
26 Aug 95	FAMINE *Ensign CDENY 663*	**51**	1

[1] Shane MacGowan and Sinead O'Connor

See also Jah Wobble's Invaders Of The Heart; Marxman.

OCTOPUS *UK / France, male vocal / instrumental group*   5 wks

22 Jun 96	YOUR SMILE *Food CDFOOD 78*	**42**	2
14 Sep 96	SAVED *Food CDFOODS 84*	**40**	2
23 Nov 96	JEALOUSY *Food CDFOODS 87*	**59**	1

Alan O'DAY *US, male vocalist*   3 wks

2 Jul 77	UNDERCOVER ANGEL *Atlantic K 10926*	**43**	3

ODETTA – *See Harry BELAFONTE*

Daniel O'DONNELL *Ireland, male vocalist*   33 wks

12 Sep 92	I JUST WANT TO DANCE WITH YOU *Ritz RITZ 250P*	**20**	7
2 Jan 93	THE THREE BELLS *Ritz RITZCD 239*	**71**	1
8 May 93	THE LOVE IN YOUR EYES *Ritz RITZCD 257*	**47**	3
7 Aug 93	WHAT EVER HAPPENED TO OLD FASHIONED LOVE *Ritz RITZCD 262*	**21**	5
16 Apr 94	SINGING THE BLUES *Ritz RITZCD 270*	**23**	3
26 Nov 94	THE GIFT *Ritz RITZCD 275*	**46**	3
10 Jun 95	SECRET LOVE *Ritz RITZCD 285* [1]	**28**	3
9 Mar 96	TIMELESS *Ritz RITZCD 293* [1]	**32**	3
28 Sep 96	FOOTSTEPS *Ritz RITZCD 300*	**25**	5

[1] Daniel O'Donnell and Mary Duff

ODYSSEY *US, male / female vocal group*   82 wks

24 Dec 77	● NATIVE NEW YORKER *RCA PC 1129*	**5**	11
21 Jun 80	★ USE IT UP AND WEAR IT OUT *RCA PB 1962*	**1**	12
13 Sep 80	● IF YOU'RE LOOKIN' FOR A WAY OUT *RCA 5*	**6**	15
17 Jan 81	HANG TOGETHER *RCA 23*	**36**	7
30 May 81	● GOING BACK TO MY ROOTS *RCA 85*	**4**	12
19 Sep 81	IT WILL BE ALRIGHT *RCA 128*	**43**	5
12 Jun 82	INSIDE OUT *RCA 226*	**3**	11
11 Sep 82	MAGIC TOUCH *RCA 275*	**41**	5
17 Aug 85	(JOY) I KNOW IT *Mirror BUTCH 12*	**51**	4

Esther and Abi OFARIM *Israel, female / male vocal duo*   22 wks

14 Feb 68	★ CINDERELLA ROCKEFELLA *Philips BF 1640*	**1**	13
19 Jun 68	ONE MORE DANCE *Philips BF 1678*	**13**	9

OFF-SHORE *Germany, male instrumental / production duo*   12 wks

22 Dec 90	● I CAN'T TAKE THE POWER *CBS 6565707*	**7**	11
17 Aug 91	I GOT A LITTLE SONG *Dance Pool 6568257*	**64**	1

Wiston OFFICE – *See Frank K featuring Wiston OFFICE*

OFFSPRING *US, male vocal / instrumental group*   5 wks

25 Feb 95	SELF ESTEEM *Golf CDSHOLE 001*	**37**	3
19 Aug 95	GOTTA GET AWAY *Out Of Step WOOS 2CDS*	**43**	2

OH WELL *Germany, male producer – Ackim Faulker*   7 wks

14 Oct 89	OH WELL *Parlophone R 6236*	**28**	6
3 Mar 90	RADAR LOVE *Parlophone R 6244*	**65**	1

OHIO EXPRESS *US, male vocal / instrumental group*   15 wks

5 Jun 68	● YUMMY YUMMY YUMMY *Pye International 7N 25459*	**5**	15

OHIO PLAYERS *US, male vocal / instrumental group*   4 wks

10 Jul 76	WHO'D SHE COO *Mercury PLAY 001*	**43**	4

O'JAYS *US, male vocal group*   72 wks

23 Sep 72	BACK STABBERS *CBS 8270*	**14**	9
3 Mar 73	● LOVE TRAIN *CBS 1181*	**9**	13
31 Jan 76	I LOVE MUSIC *Philadelphia International PIR 3879*	**13**	9
12 Feb 77	DARLIN' DARLIN' BABY (SWEET, TENDER, LOVE) *Philadelphia International PIR 4834*	**24**	6
8 Apr 78	I LOVE MUSIC (re-issue) *Philadelphia International PIR 6093*	**36**	3
17 Jun 78	USE TA BE MY GIRL *Philadelphia International PIR 6332*	**12**	12
30 Sep 78	BRANDY *Philadelphia International PIR 6658*	**21**	9
29 Sep 79	SING A HAPPY SONG *Philadelphia International PIR 7825*	**39**	6
30 Jul 83	PUT OUR HEADS TOGETHER *Philadelphia International A 3642*	**45**	5

John O'KANE UK, male vocalist — 4 wks

9 May 92	**STAY WITH ME** Circa YR 88	41	4

Mike OLDFIELD
UK, male multi-instrumentalist / vocalist — 111 wks

13 Jul 74	**MIKE OLDFIELD'S SINGLE (THEME FROM TUBULAR BELLS)** Virgin VS 101	31	6
20 Dec 75	● **IN DULCE JUBILO / ON HORSEBACK** Virgin VS 131	4	10
27 Nov 76	● **PORTSMOUTH** Virgin VS 163	3	12
23 Dec 78	**TAKE 4 EP** Virgin VS 238	72	3
21 Apr 79	**GUILTY** Virgin VS 245	22	8
8 Dec 79	**BLUE PETER** Virgin VS 317	19	9
20 Mar 82	**FIVE MILES OUT** Virgin VS 464 [1]	43	5
12 Jun 82	**FAMILY MAN** Virgin VS 489 [1]	45	6
28 May 83	● **MOONLIGHT SHADOW** Virgin VS 586 [1]	4	17
14 Jan 84	**CRIME OF PASSION** Virgin VS 648 [1]	61	3
30 Jun 84	**TO FRANCE** Virgin VS 686 [1]	48	7
14 Dec 85	**PICTURES IN THE DARK** Virgin VS 836 [2]	50	6
3 Oct 92	● **SENTINEL** WEA YZ 698	10	6
19 Dec 92	**TATTOO** WEA YZ 708	33	5
17 Apr 93	**THE BELL** WEA YZ 737CD	50	2
9 Oct 93	**MOONLIGHT SHADOW (re-issue)** Virgin VSCDT 1477	52	2
17 Dec 94	**HIBERNACULUM** WEA YZ 871CD	47	3
2 Sep 95	**LET THERE BE LIGHT** WEA YZ 880CD	51	1

[1] Mike Oldfield featuring Maggie Reilly [2] Mike Oldfield featuring Aled Jones, Anita Hegerland and Barry Palmer

Tracks on Take 4 EP: Portsmouth / In Dulce Jubilo / Wrekorder Wrondo / Sailors Hornpipe. The Bell credits Viv Stanshall.

Sally OLDFIELD UK, female vocalist — 13 wks

9 Dec 78	**MIRRORS** Bronze BRO 66	19	13

Misty OLDLAND UK, female vocalist — 7 wks

16 Oct 93	**GOT ME A FELLING** Columbia 6597872	59	2
12 Mar 94	**A FAIR AFFAIR (JE T'AIME)** Columbia 6601612	49	4
9 Jul 94	**I WROTE YOU A SONG** Columbia 6603732	73	1

OLGA Italy, female vocalist — 1 wk

1 Oct 94	**I'M A BITCH** UMM UMM 144UKCD	68	1

OLIVE UK, male / female vocal / instrumental group — 4 wks

7 Sep 96	**YOU'RE NOT ALONE** RCA 74321406272	42	4

OLIVER US, male vocalist — 18 wks

9 Aug 69	● **GOOD MORNING STARSHINE** CBS 4435	6	16
27 Dec 69	**GOOD MORNING STARSHINE (re-entry)** CBS 4435	39	2

OLLIE and JERRY US, male vocal duo — 14 wks

23 Jun 84	● **BREAKIN' ...THERE'S NO STOPPING US** Polydor POSP 690	5	11
9 Mar 85	**ELECTRIC BOOGALOO** Polydor POSP 730	57	3

OLYMPIC ORCHESTRA UK, orchestra — 15 wks

1 Oct 83	**REILLY** Red Bus RBUS 82	26	15

OLYMPIC RUNNERS
UK, male vocal / instrumental group — 21 wks

13 May 78	**WHATEVER IT TAKES** RCA PC 5078	61	2
14 Oct 78	**GET IT WHILE YOU CAN** Polydor RUN 7	35	6
20 Jan 79	**SIR DANCEALOT** Polydor POSP 17	35	6
28 Jul 79	**THE BITCH** Polydor POSP 63	37	7

OLYMPICS US, male vocal group — 9 wks

3 Oct 58	**WESTERN MOVIES** HMV POP 528	12	8
19 Jan 61	**I WISH I COULD SHIMMY LIKE MY SISTER KATE** Vogue V 9174	40	1

OMAR UK, male vocalist — 14 wks

22 Jun 91	**THERE'S NOTHING LIKE THIS** Talkin Loud TLK 9	14	7
23 May 92	**YOUR LOSS MY GAIN** Talkin Loud TLK 22	47	2
26 Sep 92	**MUSIC** Talkin Loud TLK 28	53	2
23 Jul 94	**OUTSIDE / SATURDAY** RCA 74321213982	43	2
15 Oct 94	**KEEP STEPPIN'** RCA 74321233682	57	1

OMC New Zealand, male vocalist — 16 wks

20 Jul 96	● **HOW BIZARRE** Polydor 5776202	5	16

OMD – *See ORCHESTRAL MANOEUVRES IN THE DARK*

Michie ONE – *See Louchie LOU and Michie ONE*

ONE DOVE UK, male / female vocal / instrumental group — 9 wks

7 Aug 93	**WHITE LOVE** Boy's Own BOICD 14	43	3
16 Oct 93	**BREAKDOWN** Boy's Own BOICD 15	24	3
15 Jan 94	**WHY DON'T YOU TAKE ME** Boy's Own BOICD 16	30	3

ONE HUNDRED TON AND A FEATHER – *See Jonathan KING*

ONE THE JUGGLER UK, male vocal / instrumental group — 1 wk

19 Feb 83	**PASSION KILLER** Regard RG 107	71	1

ONE TRIBE – *See OUR TRIBE/ONE TRIBE*

ONE 2 MANY
Norway, male / female vocal / instrumental group — 11 wks

12 Nov 88	**DOWNTOWN** A & M AM 476	65	4
3 Jun 89	**DOWNTOWN (re-entry)** A & M AM 476	43	7

ONE WAY featuring Al HUDSON – *See Al HUDSON*

Alexander O'NEAL US, male vocalist — 108 wks

28 Dec 85	● **SATURDAY LOVE** Tabu A 6829 [1]	6	11
15 Feb 86	**IF YOU WERE HERE TONIGHT** Tabu A 6391	13	10
5 Apr 86	**A BROKEN HEART CAN MEND** Tabu A 6244	53	4
6 Jun 87	**FAKE** Tabu 650891 7	33	6
31 Oct 87	● **CRITICIZE** Tabu 651211 7	4	14
6 Feb 88	**NEVER KNEW LOVE LIKE THIS** Tabu 651382 7 [2]	26	4
28 May 88	**THE LOVERS** Tabu 651595 7	28	4
23 Jul 88	**(WHAT CAN I SAY) TO MAKE YOU LOVE ME** Tabu 652852 7	27	5
24 Sep 88	**FAKE '88 (re-mix)** Tabu 652949 7	16	7
10 Dec 88	**CHRISTMAS SONG (CHESTNUTS ROASTING ON AN OPEN FIRE) / THANK YOU FOR A GOOD YEAR** Tabu 653182 7	30	5
25 Feb 89	**HEARSAY '89** Tabu 654466 7	56	2

2 Sep 89	**SUNSHINE** *Tabu 655191 7*	**72**	1
9 Dec 89	**HITMIX (OFFICIAL BOOTLEG MEGA-MIX)** *Tabu 655504 7*	**19**	7
24 Mar 90	**SATURDAY LOVE (re-mix)** *Tabu 655680 7* [1]	**55**	2
12 Jan 91	**ALL TRUE MAN** *Tabu 6565717*	**18**	6
23 Mar 91	**WHAT IS THIS THING CALLED LOVE** *Tabu 6567317*	**53**	2
11 May 91	**SHAME ON ME** *Tabu 6568737*	**71**	1
9 May 92	**SENTIMENTAL** *Tabu 6580147*	**53**	2
30 Jan 93	**LOVE MAKES NO SENSE** *Tabu AMCD 7708*	**28**	6
3 Jul 93	**IN THE MIDDLE** *Tabu 5877152*	**32**	3
25 Sep 93	**ALL THAT MATTERS TO ME** *Tabu 5877232*	**67**	1
2 Nov 96	**LET'S GET TOGETHER** *EMI Premier PRESCD 11*	**38**	2

[1] Cherelle with Alexander O'Neal [2] Alexander O'Neal featuring Cherelle

Shaquille O'NEAL *US, male rapper* **1 wk**

26 Mar 94	**I'M OUTSTANDING** *Jive JIVECD 349*	**70**	1

ONLY ONES *UK, male vocal / instrumental group* **2 wks**

1 Feb 92	**ANOTHER GIRL – ANOTHER PLANET** *Columbia 6577507*	**57**	2

Yoko ONO *Japan, female vocalist* **5 wks**

28 Feb 81	**WALKING ON THIN ICE** *Geffen K 79202*	**35**	5

See also John Lennon.

ONSLAUGHT *UK, male vocal / instrumental group* **3 wks**

6 May 89	**LET THERE BE ROCK** *London LON 224*	**50**	3

ONYX *US, male rap group* **7 wks**

28 Aug 93	**SLAM** *Columbia 6596302*	**31**	4
27 Nov 93	**THROW YA GUNZ** *Columbia 6598312*	**34**	3

OO LA LA *UK, male vocal / instrumental group* **2 wks**

5 Sep 92	**OO... AH... CANTONA** *North Speed OOAH 1*	**64**	2

OPEN ARMS featuring ROWETTA
UK, male / female vocal / instrumental group **1 wk**

15 Jun 96	**HEY MR. DJ** *All Around The World CDGLOBE 136*	**62**	1

See also Various Artists (EPs and LPs) – The Further Adventures Of North EP.

OPTIMYSTIC *UK, male / female vocal group* **6 wks**

17 Sep 94	**CAUGHT UP IN MY HEART** *WEA YZ 841CD*	**49**	3
10 Dec 94	**NOTHING BUT LOVE** *WEA 864CD1*	**37**	2
13 May 95	**BEST THING IN THE WORLD** *WEA YZ 920CD*	**70**	1

OPUS *Austria, male vocal / instrumental group* **15 wks**

15 Jun 85	● **LIVE IS LIFE** *Polydor POSP 743*	**6**	15

OPUS III *UK, male / female vocal / instrumental group* **10 wks**

22 Feb 92	● **IT'S A FINE DAY** *PWL International PWL 215*	**5**	8
27 Jun 92	**I TALK TO THE WIND** *PWL Continental PWL 235*	**52**	1
11 Jun 94	**WHEN YOU MADE THE MOUNTAIN** *PWL International PWCD 302*	**71**	1

ORANGE *UK, male vocal / instrumental group* **1 wk**

8 Oct 94	**JUDY OVER THE RAINBOW** *Chrysalis CDCHS 5012*	**73**	1

ORANGE JUICE *UK, male vocal / instrumental group* **34 wks**

7 Nov 81	**L.O.V.E... LOVE** *Polydor POSP 357*	**65**	2
30 Jan 82	**FELICITY** *Polydor POSP 386*	**63**	3
21 Aug 82	**TWO HEARTS TOGETHER / HOKOYO** *Polydor POSP 470*	**60**	2
23 Oct 82	**I CAN'T HELP MYSELF** *Polydor POSP 522*	**42**	3
19 Feb 83	● **RIP IT UP** *Polydor POSP 547*	**8**	11
4 Jun 83	**FLESH OF MY FLESH** *Polydor OJ 4*	**41**	6
25 Feb 84	**BRIDGE** *Polydor OJ 5*	**67**	2
12 May 84	**WHAT PRESENCE?** *Polydor OJ 6*	**47**	4
27 Oct 84	**LEAN PERIOD** *Polydor OJ 7*	**74**	1

ORB *UK, male instrumental / production duo* **24 wks**

15 Jun 91	**PERPETUAL DAWN** *Big Life BLR 46*	**61**	1
20 Jun 92	● **BLUE ROOM** *Big Life BLR 75*	**8**	6
17 Oct 92	**ASSASSIN** *Big Life BLRT 81*	**12**	5
13 Nov 93	● **LITTLE FLUFFY CLOUDS** *Big Life BLRD 98*	**10**	5
5 Feb 94	● **PERPETUAL DAWN (re-entry)** *Big Life BLRD 46*	**18**	5
27 May 95	**OXBOW LAKES** *Island CID 609*	**38**	2

Roy ORBISON *US, male vocalist* **345 wks**

28 Jul 60	**ONLY THE LONELY** *London HLU 9149*	**36**	1
11 Aug 60	★ **ONLY THE LONELY (re-entry)** *London HLU 9149*	**1**	23
27 Oct 60	**BLUE ANGEL** *London HLU 9207*	**11**	16
25 May 61	● **RUNNING SCARED** *London HLU 9342*	**9**	15
21 Sep 61	**CRYIN'** *London HLU 9405*	**25**	9
8 Mar 62	● **DREAM BABY** *London HLU 9511*	**2**	14
28 Jun 62	**THE CROWD** *London HLU 9561*	**40**	4
8 Nov 62	**WORKIN' FOR THE MAN** *London HLU 9607*	**50**	1
28 Feb 63	● **IN DREAMS** *London HLU 9676*	**6**	23
30 May 63	● **FALLING** *London HLU 9727*	**9**	11
19 Sep 63	● **BLUE BAYOU / MEAN WOMAN BLUES** *London HLU 9777*	**3**	19
20 Feb 64	**BORNE ON THE WIND** *London HLU 9845*	**15**	10
30 Apr 64	★ **IT'S OVER** *London HLU 9882*	**1**	18
10 Sep 64	★ **OH PRETTY WOMAN** *London HLU 9919*	**1**	18
19 Nov 64	● **PRETTY PAPER** *London HLU 9930*	**6**	11
11 Feb 65	**GOODNIGHT** *London HLU 9951*	**14**	9
22 Jul 65	**(SAY) YOU'RE MY GIRL** *London HLU 9978*	**23**	8
9 Sep 65	**RIDE AWAY** *London HLU 9986*	**34**	6
4 Nov 65	**CRAWLIN' BACK** *London HLU 10000*	**19**	9
27 Jan 66	**BREAKIN' UP IS BREAKIN' MY HEART** *London HL 10015*	**22**	6
7 Apr 66	**TWINKLE TOES** *London HLU 10034*	**29**	5
16 Jun 66	**LANA** *London HLU 10051*	**15**	9
18 Aug 66	● **TOO SOON TO KNOW** *London HLU 10067*	**3**	17
1 Dec 66	**THERE WON'T BE MANY COMING HOME** *London HL 10096*	**18**	9
23 Feb 67	**SO GOOD** *London HL 10113*	**32**	6
24 Jul 68	**WALK ON** *London HLU 10206*	**39**	10
25 Sep 68	**HEARTACHE** *London HLU 10222*	**44**	4
30 Apr 69	**MY FRIEND** *London HL 10261*	**35**	4
13 Sep 69	**PENNY ARCADE** *London HL 10285*	**40**	3
11 Oct 69	**PENNY ARCADE (re-entry)** *London HL 10285*	**27**	11
14 Jan 89	● **YOU GOT IT** *Virgin VS 1166*	**3**	10
1 Apr 89	**SHE'S A MYSTERY TO ME** *Virgin VS 1173*	**27**	5
4 Jul 92	**I DROVE ALL NIGHT** *MCA MCS 1652*	**7**	10
22 Aug 92	**CRYING** *Virgin America VUS 63* [1]	**13**	6
7 Nov 92	**HEARTBREAK RADIO** *Virgin America VUS 68*	**36**	3
13 Nov 93	**I DROVE ALL NIGHT (re-issue)** *Virgin America VUSCD 79*	**47**	2

[1] Roy Orbison (duet with kd lang)

William ORBIT *UK, male producer* **1 wk**

26 Jun 93	**WATER FROM A VINE LEAF** *Guerilla VSCDT 1465*	**59**	1

ORBITAL UK, male instrumental duo   28 wks

24 Mar 90	CHIME ffrr F B5	17	7
22 Sep 90	OMEN ffrr F 145	46	3
19 Jan 91	SATAN ffrr FX 149	31	4
15 Feb 92	MUTATIONS EP ffrr FX 181	24	3
26 Sep 92	RADICCIO EP Internal LIARX 1	37	2
21 Aug 93	LUSH Internal LIECD 7	43	2
24 Sep 94	ARE WE HERE Internal LIECD 15	33	2
27 May 95	BELFAST Volume VOLCD 1	53	1
27 Apr 96	THE BOX Internal LIECD 30	11	4

Tracks on Mutations EP: Chime Chime / Oolaa / Farenheit 3D 3 / Speed Freak. Tracks on Radiccio EP: Halcyon / The Naked And The Dead / Sunday. The listed flip side of Belfast was Innocent X by Therapy?.

ORCHESTRA ON THE HALF SHELL
US, male vocal / instrumental group   6 wks

15 Dec 90	TURTLE RHAPSODY SBK SBK 17	36	6

ORCHESTRAL MANOEUVRES IN THE DARK UK, male vocal / instrumental group   199 wks

9 Feb 80	RED FRAME WHITE LIGHT Dindisc DIN 6	67	2
10 May 80	MESSAGES Dindisc DIN 15	13	11
4 Oct 80 ●	ENOLA GAY Dindisc DIN 22	8	15
29 Aug 81 ●	SOUVENIR Dindisc DIN 24	3	12
24 Oct 81 ●	JOAN OF ARC Dindisc DIN 36	5	14
23 Jan 82	MAID OF ORLEANS (THE WALTZ JOAN OF ARC) Dindisc DIN 40	4	10
19 Feb 83	GENETIC ENGINEERING Virgin VS 527	20	8
9 Apr 83	TELEGRAPH Virgin VS 580	42	4
14 Apr 84 ●	LOCOMOTION Virgin VS 660	5	11
16 Jun 84	TALKING LOUD AND CLEAR Virgin VS 685	11	10
8 Sep 84	TESLA GIRLS Virgin VS 705	21	8
10 Nov 84	NEVER TURN AWAY Virgin VS 727	70	2
25 May 85	SO IN LOVE Virgin VS 766	27	7
20 Jul 85	SECRET Virgin VS 796	34	7
26 Oct 85	LA FEMME ACCIDENT Virgin VS 811	42	4
3 May 86	IF YOU LEAVE Virgin VS 843	48	4
6 Sep 86	(FOREVER) LIVE AND DIE Virgin VS 888	11	10
15 Nov 86	WE LOVE YOU Virgin VS 911	54	5
2 May 87	SHAME Virgin VS 938	52	3
6 Feb 88	DREAMING Virgin VS 987	50	3
2 Jul 88	DREAMING (re-entry) Virgin VS 987	60	3
30 Mar 91 ●	SAILING ON THE SEVEN SEAS Virgin VS 1310	3	13
6 Jul 91 ●	PANDORA'S BOX Virgin VS 1331	7	10
14 Sep 91	THEN YOU TURN AWAY Virgin VS 1368	50	4
7 Dec 91	CALL MY NAME Virgin VS 1380	50	2
15 May 93	STAND ABOVE ME Virgin VSCDG 1444	21	4
17 Jul 93	DREAM OF ME (BASED ON LOVE'S THEME) Virgin VSCDT 1461	24	5
18 Sep 93	EVERYDAY Virgin VSCDT 1471	59	2
17 Aug 96	WALKING ON THE MILKY WAY Virgin VSCDT 1599	17	5
2 Nov 96	UNIVERSAL Virgin VSCDT 1606	55	1

Group often known as OMD.

Raul ORELLANA Spain, male producer   8 wks

30 Sep 89	THE REAL WILD HOUSE RCA BCM 322	29	8

ORIGIN UNKNOWN
UK, male instrumental / production duo   1 wk

13 Jul 96	VALLEY OF THE SHADOWS Ram RAMM 16CD	60	1

ORIGINAL US, male vocal / instrumental duo   14 wks

14 Jan 95	I LUV U BABY Ore AG 8CD	31	3
19 Aug 95 ●	I LUV U BABY (re-mix) Ore AGR 8CD	2	9
11 Nov 95	B 2 GETHER Ore AG 12CD	29	2

ORIGINOO GUNN CLAPPAZ – See HELTAH SKELTAH and ORIGINOO GUNN CLAPPAZ

Tony ORLANDO US, male vocalist   11 wks

5 Oct 61 ●	BLESS YOU Fontana H 330	5	11

See also Dawn.

ORLONS US, female / male vocal group   3 wks

27 Dec 62	DON'T HANG UP Cameo Parkway C 231	50	1
10 Jan 63	DON'T HANG UP (re-entry) Cameo Parkway C 231	39	2

ORVILLE – See Keith HARRIS

Jeffrey OSBORNE US, male vocalist   38 wks

17 Sep 83	DON'T YOU GET SO MAD A & M AM 140	54	2
14 Apr 84	STAY WITH ME TONIGHT A & M AM 188	18	11
23 Jun 84	ON THE WINGS OF LOVE A & M AM 198	11	14
20 Oct 84	DON'T STOP A & M AM 222	61	2
26 Jul 86	SOWETO A & M AM 334	44	5
6 Sep 86	SOWETO (re-entry) A & M AM 334	75	1
15 Aug 87	LOVE POWER Arista RIS 27 [1]	63	3

[1] Dionne Warwick and Jeffrey Osborne

Joan OSBORNE US, female vocalist   13 wks

10 Feb 96 ●	ONE OF US Blue Gorilla JOACD 1	6	10
8 Jun 96	ST. TERESA Blue Gorilla JOACD 3	33	3

Tony OSBORNE SOUND UK, orchestra   3 wks

23 Feb 61	MAN FROM MADRID HMV POP 827 [1]	50	1
3 Feb 73	THE SHEPHERD'S SONG Philips 6006 266	46	2

[1] Tony Osborne Sound featuring Joanne Brown

Ozzy OSBOURNE UK, male vocalist   42 wks

13 Sep 80	CRAZY TRAIN Jet 197 [1]	49	4
15 Nov 80	MR. CROWLEY Jet 7003 [1]	46	3
26 Nov 83	BARK AT THE MOON Epic A 3915	21	8
2 Jun 84	SO TIRED Epic A 4452	20	4
1 Feb 86	SHOT IN THE DARK Epic A 6859	20	6
9 Aug 86	THE ULTIMATE SIN / LIGHTNING STRIKES Epic A 7311	72	1
20 May 89	CLOSE MY EYES FOREVER Dreamland PB 49409 [2]	47	3
28 Sep 91	NO MORE TEARS Epic 6574407	32	3
30 Nov 91	MAMA I'M COMING HOME Epic 6576177	46	2
25 Nov 95	PERRY MASON Epic 6626395	23	2
31 Aug 96	I JUST WANT YOU Epic 6635702	43	1

[1] Ozzy Osbourne's Blizzard of Ozz [2] Lita Ford duet with Ozzy Osbourne

OSIBISA Ghana / Nigeria, male vocal / instrumental group   12 wks

17 Jan 76	SUNSHINE DAY Bronze BRO 20	17	6
5 Jun 76	DANCE THE BODY MUSIC Bronze BRO 26	31	6

OSMOND BOYS US, male vocal group   6 wks

9 Nov 91	BOYS WILL BE BOYS Curb 6573847	65	2
11 Jan 92	SHOW ME THE WAY Curb 6577227	60	4

Donny OSMOND *US, male vocalist* **118 wks**

17 Jun 72	★ **PUPPY LOVE** *MGM 2006 104*	**1**	17
16 Sep 72	● **TOO YOUNG** *MGM 2006 113*	**5**	12
21 Oct 72	**PUPPY LOVE (re-entry)** *MGM 2006 104*	**45**	2
11 Nov 72	● **WHY** *MGM 2006 119*	**3**	20
23 Dec 72	**PUPPY LOVE (2nd re-entry)** *MGM 2006 104*	**46**	3
23 Dec 72	**TOO YOUNG (re-entry)** *MGM 2006 113*	**47**	3
27 Jan 73	**PUPPY LOVE (3rd re-entry)** *MGM 2006 104*	**48**	1
10 Mar 73	★ **THE TWELFTH OF NEVER** *MGM 2006 199*	**1**	14
18 Aug 73	★ **YOUNG LOVE** *MGM 2006 300*	**1**	10
10 Nov 73	● **WHEN I FALL IN LOVE** *MGM 2006 365*	**4**	13
9 Nov 74	**WHERE DID ALL THE GOOD TIMES GO** *MGM 2006 468*	**18**	10
26 Sep 87	**I'M IN IT FOR LOVE** *Virgin VS 994*	**70**	1
6 Aug 88	**SOLDIER OF LOVE** *Virgin VS 1094*	**29**	8
12 Nov 88	**IF IT'S LOVE THAT YOU WANT** *Virgin VS 1140*	**70**	2
9 Feb 91	**MY LOVE IS A FIRE** *Capitol CL 600*	**64**	2

See also Donny and Marie Osmond; Osmonds.

Donny and Marie OSMOND
US, male / female vocal duo **37 wks**

3 Aug 74	● **I'M LEAVING IT (ALL) UP TO YOU** *MGM 2006 446*	**2**	12
14 Dec 74	● **MORNING SIDE OF THE MOUNTAIN** *MGM 2006 474*	**5**	10
21 Jun 75	**MAKE THE WORLD GO AWAY** *MGM 2006 523*	**18**	6
17 Jan 76	**DEEP PURPLE** *MGM 2006 561*	**25**	7

See also Donny Osmond; Marie Osmond.

Little Jimmy OSMOND *US, male vocalist* **50 wks**

25 Nov 72	★ **LONG HAIRED LOVER FROM LIVERPOOL** *MGM 2006 109*	**1**	24
31 Mar 73	● **TWEEDLE DEE** *MGM 2006 175*	**4**	13
19 May 73	**LONG HAIRED LOVER FROM LIVERPOOL (re-entry)** *MGM 2006 109*	**41**	3
23 Mar 74	**I'M GONNA KNOCK ON YOUR DOOR** *MGM 2006 389*	**11**	10

Marie OSMOND *US, female vocalist* **15 wks**

17 Nov 73	● **PAPER ROSES** *MGM 2006 315*	**2**	15

See also Donny and Marie Osmond.

OSMONDS *US, male vocal / instrumental group* **92 wks**

25 Mar 72	**DOWN BY THE LAZY RIVER** *MGM 2006 096*	**40**	5
11 Nov 72	● **CRAZY HORSES** *MGM 2006 142*	**2**	18
14 Jul 73	● **GOIN' HOME** *MGM 2006 288*	**4**	10
27 Oct 73	**LET ME IN** *MGM 2006 321*	**2**	14
20 Apr 74	**I CAN'T STOP** *MCA 129*	**12**	10
24 Aug 74	★ **LOVE ME FOR A REASON** *MGM 2006 458*	**1**	9
1 Mar 75	**HAVING A PARTY** *MGM 2006 492*	**28**	8
24 May 75	● **THE PROUD ONE** *MGM 2006 520*	**5**	8
15 Nov 75	**I'M STILL GONNA NEED YOU** *MGM 2006 551*	**32**	4
30 Oct 76	**I CAN'T LIVE A DREAM** *Polydor 2066 726*	**37**	5
23 Sep 95	**CRAZY HORSES (re-mix)** *Polydor 5793212*	**50**	1

Gilbert O'SULLIVAN *Ireland, male vocalist* **145 wks**

28 Nov 70	● **NOTHING RHYMED** *MAM 3*	**8**	11
3 Apr 71	**UNDERNEATH THE BLANKET GO** *MAM 13*	**40**	1
17 Apr 71	**UNDERNEATH THE BLANKET GO (re-entry)** *MAM 13*	**42**	3
24 Jul 71	● **WE WILL** *MAM 30*	**16**	11
27 Nov 71	● **NO MATTER HOW I TRY** *MAM 53*	**5**	15
4 Mar 72	● **ALONE AGAIN (NATURALLY)** *MAM 66*	**3**	12

17 Jun 72	● **OOH-WAKKA-DOO-WAKKA-DAY** *MAM 78*	**8**	11
21 Oct 72	★ **CLAIR** *MAM 84*	**1**	14
17 Mar 73	★ **GET DOWN** *MAM 96*	**1**	13
15 Sep 73	**OOH BABY** *MAM 107*	**18**	7
10 Nov 73	● **WHY OH WHY OH WHY** *MAM 111*	**6**	14
9 Feb 74	**HAPPINESS IS ME AND YOU** *MAM 114*	**19**	7
24 Aug 74	**A WOMAN'S PLACE** *MAM 122*	**42**	3
14 Dec 74	**CHRISTMAS SONG** *MAM 124*	**12**	6
14 Jun 75	**I DON'T LOVE YOU BUT I THINK I LIKE YOU** *MAM 130*	**14**	6
27 Sep 80	**WHAT'S IN A KISS?** *CBS 8929*	**19**	9
24 Feb 90	**SO WHAT** *Dover ROJ 3*	**70**	2

O.T. QUARTET – *See OUR TRIBE*

OTHER TWO *UK, male / female vocal / instrumental duo* **5 wks**

9 Nov 91	**TASTY FISH** *Factory FAC 3297*	**41**	3
6 Nov 93	**SELFISH** *London TWOCD 1*	**46**	2

Johnny OTIS SHOW *US, orchestra and chorus* **22 wks**

22 Nov 57	● **MA (HE'S MAKING EYES AT ME)** *Capitol CL 14794* [1]	**2**	15
10 Jan 58	**BYE BYE BABY** *Capitol CL 14817* [2]	**20**	7

[1] Johnny Otis and His Orchestra with Marie Adams and the Three Tons of Joy
[2] Johnny Otis Show, vocals by Marie Adams and Johnny Otis

OTTAWAN *France, male / female vocal duo* **45 wks**

13 Sep 80	● **D.I.S.C.O.** *Carrere CAR 161*	**2**	18
13 Dec 80	**YOU'RE O.K.** *Carrere CAR 168*	**56**	6
29 Aug 81	● **HANDS UP (GIVE ME YOUR HEART)** *Carrere CAR 183*	**3**	15
5 Dec 81	**HELP, GET ME SOME HELP!** *Carrere CAR 215*	**49**	6

John OTWAY and Wild Willy BARRETT
UK, male vocal / instrumental duo **12 wks**

3 Dec 77	**REALLY FREE** *Polydor 2058 951*	**27**	8
5 Jul 80	**DK 50-80** *Polydor 2059 250* [1]	**45**	4

[1] Otway and Barrett

OUI 3
UK / US / Switzerland, male / female vocal / instrumental group **21 wks**

20 Feb 93	**FOR WHAT IT'S WORTH** *MCA MCSTD 1736*	**28**	6
24 Apr 93	**ARMS OF SOLITUDE** *MCA MCSTD 1759*	**54**	2
17 Jul 93	**BREAK FROM THE OLD ROUTINE** *MCA MCSTD 1793*	**17**	6
23 Oct 93	**FOR WHAT IT'S WORTH (re-mix)** *MCA MCSTD 1941*	**26**	3
29 Jan 94	**FACT OF LIFE** *MCA MCSTD 1939*	**38**	2
27 May 95	**THE JOY OF LIVING** *MCA MCSTD 2057*	**55**	2

OUR DAUGHTER'S WEDDING
US, male vocal / instrumental group **6 wks**

1 Aug 81	**LAWNCHAIRS** *EMI America EA 124*	**49**	6

OUR HOUSE
Australia, male instrumental production duo **1 wk**

31 Aug 96	**FLOOR SPACE** *Perfecto PERF 125CD*	**52**	1

OUR KID *UK, male vocal group* **11 wks**

29 May 76	● **YOU JUST MIGHT SEE ME CRY** *Polydor 2058 729*	**2**	11

Ozzy Osbourne

The former Black Sabbath front-
man retired from live performance
in 1992 after a farewell tour and
short Sabbath reunion. The lure of
the crowd proved too strong,
however, and Ozzy returned to the
stage with a world tour in 1995.

Joan Osborne

Kentucky-born Joan Osborne
released a couple of singles on her
own Womanly Hips label before
joining forces with Eric Brazilian of
the Hooters who penned her
breakthrough hit 'One Of Us'.

OMC

OMC stands for Otara Millionaires
Club and is one man - Paul
Fuemana-Lawrence.

OUR TRIBE/ONE TRIBE
UK/US, male/female vocal/instrumental group　　**12 wks**

20 Jun 92	**WHAT HAVE YOU DONE (IS THIS ALL)** Inner Rhythm HEART 03 [1]	52	2
27 Mar 93	**I BELIEVE IN YOU** Ffrreedom TABCD 117 [2]	42	2
30 Apr 94	**HOLD THAT SUCKER DOWN** Cheeky CHEKCD 004 [3]	24	3
21 May 94	**LOVE COME HOME** Triangle BLUESCD 001 [4]	73	1
13 May 95	**HIGH AS A KITE** ffrr FCD 259 [5]	55	1
30 Sep 95	**HOLD THAT SUCKER DOWN (re-mix)** Cheeky CHEKCD 009 [3]	26	3

[1] One Tribe featuring Gem [2] Our Tribe [3] OT Quartet [4] Our Tribe with Frankë Pharoah and Kristine W [5] One Tribe featuring Roger

OUT OF MY HAIR *UK, male vocal/instrumental group*　　**1 wk**

1 Jul 95	**MISTER JONES** RCA 74321267812	73	1

OUTHERE BROTHERS
US, male vocal/instrumental duo　　**47 wks**

18 Mar 95	★ **DON'T STOP (WIGGLE WIGGLE)** Eternal YZ 917CD	1	15
17 Jun 95	★ **BOOM BOOM BOOM** Eternal YZ 938CD	1	15
23 Sep 95	● **LA LA LA HEY HEY** Eternal YZ 974CD	7	7
16 Dec 95	● **IF YOU WANNA PARTY** Eternal WEA 030CD [1]	9	10

[1] Molella featuring the Outhere Brothers

OUTLANDER *Belgium, male producer – Marcos Salon*　　**2 wks**

31 Aug 91	**VAMP** R&S RSUK 1	51	2

OUTLAWS *UK, male instrumental group*　　**4 wks**

13 Apr 61	**SWINGIN' LOW** HMV POP 844	46	2
8 Jun 61	**AMBUSH** HMV POP 877	43	2

See also Mike Berry.

OUTRAGE *US, male vocalist*　　**2 wks**

11 Mar 95	**TALL 'N' HANDSOME** Effective ECFL 001CD	57	1
23 Nov 96	**TALL 'N' HANDSOME (re-mix)** Positiva CDTIV 64	51	1

OVERLANDERS *UK, male vocal/instrumental group*　　**10 wks**

13 Jan 66	★ **MICHELLE** Pye 7N 17034	1	10

OVERWEIGHT POOCH – See Ce Ce PENISTON

Mark OWEN *UK, male vocalist*　　**5 wks**

30 Nov 96	● **CHILD** RCA 74321424422	3†	5

Reg OWEN *UK, orchestra*　　**10 wks**

27 Feb 59	**MANHATTAN SPIRITUAL** Pye International 7N 25009	20	8
27 Oct 60	**OBSESSION** Palette PG 9004	43	2

Sid OWEN and Patsy PALMER
UK, male/female vocal duo　　**1 wk**

16 Dec 95	**BETTER BELIEVE IT (CHILDREN IN NEED)** Trinity TDM 001CD	60	1

Robert OWENS *US, male vocalist*　　**2 wks**

7 Dec 91	**I'LL BE YOUR FRIEND** Perfecto PB 45161	75	2

See also Various Artists (EPs & LPs) – Gimme Shelter (EP).

P.I.L. – See PUBLIC IMAGE LTD.

Jazzi P *US, female vocalist*　　**12 wks**

8 Jul 89	**GET LOOSE** Breakout USA 659 [1]	25	6
9 Jun 90	**FEEL THE RHYTHM** A & M AMUSA 691	51	2
3 Aug 91	**REBEL WOMAN** DNA 7DNA 001 [2]	42	4

[1] L.A. Mix performed by Jazzi P [2] DNA performed by Jazzi P

Thom PACE *US, male vocalist*　　**15 wks**

19 May 79	**MAYBE** RSO 34	14	15

PACEMAKERS – See GERRY and the PACEMAKERS

PACK featuring Nigel BENN
UK, male vocal/instrumental group　　**2 wks**

8 Dec 90	**STAND AND FIGHT** IQ ZB 44237	61	2

PACKABEATS *UK, male instrumental group*　　**1 wk**

23 Feb 61	**GYPSY BEAT** Parlophone R 4729	49	1

Jimmy PAGE – See Robert PLANT; COVERDALE PAGE

Patti PAGE *US, female vocalist*　　**5 wks**

27 Mar 53	● **(HOW MUCH IS) THAT DOGGIE IN THE WINDOW** Oriole CB 1156	9	5

Tommy PAGE *US, male vocalist*　　**3 wks**

26 May 90	**I'LL BE YOUR EVERYTHING** Sire W 9959	53	3

PAGLIARO *Canada, male vocalist*　　**6 wks**

19 Feb 72	**LOVING YOU AIN'T EASY** Pye 7N 45111	31	6

Elaine PAIGE *UK, female vocalist*　　**39 wks**

21 Oct 78	**DON'T WALK AWAY TILL I TOUCH YOU** EMI 2862	46	5
6 Jun 81	● **MEMORY** Polydor POSP 279	6	12
30 Jan 82	**MEMORY (re-entry)** Polydor POSP 279	67	3
14 Apr 84	**SOMETIMES (THEME FROM 'CHAMPIONS')** Island IS 174	72	1
5 Jan 85	★ **I KNOW HIM SO WELL** RCA CHESS 3 [1]	1	16

| 21 Nov 87 | THE SECOND TIME (THEME FROM 'BILITIS')
WEA YZ 163 | **69** | 1 |
| 21 Jan 95 | HYMNE A L'AMOUR (IF YOU LOVE ME) *WEA YZ 899CD*.. | **68** | 1 |

[1] Elaine Paige and Barbara Dickson

Hal PAIGE and the WHALERS
US, male vocal / instrumental group **1 wk**

| 25 Aug 60 | GOING BACK TO MY HOME TOWN *Melodisc MEL 1553*.. | **50** | 1 |

Orchestre De Chambre Jean-Francois PAILLARD *France, male conductor and orchestra* **3 wks**

| 20 Aug 88 | THEME FROM 'VIETNAM' (CANON IN D)
Debut DEBT 3053 | **61** | 3 |

PALE *Ireland, male vocal / instrumental group* **2 wks**

| 13 Jun 92 | DOGS WITH NO TAILS *A & M AM 866* | **51** | 2 |

PALE FOUNTAINS *UK, male vocal / instrumental group* **6 wks**

| 27 Nov 82 | THANK YOU *Virgin VS 557* | **48** | 6 |

PALE SAINTS
UK, male / female vocal / instrumental group **1 wk**

| 6 Jul 91 | KINKY LOVE *4AD AD 1009* | **72** | 1 |

Barry PALMER – *See Mike OLDFIELD*

Patsy PALMER – *See Sid OWEN and Patsy PALMER*

Robert PALMER *UK, male vocalist* **128 wks**

20 May 78	EVERY KINDA PEOPLE *Island WIP 6425*	**53**	4
7 Jul 79	BAD CASE OF LOVIN' YOU (DOCTOR DOCTOR) *Island WIP 6481*	**61**	2
6 Sep 80	JOHNNY AND MARY *Island WIP 6638*	**44**	8
22 Nov 80	LOOKING FOR CLUES *Island WIP 6651*	**33**	9
13 Feb 82	SOME GUYS HAVE ALL THE LUCK *Island WIP 6754*..	**16**	8
2 Apr 83	YOU ARE IN MY SYSTEM *Island IS 104*	**53**	4
18 Jun 83	YOU CAN HAVE IT (TAKE MY HEART) *Island IS 121*	**66**	2
10 May 86 ●	ADDICTED TO LOVE *Island IS 270*	**5**	15
19 Jul 86 ●	I DIDN'T MEAN TO TURN YOU ON *Island IS 283*	**9**	9
1 Nov 86	DISCIPLINE OF LOVE *Island IS 242*	**68**	1
26 Mar 88	SWEET LIES *Island IS 352*	**58**	3
11 Jun 88	SIMPLY IRRESISTIBLE *EMI EM 61*	**44**	4
15 Oct 88 ●	SHE MAKES MY DAY *EMI EM 65*	**6**	12
13 May 89	CHANGE HIS WAYS *EMI EM 85*	**28**	7
26 Aug 89	IT COULD HAPPEN TO YOU *EMI EM 99*	**71**	1
3 Nov 90 ●	I'LL BE YOUR BABY TONIGHT *EMI EM 167* [1]	**6**	10
5 Jan 91 ●	MERCY MERCY ME – I WANT YOU *EMI EM 173*	**9**	9
15 Jun 91	DREAMS TO REMEMBER *EMI EM 193*	**68**	1
7 Mar 92	EVERY KINDA PEOPLE (re-issue) *Island IS 498*	**43**	3
17 Oct 92	WITCHCRAFT *EMI EM 251*	**50**	3
9 Jul 94	GIRL U WANT *EMI CDEMS 331*	**57**	2
3 Sep 94	KNOW BY NOW *EMI CDEMS 343*	**25**	5
24 Dec 94	YOU BLOW ME AWAY *EMI CDEMS 350*	**38**	4
14 Oct 95	RESPECT YOURSELF *EMI CDEMS 399*	**45**	2

[1] Robert Palmer and UB40

PAN POSITION
Italy / Venezuela, male instrumental / production group **1 wk**

| 18 Jun 94 | ELEPHANT PAW (GET DOWN TO THE FUNK)
Positiva CDTIV 13 | **55** | 1 |

PANDORA'S BOX
US, male / female vocal / instrumental group **3 wks**

| 21 Oct 89 | IT'S ALL COMING BACK TO ME NOW *Virgin VS 1216*.... | **51** | 3 |

Darryl PANDY – *See Farley 'Jackmaster' FUNK*

Johnny PANIC and the BIBLE OF DREAMS
UK, male / female vocal / instrumental group **2 wks**

| 2 Feb 91 | JOHNNY PANIC AND THE BIBLE OF DREAMS
Fontana PANIC 1 | **70** | 2 |

PANTERA *US, male vocal / instrumental group* **8 wks**

10 Oct 92	MOUTH FOR WAR *Atco A 5845T*	**73**	1
27 Feb 93	WALK *Atco B 6076CD*	**35**	2
19 Mar 94	I'M BROKEN *Atco B 5932CD1*	**19**	2
22 Oct 94	PLANET CARAVAN *East West A 5836CD1*	**26**	3

PAPER DOLLS *UK, female vocal group* **13 wks**

| 13 Mar 68 | SOMETHING HERE IN MY HEART
(KEEPS A-TELLIN' ME NO) *Pye 7N 17456* | **11** | 13 |

PAPER LACE *UK, male vocal / instrumental group* **41 wks**

23 Feb 74 ★	BILLY DON'T BE A HERO *Bus Stop BUS 1014*	**1**	14
4 May 74 ●	THE NIGHT CHICAGO DIED *Bus Stop BUS 1016*	**3**	11
24 Aug 74	THE BLACK EYED BOYS *Bus Stop BUS 1019*	**11**	10
4 Mar 78	WE'VE GOT THE WHOLE WORLD IN OUR HANDS *Warner Bros. K17110* [1]	**24**	6

[1] Nottingham Forest F.C. with Paper Lace

Vanessa PARADIS *France, female vocalist* **30 wks**

13 Feb 88 ●	JOE LE TAXI *FA Productions POSP 902*	**3**	10
10 Oct 92 ●	BE MY BABY *Remark PO 235*	**6**	15
27 Feb 93	SUNDAY MONDAYS *Remark PZCD 251*	**49**	4
24 Jul 93	JUST AS LONG AS YOU ARE THERE *Remark PZCD 272*..	**57**	1

PARADISE *UK, male vocal / instrumental group* **4 wks**

| 10 Sep 83 | ONE MIND, TWO HEARTS *Priority P 1* | **42** | 4 |

PARADISE LOST *UK, male vocal / instrumental group* **2 wks**

| 20 May 95 | THE LAST TIME *Music For Nations CDKUT 165* | **60** | 1 |
| 7 Oct 95 | FOREVER FAILURE *Music For Nations CDKUT 169* | **66** | 1 |

PARADISE ORGANISATION
UK, male instrumental / production group **1 wk**

| 23 Jan 93 | PRAYER TOWER *Cowboy RODEO 13* | **70** | 1 |

PARADOX *UK, male instrumental duo* **2 wks**

| 24 Feb 90 | JAILBREAK *Ronin 7R2* | **66** | 2 |

Norrie PARAMOR *UK, orchestra* **8 wks**

| 17 Mar 60 | THEME FROM 'A SUMMER PLACE' *Columbia DB 4419*.. | **36** | 2 |
| 22 Mar 62 | THEME FROM 'Z CARS' *Columbia DB 4789* | **33** | 6 |

See also Michael Holliday.

PARAMOUNT JAZZ BAND – *See Mr. Acker BILK and his PARAMOUNT JAZZ BAND*

PARAMOUNTS *UK, male vocal / instrumental group*   **7 wks**

16 Jan 64	**POISON IVY** *Parlophone R 5093*	**35**	7

PARCHMENT *UK, male / female vocal / instrumental group* **5 wks**

16 Sep 72	**LIGHT UP THE FIRE** *Pye 7N 45178*	**31**	5

PARIS *UK, male / female vocal group*   **4 wks**

19 Jun 82	**NO GETTING OVER YOU** *RCA 222*	**49**	4

PARIS *US, male vocalist*   **2 wks**

21 Jan 95	**GUERILLA FUNK** *Priority PTYCD 100*	**38**	2

Mica PARIS *UK, female vocalist*   **60 wks**

7 May 88	● **MY ONE TEMPTATION** *Fourth & Broadway BRW 85*	**7**	11
30 Jul 88	**LIKE DREAMERS DO** *Fourth & Broadway BRW 108* [1] ...	**26**	5
22 Oct 88	**BREATHE LIFE INTO ME** *Fourth & Broadway BRW 115*	**26**	10
21 Jan 89	**WHERE IS THE LOVE** *Fourth & Broadway BRW 122* [2] ...	**19**	7
6 Oct 90	**CONTRIBUTION** *Fourth & Broadway BRW 188*	**33**	4
1 Dec 90	**SOUTH OF THE RIVER** *Fourth & Broadway BRW 199*	**50**	2
23 Feb 91	**IF I LOVE U 2 NITE** *Fourth & Broadway BRW 207*	**43**	3
31 Aug 91	**YOUNG SOUL REBELS** *Big Life BLR 57*	**61**	3
3 Apr 93	**I NEVER FELT LIKE THIS BEFORE** *Fourth & Broadway BRCD 263*	**15**	5
5 Jun 93	**I WANNA HOLD ON TO YOU** *Fourth & Broadway BRCD 275*	**27**	3
7 Aug 93	**TWO IN A MILLION** *Fourth & Broadway BRCD 285*	**51**	2
4 Dec 93	**WHISPER A PRAYER** *Fourth & Broadway BRCD 287*	**65**	1
8 Apr 95	**ONE** *Cooltempo CDCOOL 304*	**29**	4

[1] Mica Paris featuring Courtney Pine   [2] Mica Paris and Will Downing

Ryan PARIS *France, male vocalist*   **10 wks**

3 Sep 83	● **DOLCE VITA** *Carrere CAR 289*	**5**	10

PARIS ANGELS
UK, male / female vocal / instrumental group   **5 wks**

3 Nov 90	**SCOPE** *Sheer Joy SHEER 0047*	**75**	1
20 Jul 91	**PERFUME** *Virgin VS 1360*	**55**	3
21 Sep 91	**FADE** *Virgin VS 1365*	**70**	1

PARIS RED
US / Germany, male / female vocal / instrumental duo   **2 wks**

29 Feb 92	**GOOD FRIEND** *Columbia 6569417*	**61**	1
15 May 93	**PROMISES** *Columbia 6592342*	**59**	1

John PARISH – *See PJ HARVEY*

Simon PARK *UK, orchestra*   **24 wks**

25 Nov 72	**EYE LEVEL** *Columbia DB 8946*	**41**	2
15 Sep 73	★ **EYE LEVEL (re-entry)** *Columbia DB 8946*	**1**	22

Graham PARKER and the RUMOUR
UK, male vocal / instrumental group   **16 wks**

19 Mar 77	**THE PINK PARKER EP** *Vertigo PARK 001*	**24**	5
22 Apr 78	**HEY LORD DON'T ASK ME QUESTIONS** *Vertigo PARK 002*	**32**	7
20 Mar 82	**TEMPORARY BEAUTY** *RCA PARK 100* [1]	**50**	4

[1] Graham Parker

Tracks on The Pink Parker EP: Hold Back The Night / (Let Me Get) Sweet On You / White Honey / Soul Shoes.

Ray PARKER Jr. *US, male vocalist*   **47 wks**

25 Aug 84	● **GHOSTBUSTERS** *Arista ARIST 580*	**2**	31
18 Jan 86	**GIRLS ARE MORE FUN** *Arista ARIST 641*	**46**	4
3 Oct 87	**I DON'T THINK THAT MAN SHOULD SLEEP ALONE** *Geffen GEF 27*	**13**	10
30 Jan 88	**OVER YOU** *Geffen GEF 33*	**65**	2

Robert PARKER *US, male vocalist*   **8 wks**

4 Aug 66	**BAREFOOTIN'** *Island WI 286*	**24**	8

Jimmy PARKINSON *Australia, male vocalist*   **19 wks**

2 Mar 56	● **THE GREAT PRETENDER** *Columbia DB 3729*	**9**	13
17 Aug 56	**WALK HAND IN HAND** *Columbia DB 3775*	**30**	1
5 Oct 56	**WALK HAND IN HAND (re-entry)** *Columbia DB 3775*	**26**	1
9 Nov 56	**IN THE MIDDLE OF THE HOUSE** *Columbia DB 3833*	**26**	2
30 Nov 56	**IN THE MIDDLE OF THE HOUSE (re-entry)** *Columbia DB 3833*	**20**	2

John PARR *UK, male vocalist*   **22 wks**

14 Sep 85	● **ST ELMO'S FIRE (MAN IN MOTION)** *London LON 73*	**6**	13
18 Jan 86	**NAUGHTY NAUGHTY** *London LON 80*	**58**	3
30 Aug 86	**ROCK 'N' ROLL MERCENARIES** *Arista ARIST 666* [1]	**31**	6

[1] Meat Loaf featuring John Parr

Dean PARRISH *US, male vocalist*   **5 wks**

8 Feb 75	**I'M ON MY WAY** *UK USA 2*	**38**	5

Man PARRISH *US, mixer*   **26 wks**

26 Mar 83	**HOP HOP, BE BOP (DON'T STOP)** *Polydor POSP 575*	**41**	6
23 Mar 85	**BOOGIE DOWN (BRONX)** *Boiling Point POSP 731*	**56**	4
13 Sep 86	**MALE STRIPPER** *Bolts BOLTS 4* [1]	**64**	3
3 Jan 87	**MALE STRIPPER (re-entry)** *Bolts BOLTS 4* [1]	**63**	1
7 Feb 87	● **MALE STRIPPER (2nd re-entry)** *Bolts BOLTS 4* [1]	**4**	12

[1] Man 2 Man meet Man Parrish

Bill PARSONS *US, male vocalist*   **2 wks**

10 Apr 59	**ALL AMERICAN BOY** *London HL 8798*	**22**	2

Record erroneously credited to Bill Parsons, actual vocalist is Bobby Bare.

Alan PARSONS PROJECT
UK, male vocal / instrumental group   **4 wks**

15 Jan 83	**OLD AND WISE** *Arista ARIST 494*	**74**	1
10 Mar 84	**DON'T ANSWER ME** *Arista ARIST 553*	**58**	3

PARTNERS – *See Al HUDSON*

PARTNERS IN KRYME
US, male vocal / instrumental duo **10 wks**

| 21 Jul 90 | ★ TURTLE POWER *SBK TURTLE 1* | 1 | 10 |

David PARTON *UK, male vocalist* **9 wks**

| 15 Jan 77 | ● ISN'T SHE LOVELY *Pye 7N 45663* | 4 | 9 |

Dolly PARTON *US, female vocalist* **33 wks**

15 May 76	● JOLENE *RCA 2675*	7	10
21 Feb 81	● 9 TO 5 *RCA 25*	47	5
12 Nov 83	● ISLANDS IN THE STREAM *RCA 378* [1]	7	15
7 Apr 84	HERE YOU COME AGAIN *RCA 395*	75	1
16 Apr 94	THE DAY I FALL IN LOVE *Columbia 6600282* [2]	64	2

[1] Kenny Rogers and Dolly Parton [2] Dolly Parton and James Ingram

Stella PARTON *US, female vocalist* **4 wks**

| 22 Oct 77 | THE DANGER OF A STRANGER *Elektra K 12272* | 35 | 4 |

Don PARTRIDGE *UK, male vocalist* **32 wks**

7 Feb 68	● ROSIE *Columbia DB 8330*	4	12
29 May 68	● BLUE EYES *Columbia DB 8416*	3	13
19 Feb 69	BREAKFAST ON PLUTO *Columbia DB 8538*	26	7

PARTRIDGE FAMILY *US, male / female vocal group* **53 wks**

13 Feb 71	I THINK I LOVE YOU *Bell 1130* [1]	18	9
26 Feb 72	IT'S ONE OF THOSE NIGHTS (YES LOVE) *Bell 1203* [1]	11	11
8 Jul 72	● BREAKING UP IS HARD TO DO *Bell MABEL 1* [1]	3	13
3 Feb 73	● LOOKING THROUGH THE EYES OF LOVE *Bell 1278* [2]	9	9
19 May 73	● WALKING IN THE RAIN *Bell 1293* [2]	10	11

[1] Partridge Family starring Shirley Jones featuring David Cassidy
[2] Partridge Family starring David Cassidy

PARTY ANIMALS
Holland, male instrumental / production duo **3 wks**

| 1 Jun 96 | HAVE YOU EVER BEEN MELLOW *Mokum DB 17553* | 56 | 1 |
| 19 Oct 96 | HAVE YOU EVER BEEN MELLOW (EP) *Mokum DB 17413* | 43 | 2 |

Tracks on Have You Ever Been Mellow (EP): *Have You Ever Been Mellow / Hava Nequilla / Aquarius.*

PARTY FAITHFUL
UK, male / female vocal / instrumental group **1 wk**

| 22 Jul 95 | BRASS: LET THERE BE HOUSE *Ore AG 10CD* | 54 | 1 |

PASADENAS *UK, male vocal group* **57 wks**

28 May 88	● TRIBUTE (RIGHT ON) *CBS PASA 1*	5	14
17 Sep 88	RIDING ON A TRAIN *CBS PASA 2*	13	9
26 Nov 88	ENCHANTED LADY *CBS PASA 3*	31	6
12 May 90	LOVE THING *CBS PASA 4*	22	5
14 Jul 90	REELING *CBS PASA 5*	75	1
1 Feb 92	● I'M DOING FINE NOW *Columbia 6577187*	4	10
4 Apr 92	MAKE IT WITH YOU *Columbia 6579257*	20	4
6 Jun 92	I BELIEVE IN MIRACLES *Columbia 6580567*	34	3
29 Aug 92	MOVING IN THE RIGHT DIRECTION *Columbia 6583417*	49	2
21 Nov 92	LET'S STAY TOGETHER *Columbia 6587747*	22	3

PASSENGERS
Ireland / UK / Italy, male vocal / instrumental group **9 wks**

| 2 Dec 95 | ● MISS SARAJEVO *Island CID 625* | 6 | 9 |

PASSIONS *UK, male / female vocal / instrumental group* **8 wks**

| 31 Jan 81 | I'M IN LOVE WITH A GERMAN FILM STAR *Polydor POSP 222* | 25 | 8 |

PAT and MICK *UK, male vocal duo* **27 wks**

9 Apr 88	LET'S ALL CHANT / ON THE NIGHT *PWL PWL 10* [1]	11	9
25 Mar 89	● I HAVEN'T STOPPED DANCING YET *PWL PWL 33*	9	8
14 Apr 90	USE IT UP AND WEAR IT OUT *PWL PWL 55*	22	6
23 Mar 91	GIMME SOME *PWL PWL 75*	53	2
15 May 93	HOT HOT HOT *PWL International PARKCD 1*	47	2

[1] Mick and Pat

On The Night *only listed from 4 Jun 88. It peaked at position 70.*

PATIENCE and PRUDENCE *US, female vocal duo* **8 wks**

2 Nov 56	TONIGHT YOU BELONG TO ME *London HLU 8321*	28	3
1 Mar 57	GONNA GET ALONG WITHOUT YA NOW *London HLU 8369*	22	4
12 Apr 57	GONNA GET ALONG WITHOUT YA NOW (re-entry) *London HLU 8369*	24	1

PATRA *Jamaica, female vocalist* **11 wks**

25 Dec 93	FAMILY AFFAIR *Polydor PZCD 304* [1]	18	8
30 Sep 95	PULL UP TO THE BUMPER *Epic 6623942*	50	2
10 Aug 96	WORK MI BODY *Heavenly HVN 53CD* [2]	75	1

[1] Shabba Ranks featuring Patra and Terry & Monica [2] Monkey Mafia featuring Patra

PATRIC *UK, male vocalist* **2 wks**

| 9 Jul 94 | LOVE ME *Bell 7432125352* | 54 | 2 |

Kellee PATTERSON *US, female vocalist* **7 wks**

| 18 Feb 78 | IF IT DON'T FIT DON'T FORCE IT *EMI International INT 544* | 44 | 7 |

Billy PAUL *US, male vocalist* **44 wks**

13 Jan 73	ME AND MRS JONES *Epic EPC 1055*	12	9
12 Jan 74	THANKS FOR SAVING MY LIFE *Philadelphia International PIR 1928*	33	6
22 May 76	LET'S MAKE A BABY *Philadelphia International PIR 4144*	30	5
30 Apr 77	LET 'EM IN *Philadelphia International PIR 5143*	26	5
16 Jul 77	YOUR SONG *Philadelphia International PIR 5391*	37	7
19 Nov 77	ONLY THE STRONG SURVIVE *Philadelphia International PIR 5699*	33	7
14 Jul 79	BRING THE FAMILY BACK *Philadelphia International PIR 7456*	51	5

Chris PAUL *UK, male instrumentalist – guitar* **8 wks**

| 31 May 86 | EXPANSIONS '86 (EXPAND YOUR MIND) *Fourth & Broadway BRW 48* [1] | 58 | 5 |

| 21 Nov 87 | **BACK IN MY ARMS** Syncopate SY 5 | **74** | 2 |
| 13 Aug 88 | **TURN THE MUSIC UP** Syncopate SY 13 | **73** | 1 |

1 Chris Paul featuring David Joseph

Frankie PAUL – See APACHE INDIAN

Les PAUL and Mary FORD
US, male instrumentalist – guitar, and female vocalist   **4 wks**

| 20 Nov 53 ● | **VAYA CON DIOS** Capitol CL 13943 | **7** | 4 |

Lyn PAUL *UK, female vocalist*   **6 wks**

| 28 Jun 75 | **IT OUGHTA SELL A MILLION** Polydor 2058 602 | **37** | 6 |

See also New Seekers.

Owen PAUL *UK, male vocalist*   **14 wks**

| 31 May 86 ● | **MY FAVOURITE WASTE OF TIME** Epic A 7125 | **3** | 14 |

PAUL and PAULA *US, male / female vocal duo*   **31 wks**

14 Feb 63 ●	**HEY PAULA** Philips 304012 BF	**8**	12
18 Apr 63 ●	**YOUNG LOVERS** Philips 304016 BF	**9**	14
16 May 63	**HEY PAULA (re-entry)** Philips 304012 BF	**37**	5

Luciano PAVAROTTI *Italy, male vocalist*   **23 wks**

16 Jun 90 ●	**NESSUN DORMA** Decca PAV 03	**2**	11
24 Oct 92	**MISERERE** London LON 329 1	**15**	5
30 Jul 94	**LIBIAMO / LA DONNA E MOBILE** Teldec YZ 843CD 2	**21**	4
14 Dec 96 ●	**LIVE LIKE HORSES** Rocket LLHDD 1 3	**9**	3

1 Zucchero with Luciano Pavarotti 2 José Carreras, Placido Domingo and Luciano Pavarotti 3 Elton John and Luciano Pavarotti

PAVEMENT *UK, male vocal / instrumental group*   **2 wks**

| 28 Nov 92 | **WATERY DOMESTIC EP** Big Cat ABB 38T | **58** | 1 |
| 12 Feb 94 | **CUT YOUR HAIR** Big Cat ABB 55SCD | **52** | 1 |

Tracks on Watery Domestic EP: Brick Wall / Sick Profile / Annual Report / Fear The Panzers.

Rita PAVONE *Italy, female vocalist*   **19 wks**

| 1 Dec 66 | **HEART** RCA 1553 | **27** | 12 |
| 19 Jan 67 | **YOU ONLY YOU** RCA 1561 | **21** | 7 |

Freda PAYNE *US, female vocalist*   **30 wks**

5 Sep 70 ★	**BAND OF GOLD** Invictus INV 502	**1**	19
21 Nov 70	**DEEPER AND DEEPER** Invictus INV 505	**33**	9
27 Mar 71	**CHERISH WHAT IS DEAR TO YOU** Invictus INV 509	**46**	2

Tammy PAYNE *UK, female vocalist*   **2 wks**

| 20 Jul 91 | **TAKE ME NOW** Talkin Loud TLK 12 | **55** | 2 |

PEACE BY PIECE *UK, male vocal group*   **1 wk**

| 21 Sep 96 | **SWEET SISTER** Blanco Y Negro NEG 94CD | **46** | 1 |

PEACHES and HERB *US, female / male vocal duo*   **23 wks**

| 20 Jan 79 | **SHAKE YOUR GROOVE THING** Polydor 2066 992 | **26** | 10 |
| 21 Apr 79 ● | **REUNITED** Polydor POSP 43 | **4** | 13 |

Mary PEARCE – See UP YER RONSON featuring Mary PEARCE

PEARL JAM *US, male vocal / instrumental group*   **32 wks**

15 Feb 92	**ALIVE** Epic 6575727	**16**	6
18 Apr 92	**EVEN FLOW** Epic 6578577	**27**	3
26 Sep 92	**JEREMY** Epic 6582587	**15**	4
1 Jan 94	**DAUGHTER** Epic 6600202	**18**	5
28 May 94	**DISSIDENT** Epic 6604415	**14**	4
26 Nov 94 ●	**SPIN THE BLACK CIRCLE** Epic 6610362	**10**	3
25 Feb 95	**NOT FOR YOU** Epic 6612032	**34**	2
16 Dec 95	**I GOT ID** Epic 6627162	**25**	3
17 Aug 96	**WHO YOU ARE** Epic 6635392	**18**	2

PEARLS *UK, female vocal duo*   **24 wks**

27 May 72	**THIRD FINGER, LEFT HAND** Bell 1217	**31**	6
23 Sep 72	**YOU CAME YOU SAW YOU CONQUERED** Bell 1254	**32**	5
24 Mar 73	**YOU ARE EVERYTHING** Bell 1284	**41**	3
1 Jun 74 ●	**GUILTY** Bell 1352	**10**	10

Johnny PEARSON
UK, orchestra, Johnny Pearson featured pianist   **15 wks**

| 18 Dec 71 ● | **SLEEPY SHORES** Penny Farthing PEN 778 | **8** | 15 |

PEBBLES *US, female vocalist*   **17 wks**

19 Mar 88 ●	**GIRLFRIEND** MCA MCA 1233	**8**	11
28 May 88	**MERCEDES BOY** MCA MCA 1248	**42**	4
27 Oct 90	**GIVING YOU THE BENEFIT** MCA MCA 1448	**73**	2

PEDDLERS *UK, male vocal / instrumental group*   **14 wks**

7 Jan 65	**LET THE SUNSHINE IN** Philips BF 1375	**50**	1
23 Aug 69	**BIRTH** CBS 4449	**17**	9
31 Jan 70	**GIRLIE** CBS 4720	**34**	4

PEE BEE SQUAD *UK, male vocalist – Paul Burnett*   **3 wks**

| 5 Oct 85 | **RUGGED AND MEAN, BUTCH AND ON SCREEN** Project PRO 3 | **52** | 3 |

Ann PEEBLES *US, female vocalist*   **3 wks**

| 20 Apr 74 | **I CAN'T STAND THE RAIN** London HL 10428 | **50** | 1 |
| 4 May 74 | **I CAN'T STAND THE RAIN (re-entry)** London HL 10428 | **41** | 2 |

PEECH BOYS *UK, male vocal / instrumental group*   **3 wks**

| 30 Oct 82 | **DON'T MAKE ME WAIT** TMT QTMT 7001 | **49** | 3 |

Donald PEERS *UK, male vocalist*   **27 wks**

18 Dec 68 ●	**PLEASE DON'T GO** Columbia DB 8502	**3**	18
30 Apr 69	**PLEASE DON'T GO (re-entry)** Columbia DB 8502	**38**	3
24 Jun 72	**GIVE ME ONE MORE CHANCE** Decca F 13302	**36**	6

PELE UK, male / female vocal / instrumental group ·   3 wks

15 Feb 92	**MEGALOMANIA** M & G MAGS 20	**73** 1
13 Jun 92	**FAIR BLOWS THE WIND FOR FRANCE** M & G MAGS 24	**62** 1
31 Jul 93	**FAT BLACK HEART** M & G MAGCD 43	**75** 1

Teddy PENDERGRASS US, male vocalist   24 wks

21 May 77	**THE WHOLE TOWN'S LAUGHING AT ME** Philadelphia International PIR 5116	**44** 3
28 Oct 78	**ONLY YOU / CLOSE THE DOOR** Philadelphia International PIR 6713	**41** 6
23 May 81	**TWO HEARTS** 20th Century TC 2492 [1]	**49** 5
25 Jan 86	**HOLD ME** Asylum EKR 32 [2]	**44** 5
28 May 88	**JOY** Elektra EKR 75	**58** 3
19 Nov 94	**THE MORE I GET THE MORE I WANT** X-clusive XCLU 011CD [3]	**35** 2

[1] Stephanie Mills featuring Teddy Pendergrass [2] Teddy Pendergrass with Whitney Houston [3] KWS featuring Teddy Pendergrass

See also Harold Melvin and the Bluenotes.

Ce Ce PENISTON US, female vocalist   44 wks

12 Oct 91	**FINALLY** A & M AM 822	**29** 7
11 Jan 92	● **WE GOT A LOVE THANG** A & M AM 846	**6** 8
18 Jan 92	**I LIKE IT** A & M AM 847 [1]	**58** 2
21 Mar 92	● **FINALLY (re-issue)** A & M AM 858	**2** 8
23 May 92	● **KEEP ON WALKIN'** A & M AM 878	**10** 6
5 Sep 92	**CRAZY LOVE** A & M AM 0060	**44** 3
12 Dec 92	**INSIDE THAT I CRIED** A & M AM 0121	**42** 2
15 Jan 94	**I'M IN THE MOOD** A & M 5804552	**16** 4
2 Apr 94	**KEEP GIVIN' ME YOUR LOVE** A & M 5805492	**36** 2
6 Aug 94	**HIT BY LOVE** A & M 5806932	**33** 2

[1] Overweight Pooch featuring Ce Ce Peniston

Dawn PENN Jamaica, female vocalist   12 wks

11 Jun 94	● **YOU DON'T LOVE ME (NO, NO, NO)** Big Beat A 8295CD	**3** 12

Barbara PENNINGTON US, female vocalist   8 wks

27 Apr 85	**FAN THE FLAME** Record Shack SOHO 37	**62** 3
27 Jul 85	**ON A CROWDED STREET** Record Shack SOHO 49	**57** 5

Tricia PENROSE UK, female vocalist   1 wk

7 Dec 96	**WHERE DID OUR LOVE GO** RCA 74321428152	**71** 1

PENTANGLE UK, male / female vocal / instrumental group   4 wks

28 May 69	**ONCE I HAD A SWEETHEART** Big T BIG 124	**46** 1
14 Feb 70	**LIGHT FLIGHT** Big T BIG 128	**43** 1
28 Feb 70	**LIGHT FLIGHT (re-entry)** Big T BIG 128	**45** 2

PENTHOUSE 4 UK, male vocal / instrumental duo   3 wks

23 Apr 88	**BUST THIS HOUSE DOWN** Syncopate SY 10	**56** 3

PEOPLES CHOICE US, male vocal / instrumental group   9 wks

20 Sep 75	**DO IT ANYWAY YOU WANNA** Philadelphia International PIR 3500	**36** 5
21 Jan 78	**JAM JAM JAM** Philadelphia International PIR 5891	**40** 4

Danny PEPPERMINT and the JUMPING JACKS US, male vocal / instrumental group   8 wks

18 Jan 62	**PEPPERMINT TWIST** London HLL 9478	**26** 8

PEPPERS France, male instrumental group   12 wks

26 Oct 74	● **PEPPER BOX** Spark SRL 1100	**6** 12

PEPSI and SHIRLIE UK, female vocal duo   24 wks

17 Jan 87	● **HEARTACHE** Polydor POSP 837	**2** 12
30 May 87	● **GOODBYE STRANGER** Polydor POSP 865	**9** 7
26 Sep 87	**CAN'T GIVE ME LOVE** Polydor POSP 885	**58** 3
12 Dec 87	**ALL RIGHT NOW** Polydor POSP 896	**50** 2

PERCEPTION UK, male vocal group   2 wks

7 Mar 92	**FEED THE FEELING** Talkin Loud TLK 17	**58** 2

The listed flip side of Feed The Feeling was Three Times A Maybe by K-Creative.

Lance PERCIVAL UK, male vocalist   3 wks

28 Oct 65	**SHAME AND SCANDAL IN THE FAMILY** Parlophone R 5335	**37** 3

PERFECT DAY UK, male vocal / instrumental group   4 wks

21 Jan 89	**LIBERTY TOWN** London LON 214	**58** 3
1 Apr 89	**JANE** London LON 188	**68** 1

PERFECTLY ORDINARY PEOPLE
UK, male vocal / instrumental group   3 wks

22 Oct 88	**THEME FROM P.O.P.** Urban URB 25	**61** 3

PERFECTO ALLSTARZ
UK, male instrumental / production duo   11 wks

4 Feb 95	● **REACH UP (PAPA'S GOT A BRAND NEW PIG BAG)** Perfecto YZ 892CD	**6** 11

PERFUME UK, male vocal / instrumental group   1 wk

10 Feb 96	**HAVEN'T SEEN YOU** Aromasound AROMA 005CDS	**71** 1

Emilio PERICOLI Italy, male vocalist   14 wks

28 Jun 62	**AL DI LA** Warner Bros. WB 69	**30** 14

Carl PERKINS US, male vocalist   8 wks

18 May 56	● **BLUE SUEDE SHOES** London HLU 8271	**10** 8

Steve PERRY UK, male vocalist   1 wk

4 Aug 60	**STEP BY STEP** HMV POP 745	**41** 1

Jon PERTWEE UK, male vocalist   7 wks

1 Mar 80	**WORZEL'S SONG** Decca F 13885	**33** 7

PET SHOP BOYS UK, male vocal / instrumental duo   208 wks

23 Nov 85	★ WEST END GIRLS *Parlophone R 6115*	1	15
8 Mar 86	LOVE COMES QUICKLY *Parlophone R 6116*	19	9
31 May 86	OPPORTUNITIES (LET'S MAKE LOTS OF MONEY) *Parlophone R 6129*	11	8
4 Oct 86	● SUBURBIA *Parlophone R 6140*	8	9
27 Jun 87	★ IT'S A SIN *Parlophone R 6158*	1	11
22 Aug 87	● WHAT HAVE I DONE TO DESERVE THIS *Parlophone R 6163* [1]	2	9
24 Oct 87	● RENT *Parlophone R 6168*	8	7
12 Dec 87	★ ALWAYS ON MY MIND *Parlophone R 6171*	1	11
2 Apr 88	★ HEART *Parlophone R 6177*	1	10
24 Sep 88	● DOMINO DANCING *Parlophone R 6190*	7	8
26 Nov 88	● LEFT TO MY OWN DEVICES *Parlophone R 6198*	4	8
8 Jul 89	● IT'S ALRIGHT *Parlophone R 6220*	5	8
6 Oct 90	● SO HARD *Parlophone R 6269*	4	6
24 Nov 90	● BEING BORING *Parlophone R 6275*	20	8
23 Mar 91	● WHERE THE STREETS HAVE NO NAME – CAN'T TAKE MY EYES OFF YOU / HOW CAN YOU EXPECT TO BE TAKEN SERIOUSLY *Parlophone R 6285*	4	8
8 Jun 91	JEALOUSY *Parlophone R 6283*	12	5
26 Oct 91	DJ CULTURE *Parlophone R 6301*	13	3
23 Nov 91	DJ CULTURE (re-mix) *Parlophone 12RX 6301*	40	2
21 Dec 91	WAS IT WORTH IT *Parlophone R 6306*	24	4
12 Jun 93	● CAN YOU FORGIVE HER *Parlophone CDR 6348*	7	7
18 Sep 93	● GO WEST *Parlophone CDR 6356*	2	9
11 Dec 93	I WOULDN'T NORMALLY DO THIS KIND OF THING *Parlophone CDR 6370*	13	7
16 Apr 94	LIBERATION *Parlophone CDR 6377*	14	7
11 Jun 94	● ABSOLUTELY FABULOUS *Spaghetti CDR 6382* [2]	6	7
10 Sep 94	YESTERDAY WHEN I WAS MAD *Parlophone CDR 6386*	13	4
5 Aug 95	PANINARO *Parlophone CDR 6414*	15	4
4 May 96	● BEFORE *Parlophone CDR 6431*	7	5
24 Aug 96	● SE A VIDE E (THAT'S THE WAY LIFE IS) *Parlophone CDR 6443*	8	8
23 Nov 96	SINGLE *Parlophone CDR 6452*	14	3

[1] Pet Shop Boys and Dusty Springfield [2] Absolutely Fabulous

PETER and GORDON UK, male vocal duo   77 wks

12 Mar 64	★ A WORLD WITHOUT LOVE *Columbia DB 7225*	1	14
4 Jun 64	● NOBODY I KNOW *Columbia DB 7292*	10	11
8 Apr 65	● TRUE LOVE WAYS *Columbia DB 7524*	2	15
24 Jun 65	● TO KNOW YOU IS TO LOVE YOU *Columbia DB 7617*	5	10
21 Oct 65	BABY I'M YOURS *Columbia DB 7729*	19	9
24 Feb 66	WOMAN *Columbia DB 7834*	28	7
22 Sep 66	LADY GODIVA *Columbia DB 8003*	16	11

PETER, PAUL and MARY
US, male / female vocal / instrumental group   38 wks

10 Oct 63	BLOWING IN THE WIND *Warner Bros. WB 104*	13	16
16 Apr 64	TELL IT ON THE MOUNTAIN *Warner Bros. WB 127*	33	4
15 Oct 64	THE TIMES THEY ARE A-CHANGIN' *Warner Bros. WB 142*	44	2
17 Jan 70	● LEAVIN' ON A JET PLANE *Warner Bros. WB 7340*	2	16

PETERS and LEE UK, male / female vocal duo   57 wks

26 May 73	★ WELCOME HOME *Philips 6006 307*	1	24
3 Nov 73	BY YOUR SIDE *Philips 6006 339*	39	4
20 Apr 74	● DON'T STAY AWAY TOO LONG *Philips 6006 388*	3	15
17 Aug 74	RAINBOW *Philips 6006 406*	17	7
6 Mar 76	HEY MR. MUSIC MAN *Philips 6006 502*	16	7

Ray PETERSON US, male vocalist   9 wks

4 Sep 59	THE WONDER OF YOU *RCA 1131*	23	1
24 Mar 60	ANSWER ME *RCA 1175*	47	1
19 Jan 61	CORRINE, CORRINA *London HLX 9246*	48	1
2 Feb 61	CORRINE, CORRINA (re-entry) *London HLX 9246*	41	6

Tom PETTY and the HEARTBREAKERS
US, male vocal / instrumental group   43 wks

25 Jun 77	ANYTHING THAT'S ROCK 'N' ROLL *Shelter WIP 6396*	36	3
13 Aug 77	AMERICAN GIRL *Shelter WIP 6403*	40	5
15 Aug 81	STOP DRAGGIN' MY HEART AROUND *WEA K 79231* [1]	50	4
13 Apr 85	DON'T COME AROUND HERE NO MORE *MCA MCA 926*	50	4
13 May 89	I WON'T BACK DOWN *MCA MCA 1334* [2]	28	10
12 Aug 89	RUNNIN' DOWN A DREAM *MCA MCA 1359* [2]	55	2
25 Nov 89	FREE FALLIN' *MCA MCA 1381* [2]	64	2
29 Jun 91	LEARNING TO FLY *MCA MCS 1555*	46	4
4 Apr 92	TOO GOOD TO BE TRUE *MCA MCS 1616*	34	3
30 Oct 93	SOMETHING IN THE AIR *MCA MCSTD 1945* [2]	53	2
12 Mar 94	MARY JANE'S LAST DANCE *MCA MCSTD 1966*	52	2

[1] Stevie Nicks with Tom Petty and the Heartbreakers [2] Tom Petty

PHANTOMS – *See Johnny BRANDON*

PHARAO
Germany, male / female vocal / instrumental group   2 wks

4 Mar 95	THERE IS A STAR *Epic 6611832*	43	2

PHARAOHS – *See SAM THE SHAM and the PHARAOHS*

PHARCYDE US, male rap group   6 wks

31 Jul 93	PASSIN' ME BY *Atlantic A 8360CD*	55	3
6 Apr 96	RUNNIN' *Go.Beat GODCD 142*	36	2
10 Aug 96	SHE SAID *Go.Beat GODCD 144*	51	1

Frankë PHAROAH – *See FRANKE*

PhD UK, male vocal / instrumental duo   14 wks

3 Apr 82	● I WON'T LET YOU DOWN *WEA K 79209*	3	14

Barrington PHELOUNG Australia, male composer   2 wks

13 Mar 93	'INSPECTOR MORSE' THEME *Virgin VSCDT 1458*	61	2

PHILADELPHIA INTERNATIONAL ALL-STARS
US, amalgamation of various acts   8 wks

13 Aug 77	LET'S CLEAN UP THE GHETTO *Philadelphia International PIR 5451*	34	8

PHILHARMONIA ORCHESTRA, conductor
Lorin MAAZEL UK, orchestra, US, male conductor   7 wks

30 Jul 69	THUS SPAKE ZARATHUSTRA *Columbia DB 8607*	33	7

Chynna PHILLIPS US, female vocalist   1 wk

3 Feb 96	NAKED AND SACRED *EMI CDEM 409*	62	1

Esther PHILLIPS US, female vocalist   8 wks

4 Oct 75	● WHAT A DIFFERENCE A DAY MADE *Kudu 925*	6	8

Paul PHOENIX UK, male vocalist   4 wks

3 Nov 79	**NUNC DIMITTIS** *Different HAVE 20*	**56**	4

Full artist credit on hit as follows: Paul Phoenix (treble) with Instrumental Ensemble –
James Watson (trumpet), John Scott (organ), conducted by Barry Rose.

PHOTOS UK, male/female vocal/instrumental group   4 wks

17 May 80	**IRENE** *Epic EPC 8517*	**56**	4

PHUTURE ASSASSINS
UK, male instrumental/production group   1 wk

6 Jun 92	**FUTURE SOUND (EP)** *Suburban Base SUBBASE 010*	**64**	1

Tracks on Future Sound (EP): Future Sound / African Sanctus / Rydim Come Foward /
Freedom Sound.

PIA – *See Pia ZADORA*

Edith PIAF France, female vocalist   15 wks

12 May 60	**MILORD** *Columbia DC 754*	**41**	4
3 Nov 60	**MILORD (re-entry)** *Columbia DC 754*	**24**	11

PIANOMAN US, male producer – James Salmon   7 wks

15 Jun 96	● **BLURRED** *Ffrreedom TABCD 243*	**6**	7

See also Bass Boyz.

Bobby 'Boris' PICKETT and the CRYPT-KICKERS US, male vocalist, male vocal/instrumental backing group   13 wks

1 Sep 73	● **MONSTER MASH** *London HL 10320*	**3**	13

Wilson PICKETT US, male vocalist   61 wks

23 Sep 65	**IN THE MIDNIGHT HOUR** *Atlantic AT 4036*	**12**	11
25 Nov 65	**DON'T FIGHT IT** *Atlantic AT 4052*	**29**	8
10 Mar 66	**634-5789** *Atlantic AT 4072*	**36**	5
1 Sep 66	**LAND OF 1000 DANCES** *Atlantic 584-039*	**22**	9
15 Dec 66	**MUSTANG SALLY** *Atlantic 584-066*	**28**	7
27 Sep 67	**FUNKY BROADWAY** *Atlantic 584-130*	**43**	3
11 Sep 68	**I'M A MIDNIGHT MOVER** *Atlantic 584-203*	**38**	6
8 Jan 69	**HEY JUDE** *Atlantic 584-236*	**16**	9
21 Nov 87	**IN THE MIDNIGHT HOUR** *Motown ZB 41583*	**62**	3

In The Midnight Hour on Motown is a re-recording.

PICKETTYWITCH
UK, male/female vocal/instrumental group   34 wks

28 Feb 70	● **THAT SAME OLD FEELING** *Pye 7N 17887*	**5**	14
4 Jul 70	**(IT'S LIKE A) SAD OLD KINDA MOVIE** *Pye 7N 17951*	**16**	10
7 Nov 70	**BABY I WON'T LET YOU DOWN** *Pye 7N 45002*	**27**	10

PIGBAG UK, male instrumental group   20 wks

7 Nov 81	**SUNNY DAY** *Y Records Y 12*	**53**	3
27 Feb 82	**GETTING UP** *Y Records Y 16*	**61**	3
3 Apr 82	● **PAPA'S GOT A BRAND NEW PIGBAG** *Y Records Y 10*	**3**	11
10 Jul 82	**THE BIG BEAN** *Y Records Y 24*	**40**	3

Nelson PIGFORD – *See De Etta LITTLE and Nelson PIGFORD*

PIGLETS UK, female vocal group   12 wks

6 Nov 71	● **JOHNNY REGGAE** *Bell 1180*	**3**	12

Dick PIKE – *See Ruby WRIGHT*

PILOT UK, male vocal/instrumental group   29 wks

2 Nov 74	**MAGIC** *EMI 2217*	**11**	11
18 Jan 75	★ **JANUARY** *EMI 2255*	**1**	10
19 Apr 75	**CALL ME ROUND** *EMI 2287*	**34**	4
27 Sep 75	**JUST A SMILE** *EMI 2338*	**31**	4

PILTDOWN MEN US, male instrumental group   36 wks

8 Sep 60	**MACDONALD'S CAVE** *Capitol CL 15149*	**14**	18
12 Jan 61	**PILTDOWN RIDES AGAIN** *Capitol CL 15175*	**14**	10
9 Mar 61	**GOODNIGHT MRS. FLINTSTONE** *Capitol CL 15186*	**18**	8

Courtney PINE UK, male instrumentalist – saxophone   6 wks

30 Jul 88	**LIKE DREAMERS DO** *Fourth & Broadway BRW 108*	1	**26**	5
7 Jul 90	**I'M STILL WAITING** *Mango MNG 749*	2	**66**	1

1 Mica Paris featuring Courtney Pine 2 Courtney Pine featuring
Carroll Thompson

See also Movement 98 featuring Carroll Thompson.

PING PING and Al VERLAINE
Belgium, male vocal duo   4 wks

28 Sep 61	**SUCU SUCU** *Oriole CB 1589*	**41**	4

PINK FLOYD UK, male vocal/instrumental group   55 wks

30 Mar 67	**ARNOLD LAYNE** *Columbia DB 8156*	**20**	8
22 Jun 67	● **SEE EMILY PLAY** *Columbia DB 8214*	**6**	12
1 Dec 79	★ **ANOTHER BRICK IN THE WALL (PART 2)** *Harvest HAR 5194*	**1**	12
7 Aug 82	**WHEN THE TIGERS BROKE FREE** *Harvest HAR 5222*	**39**	5
7 May 83	**NOT NOW JOHN** *Harvest HAR 5224*	**30**	4
19 Dec 87	**ON THE TURNING AWAY** *EMI EM 34*	**55**	4
25 Jun 88	**ONE SLIP** *EMI EM 52*	**50**	4
4 Jun 94	**TAKE IT BACK** *EMI CDEMS 309*	**23**	4
29 Oct 94	**HIGH HOPES / KEEP TALKING** *EMI CDEMS 342*	**26**	3

PINKEES UK, male vocal/instrumental group   9 wks

18 Sep 82	● **DANGER GAMES** *Creole CR 39*	**8**	9

PINKERTON'S ASSORTED COLOURS
UK, male vocal/instrumental group   12 wks

13 Jan 66	● **MIRROR MIRROR** *Decca F 12307*	**9**	11
21 Apr 66	**DON'T STOP LOVIN' ME BABY** *Decca F 12377*	**50**	1

PINKY and PERKY UK, puppet duo   3 wks

29 May 93	**REET PETITE** *Telstar CDPIGGY 1*	**47**	3

PIONEERS Jamaica, male vocal/instrumental group   34 wks

18 Oct 69	**LONG SHOT KICK DE BUCKET** *Trojan TR 672*	**21**	10
10 Jan 70	**LONG SHOT KICK DE BUCKET (re-entry)** *Trojan TR 672*	**40**	1
31 Jul 71	● **LET YOUR YEAH BE YEAH** *Trojan TR 7825*	**5**	12

15 Jan 72	GIVE AND TAKE Trojan TR 7846	35	6
29 Mar 80	LONG SHOT KICK DE BUCKET (re-issue)		
	Trojan TRO 9063	42	5

Re-issue of Long Shot Kick De Bucket *coupled with re-issue of* Liquidator *by Harry J. All Stars.*

PIPKINS *UK, male vocal duo* **10 wks**

| 28 Mar 70 ● | GIMME DAT DING Columbia DB 8662 .... | 6 | 10 |

PIPS – *See Gladys KNIGHT and the PIPS*

PIRANHAS *UK, male vocal / instrumental group* **21 wks**

| 2 Aug 80 ● | TOM HARK Sire SIR 4044 .... | 6 | 12 |
| 16 Oct 82 | ZAMBESI Dakota DAK 6 [1] .... | 17 | 9 |

[1] Piranhas featuring Boring Bob Grover

PIRATES – *See Johnny KIDD and the PIRATES*

Gene PITNEY *US, male vocalist* **212 wks**

23 Mar 61	(I WANNA) LOVE MY LIFE AWAY London HL 9270	26	11
8 Mar 62	TOWN WITHOUT PITY HMV POP 952	32	6
5 Dec 63 ●	TWENTY FOUR HOURS FROM TULSA		
	United Artists UP 1035	5	19
5 Mar 64 ●	THAT GIRL BELONGS TO YESTERDAY		
	United Artists UP 1045	7	12
15 Oct 64	IT HURTS TO BE IN LOVE United Artists UP 1063	36	4
12 Nov 64 ●	I'M GONNA BE STRONG Stateside SS 358	2	14
18 Feb 65 ●	I MUST BE SEEING THINGS Stateside SS 390	6	10
10 Jun 65 ●	LOOKING THROUGH THE EYES OF LOVE		
	Stateside SS 420	3	12
4 Nov 65 ●	PRINCESS IN RAGS Stateside SS 471	9	12
17 Feb 66 ●	BACKSTAGE Stateside SS 490	4	10
9 Jun 66 ●	NOBODY NEEDS YOUR LOVE Stateside SS 518	2	13
10 Nov 66 ●	JUST ONE SMILE Stateside SS 558	8	12
23 Feb 67	(IN THE) COLD LIGHT OF DAY Stateside SS 597	38	6
15 Nov 67 ●	SOMETHING'S GOTTEN HOLD OF MY HEART		
	Stateside SS 2060	5	13
3 Apr 68	SOMEWHERE IN THE COUNTRY Stateside SS 2103	19	9
27 Nov 68	YOURS UNTIL TOMORROW Stateside SS 2131	34	7
5 Mar 69	MARIA ELENA Stateside SS 2142	25	6
14 Mar 70	A STREET CALLED HOPE Stateside SS 2164	37	5
3 Oct 70	SHADY LADY Stateside SS 2177	29	8
28 Apr 73	24 SYCAMORE Pye International 7N 25606	34	7
2 Nov 74	BLUE ANGEL Bronze BRO 11	49	1
16 Nov 74	BLUE ANGEL (re-entry) Bronze BRO 11	39	3
14 Jan 89 ★	SOMETHING'S GOTTEN HOLD OF MY HEART		
	Parlophone R 6201 [1]	1	12

[1] Marc Almond featuring special guest star Gene Pitney

PIXIES *US, male / female vocal / instrumental group* **11 wks**

1 Apr 89	MONKEY GONE TO HEAVEN 4AD AD 904	60	3
1 Jul 89	HERE COMES YOUR MAN 4AD AD 909	54	1
28 Jul 90	VELOURIA 4AD AD 0009	28	3
10 Nov 90	DIG FOR FIRE 4AD AD 0014	62	1
8 Jun 91	PLANET OF SOUND 4AD AD 1008	27	3

PIZZAMAN *UK, male instrumental / production group* **18 wks**

27 Aug 94	TRIPPIN' ON SUNSHINE Loaded CDLOAD 16	33	2
10 Jun 95	SEX ON THE STREETS Loaded CDLOAD 24	24	4
18 Nov 95	HAPPINESS Loaded CDLOAD 29	19	4
6 Jan 96	SEX ON THE STREETS (re-entry) Loaded CDLOAD 24	23	4
1 Jun 96	TRIPPIN' ON SUNSHINE (re-issue) Loaded CDLOAD 32 ..	18	3
14 Sep 96	HELLO HONKY TONKS (ROCK YOUR BODY)		
	Loaded CDLOAD 39	41	1

Joe PIZZULO – *See Sergio MENDES*

PJ and DUNCAN *UK, male vocal duo* **70 wks**

18 Dec 93	TONIGHT I'M FREE Telstar CDSTAS 2706	62	3
23 Apr 94	WHY ME Telstar CDSTAS 2719	27	4
23 Jul 94 ●	LET'S GET READY TO RHUMBLE XSrhythm CDANT 1	9	11
8 Oct 94	IF I GIVE YOU MY NUMBER XSrhythm CDANT 2	15	7
3 Dec 94	ETERNAL LOVE XSrhythm CDANT 3	12	9
25 Feb 95	OUR RADIO ROCKS XSrhythm CDANT 4	15	5
29 Jul 95	STUCK ON U XSrhythm CDANT 5	12	5
14 Oct 95	U KRAZY KATZ XSrhythm CDANT 6	15	4
2 Dec 95	PERFECT Telstar CDANT 7	16	7
20 Mar 96	STEPPING STONE Telstar CDANT 8	11	5
24 Aug 96 ●	BETTER WATCH OUT Telstar CDANT 9 [1]	10	4
23 Nov 96	WHEN I FALL IN LOVE Telstar CDANT 10 [1]	12†	6

[1] Ant and Dec

PJ HARVEY – *See PJ HARVEY*

PJ POWERS – *See LADYSMITH BLACK MAMBAZO*

PJB featuring HANNAH and her SISTERS – *See Hannah JONES*

PKA *UK, male producer – Phil Kelsey* **2 wks**

| 20 Apr 91 | TEMPERATURE RISING Stress SS 4 .... | 68 | 1 |
| 7 Mar 92 | POWERGEN (ONLY YOUR LOVE) Stress PKA 1 .... | 70 | 1 |

PLACEBO
US / Sweden, male instrumental / production group **3 wks**

| 28 Sep 96 | TEENAGE ANGST Elevator Music FLOORCD 3 .... | 30 | 3 |

PLANET PATROL *US, male vocal / instrumental group* **3 wks**

| 17 Sep 83 | CHEAP THRILLS Polydor POSP 639 .... | 64 | 3 |

PLANETS *UK, male vocal / instrumental group* **8 wks**

| 18 Aug 79 | LINES Rialto TREB 104 .... | 36 | 6 |
| 25 Oct 80 | DON'T LOOK DOWN Rialto TREB 116 .... | 66 | 2 |

Robert PLANT *UK, male vocalist* **31 wks**

9 Oct 82	BURNING DOWN ONE SIDE Swansong SSK 19429	73	1
16 Jul 83	BIG LOG WEA B 9848	11	10
30 Jan 88	HEAVEN KNOWS Es Paranza A 9373	33	5
28 Apr 90	HURTING KIND (I'VE GOT MY EYES ON YOU)		
	Es Paranza A 8985	45	3
8 May 93	29 PALMS Fontana FATEX 1	21	5
3 Jul 93	I BELIEVE Fontana FATEX 2	64	2
25 Dec 93	IF I WERE A CARPENTER Fontana FATEX 4	63	2
17 Dec 94	GALLOWS POLE Fontana PPCD 2 [1]	35	3

[1] Jimmy Page and Robert Plant

PLASMATICS *US, female / male vocal / instrumental group* **4 wks**

| 26 Jul 80 | BUTCHER BABY Stiff BUY 76 .... | 55 | 4 |

PLASTIC BERTRAND *Belgium, male vocalist* **17 wks**

| 13 May 78 ● | CA PLANE POUR MOI Sire 6078 616 .... | 8 | 12 |
| 5 Aug 78 | SHA LA LA LA LEE Vertigo 6059 209 .... | 39 | 5 |

PLASTIC JAM – *See BUG KANN and PLASTIC JAM*

PLASTIC ONO BAND – *See John LENNON*

PLASTIC PENNY *UK, male vocal / instrumental group* **10 wks**

3 Jan 68	● EVERYTHING I AM *Page One POF 051*	**6** 10

PLASTIC POPULATION – *See YAZZ*

PLATINUM HOOK *US, male vocal / instrumental group* **1 wk**

2 Sep 78	STANDING ON THE VERGE (OF GETTING IT ON) *Motown TMG 1115*	**72** 1

PLATTERS *US, male / female vocal group* **91 wks**

7 Sep 56	● THE GREAT PRETENDER / ONLY YOU *Mercury MT 117*	**5** 12
2 Nov 56	● MY PRAYER *Mercury MT 120*	**4** 10
7 Dec 56	THE GREAT PRETENDER / ONLY YOU (re-entry) *Mercury MT 117*	**21** 1
18 Jan 57	MY PRAYER (re-entry) *Mercury MT 120*	**28** 2
25 Jan 57	YOU'LL NEVER NEVER KNOW / IT ISN'T RIGHT *Mercury MT 130*	**23** 1
8 Feb 57	YOU'LL NEVER NEVER KNOW / IT ISN'T RIGHT (re-entry) *Mercury MT 130*	**29** 1
29 Mar 57	MY PRAYER (2nd re-entry) *Mercury MT 120*	**22** 1
29 Mar 57	ONLY YOU (2nd re-entry) *Mercury MT 117*	**18** 3
12 Apr 57	YOU'LL NEVER NEVER KNOW / IT ISN'T RIGHT (2nd re-entry) *Mercury MT 130*	**29** 1
17 May 57	I'M SORRY *Mercury MT 145*	**18** 6
5 Jul 57	I'M SORRY (re-entry) *Mercury MT 145*	**23** 1
19 Jul 57	I'M SORRY (2nd re-entry) *Mercury MT 145*	**22** 1
16 May 58	● TWILIGHT TIME *Mercury MT 214*	**3** 18
16 Jan 59	★ SMOKE GETS IN YOUR EYES *Mercury AMT 1016*	**1** 20
28 Aug 59	REMEMBER WHEN *Mercury AMT 1053*	**25** 2
29 Jan 60	HARBOUR LIGHTS *Mercury AMT 1081*	**11** 11

PLAVKA – *See JAM and SPOON featuring PLAVKA*

PLAYBOY BAND – *See John FRED and the PLAYBOY BAND*

PLAYBOYS – *See Gary LEWIS and the PLAYBOYS*

PLAYER *US / UK, male vocal / instrumental group* **7 wks**

25 Feb 78	BABY COME BACK *RSO 2090 254*	**32** 7

PLAYERS ASSOCIATION
US, male / female vocal / instrumental group **17 wks**

10 Mar 79	● TURN THE MUSIC UP *Vanguard VS 5011*	**8** 9
5 May 79	RIDE THE GROOVE *Vanguard VS 5012*	**42** 5
9 Feb 80	WE GOT THE GROOVE *Vanguard VS 5016*	**61** 3

PLUS ONE featuring SIRRON
UK, male / female vocal / instrumental group **4 wks**

19 May 90	IT'S HAPPENIN' *MCA MCA 1405*	**40** 4

PLUTO – *See Pluto SHERVINGTON*

PLUX featuring Georgia JONES
US, male / female vocal / instrumental group **2 wks**

4 May 96	OVER AND OVER *ffrr FCD 277*	**33** 2

PM DAWN *US, male vocal / instrumental duo* **38 wks**

8 Jun 91	A WATCHER'S POINT OF VIEW *Gee Street GEE 32*	**36** 5
17 Aug 91	● SET ADRIFT ON MEMORY BLISS *Gee Street GEE 33*	**3** 8
19 Oct 91	PAPER DOLL *Gee Street GEE 35*	**49** 3
22 Feb 92	REALITY USED TO BE A FRIEND OF MINE *Gee Street GEE 37*	**29** 4
7 Nov 92	I'D DIE WITHOUT YOU *Gee Street GEE 39*	**30** 5
13 Mar 93	LOOKING THROUGH PATIENT EYES *Gee Street GESCD 47*	**11** 7
12 Jun 93	MORE THAN LIKELY *Gee Street GESCD 49* [1]	**40** 3
30 Sep 95	DOWNTOWN VENUS *Gee Street GESCD 63*	**58** 2
6 Apr 96	SOMETIMES I MISS YOU SO MUCH *Gee Street GESCD 65*	**58** 1

[1] PM Dawn featuring Boy George

POETS *UK, male vocal / instrumental group* **5 wks**

29 Oct 64	NOW WE'RE THRU *Decca F 11995*	**31** 5

POGUES
Ireland / UK, male / female vocal / instrumental group **70 wks**

6 Apr 85	A PAIR OF BROWN EYES *Stiff BUY 220*	**72** 2
22 Jun 85	SALLY MACLENNANE *Stiff BUY 224*	**51** 4
14 Sep 85	DIRTY OLD TOWN *Stiff BUY 229*	**62** 3
8 Mar 86	POGUETRY IN MOTION EP *Stiff BUY 243*	**29** 6
30 Aug 86	HAUNTED *MCA MCA 1084*	**42** 4
28 Mar 87	● THE IRISH ROVER *Stiff BUY 258* [1]	**8** 8
5 Dec 87	● FAIRYTALE OF NEW YORK *Pogue Mahone NY 7* [2]	**2** 9
5 Mar 88	IF I SHOULD FALL FROM GRACE WITH GOD *Pogue Mahone PG 1*	**58** 3
16 Jul 88	FIESTA *Pogue Mahone PG 2*	**24** 5
17 Dec 88	YEAH YEAH YEAH YEAH YEAH *Pogue Mahone YZ 355*	**43** 4
8 Jul 89	MISTY MORNING, ALBERT BRIDGE *PM YZ 407*	**41** 3
16 Jun 90	JACK'S HEROES / WHISKEY IN THE JAR *PM YZ 500* [1]	**63** 2
15 Sep 90	SUMMER IN SIAM *PM YZ 519*	**64** 2
21 Sep 91	A RAINY NIGHT IN SOHO *PM YZ 603*	**67** 1
14 Dec 91	FAIRYTALE OF NEW YORK (re-issue) *PM YZ 628* [2]	**36** 5
30 May 92	HONKY TONK WOMEN *PM YZ 673*	**56** 2
21 Aug 93	TUESDAY MORNING *PM YZ 758 CD*	**18** 5
22 Jan 94	ONCE UPON A TIME *PM YZ 771CD*	**66** 2

[1] Pogues and the Dubliners [2] Pogues featuring Kirsty MacColl

Tracks on Poguetry In Motion EP: London Girl / The Body of an American / A Rainy Night in Soho / Planxty Noel Hill.

POINTER SISTERS *US, female vocal group* **87 wks**

3 Feb 79	EVERYBODY IS A STAR *Planet K 12324*	**61** 3
17 Mar 79	FIRE *Planet K 12339*	**34** 8
22 Aug 81	● SLOWHAND *Planet K 12530*	**10** 11
5 Dec 81	SHOULD I DO IT? *Reprise K 12578*	**50** 5
14 Apr 84	● AUTOMATIC *Planet RPS 105*	**2** 15
23 Jun 84	● JUMP (FOR MY LOVE) *Planet RPS 106*	**6** 10
11 Aug 84	I NEED YOU *Planet RPS 107*	**25** 9
27 Oct 84	I'M SO EXCITED *Planet RPS 108*	**11** 11
12 Jan 85	NEUTRON DANCE *Planet RPS 109*	**31** 7
20 Jul 85	DARE ME *RCA PB 49957*	**17** 8

POISON *US, male vocal / instrumental group* **43 wks**

23 May 87	TALK DIRTY TO ME *Music For Nations KUT 125*	**67** 1
7 May 88	NOTHIN' BUT A GOOD TIME *Capitol CL 486*	**35** 3
5 Nov 88	FALLEN ANGEL *Capitol CL 500*	**59** 1
11 Feb 89	EVERY ROSE HAS ITS THORN *Capitol CL 520*	**13** 9
29 Apr 89	YOUR MAMA DON'T DANCE *Capitol CL 523*	**13** 7
23 Sep 89	NOTHIN' BUT A GOOD TIME (re-issue) *Capitol CL 539*	**48** 3
30 Jun 90	UNSKINNY BOP *Capitol CL 582*	**15** 7
27 Oct 90	SOMETHING TO BELIEVE IN *Enigma CL 594*	**35** 4
23 Nov 91	SO TELL ME WHY *Capitol CL 640*	**25** 2

| 13 Feb 93 | **STAND** Capitol CDCL 679 .... | **25** 3 |
| 24 Apr 93 | **UNTIL YOU SUFFER SOME (FIRE AND ICE)** Capitol CDCL 685 | **32** 3 |

POLECATS UK, male vocal / instrumental group — 18 wks

7 Mar 81	**JOHN I'M ONLY DANCING / BIG GREEN CAR** Mercury POLE 1	**35** 8
16 May 81	**ROCKABILLY GUY** Mercury POLE 2	**35** 6
22 Aug 81	**JEEPSTER / MARIE CELESTE** Mercury POLE 3	**53** 4

POLICE UK / US, male vocal / instrumental group — 144 wks

7 Oct 78	**CAN'T STAND LOSING YOU** A & M AMS 7381	**42** 5
28 Apr 79	**ROXANNE** A & M AMS 7348	**12** 9
7 Jul 79	● **CAN'T STAND LOSING YOU (re-entry)** A & M AMS 7381	**2** 11
22 Sep 79	★ **MESSAGE IN A BOTTLE** A & M AMS 7474	**1** 11
17 Nov 79	**FALL OUT** Illegal IL 001	**47** 1
1 Dec 79	★ **WALKING ON THE MOON** A & M AMS 7494	**1** 10
16 Feb 80	● **SO LONELY** A & M AMS 7402	**6** 10
14 Jun 80	**SIX PACK** A & M AMPP 6001	**17** 4
27 Sep 80	★ **DON'T STAND SO CLOSE TO ME** A & M AMS 7564	**1** 10
13 Dec 80	● **DE DO DO DO, DE DA DA DA** A & M AMS 7578	**5** 8
26 Sep 81	● **INVISIBLE SUN** A & M AMS 8164	**2** 8
24 Oct 81	★ **EVERY LITTLE THING SHE DOES IS MAGIC** A & M AMS 8174	**1** 13
12 Dec 81	**SPIRITS IN THE MATERIAL WORLD** A & M AMS 8194	**12** 8
28 May 83	★ **EVERY BREATH YOU TAKE** A & M AM 117	**1** 11
23 Jul 83	● **WRAPPED AROUND YOUR FINGER** A & M AM 127	**7** 7
5 Nov 83	**SYNCHRONICITY II** A & M AM 153	**17** 4
14 Jan 84	**KING OF PAIN** A & M AM 176	**17** 5
11 Oct 86	**DON'T STAND SO CLOSE TO ME '86 (re-mix)** A & M AM 354	**24** 4
13 May 95	**CAN'T STAND LOSING YOU (LIVE)** A & M 5810372	**27** 2

Six Pack consists of six separate Police singles as follows: The Bed's Too Big Without You / Roxanne / Message In A Bottle / Walking On The Moon / So Lonely / Can't Stand Losing You. The last five titles were re-issues.

Su POLLARD UK, female vocalist — 11 wks

| 5 Oct 85 | **COME TO ME (I AM WOMAN)** Rainbow RBR 1 .... | **71** 1 |
| 1 Feb 86 | ● **STARTING TOGETHER** Rainbow RBR 4 .... | **2** 10 |

Jimi POLO US, male producer — 4 wks

| 9 Nov 91 | **NEVER GOIN' DOWN** MCA MCS 1578 [1] .... | **51** 2 |
| 1 Aug 92 | **EXPRESS YOURSELF** Perfecto 74321101827 .... | **59** 2 |

[1] Adamski featuring Jimi Polo

The listed flip side of Never Goin' Down was Born To Be Alive by Adamski featuring Soho.

Marco POLO Italy, male instrumental / production duo — 1 wk

| 8 Apr 95 | **A PRAYER TO THE MUSIC** Hi-Life HICD 7 .... | **65** 1 |

POLTERGEIST UK, male producer – Simon Berry — 2 wks

| 6 Jul 96 | **VICIOUS CIRCLES** Manifesto FESCD 8 .... | **32** 2 |

Peter POLYCARPOU UK, male vocalist — 4 wks

| 20 Feb 93 | **LOVE HURTS** Soundtrack Music CDEM 259 .... | **26** 4 |

POLYGON WINDOW UK, male producer – Richard James — 1 wk

| 3 Apr 93 | **QUOTH** Warp WAP 33CD .... | **49** 1 |

See also Aphex Twin.

PONI-TAILS US, female vocal group — 14 wks

| 19 Sep 58 | ● **BORN TOO LATE** HMV POP 516 .... | **5** 11 |
| 10 Apr 59 | **EARLY TO BED** HMV POP 596 .... | **26** 3 |

Brian POOLE and the TREMELOES
UK, male vocalist, male vocal / instrumental backing group — 90 wks

4 Jul 63	● **TWIST AND SHOUT** Decca F 11694	**4** 14
12 Sep 63	★ **DO YOU LOVE ME** Decca F 11739	**1** 14
28 Nov 63	**I CAN DANCE** Decca F 11771	**31** 8
30 Jan 64	● **CANDY MAN** Decca F 11823	**6** 13
7 May 64	● **SOMEONE SOMEONE** Decca F 11893	**2** 17
20 Aug 64	**TWELVE STEPS TO LOVE** Decca F 11951	**32** 7
7 Jan 65	**THREE BELLS** Decca F 12037	**17** 9
22 Jul 65	**I WANT CANDY** Decca F 12197	**25** 8

See also Tremeloes.

Glyn POOLE UK, male vocalist — 8 wks

| 20 Oct 73 | **MILLY MOLLY MANDY** York SYK 565 .... | **35** 8 |

Iggy POP US, male vocalist — 25 wks

13 Dec 86	● **REAL WILD CHILD (WILD ONE)** A & M AM 368	**10** 11
10 Feb 90	**LIVIN' ON THE EDGE OF THE NIGHT** Virgin America VUS 18	**51** 4
13 Oct 90	**CANDY** Virgin America VUS 29	**67** 1
5 Jan 91	**WELL DID YOU EVAH!** Chrysalis CHS 3646 [1]	**42** 4
4 Sep 93	**THE WILD AMERICA (EP)** Virgin America VUSCD 74	**63** 1
21 May 94	**BESIDE YOU** Virgin America VUSCD 77	**47** 2
23 Nov 96	**LUST FOR LIFE** Virgin America VUSCD 116	**26** 2

[1] Deborah Harry and Iggy Pop

Tracks on The Wild America (EP): Wild America / Credit Card / Come Back Tomorrow / My Angel.

POP TOPS Spain, male vocal group — 6 wks

| 9 Oct 71 | **MAMY BLUE** A & M AMS 859 .... | **35** 6 |

POP WILL EAT ITSELF
UK, male vocal / instrumental group — 43 wks

30 Jan 88	**THERE IS NO LOVE BETWEEN US ANYMORE** Chapter 22 CHAP 20	**66** 1
23 Jul 88	**DEF. CON ONE** Chapter 22 PWE 001	**63** 4
11 Feb 89	**CAN U DIG IT** RCA PB 42621	**38** 4
22 Apr 89	**WISE UP! SUCKER** RCA PB 42761	**41** 3
2 Sep 89	**VERY METAL NOISE POLLUTION EP** RCA PB 42883	**45** 3
9 Jun 90	**TOUCHED BY THE HAND OF CICCIOLINA** RCA PB 43735	**28** 4
13 Oct 90	**DANCE OF THE MAD** RCA PB 44023	**32** 2
12 Jan 91	**X Y & ZEE** RCA PB 44243	**15** 4
1 Jun 91	**92 DEGREES** RCA PB 44555	**23** 3
6 Jun 92	**KARMADROME / EAT ME DRINK ME LOVE ME KILL ME** RCA PB 45467	**17** 2
29 Aug 92	**BULLETPROOF!** RCA 74321110137	**24** 3
16 Jan 93	● **GET THE GIRL! KILL THE BADDIES!** RCA 74321128802	**9** 4
16 Oct 93	**RSVP / FAMILIUS HORRIBILUS** Infectious INFECT 1CD	**27** 2
12 Mar 94	**ICH BIN EIN AUSLANDER** Infectious INFECT 4CD	**28** 2
10 Sep 94	**EVERYTHING'S COOL** Infectious INFECT 9CD	**23** 2

Tracks on Very Metal Noise Pollution EP: Def Con. 1989 AD including the Twilight Zone / Preaching To The Perverted / P.W.E.I.-zation / 92°F. See also Various Artists (EPs & LPs) – Gimme Shelter (EP).

POPES – *See Shane MacGOWAN and the POPES*

Presidents Of The United States Of America

In 1994 the Presidents Of The United States Of America played a Democratic Party rally in their hometown of Seattle for the real president, Bill Clinton.

Public Image Ltd

After the break up of the Sex Pistols, lead singer Johnny Rotten reverted to his real name, John Lydon, and formed PIL.

Pulp

The release of Pulp's 1994 single 'Do You Remember The First Time' was accompanied by a short film in which celebrities were quizzed about the loss of their virginity.

POPPY FAMILY
Canada, male / female vocal / instrumental group **14 wks**

15 Aug 70	● **WHICH WAY YOU GOIN' BILLY** *Decca F 22976*	**7**	14

PORN KINGS *UK, male instrumental / production group* **2 wks**

28 Sep 96	**UP TO NO GOOD** *All Around The World CDGLOBE 145*	**28**	2

PORNO FOR PYROS
US, male vocal / instrumental group **2 wks**

5 Jun 93	**PETS** *Warner Bros. 0777CDX*	**53**	2

PORTISHEAD *UK, male / female vocal / instrumental duo* **12 wks**

13 Aug 94	**SOUR TIMES** *Go.Beat GODCD 116*	**57**	1
14 Jan 95	**GLORY BOX** *Go.Beat GODCD 120*	**13**	7
22 Apr 95	**SOUR TIMES (re-entry)** *Go.Beat GODCD 116*	**13**	4

Gary PORTNOY *US, male vocalist* **3 wks**

25 Feb 84	**THEME FROM 'CHEERS'** *Starblend CHEER 1*	**58**	3

PORTRAIT *US, male vocal group* **6 wks**

27 Mar 93	**HERE WE GO AGAIN** *Capitol CDCL 683*	**37**	3
8 Apr 95	**I CAN CALL YOU** *Capitol CDCL 740*	**61**	1
8 Jul 95	**HOW DEEP IS YOUR LOVE** *Capitol CDCL 751*	**41**	2

PORTSMOUTH SINFONIA *UK, orchestra* **4 wks**

12 Sep 81	**CLASSICAL MUDDLEY** *Island WIP 6736*	**38**	4

Sandy POSEY *US, female vocalist* **32 wks**

15 Sep 66	**BORN A WOMAN** *MGM 1321*	**24**	11
5 Jan 67	**SINGLE GIRL** *MGM 1330*	**15**	13
13 Apr 67	**WHAT A WOMAN IN LOVE WON'T DO** *MGM 1335*	**48**	3
6 Sep 75	**SINGLE GIRL (re-issue)** *MGM 2006 533*	**35**	5

POSIES *US, male vocal / instrumental group* **1 wk**

19 Mar 94	**DEFINITE DOOR** *Geffen GFSTD 68*	**67**	1

POSITIVE FORCE *US, female vocal duo* **9 wks**

22 Dec 79	**WE GOT THE FUNK** *Sugarhill SHL 102*	**18**	9

POSITIVE GANG
UK, male / female instrumental / vocal group **5 wks**

17 Apr 93	**SWEET FREEDOM** *PWL Continental PWCD 261*	**34**	4
31 Jul 93	**SWEET FREEDOM PART 2** *PWL Continental PWCD 264*	**67**	1

POSITIVE K *US, male rapper* **2 wks**

15 May 93	**I GOT A MAN** *Fourth & Broadway BRCD 280*	**43**	2

Mike POST *US, orchestra* **18 wks**

9 Aug 75	**AFTERNOON OF THE RHINO** *Warner Bros. K 16588* [1]	**48**	1
23 Aug 75	**AFTERNOON OF THE RHINO (re-entry)** *Warner Bros. K 16588* [1]	**47**	1
16 Jan 82	**THEME FROM 'HILL STREET BLUES'** *Elektron K 12576* [2]	**25**	11
29 Sep 84	**THE A TEAM** *RCA 443*	**45**	5

[1] Mike Post Coalition [2] Mike Post featuring Larry Carlton

POTTERS *UK, male vocal group* **2 wks**

1 Apr 72	**WE'LL BE WITH YOU** *Pye JT 100*	**34**	2

P.O.V. – *See JADE*

POWDER
UK, male / female vocal / instrumental group **1 wk**

24 Jun 95	**AFRODISIAC** *Parkway PARK 002CD*	**72**	1

Bryan POWELL *UK, male vocalist* **3 wks**

13 Mar 93	**IT'S ALRIGHT** *Talkin Loud TLKCD 34*	**73**	1
15 May 93	**I THINK OF YOU** *Talkin Loud TLKCD 38*	**61**	1
7 Aug 93	**NATURAL** *Talkin Loud TLKCD 41*	**73**	1

Cozy POWELL *UK, male instrumentalist – drums* **38 wks**

8 Dec 73	● **DANCE WITH THE DEVIL** *RAK 164*	**3**	15
25 May 74	**THE MAN IN BLACK** *RAK 173*	**18**	8
10 Aug 74	● **NA NA NA** *RAK 180*	**10**	10
10 Nov 79	**THEME ONE** *Ariola ARO 189*	**62**	2
19 Jun 93	**RESURRECTION** *Parlophone CDRS 6351* [1]	**23**	3

[1] Brian May with Cozy Powell

Kobie POWELL – *See US3*

POWER OF DREAMS
Ireland, male vocal / instrumental group **2 wks**

19 Jan 91	**AMERICAN DREAM** *Polydor PO 117*	**74**	1
11 Apr 92	**THERE I GO AGAIN** *Polydor PO 200*	**65**	1

POWER STATION
UK / US, male vocal / instrumental group **17 wks**

16 Mar 85	**SOME LIKE IT HOT** *Parlophone R 6091*	**14**	8
11 May 85	**GET IT ON** *Parlophone R 6096*	**22**	7
9 Nov 85	**COMMUNICATION** *Parlophone R 6114*	**75**	1
12 Oct 96	**SHE CAN ROCK IT** *Chrysalis CDCHS 5039*	**63**	1

POWERCUT featuring NUBIAN PRINZ
US, male vocal / instrumental group **4 wks**

22 Jun 91	**GIRLS** *Eternal YZ 570*	**50**	4

POWERPILL
UK, male instrumental / production group **3 wks**

6 Jun 92	**PAC-MAN** *Ffrreedom TABX 110*	**43**	3

Will POWERS *US, female vocalist – Lyn Goldsmith* **9 wks**

1 Oct 83	**KISSING WITH CONFIDENCE** *Island IS 134*	**17**	9

Hit features uncredited vocals by Carly Simon.

Perez PRADO *Cuba, orchestra* **57 wks**

25 Mar 55	★ **CHERRY PINK AND APPLE BLOSSOM WHITE**		
	HMV B 10833 [1]	**1**	17
25 Jul 58	● **PATRICIA** *RCA 1067*	**8**	16
10 Dec 94	● **GUAGLIONE** *RCA 74321250192* [2]	**41**	6
8 Apr 95	**GUAGLIONE (re-entry)** *RCA 74321250192* [2]	**58**	2
6 May 95	● **GUAGLIONE (2nd re-entry)** *RCA 74321250192* [2]	**2**	16

[1] Perez 'Prez' Prado and his Orchestra, the King of the Mambo
[2] Perez 'Prez' Prado and his Orchestra

PRAISE
UK/South Africa, male / female vocal / instrumental group **7 wks**

2 Feb 91	● **ONLY YOU** *Epic 6566117*	**4**	7

PRATT and McCLAIN with BROTHERLOVE
US, male vocal duo with male instrumental group **6 wks**

1 Oct 77	**HAPPY DAYS** *Reprise K 14435*	**31**	6

PRAXIS featuring Kathy BROWN
UK, male / female vocal / instrumental group **2 wks**

25 Nov 95	**TURN ME OUT** *Stress CDSTR 40*	**44**	2

PRAYING MANTIS *UK, male vocal / instrumental group* **2 wks**

31 Jan 81	**CHEATED** *Arista ARIST 378*	**69**	2

PREFAB SPROUT
UK, male / female vocal / instrumental group **57 wks**

28 Jan 84	**DON'T SING** *Kitchenware SK 9*	**62**	2
20 Jul 85	**FARON YOUNG** *Kitchenware SK 22*	**74**	1
9 Nov 85	**WHEN LOVE BREAKS DOWN** *Kitchenware SK 21*	**25**	10
8 Feb 86	**JOHNNY JOHNNY** *Kitchenware SK 24*	**64**	2
13 Feb 88	**CARS AND GIRLS** *Kitchenware SK 35*	**44**	5
30 Apr 88	● **THE KING OF ROCK 'N' ROLL** *Kitchenware SK 37*	**7**	10
23 Jul 88	**HEY MANHATTAN!** *Kitchenware SK 38*	**72**	2
18 Aug 90	**LOOKING FOR ATLANTIS** *Kitchenware SK 47*	**51**	3
20 Oct 90	**WE LET THE STARS GO** *Kitchenware SK 48*	**50**	4
5 Jan 91	**JORDAN: THE EP** *Kitchenware SK 49*	**35**	4
13 Jun 92	**THE SOUND OF CRYING** *Kitchenware SK 58*	**23**	5
8 Aug 92	**IF YOU DON'T LOVE ME** *Kitchenware SK 60*	**33**	4
3 Oct 92	**ALL THE WORLD LOVES LOVERS** *Kitchenware SK 62* ...	**61**	2
9 Jan 93	**LIFE OF SURPRISES** *Kitchenware SKCD 63*	**24**	4

Tracks on Jordan: The EP: Carnival 2000 / The Ice Maiden / One Of The Broken / Jordan: The Comeback.

PRELUDE *UK, male / female vocal group* **26 wks**

26 Jan 74	**AFTER THE GOLDRUSH** *Dawn DNS 1052*	**21**	9
26 Apr 80	**PLATINUM BLONDE** *EMI 5046*	**45**	7
22 May 82	**AFTER THE GOLDRUSH (re-issue)** *After Hours AFT 02* ..	**28**	7
31 Jul 82	**ONLY THE LONELY** *After Hours AFT 06*	**55**	3

AFT 02 was a re-recording of DNS 1052. Both songs are a capella.

PRESIDENT BROWN – See SABRE featuring PRESIDENT BROWN

PRESIDENTS OF THE UNITED STATES OF AMERICA *US, male vocal / instrumental group* **20 wks**

6 Jan 96	**LUMP** *Columbia 6624962*	**15**	7
20 Apr 96	● **PEACHES** *Columbia 6631072*	**8**	7

20 Jul 96	**DUNE BUGGY** *Columbia 6634892*	**15**	4
2 Nov 96	**MACH 5** *Columbia 6638812*	**29**	2

Elvis PRESLEY *US, male vocalist* **1149 wks**

11 May 56	● **HEARTBREAK HOTEL** *HMV POP 182*	**2**	21
25 May 56	● **BLUE SUEDE SHOES** *HMV POP 213*	**9**	8
13 Jul 56	**I WANT YOU I NEED YOU I LOVE YOU** *HMV POP 235* ..	**25**	2
3 Aug 56	**I WANT YOU I NEED YOU I LOVE YOU (re-entry)** *HMV POP 235*	**14**	9
17 Aug 56	**BLUE SUEDE SHOES (re-entry)** *HMV POP 213*	**26**	2
21 Sep 56	● **HOUND DOG** *HMV POP 249*	**2**	23
26 Oct 56	**HEARTBREAK HOTEL (re-entry)** *HMV POP 182*	**23**	1
16 Nov 56	● **BLUE MOON** *HMV POP 272*	**9**	11
23 Nov 56	**I DON'T CARE IF THE SUN DON'T SHINE** *HMV POP 272* ..	**29**	1
7 Dec 56	**LOVE ME TENDER** *HMV POP 253*	**11**	9
21 Dec 56	**I DON'T CARE IF THE SUN DON'T SHINE (re-entry)** *HMV POP 272*	**23**	3
15 Feb 57	**MYSTERY TRAIN** *HMV POP 295*	**25**	5
8 Mar 57	**RIP IT UP** *HMV POP 305*	**27**	1
10 May 57	● **TOO MUCH** *HMV POP 330*	**6**	8
14 Jun 57	**ALL SHOOK UP** *HMV POP 359*	**24**	1
28 Jun 57	★ **ALL SHOOK UP (re-entry)** *HMV POP 359* ..	**1**	20
12 Jul 57	● **TEDDY BEAR** *RCA 1013*	**3**	19
12 Jul 57	**TOO MUCH (re-entry)** *HMV POP 330*	**26**	1
30 Aug 57	● **PARALYSED** *HMV POP 378*	**8**	10
4 Oct 57	● **PARTY** *RCA 1020*	**2**	15
18 Oct 57	**GOT A LOT O' LIVIN' TO DO** *RCA 1020* ...	**17**	4
1 Nov 57	**LOVING YOU** *RCA 1013*	**24**	2
1 Nov 57	**TRYING TO GET TO YOU** *HMV POP 408*	**16**	4
8 Nov 57	**LAWDY MISS CLAWDY** *HMV POP 408*	**15**	5
15 Nov 57	● **SANTA BRING MY BABY BACK (TO ME)** *RCA 1025*	**7**	8
17 Jan 58	**I'M LEFT YOU'RE RIGHT SHE'S GONE** *HMV POP 428* ...	**21**	7
24 Jan 58	★ **JAILHOUSE ROCK** *RCA 1028*	**1**	14
31 Jan 58	**JAILHOUSE ROCK EP** *RCA RCX 106*	**18**	5
7 Feb 58	**I'M LEFT YOU'RE RIGHT SHE'S GONE (re-entry)** *HMV POP 428*	**29**	1
28 Feb 58	● **DON'T** *RCA 1043*	**2**	11
2 May 58	● **WEAR MY RING AROUND YOUR NECK** *RCA 1058*	**3**	10
25 Jul 58	● **HARD HEADED WOMAN** *RCA 1070*	**2**	11
3 Oct 58	● **KING CREOLE** *RCA 1081*	**2**	15
23 Jan 59	★ **ONE NIGHT / I GOT STUNG** *RCA 1100* ..	**1**	12
24 Apr 59	★ **A FOOL SUCH AS I / I NEED YOUR LOVE TONIGHT** *RCA 1113*	**1**	15
24 Jul 59	● **A BIG HUNK O' LOVE** *RCA 1136*	**4**	9
12 Feb 60	**STRICTLY ELVIS EP** *RCA RCX 175*	**26**	1
7 Apr 60	● **STUCK ON YOU** *RCA 1187*	**3**	14
28 Jul 60	● **A MESS OF BLUES** *RCA 1194*	**2**	18
3 Nov 60	★ **IT'S NOW OR NEVER** *RCA 1207*	**1**	19
19 Jan 61	★ **ARE YOU LONESOME TONIGHT** *RCA 1216*	**1**	15
9 Mar 61	★ **WOODEN HEART** *RCA 1226*	**1**	27
25 May 61	★ **SURRENDER** *RCA 1227*	**1**	15
7 Sep 61	● **WILD IN THE COUNTRY / I FEEL SO BAD** *RCA 1244*	**4**	12
2 Nov 61	● **HIS LATEST FLAME / LITTLE SISTER** *RCA 1258* ..	**1**	13
1 Feb 62	★ **ROCK A HULA BABY / CAN'T HELP FALLING IN LOVE** *RCA 1270*	**1**	20
10 May 62	● **GOOD LUCK CHARM** *RCA 1280*	**1**	17
21 Jun 62	**FOLLOW THAT DREAM EP** *RCA RCX 211*	**34**	2
30 Aug 62	★ **SHE'S NOT YOU** *RCA 1303*	**1**	14
29 Nov 62	★ **RETURN TO SENDER** *RCA 1320*	**1**	14
28 Feb 63	**ONE BROKEN HEART FOR SALE** *RCA 1337*	**12**	9
4 Jul 63	● **DEVIL IN DISGUISE** *RCA 1355*	**1**	12
24 Oct 63	**BOSSA NOVA BABY** *RCA 1374*	**13**	8
19 Dec 63	**KISS ME QUICK** *RCA 1375*	**14**	10
12 Mar 64	**VIVA LAS VEGAS** *RCA 1390*	**17**	12
25 Jun 64	● **KISSIN' COUSINS** *RCA 1404*	**10**	11
20 Aug 64	**SUCH A NIGHT** *RCA 1411*	**13**	10
29 Oct 64	**AIN'T THAT LOVIN' YOU BABY** *RCA 1422*	**15**	8
3 Dec 64	**BLUE CHRISTMAS** *RCA 1430*	**11**	7
11 Mar 65	**DO THE CLAM** *RCA 1443*	**19**	8
27 May 65	★ **CRYING IN THE CHAPEL** *RCA 1455*	**1**	15
11 Nov 65	**TELL ME WHY** *RCA 1489*	**15**	10
24 Feb 66	**BLUE RIVER** *RCA 1504*	**22**	7
7 Apr 66	**FRANKIE AND JOHNNY** *RCA 1509*	**21**	9
7 Jul 66	● **LOVE LETTERS** *RCA 1526*	**6**	10

Date	Title	Pos	Wks
13 Oct 66	ALL THAT I AM RCA 1545	18	8
1 Dec 66	IF EVERY DAY WAS LIKE CHRISTMAS RCA 1557	13	7
9 Feb 67	INDESCRIBABLY BLUE RCA 1565	21	5
11 May 67	YOU GOTTA STOP / LOVE MACHINE RCA 1593	38	5
16 Aug 67	LONG LEGGED GIRL RCA RCA 1616	49	1
21 Feb 68	GUITAR MAN RCA 1663	19	9
15 May 68	U.S. MALE RCA 1688	15	8
17 Jul 68	YOUR TIME HASN'T COME YET BABY RCA 1714	22	11
16 Oct 68	YOU'LL NEVER WALK ALONE RCA 1747	44	3
26 Feb 69	IF I CAN DREAM RCA 1795	11	10
11 Jun 69	● IN THE GHETTO RCA 1831	2	16
6 Sep 69	CLEAN UP YOUR OWN BACK YARD RCA 1869	21	7
18 Oct 69	IN THE GHETTO (re-entry) RCA 1831	50	1
29 Nov 69	● SUSPICIOUS MINDS RCA 1900	2	14
28 Feb 70	● DON'T CRY DADDY RCA 1916	8	11
16 May 70	KENTUCKY RAIN RCA 1949	21	11
11 Jul 70	★ THE WONDER OF YOU RCA 1974	1	20
8 Aug 70	KENTUCKY RAIN (re-entry) RCA 1949	46	1
14 Nov 70	● I'VE LOST YOU RCA 1999	9	12
9 Jan 71	● YOU DON'T HAVE TO SAY YOU LOVE ME RCA 2046	9	7
23 Jan 71	THE WONDER OF YOU (re-entry) RCA 1974	47	1
6 Mar 71	YOU DON'T HAVE TO SAY YOU LOVE ME (re-entry) RCA 2046	35	3
20 Mar 71	● THERE GOES MY EVERYTHING RCA 2060	6	11
15 May 71	● RAGS TO RICHES RCA 2084	9	11
17 Jul 71	HEARTBREAK HOTEL / HOUND DOG (re-issue) RCA Maximillion 2104	10	12
2 Oct 71	I'M LEAVIN' RCA 2125	23	9
4 Dec 71	● I JUST CAN'T HELP BELIEVING RCA 2158	6	16
11 Dec 71	JAILHOUSE ROCK (re-issue) RCA Maximillion 2153	42	5
1 Apr 72	● UNTIL IT'S TIME FOR YOU TO GO RCA 2188	5	9
17 Jun 72	● AMERICAN TRILOGY RCA 2229	8	11
30 Sep 72	● BURNING LOVE RCA 2267	7	9
16 Dec 72	● ALWAYS ON MY MIND RCA 2304	9	13
26 May 73	POLK SALAD ANNIE RCA 2359	23	7
11 Aug 73	FOOL RCA 2393	15	10
24 Nov 73	RAISED ON ROCK RCA 2435	36	7
16 Mar 74	I'VE GOT A THING ABOUT YOU BABY RCA APBO 0196	33	5
13 Jul 74	IF YOU TALK IN YOUR SLEEP RCA APBO 0280	40	3
16 Nov 74	● MY BOY RCA 2458	5	13
18 Jan 75	● PROMISED LAND RCA PB 10074	9	8
24 May 75	T.R.O.U.B.L.E. RCA 2562	31	4
29 Nov 75	GREEN GREEN GRASS OF HOME RCA 2635	29	7
1 May 76	HURT RCA 2674	37	5
4 Sep 76	● GIRL OF MY BEST FRIEND RCA 2729	9	12
25 Dec 76	● SUSPICION RCA 2768	9	12
5 Mar 77	● MOODY BLUE RCA PB 0857	6	9
13 Aug 77	★ WAY DOWN RCA PB 0998	1	13
3 Sep 77	ALL SHOOK UP (re-issue) RCA PB 2694	41	2
3 Sep 77	ARE YOU LONESOME TONIGHT (re-issue) RCA PB 2699	46	1
3 Sep 77	CRYING IN THE CHAPEL (re-issue) RCA PB 2708	43	2
3 Sep 77	IT'S NOW OR NEVER (re-issue) RCA PB 2698	39	2
3 Sep 77	JAILHOUSE ROCK (2nd re-issue) RCA PB 2695	44	2
3 Sep 77	RETURN TO SENDER (re-issue) RCA PB 2706	42	3
3 Sep 77	THE WONDER OF YOU (re-issue) RCA PB 2709	48	1
3 Sep 77	WOODEN HEART (re-issue) RCA PB 2700	49	1
10 Dec 77	● MY WAY RCA PB 1165	9	8
24 Jun 78	DON'T BE CRUEL RCA PB 9265	24	12
15 Dec 79	IT WON'T SEEM LIKE CHRISTMAS (WITHOUT YOU) RCA PB 9464	13	6
30 Aug 80	● IT'S ONLY LOVE / BEYOND THE REEF RCA 4	3	10
6 Dec 80	SANTA CLAUS IS BACK IN TOWN RCA 16	41	6
14 Feb 81	GUITAR MAN RCA 43	43	4
18 Apr 81	LOVING ARMS RCA 48	47	6
13 Mar 82	ARE YOU LONESOME TONIGHT RCA 196	25	7
26 Jun 82	THE SOUND OF YOUR CRY RCA 232	59	2
5 Feb 83	JAILHOUSE ROCK (re-entry) RCA 1028	27	6
7 May 83	BABY I DON'T CARE RCA 332	61	3
3 Dec 83	I CAN HELP RCA 369	30	9
10 Nov 84	THE LAST FAREWELL RCA 459	48	6
19 Jan 85	THE ELVIS MEDLEY RCA 476	51	3
10 Aug 85	ALWAYS ON MY MIND RCA PB 49944	59	4
11 Apr 87	AIN'T THAT LOVIN' YOU BABY / BOSSA NOVA BABY RCA ARON 1	47	5
22 Aug 87	LOVE ME TENDER / IF I CAN DREAM (re-issue) RCA ARON 2	56	3
16 Jan 88	STUCK ON YOU (re-issue) RCA PB 49595	58	2
17 Aug 91	ARE YOU LONESOME TONIGHT (LIVE) (re-issue) RCA PB 49177	68	2
29 Aug 92	DON'T BE CRUEL (re-issue) RCA 74321110777	42	2
11 Nov 95	THE TWELFTH OF NEVER RCA 74321320122	21	3
18 May 96	HEARTBREAK HOTEL (2nd re-issue) / I WAS THE ONE RCA 74321336862	45	1

Tracks on Jailhouse Rock (EP): Jailhouse Rock / Young And Beautiful / I Want To Be Free / Don't Leave Me Now / Baby I Don't Care. On Strictly Elvis (EP): Old Shep / Any Place Is Paradise / Paralysed / Is It So Strange. On Follow That Dream (EP): Follow That Dream / Angel / What A Wonderful Life / I'm Not The Marrying Kind. On 5 July 62 a note on the Top 50 for that week stated 'Due to difficulties in assessing returns of Follow That Dream EP, it has been decided not to include it in Britain's Top 50. It is of course No.1 in the EP charts'. Therefore this EP only had a two week run on the chart when its sales would certainly have justified a much longer one. Beyond The Reef listed only 30 Aug to 13 Sep 80. It peaked at position 7. Are You Lonesome Tonight on RCA 196 is a live version. RCA BP 49177 is a re-issue of RCA 196. Can't Help Falling In Love credited from 1 Mar 62. Tracks on The Elvis Medley: Jailhouse Rock / Teddy Bear / Hound Dog / Don't Be Cruel / Burning Love / Suspicious Minds. Both sides of RCA ARON 1 are alternate versions to the original hits. RCA PB 49944 is also an alternate version.

Billy PRESTON
US, male vocalist / instrumentalist – keyboards   51 wks

Date	Title	Pos	Wks
23 Apr 69	★ GET BACK Apple R 5777 [1]	1	17
2 Jul 69	THAT'S THE WAY GOD PLANNED IT Apple 12	11	10
16 Sep 72	OUTA SPACE A & M AMS 7007	44	3
3 Apr 76	GET BACK (re-entry) Apple R 5777 [1]	28	5
15 Dec 79	● WITH YOU I'M BORN AGAIN Motown TMG 1159 [2]	2	11
8 Mar 80	IT WILL COME IN TIME Motown TMG 1175 [2]	47	4
22 Apr 89	GET BACK (2nd re-entry) Apple R 5777 [1]	74	1

[1] Beatles with Billy Preston   [2] Billy Preston and Syreeta

See also Various Artists (LPs & EPs) – The Apple EP.

Johnny PRESTON   US, male vocalist   45 wks

Date	Title	Pos	Wks
12 Feb 60	★ RUNNING BEAR Mercury AMT 1079	1	14
21 Apr 60	● CRADLE OF LOVE Mercury AMT 1092	2	16
2 Jun 60	RUNNING BEAR (re-entry) Mercury AMT 1079	41	1
28 Jul 60	I'M STARTING TO GO STEADY Mercury AMT 1104	49	1
11 Aug 60	FEEL SO FINE Mercury AMT 1104	18	10
8 Dec 60	CHARMING BILLY Mercury AMT 1114	34	1
22 Dec 60	CHARMING BILLY (re-entry) Mercury AMT 1114	42	2

Mike PRESTON   UK, male vocalist   33 wks

Date	Title	Pos	Wks
30 Oct 59	MR. BLUE Decca F 11167	12	8
25 Aug 60	I'D DO ANYTHING Decca F 11255	23	10
22 Dec 60	TOGETHERNESS Decca F 11287	41	5
9 Mar 61	MARRY ME Decca F 11335	14	10

PRETENDERS/Chrissie HYNDE
US, female vocalist with UK male backing band   164 wks

Date	Title	Pos	Wks
10 Feb 79	STOP YOUR SOBBING Real ARE 6	34	9
14 Jul 79	KID Real ARE 9	33	7
17 Nov 79	★ BRASS IN POCKET Real ARE 11	1	17
5 Apr 80	● TALK OF THE TOWN Real ARE 12	8	8
14 Feb 81	MESSAGE OF LOVE Real ARE 15	11	7
12 Sep 81	DAY AFTER DAY Real ARE 17	45	4
14 Nov 81	● I GO TO SLEEP Real ARE 18	7	10
2 Oct 82	BACK ON THE CHAIN GANG Real ARE 19	17	9
26 Nov 83	2000 MILES Real ARE 20	15	9
9 Jun 84	THIN LINE BETWEEN LOVE AND HATE Real ARE 22	49	3
3 Aug 85	★ I GOT YOU BABE DEP International DEP 20 [1]	1	13
11 Oct 86	● DON'T GET ME WRONG Real YZ 85	10	9
13 Dec 86	● HYMN TO HER Real YZ 93	8	12

15 Aug 87	**IF THERE WAS A MAN** *Real YZ 149* [2]	**49**	6
18 Jun 88	● **BREAKFAST IN BED** *DEP International DEP 29* [1]	**6**	11
12 Oct 91	**SPIRITUAL HIGH (STATE OF INDEPENDENCE)** *Arista 114528* [3]	**66**	2
23 Jan 93	**SPIRITUAL HIGH (STATE OF INDEPENDENCE) (re-issue)** *Arista 74321127712* [3]	**47**	2
23 Apr 94	● **I'LL STAND BY YOU** *WEA YZ 815CD*	**10**	10
2 Jul 94	**NIGHT IN MY VEINS** *WEA YZ 825CD*	**25**	5
15 Oct 94	**977** *WEA YZ 848CD1*	**66**	2
18 Mar 95	★ **LOVE CAN BUILD A BRIDGE** *London COCD 1* [4]	**1**	8
14 Oct 95	**KID** *WEA 014CD*	**73**	1

[1] UB40 featuring Chrissie Hynde [2] Pretenders For 007 [3] Moodswings featuring Chrissie Hynde [4] Cher, Chrissie Hynde and Neneh Cherry with Eric Clapton

Kid in 95 is a re-recording.

PRETTY BOY FLOYD
US, male vocal / instrumental group　　　　　　**1 wk**

10 Mar 90	**ROCK AND ROLL (IS GONNA SET THE NIGHT ON FIRE)** *MCA MCA 1393*	**75**	1

PRETTY THINGS *UK, male vocal / instrumental group*　**41 wks**

18 Jun 64	**ROSALYN** *Fontana TF 469*	**41**	5
22 Oct 64	● **DON'T BRING ME DOWN** *Fontana TF 503*	**10**	11
25 Feb 65	**HONEY I NEED** *Fontana TF 537*	**13**	10
15 Jul 65	**CRY TO ME** *Fontana TF 585*	**28**	7
20 Jan 66	**MIDNIGHT TO SIX MAN** *Fontana TF 647*	**46**	4
5 May 66	**COME SEE ME** *Fontana TF 688*	**43**	5
21 Jul 66	**A HOUSE IN THE COUNTRY** *Fontana TF 722*	**50**	1
4 Aug 66	**A HOUSE IN THE COUNTRY (re-entry)** *Fontana TF 722* ..	**50**	1

Alan PRICE
UK, male vocalist / instrumentalist – keyboards　　**87 wks**

31 Mar 66	● **I PUT A SPELL ON YOU** *Decca F 12367* [1]	**9**	10
14 Jul 66	**HI LILI HI LO** *Decca F 12442* [1]	**11**	12
2 Mar 67	● **SIMON SMITH AND HIS AMAZING DANCING BEAR** *Decca F 12570* [1]	**4**	12
2 Aug 67	● **THE HOUSE THAT JACK BUILT** *Decca F 12641* [1]	**4**	10
15 Nov 67	**SHAME** *Decca F 12691* [1]	**45**	2
31 Jan 68	**DON'T STOP THE CARNIVAL** *Decca F 12731* [1]	**13**	8
10 Apr 71	**ROSETTA** *CBS 7108* [2]	**11**	10
25 May 74	● **JARROW SONG** *Warner Bros. K 16372*	**6**	9
29 Apr 78	**JUST FOR YOU** *Jet UP 36358*	**43**	7
17 Feb 79	**BABY OF MINE / JUST FOR YOU (re-issue)** *Jet 135* ..	**32**	3
30 Apr 88	**CHANGES** *Ariola 109911*	**54**	4

[1] Alan Price Set [2] Fame and Price Together

Lloyd PRICE *US, male vocalist*　　　　　　**36 wks**

13 Feb 59	● **STAGGER LEE** *HMV POP 580*	**7**	14
15 May 59	**WHERE WERE YOU** *HMV POP 598*	**15**	6
12 Jun 59	● **PERSONALITY** *HMV POP 626*	**9**	8
14 Aug 59	**PERSONALITY (re-entry)** *HMV POP 626*	**25**	2
11 Sep 59	**I'M GONNA GET MARRIED** *HMV POP 650*	**23**	5
21 Apr 60	**LADY LUCK** *HMV POP 712*	**45**	1

Dickie PRIDE *UK, male vocalist*　　　　　　**1 wk**

30 Oct 59	**PRIMROSE LANE** *Columbia DB 4340*	**28**	1

Maxi PRIEST *UK, male vocalist*　　　　　**106 wks**

29 Mar 86	**STROLLIN' ON** *10 TEN 84*	**32**	9
12 Jul 86	**IN THE SPRINGTIME** *10 TEN 127*	**54**	3
8 Nov 86	**CRAZY LOVE** *10 TEN 135*	**67**	5
4 Apr 87	**LET ME KNOW** *10 TEN 156*	**49**	4
24 Oct 87	**SOME GUYS HAVE ALL THE LUCK** *10 TEN 198*	**12**	12
20 Feb 88	**HOW CAN WE EASE THE PAIN** *10 TEN 207* [1]	**41**	6
4 Jun 88	● **WILD WORLD** *10 TEN 221*	**5**	9
27 Aug 88	**GOODBYE TO LOVE AGAIN** *10 TEN 238*	**57**	3
9 Jun 90	● **CLOSE TO YOU** *10 TEN 294*	**7**	10
1 Sep 90	**PEACE THROUGHOUT THE WORLD** *10 TEN 317* [2]	**41**	4
1 Dec 90	**HUMAN WORK OF ART** *10 TEN 328*	**75**	1
15 Dec 90	**HUMAN WORK OF ART (re-entry)** *10 TEN 328*	**71**	1
24 Aug 91	**HOUSECALL** *Epic 6573477* [3]	**31**	7
5 Oct 91	**THE MAXI PRIEST EP** *Ten TEN 343*	**62**	3
26 Sep 92	**GROOVIN' IN THE MIDNIGHT** *Ten TEN 412*	**50**	2
28 Nov 92	**JUST WANNA KNOW / FE' REAL** *Ten TEN 416* [4]	**33**	3
20 Mar 93	**ONE MORE CHANCE** *Ten TENCD 420*	**40**	3
8 May 93	● **HOUSECALL (re-mix)** *Epic 6592842* [3]	**8**	8
31 Jul 93	**WAITING IN VAIN** *GRP MCSC 1921* [5]	**65**	2
22 Jun 96	**THAT GIRL** *Virgin America VUSCD 106* [6]	**15**	7
21 Sep 96	**WATCHING THE WORLD GO BY** *Virgin America VUSCD 108*	**36**	2

[1] Maxi Priest featuring Beres Hammond [2] Maxi Priest featuring Jazzie B [3] Shabba Ranks featuring Maxi Priest [4] Maxi Priest/Maxi Priest featuring Apache Indian [5] Lee Ritenour and Maxi Priest [6] Maxi Priest featuring Shaggy

Tracks on The Maxi Priest EP: Just A Little Bit Longer / Best Of Me / Searching / Fever.

Louis PRIMA *US, male vocalist*　　　　　**1 wk**

21 Feb 58	**BUONA SERA** *Capitol CL 14841*	**25**	1

PRIMA DONNA *UK, male / female vocal group*　**4 wks**

26 Apr 80	**LOVE ENOUGH FOR TWO** *Ariola ARO 221*	**48**	4

PRIMAL SCREAM *UK, male vocal / instrumental group* **36 wks**

3 Mar 90	**LOADED** *Creation CRE 070*	**16**	9
18 Aug 90	**COME TOGETHER** *Creation CRE 0778*	**26**	6
22 Jun 91	**HIGHER THAN THE SUN** *Creation CRE 096*	**40**	2
24 Aug 91	**DON'T FIGHT IT FEEL IT** *Creation CRE 110* [1]	**41**	2
8 Feb 92	**DIXIE-NARCO EP** *Creation CRE 117*	**11**	6
12 Mar 94	**ROCKS / FUNKY JAM** *Creation CRESCD 129* [5]	**7**	5
18 Jun 94	**JAILBIRD** *Creation CRESCD 145*	**29**	2
10 Dec 94	**(I'M GONNA) CRY MYSELF BLIND** *Creation CRESCD 183*	**49**	2
15 Jun 96	**THE BIG MAN AND THE SCREAM TEAM MEET THE BARMY ARMY UPTOWN** *Creation CRESCD 194* [2]	**17**	2

[1] Primal Scream featuring Denise Johnson [2] Primal Scream, Irvine Welsh and On-U Sound

*Tracks on Dixie-Narco EP: Movin' On Up / Stone My Soul / Carry Me Home / Screamadelica.
See also Gary Clail On-U Sound System.*

PRIME MOVERS *US, male vocal / instrumental group*　**1 wk**

8 Feb 86	**ON THE TRAIL** *Island IS 263*	**74**	1

PRIMITIVE RADIO GODS
US, male vocalist – Chris O'Connor　　　　**1 wk**

30 Mar 96	**STANDING OUTSIDE A BROKEN PHONE BOOTH WITH MONEY IN MY HAND** *Columbia 6627692*	**74**	1

PRIMITIVES
UK, male / female vocal / instrumental group　　**27 wks**

27 Feb 88	● **CRASH** *Lazy PB 41761*	**5**	10
30 Apr 88	**OUT OF REACH** *Lazy PB 42011*	**25**	4

3 Sep 88	WAY BEHIND ME Lazy PB 42209	36	4
29 Jul 89	SICK OF IT Lazy PB 42947	24	4
30 Sep 89	SECRETS Lazy PB 43173	49	3
3 Aug 91	YOU ARE THE WAY RCA PB 44481	58	2

♀ PRINCE US, male vocalist — **288 wks**

19 Jan 80	I WANNA BE YOUR LOVER Warner Bros. K 17537	41	3
29 Jan 83	1999 Warner Bros. W 9896	25	7
30 Apr 83	LITTLE RED CORVETTE Warner Bros. W 9688	54	4
26 Nov 83	LITTLE RED CORVETTE (re-issue) Warner Bros. W 9436	66	2
30 Jun 84	● WHEN DOVES CRY Warner Bros. W 9286	4	15
22 Sep 84	● PURPLE RAIN Warner Bros. W 9174 [1]	8	9
8 Dec 84	I WOULD DIE 4 U Warner Bros. W 9121 [1]	58	6
19 Jan 85	● 1999 / LITTLE RED CORVETTE (re-issue) Warner Bros. W 1999	2	10
23 Feb 85	● LET'S GO CRAZY / TAKE ME WITH YOU Warner Bros. W 2000 [1]	7	9
25 May 85	PAISLEY PARK WEA W 9052 [1]	18	10
27 Jul 85	RASPBERRY BERET WEA W 8929 [1]	25	8
26 Oct 85	POP LIFE Paisley Park W 8858 [1]	60	2
8 Mar 86	● KISS Paisley Park W 8751 [1]	6	9
14 Jun 86	MOUNTAINS Paisley Park W 8711 [1]	45	4
16 Aug 86	GIRLS AND BOYS Paisley Park W 8586 [1]	11	8
1 Nov 86	ANOTHERLOVERHOLENYOHEAD Paisley Park W 8521 [1]	36	3
14 Mar 87	● SIGN 'O' THE TIMES Paisley Park W 8399	10	9
20 Jun 87	IF I WAS YOUR GIRLFRIEND Paisley Park W 8334	20	6
15 Aug 87	U GOT THE LOOK Paisley Park W 8289	11	9
28 Nov 87	I COULD NEVER TAKE THE PLACE OF YOUR MAN Paisley Park W 8288	29	6
7 May 88	● ALPHABET STREET Paisley Park W 7900	9	6
23 Jul 88	GLAM SLAM Paisley Park W 7806	29	4
5 Nov 88	I WISH U HEAVEN Paisley Park W 7745	24	5
24 Jun 89	● BATDANCE Warner Bros. W 2924	2	10
9 Sep 89	PARTYMAN Warner Bros. W 2814	14	6
18 Nov 89	THE ARMS OF ORION Warner Bros. W 2757 [2]	27	5
4 Aug 90	● THIEVES IN THE TEMPLE Paisley Park W 9751	7	6
10 Nov 90	NEW POWER GENERATION Paisley Park W 9525	26	4
31 Aug 91	● GETT OFF Paisley Park W 0056 [3]	4	8
21 Sep 91	CREAM Paisley Park W 0061 [3]	15	7
7 Dec 91	DIAMONDS AND PEARLS Paisley Park W 0075 [3]	25	6
28 Mar 92	MONEY DON'T MATTER 2 NIGHT Paisley Park W 0091 [3]	19	5
27 Jun 92	THUNDER Paisley Park W 01132P [3]	28	3
18 Jul 92	● SEXY MF / STROLLIN' Paisley Park W 0123 [3]	4	7
10 Oct 92	● MY NAME IS PRINCE Paisley Park W 0132 [3]	7	5
14 Nov 92	MY NAME IS PRINCE (re-mix) Paisley Park W 0142T [3]	51	1
5 Dec 92	7 Paisley Park W 0147 [3]	27	6
13 Mar 93	THE MORNING PAPERS Paisley Park W 0162CD [3]	52	3
16 Oct 93	PEACH Paisley Park W 0210CD	14	5
11 Dec 93	● CONTROVERSY Paisley Park W 0215CD1	5	5
9 Apr 94	★ THE MOST BEAUTIFUL GIRL IN THE WORLD NPG NPG 60155 [4]	1	12
4 Jun 94	THE BEAUTIFUL EXPERIENCE (re-mix) NPG NPG 60212	18	3
10 Sep 94	LETITGO Warner Bros. W 0260CD	30	4
18 Mar 95	PURPLE MEDLEY Warner Bros. W 0289CD	33	2
23 Sep 95	EYE HATE U Warner Bros. W 0315CD [4]	20	3
9 Dec 95	● GOLD Warner Bros. W 0325CD [4]	10	9
3 Aug 96	DINNER WITH DELORES Warner Bros. 9362437422	36	2
14 Dec 96	BETCHA BY GOLLY WOW NPG CDEM 463	11†	3

[1] Prince and the Revolution [2] Prince with Sheena Easton [3] Prince and the New Power Generation [4] ♀

Although uncredited, Sheena Easton also vocalises on U Got The Look. The Beautiful Experience *was a seven track CD featuring* The Most Beautiful Girl In The World *and six further mixes of the track.*

PRINCE BUSTER Jamaica, male vocalist — **13 wks**

| 23 Feb 67 | AL CAPONE Blue Beat BB 324 | 18 | 13 |

PRINCE CHARLES and the CITY BEAT BAND
US, male vocalist with male vocal / instrumental group — **2 wks**

| 22 Feb 86 | WE CAN MAKE IT HAPPEN PRT 7P 348 | 56 | 2 |

PRINCE NASEEM – See KALEEF

PRINCESS UK, female vocalist — **44 wks**

3 Aug 85	● SAY I'M YOU'RE NO. 1 Supreme SUPE 101	7	12
9 Nov 85	AFTER THE LOVE HAS GONE Supreme SUPE 103	28	13
19 Apr 86	I'LL KEEP ON LOVING YOU Supreme SUPE 105	16	8
5 Jul 86	TELL ME TOMORROW Supreme SUPE 106	34	5
25 Oct 86	IN THE HEAT OF A PASSIONATE MOMENT Supreme SUPE 109	74	1
13 Jun 87	RED HOT Polydor POSP 868	58	5

PRINCESS IVORI US, female rapper — **2 wks**

| 17 Mar 90 | WANTED Supreme SUPE 163 | 69 | 2 |

Patrick PRINZ – See ARTEMESIA; ETHICS; MOVIN' MELODIES; SUBLIMINAL CUTS

Maddy PRIOR – See STATUS QUO

PRIVATE LIVES UK, male vocal / instrumental duo — **4 wks**

| 11 Feb 84 | LIVING IN A WORLD (TURNED UPSIDE DOWN) EMI PRIV 2 | 53 | 4 |

PRIZNA featuring DEMOLITION MAN
UK, male vocal / instrumental group — **2 wks**

| 29 Apr 95 | FIRE Labello Blanco NLBCDX 18 | 33 | 2 |

PJ PROBY US, male vocalist — **90 wks**

28 May 64	● HOLD ME Decca F 11904	3	15
3 Sep 64	● TOGETHER Decca F 11967	8	11
10 Dec 64	● SOMEWHERE Liberty LIB 10182	6	12
25 Feb 65	I APOLOGISE Liberty LIB 10188	11	8
8 Jul 65	LET THE WATER RUN DOWN Liberty LIB 10206	19	8
30 Sep 65	THAT MEANS A LOT Liberty LIB 10215	30	6
25 Nov 65	● MARIA Liberty LIB 10218	8	9
10 Feb 66	YOU'VE COME BACK Liberty LIB 10223	25	7
16 Jun 66	TO MAKE A BIG MAN CRY Liberty LIB 10236	34	3
27 Oct 66	I CAN'T MAKE IT ALONE Liberty LIB 10250	37	5
6 Mar 68	IT'S YOUR DAY TODAY Liberty LBF 15046	32	5
28 Dec 96	YESTERDAY HAS GONE EMI Premier CDPRESX 13 [1]	58†	1

[1] PJ Proby and Marc Almond

PROCLAIMERS UK, male vocal / instrumental duo — **50 wks**

14 Nov 87	● LETTER FROM AMERICA Chrysalis CHS 3178	3	10
5 Mar 88	MAKE MY HEART FLY Chrysalis CLAIM 1	63	3
27 Aug 88	I'M GONNA BE Chrysalis CLAIM 2	11	11
12 Nov 88	SUNSHINE ON LEITH Chrysalis CLAIM 3	41	5
11 Feb 89	I'M ON MY WAY Chrysalis CLAIM 4	43	4
24 Nov 90	KING OF THE ROAD (EP) Chrysalis CLAIM 5	9	8
19 Feb 94	LET'S GET MARRIED Chrysalis CDCLAIMS 6	21	4
16 Apr 94	WHAT MAKES YOU CRY Chrysalis CDCLAIMS 7	38	3
22 Oct 94	THESE ARMS OF MINE Chrysalis CDCLAIM 8	51	2

Tracks on King Of The Road (EP): King Of The Road / Long Black Veil / Lulu Selling Tea / Not Ever.

PROCOL HARUM UK, male vocal / instrumental group   56 wks

25 May 67	★ A WHITER SHADE OF PALE Deram DM 126	1	15
4 Oct 67	● HOMBURG Regal Zonophone RZ 3003	6	10
24 Apr 68	QUITE RIGHTLY SO Regal Zonophone RZ 3007	50	1
18 Jun 69	SALTY DOG Regal Zonophone RZ 3019	44	1
2 Jul 69	SALTY DOG (re-entry) Regal Zonophone RZ 3019	44	1
16 Jul 69	SALTY DOG (2nd re-entry) Regal Zonophone RZ 3019	44	1
22 Apr 72	A WHITER SHADE OF PALE (re-issue) Fly Magnifly ECHO 101	13	13
5 Aug 72	CONQUISTADOR Chrysalis CHS 2003	22	7
23 Aug 75	PANDORA'S BOX Chrysalis CHS 2073	16	7

Michael PROCTOR – See URBAN BLUES PROJECT present Michael PROCTOR

PRODIGY UK, male vocal / instrumental group   109 wks

24 Aug 91	● CHARLY XL XLS 21	3	10
4 Jan 92	● EVERYBODY IN THE PLACE (EP) XL XLS 26	2	9
26 Sep 92	FIRE / JERICHO XL XLS 30	11	4
21 Nov 92	● OUT OF SPACE / RUFF IN THE JUNGLE BIZNESS XL XLS 35	5	12
17 Apr 93	WIND IT UP (REWOUND) XL XLS 39CD	11	7
16 Oct 93	● ONE LOVE XL XLS 47CD	8	6
28 May 94	● NO GOOD (START THE DANCE) XL XLS 51CD	4	12
24 Sep 94	VOODOO PEOPLE XL XLS 54CD	13	5
18 Mar 95	POISON XL XLS 58CD	15	6
30 Mar 96	★ FIRESTARTER XL XLS 70CD	1	19
20 Apr 96	OUT OF SPACE / RUFF IN THE JUNGLE BIZNESS (re-entry) XL XLS 35CD	52	2
20 Apr 96	NO GOOD (START THE DANCE) (re-entry) XL XLS 51CD	57	2
20 Apr 96	POISON (re-entry) XL XLS 58CD	62	1
20 Apr 96	FIRE / JERICHO (re-entry) XL XLS 30CD	63	1
20 Apr 96	CHARLY (re-entry) XL XLS 21CD	66	1
20 Apr 96	WIND IT UP (REWOUND) (re-entry) XL XLS 39CD	71	1
20 Apr 96	VOODOO PEOPLE (re-entry) XL XLS 54CD	75	1
27 Apr 96	EVERYBODY IN THE PLACE (EP) (re-entry) XL XLS 26CD1	69	1
23 Nov 96	★ BREATHE XL XLS 80CD	1†	6
14 Dec 96	FIRESTARTER (re-entry) XL XLS 70CD	70†	3

Tracks on Everybody In The Place (EP): Everybody In The Place / Crazy Man / G-Force / Rip Up The Sound System. Ruff In The Jungle Bizness only listed 27 Nov and 5 Dec 92.

PROFESSIONALS UK, male vocal / instrumental group   4 wks

11 Oct 80	1-2-3 Virgin VS 376	43	4

PROFESSOR – See DJ PROFESSOR

PROFESSOR T – See SHUT UP AND DANCE

PROGRAM 2 BELTRAM – See BELTRAM

PROJECT 1 UK, male producer – Mark Williams   3 wks

16 May 92	ROUGHNECK EP Rising High RSN 22	49	2
29 Aug 92	DON CARGON COMIN' Rising High RSN 35	64	1

Tracks on Roughneck EP: Come My Selector / Can't Take The Heartbreak / Live Vibe 4 (Summer Vibes).

PROJECT featuring GERIDEAU
US, male vocal / instrumental duo   1 wk

27 Aug 94	BRING IT BACK 2 LUV Fruittree FTREE 10CD	65	1

PRONG US, male vocal / instrumental group   1 wk

25 Apr 92	WHOSE FIST IS THIS ANYWAY EP Epic 6580026	58	1

Tracks on Whose Fist Is This Anyway EP: Prove You Wrong / Hell If I Could / (Get A) Grip (On Yourself) / Prove You Wrong (re-mix) .

PROPAGANDA
Germany, male / female vocal / instrumental group   35 wks

17 Mar 84	DR MABUSE ZTT ZTAS 2	27	9
4 May 85	DUEL ZTT ZTAS 8	21	12
10 Aug 85	P MACHINERY ZTT ZTAS 12	50	5
28 Apr 90	HEAVEN GIVE ME WORDS Virgin VS 1245	36	5
8 Sep 90	ONLY ONE WORD Virgin VS 1271	71	4

PROPELLERHEADS
UK, male instrumental / production duo   1 wk

7 Dec 96	TAKE CALIFORNIA Wall Of Sound WALLD 024	69	1

Brian PROTHEROE UK, male vocalist   6 wks

7 Sep 74	PINBALL Chrysalis CHS 2043	22	6

Dorothy PROVINE US, female vocalist   15 wks

7 Dec 61	DON'T BRING LULU Warner Bros. WB 53	17	12
28 Jun 62	CRAZY WORDS CRAZY TUNE Warner Bros. WB 70	45	3

PSEUDO ECHO
Australia, male vocal / instrumental group   12 wks

18 Jul 87	● FUNKY TOWN RCA PB 49705	8	12

PSYCHEDELIC FURS
UK, male vocal / instrumental group   31 wks

2 May 81	DUMB WAITERS CBS 1166	59	2
27 Jun 81	PRETTY IN PINK CBS A 1327	43	3
31 Jul 82	LOVE MY WAY CBS A 2549	42	6
31 Mar 84	HEAVEN CBS A 4300	29	6
16 Jun 84	GHOST IN YOU CBS A 4470	68	2
23 Aug 86	PRETTY IN PINK CBS A 7242	18	9
9 Jul 88	ALL THAT MONEY WANTS CBS FURS 4	75	1

A 7242 was a re-recording of A 1327.

PSYCHIC TV UK, male / female vocal / instrumental group   4 wks

26 Apr 86	GODSTAR Temple TOPY 009 [1]	67	2
20 Sep 86	GOOD VIBRATIONS / ROMAN P. Temple TOPY 23	65	2

[1] Psychic TV and the Angels of Light

PSYCHOTROPIC – See FREEFALL featuring PSYCHOTROPIC; SALT-N-PEPA

PUBLIC ANNOUNCEMENT – See R KELLY and PUBLIC ANNOUNCEMENT

PUBLIC ENEMY US, male rap group   48 wks

21 Nov 87	REBEL WITHOUT A PAUSE Def Jam 651245 7	37	5
2 Jan 88	REBEL WITHOUT A PAUSE (re-entry) Def Jam 651245 7	71	2
9 Jan 88	BRING THE NOISE Def Jam 651335 7	32	5
2 Jul 88	DON'T BELIEVE THE HYPE Def Jam 652833 7	18	5
15 Oct 88	NIGHT OF THE LIVING BASEHEADS Def Jam 6530460	63	2
24 Jun 89	FIGHT THE POWER Motown ZB 42877	29	5
20 Jan 90	WELCOME TO THE TERRORDOME Def Jam 655476 0	18	3
7 Apr 90	911 IS A JOKE Def Jam 655830 7	41	3
23 Jun 90	BROTHERS GONNA WORK IT OUT Def Jam 656018 1	46	2
3 Nov 90	CAN'T DO NUTTIN' FOR YA MAN Def Jam 656385 7	53	2
12 Oct 91	CAN'T TRUSS IT Def Jam 6575307	22	4
25 Jan 92	SHUT 'EM DOWN Def Jam 6577617	21	3
11 Apr 92	NIGHTTRAIN Def Jam 6578647	55	2
13 Aug 94	GIVE IT UP Def Jam DEFCD 1	18	3
29 Jul 95	SO WATCHA GONNA DO NOW Def Jam DEFCD 5	50	1

PUBLIC IMAGE LTD.
UK, male vocal / instrumental group   **61 wks**

21 Oct 78	●	**PUBLIC IMAGE** *Virgin VS 228*..................	**9** 8
7 Jul 79		**DEATH DISCO** *Virgin VS 274*	**20** 7
20 Oct 79		**MEMORIES** *Virgin VS 299*	**60** 2
4 Apr 81		**FLOWERS OF ROMANCE** *Virgin VS 397*	**24** 7
17 Sep 83	●	**THIS IS NOT A LOVE SONG** *Virgin VS 529*	**5** 10
19 May 84		**BAD LIFE** *Virgin VS 675*	**71** 2
1 Feb 86		**RISE** *Virgin VS 841*	**11** 8
3 May 86		**HOME** *Virgin VS 855*	**75** 1
22 Aug 87		**SEATTLE** *Virgin VS 988*	**47** 4
6 May 89		**DISAPPOINTED** *Virgin VS 1181*	**38** 5
20 Oct 90		**DON'T ASK ME** *Virgin VS 1231*	**22** 5
22 Feb 92		**CRUEL** *Virgin VS 1390*	**49** 2

Group often known as P.I.L.

Gary PUCKETT – *See UNION GAP featuring Gary PUCKETT*

Tito PUENTE Jr. and the LATIN RHYTHM featuring Tito PUENTE, INDIA and Cali ALEMAN *US, male / female vocal / instrumental group*   **2 wks**

16 Mar 96	**OYE COMO VA** *Media MCSTD 40013*	**36** 2

Tito PUENTE – *See Tito PUENTE JR and the LATIN RHYTHM featuring Tito PUENTE, INDIA and Cali ALEMAN*

PULP *UK, male / female vocal / instrumental group*   **53 wks**

27 Nov 93		**LIP GLOSS** *Island CID 567*	**50** 2
2 Apr 94		**DO YOU REMEMBER THE FIRST TIME** *Island CID 574*	**33** 4
4 Jun 94		**THE SISTERS EP** *Island CID 595*	**19** 4
3 Jun 95	●	**COMMON PEOPLE** *Island CID 613*	**2** 13
7 Oct 95	●	**MIS-SHAPES / SORTED FOR E'S AND WIZZ** *Island CID 620*	**2** 8
9 Dec 95	●	**DISCO 2000** *Island CID 623*	**7** 11
30 Dec 95		**MIS-SHAPES / SORTED FOR E'S AND WIZZ (re-entry)** *Island CID 620*	**62** 3
6 Apr 96	●	**SOMETHING CHANGED** *Island CID 632*	**10** 5
8 Jun 96		**SOMETHING CHANGED (re-entry)** *Island CID 632*	**62** 1
22 Jun 96		**SOMETHING CHANGED (2nd re-entry)** *Island CID 632*..	**61** 1
7 Sep 96		**DO YOU REMEMBER THE FIRST TIME (re-entry)** *Island CID 574*	**73** 1

Tracks on The Sisters EP: Babies / Your Sister's Clothes / Seconds / His 'N' Hers.

PULSE featuring Antoinette ROBERSON
US, male / female vocal / instrumental duo   **3 wks**

25 May 96	**THE LOVER THAT YOU ARE** *ffrr FCD 278*	**22** 3

Pulse is David Morales; see also David Morales.

James and Bobby PURIFY *US, male vocal duo*   **16 wks**

24 Apr 76	**I'M YOUR PUPPET** *Mercury 6167 324*	**12** 10
7 Aug 76	**MORNING GLORY** *Mercury 6167 380*	**27** 6

PURPLE HEARTS *UK, male vocal / instrumental group*   **5 wks**

22 Sep 79	**MILLIONS LIKE US** *Fiction FICS 003*	**57** 3
8 Mar 80	**JIMMY** *Fiction FICS 9*	**60** 2

PURPLE KINGS *UK, male vocal / instrumental duo*   **3 wks**

15 Oct 94	**THAT'S THE WAY YOU DO IT** *Positiva CDTIV 21*	**26** 3

PUSSYCAT
Holland, male / female vocal / instrumental group   **30 wks**

28 Aug 76	★	**MISSISSIPPI** *Sonet SON 2077*	**1** 22
25 Dec 76		**SMILE** *Sonet SON 2096*	**24** 8

PYRAMIDS *Jamaica, male vocal / instrumental group*   **4 wks**

22 Nov 67	**TRAIN TOUR TO RAINBOW CITY** *President PT 161*	**35** 4

PYTHON LEE JACKSON
Australia, male vocal / instrumental group   **12 wks**

30 Sep 72	●	**IN A BROKEN DREAM** *Youngblood YB 1002*	**3** 12

Uncredited lead vocals by Rod Stewart.

Q *UK, male instrumental / production duo*   **9 wks**

5 Jun 93	**GET HERE** *Arista 74321145972* [1]	**37** 4
12 Mar 94	**(EVERYTHING I DO) I DO IT FOR YOU** *Bell 74321193062* [2]	**47** 2

[1] Q featuring Tracy Ackerman [2] Q featuring Tony Jackson

Q-BASS *UK, male production / instrumental group*   **1 wk**

8 Feb 92	**HARDCORE WILL NEVER DIE** *Suburban Base SUBBASE 007*	**64** 1

Q BASS – *See VARIOUS ARTISTS (EPs & LPs) – Subplates Volume 1 EP*

Q-CLUB *Italy, male / female vocal / instrumental group*   **3 wks**

6 Jan 96	**TELL IT TO MY HEART** *Manifesto FESCD 5*	**28** 3

Q-TEE *UK, female rapper*   **7 wks**

21 Apr 90	**AFRIKA** *SBK SBK 7008* [1]	**42** 5
10 Feb 96	**GIMME THAT BODY** *Heavenly HVN 48CD*	**40** 2

[1] History featuring Q-Tee

Q-TEX *UK, male / female vocal / instrumental group*   **6 wks**

9 Apr 94	**THE POWER OF LOVE** *Stoatin' STOAT 002CD*	**65** 1
26 Nov 94	**BELIEVE** *23rd Precinct THIRD 2CD*	**41** 2
15 Jun 96	**LET THE LOVE** *23rd Precinct THIRD 4CD*	**30** 2
30 Nov 96	**DO YOU WANT ME** *23rd Precinct THIRD 5CD*	**48** 1

Q UNIQUE – *See C&C MUSIC FACTORY/CLIVILLES & COLE*

QFX *UK, male producer – Kirk Turnbull*   **10 wks**

6 May 95	**FREEDOM (EP)** *Epidemic EPICD 004*	**41** 3

Otis Reading

Otis Reading's debut came with a cover of Smokey Robinson-penned 'My Girl'. It had previously been an American number one by the Temptations.

Demis Roussos

Demis Roussos first charted 1968 with the band Aphrodite's Child, the band also included Vangelis Papathanassiou, composer of the Bladerunner soundrack.

Prodigy

The Prodigy's 'Firestarter' was their first single to feature a full vocal, this was delivered by Keith Flint (second from left).

Shabba Ranks

Shabba Ranks won the Grammy award for Best Reggae Album in 1991 and repeated the feat the following year.

3 Feb 96	**EVERYTIME YOU TOUCH ME** *Epidemic EPICD 006* **22** 4	
3 Aug 96	**YOU GOT THE POWER** *Epidemic EPICD 007* **33** 3	

Tracks on Freedom (EP): Freedom / Metropolis / Sianora Baby / The Machine.

QUADROPHONIA
Belgium, male instrumental / production group   **15 wks**

13 Apr 91	**QUADROPHONIA** *ARS 6567687* **14** 9	
6 Jul 91	**THE WAVE OF THE FUTURE** *ARS 6569937* **40** 3	
21 Dec 91	**FIND THE TIME (PART ONE)** *ARS 6576260*.........**41** 3	

QUADS *UK, male vocal / instrumental group*   **2 wks**

22 Sep 79	**THERE MUST BE THOUSANDS** *Big Bear BB 23* **66** 2	

QUANTUM JUMP *UK, male vocal / instrumental group*   **10 wks**

2 Jun 79	● **THE LONE RANGER** *Electric WOT 33*....................**5** 10	

QUARTERFLASH
US, male / female vocal / instrumental group   **5 wks**

27 Feb 82	**HARDEN MY HEART** *Geffen GEF A 1838* **49** 5	

QUARTZ *UK, male instrumental group*   **19 wks**

17 Mar 90	**WE'RE COMIN' AT YA** *Mercury ITMR 2* [1] **65** 2	
2 Feb 91	● **IT'S TOO LATE** *Mercury ITM 3* [2] **8** 14	
15 Jun 91	**NAKED LOVE (JUST SAY YOU WANT ME)** *Mercury ITM 4* [3] **39** 3	

[1] Quartz featuring Stepz [2] Quartz introducing Dina Carroll [3] Quartz and Dina Carroll

Jakie QUARTZ *France, female vocalist*   **3 wks**

11 Mar 89	**A LA VIE, A L'AMOUR** *PWL PWL 30* **55** 3	

QUARTZ LOCK – *See Lonnie GORDON*

Suzi QUATRO
US, female vocalist / instrumentalist – bass guitar   **122 wks**

19 May 73	★ **CAN THE CAN** *RAK 150* **1** 14	
28 Jul 73	**48 CRASH** *RAK 158* **3** 9	
27 Oct 73	**DAYTONA DEMON** *RAK 161* **14** 13	
9 Feb 74	★ **DEVIL GATE DRIVE** *RAK 167* **1** 11	
29 Jun 74	**TOO BIG** *RAK 175* **14** 6	
9 Nov 74	● **THE WILD ONE** *RAK 185* **7** 10	
8 Feb 75	**YOUR MAMA WON'T LIKE ME** *RAK 191* **31** 5	
5 Mar 77	**TEAR ME APART** *RAK 248* **27** 6	
18 Mar 78	● **IF YOU CAN'T GIVE ME LOVE** *RAK 271*.........**4** 13	
22 Jul 78	**THE RACE IS ON** *RAK 278* **43** 5	
11 Nov 78	**STUMBLIN' IN** *RAK 285* [1] **41** 8	
20 Oct 79	**SHE'S IN LOVE WITH YOU** *RAK 299* **11** 9	
19 Jan 80	**MAMA'S BOY** *RAK 303* **34** 5	
5 Apr 80	**I'VE NEVER BEEN IN LOVE** *RAK 307* **56** 3	
25 Oct 80	**ROCK HARD** *Dreamland DLSP 6* **68** 2	
13 Nov 82	**HEART OF STONE** *Polydor POSP 477* **60** 3	

[1] Suzi Quatro and Chris Norman

QUEEN *UK, male vocal / instrumental group*   **389 wks**

9 Mar 74	● **SEVEN SEAS OF RHYE** *EMI 2121* **10** 10	
26 Oct 74	● **KILLER QUEEN** *EMI 2229* **2** 12	
25 Jan 75	**NOW I'M HERE** *EMI 2256* **11** 7	

8 Nov 75	★ **BOHEMIAN RHAPSODY** *EMI 2375* **1** 17	
3 Jul 76	● **YOU'RE MY BEST FRIEND** *EMI 2494* **7** 8	
27 Nov 76	● **SOMEBODY TO LOVE** *EMI 2565* **2** 9	
19 Mar 77	**TIE YOUR MOTHER DOWN** *EMI 2593* **31** 4	
4 Jun 77	**QUEEN'S FIRST EP** *EMI 2623* **17** 10	
22 Oct 77	● **WE ARE THE CHAMPIONS** *EMI 2708* **2** 11	
25 Feb 78	**SPREAD YOUR WINGS** *EMI 2757* **34** 4	
28 Oct 78	**BICYCLE RACE / FAT BOTTOMED GIRLS** *EMI 2870*.........**11** 12	
10 Feb 79	● **DON'T STOP ME NOW** *EMI 2910* **9** 12	
14 Jul 79	**LOVE OF MY LIFE** *EMI 2959* **63** 2	
20 Oct 79	● **CRAZY LITTLE THING CALLED LOVE** *EMI 5001* **2** 14	
2 Feb 80	**SAVE ME** *EMI 5022* **11** 6	
14 Jun 80	**PLAY THE GAME** *EMI 5076* **14** 8	
6 Sep 80	● **ANOTHER ONE BITES THE DUST** *EMI 5102* **7** 9	
6 Dec 80	● **FLASH** *EMI 5126* **10** 13	
14 Nov 81	★ **UNDER PRESSURE** *EMI 5250* [1] **1** 11	
1 May 82	**BODY LANGUAGE** *EMI 5293* **25** 6	
12 Jun 82	**LAS PALABRAS DE AMOR** *EMI 5316* **17** 8	
21 Aug 82	**BACKCHAT** *EMI 5325* **40** 4	
4 Feb 84	● **RADIO GAGA** *EMI QUEEN 1* **2** 9	
14 Apr 84	● **I WANT TO BREAK FREE** *EMI QUEEN 2* **3** 15	
28 Jul 84	● **IT'S A HARD LIFE** *EMI QUEEN 3* **6** 9	
22 Sep 84	**HAMMER TO FALL** *EMI QUEEN 4* **13** 7	
8 Dec 84	**THANK GOD IT'S CHRISTMAS** *EMI QUEEN 5* **21** 6	
16 Nov 85	● **ONE VISION** *EMI QUEEN 6* **7** 10	
29 Mar 86	● **A KIND OF MAGIC** *EMI QUEEN 7* **3** 11	
21 Jun 86	**FRIENDS WILL BE FRIENDS** *EMI QUEEN 8*.........**14** 8	
27 Sep 86	**WHO WANTS TO LIVE FOREVER** *EMI QUEEN 9* **24** 5	
13 May 89	● **I WANT IT ALL** *Parlophone QUEEN 10* **3** 7	
1 Jul 89	● **BREAKTHRU'** *Parlophone QUEEN 11* **7** 7	
19 Aug 89	**THE INVISIBLE MAN** *Parlophone QUEEN 12* **12** 6	
21 Oct 89	**SCANDAL** *Parlophone QUEEN 14* **25** 4	
9 Dec 89	**THE MIRACLE** *Parlophone QUEEN 15* **21** 5	
26 Jan 91	★ **INNUENDO** *Parlophone QUEEN 16* **1** 6	
16 Mar 91	**I'M GOING SLIGHTLY MAD** *Parlophone QUEEN 17* **22** 5	
25 May 91	**HEADLONG** *Parlophone QUEEN 18* **14** 4	
26 Oct 91	**THE SHOW MUST GO ON** *Parlophone QUEEN 19* **16** 5	
7 Dec 91	**THE SHOW MUST GO ON (re-entry)** *Parlophone QUEEN 19* **27** 5	
21 Dec 91	★ **BOHEMIAN RHAPSODY (re-issue) / THESE ARE THE DAYS OF OUR LIVES** *Parlophone QUEEN 20* **1** 14	
1 May 93	★ **FIVE LIVE EP** *Parlophone CDRS 6340* [2] **1** 11	
24 Jul 93	**FIVE LIVE EP (re-entry)** *Parlophone CDRS 6340* **74** 1	
4 Nov 95	● **HEAVEN FOR EVERYONE** *Parlophone CDQUEEN 21* **2** 12	
23 Dec 95	**A WINTER'S TALE** *Parlophone CDQUEEN 22* **6** 6	
9 Mar 96	**TOO MUCH LOVE WILL KILL YOU** *Parlophone CDQUEEN 23* **15** 6	
29 Jun 96	● **LET ME LIVE** *Parlophone CDQUEEN 24* **9** 4	
30 Nov 96	**YOU DON'T FOOL ME** *Parlophone CDQUEEN 25* **17** 4	

[1] Queen and David Bowie [2] George Michael and Queen with Lisa Stansfield

Tracks on Queen's First EP: Good Old Fashioned Lover Boy / Death On Two Legs (Dedicated To...) / Tenement Funster / White Queen (As it Began). Tracks on Five Live EP: Somebody To Love / These Are The Days Of Our Lives / Calling You / Papa Was A Rolling Stone – Killer (medley). Queen only appear on the first two tracks. The first credits George Michael and Queen and the second George Michael with Lisa Stansfield.

QUEEN LATIFAH *US, female rapper*   **15 wks**

24 Mar 90	**MAMA GAVE BIRTH TO THE SOUL CHILDREN** *Gee Street GEE 26* [1] **14** 7	
26 May 90	**FIND A WAY** *Ahead Of Our Time CCUT 8* [2] **52** 2	
31 Aug 91	**FLY GIRL** *Gee Street GEE 34* **67** 1	
26 Jun 93	**WHAT'CHA GONNA DO** *Epic 6593072* [3] **21** 4	
26 Mar 94	**U.N.I.T.Y.** *Motown TMGCD 1422* **74** 1	

[1] Queen Latifah + De La Soul [2] Coldcut featuring Queen Latifah [3] Shabba Ranks featuring Queen Latifah

QUEENSRYCHE *US, male vocal / instrumental group*   **21 wks**

13 May 89	**EYES OF A STRANGER** *EMI USA MT 65* **59** 1	
10 Nov 90	**EMPIRE** *EMI USA MT 90* **61** 1	

20 Apr 91	**SILENT LUCIDITY** *EMI USA MT 94* **34**	5
6 Jul 91	**BEST I CAN** *EMI USA MT 97* **36**	3
7 Sep 91	**JET CITY WOMAN** *EMI USA MT 98* **39**	2
8 Aug 92	**SILENT LUCIDITY (re-issue)** *EMI USA MT 104* ...**18**	4
28 Jan 95	**I AM I** *EMI CDMT 109* **40**	2
25 Mar 95	**BRIDGE** *EMI CDMT 111* **40**	3

QUENCH *Australia, male instrumental / production duo* **1 wk**

| 17 Feb 96 | **DREAMS** *Infectious INFECT 3CD* ....**75** | 1 |

QUENTIN and ASH *UK, female vocal duo* **3 wks**

| 6 Jul 96 | **TELL HIM** *East West EW 049CD* ....**25** | 3 |

? (QUESTION MARK) and the MYSTERIANS
US, male vocal / instrumental group **4 wks**

| 17 Nov 66 | **96 TEARS** *Cameo Parkway C428* ....**37** | 4 |

QUESTIONS *UK, male vocal / instrumental group* **8 wks**

23 Apr 83	**PRICE YOU PAY** *Respond KOB 702* **56**	3
17 Sep 83	**TEAR SOUP** *Respond KOB 705* **66**	1
10 Mar 84	**TUESDAY SUNSHINE** *Respond KOB 707* **46**	4

QUICK *UK, male vocal / instrumental group* **7 wks**

| 15 May 82 | **RHYTHM OF THE JUNGLE** *Epic EPC A 2013* ....**41** | 7 |

Tommy QUICKLY *UK, male vocalist* **8 wks**

| 22 Oct 64 | **WILD SIDE OF LIFE** *Pye 7N 15708* ....**33** | 8 |

Quiet FIVE *UK, male vocal / instrumental group* **3 wks**

| 13 May 65 | **WHEN THE MORNING SUN DRIES THE DEW** *Parlophone R 5273* ....**45** | 1 |
| 21 Apr 66 | **HOMEWARD BOUND** *Parlophone R 5421* ....**44** | 2 |

QUIET RIOT *US, male vocal / instrumental group* **5 wks**

| 3 Dec 83 | **METAL HEALTH / CUM ON FEEL THE NOIZE** *Epic A 3968* ..**45** | 5 |

Cum on Feel the Noize only credited from 10 Dec 83.

Eimear QUINN *Ireland, female vocalist* **2 wks**

| 15 Jun 96 | **THE VOICE** *Polydor 5768842* ....**40** | 2 |

Paul QUINN – *See Edwyn COLLINS*

QUIREBOYS *UK, male vocal / instrumental group* **27 wks**

4 Nov 89	**7 O'CLOCK** *Parlophone R 6230* **36**	4
6 Jan 90	**HEY YOU** *Parlophone R 6241* **14**	7
7 Apr 90	**I DON'T LOVE YOU ANYMORE** *Parlophone R 6248* **24**	6
8 Sep 90	**THERE SHE GOES AGAIN / MISLED** *Parlophone R 6267* ..**37**	4
10 Oct 92	**TRAMPS AND THIEVES** *Parlophone RS 6323* **41**	3
20 Feb 93	**BROTHER LOUIE** *Parlophone CDR 6335* **31**	3

QUIVER – *See SUTHERLAND BROTHERS and QUIVER*

QUIVVER *UK, male instrumental / production duo* **3 wks**

| 5 Mar 94 | **SAXY LADY** *A & M 5805152* ....**56** | 2 |
| 18 Nov 95 | **BELIEVE IN ME** *Perfecto PERF 111CD* ....**56** | 1 |

R

Eddie RABBITT *US, male vocalist* **14 wks**

| 27 Jan 79 | **EVERY WHICH WAY BUT LOOSE** *Elektra K 12331* ....**41** | 9 |
| 28 Feb 81 | **I LOVE A RAINY NIGHT** *Elektra K 12498* ....**53** | 5 |

Steve RACE *UK, male instrumentalist – piano* **9 wks**

| 28 Feb 63 | **PIED PIPER (THE BEEJE)** *Parlophone R 4981* ....**29** | 9 |

RACEY *UK, male vocal / instrumental group* **44 wks**

25 Nov 78	● **LAY YOUR LOVE ON ME** *RAK 284* **3**	14
31 Mar 79	● **SOME GIRLS** *RAK 291* **2**	11
18 Aug 79	**BOY OH BOY** *RAK 297* **22**	9
20 Dec 80	**RUNAROUND SUE** *RAK 325* **13**	10

RACING CARS *UK, male vocal / instrumental group* **7 wks**

| 12 Feb 77 | **THEY SHOOT HORSES DON'T THEY** *Chrysalis CHS 2129* ..**14** | 7 |

RACKETEERS – *See Elbow BONES and the RACKETEERS*

Jimmy RADCLIFFE *US, male vocalist* **2 wks**

| 4 Feb 65 | **LONG AFTER TONIGHT IS ALL OVER** *Stateside SS 374* ....**40** | 2 |

RADHA KRISHNA TEMPLE
Oxford Street, male / female vocal / instrumental group **17 wks**

| 13 Sep 69 | **HARE KRISHNA MANTRA** *Apple 15* ....**12** | 9 |
| 28 Mar 70 | **GOVINDA** *Apple 25* ....**23** | 8 |

RADICAL ROB *UK, male producer – Rob McLuan* **1 wk**

| 11 Jan 92 | **MONKEY WAH** *R&S RSUK 8* ....**67** | 1 |

Jack RADICS – *See Chaka DEMUS and PLIERS; SUPERCAT*

RADIO HEART – *See Gary NUMAN*

RADIO 1 DJ POSSE – *See Liz KERSHAW and Bruno BROOKES*

RADIO REVELLERS – *See Anthony STEEL and the RADIO REVELLERS*

RADIO STARS *UK, male vocal / instrumental group* **3 wks**

| 4 Feb 78 | **NERVOUS WRECK** *Chiswick NS 23* ....**39** | 3 |

RADIOHEAD *UK, male vocal / instrumental group* **27 wks**

| 13 Feb 93 | **ANYONE CAN PLAY GUITAR** *Parlophone CDR 6333* ....**32** | 2 |
| 22 May 93 | **POP IS DEAD** *Parlophone CDR 6345* ....**42** | 2 |

18 Sep 93	● CREEP *Parlophone CDR 6359*	7	6
8 Oct 94	MY IRON LUNG *Parlophone CDR 6394*	24	2
11 Mar 95	HIGH AND DRY / PLANET TELEX *Parlophone CDR 6405*	17	4
27 May 95	FAKE PLASTIC TREES *Parlophone CDR 6411*	20	4
2 Sep 95	JUST *Parlophone CDR 6415*	19	3
3 Feb 96	● STREET SPIRIT (FADE OUT) *Parlophone CDR 6419*	5	4

Fonda RAE US, female vocalist   4 wks

6 Oct 84	TUCH ME *Streetwave KHAN 28*	49	4

Jesse RAE UK, male vocalist   2 wks

11 May 85	OVER THE SEA *Scotland-Video YZ 36*	65	2

RAF Italy, male producer – Mauro Picotto   6 wks

14 Mar 92	WE'VE GOT TO LIVE TOGETHER *PWL Continental PWL 218*	34	3
5 Mar 94	TAKE ME HIGHER *Media MRLCD 0012*	71	1
23 Mar 96	TAKE ME HIGHER (re-mix) *Media MCSTD 40026*	59	1
27 Jul 96	ANGEL'S SYMPHONY [1] *Media MCSTD 40051*	73	1

[1] RAF by Picotto and Gigi D'Agostino

Gerry RAFFERTY UK, male vocalist   47 wks

18 Feb 78	● BAKER STREET *United Artists UP 36346*	3	15
26 May 79	● NIGHT OWL *United Artists UP 36512*	5	13
18 Aug 79	GET IT RIGHT NEXT TIME *United Artists BP 301*	30	9
22 Mar 80	BRING IT ALL HOME *United Artists BP 340*	54	4
21 Jun 80	ROYAL MILE *United Artists BP 354*	67	2
10 Mar 90	BAKER STREET (re-mix) *EMI EM 132*	53	4

RAGE UK, male vocal / instrumental group   15 wks

31 Oct 92	● RUN TO YOU *Pulse 8 LOSE 33*	3	11
27 Feb 93	WHY DON'T YOU *Pulse 8 CDLOSE 39*	44	2
15 May 93	HOUSE OF THE RISING SUN *Pulse 8 CDLOSE 43*	41	2

RAGE AGAINST THE MACHINE
US, male vocal / instrumental group   15 wks

27 Feb 93	KILLING IN THE NAME *Epic 6584922*	25	4
8 May 93	BULLET IN THE HEAD *Epic 6592582*	16	4
4 Sep 93	BOMBTRACK *Epic 6594712*	37	2
13 Apr 96	● BULLS ON PARADE *Epic 6631522*	8	3
7 Sep 96	PEOPLE OF THE SUN *Epic 6636282*	26	2

RAGGA TWINS UK, male vocal group   10 wks

10 Nov 90	ILLEGAL GUNSHOT / SPLIFFHEAD *Shut Up And Dance SUAD 7*	51	2
6 Apr 91	WIPE THE NEEDLE / JUGGLING *Shut Up And Dance SUAD 12S*	71	2
6 Jul 91	HOOLIGAN 69 *Shut Up And Dance SUAD 16S*	56	2
7 Mar 92	MIXED TRUTH / BRING UP THE MIC SOME MORE *Shut Up And Dance SUAD 27S*	65	2
11 Jul 92	SHINE EYE *Shut Up And Dance SUAD 32S* [1]	63	2

[1] Ragga Twins featuring Junior Reid

RAGTIMERS UK, male instrumental group   8 wks

16 Mar 74	THE STING *Pye 7N 45323*	46	1
30 Mar 74	THE STING (re-entry) *Pye 7N 45323*	31	7

RAH BAND UK, male / female vocal / instrumental group   50 wks

9 Jul 77	● THE CRUNCH *Good Earth GD 7*	6	12
1 Nov 80	FALCON *DJM DJS 10954*	35	7
7 Feb 81	SLIDE *DJM DJS 10964*	50	7
1 May 82	PERFUMED GARDEN *KR KR 5*	45	7
9 Jul 83	MESSAGES FROM THE STARS *TMT TMT 5*	42	5
19 Jan 85	ARE YOU SATISFIED? (FUNKA NOVA) *RCA RCA 470*	70	2
30 Mar 85	● CLOUDS ACROSS THE MOON *RCA PB 40025*	6	10

RAHSAAN – *See US3*

RAILWAY CHILDREN
UK, male vocal / instrumental group   13 wks

24 Mar 90	EVERY BEAT OF THE HEART *Virgin VS 1237*	68	2
2 Jun 90	MUSIC STOP *Virgin VS 1255*	66	2
20 Oct 90	SO RIGHT *Virgin VS 1289*	68	1
2 Feb 91	EVERY BEAT OF THE HEART (re-entry) *Virgin VS 1237*	24	6
20 Apr 91	SOMETHING SO GOOD *Virgin VS 1318*	57	2

RAIN – *See Stephanie DE SYKES*

RAIN TREE CROW
UK, male vocal / instrumental group – Japan under an assumed name   1 wk

30 Mar 91	BLACKWATER *Virgin VS 1340*	62	1

See also Japan.

RAINBOW UK, male vocal / instrumental group   62 wks

17 Sep 77	KILL THE KING *Polydor 2066 845*	44	3
8 Apr 78	LONG LIVE ROCK 'N' ROLL *Polydor 2066 913*	33	3
30 Sep 78	L.A. CONNECTION *Polydor 2066 968*	40	4
15 Sep 79	● SINCE YOU'VE BEEN GONE *Polydor POSP 70*	6	10
16 Feb 80	● ALL NIGHT LONG *Polydor POSP 104*	5	11
31 Jan 81	● I SURRENDER *Polydor POSP 221*	3	10
20 Jun 81	CAN'T HAPPEN HERE *Polydor POSP 251*	20	8
11 Jul 81	KILL THE KING (re-issue) *Polydor POSP 274*	41	4
3 Apr 82	STONE COLD *Polydor POSP 421*	34	4
27 Aug 83	STREET OF DREAMS *Polydor POSP 631*	52	3
5 Nov 83	CAN'T LET YOU GO *Polydor POSP 654*	43	2

RAINBOW COTTAGE
UK, male vocal / instrumental group   4 wks

6 Mar 76	SEAGULL *Penny Farthing PEN 906*	33	4

RAINMAKERS US, male vocal / instrumental group   11 wks

7 Mar 87	LET MY PEOPLE GO-GO *Mercury MER 238*	18	11

Marvin RAINWATER US, male vocalist   22 wks

7 Mar 58	★ WHOLE LOTTA WOMAN *MGM 974*	1	15
6 Jun 58	I DIG YOU BABY *MGM 980*	19	7

Bonnie RAITT US, female vocalist   9 wks

14 Dec 91	I CAN'T MAKE YOU LOVE ME *Capitol CL 639*	50	4
9 Apr 94	LOVE SNEAKIN' UP ON YOU *Capitol CDCL 713*	69	1
18 Jun 94	YOU *Capitol CDCLS 718*	31	2
11 Nov 95	ROCK STEADY *Capitol CDCL 763* [1]	50	2

[1] Bonnie Raitt and Bryan Adams

RAJA NEE US, female vocalist   2 wks

4 Mar 95	**TURN IT UP** Perspective 5874872	....	**42**	2

Tony RALLO and the MIDNIGHT BAND
France / US, male vocal / instrumental group   8 wks

23 Feb 80	**HOLDIN' ON** Calibre CAB 150	....	**34**	8

Sheryl Lee RALPH US, female vocalist   2 wks

26 Jan 85	**IN THE EVENING** Arista ARIST 595	....	**64**	2

RAM JAM US, male vocal / instrumental group   20 wks

10 Sep 77	● **BLACK BETTY** Epic EPC 5492	....	**7**	12
17 Feb 90	**BLACK BETTY (re-mix)** Epic 655430 7	....	**13**	8

RAM JAM BAND – See Geno WASHINGTON and the RAM JAM BAND

RAMBLERS (from the Abbey Hey Junior School) UK, children's choir   15 wks

13 Oct 79	**THE SPARROW** Decca F 13860	....	**11**	15

RAMONES US, male vocal / instrumental group   32 wks

21 May 77	**SHEENA IS A PUNK ROCKER** Sire RAM 001	......	**22**	7
6 Aug 77	**SWALLOW MY PRIDE** Sire 6078 607	....	**36**	3
30 Sep 78	**DON'T COME CLOSE** Sire SRE 1031	......	**39**	5
8 Sep 79	**ROCK 'N' ROLL HIGH SCHOOL** Sire SIR 4021	......	**67**	2
26 Jan 80	● **BABY I LOVE YOU** Sire SIR 4031	....	**8**	9
19 Apr 80	**DO YOU REMEMBER ROCK 'N' ROLL RADIO** Sire SIR 4037	....	**54**	3
10 May 86	**SOMEBODY PUT SOMETHING IN MY DRINK / SOMETHING TO BELIEVE IN** Beggars Banquet BEG 157	......	**69**	1
19 Dec 92	**POISON HEART** Chrysalis CHS 3917	......	**69**	2

RAMP UK, male instrumental / production duo   1 wk

8 Jun 96	**ROCK THE DISCOTEK** Loaded LOADCD 30	......	**49**	1

RAMPAGE UK, male vocal / instrumental duo   1 wk

25 Nov 95	**THE MONKEES** Almo Sounds CDALMOS 017	......	**51**	1

RAMRODS US, male / female instrumental group   12 wks

23 Feb 61	● **RIDERS IN THE SKY** London HLU 9282	......	**8**	12

RANCID US, male vocal / instrumental group   1 wk

7 Oct 95	**TIME BOMB** Out Of Step WOOS 8CDS	......	**56**	1

RANGE – See Bruce HORNSBY and the RANGE

RANKING ANN – See SCRITTI POLITTI

RANKING ROGER – See VARIOUS ARTISTS (EPs & LPs) – Gimme Shelter (EP); Pato BANTON

Shabba RANKS Jamaica, male vocalist   67 wks

16 Mar 91	**SHE'S A WOMAN** Virgin VS 1333 [1]	......	**20**	7
18 May 91	**TRAILER LOAD A GIRLS** Epic 6568747	......	**63**	2
24 Aug 91	**HOUSECALL** Epic 6573477 [2]	......	**31**	7
8 Aug 92	**MR LOVERMAN** Epic 6582517	......	**23**	7
28 Nov 92	**SLOW AND SEXY** Epic 6587727 [3]	......	**17**	7
6 Mar 93	**I WAS A KING** Motown TMGCD 1414 [4]	......	**64**	1
13 Mar 93	● **MR. LOVERMAN (re-issue)** Epic 6590782	......	**3**	11
8 May 93	● **HOUSECALL (re-mix)** Epic 6592842 [2]	......	**8**	8
26 Jun 93	**WHAT'CHA GONNA DO** Epic 6593072 [5]	......	**21**	4
25 Dec 93	**FAMILY AFFAIR** Polydor PZCD 304 [6]	......	**18**	8
29 Apr 95	**LET'S GET IT ON** Epic 6614122	......	**22**	3
5 Aug 95	**SHINE EYE GAL** Epic 6622332 [7]	......	**46**	2

[1] Scritti Politti featuring Shabba Ranks [2] Shabba Ranks featuring Maxi Priest [3] Shabba Ranks featuring Johnny Gill [4] Eddie Murphy featuring Shabba Ranks [5] Shabba Ranks featuring Queen Latifah [6] Shabba Ranks featuring Patra and Terry & Monica [7] Shabba Ranks (featuring Mykal Rose)

RAPINATION
Italy, male instrumental / production duo   12 wks

26 Dec 92	**LOVE ME THE RIGHT WAY** Logic 74321128097 [1]	......	**22**	10
10 Jul 93	**HERE'S MY A** Logic 74321153092 [2]	......	**69**	1
28 Sep 96	**LOVE ME THE RIGHT WAY (re-mix)** Logic 7432140442 [1]	......	**55**	1

[1] Rapination featuring Kym Mazelle [2] Rapination featuring Carol Kenyon

RAPPIN' 4-TAY US, male rapper   5 wks

24 Jun 95	**I'LL BE AROUND** Cooltempo CDCOOL 306 [1]	......	**30**	4
30 Sep 95	**PLAYAZ CLUB** Cooltempo CDCOOL 310	......	**63**	1

[1] Rappin' 4-Tay featuring the Spinners

The Spinners on I'll Be Around are the Detroit Spinners.

RARE UK, male / female vocal / instrumental group   1 wk

17 Feb 96	**SOMETHING WILD** Equator AXISCD 011	......	**57**	1

RARE BIRD UK, male vocal / instrumental group   8 wks

14 Feb 70	**SYMPATHY** Charisma CB 120	......	**27**	8

O. RASBURY – See Rahni HARRIS and F.L.O.

Roland RAT SUPERSTAR UK, male rat vocalist   20 wks

19 Nov 83	**RAT RAPPING** Rodent RAT 1	......	**14**	12
28 Apr 84	**LOVE ME TENDER** Rodent RAT 2	......	**32**	7
2 Mar 85	**NO. 1 RAT FAN** Rodent RAT 4	......	**72**	1

RATPACK UK, male instrumental / production duo   3 wks

6 Jun 92	**SEARCHIN' FOR MY RIZLA** Big Giant BIGT 02	......	**58**	3

RATTLES Germany, male vocal / instrumental group   15 wks

3 Oct 70	● **THE WITCH** Decca F 23058	......	**8**	15

RAVESIGNAL III
UK, male producer – Christian Bolland   2 wks

14 Dec 91	**HORSEPOWER** R&S RSUK 6	......	**61**	2

See also CJ Bolland.

RAW – See Erick 'More' Morillo presents RAW

RAW SILK US, female vocal group — 12 wks

| 16 Oct 82 | DO IT TO THE MUSIC KR KR 14 | 18 | 9 |
| 10 Sep 83 | JUST IN TIME West End WEND 2 | 49 | 3 |

RAW STYLUS UK, male / female vocal / instrumental duo — 1 wk

| 26 Oct 96 | BELIEVE IN ME Wired WIRED 234 | 66 | 1 |

Lou RAWLS US, male vocalist — 10 wks

| 31 Jul 76 | ● YOU'LL NEVER FIND ANOTHER LOVE LIKE MINE Philadelphia International PIR 4372 | 10 | 10 |

Gene Anthony RAY – See KIDS FROM FAME

Johnnie RAY US, male vocalist — 152 wks

14 Nov 52	WALKING MY BABY BACK HOME Columbia DB 3060	12	1
19 Dec 52	● FAITH CAN MOVE MOUNTAINS Columbia DB 3154 [1]	7	2
9 Jan 53	● FAITH CAN MOVE MOUNTAINS (re-entry) Columbia DB 3154 [1]	9	1
3 Apr 53	MA SAYS PA SAYS Columbia DB 3242 [2]	12	1
10 Apr 53	● SOMEBODY STOLE MY GAL Philips PB 123	6	1
17 Apr 53	FULL TIME JOB Columbia DB 3242 [2]	11	1
24 Apr 53	● SOMEBODY STOLE MY GAL (re-entry) Philips PB 123	6	4
29 May 53	SOMEBODY STOLE MY GAL (2nd re-entry) Philips PB 123	12	1
24 Jul 53	● LET'S WALK THAT-A-WAY Philips PB 157 [2]	4	14
7 Aug 53	SOMEBODY STOLE MY GAL (3rd re-entry) Philips PB 123	11	1
9 Apr 54	★ SUCH A NIGHT Philips PB 244	1	18
8 Apr 55	IF YOU BELIEVE Philips PB 379	15	1
13 May 55	IF YOU BELIEVE (re-entry) Philips PB 379	7	10
20 May 55	PATHS OF PARADISE Philips PB 441	20	1
7 Oct 55	HERNANDO'S HIDEAWAY Philips PB 495	11	5
14 Oct 55	● HEY THERE Philips PB 495	5	9
28 Oct 55	SONG OF THE DREAMER Philips PB 516	10	5
17 Feb 56	WHO'S SORRY NOW Philips PB 546	17	2
20 Apr 56	AIN'T MISBEHAVIN' Philips PB 580	17	6
8 Jun 56	AIN'T MISBEHAVIN' (re-entry) Philips PB 580	24	1
12 Oct 56	★ JUST WALKIN' IN THE RAIN Philips PB 624	1	19
18 Jan 57	YOU DON'T OWE ME A THING Philips PB 655	12	15
8 Feb 57	● LOOK HOMEWARD ANGEL Philips PB 655	7	16
10 May 57	★ YES TONIGHT JOSEPHINE Philips PB 686	1	16
6 Sep 57	BUILD YOUR LOVE Philips PB 721	17	7
4 Oct 57	GOOD EVENING FRIENDS / UP ABOVE MY HEAD I HEAR MUSIC IN THE AIR Philips PB 708 [3]	25	4
4 Dec 59	I'LL NEVER FALL IN LOVE AGAIN Philips PB 952	26	4
8 Jan 60	I'LL NEVER FALL IN LOVE AGAIN (re-entry) Philips PB 952	26	1
5 Feb 60	I'LL NEVER FALL IN LOVE AGAIN (2nd re-entry) Philips PB 952	28	1

[1] Johnnie Ray and the Four Lads [2] Doris Day and Johnnie Ray
[3] Frankie Laine and Johnnie Ray

The chart history of You Don't Owe Me A Thing / Look Homeward Angel is complicated, as follows: You Don't Owe Me A Thing entered the chart by itself on 18 Jan 57. On 8 and 15 Feb 57 Look Homeward Angel was coupled with You Don't Owe Me A Thing but from 22 Feb 57 the two sides went their individual ways on the chart and were listed separately, You Don't Owe Me A Thing for a further ten weeks and Look Homeward Angel for a further 14.

RAYDIO US, male / female vocal / instrumental group — 21 wks

| 8 Apr 78 | JACK AND JILL Arista 161 | 11 | 12 |
| 8 Jul 78 | IS THIS A LOVE THING Arista 193 | 27 | 9 |

RAYVON – See SHAGGY

RAZE US, male / female vocal / instrumental group — 47 wks

1 Nov 86	JACK THE GROOVE Champion CHAMP 23	57	7
3 Jan 87	JACK THE GROOVE (re-entry) Champion CHAMP 23	20	8
28 Feb 87	LET THE MUSIC MOVE U Champion CHAMP 27	57	3
31 Dec 88	BREAK 4 LOVE Champion CHAMP 67	28	11
15 Jul 89	LET IT ROLL Atlantic A 8866 [1]	27	5
2 Sep 89	BREAK 4 LOVE (re-entry) Champion CHAMP 67	59	5
27 Jan 90	ALL 4 LOVE (BREAK 4 LOVE 1990) (re-mix) Champion CHAMP 228 [2]	30	5
10 Feb 90	CAN YOU FEEL IT / CAN YOU FEEL IT Champion CHAMP 227 [3]	62	1
24 Sep 94	BREAK 4 LOVE (2nd re-mix) Champion CHAMPCD 314	44	2

[1] Raze presents Doug Lazy [2] Raze featuring Lady J and Secretary of Entertainment [3] Raze / Championship Legend

Can You Feel It by Champion Legend is a montage of six Raze tracks.

Chris REA UK, male vocalist — 119 wks

7 Oct 78	FOOL (IF YOU THINK IT'S OVER) Magnet MAG 111	30	7
21 Apr 79	DIAMONDS Magnet MAG 144	44	3
27 Mar 82	LOVING YOU Magnet MAG 215	65	3
1 Oct 83	I CAN HEAR YOUR HEARTBEAT Magnet MAG 244	60	2
17 Mar 84	I DON'T KNOW WHAT IT IS BUT I LOVE IT Magnet MAG 255	65	2
30 Mar 85	STAINSBY GIRLS Magnet MAG 276	26	10
29 Jun 85	JOSEPHINE Magnet MAG 280	67	2
29 Mar 86	IT'S ALL GONE Magnet MAG 283	69	1
31 May 86	ON THE BEACH Magnet MAG 294	57	3
28 Jun 86	ON THE BEACH (re-entry) Magnet MAG 294	75	1
12 Jul 86	ON THE BEACH (2nd re-entry) Magnet MAG 294	66	4
6 Jun 87	LET'S DANCE Magnet MAG 299	12	10
29 Aug 87	LOVING YOU AGAIN Magnet MAG 300	47	4
5 Dec 87	JOYS OF CHRISTMAS Magnet MAG 314	67	1
13 Feb 88	QUE SERA Magnet MAG 318	73	2
13 Aug 88	ON THE BEACH SUMMER '88 WEA YZ 195	12	6
22 Oct 88	I CAN HEAR YOUR HEARTBEAT WEA YZ 320	74	2
17 Dec 88	DRIVING HOME FOR CHRISTMAS EP WEA YZ 325	53	3
18 Feb 89	WORKING ON IT WEA YZ 50	53	3
14 Oct 89	● THE ROAD TO HELL (PART 2) WEA YZ 431	10	9
10 Feb 90	TELL ME THERE'S A HEAVEN East West YZ 455	24	6
5 May 90	TEXAS East West YZ 468	69	1
16 Feb 91	AUBERGE East West YZ 555	16	6
6 Apr 91	HEAVEN East West YZ 566	57	2
29 Jun 91	LOOKING FOR THE SUMMER East West YZ 584	49	3
9 Nov 91	WINTER SONG East West YZ 629	27	4
24 Oct 92	NOTHING TO FEAR East West YZ 699	16	4
28 Nov 92	GOD'S GREAT BANANA SKIN East West YZ 706	31	3
30 Jan 93	SOFT TOP HARD SHOULDER East West YZ 710CD	53	2
23 Oct 93	JULIA East West YZ 772CD	18	5
12 Nov 94	YOU CAN GO YOUR OWN WAY ast West YZ 835CD	28	3
24 Dec 94	TELL ME THERE'S A HEAVEN (re-issue) East West YZ 885CD	70	1
16 Nov 96	'DISCO' LA PASSIONE East West EW 072CD [1]	41	1

[1] Chris Rea and Shirley Bassey

Both On The Beach Summer '88 and I Can Hear Your Heartbeat in 88 are re-recordings. Tracks on Driving Home For Christmas EP: Driving Home For Christmas / Footsteps In The Snow / Joys Of Christmas / Smile.

Eileen READ – See CADETS

Eddi READER UK, female vocalist — 13 wks

4 Jun 94	PATIENCE OF ANGELS Blanco Y Negro NEG 68CD	33	5
13 Aug 94	JOKE (I'M LAUGHING) Blanco Y Negro NEG 72CD	42	3
5 Nov 94	DEAR JOHN Blanco Y Negro NEG 75CD1	48	2
22 Jun 96	TOWN WITHOUT PITY Blanco Y Negro NEG 90CD	26	3

READY FOR THE WORLD
US, male vocal / instrumental group **8 wks**

26 Oct 85	**OH SHEILA** *MCA MCA 1005*	**50**	5
14 Mar 87	**LOVE YOU DOWN** *MCA MCA 1110*	**60**	3

REAL McCOY
Germany / US, male / female vocal / instrumental duo **36 wks**

6 Nov 93	**ANOTHER NIGHT** *Logic 74321173732*	**61**	1
5 Nov 94	● **ANOTHER NIGHT (re-issue)** *Logic 74321236992* 1	**2**	12
28 Jan 95	● **RUN AWAY** *Logic 74321258822* 1	**6**	10
22 Apr 95	**LOVE AND DEVOTION** *Logic 74321272702*	**11**	8
26 Aug 95	**COME AND GET YOUR LOVE** *Logic 74321301272*	**19**	4
11 Nov 95	**AUTOMATIC LOVER (CALL FOR LOVE)** *Logic 74321325042*	**58**	1

1 (MC Sar &) the Real McCoy

REAL EMOTION
UK, male / female vocal / instrumental group **1 wk**

1 Jul 95	**BACK FOR GOOD** *Living Beat LBECD 34*	**67**	1

REAL PEOPLE *UK, male vocal / instrumental group* **8 wks**

16 Feb 91	**OPEN UP YOUR MIND (LET ME IN)** *CBS 6566127*	**70**	1
20 Apr 91	**THE TRUTH** *Columbia 6567877*	**73**	1
6 Jul 91	**WINDOW PANE (EP)** *Columbia 6569327*	**60**	1
11 Jan 92	**THE TRUTH (re-issue)** *Columbia 6576987*	**41**	3
23 May 92	**BELIEVER** *Columbia 6580067*	**38**	2

Tracks on Window Pane (EP): Window Pane / See Through You / Everything Must Change.

REAL ROXANNE *US, female vocalist* **10 wks**

28 Jun 86	**BANG ZOOM (LET'S GO GO)** *Cooltempo COOL 124* 1 ..**11**	9
12 Nov 88	**RESPECT** *Cooltempo COOL 176*	**71**	1

1 Real Roxanne with Hitman Howie Tee

REAL THING *UK, male vocal / instrumental group* **114 wks**

5 Jun 76	★ **YOU TO ME ARE EVERYTHING** *Pye International 7N 25709*	**1**	11
4 Sep 76	● **CAN'T GET BY WITHOUT YOU** *Pye 7N 45618*	**2**	10
12 Feb 77	**YOU'LL NEVER KNOW WHAT YOU'RE MISSING** *Pye 7N 45662*	**16**	9
30 Jul 77	**LOVE'S SUCH A WONDERFUL THING** *Pye 7N 45701*	**33**	5
4 Mar 78	**WHENEVER YOU WANT MY LOVE** *Pye 7N 46045*	**18**	9
3 Jun 78	**LET'S GO DISCO** *Pye 7N 46078*	**39**	7
12 Aug 78	**RAININ' THROUGH MY SUNSHINE** *Pye 7N 46113*	**40**	8
17 Feb 79	● **CAN YOU FEEL THE FORCE** *Pye 7N 46147*	**5**	11
21 Jul 79	**BOOGIE DOWN (GET FUNKY NOW)** *Pye 7P 109*	**33**	6
22 Nov 80	**SHE'S A GROOVY FREAK** *Calibre CAB 105*	**52**	4
8 Mar 86	● **YOU TO ME ARE EVERYTHING (THE DECADE REMIX 76-86)** *PRT 7P 349*	**5**	12
24 May 86	● **CAN'T GET BY WITHOUT YOU (THE SECOND DECADE REMIX)** *PRT 7P 352*	**6**	13
7 Jun 86	**YOU TO ME ARE EVERYTHING (THE DECADE REMIX 76-86) (re-entry)** *PRT 7P 349*	**72**	1
2 Aug 86	**CAN YOU FEEL THE FORCE ('86 REMIX)** *PRT 7P 358*	**24**	6
25 Oct 86	**STRAIGHT TO THE HEART** *Jive JIVE 129*	**71**	2

REAL TO REEL *US, male vocal / instrumental group* **2 wks**

21 Apr 84	**LOVE ME LIKE THIS** *Arista ARIST 565*	**68**	2

REBEL MC *UK, male vocalist* **52 wks**

27 May 89	**JUST KEEP ROCKIN'** *Desire WANT 9* 1	**11**	12
7 Oct 89	● **STREET TUFF** *Desire WANT 18* 2	**3**	14
31 Mar 90	**BETTER WORLD** *Desire WANT 25*	**20**	6
2 Jun 90	**REBEL MUSIC** *Desire WANT 31*	**53**	2
6 Apr 91	**WICKEDEST SOUND** *Desire WANT 40* 3	**43**	6
15 Jun 91	**TRIBAL BASE** *Desire WANT 44* 4	**20**	6
31 Aug 91	**BLACK MEANING GOOD** *Desire WANT 47*	**73**	1
21 Mar 92	**RICH AH GETTING RICHER** *Big Life BLR 70* 5	**48**	4
8 Aug 92	**HUMANITY** *Big Life BLR 78* 6	**62**	1

1 Double Trouble and the Rebel MC 2 Rebel MC and Double Trouble
3 Rebel MC featuring Tenor Fly 4 Rebel MC featuring Tenor Fly and
Barrington Levy 5 Rebel MC introducing Little T 6 Rebel MC featuring
Lincoln Thompson

REBEL ROUSERS – *See Cliff BENNETT and the REBEL ROUSERS*

REBELETTES – *See Duane EDDY*

REBELS – *See Duane EDDY*

Ezz RECO and the LAUNCHERS with Boysie GRANT *Jamaica, male vocal / instrumental group* **4 wks**

5 Mar 64	**KING OF KINGS** *Columbia DB 7217*	**44**	4

RECOIL *UK, male vocal / instrumental group* **1 wk**

21 Mar 92	**FAITH HEALER** *Mute MUTE 110*	**60**	1

RED BOX *UK, male vocal / instrumental duo* **28 wks**

24 Aug 85	● **LEAN ON ME (AH-LI-AYO)** *Sire W 8926*	**3**	14
25 Oct 86	● **FOR AMERICA** *Sire YZ 84*	**10**	12
31 Jan 87	**HEART OF THE SUN** *Sire YZ 100*	**71**	2

RED CAR AND THE BLUE CAR
UK, male vocal / instrumental group **4 wks**

14 Dec 91	**HOME FOR CHRISTMAS DAY** *Virgin VS 1394*	**44**	4

RED DRAGON with Brian and Tony GOLD
Jamaica, male vocal group **15 wks**

30 Jul 94	● **COMPLIMENTS ON YOUR KISS** *Mango CIDM 820*	**2**	13
31 Dec 94	**COMPLIMENTS ON YOUR KISS (re-entry)** *Mango CIDM 820*	**49**	2

RED EYE *UK, male instrumental / production duo* **1 wk**

3 Dec 94	**KUT IT** *Champion CHAMPCD 315*	**62**	1

RED HILL CHILDREN *UK, male / female vocal group* **2 wks**

30 Nov 96	**WHEN CHILDREN RULE THE WORLD** *Really Useful 5797262*	**40**	2

RED HOT CHILI PEPPERS
US, male vocal / instrumental group **33 wks**

10 Feb 90	**HIGHER GROUND** *EMI-USA MT 75*	**55**	3
23 Jun 90	**TASTE THE PAIN** *EMI-USA MT 85*	**29**	3
8 Sep 90	**HIGHER GROUND (re-issue)** *EMI-USA MT 88*	**54**	3
14 Mar 92	**UNDER THE BRIDGE** *Warner Bros. W 0084*	**26**	4
15 Aug 92	**BREAKING THE GIRL** *Warner Bros. W 0126*	**41**	3

5 Feb 94	● **GIVE IT AWAY** Warner Bros. W 0225CD1	**9** 4
30 Apr 94	**UNDER THE BRIDGE** (re-issue)	
	Warner Bros. W 0237CD	**13** 6
2 Sep 95	**WARPED** Warner Bros. W 0316CD	**31** 2
21 Oct 95	**MY FRIENDS** Warner Bros. W 0317CD	**29** 2
17 Feb 96	**AEROPLANE** Warner Bros. W 0331CD	**11** 3

RED RAW featuring 007
UK, male vocal / instrumental duo   **1 wk**

28 Oct 95	**OOH LA LA LA** Media MCSTD 2065	**59** 1

REDBONE *US, male vocal / instrumental group*   **12 wks**

25 Sep 71	● **THE WITCH QUEEN OF NEW ORLEANS** Epic EPC 7351	**2** 12

Sharon REDD *US, female vocalist*   **32 wks**

28 Feb 81	**CAN YOU HANDLE IT** Epic EPC 9572	**31** 8
2 Oct 82	**NEVER GIVE YOU UP** Prelude PRL A2755	**20** 9
15 Jan 83	**IN THE NAME OF LOVE** Prelude PRL A2905	**31** 5
22 Oct 83	**LOVE HOW YOU FEEL** Prelude A3868	**39** 5
1 Feb 92	**CAN YOU HANDLE IT** EMI EM 219 [1]	**17** 5

[1] DNA featuring Sharon Redd

REDD KROSS *US, male vocal / instrumental group*   **3 wks**

5 Feb 94	**VISIONARY** This Way Up WAY 2733	**75** 1
10 Sep 94	**YESTERDAY ONCE MORE** A & M 5807932	**45** 2

The listed flip side of Yesterday Once More was Superstar by Sonic Youth.

Otis REDDING *US, male vocalist*   **124 wks**

25 Nov 65	**MY GIRL** Atlantic AT 4050	**11** 16
7 Apr 66	**SATISFACTION** Atlantic AT 4080	**33** 4
14 Jul 66	**MY LOVER'S PRAYER** Atlantic 584 019	**37** 6
25 Aug 66	**I CAN'T TURN YOU LOOSE** Atlantic 584 030	**29** 8
24 Nov 66	**FA FA FA FA FA (SAD SONG)** Atlantic 584 049	**23** 9
26 Jan 67	**TRY A LITTLE TENDERNESS** Atlantic 584 070	**46** 4
23 Mar 67	**DAY TRIPPER** Stax 601 005	**43** 6
4 May 67	**LET ME COME ON HOME** Stax 601 007	**48** 1
15 Jun 67	**SHAKE** Stax 601 011	**28** 10
19 Jul 67	**TRAMP** Stax 601 012 [1]	**18** 11
11 Oct 67	**KNOCK ON WOOD** Stax 601 021 [1]	**35** 5
14 Feb 68	**MY GIRL** (re-issue) Atlantic 584 092	**36** 9
21 Feb 68	● **(SITTIN' ON) THE DOCK OF THE BAY** Stax 601 031	**3** 15
29 May 68	**HAPPY SONG** Stax 601 040	**24** 5
31 Jul 68	**HARD TO HANDLE** Atlantic 584 199	**15** 12
9 Jul 69	**LOVE MAN** Atco 226 001	**43** 3

[1] Otis Redding and Carla Thomas

Helen REDDY *Australia, female vocalist*   **18 wks**

18 Jan 75	● **ANGIE BABY** Capitol CL 15799	**5** 10
28 Nov 81	**I CAN'T SAY GOODBYE TO YOU** MCA 744	**43** 8

REDHEAD KINGPIN and the FBI
US, male vocalist   **11 wks**

22 Jul 89	**DO THE RIGHT THING** 10 TEN 271	**13** 10
2 Dec 89	**SUPERBAD SUPERSLICK** 10 TEN 286	**68** 1

REDNEX *Sweden, male / female vocal / instrumental group*   **23 wks**

17 Dec 94	★ **COTTON EYE JOE** Internal Affairs KGBCD 016	**1** 16

25 Mar 95	**OLD POP IN AN OAK**	
	Internal Affairs KGBD 019	**12** 6
21 Oct 95	**WILD 'N FREE** Internal Affairs KGBD 024	**55** 1

REDSKINS *UK, male vocal / instrumental duo*   **12 wks**

10 Nov 84	**KEEP ON KEEPIN' ON** Decca F 1	**43** 5
22 Jun 85	**BRING IT DOWN (THIS INSANE THING)**	
	Decca F 2	**33** 5
22 Feb 86	**THE POWER IS YOURS** Decca F 3	**59** 2

Alex REECE *UK, male producer*   **7 wks**

16 Dec 95	**FEEL THE SUNSHINE**	
	Blunted Vinyl BLNCD 016	**69** 1
11 May 96	**FEEL THE SUNSHINE** (re-mix)	
	Fourth & Broadway BRCD 332	**26** 3
27 Jul 96	**CANDLES** Fourth & Broadway BRCD 333	**33** 2
18 Nov 96	**ACID LAB** Fourth & Broadway BRCD 344	**64** 1

Jimmy REED *US, male vocalist*   **2 wks**

10 Sep 64	**SHAME SHAME SHAME** Stateside SS 330	**45** 2

Lou REED *US, male vocalist*   **19 wks**

12 May 73	● **WALK ON THE WILD SIDE** RCA 2303	**10** 9
17 Jan 87	**SOUL MAN** A & M AM 364 [1]	**30** 10

[1] Sam Moore and Lou Reed

Dan REED NETWORK
US, male vocal / instrumental group   **16 wks**

20 Jan 90	**COME BACK BABY** Mercury DRN 2	**51** 3
17 Mar 90	**RAINBOW CHILD** Mercury DRN 3	**60** 3
21 Jul 90	**STARDATE 1990 / RAINBOW CHILD** (re-issue)	
	Mercury DRN 4	**39** 4
8 Sep 90	**LOVER / MONEY** Mercury DRN 5	**45** 3
13 Jul 91	**MIX IT UP** Mercury MER 345	**49** 2
21 Sep 91	**BABY NOW I** Mercury MER 352	**65** 1

Michael REED ORCHESTRA – *See Richard HARTLEY / Michael REED ORCHESTRA*

REEF *UK, male vocal / instrumental group*   **19 wks**

15 Apr 95	**GOOD FEELING** Sony S2 6613602	**24** 4
3 Jun 95	**NAKED** Sony S2 6620622	**11** 5
5 Aug 95	**WEIRD** Sony S2 6622772	**19** 3
2 Nov 96	● **PLACE YOUR HANDS** Sony S2 6635712	**6** 7

REEL 2 REAL *US, male vocal / instrumental duo*   **53 wks**

12 Feb 94	● **I LIKE TO MOVE IT** Positiva CDTIV 10 [1]	**5** 20
2 Jul 94	● **GO ON MOVE** Positiva CDTIV 15 [1]	**7** 9
1 Oct 94	**CAN YOU FEEL IT** Positiva CDTIV 22 [1]	**13** 5
3 Dec 94	**RAISE YOUR HANDS** Positiva CDTIV 27 [1]	**14** 6
1 Apr 95	**CONWAY** Positiva CDTIVS 30 [1]	**27** 4
6 Jul 96	● **JAZZ IT UP** Positiva CDTIV 59	**7** 7
5 Oct 96	**ARE YOU READY FOR SOME MORE**	
	Positiva CDTIV 56	**24** 2

[1] Reel 2 Real featuring the Mad Stuntman

Tony REES and the COTTAGERS
UK, male vocal group   **1 wk**

10 May 75	**VIVA EL FULHAM** Sonet SON 2059	**46** 1

REESE PROJECT US, male producer – Kevin Saunderson **7 wks**

8 Aug 92	THE COLOUR OF LOVE Network NWK 51	**52**	2
12 Dec 92	I BELIEVE Network NWKT 63	**74**	1
13 Mar 93	SO DEEP Network NWKCD 68	**54**	2
24 Sep 94	THE COLOUR OF LOVE (re-mix) Network NWKCD 81	**55**	1
6 May 95	DIRECT-ME Network NEKCD 87	**44**	1

Jim REEVES US, male vocalist **322 wks**

24 Mar 60	HE'LL HAVE TO GO RCA 1168	**36**	1
7 Apr 60	HE'LL HAVE TO GO (re-entry) RCA 1168	**12**	30
16 Mar 61	WHISPERING HOPE RCA 1223	**50**	1
23 Nov 61	YOU'RE THE ONLY GOOD THING RCA 1261	**17**	19
28 Jun 62	ADIOS AMIGO RCA 1293	**23**	21
22 Nov 62	I'M GONNA CHANGE EVERYTHING RCA 1317	**42**	2
13 Jun 63 ●	WELCOME TO MY WORLD RCA 1342	**6**	15
17 Oct 63	GUILTY RCA 1364	**29**	7
20 Feb 64 ●	I LOVE YOU BECAUSE RCA 1385	**5**	39
18 Jun 64 ●	I WON'T FORGET YOU RCA 1400	**3**	25
5 Nov 64 ●	THERE'S A HEARTACHE FOLLOWING ME RCA 1423	**6**	13
7 Jan 65	I WON'T FORGET YOU (re-entry) RCA 1400	**47**	1
4 Feb 65 ●	IT HURTS SO MUCH RCA 1437	**8**	10
15 Apr 65	NOT UNTIL THE NEXT TIME RCA 1446	**13**	12
6 May 65	HOW LONG HAS IT BEEN RCA 1445	**45**	5
15 Jul 65	THIS WORLD IS NOT MY HOME RCA 1412	**22**	9
11 Nov 65	IS IT REALLY OVER RCA 1488	**17**	9
18 Aug 66 ★	DISTANT DRUMS RCA 1537	**1**	25
2 Feb 67	I WON'T COME IN WHILE HE'S THERE RCA 1563	**12**	11
26 Jul 67	TRYING TO FORGET RCA 1611	**33**	5
22 Nov 67	I HEARD A HEART BREAK LAST NIGHT RCA 1643	**38**	6
27 Mar 68	PRETTY BROWN EYES RCA 1672	**33**	5
25 Jun 69	WHEN TWO WORLDS COLLIDE RCA 1830	**17**	17
6 Dec 69	BUT YOU LOVE ME DADDY RCA 1899	**15**	16
21 Mar 70	NOBODY'S FOOL RCA 1915	**32**	5
12 Sep 70	ANGELS DON'T LIE RCA 1997	**44**	1
26 Sep 70	ANGELS DON'T LIE (re-entry) RCA 1997	**32**	2
26 Jun 71	I LOVE YOU BECAUSE / HE'LL HAVE TO GO / MOONLIGHT & ROSES (re-issues) RCA Maximillion 2092	**34**	8
19 Feb 72	YOU'RE FREE TO GO RCA 2174	**48**	2

Martha REEVES and the VANDELLAS
US, female vocal group **85 wks**

29 Oct 64	DANCING IN THE STREET Stateside SS 345 [1]	**28**	8
1 Apr 65	NOWHERE TO RUN Tamla Motown TMG 502 [1]	**26**	8
1 Dec 66	I'M READY FOR LOVE Tamla Motown TMG 582 [1]	**29**	8
30 Mar 67	JIMMY MACK Tamla Motown TMG 599 [1]	**21**	9
17 Jan 68	HONEY CHILE Tamla Motown TMG 636	**30**	9
15 Jan 69 ●	DANCING IN THE STREET (re-issue) Tamla Motown TMG 684	**4**	12
16 Apr 69	NOWHERE TO RUN (re-issue) Tamla Motown TMG 694	**42**	3
29 Aug 70	JIMMY MACK (re-entry) Tamla Motown TMG 599	**21**	12
13 Feb 71	FORGET ME NOT Tamla Motown TMG 762	**11**	8
8 Jan 72	BLESS YOU Tamla Motown TMG 794	**33**	5
23 Jul 88	NOWHERE TO RUN (2nd re-issue) A & M AM 444	**52**	3

[1] Martha and the Vandellas

The listed flip side of Nowhere To Run *in 88 was* I Got You (I Feel Good) *by James Brown.*

Vic REEVES UK, male vocalist **29 wks**

27 Apr 91 ●	BORN FREE Sense SIGH 710 [1]	**6**	6
26 Oct 91 ★	DIZZY Sense SIGH 712 [2]	**1**	12
14 Dec 91	ABIDE WITH ME Sense SIGH 713	**47**	3
8 Jul 95 ●	I'M A BELIEVER Parlophone CDR 6412 [3]	**3**	8

[1] Vic Reeves and the Roman Numerals [2] Vic Reeves and the Wonder Stuff
[3] EMF and Reeves and Mortimer

RE-FLEX UK, male vocal / instrumental group **9 wks**

28 Jan 84	THE POLITICS OF DANCING EMI FLEX 2	**28**	9

Joan REGAN UK, female vocalist **62 wks**

11 Dec 53 ●	RICOCHET Decca F 10193 [1]	**8**	1
8 Jan 54 ●	RICOCHET (re-entry) Decca F 10193 [1]	**9**	4
14 May 54 ●	SOMEONE ELSE'S ROSES Decca F 10257	**5**	8
1 Oct 54 ●	IF I GIVE MY HEART TO YOU Decca F 10373	**20**	1
29 Oct 54 ●	IF I GIVE MY HEART TO YOU (re-entry) Decca F 10373	**3**	10
5 Nov 54	WAIT FOR ME DARLING Decca F 10362 [2]	**18**	1
25 Mar 55 ●	PRIZE OF GOLD Decca F 10432	**6**	8
6 May 55	OPEN UP YOUR HEART Decca F 10474	**19**	1
1 May 59 ●	MAY YOU ALWAYS HMV POP 593	**9**	16
5 Feb 60	HAPPY ANNIVERSARY Pye 7N 15238	**29**	1
19 Feb 60	HAPPY ANNIVERSARY (re-entry) Pye 7N 15238	**29**	1
28 Jul 60	PAPA LOVES MAMA Pye 7N 15278	**29**	8
24 Nov 60	ONE OF THE LUCKY ONES Pye 7N 15310	**47**	1
5 Jan 61	IT MUST BE SANTA Pye 7N 15303	**42**	1

[1] Joan Regan with the Squadronaires [2] Joan Regan and the Johnston Brothers

See also Various Artists (EPs & LPs) – All Star Hit Parade.

REGENTS UK, male / female vocal / instrumental group **14 wks**

22 Dec 79	7 TEEN Rialto TREB 111	**11**	12
7 Jun 80	SEE YOU LATER Arista ARIST 350	**55**	2

REGGAE PHILHARMONIC ORCHESTRA
UK, male / female vocal / instrumental group **11 wks**

19 Nov 88	MINNIE THE MOOCHER Mango IS 378	**35**	9
28 Jul 90	LOVELY THING Mango MNG 742	**71**	2

REGGAE REVOLUTION – *See Pato BANTON*

REGINA US, female vocalist **3 wks**

1 Feb 86	BABY LOVE Funkin' Marvellous MARV 01	**50**	3

REID UK, male vocal group **12 wks**

8 Oct 88	ONE WAY OUT Syncopate SY 16	**66**	2
11 Feb 89	REAL EMOTION Syncopate SY 24	**65**	2
15 Apr 89	GOOD TIMES Syncopate SY 27	**55**	6
21 Oct 89	LOVIN' ON THE SIDE Syncopate REID 1	**71**	2

Ellen REID – *See CRASH TEST DUMMIES*

John REID – *See NIGHTCRAWLERS*

Junior REID – *See COLDCUT; RAGGA TWINS; SOUPDRAGONS*

Mike REID UK, male vocalist **8 wks**

22 Mar 75 ●	THE UGLY DUCKLING Pye 7N 45434	**10**	8

Neil REID UK, male vocalist **26 wks**

1 Jan 72 ●	MOTHER OF MINE Decca F 13264	**2**	20
8 Apr 72	THAT'S WHAT I WANT TO BE Decca F 13300	**49**	1
22 Apr 72	THAT'S WHAT I WANT TO BE (re-entry) Decca F 13300	**45**	5

Maggie REILLY – *See Mike OLDFIELD*

Keith RELF *UK, male vocalist*   **1 wk**

26 May 66 **MR. ZERO** *Columbia DB 7920* **50** 1

R.E.M. *US, male vocal / instrumental group*   **126 wks**

28 Nov 87 **THE ONE I LOVE** *IRS IRM 46* **51** 8
30 Apr 88 **FINEST WORKSONG** *IRS IRM 161* **50** 2
4 Feb 89 **STAND** *Warner Bros. W 7577* **51** 3
3 Jun 89 **ORANGE CRUSH** *Warner Bros. W 2960* **28** 5
12 Aug 89 **STAND (re-issue)** *Warner Bros. W 2833* **48** 2
9 Mar 91 **LOSING MY RELIGION** *Warner Bros. W 0015* **19** 9
18 May 91 ● **SHINY HAPPY PEOPLE** *Warner Bros. W 0027* **6** 11
17 Aug 91 **NEAR WILD HEAVEN** *Warner Bros. W 0055*........**27** 4
21 Sep 91 **THE ONE I LOVE (re-issue)** *IRS IRM 178* **16** 6
16 Nov 91 **RADIO SONG** *Warner Bros. W 0072* **28** 3
14 Dec 91 **IT'S THE END OF THE WORLD AS WE KNOW IT**
IRS IRM 180 ....**39** 4
3 Oct 92 **DRIVE** *Warner Bros. W 0136*...........................**11** 5
28 Nov 92 **MAN ON THE MOON** *Warner Bros. W 0143*........**18** 8
20 Feb 93 **THE SIDEWINDER SLEEPS TONITE**
Warner Bros. W 0152CD1 ....**17** 6
17 Apr 93 ● **EVERYBODY HURTS** *Warner Bros W 0169CD1* **7** 12
24 Jul 93 **NIGHTSWIMMING** *Warner Bros. W 0184CD*........**27** 5
11 Dec 93 **FIND THE RIVER** *Warner Bros. W 0211CD* **54** 1
17 Sep 94 ● **WHAT'S THE FREQUENCY, KENNETH**
Warner Bros. W 0265CD **9** 7
12 Nov 94 **BANG AND BLAME** *Warner Bros. W 0275CD* **15** 4
4 Feb 95 **CRUSH WITH EYELINER** *Warner Bros. W 0281CD* **23** 3
15 Apr 95 ● **STRANGE CURRENCIES** *Warner Bros. W 0290CD* **9** 4
29 Jul 95 **TONGUE** *Warner Bros. W 0308CD* **13** 5
31 Aug 96 ● **E-BOW THE LETTER** *Warner Bros. W 0369CD* **4** 5
2 Nov 96 **BITTERSWEET ME** *Warner Bros. W 0377CD* **19** 2
14 Dec 96 **ELECTROLITE** *Warner Bros. W 0383CD* **29** 2

REMBRANDTS *US, male vocal / instrumental group*   **13 wks**

2 Sep 95 ● **I'LL BE THERE FOR YOU (THEME FROM FRIENDS)**
East West A 4390CD **3** 12
20 Jan 96 **THIS HOUSE IS NOT A HOME**
East West A 4336CD **58** 1

RENAISSANCE *UK, male / female vocal / instrumental group*   **11 wks**

15 Jul 78 ● **NORTHERN LIGHTS** *Warner Bros. K 17177* **10** 11

RENÉ and ANGELA *US, male / female vocal duo*   **15 wks**

15 Jun 85 **SAVE YOUR LOVE (FOR NUMBER 1)**
Club JAB 14 [1] **66** 2
7 Sep 85 **I'LL BE GOOD** *Club JAB 18* **22** 10
2 Nov 85 **SECRET RENDEZVOUS** *Champion CHAMP 5* **54** 3

[1] Rene and Angela featuring Kuris Blow

RENÉ and YVETTE *UK, male / female vocal duo*   **4 wks**

22 Nov 86 **JE T'AIME (ALLO ALLO) / RENE D.M.C.
(DEVASTATING MACHO CHARISMA)**
Sedition EDIT 3319 ....**57** 4

RENÉE and RENATO
UK / Italy, female / male vocal duo   **22 wks**

30 Oct 82 ★ **SAVE YOUR LOVE** *Hollywood HWD 003* **1** 16
12 Feb 83 **JUST ONE MORE KISS**
Hollywood HWD 006 ....**48** 6

RENEGADE SOUNDWAVE
UK, male vocal / instrumental group   **7 wks**

3 Feb 90 **PROBABLY A ROBBERY** *Mute MUTE 102* **38** 6
5 Feb 94 **RENEGADE SOUNDWAVE** *Mute CDMUTE 146* **64** 1

REO SPEEDWAGON
US, male vocal / instrumental group   **38 wks**

11 Apr 81 ● **KEEP ON LOVING YOU** *Epic EPC 9544* **7** 14
27 Jun 81 **TAKE IT ON THE RUN** *Epic EPC A 1207* **19** 14
16 Mar 85 **CAN'T FIGHT THIS FEELING** *Epic A 4880* **16** 10

REPARATA and the DELRONS
US, female vocal group   **12 wks**

20 Mar 68 **CAPTAIN OF YOUR SHIP** *Bell 1002* **13** 10
18 Oct 75 **SHOES** *Polydor 2066 562* [1] **43** 2

[1] Reparata

REPUBLICA
UK, male / female vocal / instrumental group   **2 wks**

27 Apr 96 **READY TO GO** *Deconstruction 74321326132* **43** 2

REUNION *US, male vocal group*   **4 wks**

21 Sep 74 **LIFE IS A ROCK (BUT THE RADIO ROLLED ME)**
RCA PB 10056 ....**33** 4

REVILLOS – *See REZILLOS*

REVOLTING COCKS
US, male vocal / instrumental group   **1 wk**

18 Sep 93 **DA YA THINK I'M SEXY** *Devotion CDDVN 111* **61** 1

REVOLUTION – *See PRINCE*

Debbie REYNOLDS *US, female vocalist*   **17 wks**

30 Aug 57 ● **TAMMY** *Vogue-Coral Q 72274* **2** 17

Jody REYNOLDS *US, male vocalist*   **1 wk**

14 Apr 79 **ENDLESS SLEEP** *Lightning LIG 9015* **66** 1

Endless Sleep *was coupled with* To Know Him Is To Love Him *by the Teddy Bears as
a double A-side.*

LJ REYNOLDS *US, male vocalist*   **3 wks**

30 Jun 84 **DON'T LET NOBODY HOLD YOU DOWN** *Club JAB 5* **53** 3

REYNOLDS GIRLS *UK, female vocal duo*   **12 wks**

25 Feb 89 ● **I'D RATHER JACK** *PWL PWL 25* **8** 12

REZILLOS *UK, male / female vocal / instrumental group*   **21 wks**

12 Aug 78 **TOP OF THE POPS** *Sire SIR 4001* **17** 9
25 Nov 78 **DESTINATION VENUS** *Sire SIR 4008* **43** 4
18 Aug 79 **I WANNA BE YOUR MAN / I CAN'T STAND
MY BABY** *Sensible SAB 1* **71** 1

293

1 Sep 79	**I WANNA BE YOUR MAN / I CAN'T STAND MY BABY (re-entry)** *Sensible SAB 1*	**75** 1
26 Jan 80	**MOTORBIKE BEAT** *Dindisc DIN 5* [1]	**45** 6

[1] Revillos

RHC *Belgium, male / female vocal / instrumental duo* **1 wk**

11 Jan 92	**FEVER CALLED LOVE** *R&S RSUK 9*	**65** 1

RHODA – See SPECIALS

Busta RHYMES *US, male rapper* **9 wks**

11 May 96	● **WOO-HAH!! GOT YOU ALL IN CHECK** *Elektra EKR 220CD*	**8** 7
21 Sep 96	**IT'S A PARTY** *Elektra EKR 226CD* [1]	**23** 2

[1] Busta Rhymes featuring Zhane

RHYTHM ETERNITY
UK, male / female vocal / instrumental group **1 wk**

23 May 92	**PINK CHAMPAGNE** *Dead Dead Good GOOD 15T*	**72** 1

RHYTHM FACTOR
US, male / female vocal / instrumental group **2 wks**

29 Apr 95	**YOU BRING ME JOY** *Multiply CDMULTY 4*	**53** 2

RHYTHM IS RHYTHM *US, male instrumental duo* **1 wk**

11 Nov 89	**STRINGS OF LIFE** *Kool Kat KOOL 509*	**74** 1

RHYTHM-N-BASS *UK, male rap group* **4 wks**

19 Sep 92	**ROSES** *Epic 6582907*	**56** 2
3 Jul 93	**CAN'T STOP THIS FEELING** *Epic 6592002*	**59** 2

RHYTHM ON THE LOOSE
UK, male producer – Geoff Hibbert **2 wks**

19 Aug 95	**BREAK OF DAWN** *Six6 SIXCD 126*	**36** 2

RHYTHM QUEST *UK, male producer – Mark Hadfield* **2 wks**

20 Jun 92	**CLOSER TO ALL YOUR DREAMS** *Network NWK 40*	**45** 2

RHYTHM SECTION *UK, male vocal / instrumental group* **1 wk**

18 Jul 92	**MIDSUMMER MADNESS EP** *Rhythm Section RSEC 006*	**66** 1

Tracks on Midsummer Madness EP: Dreamworld / Burnin' Up / Perfect Love 2am / Perfect Love 8am.

RHYTHM SOURCE
UK, male / female vocal / instrumental group **1 wk**

17 Jun 95	**LOVE SHINE** *A & M 5810672*	**74** 1

RHYTHMATIC *UK, male instrumental group* **3 wks**

12 May 90	**TAKE ME BACK** *Network NWK 8*	**74** 1
26 May 90	**TAKE ME BACK (re-entry)** *Network NWK 8*	**71** 1
3 Nov 90	**FREQUENCY** *Network NWK 13*	**62** 1

Reva RICE and Greg ELLIS
UK, male / female vocal duo **2 wks**

27 Mar 93	**NEXT TIME YOU FALL IN LOVE** *Really Useful RURCD 12*	**59** 2

Charlie RICH *US, male vocalist* **29 wks**

16 Feb 74	● **THE MOST BEAUTIFUL GIRL** *CBS 1897*	**2** 14
13 Apr 74	**BEHIND CLOSED DOORS** *Epic EPC 1539*	**16** 10
1 Feb 75	**WE LOVE EACH OTHER** *Epic EPC 2868*	**37** 5

Kelli RICH – See NU SOUL featuring Kelli RICH

Richie RICH *UK, male vocalist* **15 wks**

16 Jul 88	**TURN IT UP** *Club JAB 68*	**48** 3
22 Oct 88	**I'LL HOUSE YOU** *Gee Street GEE 003* [1]	**22** 5
10 Dec 88	**MY DJ (PUMP IT UP SOME)** *Gee Street GEE 7*	**74** 1
2 Sep 89	**SALSA HOUSE** *ffrr F 113*	**50** 3
9 Mar 91	**YOU USED TO SALSA** *ffrr F 156* [2]	**52** 3

[1] Richie Rich meets the Jungle Brothers [2] Richie Rich's Salsa House featuring Ralphi Rosario

RICH KIDS *UK, male vocal / instrumental group* **5 wks**

28 Jan 78	**RICH KIDS** *EMI 2738*	**24** 5

Tony RICH PROJECT *US, male vocalist* **22 wks**

4 May 96	● **NOBODY KNOWS** *LaFace 74321356422*	**4** 17
31 Aug 96	**LIKE A WOMAN** *LaFace 74321401612*	**27** 4
14 Dec 96	**LEAVIN'** *LaFace 74321438382*	**52** 1

Cliff RICHARD *UK, male vocalist* **1113 wks**

12 Sep 58	● **MOVE IT** *Columbia DB 4178*	**2** 17
21 Nov 58	● **HIGH CLASS BABY** *Columbia DB 4203*	**7** 10
30 Jan 59	**LIVIN' LOVIN' DOLL** *Columbia DB 4249*	**20** 6
8 May 59	● **MEAN STREAK** *Columbia DB 4290*	**10** 9
15 May 59	**NEVER MIND** *Columbia DB 4290*	**21** 2
10 Jul 59	★ **LIVING DOLL** *Columbia DB 4306*	**1** 21
9 Oct 59	★ **TRAVELLIN' LIGHT** *Columbia DB 4351*	**1** 17
9 Oct 59	**DYNAMITE** *Columbia DB 4351*	**16** 2
30 Oct 59	**DYNAMITE (re-entry)** *Columbia DB 4351*	**21** 2
11 Dec 59	**LIVING DOLL (re-entry)** *Columbia DB 4306*	**26** 1
1 Jan 60	**LIVING DOLL (2nd re-entry)** *Columbia DB 4306*	**28** 1
15 Jan 60	**EXPRESSO BONGO EP** *Columbia SEG 7971*	**14** 7
22 Jan 60	● **VOICE IN THE WILDERNESS** *Columbia DB 4398*	**2** 13
24 Mar 60	● **FALL IN LOVE WITH YOU** *Columbia DB 4431*	**2** 15
5 May 60	**VOICE IN THE WILDERNESS (re-entry)** *Columbia DB 4398*	**36** 2
30 Jun 60	★ **PLEASE DON'T TEASE** *Columbia DB 4479*	**1** 18
22 Sep 60	● **NINE TIMES OUT OF TEN** *Columbia DB 4506*	**3** 12
1 Dec 60	★ **I LOVE YOU** *Columbia DB 4547*	**1** 16
2 Mar 61	● **THEME FOR A DREAM** *Columbia DB 4593*	**3** 14
30 Mar 61	● **GEE WHIZ IT'S YOU** *Columbia DC 756*	**4** 14
22 Jun 61	● **A GIRL LIKE YOU** *Columbia DB 4667*	**3** 14
19 Oct 61	● **WHEN THE GIRL IN YOUR ARMS IS THE GIRL IN YOUR HEART** *Columbia DB 4716*	**3** 15
11 Jan 62	★ **THE YOUNG ONES** *Columbia DB 4761*	**1** 21
10 May 62	● **I'M LOOKING OUT THE WINDOW / DO YOU WANNA DANCE** *Columbia DB 4828*	**2** 17
6 Sep 62	● **IT'LL BE ME** *Columbia DB 4886*	**2** 12
6 Dec 62	★ **THE NEXT TIME / BACHELOR BOY** *Columbia DB 4950*	**1** 18
21 Feb 63	★ **SUMMER HOLIDAY** *Columbia DB 4977*	**1** 18
9 May 63	● **LUCKY LIPS** *Columbia DB 7034*	**4** 15
22 Aug 63	● **IT'S ALL IN THE GAME** *Columbia DB 7089*	**2** 13
7 Nov 63	● **DON'T TALK TO HIM** *Columbia DB 7150*	**2** 13
6 Feb 64	● **I'M THE LONELY ONE** *Columbia DB 7203*	**8** 10

13 Feb 64	DON'T TALK TO HIM (re-entry) Columbia DB 7150	50	1
30 Apr 64	● CONSTANTLY Columbia DB 7272	4	13
2 Jul 64	● ON THE BEACH Columbia DB 7305	7	13
8 Oct 64	● THE TWELFTH OF NEVER Columbia DB 7372	8	11
10 Dec 64	● I COULD EASILY FALL Columbia DB 7420	9	11
11 Mar 65	★ THE MINUTE YOU'RE GONE Columbia DB 7496	1	14
10 Jun 65	ON MY WORD Columbia DB 7596	12	10
19 Aug 65	THE TIME IN BETWEEN Columbia DB 7660	22	8
4 Nov 65	● WIND ME UP (LET ME GO) Columbia DB 7745	2	13
24 Mar 66	BLUE TURNS TO GREY Columbia DB 7866	15	9
21 Jul 66	VISIONS Columbia DB 7968	7	12
13 Oct 66	● TIME DRAGS BY Columbia DB 8017	10	12
15 Dec 66	● IN THE COUNTRY Columbia DB 8094	6	10
16 Mar 67	● IT'S ALL OVER Columbia DB 8150	9	10
8 Jun 67	I'LL COME RUNNING Columbia DB 8210	26	8
16 Aug 67	● THE DAY I MET MARIE Columbia DB 8245	10	14
15 Nov 67	● ALL MY LOVE Columbia DB 8293	6	12
20 Mar 68	★ CONGRATULATIONS Columbia DB 8376	1	13
26 Jun 68	I'LL LOVE YOU FOREVER TODAY Columbia DB 8437	27	6
25 Sep 68	MARIANNE Columbia DB 8476	22	8
27 Nov 68	DON'T FORGET TO CATCH ME Columbia DB 8503	21	7
26 Feb 69	GOOD TIMES (BETTER TIMES) Columbia DB 8548	12	11
28 May 69	BIG SHIP Columbia DB 8581	8	10
13 Sep 69	● THROW DOWN A LINE Columbia DB 8615 [1]	7	9
6 Dec 69	WITH THE EYES OF A CHILD Columbia DB 8641	20	11
21 Feb 70	JOY OF LIVING Columbia DB 8657 [1]	25	8
6 Jun 70	GOODBYE SAM HELLO SAMANTHA Columbia DB 8685	6	15
5 Sep 70	I AIN'T GOT TIME ANYMORE Columbia DB 8708	21	7
23 Jan 71	SUNNY HONEY GIRL Columbia DB 8747	19	8
10 Apr 71	SILVERY RAIN Columbia DB 8774	27	6
17 Jul 71	FLYING MACHINE Columbia DB 8797	37	7
13 Nov 71	SING A SONG OF FREEDOM Columbia DB 8836	13	12
11 Mar 72	JESUS Columbia DB 8864	35	3
26 Aug 72	LIVING IN HARMONY Columbia DB 8917	12	10
17 Mar 73	● POWER TO ALL OUR FRIENDS EMI 2012	4	13
12 May 73	HELP IT ALONG / TOMORROW RISING EMI 2022	29	6
1 Dec 73	TAKE ME HIGH EMI 2088	27	12
18 May 74	(YOU KEEP ME) HANGIN' ON EMI 2150	13	8
7 Feb 76	MISS YOU NIGHTS EMI 2376	15	10
8 May 76	● DEVIL WOMAN EMI 2458	9	8
21 Aug 76	I CAN'T ASK FOR ANYMORE THAN YOU EMI 2499	17	8
4 Dec 76	HEY MR. DREAM MAKER EMI 2559	31	5
5 Mar 77	MY KINDA LIFE EMI 2584	15	8
16 Jul 77	WHEN TWO WORLDS DRIFT APART EMI 2633	46	3
31 Mar 79	GREEN LIGHT EMI 2920	57	3
21 Jul 79	★ WE DON'T TALK ANYMORE EMI 2975	1	14
3 Nov 79	HOT SHOT EMI 5003	46	5
2 Feb 80	● CARRIE EMI 5006	4	10
16 Aug 80	● DREAMIN' EMI 5095	8	10
25 Oct 80	SUDDENLY Jet 7002 [2]	15	7
24 Jan 81	A LITTLE IN LOVE EMI 5123	15	8
29 Aug 81	● WIRED FOR SOUND EMI 5221	4	9
21 Nov 81	● DADDY'S HOME EMI 5251	2	12
17 Jul 82	● THE ONLY WAY OUT EMI 5318	10	9
25 Sep 82	WHERE DO WE GO FROM HERE EMI 5341	60	3
4 Dec 82	LITTLE TOWN EMI 5348	11	7
19 Feb 83	● SHE MEANS NOTHING TO ME Capitol CL 276 [3]	9	9
16 Apr 83	● TRUE LOVE WAYS EMI 5385 [4]	8	8
4 Jun 83	DRIFTING DJM SHEIL 1 [5]	64	2
3 Sep 83	NEVER SAY DIE (GIVE A LITTLE BIT MORE) EMI 5415	15	7
26 Nov 83	● PLEASE DON'T FALL IN LOVE EMI 5437	7	9
31 Mar 84	BABY YOU'RE DYNAMITE / OCEAN DEEP EMI 5457	27	6
19 May 84	OCEAN DEEP / BABY YOU'RE DYNAMITE (re-entry) EMI 5457	72	1
3 Nov 84	SHOOTING FROM THE HEART EMI RICH 1	51	4
9 Feb 85	HEART USER EMI RICH 2	46	3
14 Sep 85	SHE'S SO BEAUTIFUL EMI 5531	17	4
7 Dec 85	IT'S IN EVERY ONE OF US EMI 5537	45	6
22 Mar 86	★ LIVING DOLL WEA YZ 65 [6]	1	11
4 Oct 86	● ALL I ASK OF YOU Polydor POSP 802 [7]	3	16
29 Nov 86	SLOW RIVERS Rocket EJS 13 [8]	44	6
20 Jun 87	● MY PRETTY ONE EMI EM 4	6	10
29 Aug 87	● SOME PEOPLE EMI EM 18	3	10
31 Oct 87	REMEMBER ME EMI EM 31	35	4

13 Feb 88	TWO HEARTS EMI EM 42	34	3
3 Dec 88	★ MISTLETOE AND WINE EMI EM 78	1	8
10 Jun 89	● THE BEST OF ME EMI EM 78	2	7
26 Aug 89	● I JUST DON'T HAVE THE HEART EMI EM 101	3	8
14 Oct 89	LEAN ON YOU EMI EM 105	17	6
9 Dec 89	WHENEVER GOD SHINES HIS LIGHT Polydor VANS 2 [9]	20	6
24 Feb 90	STRONGER THAN THAT EMI EM 129	14	5
25 Aug 90	● SILHOUETTES EMI EM 152	10	7
13 Oct 90	FROM A DISTANCE EMI EM 155	11	6
8 Dec 90	★ SAVIOUR'S DAY EMI XMAS 90	1	7
14 Sep 91	MORE TO LIFE EMI EM 205	23	5
7 Dec 91	● WE SHOULD BE TOGETHER EMI XMAS 91	10	6
11 Jan 92	THIS NEW YEAR EMI EMS 216	30	2
5 Dec 92	● I STILL BELIEVE IN YOU EMI EM 255	7	6
27 Mar 93	● PEACE IN OUR TIME EMI CDEM 265	8	5
12 Jun 93	HUMAN WORK OF ART EMI CDEM 267	24	4
2 Oct 93	NEVER LET GO EMI CDEM 281	32	3
18 Dec 93	HEALING LOVE EMI CDEM 294	19	5
10 Dec 94	ALL I HAVE TO DO IS DREAM / MISS YOU NIGHTS (re-issue) EMI CDEM 359 [10]	14	6
25 Feb 95	ALL I HAVE TO DO IS DREAM / MISS YOU NIGHTS (re-entry of re-issue) EMI CDEM 359 [10]	58	3
2 Oct 95	MISUNDERSTOOD MAN EMI CDEM 394	19	3
9 Dec 95	HAD TO BE EMI CDEM 410 [11]	22	4
30 Mar 96	THE WEDDING EMI CDEM 422 [12]	40	1

[1] Cliff and Hank [2] Olivia Newton-John and Cliff Richard [3] Phil Everly and Cliff Richard [4] Cliff Richard with the London Philharmonic Orchestra [5] Sheila Walsh and Cliff Richard [6] Cliff Richard and the Young Ones featuring Hank B. Marvin [7] Cliff Richard and Sarah Brightman [8] Elton John and Cliff Richard [9] Van Morrison with Cliff Richard [10] Cliff Richard with Phil Everly/Cliff Richard [11] Cliff Richard and Olivia Newton-John [12] Cliff Richard featuring Helen Hobson

The Shadows appear on all Cliff's hits from Move It to A Girl Like You. After that they are on the following hits: The Young Ones, Do You Wanna Dance, It'll Be Me, The Next Time, Bachelor Boy, Summer Holiday, Lucky Lips, Don't Talk To Him, I'm The Lonely One, On The Beach, I Could Easily Fall, The Time In Between, Blue Turns To Grey, In The Country and Don't Forget To Catch Me. Tracks on the Expresso Bongo EP: Love / A Voice in The Wilderness / The Shrine On The Second Floor / Bongo Blues. Bongo Blues features only the Shadows. The Shadows were the Drifters on Cliff's hits before Living Doll. Bachelor Boy was only listed with The Next Time from 10 Jan 63. Ocean Deep listed from 28 Apr 84 onwards. It peaked at position 41.

Wendy RICHARD – See Mike SARNE

Lionel RICHIE US, male vocalist — 165 wks

12 Sep 81	● ENDLESS LOVE Motown TMG 1240 [1]	7	12
20 Nov 82	● TRULY Motown TMG 1284	6	11
29 Jan 83	YOU ARE Motown TMG 1290	43	7
7 May 83	MY LOVE Motown TMG 1300	70	3
1 Oct 83	● ALL NIGHT LONG (ALL NIGHT) Motown TMG 1319	2	16
3 Dec 83	● RUNNING WITH THE NIGHT Motown TMG 1324	9	12
10 Mar 84	★ HELLO Motown TMG 1330	1	15
23 Jun 84	STUCK ON YOU Motown TMG 1341	12	12
20 Oct 84	PENNY LOVER Motown TMG 1356	18	7
16 Nov 85	● SAY YOU, SAY ME Motown ZB 40421	8	11
26 Jul 86	● DANCING ON THE CEILING Motown L10 1	7	11
11 Oct 86	LOVE WILL CONQUER ALL Motown L10 2	45	5
20 Dec 86	BALLERINA GIRL / DEEP RIVER WOMAN Motown L10 3	17	8
28 Mar 87	SELA Motown L10 4	43	6
9 May 92	DO IT TO ME Motown TMG 1407	33	6
22 Aug 92	● MY DESTINY Motown TMG 1408	7	13
28 Nov 92	LOVE OH LOVE Motown TMG 1413	52	3
26 Dec 92	LOVE OH LOVE (re-entry) Motown TMG 1413	73	1
6 Apr 96	DON'T WANNA LOSE YOU Mercury MERCD 461	17	5
23 Nov 96	STILL IN LOVE Mercury MERCD 477	66	1

[1] Diana Ross and Lionel Richie

Deep River Woman was only listed from 17 Jan 87. It has the credit: background vocal 'Alabama'.

Jonathan RICHMAN and the MODERN LOVERS US, male vocal / instrumental group 27 wks

16 Jul 77	**ROADRUNNER** Beserkley BZZ 1	**11**	9
29 Oct 77	● **EGYPTIAN REGGAE** Beserkley BZZ 2	**5**	14
21 Jan 78	**MORNING OF OUR LIVES** Beserkley BZZ 7 `1`	**29**	4

`1` Modern Lovers

Ricky DILLARD – See Farley 'Jackmaster' FUNK

RICO – See SPECIALS

RIDE UK, male vocal / instrumental group 22 wks

27 Jan 90	**RIDE EP** Creation CRE 07T2	**71**	2
14 Apr 90	**PLAY EP** Creation CRE 075T	**32**	3
29 Sep 90	**FALL EP** Creation CRE 087T	**34**	3
16 Mar 91	**TODAY FOREVER** Creation CRE 100T	**14**	4
15 Feb 92	● **LEAVE THEM ALL BEHIND** Creation CRE 123T	**9**	3
25 Apr 92	**TWISTERELLA** Creation CRE 150T	**36**	2
30 Apr 94	**BIRDMAN** Creation CRESCD 155	**38**	2
25 Jun 94	**HOW DOES IT FEEL TO FEEL** Creation CRESCD 184	**58**	1
8 Oct 94	**I DON'T KNOW WHERE IT COMES FROM** Creation CRESCD 189R	**46**	1
24 Feb 96	**BLACK NITE CRASH** Creation CRESCD 199	**67**	1

Tracks on Ride EP: Chelsea Girl / Drive Blind / All I See / Close My Eyes. Tracks on Play EP: Like A Daydream / Silver / Furthest Sense / Perfect Time. Tracks on Fall EP: Dreams Burn Down / Taste / Hear And Now / Nowhere.

Andrew RIDGELEY UK, male vocalist 3 wks

31 Mar 90	**SHAKE** Epic AJR 1	**58**	3

Stan RIDGWAY US, male vocalist 12 wks

5 Jul 86	● **CAMOUFLAGE** IRS IRM 114	**4**	12

RIGHEIRA Italy, male vocal duo 3 wks

24 Sep 83	**VAMOS A LA PLAYA** A & M AM 137	**53**	3

RIGHT SAID FRED
UK, male vocal / instrumental group 61 wks

27 Jul 91	● **I'M TOO SEXY** Tug SNOG 1	**2**	16
7 Dec 91	● **DON'T TALK JUST KISS** Tug SNOG 2 `1`	**3**	11
21 Mar 92	★ **DEEPLY DIPPY** Tug SNOG 3	**1**	14
1 Aug 92	**THOSE SIMPLE THINGS / DAYDREAM** Tug SNOG 4	**29**	5
27 Feb 93	**STICK IT OUT** Tug CDCOMIC 1 `2`	**4**	7
23 Oct 93	**BUMPED** Tug CDSNOG 7	**32**	4
18 Dec 93	**HANDS UP (4 LOVERS)** Tug CDSNOG 8	**60**	3
19 Mar 94	**WONDERMAN** Tug CDSNOG 9	**55**	1

`1` Right Said Fred, guest vocals: Jocelyn Brown `2` Right Said Fred and Friends

RIGHTEOUS BROTHERS US, male vocal duo 86 wks

14 Jan 65	★ **YOU'VE LOST THAT LOVIN' FEELIN'** London HLU 9943	**1**	10
12 Aug 65	**UNCHAINED MELODY** London HL 9975	**14**	12
13 Jan 66	**EBB TIDE** London HL 10011	**48**	2
14 Apr 66	**(YOU'RE MY) SOUL AND INSPIRATION** Verve VS 535	**15**	10
10 Nov 66	**WHITE CLIFFS OF DOVER** London HL 10086	**21**	9
22 Dec 66	**ISLAND IN THE SUN** Verve VS 547	**36**	5
12 Feb 69	● **YOU'VE LOST THAT LOVIN' FEELIN'** (re-issue) London HL 10241	**10**	11
19 Nov 77	**YOU'VE LOST THAT LOVIN' FEELIN'** (2nd re-issue) Phil Spector International 2010 022	**42**	4
27 Oct 90	★ **UNCHAINED MELODY** (re-issue) Verve/Polydor PO 101	**1**	14
15 Dec 90	● **YOU'VE LOST THAT LOVIN' FEELIN'** (3rd re-issue) / **EBB TIDE** (re-issue) Verve/Polydor PO 116	**3**	9

Cheryl Pepsii RILEY US, female vocalist 1 wk

28 Jan 89	**THANKS FOR MY CHILD** CBS 653153 7	**75**	1

Jeannie C RILEY US, female vocalist 15 wks

16 Oct 68	**HARPER VALLEY P.T.A.** Polydor 56748	**12**	15

Teddy RILEY US, male producer 5 wks

21 Mar 92	**IS IT GOOD TO YOU** MCA MCS 1611 `1`	**53**	2
19 Jun 93	**BABY BE MINE** MCA MCSTD 1772 `2`	**37**	3

`1` Teddy Riley featuring Tammy Lucas `2` Blackstreet featuring Teddy Riley

RIMSHOTS US, male instrumental / vocal group 5 wks

19 Jul 75	**7-6-5-4-3-2-1 (BLOW YOUR WHISTLE)** All Platinum 6146 304	**26**	5

RIO and MARS
France / UK, male / female vocal / instrumental duo 3 wks

28 Jan 95	**BOY I GOTTA HAVE YOU** Dome CDDOME 1014	**43**	2
13 Apr 96	**BOY I GOTTA HAVE YOU** (re-issue) Feverpitch CDFVR 1007	**46**	1

Miguel RIOS Spain, male vocalist 12 wks

11 Jul 70	**SONG OF JOY** A & M AMS 790	**16**	12

Waldo de los RIOS Argentina, orchestra 16 wks

10 Apr 71	● **MOZART SYMPHONY NO. 40 IN G MINOR K550 1ST MOVEMENT (ALLEGRO MOLTO)** A & M AMS 836	**5**	16

Minnie RIPERTON US, female vocalist 10 wks

12 Apr 75	● **LOVING YOU** Epic EPC 3121	**2**	10

RITCHIE FAMILY US, female vocal group 19 wks

23 Aug 75	**BRAZIL** Polydor 2058 625	**41**	4
18 Sep 76	● **THE BEST DISCO IN TOWN** Polydor 2058 777	**10**	9
17 Feb 79	**AMERICAN GENERATION** Mercury 6007 199	**49**	6

Lee RITENOUR – See Maxi PRIEST

Tex RITTER US, male vocalist 14 wks

22 Jun 56	● **WAYWARD WIND** Capitol CL 14581	**8**	14

RIVER CITY PEOPLE
UK, male / female vocal / instrumental group 27 wks

12 Aug 89	**(WHAT'S WRONG WITH) DREAMING** EMI EM 95	**70**	3
3 Mar 90	**WALKING ON ICE** EMI EM 130	**62**	2
30 Jun 90	**CARRY THE BLAME / CALIFORNIA DREAMIN'** EMI EM 145	**13**	10
22 Sep 90	**(WHAT'S WRONG WITH) DREAMING** (re-issue) EMI EM 156	**40**	3

Alexei Sayle

Alexei Sayle charted two full years before the Young Ones, with whom he appeared in the TV show of the same name.

Joan Regan

Joan Regan's first two releases, 'Ricochet' and the uncharted 'Till I Waltzed With You' were both covers of American hits for Teresa Brewer.

Shampoo

Shampoo's 'Trouble' was re-issued in 1995 after its inclusion in the *Mighty Morph'n Power Rangers* movie.

2 Mar 91	**WHEN I WAS YOUNG** *EMI EM 176*	**62**	2
28 Sep 91	**SPECIAL WAY** *EMI EM 207*	**44**	3
22 Feb 92	**STANDING IN THE NEED OF LOVE** *EMI EM 216*	**36**	4

RIVER DETECTIVES *UK, male vocal / instrumental duo*   **4 wks**

29 Jul 89	**CHAINS** *WEA YZ 383*	**51**	4

RIVER OCEAN – *See INDIA*

Danny RIVERS *UK, male vocalist*   **3 wks**

12 Jan 61	**CAN'T YOU HEAR MY HEART** *Decca F 11294*	**36**	3

ROACH MOTEL
UK, male instrumental / production group   **2 wks**

21 Aug 93	**AFRO SLEEZE / TRANSATLANTIC** *Junior Boy's Own JBO 1412*	**73**	1
10 Dec 94	**HAPPY BIZZNESS / WILD LUV** *Junior Boy's Own JBO 24* ..	**75**	1

ROACHFORD
UK, male / female vocal / instrumental group   **52 wks**

18 Jun 88	**CUDDLY TOY** *CBS ROA 2*	**61**	4
14 Jan 89	● **CUDDLY TOY (re-issue)** *CBS ROA 4*	**4**	9
18 Mar 89	**FAMILY MAN** *CBS ROA 5*	**25**	6
1 Jul 89	**KATHLEEN** *CBS ROA 6.*	**43**	5
13 Apr 91	**GET READY!** *Columbia 6567057*	**22**	8
19 Mar 94	**ONLY TO BE WITH YOU** *Columbia 6601562*	**21**	7
18 Jun 94	**LAY YOUR LOVE ON ME** *Columbia 6603722*	**36**	4
20 Aug 94	**THIS GENERATION** *Columbia 6607452*	**38**	4
3 Dec 94	**CRY FOR ME** *Columbia 6610742*	**46**	2
1 Apr 95	**I KNOW YOU DON'T LOVE ME** *Columbia 6612525*	**42**	2

ROB 'N' RAZ – *See Leila K*

Kate ROBBINS and BEYOND
UK, female / male vocal / instrumental group   **10 wks**

30 May 81	● **MORE THAN IN LOVE** *RCA 69*	**2**	10

Marty ROBBINS *US, male vocalist*   **32 wks**

29 Jan 60	**EL PASO** *Fontana H 233*	**19**	7
7 Apr 60	**EL PASO (re-entry)** *Fontana H 233*	**44**	1
26 May 60	**BIG IRON** *Fontana H 229*	**48**	1
27 Sep 62	● **DEVIL WOMAN** *CBS AAG 114*	**5**	17
17 Jan 63	**RUBY ANN** *CBS AAG 128*	**24**	6

Antoinette ROBERSON – *See PULSE featuring Antoinette ROBERSON*

Al ROBERTS – *See FOUR ACES*

Austin ROBERTS *US, male vocalist*   **7 wks**

25 Oct 75	**ROCKY** *Private Stock PVT 33*	**22**	7

Joe ROBERTS *UK, male vocalist*   **17 wks**

28 Aug 93	**BACK IN MY LIFE** *ffrr FCD 215*	**59**	1
29 Jan 94	**LOVER** *ffrr FCD 220*	**22**	5
14 May 94	**BACK IN MY LIFE (re-issue)** *ffrr FCD 230*	**39**	3
6 Aug 94	**ADORE** *ffrr FCD 240*	**45**	3
18 Feb 95	**YOU ARE EVERYTHING** *Columbia 6611755* [1]	**28**	4
24 Feb 96	**HAPPY DAYS** *Grass Green GRASS 10CD* [2]	**63**	1

[1] Melanie Williams and Joe Roberts [2] Sweet Mercy featuring Joe Roberts

Juliet ROBERTS *UK, female vocalist*   **20 wks**

31 Jul 93	**CAUGHT IN THE MIDDLE** *Cooltempo CDCOOL 272*	**24**	6
6 Nov 93	**FREE LOVE** *Cooltempo CDCOOL 281*	**25**	3
19 Mar 94	**AGAIN / I WANT YOU** *Cooltempo CDCOOL 285*	**33**	3
2 Jul 94	**CAUGHT IN THE MIDDLE (re-mix)** *Cooltempo CDCOOL 291*	**14**	5
15 Oct 94	**I WANT YOU (re-issue)** *Cooltempo CDCOOL 297*	**28**	3

Malcolm ROBERTS *UK, male vocalist*   **29 wks**

11 May 67	**TIME ALONE WILL TELL** *RCA 1578*	**45**	2
30 Oct 68	● **MAY I HAVE THE NEXT DREAM WITH YOU** *Major Minor MM 581*	**8**	14
12 Feb 69	**MAY I HAVE THE NEXT DREAM WITH YOU (re-entry)** *Major Minor MM 581*	**45**	1
22 Nov 69	**LOVE IS ALL** *Major Minor MM 637*	**12**	12

B.A. ROBERTSON *UK, male vocalist*   **60 wks**

28 Jul 79	● **BANG BANG** *Asylum K 13152*	**2**	12
27 Oct 79	● **KNOCKED IT OFF** *Asylum K 12396*	**8**	12
1 Mar 80	**KOOL IN THE KAFTAN** *Asylum K 12427*	**17**	12
31 May 80	● **TO BE OR NOT TO BE** *Asylum K 12449*	**9**	11
17 Oct 81	**HOLD ME** *Swansong BAM 1* [1]	**11**	8
17 Dec 83	**TIME** *Epic A 3983* [2]	**45**	5

[1] B.A. Robertson and Maggie Bell [2] Frida and B.A. Robertson

Don ROBERTSON
US, male instrumentalist – piano and whistler   **9 wks**

11 May 56	● **THE HAPPY WHISTLER** *Capitol CL 14575*	**8**	9

Robbie ROBERTSON *Canada, male vocalist*   **10 wks**

23 Jul 88	**SOMEWHERE DOWN THE CRAZY RIVER** *Geffen GEF 40*	**15**	10

Ivo ROBIC *Yugoslavia, male vocalist*   **1 wk**

6 Nov 59	**MORGEN** *Polydor 23923*	**23**	1

Floyd ROBINSON *US, male vocalist*   **9 wks**

16 Oct 59	● **MAKIN' LOVE** *RCA 1146*	**9**	9

Smokey ROBINSON *US, male vocalist*   **41 wks**

23 Feb 74	**JUST MY SOUL RESPONDING** *Tamla Motown TMG 883* ..	**35**	6
24 Feb 79	**POPS WE LOVE YOU** *Motown TMG 1136* [1]	**66**	5
9 May 81	★ **BEING WITH YOU** *Motown TMG 1223*	**1**	13
13 Mar 82	**TELL ME TOMORROW** *Motown TMG 1255*	**51**	4
28 Mar 87	**JUST TO SEE HER** *Motown ZB 41147*	**52**	6
25 Feb 89	**INDESTRUCTIBLE** *Arista 112074* [2]	**30**	7

[1] Diana Ross, Marvin Gaye, Smokey Robinson and Stevie Wonder
[2] Four Tops featuring Smokey Robinson

See also Smokey Robinson and the Miracles.

Smokey ROBINSON and the MIRACLES
US, male vocal group   **71 wks**

24 Feb 66	**GOING TO A GO-GO** *Tamla Motown TMG 547*	**44**	5
22 Dec 66	**(COME 'ROUND HERE) I'M THE ONE YOU NEED** *Tamla Motown TMG 584*	**45**	2

27 Dec 67	**I SECOND THAT EMOTION** Tamla Motown TMG 631	**27** 11
3 Apr 68	**IF YOU CAN WANT** Tamla Motown TMG 648	**50** 1
7 May 69	● **THE TRACKS OF MY TEARS** Tamla Motown TMG 696	**9** 13
1 Aug 70	★ **THE EARS OF A CLOWN** Tamla Motown TMG 745	**1** 14
30 Jan 71	**(COME 'ROUND HERE) I'M THE ONE YOU NEED (re-issue)** Tamla Motown TMG 761	**13** 9
5 Jun 71	**I DON'T BLAME YOU AT ALL** Tamla Motown TMG 774	**11** 10
2 Oct 76	**THE TEARS OF A CLOWN (re-issue)** Tamla Motown TMG 1048	**34** 6

See also Miracles; Smokey Robinson.

Tom ROBINSON UK, male vocalist — **41 wks**

22 Oct 77	● **2-4-6-8 MOTORWAY** EMI 2715 [1]	**5** 9
18 Feb 78	**DON'T TAKE NO FOR AN ANSWER** EMI 2749 [1]	**18** 6
13 May 78	**UP AGAINST THE WALL** EMI 2787 [1]	**33** 6
17 Mar 79	**BULLY FOR YOU** EMI 2916 [1]	**68** 2
25 Jun 83	● **WAR BABY** Panic NIC 2	**6** 9
12 Nov 83	**LISTEN TO THE RADIO: ATMOSPHERICS** Panic NIC 3	**39** 6
15 Sep 84	**RIKKI DON'T LOSE THAT NUMBER** Castaway TR 2	**58** 3

[1] Tom Robinson Band

ROBSON and JEROME UK, male vocal duo — **39 wks**

20 May 95	★ **UNCHAINED MELODY/(THERE'LL BE BLUEBIRDS OVER) THE WHITE CLIFFS OF DOVER** RCA 74321284362 [1]	**1** 16
4 Nov 95	**UNCHAINED MELODY/(THERE'LL BE BLUEBIRDS OVER) THE WHITE CLIFFS OF DOVER (re-entry)** RCA 74321284362 [1]	**63** 1
11 Nov 95	★ **I BELIEVE / UP ON THE ROOF** RCA 74321326882	**1** 14
9 Nov 96	★ **WHAT BECOMES OF THE BROKENHEARTED / SATURDAY NIGHT AT THE MOVIES / YOU'LL NEVER WALK ALONE** RCA 74321424732	**1†** 8

[1] Robson Green and Jerome Flynn

ROBYN Sweden, female vocalist — **1 wk**

| 20 Jul 96 | **YOU'VE GOT THAT SOMETHIN'** RCA 74321393462 | **54** 1 |

John ROCCA – *See FREEEZ*

ROCHELLE US, female vocalist — **6 wks**

| 1 Feb 86 | **MY MAGIC MAN** Warner Bros. W 8838 | **27** 6 |

ROCK AID ARMENIA UK, male vocal / instrumental charity ensemble — **5 wks**

| 16 Dec 89 | **SMOKE ON THE WATER** Life Aid Armenia ARMEN 001 | **39** 5 |

ROCK CANDY UK, male vocal / instrumental group — **6 wks**

| 11 Sep 71 | **REMEMBER** MCA MK 5069 | **32** 6 |

Chubb ROCK US, male rapper — **1 wk**

| 19 Jan 91 | **TREAT 'EM RIGHT** Champion CHAMP 272 | **67** 1 |

ROCK GODDESS UK, female vocal / instrumental group — **5 wks**

| 5 Mar 83 | **MY ANGEL** A & M AMS 8311 | **64** 2 |
| 24 Mar 84 | **I DIDN'T KNOW I LOVED YOU (TILL I SAW YOU ROCK 'N' ROLL)** A & M AMS 185 | **57** 3 |

Sir Monti ROCK III – *See DISCO TEX and the SEX-O-LETTES*

ROCKER'S REVENGE US, male / female vocal / instrumental group — **20 wks**

| 14 Aug 82 | ● **WALKING ON SUNSHINE** London LON 11 [1] | **4** 13 |
| 29 Jan 83 | **THE HARDER THEY COME** London LON 18 | **30** 7 |

[1] Rocker's Revenge featuring Donnie Calvin

ROCKET FROM THE CRYPT US, male vocal / instrumental group — **6 wks**

27 Jan 96	**BORN IN 69** Elemental ELM 32CD	**68** 1
13 Apr 96	**YOUNG LIVERS** Elemental ELM 33CDS	**67** 1
14 Sep 96	**ON A ROPE** Elemental ELM 38CDS1	**12** 4

ROCKETS – *See Tony CROMBIE and his ROCKETS*

ROCKFORD FILES UK, male instrumental / production duo — **4 wks**

| 11 Mar 95 | **YOU SEXY DANCER** Escapade CDJAPE 7 | **34** 3 |
| 6 Apr 96 | **YOU SEXY DANCER (re-issue)** Escapade CDJAPE 14 | **59** 1 |

ROCKIN' BERRIES UK, male vocal / instrumental group — **41 wks**

1 Oct 64	**I DIDN'T MEAN TO HURT YOU** Piccadilly 7N 35197	**43** 1
15 Oct 64	● **HE'S IN TOWN** Piccadilly 7N 35203	**3** 13
21 Jan 65	**WHAT IN THE WORLD'S COME OVER YOU** Piccadilly 7N 35217	**23** 7
13 May 65	● **POOR MAN'S SON** Piccadilly 7N 35236	**5** 11
26 Aug 65	**YOU'RE MY GIRL** Piccadilly 7N 35254	**40** 7
6 Jan 66	**THE WATER IS OVER MY HEAD** Piccadilly 7N 35270	**43** 1
20 Jan 66	**THE WATER IS OVER MY HEAD (re-entry)** Piccadilly 7N 35270	**50** 1

ROCKNEY – *See CHAS and DAVE*

ROCKSTEADY CREW US, male / female vocal group — **16 wks**

| 1 Oct 83 | ● **(HEY YOU) THE ROCKSTEADY CREW** Charisma/Virgin RSC 1 | **6** 12 |
| 5 May 84 | **UPROCK** Charisma/Virgin RSC 2 | **64** 4 |

ROCKWELL US, male vocalist — **11 wks**

| 4 Feb 84 | ● **SOMEBODY'S WATCHING ME** Motown TMG 1331 | **6** 11 |

ROCKY V – *See Joey B ELLIS*

ROCOCO UK / Italy, male / female vocal / instrumental group — **5 wks**

| 16 Dec 89 | **ITALO HOUSE MIX** Mercury MER 314 | **54** 5 |

RODEO JONES UK / Grenada, male / female vocal / instrumental group — **2 wks**

| 30 Jan 93 | **NATURAL WORLD** A & M AMCD 0165 | **75** 1 |
| 3 Apr 93 | **SHADES OF SUMMER** A & M AMCD 212 | **59** 1 |

Clodagh RODGERS Ireland, female vocalist — **59 wks**

26 Mar 69	● **COME BACK AND SHAKE ME** RCA 1792	**3** 14
9 Jul 69	● **GOODNIGHT MIDNIGHT** RCA 1852	**4** 11
4 Oct 69	**GOODNIGHT MIDNIGHT (re-entry)** RCA 1852	**48** 1
8 Nov 69	**BILJO** RCA 1891	**22** 9

4 Apr 70	EVERYBODY GO HOME THE PARTY'S OVER RCA 1930	47	2
20 Mar 71 ●	JACK IN THE BOX RCA 2066	4	10
9 Oct 71	LADY LOVE BUG RCA 2117	28	12

Jimmie RODGERS US, male vocalist — 37 wks

1 Nov 57	HONEYCOMB Columbia DB 3986	30	1
20 Dec 57 ●	KISSES SWEETER THAN WINE Columbia DB 4052	7	11
28 Mar 58	OH OH, I'M FALLING IN LOVE AGAIN Columbia DB 4078	18	6
19 Dec 58	WOMAN FROM LIBERIA Columbia DB 4206	18	6
14 Jun 62 ●	ENGLISH COUNTRY GARDEN Columbia DB 4847	5	13

Paul RODGERS UK, male vocalist — 2 wks

12 Feb 94	MUDDY WATER BLUES Victory ROGCD 1	45	2

RODS – See EDDIE and the HOT RODS

Tommy ROE US, male vocalist — 74 wks

6 Sep 62 ●	SHEILA HMV POP 1060	3	14
6 Dec 62	SUSIE DARLIN' HMV POP 1092	37	5
21 Mar 63 ●	THE FOLK SINGER HMV POP 1138	4	13
26 Sep 63 ●	EVERYBODY HMV POP 1207	9	11
19 Dec 63	EVERYBODY (re-entry) HMV POP 1207	49	3
16 Apr 69 ★	DIZZY Stateside SS 2143	1	19
23 Jul 69	HEATHER HONEY Stateside SS 2152	24	9

ROFO UK, male instrumental / production duo — 3 wks

1 Aug 92	ROFO'S THEME PWL Continental PWLT 236	44	3

ROGER US, male vocalist — 8 wks

17 Oct 87	I WANT TO BE YOUR MAN Reprise W 8229	61	4
12 Nov 88	BOOM! THERE SHE WAS Virgin VS 1143 [1]	55	3
13 May 95	HIGH AS A KITE ffrr FCD 259 [2]	55	1

[1] Scritti Politti featuring Roger [2] One Tribe featuring Roger

Julie ROGERS UK, female vocalist — 38 wks

13 Aug 64 ●	THE WEDDING Mercury MF 820	3	23
10 Dec 64	LIKE A CHILD Mercury MF 838	21	9
25 Mar 65	HAWAIIAN WEDDING SONG Mercury MF 849	31	6

Kenny ROGERS US, male vocalist — 109 wks

18 Oct 69 ●	RUBY DON'T TAKE YOUR LOVE TO TOWN Reprise RS 20829 [1]	2	23
7 Feb 70 ●	SOMETHING'S BURNING Reprise RS 20888 [1]	8	14
30 Apr 77 ★	LUCILLE United Artists UP 36242	1	14
17 Sep 77	DAYTIME FRIENDS United Artists UP 36289	39	4
2 Jun 79	SHE BELIEVES IN ME United Artists UP 36533	42	7
26 Jan 80 ★	COWARD OF THE COUNTY United Artists UP 614	1	12
15 Nov 80	LADY United Artists UP635	12	12
12 Feb 83	WE'VE GOT TONIGHT Liberty UP 658 [2]	28	7
22 Oct 83	EYES THAT SEE IN THE DARK RCA 358	61	1
12 Nov 83 ●	ISLANDS IN THE STREAM RCA 378 [3]	7	15

[1] Kenny Rogers and the First Edition [2] Kenny Rogers and Sheena Easton
[3] Kenny Rogers and Dolly Parton

ROKOTTO UK, male vocal / instrumental group — 10 wks

22 Oct 77	BOOGIE ON UP State STAT 62	40	4
10 Jun 78	FUNK THEORY State STAT 80	49	6

ROLLING STONES UK, male vocal / instrumental group — 360 wks

25 Jul 63	COME ON Decca F 11675	21	14
14 Nov 63	I WANNA BE YOUR MAN Decca F 11764	12	16
27 Feb 64 ●	NOT FADE AWAY Decca F 11845	3	15
2 Jul 64 ★	IT'S ALL OVER NOW Decca F 11934	1	15
19 Nov 64 ★	LITTLE RED ROOSTER Decca F 12014	1	12
4 Mar 65 ★	THE LAST TIME Decca F 12104	1	13
26 Aug 65 ★	(I CAN'T GET NO) SATISFACTION Decca F 12220	1	12
28 Oct 65 ★	GET OFF OF MY CLOUD Decca F 12263	1	12
10 Feb 66 ●	NINETEENTH NERVOUS BREAKDOWN Decca F 12331	2	8
19 May 66 ★	PAINT IT, BLACK Decca F 12395	1	10
29 Sep 66 ●	HAVE YOU SEEN YOUR MOTHER BABY STANDING IN THE SHADOW Decca F 12497	5	8
19 Jan 67 ●	LET'S SPEND THE NIGHT TOGETHER / RUBY TUESDAY Decca F 12546	3	10
23 Aug 67 ●	WE LOVE YOU / DANDELION Decca F 12654	8	8
29 May 68 ★	JUMPING JACK FLASH Decca F 12782	1	11
9 Jul 69 ★	HONKY TONK WOMEN Decca F 12952	1	17
24 Apr 71 ●	BROWN SUGAR / BITCH / LET IT ROCK Rolling Stones RS 19100	2	13
3 Jul 71	STREET FIGHTING MAN Decca F 13195	21	8
29 Apr 72 ●	TUMBLING DICE Rolling Stones RS 19103	5	8
1 Sep 73 ●	ANGIE Rolling Stones RS 19105	5	10
3 Aug 74 ●	IT'S ONLY ROCK AND ROLL Rolling Stones RS 19114	10	7
20 Sep 75	OUT OF TIME Decca F 13597	45	2
1 May 76 ●	FOOL TO CRY Rolling Stones RS 19121	6	10
3 Jun 78 ●	MISS YOU / FAR AWAY EYES Rolling Stones EMI 2802	3	13
30 Sep 78	RESPECTABLE Rolling Stones EMI 2861	23	9
5 Jul 80 ●	EMOTIONAL RESCUE Rolling Stones RSR 105	9	8
4 Oct 80	SHE'S SO COLD Rolling Stones RSR 106	33	6
29 Aug 81 ●	START ME UP Rolling Stones RSR 108	7	9
12 Dec 81	WAITING ON A FRIEND Rolling Stones RSR 109	50	6
12 Jun 82	GOING TO A GO GO Rolling Stones RSR 110	26	6
2 Oct 82	TIME IS ON MY SIDE Rolling Stones RSR 111	62	2
12 Nov 83	UNDERCOVER OF THE NIGHT Rolling Stones RSR 113	11	9
11 Feb 84	SHE WAS HOT Rolling Stones RSR 114	42	4
21 Jul 84	BROWN SUGAR (re-issue) Rolling Stones SUGAR 1	58	2
15 Mar 86	HARLEM SHUFFLE Rolling Stones A 6864	13	7
2 Sep 89	MIXED EMOTIONS Rolling Stones 655193 7	36	5
2 Dec 89	ROCK AND A HARD PLACE Rolling Stones 655422 7	63	1
23 Jun 90	PAINT IT, BLACK (re-issue) London LON 264	61	3
30 Jun 90	ALMOST HEAR YOU SIGH Rolling Stones 656065 7	31	5
30 Mar 91	HIGHWIRE Rolling Stones 6567567	29	4
1 Jun 91	RUBY TUESDAY (LIVE) Rolling Stones 6568927	59	2
16 Jul 94	LOVE IS STRONG Virgin VSCDT 1503	14	5
8 Oct 94	YOU GOT ME ROCKING Virgin VSCDG 1518	23	3
10 Dec 94	OUT OF TEARS Virgin VSCDT 1524	36	4
15 Jul 95	I GO WILD Virgin VSCDX 1539	29	3
11 Nov 95	LIKE A ROLLING STONE Virgin VSCDT 1562	12	5

Far Away Eyes was listed from 15 Jul 78 with a peak position of 10.

ROLLINS BAND US, male vocal / instrumental group — 4 wks

12 Sep 92	TEARING Imago 72787250187	54	2
10 Sep 94	LIAR / DISCONNECTED Imago 74321213052	27	2

ROLLO UK, male producer – Rollo Armstrong — 8 wks

29 Jan 94	GET OFF YOUR HIGH HORSE Cheeky CHEKCD 003 [1]	43	2
1 Oct 94	GET OFF YOUR HIGH HORSE (re-entry) Cheeky CHEKCD 003 [1]	47	2
10 Jun 95	LOVE LOVE LOVE – HERE I COME Cheeky CHEKCD 007 [2]	32	2
8 Jun 96	LET THIS BE A PRAYER Cheeky CHEKCD 013 [3]	26	2

[1] Rollo Goes Camping [2] Rollo Goes Mystic [3] Rollo Goes Spiritual with Pauline Taylor

ROMAN HOLIDAY
UK, male vocal / instrumental group　　　　**19 wks**

2 Apr 83	**STAND BY** *Jive JIVE 31*	**61**	3
2 Jul 83	**DON'T TRY TO STOP IT** *Jive JIVE 39*	**14**	9
24 Sep 83	**MOTORMANIA** *Jive JIVE 49*	**40**	7

ROMAN NUMERALS – *See Vic REEVES*

ROMANTICS – *See RUBY and the ROMANTICS*

Max ROMEO *Jamaica, male vocalist*　　　　**25 wks**

28 May 69	● **WET DREAM** *Unity UN 503*	**10**	24
29 Nov 69	**WET DREAM (re-entry)** *Unity UN 503*	**50**	1

RONDO VENEZIANO *Italy, orchestra*　　　　**3 wks**

22 Oct 83	**LA SERENISSIMA (THEME FROM 'VENICE IN PERIL')** *Ferroway 7 RON 1*	**58**	3

RONETTES *US, female vocal group*　　　　**34 wks**

17 Oct 63	● **BE MY BABY** *London HLU 9793*	**4**	13
9 Jan 64	**BABY I LOVE YOU** *London HLU 9826*	**11**	14
27 Aug 64	**BEST PART OF BREAKING UP** *London HLU 9905*	**43**	4
8 Oct 64	**DO I LOVE YOU** *London HLU 9922*	**35**	4

RONNETTE – *See FIDELFATTI featuring RONNETTE*

Mick RONSON with Joe ELLIOTT
UK, male instrumental / vocal duo　　　　**1 wk**

7 May 94	**DON'T LOOK DOWN** *Epic 6603582*	**55**	1

Linda RONSTADT *US, female vocalist*　　　　**34 wks**

8 May 76	**TRACKS OF MY TEARS** *Asylum K 13034*	**42**	3
28 Jan 78	**BLUE BAYOU** *Asylum K 13106*	**35**	4
26 May 79	**ALISON** *Asylum K 13149*	**66**	2
11 Jul 87	● **SOMEWHERE OUT THERE (FROM THE MOVIE 'AN AMERICAN TAIL')** *MCA MCA 1132* [1]	**8**	13
11 Nov 89	● **DON'T KNOW MUCH** *Elektra EKR 100* [2]	**2**	12

[1] Linda Ronstadt and James Ingram [2] Linda Ronstadt featuring Aaron Neville

ROOFTOP SINGERS *US, male / female vocal group*　　　　**12 wks**

31 Jan 63	● **WALK RIGHT IN** *Fontana TF 271700*	**10**	12

Ralphi ROSARIO – *See Richie RICH*

Mykal ROSE – *See Shabba RANKS*

ROSE MARIE *UK, female vocalist*　　　　**5 wks**

19 Nov 83	**WHEN I LEAVE THE WORLD BEHIND** *A1 284*	**75**	1
3 Dec 83	**WHEN I LEAVE THE WORLD BEHIND (re-entry)** *A1 284*	**63**	2
24 Dec 83	**WHEN I LEAVE THE WORLD BEHIND (2nd re-entry)** *A1 284*	**66**	2

ROSE OF ROMANCE ORCHESTRA *UK, orchestra*　　　　**1 wk**

9 Jan 82	**TARA'S THEME FROM 'GONE WITH THE WIND'** *BBC RESL 108*	**71**	1

ROSE ROYCE
US, male / female vocal / instrumental group　　　　**110 wks**

25 Dec 76	● **CAR WASH** *MCA 267*	**9**	12
22 Jan 77	**PUT YOUR MONEY WHERE YOUR MOUTH IS** *MCA 259* ..	**44**	5
2 Apr 77	**I WANNA GET NEXT TO YOU** *MCA 278*	**14**	8
24 Sep 77	**DO YOUR DANCE** *Whitfield K 17006*	**30**	6
14 Jan 78	● **WISHING ON A STAR** *Warner Bros. K 17060*	**3**	14
6 May 78	**IT MAKES YOU FEEL LIKE DANCIN'** *Warner Bros. K 17148*	**16**	10
16 Sep 78	● **LOVE DON'T LIVE HERE ANYMORE** *Whitfield K 17236* ..	**2**	10
3 Feb 79	**I'M IN LOVE (AND I LOVE THE FEELING)** *Whitfield K 17291*	**51**	4
17 Nov 79	**IS IT LOVE YOU'RE AFTER** *Whitfield K 17456*	**13**	13
8 Mar 80	**OOH BOY** *Whitfield K 17575*	**46**	7
21 Nov 81	**ROSE ROYCE EXPRESS** *Warner Bros. K 17875*	**52**	3
1 Sep 84	**MAGIC TOUCH** *Streetwave KHAN 21*	**43**	8
6 Apr 85	**LOVE ME RIGHT NOW** *Streetwave KHAN 39*	**60**	3
11 Jun 88	**CAR WASH / IS IT LOVE YOU'RE AFTER (re-issues)** *MCA MCA 1253*	**20**	7

ROSE TATTOO *Australia, male vocal / instrumental group*　　　　**4 wks**

11 Jul 81	**ROCK 'N' ROLL OUTLAW** *Carrere CAR 200*	**60**	4

Jimmy ROSELLI *US, male vocalist*　　　　**8 wks**

5 Mar 83	**WHEN YOUR OLD WEDDING RING WAS NEW** *A1 282* ..	**51**	5
20 Jun 87	**WHEN YOUR OLD WEDDING RING WAS NEW (re-issue)** *First Night SCORE 9*	**52**	3

Diana ROSS *US, female vocalist*　　　　**428 wks**

18 Jul 70	**REACH OUT AND TOUCH (SOMEBODY'S HAND)** *Tamla Motown TMG 743*	**33**	5
12 Sep 70	● **AIN'T NO MOUNTAIN HIGH ENOUGH** *Tamla Motown TMG 751*	**6**	12
3 Apr 71	● **REMEMBER ME** *Tamla Motown TMG 768*	**7**	12
31 Jul 71	★ **I'M STILL WAITING** *Tamla Motown TMG 781*	**1**	14
30 Oct 71	● **SURRENDER** *Tamla Motown TMG 792*	**10**	11
13 May 72	**DOOBEDOOD'NDOOBE DOOBEDOOD'NDOOBE** *Tamla Motown TMG 812*	**12**	9
14 Jul 73	● **TOUCH ME IN THE MORNING** *Tamla Motown TMG 861*	**9**	12
13 Oct 73	**TOUCH ME IN THE MORNING (re-entry)** *Tamla Motown TMG 861*	**50**	1
5 Jan 74	● **ALL OF MY LIFE** *Tamla Motown TMG 880*	**9**	13
23 Mar 74	● **YOU ARE EVERYTHING** *Tamla Motown TMG 890* [1]	**5**	12
4 May 74	**LAST TIME I SAW HIM** *Tamla Motown TMG 893*	**35**	4
20 Jul 74	**STOP LOOK LISTEN (TO YOUR HEART)** *Tamla Motown TMG 906* [1]	**25**	8
28 Sep 74	**LOVE ME** *Tamla Motown TMG 917*	**38**	5
29 Mar 75	**SORRY DOESN'T ALWAYS MAKE IT RIGHT** *Tamla Motown TMG 941*	**23**	9
3 Apr 76	● **THEME FROM MAHOGANY (DO YOU KNOW WHERE YOU'RE GOING TO)** *Tamla Motown TMG 1010*	**5**	8
24 Apr 76	● **LOVE HANGOVER** *Tamla Motown TMG 1024*	**10**	10
10 Jul 76	**I THOUGHT IT TOOK A LITTLE TIME** *Tamla Motown TMG 1032*	**32**	5
16 Oct 76	**I'M STILL WAITING (re-issue)** *Tamla Motown TMG 1041*	**41**	4
19 Nov 77	**GETTIN' READY FOR LOVE** *Motown TMG 1090*	**23**	7
22 Jul 78	**LOVIN' LIVIN' AND GIVIN'** *Motown TMG 1112*	**54**	6
18 Nov 78	**EASE ON DOWN THE ROAD** *MCA 396* [2]	**45**	4
24 Feb 79	**POPS WE LOVE YOU** *Motown TMG 1136* [3]	**66**	5
21 Jul 79	**THE BOSS** *Motown TMG 1150*	**40**	7
6 Oct 79	**NO ONE GETS THE PRIZE** *Motown TMG 1160*	**59**	3
24 Nov 79	**IT'S MY HOUSE** *Motown TMG 1169*	**32**	10
19 Jul 80	● **UPSIDE DOWN** *Motown TMG 1195*	**2**	12
20 Sep 80	● **MY OLD PIANO** *Motown TMG 1202*	**5**	9
15 Nov 80	**I'M COMING OUT** *Motown TMG 1210*	**13**	10
17 Jan 81	**IT'S MY TURN** *Motown TMG 1217*	**16**	8
28 Mar 81	**ONE MORE CHANCE** *Motown TMG 1227*	**49**	5

13 Jun 81	CRYIN' MY HEART OUT FOR YOU *Motown TMG 1233* ..58		3
12 Sep 81	● ENDLESS LOVE *Motown TMG 1240* [4] 7		12
7 Nov 81	● WHY DO FOOLS FALL IN LOVE *Capitol CL 226* 4		12
23 Jan 82	TENDERNESS *Motown TMG 1248* 73		1
30 Jan 82	MIRROR MIRROR *Capitol CL 234* 36		5
6 Feb 82	TENDERNESS (re-entry) *Motown TMG 1248* 75		1
29 May 82	● WORK THAT BODY *Capitol CL 241* 7		11
7 Aug 82	IT'S NEVER TOO LATE *Capitol CL 256* 41		4
23 Oct 82	MUSCLES *Capitol CL 268* 15		9
15 Jan 83	SO CLOSE *Capitol CL 277* 43		4
23 Jul 83	PIECES OF ICE *Capitol CL 298* 46		3
7 Jul 84	ALL OF YOU *CBS A 4522* [5] 43		8
15 Sep 84	TOUCH BY TOUCH *Capitol CL 337* 47		6
28 Sep 85	EATEN ALIVE *Capitol CL 372* 71		1
25 Jan 86	★ CHAIN REACTION *Capitol CL 386* 1		17
3 May 86	EXPERIENCE *Capitol CL 400* 47		3
13 Jun 87	DIRTY LOOKS *EMI EM 2* 49		3
8 Oct 88	MR. LEE *EMI EM 73* 58		2
26 Nov 88	LOVE HANGOVER (re-mix) *Motown ZB 42307* 75		1
6 May 89	WORKIN' OVERTIME *EMI EM 91* 32		5
29 Jul 89	PARADISE *EMI EM 94* 61		2
7 Jul 90	I'M STILL WAITING (re-mix) *Motown ZB 43781* ..21		6
30 Nov 91	● WHEN YOU TELL ME THAT YOU LOVE ME *EMI EM 217* ..2		11
15 Feb 92	THE FORCE BEHIND THE POWER *EMI EM 221* 27		3
20 Jun 92	● ONE SHINING MOMENT *EMI EM 239* 10		8
28 Nov 92	IF WE HOLD ON TOGETHER *EMI EM 257* 11		10
13 Mar 93	HEART (DON'T CHANGE MY MIND) *EMI CDEM 261* 31		3
9 Oct 93	CHAIN REACTION (re-issue) *EMI CDEM 290* 20		5
11 Dec 93	YOUR LOVE *EMI CDEM 299* 14		8
2 Apr 94	THE BEST YEARS OF MY LIFE *EMI CDEM 305* 28		4
9 Jul 94	WHY DO FOOLS FALL IN LOVE (re-mix) / I'M COMING OUT (re-issue) *EMI CDEM 332* 36		4
2 Sep 95	TAKE ME HIGHER *EMI CDEM 388* 32		4
25 Nov 95	I'M GONE *EMI CDEM 402* 36		3
17 Feb 96	I WILL SURVIVE *EMI CDEM 415* [6] 14		4
21 Dec 96	IN THE ONES YOU LOVE *EMI CDEM 457* 34		2

[1] Diana Ross and Marvin Gaye [2] Diana Ross and Michael Jackson
[3] Diana Ross, Marvin Gaye, Smokey Robinson and Stevie Wonder
[4] Diana Ross and Lionel Richie [5] Julio Iglesias and Diana Ross [6] Diana

See also Supremes.

Ricky ROSS *UK, male vocalist*   3 wks

18 May 96	RADIO ON *Epic 6631352* 35		2
10 Aug 96	GOOD EVENING PHILADELPHIA *Epic 6635335* 58		1

Francis ROSSI *UK, male vocalist*   6 wks

11 May 85	MODERN ROMANCE (I WANT TO FALL IN LOVE AGAIN) *Vertigo FROS 1* [1] 54		4
3 Aug 96	GIVE MYSELF TO LOVE *Virgin VSCDT 1594* [2] 42		2

[1] Francis Rossi and Bernard Frost [2] Francis Rossi of Status Quo

See also Status Quo.

Laurent ROSSI – See *BIMBO JET*

Nini ROSSO *Italy, male instrumentalist – trumpet*   14 wks

26 Aug 65	● IL SILENZIO *Durium DRS 54000* 8		14

David Lee ROTH *US, male vocalist*   15 wks

23 Feb 85	CALIFORNIA GIRLS *Warner Bros. W 9102* 68		2
5 Mar 88	JUST LIKE PARADISE *Warner Bros. W 8119* 27		7
3 Sep 88	DAMN GOOD / STAND UP *Warner Bros. W 7753* 72		1
12 Jan 91	A LIL' AIN'T ENOUGH *Warner Bros. W 0002* 32		3
19 Feb 94	SHE'S MY MACHINE *Reprise W 0229CD* 64		1
28 May 94	NIGHT LIFE *Reprise W 0249CD* 72		1

ROTTERDAM TERMINATION SOURCE
Holland, male instrumental / production duo   6 wks

7 Nov 92	POING *SEP EDGE 74* 27		4
25 Dec 93	MERRY X-MESS *React CDREACT 33* 73		2

ROULA – See *20 FINGERS*

ROULETTES – See Adam *FAITH*

Robert ROUNSEVILLE – See *VARIOUS ARTISTS (EPs & LPs)* – Carousel Soundtrack

Demis ROUSSOS *Greece, male vocalist*   44 wks

22 Nov 75	● HAPPY TO BE ON AN ISLAND IN THE SUN *Philips 6042 033* 5		10
28 Feb 76	CAN'T SAY HOW MUCH I LOVE YOU *Philips 6042 114* ..35		5
26 Jun 76	★ THE ROUSSOS PHENOMENON EP *Philips DEMIS 001* 1		12
2 Oct 76	● WHEN FOREVER HAS GONE *Philips 6042 186* 2		10
19 Mar 77	BECAUSE *Philips 6042 245* 39		4
18 Jun 77	KYRILA (EP) *Philips Demis 002* 33		3

Tracks on The Roussos Phenomenon EP: Forever And Ever / Sing An Ode To Love / So Dreamy / My Friend The Wind. Tracks on Kyrila (EP): Kyrila / I'm Gonna Fall In Love / I Dig You / Sister Emilyne.

ROUTERS *US, male instrumental group*   7 wks

27 Dec 62	LET'S GO *Warner Bros. WB 77* 32		7

Maria ROWE *UK, female vocalist*   2 wks

20 May 95	SEXUAL *ffrr FCD 248* 67		2

ROWETTA – See *OPEN ARMS featuring ROWETTA; VARIOUS ARTISTS (EPs and LPs)* – The Further Adventures Of North EP

Kevin ROWLAND – See *DEXY'S MIDNIGHT RUNNERS*

John ROWLES *New Zealand, male vocalist*   28 wks

13 Mar 68	● IF I ONLY HAD TIME *MCA MU 1000* 3		18
19 Jun 68	HUSH NOT A WORD TO MARY *MCA MU 1023* 12		10

ROXETTE *Sweden, male / female vocal / instrumental duo* 135 wks

22 Apr 89	● THE LOOK *EMI EM 87* 7		10
15 Jul 89	DRESSED FOR SUCCESS *EMI EM 96* 48		5
28 Oct 89	LISTEN TO YOUR HEART *EMI EM 108* 62		3
2 Jun 90	● IT MUST HAVE BEEN LOVE *EMI EM 141* 3		14
11 Aug 90	● LISTEN TO YOUR HEART (re-issue) / DANGEROUS *EMI EM 149* 6		9
27 Oct 90	DRESSED FOR SUCCESS (re-issue) *EMI EM 162* 18		7
9 Mar 91	● JOYRIDE *EMI EM 177* 4		10
11 May 91	FADING LIKE A FLOWER *EMI EM 190* 12		6
7 Sep 91	THE BIG L *EMI EM 204* 21		6
23 Nov 91	SPENDING MY TIME *EMI EM 215* 22		4
28 Mar 92	CHURCH OF YOUR HEART *EMI EM 227* 21		4
1 Aug 92	HOW DO YOU DO! *EMI EM 241* 13		7
7 Nov 92	QUEEN OF RAIN *EMI EM 253* 28		4
24 Jul 93	ALMOST UNREAL *EMI EM 268* 7		9
18 Sep 93	● IT MUST HAVE BEEN LOVE (re-issue) *EMI CDEM 285* 10		7
26 Mar 94	SLEEPING IN MY CAR *EMI CDEM 314* 14		6
4 Jun 94	CRASH! BOOM! BANG! *EMI CDEM 324* 26		5
17 Sep 94	FIREWORKS *EMI CDEM 345* 30		4
3 Dec 94	RUN TO YOU *EMI CDEM 360* 27		6
8 Apr 95	VULNERABLE *EMI CDEM 369* 44		2
25 Nov 95	THE LOOK (re-mix) *EMI CDEM 406* 28		3
30 Mar 96	YOU DON'T UNDERSTAND ME *EMI CDEM 418* 42		2
20 Jul 96	JUNE AFTERNOON *EMI CDEM 437* 52		1

ROXY MUSIC UK, male vocal / instrumental group — 155 wks

19 Aug 72	● VIRGINIA PLAIN Island WIP 6144	4	12
10 Mar 73	● PYJAMARAMA Island WIP 6159	10	12
17 Nov 73	● STREET LIFE Island WIP 6173	9	12
12 Oct 74	ALL I WANT IS YOU Island WIP 6208	12	8
11 Oct 75	● LOVE IS THE DRUG Island WIP 6248	2	10
27 Dec 75	BOTH ENDS BURNING Island WIP 6262	25	7
22 Oct 77	VIRGINIA PLAIN (re-issue) Polydor 2001 739	11	6
3 Mar 79	TRASH Polydor POSP 32	40	6
28 Apr 79	● DANCE AWAY Polydor POSP 44	2	14
11 Aug 79	● ANGEL EYES Polydor POSP 67	4	11
17 May 80	● OVER YOU Polydor POSP 93	5	9
2 Aug 80	● OH YEAH (ON THE RADIO) Polydor 2001 972	5	8
8 Nov 80	● THE SAME OLD SCENE Polydor ROXY 1	12	7
21 Feb 81	★ JEALOUS GUY EG ROXY 2	1	11
3 Apr 82	● MORE THAN THIS EG ROXY 3	6	8
19 Jun 82	AVALON EG ROXY 4	13	6
25 Sep 82	TAKE A CHANCE WITH ME EG ROXY 5	26	6
27 Apr 96	LOVE IS THE DRUG (re-mix) EG VSCDT 1580	33	2

Billy Joe ROYAL US, male vocalist — 18 wks

7 Oct 65	DOWN IN THE BOONDOCKS CBS 201802	38	4

The Central Band of the ROYAL AIR FORCE, Conductor W/Cdr. A.E. SIMS O.B.E.
UK, military band — 1 wk

21 Oct 55	THE DAMBUSTERS MARCH HMV B 10877	18	1

ROYAL GUARDSMEN
US, male vocal / instrumental group — 17 wks

19 Jan 67	● SNOOPY VS. THE RED BARON Stateside SS 574	8	13
6 Apr 67	RETURN OF THE RED BARON Stateside SS 2010	37	4

ROYAL HOUSE
US, male / female vocal / instrumental group — 18 wks

10 Sep 88	CAN YOU PARTY Champion CHAMP 79	14	14
7 Jan 89	YEAH! BUDDY Champion CHAMP 91	35	4

ROYAL PHILHARMONIC ORCHESTRA arranged and conducted by Louis CLARK UK, orchestra and conductor — 19 wks

25 Jul 81	● HOOKED ON CLASSICS RCA 109	2	11
24 Oct 81	HOOKED ON CAN-CAN RCA 151	47	3
10 Jul 82	BBC WORLD CUP GRANDSTAND BBC RESL 116	61	3
7 Aug 82	IF YOU KNEW SOUSA (AND FRIENDS) RCA 256	71	2

See also Elvis Costello. Louis Clark did not conduct the third hit.

The Pipes and Drums and Military Band of the ROYAL SCOTS DRAGOON GUARDS
UK, military band — 43 wks

1 Apr 72	★ AMAZING GRACE RCA 2191	1	24
19 Aug 72	HEYKENS SERENADE / THE DAY IS ENDED RCA 2251	30	7
2 Dec 72	LITTLE DRUMMER BOY RCA 2301	13	9
23 Dec 72	AMAZING GRACE (re-entry) RCA 2191	42	3

ROYALLE DELITE US, female vocal group — 6 wks

14 Sep 85	(I'LL BE A) FREAK FOR YOU Streetwave KHAN 51	45	6

Lita ROZA UK, female vocalist — 18 wks

13 Mar 53	★ (HOW MUCH IS) THAT DOGGIE IN THE WINDOW Decca F 10070	1	11
7 Oct 55	HEY THERE Decca F 10611	17	2
23 Mar 56	JIMMY UNKNOWN Decca F 10679	15	5

See also Various Artists (EPs & LPs) – All Star Hit Parade.

ROZALLA Zimbabwe, female vocalist — 48 wks

27 Apr 91	FAITH (IN THE POWER OF LOVE) Pulse 8 LOSE 7	65	2
7 Sep 91	● EVERYBODY'S FREE (TO FEEL GOOD) Pulse 8 LOSE 13	6	11
16 Nov 91	FAITH (IN THE POWER OF LOVE) (re-issue) Pulse 8 LOSE 15	11	6
22 Feb 92	ARE YOU READY TO FLY Pulse 8 LOSE 21	14	6
9 May 92	LOVE BREAKDOWN Pulse 8 LOSE 25	65	2
15 Aug 92	IN 4 CHOONS LATER Pulse 8 LOSE 29	50	2
30 Oct 93	DON'T PLAY WITH ME Pulse 8 CDLOSE 52	50	1
5 Feb 94	I LOVE MUSIC Epic 6598932	18	5
6 Aug 94	THIS TIME I FOUND LOVE Epic 6603742	33	3
29 Oct 94	YOU NEVER LOVE THE SAME WAY TWICE Epic 6609052	16	5
4 Mar 95	BABY Epic 6611955	26	3
31 Aug 96	EVERYBODY'S FREE (re-mix) Pulse 8 CDLOSE 110	30	2

RTE CONCERT ORCHESTRA – See Bill WHELAN featuring ANUNA and the RTE CONCERT ORCHESTRA

RUBETTES UK, male vocal / instrumental group — 68 wks

4 May 74	★ SUGAR BABY LOVE Polydor 2058 442	1	10
13 Jul 74	TONIGHT Polydor 2058 499	12	9
16 Nov 74	● JUKE BOX JIVE Polydor 2058 529	3	12
8 Mar 75	● I CAN DO IT State STAT 1	7	9
21 Jun 75	FOE-DEE-O-DEE State STAT 7	15	6
22 Nov 75	LITTLE DARLING State STAT 13	30	5
1 May 76	YOU'RE THE REASON WHY State STAT 20	28	4
25 Sep 76	UNDER ONE ROOF State STAT 27	40	3
12 Feb 77	● BABY I KNOW State STAT 37	10	10

RUBY and the ROMANTICS
US, female / male vocal group — 6 wks

28 Mar 63	OUR DAY WILL COME London HLR 9679	38	6

RUDE BOY OF HOUSE – See HOUSEMASTER BOYZ and the RUDE BOY OF HOUSE

RUDIES – See Freddie NOTES and the RUDIES

Frances RUFFELLE UK, female vocalist — 6 wks

16 Apr 94	LONELY SYMPHONY Virgin VSCDT 1499	25	6

Bruce RUFFIN Jamaica, male vocalist — 23 wks

1 May 71	RAIN Trojan TR 7814	19	11
24 Jun 72	● MAD ABOUT YOU Rhino RNO 101	9	12

David RUFFIN US, male vocalist — 10 wks

17 Jan 76	● WALK AWAY FROM LOVE Tamla Motown TMG 1017	10	8
21 Sep 85	A NIGHT AT THE APOLLO LIVE! RCA PB 49935 [1]	58	2

[1] Hall and Oates featuring David Ruffin and Eddie Kendrick

Jimmy RUFFIN *US, male vocalist* — **106 wks**

27 Oct 66	● WHAT BECOMES OF THE BROKENHEARTED		
	Tamla Motown TMG 577	**10**	15
9 Feb 67	I'VE PASSED THIS WAY BEFORE		
	Tamla Motown TMG 593	**29**	7
20 Apr 67	GONNA GIVE HER ALL THE LOVE I'VE GOT		
	Tamla Motown TMG 603	**26**	6
9 Aug 69	I'VE PASSED THIS WAY BEFORE (re-issue)		
	Tamla Motown TMG 703	**33**	6
28 Feb 70	● FAREWELL IS A LONELY SOUND		
	Tamla Motown TMG 726	**8**	16
4 Jul 70	● I'LL SAY FOREVER MY LOVE		
	Tamla Motown TMG 740	**7**	12
17 Oct 70	● IT'S WONDERFUL (TO BE LOVED BY YOU)		
	Tamla Motown TMG 753	**6**	14
27 Jul 74	● WHAT BECOMES OF THE BROKENHEARTED (re-issue)		
	Tamla Motown TMG 911	**4**	12
2 Nov 74	FAREWELL IS A LONELY SOUND (re-issue)		
	Tamla Motown TMG 922	**30**	5
16 Nov 74	TELL ME WHAT YOU WANT *Polydor 2058 433*	**39**	4
3 May 80	● HOLD ON TO MY LOVE *RSO 57*	**7**	8
26 Jan 85	THERE WILL NEVER BE ANOTHER YOU		
	EMI 5541	**68**	1

RUFFNECK featuring YAVAHN
US, male / female vocal / instrumental group — **5 wks**

| 11 Nov 95 | EVERYBODY BE SOMEBODY *Positiva CDTIV 46* | **13** | 4 |
| 7 Sep 96 | MOVE YOUR BODY *Positiva CDTIV 61* | **60** | 1 |

RUFUS – *See Chaka KHAN*

Barbara RUICK – *See VARIOUS ARTISTS (EPs & LPs) – Carousel Soundtrack*

RUKMANI – *See SNAP*

RUMOUR – *See Graham PARKER and the RUMOUR*

RUMPLE-STILTS-SKIN
US, male / female vocal / instrumental group — **4 wks**

| 24 Sep 83 | I THINK I WANT TO DANCE WITH YOU | | |
| | *Polydor POSP 649* | **51** | 4 |

RUN DMC *US, male rap group* — **38 wks**

19 Jul 86	MY ADIDAS / PETER PIPER *London LON 101*	**62**	2
6 Sep 86	● WALK THIS WAY *London LON 104*	**8**	10
7 Feb 87	YOU BE ILLIN' *Profile LON 118*	**42**	4
30 May 87	IT'S TRICKY *Profile LON 130*	**16**	7
12 Dec 87	CHRISTMAS IN HOLLIS *Profile LON 163*	**56**	4
21 May 88	RUN'S HOUSE *London LON 177*	**37**	4
2 Sep 89	GHOSTBUSTERS *MCA Profile MCA 1360*	**65**	2
1 Dec 90	WHAT'S IT ALL ABOUT *Profile PROF 315*	**48**	3
27 Mar 93	DOWN WITH THE KING *Profile PROFCD 39*	**69**	2

RUN TINGS *UK, male instrumental / production duo* — **1 wk**

| 16 May 92 | FIRES BURNING *Suburban Base SUBBASE 009* | **58** | 1 |

See also Various Artists (EPs & LPs) – Subplates Volume 1.

Todd RUNDGREN *US, male vocalist* — **8 wks**

30 Jun 73	I SAW THE LIGHT *Bearsville K 15506*	**36**	6
14 Dec 85	LOVING YOU'S A DIRTY JOB BUT SOMEBODY'S		
	GOTTA DO IT *CBS A 6662* [1]	**73**	2

[1] Bonnie Tyler, guest vocals Todd Rundgren

RUNRIG *UK, male vocal / instrumental group* — **25 wks**

29 Sep 90	CAPTURE THE HEART EP *Chrysalis CHS 3594*	**49**	2
7 Sep 91	HEARTHAMMER (EP) *Chrysalis CHS 3754*	**25**	4
9 Nov 91	FLOWER OF THE WEST *Chrysalis CHS 3805*	**43**	2
6 Mar 93	WONDERFUL *Chrysalis CDCHS 3952*	**29**	3
15 May 93	THE GREATEST FLAME *Chrysalis CDCHS 3975*	**36**	3
7 Jan 95	THIS TIME OF YEAR *Chrysalis CDCHS 5018*	**38**	2
6 May 95	AN UBHAL AS AIRDE (THE HIGHEST APPLE)		
	Chrysalis CDCHS 5021	**18**	5
4 Nov 95	THINGS THAT ARE *Chrysalis CDCHS 5029*	**40**	2
12 Oct 96	RHYTHM OF MY HEART *Chrysalis CDCHS 5035*	**24**	2

Tracks on Capture The Heart EP: Stepping Down The Glory Road / Satellite Flood / Harvest Moon / The Apple Came Down. Tracks on Hearthammer (EP): Hearthammer / Pride Of The Summer (Live) / Loch Lomond (Live) / Solus Na Madainn.

RuPAUL *US, male vocalist* — **16 wks**

26 Jun 93	SUPERMODEL (YOU BETTER WORK)		
	Union City UCRD 21	**39**	4
18 Sep 93	HOUSE OF LOVE / BACK TO MY ROOTS		
	Union City UCRD 23	**40**	2
22 Jan 94	SUPERMODEL (re-mix) / LITTLE DRUMMER BOY		
	Union City UCRD 25	**61**	2
26 Feb 94	● DON'T GO BREAKING MY HEART (re-mix)		
	Rocket EJCD 33 [1]	**7**	7
21 May 94	HOUSE OF LOVE *Union City UCRDG 29*	**68**	1

[1] Elton John with RuPaul

RUSH *Canada, male vocal / instrumental group* — **43 wks**

11 Feb 78	CLOSER TO THE HEART *Mercury RUSH 7*	**36**	3
15 Mar 80	SPIRIT OF RADIO *Mercury RADIO 7*	**13**	7
28 Mar 81	VITAL SIGNS / A PASSAGE TO BANGKOK		
	Mercury VITAL7	**41**	4
31 Oct 81	TOM SAWYER *Exit EXIT 7*	**25**	6
4 Sep 82	NEW WORLD MAN *Mercury RUSH 8*	**42**	3
30 Oct 82	SUBDIVISIONS *Mercury RUSH 9*	**53**	2
7 May 83	COUNTDOWN / NEW WORLD MAN *Mercury RUSH 10*	**36**	5
26 May 84	THE BODY ELECTRIC *Vertigo RUSH 11*	**56**	3
12 Oct 85	THE BIG MONEY *Vertigo RUSH 12*	**46**	3
31 Oct 87	TIME STAND STILL *Vertigo RUSH 13* [1]	**42**	3
23 Apr 88	PRIME MOVER *Vertigo RUSH 14*	**43**	3
7 Mar 92	ROLL THE BONES *Atlantic A 7524*	**49**	1

[1] Rush with Aimee Mann

New World Man on RUSH 10 is a live version of RUSH 8.

Donell RUSH *US, male vocalist* — **1 wk**

| 5 Dec 92 | SYMPHONY *ID 6587977* | **66** | 1 |

Jennifer RUSH *US, female vocalist* — **58 wks**

29 Jun 85	★ THE POWER OF LOVE *CBS A 5003*	**1**	32
14 Dec 85	RING OF ICE *CBS A 4745*	**14**	10
20 Dec 86	THE POWER OF LOVE (re-entry) *CBS A 5003*	**55**	4
20 Jun 87	FLAMES OF PARADISE *CBS 650865 7* [1]	**59**	3
27 May 89	TILL I LOVED YOU *CBS 654843 7* [2]	**24**	9

[1] Jennifer Rush and Elton John [2] Placido Domingo and Jennifer Rush

Patrice RUSHEN *US, female vocalist* — **25 wks**

1 Mar 80	HAVEN'T YOU HEARD *Elektra K 12414*	**62**	3
24 Jan 81	NEVER GONNA GIVE YOU UP (WON'T LET YOU BE)		
	Elektra K 12494	**66**	3

24 Apr 82	● **FORGET ME NOTS** Elektra K 13173	**8**	11
10 Jul 82	**I WAS TIRED OF BEING ALONE** Elektra K 13184	**39**	5
9 Jun 84	**FEELS SO REAL (WON'T LET GO)** Elektra E 9742	**51**	3

Brenda RUSSELL US, female vocalist　　17 wks

19 Apr 80	**SO GOOD SO RIGHT / IN THE THICK OF IT** A & M AM 7515	**51**	5
12 Mar 88	**PIANO IN THE DARK** Breakout USA 623	**23**	12

Paul RUTHERFORD UK, male vocalist　　6 wks

8 Oct 88	**GET REAL** Fourth & Broadway BRW 113	**47**	3
19 Aug 89	**OH WORLD** Fourth & Broadway BRW 136	**61**	3

RUTHLESS RAP ASSASSINS UK, male rappers　　2 wks

9 Jun 90	**JUST MELLOW** Syncopate SY 35	**75**	1
1 Sep 90	**AND IT WASN'T A DREAM** Syncopate SY 38	**75**	1

RUTLES UK, male vocal group　　5 wks

15 Apr 78	**I MUST BE IN LOVE** Warner Bros. K 17125	**39**	3
13 May 78	**I MUST BE IN LOVE (re-entry)** Warner Bros. K 17125	**64**	1
16 Nov 96	**SHANGRI-LA** Virgin America VUSCD 117	**68**	1

RUTS UK, male vocal / instrumental group　　28 wks

16 Jun 79	● **BABYLON'S BURNING** Virgin VS 271	**7**	11
8 Sep 79	**SOMETHING THAT I SAID** Virgin VS 285	**29**	5
19 Apr 80	**STARING AT THE RUDE BOYS** Virgin VS 327	**22**	8
30 Aug 80	**WEST ONE (SHINE ON ME)** Virgin VS 370	**43**	4

Barry RYAN UK, male vocalist　　33 wks

23 Oct 68	● **ELOISE** MGM 1442	**2**	12
19 Feb 69	**LOVE IS LOVE** MGM 1464	**25**	4
4 Oct 69	**HUNT** Polydor 56 348	**34**	5
21 Feb 70	**MAGICAL SPIEL** Polydor 56 370	**49**	1
16 May 70	**KITSCH** Polydor 2001 035	**37**	6
15 Jan 72	**CAN'T LET YOU GO** Polydor 2001 256	**32**	5

See also Paul and Barry Ryan.

Marion RYAN UK, female vocalist　　11 wks

24 Jan 58	● **LOVE ME FOREVER** Pye Nixa N 15121	**5**	11

Paul and Barry RYAN UK, male vocal duo　　43 wks

11 Nov 65	**DON'T BRING ME YOUR HEARTACHES** Decca F 12260	**13**	9
3 Feb 66	**HAVE PITY ON THE BOY** Decca F 12319	**18**	6
12 May 66	**I LOVE HER** Decca F 12391	**17**	8
14 Jul 66	**I LOVE HOW YOU LOVE ME** Decca F 12445	**21**	7
29 Sep 66	**HAVE YOU EVER LOVED SOMEBODY** Decca F 12494	**49**	1
8 Dec 66	**MISSY MISSY** Decca F 12520	**43**	4
2 Mar 67	**KEEP IT OUT OF SIGHT** Decca F 12567	**30**	6
29 Jun 67	**CLAIRE** Decca F 12633	**47**	2

See also Barry Ryan.

Rebekah RYAN UK, female vocalist　　4 wks

18 May 96	**YOU LIFT ME UP** MCA MCSTD 40022	**26**	3
7 Sep 96	**JUST A LITTLE BIT OF LOVE** MCA MCSTD 40063	**51**	1

Bobby RYDELL US, male vocalist　　60 wks

10 Mar 60	● **WILD ONE** Columbia DB 4429	**7**	14
23 Jun 60	**WILD ONE (re-entry)** Columbia DB 4429	**47**	1
30 Jun 60	**SWINGING SCHOOL** Columbia DB 4471	**44**	1
1 Sep 60	**VOLARE** Columbia DB 4495	**46**	1
15 Sep 60	**VOLARE (re-entry)** Columbia DB 4495	**22**	5
15 Dec 60	**SWAY** Columbia DB 4545	**12**	13
23 Mar 61	**GOOD TIME BABY** Columbia DB 4600	**42**	7
19 Apr 62	**TEACH ME TO TWIST** Columbia DB 4802 [1]	**45**	1
20 Dec 62	**JINGLE BELL ROCK** Cameo Parkway C 205 [1]	**40**	3
23 May 63	**FORGET HIM** Cameo Parkway C 108	**13**	14

[1] Chubby Checker and Bobby Rydell

Mitch RYDER and the DETROIT WHEELS
US, male vocalist, male vocal / instrumental backing group　　5 wks

10 Feb 66	**JENNY TAKE A RIDE** Stateside SS 481	**44**	1
24 Feb 66	**JENNY TAKE A RIDE (re-entry)** Stateside SS 481	**33**	4

Shaun RYDER – See HEADS with Shaun RYDER

RYTHM SYNDICATE
US, male vocal / instrumental group　　5 wks

27 Jul 91	**P.A.S.S.I.O.N.** Impact American EM 197	**58**	5

S EXPRESS UK, male / female vocal / instrumental group　　50 wks

16 Apr 88	★ **THEME FROM S-EXPRESS** Rhythm King LEFT 21	**1**	13
23 Jul 88	● **SUPERFLY GUY** Rhythm King LEFT 28	**5**	9
18 Feb 89	● **HEY MUSIC LOVER** Rhythm King LEFT 30	**6**	10
16 Sep 89	**MANTRA FOR A STATE OF MIND** Rhythm King LEFT 35	**21**	8
15 Sep 90	**NOTHING TO LOSE** Rhythm King SEXY 01	**32**	4
30 May 92	**FIND 'EM, FOOL 'EM, FORGET 'EM** Rhythm King 6580137	**43**	2
11 May 96	**THEME FROM S.EXPRESS (re-mix)** Rhythm King SEXY 9CD [1]	**14**	4

[1] Mark Moore presents S Express

Robin S US, female vocalist　　29 wks

16 Jan 93	**SHOW ME LOVE** Champion CHAMPCD 300	**59**	4
13 Mar 93	● **SHOW ME LOVE (re-entry)** Champion CHAMPCD 300	**6**	13
31 Jul 93	**LUV 4 LUV** Champion CHAMPCD 301	**11**	7
4 Dec 93	**WHAT I DO BEST** Champion CHAMPCD 307	**43**	2
19 Mar 94	**I WANT TO THANK YOU** Champion CHAMPCD 310	**48**	1
5 Nov 94	**BACK IT UP** Champion CHAMPCD 312	**43**	2

Raphael SAADIQ – See TRIBE CALLED QUEST

S

SABRE featuring PRESIDENT BROWN
Jamaica, male vocal duo　　1 wk

19 Aug 95	**WRONG OR RIGHT** Greensleeves GRECD 485	**71**	1

SABRES OF PARADISE UK, male instrumental group 8 wks

2 Oct 93	SMOKEBELCH II Sabres Of Paradise PT 009CD	55	3
9 Apr 94	THEME Sabres Of Paradise PT 014CD	56	3
17 Sep 94	WILMOT Warp WAP 50CD	36	2

SABRINA Italy, female vocalist 22 wks

6 Feb 88	BOYS (SUMMERTIME LOVE) IBIZA IBIZ 1	60	3
11 Jun 88 ●	BOYS (SUMMERTIME LOVE) (re-entry) IBIZA IBIZ 1	3	11
1 Oct 88	ALL OF ME PWL PWL 19	25	7
1 Jul 89	LIKE A YO-YO Videogram DCUP 1	72	1

SACRED SPIRIT European, anonymous male producer
utilizing Native American chants 5 wks

15 Apr 95	YEHA-NOHA (WISHES OF HAPPINESS AND PROSPERITY) Virgin VSCDT 1514	71	1
18 Nov 95	WISHES OF HAPPINESS AND PROSPERITY (YEHA-NOHA) (re-entry) Virgin VSCDT 1514	37	2
16 Mar 96	WINTER CEREMONY (TOR-CHENEY-NAHANA) Virgin VSCDT 1574	45	2

SAD CAFE UK, male vocal / instrumental group 44 wks

22 Sep 79 ●	EVERY DAY HURTS RCA PB 5180	3	12
19 Jan 80	STRANGE LITTLE GIRL RCA PB 5202	32	5
15 Mar 80	MY OH MY RCA SAD 3	14	11
21 Jun 80	NOTHING LEFT TOULOUSE RCA SAD 4	62	4
27 Sep 80	LA-DI-DA RCA SAD 5	41	6
20 Dec 80	I'M IN LOVE AGAIN RCA SAD 6	40	6

SADE UK, female / male vocal / instrumental group 63 wks

25 Feb 84 ●	YOUR LOVE IS KING Epic A 4137	6	11
19 May 84	YOUR LOVE IS KING (re-entry) Epic A 4137	75	1
26 May 84	WHEN AM I GONNA MAKE A LIVING Epic A 4437	36	5
15 Sep 84	SMOOTH OPERATOR Epic A 4655	19	10
12 Oct 85	THE SWEETEST TABOO Epic A 6609	31	5
11 Jan 86	IS IT A CRIME Epic A 6742	49	3
2 Apr 88	LOVE IS STRONGER THAN PRIDE Epic SADE 1	44	3
4 Jun 88	PARADISE Epic SADE 2	29	7
10 Oct 92	NO ORDINARY LOVE Epic 6583567	26	3
28 Nov 92	FEEL NO PAIN Epic 6588297	56	2
8 May 93	KISS OF LIFE Epic 6591162	44	3
5 Jun 93	NO ORDINARY LOVE (re-entry) Epic 6583562	14	8
31 Jul 93	CHERISH THE DAY Epic 6594812	53	2

Staff Sergeant Barry SADLER US, male vocalist 8 wks

24 Mar 66	BALLAD OF THE GREEN BERETS RCA 1506	24	8

SAFFRON UK, female vocalist 2 wks

16 Jan 93	CIRCLES WEA SAFF 9CD	60	2

SAFFRONS - See CINDY and the SAFFRONS

Mike SAGAR UK, male vocalist 5 wks

8 Dec 60	DEEP FEELING HMV POP 819	44	5

SAGAT US, male rapper 6 wks

4 Dec 93	FUNK DAT ffrr FCD 224	25	5
3 Dec 94	LUVSTUFF ffrr FCD 250	71	1

Carole Bayer SAGER US, female vocalist 9 wks

28 May 77 ●	YOU'RE MOVING OUT TODAY Elektra K 12257	6	9

Bally SAGOO India, male producer 5 wks

3 Sep 94	CHURA LIYA Columbia 6607092	64	1
22 Apr 95	CHOLI KE PEECHE Columbia 6613352	45	1
19 Oct 96	DIL CHEEZ (MY HEART...) Higher Ground 6634882	12	3

SAILOR UK, male vocal / instrumental group 24 wks

6 Dec 75 ●	A GLASS OF CHAMPAGNE Epic EPC 3770	2	12
27 Mar 76 ●	GIRLS GIRLS GIRLS Epic EPC 3858	7	8
19 Feb 77	ONE DRINK TOO MANY Epic EPC 4804	35	4

ST. ANDREWS CHORALE UK, church choir 5 wks

14 Feb 76	CLOUD 99 Decca F 13617	31	5

ST. CECILIA UK, male vocal / instrumental group 17 wks

19 Jun 71	LEAP UP AND DOWN (WAVE YOUR KNICKERS IN THE AIR) Polydor 2058 104	12	17

SAINT ETIENNE
UK, male / female vocal / instrumental group 39 wks

18 May 91	NOTHING CAN STOP US / SPEEDWELL Heavenly HVN 009	54	3
7 Sep 91	ONLY LOVE CAN BREAK YOUR HEART / FILTHY Heavenly HVN 12	39	4
16 May 92	JOIN OUR CLUB / PEOPLE GET REAL Heavenly HVN 15	21	3
17 Oct 92	AVENUE Heavenly HVN 2312	40	2
13 Feb 93	YOU'RE IN A BAD WAY Heavenly HVN 25CD	12	5
22 May 93	HOBART PAVING / WHO DO YOU THINK YOU ARE Heavenly HVN 29CD	23	5
18 Dec 93	I WAS BORN ON CHRISTMAS DAY Heavenly HVN 36CD	37	5
19 Feb 94	PALE MOVIE Heavenly HVN 37CD	28	3
28 May 94	LIKE A MOTORWAY Heavenly HVN 40CD	47	2
1 Oct 94	HUG MY SOUL Heavenly HVN 42CD	32	2
11 Nov 95	HE'S ON THE PHONE Heavenly HVN 50CDR 1	11	5

1 Saint Etienne featuring Etienne Daho

See also Various Artists (EPs & LPs) – The Fred EP.

ST. GERMAIN France, male producer 1 wk

31 Aug 96	ALABAMA BLUES (REVISITED) F Communications F 050CD	50	1

Barry ST. JOHN UK, female vocalist 1 wk

9 Dec 65	COME AWAY MELINDA Columbia DB 7783	47	1

ST. JOHN'S COLLEGE SCHOOL CHOIR and the Band of the GRENADIER GUARDS
UK, school choir and military band 3 wks

3 May 86	THE QUEEN'S BIRTHDAY SONG Columbia Q1	40	3

ST. LOUIS UNION UK, male vocal / instrumental group 10 wks

13 Jan 66	GIRL Decca F 12318	11	10

Crispian ST. PETERS UK, male vocalist — **31 wks**

6 Jan 66	● **YOU WERE ON MY MIND** Decca F 12287	2	14
31 Mar 66	● **PIED PIPER** Decca F 12359	5	13
15 Sep 66	**CHANGES** Decca F 12480	49	1
29 Sep 66	**CHANGES (re-entry)** Decca F 12480	47	3

ST. PHILIPS CHOIR UK, choir — **4 wks**

12 Dec 87	**SING FOR EVER** BBC RESL 222	49	4

ST. THOMAS MORE SCHOOL CHOIR - See Scott FITZGERALD

ST. WINIFRED'S SCHOOL CHOIR
UK, school choir — **11 wks**

22 Nov 80	★ **NO ONE QUITE LIKE GRANDMA** MFP FP 900	1	11

Buffy SAINTE-MARIE Canada, female vocalist — **29 wks**

17 Jul 71	● **SOLDIER BLUE** RCA 2081	7	18
18 Mar 72	**I'M GONNA BE A COUNTRY GIRL AGAIN** Vanguard VRS 35143	34	5
8 Feb 92	**THE BIG ONES GET AWAY** Ensign ENY 650	39	5
4 Jul 92	**FALLEN ANGELS** Ensign ENY 655	57	1

SAINTS Australia, male vocal / instrumental group — **4 wks**

16 Jul 77	**THIS PERFECT DAY** Harvest HAR 5130	34	4

Kyu SAKAMOTO Japan, male vocalist — **13 wks**

27 Jun 63	● **SUKIYAKI** HMV POP 1171	6	13

Riuichi SAKAMOTO – See David SYLVIAN

SAKKARIN – See Jonathan KING

SALAD
UK / Holland, male / female vocal / instrumental group — **4 wks**

11 Mar 95	**DRINK THE ELIXIR** Island Red CIRD 104	66	1
13 May 95	**MOTORBIKE TO HEAVEN** Island Red CIRD 106	42	1
16 Sep 95	**GRANITE STATUE** Island Red CIRD 108	50	1
26 Oct 96	**I WANT YOU** Island CID 646	60	1

SALFORD JETS UK, male vocal / instrumental group — **2 wks**

31 May 80	**WHO YOU LOOKING AT** RCA PB 5239	72	2

SALSOUL ORCHESTRA – See CHARO and the SALSOUL ORCHESTRA

SALT TANK UK, male instrumental group — **2 wks**

11 May 96	**EUGINA** Internal LIECD 29	40	2

SALT-N-PEPA US, female rap duo — **113 wks**

26 Mar 88	**PUSH IT / I AM DOWN** ffrr FFR 2	41	6
25 Jun 88	● **PUSH IT / TRAMP** Champion CHAMP 51 & ffrr FFR 2	2	13
3 Sep 88	**SHAKE YOUR THANG (IT'S YOUR THING)** ffrr FFR 11 [1]	22	8
12 Nov 88	● **TWIST AND SHOUT** ffrr FFR 16	4	9
14 Apr 90	**EXPRESSION** ffrr F 127	40	6
25 May 91	● **DO YOU WANT ME** ffrr F 151	5	12
31 Aug 91	● **LET'S TALK ABOUT SEX** ffrr F 162 [2]	2	13
30 Nov 91	**YOU SHOWED ME** ffrr F 174	15	9
28 Mar 92	**EXPRESSION (re-issue)** ffrr F 182	23	6
3 Oct 92	**START ME UP** ffrr F 196	39	3
9 Oct 93	**SHOOP** ffrr FCD 219	29	3
19 Mar 94	● **WHATTA MAN** ffrr FCD 222 [3]	7	10
28 May 94	**SHOOP (re-mix)** ffrr FCD 234	13	8
12 Nov 94	**NONE OF YOUR BUSINESS** ffrr FCD 244	19	4
7 Jan 95	**NONE OF YOUR BUSINESS (re-entry)** ffrr FCD 244	64	1
21 Dec 96	**CHAMPAGNE** MCA MCSTD 48025	23†	2

[1] Salt-N-Pepa featuring E.U. [2] Salt-N-Pepa featuring Psychotropic [3] Salt-N-Pepa with En Vogue

I Am Down only listed from 2 April 88. The disc re-entered on 25 June when it was made available on Champion with a different flip side. Sales for both discs were amalgamated.

SAM and DAVE US, male vocal duo — **39 wks**

16 Mar 67	**SOOTHE ME** Stax 601 004	48	2
13 Apr 67	**SOOTHE ME (re-entry)** Stax 601 004	35	6
1 Nov 67	**SOUL MAN** Stax 601 023	24	14
13 Mar 68	**I THANK YOU** Stax 601 030	34	9
29 Jan 69	**SOUL SISTER BROWN SUGAR** Atlantic 584 237	15	8

See also Lou Reed.

SAM THE SHAM and the PHARAOHS
US, male vocal / instrumental group — **18 wks**

24 Jun 65	**WOOLY BULLY** MGM 1269	11	15
4 Aug 66	**LIL' RED RIDING HOOD** MGM 1315	48	1
18 Aug 66	**LIL' RED RIDING HOOD (re-entry)** MGM 1315	46	2

Richie SAMBORA
US, male vocalist / instrumentalist – bass — **1 wk**

7 Sep 91	**BALLAD OF YOUTH** Mercury MER 350	59	1

Mike SAMMES SINGERS
UK, male / female vocal group — **38 wks**

15 Sep 66	**SOMEWHERE MY LOVE** HMV POP 1546	22	19
12 Jul 67	**SOMEWHERE MY LOVE (re-entry)** HMV POP 1546	14	19

Dave SAMPSON UK, male vocalist — **6 wks**

19 May 60	**SWEET DREAMS** Columbia DB 4449	48	1
2 Jun 60	**SWEET DREAMS (re-entry)** Columbia DB 4449	29	5

SAMSON UK, male vocal / instrumental group — **6 wks**

4 Jul 81	**RIDING WITH THE ANGELS** RCA 67	55	3
24 Jul 82	**LOSING MY GRIP** Polydor POSP 471	63	2
5 Mar 83	**RED SKIES** Polydor POSP 554	65	1

SAN JOSÉ featuring Rodriguez ARGENTINA
UK, male instrumental group — **8 wks**

17 Jun 78	**ARGENTINE MELODY (CANCION DE ARGENTINA)** MCA 369	14	8

Rodriguez Argentina is Rod Argent. See also Argent; Silsoe.

SAN REMO STRINGS US, orchestra — **8 wks**

18 Dec 71	**FESTIVAL TIME** Tamla Motown TMG 795	39	8

Chris SANDFORD · UK, male vocalist · 9 wks

12 Dec 63	NOT TOO LITTLE NOT TOO MUCH Decca F 11778	17	9

SANDPIPERS · US, male vocal group · 33 wks

15 Sep 66	● GUANTANAMERA Pye International 7N 25380	7	17
5 Jun 68	QUANDO M'INNAMORO (A MAN WITHOUT LOVE) A & M AMS 723	33	6
26 Mar 69	KUMBAYA A & M AMS 744	38	1
9 Apr 69	KUMBAYA (re-entry) A & M AMS 744	49	1
27 Nov 76	HANG ON SLOOPY Satril SAT 114	32	8

SANDRA · Germany, female vocalist · 8 wks

17 Dec 88	EVERLASTING LOVE Siren SRN 85	45	8

Jodie SANDS · US, female vocalist · 10 wks

17 Oct 58	SOMEDAY (YOU'LL WANT ME TO WANT YOU) HMV POP 533	14	10

Tommy SANDS · US, male vocalist · 7 wks

4 Aug 60	OLD OAKEN BUCKET Capitol CL 15143	25	7

Samantha SANG · Australia, female vocalist · 13 wks

4 Feb 78	EMOTION Private Stock PVT 128	11	13

SANTA CLAUS and the CHRISTMAS TREES
UK, male vocal / instrumental group · 10 wks

11 Dec 82	SINGALONG-A-SANTA Polydor IVY 1	19	5
10 Dec 83	SINGALONG-A-SANTA AGAIN Polydor IVY 2	39	5

SANTA ESMERALDA and Leroy GOMEZ
US / France, male / female vocal / instrumental group · 5 wks

12 Nov 77	DON'T LET ME BE MISUNDERSTOOD Philips 6042 325	41	5

SANTANA · US, male vocal / instrumental group · 25 wks

28 Sep 74	SAMBA PA TI CBS 2561	27	7
15 Oct 77	SHE'S NOT THERE CBS 5671	11	12
25 Nov 78	WELL ALL RIGHT CBS 6755	53	3
22 Mar 80	ALL I EVER WANTED CBS 8160	57	3

SANTO and JOHNNY
US, male instrumental duo – steel and electric guitars · 5 wks

16 Oct 59	SLEEP WALK Pye International 7N 25037	22	4
31 Mar 60	TEARDROP Parlophone R 4619	50	1

Mike SARNE · UK, male vocalist · 43 wks

10 May 62	★ COME OUTSIDE Parlophone R 4902 [1]	1	19
30 Aug 62	WILL I WHAT Parlophone R 4932 [2]	18	10
10 Jan 63	JUST FOR KICKS Parlophone R 4974	22	7
28 Mar 63	CODE OF LOVE Parlophone R 5010	29	7

[1] Mike Sarne with Wendy Richard [2] Mike Sarne with Billie Davis

Joy SARNEY · UK, female vocalist · 6 wks

7 May 77	NAUGHTY NAUGHTY NAUGHTY Alaska ALA 2005	26	6

SARR BAND
Italy / UK / France, male / female vocal / instrumental group · 1 wk

16 Sep 78	MAGIC MANDRAKE Calendar Day 111	68	1

Peter SARSTEDT · UK, male vocalist · 25 wks

5 Feb 69	★ WHERE DO YOU GO TO MY LOVELY United Artists UP 2262	1	16
4 Jun 69	● FROZEN ORANGE JUICE United Artists UP 35021	10	9

Robin SARSTEDT · UK, male vocalist · 9 wks

8 May 76	● MY RESISTANCE IS LOW Decca F 13624	3	9

SARTORELLO · Italy, male / female vocal / instrumental duo · 1 wk

10 Aug 96	MOVE BABY MOVE Multiply CDMULTY 12	56	1

SASHA · UK, male producer · 12 wks

31 Jul 93	TOGETHER ffrr FCD 212 [1]	57	1
19 Feb 94	HIGHER GROUND Deconstruction 74321189002	19	3
27 Aug 94	MAGIC Deconstruction 74321221862 [2]	32	4
9 Mar 96	BE AS ONE Deconstruction 74321342962 [3]	17	4

[1] Danny Campbell and Sasha [2] Sasha with Sam Mollison [3] Sasha and Maria

Joe SATRIANI · US, male / vocalist / instrumentalist – guitar · 1 wk

13 Feb 93	THE SATCH EP Relativity 6589532	53	1

Tracks on The Satch EP: The Extremist / Banana Mango / Summer Song / Crazy.

SATURDAY NIGHT BAND
US, male vocal / instrumental group · 9 wks

1 Jul 78	COME ON DANCE DANCE CBS 6367	16	9

Deion SAUNDERS – See HAMMER

Kevin SAUNDERSON – See INNER CITY

Chantay SAVAGE · US, female vocalist · 8 wks

4 May 96	I WILL SURVIVE RCA 74321377682	12	8

Edna SAVAGE · UK, female vocalist · 1 wk

13 Jan 56	ARRIVEDERCI DARLING Parlophone R 4097	19	1

Telly SAVALAS · US, male vocalist · 12 wks

22 Feb 75	★ IF MCA 174	1	9
31 May 75	YOU'VE LOST THAT LOVIN' FEELING MCA 189	47	3

SAVANNA · US, male vocalist / instrumentalist – guitar · 4 wks

10 Oct 81	I CAN'T TURN AWAY R & B RBS 203	61	4

SAW DOCTORS *Ireland, male vocal / instrumental group* **8 wks**

12 Nov 94	**SMALL BIT OF LOVE** Shamtown SAW 001CD	**24** 3
27 Jan 96	**WORLD OF GOOD** Shamtown SAW 002CD	**15** 3
13 Jul 96	**TO WIN JUST ONCE** Shamtown SAW 004CD	**14** 2

SAXON *UK, male vocal / instrumental group* **61 wks**

22 Mar 80	**WHEELS OF STEEL** Carrere CAR 143	**20** 11
21 Jun 80	**747 (STRANGERS IN THE NIGHT)** Carrere CAR 151	**13** 9
28 Jun 80	**BACKS TO THE WALL** Carrere HM 6	**64** 2
28 Jun 80	**BIG TEASER / RAINBOW THEME** Carrere HM 5	**66** 2
29 Nov 80	**STRONG ARM OF THE LAW** Carrere CAR 170	**63** 3
11 Apr 81	**AND THE BANDS PLAYED ON** Carrere CAR 180	**12** 8
18 Jul 81	**NEVER SURRENDER** Carrere CAR 204	**18** 6
31 Oct 81	**PRINCESS OF THE NIGHT** Carrere CAR 208	**57** 3
23 Apr 83	**POWER AND THE GLORY** Carrere SAXON 1	**32** 5
30 Jul 83	**NIGHTMARE** Carrere CAR 284	**50** 3
31 Aug 85	**BACK ON THE STREETS** Parlophone R 6103	**75** 1
29 Mar 86	**ROCK 'N' ROLL GYPSY** Parlophone R 6112	**71** 1
30 Aug 86	**WAITING FOR THE NIGHT** EMI EMI 5575	**66** 2
5 Mar 88	**RIDE LIKE THE WIND** EMI EM 43	**52** 4
30 Apr 88	**I CAN'T WAIT ANYMORE** EMI EM 54	**71** 1

Al SAXON *UK, male vocalist* **10 wks**

16 Jan 59	**YOU'RE THE TOP CHA** Fontana H 164	**17** 4
28 Aug 59	**ONLY SIXTEEN** Fontana H 205	**24** 3
22 Dec 60	**BLUE-EYED BOY** Fontana H 278	**39** 2
7 Sep 61	**THERE I'VE SAID IT AGAIN** Piccadilly 7N 35011	**48** 1

Leo SAYER *UK, male vocalist* **148 wks**

15 Dec 73	● **THE SHOW MUST GO ON** Chrysalis CHS 2023	**2** 13
15 Jun 74	● **ONE MAN BAND** Chrysalis CHS 2045	**6** 9
14 Sep 74	● **LONG TALL GLASSES** Chrysalis CHS 2052	**4** 9
30 Aug 75	● **MOONLIGHTING** Chrysalis CHS 2076	**2** 8
30 Oct 76	● **YOU MAKE ME FEEL LIKE DANCING** Chrysalis CHS 2119	**2** 12
29 Jan 77	★ **WHEN I NEED YOU** Chrysalis CHS 2127	**1** 13
9 Apr 77	● **HOW MUCH LOVE** Chrysalis CHS 2140	**10** 8
10 Sep 77	**THUNDER IN MY HEART** Chrysalis CHS 2163	**22** 8
16 Sep 78	● **I CAN'T STOP LOVIN' YOU (THOUGH I TRY)** Chrysalis CHS 2240	**6** 11
25 Nov 78	**RAINING IN MY HEART** Chrysalis CHS 2277	**21** 10
5 Jul 80	● **MORE THAN I CAN SAY** Chrysalis CHS 2442	**2** 11
13 Mar 82	● **HAVE YOU EVER BEEN IN LOVE** Chrysalis CHS 2596	**10** 9
19 Jun 82	**HEART (STOP BEATING IN TIME)** Chrysalis CHS 2616	**22** 10
12 Mar 83	**ORCHARD ROAD** Chrysalis CHS 2677	**16** 8
15 Oct 83	**TILL YOU COME BACK TO ME** Chrysalis LEO 01	**51** 3
8 Feb 86	**UNCHAINED MELODY** Chrysalis LEO 3	**54** 4
13 Feb 93	**WHEN I NEED YOU (re-issue)** Chrysalis CDCHS 3926	**65** 2

Alexei SAYLE *UK, male vocalist* **8 wks**

25 Feb 84	**'ULLO JOHN GOT A NEW MOTOR?** Island IS 162	**15** 8

SCAFFOLD *UK, male vocal group* **62 wks**

22 Nov 67	● **THANK U VERY MUCH** Parlophone R 5643	**4** 12
27 Mar 68	**DO YOU REMEMBER** Parlophone R 5679	**34** 5
6 Nov 68	★ **LILY THE PINK** Parlophone R 5734	**1** 24
1 Nov 69	**GIN GAN GOOLIE** Parlophone R 5812	**38** 11
24 Jan 70	**GIN GAN GOOLIE (re-entry)** Parlophone R 5812	**50** 1
1 Jun 74	● **LIVERPOOL LOU** Warner Bros. K 16400	**7** 9

Boz SCAGGS *US, male vocalist* **31 wks**

30 Oct 76	**LOWDOWN** CBS 4563	**28** 4
22 Jan 77	● **WHAT CAN I SAY** CBS 4869	**10** 10
14 May 77	**LIDO SHUFFLE** CBS 5136	**13** 9
10 Dec 77	**HOLLYWOOD** CBS 5836	**33** 8

SCARFACE *US, male rapper* **4 wks**

11 Mar 95	**HAND OF THE DEAD BODY** Virgin America VUSCD 88 [1]	**41** 2
5 Aug 95	**I SEEN A MAN DIE** Virgin America VUSCD 94	**55** 2

[1] Scarface featuring Ice Cube

SCARLET *UK, female vocal / instrumental duo* **18 wks**

21 Jan 95	**INDEPENDENT LOVE SONG** WEA YZ 820CD	**12** 12
29 Apr 95	**I WANNA BE FREE (TO BE WITH HIM)** WEA YZ 913CD	**21** 4
5 Aug 95	**LOVE HANGOVER** WEA YZ 969CD	**54** 1
6 Jul 96	**BAD GIRL** WEA WEA 046CD	**54** 1

SCARLET FANTASTIC
UK, male / female vocal / instrumental group **12 wks**

3 Oct 87	**NO MEMORY** Arista RIS 36	**24** 10
23 Jan 88	**PLUG ME IN (TO THE CENTRAL LOVE LINE)** Arista 109693	**67** 2

SCARLET PARTY *UK, male vocal / instrumental group* **5 wks**

16 Oct 82	**101 DAM-NATIONS** Parlophone R 6058	**44** 5

SCATMAN JOHN *US, male vocalist* **19 wks**

13 May 95	● **SCATMAN (SKI-BA-BOP-BA-DOP-BOP)** RCA 74321281712	**3** 12
2 Sep 95	● **SCATMAN'S WORLD** RCA 74321289952	**10** 7

Michael SCHENKER GROUP
Germany / UK, male vocal / instrumental group **9 wks**

13 Sep 80	**ARMED AND READY** Chrysalis CHS 2455	**53** 3
8 Nov 80	**CRY FOR THE NATIONS** Chrysalis CHS 2471	**56** 3
11 Sep 82	**DANCER** Chrysalis CHS 2636	**52** 3

Lalo SCHIFRIN *US, orchestra* **9 wks**

9 Oct 76	**JAWS** CTI CTSP 005	**14** 9

Peter SCHILLING *Germany, male vocalist* **6 wks**

5 May 84	**MAJOR TOM (COMING HOME)** PSP/WEA X 9438	**42** 5
16 Jun 84	**MAJOR TOM (COMING HOME) (re-entry)** PSP/WEA X 9438	**73** 1

Phillip SCHOFIELD *UK, male vocalist* **6 wks**

5 Dec 92	**CLOSE EVERY DOOR** Really Useful RUR 11	**27** 6

SCIENTIST *UK, male instrumentalist* **13 wks**

6 Oct 90	**THE EXORCIST** Kickin KICK 1	**62** 3
1 Dec 90	**THE EXORCIST (re-mix)** Kickin KICK 1TR	**46** 3

15 Dec 90	**THE BEE** *Kickin KICK 3S*	**52**	3
26 Jan 91	**THE BEE (re-entry)** *Kickin KICK 3S*	**47**	3
11 May 91	**SPIRAL SYMPHONY** *Kickin KICK 5*	**74**	1

SCOOTER *UK / Germany, male vocal / instrumental group* **12 wks**

21 Oct 95	**MOVE YOUR ASS** *Club Tools 0061675 CLU*	**23**	4
17 Feb 96	**BACK IN THE UK** *Club Tools 0061955 CLU*	**18**	3
25 May 96	**REBEL YELL** *Club Tools 0062575 CLU*	**30**	2
19 Oct 96	**I'M RAVING** *Club Tools 0063015 CLU*	**33**	3

SCORPIONS *Germany, male vocal / instrumental group* **35 wks**

26 May 79	**IS THERE ANYBODY THERE / ANOTHER PIECE OF MEAT** *Harvest HAR 5185*	**39**	4
25 Aug 79	**LOVEDRIVE** *Harvest HAR 5188*	**69**	2
31 May 80	**MAKE IT REAL** *Harvest HAR 5206*	**72**	2
20 Sep 80	**THE ZOO** *Harvest HAR 5212*	**75**	1
3 Apr 82	**NO ONE LIKE YOU** *Harvest HAR 5219*	**65**	3
1 May 82	**NO ONE LIKE YOU (re-entry)** *Harvest HAR 5219*	**64**	1
17 Jul 82	**CAN'T LIVE WITHOUT YOU** *Harvest HAR 5221*	**63**	2
4 Jun 88	**RHYTHM OF LOVE** *Harvest HAR 5240*	**59**	2
18 Feb 89	**PASSION RULES THE GAME** *Harvest 5242*	**74**	1
1 Jun 91	**WIND OF CHANGE** *Vertigo VER 54*	**53**	3
28 Sep 91	● **WIND OF CHANGE (re-issue)** *Vertigo VER 58*	**2**	9
30 Nov 91	**SEND ME AN ANGEL** *Vertigo VER 60*	**27**	3
28 Dec 91	**SEND ME AN ANGEL (re-entry)** *Vertigo VER 60*	**68**	2

SCOT PROJECT *Germany, male producer – Frank De Zenk* **1 wk**

27 Jul 96	**U (I GOT A FEELING)** *Positiva CDTIV 55*	**66**	1

SCOTLAND WORLD CUP SQUAD
UK, male football team vocalists **27 wks**

22 Jun 74	**EASY EASY** *Polydor 2058 452*	**20**	4
27 May 78	● **OLE OLA (MULHER BRASILEIRA)** *Riva 15* [1]	**4**	6
1 May 82	● **WE HAVE A DREAM** *WEA K 19145*	**5**	9
9 Jun 90	**SAY IT WITH PRIDE** *RCA PB 43791*	**45**	3
15 Jun 96	**PURPLE HEATHER** *Warner Bros. W 0354CD* [2]	**16**	5

[1] Rod Stewart featuring the Scottish World Cup Football Squad
[2] Rod Stewart with the Scottish Euro '96 Squad

Jack SCOTT *Canada, male vocalist* **28 wks**

10 Oct 58	● **MY TRUE LOVE** *London HLU 8626*	**9**	10
25 Sep 59	**THE WAY I WALK** *London HLL 8912*	**30**	1
10 Mar 60	**WHAT IN THE WORLD'S COME OVER YOU** *Top Rank JAR 280*	**11**	15
2 Jun 60	**BURNING BRIDGES** *Top Rank JAR 375*	**32**	2

Linda SCOTT *US, female vocalist* **14 wks**

18 May 61	● **I'VE TOLD EVERY LITTLE STAR** *Columbia DB 4638*	**7**	13
14 Sep 61	**DON'T BET MONEY HONEY** *Columbia DB 4692*	**50**	1

Mike SCOTT *UK, male vocalist / multi-instrumentalist* **2 wks**

16 Sep 95	**BRING 'EM ALL IN** *Chrysalis CDCHS 5025*	**56**	1
11 Nov 95	**BUILDING THE CITY OF LIGHT** *Chrysalis CDCHS 5026*	**60**	1

Millie SCOTT *US, female vocalist* **11 wks**

12 Apr 86	**PRISONER OF LOVE** *Fourth & Broadway BRW 45*	**52**	4
23 Aug 86	**AUTOMATIC** *Fourth & Broadway BRW 51*	**56**	3
21 Feb 87	**EV'RY LITTLE BIT** *Fourth & Broadway BRW 58*	**63**	4

Simon SCOTT *UK, male vocalist* **8 wks**

13 Aug 64	**MOVE IT BABY** *Parlophone R 5164*	**37**	8

Tony SCOTT *US, male vocalist* **6 wks**

15 Apr 89	**THAT'S HOW I'M LIVING / THE CHIEF** *Champion CHAMP 97*	**48**	4
10 Feb 90	**GET INTO IT / THAT'S HOW I'M LIVING (re-issue)** *Champion CHAMP 232*	**63**	2

The Chief only listed from 22 Apr 89.

SCOTTISH RUGBY TEAM with Ronnie BROWNE *UK, male rugby team vocalists* **1 wk**

2 Jun 90	**FLOWER OF SCOTLAND** *Greentrax STRAX 1001*	**73**	1

SCREAMING BLUE MESSIAHS
UK, male vocal / instrumental group **6 wks**

16 Jan 88	**I WANNA BE A FLINTSTONE** *WEA YZ 166*	**28**	6

SCREAMING TREES
US, male vocal / instrumental group **2 wks**

6 Mar 93	**NEARLY LOST YOU** *Epic 6582372*	**50**	1
1 May 93	**DOLLAR BILL** *Epic 6591792*	**52**	1

SCRITTI POLITTI *UK, male vocal / instrumental group* **77 wks**

21 Nov 81	**THE SWEETEST GIRL** *Rough Trade RT 091*	**64**	3
22 May 82	**FAITHLESS** *Rough Trade RT 101*	**56**	4
7 Aug 82	**ASYLUMS IN JERUSALEM / JACQUES DERRIDA** *Rough Trade RT 111*	**43**	5
10 Mar 84	● **WOOD BEEZ (PRAY LIKE ARETHA FRANKLIN)** *Virgin VS 657*	**10**	12
9 Jun 84	**ABSOLUTE** *Virgin VS 680*	**17**	9
17 Nov 84	**HYPNOTIZE** *Virgin VS 725*	**68**	2
11 May 85	● **THE WORD GIRL** *Virgin VS 747* [1]	**6**	12
7 Sep 85	**PERFECT WAY** *Virgin VS 780*	**48**	5
7 May 88	**OH PATTI (DON'T FEEL SORRY FOR LOVERBOY)** *Virgin VS 1006*	**13**	9
27 Aug 88	**FIRST BOY IN THIS TOWN (LOVE SICK)** *Virgin VS 1082*	**63**	3
12 Nov 88	**BOOM! THERE SHE WAS** *Virgin VS 1143* [2]	**55**	3
16 Mar 91	**SHE'S A WOMAN** *Virgin VS 1333* [3]	**20**	7
3 Aug 91	**TAKE ME IN YOUR ARMS AND LOVE ME** *Virgin VS 1346*	**47**	3

[1] Scritti Politti featuring Ranking Ann [2] Scritti Politti featuring Roger
[3] Scritti Politti featuring Shabba Ranks

Sweetie Irie is credited on the sleeve only of Take Me In Your Arms And Love Me.

Earl SCRUGGS – See Lester FLATT and Earl SCRUGGS

SEA LEVEL *US, male instrumental group* **4 wks**

17 Feb 79	**FIFTY-FOUR** *Capricorn POSP 28*	**63**	4

SEAL *UK, male vocalist* **64 wks**

8 Dec 90	● **CRAZY** *ZTT ZANG 8*	**2**	15
4 May 91	**FUTURE LOVE EP** *ZTT ZANG 11*	**12**	6
20 Jul 91	**THE BEGINNING** *ZTT ZANG 21*	**24**	6
16 Nov 91	● **KILLER (EP)** *ZTT ZANG 23*	**8**	8
29 Feb 92	**VIOLET** *ZTT ZANG 27*	**39**	2

21 May 94		PRAYER FOR THE DYING ZTT ZANG 51CD	**14** 5
30 Jul 94		KISS FROM A ROSE ZTT ZANG 52CD1	**20** 5
5 Nov 94		NEWBORN FRIEND ZTT ZANG 58CD	**45** 2
15 Jul 95	●	KISS FROM A ROSE (re-issue) / I'M ALIVE ZTT ZANG 70CD	**4** 13
9 Dec 95		DON'T CRY / PRAYER FOR THE DYING (re-issue) ZTT ZANG 75CD	**51** 2

Tracks on Future Love EP: Future Love Paradise / A Minor Groove / Violet. Tracks on Killer (EP): Killer / Hey Joe / Come See What Love Has Done. See also Adamski.

SEARCHERS UK, male vocal / instrumental group — 128 wks

27 Jun 63	★	SWEETS FOR MY SWEET Pye 7N 15533	**1** 16
10 Oct 63		SWEET NOTHINS Philips BF 1274	**48** 2
24 Oct 63	●	SUGAR AND SPICE Pye 7N 15566	**2** 13
16 Jan 64	★	NEEDLES AND PINS Pye 7N 15594	**1** 15
16 Apr 64	★	DON'T THROW YOUR LOVE AWAY Pye 7N 15630	**1** 11
16 Jul 64		SOMEDAY WE'RE GONNA LOVE AGAIN Pye 7N 15670	**11** 8
17 Sep 64	●	WHEN YOU WALK IN THE ROOM Pye 7N 15694	**3** 12
3 Dec 64		WHAT HAVE THEY DONE TO THE RAIN Pye 7N 15739	**13** 11
4 Mar 65	●	GOODBYE MY LOVE Pye 7N 15794	**4** 11
8 Jul 65		HE'S GOT NO LOVE Pye 7N 15878	**12** 10
14 Oct 65		WHEN I GET HOME Pye 7N 15950	**35** 3
16 Dec 65		TAKE ME FOR WHAT I'M WORTH Pye 7N 15992	**20** 8
21 Apr 66		TAKE IT OR LEAVE IT Pye 7N 17094	**31** 6
13 Oct 66		HAVE YOU EVER LOVED SOMEBODY Pye 7N 17170	**48** 2

SEASHELLS UK, female vocal group — 5 wks

9 Sep 72		MAYBE I KNOW CBS 8218	**32** 5

SEB UK, male instrumentalist – keyboards — 1 wk

18 Feb 95		SUGAR SHACK React CDREACT 50	**61** 1

SEBADOH US, male vocal / instrumental group — 1 wk

27 Jul 96		BEAUTY OF THE RIDE Domino RUG 47CD	**74** 1

Jon SECADA US, male vocalist — 41 wks

18 Jul 92	●	JUST ANOTHER DAY SBK SBK 35	**5** 15
31 Oct 92		DO YOU BELIEVE IN US SBK SBK 37	**30** 4
6 Feb 93		ANGEL SBK CDSBK 39	**23** 5
17 Jul 93		DO YOU REALLY WANT ME SBK CDSBK 41	**30** 4
16 Oct 93		I'M FREE SBK CDSBK 44	**50** 2
14 May 94		IF YOU GO SBK CDSBK 51	**39** 4
2 Jul 94		IF YOU GO (re-entry) SBK CDSBK 51	**71** 1
4 Feb 95		MENTAL PICTURE SBK CDSBK 54	**44** 2
16 Dec 95		IF I NEVER KNEW YOU (LOVE THEME FROM 'POCAHONTAS') Walt Disney WD 7023C [1]	**51** 4

[1] Jon Secada and Shanice

SECCHI featuring Orlando JOHNSON
Italy / US, male vocal / instrumental duo — 3 wks

4 May 91		I SAY YEAH Epic 6568467	**46** 3

Harry SECOMBE UK, male vocalist — 35 wks

9 Dec 55		ON WITH THE MOTLEY Philips PB 523	**16** 3
3 Oct 63		IF I RULED THE WORLD Philips BF 1261	**44** 2
21 Nov 63		IF I RULED THE WORLD (re-entry) Philips BF 1261	**18** 15
23 Feb 67	●	THIS IS MY SONG Philips BF 1539	**2** 15

SECOND CITY SOUND UK, male instrumental group — 8 wks

20 Jan 66		TCHAIKOVSKY ONE Decca F 12310	**22** 7
2 Apr 69		DREAM OF OLWEN Major Minor MM 600	**43** 1

SECOND IMAGE UK, male vocal / instrumental group — 11 wks

24 Jul 82		STAR Polydor POSP 457	**60** 2
2 Apr 83		BETTER TAKE TIME Polydor POSP 565	**67** 2
26 Nov 83		DON'T YOU MCA 848	**68** 2
11 Aug 84		SING AND SHOUT MCA MCA 882	**53** 3
2 Feb 85		STARTING AGAIN MCA 936	**65** 2

SECOND PHASE US, male producer – Joey Beltram — 2 wks

21 Sep 91		MENTASM R&S RSUK 2	**48** 2

SECRET AFFAIR UK, male vocal / instrumental group — 34 wks

1 Sep 79		TIME FOR ACTION I-Spy SEE 1	**13** 10
10 Nov 79		LET YOUR HEART DANCE I-Spy SEE 3	**32** 6
8 Mar 80		MY WORLD I-Spy SEE 5	**16** 9
23 Aug 80		SOUND OF CONFUSION I-Spy SEE 8	**45** 5
17 Oct 81		DO YOU KNOW I-Spy SEE 10	**57** 4

SECRET KNOWLEDGE
UK / US, male / female vocal / instrumental duo — 2 wks

27 Apr 96		LOVE ME NOW Deconstruction 74321342432	**66** 1
24 Aug 96		SUGAR DADDY Deconstruction 74321400242	**75** 1

SECRET LIFE UK, male vocal group — 10 wks

12 Dec 92		AS ALWAYS Cowboy 7RODEO 9	**45** 4
7 Aug 93		LOVE SO STRONG Cowboy RODEO 18CD	**38** 2
7 May 94		SHE HOLDS THE KEY Pulse 8 CDLOSE 58	**63** 1
29 Oct 94		I WANT YOU Pulse 8 CDLOSE 71	**70** 1
28 Jan 95		LOVE SO STRONG (re-mix) Pulse 8 CDLOSE 79	**37** 2

SECRETARY OF ENTERTAINMENT – See RAZE

Neil SEDAKA US, male vocalist — 190 wks

24 Apr 59	●	I GO APE RCA 1115	**9** 13
13 Nov 59	●	OH CAROL RCA 1152	**3** 17
14 Apr 60	●	STAIRWAY TO HEAVEN RCA 1178	**8** 15
1 Sep 60		YOU MEAN EVERYTHING TO ME RCA 1198	**45** 3
2 Feb 61	●	CALENDAR GIRL RCA 1220	**8** 14
18 May 61	●	LITTLE DEVIL RCA 1236	**9** 12
21 Dec 61	●	HAPPY BIRTHDAY SWEET SIXTEEN RCA 1266	**3** 18
19 Apr 62		KING OF CLOWNS RCA 1282	**23** 11
19 Jul 62	●	BREAKING UP IS HARD TO DO RCA 1298	**7** 16
22 Nov 62		NEXT DOOR TO AN ANGEL RCA 1319	**29** 4
30 May 63		LET'S GO STEADY AGAIN RCA 1343	**42** 1
13 Jun 63		LET'S GO STEADY AGAIN (re-entry) RCA 1343	**43** 2
7 Oct 72		OH CAROL / BREAKING UP IS HARD TO DO / LITTLE DEVIL (re-issue) RCA Maximillion 2259	**19** 14
4 Nov 72		BEAUTIFUL YOU RCA 2269	**43** 3
24 Feb 73		THAT'S WHEN THE MUSIC TAKES ME RCA 2310	**18** 10
2 Jun 73		STANDING ON THE INSIDE MGM 2006 267	**26** 9
25 Aug 73		OUR LAST SONG TOGETHER MGM 2006 307	**31** 8
9 Feb 74		A LITTLE LOVIN' Polydor 2058 434	**34** 6
22 Jun 74		LAUGHTER IN THE RAIN Polydor 2058 494	**15** 9
22 Mar 75		THE QUEEN OF 1964 Polydor 2058 546	**35** 5

SEDUCTION US, female vocal group — 1 wk

21 Apr 90		HEARTBEAT Breakout USA 685	**75** 1

Showaddywaddy

Showaddywaddy racked up nine Top 10 singles between 1975 and 1978, each was a pop version of a rock'n'roll classic.

Shed Seven

Shed Seven were signed after an appearance at In The City, the annual UK music buisiness convention. Within a year they had knocked Take That off the top of the charts... in Thailand!

Sleeper

Taking their name from the Woody Allen film *Sleeper*, the Essex foursome haven't looked back since Radio 1's erstwhile breakfast show presenter, Chris Evans, championed their 'Inbetweener' single.

SEEKERS *Australia / Sri Lanka, male / female vocal group* **120 wks**

7 Jan 65	★ I'LL NEVER FIND ANOTHER YOU *Columbia DB 7431*	**1** 23
15 Apr 65	● A WORLD OF OUR OWN *Columbia DB 7532*	**3** 18
28 Oct 65	★ THE CARNIVAL IS OVER *Columbia DB 7711*	**1** 17
24 Mar 66	SOMEDAY ONE DAY *Columbia DB 7867*	**11** 11
8 Sep 66	● WALK WITH ME *Columbia DB 8000*	**10** 12
24 Nov 66	● MORNINGTOWN RIDE *Columbia DB 8060*	**2** 15
23 Feb 67	● GEORGY GIRL *Columbia DB 8134*	**3** 11
20 Sep 67	WHEN WILL THE GOOD APPLES FALL *Columbia DB 8273*	**11** 12
13 Dec 67	EMERALD CITY *Columbia DB 8313*	**50** 1

Bob SEGER and the SILVER BULLET BAND
US, male vocal / instrumental group **30 wks**

30 Sep 78	HOLLYWOOD NIGHTS *Capitol CL 16004* [1]	**42** 6
3 Feb 79	WE'VE GOT TONITE *Capitol CL 16028*	**41** 6
24 Oct 81	HOLLYWOOD NIGHTS *Capitol CL 223*	**49** 3
6 Feb 82	WE'VE GOT TONITE *Capitol CL 235*	**60** 4
9 Apr 83	EVEN NOW *Capitol CL 284*	**73** 2
28 Jan 95	WE'VE GOT TONIGHT (re-issue) *Capitol CDCL 734*	**22** 5
29 Apr 95	NIGHT MOVES *Capitol CDCL 741*	**45** 2
29 Jul 95	HOLLYWOOD NIGHTS (re-issue) *Capitol CDCL 749*	**52** 1
10 Feb 96	LOCK AND LOAD *Parlophone CDCL 765*	**57** 1

[1] Bob Seger

Capitol CL 223 and CL 235 were live versions of earlier studio hits

SEIKO and Donnie WAHLBERG
Japan / US, female / male vocal duo **5 wks**

18 Aug 90	THE RIGHT COMBINATION *Epic 656203 7*	**44** 5

SELECTER *UK, male / female vocal / instrumental group* **28 wks**

13 Oct 79	● ON MY RADIO *2 Tone CHSTT 4*	**8** 9
2 Feb 80	THREE MINUTE HERO *2 Tone CHSTT 8*	**16** 6
29 Mar 80	MISSING WORDS *2 Tone CHSTT 10*	**23** 8
23 Aug 80	THE WHISPER *Chrysalis CHSS 1*	**36** 5

See also Various Artists (EPs & LPs) – The Two Tone EP.

Peter SELLERS *UK, male vocalist* **39 wks**

2 Aug 57	ANY OLD IRON *Parlophone R 4337*	**21** 3
6 Sep 57	ANY OLD IRON (re-entry) *Parlophone R 4337*	**17** 8
10 Nov 60	● GOODNESS GRACIOUS ME *Parlophone R 4702* [1]	**4** 14
12 Jan 61	BANGERS AND MASH *Parlophone R 4724* [1]	**22** 5
23 Dec 65	A HARD DAY'S NIGHT *Parlophone R 5393*	**14** 7
27 Nov 93	A HARD DAY'S NIGHT (re-issue) *EMI CDEMS 293*	**52** 2

[1] Peter Sellers and Sophia Loren

Michael SEMBELLO *US, male vocalist* **6 wks**

20 Aug 83	MANIAC *Casablanca CAN 1017*	**43** 6

SEMPRINI *UK, orchestra* **8 wks**

16 Mar 61	THEME FROM 'EXODUS' *HMV POP 842*	**25** 8

SENSELESS THINGS
UK, male vocal / instrumental group **19 wks**

22 Jun 91	EVERYBODY'S GONE *Epic 6569807*	**73** 1
28 Sep 91	GOT IT AT THE DELMAR *Epic 6574497*	**50** 3

11 Jan 92	EASY TO SMILE *Epic 6576957*	**18** 4
11 Apr 92	HOLD IT DOWN *Epic 6579267*	**19** 4
5 Dec 92	HOMOPHOBIC ASSHOLE *Epic 6588337*	**52** 2
13 Feb 93	PRIMARY INSTINCT *Epic 6589402*	**41** 2
12 Jun 93	TOO MUCH KISSING *Epic 6592502*	**69** 1
5 Nov 94	CHRISTINE KEELER *Epic 6609572*	**56** 1
28 Jan 95	SOMETHING TO MISS *Epic 6611162*	**57** 1

SENSER *UK, male / female vocal / instrumental group* **5 wks**

25 Sep 93	THE KEY *Ultimate TOPP 019CD*	**47** 1
19 Mar 94	SWITCH *Ultimate TOPP 022CD*	**39** 2
23 Jul 94	AGE OF PANIC *Ultimate TOPP 027CD*	**52** 1
17 Aug 96	CHARMING DEMONS *Ultimate TOPP 045CD*	**42** 1

SEPULTURA *Brazil, male vocal / instrumental group* **12 wks**

2 Oct 93	TERRITORY *Roadrunner RR 23823*	**66** 2
26 Feb 94	REFUSE-RESIST *Roadrunner RR 23773*	**51** 2
4 Jun 94	SLAVE NEW WORLD *Roadrunner RR 23745*	**46** 2
24 Feb 96	ROOTS BLOODY ROOTS *Roadrunner RR 23205*	**19** 2
17 Aug 96	RATAMAHATTA *Roadrunner RR 23145*	**23** 2
14 Dec 96	ATTITUDE *Roadrunner RR 22995*	**46** 2

SERIOUS INTENTION
US, male vocal / instrumental group **6 wks**

16 Nov 85	YOU DON'T KNOW (OH-OH-OH) *Important TAN 8*	**75** 1
5 Apr 86	SERIOUS *Pow Wow LON 93*	**51** 5

SERIOUS ROPE
UK, male / female vocal / instrumental group **3 wks**

22 May 93	HAPPINESS *Rumour RUMACD 64* [1]	**54** 2
1 Oct 94	HAPPINESS – YOU MAKE ME HAPPY (re-mix) *Mercury MERCD 407*	**70** 1

[1] Serious Rope presents Sharon Dee Clarke

SET THE TONE *UK, male vocal / instrumental group* **4 wks**

22 Jan 83	DANCE SUCKER *Island WIP 6836*	**62** 2
26 Mar 83	RAP YOUR LOVE *Island IS 110*	**67** 2

SETTLERS *UK, male / female vocal / instrumental group* **5 wks**

16 Oct 71	THE LIGHTNING TREE *York SYK 505*	**36** 5

Taja SEVELLE *US, female vocalist* **13 wks**

20 Feb 88	● LOVE IS CONTAGIOUS *Paisley Park W 8257*	**7** 9
14 May 88	WOULDN'T YOU LOVE TO LOVE ME *Paisley Park W 8127*	**59** 4

SEVEN GRAND HOUSING AUTHORITY
UK, male producer – Terence Parker **1 wk**

23 Oct 93	THE QUESTION *Olympic ELYCD 010*	**70** 1

702 *US, female vocal group* **2 wks**

14 Dec 96	STEELO *Motown 8606072*	**41** 2

7669 *US, female rap group* **1 wk**

18 Jun 94	JOY *Motown TMGCD 1429*	**60** 1

740 BOYZ US, male vocal / instrumental duo   **1 wk**

| 4 Nov 95 | **SHIMMY SHAKE** MCA MCSTD 40002 | **54** | 1 |

7TH HEAVEN UK, male vocal group   **5 wks**

| 14 Sep 85 | **HOT FUN** Mercury MER 199 | **47** | 5 |

SEVERINE France, female vocalist   **11 wks**

| 24 Apr 71 | ● **UN BANC, UN ARBRE, UNE RUE** Philips 6009 135 | **9** | 11 |

David SEVILLE US, male vocalist   **6 wks**

| 23 May 58 | **WITCH DOCTOR** London HLU 8619 | **11** | 6 |

See also Chipmunks; Alfi and Harry.

Janette SEWELL – *See DOUBLE TROUBLE*

SEX CLUB featuring BROWN SUGAR
US, male / female vocal / instrumental duo   **1 wk**

| 28 Jan 95 | **BIG DICK MAN** Club Tools CLU 60775 | **67** | 1 |

SEX PISTOLS UK, male vocal / instrumental group   **88 wks**

18 Dec 76	● **ANARCHY IN THE U.K.** EMI 2566	**38**	4
4 Jun 77	● **GOD SAVE THE QUEEN** Virgin VS 181	**2**	9
9 Jul 77	● **PRETTY VACANT** Virgin VS 184	**6**	8
22 Oct 77	● **HOLIDAYS IN THE SUN** Virgin VS 191	**8**	6
8 Jul 78	● **NO ONE IS INNOCENT / MY WAY** Virgin VS 220 [1]	**7**	10
3 Mar 79	● **SOMETHING ELSE / FRIGGIN' IN THE RIGGIN'** Virgin VS 240	**3**	12
7 Apr 79	● **SILLY THING** Virgin VS 256	**6**	8
30 Jun 79	● **C'MON EVERYBODY** Virgin VS 272	**3**	9
13 Oct 79	**THE GREAT ROCK 'N' ROLL SWINDLE** Virgin VS 290	**21**	6
14 Jun 80	**(I'M NOT YOUR) STEPPING STONE** Virgin VS 339	**21**	8
3 Oct 92	**ANARCHY IN THE UK (re-issue)** Virgin VS 1431	**33**	3
5 Dec 92	**PRETTY VACANT (re-issue)** Virgin VS 1448	**56**	2
27 Jul 96	**PRETTY VACANT (LIVE)** Virgin America VUSCD 113	**18**	3

[1] Sex Pistols, punk prayer by Ronald Biggs

The listed flip side of Silly Thing was Who Killed Bambi by Ten Pole Tudor. The listed flip side of The Great Rock 'N' Roll Swindle was Rock Around The Clock, also by Ten Pole Tudor.

SEX-O-LETTES – *See DISCO TEX and the SEX-O-LETTES*

Denny SEYTON and the SABRES
UK, male vocal / instrumental group   **1 wk**

| 17 Sep 64 | **THE WAY YOU LOOK TONIGHT** Mercury MF 824 | **48** | 1 |

SFX UK, male instrumental / production duo   **3 wks**

| 15 May 93 | **LEMMINGS** Parlophone CDR 6343 | **51** | 3 |

SHADES OF LOVE US, male instrumental/production duo   **1 wk**

| 22 Apr 95 | **KEEP IN TOUCH (BODY TO BODY)** Vicious Muzik MUZCD 102 | **64** | 1 |

SHADES OF RHYTHM
UK, male instrumental / production group   **24 wks**

2 Feb 91	**HOMICIDE / EXORCIST** ZTT ZANG 13	**53**	3
13 Apr 91	**SWEET SENSATION** ZTT ZANG 18	**54**	4
20 Jul 91	**THE SOUND OF EDEN** ZTT ZANG 22	**35**	5
30 Nov 91	**EXTACY** ZTT ZANG 24	**16**	7
20 Feb 93	**SWEET REVIVAL (KEEP IT COMIN')** ZTT ZANG 40CD	**61**	1
11 Sep 93	**SOUND OF EDEN (re-issue)** ZTT ZANG 44CD	**37**	3
5 Nov 94	**THE WANDERING DRAGON** Public Demand PPDCD 5	**55**	1

SHADOWS UK, male instrumental / vocal group   **359 wks**

21 Jul 60	★ **APACHE** Columbia DB 4484	**1**	21
10 Nov 60	● **MAN OF MYSTERY / THE STRANGER** Columbia DB 4530	**5**	15
9 Feb 61	● **F.B.I.** Columbia DB 4580	**6**	19
11 May 61	● **FRIGHTENED CITY** Columbia DB 4637	**3**	20
7 Sep 61	★ **KON-TIKI** Columbia DB 4698	**1**	10
16 Nov 61	● **THE SAVAGE** Columbia DB 4726	**10**	8
23 Nov 61	**KON-TIKI (re-entry)** Columbia DB 4698	**37**	2
1 Mar 62	★ **WONDERFUL LAND** Columbia DB 4790	**1**	19
2 Aug 62	● **GUITAR TANGO** Columbia DB 4870	**4**	15
13 Dec 62	★ **DANCE ON** Columbia DB 4948	**1**	15
7 Mar 63	★ **FOOT TAPPER** Columbia DB 4984	**1**	16
6 Jun 63	● **ATLANTIS** Columbia DB 7047	**2**	17
19 Sep 63	● **SHINDIG** Columbia DB 7106	**6**	12
5 Dec 63	**GERONIMO** Columbia DB 7163	**11**	12
5 Mar 64	**THEME FOR YOUNG LOVERS** Columbia DB 7231	**12**	10
7 May 64	● **THE RISE AND FALL OF FLINGEL BUNT** Columbia DB 7261	**5**	14
3 Sep 64	**RHYTHM AND GREENS** Columbia DB 7342	**22**	7
3 Dec 64	**GENIE WITH THE LIGHT BROWN LAMP** Columbia DB 7416	**17**	10
11 Feb 65	**MARY ANNE** Columbia DB 7476	**17**	10
10 Jun 65	**STINGRAY** Columbia DB 7588	**19**	7
5 Aug 65	● **DON'T MAKE MY BABY BLUE** Columbia DB 7650	**10**	10
25 Nov 65	**WAR LORD** Columbia DB 7769	**18**	9
17 Mar 66	**I MET A GIRL** Columbia DB 7853	**22**	5
7 Jul 66	**A PLACE IN THE SUN** Columbia DB 7952	**24**	6
3 Nov 66	**THE DREAMS I DREAM** Columbia DB 8034	**42**	6
13 Apr 67	**MAROC 7** Columbia DB 8170	**24**	8
8 Mar 75	**LET ME BE THE ONE** EMI 2269	**12**	9
16 Dec 78	● **DON'T CRY FOR ME ARGENTINA** EMI 2890	**5**	14
28 Apr 79	● **THEME FROM 'THE DEER HUNTER' (CAVATINA)** EMI 2939	**9**	14
26 Jan 80	**RIDERS IN THE SKY** EMI 5027	**12**	12
23 Aug 80	**EQUINOXE (PART V)** Polydor POSP 148	**50**	3
2 May 81	**THE THIRD MAN** Polydor POSP 255	**44**	4

All the above hits were instrumentals except for Mary Anne, Don't Make My Baby Blue, I Met A Girl, The Dream I Dream and Let Me Be The One. See also Cliff Richard.

SHAFT UK, male instrumental / production duo   **9 wks**

| 21 Dec 91 | ● **ROOBARB AND CUSTARD** Ffrreedom TAB 100 | **7** | 8 |
| 25 Jul 92 | **MONKEY** Ffrreedom TAB 114 | **61** | 1 |

SHAG – *See Jonathan KING*

SHAGGY Jamaica, male vocalist   **60 wks**

6 Feb 93	★ **OH CAROLINA** Greensleeves GRECD 361	**1**	19
10 Jul 93	**SOON BE DONE** Greensleeves GRECD 380	**46**	3
8 Jul 95	● **IN THE SUMMERTIME** Virgin VSCDT 1542 [1]	**5**	9
23 Sep 95	★ **BOOMBASTIC** Virgin VSCDT 1536	**1**	12
13 Jan 96	**WHY YOU TREAT ME SO BAD** Virgin VSCDT 1566 [2]	**11**	5
23 Mar 96	**SOMETHING DIFFERENT / THE TRAIN IS COMING** Virgin VSCDT 1581 [3]	**21**	5
22 Jun 96	**THAT GIRL** Virgin America VUSCDX 106 [4]	**15**	7

[1] Shaggy featuring Rayvon [2] Shaggy featuring Grand Puba [3] Shaggy featuring Wayne Wonder /Shaggy [4] Maxi Priest featuring Shaggy

SHAI US, male vocal group — 6 wks

19 Dec 92	IF I EVER FALL IN LOVE *MCA MCS 1727*	**36** 6

SHAKATAK UK, male/female vocal/instrumental group — 85 wks

8 Nov 80	FEELS LIKE THE RIGHT TIME *Polydor POSP 188*	**41** 5
7 Mar 81	LIVING IN THE U.K. *Polydor POSP 230*	**52** 4
25 Jul 81	BRAZILIAN DAWN *Polydor POSP 282*	**48** 3
21 Nov 81	EASIER SAID THAN DONE *Polydor POSP 375*	**12** 17
3 Apr 82	● NIGHT BIRDS *Polydor POSP 407*	**9** 8
19 Jun 82	STREETWALKIN' *Polydor POSP 452*	**38** 6
4 Sep 82	INVITATIONS *Polydor POSP 502*	**24** 7
6 Nov 82	STRANGER *Polydor POSP 530*	**43** 3
4 Jun 83	DARK IS THE NIGHT *Polydor POSP 595*	**15** 8
27 Aug 83	IF YOU COULD SEE ME NOW *Polydor POSP 635*	**49** 4
7 Jul 84	● DOWN ON THE STREET *Polydor POSP 688*	**9** 11
15 Sep 84	DON'T BLAME IT ON LOVE *Polydor POSP 699*	**55** 3
16 Nov 85	DAY BY DAY *Polydor POSP 770* [1]	**53** 3
24 Oct 87	MR. MANIC AND SISTER COOL *Polydor MANIC 1*	**56** 3

[1] Shakatak with Al Jarreau

SHAKESPEARS SISTER
UK/US, female vocal/instrumental duo — 52 wks

29 Jul 89	● YOU'RE HISTORY *ffrr F 112*	**7** 9
14 Oct 89	RUN SILENT *ffrr F 119*	**54** 3
10 Mar 90	DIRTY MIND *ffrr F 128*	**71** 1
12 Oct 91	GOODBYE CRUEL WORLD *London LON 309*	**59** 2
25 Jan 92	★ STAY *London LON 314*	**1** 16
16 May 92	● I DON'T CARE *London LON 318*	**7** 7
18 Jul 92	GOODBYE CRUEL WORLD (re-issue) *London LON 322*	**32** 4
7 Nov 92	HELLO (TURN YOUR RADIO ON) *London LON 330*	**14** 6
27 Feb 93	MY 16TH APOLOGY (EP) *London LONCD 337*	**61** 1
22 Jun 96	I CAN DRIVE *London LONCD 383*	**30** 3

Tracks on My 16th Apology (EP): *My 16th Apology / Catwoman / Dirty Mind / Hot Love.*
From 96 Shakespears Sister were essentially just vocalist Siobhan Fahey.

SHAKY and BONNIE – See Shakin' STEVENS; Bonnie TYLER

SHALAMAR US, male/female vocal group — 134 wks

14 May 77	UPTOWN FESTIVAL *Soul Train FB 0885*	**30** 5
9 Dec 78	TAKE THAT TO THE BANK *RCA FB 1379*	**20** 12
24 Nov 79	THE SECOND TIME AROUND *Solar FB 1709*	**45** 9
9 Feb 80	RIGHT IN THE SOCKET *Solar SO2*	**44** 6
30 Aug 80	I OWE YOU ONE *Solar SO 11*	**13** 10
28 Mar 81	MAKE THAT MOVE *Solar SO 17*	**30** 10
27 Mar 82	● I CAN MAKE YOU FEEL GOOD *Solar K 12599*	**7** 11
12 Jun 82	● A NIGHT TO REMEMBER *Solar K 13162*	**5** 12
4 Sep 82	● THERE IT IS *Solar K 13194*	**5** 10
27 Nov 82	FRIENDS *Solar CHUM 1*	**12** 10
11 Jun 83	● DEAD GIVEAWAY *Solar E 9819*	**8** 10
13 Aug 83	DISAPPEARING ACT *Solar E 9807*	**18** 8
15 Oct 83	OVER AND OVER *Solar E 9792*	**23** 6
24 Mar 84	DANCING IN THE SHEETS *CBS A 4171*	**41** 3
31 Mar 84	DEADLINE USA *MCA MCA 866*	**52** 3
24 Nov 84	AMNESIA *Solar/MCA SHal 1*	**61** 2
2 Feb 85	MY GIRL LOVES ME *MCA SHal 2*	**45** 3
26 Apr 86	A NIGHT TO REMEMBER (re-mix) *MCA SHal 3*	**52** 4

SHAM 69 UK, male vocal/instrumental group — 53 wks

13 May 78	ANGELS WITH DIRTY FACES *Polydor 2059 023*	**19** 10
29 Jul 78	● IF THE KIDS ARE UNITED *Polydor 2059 050*	**9** 9
14 Oct 78	● HURRY UP HARRY *Polydor POSP 7*	**10** 8
24 Mar 79	QUESTIONS AND ANSWERS *Polydor POSP 27*	**18** 9
4 Aug 79	● HERSHAM BOYS *Polydor POSP 64*	**6** 9

27 Oct 79	YOU'RE A BETTER MAN THAN I *Polydor POSP 82*	**49** 5
12 Apr 80	TELL THE CHILDREN *Polydor POSP 136*	**45** 3

SHAMEN UK, male vocal/instrumental duo — 76 wks

7 Apr 90	PRO-GEN *One Little Indian 36 TP7*	**55** 4
22 Sep 90	MAKE IT MINE *One Little Indian 46 TP7*	**42** 5
6 Apr 91	HYPERREAL *One Little Indian 48 TP7*	**29** 5
27 Jul 91	● MOVE ANY MOUNTAIN (re-mix) *One Little Indian 52 TP7*	**4** 10
18 Jul 92	● LSI *One Little Indian 68 TP7*	**6** 8
5 Sep 92	★ EBENEEZER GOODE *One Little Indian 78 TP7*	**1** 10
7 Nov 92	● BOSS DRUM *One Little Indian 88 TP7*	**4** 7
7 Nov 92	BOSS DRUM (re-mix) *One Little Indian 88 TP12*	**58** 1
19 Dec 92	● PHOREVER PEOPLE *One Little Indian 98 TP7*	**5** 10
6 Mar 93	RE: EVOLUTION *One Little Indian 118 TP7CD* [1]	**18** 2
6 Nov 93	THE SOS EP *One Little Indian 108 TP7CD*	**14** 4
19 Aug 95	DESTINATION ESCHATON *One Little Indian 128 TP7CDL*	**15** 4
21 Oct 95	TRANSAMAZONIA *One Little Indian 138 TP7CD*	**28** 2
10 Feb 96	HEAL (THE SEPARATION) *One Little Indian 158 TP7CDL*	**31** 2
21 Dec 96	MOVE ANY MOUNTAIN (2nd re-mix) *One Little Indian 169 TP7CD*	**35** 2

[1] Shamen with Terence McKenna

Move Any Mountain *is a re-mix of Pro-Gen. Tracks on SOS EP: Comin' On / Make It Mine / Possible Worlds. Make It Mine on the EP is a re-mix of their second hit.*

SHAMPOO UK, female vocal duo — 28 wks

30 Jul 94	TROUBLE *Food CDFOOD 51*	**11** 12
15 Oct 94	VIVA LA MEGABABES *Food CDFOOD 54*	**27** 4
18 Feb 95	DELICIOUS *Food CDFOOD 58*	**21** 4
5 Aug 95	TROUBLE (re-issue) *Food CDFOOD 66*	**36** 3
13 Jul 96	GIRL POWER *Food CDFOOD 76*	**25** 4
21 Sep 96	I KNOW WHAT BOYS LIKE *Food CDFOOD 83*	**42** 1

Jimmy SHAND UK, male dance band — 2 wks

23 Dec 55	BLUEBELL POLKA *Parlophone F 3436*	**20** 2

Paul SHANE and the YELLOWCOATS
UK, male vocalist with male/female vocal group — 5 wks

16 May 81	HI DE HI (HOLIDAY ROCK) *EMI 5180*	**36** 5

SHANGRI-LAS US, female vocal group — 48 wks

8 Oct 64	REMEMBER (WALKIN' IN THE SAND) *Red Bird RB 10008*	**14** 13
14 Jan 65	LEADER OF THE PACK *Red Bird RB 10014*	**11** 9
14 Oct 72	● LEADER OF THE PACK (re-issue) *Kama Sutra 2013 024*	**3** 14
5 Jun 76	● LEADER OF THE PACK (2nd re-issue) *Charly CS 1009*	**7** 11
12 Jun 76	● LEADER OF THE PACK (3rd re-issue) *Contempo CS 9032*	**7** 10

From 19 Jun 76 until 14 Aug 76, the last week of the disc's chart run, the Charly and Contempo releases of Leader Of The Pack were bracketed together on the chart.

SHANICE US, female vocalist — 24 wks

23 Nov 91	I LOVE YOUR SMILE *Motown ZB 44907*	**55** 4
22 Feb 92	● I LOVE YOUR SMILE (re-mix) *Motown TMG 1401*	**2** 10
14 Nov 92	LOVIN' YOU *Motown TMG 1409*	**54** 1
16 Jan 93	SAVING FOREVER FOR YOU *Giant W 0148CD*	**42** 3
13 Aug 94	I LIKE *Motown TMGCD 1427*	**49** 2
16 Dec 95	IF I NEVER KNEW YOU (LOVE THEME FROM 'POCAHONTAS') *Walt Disney WD 7023CD* [1]	**51** 4

[1] Jon Secada and Shanice

SHANNON US, female vocalist — 36 wks

19 Nov 83	**LET THE MUSIC PLAY** Club LET 1	**51**	3
28 Jan 84	**LET THE MUSIC PLAY (re-entry)** Club LET 1	**14**	12
7 Apr 84	**GIVE ME TONIGHT** Club JAB 1	**24**	7
30 Jun 84	**SWEET SOMEBODY** Club JAB 3	**25**	8
20 Jul 85	**STRONGER TOGETHER** Club JAB 15	**46**	6

Del SHANNON US, male vocalist — 147 wks

27 Apr 61	★ **RUNAWAY** London HLX 9317	**1**	22
14 Sep 61	● **HATS OFF TO LARRY** London HLX 9402	**6**	12
7 Dec 61	● **SO LONG BABY** London HLX 9462	**10**	11
15 Mar 62	● **HEY LITTLE GIRL** London HLX 9515	**2**	15
6 Sep 62	● **CRY MYSELF TO SLEEP** London HLX 9587	**29**	6
11 Oct 62	● **SWISS MAID** London HLX 9609	**2**	17
17 Jan 63	● **LITTLE TOWN FLIRT** London HLX 9653	**4**	13
25 Apr 63	● **TWO KINDS OF TEARDROPS** London HLX 9710	**5**	13
22 Aug 63	**TWO SILHOUETTES** London HLX 9761	**23**	8
24 Oct 63	**SUE'S GOTTA BE MINE** London HLU 9800	**21**	8
12 Mar 64	**MARY JANE** Stateside SS 269	**35**	5
30 Jul 64	**HANDY MAN** Stateside SS 317	**36**	4
14 Jan 65	● **KEEP SEARCHIN' (WE'LL FOLLOW THE SUN)** Stateside SS 368	**3**	11
18 Mar 65	**STRANGER IN TOWN** Stateside SS 395	**40**	2

Roxanne SHANTE US, female rapper — 10 wks

1 Aug 87	**HAVE A NICE DAY** Breakout USA 612	**58**	3
4 Jun 88	**GO ON GIRL** Breakout USA 633	**55**	3
29 Oct 88	**SHARP AS A KNIFE** Club JAB 73 [1]	**45**	3
14 Apr 90	**GO ON GIRL (re-mix)** Breakout USA 689	**74**	1

[1] Brandon Cooke featuring Roxanne Shante

Helen SHAPIRO UK, female vocalist — 119 wks

23 Mar 61	● **DON'T TREAT ME LIKE A CHILD** Columbia DB 4589	**3**	20
29 Jun 61	★ **YOU DON'T KNOW** Columbia DB 4670	**1**	23
28 Sep 61	★ **WALKIN' BACK TO HAPPINESS** Columbia DB 4715	**1**	19
15 Feb 62	● **TELL ME WHAT HE SAID** Columbia DB 4782	**2**	15
3 May 62	**LET'S TALK ABOUT LOVE** Columbia DB 4824	**23**	7
12 Jul 62	● **LITTLE MISS LONELY** Columbia DB 4869	**8**	11
18 Oct 62	**KEEP AWAY FROM OTHER GIRLS** Columbia DB 4908	**40**	6
7 Feb 63	**QUEEN FOR TONIGHT** Columbia DB 4966	**33**	5
25 Apr 63	**WOE IS ME** Columbia DB 7026	**35**	6
24 Oct 63	**LOOK WHO IT IS** Columbia DB 7130	**47**	3
23 Jan 64	**FEVER** Columbia DB 7190	**38**	4

SHARADA HOUSE GANG
Italy, male / female vocal / instrumental group — 3 wks

12 Aug 95	**KEEP IT UP** Media MCSTD 2071	**36**	2
11 May 96	**LET THE RHYTHM MOVE YOU** Media MCSTD 40035	**50**	1

Feargal SHARKEY UK, male vocalist — 58 wks

13 Oct 84	**LISTEN TO YOUR FATHER** Zarjazz JAZZ 1	**23**	7
29 Jun 85	**LOVING YOU** Virgin VS 770	**26**	10
12 Oct 85	★ **A GOOD HEART** Virgin VS 808	**1**	16
4 Jan 86	● **YOU LITTLE THIEF** Virgin VS 840	**5**	9
5 Apr 86	**SOMEONE TO SOMEBODY** Virgin VS 828	**64**	3
16 Jan 88	**MORE LOVE** Virgin VS 992	**44**	5
16 Mar 91	**I'VE GOT NEWS FOR YOU** Virgin VS 1294	**12**	8

SHARONETTES UK, female vocal group — 8 wks

26 Apr 75	**PAPA OOM MOW MOW** Black Magic BM 102	**26**	5
12 Jul 75	**GOING TO A GO-GO** Black Magic BM 104	**46**	3

Debbie SHARP – See DREAM FREQUENCY

Dee Dee SHARP US, female vocalist — 2 wks

25 Apr 63	**DO THE BIRD** Cameo Parkway C 244	**46**	2

Barrie K. SHARPE – See Diana BROWN and Barrie K. SHARPE

SHARPE and NUMAN – See Gary NUMAN

Rocky SHARPE and the REPLAYS
UK, male / female vocal group — 41 wks

16 Dec 78	**RAMA LAMA DING DONG** Chiswick CHIS 104	**17**	10
24 Mar 79	**IMAGINATION** Chiswick CHIS 110	**39**	6
25 Aug 79	**LOVE WILL MAKE YOU FAIL IN SCHOOL** Chiswick CHIS 114 [1]	**60**	4
9 Feb 80	**MARTIAN HOP** Chiswick CHIS 121 [1]	**55**	4
17 Apr 82	**SHOUT SHOUT (KNOCK YOURSELF OUT)** Chiswick DICE 3	**19**	9
7 Aug 82	**CLAP YOUR HANDS** RAK 345	**54**	3
26 Feb 83	**IF YOU WANNA BE HAPPY** Polydor POSP 560	**46**	5

[1] Rocky Sharpe and the Replays featuring the Top Liners

Mark SHAW UK, male vocalist — 1 wk

17 Nov 90	**LOVE SO BRIGHT** EMI EM 161	**54**	1

Sandie SHAW UK, female vocalist — 165 wks

8 Oct 64	★ **(THERE'S) ALWAYS SOMETHING THERE TO REMIND ME** Pye 7N 15704	**1**	11
10 Dec 64	● **GIRL DON'T COME** Pye 7N 15743	**3**	12
18 Feb 65	● **I'LL STOP AT NOTHING** Pye 7N 15783	**4**	11
13 May 65	★ **LONG LIVE LOVE** Pye 7N 15841	**1**	14
23 Sep 65	● **MESSAGE UNDERSTOOD** Pye 7N 15940	**6**	10
18 Nov 65	**HOW CAN YOU TELL** Pye 7N 15987	**21**	9
27 Jan 66	● **TOMORROW** Pye 7N 17036	**9**	9
19 May 66	**NOTHING COMES EASY** Pye 7N 17086	**14**	9
8 Sep 66	**RUN** Pye 7N 17163	**32**	5
24 Nov 66	**THINK SOMETIMES ABOUT ME** Pye 7N 17212	**32**	4
19 Jan 67	**I DON'T NEED ANYTHING** Pye 7N 17239	**50**	1
16 Mar 67	★ **PUPPET ON A STRING** Pye 7N 17272	**1**	18
12 Jul 67	**TONIGHT IN TOKYO** Pye 7N 17346	**21**	6
4 Oct 67	**YOU'VE NOT CHANGED** Pye 7N 17378	**18**	12
7 Feb 68	**TODAY** Pye 7N 17441	**27**	7
12 Feb 69	● **MONSIEUR DUPONT** Pye 7N 17675	**6**	15
14 May 69	**THINK IT ALL OVER** Pye 7N 17726	**42**	4
21 Apr 84	**HAND IN GLOVE** Rough Trade RT 130	**27**	5
14 Jun 86	**ARE YOU READY TO BE HEARTBROKEN** Polydor POSP 793	**68**	1
12 Nov 94	**NOTHING LESS THAN BRILLIANT** Virgin VSCDT 1521	**66**	2

See also Various Artists (EPs & LPs) – Gimme Shelter (EP).

Winifred SHAW US, female vocalist — 4 wks

14 Aug 76	**LULLABY OF BROADWAY** United Artists UP 36131	**42**	4

SHE – See URBAN DISCHARGE featuring SHE

SHE ROCKERS UK, female vocal duo — 2 wks

13 Jan 90	**JAM IT JAM** Jive JIVE 233	**58**	2

George SHEARING UK, male instrumentalist – piano — 15 wks

19 Jul 62	**LET THERE BE LOVE** Capitol CL 15257 [1]	**11**	14

4 Oct 62   **BAUBLES BANGLES AND BEADS** Capitol CL 15269 ....**49** 1

1 Nat 'King' Cole with George Shearing

Gary SHEARSTON Australia, male vocalist   **8 wks**

5 Oct 74   ● **I GET A KICK OUT OF YOU** Charisma CB 234 ....**7** 8

SHED SEVEN UK, male vocal / instrumental group   **31 wks**

25 Jun 94	**DOLPHIN** Polydor YORCD 2 ....**28** 4
27 Aug 94	**SPEAKEASY** Polydor YORCD 3 ....**24** 3
12 Nov 94	**OCEAN PIE** Polydor YORCD 4 ....**33** 2
13 May 95	**WHERE HAVE YOU BEEN TONIGHT** Polydor YORCD 5...**23** 2
27 Jan 96	**GETTING BETTER** Polydor 5778912 ....**14** 3
23 Mar 96	● **GOING FOR GOLD** Polydor 5762152 ....**8** 5
18 May 96	**BULLY BOY** Polydor 5765972 ....**22** 3
31 Aug 96	**ON STANDBY** Polydor 5752732 ....**12** 4
23 Nov 96	**CHASING RAINBOWS** Polydor 5759292 ....**17** 5

SHEEP ON DRUGS UK, male vocal / instrumental duo   **5 wks**

27 Mar 93	**15 MINUTES OF FAME** Transglobal CID 564 ....**44** 2
30 Oct 93	**FROM A TO H AND BACK AGAIN** Transglobal CID 575..**40** 2
14 May 94	**LET THE GOOD TIMES ROLL** Transglobal CID 576..........**56** 1

SHEER BRONZE featuring Lisa MILLETT
UK, male / female vocal / instrumental duo   **1 wk**

3 Sep 94   **WALKIN' ON** Go.Beat GODCD 115 ....**63** 1

SHEER ELEGANCE UK, male vocal group   **23 wks**

20 Dec 75	**MILKY WAY** Pye International 7N 25697 ....**18** 10
3 Apr 76	● **LIFE IS TOO SHORT GIRL** Pye International 7N 25703 ......**9** 9
24 Jul 76	**IT'S TEMPTATION** Pye International 7N 25715..........**41** 4

Doug SHELDON UK, male vocalist   **15 wks**

9 Nov 61	**RUNAROUND SUE** Decca F 11398 ....**36** 3
4 Jan 62	**YOUR MA SAID YOU CRIED IN YOUR SLEEP**
	LAST NIGHT Decca F 11416 ....**29** 6
7 Feb 63	**I SAW LINDA YESTERDAY** Decca F 11564 ....**36** 6

Pete SHELLEY UK, male vocalist   **1 wk**

12 Mar 83   **TELEPHONE OPERATOR** Genetic XX1 ....**66** 1

Peter SHELLEY UK, male vocalist   **20 wks**

| 14 Sep 74 | ● **GEE BABY** Magnet MAG 12 ....**4** 10 |
| 22 Mar 75 | ● **LOVE ME LOVE MY DOG** Magnet MAG 22 ....**3** 10 |

Anne SHELTON UK, female vocalist   **31 wks**

16 Dec 55	**ARRIVEDERCI DARLING** HMV POP 146 ....**17** 4
13 Apr 56	**SEVEN DAYS** Philips PB 567 ....**20** 4
24 Aug 56	★ **LAY DOWN YOUR ARMS** Philips PB 616 ....**1** 14
20 Nov 59	**VILLAGE OF ST. BERNADETTE** Philips PB 969 ....**27** 1
26 Jan 61	● **SAILOR** Philips PB 1096 ....**10** 8

Vikki SHEPARD – See SLEAZESISTERS with Vikki SHEPARD

SHEPHERD SISTERS US, female vocal group   **6 wks**

| 15 Nov 57 | **ALONE** HMV POP 411 ....**14** 5 |
| 3 Jan 58 | **ALONE (re-entry)** HMV POP 411 ....**22** 1 |

SHERBET Australia, male vocal / instrumental group   **10 wks**

25 Sep 76   ● **HOWZAT** Epic EPC 4574 ....**4** 10

Tony SHERIDAN – See BEATLES

Allan SHERMAN US, male vocalist   **10 wks**

12 Sep 63   **HELLO MUDDAH HELLO FADDAH** Warner Bros. WB 106..**14** 10

Bobby SHERMAN US, male vocalist   **4 wks**

31 Oct 70   **JULIE DO YA LOVE ME** CBS 5144 ....**28** 4

SHERRICK US, male vocalist   **10 wks**

| 1 Aug 87 | **JUST CALL** Warner Bros. W 8380 ....**23** 8 |
| 21 Nov 87 | **LET'S BE LOVERS TONIGHT** Warner Bros. W 8146 ....**63** 2 |

Pluto SHERVINGTON Jamaica, male vocalist   **20 wks**

7 Feb 76	● **DAT** Opal Pal 5 ....**6** 8
10 Apr 76	**RAM GOAT LIVER** Trojan TR 7978..........**43** 4
6 Mar 82	**YOUR HONOUR** KR KR 4 1 ....**19** 8

1 Pluto

Holly SHERWOOD US, female vocalist   **7 wks**

5 Feb 72   **DAY BY DAY** Bell 1182 ....**29** 7

Tony SHEVETON UK, male vocalist   **1 wk**

13 Feb 64   **MILLION DRUMS** Oriole CB 1895 ....**49** 1

SHINEHEAD Jamaica, male vocalist   **6 wks**

| 3 Apr 93 | **JAMAICAN IN NEW YORK** Elektra EKR 161CD ....**30** 5 |
| 26 Jun 93 | **LET 'EM IN** Elektra EKR 168CD ....**70** 1 |

SHIRELLES US, female vocal group   **29 wks**

9 Feb 61	● **WILL YOU LOVE ME TOMORROW** Top Rank JAR 540 ......**4** 15
31 May 62	**SOLDIER BOY** HMV POP 1019 ....**23** 9
23 May 63	**FOOLISH LITTLE GIRL** Stateside SS 181..........**38** 5

SHIRLEY and COMPANY
US, female vocalist and male vocal / instrumental backing group   **9 wks**

8 Feb 75   ● **SHAME SHAME SHAME** All Platinum 6146 301 ....**6** 9

SHIVA UK, male / female vocal / instrumental group   **5 wks**

| 13 May 95 | **WORK IT OUT** ffrr FCD 261 ....**36** 2 |
| 19 Aug 95 | **FREEDOM** ffrr FCD 263 ....**18** 3 |

SHO NUFF US, male vocal / instrumental group   **4 wks**

24 May 80   **IT'S ALRIGHT** Ensign ENY 37 ....**53** 4

Michelle SHOCKED US, female vocalist   **10 wks**

8 Oct 88   **ANCHORAGE** Cooking Vinyl LON 193 ....**60** 4

14 Jan 89	**IF LOVE WAS A TRAIN** Cooking Vinyl LON 212	**63** 3
11 Mar 89	**WHEN I GROW UP** Cooking Vinyl LON 219	**67** 3

SHOCKING BLUE
Holland, male / female vocal / instrumental group **14 wks**

17 Jan 70	● **VENUS** Penny Farthing PEN 702	**8** 11
25 Apr 70	**MIGHTY JOE** Penny Farthing PEN 713	**43** 3

Troy SHONDELL *US, male vocalist* **11 wks**

2 Nov 61	**THIS TIME** London HLG 9432	**22** 11

SHONDELLS – *See Tommy JAMES and the SHONDELLS*

SHOOTING PARTY *UK, male vocal duo* **2 wks**

31 Mar 90	**LET'S HANG ON** Lisson DOLE 15	**66** 2

SHOWADDYWADDY
UK, male vocal / instrumental group **209 wks**

18 May 74	● **HEY ROCK AND ROLL** Bell BELL 1357	**2** 14
17 Aug 74	**ROCK 'N' ROLL LADY** Bell BELL 1374	**15** 9
30 Nov 74	**HEY MISTER CHRISTMAS** Bell BELLl 1387	**13** 8
22 Feb 75	**SWEET MUSIC** Bell BELL 1403	**14** 9
17 May 75	● **THREE STEPS TO HEAVEN** Bell BELL 1426	**2** 11
6 Sep 75	● **HEARTBEAT** Bell BELL 1450	**7** 7
15 Nov 75	**HEAVENLY** Bell BELL 1460	**34** 6
29 May 76	**TROCADERO** Bell BELL 1476	**32** 3
6 Nov 76	★ **UNDER THE MOON OF LOVE** Bell BELL 1495	**1** 15
5 Mar 77	● **WHEN** Arista ARIST 91	**3** 11
23 Jul 77	● **YOU GOT WHAT IT TAKES** Arista ARIST 126	**2** 10
5 Nov 77	● **DANCIN' PARTY** Arista ARIST 149	**4** 11
25 Mar 78	● **I WONDER WHY** Arista ARIST 174	**2** 11
24 Jun 78	● **A LITTLE BIT OF SOAP** Arista ARIST 191	**5** 12
4 Nov 78	● **PRETTY LITTLE ANGEL EYES** Arista ARIST 222	**5** 12
31 Mar 79	**REMEMBER THEN** Arista ARIST 247	**17** 8
28 Jul 79	**SWEET LITTLE ROCK 'N' ROLLER** Arista ARIST 278	**15** 9
10 Nov 79	**A NIGHT AT DADDY GEE'S** Arista ARIST 314	**39** 5
27 Sep 80	**WHY DO LOVERS BREAK EACH OTHER'S HEARTS** Arista ARIST 359	**22** 10
29 Nov 80	**BLUE MOON** Arista ARIST 379	**32** 9
13 Jun 81	**MULTIPLICATION** Arista ARIST 416	**39** 4
28 Nov 81	**FOOTSTEPS** Bell BELL 1499	**31** 9
28 Aug 82	**WHO PUT THE BOMP (IN THE BOMP-A-BOMP-A-BOMP)** RCA 236	**37** 6

SHOWDOWN *US, male vocal / instrumental group* **3 wks**

17 Dec 77	**KEEP DOIN' IT** State STAT 63	**41** 3

SHOWDOWN – *See Garry LEE and SHOWDOWN*

SHOWSTOPPERS *US, male vocal group* **25 wks**

13 Mar 68	**AIN'T NOTHING BUT A HOUSEPARTY** Beacon 3-100	**11** 15
13 Nov 68	**EENY MEENY** MGM 1436	**33** 7
30 Jan 71	**AIN'T NOTHING BUT A HOUSEPARTY (re-issue)** Beacon BEA 100	**43** 1
13 Feb 71	**AIN'T NOTHING BUT A HOUSEPARTY (re-entry of re-issue)** Beacon BEA 100	**33** 1
27 Feb 71	**AIN'T NOTHING BUT A HOUSEPARTY (2nd re-entry of re-issue)** Beacon BEA 100	**36** 1

SHRIEKBACK *UK, male vocal / instrumental group* **4 wks**

28 Jul 84	**HAND ON MY HEART** Arista SHRK 1	**52** 4

SHUT UP AND DANCE
UK, male vocal / production group **14 wks**

21 Apr 90	**£20 TO GET IN** Shut Up And Dance SUAD 3	**56** 3
28 Jul 90	**LAMBORGHINI** Shut Up And Dance SUAD 4	**55** 2
8 Feb 92	**AUTOBIOGRAPHY OF A CRACKHEAD / THE GREEN MAN** Shut Up And Dance SUAD 21	**43** 2
30 May 92	● **RAVING I'M RAVING** Shut Up And Dance SUAD 30S [1]	**2** 2
15 Aug 92	**THE ART OF MOVING BUTTS** Shut Up And Dance SUAD 34S [2]	**69** 1
1 Apr 95	**SAVE IT 'TIL THE MOURNING AFTER** Pulse 8 PULS 84CD	**25** 3
8 Jul 95	**I LUV U** Pulse 8 PULS 90CD [3]	**68** 1

[1] Shut Up And Dance featuring Peter Bouncer [2] Shut Up And Dance featuring Erin [3] Shut Up And Dance featuring Richie Davis and Professor T

SHY *UK, male vocal / instrumental group* **3 wks**

19 Apr 80	**GIRL (IT'S ALL I HAVE)** Gallery GA 1	**60** 3

SHY FX – *See UK APACHI with SHY FX*

SHYHEIM *US, male rapper* **1 wk**

8 Jun 96	**THIS IZ REAL** Noo Trybe VUSCD 105	**61** 1

Labi SIFFRE *UK, male vocalist* **44 wks**

27 Nov 71	**IT MUST BE LOVE** Pye International 7N 25572	**14** 12
25 Mar 72	**CRYING LAUGHING LOVING LYING** Pye International 7N 25576	**11** 9
29 Jul 72	**WATCH ME** Pye International 7N 25586	**29** 6
4 Apr 87	● **(SOMETHING INSIDE) SO STRONG** China WOK 12	**4** 13
21 Nov 87	**NOTHIN'S GONNA CHANGE** China WOK 16	**52** 4

SIGUE SIGUE SPUTNIK
UK, male vocal / instrumental group **20 wks**

1 Mar 86	● **LOVE MISSILE F1-11** Parlophone SSS 1	**3** 9
7 Jun 86	**TWENTY-FIRST CENTURY BOY** Parlophone SSS 2	**20** 5
19 Nov 88	**SUCCESS** Parlophone SSS 3	**31** 3
1 Apr 89	**DANCERAMA** Parlophone SSS 5	**50** 2
20 May 89	**ALBINONI VS STAR WARS** Parlophone SSS 4	**75** 1

SILENCERS *UK, male vocal / instrumental group* **7 wks**

25 Jun 88	**PAINTED MOON** RCA HUSH 1	**57** 4
27 May 89	**SCOTTISH RAIN** RCA PB 42701	**71** 2
15 May 93	**I CAN FEEL IT** RCA 74321147112	**62** 1

SILENT UNDERDOG
UK, male instrumentalist – Paul Hardcastle **1 wk**

16 Feb 85	**PAPA'S GOT A BRAND NEW PIGBAG** Kaz KAZ 50	**73** 1

SILJE *Norway, female vocalist* **6 wks**

15 Dec 90	**TELL ME WHERE YOU'RE GOING** EMI EM 159	**55** 6

SILK *US, male vocal group* **10 wks**

24 Apr 93	**FREAK ME** Elektra EKR 165CD	**46** 5
5 Jun 93	**GIRL U FOR ME** Elektra EKR 167CD	**67** 2
9 Oct 93	**BABY IT'S YOU** Elektra EKR 173CD	**44** 2
26 Feb 94	**FREAK ME (re-entry)** Elektra EKR 165CD	**72** 1

SILKIE UK, male / female vocal / instrumental group — 6 wks

23 Sep 65	**YOU'VE GOT TO HIDE YOUR LOVE AWAY** Fontana TF 603	**28**	6

SILSOE UK, male instrumentalist – keyboards — 4 wks

21 Jun 86	**AZTEC GOLD** CBS A 7231	**48**	4

Aztec Gold was the ITV theme to the 1986 World Cup Finals and was performed by Rod Argent under the title Silsoe. See also Argent; San José featuring Rodriguez Argentina.

SILVER BULLET UK, male vocal / instrumental duo — 20 wks

2 Sep 89	**BRING FORTH THE GUILLOTINE** Tam Tam TTT 013	**70**	1
9 Dec 89	**20 SECONDS TO COMPLY** Tam Tam 7TTT 019	**11**	10
3 Mar 90	**BRING FORTH THE GUILLOTINE (re-entry)** Tam Tam TTT 013	**45**	5
13 Apr 91	**UNDERCOVER ANARCHIST** Parlophone R 6284	**33**	4

SILVER BULLET BAND – See Bob SEGER and the SILVER BULLET BAND

SILVER CITY UK, male / female vocal / instrumental duo — 1 wk

30 Oct 93	**LOVE INFINITY** Silver City GFJMCD 1	**62**	1

SILVER CONVENTION
Germany / US, female vocal group — 35 wks

5 Apr 75	**SAVE ME** Magnet MAG 26	**30**	7
15 Nov 75	**FLY ROBIN FLY** Magnet MAG 43	**28**	8
3 Apr 76	● **GET UP AND BOOGIE (THAT'S RIGHT)** Magnet MAG 55	**7**	11
19 Jun 76	**TIGER BABY / NO NO JOE** Magnet MAG 69	**41**	4
29 Jan 77	**EVERYBODY'S TALKIN' 'BOUT LOVE** Magnet MAG 81	**25**	5

SILVER SUN UK, male vocal / instrumental group — 1 wk

2 Nov 96	**LAVA** Polydor 5756872	**54**	1

SILVERCHAIR
Australia, male vocal / instrumental group — 3 wks

29 Jul 95	**PURE MASSACRE** Murmur 6622642	**71**	1
9 Sep 95	**TOMORROW** Murmur 6623952	**59**	2

Dooley SILVERSPOON US, male vocalist — 3 wks

31 Jan 76	**LET ME BE THE NUMBER 1 (LOVE OF YOUR LIFE)** Seville SEV 1020	**44**	3

Harry SIMEONE CHORALE US, choir — 14 wks

13 Feb 59	**LITTLE DRUMMER BOY** Top Rank JAR 101	**13**	7
22 Dec 60	**ONWARD CHRISTIAN SOLDIERS** Ember EMBS 118	**35**	1
5 Jan 61	**ONWARD CHRISTIAN SOLDIERS (re-entry)** Ember EMBS 118	**38**	1
21 Dec 61	**ONWARD CHRISTIAN SOLDIERS (2nd re-entry)** Ember EMBS 118	**36**	3
20 Dec 62	**ONWARD CHRISTIAN SOLDIERS (re-issue)** Ember EMBS 144	**38**	2

Gene SIMMONS US, male vocalist — 4 wks

27 Jan 79	**RADIOACTIVE** Casablanca CAN 134	**41**	4

Carly SIMON US, female vocalist — 76 wks

16 Dec 72	● **YOU'RE SO VAIN** Elektra K 12077	**3**	15
31 Mar 73	**THE RIGHT THING TO DO** Elektra K 12095	**17**	9
16 Mar 74	**MOCKINGBIRD** Elektra K 12134 [1]	**34**	5
6 Aug 77	● **NOBODY DOES IT BETTER** Elektra K 12261	**7**	12
21 Aug 82	● **WHY** WEA K 79300	**10**	13
24 Jan 87	● **COMING AROUND AGAIN** Arista ARIST 687	**10**	12
10 Jun 89	**WHY (re-issue)** WEA U 7501	**56**	5
20 Apr 91	**YOU'RE SO VAIN (re-issue)** Elektra EKR 123	**41**	5

[1] Carly Simon and James Taylor

See also Will Powers.

Joe SIMON US, male vocalist — 10 wks

16 Jun 73	**STEP BY STEP** Mojo 2093 030	**14**	10

Paul SIMON US, male vocalist — 85 wks

19 Feb 72	● **MOTHER AND CHILD REUNION** CBS 7793	**5**	12
29 Apr 72	**ME AND JULIO DOWN BY THE SCHOOLYARD** CBS 7964	**15**	9
16 Jun 73	● **TAKE ME TO THE MARDI GRAS** CBS 1578	**7**	11
22 Sep 73	**LOVES ME LIKE A ROCK** CBS 1700	**39**	5
10 Jan 76	**50 WAYS TO LEAVE YOUR LOVER** CBS 3887	**23**	6
3 Dec 77	**SLIP SLIDIN' AWAY** CBS 5770	**36**	5
6 Sep 80	**LATE IN THE EVENING** Warner Bros. K 17666	**58**	4
13 Sep 86	● **YOU CAN CALL ME AL** Warner Bros. W 8667	**4**	13
13 Dec 86	**THE BOY IN THE BUBBLE** Warner Bros. W 8509	**26**	8
6 Oct 90	**THE OBVIOUS CHILD** Warner Bros W 9549	**15**	10
9 Dec 95	**SOMETHING SO RIGHT** RCA 74321332392 [1]	**44**	2

[1] Annie Lennox featuring Paul Simon

See also Simon and Garfunkel.

Ronni SIMON UK, male vocalist — 2 wks

13 Aug 94	**B GOOD 2 ME** Network NWKCD 80	**73**	1
10 Jun 95	**TAKE YOU THERE** Network NWKCD 85	**58**	1

Tito SIMON Jamaica, male vocalist — 4 wks

8 Feb 75	**THIS MONDAY MORNING FEELING** Horse HOSS 57	**45**	4

SIMON and GARFUNKEL US, male vocal duo — 87 wks

24 Mar 66	● **HOMEWARD BOUND** CBS 202045	**9**	12
16 Jun 66	**I AM A ROCK** CBS 202303	**17**	10
10 Jul 68	● **MRS. ROBINSON** CBS 3443	**4**	12
8 Jan 69	● **MRS. ROBINSON (EP)** CBS EP 6400	**9**	5
30 Apr 69	● **THE BOXER** CBS 4162	**6**	14
21 Feb 70	★ **BRIDGE OVER TROUBLED WATER** CBS 4790	**1**	19
15 Aug 70	**BRIDGE OVER TROUBLED WATER (re-entry)** CBS 4790	**45**	1
7 Oct 72	**AMERICA** CBS 8336	**25**	7
7 Dec 91	**A HAZY SHADE OF WINTER / SILENT NIGHT – SEVEN O'CLOCK NEWS** Columbia 6576537	**30**	6
15 Feb 92	**THE BOXER (re-issue)** Columbia 6578067	**75**	1

Tracks on Mrs. Robinson (EP): Mrs. Robinson / Scarborough Fair – Canticle / Sounds of Silence / April Come She Will. This EP would have stayed more than five weeks on chart had a decision to exclude EPs from chart in Feb 69 not been taken. See also Paul Simon; Art Garfunkel.

SIMONE US, female vocalist — 1 wk

23 Nov 91	**MY FAMILY DEPENDS ON ME** Strictly Rhythm A 8678	**75**	1

Nina SIMONE US, female vocalist — 46 wks

5 Aug 65	I PUT A SPELL ON YOU *Philips BF 1415*	49	1
16 Oct 68	● AIN'T GOT NO – I GOT LIFE / DO WHAT YOU GOTTA DO *RCA 1743*	2	18
15 Jan 69	TO LOVE SOMEBODY *RCA 1779*	5	9
15 Jan 69	I PUT A SPELL ON YOU (re-issue) *Philips BF 1736*	28	4
31 Oct 87	● MY BABY JUST CARES FOR ME *Charly CYZ 7112*	5	11
9 Jul 94	FEELING GOOD *Mercury MERCD 403*	40	3

Do What You Gotta Do was only listed for the first eight weeks of the record's chart run. It peaked at position 7.

Victor SIMONELLI presents SOLUTION
US, male producer — 1 wk

2 Nov 96	FEELS SO RIGHT *Soundproof MCSTD 40068*	63	1

SIMPLE MINDS UK, male vocal / instrumental group — 184 wks

12 May 79	LIFE IN A DAY *Zoom ZUM 10*	62	2
23 May 81	THE AMERICAN *Virgin VS 410*	59	3
15 Aug 81	LOVE SONG *Virgin VS 434*	47	4
7 Nov 81	SWEAT IN BULLET *Virgin VS 451*	52	3
10 Apr 82	PROMISED YOU A MIRACLE *Virgin VS 488*	13	11
28 Aug 82	GLITTERING PRIZE *Virgin VS 511*	16	11
13 Nov 82	SOMEONE SOMEWHERE (IN SUMMERTIME) *Virgin VS 538*	36	5
26 Nov 83	WATERFRONT *Virgin VS 636*	13	10
28 Jan 84	SPEED YOUR LOVE TO ME *Virgin VS 649*	20	4
24 Mar 84	UP ON THE CATWALK *Virgin VS 661*	27	5
20 Apr 85	● DON'T YOU (FORGET ABOUT ME) *Virgin VS 749*	7	11
17 Aug 85	DON'T YOU (FORGET ABOUT ME) (re-entry) *Virgin VS 749*	61	8
12 Oct 85	● ALIVE AND KICKING *Virgin VS 817*	7	9
28 Dec 85	DON'T YOU (FORGET ABOUT ME) (2nd re-entry) *Virgin VS 749*	74	1
4 Jan 86	ALIVE AND KICKING (re-entry) *Virgin VS 817*	60	2
1 Feb 86	● SANCTIFY YOURSELF *Virgin SM 1*	10	7
15 Feb 86	DON'T YOU (FORGET ABOUT ME) (3rd re-entry) *Virgin VS 779*	62	3
15 Mar 86	DON'T YOU (FORGET ABOUT ME) (4th re-entry) *Virgin VS 779*	68	1
12 Apr 86	● ALL THE THINGS SHE SAID *Virgin VS 860*	9	8
14 Jun 86	ALL THE THINGS SHE SAID (re-entry) *Virgin VS 860*	73	1
15 Nov 86	GHOSTDANCING *Virgin VS 907*	13	6
3 Jan 87	GHOSTDANCING (re-entry) *Virgin VS 907*	68	2
20 Jun 87	PROMISED YOU A MIRACLE *Virgin SM 2*	19	7
18 Feb 89	★ BELFAST CHILD *Virgin SMX 3*	1	11
22 Apr 89	THIS IS YOUR LAND *Virgin SMX4*	13	4
29 Jul 89	KICK IT IN *Virgin SM 5*	15	5
9 Dec 89	THE AMSTERDAM EP *Virgin SMX 6*	18	6
23 Mar 91	● LET THERE BE LOVE *Virgin VS 1332*	6	7
25 May 91	SEE THE LIGHTS *Virgin VS 1343*	20	4
31 Aug 91	STAND BY LOVE *Virgin VS 1358*	13	4
26 Oct 91	REAL LIFE *Virgin VS 1382*	34	3
10 Oct 92	● LOVE SONG / ALIVE AND KICKING (re-issues) *Virgin VS 1440*	6	4
28 Jan 95	SHE'S A RIVER *Virgin VSCDX 1509*	9	5
8 Apr 95	HYPNOTISED *Virgin VSCDX 1534*	18	5

The 1987 version of Promised You A Miracle was a live recording. Tracks on The Amsterdam EP: Let It All Come Down / Jerusalem / Sign Of The Times.

SIMPLICIOUS US, male vocal group — 9 wks

29 Sep 84	LET HER FEEL IT *Fourth & Broadway BRW 13*	65	3
2 Feb 85	LET HER FEEL IT (re-issue) *Fourth & Broadway BRW 18*	34	6

The re-issue of Let Her Feel It was listed with Personality by Eugene Wilde.

SIMPLY RED UK, male vocal / instrumental group — 177 wks

15 Jun 85	MONEY'S TOO TIGHT (TO MENTION) *Elektra EKR 9*	13	12
21 Sep 85	COME TO MY AID *Elektra EKR 19*	66	2
16 Nov 85	HOLDING BACK THE YEARS *Elektra EKR 29*	51	4
8 Mar 86	JERICHO *WEA YZ 63*	53	3
17 May 86	● HOLDING BACK THE YEARS (re-issue) *WEA YZ 70*	2	13
9 Aug 86	OPEN UP THE RED BOX *WEA YZ 75*	61	4
14 Feb 87	THE RIGHT THING *WEA YZ 103*	11	10
23 May 87	INFIDELITY *Elektra YZ 114*	31	5
28 Nov 87	EV'RY TIME WE SAY GOODBYE *Elektra YZ 161*	11	9
12 Mar 88	I WON'T FEEL BAD *Elektra YZ 172*	68	3
28 Jan 89	IT'S ONLY LOVE *Elektra YZ 349*	13	6
8 Apr 89	● IF YOU DON'T KNOW ME BY NOW *Elektra YZ 377*	2	10
8 Jul 89	A NEW FLAME *WEA YZ 404*	17	8
28 Oct 89	YOU'VE GOT IT *Elektra YZ 424*	46	3
21 Sep 91	SOMETHING GOT ME STARTED *East West YZ 614*	11	8
30 Nov 91	● STARS *East West YZ 626*	8	10
8 Feb 92	● FOR YOUR BABIES *East West YZ 642*	9	8
2 May 92	THRILL ME *East West YZ 671*	33	5
25 Jul 92	YOUR MIRROR *East West YZ 689*	17	4
21 Nov 92	MONTREUX EP *East West YZ 716*	11	4
30 Sep 95	★ FAIRGROUND *East West EW 001CD1*	1	14
16 Dec 95	REMEMBERING THE FIRST TIME *East West EW 015CD1*	22	6
24 Feb 96	NEVER NEVER LOVE *East West EW 029CD1*	18	4
22 Jun 96	WE'RE IN THIS TOGETHER *East West EW 046CD1*	11	6
9 Nov 96	● ANGEL *East West EW 074CD1*	4†	6

Tracks on Montreux EP: Drowning In My Own Tears / Granma's Hands / Lady Godiva's Room / Love For Sale.

SIMPLY RED AND WHITE UK, male vocal group — 4 wks

6 Apr 96	DAYDREAM BELIEVER (CHEER UP PETER REID) *Ropery SHAYISGOD 1D*	41	3
4 May 96	DAYDREAM BELIEVER (CHEER UP PETER REID) (re-entry) *Ropery SHAYISGOD 1D*	74	1

Paul SIMPSON – See ADEVA

Vida SIMPSON US, female vocalist — 1 wk

18 Feb 95	OOHHH BABY *Hi-Life HICD 6*	70	1

SIMPSONS US, male / female cartoon group — 19 wks

26 Jan 91	★ DO THE BARTMAN *Geffen GEF 87*	1	12
6 Apr 91	● DEEP DEEP TROUBLE *Geffen GEF 88* [1]	7	7

[1] Simpsons featuring Bart and Homer

W/Cdr. A.E. SIMS – See Central Band of the ROYAL AIR FORCE, conductor W/Cdr. A.E. SIMS, O.B.E.

Joyce SIMS US, female vocalist — 36 wks

19 Apr 86	ALL AND ALL *London LON 94*	16	10
13 Jun 87	LIFETIME LOVE *London LON 137*	34	6
9 Jan 88	● COME INTO MY LIFE *London LON 161*	7	9
23 Apr 88	WALK AWAY *London LON 176*	24	6
17 Jun 89	LOOKING FOR A LOVE *ffrr F 109*	39	4
27 May 95	COME INTO MY LIFE (re-mix) *Club Tools 0060435 CLU*	72	1

Kym SIMS US, female vocalist — 23 wks

7 Dec 91	● TOO BLIND TO SEE IT *Atco B 8667*	5	12
28 Mar 92	TAKE MY ADVICE *Atco B 8591*	13	7
27 Jun 92	A LITTLE BIT MORE *Atco B 8528*	30	3
8 Jun 96	WE GOTTA LOVE *Pulse 8 CDLOSE 104*	58	1

SIN WITH SEBASTIAN
Germany, male vocalist – Sebastian Roth **2 wks**

16 Sep 95	**SHUT UP (AND SLEEP WITH ME)** *Sing Sing 74321253592* ..**44**	1
27 Jan 96	**SHUT UP (AND SLEEP WITH ME) (re-mix)** *Sing Sing 74321337972* **46**	1

Frank SINATRA *US, male vocalist* **439 wks**

9 Jul 54	**YOUNG AT HEART** *Capitol CL 14064* **12**	1
16 Jul 54	★ **THREE COINS IN THE FOUNTAIN** *Capitol CL 14120* **1**	19
10 Jun 55	**YOU MY LOVE** *Capitol CL 14240* **13**	3
22 Jul 55	**YOU MY LOVE (re-entry)** *Capitol CL 14240* **17**	2
5 Aug 55	● **LEARNIN' THE BLUES** *Capitol CL 14296* **2**	13
12 Aug 55	**YOU MY LOVE (2nd re-entry)** *Capitol CL 14240* **17**	2
2 Sep 55	**NOT AS A STRANGER** *Capitol CL 14326*.............**18**	1
13 Jan 56	● **LOVE AND MARRIAGE** *Capitol CL 14503* **3**	8
20 Jan 56	**(LOVE IS) THE TENDER TRAP** *Capitol CL 14511* **2**	9
15 Jun 56	**SONGS FOR SWINGING LOVERS (LP)** *Capitol LCT 6106*..**12**	8
22 Nov 57	**ALL THE WAY** *Capitol CL 14800* **29**	1
29 Nov 57	**CHICAGO** *Capitol CL 14800* **25**	1
6 Dec 57	**ALL THE WAY / CHICAGO (re-entry)** *Capitol CL 14800* ..**21**	1
13 Dec 57	● **ALL THE WAY (2nd re-entry)** *Capitol CL 14800* **3**	17
7 Feb 58	**WITCHCRAFT** *Capitol CL 14819* **12**	8
14 Nov 58	**MR. SUCCESS** *Capitol CL 14956* **29**	1
12 Dec 58	**MR. SUCCESS (re-entry)** *Capitol CL 14956* **25**	2
2 Jan 59	**MR. SUCCESS (2nd re-entry)** *Capitol CL 14956* **26**	1
10 Apr 59	**FRENCH FOREIGN LEGION** *Capitol CL 14997* **18**	5
15 May 59	**COME DANCE WITH ME (LP)** *Capitol LCT 6179* **30**	1
28 Aug 59	**HIGH HOPES** *Capitol CL 15052* **28**	1
11 Sep 59	● **HIGH HOPES (re-entry)** *Capitol CL 15052* **6**	13
10 Mar 60	**HIGH HOPES (2nd re-entry)** *Capitol CL 15052* **42**	1
7 Apr 60	**IT'S NICE TO GO TRAV'LING** *Capitol CL 15116* **48**	2
16 Jun 60	**RIVER STAY 'WAY FROM MY DOOR** *Capitol CL 15135* ..**18**	3
8 Sep 60	**NICE 'N EASY** *Capitol CL 15150* **15**	12
24 Nov 60	**OL' MACDONALD** *Capitol CL 15168* **11**	8
20 Apr 61	**MY BLUE HEAVEN** *Capitol CL 15193* **33**	7
28 Sep 61	**GRANADA** *Reprise R 20010* **15**	8
23 Nov 61	**THE COFFEE SONG** *Reprise R 20035* **39**	3
5 Apr 62	**EVERYBODY'S TWISTING** *Reprise R 20063* **22**	12
13 Dec 62	**ME AND MY SHADOW** *Reprise R 20128* [1] **20**	7
7 Feb 63	**ME AND MY SHADOW (re-entry)** *Reprise R 20128* [1] ..**47**	2
7 Mar 63	**MY KIND OF GIRL** *Reprise R 20148* [2] **35**	6
24 Sep 64	**HELLO DOLLY** *Reprise R 20351* [2] **47**	1
12 May 66	★ **STRANGERS IN THE NIGHT** *Reprise R 23052* **1**	20
29 Sep 66	**SUMMER WIND** *Reprise RS 20509* **36**	5
15 Dec 66	**THAT'S LIFE** *Reprise RS 20531* **46**	5
23 Mar 67	★ **SOMETHIN' STUPID** *Reprise RS 23166* [3] **1**	18
23 Aug 67	**THE WORLD WE KNEW OVER AND OVER)** *Reprise RS 20610* **33**	11
2 Apr 69	● **MY WAY** *Reprise RS 20817* **5**	42
4 Oct 69	● **LOVE'S BEEN GOOD TO ME** *Reprise RS 20852* **8**	18
31 Jan 70	**MY WAY (re-entry)** *Reprise RS 20817* **49**	1
28 Feb 70	**MY WAY (2nd re-entry)** *Reprise RS 20817* **30**	5
11 Apr 70	**MY WAY (3rd re-entry)** *Reprise RS 20817* **33**	9
27 Jun 70	**MY WAY (4th re-entry)** *Reprise RS 20817* **28**	21
28 Nov 70	**MY WAY (5th re-entry)** *Reprise RS 20817* **18**	16
6 Mar 71	**I WILL DRINK THE WINE** *Reprise RS 23487* **16**	12
27 Mar 71	**MY WAY (6th re-entry)** *Reprise RS 20817* **22**	19
4 Sep 71	**MY WAY (7th re-entry)** *Reprise RS 20817* **39**	8
1 Jan 72	**MY WAY (8th re-entry)** *Reprise RS 20817* **50**	1
20 Dec 75	**I BELIEVE I'M GONNA LOVE YOU** *Reprise K 14400* **34**	7
9 Aug 80	**THEME FROM NEW YORK, NEW YORK** *Reprise K 14502* **59**	4
22 Feb 86	● **THEME FROM NEW YORK, NEW YORK (re-entry)** *Reprise K 14502* **4**	10
4 Dec 93	● **I'VE GOT YOU UNDER MY SKIN** *Island CID 578* [4] **4**	9
16 Apr 94	**MY WAY (re-issue)** *Reprise W 0163CD* **45**	2

[1] Frank Sinatra and Sammy Davis Jr. [2] Frank Sinatra with Count Basie [3] Nancy Sinatra and Frank Sinatra [4] Frank Sinatra with Bono

Tracks on Songs For Swinging Lovers LP*: You Make Me Feel So Young / It Happened In Monterey / You're Getting To Be A Habit With Me / You Brought A New Kind Of Love To Me / Too Marvellous For Words / Old Devil Moon / Pennies From Heaven / Love Is Here To Stay / I've Got You Under My Skin / I Thought About You / We'll Be Together Again / Making Whoopee / Swingin' Down The Lane / Anything Goes / How About You.* Tracks on* Come Dance With Me LP*: Something's Gotta Give / Just In Time / Dancing In The Dark / Too Close For Comfort / I Could Have Danced All Night / Saturday Night Is The Loneliest Night Of The Week / Day In Day Out / Cheek To Cheek / Baubles Bangles And Beads / The Song Is You / The Last Dance.* All The Way *and* Chicago*, Capitol CL14800, were at first billed separately, then together for one week, then* All The Way *on its own.* I've Got You Under My Skin *was the listed B-side of* Stay (Faraway So Close) *by U2.*

See also U2.

Nancy SINATRA *US, female vocalist* **99 wks**

27 Jan 66	★ **THESE BOOTS ARE MADE FOR WALKING** *Reprise R 20432* **1**	14
28 Apr 66	**HOW DOES THAT GRAB YOU DARLIN'** *Reprise R 20461* ..**19**	8
19 Jan 67	● **SUGAR TOWN** *Reprise RS 20527* **8**	10
23 Mar 67	★ **SOMETHIN' STUPID** *Reprise RS 23166* [1] **1**	18
5 Jul 67	**YOU ONLY LIVE TWICE /JACKSON** *Reprise RS 20595* [2] **11**	19
8 Nov 67	**LADYBIRD** *Reprise RS 20629* [3] **47**	1
29 Nov 69	**HIGHWAY SONG** *Reprise RS 20869* **21**	10
21 Aug 71	● **DID YOU EVER** *Reprise K 14093* [4] **2**	19

[1] Nancy Sinatra and Frank Sinatra [2] Nancy Sinatra / Nancy Sinatra and Lee Hazlewood [3] Nancy Sinatra and Lee Hazlewood [4] Nancy and Lee

Jackson *listed with* You Only Live Twice *from 12 Jul 67.*

SINCLAIR *UK, male vocalist* **8 wks**

21 Aug 93	**AIN'T NO CASANOVA** *Dome CDDOME 1004*..............**28**	5
26 Feb 94	**(I WANNA KNOW) WHY** *Dome CDDOME 1009* **58**	2
6 Aug 94	**DON'T LIE** *Dome CDDOME 1010* **70**	1

SINDY *UK, female vocalist* **1 wk**

5 Oct 96	**SATURDAY NIGHT** *Love This LUVTHISCD 13*..................**70**	1

SINE *US, disco aggregation* **9 wks**

10 Jun 78	**JUST LET ME DO MY THING** *CBS 6351*.............**33**	9

SINFONIA OF LONDON – *See Peter AUTY and the SINFONIA OF LONDON*

SINGING CORNER – *See DONOVAN*

SINGING DOGS *Denmark, canine vocal group* **4 wks**

25 Nov 55	**THE SINGING DOGS (MEDLEY)** *Nixa N 15009* **13**	4

Medley songs: Pat-a-Cake / Three Blind Mice / Jingle Bells / Oh Susanna.

SINGING NUN (Soeur Sourire)
Belgium, female vocalist **14 wks**

5 Dec 63	● **DOMINIQUE** *Philips BF 1293*.........................**7**	14

SINGING SHEEP *UK, computerized sheep noises* **5 wks**

18 Dec 82	**BAA BAA BLACK SHEEP** *Sheep BAA 1* **42**	5

Maxine SINGLETON *US, female vocalist* **3 wks**

2 Apr 83	**YOU CAN'T RUN FROM LOVE** *Creole CR 50* **57**	3

SINITTA US, female vocalist   104 wks

8 Mar 86		**SO MACHO / CRUISING** Fanfare FAN 7	**47** 11
28 Jun 86	●	**SO MACHO / CRUISING (re-entry)** Fanfare FAN 7	**2** 17
11 Oct 86		**FEELS LIKE THE FIRST TIME** Fanfare FAN 8	**45** 5
25 Jul 87	●	**TOY BOY** Fanfare FAN 12	**4** 14
12 Dec 87		**G.T.O** Fanfare FAN 14	**15** 9
19 Mar 88	●	**CROSS MY BROKEN HEART** Fanfare FAN 15	**6** 9
24 Sep 88		**I DON'T BELIEVE IN MIRACLES** Fanfare FAN 16	**22** 8
3 Jun 89	●	**RIGHT BACK WHERE WE STARTED FROM** Fanfare FAN18	**4** 10
7 Oct 89		**LOVE ON A MOUNTAIN TOP** Fanfare FAN 21	**20** 6
21 Apr 90		**HITCHIN' A RIDE** Fanfare FAN 24	**24** 6
22 Sep 90		**LOVE AND AFFECTION** Fanfare FAN 31	**62** 3
4 Jul 92		**SHAME SHAME SHAME** Arista 74321100327	**28** 4
17 Apr 93		**THE SUPREME EP** Arista 74321139592	**49** 2

Tracks on The Supreme EP: Where Did Our Love Go / Stop! In The Name Of Love / You Can't Hurry Love / Remember Me.

SINNAMON US, male vocal / instrumental group   1 wk

28 Sep 96		**I NEED YOU NOW** Worx WORXCD 003	**70** 1

SIOUXSIE and the BANSHEES
UK, female / male vocal / instrumental group   150 wks

26 Aug 78	●	**HONG KONG GARDEN** Polydor 2059 052	**7** 10
31 Mar 79		**THE STAIRCASE (MYSTERY)** Polydor POSP 9	**24** 8
7 Jul 79		**PLAYGROUND TWIST** Polydor POSP 59	**28** 6
29 Sep 79		**MITTAGEISEN (METAL POSTCARD)** Polydor 2059 151	**47** 3
15 Mar 80		**HAPPY HOUSE** Polydor POSP 117	**17** 8
7 Jun 80		**CHRISTINE** Polydor 2059 249	**22** 8
6 Dec 80		**ISRAEL** Polydor POSP 205	**41** 8
30 May 81		**SPELLBOUND** Polydor POSP 273	**22** 8
1 Aug 81		**ARABIAN KNIGHTS** Polydor POSP 309	**32** 7
29 May 82		**FIRE WORKS** Polydor POSPG 450	**22** 6
9 Oct 82		**SLOWDIVE** Polydor POSP 510	**41** 4
4 Dec 82		**MELT / IL EST NE LE DIVIN ENFANT** Polydor POSP 539	**49** 5
1 Oct 83	●	**DEAR PRUDENCE** Wonderland SHE 4	**3** 8
24 Mar 84		**SWIMMING HORSES** Wonderland SHE 6	**28** 4
2 Jun 84		**DAZZLE** Wonderland SHE 7	**33** 3
27 Oct 84		**THE THORN EP** Wonderland SHEEP 8	**47** 3
26 Oct 85		**CITIES IN DUST** Wonderland SHE 9	**21** 6
8 Mar 86		**CANDYMAN** Wonderland SHE 10	**34** 5
17 Jan 87		**THIS WHEEL'S ON FIRE** Wonderland SHE 11	**14** 6
28 Mar 87		**THE PASSENGER** Wonderland SHE 12	**41** 6
25 Jul 87		**SONG FROM THE EDGE OF THE WORLD** Wonderland SHE 13	**59** 3
30 Jul 88		**PEEK-A-BOO** Wonderland SHE 14	**16** 6
8 Oct 88		**THE KILLING JAR** Wonderland SHE 15	**41** 3
3 Dec 88		**THE LAST BEAT OF MY HEART** Wonderland SHE 16	**44** 1
25 May 91		**KISS THEM FOR ME** Wonderland SHE 19	**32** 4
13 Jul 91		**SHADOWTIME** Wonderland SHE 20	**57** 1
25 Jul 92		**FACE TO FACE** Wonderland SHE 21	**21** 4
20 Aug 94		**INTERLUDE** Parlophone CDR 6365 [1]	**25** 2
7 Jan 95		**O BABY** Wonderland SHECD 22	**34** 3
18 Feb 95		**STARGAZER** Wonderland SHECD 23	**64** 1

[1] Morrissey and Siouxsie

Tracks on The Thorn EP: Overground / Voices / Placebo Effect / Red Over White.

SIR DOUGLAS QUINTET
US, male vocal / instrumental group   10 wks

17 Jun 65		**SHE'S ABOUT A MOVER** London HLU 9964	**15** 10

SIR MIX-A-LOT US, male rapper   2 wks

8 Aug 92		**BABY GOT BACK** Def American DEFA 20	**56** 2

SIRRON – See PLUS ONE featuring SIRRON

SISTA – See VARIOUS ARTISTS (EPs and LPs) – The Dangerous Minds EP

SISTER BLISS with COLETTE
UK, female vocal / instrumental duo   7 wks

15 Oct 94	**CANTGETAMAN CANTGETAJOB (LIFE'S A BITCH)** Go.Beat GODCD 124	**31** 4
15 Jul 95	**OH! WHAT A WORLD** Go.Beat GODCD 126	**40** 2
29 Jun 96	**BADMAN** Junk Dog JDOGCD 1 [1]	**51** 1

[1] Sister Bliss

SISTER SLEDGE US, female vocal group   111 wks

21 Jun 75		**MAMA NEVER TOLD ME** Atlantic K 10619	**20** 6
17 Mar 79	●	**HE'S THE GREATEST DANCER** Atlantic/Cotillion K 11257	**6** 11
26 May 79	●	**WE ARE FAMILY** Atlantic/Cotillion K 11293	**8** 10
11 Aug 79		**LOST IN MUSIC** Atlantic/Cotillion K 11337	**17** 10
19 Jan 80		**GOT TO LOVE SOMEBODY** Atlantic/Cotillion K 11404	**34** 4
28 Feb 81		**ALL AMERICAN GIRLS** Atlantic K 11656	**41** 5
26 May 84		**THINKING OF YOU** Cotillion K 11571	**11** 13
8 Sep 84	●	**LOST IN MUSIC (re-mix)** Cotillion/Atlantic B 9718	**4** 12
17 Nov 84		**WE ARE FAMILY (re-mix)** Cotillion/Atlantic B 9692	**33** 4
1 Jun 85	★	**FRANKIE** Atlantic A 9547	**1** 16
31 Aug 85		**DANCING ON THE JAGGED EDGE** Atlantic A 9520	**50** 3
23 Jan 93	●	**WE ARE FAMILY (2nd re-mix)** Atlantic A 4508CD	**5** 8
13 Mar 93		**LOST IN MUSIC (2nd re-mix)** Atlantic A 4509CD	**14** 5
12 Jun 93		**THINKING OF YOU (re-mix)** Atlantic A 4515CD	**17** 4

SISTERS OF MERCY
UK, male vocalist Andrew Eldritch and backing musicians   40 wks

16 Jun 84		**BODY AND SOUL / TRAIN** Merciful Release MR 029	**46** 3
20 Oct 84		**WALK AWAY** Merciful Release MR 033	**45** 3
9 Mar 85		**NO TIME TO CRY** Merciful Release MR 035	**63** 2
3 Oct 87	●	**THIS CORROSION** Merciful Release MR 39	**7** 6
27 Feb 88		**DOMINION** Merciful Release MR 43	**13** 6
18 Jun 88		**LUCRETIA MY REFLECTION** Merciful Release MR 45	**20** 4
13 Oct 90		**MORE** Merciful Release MR 47	**14** 4
22 Dec 90		**DOCTOR JEEP** Merciful Release MR 51	**37** 4
2 May 92	●	**TEMPLE OF LOVE** Merciful Release MR 53	**3** 5
28 Aug 93		**UNDER THE GUN** Merciful Release MR 59CDX	**19** 3

SIVUCA Brazil, male vocalist   3 wks

28 Jul 84		**AIN'T NO SUNSHINE** London LON 51	**56** 3

6 BY SIX UK, male instrumental / production duo   1 wk

4 May 96		**INTO YOUR HEART** Six6 SIXCD 130	**51** 1

60FT DOLLS UK, male vocal / instrumental group   3 wks

3 Feb 96		**STAY** Indolent DOLLS 002CD	**48** 1
11 May 96		**TALK TO ME** Indolent DOLLS 003CD	**37** 1
20 Jul 96		**HAPPY SHOPPER** Indolent DOLLS 005CD	**38** 1

SIZE 9 US, male producer – Josh Wink   4 wks

17 Jun 95		**I'M READY** Virgin America VUSCD 92	**52** 1
11 Nov 95		**I'M READY (re-issue)** VC VCRD 2 [1]	**30** 3

[1] Josh Wink's Size 9

See also Josh Wink.

Skunk Anansie

Skunk Anansie are both characters from a Jamaican folk tale, Anansie being a spider.

Small Faces

The Small Faces are one of the bands most often cited as the inspiration for the current crop of British guitar acts. Paul Weller, Ocean Colour Scene and Dodgy are just some of the artists who contributed to the Small Faces tribute album released in 1996.

Simply Red

Simply Red's cover of Aretha Franklin's 'Angel' also featured Wyclef Jean and Prakazrel Michel of the Fugees.

SKATALITES *Jamaica, male instrumental group* — 6 wks

20 Apr 67	**GUNS OF NAVARONE** *Island WI 168*	**36**	6

SKEE-LO *US, male rapper* — 10 wks

9 Dec 95	**I WISH** *Wild Card 5777752*	**15**	8
27 Apr 96	**TOP OF THE STAIRS** *Wild Card 5763352*	**38**	2

Beverli SKEETE – *See DE-CODE featuring Beverli SKEETE*

Peter SKELLERN *UK, male vocalist* — 24 wks

23 Sep 72	● **YOU'RE A LADY** *Decca F 13333*	**3**	11
29 Mar 75	**HOLD ON TO LOVE** *Decca F 13568*	**14**	9
28 Oct 78	**LOVE IS THE SWEETEST THING** *Mercury 6008 603* [1]	**60**	4

[1] Peter Skellern featuring Grimethorpe Colliery Band

SKID ROW *US, male vocal / instrumental group* — 27 wks

18 Nov 89	**YOUTH GONE WILD** *Atlantic A 8935*	**42**	3
3 Feb 90	**18 AND LIFE** *Atlantic A 8883*	**12**	6
31 Mar 90	**I REMEMBER YOU** *East West A 8836*	**36**	4
15 Jun 91	**MONKEY BUSINESS** *Atlantic A 7673*	**19**	3
14 Sep 91	**SLAVE TO THE GRIND** *Atlantic A 7603*	**43**	2
23 Nov 91	**WASTED TIME** *Atlantic A 7570*	**20**	3
29 Aug 92	**YOUTH GONE WILD (re-issue) / DELIVERING THE GOODS** *Atlantic A 7444*	**22**	4
18 Nov 95	**BREAKIN' DOWN** *Atlantic A 7135CD1*	**48**	2

SKIDS *UK, male vocal / instrumental group* — 60 wks

23 Sep 78	**SWEET SUBURBIA** *Virgin VS 227*	**70**	1
7 Oct 78	**SWEET SUBURBIA (re-entry)** *Virgin VS 227*	**71**	2
4 Nov 78	**THE SAINTS ARE COMING** *Virgin VS 232*	**48**	3
17 Feb 79	● **INTO THE VALLEY** *Virgin VS 241*	**10**	11
26 May 79	**MASQUERADE** *Virgin VS 262*	**14**	9
29 Sep 79	**CHARADE** *Virgin VS 288*	**31**	6
24 Nov 79	**WORKING FOR THE YANKEE DOLLAR** *Virgin VS 306*	**20**	11
1 Mar 80	**ANIMATION** *Virgin VS 323*	**56**	3
16 Aug 80	**CIRCUS GAMES** *Virgin VS 359*	**32**	7
18 Oct 80	**GOODBYE CIVILIAN** *Virgin VS 373*	**52**	4
6 Dec 80	**WOMEN IN WINTER** *Virgin VSK 101*	**49**	3

SKIN *UK / Germany, male vocal / instrumental group* — 19 wks

25 Dec 93	**THE SKIN UP EP** *Parlophone CDR 6363*	**67**	2
12 Mar 94	**HOUSE OF LOVE** *Parlophone CDR 6374*	**45**	2
30 Apr 94	**MONEY / UNBELIEVEABLE** *Parlophone CDR 6381*	**18**	3
23 Jul 94	**TOWER OF STRENGTH** *Parlophone CDR 6387*	**19**	3
15 Oct 94	**LOOK BUT DON'T TOUCH (EP)** *Parlophone CDR 6391*	**33**	3
20 May 95	**TAKE ME DOWN TO THE RIVER** *Parlophone CDR 6409*	**26**	2
23 Mar 96	**HOW LUCKY YOU ARE** *Parlophone CDR 6426*	**32**	2
18 May 96	**PERFECT DAY** *Parlophone CDR 6433*	**33**	2

Tracks on The Skin Up EP: *Look But Don't Touch / Shine Your Light / Monkey*. Tracks on Look But Don't Touch (EP): *Look But Don't Touch / Should I Stay Or Should I Go / Pump It Up / Monkey*. The first and last tracks on this EP are, of course, re-issues of two tracks from The Skin Up EP.

SKIN UP *UK, male producer* — 9 wks

7 Sep 91	**IVORY** *Love EVOL 4*	**48**	3
14 Mar 92	**A JUICY RED APPLE** *Love EVOL 11*	**32**	4
18 Jul 92	**ACCELERATE** *Love EVOL 17*	**45**	2

SKINNER – *See LIGHTNING SEEDS*

SKIPWORTH and TURNER *US, male vocal duo* — 12 wks

27 Apr 85	**THINKING ABOUT YOUR LOVE** *Fourth & Broadway BRW 23*	**24**	10
21 Jan 89	**MAKE IT LAST** *Fourth & Broadway BRW 118*	**60**	2

SKUNK ANANSIE
UK, male / female vocal / instrumental group — 21 wks

25 Mar 95	**SELLING JESUS** *One Little Indian 101 TP7CD*	**46**	1
17 Jun 95	**I CAN DREAM** *One Little Indian 121 TP7CD*	**41**	2
2 Sep 95	**CHARITY** *One Little Indian 131 TP7CD*	**40**	2
27 Jan 96	**WEAK** *One Little Indian 141 TP7CD*	**20**	5
27 Apr 96	**CHARITY (re-issue)** *One Little Indian 151 TP7CD*	**20**	3
28 Sep 96	**ALL I WANT** *One Little Indian 161 TP7CD*	**14**	4
30 Nov 96	**TWISTED (EVERYDAY HURTS)** *One Little Indian 171 TP7CD*	**26**	4

SKY *UK / Australia, male instrumental group* — 11 wks

5 Apr 80	● **TOCCATA** *Ariola ARO 300*	**5**	11

SKYHOOKS *Australia, male vocal / instrumental group* — 1 wk

9 Jun 79	**WOMEN IN UNIFORM** *United Artists UP 36508*	**73**	1

SLADE *UK, male vocal / instrumental group* — 276 wks

19 Jun 71	**GET DOWN AND GET WITH IT** *Polydor 2058 112*	**16**	14
30 Oct 71	★ **COZ I LUV YOU** *Polydor 2058 155*	**1**	15
5 Feb 72	● **LOOK WOT YOU DUN** *Polydor 2058 195*	**4**	10
3 Jun 72	★ **TAKE ME BAK 'OME** *Polydor 2058 231*	**1**	13
2 Sep 72	★ **MAMA WEER ALL CRAZEE NOW** *Polydor 2058 274*	**1**	10
25 Nov 72	● **GUDBUY T'JANE** *Polydor 2058 312*	**2**	13
3 Mar 73	★ **CUM ON FEEL THE NOIZE** *Polydor 2058 339*	**1**	12
30 Jun 73	★ **SKWEEZE ME PLEEZE ME** *Polydor 2058 377*	**1**	10
6 Oct 73	● **MY FREND STAN** *Polydor 2058 407*	**2**	8
15 Dec 73	★ **MERRY XMAS EVERYBODY** *Polydor 2058 422*	**1**	9
6 Apr 74	● **EVERYDAY** *Polydor 2058 453*	**3**	7
6 Jul 74	● **BANGIN' MAN** *Polydor 2058 492*	**3**	7
19 Oct 74	● **FAR FAR AWAY** *Polydor 2058 522*	**2**	6
15 Feb 75	**HOW DOES IT FEEL** *Polydor 2058 547*	**15**	7
17 May 75	● **THANKS FOR THE MEMORY (WHAM BAM THANK YOU MAM)** *Polydor 2058 585*	**7**	7
22 Nov 75	**IN FOR A PENNY** *Polydor 2058 663*	**11**	8
7 Feb 76	**LET'S CALL IT QUITS** *Polydor 2058 690*	**11**	7
5 Feb 77	**GYPSY ROAD HOG** *Barn 2014 105*	**48**	2
29 Oct 77	**MY BABY LEFT ME – THAT'S ALL RIGHT (MEDLEY)** *Barn 2014 114*	**32**	4
18 Oct 80	**SLADE ALIVE AT READING '80 EP** *Cheapskate CHEAP 5*	**44**	5
27 Dec 80	**MERRY XMAS EVERYBODY** *Cheapskate CHEAP 11* [1]	**70**	2
31 Jan 81	● **WE'LL BRING THE HOUSE DOWN** *Cheapskate CHEAP 16*	**10**	9
4 Apr 81	**WHEELS AIN'T COMING DOWN** *Cheapskate CHEAP 21*	**60**	3
19 Sep 81	**LOCK UP YOUR DAUGHTERS** *RCA 124*	**29**	8
19 Dec 81	**MERRY XMAS EVERYBODY (re-entry)** *Polydor 2058 422*	**32**	4
27 Mar 82	**RUBY RED** *RCA 191*	**51**	3
27 Nov 82	**(AND NOW – THE WALTZ) C'EST LA VIE** *RCA 291*	**50**	6
25 Dec 82	**MERRY XMAS EVERYBODY (2nd re-entry)** *Polydor 2058 422*	**67**	3
19 Nov 83	● **MY OH MY** *RCA 373*	**2**	11
10 Dec 83	**MERRY XMAS EVERYBODY (3rd re-entry)** *Polydor 2058 422*	**20**	5
4 Feb 84	● **RUN RUN AWAY** *RCA 385*	**7**	10
17 Nov 84	**ALL JOIN HANDS** *RCA 455*	**15**	9
15 Dec 84	**MERRY XMAS EVERYBODY (4th re-entry)** *Polydor 2058 422*	**47**	4
26 Jan 85	**7 YEAR BITCH** *RCA 475*	**60**	3
23 Mar 85	**MYZSTERIOUS MIZTER JONES** *RCA PB 40027*	**50**	5

30 Nov 85	**DO YOU BELIEVE IN MIRACLES** RCA PB 40449	**54**	6
21 Dec 85	**MERRY XMAS EVERYBODY (re-issue)**		
	Polydor POSP 780	**48**	3
27 Dec 86	**MERRY XMAS EVERYBODY (re-entry of re-issue)**		
	Polydor POSP 780	**71**	1
21 Feb 87	**STILL THE SAME** RCA PB 41137	**73**	2
19 Oct 91	**RADIO WALL OF SOUND** Polydor PO 180	**21**	5

1 Slade and the Reading Choir

Tracks on Slade Alive At Reading '80 EP: *When I'm Dancin' / I Ain't Fightin' / Born To Be Wild / Somethin' Else / Pistol Packin' Mama / Keep A Rollin'.*

SLAMM *UK, male vocal / instrumental group* **6 wks**

17 Jul 93	**ENERGIZE** PWL International PWCD 266 .... **57**	2
23 Oct 93	**VIRGINIA PLAIN** PWL International PWCD 274 .... **60**	1
22 Oct 94	**THAT'S WHERE MY MIND GOES**	
	PWL International PWCD 310 .... **68**	1
4 Feb 95	**CAN'T GET BY** PWL International PWCD 316 .... **47**	2

SLAUGHTER *US, male vocal / instrumental group* **2 wks**

29 Sep 90	**UP ALL NIGHT** Chrysalis CHS 3556 .... **62**	1
2 Feb 91	**FLY TO THE ANGELS** Chrysalis CHS 3634 .... **55**	1

SLAVE *US, male vocal / instrumental group* **3 wks**

8 Mar 80	**JUST A TOUCH OF LOVE** Atlantic /Cotillion K 11442 .... **64**	3

SLAYER *US, male vocal / instrumental group* **3 wks**

13 Jun 87	**CRIMINALLY INSANE** Def Jam LON 133 .... **64**	1
26 Oct 91	**SEASONS IN THE ABYSS** Def American DEFA 9 .... **51**	1
9 Sep 95	**SERENITY IN MURDER** American 74321312482 .... **50**	1

SLEAZESISTERS with Vikki SHEPARD
US / UK, male / female vocal / instrumental group **2 wks**

29 Jul 95	**SEX** Pulse 8 CDLOSE 92 .... **53**	1
30 Mar 96	**LET'S WHIP IT UP (YOU GO GIRL)** Pulse 8 CDLOSE 102 ..**46**	1

Kathy SLEDGE *US, female vocalist* **3 wks**

16 May 92	**TAKE ME BACK TO LOVE AGAIN** Epic 6579837 .... **62**	2
18 Feb 95	**ANOTHER STAR** NRC DEACD 002 .... **54**	1

Percy SLEDGE *US, male vocalist* **34 wks**

12 May 66	● **WHEN A MAN LOVES A WOMAN** Atlantic 584 001 ......**4**	17
4 Aug 66	**WARM AND TENDER LOVE** Atlantic 584 034 .... **34**	7
14 Feb 87	● **WHEN A MAN LOVES A WOMAN (re-issue)**	
	Atlantic YZ 96 .... **2**	10

SLEEPER *UK, male / female vocal / instrumental group* **25 wks**

21 May 94	**DELICIOUS** Indolent SLEEP 003CD **75**	1
21 Jan 95	**INBETWEENER** Indolent SLEEP 006CD **16**	4
8 Apr 95	**VEGAS** Indolent SLEEP 008CD **33**	3
7 Oct 95	**WHAT DO I DO NOW** Indolent SLEEP 009CD1 .... **14**	4
4 May 96	● **SALE OF THE CENTURY** Indolent SLEEP 011CD **10**	5
13 Jul 96	● **NICE GUY EDDIE** Indolent SLEEP 013CD **10**	5
5 Oct 96	**STATUESQUE** Indolent SLEEP 014CD1 .... **17**	3

SLICK *US, male / female vocal / instrumental group* **15 wks**

16 Jun 79	**SPACE BASS** Fantasy FTC 176 .... **16**	10
15 Sep 79	**SEXY CREAM** Fantasy FTC 182 .... **47**	5

Grace SLICK *US, female vocalist* **4 wks**

24 May 80	**DREAMS** RCA PB 9534 .... **50**	4

SLICK RICK – *See Montell JORDAN*

SLIK *UK, male vocal / instrumental group* **18 wks**

17 Jan 76	★ **FOREVER AND EVER** Bell 1464 .... **1**	9
8 May 76	**REQUIEM** Bell 1478 .... **24**	9

SLIM CHANCE – *See Ronnie LANE and SLIM CHANCE*

SLIPSTREAM *UK, male vocal group* **7 wks**

19 Dec 92	**WE ARE RAVING – THE ANTHEM** Boogie Food 7BF 1 ....**18**	7

SLITS *UK, female vocal / instrumental group* **3 wks**

13 Oct 79	**TYPICAL GIRLS / I HEARD IT THROUGH THE**	
	GRAPEVINE Island WIP 6505 .... **60**	3

SLO-MOSHUN *UK, male instrumental / production duo* **4 wks**

5 Feb 94	**BELLS OF NY** Six6 SIXCD 108 .... **29**	3
30 Jul 94	**HELP MY FRIEND** Six6 SIXCD 117 .... **52**	1

PF SLOAN *US, male vocalist* **3 wks**

4 Nov 65	**SINS OF THE FAMILY** RCA 1482 .... **38**	3

SLOWDIVE *UK, male / female vocal / instrumental group* **2 wks**

15 Jun 91	**CATCH THE BREEZE / SHINE** Creation CRE 112 .... **52**	1
29 May 93	**OUTSIDE YOUR ROOM (EP)** Creation CRESCD 119 .... **69**	1

Tracks on Outside Your Room (EP): *Outside Your Room / Alison / So Tired / Souvlaki Space Station.*

SL2 *UK, male instrumental / production duo* **23 wks**

2 Nov 91	**DJS TAKE CONTROL / WAY IN MY BRAIN** XL XLS 24 ....**11**	5
4 Jan 92	**DJS TAKE CONTROL / WAY IN MY BRAIN (re-entry)**	
	XL XLS 24 .... **71**	1
18 Apr 92	● **ON A RAGGA TIP** XL XLS 29 .... **2**	11
19 Dec 92	**WAY IN MY BRAIN (re-mix) / DRUMBEATS** XL XLS 36 ..**26**	6

SLY and the FAMILY STONE
US, male / female vocal / instrumental group **42 wks**

10 Jul 68	● **DANCE TO THE MUSIC** Direction 58 3568 .... **7**	14
2 Oct 68	**M'LADY** Direction 58 3707 .... **32**	7
19 Mar 69	**EVERYDAY PEOPLE** Direction 58 3938 .... **36**	1
9 Apr 69	**EVERYDAY PEOPLE (re-entry)** Direction 58 3938 .... **37**	4
8 Jan 72	**FAMILY AFFAIR** Epic EPC 7632 .... **15**	8
15 Apr 72	**RUNNIN' AWAY** Epic EPC 7810 .... **17**	8

SLY FOX *US, male / female vocal / instrumental duo* **16 wks**

31 May 86	● **LET'S GO ALL THE WAY** Capitol CL 403 .... **3**	16

SLY and ROBBIE
Jamaica, male vocal / instrumental duo **15 wks**

4 Apr 87	**BOOPS (HERE TO GO)** Fourth & Broadway BRW 61 ....**12**	11
25 Jul 87	**FIRE** Fourth & Broadway BRW 71 .... **60**	4

SMALL ADS *UK, male vocal / instrumental group* **3 wks**

| 18 Apr 81 | **SMALL ADS** *Bronze BRO 115*..........................**63** 3 |

SMALL FACES *UK, male vocal / instrumental group* **137 wks**

2 Sep 65	**WHATCHA GONNA DO ABOUT IT?**
	Decca F 12208 ....**14** 12
10 Feb 66 ●	**SHA LA LA LA LEE** *Decca F 12317*.....................**3** 11
12 May 66 ●	**HEY GIRL** *Decca F 12393* **10** 9
11 Aug 66 ★	**ALL OR NOTHING** *Decca F 12470* **1** 12
17 Nov 66 ●	**MY MIND'S EYE** *Decca F 12500* **4** 11
9 Mar 67	**I CAN'T MAKE IT** *Decca F 12565* **26** 7
8 Jun 67	**HERE COME THE NICE** *Immediate IM 050* **12** 10
9 Aug 67 ●	**ITCHYCOO PARK** *Immediate IM 057* **3** 14
6 Dec 67 ●	**TIN SOLDIER** *Immediate IM 062* **9** 12
17 Apr 68 ●	**LAZY SUNDAY** *Immediate IM 064* **2** 11
10 Jul 68 ●	**UNIVERSAL** *Immediate IM 069* **16** 11
19 Mar 69	**AFTERGLOW OF YOUR LOVE**
	Immediate IM 077 ....**36** 1
13 Dec 75 ●	**ITCHYCOO PARK (re-issue)** *Immediate IMS 102* **9** 11
20 Mar 76	**LAZY SUNDAY (re-issue)** *Immediate IMS 106* **39** 5

SMALLER *UK, male vocal / instrumental group* **1 wk**

| 28 Sep 96 | **WASTED** *Better BETSCD 006*..........................**72** 1 |

SMART E'S *UK, male instrumental / production group* **9 wks**

| 11 Jul 92 ● | **SESAME'S TREET** *Suburban Base SUBBASE 12S*.................**2** 9 |

S*M*A*S*H *UK, male vocal / instrumental group* **1 wk**

| 6 Aug 94 | **(I WANT TO) KILL SOMEBODY** *Hi-Rise FLATSCD 5* ....**26** 1 |

SMASHING PUMPKINS
US, male / female vocal / instrumental group **22 wks**

5 Sep 92	**I AM ONE** *Hut HUTT 18* **73** 1
3 Jul 93	**CHERUB ROCK** *Hut HUTCD 31* **31** 2
25 Sep 93	**TODAY** *Hut HUTCD 37* **44** 2
5 Mar 94	**DISARM** *Hut HUTCD 43* **11** 3
28 Oct 95	**BULLET WITH BUTTERFLY WINGS** *Hut HUTCD 63* **20** 3
10 Feb 96	**1979** *Hut HUTCD 67* **16** 3
18 May 96 ●	**TONIGHT TONIGHT** *Hut HUTDX 69* **7** 6
23 Nov 96	**THIRTY THREE** *Hut HUTCD 78* **21** 2

SMEAR CAMPAIGN – *See MR. BEAN and SMEAR CAMPAIGN featuring Bruce DICKINSON*

SMELLS LIKE HEAVEN
Italy, male producer – Fabi Paras **1 wk**

| 10 Jul 93 | **LONDRES STRUTT** |
| | *Deconstruction 74321154312* ....**57** 1 |

'Fast' Eddie SMITH – *See DJ 'FAST' EDDIE*

Ann-Marie SMITH *UK, female vocalist* **5 wks**

23 Jan 93	**MUSIC** *Synthetic CDR 6334* [1] **34** 2
18 Mar 95	**ROCKIN' MY BODY** *Media MCSTD 2021* [2] **31** 2
15 Jul 95	**(YOU'RE MY ONE AND ONLY) TRUE LOVE**
	Media MCSTD 2060 ....**46** 1

[1] Fargetta and Anne-Marie Smith [2] 49ers featuring Ann-Marie Smith

Hurricane SMITH *UK, male vocalist* **35 wks**

12 Jun 71 ●	**DON'T LET IT DIE** *Columbia DB 8785* **2** 12
29 Apr 72 ●	**OH BABE WHAT WOULD YOU SAY?** *Columbia DB 8878* ..**4** 16
2 Sep 72	**WHO WAS IT** *Columbia DB 8916* **23** 7

Jimmy SMITH *US, male instrumentalist – organ* **3 wks**

| 28 Apr 66 | **GOT MY MOJO WORKING** *Verve VS 536* ....**48** 2 |
| 19 May 66 | **GOT MY MOJO WORKING (re-entry)** *Verve VS 536* ......**48** 1 |

Keely SMITH *US, female vocalist* **10 wks**

| 18 Mar 65 | **YOU'RE BREAKIN' MY HEART** *Reprise R 20346* ....**14** 10 |

Mandy SMITH *UK, female vocalist* **2 wks**

| 20 May 89 | **DON'T YOU WANT ME BABY** *PWL PWL 37*....................**59** 2 |

Mark E SMITH *UK, male vocalist* **4 wks**

| 5 Mar 94 | **I WANT YOU** *Cow DUNG 24CD* [1] ....**18** 3 |
| 23 Mar 96 | **PLUG MYSELF IN** *Coliseum TOGA 001CD1* [2] ....**50** 1 |

[1] Inspiral Carpets featuring Mark E Smith [2] DOSE featuring Mark E Smith

See also Fall.

Mel SMITH *UK, male vocalist* **10 wks**

| 5 Dec 87 ● | **ROCKIN' AROUND THE CHRISTMAS TREE** *10 TEN 2* [1] ....**3** 7 |
| 21 Dec 91 | **ANOTHER BLOOMING CHRISTMAS** *Epic 6576877* ....**59** 3 |

[1] Mel and Kim

Muriel SMITH *UK, female vocalist* **17 wks**

| 15 May 53 ● | **HOLD ME THRILL ME KISS ME** *Philips PB 122* ....**3** 17 |

OC SMITH *US, male vocalist* **23 wks**

| 29 May 68 ● | **SON OF HICKORY HOLLER'S TRAMP** *CBS 3343* ....**2** 15 |
| 26 Mar 77 | **TOGETHER** *Caribou CRB 4910* ....**25** 8 |

Rex SMITH – *See Rachel SWEET*

Richard Jon SMITH *South Africa, male vocalist* **2 wks**

| 16 Jul 83 | **SHE'S THE MASTER OF THE GAME** *Jive JIVE 38*.............**63** 2 |

Whistling Jack SMITH *UK, male whistler* **12 wks**

| 2 Mar 67 ● | **I WAS KAISER BILL'S BATMAN** *Deram DM 112* ....**5** 12 |

Patti SMITH GROUP
US, female vocalist, male instrumental backing group **16 wks**

29 Apr 78 ●	**BECAUSE THE NIGHT** *Arista 181* **5** 12
19 Aug 78	**PRIVILEGE (SET ME FREE)** *Arista 197* **72** 1
2 Jun 79	**FREDERICK** *Arista 264* **63** 3

SMITHS *UK, male vocal / instrumental group* **105 wks**

| 12 Nov 83 | **THIS CHARMING MAN** *Rough Trade RT 136* ....**25** 12 |
| 28 Jan 84 | **WHAT DIFFERENCE DOES IT MAKE** *Rough Trade RT 146*..**12** 9 |

2 Jun 84 ●	**HEAVEN KNOWS I'M MISERABLE NOW** *Rough Trade RT 156*	**10** 8
1 Sep 84	**WILLIAM, IT WAS REALLY NOTHING** *Rough Trade RT 166*	**17** 6
9 Feb 85	**HOW SOON IS NOW?** *Rough Trade RT 176*	**24** 6
30 Mar 85	**SHAKESPEARE'S SISTER** *Rough Trade RT 181*	**26** 4
13 Jul 85	**THAT JOKE ISN'T FUNNY ANYMORE** *Rough Trade RT 186*	**49** 3
5 Oct 85	**THE BOY WITH THE THORN IN HIS SIDE** *Rough Trade RT 191*	**23** 5
31 May 86	**BIG MOUTH STRIKES AGAIN** *Rough Trade RT 192*	**26** 4
2 Aug 86	**PANIC** *Rough Trade RT 193*	**11** 8
1 Nov 86	**ASK** *Rough Trade RT 194*	**14** 5
7 Feb 87	**SHOPLIFTERS OF THE WORLD UNITE** *Rough Trade RT195*	**12** 4
25 Apr 87 ●	**SHEILA TAKE A BOW** *Rough Trade RT 196*	**10** 5
22 Aug 87	**GIRLFRIEND IN A COMA** *Rough Trade RT 197*	**13** 5
14 Nov 87	**I STARTED SOMETHING I COULDN'T FINISH** *Rough Trade RT 198*	**23** 4
19 Dec 87	**LAST NIGHT I DREAMT THAT SOMEBODY LOVED ME** *Rough Trade RT 200*	**30** 4
15 Aug 92 ●	**THIS CHARMING MAN (re-issue)** *WEA YZ 0001*	**8** 5
12 Sep 92	**HOW SOON IS NOW (re-issue)** *WEA YZ 0002*	**16** 4
24 Oct 92	**THERE IS A LIGHT THAT NEVER GOES OUT** *WEA YZ 0003*	**25** 3
18 Feb 95	**ASK (re-issue)** *WEA YZ 0004CDX*	**62** 1

SMOKE *UK, male vocal / instrumental group* **3 wks**

9 Mar 67	**MY FRIEND JACK** *Columbia DB 8115*	**45** 3

SMOKIE *UK, male vocal / instrumental group* **125 wks**

19 Jul 75 ●	**IF YOU THINK YOU KNOW HOW TO LOVE ME** *RAK 206* [1]	**3** 9
4 Oct 75 ●	**DON'T PLAY YOUR ROCK 'N ROLL TO ME** *RAK 217* [1]	**8** 7
31 Jan 76	**SOMETHING'S BEEN MAKING ME BLUE** *RAK 227*	**17** 8
25 Sep 76	**I'LL MEET YOU AT MIDNIGHT** *RAK 241*	**11** 9
4 Dec 76 ●	**LIVING NEXT DOOR TO ALICE** *RAK 244*	**5** 11
19 Mar 77	**LAY BACK IN THE ARMS OF SOMEONE** *RAK 251*	**12** 9
16 Jul 77 ●	**IT'S YOUR LIFE** *RAK 260*	**5** 9
15 Oct 77 ●	**NEEDLES AND PINS** *RAK 263*	**10** 9
28 Jan 78	**FOR A FEW DOLLARS MORE** *RAK 267*	**17** 6
20 May 78 ●	**OH CAROL** *RAK 276*	**5** 13
23 Sep 78	**MEXICAN GIRL** *RAK 283*	**19** 9
19 Apr 80	**TAKE GOOD CARE OF MY BABY** *RAK 309*	**34** 7
13 May 95	**LIVING NEXT DOOR TO ALICE (WHO THE F**K IS ALICE)** *NOW CDWAG 245* [2]	**64** 2
26 Aug 95 ●	**LIVING NEXT DOOR TO ALICE (WHO THE F**K IS ALICE) (re-entry)** *NOW CDWAG 245* [2]	**3** 17

[1] Smokey [2] Smokie featuring Roy 'Chubby' Brown

Living Next Door To Alice (Who The F**k Is Alice) *is a re-recorded version of* Living Next Door To Alice.

SMOKIN' MOJO FILTERS
UK / US, male / female vocal / instrumental group **5 wks**

23 Dec 95	**COME TOGETHER (WAR CHILD)** *Go! Discs GODCD 136*	**19** 5

SMOOTH *US, female vocalist* **7 wks**

22 Jul 95	**MIND BLOWIN'** *Jive JIVECD 379*	**36** 2
7 Oct 95	**IT'S SUMMERTIME (LET IT GET INTO YOU)** *Jive JIVECD 383*	**46** 1
16 Mar 96	**WE GOT IT** *MCA MCSTD 48009* [1]	**26** 2
16 Mar 96	**LOVE GROOVE (GROOVE WITH YOU)** *Jive JIVECD 390*	**46** 1
6 Jul 96	**UNDERCOVER LOVER** *Jive JIVECD 397*	**41** 1

[1] Immature featuring Smooth

Joe SMOOTH *US, male vocalist* **4 wks**

4 Feb 89	**PROMISED LAND** *DJ International DJIN 6*	**56** 4

SMOOTH TOUCH
US, male instrumental / production duo **1 wk**

2 Apr 94	**HOUSE OF LOVE (IN MY HOUSE)** *Six6 SIXCD 112*	**58** 1

SMURFS *Holland, small blue creatures* **48 wks**

3 Jun 78 ●	**THE SMURF SONG** *Decca F 13759* [1]	**2** 17
30 Sep 78	**DIPPETY DAY** *Decca F 13798*	**13** 12
2 Dec 78	**CHRISTMAS IN SMURFLAND** *Decca F 13819*	**19** 7
7 Sep 96 ●	**I'VE GOT A LITTLE PUPPY** *EMI TV CDSMURF 100*	**4** 10
21 Dec 96 ●	**YOUR CHRISTMAS WISH** *EMI TV CDSMURF 102*	**8†** 2

[1] Father Abraham and the Smurfs

Patty SMYTH – *See Don HENLEY*

SNAP
US / Germany, male / female vocal / instrumental group **115 wks**

24 Mar 90 ★	**THE POWER** *Arista 113133*	**1** 15
16 Jun 90 ●	**OOOPS UP** *Arista 113296*	**5** 12
22 Sep 90 ●	**CULT OF SNAP** *Arista 113596*	**8** 7
8 Dec 90 ●	**MARY HAD A LITTLE BOY** *Arista 113831*	**8** 10
30 Mar 91 ●	**SNAP MEGAMIX** *Arista 114169*	**10** 6
21 Dec 91	**THE COLOUR OF LOVE** *Arista 114678*	**54** 3
4 Jul 92 ★	**RHYTHM IS A DANCER** *Arista 115309*	**1** 19
9 Jan 93 ●	**EXTERMINATE!** *Arista 74321106962* [1]	**2** 11
12 Jun 93 ●	**DO YOU SEE THE LIGHT (LOOKING FOR)** *Arista 74321147622* [1]	**10** 8
17 Sep 94 ●	**WELCOME TO TOMORROW** *Arista 74321223852* [2]	**6** 13
14 Jan 95	**WELCOME TO TOMORROW (re-entry)** *Arista 74321223852* [2]	**75** 1
1 Apr 95	**THE FIRST THE LAST ETERNITY (TIL THE END)** *Arista 74321254672* [2]	**15** 7
28 Oct 95	**THE WORLD IN MY HANDS** *Arista 74321314792* [2]	**44** 1
13 Apr 96	**RAME** *Arista 74321368902* [3]	**50** 1
24 Aug 96	**THE POWER** *Arista 74321398672* [4]	**42** 1

[1] Snap featuring Niki Haris [2] Snap featuring Summer [3] Snap featuring Rukmani [4] Snap featuring Einstein

The Power *in 96 is a re-recording.*

SNEAKER PIMPS
UK, male / female vocal / instrumental group **4 wks**

19 Oct 96	**6 UNDERGROUND** *Clean Up CUP 023CDS*	**15** 4

SNIFF 'N' THE TEARS
UK, male vocal / instrumental group **5 wks**

23 Jun 79	**DRIVER'S SEAT** *Chiswick CHIS 105*	**42** 5

SNOOP DOGGY DOGG *US, male rapper* **17 wks**

4 Dec 93	**WHAT'S MY NAME?** *Death Row A 8337CD*	**20** 8
12 Feb 94	**GIN AND JUICE** *Death Row A 8316CD*	**39** 3
20 Aug 94	**DOGGY DOGG WORLD** *Death Row A 8289CD*	**32** 3
14 Dec 96	**SNOOP'S UPSIDE YOUR HEAD** *Interscope IND 95520* [1]	**12†** 3

[1] Snoop Doggy Dogg featuring Charlie Wilson

SNOW *Canada, male rapper* — **18 wks**

13 Mar 93	● INFORMER *East West America A 8436CD*	.2	15
5 Jun 93	GIRL I'VE BEEN HURT		
	East West America A 8417CD	.48	2
4 Sep 93	UHH IN YOU *Atlantic A 8378CD*	.67	1

Mark SNOW *US, male instrumentalist – keyboards* — **15 wks**

| 30 Mar 96 | ● THE X-FILES *Warner Bros. W 0341CD* | .2 | 15 |

Phoebe SNOW *US, female vocalist* — **7 wks**

| 6 Jan 79 | EVERY NIGHT *CBS 6842* | .37 | 7 |

SNOWMAN – *See Peter AUTY*

SNOWMEN *UK, male vocal / instrumental group* — **12 wks**

| 12 Dec 81 | HOKEY COKEY *Stiff ODB 1* | .18 | 8 |
| 18 Dec 82 | XMAS PARTY *Solid STOP 006* | .44 | 4 |

SO *UK, male vocal / instrumental group* — **3 wks**

| 13 Feb 88 | ARE YOU SURE *Parlophone R 6173* | .62 | 3 |

SOAPY *UK, male instrumental / production duo* — **2 wks**

| 14 Sep 96 | HORNY AS FUNK *WEA WEA 074CD* | .35 | 2 |

Gino SOCCIO
Canada, male instrumentalist – keyboards — **5 wks**

| 28 Apr 79 | DANCER *Warner Bros. K 17357* | .46 | 5 |

SOEUR SOURIRE – *See SINGING NUN*

SOFT CELL *UK, male vocal / instrumental duo* — **107 wks**

1 Aug 81	★ TAINTED LOVE *Some Bizzare BZS 2*	.1	16
14 Nov 81	● BED SITTER *Some Bizzare BZS 6*	.4	12
9 Jan 82	TAINTED LOVE (re-entry) *Some Bizzare BZS 2*	.43	10
6 Feb 82	● SAY HELLO WAVE GOODBYE *Some Bizzare BZS 7*	.3	9
29 May 82	● TORCH *Some Bizzare BZS 9*	.2	9
24 Jul 82	TAINTED LOVE (2nd re-entry) *Some Bizzare BZS 2*	.50	4
21 Aug 82	● WHAT *Some Bizzare BZS 11*	.3	8
4 Dec 82	WHERE THE HEART IS *Some Bizzare BZS 16*	.21	7
5 Mar 83	NUMBERS / BARRIERS *Some Bizzare BZS 17*	.25	4
24 Sep 83	SOUL INSIDE *Some Bizzare BZS 20*	.16	5
25 Feb 84	DOWN IN THE SUBWAY *Some Bizzare BZS 22*	.24	6
9 Feb 85	TAINTED LOVE (3rd re-entry) *Some Bizzare BZS 2*	.43	6
23 Mar 91	SAY HELLO WAVE GOODBYE '91		
	Mercury SOFT 1 [1]	.38	3
18 May 91	● TAINTED LOVE *Mercury SOFT 2* [1]	.5	8

[1] Soft Cell / Marc Almond

SOHO *UK, male / female vocal / instrumental group* — **11 wks**

5 May 90	HIPPY CHICK *Savage 7SAV 106*	.67	1
19 Jan 91	● HIPPY CHICK (re-entry) *Savage 7SAV 106*	.8	8
9 Nov 91	BORN TO BE ALIVE *MCA MCS 1578* [1]	.51	2

[1] Adamski featuring Soho

The listed flip side of Born To Be Alive was Never Goin' Down by Adamski featuring Jimi Polo.

SOLO *UK, male producer – Stuart Crichton* — **4 wks**

20 Jul 91	RAINBOW (SAMPLE FREE) *Reverb RVBT 003*	.59	2
18 Jan 92	COME ON! *Reverb RVBT 008*	.75	1
11 Sep 93	COME ON! (re-mix) *Stoatin' STOAT 003CD*	.63	1

SOLO (US) *US, male vocal group* — **3 wks**

3 Feb 96	HEAVEN *Perspective 5875212*	.35	2
30 Mar 96	WHERE DO U WANT ME TO PUT IT		
	Perspective 5875312	.45	1

Sal SOLO *UK, male vocalist* — **13 wks**

| 15 Dec 84 | SAN DAMIANO (HEART AND SOUL) *MCA MCA 930* | .15 | 10 |
| 6 Apr 85 | MUSIC AND YOU *MCA MCA 946* [1] | .52 | 3 |

[1] Sal Solo with the London Community Gospel Choir

SOLUTION – *See Victor SIMONELLI presents SOLUTION*

Belouis SOME *UK, male vocalist* — **26 wks**

27 Apr 85	IMAGINATION *Parlophone R 6097*	.50	7
18 Jan 86	IMAGINATION (re-issue) *Parlophone R 1986*	.17	10
12 Apr 86	SOME PEOPLE *Parlophone R 6130*	.33	7
16 May 87	LET IT BE WITH YOU *Parlophone R 6154*	.53	2

Jimmy SOMERVILLE *UK, male vocalist* — **52 wks**

11 Nov 89	COMMENT TE DIRE ADIEU *London LON 241* [1]	.14	9
13 Jan 90	● YOU MAKE ME FEEL (MIGHTY REAL)		
	London LON 249	.5	8
17 Mar 90	READ MY LIPS (ENOUGH IS ENOUGH) *London LON 254*	.26	6
3 Nov 90	● TO LOVE SOMEBODY *London LON 281*	.8	11
2 Feb 91	SMALLTOWN BOY *London LON 287* [2]	.32	4
10 Aug 91	RUN FROM LOVE *London LON 301*	.52	2
28 Jan 95	HEARTBEAT *London LONCD 358*	.24	4
27 May 95	HURT SO GOOD *London LONCD 364*	.15	6
28 Oct 95	BY YOUR SIDE *London LONCD 372*	.41	2

[1] Jimmy Somerville featuring June Miles-Kingston [1] Jimmy Somerville with Bronski Beat

See also Bronski Beat; Various Artists (EPs & LPs) – Gimme Shelter (EP).

SONIA *UK, female vocalist* — **78 wks**

24 Jun 89	★ YOU'LL NEVER STOP ME LOVING YOU		
	Chrysalis CHS 3385	.1	13
7 Oct 89	CAN'T FORGET YOU *Chrysalis CHS 3419*	.17	6
9 Dec 89	● LISTEN TO YOUR HEART *Chrysalis CHS 3465*	.10	10
7 Apr 90	COUNTING EVERY MINUTE *Chrysalis CHS 3492*	.16	7
23 Jun 90	YOU'VE GOT A FRIEND *Jive CHILD 90* [1]	.14	6
25 Aug 90	END OF THE WORLD *Chrysalis/PWL CHS 3557*	.18	7
1 Jun 91	● ONLY FOOLS (NEVER FALL IN LOVE) *IQ ZB 44613*	.10	8
31 Aug 91	BE YOUNG BE FOOLISH BE HAPPY *IQ ZB 44935*	.22	5
16 Nov 91	YOU TO ME ARE EVERYTHING *IQ ZB 45121*	.13	5
12 Sep 92	BOOGIE NIGHTS *Arista 74321113467*	.30	3
1 May 93	BETTER THE DEVIL YOU KNOW *Arista 74321146872*	.15	7
30 Jul 94	HOPELESSLY DEVOTED TO YOU *Cockney COCCD 2*	.61	1

[1] Big Fun and Sonia

SONIC SOLUTION *UK, male / producer – Steve Cop* — **1 wk**

| 4 Apr 92 | BEATSTIME *R&S RSUK 11* | .59 | 1 |

SONIC SURFERS
Holland, male instrumental / production duo　　　　**2 wks**

20 Mar 93	**TAKE ME UP** *A & M AMCD 210* [1]	**61** 1
30 Jul 94	**DON'T GIVE IT UP** *Brilliant CDBRIL 6*	**54** 1

[1] Sonic Surfers featuring Jocelyn Brown

SONIC THE HEDGEHOG – See HWA featuring SONIC THE HEDGEHOG

SONIC YOUTH
US, male / female vocal / instrumental group　　　　**13 wks**

11 Jul 92	**100%** *DGC DGCS 11*	**28** 4
7 Nov 92	**YOUTH AGAINST FASCISM** *Geffen GFS 26*	**52** 2
3 Apr 93	**SUGAR KANE** *Geffen GFSTD 37*	**26** 3
7 May 94	**BULL IN THE HEATHER** *Geffen GFSTD 72*	**24** 2
10 Sep 94	**SUPERSTAR** *A & M 5807932*	**45** 2

The listed flip side of Superstar was Yesterday Once More by Redd Kross.

SONNY
US, male vocalist　　　　**11 wks**

19 Aug 65	● **LAUGH AT ME** *Atlantic AT 4038*	**9** 11

See also Sonny and Cher.

SONNY and CHER
US, male / female vocal duo　　　　**78 wks**

12 Aug 65	★ **I GOT YOU BABE** *Atlantic AT 4035*	**1** 12
16 Sep 65	**BABY DON'T GO** *Reprise R 20309*	**11** 9
21 Oct 65	**BUT YOU'RE MINE** *Atlantic AT 4047*	**17** 8
17 Feb 66	**WHAT NOW MY LOVE** *Atlantic AT 4069*	**13** 11
30 Jun 66	**HAVE I STAYED TOO LONG** *Atlantic 584 018*	**42** 3
8 Sep 66	● **LITTLE MAN** *Atlantic 584 040*	**4** 10
17 Nov 66	**LIVING FOR YOU** *Atlantic 584 057*	**44** 4
2 Feb 67	**THE BEAT GOES ON** *Atlantic 584 078*	**29** 8
15 Jan 72	● **ALL I EVER NEED IS YOU** *MCA MU 1145*	**8** 12
22 May 93	**I GOT YOU BABE (re-issue)** *Epic 6592402*	**66** 1

See also Sonny; Cher.

SON'Z OF A LOOP DA LOOP ERA
UK, male producer – Danny Breaks　　　　**4 wks**

15 Feb 92	**FAR OUT** *Suburban Base SUBBASE 008*	**36** 3
17 Oct 92	**PEACE + LOVEISM** *Suburban Base SUBBASE 14*	**60** 1

See also Various Artists (EPs & LPs) – Subplates Volume 1 EP.

SORROWS
UK, male vocal / instrumental group　　　　**8 wks**

16 Sep 65	**TAKE A HEART** *Piccadilly 7N 35260*	**21** 8

S.O.S. BAND
US, male / female vocal / instrumental group　　　　**46 wks**

19 Jul 80	**TAKE YOUR TIME (DO IT RIGHT) PART 1** *Tabu TBU 8564*	**51** 4
26 Feb 83	**GROOVIN' (THAT'S WHAT WE'RE DOIN')** *Tabu TBU A3120*	**72** 1
7 Apr 84	**JUST BE GOOD TO ME** *Tabu A 3626*	**13** 11
4 Aug 84	**JUST THE WAY YOU LIKE IT** *Tabu A 4621*	**32** 7
13 Oct 84	**WEEKEND GIRL** *Tabu A 4785*	**51** 5
29 Mar 86	**THE FINEST** *Tabu A 6997*	**17** 10
5 Jul 86	**BORROWED LOVE** *Tabu A 7241*	**50** 5
2 May 87	**NO LIES** *Tabu 650444 7*	**64** 3

David SOUL
US, male vocalist　　　　**56 wks**

18 Dec 76	★ **DON'T GIVE UP ON US** *Private Stock PVT 84*	**1** 16
26 Mar 77	● **GOING IN WITH MY EYES OPEN** *Private Stock PVT 99*	**2** 8
27 Aug 77	★ **SILVER LADY** *Private Stock PVT 115*	**1** 14
17 Dec 77	● **LET'S HAVE A QUIET NIGHT IN** *Private Stock PVT 130*	**8** 9
27 May 78	**IT SURE BRINGS OUT THE LOVE IN YOUR EYES** *Private Stock PVT 137*	**12** 9

Jimmy SOUL
US, male vocalist　　　　**5 wks**

11 Jul 63	**IF YOU WANNA BE HAPPY** *Stateside SS 178*	**39** 2
15 Jun 91	**IF YOU WANNA BE HAPPY (re-issue)** *Epic 6569647*	**68** 3

SOUL ASYLUM
US, male vocal / instrumental group　　　　**33 wks**

19 Jun 93	**RUNAWAY TRAIN** *Columbia 6593902*	**37** 8
4 Sep 93	**SOMEBODY TO SHOVE** *Columbia 6596492*	**34** 3
13 Nov 93	● **RUNAWAY TRAIN (re-entry)** *Columbia 6593902*	**7** 11
22 Jan 94	**BLACK GOLD** *Columbia 6598442*	**26** 4
26 Mar 94	**SOMEBODY TO SHOVE (re-issue)** *Columbia 6602245*	**32** 3
15 Jul 95	**MISERY** *Columbia 6621092*	**30** 3
2 Dec 95	**JUST LIKE ANYONE** *Columbia 6624785*	**52** 1

SOUL BROTHERS
UK, male vocal / instrumental group　　　　**3 wks**

22 Apr 65	**I KEEP RINGING MY BABY** *Decca F 12116*	**42** 3

SOUL CITY ORCHESTRA
UK, male instrumental / production group　　　　**1 wk**

11 Dec 93	**IT'S JURASSIC** *London JURCD 1*	**70** 1

SOUL CITY SYMPHONY – See Van McCOY

SOUL FAMILY SENSATION
UK / US, male / female vocal / instrumental group　　　　**4 wks**

11 May 91	**I DON'T EVEN KNOW IF I SHOULD CALL YOU BABY** *One Little Indian 47 TP7*	**49** 4

SOUL FOR REAL
US, male vocal group　　　　**4 wks**

8 Jul 95	**CANDY RAIN** *Uptown MCSTD 2052*	**23** 2
23 Mar 96	**EVERY LITTLE THING I DO** *Uptown MCSTD 48005*	**31** 2

SOUL II SOUL
UK, male producer – Jazzie B　　　　**86 wks**

21 May 88	**FAIRPLAY** *10 TEN 228* [1]	**63** 3
17 Sep 88	**FEEL FREE** *10 TEN 236* [2]	**64** 2
18 Mar 89	● **KEEP ON MOVING** *10 TEN 263* [3]	**5** 12
10 Jun 89	★ **BACK TO LIFE (HOWEVER DO YOU WANT ME)** *10 TEN 265* [3]	**1** 14
9 Dec 89	● **GET A LIFE** *10 TEN 284*	**3** 13
5 May 90	● **A DREAM'S A DREAM** *10 TEN 300*	**6** 9
24 Nov 90	**MISSING YOU** *10 TEN 345* [4]	**22** 7
4 Apr 92	● **JOY** *Ten TEN 350*	**4** 7
13 Jun 92	**MOVE ME NO MOUNTAIN** *Ten TEN 400* [5]	**31** 2
26 Sep 92	**JUST RIGHT** *Ten TEN 410*	**38** 2
6 Nov 93	**WISH** *Virgin VSCDG 1480*	**24** 4
22 Jul 95	**LOVE ENUFF** *Virgin VSCDT 1527*	**12** 6
21 Oct 95	**I CARE (SOUL II SOUL)** *Virgin VSCDT 1560*	**17** 4
19 Oct 96	**KEEP ON MOVIN' (re-mix)** *Virgin VSCDT 1612*	**31** 2

[1] Soul II Soul featuring Rose Windross [2] Soul II Soul featuring Do'reen [3] Soul II Soul featuring Caron Wheeler [4] Soul II Soul featuring Kym Mazelle [5] Soul II Soul, lead vocals Kofi

S.O.U.L. S.Y.S.T.E.M. introducing Michelle VISAGE *US, male / female vocal / instrumental group* **5 wks**

16 Jan 93	**IT'S GONNA BE A LOVELY DAY** Arista 74321125692	**17**	5

SOULED OUT
Italy / US / UK, male / female vocal / instrumental group **1 wk**

9 May 92	**IN MY LIFE** Columbia 6578367	**75**	1

SOUND 9418 – *See Jonathan KING*

SOUND FACTORY *Sweden, male vocal / instrumental duo* **1 wk**

5 Jun 93	**2 THE RHYTHM** Logic 74321149422	**72**	1

SOUND OF ONE *US, male / female vocal / instrumental duo* **1 wk**

20 Nov 93	**AS I AM** Cooltempo CDCOOL 280	**65**	1

SOUNDGARDEN *US, male vocal / instrumental group* **23 wks**

11 Apr 92	**JESUS CHRIST POSE** A & M AM 862	**30**	3
20 Jun 92	**RUSTY CAGE** A & M AM 874	**41**	1
21 Nov 92	**OUTSHINED** A & M AM 0102	**50**	1
26 Feb 94	**SPOONMAN** A & M 5805392	**20**	3
30 Apr 94	**THE DAY I TRIED TO LIVE** A & M 5805952	**42**	2
20 Aug 94	**BLACK HOLE SUN** A & M 5807532	**12**	5
28 Jan 95	**FELL ON BLACK DAYS** A & M 5809472	**24**	2
18 May 96	**PRETTY NOOSE** A & M 5816202	**14**	3
28 Sep 96	**BURDEN IN MY HAND** A & M 5818552	**33**	2
28 Dec 96	**BLOW UP THE OUTSIDE WORLD** A & M 5819862	**40†**	1

SOUNDMAN and David LLOYDIE with Elizabeth TROY
UK, male / female vocal / instrumental group **2 wks**

25 Feb 95	**GREATER LOVE** Sound Of Underground SOURCD 016	**49**	2

SOUNDS INCORPORATED
UK, male instrumental group **11 wks**

23 Apr 64	**THE SPARTANS** Columbia DB 7239	**30**	6
30 Jul 64	**SPANISH HARLEM** Columbia DB 7321	**35**	5

SOUNDS NICE *UK, male instrumental group* **11 wks**

6 Sep 69	**LOVE AT FIRST SIGHT (JE T'AIME... MOI NON PLUS)** Parlophone R 5797	**18**	11

Has credit: Tim Mycroft on organ.

SOUNDS OF BLACKNESS
US, male / female gospel choir **29 wks**

22 Jun 91	**OPTIMISTIC** Perspective PERSS 786	**45**	4
28 Sep 91	**THE PRESSURE PART 1** Perspective PERSS 816	**71**	1
15 Feb 92	**OPTIMISTIC (re-issue)** Perspective PERSS 849	**28**	4
25 Apr 92	**THE PRESSURE PART 1 (re-issue)** Perspective PERSS 867	**49**	2
8 May 93	**I'M GOING ALL THE WAY** Perspective 5874252	**27**	3
26 Mar 94	**I BELIEVE** A & M 5874512	**17**	4
2 Jul 94	**GLORYLAND** Mercury MERCD 404 [1]	**36**	4
20 Aug 94	**EVERYTHING IS GONNA BE ALRIGHT** A & M 5874672	**29**	3
14 Jan 95	**I'M GOING ALL THE WAY (re-issue)** A & M 5874832	**14**	4

[1] Daryl Hall and the Sounds of Blackness

SOUNDS ORCHESTRAL *UK, orchestra* **18 wks**

3 Dec 64	● **CAST YOUR FATE TO THE WIND** Piccadilly 7N 35206	**5**	16
8 Jul 65	**MOONGLOW** Piccadilly 7N 35248	**43**	2

SOUNDSATION *UK, male producer* **1 wk**

14 Jan 95	**PEACE AND JOY** Ffrreedom TABCD 224	**48**	1

SOUNDSOURCE
Sweden / UK, male instrumental / production group **1 wk**

11 Jan 92	**TAKE ME UP** ffrr FX 177	**62**	1

SOUP DRAGONS *UK, male vocal / instrumental group* **23 wks**

20 Jun 87	**CAN'T TAKE NO MORE** Raw TV RTV 3	**65**	1
5 Sep 87	**SOFT AS YOUR FACE** Raw TV RTV 4	**66**	2
14 Jul 90	● **I'M FREE** Raw TV RTV 9 [1]	**5**	12
20 Oct 90	**MOTHER UNIVERSE** Big Life BLR 30	**26**	5
11 Apr 92	**DIVINE THING** Big Life BLR 68	**53**	3

[1] Soup Dragons featuring Junior Reid

SOURCE *UK, male producer – John Truelove* **12 wks**

2 Feb 91	● **YOU GOT THE LOVE** Truelove TLOVE 7001 [1]	**4**	11
26 Dec 92	**ROCK THE HOUSE** React 12REACT 12 [2]	**63**	1

[1] Source featuring Candi Staton [2] Source featuring Nicole

Joe SOUTH *US, male vocalist* **11 wks**

5 Mar 69	● **GAMES PEOPLE PLAY** Capitol CL 15579	**6**	11

Jeri SOUTHERN *US, female vocalist* **3 wks**

21 Jun 57	**FIRE DOWN BELOW** Brunswick 05665	**22**	3

SOUTHLANDERS *UK, male vocal group* **10 wks**

22 Nov 57	**ALONE** Decca F 10946	**17**	10

SOVEREIGN COLLECTION *UK, orchestra* **6 wks**

3 Apr 71	**MOZART 40** Capitol CL 15676	**27**	6

Red SOVINE *US, male vocalist* **8 wks**

13 Jun 81	● **TEDDY BEAR** Starday SD 142	**4**	8

SOX *UK, female vocal group* **1 wk**

15 Apr 95	**GO FOR THE HEART** Living Beat LBECD 33	**47**	1

Bob B. SOXX and the BLUE JEANS
US, male / female vocal group **2 wks**

31 Jan 63	**ZIP-A-DEE-DOO-DAH** London HLU 9646	**45**	2

SPACE *France, male instrumental group* **12 wks**

13 Aug 77	● **MAGIC FLY** Pye International 7N 25746	**2**	12

SPACE UK, male vocal / instrumental group — 23 wks

6 Apr 96	**NEIGHBOURHOOD** Gut CDGUT 1	**56** 1
8 Jun 96	**FEMALE OF THE SPECIES** Gut CDGUT 2	**14** 10
7 Sep 96	● **ME AND YOU VERSUS THE WORLD)** Gut CDGUT 4	**9** 6
2 Nov 96	**NEIGHBOURHOOD (re-issue)** Gut CDGUT 5	**11** 6

SPACE KITTENS
UK, male instrumental / production group — 1 wk

13 Apr 96	**STORM** Hooj Choons HOOJCD 41	**58** 1

SPACE MONKEY UK, male producer – Paul Goodchild — 4 wks

8 Oct 83	**CAN'T STOP RUNNING** Innervision A 3742	**53** 4

SPACE 2000 UK, male vocal / instrumental duo — 1 wk

12 Aug 95	**DO U WANNA FUNK** Wired WIRED 218	**50** 1

SPACEBABY UK, male producer – Matt Darey — 1 wk

8 Jul 95	**FREE YOUR MIND** Hooj Choons HOOJ 34CD	**55** 1

SPACEHOG UK, male vocal / instrumental group — 2 wks

11 May 96	**IN THE MEANTIME** Sire 7559643162	**70** 1
28 Dec 96	**IN THE MEANTIME (re-entry)** Sire 7559643162	**29†** 1

SPAGHETTI SURFERS
UK, male instrumental / production duo — 1 wk

22 Jul 95	**MISIRLOU (THE THEME TO THE MOTION PICTURE PULP FICTION)** Tempo Toons CDTOON 4	**55** 1

SPAGNA Italy, female vocalist — 23 wks

25 Jul 87	● **CALL ME** CBS 650279 7	**2** 12
17 Oct 87	**EASY LADY** CBS 651169 7	**62** 3
20 Aug 88	**EVERY GIRL AND BOY** CBS SPAG 1	**23** 8

SPANDAU BALLET
UK, male vocal / instrumental group — 159 wks

15 Nov 80	● **TO CUT A LONG STORY SHORT** Reformation CHS 2473	**5** 11
24 Jan 81	**THE FREEZE** Reformation CHS 2486	**17** 8
4 Apr 81	● **MUSCLEBOUND / GLOW** Reformation CHS 2509	**10** 10
18 Jul 81	● **CHANT NO. 1 (I DON'T NEED THIS PRESSURE ON)** Reformation CHS 2528	**3** 10
14 Nov 81	**PAINT ME DOWN** Chrysalis CHS 2560	**30** 5
30 Jan 82	**SHE LOVED LIKE DIAMOND** Chrysalis CHS 2585	**49** 4
10 Apr 82	● **INSTINCTION** Chrysalis CHS 2602	**10** 11
2 Oct 82	● **LIFELINE** Chrysalis CHS 2642	**7** 9
12 Feb 83	**COMMUNICATION** Reformation CHS 2662	**12** 10
23 Apr 83	★ **TRUE** Reformation SPAN 1	**1** 12
13 Aug 83	● **GOLD** Reformation SPAN 2	**2** 9
9 Jun 84	● **ONLY WHEN YOU LEAVE** Reformation SPAN 3	**3** 9
18 Aug 84	**ONLY WHEN YOU LEAVE (re-entry)** Reformation SPAN 3	**74** 1
25 Aug 84	● **I'LL FLY FOR YOU** Reformation SPAN 4	**9** 9
20 Oct 84	**HIGHLY STRUNG** Reformation SPAN 5	**15** 5
8 Dec 84	**ROUND AND ROUND** Reformation SPAN 6	**18** 8
26 Jul 86	**FIGHT FOR OURSELVES** Reformation A 7264	**15** 7
8 Nov 86	● **THROUGH THE BARRICADES** Reformation SPANS 1	**6** 10
14 Feb 87	**HOW MANY LIES** Reformation SPANS 2	**34** 4
3 Sep 88	**RAW** CBS SPANS 3	**47** 3
26 Aug 89	**BE FREE WITH YOUR LOVE** CBS SPANS 4	**42** 4

SPARKLEHORSE US, male vocal / instrumental group — 1 wk

31 Aug 96	**RAINMAKER** Capitol CDCL 777	**61** 1

SPARKS US, male vocal / instrumental duo — 78 wks

4 May 74	● **THIS TOWN AIN'T BIG ENOUGH FOR BOTH OF US** Island WIP 6193	**2** 10
20 Jul 74	● **AMATEUR HOUR** Island WIP 6203	**7** 9
19 Oct 74	**NEVER TURN YOUR BACK ON MOTHER EARTH** Island WIP 6211	**13** 7
18 Jan 75	**SOMETHING FOR THE GIRL WITH EVERYTHING** Island WIP 6221	**17** 7
19 Jul 75	**GET IN THE SWING** Island WIP 6236	**27** 7
4 Oct 75	**LOOKS LOOKS LOOKS** Island WIP 6249	**26** 4
21 Apr 79	**THE NUMBER ONE SONG IN HEAVEN** Virgin VS 244	**14** 12
21 Jul 79	● **BEAT THE CLOCK** Virgin VS 270	**10** 9
27 Oct 79	**TRYOUTS FOR THE HUMAN RACE** Virgin VS 289	**45** 5
29 Oct 94	**WHEN DO I GET TO SING 'MY WAY'** Logic 74321234472	**38** 3
11 Mar 95	**WHEN I KISS YOU (I HEAR CHARLIE PARKER PLAYING)** Logic 74321264272	**36** 2
20 May 95	**WHEN DO I GET TO SING 'MY WAY' (re-issue)** Logic 74321274002	**32** 2
9 Mar 96	**NOW THAT I OWN THE BBC** Logic 74321348672	**60** 1

Group were a UK / US group for first six hits.

SPEAR OF DESTINY
UK, male vocal / instrumental group — 43 wks

21 May 83	**THE WHEEL** Epic A 3372	**59** 5
21 Jan 84	**PRISONER OF LOVE** Epic A 4068	**59** 3
14 Apr 84	**LIBERATOR** Epic A 4310	**67** 2
15 Jun 85	**ALL MY LOVE (ASK NOTHING)** Epic A 6333	**61** 3
10 Aug 85	**COME BACK** Epic 6445	**55** 3
7 Feb 87	**STRANGERS IN OUR TOWN** 10 TEN 148	**49** 4
4 Apr 87	● **NEVER TAKE ME ALIVE** 10 TEN 162	**14** 11
25 Jul 87	**WAS THAT YOU** 10 TEN 173	**55** 4
3 Oct 87	**THE TRAVELLER** 10 TEN 189	**44** 3
24 Sep 88	**SO IN LOVE WITH YOU** Virgin VS 1123	**36** 5

SPEARHEAD US, male vocal / instrumental group — 4 wks

17 Dec 94	**OF COURSE YOU CAN** Capitol CDCL 733	**74** 1
22 Apr 95	**HOLE IN THE BUCKET** Capitol CDCL 742	**55** 1
15 Jul 95	**PEOPLE IN THA MIDDLE** Capitol CDCLS 752	**49** 2

Billie Jo SPEARS US, female vocalist — 40 wks

12 Jul 75	● **BLANKET ON THE GROUND** United Artists UP 35805	**6** 13
17 Jul 76	● **WHAT I'VE GOT IN MIND** United Artists UP 36118	**4** 13
11 Dec 76	**SING ME AN OLD FASHIONED SONG** United Artists UP 36179	**34** 9
21 Jul 79	**I WILL SURVIVE** United Artists UP 601	**47** 5

SPECIALS UK, male vocal / instrumental group — 101 wks

28 Jul 79	● **GANGSTERS** 2 Tone CHSTT 1 [1]	**6** 12
27 Oct 79	● **A MESSAGE TO YOU RUDY / NITE CLUB** 2 Tone CHSTT 5 [2]	**10** 14
26 Jan 80	★ **TOO MUCH TOO YOUNG (LIVE) EP** 2 Tone CHSTT 7 [1]	**1** 10
24 May 80	● **RAT RACE / RUDE BOYS OUTA JAIL** 2 Tone CHSTT 11	**5** 9
20 Sep 80	● **STEREOTYPE / INTERNATIONAL JET SET** 2 Tone CHSTT 13	**6** 8
13 Dec 80	● **DO NOTHING / MAGGIE'S FARM** 2 Tone CHSTT 16	**4** 11
20 Jun 81	★ **GHOST TOWN** 2 Tone CHSTT 17	**1** 14
23 Jan 82	**THE BOILER** 2 Tone CHSTT 18 [3]	**35** 5
3 Sep 83	**RACIST FRIEND / BRIGHT LIGHTS** 2 Tone CHSTT 25 [1]	**60** 3
17 Mar 84	● **NELSON MANDELA** 2 Tone CHSTT 26 [1]	**9** 10

| 8 Sep 84 | **WHAT I LIKE MOST ABOUT YOU IS YOUR GIRLFRIEND** *2 Tone CHSTT 27* [1] | **51** 4 |
| 10 Feb 96 | **HYPOCRITE** *Kuff KUFFD 3* | **66** 1 |

[1] Special A.K.A. [2] Specials (featuring Rico+) [3] Rhoda with the Special A.K.A.

Tracks on The Special A.K.A. Live! EP: *Too Much Too Young / Guns Of Navarone / Long Shot Kick De Bucket / Liquidator / Skinhead Moonstomp*. Maggie's Farm only listed with Do Nothing *from 10 Jan 81*. Group were male / female for last four hits. See also Various Artists (EPs & LPs) – The Two Tone EP.

SPECTRUM UK, male producer   **1 wk**

| 26 Sep 92 | **TRUE LOVE WILL FIND YOU IN THE END** *Silvertone ORE 44* | **70** 1 |

Chris SPEDDING
UK, male vocalist / instrumentalist – guitar   **8 wks**

| 23 Aug 75 | **MOTOR BIKING** *RAK 210* | **14** 8 |

SPEECH US, male vocalist   **2 wks**

| 17 Feb 96 | **LIKE MARVIN GAYE SAID (WHAT'S GOING ON)** *Cooltempo CDCOOL 314* | **35** 2 |

SPEEDY UK, male vocal / instrumental group   **1 wk**

| 9 Nov 96 | **BOY WONDER** *Boiler House! BOIL 2CD* | **56** 1 |

Johnnie SPENCE UK, orchestra   **15 wks**

| 1 Mar 62 | **THEME FROM 'DR. KILDARE'** *Parlophone R 4872* | **15** 15 |

Don SPENCER UK, male vocalist   **12 wks**

| 21 Mar 63 | **FIREBALL** *HMV POP 1087* | **32** 11 |
| 13 Jun 63 | **FIREBALL (re-entry)** *HMV POP 1087* | **49** 1 |

Tracie SPENCER US, female vocalist   **2 wks**

| 4 May 91 | **THIS HOUSE** *Capitol CL 612* | **65** 2 |

SPHINX UK / US, male vocal / instrumental group   **2 wks**

| 25 Mar 95 | **WHAT HOPE HAVE I** *Champion CHAMPCD 318* | **43** 2 |

SPICE GIRLS UK, female vocal group   **35 wks**

20 Jul 96	★ **WANNABE** *Virgin VSCDX 1588*	**1**† 24
26 Oct 96	★ **SAY YOU'LL BE THERE** *Virgin VSCDT 1601*	**1**† 10
28 Dec 96	★ **2 BECOME 1** *Virgin VSCDT 1607*	**1**† 1

SPIDER UK, male vocal / instrumental group   **5 wks**

| 5 Mar 83 | **WHY D'YA LIE TO ME** *RCA 313* | **65** 2 |
| 10 Mar 84 | **HERE WE GO ROCK 'N' ROLL** *A & M AM 180* | **57** 3 |

SPIN DOCTORS US, male vocal / instrumental group   **28 wks**

15 May 93	● **TWO PRINCES** *Epic 6591452*	**3** 15
14 Aug 93	**LITTLE MISS CAN'T BE WRONG** *Epic 6584892*	**23** 5
9 Oct 93	**JIMMY OLSEN'S BLUES** *Epic 6597582*	**40** 2
4 Dec 93	**WHAT TIME IS IT** *Epic 6599552*	**56** 1

25 Jun 94	**CLEOPATRA'S CAT** *Epic 6604192*	**29** 2
30 Jul 94	**YOU LET YOUR HEART GO TOO FAST** *Epic 6606612*	**66** 1
29 Oct 94	**MARY JANE** *Epic 6609772*	**55** 1
8 Jun 96	**SHE USED TO BE MINE** *Epic 6632682*	**55** 1

SPINAL TAP US / UK, male vocal / instrumental group   **3 wks**

| 28 Mar 92 | **BITCH SCHOOL** *MCA MCS 1624* | **35** 2 |
| 2 May 92 | **THE MAJESTY OF ROCK** *MCA MCS 1629* | **61** 1 |

SPINNERS – See DETROIT SPINNERS

SPIRAL TRIBE UK, male / female vocal / instrumental group   **2 wks**

| 29 Aug 92 | **BREACH THE PEACE (EP)** *Butterfly BLRT 79* | **66** 1 |
| 21 Nov 92 | **FORWARD THE REVOLUTION** *Butterfly BLRT 85* | **70** 1 |

Tracks on Breach The Peace (EP): *Breach The Peace / Do Et / Seven / 25 Minute Warning.*

SPIRITS UK, male / female vocal duo   **5 wks**

| 19 Nov 94 | **DON'T BRING ME DOWN** *MCA MCSTD 2018* | **31** 3 |
| 8 Apr 95 | **SPIRIT INSIDE** *MCA MCSTD 2045* | **39** 2 |

SPIRITUAL COWBOYS – See David A. STEWART

SPIRITUALIZED UK, male vocal / instrumental group   **6 wks**

30 Jun 90	**ANYWAY YOU WANT ME / STEP INTO THE BREEZE** *Dedicated ZB 43783*	**75** 1
17 Aug 91	**RUN** *Dedicated SPIRIT 002*	**59** 1
25 Jul 92	**MEDICATION** *Dedicated SPIRIT 005T*	**55** 1
23 Oct 93	**GOOD TIMES** *Dedicated SPIRIT 007CD*	**49** 1
4 Feb 95	**LET IT FLOW** *Dedicated SPIRIT 009CD* [1]	**30** 2

[1] Spiritualized Electric Mainline

SPIRO and WIX UK, male instrumental duo   **2 wks**

| 10 Aug 96 | **TARA'S THEME** *EMI Premier PRESCD 4* | **29** 2 |

SPITTING IMAGE UK, male / female puppets   **18 wks**

10 May 86	★ **THE CHICKEN SONG** *Virgin SPIT 1*	**1** 10
26 Jul 86	**THE CHICKEN SONG (re-entry)** *Virgin SPIT 1*	**67** 1
6 Dec 86	**SANTA CLAUS IS ON THE DOLE / FIRST ATHEIST TABERNACLE CHOIR** *Virgin VS 921*	**22** 7

SPLINTER UK, male vocal / instrumental duo   **10 wks**

| 2 Nov 74 | **COSTAFINE TOWN** *Dark Horse AMS 7135* | **17** 10 |

SPLIT ENZ
New Zealand / UK, male vocal / instrumental group   **15 wks**

| 16 Aug 80 | **I GOT YOU** *A & M AMS 7546* | **12** 11 |
| 23 May 81 | **HISTORY NEVER REPEATS** *A & M AMS 8128* | **63** 4 |

A SPLIT SECOND
Belgium / Italy, male instrumental / production group   **1 wk**

| 14 Dec 91 | **FLESH** *ffrr FX 178* | **68** 1 |

SPLODGENESSABOUNDS
UK, male vocal / instrumental group   **17 wks**

| 14 Jun 80 | ● **SIMON TEMPLAR / TWO PINTS OF LAGER AND A PACKET OF CRISPS PLEASE** *Deram BUM 1* | **7** 8 |

6 Sep 80	TWO LITTLE BOYS / HORSE *Deram ROLF 1*	26	7
13 Jun 81	COWPUNK MEDLUM *Deram BUM 3*	69	2

SPONGE *US, male vocal / instrumental group*   **1 wk**

19 Aug 95	PLOWED *Work 6623162*	74	1

SPOOKY *UK, male vocal / instrumental duo*   **1 wk**

13 Mar 93	SCHMOO *Guerilla GRRR 45CD*	72	1

SPOTNICKS *Sweden, male instrumental group*   **37 wks**

14 Jun 62	ORANGE BLOSSOM SPECIAL *Oriole CB 1724*	29	10
6 Sep 62	ROCKET MAN *Oriole CB 1755*	38	9
31 Jan 63	HAVA NAGILA *Oriole CB 1790*	13	12
25 Apr 63	JUST LISTEN TO MY HEART *Oriole CB 1818*	36	6

Dusty SPRINGFIELD *UK, female vocalist*   **211 wks**

21 Nov 63	● I ONLY WANT TO BE WITH YOU *Philips BF 1292*	4	18
20 Feb 64	STAY AWHILE *Philips BF 1313*	13	10
2 Jul 64	● I JUST DON'T KNOW WHAT TO DO WITH MYSELF *Philips BF 1348*	3	12
22 Oct 64	● LOSING YOU *Philips BF 1369*	9	13
18 Feb 65	YOUR HURTIN' KIND OF LOVE *Philips BF 1396*	37	4
1 Jul 65	IN THE MIDDLE OF NOWHERE *Philips BF 1418*	8	10
16 Sep 65	● SOME OF YOUR LOVIN' *Philips BF 1430*	8	12
27 Jan 66	LITTLE BY LITTLE *Philips BF 1466*	17	9
31 Mar 66	★ YOU DON'T HAVE TO SAY YOU LOVE ME *Philips BF 1482*	1	13
7 Jul 66	GOING BACK *Philips BF 1502*	10	10
15 Sep 66	● ALL I SEE IS YOU *Philips BF 1510*	9	12
23 Feb 67	I'LL TRY ANYTHING *Philips BF 1553*	13	9
25 May 67	GIVE ME TIME *Philips BF 1577*	24	6
10 Jul 68	● I CLOSE MY EYES AND COUNT TO TEN *Philips BF 1682*	4	12
4 Dec 68	SON OF A PREACHER MAN *Philips BF 1730*	9	9
20 Sep 69	AM I THE SAME GIRL *Philips BF 1811*	43	3
18 Oct 69	AM I THE SAME GIRL (re-entry) *Philips BF 1811*	46	1
19 Sep 70	HOW CAN I BE SURE *Philips 6006 045*	36	4
20 Oct 79	BABY BLUE *Mercury DUSTY 4*	61	5
22 Aug 87	● WHAT HAVE I DONE TO DESERVE THIS *Parlophone R 6163* [1]	2	9
25 Feb 89	NOTHING HAS BEEN PROVED *Parlophone R 6207*	16	7
2 Dec 89	IN PRIVATE *Parlophone R 6234*	14	10
26 May 90	REPUTATION *Parlophone R 6253*	38	6
24 Nov 90	ARRESTED BY YOU *Parlophone R 6266*	70	2
30 Oct 93	HEART AND SOUL *Columbia 6598562* [2]	75	1
10 Jun 95	WHEREVER WOULD I BE *Columbia 6620592* [3]	44	3
4 Nov 95	ROLL AWAY *Columbia 6623682*	68	1

[1] Pet Shop Boys and Dusty Springfield [2] Cilla Black with Dusty Springfield [3] Dusty Springfield and Daryl Hall

See also Springfields.

Rick SPRINGFIELD *Australia, male vocalist*   **13 wks**

14 Jan 84	HUMAN TOUCH / SOULS *RCA RICK 1*	23	7
24 Mar 84	JESSIE'S GIRL *RCA RICK 2*	43	6

Souls only listed from 11 Feb 84. It peaked at position 24.

SPRINGFIELDS
UK, male / female vocal / instrumental group   **66 wks**

31 Aug 61	BREAKAWAY *Philips BF 1168*	31	8
16 Nov 61	BAMBINO *Philips BF 1178*	16	11
13 Dec 62	● ISLAND OF DREAMS *Philips 326557 BF*	5	26
28 Mar 63	● SAY I WON'T BE THERE *Philips 326577 BF*	5	15
25 Jul 63	COME ON HOME *Philips BF 1263*	31	6

Bruce SPRINGSTEEN *US, male vocalist*   **140 wks**

22 Nov 80	HUNGRY HEART *CBS 9309*	44	4
13 Jun 81	THE RIVER *CBS A 1179*	35	6
26 May 84	DANCING IN THE DARK *CBS A 4436*	28	7
6 Oct 84	COVER ME *CBS 4662*	38	5
12 Jan 85	● DANCING IN THE DARK (re-entry) *CBS A 4436*	4	16
23 Mar 85	COVER ME (re-entry) *CBS A 4662*	16	8
15 Jun 85	I'M ON FIRE / BORN IN THE USA *CBS A 6342*	5	12
3 Aug 85	GLORY DAYS *CBS A 6375*	17	6
14 Dec 85	● SANTA CLAUS IS COMIN' TO TOWN / MY HOMETOWN *CBS A 6773*	9	5
29 Nov 86	WAR *CBS 650193 7*	18	7
7 Feb 87	FIRE *CBS 650381 7*	54	2
23 May 87	BORN TO RUN *CBS BRUCE 2*	16	4
3 Oct 87	BRILLIANT DISGUISE *CBS 651141 7*	20	5
12 Dec 87	TUNNEL OF LOVE *CBS 651295 7*	45	4
18 Jun 88	TOUGHER THAN THE REST *CBS BRUCE 3*	13	8
24 Sep 88	SPARE PARTS *CBS BRUCE 4*	32	3
21 Mar 92	HUMAN TOUCH *Columbia 6578727*	11	5
23 May 92	BETTER DAYS *Columbia 6578907*	34	3
25 Jul 92	57 CHANNELS (AND NOTHIN' ON) *Columbia 6581387*	32	4
24 Oct 92	LEAP OF FAITH *Columbia 6583697*	46	3
10 Apr 93	LUCKY TOWN (LIVE) *Columbia 6592282*	48	3
19 Mar 94	● STREETS OF PHILADELPHIA *Columbia 6600652*	2	12
22 Apr 95	SECRET GARDEN *Columbia 6612955*	44	3
11 Nov 95	HUNGRY HEART (re-issue) *Columbia 6626252*	28	3
4 May 96	THE GHOST OF TOM JOAD *Columbia 6630315*	26	2

SPRINGWATER
UK, male instrumentalist – Phil Cordell   **12 wks**

23 Oct 71	● I WILL RETURN *Polydor 2058 141*	5	12

SPYRO GYRA *US, male instrumental group*   **10 wks**

21 Jul 79	MORNING DANCE *Infinity INF 111*	17	10

SQUADRONAIRES – *See Joan REGAN*

SQUEEZE *UK, male vocal / instrumental group*   **123 wks**

8 Apr 78	TAKE ME I'M YOURS *A & M AMS 7335*	19	9
10 Jun 78	BANG BANG *A & M AMS 7360*	49	5
18 Nov 78	GOODBYE GIRL *A & M AMS 7398*	63	2
24 Mar 79	● COOL FOR CATS *A & M AMS 7426*	2	11
2 Jun 79	● UP THE JUNCTION *A & M AMS 7444*	2	11
8 Sep 79	SLAP AND TICKLE *A & M AMS 7466*	24	8
1 Mar 80	ANOTHER NAIL IN MY HEART *A & M AMS 7507*	17	9
10 May 80	PULLING MUSSELS (FROM THE SHELL) *A & M AMS 7523*	44	6
16 May 81	IS THAT LOVE *A & M AMS 8129*	35	8
25 Jul 81	TEMPTED *A & M AMS 8147*	41	5
10 Oct 81	● LABELLED WITH LOVE *A & M AMS 8166*	4	10
24 Apr 82	BLACK COFFEE IN BED *A & M AMS 8219*	51	4
23 Oct 82	ANNIE GET YOUR GUN *A & M AMS 8259*	43	4
15 Jun 85	LAST TIME FOREVER *A & M AM 255*	45	5
8 Aug 87	HOURGLASS *A & M AM 400*	16	10
17 Oct 87	TRUST ME TO OPEN MY MOUTH *A & M AM 412*	72	1
25 Apr 92	COOL FOR CATS (re-issue) *A & M AM 860*	62	2
24 Jul 93	THIRD RAIL *A & M 5803372*	39	3
11 Sep 93	SOME FANTASTIC PLACE *A & M 5803792*	73	1
9 Sep 95	THIS SUMMER *A & M 5811912*	36	3
18 Nov 95	ELECTRIC TRAINS *A & M 5812692*	44	2
15 Jun 96	HEAVEN KNOWS *A & M 5816052*	27	2
24 Aug 96	THIS SUMMER (re-mix) *A & M 5818372*	32	2

Billy SQUIER *US, male vocalist*   **3 wks**

3 Oct 81	THE STROKE *Capitol CL 214*	52	3

Dorothy SQUIRES *UK, female vocalist*   **56 wks**

5 Jun 53	**I'M WALKING BEHIND YOU** *Polygon P 1068* **12** 1
24 Aug 61	**SAY IT WITH FLOWERS** *Columbia DB 4665* [1] **23** 10
20 Sep 69	**FOR ONCE IN MY LIFE** *President PT 267* **24** 10
20 Dec 69	**FOR ONCE IN MY LIFE (re-entry)** *President PT 267*......**48** 1
21 Feb 70	**TILL** *President PT 281* **25** 10
9 May 70	**TILL (re-entry)** *President PT 281* **48** 1
8 Aug 70	**MY WAY** *President PT 305* **40** 5
19 Sep 70	**MY WAY (re-entry)** *President PT 305*...............**34** 8
28 Nov 70	**MY WAY (2nd re-entry)** *President PT 305*.........**25** 10

[1] Dorothy Squires and Russ Conway

STABBS
Finland / US / Cameroon, male instrumental / production group   **1 wk**

| 24 Dec 94 | **JOY AND HAPPINESS** *Hi-Life HICD 3* ....**65** 1 |

STACCATO
UK / Holland, male / female vocal / instrumental duo   **1 wk**

| 20 Jul 96 | **I WANNA KNOW** *Multiply CDMULTY 11* ....**65** 1 |

Jim STAFFORD *US, male vocalist*   **16 wks**

| 27 Apr 74 | **SPIDERS AND SNAKES** *MGM 2006 374* ....**14** 8 |
| 6 Jul 74 | **MY GIRL BILL** *MGM 2006 423* ....**20** 8 |

Jo STAFFORD *US, female vocalist*   **28 wks**

14 Nov 52	★ **YOU BELONG TO ME** *Columbia DB 3152* **1** 19
19 Dec 52	**JAMBALAYA** *Columbia DB 3169* **11** 2
7 May 54	● **MAKE LOVE TO ME** *Philips PB 233* **8** 1
9 Dec 55	**SUDDENLY THERE'S A VALLEY** *Philips PB 509* **12** 5
3 Feb 56	**SUDDENLY THERE'S A VALLEY (re-entry)** *Philips PB 509* **19** 1

Terry STAFFORD *US, male vocalist*   **9 wks**

| 7 May 64 | **SUSPICION** *London HLU 9871* ....**31** 9 |

STAIFFI and his MUSTAFAS
France, male vocal / instrumental group   **1 wk**

| 28 Jul 60 | **MUSTAFA CHA CHA CHA ORIENTAL** *Pye International 7N 25057* ....**43** 1 |

STAKKA BO *Sweden, male producer*   **12 wks**

| 25 Sep 93 | **HERE WE GO** *Polydor PZCD 280* ....**13** 8 |
| 18 Dec 93 | **DOWN THE DRAIN** *Polydor PZCD 301* ....**64** 4 |

Frank STALLONE *US, male vocalist*   **2 wks**

| 22 Oct 83 | **FAR FROM OVER** *RSO 95* ....**68** 2 |

STAMFORD BRIDGE *UK, male vocal group*   **1 wk**

| 16 May 70 | **CHELSEA** *Penny Farthing PEN 715*...............**47** 1 |

STAN *UK, male vocal / instrumental duo*   **3 wks**

| 31 Jul 93 | **SUNTAN** *Hug CDBUM 1* ....**40** 3 |

Lisa STANSFIELD *UK, female vocalst*   **109 wks**

25 Mar 89	**PEOPLE HOLD ON** *Ahead Of Our Time CCUT 5* [1] **11** 9
12 Aug 89	**THIS IS THE RIGHT TIME** *Arista 112512* **13** 8
28 Oct 89	★ **ALL AROUND THE WORLD** *Arista 112693* **1** 14
10 Feb 90	● **LIVE TOGETHER** *Arista 112914* **10** 6
12 May 90	**WHAT DID I DO TO YOU (EP)** *Arista 113168* **25** 4
19 Oct 91	● **CHANGE** *Arista 114820* **10** 7
21 Dec 91	**ALL WOMAN** *Arista 115000* **20** 8
14 Mar 92	**TIME TO MAKE YOU MINE** *Arista 115113* **14** 8
6 Jun 92	**SET YOUR LOVING FREE** *Arista 74321100587* **28** 4
19 Dec 92	● **SOMEDAY (I'M COMING BACK)** *Arista 74321123567* ...**10** 9
1 May 93	★ **FIVE LIVE EP** *Parlophone CDRS 6340* [2] **1** 9
5 Jun 93	● **IN ALL THE RIGHT PLACES** *MCA MCSTD 1780* **8** 11
24 Jul 93	**FIVE LIVE EP (re-entry)** *Parlophone CDRS 6340* [2] **74** 1
23 Oct 93	**SO NATURAL** *Arista 74321169132* **15** 5
11 Dec 93	**LITTLE BIT OF HEAVEN** *Arista 74321178202* **32** 4

[1] Coldcut featuring Lisa Stansfield [2] George Michael and Queen with Lisa Stansfield

Tracks on What Did I Do To You (EP): What Did I Do To You / My Apple Heart / Lay Me Down / Something's Happenin'. Tracks on Five Live EP: Somebody To Love / These Are The Days Of Our Lives / Calling You / Papa Was A Rolling Stone – Killer (medley). Lisa Stansfield appears only on the second track.

Viv STANSHALL – See Mike OLDFIELD

STAPLE SINGERS *US, male / female vocal group*   **14 wks**

| 10 Jun 72 | **I'LL TAKE YOU THERE** *Stax 2025 110* ....**30** 8 |
| 8 Jun 74 | **IF YOU'RE READY (COME GO WITH ME)** *Stax 2025 224* ....**34** 6 |

Cyril STAPLETON *UK, orchestra*   **27 wks**

27 May 55	**ELEPHANT TANGO** *Decca F 10488*...............**20** 2
1 Jul 55	**ELEPHANT TANGO (re-entry)** *Decca F 10488* **20** 1
22 Jul 55	**ELEPHANT TANGO (2nd re-entry)** *Decca F 10488* **19** 1
23 Sep 55	● **BLUE STAR (THE MEDIC THEME)** *Decca F 10559* [1] **2** 12
6 Apr 56	**THE ITALIAN THEME** *Decca F 10703* **18** 2
1 Jun 56	**THE HAPPY WHISTLER** *Decca F 10735* [2] **22** 4
19 Jul 57	**FORGOTTEN DREAMS** *Decca F 10912*...............**27** 5

[1] Cyril Stapleton Orchestra featuring Julie Dawn [2] Cyril Stapleton Orchestra featuring Desmond Lane, penny whistle

See also David Whitfield.

STARDUST *Sweden, male / female vocal / instrumental group*   **3 wks**

| 8 Oct 77 | **ARIANA** *Satril SAT 120* ....**42** 3 |

Alvin STARDUST *UK, male vocalist*   **119 wks**

3 Nov 73	● **MY COO-CA-CHOO** *Magnet MAG 1* **2** 21
16 Feb 74	★ **JEALOUS MIND** *Magnet MAG 5* **1** 11
4 May 74	**RED DRESS** *Magnet MAG 8* **7** 8
31 Aug 74	● **YOU YOU YOU** *Magnet MAG 13* **6** 10
30 Nov 74	**TELL ME WHY** *Magnet MAG 19* **16** 8
1 Feb 75	**GOOD LOVE CAN NEVER DIE** *Magnet MAG 21* **11** 9
12 Jul 75	**SWEET CHEATIN' RITA** *Magnet MAG 32* **37** 4
5 Sep 81	● **PRETEND** *Stiff BUY 124* **4** 10
21 Nov 81	**A WONDERFUL TIME UP THERE** *Stiff BUY 132*...........**56** 8
5 May 84	● **I FEEL LIKE BUDDY HOLLY** *Chrysalis CHS 2784* **7** 11
27 Oct 84	● **I WON'T RUN AWAY** *Chrysalis CHS 2829* **7** 13
15 Dec 84	**SO NEAR TO CHRISTMAS** *Chrysalis CHS 2835* **29** 4
23 Mar 85	**GOT A LITTLE HEARTACHE** *Chrysalis CHS 2856* **55** 2

Alvin started his career as Shane Fenton. See also Shane Fenton and the Fentones.

STARGARD US, female vocal group — 14 wks

28 Jan 78	THEME FROM 'WHICH WAY IS UP' MCA 346	19	7
15 Apr 78	LOVE IS SO EASY MCA 354	45	1
9 Sep 78	WHAT YOU WAITING FOR MCA 382	39	6

STARGAZERS UK, male vocal / instrumental group — 53 wks

13 Feb 53	BROKEN WINGS Decca F 10047	11	1
27 Feb 53	★ BROKEN WINGS (re-entry) Decca F 10047	1	11
19 Feb 54	★ I SEE THE MOON Decca F 10213	1	15
9 Apr 54	HAPPY WANDERER Decca F 10259	12	1
4 Mar 55	SOMEBODY Decca F 10437	20	1
3 Jun 55	CRAZY OTTO RAG Decca F 10523	18	3
9 Sep 55	● CLOSE THE DOOR Decca F 10594	6	9
11 Nov 55	● TWENTY TINY FINGERS Decca F 10626	4	11
22 Jun 56	HOT DIGGITY Decca F 10731	28	1

See also Dickie Valentine.

STARGAZERS UK, male vocal / instrumental group — 3 wks

6 Feb 82	GROOVE BABY GROOVE (EP) Epic EPC A 1924	56	3

Tracks on Groove Baby Groove (EP): Groove Baby Groove / Jump Around / La Rock 'N' Roll (Quelques Uns A La Lune) / Red Light Green Light.

STARJETS UK, male vocal / instrumental group — 5 wks

8 Sep 79	WAR STORIES Epic EPC 7770	51	5

STARLAND VOCAL BAND
US, male / female vocal group — 10 wks

7 Aug 76	AFTERNOON DELIGHT RCA 2716	18	10

STARLIGHT
Italy, male instrumental / production group — 11 wks

19 Aug 89	● NUMERO UNO Citybeat CBE 742	9	11

STARLITERS – See Joey DEE and the STARLITERS

Edwin STARR US, male vocalist — 70 wks

12 May 66	STOP HER ON SIGHT (SOS) Polydor BM 56 702	35	8
18 Aug 66	HEADLINE NEWS Polydor 56 717	39	3
11 Dec 68	STOP HER ON SIGHT (SOS) / HEADLINE NEWS (re-issue) Polydor 56 753	11	11
13 Sep 69	25 MILES Tamla Motown TMG 672	36	6
24 Oct 70	● WAR Tamla Motown TMG 754	3	12
20 Feb 71	STOP THE WAR NOW Tamla Motown TMG 764	33	1
27 Jan 79	● CONTACT 20th Century BTC 2396	6	12
26 May 79	● H.A.P.P.Y. RADIO RCA TC 2408	9	11
1 Jun 85	IT AIN'T FAIR Hippodrome HIP 101	56	4
30 Oct 93	WAR Weekend CDWEEK 103 [1]	69	2

[1] Edwin Starr and Shadow

Headline News not listed with SOS from 22 Jan 69 to 19 Feb 69. It therefore peaked at position 16. War in 93 was a re-recording and was listed with the flip side Wild Thing by the Troggs and Wolf.

Freddie STARR UK, male vocalist — 14 wks

23 Feb 74	● IT'S YOU Tiffany 6121 501	9	10
20 Dec 75	WHITE CHRISTMAS Thunderbird THE 102	41	4

Kay STARR US, female vocalist — 58 wks

5 Dec 52	★ COMES A-LONG A-LOVE Capitol CL 13808	1	16
24 Apr 53	● SIDE BY SIDE Capitol CL 13871	7	4
19 Mar 54	● CHANGING PARTNERS Capitol CL 14050	4	14
15 Oct 54	AM I A TOY OR A TREASURE Capitol CL 14151	17	3
12 Nov 54	AM I A TOY OR A TREASURE (re-entry) Capitol CL 14151	20	1
17 Feb 56	★ ROCK AND ROLL WALTZ HMV POP 168	1	20

Ringo STARR UK, male vocalist — 56 wks

17 Apr 71	● IT DON'T COME EASY Apple R 5898	4	11
1 Apr 72	● BACK OFF BOOGALOO Apple R 5944	2	10
27 Oct 73	● PHOTOGRAPH Apple R 5992	8	13
23 Feb 74	● YOU'RE SIXTEEN Apple R 5995	4	10
30 Nov 74	ONLY YOU Apple R 6000	28	11
6 Jun 92	WEIGHT OF THE WORLD Private Music 115392	74	1

STARSHIP US, female / male vocal / instrumental group — 41 wks

26 Jan 80	JANE Grunt FB 1750 [1]	21	9
16 Nov 85	WE BUILT THIS CITY RCA PB 49929	12	12
8 Feb 86	SARA RCA FB 49893	66	3
11 Apr 87	★ NOTHING'S GONNA STOP US NOW Grunt FB 49757	1	17

[1] Jefferson Starship

STARSOUND Holland, producer Jaap Eggermont with male / female session singers — 37 wks

18 Apr 81	● STARS ON 45 CBS A 1102	2	14
4 Jul 81	● STARS ON 45 VOL. 2 CBS A 1407	2	10
19 Sep 81	STARS ON 45 VOL. 3 CBS A 1521	17	6
27 Feb 82	STARS ON STEVIE CBS A 2041	14	7

STARTRAX UK, male / female session group — 8 wks

1 Aug 81	STARTRAX CLUB DISCO Picksy KSY 1001	18	8

STARTURN ON 45 (PINTS) UK, male vocal group — 9 wks

24 Oct 81	STARTURN ON 45 (PINTS) V Tone V TONE 003	45	4
30 Apr 88	PUMP UP THE BITTER Pacific DRINK 1	12	5

STARVATION Multi-national, male / female vocal / instrumental charity assembly — 6 wks

9 Mar 85	STARVATION / TAM -TAM POUR L'ETHIOPE Zarjazz JAZZ 3	33	6

STARVING SOULS UK, male vocal / instrumental group — 1 wk

21 Oct 95	I BE THE PROPHET Durban Poison DPCD 1	66	1

STATLER BROTHERS US, male vocal group — 4 wks

24 Feb 66	FLOWERS ON THE WALL CBS 201976	38	4

Candi STATON US, female vocalist — 58 wks

29 May 76	● YOUNG HEARTS RUN FREE Warner Bros. K 16730	2	13
18 Sep 76	DESTINY Warner Bros. K 16806	41	3
23 Jul 77	● NIGHTS ON BROADWAY Warner Bros. K 16972	6	12
3 Jun 78	HONEST I DO LOVE YOU Warner Bros. K 17164	48	5
24 Apr 82	SUSPICIOUS MINDS Sugarhill SH 112	31	9

1. alphabetically by artist

Sting

Sting wrote 'This Cowboy Song' for Jimmy Nail's *Crocodile Shoes* project, but submitted it too late for inlcusion on either the album or the TV show.

Smashing Pumpkins

This US quartet received an MTV award in 1996 for the video to their only UK Top 10 hit to date, 'Tonight Tonight'.

Strawberry Switchblade

'Since Yesterday' memorably borrowed the hook from 'Beach Baby', a hit for First Class in 1974.

336

31 May 86	**YOUNG HEARTS RUN FREE (re-mix)**		
	Warner Bros. W 8680	**47**	5
2 Feb 91	● **YOU GOT THE LOVE** *Truelove TLOVE 7001* 1	**4**	11

1 Source featuring Candi Staton

STATUS IV US, male vocal group — 3 wks

9 Jul 83	**YOU AIN'T REALLY DOWN** *TMT TMT 4*	**56**	3

STATUS QUO UK, male vocal / instrumental group — 408 wks

24 Jan 68	● **PICTURES OF MATCHSTICK MEN** *Pye 7N 17449*	**7**	12
21 Aug 68	● **ICE IN THE SUN** *Pye 7N 17581*	**8**	12
28 May 69	**ARE YOU GROWING TIRED OF MY LOVE** *Pye 7N 17728*	**46**	2
18 Jun 69	**ARE YOU GROWING TIRED OF MY LOVE (re-entry)**		
	Pye 7N 17728	**50**	1
2 May 70	**DOWN THE DUSTPIPE** *Pye 7N 17907*	**12**	17
7 Nov 70	**IN MY CHAIR** *Pye 7N 17998*	**21**	14
13 Jan 73	● **PAPER PLANE** *Vertigo 6059 071*	**8**	11
14 Apr 73	**MEAN GIRL** *Pye 7N 45229*	**20**	11
8 Sep 73	● **CAROLINE** *Vertigo 6059 085*	**5**	13
4 May 74	● **BREAK THE RULES** *Vertigo 6059 101*	**8**	8
7 Dec 74	★ **DOWN DOWN** *Vertigo 6059 114*	**1**	11
17 May 75	● **ROLL OVER LAY DOWN** *Vertigo QUO 13*	**9**	8
14 Feb 76	● **RAIN** *Vertigo 6059 133*	**7**	7
10 Jul 76	**MYSTERY SONG** *Vertigo 6059 146*	**11**	9
11 Dec 76	● **WILD SIDE OF LIFE** *Vertigo 6059 153*	**9**	12
8 Oct 77	● **ROCKIN' ALL OVER THE WORLD** *Vertigo 6059 184*	**3**	16
2 Sep 78	**AGAIN AND AGAIN** *Vertigo QUO 1*	**13**	9
25 Nov 78	**ACCIDENT PRONE** *Vertigo QUO 2*	**36**	8
22 Sep 79	● **WHATEVER YOU WANT** *Vertigo 6059 242*	**4**	9
24 Nov 79	**LIVING ON AN ISLAND** *Vertigo 6059 248*	**16**	10
11 Oct 80	● **WHAT YOU'RE PROPOSING** *Vertigo QUO 3*	**2**	11
6 Dec 80	**LIES / DON'T DRIVE MY CAR** *Vertigo QUO 4*	**11**	10
28 Feb 81	● **SOMETHING 'BOUT YOU BABY I LIKE** *Vertigo QUO 5*	**9**	7
28 Nov 81	● **ROCK 'N' ROLL** *Vertigo QUO 6*	**8**	11
27 Mar 82	● **DEAR JOHN** *Vertigo QUO 7*	**10**	8
12 Jun 82	**SHE DON'T FOOL ME** *Vertigo QUO 8*	**36**	5
30 Oct 82	**CAROLINE (LIVE AT THE N.E.C.)** *Vertigo QUO 10*	**13**	7
10 Sep 83	● **OL' RAG BLUES** *Vertigo QUO 11*	**9**	8
5 Nov 83	● **A MESS OF THE BLUES** *Vertigo QUO 12*	**15**	6
10 Dec 83	● **MARGUERITA TIME** *Vertigo QUO 14*	**3**	11
19 May 84	**GOING DOWN TOWN TONIGHT** *Vertigo QUO 15*	**20**	6
27 Oct 84	● **THE WANDERER** *Vertigo QUO 16*	**7**	11
17 May 86	● **ROLLIN' HOME** *Vertigo QUO 18*	**9**	6
26 Jul 86	**RED SKY** *Vertigo QUO 19*	**19**	8
4 Oct 86	● **IN THE ARMY NOW** *Vertigo QUO 20*	**2**	14
6 Dec 86	**DREAMIN'** *Vertigo QUO 21*	**15**	8
28 Mar 88	**AIN'T COMPLAINING** *Vertigo QUO 22*	**19**	6
21 May 88	**WHO GETS THE LOVE** *Vertigo QUO 23*	**34**	4
20 Aug 88	**RUNNING ALL OVER THE WORLD** *Vertigo QUAID 1*	**17**	6
3 Dec 88	● **BURNING BRIDGES (ON AND OFF AND ON AGAIN)**		
	Vertigo QUO 25	**5**	10
28 Oct 89	**NOT AT ALL** *Vertigo QUO 26*	**50**	2
29 Sep 90	● **THE ANNIVERSARY WALTZ – PART 1** *Vertigo QUO 28*	**2**	9
15 Dec 90	**THE ANNIVERSARY WALTZ – PART 2** *Vertigo QUO 29*	**16**	7
7 Sep 91	**CAN'T GIVE YOU MORE** *Vertigo QUO 30*	**37**	3
18 Jan 92	**ROCK 'TIL YOU DROP** *Vertigo QUO 32*	**38**	3
10 Oct 92	**ROADHOUSE MEDLEY (ANNIVERSARY**		
	WALTZ PART 25) *Polydor QUO 33*	**21**	4
6 Aug 94	**I DIDN'T MEAN IT** *Polydor QUOCD 34*	**21**	4
22 Oct 94	**SHERRI DON'T FAIL ME NOW** *Polydor QUOCD 35*	**38**	2
3 Dec 94	**RESTLESS** *Polydor QUOCD 36*	**39**	2
4 Nov 95	**WHEN YOU WALK IN THE ROOM** *PolyGram TV 5775122*	**34**	2
2 Mar 96	**FUN FUN FUN** *PolyGram TV 5762632* 1	**24**	4
13 Apr 96	**DON'T STOP** *PolyGram TV 5766352*	**35**	2
9 Nov 96	**ALL AROUND MY HAT** *PolyGram TV 5759452* 2	**47**	1

1 Status Quo with the Beach Boys 2 Status Quo with Maddy Prior from Steeleye Span

Don't Drive My Car *listed from 20 Dec 80 only. Running All Over The World* is a re-recorded version of Rockin' All Over The World, *with a slightly changed lyric, released to promote the Race Against Time of 28 Aug 88. See also Francis Rossi.*

STAXX UK, male / female vocal / instrumental group — 7 wks

2 Oct 93	**JOY** *Champion CHAMPCD 303*	**25**	6
20 May 95	**YOU** *Champion CHAMPCD 316* 1	**50**	1

1 Staxx featuring Carol Leeming

STEALER'S WHEEL UK, male vocal/instrumental group — 22 wks

26 May 73	● **STUCK IN THE MIDDLE WITH YOU** *A & M AMS 7036*	**8**	10
1 Sep 73	**EVERYTHING'L TURN OUT FINE** *A & M AMS 7079*	**33**	6
26 Jan 74	**STAR** *A & M AMS 7094*	**25**	6

STEAM US, male vocal / instrumental group — 14 wks

31 Jan 70	● **NA NA HEY HEY KISS HIM GOODBYE** *Fontana TF 1058*	**9**	14

Anthony STEEL and the RADIO REVELLERS
UK, male vocalist / male instrumental group — 6 wks

10 Sep 54	**WEST OF ZANZIBAR** *Polygon P 1114*	**11**	6

STEEL PULSE UK, male vocal / instrumental group — 12 wks

1 Apr 78	**KU KLUX KLAN** *Island WIP 6428*	**41**	4
8 Jul 78	**PRODIGAL SON** *Island WIP 6449*	**35**	6
23 Jun 79	**SOUND SYSTEM** *Island WIP 6490*	**71**	2

Tommy STEELE UK, male vocalist — 145 wks

26 Oct 56	**ROCK WITH THE CAVEMAN** *Decca F 10795* 1	**13**	4
30 Nov 56	**ROCK WITH THE CAVEMAN (re-entry)**		
	Decca F 10795 1	**23**	1
14 Dec 56	★ **SINGING THE BLUES** *Decca F 10819* 1	**1**	13
15 Feb 57	**KNEE DEEP IN THE BLUES** *Decca F 10849* 1	**15**	9
19 Apr 57	**SINGING THE BLUES (re-entry)** *Decca F 10819* 1	**24**	1
3 May 57	**BUTTERFINGERS** *Decca F 10877* 1	**25**	1
17 May 57	● **BUTTERFINGERS (re-entry)** *Decca F 10877* 1	**8**	17
17 May 57	**SINGING THE BLUES (2nd re-entry)** *Decca F 10819* 1	**29**	1
16 Aug 57	● **WATER WATER / HANDFUL OF SONGS** *Decca F 10923* 1	**5**	16
30 Aug 57	**SHIRALEE** *Decca F 10896* 1	**11**	4
22 Nov 57	**HEY YOU** *Decca F 10941* 1	**28**	1
13 Dec 57	**WATER WATER / HANDFUL OF SONGS (re-entry)**		
	Decca F 10923 1	**28**	1
7 Mar 58	● **NAIROBI** *Decca F 10991*	**3**	11
25 Apr 58	**HAPPY GUITAR** *Decca F 10976*	**20**	5
18 Jul 58	**THE ONLY MAN ON THE ISLAND** *Decca F 11041* 1	**16**	8
14 Nov 58	● **COME ON LET'S GO** *Decca F 11072*	**10**	13
14 Aug 59	**TALLAHASSEE LASSIE** *Decca F 11152*	**16**	4
28 Aug 59	**GIVE GIVE GIVE** *Decca F 11152*	**28**	2
25 Sep 59	**TALLAHASSEE LASSIE (re-entry)** *Decca F 11152*	**25**	1
4 Dec 59	● **LITTLE WHITE BULL** *Decca F 11177*	**6**	12
10 Mar 60	**LITTLE WHITE BULL (re-entry)** *Decca F 11177*	**30**	5
23 Jun 60	● **WHAT A MOUTH** *Decca F 11245*	**5**	11
29 Dec 60	**MUST BE SANTA** *Decca F 11299*	**40**	1
17 Aug 61	**WRITING ON THE WALL** *Decca F 11372*	**30**	5

1 Tommy Steele and the Steelmen

Handful Of Songs *listed together with* Water Water *from week of 23 Aug 57. See also Various Artists (EPs & LPs) – All Star Hit Parade No.2.*

STEELEYE SPAN
UK, male / female vocal / instrumental group — 18 wks

8 Dec 73	**GAUDETE** *Chrysalis CHS 2007*	**14**	9
15 Nov 75	● **ALL AROUND MY HAT** *Chrysalis CHS 2078*	**5**	9

See also Status Quo.

STEELY DAN US, male vocal / instrumental group · 21 wks

30 Aug 75	**DO IT AGAIN** ABC 4075	**39**	4
11 Dec 76	**HAITIAN DIVORCE** ABC 4152	**17**	9
29 Jul 78	**FM (NO STATIC AT ALL)** MCA 374	**49**	4
2 Sep 78	**FM (NO STATIC AT ALL) (re-entry)** MCA 374	**75**	1
10 Mar 79	**RIKKI DON'T LOSE THAT NUMBER** ABC 4241	**58**	3

Jim STEINMAN US, male vocalist · 9 wks

4 Jul 81	**ROCK 'N' ROLL DREAMS COME THROUGH** Epic EPC A 1236 [1]	**52**	7
23 Jun 84	**TONIGHT IS WHAT IT MEANS TO BE YOUNG** MCA MCA 889 [2]	**67**	2

[1] Jim Steinman, vocals by Rory Dodd [2] Jim Steinman and Fire Inc.

STEINSKI and MASS MEDIA
US, male producer and rapper · 2 wks

31 Jan 87	**WE'LL BE RIGHT BACK** Fourth & Broadway BRW 59	**63**	2

Mike STEIPHENSON – See BURUNDI STEIPHENSON BLACK

Doreen STEPHENS – See Billy COTTON and his BAND

Ritchie STEPHENS – See MAD COBRA featuring Ritchie STEPHENS

Martin STEPHENSON and the DAINTEES
UK, male vocal / instrumental group · 7 wks

8 Nov 86	**BOAT TO BOLIVIA** Kitchenware SL 27	**70**	2
17 Jan 87	**TROUBLE TOWN** Kitchenware SK 13 [1]	**58**	3
27 Jun 92	**BIG SKY NEW LIGHT** Kitchenware SK 57	**71**	2

[1] Daintees

STEPPENWOLF
US / Canada, male vocal / instrumental group · 9 wks

11 Jun 69	**BORN TO BE WILD** Stateside SS 8017	**30**	7
9 Aug 69	**BORN TO BE WILD (re-entry)** Stateside SS 8017	**50**	2

STEREO MC'S UK, male rap group · 31 wks

29 Sep 90	**ELEVATE MY MIND** Fourth & Broadway BRW 186	**74**	1
9 Mar 91	**LOST IN MUSIC** Fourth & Broadway BRW 198	**46**	3
26 Sep 92	**CONNECTED** Fourth & Broadway BRW 262	**18**	6
5 Dec 92	**STEP IT UP** Fourth & Broadway BRW 266	**12**	12
20 Feb 93	**GROUND LEVEL** Fourth & Broadway BRCD 268	**19**	5
29 May 93	**CREATION** Fourth & Broadway BRCD 276	**19**	4

STEREO NATION UK, male vocal duo · 1 wk

17 Aug 96	**I'VE BEEN WAITING** EMI Premier PRESCD 5	**53**	1

STEREOLAB
UK / France, male / female vocal / instrumental group · 5 wks

8 Jan 94	**JENNY ONDIOLINE / FRENCH DISKO** Duophonic UHF DUHFD 01	**75**	1
30 Jul 94	**PING PONG** Duophonic UHF DUHFCD 04	**45**	2
12 Nov 94	**WOW AND FLUTTER** Duophonic UHF DUHFCD 07	**70**	1
2 Mar 96	**CYBELE'S REVERIE** Duophonic UHF DUHFCD 10	**62**	1

STETASONIC US, male rap group · 2 wks

24 Sep 88	**TALKIN' ALL THAT JAZZ** Breakout USA 640	**73**	2

STEVE and EYDIE – See Steve LAWRENCE; Eydie GORMÉ

April STEVENS – See Nino TEMPO and April STEVENS

Cat STEVENS UK, male vocalist · 96 wks

20 Oct 66	**I LOVE MY DOG** Deram DM 102	**28**	7
12 Jan 67 ●	**MATTHEW AND SON** Deram DM 110	**2**	10
30 Mar 67	**I'M GONNA GET ME A GUN** Deram DM 118	**6**	10
2 Aug 67	**A BAD NIGHT** Deram DM 140	**20**	8
20 Dec 67	**KITTY** Deram DM 156	**47**	1
27 Jun 70 ●	**LADY D'ARBANVILLE** Island WIP 6086	**8**	13
28 Aug 71	**MOON SHADOW** Island WIP 6092	**22**	11
1 Jan 72 ●	**MORNING HAS BROKEN** Island WIP 6121	**9**	13
9 Dec 72	**CAN'T KEEP IT IN** Island WIP 6152	**13**	12
24 Aug 74	**ANOTHER SATURDAY NIGHT** Island WIP 6206	**19**	8
2 Jul 77	**(REMEMBER THE DAYS OF THE) OLD SCHOOL YARD** Island WIP 6387	**44**	3

Connie STEVENS US, female vocalist · 20 wks

5 May 60 ●	**SIXTEEN REASONS** Warner Bros. WB 3	**9**	11
5 May 60	**KOOKIE KOOKIE (LEND ME YOUR COMB)** Warner Bros. WB 5 [1]	**27**	8
4 Aug 60	**SIXTEEN REASONS (re-entry)** Warner Bros. WB 3	**45**	1

[1] Edward Byrnes and Connie Stevens

Ray STEVENS US, male vocalist · 64 wks

16 May 70 ●	**EVERYTHING IS BEAUTIFUL** CBS 4953	**6**	16
13 Mar 71 ●	**BRIDGET THE MIDGET (THE QUEEN OF THE BLUES)** CBS 7070	**2**	14
25 Mar 72	**TURN YOUR RADIO ON** CBS 7634	**33**	4
25 May 74 ★	**THE STREAK** Janus 6146 201	**1**	12
21 Jun 75 ●	**MISTY** Janus 6146 204	**2**	10
27 Sep 75	**INDIAN LOVE CALL** Janus 6146 205	**34**	4
5 Mar 77	**IN THE MOOD** Warner Bros. K 16875	**31**	4

In The Mood *features Ray Stevens not as a conventional vocalist, but as a group of chickens.*

Ricky STEVENS UK, male vocalist · 7 wks

14 Dec 61	**I CRIED FOR YOU** Columbia DB 4739	**34**	7

Shakin' STEVENS UK, male vocalist · 277 wks

16 Feb 80	**HOT DOG** Epic EPC 8090	**24**	9
16 Aug 80	**MARIE MARIE** Epic EPC 8725	**19**	10
28 Feb 81 ★	**THIS OLE HOUSE** Epic EPC 9555	**1**	17
2 May 81 ●	**YOU DRIVE ME CRAZY** Epic A 1165	**2**	12
25 Jul 81 ★	**GREEN DOOR** Epic A 1354	**1**	12
10 Oct 81 ●	**IT'S RAINING** Epic A 1643	**10**	9
16 Jan 82 ★	**OH JULIE** Epic EPC A 1742	**1**	10
24 Apr 82 ●	**SHIRLEY** Epic EPC A 2087	**6**	6
21 Aug 82	**GIVE ME YOUR HEART TONIGHT** Epic EPC A 2656	**11**	10
16 Oct 82 ●	**I'LL BE SATISFIED** Epic EPC A 2846	**10**	8
11 Dec 82 ●	**THE SHAKIN' STEVENS EP** Epic SHAKY 1	**2**	7
23 Jul 83	**IT'S LATE** Epic A 3565	**11**	7
5 Nov 83 ●	**CRY JUST A LITTLE BIT** Epic A 3774	**3**	12
7 Jan 84 ●	**A ROCKIN' GOOD WAY** Epic A 4071 [1]	**5**	9
24 Mar 84 ●	**A LOVE WORTH WAITING FOR** Epic A 4291	**2**	10
15 Sep 84 ●	**A LETTER TO YOU** Epic A 4677	**10**	8
24 Nov 84 ●	**TEARDROPS** Epic A 4882	**5**	9
2 Mar 85	**BREAKING UP MY HEART** Epic A 6072	**14**	7
12 Oct 85	**LIPSTICK POWDER AND PAINT** Epic A 6610	**11**	9
7 Dec 85 ★	**MERRY CHRISTMAS EVERYONE** Epic A 6769	**1**	8
8 Feb 86	**TURNING AWAY** Epic A 6819	**15**	7
1 Nov 86 ●	**BECAUSE I LOVE YOU** Epic SHAKY 2	**14**	10
20 Dec 86	**MERRY CHRISTMAS EVERYONE (re-entry)** Epic A 6769	**58**	3

27 Jun 87		A LITTLE BOOGIE WOOGIE (IN THE BACK OF MY MIND) *Epic SHAKY 3*	12	10
19 Sep 87		COME SEE ABOUT ME *Epic SHAKY 4*	24	6
28 Nov 87	●	WHAT DO YOU WANT TO MAKE THOSE EYES AT ME FOR *Epic SHAKY 5*	5	8
23 Jul 88		FEEL THE NEED IN ME *Epic SHAKY 6*	26	5
15 Oct 88		HOW MANY TEARS CAN YOU HIDE *Epic SHAKY 7*	47	4
10 Dec 88		TRUE LOVE *Epic SHAKY 8*	23	6
18 Feb 89		JEZEBEL *Epic SHAKY 9*	58	2
13 May 89		LOVE ATTACK *Epic SHAKY 10*	28	4
24 Feb 90		I MIGHT *Epic SHAKY 11*	18	6
12 May 90		YES I DO *Epic SHAKY 12*	60	2
18 Aug 90		PINK CHAMPAGNE *Epic SHAKY 13*	59	2
13 Oct 90		MY CUTIE CUTIE *Epic SHAKY 14*	75	1
15 Dec 90		THE BEST CHRISTMAS OF THEM ALL *Epic SHAKY 15*	19	4
7 Dec 91		I'LL BE HOME THIS CHRISTMAS *Epic 6576507*	34	5
10 Oct 92		RADIO *Epic 6584367* [2]	37	3

[1] Shaky and Bonnie [2] Shaky featuring Roger Taylor

Tracks on The Shakin' Stevens EP: Blue Christmas / Que Sera Sera / Josephine / Lawdy Miss Clawdy.

STEVENSON'S ROCKET
UK, male vocal / instrumental group   **5 wks**

29 Nov 75		ALRIGHT BABY *Magnet MAG 47*	37	2
20 Dec 75		ALRIGHT BABY (re-entry) *Magnet MAG 47*	45	3

Al STEWART *UK, male vocalist*   **6 wks**

29 Jan 77		YEAR OF THE CAT *RCA 2771*	31	6

Amii STEWART *US, female vocalist*   **61 wks**

7 Apr 79	●	KNOCK ON WOOD *Atlantic / Hansa K 11214*	6	12
16 Jun 79	●	LIGHT MY FIRE / 137 DISCO HEAVEN (MEDLEY) *Atlantic / Hansa K 11278*	5	11
3 Nov 79		JEALOUSY *Atlantic / Hansa K 11386*	58	3
19 Jan 80		THE LETTER / PARADISE BIRD *Atlantic / Hansa K 11424*	39	4
19 Jul 80		MY GU – MY GIRL (MEDLEY) *Atlantic / Hansa K 11550* [1]	39	5
29 Dec 84		FRIENDS *RCA 471*	12	11
17 Aug 85	●	KNOCK ON WOOD / LIGHT MY FIRE (re-mix) *Sedition EDIT 3303*	7	12
25 Jan 86		MY GUY – MY GIRL (MEDLEY) *Sedition EDIT 3310* [2]	63	3

[1] Amii Stewart and Johnny Bristol [2] Amii Stewart and Deon Estus

Andy STEWART *UK, male vocalist*   **67 wks**

15 Dec 60		DONALD WHERE'S YOUR TROOSERS *Top Rank JAR 427*	37	1
12 Jan 61		A SCOTTISH SOLDIER *Top Rank JAR 512*	19	38
1 Jun 61		THE BATTLE'S O'ER *Top Rank JAR 565*	28	13
12 Oct 61		A SCOTTISH SOLDIER (re-entry) *Top Rank JAR 512*	43	2
12 Aug 65		DR. FINLAY *HMV POP 1454*	50	1
26 Aug 65		DR. FINLAY (re-entry) *HMV POP 1454*	43	4
9 Dec 89	●	DONALD WHERE'S YOUR TROOSERS (re-issue) *Stone SON 2353*	4	8

Billy STEWART *US, male vocalist*   **2 wks**

8 Sep 66		SUMMERTIME *Chess CRS 8040*	39	2

Dave STEWART *UK, male instrumentalist – keyboards*   **30 wks**

14 Mar 81		WHAT BECOMES OF THE BROKEN HEARTED *Stiff BROKEN 1* [1]	13	10
19 Sep 81	★	IT'S MY PARTY *Broken BROKEN 2* [2]	1	13
13 Aug 83		BUSY DOING NOTHING *Broken BROKEN 5* [2]	49	4
14 Jun 86		THE LOCOMOTION *Broken BROKEN 8* [2]	70	3

[1] Dave Stewart. Guest vocals Colin Blunstone [2] Dave Stewart with Barbara Gaskin

Dave STEWART
UK, male vocalist / instrumentalist – guitar   **19 wks**

24 Feb 90	●	LILY WAS HERE *RCA ZB 43045* [1]	6	12
18 Aug 90		JACK TALKING *RCA PB 43907* [2]	69	2
3 Sep 94		HEART OF STONE *East West YZ 845CD*	36	5

[1] David A. Stewart featuring Candy Dulfer [2] Dave Stewart and the Spiritual Cowboys

Jermaine STEWART *US, male vocalist*   **42 wks**

9 Aug 86	●	WE DON'T HAVE TO... *10 TEN 96*	2	14
1 Nov 86		JODY *10 TEN 143*	50	4
16 Jan 88	●	SAY IT AGAIN *10 TEN 188*	7	12
2 Apr 88		GET LUCKY *Siren SRN 82*	13	9
24 Sep 88		DON'T TALK DIRTY TO ME *Siren SRN 86*	61	3

John STEWART *US, male vocalist*   **6 wks**

30 Jun 79		GOLD *RSO 35*	43	6

Rod STEWART *UK, male vocalist*   **449 wks**

4 Sep 71		REASON TO BELIEVE *Mercury 6052 097*	19	2
18 Sep 71	★	MAGGIE MAY *Mercury 6052 097*	1	19
12 Aug 72	★	YOU WEAR IT WELL *Mercury 6052 171*	1	12
18 Nov 72	●	ANGEL / WHAT MADE MILWAUKEE FAMOUS (HAS MADE A LOSER OUT OF ME) *Mercury 6052 198*	4	11
5 May 73		I'VE BEEN DRINKING *RAK RR 4* [1]	27	6
8 Sep 73	●	OH NO NOT MY BABY *Mercury 6052 371*	6	9
5 Oct 74	●	FAREWELL – BRING IT ON HOME TO ME / YOU SEND ME *Mercury 6167 033*	7	7
16 Aug 75	★	SAILING *Warner Bros. K 16600*	1	11
15 Nov 75	●	THIS OLD HEART OF MINE *Riva 1*	4	9
5 Jun 76	●	TONIGHT'S THE NIGHT (GONNA BE ALRIGHT) *Riva 3*	5	9
21 Aug 76	●	THE KILLING OF GEORGIE (PARTS 1 & 2) *Riva 4*	2	10
4 Sep 76	●	SAILING (re-entry) *Warner Bros. K 16600*	3	20
20 Nov 76		GET BACK *Riva 6*	11	9
4 Dec 76		MAGGIE MAY (re-entry) *Mercury 6160 006*	31	7
23 Apr 77	★	I DON'T WANT TO TALK ABOUT IT / FIRST CUT IS THE DEEPEST *Riva 7*	1	13
15 Oct 77	●	YOU'RE IN MY HEART *Riva 11*	3	10
28 Jan 78	●	HOTLEGS / I WAS ONLY JOKING *Riva 10*	5	8
27 May 78	●	OLE OLA (MULHER BRASILEIRA) *Riva 15* [2]	4	6
18 Nov 78	★	DA YA THINK I'M SEXY? *Riva 17*	1	13
3 Feb 79	●	AIN'T LOVE A BITCH *Riva 18*	11	8
5 May 79		BLONDES (HAVE MORE FUN) *Riva 19*	63	3
31 May 80		IF LOVING YOU IS WRONG (I DON'T WANT TO BE RIGHT) *Riva 23*	23	9
8 Nov 80	●	PASSION *Riva 26*	17	10
20 Dec 80		MY GIRL *Riva 28*	32	7
17 Oct 81	●	TONIGHT I'M YOURS (DON'T HURT ME) *Riva 33*	8	13
12 Dec 81		YOUNG TURKS *Riva 34*	11	9
27 Feb 82		HOW LONG *Riva 35*	41	4
4 Jun 83	★	BABY JANE *Warner Bros. W 9608*	1	14
27 Aug 83	●	WHAT AM I GONNA DO *Warner Bros. W 9564*	3	8
10 Dec 83		SWEET SURRENDER *Warner Bros. W 9440*	23	9
26 May 84		INFATUATION *Warner Bros. W 9256*	27	7
28 Jul 84		SOME GUYS HAVE ALL THE LUCK *Warner Bros. W 9204*	15	10
24 May 86		LOVE TOUCH *Warner Bros. W 8668*	27	5
5 Jul 86		LOVE TOUCH (re-entry) *Warner Bros. W 8668*	69	3
12 Jul 86	●	EVERY BEAT OF MY HEART *Warner Bros. W 8625*	2	9
20 Sep 86		ANOTHER HEARTACHE *Warner Bros. W 8631*	54	2
28 Mar 87		SAILING (2nd re-entry) *Warner Bros. K 16600*	41	3
28 May 88		LOST IN YOU *Warner Bros. W 7927*	21	6

13 Aug 88	FOREVER YOUNG *Warner Bros. W 7796*	57	3
6 May 89	MY HEART CAN'T TELL YOU NO *Warner Bros. W 7729*	49	4
11 Nov 89	THIS OLD HEART OF MINE *Warner Bros. W 2686* [3]	51	3
13 Jan 90	● DOWNTOWN TRAIN *Warner Bros. W 2647*	10	12
24 Nov 90	● IT TAKES TWO *Warner Bros. ROD 1* [4]	5	8
16 Mar 91	● RHYTHM OF MY HEART *Warner Bros. W 0017*	3	11
15 Jun 91	● THE MOTOWN SONG *Warner Bros. W 0030*	10	8
7 Sep 91	BROKEN ARROW *Warner Bros. W 0059*	54	3
7 Mar 92	PEOPLE GET READY *Epic 6577567* [1]	49	3
18 Apr 92	YOUR SONG / BROKEN ARROW (re-issue) *Warner Bros. W 0104*	41	4
5 Dec 92	● TOM TRAUBERT'S BLUES (WALTZING MATILDA) *Warner Bros. W 0144*	6	9
20 Feb 93	RUBY TUESDAY *Warner Bros. W 0158CD*	11	6
17 Apr 93	SHOTGUN WEDDING *Warner Bros. W 0171CD*	21	4
26 Jun 93	● HAVE I TOLD YOU LATELY *Warner Bros. W 0185CD*	5	9
21 Aug 93	REASON TO BELIEVE *Warner Bros. W 0198CD1*	51	3
18 Dec 93	PEOPLE GET READY *Warner Bros. W 0226CD1*	45	4
15 Jan 94	● ALL FOR LOVE *A & M 5804772* [5]	2	13
20 May 95	YOU'RE THE STAR *Warner Bros. W 0296CD*	19	5
19 Aug 95	LADY LUCK *Warner Bros. W 0310CD1*	56	1
15 Jun 96	PURPLE HEATHER *Warner Bros. W 0354CD* [6]	16	5
14 Dec 96	IF WE FALL IN LOVE TONIGHT *Warner Bros. W 0380CD*	58	1

[1] Jeff Beck and Rod Stewart [2] Rod Stewart featuring the Scottish World Cup Football Squad [3] Rod Stewart featuring Ronald Isley [4] Rod Stewart and Tina Turner [5] Bryan Adams, Rod Stewart and Sting [6] Rod Stewart with the Scottish Euro '96 Squad

Reason To Believe and People Get Ready in '93 were re-recordings. Reason To Believe additionally credits Ronnie Wood on the sleeve. See also Faces; Glass Tiger; Python Lee Jackson.

STEX *UK, male vocal group* **2 wks**

19 Jan 91	STILL FEEL THE RAIN *Some Bizzare SBZ 7002*	63	2

STIFF LITTLE FINGERS
UK, male vocal / instrumental group **39 wks**

29 Sep 79	STRAW DOGS *Chrysalis CHS 2368*	44	4
16 Feb 80	AT THE EDGE *Chrysalis CHS 2406*	15	9
24 May 80	NOBODY'S HERO / TIN SOLDIERS *Chrysalis CHS 2424*	36	5
2 Aug 80	BACK TO FRONT *Chrysalis CHS 2447*	49	4
28 Mar 81	JUST FADE AWAY *Chrysalis CHS 2510*	47	6
30 May 81	SILVER LINING *Chrysalis CHS 2517*	68	3
23 Jan 82	LISTEN EP *Chrysalis CHS 2580*	33	6
18 Sep 82	BITS OF KIDS *Chrysalis CHS 2637*	73	2

Tracks on Listen EP: That's When Your Blood Bumps / Two Guitars Clash / Listen / Sad-Eyed People.

Curtis STIGERS *US, male vocalist* **34 wks**

18 Jan 92	● I WONDER WHY *Arista 114716*	5	10
28 Mar 92	● YOU'RE ALL THAT MATTERS TO ME *Arista 115273*	6	12
11 Jul 92	SLEEPING WITH THE LIGHTS ON *Arista 74321102307*	34	4
17 Oct 92	NEVER SAW A MIRACLE *Arista 74321117257*	53	4
3 Jun 95	THIS TIME *Arista 74321286962*	28	3
2 Dec 95	KEEP ME FROM THE COLD *Arista 74321319162*	57	1

Stephen STILLS *US, male vocalist* **4 wks**

13 Mar 71	LOVE THE ONE YOU'RE WITH *Atlantic 2091 046*	37	4

See also Crosby, Stills, Nash and Young.

STILTSKIN *UK, male vocal / instrumental group* **15 wks**

7 May 94	★ INSIDE *White Water LEV 1CD*	1	13
24 Sep 94	FOOTSTEPS *White Water WWRD 2*	34	2

STING *UK, male vocalist* **131 wks**

14 Aug 82	SPREAD A LITTLE HAPPINESS *A & M AMS 8242*	16	8
8 Jun 85	IF YOU LOVE SOMEBODY SET THEM FREE *A & M AM 258*	26	7
24 Aug 85	LOVE IS THE SEVENTH WAVE *A & M AM 272*	41	5
19 Oct 85	FORTRESS AROUND YOUR HEART *A & M AM 286*	49	3
7 Dec 85	RUSSIANS *A & M AM 292*	12	11
15 Feb 86	MOON OVER BOURBON STREET *A & M AM 305*	44	4
1 Mar 86	RUSSIANS (re-entry) *A & M AM 292*	71	1
7 Nov 87	WE'LL BE TOGETHER *A & M AM 410*	41	4
20 Feb 88	ENGLISHMAN IN NEW YORK *A & M AM 431*	51	3
9 Apr 88	FRAGILE *A & M AM 439*	70	2
11 Aug 90	ENGLISHMAN IN NEW YORK (re-mix) *A & M AM 580*	15	7
12 Jan 91	ALL THIS TIME *A & M AM 713*	22	4
9 Mar 91	MAD ABOUT YOU *A & M AM 721*	56	2
4 May 91	THE SOUL CAGES *A & M AM 759*	57	1
29 Aug 92	IT'S PROBABLY ME *A & M AM 883* [1]	30	5
13 Feb 93	IF I EVER LOSE MY FAITH IN YOU *A & M AMCD 0172*	14	6
24 Apr 93	SEVEN DAYS *A & M 5802232*	25	4
19 Jun 93	FIELDS OF GOLD *A & M 5803012*	16	6
4 Sep 93	SHAPE OF MY HEART *A & M 5803532*	57	1
20 Nov 93	DEMOLITION MAN *A & M 5804512*	21	4
15 Jan 94	● ALL FOR LOVE *A & M 5804772* [2]	2	13
26 Feb 94	NOTHING 'BOUT ME *A & M 5805292*	32	3
29 Oct 94	● WHEN WE DANCE *A & M 5808612*	9	7
11 Feb 95	THIS COWBOY SONG *A & M 5809652*	15	6
20 Jan 96	SPIRITS IN THE MATERIAL WORLD *MCA MCSTD 2113* [3]	36	2
2 Mar 96	LET YOUR SOUL BE YOUR PILOT *A & M 5813312*	15	4
11 May 96	YOU STILL TOUCH ME *A & M 5815472*	27	3
22 Jun 96	LIVE AT TFI FRIDAY EP *A & M 5817652*	53	2
14 Sep 96	I WAS BROUGHT TO MY SENSES *A & M 5818912*	31	2
30 Nov 96	I'M SO HAPPY I CAN'T STOP CRYING *A & M 5820312*	54	1

[1] Sting with Eric Clapton [2] Bryan Adams, Rod Stewart and Sting [3] Pato Banton with Sting

Pato Banton provides uncredited vocals on This Cowboy Song. Tracks on Live At TFI Friday EP: You Still Touch Me / Lithium Sunset / Message In A Bottle.

STINGERS – *See B. BUMBLE and the STINGERS*

STIX 'N' STONED
UK, male instrumental / production duo **2 wks**

20 Jul 96	OUTRAGEOUS *Positiva CDTIV 52*	39	2

Catherine STOCK *UK, female vocalist* **6 wks**

18 Oct 86	TO HAVE AND TO HOLD *Sierra FED 29*	17	6

STOCK AITKEN WATERMAN *UK, male producers* **36 wks**

25 Jul 87	ROADBLOCK *Breakout USA 611*	13	9
24 Oct 87	● MR. SLEAZE *London NANA 14*	3	10
12 Dec 87	PACKJAMMED (WITH THE PARTY POSSE) *Breakout USA 620*	41	6
21 May 88	ALL THE WAY *MCA GOAL 1* [1]	64	2
3 Dec 88	SS PAPARAZZI *PWL PWL 22*	68	2
20 May 89	★ FERRY 'CROSS THE MERSEY *PWL PWL 41* [2]	1	7

[1] England Football Team with the 'sound' of Stock Aitken and Waterman [2] Christians, Holly Johnson, Paul McCartney, Gerry Marsden and Stock Aitken Waterman

The listed flip side of Mr. Sleaze was Love In The First Degree by Bananarama.

Rhet STOLLER *UK, male instrumentalist – guitar* **8 wks**

12 Jan 61	CHARIOT *Decca F 11302*	26	8

Morris STOLOFF US, orchestra   **11 wks**

| 1 Jun 56 | ● | MOONGLOW / THEME FROM 'PICNIC' *Brunswick 05553* ..**7** | 11 |

R & J STONE UK / US, male / female vocal duo   **9 wks**

| 10 Jan 76 | ● | WE DO IT *RCA 2616* ....**5** | 9 |

STONE ROSES UK, male vocal / instrumental group   **74 wks**

29 Jul 89		SHE BANGS THE DRUMS *Silvertone ORE 6* **36**	3
25 Nov 89	●	WHAT THE WORLD IS WAITING FOR / FOOL'S GOLD *Silvertone ORE 13* **8**	14
6 Jan 90		SALLY CINNAMON *Revolver REV 36* **75**	1
20 Jan 90		SALLY CINNAMON (re-entry) *Revolver REV 36* **46**	4
3 Mar 90	●	ELEPHANT STONE *Silvertone ORE 1* **8**	6
17 Mar 90		MADE OF STONE *Silvertone ORE 2* **20**	4
31 Mar 90		SHE BANGS THE DRUMS (re-entry) *Silvertone ORE 6* **34**	3
14 Jul 90	●	ONE LOVE *Silvertone ORE 17* **4**	7
15 Sep 90		WHAT THE WORLD IS WAITING FOR / FOOL'S GOLD (re-entry) *Silvertone ORE 13* **22**	5
14 Sep 91		I WANNA BE ADORED *Silvertone ORE 31* **20**	3
11 Jan 92		WATERFALL *Silvertone ORE 35* **27**	4
11 Apr 92		I AM THE RESURRECTION *Silvertone ORE 40* **33**	2
30 May 92		FOOL'S GOLD (re-mix) *Silvertone ORET 13* **73**	1
3 Dec 94	●	LOVE SPREADS *Geffen GFSTD 84* **2**	8
11 Mar 95		TEN STOREY LOVE SONG *Geffen GFSTD 87* **11**	3
29 Apr 95		FOOL'S GOLD (2nd re-mix) *Silvertone ORECD 71* **25**	3
11 Nov 95		BEGGING YOU *Geffen GFSTD 22060* **15**	3

STONE TEMPLE PILOTS
US, male vocal / instrumental group   **11 wks**

27 Mar 93	SEX TYPE THING *Atlantic A 5769CD* **60**	2
4 Sep 93	PLUSH *Atlantic A 7349CD* **23**	4
27 Nov 93	SEX TYPE THING (re-issue) *Atlantic A 7293CD* **55**	2
20 Aug 94	VASOLINE *Atlantic A 5650CD* **48**	2
10 Dec 94	INTERSTATE LOVE SONG *Atlantic A 7192CD* **53**	1

STONEBRIDGE McGUINNESS
UK, male vocal / instrumental duo   **2 wks**

| 14 Jul 79 | OO-EEH BABY *RCA PB 5163* ....**54** | 2 |

STONEFREE UK, male vocalist   **1 wk**

| 23 May 87 | CAN'T SAY 'BYE *Ensign ENY 607* ....**73** | 1 |

STONKERS – *See HALE and PACE and the STONKERS*

STOP THE VIOLENCE
US, male / female rap charity ensemble   **1 wk**

| 18 Feb 89 | SELF DESTRUCTION *Jive BDPST 1* ....**75** | 1 |

Axel STORDAHL – *See June HUTTON and Axel STORDAHL*

STORM UK, male / female vocal / instrumental group   **10 wks**

| 17 Nov 79 | IT'S MY HOUSE *Scope SC 10* ....**36** | 10 |

Danny STORM UK, male vocalist   **4 wks**

| 12 Apr 62 | HONEST I DO *Piccadilly 7N 35025* ....**42** | 4 |

Rebecca STORM UK, female vocalist   **13 wks**

| 13 Jul 85 | THE SHOW (THEME FROM 'CONNIE') *Towerbell TVP 3* ..**22** | 13 |

STORYVILLE JAZZ BAND – *See Bob WALLIS and his STORYVILLE JAZZ BAND*

Izzy STRADLIN' US, male vocalist / instrumentalist – guitar   **2 wks**

| 26 Sep 92 | PRESSURE DROP *Geffen GFS 25* ....**45** | 2 |

Nick STRAKER BAND
UK, male vocal / instrumental group   **15 wks**

| 2 Aug 80 | A WALK IN THE PARK *CBS 8525* ....**20** | 12 |
| 15 Nov 80 | LEAVING ON THE MIDNIGHT TRAIN *CBS 9088* ....**61** | 3 |

Peter STRAKER and the HANDS OF
DR. TELENY *UK, male vocalist and male vocal / instrumental group*   **4 wks**

| 19 Feb 72 | THE SPIRIT IS WILLING *RCA 2163* ....**40** | 4 |

STRANGE BEHAVIOUR – *See Jane KENNAWAY and STRANGE BEHAVIOUR*

STRANGELOVE UK, male vocal / instrumental group   **4 wks**

20 Apr 96	LIVING WITH THE HUMAN MACHINES *Food CDFOOD 70* **53**	1
15 Jun 96	BEAUTIFUL ALONE *Food CDFOOD 81* **35**	2
19 Oct 96	SWAY *Food CDFOOD 82* **47**	1

STRANGLERS UK, male vocal / instrumental group   **194 wks**

19 Feb 77		(GET A) GRIP (ON YOURSELF) *United Artists UP 36211* ..**44**	4
21 May 77	●	PEACHES / GO BUDDY GO *United Artists UP 36248* **8**	14
30 Jul 77	●	SOMETHING BETTER CHANGE / STRAIGHTEN OUT *United Artists UP 36277* **9**	8
24 Sep 77	●	NO MORE HEROES *United Artists UP 36300* **8**	9
4 Feb 78		FIVE MINUTES *United Artists UP 36350* **11**	9
6 May 78		NICE 'N SLEAZY *United Artists UP 36379* **18**	8
12 Aug 78		WALK ON BY *United Artists UP 36429* **21**	8
18 Aug 79		DUCHESS *United Artists BP 308* **14**	9
20 Oct 79		NUCLEAR DEVICE (THE WIZARD OF AUS) *United Artists BP 318* **36**	4
1 Dec 79		DON'T BRING HARRY (EP) *United Artists STR 1* **41**	3
22 Mar 80		BEAR CAGE *United Artists BP 344* **36**	5
7 Jun 80		WHO WANTS THE WORLD *United Artists BPX 355* **39**	4
31 Jan 81		THROWN AWAY *Liberty BP 383* **42**	4
14 Nov 81		LET ME INTRODUCE YOU TO THE FAMILY *United Artists BP 405* **42**	3
9 Jan 82	●	GOLDEN BROWN *Liberty BP 407* **2**	12
24 Apr 82		LA FOLIE *Liberty BP 410* **47**	3
24 Jul 82	●	STRANGE LITTLE GIRL *Liberty BP 412* **7**	9
8 Jan 83	●	EUROPEAN FEMALE *Epic EPC A 2893* **9**	6
26 Feb 83		MIDNIGHT SUMMER DREAM *Epic EPC A 3167* **35**	4
6 Aug 83		PARADISE *Epic A 3387* **48**	3
6 Oct 84		SKIN DEEP *Epic A 4738* **15**	7
1 Dec 84		NO MERCY *Epic A 4921* **37**	7
16 Feb 85		LET ME DOWN EASY *Epic A 6045* **48**	4
23 Aug 86		NICE IN NICE *Epic 650057* **30**	5
18 Oct 86		ALWAYS THE SUN *Epic SOLAR 1* **30**	5
13 Dec 86		BIG IN AMERICA *Epic HUGE 1* **48**	6
7 Mar 87		SHAKIN' LIKE A LEAF *Epic SHEIK 1* **58**	4
9 Jan 88	●	ALL DAY AND ALL OF THE NIGHT *Epic VICE 1* **7**	7
28 Jan 89		GRIP '89 (GET A) GRIP (ON YOURSELF) (re-mix) *EMI EM 84* **33**	3
17 Feb 90		96 TEARS *Epic TEARS 1* **17**	6
21 Apr 90		SWEET SMELL OF SUCCESS *Epic TEARS 2* **65**	1
5 Jan 91		ALWAYS THE SUN (re-mix) *Epic 6564307* **29**	5
30 Mar 91		GOLDEN BROWN (re-mix) *Epic 6567617* **68**	2
22 Aug 92		HEAVEN OR HELL *Psycho WOK 2025* **46**	2

Go Buddy Go *credited with* Peaches *from 11 Jun 77.* Straighten Out *credited with* Something Better Change *from 13 Aug 77. Tracks on* Don't Bring Harry (EP)*: Don't Bring Harry / Wired / Crabs (Live) / In The Shadows (Live).*

STRAWBERRY SWITCHBLADE
UK, female vocal duo **26 wks**

17 Nov 84 ●	**SINCE YESTERDAY** Korova KOW 38	**5**	17
23 Mar 85	**LET HER GO** Korova KOW 39	**59**	5
21 Sep 85	**JOLENE** Korova KOW 42	**53**	4

STRAWBS *UK, male vocal / instrumental group* **27 wks**

28 Oct 72	**LAY DOWN** A & M AMS 7035	**12**	13
27 Jan 73 ●	**PART OF THE UNION** A & M AMS 7047	**2**	11
6 Oct 73	**SHINE ON SILVER SUN** A & M AMS 7082	**34**	3

STRAY CATS *US, male vocal / instrumental group* **49 wks**

29 Nov 80 ●	**RUNAWAY BOYS** Arista SCAT 1	**9**	10
7 Feb 81 ●	**ROCK THIS TOWN** Arista SCAT 2	**9**	8
25 Apr 81	**STRAY CAT STRUT** Arista SCAT 3	**11**	10
20 Jun 81	**THE RACE IS ON** Swansong SSK 19425 [1]	**34**	6
7 Nov 81	**YOU DON'T BELIEVE ME** Arista SCAT 4	**57**	3
6 Aug 83	**(SHE'S) SEXY AND 17** Arista SCAT 6	**29**	9
4 Mar 89	**BRING IT BACK AGAIN** EMI USA MT 62	**64**	3

[1] Dave Edmunds and the Stray Cats

STRAY MOB – *See MC SKAT KAT and the STRAY MOB*

STREETBAND *UK, male vocal / instrumental group* **6 wks**

4 Nov 78	**TOAST / HOLD ON** Logo GO 325	**18**	6

Barbra STREISAND *US, female vocalist* **130 wks**

20 Jan 66	**SECOND HAND ROSE** CBS 202025	**14**	13
30 Jan 71	**STONEY END** CBS 5321	**46**	1
13 Feb 71	**STONEY END (re-entry)** CBS 5321	**27**	10
30 Mar 74	**THE WAY WE WERE** CBS 1915	**31**	6
9 Apr 77 ●	**LOVE THEME FROM 'A STAR IS BORN' (EVERGREEN)** CBS 4855	**3**	19
25 Nov 78 ●	**YOU DON'T BRING ME FLOWERS** CBS 6803 [1]	**5**	12
3 Nov 79 ●	**NO MORE TEARS (ENOUGH IS ENOUGH)** Casablanca CAN 174/ CBS 8000 [2]	**3**	13
4 Oct 80 ★	**WOMAN IN LOVE** CBS 8966	**1**	16
6 Dec 80	**GUILTY** CBS 9315 [3]	**34**	10
30 Jan 82	**COMIN' IN AND OUT OF YOUR LIFE** CBS A 1789	**66**	3
20 Mar 82	**MEMORY** CBS A 1903	**34**	6
5 Nov 88	**TILL I LOVED YOU (LOVE THEME FROM 'GOYA')** CBS BARB 2 [4]	**16**	7
7 Mar 92	**PLACES THAT BELONG TO YOU** Columbia 6577947	**17**	5
5 Jun 93	**WITH ONE LOOK** Columbia 6593422	**30**	3
5 Jan 94	**THE MUSIC OF THE NIGHT** Columbia 6597382 [5]	**54**	3
30 Apr 94	**AS IF WE NEVER SAID GOODBYE (FROM 'SUNSET BOULEVARD')** Columbia 6603572	**20**	3

[1] Barbra and Neil [2] Donna Summer and Barbra Streisand
[3] Barbra Streisand and Barry Gibb [4] Barbra Streisand and Don Johnson
[5] Barbra Streisand (duet with Michael Crawford)

Neil was Neil Diamond. No More Tears (Enough Is Enough) was released simultaneously on two different labels, a 7-inch single on Casablanca and a 12-inch on CBS.

STRESS *UK, male vocal / instrumental group* **1 wk**

13 Oct 90	**BEAUTIFUL PEOPLE** Eternal YZ 495	**74**	1

STRETCH *UK, male vocal / instrumental group* **9 wks**

8 Nov 75	**WHY DID YOU DO IT** Anchor ANC 1021	**16**	9

STRETCH AND VERN present MADDOG
UK, male instrumental / production duo **9 wks**

14 Sep 96 ●	**I'M ALIVE** ffrr FCD 284	**6**	9

STRIKE
UK / Australia, male / female vocal / instrumental group **19 wks**

24 Dec 94	**U SURE DO** Fresh FRSHD 19	**31**	5
1 Apr 95 ●	**U SURE DO (re-entry)** Fresh FRSHD 19	**4**	9
23 Sep 95	**THE MORNING AFTER (FREE AT LAST)** Fresh FRSHD 37	**38**	1
29 Jun 96	**INSPIRATION** Fresh FRSHD 45	**27**	2
16 Nov 96	**MY LOVE IS FOR REAL** Fresh FRSHD 46	**35**	2

STRIKERS *US, male vocal / instrumental group* **5 wks**

6 Jun 81	**BODY MUSIC** Epic EPC A 1290	**45**	5

STRING-A-LONGS *US, male instrumental group* **16 wks**

23 Feb 61 ●	**WHEELS** London HLU 9278	**8**	16

STRINGS OF LOVE
Italy, male / female vocal / instrumental group **2 wks**

3 Mar 90	**NOTHING HAS BEEN PROVED** Breakout USA 688	**59**	2

Joe STRUMMER *UK, male vocalist* **13 wks**

2 Aug 86	**LOVE KILLS** CBS A 7244	**69**	1
23 Dec 95	**JUST THE ONE** China WOKCD 2076 [1]	**12**	8
29 Jun 96 ●	**ENGLAND'S IRIE** Radioactive RAXTD 25 [2]	**6**	4

[1] Levellers, special guest Joe Strummer [2] Black Grape featuring Joe Strummer and Keith Allen

STRYKER – *See MANCHESTER UNITED FOOTBALL SQUAD*

Chad STUART and Jeremy CLYDE
UK, male vocal duo **7 wks**

28 Nov 63	**YESTERDAY'S GONE** Ember EMB S 180	**37**	7

STUMP *UK, male vocal / instrumental group* **1 wk**

13 Aug 88	**CHARLTON HESTON** Ensign ENY 614	**72**	1

STUTZ BEARCATS and the Denis KING ORCHESTRA *UK, male / female vocal group with orchestra* **6 wks**

24 Apr 82	**THE SONG THAT I SING (THEME FROM 'WE'LL MEET AGAIN')** Multi-Media Tapes MMT 6	**36**	6

STYLE COUNCIL *UK, male vocal / instrumental duo* **103 wks**

19 Mar 83 ●	**SPEAK LIKE A CHILD** Polydor TSC 1	**4**	8
28 May 83	**MONEY GO ROUND (PART 1)** Polydor TSC 2	**11**	6
13 Aug 83 ●	**LONG HOT SUMMER / PARIS MATCH** Polydor TSC 3	**3**	9
20 Aug 83	**MONEY GO ROUND (PART 1) (re-entry)** Polydor TSC 2	**74**	1
19 Nov 83 ●	**SOLID BOND IN YOUR HEART** Polydor TSC 4	**11**	8
18 Feb 84 ●	**MY EVER CHANGING MOODS** Polydor TSC 5	**5**	7
26 May 84 ●	**GROOVIN' (YOU'RE THE BEST THING) / BIG BOSS GROOVE** Polydor TSC 6	**5**	8
13 Oct 84 ●	**SHOUT TO THE TOP** Polydor TSC 7	**7**	8

11 May 85	● **WALLS COME TUMBLING DOWN!** *Polydor TSC 8*............**6**	7
6 Jul 85	**COME TO MILTON KEYNES** *Polydor TSC 9* **23**	5
28 Sep 85	**THE LODGERS** *Polydor TSC 10* **13**	6
5 Apr 86	**HAVE YOU EVER HAD IT BLUE** *Polydor CINE 1*...............**14**	6
17 Jan 87	**IT DIDN'T MATTER** *Polydor TSC 12* **9**	5
14 Mar 87	**WAITING** *Polydor TSC 13* **52**	3
31 Oct 87	**WANTED** *Polydor TSC 14* **20**	4
28 May 88	**LIFE AT A TOP PEOPLE'S HEALTH FARM**	
	Polydor TSC 15 ....**28**	3
23 Jul 88	**HOW SHE THREW IT ALL AWAY (EP)** *Polydor TSC 16* **41**	2
18 Feb 89	**PROMISED LAND** *Polydor TSC 17* **27**	5
27 May 89	**LONG HOT SUMMER 89 (re-mix)** *Polydor LHS 1* **48**	2

Paris Match was listed with Long Hot Summer from 3 Sep 83. It peaked at position 7. Tracks on How She Threw It All Away (EP): How She Threw It All Away / Love The First Time / Long Hot Summer / I Do Like To Be B-Side The A-Side. The version of Long Hot Summer on the EP is a re-recording of their third hit.

STYLISTICS US, male vocal group   143 wks

24 Jun 72	**BETCHA BY GOLLY WOW** *Avco 6105 011* **13**	12
4 Nov 72	● **I'M STONE IN LOVE WITH YOU** *Avco 6105 015* **9**	10
17 Mar 73	**BREAK UP TO MAKE UP** *Avco 6105 020* **34**	5
30 Jun 73	**PEEK-A-BOO** *Avco 6105 023* **35**	6
19 Jan 74	**ROCKIN' ROLL BABY** *Avco 6105 026* **6**	9
13 Jul 74	● **YOU MAKE ME FEEL BRAND NEW** *Avco 6105 028* **2**	14
19 Oct 74	● **LET'S PUT IT ALL TOGETHER** *Avco 6105 032* **9**	9
25 Jan 75	**STAR ON A TV SHOW** *Avco 6105 035* **12**	8
10 May 75	● **SING BABY SING** *Avco 6105 036* **3**	10
26 Jul 75	★ **CAN'T GIVE YOU ANYTHING (BUT MY LOVE)**	
	Avco 6105 039 ....**1**	11
15 Nov 75	● **NA NA IS THE SADDEST WORD** *Avco 6105 041* **5**	10
14 Feb 76	● **FUNKY WEEKEND** *Avco 6105 044* **10**	7
24 Apr 76	● **CAN'T HELP FALLING IN LOVE** *H & L 6105 050* **4**	7
7 Aug 76	● **16 BARS** *H & L 6105 059* **7**	9
27 Nov 76	**YOU'LL NEVER GET TO HEAVEN EP** *H & L STYL 001* **24**	9
26 Mar 77	**7000 DOLLARS AND YOU** *H & L 6105 073* **24**	7

Tracks on You'll Never Get To Heaven EP: You'll Never Get To Heaven / Country Living / You Are Beautiful / The Miracle.

STYX US, male vocal / instrumental group   18 wks

5 Jan 80	● **BABE** *A & M AMS 7489* **6**	10
24 Jan 81	**THE BEST OF TIMES** *A & M AMS 8102* **42**	5
18 Jun 83	**DON'T LET IT END** *A & M AM 120* **56**	3

SUB SUB UK, male instrumental / production group   12 wks

10 Apr 93	● **AIN'T NO LOVE (AIN'T NO USE)** *Rob's CDROB 9* [1] **3**	11
19 Feb 94	**RESPECT** *Rob's CDROB 19* **49**	1

[1] Sub Sub featuring Melanie Williams

SUBLIMINAL CUTS
Holland, male producer – Patrick Prinz   3 wks

15 Oct 94	**LE VOIE LE SOLEIL** *XL XLS 53CD* **69**	1
20 Jul 96	**LE VOIE LE SOLEIL (re-mix)** *XL XLSR 53CD* **23**	2

See also Artemesia; Ethics; Movin' Melodies.

SUBSONIC 2 UK, male rap duo   3 wks

13 Jul 91	**THE UNSUNG HEROES OF HIP HOP** *Unity 6577947* **63**	3

SUBTERRANIA featuring Ann CONSUELO
Sweden, male / female vocal / instrumental duo   1 wk

5 Jun 93	**DO IT FOR LOVE** *Champion CHAMPCD 297* **68**	1

SUEDE UK, male vocal / instrumental group   43 wks

23 May 92	**THE DROWNERS / TO THE BIRDS** *Nude NUD 1S* **49**	2
26 Sep 92	**METAL MICKEY** *Nude NUD 3S* **17**	3
6 Mar 93	● **ANIMAL NITRATE** *Nude NUD 4CD* **7**	7
29 May 93	**SO YOUNG** *Nude NUD 5CD* **22**	3
26 Feb 94	● **STAY TOGETHER** *Nude NUD 9CD* **3**	6
24 Sep 94	**WE ARE THE PIGS** *Nude NUD 10CD* **18**	3
19 Nov 94	**THE WILD ONES** *Nude NUD 11CD* **18**	4
11 Feb 95	**NEW GENERATION** *Nude NUD 12CD1* **21**	3
11 Mar 95	**NEW GENERATION (re-entry)** *Nude NUD 12CD1* **75**	1
10 Aug 96	● **TRASH** *Nude NUD 21CD1* **3**	6
26 Oct 96	● **BEAUTIFUL ONES** *Nude NUD 23CD1* **8**	5

SUENO LATINO featuring Carolina DAMAS
Italy, male production duo and female vocalist   5 wks

23 Sep 89	**SUENO LATINO** *BCM BCM 323*..............................**47**	5

SUGAR US, male vocal / instrumental group   7 wks

31 Oct 92	**A GOOD IDEA** *Creation CRE 143* **65**	1
30 Jan 93	**IF I CAN'T CHANGE YOUR MIND**	
	Creation CRESCD 149 ....**30**	2
21 Aug 93	**TILTED** *Creation CRECD 156* **48**	1
3 Sep 94	**YOUR FAVORITE THING** *Creation CRESCD 186* **40**	2
29 Oct 94	**BELIEVE WHAT YOU'RE SAYING**	
	Creation CRESCD 193 ....**73**	1

SUGAR CANE US, male / female vocal group   5 wks

30 Sep 78	**MONTEGO BAY** *Ariola Hansa AHA 524* **54**	5

SUGARCUBES
Iceland, male / female vocal / instrumental group   22 wks

14 Nov 87	**BIRTHDAY** *One Little Indian TP 7*............................**65**	3
30 Jan 88	**COLD SWEAT** *One Little Indian 7TP 9* **56**	4
16 Apr 88	**DEUS** *One Little Indian 7TP 10* **51**	3
3 Sep 88	**BIRTHDAY** *One Little Indian 7TP 11* **65**	3
16 Sep 89	**REGINA** *One Little Indian 26TP7* **55**	2
11 Jan 92	**HIT** *One Little Indian 62 TP7* **17**	6
3 Oct 92	**BIRTHDAY (re-mix)** *One Little Indian 104 TP12*............**64**	1

7TP 11 is a re-recording of their first hit.

SUGARHILL GANG US, male rap group   16 wks

1 Dec 79	● **RAPPER'S DELIGHT** *Sugarhill SHL 101* **3**	11
11 Sep 82	**THE LOVER IN YOU** *Sugarhill SH 116* **54**	3
25 Nov 89	**RAPPER'S DELIGHT (re-mix)** *Sugarhill SHRD 0007*........**58**	2

SUGGS UK, male vocalist   38 wks

12 Aug 95	● **I'M ONLY SLEEPING / OFF ON HOLIDAY**	
	WEA YZ 975CD **7**	6
14 Oct 95	**CAMDEN TOWN** *WEA WEA 019CD* **14**	6
16 Dec 95	**THE TUNE** *WEA WEA 031CD* **33**	3
13 Apr 96	● **CECILIA** *WEA WEA 042CD1* [1] **4**	17
24 Aug 96	**CECILIA (re-entry)** *WEA WEA 042CD1* [1] **65**	1
7 Sep 96	**CECILIA (2nd re-entry)** *WEA WEA 042CD1* [1] **59**	1
21 Sep 96	**NO MORE ALCOHOL** *WEA WEA 065CD1* [1] **24**	4

[1] Suggs featuring Louchie Lou and Michie One

SULTANA Italy, male instrumental / production group   1 wk

26 Mar 94	**TE AMO** *Union City UCRD 28* **57**	1

SULTANS OF PING
Ireland, male vocal / instrumental group   **12 wks**

8 Feb 92	**WHERE'S ME JUMPER** *Divine ATHY 01* [1]	**67**	2
9 May 92	**STUPID KID** *Divine ATHY 02* [1]	**67**	1
10 Oct 92	**VERONICA** *Divine ATHY 03* [1]	**69**	1
9 Jan 93	**YOU TALK TOO MUCH** *Rhythm King 6588872* [1]	**26**	3
11 Sep 93	**TEENAGE PUNKS** *Epic 6595792*	**49**	2
30 Oct 93	**MICHIKO** *Epic 6598222*	**43**	2
19 Feb 94	**WAKE UP AND SCRATCH ME** *Epic 6601122*	**50**	1

[1] Sultans Of Ping FC

SUMMER – *See SNAP*

SUMMER DAZE
UK, male instrumental / production duo   **1 wk**

26 Oct 96	**SAMBA MAGIC** *VC VCRD 14*	**61**	1

Donna SUMMER *US, female vocalist*   **297 wks**

17 Jan 76	● **LOVE TO LOVE YOU BABY** *GTO GT 17*	**4**	9
29 May 76	**COULD IT BE MAGIC** *GTO GT 60*	**40**	7
25 Dec 76	**WINTER MELODY** *GTO GT 76*	**27**	6
9 Jul 77	★ **I FEEL LOVE** *GTO GT 100*	**1**	11
20 Aug 77	● **DOWN DEEP INSIDE (THEME FROM 'THE DEEP')** *Casablanca CAN 111*	**5**	10
24 Sep 77	**I REMEMBER YESTERDAY** *GTO GT 107*	**14**	7
3 Dec 77	● **LOVE'S UNKIND** *GTO GT 113*	**3**	13
10 Dec 77	● **I LOVE YOU** *Casablanca CAN 114*	**10**	9
25 Feb 78	**RUMOUR HAS IT** *Casablanca CAN 122*	**19**	8
22 Apr 78	**BACK IN LOVE AGAIN** *GTO GT 117*	**29**	7
10 Jun 78	**LAST DANCE** *Casablanca TGIF 2*	**70**	1
24 Jun 78	**LAST DANCE (re-entry)** *Casablanca TGIF 2*	**51**	8
14 Oct 78	● **MACARTHUR PARK** *Casablanca CAN 131*	**5**	10
17 Feb 79	**HEAVEN KNOWS** *Casablanca CAN 141*	**34**	8
12 May 79	**HOT STUFF** *Casablanca CAN 151*	**11**	10
7 Jul 79	**BAD GIRLS** *Casablanca CAN 155*	**14**	10
1 Sep 79	**DIM ALL THE LIGHTS** *Casablanca CAN 162*	**29**	9
3 Nov 79	● **NO MORE TEARS (ENOUGH IS ENOUGH)** *Casablanca CAN 174/ CBS 8000* [1]	**3**	13
16 Feb 80	**ON THE RADIO** *Casablanca NB 2236*	**32**	6
21 Jun 80	**SUNSET PEOPLE** *Casablanca CAN 198*	**46**	5
27 Sep 80	**THE WANDERER** *Geffen K 79180*	**48**	6
17 Jan 81	**COLD LOVE** *Geffen K 79193*	**44**	3
10 Jul 82	**LOVE IS IN CONTROL (FINGER ON THE TRIGGER)** *Warner Bros. K 79302*	**18**	11
6 Nov 82	**STATE OF INDEPENDENCE** *Warner Bros. K 79344*	**14**	11
4 Dec 82	**I FEEL LOVE (re-mix)** *Casablanca FEEL 7*	**21**	10
5 Mar 83	**THE WOMAN IN ME** *Warner Bros. U 9983*	**62**	2
18 Jun 83	**SHE WORKS HARD FOR THE MONEY** *Mercury DONNA 1*	**25**	8
24 Sep 83	**UNCONDITIONAL LOVE** *Mercury DONNA 2*	**14**	12
21 Jan 84	**STOP LOOK AND LISTEN** *Mercury DONNA 3*	**57**	2
24 Oct 87	**DINNER WITH GERSHWIN** *Warner Bros. U 8237*	**13**	11
23 Jan 88	**ALL SYSTEMS GO** *WEA U 8122*	**54**	3
25 Feb 89	● **THIS TIME I KNOW IT'S FOR REAL** *Warner Bros. U 7780*	**3**	14
27 May 89	● **I DON'T WANNA GET HURT** *Warner Bros. U 7567*	**7**	9
26 Aug 89	**LOVE'S ABOUT TO CHANGE MY HEART** *Warner Bros. U 7494*	**20**	6
25 Nov 89	**WHEN LOVE TAKES OVER YOU** *WEA U 7361*	**72**	1
17 Nov 90	**STATE OF INDEPENDENCE (re-issue)** *Warner Bros. U 2857*	**45**	3
12 Jan 91	**BREAKAWAY** *Warner Bros. U 3308*	**49**	4
30 Nov 91	**WORK THAT MAGIC** *Warner Bros. U 5937*	**74**	1
12 Nov 94	**MELODY OF LOVE (WANNA BE LOVED)** *Mercury MERCD 418*	**21**	3
9 Sep 95	● **I FEEL LOVE** *Manifesto FESCD 1*	**8**	5
6 Apr 96	**STATE OF INDEPENDENCE (re-mix)** *Manifesto FESCD 7* [2]	**13**	5

[1] Donna Summer and Barbra Streisand [2] Donna Summer featuring the All Star Choir

No More Tears (Enough Is Enough) was released simultaneously on two different labels, a 7-inch single on Casablanca and 12-inch on CBS. Unconditional Love features the additional vocals of Musical Youth. I Feel Love in 95 is a re-recording.

Mark SUMMERS *UK, male producer*   **6 wks**

26 Jan 91	**SUMMER'S MAGIC** *Fourth & Broadway BRW 205*	**27**	6

SUNDANCE – *See DJ 'FAST' EDDIE*

SUNDAYS *UK, male / female vocal / instrumental group*   **7 wks**

11 Feb 89	**CAN'T BE SURE** *Rough Trade RT 218*	**45**	5
3 Oct 92	**GOODBYE** *Parlophone R 6319*	**27**	2

SUNDRAGON *UK, male vocal / instrumental duo*   **1 wk**

21 Feb 68	**GREEN TAMBOURINE** *MGM 1380*	**50**	1

SUNFIRE *US, male vocal / instrumental group*   **11 wks**

12 Mar 83	**YOUNG, FREE AND SINGLE** *Warner Bros. W 9897*	**20**	11

SUNNY *UK, female vocalist*   **10 wks**

30 Mar 74	● **DOCTOR'S ORDERS** *CBS 2068*	**7**	10

SUNSCREEM
UK, male / female vocal / instrumental group   **32 wks**

29 Feb 92	**PRESSURE** *Sony S2 6578017*	**60**	2
18 Jul 92	**LOVE U MORE** *Sony S2 6581727*	**23**	6
17 Oct 92	**PERFECT MOTION** *Sony S2 6584057*	**18**	5
9 Jan 93	**BROKEN ENGLISH** *Sony S2 6589032*	**13**	5
27 Mar 93	**PRESSURE US (re-mix)** *Sony S2 6591102*	**19**	5
2 Sep 95	**WHEN** *Sony S2 6623222*	**47**	2
18 Nov 95	**EXODUS** *Sony S2 6625342*	**40**	2
20 Jan 96	**WHITE SKIES** *Sony S2 6627425*	**25**	3
23 Mar 96	**SECRETS** *Sony S2 6629342*	**36**	2

SUNSHINE BAND – *See KC and the SUNSHINE BAND*

Monty SUNSHINE – *See Chris BARBER*

SUPER FURRY ANIMALS
UK, male vocal / instrumental group   **10 wks**

9 Mar 96	**HOMETOWN UNICORN** *Creation CRESCD 222*	**47**	1
11 May 96	**GOD! SHOW ME MAGIC** *Creation CRESCD 231*	**33**	2
13 Jul 96	**SOMETHING 4 THE WEEKEND** *Creation CRESCD 235*	**18**	3
12 Oct 96	**IF YOU DON'T WANT ME TO DESTROY YOU** *Creation CRESCD 243*	**18**	2
14 Dec 96	**THE MAN DON'T GIVE A FUCK** *Creation CRESCD 247*	**22**	2

SUPERCAT *Jamaica, male vocalist*   **5 wks**

1 Aug 92	**IT FE DONE** *Columbia 6582737*	**66**	1
6 May 95	**MY GIRL JOSEPHINE** *Columbia 6614702* [1]	**22**	4

[1] Supercat featuring Jack Radics

Suede

After the departure of guitarist Bernard Butler in 1994, the future for Suede looked uncertain. However, with his replacement, Richard Oakes (3rd from left), and keyboard player Neil Codling (2nd left), the band have experienced consistent singles success.

Suggs

Tracks from Simon and Garfunkel's *Bridge Over Troubled Water* have been a source of material for hundreds of artists, Suggs, though, lis the first to take a cover of a track from the album into the Top 10.

Supergrass

Oxford trio Supergrass started life as the Jennifers, releasing one single, 'Just Got Back Today', for the then fledgling Nude label in 1992.

SUPERGRASS *UK, male vocal / instrumental group* **25 wks**

29 Oct 94	**CAUGHT BY THE FUZZ** Parlophone CDR 6396	**43**	2
18 Feb 95	**MANSIZE ROOSTER** Parlophone CDR 6402	**20**	3
25 Mar 95	**LOSE IT** Sub Pop SP 281	**75**	1
13 May 95	● **LENNY** Parlophone CDR 6410	**10**	3
15 Jul 95	● **ALRIGHT / TIME** Parlophone CDR 6413	**2**	10
9 Mar 96	● **GOING OUT** Parlophone CDR 6428	**5**	6

SUPERNATURALS *UK, male vocal / instrumental group* **2 wks**

26 Oct 96	**LAZY LOVER** Food CDFOOD 85	**34**	2

SUPERNOVA *UK, male / female vocal / instrumental duo* **1 wk**

11 May 96	**SOME MIGHT SAY** Sing Sing 74321369442	**55**	1

SUPERTRAMP *UK / US, male vocal / instrumental group* **52 wks**

15 Feb 75	**DREAMER** A & M AMS 7132	**13**	10
25 Jun 77	**GIVE A LITTLE BIT** A & M AMS 7293	**29**	7
31 Mar 79	● **THE LOGICAL SONG** A & M AMS 7427	**7**	12
30 Jun 79	**BREAKFAST IN AMERICA** A & M AMS 7451	**9**	10
27 Oct 79	**GOODBYE STRANGER** A & M AMS 7481	**57**	3
30 Oct 82	**IT'S RAINING AGAIN** A & M AMS 8255 [1]	**26**	11

[1] Supertramp featuring vocals by Roger Hodgson

SUPREMES *US, female vocal group* **306 wks**

3 Sep 64	● **WHERE DID OUR LOVE GO** Stateside SS 327	**3**	14
22 Oct 64	★ **BABY LOVE** Stateside SS 350	**1**	15
21 Jan 65	**COME SEE ABOUT ME** Stateside SS 376	**27**	6
25 Mar 65	● **STOP IN THE NAME OF LOVE** Tamla Motown TMG 501	**7**	12
10 Jun 65	**BACK IN MY ARMS AGAIN** Tamla Motown TMG 516	**40**	5
9 Dec 65	**I HEAR A SYMPHONY** Tamla Motown TMG 543	**50**	1
23 Dec 65	**I HEAR A SYMPHONY (re-entry)** Tamla Motown TMG 543	**39**	4
8 Sep 66	● **YOU CAN'T HURRY LOVE** Tamla Motown TMG 575	**3**	12
1 Dec 66	● **YOU KEEP ME HANGIN' ON** Tamla Motown TMG 585	**8**	10
2 Mar 67	**LOVE IS HERE AND NOW YOU'RE GONE** Tamla Motown TMG 597	**17**	10
11 May 67	● **THE HAPPENING** Tamla Motown TMG 607	**6**	12
30 Aug 67	● **REFLECTIONS** Tamla Motown TMG 616 [1]	**5**	14
29 Nov 67	**IN AND OUT OF LOVE** Tamla Motown TMG 632 [1]	**13**	13
10 Apr 68	**FOREVER CAME TODAY** Tamla Motown TMG 650 [1]	**28**	8
3 Jul 68	**SOME THINGS YOU NEVER GET USED TO** Tamla Motown TMG 662 [1]	**34**	6
20 Nov 68	**LOVE CHILD** Tamla Motown TMG 677 [1]	**15**	14
29 Jan 69	● **I'M GONNA MAKE YOU LOVE ME** Tamla Motown TMG 685 [2]	**3**	11
23 Apr 69	**I'M GONNA MAKE YOU LOVE ME (re-entry)** Tamla Motown TMG 685 [2]	**49**	1
23 Apr 69	**I'M LIVING IN SHAME** Tamla Motown TMG 695 [1]	**14**	9
2 Jul 69	**I'M LIVING IN SHAME (re-entry)** Tamla Motown TMG 695 [1]	**50**	1
16 Jul 69	**NO MATTER WHAT SIGN YOU ARE** Tamla Motown TMG 704 [1]	**37**	7
20 Sep 69	**I SECOND THAT EMOTION** Tamla Motown TMG 709 [2]	**18**	8
13 Dec 69	**SOMEDAY WE'LL BE TOGETHER** Tamla Motown TMG 721 [1]	**13**	13
21 Mar 70	**WHY (MUST WE FALL IN LOVE)** Tamla Motown TMG 730 [2]	**31**	7
2 May 70	● **UP THE LADDER TO THE ROOF** Tamla Motown TMG 735	**6**	15
16 Jan 71	● **STONED LOVE** Tamla Motown TMG 760	**3**	13
26 Jun 71	**RIVER DEEP MOUNTAIN HIGH** Tamla Motown TMG 777	**11**	10
21 Aug 71	● **NATHAN JONES** Tamla Motown TMG 782	**5**	11
20 Nov 71	**YOU GOTTA HAVE LOVE IN YOUR HEART** Tamla Motown TMG 793 [3]	**25**	10
4 Mar 72	● **FLOY JOY** Tamla Motown TMG 804	**9**	10
15 Jul 72	● **AUTOMATICALLY SUNSHINE** Tamla Motown TMG 821	**10**	9
21 Apr 73	**BAD WEATHER** Tamla Motown TMG 847	**37**	4
24 Aug 74	**BABY LOVE (re-issue)** Tamla Motown TMG 915 [1]	**12**	10
18 Feb 89	**STOP! IN THE NAME OF LOVE (re-issue)** Motown ZB 41963 [1]	**62**	1

[1] Diana Ross and the Supremes [2] Diana Ross and the Supremes and the Temptations [3] Supremes and the Four Tops

Al B SURE! *US, male vocalist* **13 wks**

16 Apr 88	**NITE AND DAY** Uptown W 8192	**44**	5
30 Jul 88	**OFF ON YOUR OWN (GIRL)** Uptown W 7870	**70**	2
10 Jun 89	**IF I'M NOT YOUR LOVER** Warner Bros. W 2908	**54**	3
31 Mar 90	**SECRET GARDEN** Qwest W 9992 [1]	**67**	1
12 Jun 93	**BLACK TIE WHITE NOISE** Arista 74321148682 [2]	**36**	2

[1] Quincy Jones featuring Al B. Sure!, James Ingram, El DeBarge and Barry White [2] David Bowie featuring Al B. Sure!

SURFACE *US, male vocal / instrumental duo* **14 wks**

23 Jul 83	**FALLING IN LOVE** Salsoul SAL 104	**67**	3
23 Jun 84	**WHEN YOUR 'EX' WANTS YOU BACK** Salsoul SAL 106	**52**	5
28 Feb 87	**HAPPY** CBS 650393 7	**56**	5
12 Jan 91	**THE FIRST TIME** Columbia 6564767	**60**	2

SURFACE NOISE *UK, male instrumental group* **11 wks**

31 May 80	**THE SCRATCH** WEA K 18291	**26**	8
30 Aug 80	**DANCIN' ON A WIRE** Groove GP102	**59**	3

SURFARIS *US, male instrumental group* **14 wks**

25 Jul 63	● **WIPE OUT** London HLD 9751	**5**	14

SURPRISE SISTERS *UK, female vocal group* **3 wks**

13 Mar 76	**LA BOOGA ROOGA** Good Earth GD 1	**38**	3

SURVIVOR *US, male vocal / instrumental group* **26 wks**

31 Jul 82	★ **EYE OF THE TIGER** Scotti Brothers SCT A 2411	**1**	15
1 Feb 86	● **BURNING HEART** Scotti Brothers A 6708	**5**	11

SUTHERLAND BROTHERS and QUIVER
UK, male vocal / instrumental group **20 wks**

3 Apr 76	● **ARMS OF MARY** CBS 4001	**5**	12
20 Nov 76	**SECRETS** CBS 4668	**35**	4
2 Jun 79	**EASY COME EASY GO** CBS 7121 [1]	**50**	4

[1] Sutherland Brothers

Pat SUZUKI *US, female vocalist* **1 wk**

14 Apr 60	**I ENJOY BEING A GIRL** RCA 1171	**49**	1

Billy SWAN *US, male vocalist* **13 wks**

14 Dec 74	● **I CAN HELP** Monument MNT 2752	**6**	9
24 May 75	**DON'T BE CRUEL** Monument MNT 3244	**42**	4

SWAN LAKE *US, male vocalist / multi-instrumentalist* **4 wks**

17 Sep 88	**IN THE NAME OF LOVE** Champion CHAMP 86	**53**	4

SWANS WAY UK, male/female vocal/instrumental group　12 wks

4 Feb 84	SOUL TRAIN Exit EXT 3	20	7
26 May 84	ILLUMINATIONS Balgier PH 5	57	5

Patrick SWAYZE featuring Wendy FRASER
US, male/female vocal duo　11 wks

26 Mar 88	SHE'S LIKE THE WIND RCA PB 49565	17	11

Keith SWEAT US, male vocalist　18 wks

20 Feb 88	I WANT HER Vintertainment EKR 68	26	10
14 May 88	SOMETHING JUST AIN'T RIGHT Vintertainment EKR 72	55	3
14 May 94	HOW DO YOU LIKE IT Elektra EKR 185CD	71	1
22 Jun 96	TWISTED Elektra EKR 223CD	39	2
23 Nov 96	JUST A TOUCH Elektra EKR 227CD	35	2

Michelle SWEENEY US, female vocalist　1 wk

29 Oct 94	THIS TIME Big Beat A 8229CD	57	1

SWEET UK, male vocal/instrumental group　159 wks

13 Mar 71	FUNNY FUNNY RCA 2051	13	14
12 Jun 71 ●	CO-CO RCA 2087	2	15
16 Oct 71	ALEXANDER GRAHAM BELL RCA 2121	33	5
5 Feb 72	POPPA JOE RCA 2164	11	12
10 Jun 72 ●	LITTLE WILLY RCA 2225	4	14
9 Sep 72 ●	WIG-WAM BAM RCA 2260	4	13
13 Jan 73 ★	BLOCKBUSTER RCA 2305	1	15
5 May 73 ●	HELL RAISER RCA 2357	2	11
22 Sep 73 ●	THE BALLROOM BLITZ RCA 2403	2	9
19 Jan 74 ●	TEENAGE RAMPAGE RCA LPBO 5004	2	8
13 Jul 74 ●	THE SIX TEENS RCA LPBO 5037	9	7
9 Nov 74	TURN IT DOWN RCA 2480	41	2
15 Mar 75 ●	FOX ON THE RUN RCA 2524	2	10
12 Jul 75	ACTION RCA 2578	15	6
24 Jan 76	THE LIES IN YOUR EYES RCA 2641	35	4
28 Jan 78 ●	LOVE IS LIKE OXYGEN Polydor POSP 1	9	9
26 Jan 85	IT'S IT'S THE SWEET MIX Anagram ANA 28	45	5

It's It's The Sweet Mix is a medley of the following songs: Blockbuster / Fox On The Run / Teenage Rampage / Hell Raiser / Ballroom Blitz.

Rachel SWEET US, female vocalist　15 wks

9 Dec 78	B-A-B-Y Stiff BUY 39	35	8
22 Aug 81	EVERLASTING LOVE CBS A 1405　[1]	35	7

[1] Rex Smith and Rachel Sweet

SWEET DREAMS UK, male/female vocal duo　12 wks

20 Jul 74 ●	HONEY HONEY Bradley's BRAD 7408	10	12

SWEET DREAMS UK, male/female vocal group　7 wks

9 Apr 83	I'M NEVER GIVING UP Ariola ARO 333	21	7

SWEET MERCY - See Joe ROBERTS

SWEET PEOPLE France, male vocal/instrumental group　10 wks

4 Oct 80 ●	ET LES OISEAUX CHANTAIENT (AND THE BIRDS WERE SINGING) Polydor POSP 179	4	8
29 Aug 87	ET LES OISEAUX CHANTAIENT (AND THE BIRDS WERE SINGING) (re-entry) Polydor POSP 179	73	2

SWEET PUSSY PAULINE - See CANDY GIRLS

SWEET SENSATION UK, male vocal group　17 wks

14 Sep 74 ★	SAD SWEET DREAMER Pye 7N 45385	1	10
18 Jan 75	PURELY BY COINCIDENCE Pye 7N 45421	11	7

SWEET TEE US, female rapper　8 wks

16 Jan 88	IT'S LIKE THAT Y'ALL / I GOT DA FEELIN' Cooltempo COOL 160	31	6
13 Aug 94	THE FEELING Deep Distraxion OILYCD 029　[1]	32	2

[1] Tin Tin Out featuring Sweet Tee

Sally SWEETLAND - See Eddie FISHER

SWERVEDRIVER UK, male vocal/instrumental group　3 wks

10 Aug 91	SANDBLASTED EP Creation CRE 102	67	1
30 May 92	NEVER LOSE THAT FEELING Creation CRE 120	62	1
14 Aug 93	DUEL Creation CRESCD 136	60	1

Tracks on Sandblasted EP: Sandblaster / Flawed / Out / Laze It Up.

SWIMMING WITH SHARKS
Germany, female vocal duo　3 wks

7 May 88	CARELESS LOVE WEA YZ 173	63	3

SWING - See DR. ALBAN

SWING 52 US, male vocal/instrumental group　1 wk

25 Feb 95	COLOR OF MY SKIN ffrr FCD 256	60	1

SWING KIDS - See K7

SWING OUT SISTER
UK, male/female vocal/instrumental group　55 wks

25 Oct 86 ●	BREAKOUT Mercury SWING 2	4	14
10 Jan 87 ●	SURRENDER Mercury SWING 3	7	8
18 Apr 87	TWILIGHT WORLD Mercury SWING 4	32	6
11 Jul 87	FOOLED BY A SMILE Mercury SWING 5	43	4
8 Apr 89	YOU ON MY MIND Fontana SWING 6	28	9
8 Jul 89	WHERE IN THE WORLD Fontana SWING 7	47	4
11 Apr 92	AM I THE SAME GIRL Fontana SWING 9	21	6
20 Jun 92	NOTGONNACHANGE Fontana SWING 10	49	2
27 Aug 94	LA LA (MEANS I LOVE YOU) Fontana SWIDD 11	37	2

SWINGING BLUE JEANS
UK, male vocal/instrumental group　57 wks

20 Jun 63	IT'S TOO LATE NOW HMV POP 1170	30	6
8 Aug 63	IT'S TOO LATE NOW (re-entry) HMV POP 1170	46	3
12 Dec 63 ●	HIPPY HIPPY SHAKE HMV POP 1242	2	11
19 Mar 64	GOOD GOLLY MISS MOLLY HMV POP 1273	11	10
4 Jun 64 ●	YOU'RE NO GOOD HMV POP 1304	3	13
20 Jan 66	DON'T MAKE ME OVER HMV POP 1501	31	8

SWITCH US, male vocal/instrumental group　3 wks

10 Nov 84	KEEPING SECRETS Total Experience RCA XE 502	61	3

SWV US, female vocal group　34 wks

1 May 93	I'M SO INTO YOU RCA 74321144972	17	6

26 Jun 93	**WEAK** RCA 74321153352	**33**	3
28 Aug 93 ●	**RIGHT HERE** RCA 74321160482	**3**	12
26 Feb 94	**DOWNTOWN** RCA 74321189012	**19**	5
11 Jun 94	**ANYTHING** RCA 74321212212	**24**	3
25 May 96	**YOU'RE THE ONE** RCA 74321383312	**13**	3
21 Dec 96	**IT'S ALL ABOUT U** RCA 74321442152	**36†**	2

SYBIL US, female vocalist   67 wks

1 Nov 86	**FALLING IN LOVE** Champion CHAMP 22	**68**	3
25 Apr 87	**LET YOURSELF GO** Champion CHAMP 42	**32**	6
29 Aug 87	**MY LOVE IS GUARANTEED** Champion CHAMP 55	**42**	5
22 Jul 89	**DON'T MAKE ME OVER** Champion CHAMP 213	**59**	5
14 Oct 89	**DON'T MAKE ME OVER** (re-entry) Champion CHAMP 213	**19**	6
27 Jan 90 ●	**WALK ON BY** PWL PWL 48	**6**	9
21 Apr 90	**CRAZY FOR YOU** PWL PWL 53	**71**	1
16 Jan 93 ●	**THE LOVE I LOST** PWL Sanctuary PWCD 253 [1]	**3**	13
20 Mar 93 ●	**WHEN I'M GOOD AND READY** PWL International PWCD 260	**5**	13
26 Jun 93	**BEYOND YOUR WILDEST DREAMS** PWL International PWCD 265	**41**	2
11 Sep 93	**STRONGER TOGETHER** PWL International PWCD 269	**41**	2
11 Dec 93	**MY LOVE IS GUARANTEED** (re-mix) PWL International PWCD 227	**48**	1
9 Mar 96	**SO TIRED OF BEING ALONE** PWL International PWL 324CD	**53**	1

[1] West End featuring Sybil

SYLVESTER US, male vocalist   45 wks

19 Aug 78 ●	**YOU MAKE ME FEEL (MIGHTY REAL)** Fantasy FTC 160	**8**	15
18 Nov 78	**DANCE (DISCO HEAT)** Fantasy FTC 163	**29**	12
31 Mar 79	**I (WHO HAVE NOTHING)** Fantasy FTC 171	**46**	5
7 Jul 79	**STARS** Fantasy FTC 177	**47**	3
11 Sep 82	**DO YOU WANNA FUNK** London LON 13 [1]	**32**	8
3 Sep 83	**BAND OF GOLD** London LON 33	**67**	2

[1] Sylvester with Patrick Cowley

SYLVIA US, female vocalist   11 wks

23 Jun 73	**PILLOW TALK** London HL 10415	**14**	11

SYLVIA Sweden, female vocalist   33 wks

10 Aug 74 ●	**Y VIVA ESPANA** Sonet SON 2037	**4**	19
4 Jan 75	**Y VIVA ESPANA** (re-entry) Sonet SON 2037	**35**	9
26 Apr 75	**HASTA LA VISTA** Sonet SON 2055	**38**	5

David SYLVIAN UK, male vocalist   34 wks

7 Aug 82	**BAMBOO HOUSES / BAMBO MUSIC** Virgin VS 510 [1]	**30**	4
2 Jul 83	**FORBIDDEN COLOURS** Virgin VS 601 [2]	**16**	8
2 Jun 84	**RED GUITAR** Virgin VS 633	**17**	5
18 Aug 84	**THE INK IN THE WELL** Virgin VS 700	**36**	3
3 Nov 84	**PULLING PUNCHES** Virgin VS 717	**56**	2
14 Dec 85	**WORDS WITH THE SHAMAN** Virgin VS 835	**72**	1
9 Aug 86	**TAKING THE VEIL** Virgin VS 815	**53**	3
17 Jan 87	**BUOY** Virgin VS 910 [3]	**63**	2
10 Oct 87	**LET THE HAPPINESS IN** Virgin VS 1001	**66**	1
13 Jun 92	**HEARTBEAT (TAINAI KAIKI II) RETURNING TO THE WOMB** Virgin America VUS 57 [4]	**58**	3
28 Aug 93	**JEAN THE BIRDMAN** Virgin VSCDG 1462 [5]	**68**	2

[1] Sylvian Sakamoto [2] David Sylvian and Riuichi Sakamoto [3] Mick Karn featuring David Sylvian [4] David Sylvian and Riuichi Sakamoto featuring Ingrid Chavez [5] David Sylvian and Robert Fripp

SYMARIP UK, male vocal / instrumental group   3 wks

2 Feb 80	**SKINHEAD MOONSTOMP** Trojan TRO 9062	**54**	3

SYMBOLS UK, male vocal / instrumental group   15 wks

2 Aug 67	**BYE BYE BABY** President PT 144	**44**	3
3 Jan 68	**BEST PART OF BREAKING UP** President PT 173	**25**	12

Terri SYMON UK, female vocalist   1 wk

10 Jun 95	**I WANT TO KNOW WHAT LOVE IS** A & M 5810592	**54**	1

SYREETA US, female vocalist   30 wks

21 Sep 74	**SPINNIN' AND SPINNIN'** Tamla Motown TMG 912	**49**	3
1 Feb 75	**YOUR KISS IS SWEET** Tamla Motown TMG 933	**12**	8
12 Jul 75	**HARMOUR LOVE** Tamla Motown TMG 954	**32**	4
15 Dec 79 ●	**WITH YOU I'M BORN AGAIN** Motown TMG 1159 [1]	**2**	11
8 Mar 80	**IT WILL COME IN TIME** Motown TMG 1175 [1]	**47**	4

[1] Billy Preston and Syreeta

SYSTEM US, male vocal / instrumental duo   2 wks

9 Jun 84	**I WANNA MAKE YOU FEEL GOOD** Polydor POSP 685	**73**	2

SYSTEM 7 UK / France, male / female instrumental duo   2 wks

13 Feb 93	**7:7 EXPANSION** Butterfly BFLD 2	**39**	1
17 Jul 93	**SINBAD QUEST** Butterfly BFLD 8	**74**	1

T

T-BOZ US, female vocalist   1 wk

23 Nov 96	**TOUCH MYSELF** LaFace 74321422882	**48**	1

T-EMPO UK, male / female vocal / instrumental group   4 wks

7 May 94	**SATURDAY NIGHT SUNDAY MORNING** ffrr FCD 232	**19**	3
9 Nov 96	**THE LOOK OF LOVE / THE BLUE ROOM** ffrr FCD 281	**71**	1

T-POWER UK, male producer – Mark Royal   1 wk

13 Apr 96	**POLICE STATE** Sound Of Underground TPOWCD 001	**63**	1

T. REX UK, male vocal / instrumental group   235 wks

8 May 68	**DEBORA** Regal Zonophone RZ 3008 [1]	**34**	7
4 Sep 68	**ONE INCH ROCK** Regal Zonophone RZ 3011 [1]	**28**	7
9 Aug 69	**KING OF THE RUMBLING SPIRES** Regal Zonophone RZ 3022 [1]	**44**	1
24 Oct 70 ●	**RIDE A WHITE SWAN** Fly BUG 1	**2**	20

27 Feb 71	★ HOT LOVE *Fly BUG 6*	**1**	17
10 Jul 71	★ GET IT ON *Fly BUG 10*	**1**	13
13 Nov 71	● JEEPSTER *Fly BUG 16*	**2**	15
29 Jan 72	★ TELEGRAM SAM *T. Rex 101*	**1**	12
1 Apr 72	● DEBORA / ONE INCH ROCK (re-issue)		
	Magnifly ECHO 102 [1]	**7**	10
13 May 72	★ METAL GURU *EMI MARC 1*	**1**	14
16 Sep 72	● CHILDREN OF THE REVOLUTION *EMI MARC 2*	**2**	10
9 Dec 72	● SOLID GOLD EASY ACTION *EMI MARC 3*	**2**	11
10 Mar 73	● 20TH CENTURY BOY *EMI MARC 4*	**3**	9
16 Jun 73	● THE GROOVER *EMI MARC 5*	**4**	9
24 Nov 73	TRUCK ON (TYKE) *EMI MARC 6*	**12**	11
9 Feb 74	TEENAGE DREAM *EMI MARC 7* [2]	**13**	5
13 Jul 74	LIGHT OF LOVE *EMI MARC 8*	**22**	4
16 Nov 74	ZIP GUN BOOGIE *EMI MARC 9*	**41**	3
12 Jul 75	NEW YORK CITY *EMI MARC 10*	**15**	8
11 Oct 75	DREAMY LADY *EMI MARC 11* [3]	**30**	5
6 Mar 76	LONDON BOYS *EMI MARC 13*	**40**	4
19 Jun 76	I LOVE TO BOOGIE *EMI MARC 14*	**13**	9
2 Oct 76	LASER LOVE *EMI MARC 15*	**41**	4
2 Apr 77	THE SOUL OF MY SUIT *EMI MARC 16*	**42**	3
9 May 81	RETURN OF THE ELECTRIC WARRIOR EP		
	Rarn MBSF 001 [4]	**50**	4
19 Sep 81	YOU SCARE ME TO DEATH *Cherry Red CHERRY 29* [4]	**51**	4
27 Mar 82	TELEGRAM SAM (re-entry) *T. Rex 101*	**69**	2
18 May 85	MEGAREX *Marc On Wax TANX 1* [2]	**72**	2
9 May 87	GET IT ON (re-mix) *Marc On Wax MARC 10* [2]	**54**	4
24 Aug 91	20TH CENTURY BOY (re-issue)		
	Marc On Wax MARC 501 [2]	**13**	8

[1] Tyrannosaurus Rex [2] Marc Bolan and T. Rex [3] T. Rex Disco Party
[4] Marc Bolan

Tracks on Return Of The Electric Warrior EP: Sing Me A Song / Endless Sleep / The Lilac Hand Of Menihol Dan. Megarex is a medley of extracts from the following T. Rex hits: Truck On (Tyke) / The Groover / Telegram Sam / Shock Rock / Metal Guru / 20th Century Boy / Children Of The Revolution / Hot Love.

TABERNACLE *UK, male instrumental / production group*   **2 wks**

4 Mar 95	I KNOW THE LORD *Good Groove CDGG 1*	**62**	1
3 Feb 96	I KNOW THE LORD (re-mix) *Good Groove CDGGX 1*	**55**	1

TACK HEAD *US, male rapper*   **3 wks**

30 Jun 90	DANGEROUS SEX *SBK SBK 7014*	**48**	3

TAFFY *UK, female vocalist*   **14 wks**

10 Jan 87	● I LOVE MY RADIO (MY DEE JAY'S RADIO)		
	Transglobal TYPE 1	**6**	10
18 Jul 87	STEP BY STEP *Transglobal TYPE 5*	**59**	4

TAG TEAM *US, male rap duo*   **8 wks**

8 Jan 94	WHOOMP! (THERE IT IS) *Club Tools SHXCD 1*	**34**	5
29 Jan 94	ADDAMS FAMILY (WHOOMP!) *Atlas PZCD 305*	**53**	1
10 Sep 94	WHOOMP! (THERE IT IS) (re-mix) *Club Tools SHXR 1*	**48**	2

TAK TIX *US, female vocalist*   **2 wks**

20 Jan 96	FEEL LIKE SINGING *A & M 5813212*	**33**	2

TAKE THAT *UK, male vocal group*   **158 wks**

23 Nov 91	PROMISES *RCA PB 45085*	**38**	2
8 Feb 92	ONCE WHEN YOU'VE TASTED LOVE *RCA PB 45257*	**47**	3
6 Jun 92	● IT ONLY TAKES A MINUTE *RCA 74321101007*	**7**	8
15 Aug 92	I FOUND HEAVEN *RCA 74321108137*	**15**	6
10 Oct 92	● A MILLION LOVE SONGS *RCA 74321116307*	**7**	9

12 Dec 92	● COULD IT BE MAGIC *RCA 74321123137*	**3**	12
20 Feb 93	● WHY CAN'T I WAKE UP WITH YOU *RCA 74321133102*	**2**	10
17 Jul 93	★ PRAY *RCA 74321154502*	**1**	11
9 Oct 93	★ RELIGHT MY FIRE *RCA 74321167722* [1]	**1**	14
18 Dec 93	★ BABE *RCA 74321182122*	**1**	10
9 Apr 94	● EVERYTHING CHANGES *RCA 74321167732*	**1**	10
9 Jul 94	● LOVE AIN'T HERE ANYMORE *RCA 74321214832*	**3**	10
15 Oct 94	★ SURE *RCA 74321236622*	**1**	15
15 Oct 94	LOVE AIN'T HERE ANYMORE (re-entry)		
	RCA 74321214832	**55**	2
8 Apr 95	★ BACK FOR GOOD *RCA 74321271462*	**1**	13
5 Aug 95	★ NEVER FORGET *RCA 74321299572*	**1**	9
9 Mar 96	★ HOW DEEP IS YOUR LOVE *RCA 74321355592*	**1**	13
15 Jun 96	HOW DEEP IS YOUR LOVE (re-entry) *RCA 74321355592*	**71**	1

[1] Take That featuring Lulu

Billy TALBOT – See Ian McNABB

TALK TALK *UK, male vocal / instrumental group*   **73 wks**

24 Apr 82	TALK TALK *EMI 5284*	**52**	4
24 Jul 82	TODAY *EMI 5314*	**14**	13
13 Nov 82	TALK TALK (re-mix) *EMI 5352*	**23**	10
19 Mar 83	MY FOOLISH FRIEND *EMI 5373*	**57**	3
14 Jan 84	IT'S MY LIFE *EMI 5443*	**46**	5
7 Apr 84	SUCH A SHAME *EMI 5433*	**49**	6
11 Aug 84	DUM DUM GIRL *EMI 5480*	**74**	1
18 Jan 86	LIFE'S WHAT YOU MAKE IT *EMI EMI 5540*	**16**	9
15 Mar 86	LIVING IN ANOTHER WORLD *EMI EMI 5551*	**48**	4
17 May 86	GIVE IT UP *Parlophone R 6131*	**59**	3
19 May 90	IT'S MY LIFE (re-issue) *Parlophone R 6254*	**13**	9
1 Sep 90	LIFE'S WHAT YOU MAKE IT (re-issue)		
	Parlophone R 6264	**23**	6

TALKING HEADS *US / UK, male / female vocal / instrumental group*   **54 wks**

7 Feb 81	ONCE IN A LIFETIME *Sire SIR 4048*	**14**	10
9 May 81	HOUSES IN MOTION *Sire SIR 4050*	**50**	3
21 Jan 84	THIS MUST BE THE PLACE *Sire W 9451*	**51**	3
3 Nov 84	SLIPPERY PEOPLE *EMI 5504*	**68**	2
12 Oct 85	● ROAD TO NOWHERE *EMI EMI 5530*	**6**	16
8 Feb 86	AND SHE WAS *EMI EMI 5543*	**17**	8
6 Sep 86	WILD WILD LIFE *EMI EMI 5567*	**43**	4
16 May 87	RADIO HEAD *EMI EM 1*	**52**	2
13 Aug 88	BLIND *EMI EM 68*	**59**	3
10 Oct 92	LIFETIME PILING UP *EMI EM 250*	**50**	3

See also Heads with Shaun Ryder.

TAMS *US, male vocal group*   **31 wks**

14 Feb 70	BE YOUNG BE FOOLISH BE HAPPY *Stateside SS 2123*	**32**	7
31 Jul 71	★ HEY GIRL DON'T BOTHER ME *Probe PRO 532*	**1**	17
21 Nov 87	THERE AIN'T NOTHING LIKE SHAGGIN' *Virgin VS 1029*	**21**	7

Norma TANEGA *US, female vocalist*   **8 wks**

7 Apr 66	WALKING MY CAT NAMED DOG *Stateside SS 496*	**22**	8

The Children of TANSLEY SCHOOL
UK, children's choir   **4 wks**

28 Mar 81	MY MUM IS ONE IN A MILLION *EMI 5151*	**27**	4

Jimmy TARBUCK *UK, male vocalist*   **2 wks**

16 Nov 85	AGAIN *Safari SAFE 68*	**74**	1
30 Nov 85	AGAIN (re-entry) *Safari SAFE 68*	**68**	1

Bill TARMEY UK, male vocalist — 9 wks

3 Apr 93	**ONE VOICE** Arista 74321140852	**16**	4
19 Feb 94	**WIND BENEATH MY WINGS** EMI CDEM 304	**40**	3
19 Nov 94	**IOU** EMI CDEM 361	**55**	2

TARRIERS US, male vocal / instrumental group — 6 wks

14 Dec 56	**CINDY OH CINDY** London HLN 8340 [1]	**26**	1
1 Mar 57	**BANANA BOAT SONG** Columbia DB 3891	**15**	5

[1] Vince Martin and the Tarriers

A TASTE OF HONEY US, female vocal duo — 19 wks

17 Jun 78	● **BOOGIE OOGIE OOGIE** Capitol CL 15988	**3**	16
18 May 85	**BOOGIE OOGIE OOGIE (re-mix)** Capitol CL 357	**59**	3

TATJANA Croatia, female vocalist — 2 wks

21 Sep 96	**SANTA MARIA** Love This LUVTHISCDX 4	**40**	2

TAVARES US, male vocal group — 77 wks

10 Jul 76	● **HEAVEN MUST BE MISSING AN ANGEL** Capitol CL 15876	**4**	11
9 Oct 76	● **DON'T TAKE AWAY THE MUSIC** Capitol CL 15886	**4**	10
5 Feb 77	**MIGHTY POWER OF LOVE** Capitol CL 15905	**25**	6
9 Apr 77	● **WHODUNIT** Capitol CL 15914	**5**	10
2 Jul 77	**ONE STEP AWAY** Capitol CL 15930	**16**	7
18 Mar 78	**THE GHOST OF LOVE** Capitol CL 15968	**29**	6
6 May 78	● **MORE THAN A WOMAN** Capitol CL 15977	**7**	11
12 Aug 78	**SLOW TRAIN TO PARADISE** Capitol CL 15996	**62**	3
22 Feb 86	**HEAVEN MUST BE MISSING AN ANGEL (re-issue)** Capitol TAV 1	**12**	9
3 May 86	**IT ONLY TAKES A MINUTE** Capitol TAV 2	**46**	4

TAXMAN – See KICKING BACK with TAXMAN

TAYLOR – See LIBRA presents TAYLOR

Andy TAYLOR UK, male vocalist — 2 wks

20 Oct 90	**LOLA** A & M AM 596	**60**	2

Dina TAYLOR – See BBG

Felice TAYLOR US, female vocalist — 13 wks

25 Oct 67	**I FEEL LOVE COMIN' ON** President PT 155	**11**	13

James TAYLOR US, male vocalist — 23 wks

21 Nov 70	**FIRE AND RAIN** Warner Bros. WB 6104	**42**	3
28 Aug 71	● **YOU'VE GOT A FRIEND** Warner Bros. WB 16085	**4**	15
16 Mar 74	**MOCKINGBIRD** Elektra K 12134 [1]	**34**	5

[1] Carly Simon and James Taylor

John TAYLOR UK, male vocalist — 4 wks

15 Mar 86	**I DO WHAT I DO... THEME FOR '9 ½ WEEKS'** Parlophone R 6125	**42**	4

Johnnie TAYLOR US, male vocalist — 7 wks

24 Apr 76	**DISCO LADY** CBS 4044	**25**	7

JT TAYLOR US, male vocalist — 5 wks

24 Aug 91	**LONG HOT SUMMER NIGHT** MCA MCS 1567	**63**	2
30 Nov 91	**FEEL THE NEED** MCA MCS 1592	**57**	1
18 Apr 92	**FOLLOW ME** MCA MCS 1617	**59**	2

Pauline TAYLOR UK, female vocalist — 3 wks

8 Jun 96	**LET THIS BE A PRAYER** Cheeky CHEKCD 013 [1]	**26**	2
9 Nov 96	**CONSTANTLY WAITING** Cheeky CHEKCD 015	**51**	1

[1] Rollo Goes Spiritual with Pauline Taylor

R Dean TAYLOR Canada, male vocalist — 48 wks

19 Jun 68	**GOTTA SEE JANE** Tamla Motown TMG 656	**17**	12
3 Apr 71	● **INDIANA WANTS ME** Tamla Motown TMG 763	**2**	15
11 May 74	● **THERE'S A GHOST IN MY HOUSE** Tamla Motown TMG 896	**3**	12
31 Aug 74	**WINDOW SHOPPING** Polydor 2058 502	**36**	5
21 Sep 74	**GOTTA SEE JANE (re-issue)** Tamla Motown TMG 918	**41**	4

Roger TAYLOR UK, male vocalist — 15 wks

18 Apr 81	**FUTURE MANAGEMENT** EMI 5157	**49**	4
16 Jun 84	**MAN ON FIRE** EMI 5478	**66**	2
10 Oct 92	**RADIO** Epic 6584367 [1]	**37**	3
14 May 94	**NAZIS** Parlophone CDR 6379	**22**	2
1 Oct 94	**FOREIGN SAND** Parlophone CDR 6389 [2]	**26**	2
26 Nov 94	**HAPPINESS** Parlophone CDR 6399	**32**	2

[1] Shaky featuring Roger Taylor [2] Roger Taylor and Yoshiki

James TAYLOR QUARTET – See JTQ

TC Italy, male instrumental / production duo — 5 wks

14 Mar 92	**BERRY** Union City UCRT 1 [1]	**73**	1
21 Nov 92	**FUNKY GUITAR** Union City UCRT 13 [2]	**40**	2
10 Jul 93	**HARMONY** Union UCRD 20 [3]	**51**	2

[1] TC 1991 [2] TC 1992 [3] TC 1993

T-CONNECTION
US, male vocal / instrumental group — 27 wks

18 Jun 77	**DO WHAT YOU WANNA DO** TK XC 9109	**11**	8
14 Jan 78	**ON FIRE** TK TKR 6006	**16**	5
10 Jun 78	**LET YOURSELF GO** TK TKR 6024	**52**	3
24 Feb 79	**AT MIDNIGHT** TK TKR 7517	**53**	5
5 May 79	**SATURDAY NIGHT** TK TKR 7536	**41**	6

T-COY – See VARIOUS ARTISTS (EPs & LPs) – The Further Adventures Of North EP

Kiri TE KANAWA New Zealand, female vocalist — 11 wks

28 Sep 91	● **WORLD IN UNION** Columbia 6574817	**4**	11

TEACH-IN
Holland, male / female vocal / instrumental group — 7 wks

12 Apr 75	**DING-A-DONG** Polydor 2058 570	**13**	7

TEAM UK, male vocal / instrumental group — 5 wks

1 Jun 85	**WICKI WACKY HOUSE PARTY** EMI 5519	**55**	5

TEARDROP EXPLODES
UK, male vocal / instrumental group　　　　　　**50 wks**

27 Sep 80	**WHEN I DREAM** *Mercury TEAR 1*	47	6
31 Jan 81	● **REWARD** *Vertigo TEAR 2*	6	13
2 May 81	**TREASON (IT'S JUST A STORY)** *Mercury TEAR 3*	18	8
29 Aug 81	**PASSIONATE FRIEND** *Zoo TEAR 5*	25	10
21 Nov 81	**COLOURS FLY AWAY** *Mercury TEAR 6*	54	3
19 Jun 82	**TINY CHILDREN** *Mercury TEAR 7*	44	7
19 Mar 83	**YOU DISAPPEAR FROM VIEW** *Mercury TEAR 8*	41	3

TEARS FOR FEARS *UK, male vocal / instrumental duo* **143 wks**

2 Oct 82	● **MAD WORLD** *Mercury IDEA 3*	3	16
5 Feb 83	● **CHANGE** *Mercury IDEA 4*	4	9
30 Apr 83	● **PALE SHELTER** *Mercury IDEA 5*	5	8
3 Dec 83	**THE WAY YOU ARE** *Mercury IDEA 6*	24	8
18 Aug 84	**MOTHER'S TALK** *Mercury IDEA 7*	14	8
1 Dec 84	● **SHOUT** *Mercury IDEA 8*	4	16
30 Mar 85	● **EVERYBODY WANTS TO RULE THE WORLD** *Mercury IDEA 9*	2	14
22 Jun 85	**HEAD OVER HEELS** *Mercury IDEA 10*	12	9
31 Aug 85	**SUFFER THE CHILDREN** *Mercury IDEA 1*	52	4
7 Sep 85	**PALE SHELTER (re-issue)** *Mercury IDEA 2*	73	2
12 Oct 85	**I BELIEVE (A SOULFUL RE-RECORDING)** *Mercury IDEA 11*	23	4
22 Feb 86	**EVERYBODY WANTS TO RULE THE WORLD (re-entry)** *Mercury IDEA 9*	73	1
31 May 86	● **EVERYBODY WANTS TO RUN THE WORLD** *Mercury RACE 1*	5	6
19 Jul 86	**EVERYBODY WANTS TO RUN THE WORLD (re-entry)** *Mercury RACE 1*	73	1
2 Sep 89	● **SOWING THE SEEDS OF LOVE** *Fontana IDEA 12*	5	9
18 Nov 89	**WOMAN IN CHAINS** *Fontana IDEA 13*	26	8
3 Mar 90	**ADVICE FOR THE YOUNG AT HEART** *Fontana IDEA 14*	36	4
22 Feb 92	**LAID SO LOW (TEARS ROLL DOWN)** *Fontana IDEA 17*	17	5
25 Apr 92	**WOMAN IN CHAINS (re-issue)** *Fontana IDEA 16* 1	57	1
29 May 93	**BREAK IT DOWN AGAIN** *Mercury IDECD 18*	20	5
31 Jul 93	**COLD** *Mercury IDECD 19*	72	1
7 Oct 95	**RAOUL AND THE KINGS OF SPAIN** *Epic 6624765*	31	3
29 Jun 96	**GOD'S MISTAKE** *Epic 6634185*	61	1

1 Tears For Fears featuring Oleta Adams

Mercury RACE 1 was a slightly changed version of Mercury IDEA 9, released to promote the Race Against Time of 15 May 1986. Oleta Adams is given no label credit on the original release of Woman In Chains. From '92 Tears For Fears were essentially a male vocalist / multi-instrumentalist – Roland Orzabal.

TECHNICIAN 2 *UK, male instrumental / production group* **1 wk**

14 Nov 92	**PLAYING WITH THE BOY** *MCA MCS 1710*	70	1

TECHNO TWINS *UK, male / female vocal duo* **2 wks**

16 Jan 82	**FALLING IN LOVE AGAIN** *PRT 7P 224*	75	1
30 Jan 82	**FALLING IN LOVE AGAIN (re-entry)** *PRT 7P 224*	70	1

TECHNOCAT – *See Tom WILSON*

TECHNOHEAD
UK, male / female vocal / instrumental duo **20 wks**

3 Feb 96	● **I WANNA BE A HIPPY** *Mokum DB 17703*	6	14
27 Apr 96	**HAPPY BIRTHDAY** *Mokum DB 17593*	18	5
12 Oct 96	**BANANA-NA-NA (DUMB DI DUMB)** *Mokum DB 17473*	64	1

See also Tricky Disco; GTO. They are all the same act.

TECHNOTRONIC
Belgium, male producer – Jo Bogaert **66 wks**

2 Sep 89	● **PUMP UP THE JAM** *Swanyard SYR 4* 1	2	15
3 Feb 90	● **GET UP (BEFORE THE NIGHT IS OVER)** *Swanyard SYR 8* 2	2	10
7 Apr 90	**THIS BEAT IS TECHNOTRONIC** *Swanyard SYR 9* 3	14	7
14 Jul 90	● **ROCKIN' OVER THE BEAT** *Swanyard SYR 14* 2	9	9
6 Oct 90	● **MEGAMIX** *Swanyard SYR 19*	6	8
15 Dec 90	**TURN IT UP** *Swanyard SYD 9* 4	42	4
25 May 91	**MOVE THAT BODY** *ARS 6568377* 5	12	7
3 Aug 91	**WORK** *ARS 6573317* 5	40	4
14 Dec 96	**PUMP UP THE JAM (re-mix)** *Worx WORXCD 004*	36	2

1 Technotronic featuring Felly 2 Technotronic featuring Ya Kid K 3 Technotronic featuring MC Eric 4 Technotronic featuring Melissa and Einstein 5 Technotronic featuring Reggie

See also Hi-Tek 3 featuring Ya Kid K.

TEDDY BEARS *US, male / female vocal group* **17 wks**

19 Dec 58	● **TO KNOW HIM IS TO LOVE HIM** *London HLN 8733*	2	16
14 Apr 79	**TO KNOW HIM IS TO LOVE HIM (re-issue)** *Lightning LIG 9015*	66	1

To Know Him Is To Love Him re-issue was coupled with Endless Sleep by Jody Reynolds as a double A-side.

TEENAGE FANCLUB
UK, male vocal / instrumental group **15 wks**

24 Aug 91	**STAR SIGN** *Creation CRE 105*	44	2
2 Nov 91	**THE CONCEPT** *Creation CRE 111*	51	1
8 Feb 92	**WHAT YOU DO TO ME (EP)** *Creation CRE 115*	31	2
26 Jun 93	**RADIO** *Creation CRESCD 130*	31	2
2 Oct 93	**NORMAN 3** *Creation CRESCD 142*	50	1
2 Apr 94	**FALLIN'** *Epic 6602622* 1	59	1
8 Apr 95	**MELLOW DOUBT** *Creation CRESCD 175*	34	2
27 May 95	**SPARKY'S DREAM** *Creation CRESCD 201*	40	2
2 Sep 95	**NEIL JUNG** *Creation CRESCD 210*	62	1
16 Dec 95	**HAVE LOST IT EP** *Creation CRESCD 216*	53	1

1 Teenage Fanclub and De La Soul

Tracks on What You Do To Me (EP): What You Do To Me / B-Side / Life's A Gas / Filler. Tracks On Have Lost It EP: 120 Mins / Don't Look Back / Everything Flows / Star Sign. This last track is a re-recorded version of their first hit.

TEENAGERS – *See Frankie LYMON and the TEENAGERS*

TEKNO TOO
UK, male instrumental / production duo **2 wks**

13 Jul 91	**JET-STAR** *D-Zone DANCE 012*	56	2

TELEVISION *US, male vocal / instrumental group* **10 wks**

16 Apr 77	**MARQUEE MOON** *Elektra K 12252*	30	4
30 Jul 77	**PROVE IT** *Elektra K 12262*	25	4
22 Apr 78	**FOXHOLE** *Elektra K 12287*	36	2

TELEX *Belgium, male vocal / instrumental duo* **7 wks**

21 Jul 79	**ROCK AROUND THE CLOCK** *Sire SIR 4020*	34	7

Sylvia TELLA – *See BLOW MONKEYS*

TLC

TLC is an acronym for the nicknames of the group's three members: T-Boz, Left Eye and Chilli.

Technohead

'I Wanna Be A Hippy' by Technohead topped the chart in Germany a full year before garnering a UK release. In Britain, the song was a bigger hit for the Smurfs than the song's originators.

Terrorvision

Terrorvision were one of the first wave of new Brit rock acts to win the vote of the heavy metal rock press without resorting to the usual denim and leather cliches.

TEMPERANCE SEVEN
UK, male vocal / instrumental band   **45 wks**

30 Mar 61	★ YOU'RE DRIVING ME CRAZY *Parlophone R 4757*	**1**	16
15 Jun 61	● PASADENA *Parlophone R 4781*	**4**	17
28 Sep 61	HARD HEARTED HANNAH / CHILI BOM BOM		
	Parlophone R 4823	**28**	4
7 Dec 61	CHARLESTON *Parlophone R 4851*	**22**	8

Chili Bom Bom only listed with Hard Hearted Hannah for the weeks of 12 and 19 Oct 61.

TEMPLE OF THE DOG
US, male vocal / instrumental group   **2 wks**

24 Oct 92	HUNGER STRIKE *A & M AM 0091*	**51**	2

Nino TEMPO and April STEVENS
US, male / female vocal duo   **19 wks**

7 Nov 63	DEEP PURPLE *London HLK 9782*	**17**	11
16 Jan 64	WHISPERING *London HLK 9829*	**20**	8

TEMPTATIONS *US, male vocal group*   **203 wks**

18 Mar 65	MY GIRL *Stateside SS 378*	**43**	1
1 Apr 65	IT'S GROWING *Tamla Motown TMG 504*	**49**	1
15 Apr 65	IT'S GROWING (re-entry) *Tamla Motown TMG 504*	**45**	1
14 Jul 66	AIN'T TOO PROUD TO BEG *Tamla Motown TMG 565*	**21**	11
6 Oct 66	BEAUTY IS ONLY SKIN DEEP *Tamla Motown TMG 578*	**18**	10
15 Dec 66	(I KNOW) I'M LOSING YOU *Tamla Motown TMG 587*	**19**	9
6 Sep 67	YOU'RE MY EVERYTHING *Tamla Motown TMG 620*	**26**	15
6 Mar 68	I WISH IT WOULD RAIN *Tamla Motown TMG 641*	**45**	1
12 Jun 68	I COULD NEVER LOVE ANOTHER		
	Tamla Motown TMG 658	**47**	1
29 Jan 69	● I'M GONNA MAKE YOU LOVE ME		
	Tamla Motown TMG 685 [1]	**3**	11
5 Mar 69	● GET READY *Tamla Motown TMG 688*	**10**	9
23 Apr 69	I'M GONNA MAKE YOU LOVE ME (re-entry)		
	Tamla Motown TMG 685 [1]	**49**	1
23 Aug 69	CLOUD NINE *Tamla Motown TMG 707*	**15**	10
20 Sep 69	I SECOND THAT EMOTION *Tamla Motown TMG 709* [1]	**18**	8
17 Jan 70	I CAN'T GET NEXT TO YOU *Tamla Motown TMG 722*	**13**	9
21 Mar 70	WHY (MUST WE FALL IN LOVE)		
	Tamla Motown TMG 730 [1]	**31**	7
13 Jun 70	PSYCHEDELIC SHACK *Tamla Motown TMG 741*	**33**	7
19 Sep 70	● BALL OF CONFUSION *Tamla Motown TMG 749*	**7**	12
19 Dec 70	BALL OF CONFUSION (re-entry)		
	Tamla Motown TMG 749	**48**	3
22 May 71	● JUST MY IMAGINATION (RUNNING AWAY		
	WITH ME) *Tamla Motown TMG 773*	**8**	16
5 Feb 72	SUPERSTAR (REMEMBER HOW YOU GOT		
	WHERE YOU ARE) *Tamla Motown TMG 800*	**32**	5
15 Apr 72	TAKE A LOOK AROUND *Tamla Motown TMG 808*	**13**	10
13 Jan 73	PAPA WAS A ROLLIN' STONE *Tamla Motown TMG 839*	**14**	8
29 Sep 73	LAW OF THE LAND *Tamla Motown TMG 866*	**41**	4
12 Jun 82	STANDING ON THE TOP (PART 1)		
	Motown TMG 1263 [2]	**53**	3
17 Nov 84	TREAT HER LIKE A LADY *Motown TMG 1365*	**12**	10
15 Aug 87	PAPA WAS A ROLLIN' STONE (re-mix)		
	Motown ZB 41431	**31**	6
6 Feb 88	LOOK WHAT YOU STARTED *Motown ZB 41733*	**63**	2
21 Oct 89	ALL I WANT FROM YOU *Motown ZB 43233*	**71**	1
15 Feb 92	● MY GIRL (re-issue) *Epic 6576767*	**2**	10
22 Feb 92	THE JONES' *Motown TMG 1403*	**69**	1

[1] Diana Ross and the Supremes and the Temptations [2] Temptations featuring Rick James

10 CC *UK, male vocal / instrumental group*   **133 wks**

23 Sep 72	● DONNA *UK 6*	**2**	13
19 May 73	★ RUBBER BULLETS *UK 36*	**1**	15
25 Aug 73	● THE DEAN AND I *UK 48*	**10**	8
15 Jun 74	● THE WALL STREET SHUFFLE *UK 69*	**10**	10
14 Sep 74	SILLY LOVE *UK 77*	**24**	7
5 Apr 75	● LIFE IS A MINESTRONE *Mercury 6008 010*	**7**	8
31 May 75	★ I'M NOT IN LOVE *Mercury 6008 014*	**1**	11
29 Nov 75	● ART FOR ART'S SAKE *Mercury 6008 017*	**5**	10
20 Mar 76	● I'M MANDY FLY ME *Mercury 6008 019*	**6**	9
11 Dec 76	● THE THINGS WE DO FOR LOVE *Mercury 6008 022*	**6**	11
16 Apr 77	● GOOD MORNING JUDGE *Mercury 6008 025*	**5**	12
12 Aug 78	★ DREADLOCK HOLIDAY *Mercury 6008 035*	**1**	13
7 Aug 82	RUN AWAY *Mercury MER 113*	**50**	4
18 Mar 95	I'M NOT IN LOVE *Avex UK AVEXCD 2*	**29**	2

From Things We Do For Love 10 CC were a male vocal / instrumental duo. I'm Not In Love in 95 is a re-recording.

TEN CITY *US, male vocal / instrumental group*   **21 wks**

21 Jan 89	● THAT'S THE WAY LOVE IS *Atlantic A 8963*	**8**	10
8 Apr 89	DEVOTION *Atlantic A 8916*	**29**	4
22 Jul 89	WHERE DO WE GO *Atlantic A 8864*	**60**	1
27 Oct 90	WHATEVER MAKES YOU HAPPY *Atlantic A 7819*	**60**	2
15 Aug 92	ONLY TIME WILL TELL / MY PEACE OF HEAVEN		
	East West America A 8516	**63**	2
11 Sep 93	FANTASY *Columbia 6595042*	**45**	2

TEN POLE TUDOR
UK, male vocal / instrumental group   **40 wks**

7 Apr 79	● WHO KILLED BAMBI *Virgin VS 256*	**6**	8
13 Oct 79	ROCK AROUND THE CLOCK *Virgin VS 290*	**21**	6
25 Apr 81	● SWORDS OF A THOUSAND MEN *Stiff BUY 109*	**6**	12
1 Aug 81	WUNDERBAR *Stiff BUY 120*	**16**	9
14 Nov 81	THROWING MY BABY OUT WITH THE BATHWATER		
	Stiff BUY 129	**49**	5

The listed flip side of Who Killed Bambi was Silly Thing by the Sex Pistols. The listed flip side of Rock Around The Clock was The Great Rock 'n' Roll Swindle also by the Sex Pistols.

TEN SHARP *Holland, male vocal / instrumental duo*   **15 wks**

21 Mar 92	● YOU *Columbia 6566647*	**10**	13
20 Jun 92	AIN'T MY BEATING HEART *Columbia 6580947*	**63**	2

10,000 MANIACS
US, female / male vocal / instrumental group   **7 wks**

12 Sep 92	THESE ARE DAYS *Elektra EKR 156*	**58**	3
10 Apr 93	CANDY EVERYBODY WANTS		
	Elektra EKR 160CD1	**47**	3
23 Oct 93	BECAUSE THE NIGHT *Elektra EKR 175CD*	**65**	1

TEN YEARS AFTER
UK, male vocal / instrumental group   **18 wks**

6 Jun 70	● LOVE LIKE A MAN *Deram DM 299*	**10**	18

TENNESSEE THREE – *See Johnny CASH*

TENOR FLY *UK, male vocalist*   **14 wks**

6 Apr 91	WICKEDEST SOUND *Desire WANT 40* [1]	**43**	6
15 Jun 91	TRIBAL BASE *Desire WANT 44* [2]	**20**	6
7 Jan 95	BRIGHT SIDE OF LIFE *Mango CIDM 825*	**51**	2

[1] Rebel MC featuring Tenor Fly [2] Rebel MC featuring Tenor Fly and Barrington Levy

TERMINATERS – *See ARNEE and the TERMINATERS*

TERRA FIRMA *Italy, male producer – Claudio Giussani*   **1 wk**

18 May 96	**FLOATING** *Platipus PLAT 21CD* **64**	1

Tammi TERRELL – *See Marvin GAYE*

TERRORIZE *UK, male producer – Shaun Imrei*   **6 wks**

2 May 92	**IT'S JUST A FEELING** *Hamster STER 1* **52**	3
22 Aug 92	**FEEL THE RHYTHM** *Hamster 12STER 2* **69**	1
14 Nov 92	**IT'S JUST A FEELING (re-issue)** *Hamster STER 8* **47**	2

TERRORVISION
UK, male vocal / instrumental group   **36 wks**

19 Jun 93	**AMERICAN TV** *Total Vegas CDVEGAS 3* **63**	1
30 Oct 93	**NEW POLICY ONE** *Total Vegas CDVEGAS 4* **42**	2
8 Jan 94	**MY HOUSE** *Total Vegas CDVEGAS 5* **29**	4
9 Apr 94	**OBLIVION** *Total Vegas CDVEGAS 6* **21**	5
25 Jun 94	**MIDDLEMAN** *Total Vegas CDVEGAS 7* **25**	4
3 Sep 94	**PRETEND BEST FRIEND** *Total Vegas CDVEGAS 8*.......... **25**	3
29 Oct 94	**ALICE WHAT'S THE MATTER** *Total Vegas CDVEGAS 9*...................... **24**	4
18 Mar 95	**SOME PEOPLE SAY** *Total Vegas CDVEGAS 10* **22**	3
2 Mar 96 ●	**PERSEVERANCE** *Total Vegas CDVEGAS 11* **5**	4
4 May 96	**CELEBRITY HIT LIST** *Total Vegas CDVEGAS 12* **20**	3
20 Jul 96 ●	**BAD ACTRESS** *Total Vegas CDVEGAS 13* **10**	3

Helen TERRY *UK, female vocalist*   **6 wks**

12 May 84	**LOVE LIES LOST** *Virgin VS 678* **34**	6

Tony TERRY *US, male vocalist*   **6 wks**

27 Feb 88	**LOVEY DOVEY** *Epic TONY 2* **44**	6

Todd TERRY PROJECT *US, male producer*   **12 wks**

12 Nov 88	**WEEKEND** *Sleeping Bag SBUK 1T* **56**	3
14 Oct 95	**WEEKEND (re-mix)** *Ore AG 13CD*........................ **28**	3
13 Jul 96 ●	**KEEP ON JUMPIN'** *Manifesto FESCD 11* ☐1 .... **8**	6

☐1 Todd Terry featuring Martha Wash and Jocelyn Brown

TESLA *US, male vocal / instrumental group*   **1 wk**

27 Apr 91	**SIGNS** *Geffen GFS 3* **70**	1

Joe TEX *US, male vocalist*   **11 wks**

23 Apr 77 ●	**AIN'T GONNA BUMP NO MORE (WITH NO BIG FAT WOMAN)** *Epic EPC 5035* **2**	11

TEXAS *UK, male / female vocal / instrumental group*   **40 wks**

4 Feb 89 ●	**I DON'T WANT A LOVER** *Mercury TEX 1* **8**	11
6 May 89	**THRILL HAS GONE** *Mercury TEX 2* **60**	3
5 Aug 89	**EVERYDAY NOW** *Mercury TEX 3*......................**44**	5
2 Dec 89	**PRAYER FOR YOU** *Mercury TEX 4* **73**	1
7 Sep 91	**WHY BELIEVE IN YOU** *Mercury TEX 5* **66**	1
26 Oct 91	**IN MY HEART** *Mercury TEX 6*......................**74**	1
8 Feb 92	**ALONE WITH YOU** *Mercury TEX 7* **32**	4
25 Apr 92	**TIRED OF BEING ALONE** *Mercury TEX 8* **19**	6
11 Sep 93	**SO CALLED FRIEND** *Vertigo TEXCD 9*......................**30**	3
30 Oct 93	**YOU OWE IT ALL TO ME** *Vertigo TEXCD 10* **39**	3
12 Feb 94	**SO IN LOVE WITH YOU** *Vertigo TEXCD 11*......**28**	2

THAT PETROL EMOTION
UK, male vocal / instrumental group   **24 wks**

11 Apr 87	**BIG DECISION** *Polydor TPE 1* **43**	7
11 Jul 87	**DANCE** *Polydor TPE 2* **64**	2
17 Oct 87	**GENIUS MOVE** *Virgin VS 1002* **65**	2
31 Mar 90	**ABANDON** *Virgin VS 1242* **73**	1
1 Sep 90	**HEY VENUS** *Virgin VS 1290* **49**	4
9 Feb 91	**TINGLE** *Virgin VS 1312* **49**	4
27 Apr 91	**SENSITIZE** *Virgin VS 1261* **55**	4

The THE
UK, male vocalist – Matt Johnson and backing musicians   **52 wks**

4 Dec 82	**UNCERTAIN SMILE** *Epic EPC A 2787* **68**	3
17 Sep 83	**THIS IS THE DAY** *Epic A 3710* **71**	3
9 Aug 86	**HEARTLAND** *Some Bizzare TRUTH 2* **29**	10
25 Oct 86	**INFECTED** *Some Bizzare TRUTH 3* **48**	5
24 Jan 87	**SLOW TRAIN TO DAWN** *Some Bizzare TENSE 1* **64**	2
23 May 87	**SWEET BIRD OF TRUTH** *Epic TENSE 2* **55**	2
1 Apr 89	**THE BEAT(EN) GENERATION** *Epic EMU 8*.........**18**	5
22 Jul 89	**GRAVITATE TO ME** *Epic EMU 9* **63**	3
7 Oct 89	**ARMAGEDDON DAYS ARE HERE (AGAIN)** *Epic EMU 10* **70**	2
2 Mar 91	**SHADES OF BLUE EP** *Epic 6557968* **54**	1
16 Jan 93	**DOGS OF LUST** *Epic 6584572* **25**	4
17 Apr 93	**SLOW EMOTION REPLAY** *Epic 6590772* **35**	3
19 Jun 93	**LOVE IS STRONGER THAN DEATH** *Epic 6593712* **39**	3
15 Jan 94	**DIS-INFECTED EP** *Epic 6598112* **17**	4
4 Feb 95	**I SAW THE LIGHT** *Epic 6610912* **31**	2

Tracks on Shades Of Blue EP: Jealous Of Youth / Another Boy Drowning (Live) / Solitude / Dolphins. Tracks on Dis-Infected EP: That Was The Day / Dis-Infected / Helpline Operator / Dogs Of Lust. That Was The Day and Dis-Infected on the EP are re-recordings of earlier hits, Dogs Of Lust is a re-mix.

THEATRE OF HATE *UK, male vocal / instrumental group*   **9 wks**

23 Jan 82	**DO YOU BELIEVE IN THE WESTWORLD** *Burning Rome BRR 2* **40**	7
29 May 82	**THE HOP** *Burning Rome BRR 3* **70**	2

THEM *UK, male vocal / instrumental group*   **23 wks**

7 Jan 65 ●	**BABY PLEASE DON'T GO** *Decca F 12018* **10**	9
25 Mar 65 ●	**HERE COMES THE NIGHT** *Decca F 12094* **2**	12
9 Feb 91	**BABY PLEASE DON'T GO (re-issue)** *London LON 292* **65**	2

THEN JERICO *UK, male vocal / instrumental group*   **36 wks**

31 Jan 87	**LET HER FALL** *London LON 97*...............**65**	3
25 Jul 87	**THE MOTIVE (LIVING WITHOUT YOU)** *London LON 145* **18**	12
24 Oct 87	**MUSCLE DEEP** *London LON 156* **48**	3
28 Jan 89	**BIG AREA** *London LON 204* **13**	7
8 Apr 89	**WHAT DOES IT TAKE** *London LON 223* **33**	3
12 Aug 89	**SUGAR BOX** *London LON 235* **22**	6

THERAPY? *UK, male vocal / instrumental group*   **30 wks**

31 Oct 92	**TEETHGRINDER** *A & M AM 0097* **30**	2
20 Mar 93 ●	**SHORTSHARPSHOCK EP** *A & M AMCD 208* **9**	4
12 Jun 93	**FACE THE STRANGE EP** *A & M 5803052* **18**	3
28 Aug 93	**OPAL MANTRA** *A & M 5803612* **14**	3
29 Jan 94	**NOWHERE** *A & M 5805052* **18**	4
12 Mar 94	**TRIGGER INSIDE** *A & M 5805352* **22**	3
11 Jun 94	**DIE LAUGHING** *A & M 5805892* **29**	2
27 May 95	**INNOCENT X** *Volume VOLCD 1* **53**	1
3 Jun 95	**STORIES** *A & M 5811052* **14**	3

| 29 Jul 95 | **LOOSE** A & M 5811652 | **25** | 3 |
| 18 Nov 95 | **DIANE** A & M 5812912 | **26** | 2 |

Tracks on Shortsharpshock EP: Screamager / Auto Surgery / Totally Random Man / Accelerator. Tracks on Face The Strange EP: Turn / Speedball / Bloody Blue / Neckfreak. The listed flip side of Innocent X was Belfast by Orbital.

THESE ANIMAL MEN
UK, male vocal / instrumental group **1 wk**

| 24 Sep 94 | **THIS IS THE SOUND OF YOUTH** Hi-Rise FLATSCD 7 | **72** | 1 |

THEY MIGHT BE GIANTS
US, male vocal / instrumental duo **13 wks**

| 3 Mar 90 | ● **BIRDHOUSE IN YOUR SOUL** Elektra EKR 104 | **6** | 11 |
| 2 Jun 90 | **ISTANBUL (NOT CONSTANTINOPLE)** Elektra EKR 110 | **61** | 2 |

THIN LIZZY
Ireland / UK / Canada, male vocal / instrumental group **128 wks**

20 Jan 73	● **WHISKEY IN THE JAR** Decca F 13355	**6**	12
29 May 76	● **THE BOYS ARE BACK IN TOWN** Vertigo 6059 139	**8**	10
14 Aug 76	**JAILBREAK** Vertigo 6059 150	**31**	4
15 Jan 77	**DON'T BELIEVE A WORD** Vertigo Lizzy 001	**12**	7
13 Aug 77	**DANCIN' IN THE MOONLIGHT (IT'S CAUGHT ME IN THE SPOTLIGHT)** Vertigo 6059 177	**14**	8
13 May 78	**ROSALIE – COWGIRLS' SONG (MEDLEY)** Vertigo LIZZY 2	**20**	13
3 Mar 79	● **WAITING FOR AN ALIBI** Vertigo LIZZY 003	**9**	8
16 Jun 79	**DO ANYTHING YOU WANT TO** Vertigo LIZZY 004	**14**	9
20 Oct 79	**SARAH** Vertigo LIZZY 5	**24**	13
24 May 80	**CHINATOWN** Vertigo LIZZY 6	**21**	9
27 Sep 80	● **KILLER ON THE LOOSE** Vertigo LIZZY 7	**10**	7
2 May 81	**KILLERS LIVE EP** Vertigo LIZZY 8	**19**	7
8 Aug 81	**TROUBLE BOYS** Vertigo LIZZY 9	**53**	4
6 Mar 82	**HOLLYWOOD (DOWN ON YOUR LUCK)** Vertigo LIZZY 10	**53**	3
12 Feb 83	**COLD SWEAT** Vertigo LIZZY 11	**27**	5
7 May 83	**THUNDER AND LIGHTNING** Vertigo LIZZY 12	**39**	2
6 Aug 83	**THE SUN GOES DOWN** Vertigo LIZZY 13	**52**	3
26 Jan 91	**DEDICATION** Vertigo LIZZY 14	**35**	3
23 Mar 91	**THE BOYS ARE BACK IN TOWN (re-issue)** Vertigo LIZZY 15	**63**	1

Tracks on Killers Live EP: Bad Reputation / Are You Ready / Dear Miss Lonely Hearts.

3RD BASS
US, male rap group **5 wks**

10 Feb 90	**THE GAS FACE** Def Jam 655627 0	**71**	1
7 Apr 90	**BROOKLYN-QUEENS** Def Jam 655830 7	**61**	2
22 Jun 91	**POP GOES THE WEASEL** Def Jam 6569547	**64**	2

THIRD DIMENSION featuring Julie McDERMOTT
UK, male / female vocal / instrumental group **2 wks**

| 12 Oct 96 | **DON'T GO** Soundproof MCSTD 40082 | **34** | 2 |

THIRD WORLD
Jamaica, male vocal / instrumental group **53 wks**

23 Sep 78	● **NOW THAT WE'VE FOUND LOVE** Island WIP 6457	**10**	9
6 Jan 79	**COOL MEDITATION** Island WIP 6469	**17**	10
16 Jun 79	**TALK TO ME** Island WIP 6496	**56**	5
6 Jun 81	● **DANCING ON THE FLOOR (HOOKED ON LOVE)** CBS A 1214	**10**	15
17 Apr 82	**TRY JAH LOVE** CBS A 2063	**47**	6
9 Mar 85	**NOW THAT WE'VE FOUND LOVE (re-issue)** Island IS 219	**22**	8

THIRST
UK, male vocal / instrumental group **2 wks**

| 6 Jul 91 | **THE ENEMY WITHIN** Ten TEN 379 | **61** | 2 |

1300 DRUMS featuring the UNJUSTIFIED ANCIENTS OF MU
UK, male instrumental / production group **4 wks**

| 18 May 96 | **OOH! AAH! CANTONA** Dynamo DYND 5 | **11** | 4 |

THIS ISLAND EARTH
UK, male / female vocal / instrumental group **5 wks**

| 5 Jan 85 | **SEE THAT GLOW** Magnet MAG 266 | **47** | 5 |

THIS MORTAL COIL
UK, male / female vocal / instrumental group **3 wks**

| 22 Oct 83 | **SONG TO THE SIREN** 4AD AD 310 | **66** | 2 |
| 12 Nov 83 | **SONG TO THE SIREN (re-entry)** 4AD AD 310 | **75** | 1 |

THIS WAY UP
UK, male vocal / instrumental duo **2 wks**

| 22 Aug 87 | **TELL ME WHY** Virgin VS 954 | **72** | 2 |

THIS YEAR'S BLONDE
UK, male / female vocal / instrumental group **8 wks**

| 10 Oct 81 | **PLATINUM POP** Creole CR 19 | **46** | 5 |
| 14 Nov 87 | **WHO'S THAT MIX** Debut DEBT 3034 | **62** | 3 |

BJ THOMAS
US, male vocalist **4 wks**

| 21 Feb 70 | **RAINDROPS KEEP FALLING ON MY HEAD** Wand WN1 | **38** | 3 |
| 2 May 70 | **RAINDROPS KEEP FALLING ON MY HEAD (re-entry)** Wand WN1 | **49** | 1 |

Carla THOMAS – See Otis REDDING

Evelyn THOMAS
US, female vocalist **29 wks**

24 Jan 76	**WEAK SPOT** 20th Century BTC 1014	**26**	7
17 Apr 76	**DOOMSDAY** 20th Century BTC 1017	**41**	1
1 May 76	**DOOMSDAY (re-entry)** 20th Century BTC 1017	**45**	1
21 Apr 84	● **HIGH ENERGY** Record Shack SOHO 18	**5**	17
25 Aug 84	**MASQUERADE** Record Shack SOHO 25	**60**	3

Jamo THOMAS
US, male vocalist **2 wks**

| 26 Feb 69 | **I SPY FOR THE FBI** Polydor 56755 | **48** | 1 |
| 12 Mar 69 | **I SPY FOR THE FBI (re-entry)** Polydor 56755 | **44** | 1 |

Kenny THOMAS
UK, male vocalist **54 wks**

26 Jan 91	**OUTSTANDING** Cooltempo COOL 227	**12**	10
1 Jun 91	● **THINKING ABOUT YOUR LOVE** Cooltempo COOL 235	**4**	13
5 Oct 91	**BEST OF YOU** Cooltempo COOL 243	**11**	7
30 Nov 91	**TENDER LOVE** Cooltempo COOL 247	**26**	6
10 Jul 93	**STAY** Cooltempo CDCOOL 271	**22**	6
4 Sep 93	**TRIPPIN' ON YOUR LOVE** Cooltempo CDCOOL 277	**17**	5
6 Nov 93	**PIECE BY PIECE** Cooltempo CDCOOL 283	**36**	3
14 May 94	**DESTINY** Cooltempo CDCOOL 289	**59**	1
2 Sep 95	**WHEN I THINK OF YOU** Cooltempo CDCOOL 309	**27**	3

Lillo THOMAS US, male vocalist · 10 wks

27 Apr 85	**SETTLE DOWN** Capitol CL 356	**66**	2
21 Mar 87	**SEXY GIRL** Capitol CL 445	**23**	5
30 May 87	**I'M IN LOVE** Capitol CL 450	**54**	3

Mickey THOMAS – See Elvin BISHOP

Nicky THOMAS Jamaica, male vocalist · 14 wks

13 Jun 70	● **LOVE OF THE COMMON PEOPLE** Trojan TR 7750	**9**	14

Rufus THOMAS US, male vocalist · 12 wks

11 Apr 70	**DO THE FUNKY CHICKEN** Stax 144	**18**	12

Tasha THOMAS US, female vocalist · 3 wks

20 Jan 79	**SHOOT ME (WITH YOUR LOVE)** Atlantic LV 4	**59**	3

Timmy THOMAS US, male vocalist · 20 wks

24 Feb 73	**WHY CAN'T WE LIVE TOGETHER** Mojo 2027 012	**12**	11
28 Dec 85	**NEW YORK EYES** Portrait A 6805 [1]	**41**	7
14 Jul 90	**WHY CAN'T WE LIVE TOGETHER (re-mix)** TK TKR 1	**54**	2

[1] Nicole with Timmy Thomas

THOMAS and TAYLOR US, male / female vocal duo · 5 wks

17 May 86	**YOU CAN'T BLAME LOVE** Cooltempo COOL 123	**53**	5

Amanda THOMPSON – See Lesley GARRETT and Amanda THOMPSON

Carroll THOMPSON – See MOVEMENT 98 featuring Carroll THOMPSON; Courtney PINE

Chris THOMPSON UK, male vocalist · 5 wks

27 Oct 79	**IF YOU REMEMBER ME** Planet K 12389	**42**	5

Sue THOMPSON US, female vocalist · 9 wks

2 Nov 61	**SAD MOVIES** Polydor NH 66967	**46**	1
16 Nov 61	**SAD MOVIES (re-entry)** Polydor NH 66967	**48**	1
21 Jan 65	**PAPER TIGER** Hickory 1284	**50**	1
11 Feb 65	**PAPER TIGER (re-entry)** Hickory 1284	**30**	6

THOMPSON TWINS
UK / New Zealand, male / female vocal / instrumental group · 110 wks

6 Nov 82	**LIES** Arista ARIST 486	**67**	3
29 Jan 83	● **LOVE ON YOUR SIDE** Arista ARIST 504	**9**	12
16 Apr 83	● **WE ARE DETECTIVE** Arista ARIST 526	**7**	9
16 Jul 83	**WATCHING** Arista TWINS 1	**33**	6
19 Nov 83	● **HOLD ME NOW** Arista TWINS 2	**4**	15
4 Feb 84	● **DOCTOR DOCTOR** Arista TWINS 3	**3**	10
31 Mar 84	● **YOU TAKE ME UP** Arista TWINS 4	**2**	9
7 Jul 84	**SISTER OF MERCY** Arista TWINS 5	**11**	8
8 Sep 84	**SISTER OF MERCY (re-entry)** Arista TWINS 5	**66**	1
8 Dec 84	**LAY YOUR HANDS ON ME** Arista TWINS 6	**13**	9
31 Aug 85	**DON'T MESS WITH DOCTOR DREAM** Arista TWINS 9	**15**	6
19 Oct 85	**KING FOR A DAY** Arista TWINS 7	**22**	6
7 Dec 85	**REVOLUTION** Arista TWINS 10	**56**	3
4 Jan 86	**REVOLUTION (re-entry)** Arista TWINS 10	**75**	1
21 Mar 87	**GET THAT LOVE** Arista TWINS 12	**68**	2
11 Apr 87	**GET THAT LOVE (re-entry)** Arista TWINS 12	**66**	1
15 Oct 88	**IN THE NAME OF LOVE '88** Arista 111808	**46**	3

28 Sep 91	**COME INSIDE** Warner Bros. W 0058	**56**	4
25 Jan 92	**THE SAINT** Warner Bros. W 0080	**53**	2

Tracey THORN – See MASSIVE ATTACK

David THORNE US, male vocalist · 8 wks

24 Jan 63	**ALLEY CAT SONG** Stateside SS 141	**21**	8

Ken THORNE UK, orchestra · 15 wks

18 Jul 63	● **THEME FROM THE FILM 'THE LEGION'S LAST PATROL'** HMV POP 1176	**4**	15

THOSE 2 GIRLS UK, female vocal duo · 4 wks

5 Nov 94	**WANNA MAKE YOU GO... UUH!** Final Vinyl 74321233782	**74**	1
4 Mar 95	**ALL I WANT** Final Vinyl 74321254202	**36**	3

THOUSAND YARD STARE
UK, male vocal / instrumental group · 5 wks

26 Oct 91	**SEASONSTREAM EP** Stifled Aardvark AARD 5T	**65**	1
8 Feb 92	**COMEUPPANCE** Stifled Aardvark AARD 007	**37**	2
11 Jul 92	**SPINDRIFT EP** Stifled Aardvark AARDT 010	**58**	1
8 May 93	**VERSION OF ME** Polydor AARDC 012	**57**	1

Tracks on Seasonstream EP: O-O AET / Village End / Keepsake / Worse For Wear. Tracks on Spindrift EP: Wideshire Two / Hand, Son / Happenstance / Mocca Pune.

THRASHING DOVES
UK, male vocal / instrumental group · 3 wks

24 Jan 87	**BEAUTIFUL IMBALANCE** A & M TDOVE 1	**50**	3

THREE DEGREES US, female vocal group · 111 wks

13 Apr 74	**YEAR OF DECISION** Philadelphia International PIR 2073	**13**	10
27 Apr 74	**TSOP (THE SOUND OF PHILADELPHIA)** Philadelphia International PIR 2289 [1]	**22**	9
13 Jul 74	★ **WHEN WILL I SEE YOU AGAIN** Philadelphia International PIR 2155	**1**	16
2 Nov 74	**GET YOUR LOVE BACK** Philadelphia International PIR 2737	**34**	4
12 Apr 75	● **TAKE GOOD CARE OF YOURSELF** Philadelphia International PIR 3177	**9**	9
5 Jul 75	**LONG LOST LOVER** Philadelphia International PIR 3352	**40**	4
1 May 76	**TOAST OF LOVE** Epic EPC 4215	**36**	4
7 Oct 78	**GIVIN' UP GIVIN' IN** Ariola ARO 130	**12**	10
13 Jan 79	● **WOMAN IN LOVE** Ariola ARO 141	**3**	11
24 Mar 79	**THE RUNNER** Ariola ARO 154	**10**	10
23 Jun 79	**THE GOLDEN LADY** Ariola ARO 170	**56**	3
29 Sep 79	**JUMP THE GUN** Ariola ARO 183	**48**	5
24 Nov 79	● **MY SIMPLE HEART** Ariola ARO 202	**9**	11
5 Oct 85	**THE HEAVEN I NEED** Supreme SUPE 102	**42**	5

[1] MFSB featuring the Three Degrees

THREE DOG NIGHT US, male vocal / instrumental group · 23 wks

8 Aug 70	● **MAMA TOLD ME (NOT TO COME)** Stateside SS 8052	**3**	14
29 May 71	**JOY TO THE WORLD** Probe PRO 523	**24**	9

THREE GOOD REASONS
UK, male vocal / instrumental group · 3 wks

10 Mar 66	**NOWHERE MAN** Mercury MF 899	**47**	3

THREE KAYES – See KAYE SISTERS

3T US, male vocal group — 30 wks

27 Jan 96	● ANYTHING MJJ 6627152	2	14
4 May 96	24 / 7 MJJ 6631995	11	7
24 Aug 96	● WHY MJJ 6636482 [1]	2	9

[1] 3T featuring Michael Jackson

THREE TONS OF JOY – See Johnny OTIS SHOW

THROWING MUSES
US, male / female vocal / instrumental group — 6 wks

9 Feb 91	COUNTING BACKWARDS 4AD AD 1001	70	2
1 Aug 92	FIREPILE (EP) 4AD AD 2012	46	1
24 Dec 94	BRIGHT YELLOW GUN 4AD BAD 4018CD	51	2
10 Aug 96	SHARK 4AD BAD 6016CD	53	1

Tracks on Firepile (EP): Firepile / Manic Depression / Snailhead / City Of The Dead.

THS – THE HORN SECTION
US, male / female vocal / instrumental group — 3 wks

18 Aug 84	LADY SHINE (SHINE ON) Fourth & Broadway BRW 10	54	3

Harry THUMANN
Germany, male instrumentalist – keyboards — 6 wks

21 Feb 81	UNDERWATER Decca F 13901	41	6

THUNDER
UK, male vocal / instrumental group — 44 wks

17 Feb 90	DIRTY LOVE EMI EM 126	32	4
12 May 90	BACKSTREET SYMPHONY EMI EM 137	25	4
14 Jul 90	GIMME SOME LOVIN' EMI EM 148	36	3
29 Sep 90	SHE'S SO FINE EMI EM 158	34	3
23 Feb 91	LOVE WALKED IN EMI EM 175	21	4
15 Aug 92	LOW LIFE IN HIGH PLACES EMI EM 242	22	5
10 Oct 92	EVERYBODY WANTS HER EMI EM 249	36	4
13 Feb 93	A BETTER MAN EMI CDBETTER 1	18	4
19 Jun 93	LIKE A SATELLITE (EP) EMI CDEM 272	28	2
7 Jan 95	STAND UP EMI CDEM 365	23	4
25 Feb 95	RIVER OF PAIN EMI CDEM 367	31	2
6 May 95	CASTLES IN THE SAND EMI CDEM 372	30	3
23 Sep 95	IN A BROKEN DREAM EMI CDEM 384	26	2

Tracks on Like A Satellite (EP): Like A Satellite / The Damage Is Done / Like A Satellite (Live) / Gimme Shelter. See also Various Artists (EPs & LPs) – Gimme Shelter (EP).

THUNDERBIRDS – See Chris FARLOWE

THUNDERCLAP NEWMAN
UK, male vocal / instrumental group — 13 wks

11 Jun 69	★ SOMETHING IN THE AIR Track 604-031	1	12
27 Jun 70	ACCIDENTS Track 2094 001	46	1

THUNDERTHIGHS UK, female vocal group — 5 wks

22 Jun 74	CENTRAL PARK ARREST Philips 6006 386	30	5

Bobby THURSTON US, male vocalist — 10 wks

29 Mar 80	● CHECK OUT THE GROOVE Epic EPC 8348	10	10

TIFFANY US, female vocalist — 45 wks

16 Jan 88	★ I THINK WE'RE ALONE NOW MCA MCA 1211	1	13
19 Mar 88	● COULD'VE BEEN MCA TIFF 2	4	9
4 Jun 88	● I SAW HIM STANDING THERE MCA TIFF 3	8	7
6 Aug 88	FEELINGS OF FOREVER MCA TIFF 4	52	2
12 Nov 88	RADIO ROMANCE MCA TIFF 5	13	11
11 Feb 89	ALL THIS TIME MCA TIFF 6	47	3

TIGER UK / Ireland, male / female vocal / instrumental group — 3 wks

31 Aug 96	RACE Trade 2 TRDCD 004	37	2
16 Nov 96	MY PUPPET PAL Trade 2 TRDCD 005	62	1

TIGERTAILZ US, male vocal / instrumental group — 2 wks

24 Jun 89	LOVE BOMB BABY Music For Nations KUT 132	75	1
16 Feb 91	HEAVEN Music For Nations KUT 137	71	1

TIGHT FIT UK, male / female vocal group — 49 wks

18 Jul 81	● BACK TO THE SIXTIES Jive JIVE 002	4	11
26 Sep 81	BACK TO THE SIXTIES PART II Jive JIVE 005	33	5
23 Jan 82	★ THE LION SLEEPS TONIGHT Jive JIVE 9	1	15
1 May 82	● FANTASY ISLAND Jive JIVE 13	5	12
31 Jul 82	SECRET HEART Jive JIVE 20	41	6

TIJUANA BRASS – See Herb ALPERT

TIK and TOK UK, male vocal duo — 2 wks

8 Oct 83	COOL RUNNING Survival SUR 016	69	2

Tanita TIKARAM UK, female vocalist — 29 wks

30 Jul 88	● GOOD TRADITION WEA YZ 196	10	10
22 Oct 88	TWIST IN MY SOBRIETY WEA YZ 321	22	8
14 Jan 89	CATHEDRAL SONG WEA YZ 331	48	3
18 Mar 89	WORLD OUTSIDE YOUR WINDOW WEA YZ 363	58	3
13 Jan 90	WE ALMOST GOT IT TOGETHER WEA YZ 443	52	3
9 Feb 91	ONLY THE ONES WE LOVE East West YZ 558	69	1
4 Feb 95	I MIGHT BE CRYING East West YZ 879CD	64	2

Johnny TILLOTSON US, male vocalist — 50 wks

1 Dec 60	★ POETRY IN MOTION London HLA 9231	1	15
2 Feb 61	JIMMY'S GIRL London HLA 9275	50	1
16 Feb 61	JIMMY'S GIRL (re-entry) London HLA 9275	43	1
12 Jul 62	IT KEEPS RIGHT ON A HURTIN' London HLA 9550	31	10
4 Oct 62	SEND ME THE PILLOW YOU DREAM ON London HLA 9598	21	10
27 Dec 62	I CAN'T HELP IT London HLA 9642	42	1
10 Jan 63	I CAN'T HELP IT (re-entry) London HLA 9642	47	1
24 Jan 63	I CAN'T HELP IT (2nd re-entry) London HLA 9642	41	4
9 May 63	OUT OF MY MIND London HLA 9695	34	5
14 Apr 79	POETRY IN MOTION (re-issue)/PRINCESS PRINCESS Lightning LIG 9016	67	2

TILT UK, male instrumental / production group — 1 wk

2 Dec 95	I DREAM Perfecto PERF 112CD	69	1

TIMBUK 3 US, male / female vocal / instrumental duo — 7 wks

31 Jan 87	THE FUTURE'S SO BRIGHT I GOTTA WEAR SHADES IRS IRM 126	21	7

TIME FREQUENCY
UK, male instrumental / production group   **33 wks**

6 Jun 92	**REAL LOVE** *Jive JIVET 307*	**60**	1
9 Jan 93	**NEW EMOTION** *Internal Affairs KGBCD 009*	**36**	6
12 Jun 93	**THE ULTIMATE HIGH / THE POWER ZONE** *Internal Affairs KGBD 010*	**17**	11
6 Nov 93	● **REAL LOVE (re-mix)** *Internal Affairs KGBCD 011*	**8**	6
1 Jan 94	**REAL LOVE (re-entry of re-mix)** *Internal Affairs KGBCD 011*	**71**	2
28 May 94	**SUCH A PHANTASY** *Internal Affairs KGBD 013*	**25**	4
8 Oct 94	**DREAMSCAPE '94** *Internal Affairs KGBD 015*	**32**	3

TIME OF THE MUMPH
UK, male producer – Mark Mumford   **1 wk**

11 Feb 95	**CONTROL** *Fresh FRSHD 24*	**69**	1

TIME UK
UK, male vocal / instrumental group   **3 wks**

8 Oct 83	**THE CABARET** *Red Bus/Aroadia TIM 123*	**63**	3

TIME ZONE
UK / US, male vocal / instrumental duo   **9 wks**

19 Jan 85	**WORLD DESTRUCTION** *Virgin VS 743*	**44**	9

TIMEBOX
UK, male vocal / instrumental group   **4 wks**

24 Jul 68	**BEGGIN'** *Deram DM 194*	**38**	4

TIMELORDS
UK, male / female vocal / instrumental group   **9 wks**

4 Jun 88	★ **DOCTORIN' THE TARDIS** *KLF Communications KLF 003*	**1**	9

TIMEX SOCIAL CLUB
US, male vocal / instrumental group   **9 wks**

13 Sep 86	**RUMORS** *Cooltempo COOL 133*	**13**	9

TIN MACHINE
US / UK, male vocal / instrumental group   **10 wks**

1 Jul 89	**UNDER THE GOD** *EMI-USA MT 68*	**51**	2
9 Sep 89	**TIN MACHINE / MAGGIE'S FARM (LIVE)** *EMI-USA MT 73*	**48**	2
24 Aug 91	**YOU BELONG IN ROCK 'N' ROLL** *London LON 305*	**33**	3
2 Nov 91	**BABY UNIVERSAL** *London LON 310*	**48**	3

Maggie's Farm (Live) was only listed for the week of 16 Sep.

TIN TIN OUT
UK, male instrumental / production duo   **7 wks**

13 Aug 94	**THE FEELING** *Deep Distraxion OILYCD 029* [1]	**32**	2
25 Mar 95	**ALWAYS SOMETHING THERE TO REMIND ME** *WEA YZ 911CD* [2]	**14**	5

[1] Tin Tin Out featuring Sweet Tee [2] Tin Tin Out featuring Espiritu

TINA – *See Tina TURNER*

TINDERSTICKS
UK, male vocal / instrumental group   **3 wks**

5 Feb 94	**KATHLEEN (EP)** *This Way Up WAY 2833CD*	**61**	1
18 Mar 95	**NO MORE AFFAIRS** *This Way Up WAY 3833*	**58**	1
12 Aug 95	**TRAVELLING LIGHT** *This Way Up WAY 4533*	**51**	1

Tracks on Kathleen (EP): Kathleen / Summat Moon / A Sweet Man / E-Type Joe.

TINGO TANGO
UK, male instrumental group   **2 wks**

21 Jul 90	**IT IS JAZZ** *Champion CHAMP 250*	**68**	2

TINMAN
UK, male producer – Paul Dakeyne   **9 wks**

20 Aug 94	● **EIGHTEEN STRINGS** *ffrr FCD 242*	**9**	8
3 Jun 95	**GUDVIBE** *ffrr FCD 262*	**49**	1

TINY TIM
US, male vocalist   **1 wk**

5 Feb 69	**GREAT BALLS OF FIRE** *Reprise RS 20802*	**45**	1

TITANIC
Norway / UK, male instrumental group   **12 wks**

25 Sep 71	● **SULTANA** *CBS 5365*	**5**	12

TITIYO
Sweden, female vocalist   **6 wks**

3 Mar 90	**AFTER THE RAIN** *Arista 112722*	**60**	3
6 Oct 90	**FLOWERS** *Arista 113212*	**71**	1
5 Feb 94	**TELL ME I'M NOT DREAMING** *Arista 74321185622*	**45**	2

Cara TIVEY – *See Billy BRAGG*

TLC
US, female vocal group   **44 wks**

20 Jun 92	**AIN'T 2 PROUD 2 BEG** *Arista 115265*	**13**	5
22 Aug 92	**BABY-BABY-BABY** *LaFace 74321111297*	**55**	3
24 Oct 92	**WHAT ABOUT YOUR FRIENDS** *LaFace 74321118177*	**59**	2
21 Jan 95	**CREEP** *LaFace 74321254212*	**22**	4
22 Apr 95	**RED LIGHT SPECIAL** *LaFace 74321273662*	**18**	4
5 Aug 95	● **WATERFALLS** *LaFace 74321298812*	**4**	14
4 Nov 95	**DIGGIN' ON YOU** *LaFace 74321319252*	**18**	5
13 Jan 96	● **CREEP (re-issue)** *LaFace 74321340942*	**6**	7

T99
Belgium, male instrumental / production group   **10 wks**

11 May 91	**ANASTHASIA** *XL XLS 19*	**14**	6
19 Oct 91	**NOCTURNE** *Emphasis 6574097*	**33**	4

TOADS – *See STAN FREBERG*

Art and Dotty TODD
US, male / female vocal duo   **7 wks**

13 Feb 53	● **BROKEN WINGS** *HMV B 10399*	**6**	7

TOGETHER
UK, male vocal / instrumental group   **8 wks**

4 Aug 90	**HARDCORE UPROAR** *ffrr F 143*	**12**	8

TOKENS
US, male vocal group   **12 wks**

21 Dec 61	**THE LION SLEEPS TONIGHT (WIMOWEH)** *RCA 1263*	**11**	12

TOKYO GHETTO PUSSY
Germany, male instrumental / production duo   **4 wks**

16 Sep 95	**EVERYBODY ON THE FLOOR (PUMP IT)** *Epic 6611132*	**26**	2
16 Mar 96	**I KISS YOUR LIPS** *Epic 6623212*	**55**	2

Duo are also known as Jam and Spoon. See also Jam and Spoon featuring Plavka.

TOL and TOL Holland, male vocal / instrumental duo — 2 wks

| 14 Apr 90 | ELENI Dover ROJ 5 | 73 | 2 |

TOM TOM CLUB
US, female / male vocal / instrumental group — 20 wks

20 Jun 81	● WORDY RAPPINGHOOD Island WIP 6694	7	9
10 Oct 81	GENIUS OF LOVE Island WIP 6735	65	2
7 Aug 82	UNDER THE BOARDWALK Island WIP 6762	22	9

Satoshi TOMIIE – See Frankie KNUCKLES

TONGUE 'N' CHEEK
UK, male / female vocal / instrumental group — 28 wks

27 Feb 88	NOBODY (CAN LOVE ME) Criminal BUS 6 [1]	59	6
25 Nov 89	ENCORE Syncopate SY 33	41	4
14 Apr 90	TOMORROW Syncopate SY 34	20	7
4 Aug 90	NOBODY Syncopate SY 37	37	5
19 Jan 91	FORGET ME NOTS Syncopate SY 39	26	6

[1] Tongue In Cheek

TONIGHT UK, male vocal / instrumental group — 10 wks

| 28 Jan 78 | DRUMMER MAN Target TDS 1 | 14 | 8 |
| 20 May 78 | MONEY THAT'S YOUR PROBLEM Target TDS 2 | 66 | 2 |

TONY! TONI! TONÉ! US, male vocal group — 10 wks

30 Jun 90	OAKLAND STROKE Wing WING 7	50	5
9 Mar 91	IT NEVER RAINS (IN SOUTHERN CALIFORNIA) Wing WING 10	69	2
4 Sep 93	IF I HAD NO LOOT Polydor PZCD 292	44	3

TOO TOUGH TEE – See DYNAMIX featuring TOO TOUGH TEE

TOP UK, male vocal / instrumental group — 2 wks

| 20 Jul 91 | NUMBER ONE DOMINATOR Island IS 496 | 67 | 2 |

TOP LINERS – See Rocky SHARPE and the REPLAYS

TOPOL Israel, male vocalist — 20 wks

| 20 Apr 67 | ● IF I WERE A RICH MAN CBS 202651 | 9 | 20 |

Mel TORMÉ US, male vocalist — 32 wks

27 Apr 56	MOUNTAIN GREENERY Vogue/Coral Q 72150	15	11
27 Jul 56	● MOUNTAIN GREENERY (re-entry) Vogue/Coral Q 72150	4	13
3 Jan 63	COMING HOME BABY London HLK 9643	13	8

TORNADOS UK, male instrumental group — 59 wks

30 Aug 62	★ TELSTAR Decca F 11494	1	25
10 Jan 63	● GLOBETROTTER Decca F 11562	5	11
21 Mar 63	ROBOT Decca F 11606	17	12
6 Jun 63	THE ICE CREAM MAN Decca F 11662	18	9
10 Oct 63	DRAGONFLY Decca F 11745	41	2

Mitchell TOROK US, male vocalist — 19 wks

28 Sep 56	● WHEN MEXICO GAVE UP THE RUMBA Brunswick 05586	6	17
11 Jan 57	RED LIGHT GREEN LIGHT Brunswick 05626	29	1
1 Feb 57	WHEN MEXICO GAVE UP THE RUMBA (re-entry) Brunswick 05586	30	1

Peter TOSH Jamaica, male vocalist — 12 wks

| 21 Oct 78 | (YOU GOTTA WALK) DON'T LOOK BACK Rolling Stones 2859 | 43 | 7 |
| 2 Apr 83 | JOHNNY B. GOODE EMI RIC 115 | 48 | 5 |

TOTAL US, female vocal group — 4 wks

| 15 Jul 95 | CAN'T YOU SEE Tommy Boy TBCD 700 [1] | 43 | 2 |
| 14 Sep 96 | KISSIN' YOU Arista 74321404172 | 29 | 2 |

[1] Total featuring Notorious BIG

TOTAL CONTRAST UK, male vocal / instrumental duo — 22 wks

3 Aug 85	TAKES A LITTLE TIME London LON 71	17	10
19 Oct 85	HIT AND RUN London LON 76	41	5
1 Mar 86	THE RIVER London LON 83	44	3
10 May 86	WHAT YOU GONNA DO ABOUT IT London LON 95	63	4

TOTO US, male vocal / instrumental group — 35 wks

10 Feb 79	HOLD THE LINE CBS 6784	14	11
5 Feb 83	• AFRICA CBS A 2510	3	10
9 Apr 83	ROSANNA CBS A 2079	12	8
18 Jun 83	I WON'T HOLD YOU BACK CBS A 3392	37	5
18 Nov 95	I WILL REMEMBER Columbia 6626552	64	1

TOTO COELO UK, female vocal group — 14 wks

| 7 Aug 82 | ● I EAT CANNIBALS PART 1 Radialchoice TIC 10 | 8 | 10 |
| 13 Nov 82 | DRACULA'S TANGO / MUCHO MACHO Radialchoice TIC 11 | 54 | 4 |

TOTTENHAM HOTSPUR F.A. CUP FINAL SQUAD UK, male football team vocalists — 23 wks

9 May 81	● OSSIE'S DREAM (SPURS ARE ON THEIR WAY TO WEMBLEY) Shelf SHELF 1	5	8
1 May 82	TOTTENHAM TOTTENHAM Shelf SHELF 2	19	7
9 May 87	HOT SHOT TOTTENHAM! Rainbow RBR 16	18	5
11 May 91	WHEN THE YEAR ENDS IN 1 A1 A 1324	44	3

All hits feature the vocal and instrumental talents of Chas and Dave.

TOUCH OF SOUL
UK, male / female vocal / instrumental group — 3 wks

| 19 May 90 | WE GOT THE LOVE Cooltempo COOL 204 | 46 | 3 |

TOURISTS UK, male / female vocal / instrumental group — 40 wks

9 Jun 79	BLIND AMONG THE FLOWERS Logo GO 350	52	5
8 Sep 79	THE LONELIEST MAN IN THE WORLD Logo GO 360	32	7
10 Nov 79	● I ONLY WANT TO BE WITH YOU Logo GO 370	4	14
9 Feb 80	● SO GOOD TO BE BACK HOME AGAIN Logo TOUR 1	8	9
18 Oct 80	DON'T SAY I TOLD YOU SO RCA TOUR 2	40	5

Carol Lynn TOWNES US, female vocalist — 7 wks

| 4 Aug 84 | 99 1/2 Polydor POSP 693 | 47 | 4 |
| 19 Jan 85 | BELIEVE IN THE BEAT Polydor POSP 720 | 56 | 3 |

Pete TOWNSHEND UK, male vocalist   17 wks

5 Apr 80	ROUGH BOYS Atco K 11460	39	6
21 Jun 80	LET MY LOVE OPEN THE DOOR Atco K 11486	46	6
21 Aug 82	UNIFORMS (CORPS D'ESPRIT) Atco K 11751	48	5

TOXIC TWO US, male instrumental / production duo   6 wks

7 Mar 92	RAVE GENERATOR PWL International PWL 223	13	6

TOY DOLLS UK, male vocal / instrumental group   12 wks

1 Dec 84	● NELLIE THE ELEPHANT Volume VOL 11	4	12

TOYAH UK, female vocalist   87 wks

14 Feb 81	● FOUR FROM TOYAH EP Safari TOY 1	4	14
16 May 81	● I WANT TO BE FREE Safari SAFE 34	8	11
3 Oct 81	● THUNDER IN THE MOUNTAINS Safari SAFE 38	4	9
28 Nov 81	FOUR MORE FROM TOYAH EP Safari TOY 2	14	9
22 May 82	BRAVE NEW WORLD Safari SAFE 45	21	8
17 Jul 82	IEYA Safari SAFE 28	48	5
9 Oct 82	BE PROUD BE LOUD (BE HEARD) Safari SAFE 52	30	7
24 Sep 83	REBEL RUN Safari SAFE 56	24	5
19 Nov 83	THE VOW Safari SAFE 58	50	5
27 Apr 85	DON'T FALL IN LOVE (I SAID) Portrait A 6160	22	6
29 Jun 85	SOUL PASSING THROUGH SOUL Portrait A 6359	57	3
25 Apr 87	ECHO BEACH EG EGO 31	54	5

Tracks on Four From Toyah EP: It's A Mystery / Revelations / War Boys / Angels And Demons. Tracks on Four More From Toyah EP: Good Morning Universe / Urban Tribesman / In The Fairground / The Furious Futures.

TOYS US, female vocal group   17 wks

4 Nov 65	● A LOVER'S CONCERTO Stateside SS 460	5	13
27 Jan 66	ATTACK Stateside SS 483	36	4

T'PAU UK, male / female vocal / instrumental group   77 wks

8 Aug 87	● HEART AND SOUL Siren SRN 41	4	13
24 Oct 87	★ CHINA IN YOUR HAND Siren SRN 64	1	15
30 Jan 88	● VALENTINE Siren SRN 69	9	8
2 Apr 88	SEX TALK (LIVE) Siren SRN 80	23	7
25 Jun 88	I WILL BE WITH YOU Siren SRN 87	14	6
1 Oct 88	SECRET GARDEN Siren SRN 93	18	7
3 Dec 88	ROAD TO OUR DREAM Siren SRN 100	42	6
25 Mar 89	ONLY THE LONELY Siren SRN 107	28	6
18 May 91	WHENEVER YOU NEED ME Siren SRN 140	16	6
27 Jul 91	WALK ON AIR Siren SRN 142	62	2
20 Feb 93	VALENTINE (re-issue) Virgin VALEG 1	53	1

TRACIE UK, female vocalist   24 wks

26 Mar 83	● THE HOUSE THAT JACK BUILT Respond KOB 701	9	8
16 Jul 83	GIVE IT SOME EMOTION Respond KOB 704	24	9
14 Apr 84	SOUL'S ON FIRE Respond KOB 708	73	2
9 Jun 84	(I LOVE YOU) WHEN YOU SLEEP Respond KOB 710	59	3
17 Aug 85	I CAN'T LEAVE YOU ALONE Respond SBS 1 [1]	60	2

[1] Tracie Young

TRACY – See MASSIVO featuring TRACY

Jeanie TRACY US, female vocalist   3 wks

11 Jun 94	IF THIS IS LOVE Pulse 8 CDLOSE 63	73	1
5 Nov 94	DO YOU BELIEVE IN THE WONDER Pulse 8 CDLOSE 74	57	1
13 May 95	IT'S A MAN'S MAN'S MAN'S WORLD Pulse 8 CDLOSE 89 [1]	73	1

[1] Jeanie Tracy and Bobby Womack

TRAFFIC UK, male vocal / instrumental group   40 wks

1 Jun 67	● PAPER SUN Island WIP 6002	5	10
6 Sep 67	● HOLE IN MY SHOE Island WIP 6017	2	14
29 Nov 67	● HERE WE GO ROUND THE MULBERRY BUSH Island WIP 6025	8	12
6 Mar 68	NO FACE, NO NAME, NO NUMBER Island WIP 6030	40	4

TRAMAINE US, female vocalist   2 wks

5 Oct 85	FALL DOWN (SPIRIT OF LOVE) A & M AM 281	60	2

TRAMMPS US, male vocal group   55 wks

23 Nov 74	ZING WENT THE STRINGS OF MY HEART Buddah BDS 405	29	10
1 Feb 75	SIXTY MINUTE MAN Buddah BDS 415	40	4
11 Oct 75	● HOLD BACK THE NIGHT Buddah BDS 437	5	6
13 Mar 76	THAT'S WHERE THE HAPPY PEOPLE GO Atlantic K 10703	35	8
24 Jul 76	SOUL SEARCHIN' TIME Atlantic K 10797	42	3
14 May 77	DISCO INFERNO Atlantic K 10914	16	7
24 Jun 78	DISCO INFERNO (re-issue) Atlantic K 11135	47	10
12 Dec 92	HOLD BACK THE NIGHT Network NWK 65 [1]	30	5

[1] KWS featuring guest vocals from the Trammps

TRANSFORMER 2
Belgium / Holland, male / female vocal / instrumental group   1 wk

24 Feb 96	JUST CAN'T GET ENOUGH Positiva CDTIV 49	45	1

TRANSVISION VAMP
UK, female / male vocal / instrumental group   59 wks

16 Apr 88	TELL THAT GIRL TO SHUT UP MCA TVV 2	45	3
25 Jun 88	● I WANT YOUR LOVE MCA TVV 3	5	13
17 Sep 88	REVOLUTION BABY MCA TVV 4	30	5
19 Nov 88	SISTER MOON MCA TVV 5	41	5
1 Apr 89	● BABY I DON'T CARE MCA TVV 6	3	11
10 Jun 89	THE ONLY ONE MCA TVV 7	15	6
5 Aug 89	LANDSLIDE OF LOVE MCA TVV 8	14	5
4 Nov 89	BORN TO BE SOLD MCA TVV 9	22	4
13 Apr 91	(I JUST WANNA) B WITH U MCA TVV 10	30	4
22 Jun 91	IF LOOKS COULD KILL MCA TVV 11	41	3

TRANS-X
Canada, female / male vocal / instrumental group   9 wks

13 Jul 85	● LIVING ON VIDEO Boiling Point POSP 650	9	9

TRASH UK, male vocal / instrumental group   3 wks

25 Oct 69	GOLDEN SLUMBERS / CARRY THAT WEIGHT Apple 17	35	3

TRASH CAN SINATRAS
UK, male vocal / instrumental group   1 wk

24 Apr 93	HAYFEVER Go! Discs GODCD 98	61	1

TRAVELING WILBURYS
UK / US, male vocal / instrumental group **19 wks**

29 Oct 88	**HANDLE WITH CARE** *Wilbury W 7732*	**21** 13
11 Mar 89	**END OF THE LINE** *Wilbury W 7637*	**52** 4
30 Jun 90	**NOBODY'S CHILD** *Wilbury W 9773*	**44** 2

Randy TRAVIS *US, male vocalist* **6 wks**

21 May 88	**FOREVER AND EVER, AMEN** *Warner Bros. W 8384*	**55** 6

John TRAVOLTA *US, male vocalist* **81 wks**

20 May 78	★ **YOU'RE THE ONE THAT I WANT** *RSO 006* 1	**1** 26
16 Sep 78	★ **SUMMER NIGHTS** *RSO 18* 1	**1** 19
7 Oct 78	● **SANDY** *Polydor POSP 6*	**2** 15
2 Dec 78	**GREASED LIGHTNIN'** *Polydor POSP 14*	**11** 9
22 Dec 90	● **GREASE MEGAMIX** *Polydor PO 114* 1	**3** 10
23 Mar 91	**GREASE – THE DREAM MIX** *PWL/Polydor PO 136* 2	**47** 2

1 John Travolta and Olivia Newton-John 2 Frankie Valli, John Travolta and Olivia Newton-John

TREMELOES *UK, male vocal / instrumental group* **131 wks**

2 Feb 67	● **HERE COMES MY BABY** *CBS 202519*	**4** 11
27 Apr 67	★ **SILENCE IS GOLDEN** *CBS 2723*	**1** 15
2 Aug 67	● **EVEN THE BAD TIMES ARE GOOD** *CBS 2930*	**4** 13
8 Nov 67	**BE MINE** *CBS 3043*	**39** 2
17 Jan 68	● **SUDDENLY YOU LOVE ME** *CBS 3234*	**6** 11
8 May 68	**HELULE HELULE** *CBS 2889*	**14** 9
18 Sep 68	● **MY LITTLE LADY** *CBS 3680*	**6** 12
11 Dec 68	**I SHALL BE RELEASED** *CBS 3873*	**29** 5
19 Mar 69	**HELLO WORLD** *CBS 4065*	**14** 8
1 Nov 69	● **(CALL ME) NUMBER ONE** *CBS 4582*	**2** 14
21 Mar 70	**BY THE WAY** *CBS 4815*	**35** 6
12 Sep 70	● **ME AND MY LIFE** *CBS 5139*	**4** 18
10 Jul 71	**HELLO BUDDY** *CBS 7294*	**32** 7

See also Brian Poole and the Tremeloes.

Jackie TRENT *UK, female vocalist* **17 wks**

22 Apr 65	★ **WHERE ARE YOU NOW (MY LOVE)** *Pye 7N 15776*	**1** 11
1 Jul 65	**WHEN THE SUMMERTIME IS OVER** *Pye 7N 15865*	**39** 2
2 Apr 69	**I'LL BE THERE** *Pye 7N 17693*	**38** 4

Ralph TRESVANT *US, male vocalist* **21 wks**

12 Jan 91	**SENSITIVITY** *MCA MCS 1462*	**18** 8
15 Aug 92	● **THE BEST THINGS IN LIFE ARE FREE** *Perspective PERSS 7400* 1	**2** 13

1 Luther Vandross and Janet Jackson with special guests BBD and Ralph Tresvant

TRI *UK, male vocal / instrumental group* **1 wk**

2 Sep 95	**WE GOT THE LOVE** *Epic 6623642*	**61** 1

TRIBAL HOUSE *US, male vocal / instrumental group* **2 wks**

3 Feb 90	**MOTHERLAND-A-FRI-CA** *Cooltempo COOL 198*	**57** 2

Tony TRIBE *Jamaica, male vocalist* **2 wks**

16 Jul 69	**RED RED WINE** *Downtown DT 419*	**50** 1
9 Aug 69	**RED RED WINE (re-entry)** *Downtown DT 419*	**46** 1

A TRIBE CALLED QUEST *US, male rap group* **15 wks**

18 Aug 90	**BONITA APPLEBUM** *Jive JIVE 256*	**47** 3
19 Jan 91	**CAN I KICK IT** *Jive JIVE 265*	**15** 7
11 Jun 94	**OH MY GOD** *Jive JIVECD 355*	**68** 1
13 Jul 96	**1NCE AGAIN** *Jive JIVECD 399*	**34** 2
23 Nov 96	**STRESSED OUT** *Jive JIVECD 404* 1	**33** 2

1 A Tribe Called Quest featuring Faith Evans and Raphael Saadiq

TRIBE OF TOFFS *UK, male vocal / instrumental group* **5 wks**

24 Dec 88	**JOHN KETTLEY (IS A WEATHERMAN)** *Completely Different DAFT 1*	**21** 5

TRICKBABY *UK, femal vocal / instrumental group* **2 wks**

12 Oct 96	**INDIE-YARN** *Logic 74321423152*	**47** 2

TRICKY *UK, male vocalist / multi-instrumentalist* **20 wks**

5 Feb 94	**AFTERMATH** *Fourth & Broadway BRCD 288*	**69** 1
28 Jan 95	**OVERCOME** *Fourth & Broadway BRCD 304*	**34** 3
15 Apr 95	**BLACK STEEL** *Fourth & Broadway BRCD 320*	**28** 3
5 Aug 95	**THE HELL EP** *Fourth & Broadway BRCD 326* 1	**12** 3
11 Nov 95	**PUMPKIN** *Fourth & Broadway BRCD 330*	**26** 2
9 Nov 96	**CHRISTIANSANDS** *Fourth & Broadway BRCD 340*	**36** 2
23 Nov 96	● **MILK** *Mushroom D 1494* 2	**10†** 6

1 Tricky vs the Gravediggaz 2 Garbage featuring Tricky

Tracks on The Hell EP: Hell Is Round The Corner / Hell Is Round The Corner (remix) / Psychosis / Tonite Is A Special Nite.

TRICKY DISCO
UK, male / female instrmental / production duo **10 wks**

28 Jul 90	**TRICKY DISCO** *Warp WAP 7*	**14** 8
20 Apr 91	**HOUSE FLY** *Warp 7WAP 11*	**55** 2

See also GTO; Technohead. All three are the same act.

TRIFFIDS
Australia, male / female vocal / instrumental group **1 wk**

6 Feb 88	**A TRICK OF THE LIGHT** *Island IS 350*	**73** 1

TRINIDAD OIL COMPANY
Trinidad, male / female vocal / instrumental group **5 wks**

21 May 77	**THE CALENDAR SONG** *Harvest HAR 5122*	**34** 5

TRINITY – *See Julie DRISCOLL, Brian AUGER and the TRINITY*

TRIO *Germany, male vocal / instrumental group* **10 wks**

3 Jul 82	● **DA DA DA** *Mobile Suit Corporat CORP 5*	**2** 10

TRIPPING DAISY *US, male vocal / instrumental group* **1 wk**

30 Mar 96	**PIRANHA** *Island CID 638*	**72** 1

TRIUMPH *Canada, male vocal / instrumental group* **2 wks**

22 Nov 80	**I LIVE FOR THE WEEKEND** *RCA 13*	**59** 2

TROGGS UK, male vocal / instrumental group — 87 wks

5 May 66	●	**WILD THING** Fontana TF 689	**2**	12
14 Jul 66	★	**WITH A GIRL LIKE YOU** Fontana TF 717	**1**	12
29 Sep 66	●	**I CAN'T CONTROL MYSELF** Page One POF 001	**2**	14
15 Dec 66	●	**ANY WAY THAT YOU WANT ME** Page One POF 010	**8**	10
16 Feb 67		**GIVE IT TO ME** Page One POF 015	**12**	10
1 Jun 67		**NIGHT OF THE LONG GRASS** Page One POF 022	**17**	6
26 Jul 67		**HI HI HAZEL** Page One POF 030	**42**	3
18 Oct 67	●	**LOVE IS ALL AROUND** Page One POF 040	**5**	14
28 Feb 68		**LITTLE GIRL** Page One POF 056	**37**	4
30 Oct 93		**WILD THING** Weekend CDWEEK 103 [1]	**69**	2

[1] Troggs and Wolf

Wild Thing in '93 is a re-recording and was listed with the flip side, War, by Edwin Starr and Shadow.

TRONIKHOUSE US, male producer – Kevin Saunderson — 1 wk

14 Mar 92	**UP TEMPO** KMS UK KMSUK 1	**68**	1

TROUBADOURS DU ROI BAUDOUIN
Zaire, male / female vocal group — 11 wks

19 Mar 69	**SANCTUS (MISSA LUBA)** Philips BF 1732	**28**	6
7 May 69	**SANCTUS (MISSA LUBA) (re-entry)** Philips BF 1732	**37**	5

TROUBLE FUNK US, male vocal / instrumental group — 3 wks

27 Jun 87	**WOMAN OF PRINCIPLE** Fourth & Broadway BRW 70	**65**	3

Doris TROY US, female vocalist — 12 wks

19 Nov 64	**WHATCHA GONNA DO ABOUT IT** Atlantic AT 4011	**37**	7
21 Jan 65	**WHATCHA GONNA DO ABOUT IT (re-entry)** Atlantic AT 4011	**38**	5

Elizabeth TROY – See SOUNDMAN and David LLOYDIE featuring Elizabeth TROY

TRUCE UK, female vocal group — 2 wks

2 Sep 95	**THE FINEST** Big Life BLRD 118	**54**	1
30 Mar 96	**CELEBRATION OF LIFE** Big Life BLRD 126	**51**	1

TRUCKIN' CO. – See Garnet MIMMS and TRUCKIN' CO.

Andrea TRUE CONNECTION
US, female vocalist, male instrumental backing group — 16 wks

17 Apr 76	●	**MORE MORE MORE** Buddah BDS 442	**5**	10
4 Mar 78		**WHAT'S YOUR NAME WHAT'S YOUR NUMBER** Buddah BDS 467	**34**	6

TRUE FAITH with FINAL CUT
US, male / female vocal / instrumental group — 4 wks

2 Mar 91	**TAKE ME AWAY** Network NWK 20	**51**	4

TRUE IMAGE – See Monie LOVE

TRUSSEL US, male vocal / instrumental group — 4 wks

8 Mar 80	**LOVE INJECTION** Elektra K 12412	**43**	4

TRUTH UK, male vocal duo — 6 wks

3 Feb 66	**GIRL** Pye 7N 17035	**27**	6

TRUTH UK, male vocal / instrumental group — 16 wks

11 Jun 83	**CONFUSION (HITS US EVERY TIME)** Formation TRUTH 1	**22**	7
27 Aug 83	**A STEP IN THE RIGHT DIRECTION** Formation TRUTH 2	**32**	7
4 Feb 84	**NO STONE UNTURNED** Formation TRUTH 3	**66**	2

TSD UK, female vocal group — 2 wks

17 Feb 96	**HEART AND SOUL** Avex UK AVEXCD 21	**69**	1
30 Mar 96	**BABY I LOVE YOU** Avex UK AVEXCD 34	**64**	1

TUBES US, male vocal / instrumental group — 18 wks

19 Nov 77	**WHITE PUNKS ON DOPE** A & M AMS 7323	**28**	4
28 Apr 79	**PRIME TIME** A & M AMS 7423	**34**	10
12 Sep 81	**DON'T WANT TO WAIT ANYMORE** Capitol CL 208	**60**	4

TUBEWAY ARMY – See Gary NUMAN

Barbara TUCKER US, female vocalist — 6 wks

5 Mar 94	**BEAUTIFUL PEOPLE** Positiva CDTIV 11	**23**	3
26 Nov 94	**I GET LIFTED** Positiva CDTIV 23	**33**	2
23 Sep 95	**STAY TOGETHER** Positiva CDTIV 39	**46**	1

Junior TUCKER UK, male vocalist — 2 wks

2 Jun 90	**DON'T TEST** 10 TEN 299	**54**	2

Louise TUCKER UK, female vocalist — 5 wks

9 Apr 83	**MIDNIGHT BLUE** Ariola ARO 289	**59**	5

Tommy TUCKER US, male vocalist — 10 wks

26 Mar 64	**HI-HEEL SNEAKERS** Pye 7N 25238	**23**	10

Claramae TURNER – See VARIOUS ARTISTS (EPs & LPs) – Carousel Soundtrack

Ike and Tina TURNER
US, male / female vocal instrumental duo — 44 wks

9 Jun 66	●	**RIVER DEEP MOUNTAIN HIGH** London HL 10046	**3**	13
28 Jul 66		**TELL HER I'M NOT HOME** Warner Bros. WB 5753	**48**	1
27 Oct 66		**A LOVE LIKE YOURS** London HL 10083	**16**	10
12 Feb 69		**RIVER DEEP MOUNTAIN HIGH (re-issue)** London HLU 10242	**33**	7
8 Sep 73	●	**NUTBUSH CITY LIMITS** United Artists UP 35582	**4**	13

See also Tina Turner.

Ruby TURNER UK, female vocalist — 31 wks

25 Jan 86	**IF YOU'RE READY (COME GO WITH ME)** Jive JIVE 109 [1]	**30**	7
29 Mar 86	**I'M IN LOVE** Jive JIVE 118	**61**	4
13 Sep 86	**BYE BABY** Jive JIVE 126	**52**	3
14 Mar 87	**I'D RATHER GO BLIND** Jive RTS 1	**24**	8
16 May 87	**I'M IN LOVE (re-issue)** Jive RTS 2	**57**	2
13 Jan 90	**IT'S GONNA BE ALRIGHT** Jive RTS 7	**57**	3
5 Feb 94	**STAY WITH ME BABY** M & G MAGCD 53	**39**	3
9 Dec 95	**SHAKABOOM!** Telstar HUNTCD 1 [2]	**64**	1

[1] Ruby Turner featuring Jonathan Butler [2] Hunter featuring Ruby Turner

Sammy TURNER *US, male vocalist*   **2 wks**

13 Nov 59	ALWAYS *London HLX 8963*	**26**	2

Tina TURNER *US, female vocalist*   **213 wks**

19 Nov 83	● LET'S STAY TOGETHER *Capitol CL 316*	**6**	13
25 Feb 84	HELP *Capitol CL 325*	**40**	6
16 Jun 84	WHAT'S LOVE GOT TO DO WITH IT *Capitol CL 334*	**3**	16
15 Sep 84	BETTER BE GOOD TO ME *Capitol CL 338*	**45**	5
17 Nov 84	PRIVATE DANCER *Capitol CL 343*	**26**	9
2 Mar 85	I CAN'T STAND THE RAIN *Capitol CL 352*	**57**	3
20 Jul 85	● WE DON'T NEED ANOTHER HERO (THUNDERDOME) *Capitol CL 364*	**3**	12
12 Oct 85	ONE OF THE LIVING *Capitol CL 376*	**55**	2
2 Nov 85	IT'S ONLY LOVE *A & M AM 285* [1]	**29**	6
23 Aug 86	TYPICAL MALE *Capitol CL 419*	**33**	6
8 Nov 86	TWO PEOPLE *Capitol CL 430*	**43**	4
14 Mar 87	WHAT YOU GET IS WHAT YOU SEE *Capitol CL 439*	**30**	7
13 Jun 87	BREAK EVERY RULE *Capitol CL 452*	**43**	3
20 Jun 87	TEARING US APART *Duck W 8299* [2]	**56**	3
19 Mar 88	ADDICTED TO LOVE (LIVE) *Capitol CL 484*	**71**	2
2 Sep 89	● THE BEST *Capitol CL 543*	**5**	12
18 Nov 89	● I DON'T WANNA LOSE YOU *Capitol CL 553*	**8**	11
17 Feb 90	STEAMY WINDOWS *Capitol CL 560*	**13**	6
11 Aug 90	LOOK ME IN THE HEART *Capitol CL 584*	**31**	6
13 Oct 90	BE TENDER WITH ME BABY *Capitol CL 593*	**28**	4
24 Nov 90	● IT TAKES TWO *Warner Bros. ROD 1* [3]	**5**	8
21 Sep 91	NUTBUSH CITY LIMITS *Capitol CL 630*	**23**	5
23 Nov 91	WAY OF THE WORLD *Capitol CL 637*	**13**	7
15 Feb 92	LOVE THING *Capitol CL 644*	**29**	4
6 Jun 92	I WANT YOU NEAR ME *Capitol CL 659*	**22**	4
22 May 93	● I DON'T WANNA FIGHT *Parlophone CDRS 6346*	**7**	9
28 Aug 93	DISCO INFERNO *Parlophone CDR 6357*	**12**	6
30 Oct 93	WHY MUST WE WAIT UNTIL TONIGHT *Parlophone CDR 6366*	**16**	4
18 Nov 95	● GOLDENEYE *Parlophone CDR 0071001*	**10**	9
23 Mar 96	WHATEVER YOU WANT *Parlophone CDR 6429* [4]	**23**	6
8 Jun 96	ON SILENT WINGS *Parlophone CDR 6434*	**13**	6
27 Jul 96	MISSING YOU *Parlophone CDR 6441*	**12**	5
19 Oct 96	SOMETHING BEAUTIFUL REMAINS *Parlophone CDR 6448*	**27**	2
21 Dec 96	IN YOUR WILDEST DREAMS *Parlophone CDR 6451* [5]	**32†**	2

[1] Bryan Adams and Tina Turner [2] Eric Clapton and Tina Turner
[3] Rod Stewart and Tina Turner [4] Tina [5] Tina Turner featuring
Barry White

See also Ike and Tina Turner.

TURNTABLE ORCHESTRA
US, male vocal / instrumental duo   **4 wks**

21 Jan 89	YOU'RE GONNA MISS ME *Republic LIC 012*	**52**	4

TURTLES *US, male vocal / instrumental group*   **39 wks**

23 Mar 67	HAPPY TOGETHER *London HL 10115*	**12**	12
15 Jun 67	● SHE'D RATHER BE WITH ME *London HLU 10135*	**4**	15
30 Oct 68	● ELENORE *London HL 10223*	**7**	12

TUXEDOS - *See Bobby ANGELO and the TUXEDOS*

T.W.A. *UK, male instrumental / production group*   **1 wk**

16 Sep 95	NASTY GIRLS *Mercury MERCD 441*	**51**	1

TWEETS *UK, male instrumental group*   **34 wks**

12 Sep 81	● BIRDIE SONG (THE BIRDIE DANCE) *PRT 7P 219*	**2**	23

5 Dec 81	LET'S ALL SING LIKE THE BIRDIES SING *PRT 7P 226*	**44**	6
18 Dec 82	THE BIRDIE SONG (BIRDIE DANCE) (re-entry) *PRT 7P 219*	**46**	5

20 FINGERS *US, male instrumental / production duo*   **14 wks**

26 Nov 94	SHORT DICK MAN *Multiply CDMULT 12* [1]	**21**	4
30 Sep 95	SHORT SHORT MAN (re-mix) *Multiply CXMULTY 7* [1]	**11**	7
30 Sep 95	LICK IT *Zyx ZYX 75908* [2]	**48**	3

[1] 20 Fingers featuring Gillette [2] 20 Fingers featuring Roula

TWENTY 4 SEVEN – *See CAPTAIN HOLLYWOOD PROJECT*

TWICE AS MUCH *UK, male vocal duo*   **9 wks**

16 Jun 66	SITTIN' ON A FENCE *Immediate IM 033*	**25**	9

TWIGGY *UK, female vocalist*   **10 wks**

14 Aug 76	HERE I GO AGAIN *Mercury 6007 100*	**17**	10

TWIN HYPE *US, male rap duo*   **2 wks**

15 Jul 89	DO IT TO THE CROWD *Profile PROF 255*	**65**	2

TWINKLE *UK, female vocalist*   **20 wks**

26 Nov 64	● TERRY *Decca F 12013*	**4**	15
25 Feb 65	GOLDEN LIGHTS *Decca F 12076*	**21**	5

TWISTED SISTER
US, male vocal / instrumental group   **28 wks**

26 Mar 83	I AM (I'M ME) *Atlantic A 9854*	**18**	9
28 May 83	THE KIDS ARE BACK *Atlantic A 9827*	**32**	6
20 Aug 83	YOU CAN'T STOP ROCK 'N' ROLL *Atlantic A 9792*	**43**	4
2 Jun 84	WE'RE NOT GONNA TAKE IT *Atlantic A 9657*	**58**	6
18 Jan 86	LEADER OF THE PACK *Atlantic A 9478*	**47**	3

Conway TWITTY *US, male vocalist*   **36 wks**

14 Nov 58	★ IT'S ONLY MAKE BELIEVE *MGM 992*	**1**	15
27 Mar 59	STORY OF MY LOVE *MGM 1003*	**30**	1
21 Aug 59	● MONA LISA *MGM 1029*	**5**	14
21 Jul 60	IS A BLUE BIRD BLUE *MGM 1082*	**43**	3
23 Feb 61	C'EST SI BON *MGM 1118*	**40**	3

2 BAD MICE *UK, male instrumental / production group*   **4 wks**

15 Feb 92	HOLD IT DOWN *Moving Shadow SHADOW 14*	**70**	1
8 Aug 92	HOLD IT DOWN (re-entry) *Moving Shadow SHADOW 14*	**48**	2
7 Sep 96	BOMBSCARE *Arista 74321397662*	**46**	1

TWO COWBOYS
Italy, male instrumental / production duo   **11 wks**

9 Jul 94	● EVERYBODY GONFI-GON *3 Beat TABCD 221*	**7**	11

2 FOR JOY *UK, male instrumental / production duo*   **3 wks**

1 Dec 90	IN A STATE *Mercury MER 333*	**61**	1
9 Nov 91	LET THE BASS KICK *All Around Thr World GLOBE 102*	**67**	2

2 FUNKY 2 starring Katherine DION
UK, male / female vocal / instrumental group **4 wks**

6 Nov 93	**BROTHERS AND SISTERS** *Logic 74321170772* **56** 2	
30 Nov 96	**BROTHERS AND SISTERS (re-mix)** *All Around The World CDGLOBE 138*.................**36** 2	

2 HOUSE *US, male instrumental / production duo* **1 wk**

21 Mar 92	**GO TECHNO** *Atlantic A 7519* **65** 1	

2 IN A ROOM *US, male vocal duo* **15 wks**

18 Nov 89	**SOMEBODY IN THE HOUSE SAY YEAH!** *Big Life BLR 12*..**66** 1	
26 Jan 91	● **WIGGLE IT** *SBK SBK 19* **3** 8	
6 Apr 91	**SHE'S GOT ME GOING CRAZY** *SBK SBK 23* **54** 2	
22 Oct 94	**EL TRAGO (THE DRINK)** *Positiva CDTIV 18* **34** 2	
8 Apr 95	**AHORA ES (NOW IS THE TIME)** *Positiva CDTIV 32* **43** 1	
17 Aug 96	**GIDDY-UP** *Encore CDCOR 008* **74** 1	

2 IN A TENT *UK, male instrumental / production duo* **7 wks**

17 Dec 94	**WHEN I'M CLEANING WINDOWS (TURNED OUT NICE AGAIN)** *Love This SPONCD 1* **25** 5	
13 May 95	**BOOGIE WOOGIE BUGLE BOY (DON'T STOP)** *Bald Cat BALDCD 1* ⓵ **48** 1	
6 Jan 96	**WHEN I'M CLEANING WINDOWS (TURNED OUT NICE AGAIN) (re-entry)** *Love This SPONCD 1*...............**62** 1	

⓵ 2 In A Tank

First hit features the vocals of George Formby. See also George Formby.

2 MAD *UK, male vocal / instrumental duo* **4 wks**

9 Feb 91	**THINKING ABOUT YOUR BODY** *Big Life BLR 37* **43** 4	

TWO MAN SOUND
Belgium, male vocal / instrumental group **7 wks**

20 Jan 79	**QUE TAL AMERICA** *Miracle M 1* **46** 7	

TWO MEN, A DRUM MACHINE AND A TRUMPET *UK, male instrumental duo* **17 wks**

9 Jan 88	**I'M TIRED OF GETTING PUSHED AROUND** *London LON 141* **18** 8	
25 Jun 88	**HEAT IT UP** *Jive JIVE 174* ⓵ **21** 9	

⓵ Wee Papa Girl Rappers featuring Two Men and a Drum Machine

TWO NATIONS *UK, male vocal / instrumental group* **1 wk**

20 Jun 87	**THAT'S THE WAY IT FEELS** *10 TEN 168* **74** 1	

TWO PEOPLE *UK, male vocal / instrumental group* **2 wks**

31 Jan 87	**HEAVEN** *Polydor POSP 844* **63** 2	
8 Oct 94	**I WANT THE WORLD** *Epic 6608545* **20** 5	
17 Dec 94	**I WANT TO BE ALONE** *Epic 6610852* **29** 5	

2 UNLIMITED *Holland, male / female vocal duo* **110 wks**

5 Oct 91	● **GET READY FOR THIS** *PWL Continental PWL 206* **2** 15	
25 Jan 92	● **TWILIGHT ZONE** *PWL Continental PWL 211* **2** 10	
2 May 92	● **WORKAHOLIC** *PWL Continental PWL 228*.................**4** 7	

15 Aug 92	**THE MAGIC FRIEND** *PWL Continental PWL 240* **11** 7	
30 Jan 93	★ **NO LIMIT** *PWL Continental PWCD 256* **1** 16	
8 May 93	● **TRIBAL DANCE** *PWL Continental PWCD 262* **4** 11	
4 Sep 93	● **FACES** *PWL Continental PWCD 268* **8** 7	
20 Nov 93	**MAXIMUM OVERDRIVE** *PWL Continental PWCD 276* **15** 8	
19 Feb 94	● **LET THE BEAT CONTROL YOUR BODY** *PWL Continental PWCD 280* **6** 6	
21 May 94	● **THE REAL THING** *PWL Continental PWCD 306* **6** 7	
1 Oct 94	**NO ONE** *PWL Continental PWCD 314* **17** 6	
25 Mar 95	**HERE I GO** *PWL Continental PWCD 317* **22** 3	
21 Oct 95	**DO WHAT'S GOOD FOR ME** *PWL Continental PWL 322CD1* **16** 4	

2PAC *US, male rapper* **17 wks**

13 Apr 96	● **CALIFORNIA LOVE** *Death Row DRWCD 3* ⓵ **6** 8	
27 Jul 96	**HOW DO YOU WANT IT** *Death Row DRWCD 4* ⓶ **17** 4	
30 Nov 96	**I AIN'T MAD AT CHA** *Death Row DRWCD 5* ....**13†** 5	

⓵ 2Pac featuring Dr. Dre ⓶ 2Pac featuring KC and Jojo

2WO THIRD3 *UK, male vocal / instrumental group* **15 wks**

19 Feb 94	**HEAR ME CALLING** *Epic 6600642* **48** 3	
11 Jun 94	**EASE THE PRESSURE** *Epic 6604782*.......................**45** 2	

TYGERS OF PAN TANG
UK, male vocal / instrumental group **15 wks**

14 Feb 81	**HELLBOUND** *MCA 672* **48** 3	
27 Mar 82	**LOVE POTION NO. 9** *MCA 769* **45** 6	
10 Jul 82	**RENDEZVOUS** *MCA 777* **49** 4	
11 Sep 82	**PARIS BY AIR** *MCA 790* **63** 2	

Bonnie TYLER *UK, female vocalist* **81 wks**

30 Oct 76	● **LOST IN FRANCE** *RCA 2734* **9** 10	
19 Mar 77	**MORE THAN A LOVER** *RCA PB 5008* **27** 6	
3 Dec 77	● **IT'S A HEARTACHE** *RCA PB 5057* **4** 12	
30 Jun 79	**MARRIED MEN** *RCA PB 5164*.................................**35** 6	
19 Feb 83	★ **TOTAL ECLIPSE OF THE HEART** *CBS TYLER 1* **1** 12	
7 May 83	**FASTER THAN THE SPEED OF NIGHT** *CBS A 3338* **43** 4	
25 Jun 83	**HAVE YOU EVER SEEN THE RAIN** *CBS A 3517* **47** 3	
7 Jan 84	● **A ROCKIN' GOOD WAY** *Epic A 4071* ⓵ **5** 9	
31 Aug 85	**HOLDING OUT FOR A HERO** *CBS A 4251* **2** 13	
14 Dec 85	**LOVING YOU'S A DIRTY JOB BUT SOMEBODY'S GOTTA DO IT** *CBS A 6662* ⓶ **73** 2	
28 Dec 91	**HOLDING OUT FOR A HERO (re-issue)** *Total TYLER 10*..**69** 2	
27 Jan 96	**MAKING LOVE (OUT OF NOTHING AT ALL)** *East West EW 010CD* **45** 2	

⓵ Shaky and Bonnie ⓶ Bonnie Tyler, guest vocalist Todd Rundgren

TYMES *US, male vocal group* **41 wks**

25 Jul 63	**SO MUCH IN LOVE** *Cameo Parkway P 871* **21** 8	
15 Jan 69	**PEOPLE** *Direction 58 3903* **16** 10	
21 Sep 74	**YOU LITTLE TRUST MAKER** *RCA 2456* **18** 9	
21 Dec 74	★ **MS GRACE** *RCA 2493* **1** 11	
17 Jan 76	**GOD'S GONNA PUNISH YOU** *RCA 2626* **41** 3	

TYPICALLY TROPICAL
UK, male vocal / instrumental duo **11 wks**

5 Jul 75	★ **BARBADOS** *Gull GULS 14* **1** 11	

TYREE *US, male producer* **10 wks**

25 Feb 89	**TURN UP THE BASS** *ffrr FFR 24* ⓵ **12** 7	

364

Undertones

The Undertones were championed by DJ John Peel who named 'Teenage Kicks' as his favourite record of all time.

Tricky

Tricky was born Adrian Thaus in Bristol. His first taste of chart success came in 1989 as a member of the Fresh 4 Collective, who scored a Top 10 hit with a cover of Rose Royce's 'Wishing On A Star'.

Upside Down

Upside Down were handpicked from 7,500 hopefuls who responded to ads placed in *The People* and London's *Evening Standard*.

Toyah

Toyah worked as a mime artist at the Ballet Rambert and appeared in the films *Jubilee* and *Quadrophenia* before exploding chartwise in 1981.

366

8 Sep 79	**TOMORROW'S GIRLS** *Gem GEMS 10*	**28**	6
1 Dec 79	**SHE'S NOT THERE / KICKS EP** *Gem GEMS 14*	**36**	7
8 Mar 80	**WARHEAD** *Gem GEMS 23*	**30**	4
17 May 80	**TEENAGE** *Gem GEMS 30*	**32**	5
25 Oct 80	**PARTY IN PARIS** *Gem GEMS 42*	**37**	4
18 Apr 81	**KEEP ON RUNNIN' (TILL YOU BURN)** *Gem GEMS 45*	**41**	5

Tracks on She's Not There / Kicks EP: She's Not There / Kicks / Victim / The Same Thing.

Tracey ULLMAN *UK, female vocalist* 49 wks

19 Mar 83	● **BREAKAWAY** *Stiff BUY 168*	**4**	11
24 Sep 83	● **THEY DON'T KNOW** *Stiff BUY 180*	**2**	11
3 Dec 83	● **MOVE OVER DARLING** *Stiff BUY 195*	**8**	9
3 Mar 84	**MY GUY'S MAD AT ME** *Stiff BUY 197*	**23**	6
28 Jul 84	**SUNGLASSES** *Stiff BUY 205*	**18**	9
27 Oct 84	**HELPLESS** *Stiff BUY 211*	**61**	3

ULTIMATE KAOS *UK, male vocal group* 22 wks

22 Oct 94	● **SOME GIRLS** *Wild Card CARDD 12*	**9**	8
7 Jan 95	**SOME GIRLS (re-entry)** *Wild Card CARDD 12*	**67**	1
21 Jan 95	**HOOCHIE BOOTY** *Wild Card CARDW 14*	**17**	4
1 Apr 95	**SHOW A LITTLE LOVE** *Wild Card CARDW 18*	**23**	5
1 Jul 95	**RIGHT HERE** *Wild Card 5795832*	**18**	4

ULTRA HIGH *UK, male vocalist – Michael McCloud* 3 wks

2 Dec 95	**STAY WITH ME** *MCA MCSTD 40007*	**36**	2
20 Jul 96	**ARE YOU READY FOR LOVE** *MCA MCSTD 40039*	**45**	1

ULTRA-SONIC *UK, male instrumental / production duo* 2 wks

3 Sep 94	**OBSESSION** *Clubscene DCSRT 027*	**75**	1
21 Sep 96	**DO YOU BELIEVE IN LOVE** *Clubscene DCSRT 070*	**47**	1

ULTRACYNIC *UK, male / female vocal / instrumental group* 2 wks

29 Aug 92	**NOTHING IS FOREVER** *380 PEW 2*	**50**	2

ULTRAMARINE *UK, male instrumental duo* 4 wks

24 Jul 93	**KINGDOM** *Blanco Y Negro NEG 65CD*	**46**	2
29 Jan 94	**BAREFOOT EP** *Blanco Y Negro NEG 67CD*	**61**	1
27 Apr 96	**HYMN** *Blanco Y Negro NEG 87CD* [1]	**65**	1

[1] Ultramarine featuring David McAlmont

Tracks on Barefoot EP: Hooter / The Badger / Urf / Happy Land.

ULTRAVOX *UK / Canada, male vocal / instrumental group* 142 wks

5 Jul 80	**SLEEPWALK** *Chrysalis CHS 2441*	**29**	11
18 Oct 80	**PASSING STRANGERS** *Chrysalis CHS 2457*	**57**	4
17 Jan 81	● **VIENNA** *Chrysalis CHS 2481*	**2**	14
28 Mar 81	**SLOW MOTION** *Island WIP 6691*	**33**	4
6 Jun 81	● **ALL STOOD STILL** *Chrysalis CHS 2522*	**8**	10
22 Aug 81	**THE THIN WALL** *Chrysalis CHS 2540*	**14**	8
7 Nov 81	**THE VOICE** *Chrysalis CHS 2559*	**16**	12
25 Sep 82	**REAP THE WILD WIND** *Chrysalis CHS 2639*	**12**	9
27 Nov 82	**HYMN** *Chrysalis CHS 2657*	**11**	11
19 Mar 83	**VISIONS IN BLUE** *Chrysalis CHS 2676*	**15**	6
4 Jun 83	**WE CAME TO DANCE** *Chrysalis VOX 1*	**18**	7
11 Feb 84	**ONE SMALL DAY** *Chrysalis VOX 2*	**27**	6
19 May 84	● **DANCING WITH TEARS IN MY EYES** *Chrysalis UV 1*	**3**	10
7 Jul 84	**LAMENT** *Chrysalis UV 2*	**22**	6
4 Aug 84	**DANCING WITH TEARS IN MY EYES (re-entry)** *Chrysalis UV 1*	**74**	1
25 Aug 84	**LAMENT (re-entry)** *Chrysalis UV 2*	**73**	1
20 Oct 84	**LOVE'S GREAT ADVENTURE** *Chrysalis UV 3*	**12**	9
27 Sep 86	**SAME OLD STORY** *Chrysalis UV 4*	**31**	4
22 Nov 86	**ALL FALL DOWN** *Chrysalis UV 5*	**30**	5
6 Feb 93	**VIENNA (re-issue)** *Chrysalis CDCHSS 3936*	**13**	4

UMBOZA *UK, male instrumental / production duo* 9 wks

23 Sep 95	**CRY INDIA** *Positiva CDTIV 43*	**19**	4
20 Jul 96	**SUNSHINE** *Positiva CDTIV 47*	**14**	5

Piero UMILIANI *Italy, orchestra and chorus* 8 wks

30 Apr 77	● **MAH NA MAH NA** *EMI International INT 530*	**8**	8

UNATION *UK, male / female vocal / instrumental group* 3 wks

5 Jun 93	**HIGHER AND HIGHER** *MCA MCSTD 1773*	**42**	2
7 Aug 93	**DO YOU BELIEVE IN LOVE** *MCA MCSTD 1796*	**75**	1

UNCANNY ALLIANCE
US, male / female vocal / instrumental duo 5 wks

19 Dec 92	**I GOT MY EDUCATION** *A & M AM 0128*	**39**	5

UNDERCOVER *UK, male vocal / instrumental group* 29 wks

15 Aug 92	● **BAKER STREET** *PWL International PWL 239*	**2**	14
14 Nov 92	● **NEVER LET HER SLIP AWAY** *PWL International PWL 255*	**5**	11
6 Feb 93	**I WANNA STAY WITH YOU** *PWL International PWCD 258*	**28**	3
14 Aug 93	**LOVESICK** *PWL International PWCD 271* [1]	**62**	1

[1] Undercover featuring John Matthews

UNDERTAKERS *UK, male vocal / instrumental group* 1 wk

9 Apr 64	**JUST A LITTLE BIT** *Pye 7N 15607*	**49**	1

UNDERTONES *UK, male vocal / instrumental group* 67 wks

21 Oct 78	**TEENAGE KICKS** *Sire SIR 4007*	**31**	6
3 Feb 79	**GET OVER YOU** *Sire SIR 4010*	**57**	4
28 Apr 79	**JIMMY JIMMY** *Sire SIR 4015*	**16**	10
21 Jul 79	**HERE COMES THE SUMMER** *Sire SIR 4022*	**34**	6
20 Oct 79	**YOU'VE GOT MY NUMBER (WHY DON'T YOU USE IT?)** *Sire SIR 4024*	**32**	6
5 Apr 80	● **MY PERFECT COUSIN** *Sire SIR 4038*	**9**	10
5 Jul 80	**WEDNESDAY WEEK** *Sire SIR 4042*	**11**	9
2 May 81	**IT'S GOING TO HAPPEN!** *Ardeck AROS 8*	**18**	9
25 Jul 81	**JULIE OCEAN** *Ardeck ARDS 9*	**41**	5
9 Jul 83	**TEENAGE KICKS (re-issue)** *Ardeck ARDS 1*	**60**	2

UNDERWORLD *UK, male instrumental / vocal group* 26 wks

18 Dec 93	**SPIKEE / DOGMAN GO** *Junior Boy's Own JBO 17CD*	**63**	1
25 Jun 94	**DARK AND LONG** *Junior Boy's Own JBO 19CDS*	**57**	1
13 May 95	**BORN SLIPPY** *Junior Boy's Own JBO 29CDS*	**52**	2
18 May 96	**PEARL'S GIRL** *Junior Boy's Own JBO 38CDS1*	**24**	2
13 Jul 96	● **BORN SLIPPY (re-mix)** *Junior Boy's Own JBO 44CDS*	**2**	16
9 Nov 96	**PEARL'S GIRL (re-issue)** *Junior Boy's Own JBO 45CDS1* ..	**22**	3
28 Dec 96	**BORN SLIPPY (re-entry of re-mix)** *Junior Boy's Own JBO 44CDS*	**74†**	1

UNDISPUTED TRUTH
US, male / female vocal / instrumental group 4 wks

22 Jan 77	**YOU + ME = LOVE** *Warner Bros. K 16804*	**43**	4

U96
Germany, male producer – Alex Christiansen **7 wks**

29 Aug 92	**DAS BOOT** M & G MAGS 28	**18**	5
4 Jun 94	**INSIDE YOUR DREAMS** Logic 74321209722	**44**	1
29 Jun 96	**CLUB BIZARRE** Urban 5750152	**70**	1

UNION featuring the ENGLAND WORLD CUP SQUAD
UK / Holland, male instrumental group with UK rugby team vocalists **7 wks**

12 Oct 91	**SWING LOW (RUN WITH THE BALL)** Columbia 6575317	**16**	7

UNION GAP featuring Gary PUCKETT
US, male vocal / instrumental group **47 wks**

17 Apr 68	★ **YOUNG GIRL** CBS 3365	**1**	17
7 Aug 68	● **LADY WILLPOWER** CBS 3551	**5**	16
28 Aug 68	**WOMAN WOMAN** CBS 3110 [1]	**48**	1
15 Jun 74	● **YOUNG GIRL** CBS 8202 [1]	**6**	13

[1] Gary Puckett and the Union Gap

UNIQUE
US, male / female vocal / instrumental group **7 wks**

10 Sep 83	**WHAT I GOT IS WHAT YOU NEED** Prelude A 3707	**27**	7

UNIQUE 3
UK, male rap / scratch group **12 wks**

4 Nov 89	**THE THEME** 10 TEN 285	**61**	3
14 Apr 90	**MUSICAL MELODY / WEIGHT FOR THE BASS** 10 TEN 298	**29**	5
10 Nov 90	**RHYTHM TAKES CONTROL** 10 TEN 327 [1]	**41**	3
16 Nov 91	**NO MORE** 10 TEN 387	**74**	1

[1] Unique 3 featuring Karin

UNIT FOUR PLUS TWO
UK, male vocal / instrumental group **29 wks**

13 Feb 64	**GREEN FIELDS** Decca F 11821	**48**	2
25 Feb 65	★ **CONCRETE AND CLAY** Decca F 12071	**1**	15
13 May 65	**YOU'VE NEVER BEEN IN LOVE LIKE THIS BEFORE** Decca F 12144	**14**	11
17 Mar 66	**BABY NEVER SAY GOODBYE** Decca F 12333	**49**	1

UNITED KINGDOM SYMPHONY
UK, orchestra **4 wks**

27 Jul 85	**SHADES (THEME FROM THE CROWN PAINT TELEVISION COMMERCIAL)** Food For Thought YUM 108	**68**	4

UNITONE – See Laurel AITKEN and the UNITONE

UNITONE ROCKERS featuring STEEL
UK, male vocal / instrumental group **1 wk**

26 Jun 93	**CHILDREN OF THE REVOLUTION** The Hit Label HLC 4	**60**	1

UNITY
UK, male / female vocal / instrumental group **2 wks**

31 Aug 91	**UNITY** Cardiac CNY 6	**64**	2

UNO CLIO featuring Martine McCUTCHEON
UK, male / female vocal / instrumental group **1 wk**

18 Nov 95	**ARE YOU MAN ENOUGH** Avex UK AVEXCD 14	**62**	1

UNTOUCHABLES
US, male vocal / instrumental group **16 wks**

6 Apr 85	**FREE YOURSELF** Stiff BUY 221	**26**	11
27 Jul 85	**I SPY FOR THE FBI** Stiff BUY 227	**59**	5

UP YER RONSON featuring Mary PEARCE
UK, male / female vocal / instrumental group **5 wks**

5 Aug 95	**LOST IN LOVE** Hi-Life 5795572	**27**	3
30 Mar 96	**ARE YOU GONNA BE THERE** Hi-Life 5763272	**27**	2

Phil UPCHURCH COMBO
US, male instrumental group, Phil Upchurch bass guitar **2 wks**

5 May 66	**YOU CAN'T SIT DOWN** Sue WI 4005	**39**	2

UPSETTERS
Jamaica, male instrumental group **15 wks**

4 Oct 69	● **RETURN OF DJANGO / DOLLAR IN THE TEETH** Upsetter US 301	**5**	15

UPSIDE DOWN
UK, male vocal group **16 wks**

20 Jan 96	**CHANGE YOUR MIND** World CDWORLD 1A	**11**	7
13 Apr 96	**EVERY TIME I FALL IN LOVE** World CDWORLD 2A	**18**	3
8 Jun 96	**EVERY TIME I FALL IN LOVE (re-entry)** World CDWORLD 2A	**71**	1
29 Jun 96	**NEVER FOUND A LOVE LIKE THIS BEFORE** World CDWORLD 3A	**19**	3
23 Nov 96	**IF YOU LEAVE ME NOW** World CDWORLD 4A	**27**	2

URBAN ALL STARS
UK, male / female vocal instrumental group **2 wks**

27 Aug 88	**IT BEGAN IN AFRICA** Urban URB 23	**64**	2

URBAN BLUES PROJECT present Michael PROCTOR
US, male vocal / instrumental group **1 wk**

10 Aug 96	**LOVE DON'T LIVE** AM:PM 5817932	**55**	1

URBAN COOKIE COLLECTIVE
UK, male / female vocal / instrumental group **37 wks**

10 Jul 93	● **THE KEY THE SECRET** Pulse 8 CDLOSE 48	**2**	16
13 Nov 93	● **FEELS LIKE HEAVEN** Pulse 8 CDLOSE 55	**5**	9
19 Feb 94	**SAIL AWAY** Pulse 8 CDLOSE 56	**18**	4
23 Apr 94	**HIGH ON A HAPPY VIBE** Pulse 8 CDLOSE 60	**31**	3
15 Oct 94	**BRING IT ON HOME** Pulse 8 CDLOSE 73	**56**	1
27 May 95	**SPEND THE DAY** Pulse 8 CDLOSE 85	**59**	1
9 Sep 95	**REST OF MY LOVE** Pulse 8 CDLOSE 93	**67**	1
16 Dec 95	**SO BEAUTIFUL** Pulse 8 CDLOSE 100	**68**	1
24 Aug 96	**THE KEY THE SECRET (re-mix)** Pulse 8 CDLOSE 109 [1]	**52**	1

[1] UCC

URBAN DISCHARGE featuring SHE
US, male / female vocal / instrumental group **1 wk**

27 Jan 96	**WANNA DROP A HOUSE (ON THAT BITCH)** MCA MCSTD 40020	**51**	1

URBAN HYPE
UK, male production / instrumental group **12 wks**

11 Jul 92	● **A TRIP TO TRUMPTON** Faze 2 FAZE 5	**6**	8
17 Oct 92	**THE FEELING** Faze 2 FAZE 10	**67**	1
9 Jan 93	**LIVING IN A FANTASY** Faze 2 CDFAZE 13	**57**	3

URBAN SHAKEDOWN featuring Micky FINN
UK / Italy, male vocal / instrumental group   **8 wks**

27 Jun 92	**SOME JUSTICE** Urban Shakedown URBST 1	**23**	5
12 Sep 92	**BASS SHAKE** Urban Shakedown URBST 2	**59**	2
10 Jun 95	**SOME JUSTICE** Urban Shakedown URBCD 3 [1]	**49**	1

[1] Urban Shakedown featuring D Bo General

Some Justice *in 95 is a re-recording.*

URBAN SOUL *US, male producer – Roland Clarke*   **10 wks**

30 Mar 91	**ALRIGHT** Cooltempo COOL 231	**60**	4
21 Sep 91	**ALRIGHT (re-mix)** Cooltempo COOL 244	**43**	3
28 Mar 92	**ALWAYS** Cooltempo COOL 251	**41**	3

URBAN SPECIES *UK, male vocal / instrumental group*   **9 wks**

12 Feb 94	**SPIRITUAL LOVE** Talkin Loud TLKCD 45	**35**	4
16 Apr 94	**BROTHER** Talkin Loud TLKCD 47	**40**	3
20 Aug 94	**LISTEN** Talkin Loud TLKCD 50 [1]	**47**	2

[1] Urban Species featuring MC Solaar

Midge URE *UK, male vocalist*   **56 wks**

12 Jun 82	● **NO REGRETS** Chrysalis CHS 2618	**9**	10
9 Jul 83	**AFTER A FASHION** Musicfest FEST 1 [1]	**39**	4
14 Sep 85	★ **IF I WAS** Chrysalis URE 1	**1**	11
16 Nov 85	**THAT CERTAIN SMILE** Chrysalis URE 2	**28**	4
8 Feb 86	**WASTELANDS** Chrysalis URE 3	**46**	3
7 Jun 86	**CALL OF THE WILD** Chrysalis URE 4	**27**	8
20 Aug 88	**ANSWERS TO NOTHING** Chrysalis URE 5	**49**	4
19 Nov 88	**DEAR GOD** Chrysalis URE 6	**55**	4
17 Aug 91	**COLD COLD HEART** Arista 114555	**17**	7
25 May 96	**BREATHE** Arista 74321371172	**70**	1

[1] Midge Ure and Mick Karn

URGE OVERKILL *US, male vocal / instrumental group*   **6 wks**

21 Aug 93	**SISTER HAVANA** Geffen GFSTD 51	**67**	1
16 Oct 93	**POSITIVE BLEEDING** Geffen GFSTD 57	**61**	1
19 Nov 94	**GIRL YOU'LL BE A WOMAN SOON** MCA MCSTD 2024 ..	**37**	4

USA FOR AFRICA *US, male / female vocal group*   **9 wks**

13 Apr 85	★ **WE ARE THE WORLD** CBS USAID 1	**1**	9

US3 *UK, male instrumental / production duo*   **13 wks**

10 Jul 93	**RIDDIM** Blue Note CDCL 686 [1]	**34**	6
25 Sep 93	**CANTALOOP** Blue Note CDCL 696 [2]	**23**	5
28 May 94	**I GOT IT GOIN' ON** Blue Note CDCL 708 [3]	**52**	2

[1] Us3 featuring Tukka Yoot [2] Us3 featuring Rahsaan [3] Us3 featuring Kobie Powell and Rahsaan

USHER *US, male vocalist*   **1 wk**

18 Mar 95	**THINK OF YOU** LaFace 74321269252	**70**	1

USURA *Italy, male / female vocal / instrumental group*   **12 wks**

23 Jan 93	● **OPEN YOUR MIND** Deconstruction 74321128042	**7**	9
10 Jul 93	**SWEAT** Deconstruction 74321154602	**29**	3

UTAH SAINTS *UK, male instrumental / production duo*   **35 wks**

24 Aug 91	● **WHAT CAN YOU DO FOR ME** ffrr F 164	**10**	11
6 Jun 92	● **SOMETHING GOOD** ffrr F 187	**4**	9
8 May 93	● **BELIEVE IN ME** ffrr FCD 209	**8**	6
17 Jul 93	**I WANT YOU** ffrr FCD 213	**25**	5
25 Jun 94	**I STILL THINK OF YOU** ffrr FCD 225	**32**	2
2 Sep 95	**OHIO** ffrr FCD 264	**42**	2

U2 *Ireland, male vocal / instrumental group*   **167 wks**

8 Aug 81	**FIRE** Island WIP 6679	**35**	6
17 Oct 81	**GLORIA** Island WIP 6733	**55**	4
3 Apr 82	**A CELEBRATION** Island WIP 6770	**47**	4
22 Jan 83	● **NEW YEARS DAY** Island UWIP 6848	**10**	8
2 Apr 83	**TWO HEARTS BEAT AS ONE** Island IS 109	**18**	5
15 Mar 84	● **PRIDE (IN THE NAME OF LOVE)** Island IS 202	**3**	11
4 May 85	● **THE UNFORGETTABLE FIRE** Island IS 220	**6**	6
28 Mar 87	● **WITH OR WITHOUT YOU** Island IS 319	**4**	11
6 Jun 87	● **I STILL HAVEN'T FOUND WHAT I'M LOOKING FOR** Island IS 328	**6**	11
12 Sep 87	● **WHERE THE STREETS HAVE NO NAME** Island IS 340	**4**	6
26 Dec 87	● **IN GOD'S COUNTRY (IMPORT)** Island 7-99385	**48**	4
1 Oct 88	★ **DESIRE** Island IS 400	**1**	8
17 Dec 88	● **ANGEL OF HARLEM** Island IS 402	**9**	6
15 Apr 89	● **WHEN LOVE COMES TO TOWN** Island IS 411 [1]	**6**	7
24 Jun 89	● **ALL I WANT IS YOU** Island IS 422	**4**	5
2 Nov 91	★ **THE FLY** Island IS 500	**1**	6
14 Dec 91	**MYSTERIOUS WAYS** Island IS 509	**13**	7
4 Jan 92	**THE FLY (re-entry)** Island IS 500	**62**	1
7 Mar 92	● **ONE** Island IS 515	**7**	6
20 Jun 92	**EVEN BETTER THAN THE REAL THING** Island IS 525	**12**	7
11 Jul 92	● **EVEN BETTER THAN THE REAL THING (re-mix)** Island REAL U2	**8**	7
5 Dec 92	**WHO'S GONNA RIDE YOUR WILD HORSES** Island IS 550	**14**	8
4 Dec 93	● **STAY (FARAWAY, SO CLOSE)** Island CID 578	**4**	9
17 Jun 95	● **HOLD ME THRILL ME KISS ME KILL ME** Atlantic A 7131CD	**2**	14

[1] U2 featuring BB King

Stay (Faraway, So Close), *was listed with* I've Got You Under My Skin *by Frank Sinatra with Bono, which was featured on many but not all formats.*

VAGABONDS – *See Jimmy JAMES and the VAGABONDS*

Ricky VALANCE *UK, male vocalist*   **16 wks**

25 Aug 60	★ **TELL LAURA I LOVE HER** Columbia DB 4493	**1**	16

Ritchie VALENS *US, male vocalist*   **5 wks**

6 Mar 59	**DONNA** London HL 8803	**29**	1
1 Aug 87	**LA BAMBA** RCA PB 41435	**49**	4

Caterina VALENTE *France, female vocalist*   **14 wks**

19 Aug 55	● **THE BREEZE AND I** Polydor BM 6002	**5**	14

Dickie VALENTINE UK, male vocalist — 92 wks

20 Feb 53	BROKEN WINGS Decca F 9954	12	1
13 Mar 53 ●	ALL THE TIME AND EVERYWHERE Decca F 10038	9	3
5 Jun 53 ●	IN A GOLDEN COACH Decca F 10098	7	1
5 Nov 54	ENDLESS Decca F 10346	19	1
17 Dec 54 ●	MR. SANDMAN Decca F 10415	5	12
17 Dec 54 ★	FINGER OF SUSPICION Decca F 10394 [1]	1	15
18 Feb 55 ●	A BLOSSOM FELL Decca F 10430	9	9
29 Apr 55 ●	A BLOSSOM FELL (re-entry) Decca F 10430	18	1
3 Jun 55 ●	I WONDER Decca F 10493	4	15
25 Nov 55 ★	CHRISTMAS ALPHABET Decca F 10628	1	7
16 Dec 55	OLD PIANNA RAG Decca F 10645	15	5
7 Dec 56 ●	CHRISTMAS ISLAND Decca F 10798	8	5
27 Dec 57	SNOWBOUND FOR CHRISTMAS Decca F 10950	28	1
13 Mar 59	VENUS Pye Nixa 7N 15192	28	1
3 Apr 59	VENUS (re-entry) Pye Nixa 7N 15192	25	1
17 Apr 59	VENUS (2nd re-entry) Pye Nixa 7N 15192	20	4
22 May 59	VENUS (3rd re-entry) Pye Nixa 7N 15192	25	1
19 Jun 59	VENUS (4th re-entry) Pye Nixa 7N 15192	28	1
23 Oct 59	ONE MORE SUNRISE (MORGEN) Pye 7N 15221	14	8

[1] Dickie Valentine with the Stargazers

See also Various Artists (EPs & LPs) – All Star Hit Parade.

VALENTINE BROTHERS US, male vocal duo — 1 wk

23 Apr 83	MONEY'S TOO TIGHT (TO MENTION) Energy NRG 1	73	1

Joe VALINO US, male vocalist — 2 wks

18 Jan 57	GARDEN OF EDEN HMV POP 283	23	2

Frankie VALLI US, male vocalist — 52 wks

12 Dec 70	YOU'RE READY NOW Philips 320226	11	13
1 Feb 75 ●	MY EYES ADORED YOU Private Stock PVT 1	5	11
21 Jun 75	SWEARIN' TO GOD Private Stock PVT 21	31	5
17 Apr 76	FALLEN ANGEL Private Stock PVT 51	11	7
26 Aug 78 ●	GREASE RSO 012	3	14
23 Mar 91	GREASE – THE DREAM MIX PWL/Polydor PO 136 [1]	47	2

[1] Frankie Valli, John Travolta and Olivia Newton-John

See also Four Seasons.

David VAN DAY UK, male vocalist — 3 wks

14 May 83	YOUNG AMERICANS TALKING WEA DAY 1	43	3

George VAN DUSEN UK, male vocalist — 4 wks

17 Dec 88	IT'S PARTY TIME AGAIN Bri-Tone 7BT 001	43	4

Leroy VAN DYKE US, male vocalist — 20 wks

4 Jan 62 ●	WALK ON BY Mercury AMT 1166	5	17
26 Apr 62	BIG MAN IN A BIG HOUSE Mercury AMT 1173	34	3

VAN HALEN
US / Holland, male vocal / instrumental group — 51 wks

28 Jun 80	RUNNIN' WITH THE DEVIL Warner Bros. HM 10	52	3
4 Feb 84 ●	JUMP Warner Bros. W 9384	7	13
19 May 84	PANAMA Warner Bros. W 9273	61	2
5 Apr 86 ●	WHY CAN'T THIS BE LOVE Warner Bros. W 8740	8	14
12 Jul 86	DREAMS Warner Bros. W 8642	62	2

6 Aug 88	WHEN IT'S LOVE Warner Bros. W 7816	28	7
1 Apr 89	FEELS SO GOOD Warner Bros. W 7565	63	1
22 Jun 91	POUNDCAKE Warner Bros. W 0045	74	1
19 Oct 91	TOP OF THE WORLD Warner Bros. W 0066	63	1
27 Mar 93	JUMP (LIVE) Warner Bros. W 0155CD	26	3
21 Jan 95	DON'T TELL ME Warner Bros. W 0280CD	27	2
1 Apr 95	CAN'T STOP LOVIN' YOU Warner Bros. W 0288CD	33	2

VAN TWIST
Zaire / Belgium, male / female vocal / instrumental group — 2 wks

16 Feb 85	SHAFT Polydor POSP 729	57	2

VANDELLAS – See Martha REEVES and the VANDELLAS

Luther VANDROSS US, male vocalist — 146 wks

19 Feb 83	NEVER TOO MUCH Epic EPC A 3101	44	6
26 Jul 86	GIVE ME THE REASON Epic A 7288	60	3
21 Feb 87	GIVE ME THE REASON (re-issue) Epic 650216 7	71	2
28 Mar 87	SEE ME Epic LUTH 1	60	4
11 Jul 87	I REALLY DIDN'T MEAN IT Epic LUTH 3	16	10
5 Sep 87	STOP TO LOVE Epic LUTH 2	24	7
7 Nov 87	SO AMAZING Epic LUTH 4	33	6
23 Jan 88	GIVE ME THE REASON (2nd re-issue) Epic LUTH 5	26	6
16 Apr 88	I GAVE IT UP (WHEN I FELL IN LOVE) Epic LUTH 6	28	5
9 Jul 88	THERE'S NOTHING BETTER THAN LOVE Epic LUTH 7 [1]	72	1
8 Oct 88	ANY LOVE Epic LUTH 8	31	4
4 Feb 89	SHE WON'T TALK TO ME Epic LUTH 9	34	4
22 Apr 89	COME BACK Epic LUTH 10	53	3
28 Oct 89	NEVER TOO MUCH (re-mix) Epic LUTH 12	13	7
6 Jan 90	HERE AND NOW Epic LUTH 13	43	3
27 Apr 91	POWER OF LOVE – LOVE POWER Epic 6568227	46	5
18 Jan 92	THE RUSH Epic 6577237	53	3
15 Aug 92 ●	THE BEST THINGS IN LIFE ARE FREE Perspective PERSS 7400 [2]	2	13
22 May 93	LITTLE MIRACLES (HAPPEN EVERY DAY) Epic 6590442	28	3
18 Sep 93	HEAVEN KNOWS Epic 6596522	34	3
4 Dec 93	LOVE IS ON THE WAY Epic 6599592	38	2
17 Sep 94 ●	ENDLESS LOVE Epic 6608062 [3]	3	10
26 Nov 94	LOVE THE ONE YOU'RE WITH Epic 6610612	31	4
7 Jan 95	ENDLESS LOVE (re-entry) Epic 6608062 [3]	70	1
4 Feb 95	ALWAYS AND FOREVER Epic 6611942	20	5
4 Feb 95	ENDLESS LOVE (2nd re-entry) Epic 6608062 [3]	55	4
15 Apr 95	AIN'T NO STOPPING US NOW Epic 6614242	22	3
11 Nov 95	POWER OF LOVE-LOVE POWER (re-mix) Epic 6625902	31	3
16 Dec 95 ●	THE BEST THINGS IN LIFE ARE FREE (re-mix) A & M 5813092 [4]	7	7
23 Dec 95	EVERY YEAR EVERY CHRISTMAS Epic 6627762	43	2
12 Oct 96	YOUR SECRET LOVE Epic 6638385	14	5
28 Dec 96	I CAN MAKE IT BETTER Epic 6640632	44†	1

[1] Luther Vandross, duet with Gregory Hines [2] Luther Vandross and Janet Jackson with special guests BBD and Ralph Tresvant [3] Luther Vandross and Mariah Carey [4] Luther Vandross and Janet Jackson

VANESSA-MAE UK, female instrumentalist – violin — 16 wks

28 Jan 95	TOCCATA AND FUGUE EMI Classics MAE 8816812	16	10
20 May 95	RED HOT EMI CDMAE 2	37	2
18 Nov 95	CLASSICAL GAS EMI CDEM 404	41	2
26 Oct 96	I'M A DOUN FOR LACK O' JOHNNIE (A LITTLE SCOTTISH FANTASY) EMI CDMAE 3	28	2

VANGELIS Greece, male instrumentalist – keyboards — 25 wks

9 May 81	'CHARIOTS OF FIRE' – TITLES Polydor POSP 246	12	10
11 Jul 81	HEAVEN AND HELL, THIRD MOVEMENT (THEME FROM THE BBC-TV SERIES, 'THE COSMOS') BBC 1	48	6

24 Apr 82	CHARIOTS OF FIRE – TITLES (re-entry)		
	Polydor POSP 246..41		7
31 Oct 92	CONQUEST OF PARADISE East West YZ 704 60		2

See also Jon and Vangelis.

VANILLA FUDGE US, male vocal / instrumental group   11 wks

9 Aug 67	YOU KEEP ME HANGIN' ON Atlantic 584 123 18		11

VANILLA ICE US, male rapper   32 wks

24 Nov 90	★ ICE ICE BABY SBK SBK 18 1		13
2 Feb 91	● PLAY THAT FUNKY MUSIC SBK SBK 20 10		6
30 Mar 91	I LOVE YOU SBK SBK 22 45		5
29 Jun 91	ROLLIN' IN MY 5.0 SBK SBK 27........................27		4
10 Aug 91	SATISFACTION SBK SBK 29 22		4

VANITY FARE UK, male vocal / instrumental group   34 wks

28 Aug 68	I LIVE FOR THE SUN Page One POF 075 20		9
23 Jul 69	● EARLY IN THE MORNING Page One POF 142 8		12
27 Dec 69	HITCHIN' A RIDE Page One POF 158....................16		13

Joe T. VANNELLI PROJECT Italy, male producer   2 wks

17 Jun 95	SWEETEST DAY OF MAY Positiva CDTIV 36...............45		2

Randy VANWARMER US, male vocalist   11 wks

4 Aug 79	● JUST WHEN I NEEDED YOU MOST		
	Bearsville WIP 6516 8		11

VAPORS UK, male vocal / instrumental group   23 wks

9 Feb 80	● TURNING JAPANESE United Artists BP 334 3		13
5 Jul 80	NEWS AT TEN United Artists BP 345 44		4
11 Jul 81	JIMMIE JONES Liberty BP 401 44		6

VARDIS UK, male vocal / instrumental group   4 wks

27 Sep 80	LET'S GO Logo VAR 1 59		4

VARIOUS ARTISTS (EPs and LPs)   39 wks

15 Jun 56	'CAROUSEL' – ORIGINAL SOUNDTRACK (LP)		
	Capitol LCT 6105 27		1
29 Jun 56	● ALL STAR HIT PARADE Decca F 10752 2		9
6 Jul 56	'CAROUSEL' – ORIGINAL SOUNDTRACK (LP)		
	(re-entry) Capitol LCT 6105 26		1
26 Jul 57	ALL STAR HIT PARADE NO. 2 Decca F 10915 15		7
9 Dec 89	THE FOOD CHRISTMAS EP Food FOOD 23 63		1
20 Jan 90	THE FURTHER ADVENTURES OF NORTH EP		
	Deconstruction PT 43372.............................64		2
2 Nov 91	THE APPLE EP Apple APP 1 60		1
11 Jul 92	FOURPLAY EP XL XLFP 1 45		2
7 Nov 92	THE FRED EP Heavenly HVN 19 26		3
24 Apr 93	GIMME SHELTER (EP) Food CDORDERA 1 23		4
5 Jun 93	SUBPLATES VOLUME 1 EP		
	Suburban Base SUBBASE 24CD 69		1
9 Oct 93	THE TWO TONE EP 2 Tone CHSTT 31 30		3
4 Nov 95	HELP EP Go! Discs GODCD 135.........................51		2
16 Mar 96	NEW YORK UNDERCOVER EP Uptown MCSTD 48002 39		1
30 Mar 96	DANGEROUS MINDS EP MCA MCSTD 48007 35		1

Tracks and artists on 'Carousel' are as follows: Carousel Waltz – Orchestra conducted by Alfred Newman; You're A Queer One Julie Jordan – Barbara Ruick and Shirley Jones; Mister Snow – Barbara Ruick; If I Loved You – Shirley Jones and Gordon MacRae; June Is

Busting Out All Over – Claramae Turner; Soliloquy – Gordon MacRae; Blow High Blow Low – Cameron Mitchell; When The Children Are Asleep – Robert Rounseville and Barbara Ruick; This Was A Real Nice Clambake – Barbara Ruick, Claramae Turner, Robert Rounseville and Cameron Mitchell; Stonecutters Cut It On Stone (There's Nothing So Bad For A Woman) – Cameron Mitchell; What's The Use of Wonderin' – Shirley Jones; You'll Never Walk Alone – Claramae Turner; If I Loved You – Gordon MacRae; You'll Never Walk Alone – Shirley Jones.
Tracks on All Star Hit Parade; Theme From The Threepenny Opera – Winifred Atwell; No Other Love – Dave King; My September Love – Joan Regan; A Tear Fell – Lita Roza; Out Of Town – Dickie Valentine; It's Almost Tomorrow – David Whitfield.
Tracs on All Star Hit Parade No. 2: Around The World – Johnston Brothers; Puttin' On The Style – Billy Cotton; When I Fall In Love – Jimmy Young; A White Sport Coat – Max Bygraves; Freight Train – Beverley Sisters; Butterfly – Tommy Steele.
Tracks on The Food Christmas EP: Like Princes Do – Crazyhead; I Don't Want That Kind Of Love – Jesus Jones; Info Freako – Diesel Park West.
Tracks on The Further Adventures of North EP: Dream 17 – Annette; Carino 90 – T-Coy; The Way I Feel – Frequency 9; Stop This Thing – Dynasty Of Two featuring Rowetta.
Tracks on The Apple EP: Those Were The Days – Mary Hopkin; That's The Way God Planned It – Billy Preston; Sour Milk Sea – Jackie Lomax; Come And Get It – Badfinger.
Tracks on Fourplay EP: DJs Unite – DJs Unite; Alright – Glide; Be Free – Noise Factory; True Devotion – EQ.
Tracks on The Fred EP: Deeply Dippy – Rockingbirds; Don't Talk Just Kiss – Flowered Up; I'm Too Sexy – Saint Etienne.
Gimme Shelter (EP) was available on four formats, each featuring an interview with the featured artist plus the following artists performing versions of Gimme Shelter: (cassette) Jimmy Somerville and Voice Of The Beehive; Heaven 17; (12-inch) Blue Pearl, 808 State and Robert Owens; Pop Will Eat Itself vs Gary Clail; Ranking Roger and the Mighty Diamonds; (CD) Thunder; Little Angels; Hawkwind and Sam Fox (2nd CD) Cud with Sandie Shaw; Kingmaker; New Model Army and Tom Jones.
Tracks on Subplates Volume 1 EP: Style Warz – Son'z Of A Loop Da Loop Era; Funky Dope Track – A-Bass; The Chopper – DJ Hype; Look No Further – Run Tings.
Tracks on The Two Tone EP: Gangsters – Special AKA ; The Prince – Madness; On My Radio – Selecter; Tears Of A Clown – Beat.
Tracks on Help EP: Lucky – Radiohead; 50ft Queenie (Live) – PJ Harvey; Momentum – Guru featuring Big Shug; an untitled piece of incidental music.
Tracks on New York Undercover EP: Tell Me What You Like – Guy; Dom Perignon – Little Shawn; I Miss You – Monifah; Jeeps, Lex Coups, Bimaz & Menz – Lost Boys.
Tracks on Dangerous Minds EP: Curiosity – Aaron Hall; Gin & Dance – De Vante; It's Alright   – Sista featuring Craig Mack.

VARIOUS ARTISTS (MONTAGES)   31 wks

17 May 80	CALIBRE CUTS Calibre CAB 502........................75		2
25 Nov 89	DEEP HEAT '89 Deep Heat DEEP 10 12		11
3 Mar 90	● THE BRITS 1990 RCA PB 43565.........................2		7
28 Apr 90	THE SIXTH SENSE Deep Heat DEEP 12 49		2
10 Nov 90	TIME TO MAKE THE FLOOR BURN		
	Megabass MEGAX 1 16		9

The following tracks are sampled:

Calibre Cuts: Big Apples Rock – Black Ivory; Don't Hold Back – Chanson; The River Drive – Jupiter Beyond; Dancing In The Disco – LAX; Mellow Mellow Right On – Lowrell; Pata Pata – Osibisa; I Like It – Players Association; We Got The Funk – Positive Force; Holdin' On – Tony Rallo and the Midnight Band; Can You Feel The Force – Real Thing; Miami Heatwave – Seventh Avenue; Rappers Delight – Sugarhill Gang; Que Tal America – Two Man Sound; Remakes by session musicians: Ain't No Stoppin' Us Now, Bad Girls, We Are Family, Deep Heat '89 (credited to Latino Rave): Pump Up The Jam – Technotronic; Stakker Humanoid – Humanoid; A Day In The Life – Black Riot; Work It To The Bone – LNR; I Can Make U Dance – DJ 'Fast' Eddie; Voodoo Ray – A Guy Called Gerald; Numero Uno – Starlight; Bango (To The Batmobile) – Todd Terry; Break 4 Love – Raze; Don't Scandalize Mine – Sugar Bear. The Brits 1990: Street Tuff – Double Trouble and the Rebel MC; Voodoo Ray – A Guy Called Gerald; Theme From S-Express – S Express; Hey DJ I Can't Dance To That Music You're Playing – Beatmasters; Eve Of The War – Jeff Wayne; Pacific State – 808 State; We Call It Acieed – D Mob; Got To Keep On – Cookie Crew. The Sixth Sense (credited to Latino Rave): Get Up – Technotronic; The Magic Number – De La Soul; G'Ding G'Ding (Do Wanna Wanna) – Anna G; Show 'M The Bass – MC Miker G; Turn It Out (Go Base) – Rob Base; Eve Of The War (War Of The Worlds) – Project D; Moments In Love – 2 To The Power. Time To Make The Floor Burn (credited to Megabass): Do This My Way – Kid 'N' Play; Street Tuff – Double Trouble and the Rebel MC; Sex 4 Daze – Lake Eerie; Ride On Time – Black Box; Make My Body Rock – Jomanda; Don't Miss The Partyline – Bizz Nizz; Pump Pump It Up – Hypnotek; Big Fun – Inner City; Pump That Body – Mr Lee; Pump Up The Jam – Technotronic; This Beat Is Technotronic – Technotronic; Get Busy – Mr Lee; Touch Me – 49ers; Thunderbirds Are Go – FAB.

Junior VASQUEZ US, male producer   **5 wks**

15 Jul 95	GET YOUR HANDS OFF MY MAN! *Positiva CDTIV 37* **22** 3
31 Aug 96	IF MADONNA CALLS *Multiply CDMULTY 13* **24** 2

Elaine VASSELL – *See* BEATMASTERS

Sven VÄTH Germany, male producer   **5 wks**

24 Jul 93	L'ESPERANZA *Eye Q YZ 757*....................................**63** 2
6 Nov 93	AN ACCIDENT IN PARADISE *Eye Q YZ 778CD* **57** 2
22 Oct 94	HARLEQUIN – THE BEAUTY AND THE BEAST
	Eye Q YZ 857 ....**72** 1

Frankie VAUGHAN UK, male vocalist   **232 wks**

29 Jan 54	ISTANBUL *HMV B 10599* **11** 1
28 Jan 55	HAPPY DAYS AND LONELY NIGHTS *HMV B 10783* **12** 3
22 Apr 55	TWEEDLE DEE *Philips PB 423* **17** 1
2 Dec 55	SEVENTEEN *Philips PB 511* **18** 3
3 Feb 56	MY BOY FLAT TOP *Philips PB 544* **20** 2
9 Nov 56	● GREEN DOOR *Philips PB 640* **2** 15
11 Jan 57	★ GARDEN OF EDEN *Philips PB 660* **1** 13
4 Oct 57	● MAN ON FIRE / WANDERIN' EYES *Philips PB 729* **6** 12
1 Nov 57	● GOTTA HAVE SOMETHING IN THE BANK FRANK
	Philips PB 751 [1] **8** 11
20 Dec 57	● KISSES SWEETER THAN WINE *Philips PB 775* **8** 11
7 Mar 58	CAN'T GET ALONG WITHOUT YOU / WE ARE NOT
	ALONE *Philips PB 793* **11** 6
9 May 58	● KEWPIE DOLL *Philips PB 825* **10** 12
1 Aug 58	WONDERFUL THINGS *Philips PB 834* **22** 3
12 Sep 58	WONDERFUL THINGS (re-entry) *Philips PB 834* **27** 3
10 Oct 58	AM I WASTING MY TIME ON YOU *Philips PB 865* **25** 2
9 Jan 59	AM I WASTING MY TIME ON YOU (re-entry)
	Philips PB 865 ....**27** 2
30 Jan 59	THAT'S MY DOLL *Philips PB 895* **28** 2
1 May 59	● COME SOFTLY TO ME *Philips PB 913* [1] **9** 9
24 Jul 59	● THE HEART OF A MAN *Philips PB 930* **5** 14
18 Sep 59	WALKIN' TALL *Philips PB 931* **28** 1
2 Oct 59	WALKIN' TALL (re-entry) *Philips PB 931* **29** 1
29 Jan 60	WHAT MORE DO YOU WANT *Philips PB 985* **25** 2
22 Sep 60	KOOKIE LITTLE PARADISE *Philips PB 1054* **31** 5
27 Oct 60	MILORD *Philips PB 1066* **34** 6
9 Nov 61	★ TOWER OF STRENGTH *Philips PB 1195* **1** 13
1 Feb 62	DON'T STOP TWIST *Philips 1219* **22** 7
27 Sep 62	HERCULES *Philips 326542 BF* **42** 4
24 Jan 63	● LOOP-DE-LOOP *Philips 326566 BF* **5** 12
20 Jun 63	HEY MAMA *Philips BF 1254* **21** 9
4 Jun 64	HELLO DOLLY *Philips BF 1339* **18** 11
11 Mar 65	SOMEONE MUST HAVE HURT YOU A LOT
	Philips BF 1394 ....**46** 1
23 Aug 67	● THERE MUST BE A WAY *Columbia DB 8248* **7** 21
15 Nov 67	SO TIRED *Columbia DB 8298* **21** 9
28 Feb 68	NEVERTHELESS *Columbia DB 8354*........................**29** 5

[1] Frankie Vaughan and the Kaye Sisters

Malcolm VAUGHAN UK, male vocalist   **106 wks**

1 Jul 55	● EVERY DAY OF MY LIFE *HMV B 10874* **5** 16
27 Jan 56	WITH YOUR LOVE *HMV POP 130* **20** 1
10 Feb 56	WITH YOUR LOVE (re-entry) *HMV POP 130* **18** 1
2 Mar 56	WITH YOUR LOVE (2nd re-entry)*HMV POP 130* **20** 1
26 Oct 56	ST. THERESE OF THE ROSES *HMV POP 250* **27** 1
16 Nov 56	● ST. THERESE OF THE ROSES (re-entry) *HMV POP 250* ...**3** 19
12 Apr 57	THE WORLD IS MINE *HMV POP 303* **30** 1
3 May 57	THE WORLD IS MINE (re-entry) *HMV POP 303* **29** 2
10 May 57	CHAPEL OF THE ROSES *HMV POP 325* **13** 8
31 May 57	THE WORLD IS MINE (2nd re-entry)*HMV POP 303* **26** 1
29 Nov 57	● MY SPECIAL ANGEL *HMV POP 419* **3** 14
21 Mar 58	TO BE LOVED *HMV POP 459* [1] **14** 12
17 Oct 58	● MORE THAN EVER (COME PRIMA) *HMV POP 538* [1] **5** 14

27 Feb 59	WAIT FOR ME / WILLINGLY *HMV POP 590* **28** 1
13 Mar 59	WAIT FOR ME (re-entry) *HMV POP 590* **13** 14

[1] Malcolm Vaughan with the Michael Sammes Singers

Norman VAUGHAN UK, male vocalist   **5 wks**

17 May 62	SWINGING IN THE RAIN *Pye 7N 15438* **34** 5

Sarah VAUGHAN US, female vocalist   **34 wks**

27 Sep 57	PASSING STRANGERS *Mercury MT 164* [1] **22** 2
11 Sep 59	● BROKEN HEARTED MELODY *Mercury AMT 1057* **7** 13
29 Dec 60	LET'S / SERENATA *Columbia DB 4542* **37** 3
2 Feb 61	LET'S / SERENATA (re-entry) *Columbia DB 4542* **47** 1
12 Mar 69	PASSING STRANGERS (re-issue) *Mercury MF 1082* [1] **20** 15

[1] Billy Eckstine and Sarah Vaughan

Billy VAUGHN US, orchestra and chorus   **8 wks**

27 Jan 56	SHIFTING WHISPERING SANDS *London HLD 8205* [1] **20** 1
23 Mar 56	THEME FROM THE 'THREEPENNY OPERA'
	London HLD 8238 ....**12** 7

[1] Billy Vaughn Orchestra and Chorus, narration by Ken Nordene

VDC – *See* BLAST featuring VDC

Bobby VEE US, male vocalist   **134 wks**

19 Jan 61	● RUBBER BALL *London HLG 9255* **4** 11
13 Apr 61	● MORE THAN I CAN SAY / STAYING IN
	London HLG 9316 ....**4** 16
3 Aug 61	● HOW MANY TEARS *London HLG 9389*....................**10** 13
26 Oct 61	● TAKE GOOD CARE OF MY BABY *London HLG 9438* **3** 16
21 Dec 61	● RUN TO HIM *London HLG 9470* **6** 15
8 Mar 62	PLEASE DON'T ASK ABOUT BARBARA
	Liberty LIB 55419 ....**29** 9
7 Jun 62	● SHARING YOU *Liberty LIB 55451* **10** 13
27 Sep 62	A FOREVER KIND OF LOVE *Liberty LIB 10046* **13** 19
7 Feb 63	● THE NIGHT HAS A THOUSAND EYES
	Liberty LIB 10069 ....**3** 12
20 Jun 63	BOBBY TOMORROW *Liberty LIB 55530* **21** 10

Staying In *listed with* More Than I Can Say *from 13 Apr to 4 May 61. It peaked at 13.*

Louie VEGA and Marc ANTHONY
US, male vocal / instrumental duo   **2 wks**

5 Oct 91	RIDE ON THE RHYTHM *Atlantic A 7602* [1] **71** 1
23 May 92	RIDE ON THE RHYTHM (re-issue) *Atlantic A 7486*..........**70** 1

[1] Little Louie Vega and Marc Anthony

Suzanne VEGA US, female vocalist   **51 wks**

18 Jan 86	SMALL BLUE THING *A & M AM 294*.........................**65** 3
22 Mar 86	MARLENE ON THE WALL *A & M AM 309* **21** 9
7 Jun 86	LEFT OF CENTER *A & M AM 320* [1] **32** 9
23 May 87	LUKA *A & M VEGA 1* **23** 8
18 Jul 87	TOM'S DINER *A & M VEGA 2* **58** 3
19 May 90	BOOK OF DREAMS *A & M AM 559*.........................**66** 1
28 Jul 90	● TOM'S DINER *A & M AM 592* [2] **2** 10
22 Aug 92	IN LIVERPOOL *A & M AM 0029* **52** 2
24 Oct 92	99.9˚F *A & M AM 0085* **46** 2
19 Dec 92	BLOOD MAKES NOISE *A & M AM 0112* **60** 3
6 Mar 93	WHEN HEROES GO DOWN *A & M AMCD 0158* **58** 1

[1] Suzanne Vega featuring Joe Jackson [2] DNA featuring Suzanne Vega

Tata VEGA *US, female vocalist* — 4 wks

26 May 79	GET IT UP FOR LOVE / I JUST KEEP THINKING ABOUT YOU BABY *Motown TMG 1140*	52	4

VEGAS *UK, male vocal / instrumental duo* — 10 wks

19 Sep 92	POSSESSED *RCA 74321110437*	32	4
28 Nov 92	SHE *RCA 74321124657*	43	4
3 Apr 93	WALK INTO THE WIND *RCA 74321122462*	65	2

Rosie VELA *US, female vocalist* — 7 wks

17 Jan 87	MAGIC SMILE *A & M AM 369*	27	7

Wil VELOZ – *See LOS DEL MAR featuring Wil VELOZ*

VELVELETTES *US, female vocal group* — 7 wks

31 Jul 71	THESE THINGS WILL KEEP ME LOVING YOU *Tamla Motown TMG 780*	34	7

VELVET UNDERGROUND
US / UK, male / female vocal / instrumental group — 1 wk

12 Mar 94	VENUS IN FURS *Sire W 0224CD*	71	1

VELVETS *US, male vocal group* — 2 wks

11 May 61	THAT LUCKY OLD SUN *London HLU 9328*	46	1
17 Aug 61	TONIGHT (COULD BE THE NIGHT) *London HLU 9372*	50	1

VENT 414 *UK, male vocal / instrumental group* — 1 wk

28 Sep 96	FIXER *Polydor 5753292*	71	1

VENTURES *US, male instrumental group* — 31 wks

8 Sep 60	● WALK DON'T RUN *Top Rank JAR 417*	8	13
1 Dec 60	● PERFIDIA *London HLG 9232*	4	13
9 Mar 61	RAM-BUNK-SHUSH *London HLG 9292*	45	1
11 May 61	LULLABY OF THE LEAVES *London HLG 9344*	43	4

Al VERLAINE – *See PING PING and Al VERLAINE*

VERNONS GIRLS *UK, female vocal group* — 31 wks

17 May 62	LOVER PLEASE *Decca F 11450*	16	9
23 Aug 62	LOVER PLEASE (re-entry) / YOU KNOW WHAT I MEAN (re-entry) *Decca F 11450*	39	7
6 Sep 62	LOCO-MOTION *Decca F 11495*	47	1
18 Oct 62	YOU KNOW WHAT I MEAN (re-entry) *Decca F 11450*	37	3
15 Nov 62	YOU KNOW WHAT I MEAN (2nd re-entry) *Decca F 11450*	50	1
3 Jan 63	FUNNY ALL OVER *Decca F 11549*	31	8
18 Apr 63	DO THE BIRD *Decca F 11629*	50	1
2 May 63	DO THE BIRD (re-entry) *Decca F 11629*	44	1

You Know What I Mean was not coupled with Lover Please on the chart of 23 Aug 62, but both sides of this record were listed for the following six weeks.

VERNON'S WONDERLAND
Germany, male producer – Matthias Hoffmann — 1 wk

25 May 96	VERNON'S WONDERLAND *Eye-Q Classics EYECL 004CD*	59	1

VERUCA SALT *US, male vocal / instrumental group* — 3 wks

2 Jul 94	SEETHER *Scared Hitless FRET 003CD*	61	1
3 Dec 94	SEETHER (re-issue) *Hi-Rise FLATSDG 12*	73	1
4 Feb 95	NUMBER ONE BLIND *Hi-Rise FLATSCD 16*	68	1

VERVE *UK, male vocal / instrumental group* — 10 wks

4 Jul 92	SHE'S A SUPERSTAR *Hut HUT 16*	66	1
22 May 93	BLUE *Hut HUTCD 29*	69	1
13 May 95	THIS IS MUSIC *Hut HUTCD 54*	35	3
24 Jun 95	ON YOUR OWN *Hut HUTCD 55*	28	2
30 Sep 95	HISTORY *Hut HUTCD 59*	24	3

VIBRATIONS – *See Tony JACKSON and the VIBRATIONS*

VIBRATORS *UK, male vocal / instrumental group* — 8 wks

18 Mar 78	AUTOMATIC LOVER *Epic EPC 6137*	35	5
17 Jun 78	JUDY SAYS (KNOCK YOU IN THE HEAD) *Epic EPC 6393*	70	3

VICE SQUAD *UK, male / female vocal / instrumental group* — 1 wk

13 Feb 82	OUT OF REACH *Zonophone Z 26*	68	1

VICIOUS PINK *UK, male / female vocal / instrumental duo* — 4 wks

15 Sep 84	CCCAN'T YOU SEE *Parlophone R 6074*	67	4

Mike VICKERS – *See Kenny EVERETT*

Maria VIDAL *US, female vocalist* — 13 wks

24 Aug 85	BODY ROCK *EMI America EA 189*	11	13

VIDEO KIDS *Holland, male / female vocal duo* — 1 wk

5 Oct 85	WOODPECKERS FROM SPACE *Epic A 6504*	72	1

VIDEO SYMPHONIC *UK, orchestra* — 3 wks

24 Oct 81	THE FLAME TREES OF THIKA *EMI EMI 5222*	42	3

VIENNA PHILHARMONIC ORCHESTRA
Austria, orchestra — 14 wks

18 Dec 71	THEME FROM 'THE ONEDIN LINE' *Decca F 13259*	15	14

VIEW FROM THE HILL
UK, male / female vocal / instrumental group — 6 wks

19 Jul 86	NO CONVERSATION *EMI EMI 5565*	58	3
21 Feb 87	I'M NO REBEL *EMI EM 5580*	59	3

VIKKI *UK, female vocalist* — 3 wks

4 May 85	LOVE IS... *PRT 7P 326*	49	3

VILLAGE PEOPLE *US, male vocal / instrumental group* — 63 wks

3 Dec 77	SAN FRANCISCO (YOU'VE GOT ME) *DJM DJS 10817*	45	5
25 Nov 78	★ Y.M.C.A. *Mercury 6007 192*	1	16
17 Mar 79	● IN THE NAVY *Mercury 6007 209*	2	9
16 Jun 79	GO WEST *Mercury 6007 221*	15	8

9 Aug 80	CAN'T STOP THE MUSIC *Mercury MER 16*	**11**	11
9 Feb 85	SEX OVER THE PHONE *Record Shack SOHO 34*	**59**	5
4 Dec 93	Y.M.C.A. (re-mix) *Bell 74321177182*	**12**	7
28 May 94	IN THE NAVY (re-mix) *Bell 74321198192*	**36**	2

V.I.M. *UK, male instrumental / production group* **1 wk**

26 Jan 91	MAGGIE'S LAST PARTY *F2 BOZ 1*	**68**	1

Gene VINCENT *US, male vocalist* **51 wks**

13 Jul 56	BE BOP A LULA *Capitol CL 14599*	**30**	2
24 Aug 56	BE BOP A LULA (re-entry) *Capitol CL 14599*	**16**	3
28 Sep 56	BE BOP A LULA (2nd re-entry) *Capitol CL 14599*	**23**	2
12 Oct 56	RACE WITH THE DEVIL *Capitol CL 14628*	**28**	1
19 Oct 56	BLUE JEAN BOP *Capitol CL 14637*	**16**	5
8 Jan 60	WILD CAT *Capitol CL 15099*	**21**	3
10 Mar 60	MY HEART *Capitol CL 15115*	**16**	6
10 Mar 60	WILD CAT (re-entry) *Capitol CL 15099*	**39**	3
28 Apr 60	MY HEART (re-entry) *Capitol CL 15115*	**47**	1
19 May 60	MY HEART (2nd re-entry) *Capitol CL 15115*	**36**	1
16 Jun 60	PISTOL PACKIN' MAMA *Capitol CL 15136*	**15**	9
1 Jun 61	SHE SHE LITTLE SHEILA *Capitol CL 15202*	**22**	10
17 Aug 61	SHE SHE LITTLE SHEILA (re-entry) *Capitol CL 15202*	**44**	1
31 Aug 61	I'M GOING HOME *Capitol CL 15215*	**36**	4

VINDALOO SUMMER SPECIAL
UK, male / female vocal / instrumental group **3 wks**

19 Jul 86	ROCKIN' WITH RITA (HEAD TO TOE) *Vindaloo UGH 13*	**56**	3

Bobby VINTON *US, male vocalist* **29 wks**

2 Aug 62	ROSES ARE RED *Columbia DB 4878*	**15**	8
19 Dec 63	THERE I'VE SAID IT AGAIN *Columbia DB 7179*	**34**	10
29 Sep 90	● BLUE VELVET *Epic 6505240*	**2**	10
17 Nov 90	ROSES ARE RED (MY LOVE) (re-issue) *Epic 6564677*	**71**	1

VIOLINSKI *UK, male instrumental group* **9 wks**

17 Feb 79	CLOG DANCE *Jet 136*	**17**	9

V.I.P.'S *UK, male vocal / instrumental group* **4 wks**

6 Sep 80	THE QUARTER MOON *Gem GEMS 39*	**55**	4

VIPERS SKIFFLE GROUP
UK, male vocal / instrumental group **18 wks**

25 Jan 57	● DON'T YOU ROCK ME DADDY-O *Parlophone R 4261*	**10**	9
22 Mar 57	● CUMBERLAND GAP *Parlophone R 4289*	**10**	6
31 May 57	STREAMLINE TRAIN *Parlophone R 4308*	**23**	3

VIRUS *UK, male instrumental / production duo* **1 wk**

26 Aug 95	SUN *Perfecto PERF 107CD*	**62**	1

VISAGE *UK, male vocal / instrumental group* **56 wks**

20 Dec 80	● FADE TO GREY *Polydor POSP 194*	**8**	15
14 Mar 81	MIND OF A TOY *Polydor POSP 236*	**13**	8
11 Jul 81	VISAGE *Polydor POSP 293*	**21**	7
13 Mar 82	DAMNED DON'T CRY *Polydor POSP 390*	**11**	8
26 Jun 82	NIGHT TRAIN *Polydor POSP 441*	**12**	10
13 Nov 82	PLEASURE BOYS *Polydor POSP 523*	**44**	3
1 Sep 84	LOVE GLOVE *Polydor POSP 691*	**54**	3
28 Aug 93	FADE TO GREY (re-mix) *Polydor PZCD 282*	**39**	2

Michelle VISAGE – *See S.O.U.L. S.Y.S.T.E.M. introducing Michelle VISAGE*

VISCOUNTS *UK, male vocal group* **18 wks**

13 Oct 60	SHORT'NIN' BREAD *Pye 7N 15287*	**16**	8
14 Sep 61	WHO PUT THE BOMP *Pye 7N 15379*	**21**	10

VISION *UK, male vocal / instrumental group* **1 wk**

9 Jul 83	LOVE DANCE *MVM MVM 2886*	**74**	1

VISIONMASTERS – *See Kylie MINOGUE*

VIXEN *US, female vocal / instrumental group* **21 wks**

3 Sep 88	EDGE OF A BROKEN HEART *Manhattan MT 48*	**51**	4
4 Mar 89	CRYIN' *EMI Manhattan MT 60*	**27**	4
3 Jun 89	LOVE MADE ME *EMI-USA MT 66*	**36**	4
2 Sep 89	EDGE OF A BROKEN HEART (re-entry) *EMI-USA MT 48*	**59**	2
28 Jul 90	HOW MUCH LOVE *EMI-USA MT 87*	**35**	3
20 Oct 90	LOVE IS A KILLER *EMI-USA MT 91*	**41**	2
16 Mar 91	NOT A MINUTE TOO SOON *EMI America MT 93*	**37**	2

VOGGUE *Canada, female vocal duo* **6 wks**

18 Jul 81	DANCIN' THE NIGHT AWAY *Mercury MER 76*	**39**	6

VOICE OF THE BEEHIVE
US / UK, male / female vocal / instrumental group **51 wks**

14 Nov 87	I SAY NOTHING *London LON 151*	**45**	5
5 Mar 88	I WALK THE EARTH *London LON 169*	**42**	4
14 May 88	DON'T CALL ME BABY *London LON 175*	**15**	10
23 Jul 88	I SAY NOTHING (re-issue) *London LON 190*	**22**	6
22 Oct 88	I WALK THE EARTH (re-issue) *London LON 206*	**46**	4
13 Jul 91	MONSTERS AND ANGELS *London LON 302*	**17**	10
28 Sep 91	I THINK I LOVE YOU *London LON 308*	**25**	6
11 Jan 92	PERFECT PLACE *London LON 312*	**37**	6

See also Various Artists (EPs & LPs) – Gimme Shelter (EP).

Sterling VOID *UK, male vocalist* **3 wks**

4 Feb 89	RUNAWAY GIRL / IT'S ALRIGHT *ffrr FFR 21*	**53**	3

VOLCANO
Norway / UK, male / female vocal / instrumental group **4 wks**

23 Jul 94	MORE TO LOVE *Deconstruction 74321221832*	**32**	3
18 Nov 95	THAT'S THE WAY LOVE IS *EXP EXPCD 002* [1]	**72**	1

[1] Volcano with Sam Cartwright

VOYAGE *UK / France, disco aggregation* **27 wks**

17 Jun 78	FROM EAST TO WEST / SCOTS MACHINE *GTO GT 224*	**13**	13
25 Nov 78	SOUVENIRS *GTO GT 241*	**56**	7
24 Mar 79	LET'S FLY AWAY *GTO GT 245*	**38**	7

Scots Machine credited from 24 Jun 78 until end of record's chart run.

VOYAGER *UK, male vocal / instrumental group* **8 wks**

26 May 79	HALFWAY HOTEL *Mountain VOY 001*	**33**	8

VYBE *US, female vocal group* **1 wk**

7 Oct 95	WARM SUMMER DAZE *Fourth & Broadway BRCD 315*	**60**	1

Kristine W US, female vocalist   6 wks

21 May 94	**LOVE COME HOME** Triangle BLUESCD 001 [1]	73	1
25 Jun 94	**FEEL WHAT YOU WANT**		
	Champion CHAMPCD 304	33	3
25 May 96	**ONE MORE TRY** Champion CHAMPCD 317	41	1
21 Dec 96	**LAND OF THE LIVING** Champion CHAMPCD 324	57	1

[1] Our Tribe with Frankë Pharoah and Kristine W

Bill WADDINGTON – See CORONATION STREET CAST featuring Bill WADDINGTON

Adam WADE US, male vocalist   6 wks

8 Jun 61	**TAKE GOOD CARE OF HER** HMV POP 843	38	1
22 Jun 61	**TAKE GOOD CARE OF HER (re-entry)**		
	HMV POP 843	38	5

WAG YA TAIL UK, male vocal/instrumental group   1 wk

3 Oct 92	**XPAND YA MIND (EXPANSIONS)**		
	PWL International PWL 238	49	1

WAH! UK, male vocal/instrumental group   26 wks

25 Dec 82	● **THE STORY OF THE BLUES** Eternal JF 1	3	12
19 Mar 83	**HOPE (I WISH YOU'D BELIEVE ME)** WEA X 9880	37	5
30 Jun 84	**COME BACK** Beggars Banquet BEG 111 [1]	20	9

[1] Mighty Wah

Donnie WAHLBERG – See SEIKO and Donnie WAHLBERG

WAIKIKIS Belgium, male instrumental group   2 wks

11 Mar 65	**HAWAII TATTOO** Pye International 7N 25286	41	2

WAILERS – See Bob MARLEY and the WAILERS

John WAITE UK, male vocalist   13 wks

29 Sep 84	● **MISSING YOU** EMI America EA 182	9	11
13 Feb 93	**MISSING YOU (re-issue)** Chrysalis CDCHS 3938	56	2

WAITRESSES UK, female vocal group   4 wks

18 Dec 82	**CHRISTMAS WRAPPING** Ze/Island WIP 6821	45	4

Johnny WAKELIN UK, male vocalist   20 wks

18 Jan 75	● **BLACK SUPERMAN (MUHAMMAD ALI)**		
	Pye 7N 45420 [1]	7	10
24 Jul 76	● **IN ZAIRE** Pye 7N 45595	4	10

[1] Johnny Wakelin and the Kinshasa Band

Narada Michael WALDEN
US, male vocalist/producer   28 wks

23 Feb 80	**TONIGHT I'M ALL RIGHT** Atlantic K 11437	34	9
26 Apr 80	● **I SHOULDA LOVED YA** Atlantic K 11413	8	9
23 Apr 88	● **DIVINE EMOTIONS** Reprise W 7967 [1]	8	10

[1] Narada

Gary WALKER US, male vocalist   12 wks

24 Feb 66	**YOU DON'T LOVE ME** CBS 202036	26	6
26 May 66	**TWINKIE LEE** CBS 202081	26	6

See also Walker Brothers.

John WALKER US, male vocalist   6 wks

5 Jul 67	**ANNABELLA** Philips BF 1593	48	1
19 Jul 67	**ANNABELLA (re-entry)** Philips BF 1593	24	5

See also Walker Brothers.

Junior WALKER and the ALL-STARS
US, male instrumental/vocal group   59 wks

18 Aug 66	**HOW SWEET IT IS** Tamla Motown TMG 571	22	10
2 Apr 69	**(I'M A) ROAD RUNNER** Tamla Motown TMG 691	12	12
18 Oct 69	**WHAT DOES IT TAKE (TO WIN YOUR LOVE)**		
	Tamla Motown TMG 712	13	12
26 Aug 72	**WALK IN THE NIGHT** Tamla Motown TMG 824	16	11
27 Jan 73	**TAKE ME GIRL I'M READY** Tamla Motown TMG 840	16	9
30 Jun 73	**WAY BACK HOME** Tamla Motown TMG 857	35	5

Scott WALKER US, male vocalist   30 wks

6 Dec 67	**JACKIE** Philips BF 1628	22	9
1 May 68	● **JOANNA** Philips BF 1662	7	11
11 Jun 69	**LIGHTS OF CINCINATTI** Philips BF 1793	13	10

See also Walker Brothers.

WALKER BROTHERS US, male vocal group   93 wks

29 Apr 65	**LOVE HER** Philips BF 1409	20	13
19 Aug 65	★ **MAKE IT EASY ON YOURSELF** Philips BF 1428	1	14
2 Dec 65	● **MY SHIP IS COMING IN** Philips BF 1454	3	12
3 Mar 66	★ **THE SUN AIN'T GONNA SHINE ANYMORE**		
	Philips BF 1473	1	11
14 Jul 66	**(BABY) YOU DON'T HAVE TO TELL ME**		
	Philips BF 1497	13	8
22 Sep 66	**ANOTHER TEAR FALLS** Philips BF 1514	12	8
15 Dec 66	**DEADLIER THAN THE MALE** Philips BF 1537	34	6
9 Feb 67	**STAY WITH ME BABY** Philips BF 1548	26	6
18 May 67	**WALKING IN THE RAIN** Philips BF 1576	26	6
17 Jan 76	● **NO REGRETS** GTO GT 42	7	9

See also Gary Walker; John Walker; Scott Walker.

WALL OF SOUND featuring
Gerald LETHAN US, male vocal/instrumental group   1 wk

31 Jul 93	**CRITICAL (IF YOU ONLY KNEW)** Positiva CDTIV 4	73	1

WALL OF VOODOO
US, male vocal/instrumental group   3 wks

19 Mar 83	**MEXICAN RADIO** Illegal ILS 36	64	3

Jerry WALLACE US, male vocalist — **1 wk**

23 Jun 60	**YOU'RE SINGING OUR LOVE SONG TO SOMEBODY ELSE** London HLH 9110	**46**	1

Bob WALLIS and his STORYVILLE JAZZ BAND UK, male jazz band, Bob Wallis vocalist / instrumentalist – trumpet — **7 wks**

6 Jul 61	**I'M SHY MARY ELLEN I'M SHY** Pye Jazz 7NJ 2043	**44**	2
4 Jan 62	**COME ALONG PLEASE** Pye Jazz 7NJ 2048	**33**	5

Joe WALSH US, male vocalist — **15 wks**

16 Jul 77	**ROCKY MOUNTAIN WAY EP** ABC ABE 12002	**39**	4
8 Jul 78	**LIFE'S BEEN GOOD** Asylum K 13129	**14**	11

Tracks on Rocky Mountain Way EP: Rocky Mountain Way / Turn To Stone / Meadows / Walk Away.

Maureen WALSH – See Maureen

Sheila WALSH – See Cliff RICHARD

Steve WALSH UK, male vocalist — **18 wks**

18 Jul 87	**I FOUND LOVIN'** A1 A1 299	**74**	1
29 Aug 87	● **I FOUND LOVIN' (re-entry)** A1 A1 299	**9**	12
12 Dec 87	**LET'S GET TOGETHER TONITE** A1 A1 303	**74**	1
30 Jul 88	**AIN'T NO STOPPING US NOW (PARTY FOR THE WORLD)** A1 A1 304	**44**	4

Trevor WALTERS UK, male vocalist — **22 wks**

24 Oct 81	**LOVE ME TONIGHT** Magnet MAG 198	**27**	8
21 Jul 84	● **STUCK ON YOU** Sanity IS 002	**9**	12
1 Dec 84	**NEVER LET HER SLIP AWAY** Polydor POSP 716	**73**	2

WANG CHUNG UK, male vocal / instrumental group — **12 wks**

28 Jan 84	**DANCE HALL DAYS** Geffen A 3837	**21**	12

WANNADIES Sweden, male / female vocal / instrumental group — **7 wks**

18 Nov 95	**MIGHT BE STARS** Indolent DIE 003CD1	**51**	2
24 Feb 96	**HOW DOES IT FEEL** Indolent DIE 004CD1	**53**	1
20 Apr 96	**YOU AND ME SONG** Indolent DIE 005CD	**18**	3
7 Sep 96	**SOMEONE SOMEWHERE** Indolent DIE 006CD	**38**	1

Dexter WANSELL US, male instrumentalist – keyboards — **3 wks**

20 May 78	**ALL NIGHT LONG** Philadelphia International PIR 6255	**59**	3

WAR US / Canada / Denmark, male vocal / instrumental group — **32 wks**

24 Jan 76	**LOW RIDER** Island WIP 6267	**12**	7
26 Jun 76	**ME AND BABY BROTHER** Island WIP 6303	**21**	7
14 Jan 78	**GALAXY** MCA 339	**14**	7
15 Apr 78	**HEY SENORITA** MCA 359	**40**	2
10 Apr 82	**YOU GOT THE POWER** RCA 201	**58**	4
6 Apr 85	**GROOVIN'** Bluebird BR 16	**43**	5

Anita WARD US, female vocalist — **11 wks**

2 Jun 79	★ **RING MY BELL** TK TKR 7543	**1**	11

Billy WARD US, male vocalist — **13 wks**

13 Sep 57	**STARDUST** London HLU 8465	**13**	11
29 Nov 57	**DEEP PURPLE** London HLU 8502	**30**	1
3 Jan 58	**STARDUST (re-entry)** London HLU 8465	**26**	1

Chrissy WARD US, female vocalist — **1 wk**

24 Jun 95	**RIGHT AND EXACT** Ore AG 6CD	**62**	1

Clifford T WARD UK, male vocalist — **16 wks**

30 Jun 73	● **GAYE** Charisma CB 205	**8**	11
26 Jan 74	**SCULLERY** Charisma CB 221	**37**	5

Michael WARD UK, male vocalist — **13 wks**

29 Sep 73	**LET THERE BE PEACE ON EARTH (LET IT BEGIN WITH ME)** Philips 6006 340	**15**	10
15 Dec 73	**LET THERE BE PEACE ON EARTH (LET IT BEGIN WITH ME) (re-entry)** Philips 6006 340	**50**	3

WARD BROTHERS UK, male vocal / instrumental group — **8 wks**

10 Jan 87	**CROSS THAT BRIDGE** Siren SIREN 37	**32**	8

Justin WARFIELD – See BOMB THE BASS

WARM SOUNDS UK, male vocal duo — **6 wks**

4 May 67	**BIRDS AND BEES** Deram DM 120	**27**	6

Toni WARNE UK, female vocalist — **4 wks**

25 Apr 87	**BEN** Mint CHEW 110	**50**	4

Jennifer WARNES US, female vocalist — **37 wks**

15 Jan 83	● **UP WHERE WE BELONG** Island WIP 6830 [1]	**7**	13
25 Jul 87	**FIRST WE TAKE MANHATTAN** Cypress PB 49709	**74**	1
31 Oct 87	● **(I'VE HAD) THE TIME OF MY LIFE (LOVE THEME FROM 'DIRTY DANCING')** RCA PB 49625 [2]	**6**	12
15 Dec 90	● **(I'VE HAD) THE TIME OF MY LIFE (re-entry)** RCA PB 49625 [2]	**8**	11

[1] Joe Cocker and Jennifer Warnes [2] Bill Medley and Jennifer Warnes

WARRANT US, male vocal / instrumental group — **7 wks**

17 Nov 90	**CHERRY PIE** CBS 6562587	**59**	2
9 Mar 91	**CHERRY PIE (re-issue)** Columbia 6566867	**35**	5

Alysha WARREN UK, female vocalist — **4 wks**

24 Sep 94	**I'M SO IN LOVE** Wild Card CARDD 10	**61**	1
25 Mar 95	**I THOUGHT I MEANT THE WORLD TO YOU** Wild Card CARDD 16	**40**	1
27 Jul 96	**KEEP ON PUSHING OUR LOVE** Arista 74321390422 [1]	**30**	2

[1] Nightcrawlers featuring John Reid and Alysha Warren

Ann WARREN – See Ruby MURRAY

Nikita WARREN Italy, female vocalist — **1 wk**

13 Jul 96	**I NEED YOU** VC VCRD 12	**48**	1

Dionne WARWICK US, female vocalist   101 wks

13 Feb 64	**ANYONE WHO HAD A HEART**	
	Pye International 7N 25234 ....**42**	3
16 Apr 64 ●	**WALK ON BY** *Pye International 7N 25241* **9**	14
30 Jul 64	**YOU'LL NEVER GET TO HEAVEN**	
	Pye International 7N 25256 ....**20**	8
8 Oct 64	**REACH OUT FOR ME** *Pye International 7N 25265* **23**	7
1 Apr 65	**YOU CAN HAVE HIM** *Pye International 7N 25290* **37**	5
13 Mar 68	**VALLEY OF THE DOLLS** *Pye International 7N 25445* **28**	8
15 May 68 ●	**DO YOU KNOW THE WAY TO SAN JOSÉ**	
	Pye International 7N 25457 ....**8**	10
19 Oct 74	**THEN CAME YOU** *Atlantic K 10495* [1] **29**	6
23 Oct 82 ●	**HEARTBREAKER** *Arista ARIST 496* **2**	13
11 Dec 82 ●	**ALL THE LOVE IN THE WORLD** *Arista ARIST 507* **10**	10
26 Feb 83	**YOURS** *Arista ARIST 518* **66**	2
28 May 83	**I'LL NEVER LOVE THIS WAY AGAIN** *Arista ARIST 530*....**62**	3
9 Nov 85	**THAT'S WHAT FRIENDS ARE FOR** *Arista ARIST 638* [2] **16**	9
15 Aug 87	**LOVE POWER** *Arista RIS 27* [3] **63**	3

[1] Dionne Warwicke and the Detroit Spinners [2] Dionne Warwick and Friends featuring Elton John, Stevie Wonder and Gladys Knight [3] Dionne Warwick and Jeffrey Osborne

WAS (NOT WAS) US, male vocal / instrumental duo   58 wks

3 Mar 84	**OUT COME THE FREAKS** *Ze/Geffen A 4178* **41**	5
18 Jul 87	**SPY IN THE HOUSE OF LOVE** *Fontana WAS 2* **51**	7
3 Oct 87 ●	**WALK THE DINOSAUR** *Fontana WAS 3* **10**	10
6 Feb 88	**SPY IN THE HOUSE OF LOVE (re-entry)** *Fontana WAS 2* ...**21**	8
7 May 88	**OUT COME THE FREAKS (AGAIN)** *Fontana WAS 4* **44**	3
16 Jul 88	**ANYTHING CAN HAPPEN** *Fontana WAS 5* **67**	3
26 May 90	**PAPA WAS A ROLLING STONE** *Fontana WAS 7* **12**	7
11 Aug 90	**HOW THE HEART BEHAVES** *Fontana WAS 8* **53**	3
23 May 92	**LISTEN LIKE THIEVES** *Fontana WAS 10* **58**	2
11 Jul 92 ●	**SHAKE YOUR HEAD** *Fontana WAS 11* **4**	9
26 Sep 92	**SOMEWHERE IN AMERICA (THERE'S A STREET NAMED AFTER MY DAD)** *Fontana WAS 12* **57**	1

Fontana WAS 4 was a re-recorded version of their first hit. Shake Your Head features uncredited vocals by Ozzy Osbourne and Kim Basinger. See also Ozzy Osbourne.

Martha WASH US, female vocalist   15 wks

28 Nov 92	**CARRY ON** *RCA 74321125457* **74**	1
6 Mar 93	**GIVE IT TO YOU** *RCA 74321136562* **37**	4
10 Jul 93	**RUNAROUND / CARRY ON (re-mix)** *RCA 74321153702*..**49**	2
18 Feb 95	**TAKE A TOKE** *Columbia 6612112* [1] **26**	2
13 Jul 96 ●	**KEEP ON JUMPIN'** *Manifesto FESCD 11* [2] **8**	6

[1] C & C Music Factory featuring Martha Wash [2] Todd Terry featuring Martha Wash and Jocelyn Brown

The listed flip side of Take A Toke was I Found Love by C & C Music Factory featuring Zelma Davis. See also C & C Music Factory.

Dinah WASHINGTON US, female vocalist   8 wks

30 Nov 61	**SEPTEMBER IN THE RAIN** *Mercury AMT 1162* **35**	3
18 Jan 62	**SEPTEMBER IN THE RAIN (re-entry)**	
	Mercury AMT 1162 ....**49**	1
4 Apr 92	**MAD ABOUT THE BOY** *Mercury DINAH 1* **41**	4

Geno WASHINGTON and the RAM JAM BAND UK, male vocalist, male instrumental backing group   20 wks

19 May 66	**WATER** *Piccadilly 7N 35312* **39**	8
21 Jul 66	**HI HI HAZEL** *Piccadilly 7N 35329* **45**	3
25 Aug 66	**HI HI HAZEL (re-entry)** *Piccadilly 7N 35329*.............**48**	1
6 Oct 66	**QUE SERA SERA** *Piccadilly 7N 35346* **43**	3
2 Feb 67	**MICHAEL** *Piccadilly 7N 35359* **39**	5

Grover WASHINGTON Jr.
US, male instrumentalist – saxophone   7 wks

16 May 81	**JUST THE TWO OF US** *Elektra K 12514* **34**	7

Although uncredited, Bill Withers vocalises on Just The Two Of Us.

Keith WASHINGTON – See Kylie MINOGUE

Sarah WASHINGTON UK, female vocalist   13 wks

14 Aug 93	**I WILL ALWAYS LOVE YOU**	
	Almighty CDALMY 33 ....**12**	7
27 Nov 93	**CARELESS WHISPER** *Almighty CDALMY 43* **45**	2
25 May 96	**HEAVEN** *AM:PM 5815352* **28**	2
12 Oct 96	**EVERYTHING** *AM:PM 5818872* **30**	2

W.A.S.P. US, male vocal / instrumental group   38 wks

31 May 86	**WILD CHILD** *Capitol CL 388* **71**	2
11 Oct 86	**95 – NASTY** *Capitol CL 432* **70**	1
29 Aug 87	**SCREAM UNTIL YOU LIKE IT** *Capitol CL 458* **32**	5
31 Oct 87	**I DON'T NEED NO DOCTOR (LIVE)** *Capitol CL 469*........**31**	5
20 Feb 88	**LIVE ANIMAL (F * * K LIKE A BEAST)**	
	Music For Nations KUT 109 ....**61**	5
4 Mar 89	**MEAN MAN** *Capitol CL 521* **21**	5
27 May 89	**THE REAL ME** *Capitol CL 534* **23**	5
9 Sep 89	**FOREVER FREE** *Capitol CL 546* **25**	5
4 Apr 92	**CHAINSAW CHARLIE (MURDERS IN THE NEW MORGUE)** *Parlophone RS 6308* **17**	2
6 Jun 92	**THE IDOL** *Parlophone RPD 6314* **41**	2
31 Oct 92	**I AM ONE** *Parlophone 10RG 6324* **56**	1
23 Oct 93	**SUNSET AND BABYLON** *Capitol CDCL 698* **38**	2

WATERBOYS
UK / Ireland, male vocal / instrumental group   33 wks

2 Nov 85	**THE WHOLE OF THE MOON** *Ensign ENY 520* **26**	7
14 Jan 89	**FISHERMAN'S BLUES** *Ensign ENY 621* **32**	6
1 Jul 89	**AND A BANG ON THE EAR** *Ensign ENY 624* **51**	4
6 Apr 91 ●	**THE WHOLE OF THE MOON (re-issue)**	
	Ensign ENY 642 ....**3**	9
8 Jun 91	**FISHERMAN'S BLUES (re-issue)** *Ensign ENY 645* **75**	1
15 May 93	**THE RETURN OF PAN** *Geffen GFSTD 42* **24**	3
24 Jul 93	**GLASTONBURY SONG** *Geffen GFSTD 49* **29**	3

WATERFRONT UK, male vocal / instrumental duo   19 wks

15 Apr 89	**BROKEN ARROW** *Polydor WON 3* **63**	2
27 May 89	**CRY** *Polydor WON 1* **17**	13
9 Sep 89	**NATURE OF LOVE** *Polydor WON 2* **63**	4

Dennis WATERMAN UK, male vocalist   17 wks

25 Oct 80 ●	**I COULD BE SO GOOD FOR YOU** *EMI 5009* [1] **3**	12
17 Dec 83	**WHAT ARE WE GONNA GET 'ER INDOORS**	
	EMI MIN 101 [2] **21**	5

[1] Dennis Waterman with the Dennis Waterman Band [2] Dennis Waterman and George Cole

Crystal WATERS US, female vocalist   34 wks

18 May 91 ●	**GYPSY WOMAN (LA DA DEE)** *A & M AM 772* **2**	10
7 Sep 91	**MAKIN' HAPPY** *A & M AM 790* **18**	6
11 Jan 92	**MEGAMIX** *A & M AM 843* **39**	3
3 Oct 92	**GYPSY WOMAN (re-mix)** *Epic 6584377* **35**	2
23 Apr 94	**100% PURE LOVE** *A & M 8586692* **15**	7
2 Jul 94	**GHETTO DAY** *A & M 8589592* **40**	2

Weezer

The video for Weezer's 'Buddy Holly' was shot on a re-created set of *Happy Days*. The band were seen performing the song at Arnold's Drive-In surrounded by many of the show's characters.

ZZ Top

ZZ Top's breakthrough UK hit came more than 13 years after the band's formation in 1970.

Pete Wylie

Five years before he hit the chart with Wah!, Pete Wylie was in the Crucial Three with Ian McCulloch and Julian Cope.

Luther Vandross

Besides his solo entries Luther Vandross has vocalised on hits by Change, Charme and Gregg Diamond Bionic Boogie.

| 25 Nov 95 | **RELAX** *Manifesto FESCD 4* .... | **37** | 2 |
| 24 Aug 96 | **IN DE GHETTO** *Manifesto FESCD 12* [1] ...... | **35** | 2 |

[1] David Morales and the Bad Yard Club featuring Crystal Waters and Delta

The listed flip side of Gypsy Woman (re-mix) was Peace (re-mix) by Sabrina Johnston.

Muddy WATERS
US, male vocalist / instrumentalist – guitar　　　　　**6 wks**

| 16 Jul 88 | **MANNISH BOY** *Epic MUD 1* .... | **51** | 6 |

Roger WATERS *UK, male vocalist / instrumentalist*　**8 wks**

30 May 87	**RADIO WAVES** *Harvest EM 6*	**74**	1
26 Dec 87	**THE TIDE IS TURNING (AFTER LIVE AID)** *Harvest EM 37*	**54**	4
5 Sep 92	**WHAT GOD WANTS PART 1** *Columbia 6581390*	**35**	3

Michael WATFORD *US, male vocalist*　　　**2 wks**

| 26 Feb 94 | **SO INTO YOU** *East West A 8309CD* .... | **53** | 2 |

Jody WATLEY *US, female vocalist*　　　**34 wks**

9 May 87	**LOOKING FOR A NEW LOVE** *MCA MCA 1107*	**13**	11
17 Oct 87	**DON'T YOU WANT ME** *MCA MCA 1198*	**55**	3
8 Apr 89	**REAL LOVE** *MCA MCA 1324*	**31**	7
12 Aug 89	**FRIENDS** *MCA MCA 1352* [1]	**21**	6
10 Feb 90	**EVERYTHING** *MCA MCA 1395*	**74**	2
11 Apr 92	**I'M THE ONE YOU NEED** *MCA MCS 1608*	**50**	3
21 May 94	**WHEN A MAN LOVES A WOMAN** *MCA MCSTD 1964*	**33**	2

[1] Jody Watley with Eric B. and Rakim

Johnny 'Guitar' WATSON
US, male vocalist, instrumentalist – guitar　　　**8 wks**

| 28 Aug 76 | **I NEED IT** *DJM DJS 10694* .... | **35** | 5 |
| 23 Apr 77 | **A REAL MOTHER FOR YA** *DJM DJT 10762* .... | **44** | 3 |

WAVELENGTH *UK, male vocal group*　　　**12 wks**

| 10 Jul 82 | **HURRY HOME** *Ariola ARO 281* .... | **17** | 12 |

WAX *US / UK, male vocal / instrumental duo*　　**16 wks**

| 12 Apr 86 | **RIGHT BETWEEN THE EYES** *RCA PB 40509* .... | **60** | 5 |
| 1 Aug 87 | **BRIDGE TO YOUR HEART** *RCA PB 41405* .... | **12** | 11 |

Anthony WAY *UK, choirboy*　　　**2 wks**

| 15 Apr 95 | **PANIS ANGELICUS** *Decca 4481642* .... | **55** | 2 |

A WAY OF LIFE
US, male / female vocal / instrumental group　　**3 wks**

| 21 Apr 90 | **TRIPPIN' ON YOUR LOVE** *Eternal YZ 464* .... | **55** | 3 |

WAY OF THE WEST
UK, male vocal / instrumental group　　　**5 wks**

| 25 Apr 81 | **DON'T SAY THAT'S JUST FOR WHITE BOYS** *Mercury MER 66* .... | **54** | 5 |

WAY OUT WEST *UK, male instrumental / production duo*　**8 wks**

3 Dec 94	**AJARE** *Deconstruction 74321243802*	**52**	1
2 Mar 96	**DOMINATION** *Deconstruction 74321342822*	**38**	2
14 Sep 96	**THE GIFT** *Deconstruction 74321401912* [1]	**15**	5

[1] Way Out West featuring Miss Joanna Law

Jeff WAYNE *US, orchestra*　　　**3 wks**

| 10 Jul 82 | **MATADOR** *CBS A 2493* .... | **57** | 3 |

See also Jeff Wayne's War Of The Worlds.

Jeff WAYNE'S WAR OF THE WORLDS
US / UK, male / female vocal / instrumental cast　**18 wks**

| 9 Sep 78 | **THE EVE OF THE WAR** *CBS 6496* .... | **36** | 8 |
| 25 Nov 89 | ● **THE EVE OF THE WAR (re-mix)** *CBS 6551267* .... | **3** | 10 |

See also Jeff Wayne.

WEATHER GIRLS *US, female vocal duo*　**14 wks**

| 27 Aug 83 | **IT'S RAINING MEN** *CBS A 2924* .... | **73** | 3 |
| 3 Mar 84 | ● **IT'S RAINING MEN (re-entry)** *CBS A 2924* .... | **2** | 11 |

WEATHER PROPHETS
UK, male vocal / instrumental group　　　**2 wks**

| 28 Mar 87 | **SHE COMES FROM THE RAIN** *Elevation ACID 1* .... | **62** | 2 |

WEATHERMEN – See Jonathan KING

Marti WEBB *UK, female vocalist*　　　**42 wks**

9 Feb 80	● **TAKE THAT LOOK OFF YOUR FACE** *Polydor POSP 100*	**3**	12
19 Apr 80	**TELL ME ON A SUNDAY** *Polydor POSP 111*	**67**	2
20 Sep 80	**YOUR EARS SHOULD BE BURNING NOW** *Polydor POSP 166*	**61**	4
8 Jun 85	● **BEN** *Starblend STAR 6*	**5**	11
20 Sep 86	**ALWAYS THERE** *BBC RESL 190*	**13**	12
6 Jun 87	**I CAN'T LET GO** *Rainbow RBR 12*	**65**	1

Always There features the Simon May Orchestra. See also Simon May.

Joan WEBER *US, female vocalist*　　　**1 wk**

| 18 Feb 55 | **LET ME GO LOVER** *Philips PB 389* .... | **16** | 1 |

WEDDING PRESENT
UK, male vocal / instrumental group　　　**37 wks**

5 Mar 88	**NOBODY'S TWISTING YOUR ARM** *Reception REC 009* ...	**46**	2
1 Oct 88	**WHY ARE YOU BEING SO REASONABLE NOW** *Reception REC 011*	**42**	2
7 Oct 89	**KENNEDY** *RCA PB 43117*	**33**	3
17 Feb 90	**BRASSNECK** *RCA PB 43403*	**24**	3
29 Sep 90	**3 SONGS EP** *RCA PB 44021*	**25**	4
11 May 91	**DALLIANCE** *RCA PB 44495*	**29**	3
27 Jul 91	**LOVENEST** *RCA PT 44750*	**58**	1
18 Jan 92	**BLUE EYES** *RCA PB 45185*	**26**	2
15 Feb 92	**GO-GO DANCER** *RCA PB 45183*	**20**	1
14 Mar 92	**THREE** *RCA PB 45181*	**14**	2
18 Apr 92	**SILVER SHORTS** *RCA PB 45311*	**14**	1
16 May 92	● **COME PLAY WITH ME** *RCA PB 45313*	**10**	2
13 Jun 92	**CALIFORNIA** *RCA PB 45315*	**16**	1
18 Jul 92	**FLYING SAUCER** *RCA 74321101157*	**22**	1

15 Aug 92	**BOING!** *RCA 74321101177* **19**	1
19 Sep 92	**LOVE SLAVE** *RCA 743211101167* **17**	1
17 Oct 92	**STICKY** *RCA 74321116917* **17**	1
14 Nov 92	**THE QUEEN OF OUTER SPACE** *RCA 74321116927*....**23**	1
19 Dec 92	**NO CHRISTMAS** *RCA 74321116937* **25**	1
10 Sep 94	**YEAH YEAH YEAH YEAH YEAH** *Island CID 585* **51**	2
26 Nov 94	**IT'S A GAS** *Island CID 591* **71**	1
31 Aug 96	**2, 3, GO** *Cooking Vinyl FRYCD 048* **67**	1

Tracks on 3 Songs EP: Corduroy / Crawl / Make Me Smile (Come Up And See Me).

Act were male/female for last hit.

Fred WEDLOCK *UK, male vocalist*   **10 wks**

31 Jan 81	● **OLDEST SWINGER IN TOWN** *Rocket XPRES 46* **6**	10

WEE PAPA GIRL RAPPERS *UK, female vocal duo*   **27 wks**

12 Mar 88	**FAITH** *Jive JIVE 164* **60**	4
25 Jun 88	**HEAT IT UP** *Jive JIVE 174* [1] **21**	9
1 Oct 88	● **WEE RULE** *Jive JIVE 185* **6**	9
24 Dec 88	**SOULMATE** *Jive JIVE 193* **45**	4
25 Mar 89	**BLOW THE HOUSE DOWN** *Jive JIVE 197*............**65**	1

[1] Wee Papa Girl Rappers featuring Two Men and a Drum Machine

Bert WEEDON *UK, male instrumentalist – guitar*   **38 wks**

15 May 59	● **GUITAR BOOGIE SHUFFLE** *Top Rank JAR 117* **10**	9
20 Nov 59	**NASHVILLE BOOGIE** *Top Rank JAR 221* **29**	2
10 Mar 60	**BIG BEAT BOOGIE** *Top Rank JAR 300* **37**	3
7 Apr 60	**BIG BEAT BOOGIE (re-entry)** *Top Rank JAR 300* **49**	1
9 Jun 60	**TWELFTH STREET RAG** *Top Rank JAR 360* **47**	2
28 Jul 60	**APACHE** *Top Rank JAR 415* **44**	1
11 Aug 60	**APACHE (re-entry)** *Top Rank JAR 415* **24**	3
27 Oct 60	**SORRY ROBBIE** *Top Rank JAR 517*................**28**	11
2 Feb 61	**GINCHY** *Top Rank JAR 537* **35**	5
4 May 61	**MR. GUITAR** *Top Rank JAR 559* **47**	1

WEEKEND
Multi-national, male / female vocal / instrumental group   **5 wks**

14 Dec 85	**CHRISTMAS MEDLEY/AULD LANG SYNE** *Lifestyle XY 1*..**47**	5

WEEZER *US, male vocal / instrumental group*   **12 wks**

11 Feb 95	**UNDONE – THE SWEATER SONG** *Geffen GFSTD 85* **35**	2
6 May 95	**BUDDY HOLLY** *Geffen GFSTD 88* **12**	7
22 Jul 95	**SAY IT AIN'T SO** *Geffen GFSTD 95* **37**	2
5 Oct 96	**EL SCORCHO** *Geffen GFSTD 22167* **50**	1

Frank WEIR *UK, orchestra*   **4 wks**

15 Sep 60	**CARIBBEAN HONEYMOON** *Oriole CB 1559* **42**	4

See also Vera Lynn.

Eric WEISSBERG – *See 'DELIVERANCE' SOUNDTRACK*

Denise WELCH *UK, female vocalist*   **3 wks**

4 Nov 95	**YOU DON'T HAVE TO SAY YOU LOVE ME / CRY ME A RIVER** *Virgin VSCDT 1569* **23**	3

Paul WELLER *UK, male vocalist*   **48 wks**

18 May 91	**INTO TOMORROW** *Freedom High FHP 1* [1] **36**	3
15 Aug 92	**UH HUH OH YEH** *Go! Discs GODCD 107* **18**	5
10 Oct 92	**ABOVE THE CLOUDS** *Go! Discs GOD 91* **47**	2
17 Jul 93	**SUNFLOWER** *Go! Discs GODCD 102* **16**	5
4 Sep 93	**WILD WOOD** *Go! Discs GODCD 104* **14**	5
13 Nov 93	**THE WEAVER (EP)** *Go! Discs GODCD 107* **18**	3
9 Apr 94	**HUNG UP** *Go! Discs GODCD 111* **11**	3
5 Nov 94	**OUT OF THE SINKING** *Go! Discs GODCD 121* **20**	3
6 May 95	● **THE CHANGINGMAN** *Go! Discs GODCD 127* **7**	4
22 Jul 95	● **YOU DO SOMETHING TO ME** *Go! Discs GODCD 130* **9**	6
30 Sep 95	**BROKEN STONES** *Go! Discs GODCD 132*............**20**	4
9 Mar 96	**OUT OF THE SINKING** *Go! Discs GODCD 143* **16**	2
17 Aug 96	● **PEACOCK SUIT** *Go! Discs GODCD 149* **5**	5

[1] Paul Weller Movement

Tracks on The Weaver (EP): The Weaver / There Is No Time / Another New Day / Ohio.
Out Of The Sinking in 96 is a re-recording.

Brandi WELLS *US, female vocalist*   **1 wk**

20 Feb 82	**WATCH OUT** *Virgin VS 479* **74**	1

Houston WELLS *UK, male vocalist*   **10 wks**

1 Aug 63	**ONLY THE HEARTACHES** *Parlophone R 5031* **22**	10

Mary WELLS *US, female vocalist*   **25 wks**

21 May 64	● **MY GUY** *Stateside SS 288* **5**	14
30 Jul 64	**ONCE UPON A TIME** *Stateside SS 316* [1] **50**	1
8 Jul 72	**MY GUY (re-issue)** *Tamla Motown TMG 820* **14**	10

[1] Marvin Gaye and Mary Wells

Terri WELLS *US, female vocalist*   **9 wks**

2 Jul 83	**YOU MAKE IT HEAVEN** *Phillyworld PWS 111* **53**	2
5 May 84	**I'LL BE AROUND** *Phillyworld LON 48* **17**	7

Alex WELSH *UK, male instrumentalist – trumpet*   **4 wks**

10 Aug 61	**TANSY** *Columbia DB 4686* **45**	4

Irvine WELSH – *See PRIMAL SCREAM*

WENDY and LISA *US, female vocal duo*   **31 wks**

5 Sep 87	**WATERFALL** *Virgin VS 999* **66**	5
16 Jan 88	**SIDE SHOW** *Virgin VS 1012* **49**	5
18 Feb 89	**ARE YOU MY BABY** *Virgin VS 1156* **70**	3
29 Apr 89	**LOLLY LOLLY** *Virgin VS 1175* **64**	3
8 Jul 89	**SATISFACTION** *Virgin VS 1194* **27**	8
18 Nov 89	**WATERFALL (re-mix)** *Virgin VS 1223* **69**	2
30 Jun 90	**STRUNG OUT** *Virgin VS 1272* **44**	5
10 Nov 90	**RAINBOW LAKE** *Virgin VS 1280* **70**	1

Dodie WEST *UK, female vocalist*   **4 wks**

14 Jan 65	**GOING OUT OF MY HEAD** *Decca F 12046* **39**	4

Keith WEST *UK, male vocalist*   **18 wks**

9 Aug 67	● **EXCERPT FROM A TEENAGE OPERA** *Parlophone R 5623* ..**2**	15
22 Nov 67	**SAM** *Parlophone R 5651* **38**	3

Kit WEST – *See DEGREES OF MOTION featuring BITI*

WEST END – *See SYBIL*

380

WEST END UK, female vocal group — 2 wks

| 19 Aug 95 | LOVE RULES RCA 74321292702 | 44 | 2 |

WEST HAM UNITED CUP SQUAD
UK, male football team vocalists — 2 wks

| 10 May 75 | I'M FOREVER BLOWING BUBBLES Pye 7N 45470 | 31 | 2 |

WEST STREET MOB US, male vocal group — 3 wks

| 8 Oct 83 | BREAK DANCIN' – ELECTRIC BOOGIE Sugarhill SH 128 | 71 | 1 |
| 22 Oct 83 | BREAK DANCIN' – ELECTRIC BOOGIE (re-entry) Sugarhill SH 128 | 64 | 2 |

WESTBAM Germany, male producer — 6 wks

9 Jul 94	CELEBRATION GENERATION Low Spirit PQCD 5	48	2
19 Nov 94	BAM BAM BAM Low Spirit PZCD 329	57	1
3 Jun 95	WIZARDS OF THE SONIC Urban PZCD 344	32	2
23 Mar 96	ALWAYS MUSIC Low Spirit 5779152 [1]	51	1

[1] Westbam / Koon + Stephenson

Kim WESTON – See Marvin GAYE

WESTWORLD
UK / US, male / female vocal / instrumental group — 23 wks

21 Feb 87	SONIC BOOM BOY RCA BOOM 1	11	7
2 May 87	BA-NA-NA-BAM-BOO RCA BOOM 2	37	5
25 Jul 87	WHERE THE ACTION IS RCA BOOM 3	54	4
17 Oct 87	SILVERMAC RCA BOOM 4	42	5
15 Oct 88	EVERYTHING GOOD IS BAD RCA PB 42243	72	2

WET WET WET UK, male vocal / instrumental group — 189 wks

11 Apr 87	● WISHING I WAS LUCKY Precious JEWEL 3	6	14
25 Jul 87	● SWEET LITTLE MYSTERY Precious JEWEL 4	5	12
5 Dec 87	● ANGEL EYES (HOME AND AWAY) Precious JEWEL 6	5	12
19 Mar 88	TEMPTATION Precious JEWEL 7	12	8
14 May 88	★ WITH A LITTLE HELP FROM MY FRIENDS Childline CHILD 1	1	11
30 Sep 89	● SWEET SURRENDER Precious JEWEL 9	6	8
9 Dec 89	BROKE AWAY Precious JEWEL 10	19	7
10 Mar 90	HOLD BACK THE RIVER Precious JEWEL 11	31	4
11 Aug 90	STAY WITH ME HEARTACHE / I FEEL FINE Precious JEWEL 13	30	4
14 Sep 91	MAKE IT TONIGHT Precious JEWEL 15	37	3
2 Nov 91	PUT THE LIGHT ON Precious JEWEL 16	56	2
4 Jan 92	★ GOODNIGHT GIRL Precious JEWEL 17	1	11
21 Mar 92	MORE THAN LOVE Precious JEWEL 18	19	5
11 Jul 92	LIP SERVICE (EP) Precious JEWEL 19	15	5
8 May 93	BLUE FOR YOU / THIS TIME (LIVE) Precious JWLCD 20	38	2
6 Nov 93	SHED A TEAR Precious JWLCD 21	22	5
8 Jan 94	COLD COLD HEART Precious JWLCD 22	23	4
21 May 94	★ LOVE IS ALL AROUND Precious JWLCD 23	1	37
25 Mar 95	● JULIA SAYS Precious JWLDD 24	3	9
17 Jun 95	● DON'T WANT TO FORGIVE ME NOW Precious JWLDD 25	7	8
30 Sep 95	● SOMEWHERE SOMEHOW Precious JWLDD 26	7	7
2 Dec 95	SHE'S ALL ON MY MIND Precious JWLDD 27	17	7
30 Mar 96	● MORNING Precious JWLDD 28	16	4

The listed A-side with With A Little Help From My Friends was She's Leaving Home by Billy Bragg with Cara Tivey. Tracks on Lip Service (EP): Lip Service / High On The Happy Side / Lip Service (Live) / More Than Love (Live).

WE'VE GOT A FUZZBOX AND WE'RE GONNA USE IT UK, female vocal / instrumental group — 39 wks

26 Apr 86	XX SEX / RULES AND REGULATIONS Vindaloo UGH 11	41	7
15 Nov 86	LOVE IS THE SLUG Vindaloo UGH 14	31	4
7 Feb 87	WHAT'S THE POINT Vindaloo YZ 101	51	2
25 Feb 89	INTERNATIONAL RESCUE WEA YZ 347	11	10
20 May 89	PINK SUNSHINE WEA YZ 401	14	10
5 Aug 89	SELF! WEA YZ 408	24	6

WHALE Sweden, male / female vocal / instrumental group — 7 wks

19 Mar 94	HOBO HUMPIN' SLOBO BABE East West YZ 798CD	46	2
15 Jul 95	I'LL DO YA Hut HUTDG 51	53	1
25 Nov 95	HOBO HUMPIN' SLOBO BABE (re-issue) Hut HUTCD 64	15	4

WHALERS – See Hal PAIGE and the WHALERS

WHAM! UK, male vocal duo — 137 wks

16 Oct 82	● YOUNG GUNS (GO FOR IT) Innervision IVL A2766	3	17
15 Jan 83	● WHAM RAP Innervision IVL A2442	8	11
14 May 83	● BAD BOYS Innervision A 3143	2	14
30 Jul 83	● CLUB TROPICANA Innervision A 3613	4	11
3 Dec 83	CLUB FANTASTIC MEGAMIX Innervision A 3586	15	8
26 May 84	★ WAKE ME UP BEFORE YOU GO GO Epic A 4440	1	16
13 Oct 84	★ FREEDOM Epic A 4743	1	14
15 Dec 84	● LAST CHRISTMAS / EVERYTHING SHE WANTS Epic A 4949	2	13
23 Nov 85	★ I'M YOUR MAN Epic A 6716	1	12
14 Dec 85	● LAST CHRISTMAS (re-issue) Epic WHAM 1	6	7
21 Jun 86	★ THE EDGE OF HEAVEN / WHERE DID YOUR HEART GO Epic FIN 1	1	10
20 Dec 86	LAST CHRISTMAS (2nd re-issue) Epic 650269 7	45	4

Where Did Your Heart Go only listed from 2 August 86 with a peak position of 28.

WHATNAUTS – See MOMENTS

Caron WHEELER UK, female vocalist — 42 wks

18 Mar 89	● KEEP ON MOVING 10 TEN 263 [1]	5	12
10 Jun 89	★ BACK TO LIFE (HOWEVER DO YOU WANT ME) 10 TEN 265 [1]	1	14
8 Sep 90	LIVIN' IN THE LIGHT RCA PB 43939	14	6
10 Nov 90	UK BLAK RCA PB 43719	40	4
9 Feb 91	DON'T QUIT RCA PB 44259	53	3
7 Nov 92	I ADORE YOU Perspective PERSS 7407	59	2
11 Sep 93	BEACH OF THE WAR GODDESS EMI CDEM 282	75	1

[1] Soul II Soul featuring Caron Wheeler

Bill WHELAN featuring ANUNA and the RTE CONCERT ORCHESTRA Ireland, male composer, male / female choir and orchestra — 16 wks

| 17 Dec 94 | ● RIVERDANCE Son RTEBUACD 1 | 9 | 16 |

WHEN IN ROME UK, male vocal / instrumental group — 3 wks

| 28 Jan 89 | THE PROMISE 10 TEN 244 | 58 | 3 |

WHIGFIELD Denmark, female vocalist — 51 wks

17 Sep 94	★ SATURDAY NIGHT Systematic SYSCD 3	1	18
10 Dec 94	● ANOTHER DAY Systematic SYSCD 4	7	10
10 Jun 95	● THINK OF YOU Systematic SYSCDP 10	7	11

9 Sep 95	**CLOSE TO YOU** *Systematic SYCDP 18*	**13**	7
16 Dec 95	**LAST CHRISTMAS / BIG TIME** *Systematic SYSCD 24*	**21**	5

WHIPPING BOY *Ireland, male vocal / instrumental group* **4 wks**

14 Oct 95	**WE DON'T NEED NOBODY ELSE** *Columbia 6622205*	**51**	1
3 Feb 96	**WHEN WE WERE YOUNG** *Columbia 6628062*	**46**	2
25 May 96	**TWINKLE** *Columbia 6632272*	**55**	1

Nancy WHISKEY – See Charles McDEVITT SKIFFLE GROUP featuring Nancy WHISKEY

WHISPERS *US, male vocal group* **52 wks**

2 Feb 80	● **AND THE BEAT GOES ON** *Solar SO 1*	**2**	12
10 May 80	**LADY** *Solar SO 4*	**55**	3
12 Jul 80	**MY GIRL** *Solar SO 8*	**26**	6
14 Mar 81	● **IT'S A LOVE THING** *Solar SO 16*	**9**	11
13 Jun 81	**I CAN MAKE IT BETTER** *Solar SO 19*	**44**	5
19 Jan 85	**CONTAGIOUS** *MCA MCA 937*	**56**	3
28 Mar 87	**AND THE BEAT GOES ON (re-issue)** *Solar MCA 1126* ...	**45**	4
23 May 87	**ROCK STEADY** *Solar MCA 1152*	**38**	6
15 Aug 87	**SPECIAL F/X** *Solar MCA 1178*	**69**	2

WHISTLE *US, male rap group* **8 wks**

1 Mar 86	● **(NOTHIN' SERIOUS) JUST BUGGIN'** *Champion CHAMP 12*	**7**	8

Barry WHITE *US, male vocalist* **135 wks**

9 Jun 73	**I'M GONNA LOVE YOU JUST A LITTLE BIT MORE BABY** *Pye International 7N 25610*	**23**	7
26 Jan 74	**NEVER NEVER GONNA GIVE YA UP** *Pye International 7N 25633*	**14**	11
17 Aug 74	● **CAN'T GET ENOUGH OF YOUR LOVE BABE** *Pye International 7N 25661*	**8**	12
2 Nov 74	★ **YOU'RE THE FIRST THE LAST MY EVERYTHING** *20th Century BTC 2133*	**1**	14
8 Mar 75	● **WHAT AM I GONNA DO WITH YOU** *20th Century BTC 2177*	**5**	8
24 May 75	**(FOR YOU) I'LL DO ANYTHING YOU WANT ME TO** *20th Century BTC 2208*	**20**	6
27 Dec 75	● **LET THE MUSIC PLAY** *20th Century BTC 2265*	**9**	8
6 Mar 76	● **YOU SEE THE TROUBLE WITH ME** *20th Century BTC 2277*	**2**	10
21 Aug 76	**BABY WE BETTER TRY TO GET IT TOGETHER** *20th Century BTC 2298*	**15**	7
13 Nov 76	**DON'T MAKE ME WAIT TOO LONG** *20th Century BTC 2309*	**17**	8
5 Mar 77	**I'M QUALIFIED TO SATISFY** *20th Century BTC 2328*	**37**	5
15 Oct 77	**IT'S ECSTASY WHEN YOU LAY DOWN NEXT TO ME** *20th Century BTC 2350*	**40**	3
16 Dec 78	**JUST THE WAY YOU ARE** *20th Century BTC 2380*	**12**	12
24 Mar 79	**SHA LA LA MEANS I LOVE YOU** *20th Century BTC 1041*	**55**	6
7 Nov 87	**SHO' YOU RIGHT** *Breakout USA 614*	**14**	7
16 Jan 88	**NEVER NEVER GONNA GIVE YOU UP (re-mix)** *Club JAB 59*	**63**	2
31 Mar 90	**SECRET GARDEN** *Qwest W 9992* [1]	**67**	1
21 Jan 95	**PRACTICE WHAT YOU PREACH / LOVE IS THE ICON** *A & M 5808992*	**20**	4
8 Apr 95	**I ONLY WANT TO BE WITH YOU** *A & M 5810252*	**36**	2
21 Dec 96	**IN YOUR WILDEST DREAMS** *Parlophone CDR 6451* [2]	**32†**	2

[1] Quincy Jones featuring Al B. Sure!, James Ingram, El DeBarge and Barry White [2] Tina Turner featuring Barry White

Chris WHITE *UK, male vocalist* **4 wks**

20 Mar 76	**SPANISH WINE** *Charisma CB 272*	**37**	4

Karyn WHITE *US, female vocalist* **38 wks**

5 Nov 88	**THE WAY YOU LOVE ME** *Warner Bros. W 7773*	**42**	5
18 Feb 89	**SECRET RENDEZVOUS** *Warner Bros. W 7562*	**52**	3
10 Jun 89	**SUPERWOMAN** *Warner Bros. W 2920*	**11**	13
9 Sep 89	**SECRET RENDEZVOUS (re-issue)** *Warner Bros. W 2855* ..	**22**	9
17 Aug 91	**ROMANTIC** *Warner Bros. W 0028*	**23**	5
18 Jan 92	**THE WAY I FEEL ABOUT YOU** *Warner Bros. W 0073*	**65**	2
24 Sep 94	**HUNGAH** *Warner Bros. W 0264CD*	**69**	1

Snowy WHITE
UK, male vocalist / instrumentalist – guitar **12 wks**

24 Dec 83	● **BIRD OF PARADISE** *Towerbell TOW 42*	**6**	10
28 Dec 85	**FOR YOU** *R4 FOR 3*	**65**	1
18 Jan 86	**FOR YOU (re-entry)** *R4 FOR 3*	**72**	1

Tam WHITE *UK, male vocalist* **4 wks**

15 Mar 75	**WHAT IN THE WORLD'S COME OVER YOU** *RAK 193* ...	**36**	4

Tony Joe WHITE *US, male vocalist* **10 wks**

6 Jun 70	**GROUPIE GIRL** *Monument MON 1043*	**22**	10

WHITE and TORCH *UK, male vocal / instrumental duo* **4 wks**

2 Oct 82	**PARADE** *Chrysalis CHS 2641*	**54**	4

WHITE PLAINS *UK, male vocal group* **56 wks**

7 Feb 70	● **MY BABY LOVES LOVIN'** *Deram DM 280*	**9**	11
18 Apr 70	**I'VE GOT YOU ON MY MIND** *Deram DM 291*	**17**	11
24 Oct 70	● **JULIE DO YA LOVE ME** *Deram DM 315* [1]	**8**	14
12 Jun 71	**WHEN YOU ARE A KING** *Deram DM 333*	**13**	11
17 Feb 73	**STEP INTO A DREAM** *Deram DM 371*	**21**	9

[1] White Plains with Pete Nelson

WHITE ZOMBIE *US, male vocal / instrumental group* **4 wks**

20 May 95	**MORE HUMAN THAN HUMAN** *Geffen GFSTD 92*	**51**	2
18 May 96	**ELECTRIC HEAD PART 2 (THE ECSTASY)** *Geffen GFSXD 22140*	**31**	2

WHITEHEAD BROS. *US, male vocal duo* **5 wks**

14 Jan 95	**YOUR LOVE IS A 187** *Motown TMGCD 1434*	**32**	3
13 May 95	**FORGET I WAS A G** *Motown TMGCD 1441*	**40**	2

WHITEOUT *UK, male vocal / instrumental group* **2 wks**

24 Sep 94	**DETROIT** *Silvertone ORECD 66*	**73**	1
18 Feb 95	**JACKIE'S RACING** *Silvertone ORECD 68*	**72**	1

WHITESNAKE *UK, male vocal / instrumental group* **111 wks**

24 Jun 78	**SNAKE BITE EP** *EMI International INEP 751* [1]	**61**	3
10 Nov 79	**LONG WAY FROM HOME** *United Artists BP 324*	**55**	2
26 Apr 80	**FOOL FOR YOUR LOVING** *United Artists BP 352*	**13**	9
12 Jul 80	**READY AN' WILLING (SWEET SATISFACTION)** *United Artists BP 363*	**43**	4
22 Nov 80	**AIN'T NO LOVE IN THE HEART OF THE CITY** *Sunburst/Liberty BP 381*	**51**	4
11 Apr 81	**DON'T BREAK MY HEART AGAIN** *Liberty BP 395*	**17**	9
6 Jun 81	**WOULD I LIE TO YOU** *Liberty BP 399*	**37**	6

6 Nov 82	**HERE I GO AGAIN / BLOODY LUXURY**	
	Liberty BP 416 ....**34** 10	
13 Aug 83	**GUILTY OF LOVE** *Liberty BP 420* **31** 5	
14 Jan 84	**GIVE ME MORE TIME** *Liberty BP 422* **29** 4	
28 Apr 84	**STANDING IN THE SHADOW** *Liberty BP 423* **62** 2	
9 Feb 85	**LOVE AIN'T NO STRANGER** *Liberty BP 424* **44** 4	
28 Mar 87	**STILL OF THE NIGHT** *EMI EMI 5606* **16** 8	
6 Jun 87	● **IS THIS LOVE** *EMI EM 3* **9** 11	
31 Oct 87	● **HERE I GO AGAIN (re-mix)** *EMI EM 35* **9** 11	
6 Feb 88	**GIVE ME ALL YOUR LOVE** *EMI EM 23* **18** 6	
2 Dec 89	**FOOL FOR YOUR LOVING** *EMI EM 123* **43** 2	
10 Mar 90	**THE DEEPER THE LOVE** *EMI EM 128* **35** 3	
25 Aug 90	**NOW YOU'RE GONE** *EMI EM 150* **31** 4	
6 Aug 94	**IS THIS LOVE (re-issue) / SWEET LADY LUCK**	
	EMI CDEM 329 ....**25** 4	

1 David Coverdale's Whitesnake

Tracks on Snake Bite EP: *Bloody Mary / Steal Away / Ain't No Love In The Heart Of The City / Come On. EM 123 is a re-recording of their third hit.*

David WHITFIELD *UK, male vocalist* **181 wks**

2 Oct 53	● **BRIDGE OF SIGHS** *Decca F 10129* **9** 1	
16 Oct 53	★ **ANSWER ME** *Decca F 10192* **1** 13	
11 Dec 53	**RAGS TO RICHES** *Decca F 10207* 1 ....**12** 1	
8 Jan 54	**RAGS TO RICHES (re-entry)** *Decca F 10207* 1 ....**3** 10	
29 Jan 54	**ANSWER ME (re-entry)** *Decca F 10192* **12** 1	
19 Feb 54	● **THE BOOK** *Decca F 10242* 1 ....**5** 12	
28 May 54	● **THE BOOK (re-entry)** *Decca F 10242* 1 ....**10** 3	
18 Jun 54	★ **CARA MIA** *Decca F 10327* 2 ....**1** 25	
12 Nov 54	**SANTO NATALE** *Decca F 10399* **2** 10	
11 Feb 55	**BEYOND THE STARS** *Decca F 10458* **8** 9	
27 May 55	**MAMA** *Decca F 10515* **20** 1	
24 Jun 55	**MAMA (re-entry)** *Decca F 10515* **19** 2	
8 Jul 55	**EV'RYWHERE** *Decca F 10515* 3 ....**3** 20	
29 Jul 55	**MAMA (2nd re-entry)** *Decca F 10515* **12** 8	
25 Nov 55	● **WHEN YOU LOSE THE ONE YOU LOVE**	
	Decca F 10627 2 ....**7** 11	
2 Mar 56	**MY SEPTEMBER LOVE** *Decca F 10690* **19** 2	
23 Mar 56	**MY SEPTEMBER LOVE (re-entry)** *Decca F 10690* **18** 1	
6 Apr 56	● **MY SEPTEMBER LOVE (2nd re-entry)** *Decca F 10690* ...**3** 20	
24 Aug 56	**MY SON JOHN** *Decca F 10769* **22** 4	
31 Aug 56	**MY UNFINISHED SYMPHONY** *Decca F 10769* **29** 1	
7 Sep 56	**MY SEPTEMBER LOVE (3rd re-entry)** *Decca F 10690* ...**25** 1	
25 Jan 57	● **ADORATION WALTZ** *Decca F 10833* 3 .....**9** 11	
5 Apr 57	**I'LL FIND YOU** *Decca F 10864* **28** 2	
7 Jun 57	**I'LL FIND YOU (re-entry)** *Decca F 10864* **27** 2	
14 Feb 58	**CRY MY HEART** *Decca F 10978* 2 ....**22** 3	
16 May 58	**ON THE STREET WHERE YOU LIVE**	
	Decca F 11018 4 ....**16** 14	
8 Aug 58	**THE RIGHT TO LOVE** *Decca F 11039* **30** 1	
24 Nov 60	**I BELIEVE** *Decca F 11289* **49** 1	

1 David Whitfield with Stanley Buick and his Orchestra 2 David Whitfield with chorus and Mantovani and his Orchestra 3 David Whitfield with the Roland Shaw Orchestra 4 David Whitfield with Cyril Stapleton and his Orchestra

See also Various Artists (EPs & LPs) – All-Star Hit Parade; Mantovani.

Slim WHITMAN *US, male vocalist* **75 wks**

15 Jul 55	★ **ROSE MARIE** *London HL 8061* **1** 19	
29 Jul 55	● **INDIAN LOVE CALL** *London L 1149* **7** 12	
23 Sep 55	**CHINA DOLL** *London L 1149* **15** 2	
9 Mar 56	**TUMBLING TUMBLEWEEDS** *London HLU 8230* **19** 2	
13 Apr 56	**I'M A FOOL** *London HLU 8252* **16** 3	
11 May 56	**I'M A FOOL (re-entry)** *London HLU 8252* **29** 1	
22 Jun 56	**SERENADE** *London HLU 8287* **24** 3	
27 Jul 56	● **SERENADE (re-entry)** *London HLU 8287* ...**8** 12	
12 Apr 57	● **I'LL TAKE YOU HOME AGAIN KATHLEEN**	
	London HLP 8403 ....**7** 13	
5 Oct 74	**HAPPY ANNIVERSARY** *United Artists UP 35728* **14** 10	

Roger WHITTAKER *Kenya, male vocalist* **85 wks**

8 Nov 69	**DURHAM TOWN (THE LEAVIN')** *Columbia DB 8613* **12** 18	
11 Apr 70	● **I DON'T BELIEVE IN IF ANYMORE** *Columbia DB 8664* **8** 18	
10 Oct 70	**NEW WORLD IN THE MORNING** *Columbia DB 8718* **17** 14	
3 Apr 71	**WHY** *Columbia DB 8752* **47** 1	
2 Oct 71	**MAMMY BLUE** *Columbia DB 8822* **31** 10	
26 Jul 75	● **THE LAST FAREWELL** *EMI 2294* **2** 14	
8 Nov 86	● **THE SKYE BOAT SONG** *Tembo TML 119* 1 ....**10** 10	

1 Roger Whittaker and Des O'Connor

WHO *UK, male vocal / instrumental group* **247 wks**

18 Feb 65	● **I CAN'T EXPLAIN** *Brunswick 05926* **8** 13	
27 May 65	● **ANYWAY ANYHOW ANYWHERE** *Brunswick 05935* **10** 12	
4 Nov 65	● **MY GENERATION** *Brunswick 05944* **2** 13	
10 Mar 66	● **SUBSTITUTE** *Reaction 591 001* **5** 13	
24 Mar 66	**A LEGAL MATTER** *Brunswick 05956* **32** 6	
1 Sep 66	● **I'M A BOY** *Reaction 591 004* **2** 13	
1 Sep 66	**THE KIDS ARE ALRIGHT** *Brunswick 05965* ...**41** 2	
22 Sep 66	**THE KIDS ARE ALRIGHT (re-entry)** *Brunswick 05965* ...**48** 1	
15 Dec 66	● **HAPPY JACK** *Reaction 591 010* **3** 11	
27 Apr 67	● **PICTURES OF LILY** *Track 604 002* **4** 10	
26 Jul 67	**THE LAST TIME / UNDER MY THUMB** *Track 604 006* **44** 3	
18 Oct 67	● **I CAN SEE FOR MILES** *Track 604 011* **10** 12	
19 Jun 68	**DOGS** *Track 604 023* **25** 5	
23 Oct 68	**MAGIC BUS** *Track 604 024* **26** 6	
19 Mar 69	● **PINBALL WIZARD** *Track 604 027* **4** 13	
4 Apr 70	**THE SEEKER** *Track 604 036* **19** 11	
8 Aug 70	**SUMMERTIME BLUES** *Track 2094 002* **38** 4	
10 Jul 71	● **WON'T GET FOOLED AGAIN** *Track 2094 009* ...**9** 12	
23 Oct 71	**LET'S SEE ACTION** *Track 2094 012* **16** 12	
24 Jun 72	● **JOIN TOGETHER** *Track 2094 102* **9** 9	
13 Jan 73	**RELAY** *Track 2094 106* **21** 5	
13 Oct 73	**5:15** *Track 2094 115* **20** 6	
24 Jan 76	● **SQUEEZE BOX** *Polydor 2121 275* **10** 9	
30 Oct 76	● **SUBSTITUTE (re-issue)** *Polydor 2058 803* ..**7** 7	
22 Jul 78	**WHO ARE YOU** *Polydor WHO 1* **18** 12	
28 Apr 79	**LONG LIVE ROCK** *Polydor WHO 2* **48** 5	
7 Mar 81	● **YOU BETTER YOU BET** *Polydor WHO 004* ...**9** 8	
9 May 81	**DON'T LET GO THE COAT** *Polydor WHO 005* **47** 4	
2 Oct 82	**ATHENA** *Polydor WHO 6* **40** 4	
26 Nov 83	**READY STEADY WHO EP** *Polydor WHO 7* **58** 2	
20 Feb 88	**MY GENERATION (re-issue)** *Polydor POSP 907* **68** 2	
27 Jul 96	**MY GENERATION (2nd re-issue)** *Polydor 8546372* **31** 2	

Tracks on Ready Steady Who EP: *Disguises / Circles / Batman / Bucket 'T' / Barbara Ann. See also High Numbers.*

WHODINI *US, male rap / scratch duo* **10 wks**

25 Dec 82	**MAGIC'S WAND** *Jive JIVE 28* **47** 6	
17 Mar 84	**MAGIC'S WAND (THE WHODINI ELECTRIC EP)**	
	Jive JIVE 61 ....**63** 4	

Tracks on The Whodini Electric EP: *Jive Magic Wand / Nasty Lady / Rap Machine / The Haunted House of Rock.*

WHOOLIGANZ *US, male rap duo* **2 wks**

13 Aug 94	**PUT YOUR HANDZ UP** *Positiva CDTIV 17* **53** 2	

WHYCLIFFE *UK, male vocalist* **2 wks**

20 Nov 93	**HEAVEN** *MCA MCSTD 1944* **56** 1	
2 Apr 94	**ONE MORE TIME** *MCA MCSTD 1955* **72** 1	

Jane WIEDLIN *US, female vocalist* **14 wks**

6 Aug 88	**RUSH HOUR** *Manhattan MT 36* **12** 11	
29 Oct 88	**INSIDE A DREAM** *Manhattan MT 55* **64** 3	

WIGAN'S CHOSEN FEW
US, instrumental track plus UK crowd vocal   **11 wks**

| 18 Jan 75 | ● **FOOTSEE** *Pye Disco Demand DDS 111* | **9** 11 |

WIGAN'S OVATION
UK, male vocal / instrumental group   **19 wks**

15 Mar 75	**SKIING IN THE SNOW** *Spark SRL 1122*	**12** 10
28 Jun 75	**PER-SO-NAL-LY** *Spark SRL 1129*	**38** 6
29 Nov 75	**SUPER LOVE** *Spark SRL 1133*	**41** 3

Jack WILD *UK, male vocalist*   **2 wks**

| 2 May 70 | **SOME BEAUTIFUL** *Capitol CL 15635* | **46** 2 |

WILD BOYS – *See HEINZ*

WILD CHERRY *US, male vocal / instrumental group*   **11 wks**

| 9 Oct 76 | ● **PLAY THAT FUNKY MUSIC** *Epic EPC 4593* | **7** 11 |

WILD COLOUR
UK, male / female vocal / instrumental group   **2 wks**

| 14 Oct 95 | **DREAMS** *Perfecto PERF 105CD* | **25** 2 |

WILD PAIR – *See Paula ABDUL*

WILD WEEKEND *UK, male vocal / instrumental group*   **2 wks**

| 29 Apr 89 | **BREAKIN' UP** *Parlophone R 6204* | **74** 1 |
| 5 May 90 | **WHO'S AFRAID OF THE BIG BAD LOVE** *Parlophone R 6249* | **70** 1 |

WILDCHILD *UK, male producer – Roger McKenzie*   **9 wks**

22 Apr 95	**LEGENDS OF THE DARK BLACK PART 2** *Hi-Life HICD 9*	**34** 3
21 Oct 95	**RENEGADE MASTER (re-issue)** *Hi-Life 5771312*	**11** 4
23 Nov 96	**JUMP TO MY BEAT** *Hi-Life 5757372*	**30** 2

Although titled differently first two hits are identical.

Eugene WILDE *US, male vocalist*   **15 wks**

| 13 Oct 84 | **GOTTA GET YOU HOME TONIGHT** *Fourth & Broadway BRW 15* | **18** 9 |
| 2 Feb 85 | **PERSONALITY** *Fourth & Broadway BRW 18* | **34** 6 |

Personality was coupled with Let Her Feel It *by Simplicious.*

Kim WILDE *UK, female vocalist*   **194 wks**

21 Feb 81	● **KIDS IN AMERICA** *RAK 327*	**2** 13
9 May 81	● **CHEQUERED LOVE** *RAK 330*	**4** 9
1 Aug 81	**WATER ON GLASS / BOYS** *RAK 334*	**11** 8
14 Nov 81	**CAMBODIA** *RAK 336*	**12** 12
17 Apr 82	**VIEW FROM A BRIDGE** *RAK 342*	**16** 7
16 Oct 82	**CHILD COME AWAY** *RAK 352*	**43** 4
30 Jul 83	**LOVE BLONDE** *RAK 360*	**23** 8
12 Nov 83	**DANCING IN THE DARK** *RAK 365*	**67** 2
13 Oct 84	**THE SECOND TIME** *MCA KIM 1*	**29** 6
8 Dec 84	**THE TOUCH** *MCA KIM 2*	**56** 3
27 Apr 85	**RAGE TO LOVE** *MCA KIM 3*	**19** 8
25 Oct 86	● **YOU KEEP ME HANGIN' ON** *MCA KIM 4*	**2** 14
4 Apr 87	● **ANOTHER STEP (CLOSER TO YOU)** *MCA KIM 5* [1]	**6** 11
8 Aug 87	**SAY YOU REALLY WANT ME** *MCA KIM 6*	**29** 5
5 Dec 87	● **ROCKIN' AROUND THE CHRISTMAS TREE** *10 TEN 2* [2]	**3** 7
14 May 88	● **HEY MISTER HEARTACHE** *MCA KIM 7*	**31** 5
16 Jul 88	● **YOU CAME** *MCA KIM 8*	**3** 11
1 Oct 88	● **NEVER TRUST A STRANGER** *MCA KIM 9*	**7** 9
3 Dec 88	● **FOUR LETTER WORD** *MCA KIM 10*	**6** 12
4 Mar 89	**LOVE IN THE NATURAL WAY** *MCA KIM 11*	**32** 6
14 Apr 90	**IT'S HERE** *MCA KIM 12*	**42** 4
16 Jun 90	**TIME** *MCA KIM 13*	**71** 3
15 Dec 90	**I CAN'T SAY GOODBYE** *MCA KIM 14*	**51** 3
2 May 92	**LOVE IS HOLY** *MCA KIM 15*	**16** 6
27 Jun 92	**HEART OVER MIND** *MCA KIM 16*	**34** 3
12 Sep 92	**WHO DO YOU THINK YOU ARE** *MCA KIM 17*	**49** 3
10 Jul 93	**IF I CAN'T HAVE YOU** *MCA KIMTD 18*	**12** 8
13 Nov 93	**IN MY LIFE** *MCA KIMTD 19*	**54** 1
14 Oct 95	**BREAKIN' AWAY** *MCA KIMTD 21*	**43** 2
10 Feb 96	**THIS I SWEAR** *MCA KIMTD 22*	**46** 1

[1] Kim Wilde and Junior [2] Mel and Kim

Mel is Mel Smith.

Marty WILDE *UK, male vocalist*   **117 wks**

11 Jul 58	● **ENDLESS SLEEP** *Philips PB 835*	**4** 14
6 Mar 59	● **DONNA** *Philips PB 902*	**3** 16
5 Jun 59	● **A TEENAGER IN LOVE** *Philips PB 926*	**2** 17
3 Jul 59	**DONNA (re-entry)** *Philips PB 902*	**25** 2
25 Sep 59	● **SEA OF LOVE** *Philips PB 959*	**3** 12
11 Dec 59	● **BAD BOY** *Philips PB 972*	**7** 8
10 Mar 60	**JOHNNY ROCCO** *Philips PB 1002*	**30** 4
19 May 60	**THE FIGHT** *Philips PB 1022*	**47** 1
22 Dec 60	**LITTLE GIRL** *Philips PB 1078*	**16** 9
26 Jan 61	● **RUBBER BALL** *Philips PB 1101*	**9** 9
27 Jul 61	**HIDE AND SEEK** *Philips PB 1161*	**47** 2
9 Nov 61	**TOMORROW'S CLOWN** *Philips PB 1191*	**33** 5
24 May 62	**JEZEBEL** *Philips PB 1240*	**19** 11
25 Oct 62	**EVER SINCE YOU SAID GOODBYE** *Philips 326546 BF*	**31** 7

Matthew WILDER *US, male vocalist*   **11 wks**

| 21 Jan 84 | ● **BREAK MY STRIDE** *Epic A 3908* | **4** 11 |

WILDHEARTS *UK, male vocal / instrumental group*   **20 wks**

20 Nov 93	**TV TAN** *Bronze YZ 784CD*	**53** 2
19 Feb 94	**CAFFEINE BOMB** *Bronze YZ 794CD*	**31** 3
9 Jul 94	**SUCKERPUNCH** *Bronze YZ 828CD*	**38** 2
28 Jan 95	**IF LIFE IS LIKE A LOVE BANK I WANT AN OVERDRAFT / GEORDIE IN WONDERLAND** *East West YZ 874CD*	**31** 3
6 May 95	**I WANNA GO WHERE THE PEOPLE GO** *East West YZ 923CD*	**16** 3
29 Jul 95	**JUST IN LUST** *East West YZ 967CD*	**28** 2
20 Apr 96	**SICK OF DRUGS** *Round WILD 1CD*	**14** 3
29 Jun 96	**RED LIGHT – GREEN LIGHT (EP)** *Round WILD 2CD*	**30** 2

Tracks on Red Light – Green Light (EP): Red Light – Green Light / Got It On Tuesday / Do Anything / The British All-American Homeboy Crowd.

Sue WILKINSON *UK, female vocalist*   **8 wks**

| 2 Aug 80 | **YOU GOTTA BE A HUSTLER IF YOU WANNA GET ON** *Cheapskate CHEAP 2* | **25** 8 |

WILL TO POWER
US, male / female vocal / instrumental duo   **18 wks**

| 7 Jan 89 | ● **BABY I LOVE YOUR WAY – FREEBIRD** *Epic 653094 7* | **6** 9 |
| 22 Dec 90 | **I'M NOT IN LOVE** *Epic 6565377* | **29** 9 |

Alyson WILLIAMS US, female vocalist · 28 wks

4 Mar 89		SLEEP TALK Def Jam 654656 7	17	9
6 May 89		MY LOVE IS SO RAW Def Jam 654898 7 [1]	34	5
19 Aug 89	●	I NEED YOUR LOVIN' Def Jam 655143 7	8	11
18 Nov 89		I SECOND THAT EMOTION Def Jam 655456 7	44	3

[1] Alyson Williams featuring Nikki D

Andy WILLIAMS US, male vocalist · 228 wks

19 Apr 57	★	BUTTERFLY London HLA 8399	1	15
21 Jun 57		I LIKE YOUR KIND OF LOVE London HLA 8437	16	10
30 Aug 57		BUTTERFLY (re-entry) London HLA 8399	29	1
14 Jun 62		STRANGER ON THE SHORE CBS AAG 103	30	10
21 Mar 63	●	CAN'T GET USED TO LOSING YOU CBS AAG 138	2	18
27 Feb 64		A FOOL NEVER LEARNS CBS AAG 182	40	4
16 Sep 65	●	ALMOST THERE CBS 201813	2	17
24 Feb 66		MAY EACH DAY CBS 202042	19	8
22 Sep 66		IN THE ARMS OF LOVE CBS 202300	33	7
4 May 67		MUSIC TO WATCH GIRLS BY CBS 2675	33	6
2 Aug 67		MORE AND MORE CBS 2886	45	1
13 Mar 68	●	CAN'T TAKE MY EYES OFF YOU CBS 3298	5	18
7 May 69		HAPPY HEART CBS 4062	47	1
21 May 69		HAPPY HEART (re-entry) CBS 4062	19	9
14 Mar 70	●	CAN'T HELP FALLING IN LOVE CBS 4818	3	17
1 Aug 70		IT'S SO EASY CBS 5113	13	13
7 Nov 70		IT'S SO EASY (re-entry) CBS 5113	49	1
21 Nov 70	●	HOME LOVIN' MAN CBS 5267	7	12
20 Mar 71	●	(WHERE DO I BEGIN) LOVE STORY CBS 7020	4	17
24 Jul 71		(WHERE DO I BEGIN) LOVE STORY (re-entry) CBS 7020	49	1
5 Aug 72		LOVE THEME FROM 'THE GODFATHER' CBS 8166	50	1
2 Sep 72		LOVE THEME FROM 'THE GODFATHER' (re-entry) CBS 8166	44	3
30 Sep 72		LOVE THEME FROM 'THE GODFATHER' (2nd re-entry) CBS 8166	42	5
8 Dec 73	●	SOLITAIRE CBS 1824	4	18
18 May 74		GETTING OVER YOU CBS 2181	35	5
31 May 75		YOU LAY SO EASY ON MY MIND CBS 3167	32	7
6 Mar 76		THE OTHER SIDE OF ME CBS 3903	42	3

Andy and David WILLIAMS US, male vocal duo · 5 wks

24 Mar 73	I DON'T KNOW WHY (I JUST DO) MCA MUS 1183	37	5

Do not see Andy Williams. This Andy is the nephew of the other Andy.

Billy WILLIAMS US, male vocalist · 9 wks

2 Aug 57	I'M GONNA SIT RIGHT DOWN AND WRITE MYSELF A LETTER Vogue Coral Q 72266	22	8
18 Oct 57	I'M GONNA SIT RIGHT DOWN AND WRITE MYSELF A LETTER (re-entry) Vogue Coral Q 72266	28	1

Danny WILLIAMS UK, male vocalist · 74 wks

25 May 61		WE WILL NEVER BE AS YOUNG AS THIS AGAIN HMV POP 839	44	3
6 Jul 61		THE MIRACLE OF YOU HMV POP 885	41	8
2 Nov 61	★	MOON RIVER HMV POP 932	1	19
18 Jan 62		JEANNIE HMV POP 968	14	14
12 Apr 62	●	WONDERFUL WORLD OF THE YOUNG HMV POP 1002	8	13
5 Jul 62		TEARS HMV POP 1035	22	7
28 Feb 63		MY OWN TRUE LOVE HMV POP 1112	45	3
30 Jul 77		DANCIN' EASY Ensign ENY 3	30	7

Deniece WILLIAMS US, female vocalist · 59 wks

2 Apr 77	★	FREE CBS 4978	1	10

30 Jul 77	●	THAT'S WHAT FRIENDS ARE FOR CBS 5432	8	11
12 Nov 77		BABY BABY MY LOVE'S ALL FOR YOU CBS 5779	32	5
25 Mar 78	●	TOO MUCH TOO LITTLE TOO LATE CBS 6164 [1]	3	14
29 Jul 78		YOU'RE ALL I NEED TO GET BY CBS 6483 [1]	45	6
5 May 84	●	LET'S HEAR IT FOR THE BOY CBS A 4319	2	12
4 Aug 84		LET'S HEAR IT FOR THE BOY (re-entry) CBS A 4319	75	1

[1] Johnny Mathis and Deniece Williams

Diana WILLIAMS US, female vocalist · 3 wks

25 Jul 81	TEDDY BEAR'S LAST RIDE Capitol CL 207	54	3

Don WILLIAMS US, male vocalist · 16 wks

19 Jun 76	I RECALL A GYPSY WOMAN ABC 4098	13	10
23 Oct 76	YOU'RE MY BEST FRIEND ABC 4144	35	6

Freedom WILLIAMS US, male rapper · 31 wks

15 Dec 90	●	GONNA MAKE YOU SWEAT (EVERYBODY DANCE NOW) CBS 6564540 [1]	3	12
30 Mar 91		HERE WE GO Columbia 6567537 [1]	20	7
6 Jul 91	●	THINGS THAT MAKE YOU GO HMMM... Columbia 6566907 [1]	4	11
5 Jun 93		VOICE OF FREEDOM Columbia 6593342	62	1

[1] C & C Music Factory (featuring Freedom Williams)

Geoffrey WILLIAMS UK, male vocalist · 5 wks

11 Apr 92	IT'S NOT A LOVE THING EMI EM 228	63	2
22 Aug 92	SUMMER BREEZE EMI EM 245	56	3

Iris WILLIAMS UK, female vocalist · 8 wks

27 Oct 79	HE WAS BEAUTIFUL (CAVATINA) (THE THEME FROM 'THE DEER HUNTER') Columbia DB 9070	18	8

John WILLIAMS UK, male instrumentalist – guitar · 11 wks

19 May 79	CAVATINA Cube BUG 80	13	11

John WILLIAMS
US, orchestra leader with US, orchestra · 12 wks

18 Dec 82	THEME FROM 'E.T.' (THE EXTRA-TERRESTRIAL) MCA 800	17	10
14 Aug 93	THEME FROM 'JURASSIC PARK' MCA MCSTD 1927	45	2

Kenny WILLIAMS US, male vocalist · 7 wks

19 Nov 77	(YOU'RE) FABULOUS BABE Decca FR 13731	35	7

Larry WILLIAMS US, male vocalist · 18 wks

20 Sep 57	SHORT FAT FANNIE London HLN 8472	21	8
17 Jan 58	BONY MORONIE London HLU 8532	11	10

Lenny WILLIAMS US, male vocalist · 7 wks

5 Nov 77	SHOO DOO FU FU OOH ABC 4194	38	4
16 Sep 78	YOU GOT ME BURNING ABC 4228	67	3

Mark WILLIAMS – See Karen BODDINGTON and Mark WILLIAMS

Mason WILLIAMS
US, male instrumentalist – guitar **13 wks**

28 Aug 68 ● **CLASSICAL GAS** *Warner Bros. WB 7190* **9** 13

Maurice WILLIAMS and the ZODIACS
US, male vocal group **9 wks**

5 Jan 61 **STAY** *Top Rank JAR 526* **14** 9

Melanie WILLIAMS *UK, female vocalist* **21 wks**

10 Apr 93	● **AIN'T NO LOVE (AIN'T NO USE)**		
	Rob's CDROB 9 [1]	**3**	11
9 Apr 94	**ALL CRIED OUT** *Columbia 6601872*	**60**	2
11 Jun 94	**EVERYDAY THANG** *Columbia 6604712*	**38**	3
17 Sep 94	**NOT ENOUGH** *Columbia 6607752*	**65**	1
18 Feb 95	**YOU ARE EVERYTHING** *Columbia 6611755* [2]	**28**	4

[1] Sub Sub featuring Melanie Williams [2] Melanie Williams and Joe Roberts

Robbie WILLIAMS *UK, male vocalist* **17 wks**

| 10 Aug 96 | ● **FREEDOM** *Chrysalis CDFREE 1* | **2** | 10 |
| 26 Oct 96 | **FREEDOM (re-entry)** *Chrysalis CDFREE 1* | **56** | 4 |

Vanessa WILLIAMS *US, female vocalist* **24 wks**

20 Aug 88	**THE RIGHT STUFF** *Wing WING 3*	**71**	1
25 Mar 89	**DREAMIN'** *Wing WING 4*	**74**	2
19 Aug 89	**THE RIGHT STUFF (re-mix)** *Wing WINR 3*	**62**	2
21 Apr 92	● **SAVE THE BEST FOR LAST** *Polydor PO 192*	**3**	11
8 Apr 95	**THE SWEETEST DAYS** *Mercury MERCD 422*	**41**	2
8 Jul 95	**THE WAY THAT YOU LOVE** *Mercury MERCD 439*	**52**	1
18 Sep 95	**COLOURS OF THE WIND**		
	Walt Disney WD 7677CD	**21**	5

Vesta WILLIAMS *US, female vocalist* **13 wks**

20 Dec 86 **ONCE BITTEN TWICE SHY** *A & M AM 362* **14** 13

Wendell WILLIAMS *US, male rapper* **6 wks**

| 6 Oct 90 | **EVERYBODY (RAP)** *Deconstruction PB 44701* [1] | **30** | 4 |
| 18 May 91 | **SO GROOVY** *Deconstruction PB 44567* | **74** | 2 |

[1] Criminal Element Orchestra and Wendell Williams

WILLING SINNERS – *See Marc ALMOND*

Bruce WILLIS *US, male vocalist* **30 wks**

7 Mar 87	● **RESPECT YOURSELF** *Motown ZB 41117*	**7**	10
30 May 87	● **UNDER THE BOARDWALK** *Motown ZB 41349*	**2**	15
12 Sep 87	**SECRET AGENT MAN – JAMES BOND IS BACK**		
	Motown ZB 41437	**43**	4
23 Jan 88	**COMIN' RIGHT UP** *Motown ZB 41453*	**73**	1

Chill WILLS – *See LAUREL and HARDY with the AVALON BOYS featuring Chill WILLS*

Viola WILLS *US, female vocalist* **16 wks**

6 Oct 79	● **GONNA GET ALONG WITHOUT YOU NOW**		
	Ariola/Hansa AHA 546	**8**	10
15 Mar 86	**BOTH SIDES NOW / DARE TO DREAM**		
	Streetwave KHAN 66	**35**	6

Al WILSON *US, male vocalist* **5 wks**

23 Aug 75 **THE SNAKE** *Bell 1436* **41** 5

Charlie WILSON – *see SNOOP DOGGY DOGG*

Dooley WILSON *US, male vocalist* **9 wks**

3 Dec 77 **AS TIME GOES BY** *United Artists UP 36331* **15** 9

Disc has credit 'with the voices of Humphrey Bogart and Ingrid Bergman'.

Jackie WILSON *US, male vocalist* **97 wks**

15 Nov 57	● **REET PETITE** *Coral Q 72290*	**6**	14
14 Mar 58	**TO BE LOVED** *Coral Q 72306*	**27**	1
28 Mar 58	**TO BE LOVED (re-entry)** *Coral Q 72306*	**23**	6
16 May 58	**TO BE LOVED (2nd re-entry)** *Coral Q 72306*	**23**	1
15 Sep 60	**(YOU WERE MADE FOR) ALL MY LOVE** *Coral Q 72407*	**33**	6
3 Nov 60	**(YOU WERE MADE FOR) ALL MY LOVE (re-entry)**		
	Coral Q 72407	**47**	1
22 Dec 60	**ALONE AT LAST** *Coral Q 72412*	**50**	1
14 May 69	**(YOUR LOVE KEEPS LIFTING ME) HIGHER AND**		
	HIGHER *MCA BAG 2*	**11**	11
29 Jul 72	● **I GET THE SWEETEST FEELING** *MCA MU 1160*	**9**	13
3 May 75	**I GET THE SWEETEST FEELING / (YOUR LOVE KEEPS**		
	LIFTING ME) HIGHER AND HIGHER (re-issues)		
	Brunswick BR 18	**25**	8
29 Nov 86	★ **REET PETITE (THE SWEETEST GIRL IN TOWN)**		
	(re-issue) *SMP SKM 3*	**1**	17
28 Feb 87	● **I GET THE SWEETEST FEELING (2nd re-issue)**		
	SMP SKM 1	**3**	11
4 Jul 87	**HIGHER AND HIGHER (2nd re-issue)** *SMP SKM 10*	**15**	7

Higher and Higher was not listed together with I Get The Sweetest Feeling on Brunswick until 17 May 75.

Mari WILSON *UK, female vocalist* **34 wks**

6 Mar 82	**BEAT THE BEAT** *Compact PINK 2*	**59**	3
8 May 82	**BABY IT'S TRUE** *Compact PINK 3*	**42**	6
11 Sep 82	● **JUST WHAT I ALWAYS WANTED** *Compact PINK 4*	**8**	10
13 Nov 82	**(BEWARE) BOYFRIEND** *Compact PINK 5*	**51**	4
19 Mar 83	**CRY ME A RIVER** *Compact PINK 6*	**27**	7
11 Jun 83	**WONDERFUL** *Compact PINK 7*	**47**	4

Meri WILSON *US, female vocalist* **10 wks**

27 Aug 77 ● **TELEPHONE MAN** *Pye International 7N 25747* **6** 10

Mike 'Hitman' WILSON *US, male producer* **1 wk**

22 Sep 90 **ANOTHER SLEEPLESS NIGHT** *Arista 113506* **74** 1

Precious WILSON – *See ERUPTION; MESSIAH*

Tom WILSON *UK, male producer* **4 wks**

| 2 Dec 95 | **TECHNOCAT** *Pukka CDPUKKA 4* [1] | **33** | 3 |
| 16 Mar 96 | **LET YOUR BODY GO** *Clubscene DCSRT 050* | **60** | 1 |

[1] Technocat featuring Tom Wilson

WILSON PHILLIPS *US, female vocal group* **33 wks**

26 May 90	● **HOLD ON** *SBK SBK 6*	**6**	12
18 Aug 90	**RELEASE ME** *SBK SBK 11*	**36**	5
10 Nov 90	**IMPULSIVE** *SBK SBK 16*	**42**	3

11 May 91	**YOU'RE IN LOVE** SBK SBK 25	**29** 5
23 May 92	**YOU WON'T SEE ME CRY** SBK SBK 34	**18** 5
22 Aug 92	**GIVE IT UP** SBK SBK 36	**36** 3

Chris WILTSHIRE – *See CLASS ACTION featuring Chris WILTSHIRE*

WIN *UK, male vocal / instrumental group*　　3 wks

| 4 Apr 87 | **SUPER POPOID GROOVE** Swamplands LON 128 | **63** 3 |

WINANS *US, male vocal group*　　1 wk

| 30 Nov 85 | **LET MY PEOPLE GO (PART 1)** Qwest W 8874 | **71** 1 |

Ce Ce WINANS – *See Whitney HOUSTON*

WINDJAMMER *US, male vocal / instrumental group*　　12 wks

| 30 Jun 84 | **TOSSING AND TURNING** MCA MCA 897 | **18** 12 |

Rose WINDROSS – *See SOUL II SOUL*

WING AND A PRAYER FIFE AND DRUM CORPS *US, male / female vocal / instrumental group*　　7 wks

| 24 Jan 76 | **BABY FACE** Atlantic K 10705 | **12** 7 |

WINGER *US, male vocal / instrumental group*　　3 wks

| 19 Jan 91 | **MILES AWAY** Atlantic A 7802 | **56** 3 |

Pete WINGFIELD *UK, male vocalist*　　7 wks

| 28 Jun 75 | ● **EIGHTEEN WITH A BULLET** Island WIP 6231 | **7** 7 |

WINGS – *See Paul McCARTNEY*

Josh WINK *US, male producer*　　26 wks

6 May 95	**DON'T LAUGH** XL XLS 62CD [1]	**38** 2
21 Oct 95	● **HIGHER STATE OF CONCIOUSNESS** Manifesto FESCD 3	**8** 8
30 Dec 95	**HIGHER STATE OF CONCIOUSNESS (re-entry)** Manifesto FESCD 3	**60** 4
2 Mar 96	**HYPNOTIZIN'** XL XLS 71CD [1]	**35** 2
27 Jul 96	● **HIGHER STATE OF CONCIOUSNESS (re-mix)** Manifesto FESCD 9 [1]	**7** 10

[1] Winx

See also Size 9.

Edgar WINTER GROUP *US, male instrumental group*　9 wks

| 26 May 73 | **FRANKENSTEIN** Epic EPC 1440 | **18** 9 |

Ruby WINTERS *US, female vocalist*　　35 wks

5 Nov 77	● **I WILL** Creole CR 141	**4** 13
29 Apr 78	**COME TO ME** Creole CR 153	**11** 12
26 Aug 78	**I WON'T MENTION IT AGAIN** Creole CR 160	**45** 5
16 Jun 79	**BABY LAY DOWN** Creole CR 171	**43** 5

Steve WINWOOD *UK, male vocalist*　　33 wks

| 17 Jan 81 | **WHILE YOU SEE A CHANCE** Island WIP 6655 | **45** 5 |
| 9 Oct 82 | **VALERIE** Island WIP 6818 | **51** 4 |

28 Jun 86	**HIGHER LOVE** Island IS 288	**13** 9
13 Sep 86	**FREEDOM OVERSPILL** Island IS 294	**69** 1
24 Jan 87	**BACK IN THE HIGH LIFE AGAIN** Island IS 303	**53** 2
19 Sep 87	**VALERIE (re-issue)** Island IS 336	**19** 8
11 Jun 88	**ROLL WITH IT** Virgin VS 1085	**53** 4

WINX – *See Josh WINK*

WIRE *UK, male vocal / instrumental group*　　4 wks

| 27 Jan 79 | **OUTDOOR MINER** Harvest HAR 5172 | **51** 3 |
| 13 May 89 | **EARDRUM BUZZ** Mute MUTE 87 | **68** 1 |

Norman WISDOM *UK, male vocalist*　　20 wks

| 19 Feb 54 | ● **DON'T LAUGH AT ME** Columbia DB 3133 | **3** 15 |
| 15 Mar 57 | **WISDOM OF A FOOL** Columbia DB 3903 | **13** 5 |

Bill WITHERS *US, male vocalist*　　29 wks

12 Aug 72	**LEAN ON ME** A & M AMS 7004	**18** 9
14 Jan 78	● **LOVELY DAY** CBS 5773	**7** 8
25 May 85	**OH YEAH!** CBS A 6154	**60** 3
10 Sep 88	● **LOVELY DAY (re-mix)** CBS 653001 7	**4** 9

See also Grover Washington Jr.

WIX – *See SPIRO and WIX*

WIZZARD *UK, male vocal / instrumental group*　　77 wks

9 Dec 72	● **BALL PARK INCIDENT** Harvest HAR 5062	**6** 12
21 Apr 73	★ **SEE MY BABY JIVE** Harvest HAR 5070	**1** 17
1 Sep 73	★ **ANGEL FINGERS** Harvest HAR 5076	**1** 10
8 Dec 73	● **I WISH IT COULD BE CHRISTMAS EVERYDAY** Harvest HAR 5079 [1]	**4** 9
27 Apr 74	● **ROCK 'N' ROLL WINTER** Warner Bros. K 16357	**6** 7
10 Aug 74	**THIS IS THE STORY OF MY LOVE (BABY)** Warner Bros. K 16434	**34** 4
21 Dec 74	● **ARE YOU READY TO ROCK** Warner Bros. K 16497	**8** 10
19 Dec 81	**I WISH IT COULD BE CHRISTMAS EVERYDAY (re-issue)** Harvest HAR 5173 [1]	**41** 4
15 Dec 84	**I WISH IT COULD BE CHRISTMAS EVERYDAY (re-entry of re-issue)** Harvest HAR 5173 [1]	**23** 4

[1] Wizzard featuring vocal backing by the Suedettes plus the Stockland Green Bilateral School First Year Choir with additional noises by Miss Snob and Class 3C

Jah WOBBLE'S INVADERS OF THE HEART *UK, male vocalist / multi-instrumentalist*　　10 wks

1 Feb 92	**VISIONS OF YOU** Oval OVAL 103	**35** 5
30 Apr 94	**BECOMING MORE LIKE GOD** Island CID 571	**36** 2
25 Jun 94	**THE SUN DOES RISE** Island CIDX 587	**41** 3

First hit features the uncredited vocals of Sinead O'Connor.

Terry WOGAN *Ireland, male vocalist*　　5 wks

| 7 Jan 78 | **FLORAL DANCE** Philips 6006 592 | **21** 5 |

WOLFSBANE *US, male vocal / instrumental group*　　1 wk

| 5 Oct 91 | **EZY** Def American DEFA 11 | **68** 1 |

Bobby WOMACK *US, male vocalist*　　21 wks

| 16 Jun 84 | **TELL ME WHY** Motown TMG 1339 | **60** 3 |

5 Oct 85	I WISH HE DIDN'T TRUST ME SO MUCH *MCA MCA 994*..............**64**	2
26 Sep 87	SO THE STORY GOES *Chrysalis LIB 3* [1] **34**	8
7 Nov 87	LIVING IN A BOX *MCA MCA 1210* **70**	2
3 Apr 93	I'M BACK FOR MORE *Dome CDDOME 1002* [2] **27**	5
13 May 95	IT'S A MAN'S MAN'S MAN'S WORLD	
	Pulse 8 CDLOSE 89 [3] **73**	1

[1] Living In A Box featuring Bobby Womack [2] Lulu and Bobby Womack
[3] Jeanie Tracy and Bobby Womack

See also Wilton Felder.

WOMACK and WOMACK
US, male/female vocal duo　　　　　　　　**51 wks**

28 Apr 84	LOVE WARS *Elektra E 9799* **14**	10
30 Jun 84	BABY I'M SCARED OF YOU *Elektra E 9733* **72**	2
6 Dec 86	SOUL LOVE – SOUL MAN *Manhattan MT 16* **58**	6
6 Aug 88	● TEARDROPS *Fourth & Broadway BRW 101* **3**	17
12 Nov 88	LIFE'S JUST A BALLGAME *Fourth & Broadway BRW 116* ..**32**	5
25 Feb 89	CELEBRATE THE WORLD *Fourth & Broadway BRW 125* ..**19**	8
5 Feb 94	SECRET STAR *Warner Bros. W 0222CD* [1] **46**	3

[1] House Of Zekkariyas AKA Womack and Womack

WOMBLES
UK, male vocalist, arranger and producer – Mike Batt　　**87 wks**

26 Jan 74	● THE WOMBLING SONG *CBS 1794* **4**	23
6 Apr 74	● REMEMBER YOU'RE A WOMBLE *CBS 2241* **3**	16
22 Jun 74	● BANANA ROCK *CBS 2465* **9**	13
12 Oct 74	MINUETTO ALLEGRETTO *CBS 2710* **16**	9
7 Dec 74	● WOMBLING MERRY CHRISTMAS *CBS 2842* **2**	8
10 May 75	WOMBLING WHITE TIE AND TAILS *CBS 3266* **22**	7
9 Aug 75	SUPER WOMBLE *CBS 3480* **20**	6
13 Dec 75	LET'S WOMBLE TO THE PARTY TONIGHT *CBS 3794* **34**	5

Stevie WONDER
US, male vocalist / multi-instrumentalist　　　　**409 wks**

3 Feb 66	UPTIGHT (EVERYTHING'S ALRIGHT)	
	Tamla Motown TMG 545 ....**14**	10
18 Aug 66	BLOWIN' IN THE WIND *Tamla Motown TMG 570* **36**	5
5 Jan 67	A PLACE IN THE SUN *Tamla Motown TMG 588* **20**	5
26 Jul 67	● I WAS MADE TO LOVE HER *Tamla Motown TMG 613* **5**	15
25 Oct 67	I'M WONDERING *Tamla Motown TMG 626* **22**	8
8 May 68	SHOO BE DOO BE DOO DA DAY	
	Tamla Motown TMG 653 ....**46**	4
18 Dec 68	● FOR ONCE IN MY LIFE *Tamla Motown TMG 679* **3**	13
19 Mar 69	I DON'T KNOW WHY I LOVE YOU	
	Tamla Motown TMG 690 ....**14**	10
9 Jul 69	I DON'T KNOW WHY I LOVE YOU (re-entry)	
	Tamla Motown TMG 690 ....**43**	1
16 Jul 69	● MY CHERIE AMOUR *Tamla Motown TMG 690* **4**	15
15 Nov 69	● YESTER-ME YESTER-YOU YESTERDAY	
	Tamla Motown TMG 717 ....**2**	13
28 Mar 70	● NEVER HAD A DREAM COME TRUE	
	Tamla Motown TMG 731 ....**6**	12
18 Jul 70	SIGNED SEALED DELIVERED I'M YOURS	
	Tamla Motown TMG 744 ....**15**	9
26 Sep 70	SIGNED SEALED DELIVERED I'M YOURS (re-entry)	
	Tamla Motown TMG 744 ....**49**	1
21 Nov 70	HEAVEN HELP US ALL *Tamla Motown TMG 757* **29**	11
15 May 71	WE CAN WORK IT OUT *Tamla Motown TMG 772* **27**	7
22 Jan 72	IF YOU REALLY LOVE ME	
	Tamla Motown TMG 798 ....**20**	7
3 Feb 73	SUPERSTITION *Tamla Motown TMG 841* **11**	9
19 May 73	● YOU ARE THE SUNSHINE OF MY LIFE	
	Tamla Motown TMG 852 ....**7**	11
13 Oct 73	HIGHER GROUND *Tamla Motown TMG 869* **29**	5
12 Jan 74	LIVING FOR THE CITY *Tamla Motown TMG 881* **15**	9
13 Apr 74	● HE'S MISSTRA KNOW IT ALL	
	Tamla Motown TMG 892 ....**10**	9

19 Oct 74	YOU HAVEN'T DONE NOTHIN'	
	Tamla Motown TMG 921 ....**30**	5
11 Jan 75	BOOGIE ON REGGAE WOMAN	
	Tamla Motown TMG 928 ....**12**	8
18 Dec 76	● I WISH *Tamla Motown TMG 1054* **5**	10
9 Apr 77	● SIR DUKE *Motown TMG 1068* **2**	9
10 Sep 77	ANOTHER STAR *Motown TMG 1083* **29**	5
24 Feb 79	POPS WE LOVE YOU *Motown TMG 1136* [1] **66**	5
24 Nov 79	SEND ONE YOUR LOVE *Motown TMG 1149* **52**	3
26 Jan 80	BLACK ORCHID *Motown TMG 1173* **63**	3
29 Mar 80	OUTSIDE MY WINDOW *Motown TMG 1179* **52**	4
13 Sep 80	● MASTERBLASTER (JAMMIN') *Motown TMG 1204* **2**	10
27 Dec 80	● I AIN'T GONNA STAND FOR IT *Motown TMG 1215* **10**	10
7 Mar 81	● LATELY *Motown TMG 1226* **3**	13
25 Jul 81	● HAPPY BIRTHDAY *Motown TMG 1235* **2**	11
23 Jan 82	THAT GIRL *Motown TMG 1254* **39**	6
10 Apr 82	★ EBONY AND IVORY *Parlophone R 6054* [2] **1**	10
5 Jun 82	● DO I DO *Motown TMG 1269* **10**	7
25 Sep 82	RIBBON IN THE SKY *Motown TMG 1280* **45**	4
25 Aug 84	★ I JUST CALLED TO SAY I LOVE YOU	
	Motown TMG 1349 ....**1**	24
1 Dec 84	LOVE LIGHT IN FLIGHT *Motown TMG 1364* **44**	5
29 Dec 84	DON'T DRIVE DRUNK *Motown TMG 1372* **71**	1
12 Jan 85	DON'T DRIVE DRUNK (re-entry)	
	Motown TMG 1372 ....**62**	2
7 Sep 85	● PART-TIME LOVER *Motown ZB 40351* **3**	12
9 Nov 85	THAT'S WHAT FRIENDS ARE FOR	
	Arista ARIST 638 [3] **16**	9
23 Nov 85	GO HOME *Motown ZB 40501* **67**	2
28 Dec 85	I JUST CALLED TO SAY I LOVE YOU (re-entry)	
	Motown TMG 1349 ....**64**	2
8 Mar 86	OVERJOYED *Motown ZB 40567* **17**	8
17 Jan 87	STRANGER ON THE SHORE OF LOVE	
	Motown WOND 2 ....**55**	3
31 Oct 87	SKELETONS *Motown TMG 41439* **59**	3
28 May 88	GET IT *Motown ZB 41883* [4] **37**	4
6 Aug 88	● MY LOVE *CBS JULIO 2* [5] **5**	11
20 May 89	FREE *Motown ZB 42855* **49**	5
12 Oct 91	FUN DAY *Motown ZB 44957* **63**	1
25 Feb 95	FOR YOUR LOVE *Motown TMGCD 1437* **23**	4
22 Jul 95	TOMORROW ROBINS WILL SING	
	Motown 8603732 ....**71**	1

[1] Diana Ross, Marvin Gaye, Smokey Robinson and Stevie Wonder
[2] Paul McCartney with Stevie Wonder [3] Dionne Warwick and Friends
featuring Elton John, Gladys Knight and Stevie Wonder [4] Stevie Wonder
and Michael Jackson [5] Julio Iglesias featuring Stevie Wonder

WONDER DOGS *UK, canine vocal group*　　**7 wks**

21 Aug 82	RUFF MIX *Flip FLIP 001* **31**	7

WONDER STUFF *UK, male vocal / instrumental group*　**66 wks**

30 Apr 88	GIVE GIVE GIVE ME MORE MORE MORE	
	Polydor GONE 3 ....**72**	2
16 Jul 88	A WISH AWAY *Polydor GONE 4* **43**	5
24 Sep 88	IT'S YER MONEY I'M AFTER BABY	
	Polydor GONE 5 ....**40**	3
11 Mar 89	WHO WANTS TO BE THE DISCO KING	
	Polydor GONE 6 ....**28**	3
23 Sep 89	DON'T LET ME DOWN GENTLY *Polydor GONE 7* **19**	4
11 Nov 89	GOLDEN GREEN / GET TOGETHER	
	Polydor GONE 8 ....**33**	3
12 May 90	CIRCLESQUARE *Polydor GONE 10* **20**	4
13 Apr 91	● THE SIZE OF A COW *Polydor GONE 11* **5**	7
25 May 91	CAUGHT IN MY SHADOW *Polydor GONE 12* **18**	3
7 Sep 91	SLEEP ALONE *Polydor GONE 13* **43**	2
26 Oct 91	★ DIZZY *Sense SIGH 712* [1] **1**	12
25 Jan 92	● WELCOME TO THE CHEAP SEATS (EP)	
	Polydor GONE 14 ....**8**	5
25 Sep 93	● ON THE ROPES (EP) *Polydor GONCD 15* **10**	4
27 Nov 93	FULL OF LIFE (HAPPY NOW) *Polydor GONCD 16* **28**	3
26 Mar 94	HOT LOVE NOW *Polydor GONCD 17* **19**	3

| 10 Sep 94 | **UNBEARABLE** Polydor GONCD 18 | **16** | 3 |

[1] Vic Reeves and the Wonder Stuff

Tracks on Welcome To The Cheap Seats (EP): *Welcome To The Cheap Seats / Me, My Mom, My Dad And My Brother / Will The Circle Be Unbroken / That's Entertainment. Tracks on* On The Ropes (EP): *On The Ropes / Professional Disturber Of The Peace / Hank And John.*

Wayne WONDER – *See* SHAGGY

WONDRESS – *See* MANTRONIX

Brenton WOOD *US, male vocalist*   14 wks

| 27 Dec 67 | ● **GIMME LITTLE SIGN** Liberty LBF 15021 | **8** | 14 |

Roy WOOD *UK, male vocalist / multi-instrumentalist*   41 wks

11 Aug 73	**DEAR ELAINE** Harvest HAR 5074	**18**	8
1 Dec 73	● **FOREVER** Harvest HAR 5078	**8**	13
15 Jun 74	**GOING DOWN THE ROAD** Harvest HAR 5083	**13**	7
31 May 75	**OH WHAT A SHAME** Jet 754	**13**	7
22 Nov 86	**WATERLOO** IRS IRM 125 [1]	**45**	4
23 Dec 95	**I WISH IT COULD BE CHRISTMAS EVERYDAY** Woody WOODY 001CD [2]	**59**	2

[1] Doctor and the Medics featuring Roy Wood [2] Roy Wood Big Band

WOODENTOPS *UK, male vocal / instrumental group*   1 wk

| 11 Oct 86 | **EVERYDAY LIVING** Rough Trade RT 178 | **72** | 1 |

Edward WOODWARD *UK, male vocalist*   2 wks

| 16 Jan 71 | **THE WAY YOU LOOK TONIGHT** DJM DJS 232 | **50** | 1 |
| 30 Jan 71 | **THE WAY YOU LOOK TONIGHT (re-entry)** DJM DJS 232 | **42** | 1 |

Sheb WOOLEY *US, male vocalist*   8 wks

| 20 Jun 58 | **PURPLE PEOPLE EATER** MGM 981 | **12** | 8 |

WOOLPACKERS *UK, male vocal group*   7 wks

| 16 Nov 96 | ● **HILLBILLY ROCK HILLBILLY ROLL** RCA 74321425412 | **7†** | 7 |

WORKING WEEK
UK, male / female vocal / instrumental group   2 wks

| 9 Jun 84 | **VENCEREMOS – WE WILL WIN** Virgin VS 684 | **64** | 2 |

WORLD – *See* LIL' LOUIS

WORLD OF TWIST
UK, male/female vocal / instrumental group   12 wks

24 Nov 90	**THE STORM** Circa YR 55	**42**	3
5 Jan 91	**THE STORM (re-entry)** Circa YR 55	**74**	2
23 Mar 91	**SONS OF THE STAGE** Circa YR 62	**47**	3
12 Oct 91	**SWEETS** Circa YR 72	**58**	2
22 Feb 92	**SHE'S A RAINBOW** Circa YR 82	**62**	2

WORLD PARTY
Ireland / UK, male vocal / instrumental group   27 wks

| 14 Feb 87 | **SHIP OF FOOLS** Ensign ENY 606 | **42** | 6 |

16 Jun 90	**MESSAGE IN THE BOX** Ensign ENY 631	**39**	6
15 Sep 90	**WAY DOWN NOW** Ensign ENY 634	**66**	2
18 May 91	**THANK YOU WORLD** Ensign ENY 643	**68**	1
10 Apr 93	**IS IT LIKE TODAY** Ensign CDENY 658	**19**	6
10 Jul 93	**GIVE IT ALL AWAY** Ensign CDENY 659	**43**	3
2 Oct 93	**ALL I GAVE** Ensign CDENYS 660	**37**	3

WORLD PREMIERE
US, male vocal / instrumental group   4 wks

| 28 Jan 84 | **SHARE THE NIGHT** Epic A 4133 | **64** | 4 |

WORLD WARRIOR *UK, male producer – Simon Harris*   1 wk

| 16 Apr 94 | **STREET FIGHTER II** Living Beat LBECD 27 | **70** | 1 |

See also Simon Harris

WORLD'S FAMOUS SUPREME TEAM
US, male vocal / scratch group   18 wks

4 Dec 82	● **BUFFALO GALS** Charisma MALC 1 [1]	**9**	12
25 Feb 84	**HEY DJ** Charisma TEAM 1	**52**	5
8 Dec 90	**OPERAA HOUSE** Virgin VS 1273 [2]	**75**	1

[1] Malcolm McLaren and the World's Famous Supreme Team
[2] World's Famous Supreme Team Show

WORLDS APART *UK, male vocal group*   17 wks

27 Mar 93	**HEAVEN MUST BE MISSING AN ANGEL** Arista 74321139362	**29**	3
3 Jul 93	**WONDERFUL WORLD** Arista 74321153402	**51**	1
25 Sep 93	**EVERLASTING LOVE** Bell 74321164802	**20**	4
26 Mar 94	**COULD IT BE I'M FALLING IN LOVE** Bell 74321189952	**15**	6
4 Jun 94	**BEGGIN' TO BE WRITTEN** Bell 74321211982	**29**	3

WRECKX-N-EFFECT *US, male vocal group*   18 wks

13 Jan 90	**JUICY** Motown ZB 43295 [1]	**29**	7
5 Dec 92	**RUMP SHAKER** MCA MCS 1725	**24**	7
7 May 94	**WRECKX SHOP** MCA MCSTD 1969 [2]	**26**	2
13 Aug 94	**RUMP SHAKER (re-issue)** MCA MCSTD 1989	**40**	2

[1] Wrecks-N-Effect [1] Wreckx-N-Effect featuring Apache Indian

Betty WRIGHT *US, female vocalist*   23 wks

25 Jan 75	**SHOORAH SHOORAH** RCA 2491	**27**	7
19 Apr 75	**WHERE IS THE LOVE** RCA 2548	**25**	7
8 Feb 86	**PAIN** Cooltempo COOL 117	**42**	6
9 Sep 89	**KEEP LOVE NEW** Sure Delight SD 11	**71**	3

Ian WRIGHT *UK, male vocalist*   2 wks

| 28 Aug 93 | **DO THE RIGHT THING** M & G MAGCD 45 | **43** | 2 |

Linda WRIGHT – *See* NEW ATLANTIC

Ruby WRIGHT *UK, female vocalist*   15 wks

16 Apr 54	● **BIMBO** Parlophone R 3816	**7**	4
21 May 54	**BIMBO (re-entry)** Parlophone R 3816	**12**	1
22 May 59	**THREE STARS** Parlophone R 4556	**19**	10

Three Stars is narrated by Dick Pike.

Steve WRIGHT · UK, male vocalist · 10 wks

27 Nov 82	I'M ALRIGHT RCA 296 [1]	40	6
15 Oct 83	GET SOME THERAPY RCA RCA 362 [2]	75	1
1 Dec 84	THE GAY CAVALIEROS (THE STORY SO FAR) MCA 925	61	3

[1] Young Steve and the Afternoon Boys [2] Steve Wright and the Sisters of Soul

WURZELS · UK, male vocal / instrumental group · 28 wks

2 Feb 67	DRINK UP THY ZIDER Columbia DB 8081 [1]	45	1
15 May 76	★ COMBINE HARVESTER (BRAND NEW KEY) EMI 2450	1	13
11 Sep 76	● I AM A CIDER DRINKER (PALOMA BLANCA) EMI 2520	3	9
25 Jun 77	FARMER BILL'S COWMAN (I WAS KAISER BILL'S BATMAN) EMI 2637	32	5

[1] Adge Cutler and the Wurzels.

WWF SUPERSTARS · US / UK, male wrestling vocalists · 15 wks

12 Dec 92	● SLAM JAM Arista 74321124887	4	8
13 Feb 93	SLAM JAM Arista 74321124887	75	1
3 Apr 93	WRESTLEMANIA Arista 74321136832	14	5
10 Jul 93	USA Arista 74321153092	71	1

Robert WYATT · UK, male vocalist · 11 wks

28 Sep 74	I'M A BELIEVER Virgin VS 114	29	5
7 May 83	SHIPBUILDING Rough Trade RT 115	35	6

Michael WYCOFF · US, male vocalist · 2 wks

23 Jul 83	(DO YOU REALLY LOVE ME) TELL ME LOVE RCA 348	60	2

Pete WYLIE · UK, male vocalist · 18 wks

3 May 86	SINFUL Eternal MDM 7	13	10
13 Sep 86	DIAMOND GIRL Eternal MDM 12	57	3
13 Apr 91	SINFUL! Siren SRN 138 [1]	28	5

[1] Pete Wylie with the Farm

Bill WYMAN · UK, male vocalist · 13 wks

25 Jul 81	(SI SI) JE SUIS UN ROCK STAR A & M AMS 8144	14	9
20 Mar 82	A NEW FASHION A & M AMS 8209	37	4

Jane WYMAN – See Bing CROSBY

Tammy WYNETTE · US, female vocalist · 35 wks

26 Apr 75	★ STAND BY YOUR MAN Epic EPC 7137	1	12
28 Jun 75	D.I.V.O.R.C.E. Epic EPC 3361	12	7
12 Jun 76	I DON'T WANNA PLAY HOUSE Epic EPC 4091	37	4
7 Dec 91	● JUSTIFIED AND ANCIENT KLF Communications KLF 099 [1]	2	12

[1] KLF, guest vocals: Tammy Wynette

Mark WYNTER · UK, male vocalist · 80 wks

25 Aug 60	IMAGE OF A GIRL Decca F 11263	11	10
10 Nov 60	KICKING UP THE LEAVES Decca F 11279	24	10
9 Mar 61	DREAM GIRL Decca F 11323	27	5
8 Jun 61	EXCLUSIVELY YOURS Decca F 11354	32	7
4 Oct 62	● VENUS IN BLUE JEANS Pye 7N 15466	4	15

13 Dec 62	● GO AWAY LITTLE GIRL Pye 7N 15492	6	11
6 Jun 63	SHY GIRL Pye 7N 15525	28	6
14 Nov 63	IT'S ALMOST TOMORROW Pye 7N 15577	12	12
9 Apr 64	ONLY YOU Pye 7N 15626	38	4

X

Malcolm X · US, male orator · 4 wks

7 Apr 84	NO SELL OUT Tommy Boy IS 165	60	4

Hit features credit: 'Music by Keith Le Blanc'.

X-PRESS 2 · UK, male instrumental / production group · 7 wks

5 Jun 93	LONDON X-PRESS Junior Boy's Own JBO 12	59	1
16 Oct 93	SAY WHAT! Junior Boy's Own JBO 16CD	32	2
30 Jul 94	ROCK 2 HOUSE / HIP HOUSIN' Junior Boy's Own JBO 21CD [1]	55	2
9 Mar 96	THE SOUND Junior Boy's Own JBO 36	38	1
12 Oct 96	TRANZ EURO XPRESS Junior Boy's Own JBO 42CD	45	1

[1] X-Press 2 featuring Lo-Pro

X-RAY SPEX · UK, male / female vocal / instrumental group · 33 wks

29 Apr 78	THE DAY THE WORLD TURNED DAY-GLO EMI International INT 553	23	8
22 Jul 78	IDENTITY EMI International INT 563	24	10
4 Nov 78	GERM FREE ADOLESCENCE EMI International INT 573	19	11
21 Apr 79	HIGHLY INFLAMMABLE EMI International INT 583	45	4

X-STATIC · Italy, male / female vocal / instrumental group · 2 wks

4 Feb 95	I'M STANDING (HIGHER) Positiva CDTIV 25	41	2

XAVIER · US, male vocal / instrumental group · 3 wks

20 Mar 82	WORK THAT SUCKER TO DEATH / LOVE IS THE ONE Liberty UP 651	53	3

XPANSIONS · UK, male producer – Ritchie Malone · 20 wks

6 Oct 90	ELEVATION Arista 113683	49	5
23 Feb 91	● MOVE YOUR BODY (ELEVATION) (re-entry) Arista 113 683	7	9
15 Jun 91	WHAT YOU WANT Arista 114 246 [1]	55	2
26 Aug 95	MOVE YOUR BODY (re-mix) Arista 74321294982 [2]	14	4

[1] Xpansions featuring Dale Joyner [2] Xpansions 95

XSCAPE · US, female vocal group · 11 wks

20 Nov 93	JUST KICKIN' IT Columbia 6598622	49	2
5 Nov 94	JUST KICKIN' IT (re-issue) Columbia 6608642	54	2
7 Oct 95	FEELS SO GOOD Columbia 6625022	34	2
27 Jan 96	WHO CAN I RUN TO Columbia 6628112	31	3
29 Jun 96	KEEP ON KEEPIN' ON East West A 4287CD	39	2

XTC
UK, male vocal / instrumental group   **70 wks**

12 May 79	**LIFE BEGINS AT THE HOP** *Virgin VS 259*	**54**	4
22 Sep 79	**MAKING PLANS FOR NIGEL** *Virgin VS 282*	**17**	11
6 Sep 80	**GENERALS AND MAJORS / DON'T LOSE YOUR TEMPER** *Virgin VS 365*	**32**	8
18 Oct 80	**TOWERS OF LONDON** *Virgin VS 372*	**31**	5
24 Jan 81	**SGT. ROCK (IS GOING TO HELP ME)** *Virgin VS 384*	**16**	9
23 Jan 82	● **SENSES WORKING OVERTIME** *Virgin VS 462*	**10**	9
27 Mar 82	**BALL AND CHAIN** *Virgin VS 482*	**58**	4
15 Oct 83	**LOVE ON A FARMBOY'S WAGES** *Virgin VS 613*	**50**	4
29 Sep 84	**ALL YOU PRETTY GIRLS** *Virgin VS 709*	**55**	5
28 Jan 89	**MAYOR OF SIMPLETON** *Virgin VS 1158*	**46**	5
4 Apr 92	**THE DISAPPOINTED** *Virgin VS 1404*	**33**	5
13 Jun 92	**THE BALLAD OF PETER PUMPKINHEAD** *Virgin VS 1415* ..	**71**	1

Y & T
US, male vocal / instrumental group   **4 wks**

13 Aug 83	**MEAN STREAK** *A & M AM 135*	**41**	4

Y?N-VEE
US, female vocal group   **1 wk**

17 Dec 94	**CHOCOLATE** *RAL RALCD 2*	**65**	1

YA KID K – *See HI-TEK 3 featuring YA KID K; TECHNOTRONIC*

Weird Al YANKOVIC
US, male vocalist   **8 wks**

7 Apr 84	**EAT IT** *Scotti Bros./Epic A 4257*	**36**	7
4 Jul 92	**SMELLS LIKE NIRVANA** *Scotti Bros PO 219*	**58**	1

YARBROUGH and PEOPLES
US, male / female vocal / instrumental duo   **20 wks**

27 Dec 80	● **DON'T STOP THE MUSIC** *Mercury MER 53*	**7**	12
5 May 84	**DON'T WASTE YOUR TIME** *Total Experience XE 501*	**60**	3
11 Jan 86	**GUILTY** *Total Experience FB 49905*	**53**	3
5 Jul 86	**I WOULDN'T LIE** *Total Experience FB 49841*	**61**	2

YARDBIRDS
UK, male vocal / instrumental group   **62 wks**

12 Nov 64	**GOOD MORNING LITTLE SCHOOLGIRL** *Columbia DB 7391*	**44**	4
18 Mar 65	● **FOR YOUR LOVE** *Columbia DB 7499*	**3**	12
17 Jun 65	● **HEART FULL OF SOUL** *Columbia DB 7594*	**2**	13
14 Oct 65	● **EVIL HEARTED YOU / STILL I'M SAD** *Columbia DB 7706* ..	**3**	10
3 Mar 66	● **SHAPES OF THINGS** *Columbia DB 7848*	**3**	9
2 Jun 66	● **OVER UNDER SIDEWAYS DOWN** *Columbia DB 7928*	**10**	9
27 Oct 66	**HAPPENINGS TEN YEARS TIME AGO** *Columbia DB 8024*	**43**	5

YAVAHN – *See RUFFNECK featuring YAVAHN*

YAZOO
UK, female / male vocal / instrumental duo   **53 wks**

17 Apr 82	● **ONLY YOU** *Mute MUTE 020*	**2**	14
17 Jul 82	● **DON'T GO** *Mute YAZ 001*	**3**	11

---

20 Nov 82	**THE OTHER SIDE OF LOVE** *Mute YAZ 002*	**13**	9
21 May 83	● **NOBODY'S DIARY** *Mute YAZ 003*	**3**	11
8 Dec 90	**SITUATION** *Mute YAZ 4*	**14**	8

YAZZ
UK, female vocalist   **68 wks**

20 Feb 88	● **DOCTORIN' THE HOUSE** *Ahead Of Our Time CCUT 27* [1]	**6**	9
23 Jul 88	★ **THE ONLY WAY IS UP** *Big Life BLR 4* [2]	**1**	15
29 Oct 88	● **STAND UP FOR YOUR LOVE RIGHTS** *Big Life BLR 5*	**2**	12
4 Feb 89	● **FINE TIME** *Big Life BLR 6*	**9**	8
29 Apr 89	**WHERE HAS ALL THE LOVE GONE** *Big Life BLR 8*	**16**	6
23 Jun 90	**TREAT ME GOOD** *Big Life BLR 24*	**20**	5
28 Mar 92	**ONE TRUE WOMAN** *Polydor PO 198*	**60**	2
31 Jul 93	**HOW LONG** *Polydor PZCD 252* [3]	**31**	5
2 Apr 94	**HAVE MERCY** *Polydor PZCD 309*	**42**	3
9 Jul 94	**EVERYBODY'S GOT TO LEARN SOMETIME** *Polydor PZCD 316*	**56**	2
28 Sep 96	**GOOD THING GOING** *East West EW 062CD*	**53**	1

[1] Coldcut featuring Yazz and the Plastic Population [2] Yazz and the Plastic Population [3] Yazz and Aswad

YELL!
UK, male vocal duo   **8 wks**

20 Jan 90	● **INSTANT REPLAY** *Fanfare FAN 22*	**10**	8

YELLO
Switzerland, male vocal / instrumental duo   **42 wks**

25 Jun 83	**I LOVE YOU** *Stiff BUY 176*	**41**	4
26 Nov 83	**LOST AGAIN** *Stiff BUY 191*	**73**	1
9 Aug 86	**GOLDRUSH** *Mercury MER 218*	**54**	3
22 Aug 87	**THE RHYTHM DIVINE** *Mercury MER 253* [1]	**54**	2
27 Aug 88	● **THE RACE** *Mercury YELLO 1*	**7**	11
17 Dec 88	**TIED UP** *Mercury YELLO 2*	**60**	5
25 Mar 89	**OF COURSE I'M LYING** *Mercury YELLO 3*	**23**	8
22 Jul 89	**BLAZING SADDLES** *Mercury YELLO 4*	**47**	2
8 Jun 91	**RUBBERBANDMAN** *Mercury YELLO 5*	**58**	2
5 Sep 92	**JUNGLE BILL** *Mercury MER 376*	**61**	2
7 Nov 92	**THE RACE / BOSTITCH (re-issue)** *Mercury MER 382*	**55**	1
15 Oct 94	**HOW HOW** *Mercury MERCD 414*	**59**	1

[1] Yello featuring Shirley Bassey

YELLOW DOG
US / UK, male vocal / instrumental group   **13 wks**

4 Feb 78	● **JUST ONE MORE NIGHT** *Virgin VS 195*	**8**	9
22 Jul 78	**WAIT UNTIL MIDNIGHT** *Virgin VS 217*	**54**	4

YELLOW MAGIC ORCHESTRA
Japan, male instrumental group   **11 wks**

14 Jun 80	**COMPUTER GAME (THEME FROM 'THE INVADERS')** *A & M AMS 7502*	**17**	11

YELLOWCOATS – *See Paul SHANE and the YELLOWCOATS*

YES
UK / South Africa, male vocal / instrumental group   **31 wks**

17 Sep 77	● **WONDEROUS STORIES** *Atlantic K 10999*	**7**	9
26 Nov 77	**GOING FOR THE ONE** *Atlantic K 11047*	**24**	4
9 Sep 78	**DON'T KILL THE WHALE** *Atlantic K 11184*	**36**	4
12 Nov 83	**OWNER OF A LONELY HEART** *Acto B 9817*	**28**	9
31 Mar 84	**LEAVE IT** *Acto B 9787*	**56**	4
3 Oct 87	**LOVE WILL FIND A WAY** *Atco A 9449*	**73**	1

Group were UK only for first three hits.

Melissa YIANNAKOU – *See DESIYA featuring Melissa YIANNAKOU*

YIN and YAN UK, male vocal duo   5 wks

29 Mar 75   **IF** *EMI 2282* **25** 5

Tukka YOOT – *See US3*

YOSH presents LOVEDEEJAY AKEMI
Holland, male producer   5 wks

29 Jul 95   **IT'S WHAT'S UPFRONT THAT COUNTS**
Limbo LIMB 46CD **69** 1
2 Dec 95   **IT'S WHAT'S UPFRONT THAT COUNTS (re-mix)**
Limbo LIMB 50CD **31** 2
20 Apr 96   **THE SCREAMER** *Limbo LIMB 54CD* **38** 2

YOSHIKI – *See Roger TAYLOR*

YOTHU YINDI *Australia, male vocal/instrumental group*   1 wk

15 Feb 92   **TREATY** *Hollywood HWD 116* **72** 1

YOUNG and COMPANY
US, male/female vocal/instrumental group   12 wks

1 Nov 80   **I LIKE (WHAT YOU'RE DOING TO ME)**
Excalibur EXC 501 ....**20** 12

Faron YOUNG US, male vocalist   23 wks

15 Jul 72   ● **IT'S FOUR IN THE MORNING** *Mercury 6052 140* **3** 23

Jimmy YOUNG UK, male vocalist   88 wks

9 Jan 53   **FAITH CAN MOVE MOUNTAINS** *Decca F 9986* **11** 1
21 Aug 53   ● **ETERNALLY** *Decca F 10130* **8** 9
6 May 55   ★ **UNCHAINED MELODY** *Decca F 10502* **1** 19
16 Sep 55   ★ **THE MAN FROM LARAMIE** *Decca F 10597* **1** 12
23 Dec 55   **SOMEONE ON YOUR MIND** *Decca F 10640* **13** 5
16 Mar 56   ● **CHAIN GANG** *Decca F 10694* **9** 6
8 Jun 56   **WAYWARD WIND** *Decca F 10736* **27** 1
22 Jun 56   **RICH MAN POOR MAN** *Decca F 10736* **25** 1
28 Sep 56   ● **MORE** *Decca F 10774* **4** 17
3 May 57   **ROUND AND ROUND** *Decca F 10875* **30** 1
10 Oct 63   **MISS YOU** *Columbia DB 7119* **15** 13
26 Mar 64   **UNCHAINED MELODY** *Columbia DB 7234* **43** 3

*The versions of Unchained Melody on Decca and on Columbia are different recordings.
Round and Round is with the Michael Sammes Singers. See also Various Artists (EPs & LPs)
– All Star Hit Parade No. 2.*

John Paul YOUNG Australia, male vocalist   16 wks

29 Apr 78   ● **LOVE IS IN THE AIR** *Ariola ARO 117* **5** 13
14 Nov 92   **LOVE IS IN THE AIR (re-mix)** *Columbia 6587697* **49** 3

Karen YOUNG UK, female vocalist   21 wks

6 Sep 69   ● **NOBODY'S CHILD** *Major Minor MM 625* **6** 21

Karen YOUNG US, female vocalist   8 wks

19 Aug 78   **HOT SHOT** *Atlantic K 11180* **34** 7
24 Feb 79   **HOT SHOT (re-issue)** *Atlantic LV 8* **75** 1

Neil YOUNG Canada, male vocalist   22 wks

11 Mar 72   ● **HEART OF GOLD** *Reprise K 14140* **10** 11

6 Jan 79   **FOUR STRONG WINDS** *Reprise K 14493* **57** 4
27 Feb 93   **HARVEST MOON** *Reprise W 0139CD* **36** 3
17 Jul 93   **THE NEEDLE AND THE DAMAGE DONE**
Reprise W 0191CD **75** 1
30 Oct 93   **LONG MAY YOU RUN (LIVE)** *Reprise W 0207CD* **71** 1
9 Apr 94   **PHILADELPHIA** *Reprise W 0242CD* **62** 2

See also Crosby, Stills, Nash and Young.

Paul YOUNG UK, male vocalist   132 wks

18 Jun 83   ★ **WHEREVER I LAY MY HAT (THAT'S MY HOME)**
CBS A 3371 ....**1** 15
10 Sep 83   ● **COME BACK AND STAY** *CBS A 3636* **4** 9
19 Nov 83   ● **LOVE OF THE COMMON PEOPLE** *CBS A 3585* **2** 13
13 Oct 84   ● **I'M GONNA TEAR YOUR PLAYHOUSE DOWN**
CBS A 4786 ....**9** 7
8 Dec 84   ● **EVERYTHING MUST CHANGE** *CBS A 4972* **9** 11
9 Mar 85   ● **EVERY TIME YOU GO AWAY** *CBS A 6300* **4** 11
22 Jun 85   **TOMB OF MEMORIES** *CBS A 6321* **16** 7
17 Aug 85   **TOMB OF MEMORIES (re-entry)** *CBS A 6321* **74** 1
4 Oct 86   **WONDERLAND** *CBS YOUNG 1* **24** 5
29 Nov 86   **SOME PEOPLE** *CBS YOUNG 2* **56** 3
7 Feb 87   **WHY DOES A MAN HAVE TO BE STRONG**
CBS YOUNG 3 ....**63** 2
12 May 90   **SOFTLY WHISPERING I LOVE YOU** *CBS YOUNG 4* **21** 6
7 Jul 90   **OH GIRL** *CBS YOUNG 5* **25** 6
6 Oct 90   **HEAVEN CAN WAIT** *CBS YOUNG 6* **71** 2
12 Jan 91   **CALLING YOU** *CBS YOUNG 7* **57** 2
30 Mar 91   ● **SENZA UNA DONNA (WITHOUT A WOMAN)**
London LON 294 [1] **4** 12
10 Aug 91   **BOTH SIDES NOW** *MCA MCS 1546* [2] **74** 1
26 Oct 91   **DON'T DREAM IT'S OVER** *Columbia 6574117* **20** 5
25 Sep 93   **NOW I KNOW WHAT MADE OTIS BLUE**
Columbia 6596412 ....**14** 7
27 Nov 93   **HOPE IN A HOPELESS WORLD** *Columbia 6598652* **42** 3
23 Apr 94   **IT WILL BE YOU** *Columbia 6602812* **34** 4

[1] Zucchero and Paul Young [2] Clannad and Paul Young

Retta YOUNG US, female vocalist   7 wks

24 May 75   **SENDING OUT AN S.O.S.** *All Platinum 6146 305* **28** 7

Tracie YOUNG – *See TRACIE*

YOUNG AND MOODY BAND
UK, male vocal/instrumental group   4 wks

10 Oct 81   **DON'T DO THAT** *Bronze BRO 130* **63** 4

YOUNG BLACK TEENAGERS *US, male rap group*   3 wks

9 Apr 94   **TAP THE BOTTLE** *MCA MCSTD 1967* **39** 3

YOUNG DISCIPLES
UK/US, male/female vocal/instrumental group   17 wks

13 Oct 90   **GET YOURSELF TOGETHER** *Talkin Loud TLK 2* **68** 1
23 Feb 91   **APPARENTLY NOTHIN'** *Talkin Loud TLK 5* **46** 4
3 Aug 91   **APPARENTLY NOTHIN' (re-entry)** *Talkin Loud TLK 5* **13** 7
5 Oct 91   **GET YOURSELF TOGETHER (re-issue)**
Talkin Loud TLK 15 ....**65** 2
5 Sep 92   **YOUNG DISCIPLES EP** *Talkin Loud TLK 18* **48** 3

Tracks on Young Disciples EP: Move On / Freedom / All I Have In Me / Move On (re-mix).

YOUNG IDEA UK, male vocal duo   6 wks

29 Jun 67   ● **WITH A LITTLE HELP FROM MY FRIENDS**
Columbia DB 8205 ....**10** 6

YOUNG MC *US, male rapper* **7 wks**

15 Jul 89	**BUST A MOVE** *Delicious Vinyl BRW 137*	**73**	2
17 Feb 90	**PRINCIPAL'S OFFICE** *Delicious Vinyl BRW 161*	**54**	3
17 Aug 91	**THAT'S THE WAY LOVE GOES** *Capitol CL 623*	**65**	2

YOUNG ONES – *See Cliff RICHARD*

YOUNG RASCALS
US, male vocal / instrumental group **17 wks**

25 May 67	● **GROOVIN'** *Atlantic 584 111*	**8**	13
16 Aug 67	**A GIRL LIKE YOU** *Atlantic 584 128*	**37**	4

Leon YOUNG STRING CHORALE – *See Mr Acker BILK*

Sydney YOUNGBLOOD *US, male vocalist* **31 wks**

26 Aug 89	● **IF ONLY I COULD** *Circa YR 34*	**3**	14
9 Dec 89	**SIT AND WAIT** *Circa YR 40*	**16**	8
31 Mar 90	**I'D RATHER GO BLIND** *Circa YR 43*	**44**	5
29 Jun 91	**HOOKED ON YOU** *Circa YR 65*	**72**	2
20 Mar 93	**ANYTHING** *RCA 74321138672*	**48**	2

Z

Helmut ZACHARIAS *Germany, orchestra* **11 wks**

29 Oct 64	● **TOKYO MELODY** *Polydor NH 52341*	**9**	11

Pia ZADORA *US, female vocalist* **6 wks**

27 Oct 84	**WHEN THE RAIN BEGINS TO FALL** *Arista ARIST 584* [1]	**68**	2
12 Nov 88	**DANCE OUT OF MY HEAD** *Epic 6528867* [2]	**65**	4

[1] Jermaine Jackson and Pia Zadora [2] Pia

Michael ZAGER BAND
US, male / female vocal / instrumental group **12 wks**

1 Apr 78	● **LET'S ALL CHANT** *Private Stock PVT 143*	**8**	12

ZAGER and EVANS *US, male vocal duo* **13 wks**

9 Aug 69	★ **IN THE YEAR 2525 (EXORDIUM AND TERMINUS)** *RCA 1860*	**1**	13

Georghe ZAMFIR
Romania, male instrumentalist – pipes **9 wks**

21 Aug 76	● **(THE LIGHT OF EXPERIENCE) DOINA DE JALE** *Epic EPC 4310*	**4**	9

Tommy ZANG *US, male vocalist* **1 wk**

16 Feb 61	**HEY GOOD LOOKING** *Polydor NH 66957*	**45**	1

ZAPP *US, male vocal / instrumental group* **6 wks**

25 Jan 86	**IT DOESN'T REALLY MATTER** *Warner Bros. W 8879*	**57**	3
24 May 86	**COMPUTER LOVE (PART 1)** *Warner Bros. W 8805*	**64**	3

Francesco ZAPPALA *Italy, male producer* **3 wks**

10 Aug 91	**WE GOTTA DO IT** *Fourth & Broadway BRW 225* [1]	**57**	2
2 May 92	**NO WAY OUT** *PWL Continental PWL 230*	**69**	1

[1] DJ Professor featuring Francesco Zappala

Lena ZAVARONI *UK, female vocalist* **14 wks**

9 Feb 74	● **MA (HE'S MAKING EYES AT ME)** *Philips 6006 367*	**10**	11
1 Jun 74	**PERSONALITY** *Philips 6006 391*	**33**	3

ZEE *UK, female vocalist* **2 wks**

6 Jul 96	**DREAMTIME** *Perfecto PERF 122CD*	**31**	2

ZEPHYRS *UK, male vocal / instrumental group* **1 wk**

18 Mar 65	**SHE'S LOST YOU** *Columbia DB 7481*	**48**	1

ZERO B *UK, male instrumentalist – keyboards* **6 wks**

22 Feb 92	**THE EP** *Ffrreedom TAB 102*	**32**	4
24 Jul 93	**RECONNECTION EP** *Internal LIECD 6*	**54**	2

Tracks on The EP: *Lock Up / Spinning Wheel / Module / Eclipse*. Tracks on Reconnection EP: *Lock Up / Lock Up (re-mix) / Ou Est Le Spoon / Love To Be In Love*. All three versions of *Lock Up* are different mixes of the same track.

ZERO ZERO *UK, male instrumental / production duo* **1 wk**

10 Aug 91	**ZEROXED** *Kickin KICK 9*	**71**	1

ZHANÉ *US, female vocal duo* **12 wks**

11 Sep 93	**HEY MR. DJ** *Epic 6596102*	**26**	3
4 Dec 93	**HEY MR. DJ (re-entry)** *Epic 6596102*	**50**	2
19 Mar 94	**GROOVE THANG** *Motown TMGCD 1423*	**34**	3
20 Aug 94	**VIBE** *Motown TMGCD 1430*	**67**	1
25 Feb 95	**SHAME** *Jive JIVECD 372*	**66**	1
21 Sep 96	**IT'S A PARTY** *Elektra EKR 226CD* [1]	**23**	2

[1] Busta Rhymes featuring Zhané

ZIG and ZAG *Ireland, male puppet duo* **12 wks**

24 Dec 94	● **THEM GIRLS THEM GIRLS** *RCA 74321251042*	**5**	9
1 Jul 95	**HANDS UP! HANDS UP!** *RCA 74321284392*	**21**	3

ZIGZAG JIVE FLUTES – *See ELIAS and his ZIGZAG JIVE FLUTES*

ZION TRAIN *UK, male / female vocal / instrumental group* **1 wk**

27 Jul 96	**RISE** *China WOKCD 2085*	**61**	1

ZODIACS – *See Maurice WILLIAMS and the ZODIACS*

ZOE *UK, female vocalist* **22 wks**

10 Nov 90	**SUNSHINE ON A RAINY DAY** *M & G MAGS 6*	**53**	5

| 24 Aug 91 | ● **SUNSHINE ON A RAINY DAY** (re-mix) *M & G MAGS 14* ..**4** | 11 |

24 Aug 91	● **SUNSHINE ON A RAINY DAY** (re-mix) *M & G MAGS 14*	..**4**	11
2 Nov 91	**LIGHTNING** *M & G MAGS 18*	**37**	4
29 Feb 92	**HOLY DAYS** *M & G MAGS 21*	**72**	2

ZOMBIES *UK, male vocal / instrumental group*   **16 wks**

| 13 Aug 64 | **SHE'S NOT THERE** *Decca F 11940* | **12** | 11 |
| 11 Feb 65 | **TELL HER NO** *Decca F 12072* | **42** | 5 |

ZOO EXPERIENCE featuring DESTRY
UK / US, male / female vocal / instrumental group   **1 wk**

| 22 Aug 92 | **LOVE'S GOTTA HOLD ON ME** *Cooltempo COOL 261* | **66** | 1 |

ZUCCHERO
Italy, male vocalist / instrumentalist – guitar, Adelmo Fornaciari   **24 wks**

30 Mar 91	● **SENZA UNA DONNA (WITHOUT A WOMAN)** *London LON 294* 1	**4**	12
18 Jan 92	**DIAMANTE** *London LON 313* 2	**44**	7
24 Oct 92	**MISERERE** *London LON 329* 3	**15**	5

1 Zucchero and Paul Young 2 Zucchero with Randy Crawford
3 Zucchero with Luciano Pavarotti

ZZ TOP *US, male vocal / instrumental group*   **92 wks**

3 Sep 83	**GIMME ALL YOUR LOVIN'** *Warner Bros. W 9693*	**61**	3
26 Nov 83	**SHARP DRESSED MAN** *Warner Bros. W 9576*	**53**	3
31 Mar 84	**TV DINNERS** *Warner Bros. W 9334*	**67**	3
6 Oct 84	● **GIMME ALL YOUR LOVIN'** (re-entry) *Warner Bros. W 9693*	**10**	15
15 Dec 84	**SHARP DRESSED MAN** (re-entry) *Warner Bros. W 9576*	**22**	10
23 Feb 85	**LEGS** *Warner Bros. W 9272*	**16**	7
13 Jul 85	**SUMMER HOLIDAY (EP)** *Warner Bros. W 8946*	**51**	5
19 Oct 85	**SLEEPING BAG** *Warner Bros. W 2001*	**27**	5
15 Feb 86	**STAGES** *Warner Bros. W 2002*	**43**	3
19 Apr 86	**ROUGH BOY** *Warner Bros. W 2003*	**23**	9
4 Oct 86	**VELCRO FLY** *Warner Bros. W 8650*	**54**	3
21 Jul 90	**DOUBLEBACK** *Warner Bros. W 9812*	**29**	6
13 Apr 91	**MY HEAD'S IN MISSISSIPPI** *Warner Bros W 0009*	**37**	5
11 Apr 92	● **VIVA LAS VEGAS** *Warner Bros. W 0098*	**10**	7
20 Jun 92	**ROUGH BOY** (re-issue) *Warner Bros. W 0111*	**49**	3
29 Jan 94	**PINCUSHION** *RCA 74321184732*	**15**	3
7 May 94	**BREAKAWAY** *RCA 74321192282*	**60**	1
29 Jun 96	**WHAT'S UP WITH THAT** *RCA 74321394822*	**58**	1

Tracks on Summer Holiday EP: *Tush / Got Me Under Pressure / Beer Drinkers and Hell Raisers / I'm Bad, I'm Nationwide*

2. alphabetically by title

part two

Different songs/tunes with the same title (e.g. 'Zoom' which has been a hit title for both the Commodores and Fat Larry's Band) are indicated by [A], [B] etc. Where there is no letter in brackets after the title, all hit recordings are of just one song. Individual titles of songs or tunes on EP, LP, medley or megamix singles which made the chart are not included here, with the obvious exception of titles that are actually part of the overall title of the hit in question.

The recording act named alongside each song title is the act that is billed on the record, but is not necessarily the act under whose name all the information about the title can be found in Part One. So, for example 'Zing A Little Zong' is credited correctly in Part Two to Bing Crosby and Jane Wyman, but in Part One is to be found in Bing Crosbys hits, with a footnote indicating that it was a duet with Jane Wyman. We have also simplified some act names in Part Two in the interests of saving space. For example 'Happy Xmas (War Is Over)' is credited here to John Lennon, but if you look up John Lennon in Part One, you will discover the actual credit for that hit was 'John and Yoko, the Plastic Ono Band with the Harlem Community Choir'.

The column showing the year of chart entry shows the year in which each disc made its very first appearance on the chart. Subsequent appearances are only listed here if they signify a period of success totally separate from the disc's first impact. So, for example, 'Bohemian Rhapsody' by Queen is listed as having been a hit in 1975 and 1991, but Cliff Richard's original version of 'Living Doll', which re-entered the charts for one brief week in 1960 after topping the charts in 1959, is shown only as a hit in 1959.

415

416

428

429

437

440

444

446

450

3. facts and feats

part three

All the chart achievements you need to know about are here. Which record took over from 'Hey Jude' at the top of the chart? Who has had more consecutive top ten hits than Cliff Richard? From which chart position did 'Happy Talk' leap to the top? How long did 'Tainted Love' stay on the charts? Did anybody spend more time on the charts in 1996 than Oasis? Who was the first woman to debut at number one? Who has a hit record span of over 42 years?

The answer to all these questions, as well as several even more significant, are to be found in this section. Nothing here proves that anybody produces better or worse music than anybody else, or that any particular record is more enjoyable to listen to than any other. All we are doing is listing the facts; we leave the opinions to you.

most weeks

most weeks on chart

This table lists the 133 recording acts that have spent 150 weeks or more on the British singles charts from 14 November 1952 up to the end of December 1996. It is of course possible for an act to be credited with two chart weeks in the same week if that act has two or more records on the chart at once. Double-sided hits, EPs and double singles only count as one hit each week, as do the handful of albums which have hit the singles chart over the years.

Act	number of weeks
ELVIS PRESLEY	1149
CLIFF RICHARD	1113

(includes 18 with Phil Everly, 16 with Sarah Brightman, 11 with Olivia Newton-John, 11 with Young Ones, 8 with Elton John, 6 with Van Morrison, 2 with Sheila Walsh and 1 with Helen Hobson)

ELTON JOHN	526

(includes 24 with Kiki Dee, 10 with George Michael, 9 with Dionne Warwick and Friends, 8 with Cliff Richard, 7 with RuPaul, 5 with Millie Jackson, 4 with Eric Clapton, 4 with Marcella Detroit, 4 with John Lennon, 3 with Aretha Franklin, 3 with Jennifer Rush and 3 with Luciano Pavarotti)

MICHAEL JACKSON	459

(includes 25 with Paul McCartney, 15 with Janet Jackson, 9 with 3T, 4 with Diana Ross, 4 with Stevie Wonder. + 235 as a Jackson)

BEATLES	456

(includes 23 with Billy Preston and 1 with Tony Sheridan)

ROD STEWART	449

(includes 13 with Bryan Adams and Sting, 9 with Jeff Beck, 8 with Tina Turner and 5 with the Scottish Euro 96 Squad. + 46 with Faces)

FRANK SINATRA	439

(includes 18 with Nancy Sinatra, 9 with Sammy Davis Jr. and 8 with Bono)

MADONNA	430
DIANA ROSS	428

(includes 20 with Marvin Gaye, 12 with Lionel Richie, 8 with Julio Iglesias, 5 with Marvin Gaye, Smokey Robinson and Stevie Wonder and 4 with Michael Jackson. + 197 as a Supreme, 27 with Supremes and Temptations)

DAVID BOWIE	426

(includes 12 with Mick Jagger, 11 with Queen, 8 with Bing Crosby, 7 with Pat Metheney and 2 with Al B. Sure!)

STEVIE WONDER	409

(includes 11 with Julio Iglesias, 10 with Paul McCartney, 9 with Dionne Warwick and Friends, 5 with Diana Ross, Smokey Robinson and Marvin Gaye, and 4 with Michael Jackson)

STATUS QUO	408

(includes 4 with Beach Boys and 1 with Maddy Prior)

PAUL McCARTNEY/WINGS	397

(includes 25 with Michael Jackson, 10 with Stevie Wonder, and 7 with Christians, Holly Johnson, Paul McCartney, Gerry Marsden and Stock Aitken Waterman)

QUEEN	389

(includes 12 with George Michael and Lisa Stansfield and 11 with David Bowie)

ROLLING STONES	360
SHADOWS	359

(+ 404 backing Cliff Richard)

TOM JONES	356

(includes 7 with Art Of Noise)

ROY ORBISON	345

(includes 6 with kd lang)

EVERLY BROTHERS	337

(Phil Everly had 6 more solo and 18 with Cliff Richard)

BEE GEES	322
JIM REEVES	322
LONNIE DONEGAN	321
FOUR TOPS	318

(includes 20 with Supremes)

HOLLIES	318
SHIRLEY BASSEY	316

(includes 2 with Yello and 1 with Chris Rea)

UB40	311

(includes 8 with Afrika Bambaataa and Family, 9 with Robert Palmer and 8 with 808 State)

SUPREMES	306

(includes 27 with Temptations and 20 with Four Tops)

DONNA SUMMER	297

(includes 13 with Barbra Streisand)

PAT BOONE	296
PERRY COMO	294
PRINCE	288

(includes 5 with Sheena Easton)

BEACH BOYS	281

(includes 12 with Fat Boys, 4 with Status Quo)

BILLY FURY	281
FRANKIE LAINE	281

(includes 16 with Jimmy Boyd, 16 with Four Lads, 8 with Doris Day and 4 with Johnnie Ray)

SHAKIN' STEVENS	277

(includes 9 with Bonnie Tyler)

SLADE	276
HOT CHOCOLATE	272
MADNESS	258
ELECTRIC LIGHT ORCHESTRA	255

(includes 11 with Olivia Newton-John)

ABBA	252
ADAM FAITH	251
PETULA CLARK	247
WHO (+ 4 as High Numbers)	247
CONNIE FRANCIS	241
NAT 'KING' COLE	237
ENGELBERT HUMPERDINCK	235
JACKSONS/JACKSON 5	235

(113 as Jackson 5 and 122 as Jacksons)

T. REX	235

(includes 8 billed as Marc Bolan)

KEN DODD	233
FRANKIE VAUGHAN	232

(includes 20 with Kaye Sisters)

ANDY WILLIAMS	228
OLIVIA NEWTON-JOHN	225

(includes 57 with John Travolta, 11 with Electric Light Orchestra and 11 with Cliff Richard)

FLEETWOOD MAC	223
WHITNEY HOUSTON	221

(includes 6 with Cece Winans, 5 with Teddy Pendergrass, 5 with Aretha Franklin and 5 with Bobby Brown)

OASIS	220
MANFRED MANN	217

(includes 41 as Manfred Mann's Earth Band)

DURAN DURAN	216
PHIL COLLINS	213

(includes 13 with Marilyn Martin, 12 with Philip Bailey and 3 with David Crosby)

KINKS	213
TINA TURNER	213

(includes 8 with Rod Stewart, 6 with Bryan Adams, 3 with Eric Clapton and 3 with Barry White. + 44 with Ike and Tina Turner)

GENE PITNEY	212

(includes 12 with Marc Almond)

In the last edition of British Hit Singles Oasis had spent just 21 weeks on chart. They are now the 55th most charted act of all time.

474

most weeks

HERMAN'S HERMITS 211
DUSTY SPRINGFIELD 211
   (includes 9 with Pet Shop Boys, 3 with
   Daryl Hall and 1 with Cilla Black)
BRENDA LEE 210
SHOWADDYWADDY 209
DEPECHE MODE 208
PET SHOP BOYS 208
   (includes 9 with Dusty Springfield and 7
   with Absolutely Fabulous)
KOOL AND THE GANG 207
JAM 203
TEMPTATIONS 203
   (includes 27 with Supremes)
BANANARAMA 202
   (includes 10 with Fun Boy Three and 9
   with La Na Nee Nee Noo Noo)
KYLIE MINOGUE 201
   (includes 14 with Jason Donovan, 7 with
   Keith Washington, 4 with Nick Cave,
   1 with Visionmasters)
MARVIN GAYE 200
   (includes 61 with Tammi Terrell, 20 with
   Diana Ross, 11 with Kim Weston, 5 with
   Diana Ross, Stevie Wonder and Smokey
   Robinson and 1 with Mary Wells)
ADAM ANT/ADAM AND
   THE ANTS 199
   (130 as Adam and the Ants and 69 as
   Adam Ant)
DAVID ESSEX 199
   (includes 3 with Catherine Zeta Jones)
BILL HALEY AND HIS
   COMETS 199
ORCHESTRAL MANOEUVRES
   IN THE DARK 199
EURYTHMICS 198
   (includes 11 with Aretha Franklin)
DUANE EDDY AND THE REBELS . 196
   (includes 9 with Art Of Noise)
GLORIA ESTEFAN/MIAMI SOUND
   MACHINE 196
ERASURE 195
CILLA BLACK 194
   (includes 1 with Dusty Springfield)
STRANGLERS 194
KIM WILDE 194
   (includes 11 with Junior and 7 with
   Mel Smith [Mel and Kim])
BUDDY HOLLY (+ 47 as a Cricket) . . 190
JANET JACKSON 190
   (includes 20 with Luther Vandross, 15 with
   Michael Jackson. + 7 with Herb Alpert)
NEIL SEDAKA 190
WET WET WET 189
BACHELORS 187

GLADYS KNIGHT AND THE PIPS . 187
   (includes 2 with Johnny Mathis and
   9 with Dionne Warwick and Friends)
JOHN LENNON/PLASTIC ONO
   BAND (includes 4 with Elton John) . . 184
SIMPLE MINDS 184
GENESIS 183
DAVID WHITFIELD 181
   (+ 9 as one of the artists on All Star Hit
   Parade)
NEW ORDER 179
   (includes 12 with Englandneworder)
RUSS CONWAY 178
   (includes 10 with Dorothy Squires)
GEORGE MICHAEL 178
   (includes 12 with Queen and Lisa Stansfield,
   10 with Elton John and 9 with
   Aretha Franklin)
BON JOVI (Jon Bon Jovi 13 more solo) . 177
ARETHA FRANKLIN 177
   (includes 11 with Eurythmics, 9 with
   George Michael, 5 with Whitney Houston, 3
   with George Benson and 3 with Elton John)
LEVEL 42 177
SIMPLY RED 177
DRIFTERS 176
DAVE CLARKE FIVE 174
CARPENTERS 173
CHER 171
   (includes 8 with Chrissie Hynde, Neneh
   Cherry and Eric Clapton and 3 with Beavis
   and Butt-Head. + 77 with Sonny and Cher
   and 17 uncredited with Meat Loaf)
MR ACKER BILK 171
GARY GLITTER 170
MARIAH CAREY 169
   (includes 16 with Luther Vandross and 11
   with Boyz II Men)
KATE BUSH 168
   (includes 11 with Peter Gabriel and 2 with
   Larry Adler)
ELVIS COSTELLO (AND THE
   ATTRACTIONS) 168
   (includes 7 as the Imposter and 4 as the
   Costello Show)
BONEY M 167
U2 167
LULU 165
   (includes 12 with Take That and 5 with
   Bobby Womack)
LIONEL RICHIE 165
   (includes 12 with Diana Ross)
SANDIE SHAW 165
BRYAN ADAMS 164
   (includes 13 with Rod Stewart and Sting, 6
   with Tina Turner and 2 with Bonnie Raitt)

GARY NUMAN 164
   (includes 16 with Sharpe and Numan and 8
   with Radio Heart)
PRETENDERS/CHRISSIE HYNDE . 164
   (includes 24 with UB40, 8 with Cher,
   Neneh Cherry and Eric Clapton and 4
   with Moodswings)
GUY MITCHELL 163
FRANK IFIELD 162
   (includes 4 with the Backroom Boys)
BOBBY DARIN 161
SPANDAU BALLET 159
SWEET 159
TAKE THAT (includes 14 with Lulu) . . 158
DEAN MARTIN 156
HUMAN LEAGUE 155
ROXY MUSIC 155
BLONDIE 154
BILLY OCEAN 153
JOHNNIE RAY 152
   (includes 16 with Doris Day and 4 with
   Frankie Laine)
FOUR SEASONS 151
BUCKS FIZZ 150
SIOUXSIE AND THE BANSHEES . 150
   (includes 2 with Morrissey)

Also worth mentioning are:

MIDGE URE 293
   (52 solo, 138 with Ultravox, 56 as part of
   Visage, 18 as part of Slik, 5 as a Rich Kid,
   4 with Mick Karn and 20 as leader of
   Band Aid)
STING 275
   (111 solo, 144 with Police, 13 with Bryan
   Adams and Rod Stewart, 5 with
   Eric Clapton and 2 with Pato Banton)
DONNY OSMOND 247
   (118 solo, 92 with Osmonds and 37 with
   Marie Osmond) . . . .
TREMELOES 221
   (131 and 90 backing Brian Poole)
ERIC CLAPTON 219
   (91 solo, 59 with Cream, 21 as Derek
   and the Dominoes, 16 with Yardbirds,
   9 with Delaney and Bonnie and Friends,
   8 with Cher, Chrissie Hynde and Neneh
   Cherry, 5 with Sting, 4 with Elton John,
   3 with Michael Kamen and 3 with
   Tina Turner)
MARC ALMOND 207
   (72 solo, 107 with Soft Cell, 12 with
   Bronski Beat, 12 with Gene Pitney,
   3 with Marc and the Mambas and 1
   with PJ Proby)

British and American artists account for more than 96% of the acts in this table. Only 5 acts (Abba, Kylie Minogue, U2, Boney M and Bryan Adams) originate from outside the UK or US.

3. facts and feats

most weeks on chart
(continued)

TERRY HALL 183
(5 solo, 78 with Specials, 50 with Fun Boy
Three, 20 with Bananarama, 18 with
Colourfield, 10 with Vegas, 2 with
Nearly God)

SMALL FACES/FACES 183
(137 as Small Faces)

JIMMY SOMERVILLE 174
(48 solo, 76 with Communards, 38 with
Bronski Beat and 12 with Bronski Beat
and Marc Almond)

HOLLY JOHNSON 173
(29 solo, 137 with Frankie Goes To
Hollywood and 7 with Christians,
Paul McCartney, Gerry Marsden and Stock
Aitken Waterman)

PAUL SIMON 172
(85 solo, 87 with Simon and Garfunkel)

MORRISSEY 171
(66 solo, 105 with Smiths and 2 with
Siouxsie)

MICK JONES 170
(8 with Aztec Camera, 135 with Clash
and 27 with Big Audio Dynamite)

LUTHER VANDROSS 169
(146 solo, 18 with Change, 3 with Gregg
Diamond Bionic Boogie and 2 with
Charme)

BOY GEORGE 167
(43 solo, 103 with Culture Club, 18 as
Jesus Loves You and 3 with PM Dawn)

ALAN PRICE 166
(78 solo, 78 as an Animal and 10 with
Fame and Price Together)

PHILIP LYNOTT 164
(36 solo, 128 with Thin Lizzy)

EDDY GRANT 163
(94 solo, 69 as an Equal)

JOHN LYDON 163
(5 with Leftfield Lydon, 88 with Sex Pistols,
61 with Public Image Ltd and 9 with
Time Zone)

DOLLAR 161
(128 as a duo, 33 with Guys And Dolls.
David Van Day + 3 solo)

ALISON MOYET 160
(107 solo, 53 with Yazoo)

BOB GELDOF 158
(15 solo, 123 with Boomtown Rats and
20 as the prime mover behind
Band Aid)

JODY WATLEY 157
(34 solo, 123 with Shalamar)

BOBBY BROWN 153
(108 solo, 31 with New Edition,
9 with Glenn Medeiros and 5 with
Whitney Houston)

BELINDA CARLISLE 152
(142 solo, 10 with Go-Gos)

TOMMY STEELE 152
(145 solo, 7 as one of the artists on
All Star Hit Parade)

Morrissey

Morrissey's solo hits spent an average of just three weeks on the chart. His hits with the Smiths, however, had an average chart lifespan of more than double that figure.

most weeks on chart
(by individual)

It is extremely difficult to list in correct order the individuals who have spent most weeks on chart in all guises, whether as a solo act, as part of a group or as a backing musician for another act. However, those persons who have spent 500 weeks or more in the charts, whether alone or as fully paid up members of duos or groups, are:

act	weeks
ELVIS PRESLEY	1149
CLIFF RICHARD	1119
PAUL McCARTNEY	891
HANK MARVIN	799
BRUCE WELCH	763
MICHAEL JACKSON	703
DIANA ROSS	654
JOHN LENNON	640
GEORGE HARRISON	538
ELTON JOHN	526
ROD STEWART	514
RINGO STARR	511

most consecutive years on chart
(by artist)

total	act	years
30	ELVIS PRESLEY	56 – 85
27	DIANA ROSS	70 – 96
	(+ 6 with Supremes from 64 – 69. Total: 33)	
26	ELTON JOHN	71 – 96
20	STATUS QUO	73 – 92
18	CLIFF RICHARD	79 – 96
17	CLIFF RICHARD	58 – 74
16	UB40	80 – 95
16	STRANGLERS	77 – 92
16	DAVID BOWIE	72 – 87
15	HOT CHOCOLATE	70 – 84
15	ANDY WILLIAMS	62 – 76
14	PRINCE	83 – 96
14	IRON MAIDEN	80 – 93
14	ROD STEWART	71 – 84
13	MADONNA	84 – 96
13	CHRIS REA	82 – 94
13	KIM WILDE	81 – 93
13	SHAKIN' STEVENS	80 – 92
13	JIM REEVES	60 – 72
12	WHITNEY HOUSTON	85 – 96
12	PET SHOP BOYS	85 – 96
12	BANANARAMA	82 – 93
12	STEVIE WONDER	66 – 77
12	HOLLIES	63 – 74
12	FRANKIE VAUGHAN	54 – 65
11	ROD STEWART	86 – 96
11	LUTHER VANDROSS	86 – 96
11	MARC ALMOND	83 – 93
	(Almond also hit with Soft Cell in 81 & 82. Total: 13)	
11	TINA TURNER	83 – 93
11	EURYTHMICS	81 – 91
	(Dave Stewart hit with Tourists in 79 – 80, Vegas in 92 – 93 & solo in 94. Total: 16. Annie Lennox also hit with Tourists in 79 – 80 & extended her run with solo hits in 92 & 93. Total: 15)	
11	CURE	80 – 90
11	KOOL AND THE GANG	79 – 89
11	GARY NUMAN	79 – 89
11	SIOUXSIE AND THE BANSHEES	78 – 88
11	SUPREMES	64 – 74
11	FRANK SINATRA	54 – 64
10	CHER	87 – 96
10	WET WET WET	87 – 96
10	POGUES	85 – 94
10	PAUL McCARTNEY	82 – 91
	(McCartney hit with the Beatles in 92 and again solo in 93. Total: 12)	
10	DEPECHE MODE	81 – 90
10	DURAN DURAN	81 – 90
10	NEW ORDER	81 – 90
	(+ 1 as Joy Division in 1980. Barney Sumner hit with Electronic in 91 & 92. Total: 13. Stephen Morris hit in 91 as half of the Other Two. Total: 12. The other half of the Other Two, Gillian Gilbert, joined New Order in 82.)	
10	LEVEL 42	80 – 89
10	SPANDAU BALLET	80 – 89
10	GEORGE BENSON	78 – 88
10	MADNESS	79 – 88
10	PRETENDERS/CHRISSIE HYNDE	79 – 88
10	ELVIS COSTELLO	77 – 86
10	SHALAMAR	77 – 86
10	ABBA	74 – 83
10	PAUL McCARTNEY	71 – 80
	(+ 9 with the Beatles from 62 – 70. Total: 19)	
10	T. REX	68 – 77
10	TOM JONES	65 – 74
10	CILLA BLACK	63 – 72
10	GENE PITNEY	61 – 70
10	ROY ORBISON	60 – 69
10	MAX BYGRAVES	52 – 61

Also worth mentioning:

15	PHIL COLLINS	80 – 94
	(solo: 81 – 86, 88 – 91, 93 – 94. With Genesis: 80, 87, 92)	
15	JOHN LENNON	62 – 76
	(with Beatles: 62 – 70 & 76. Solo: 71 – 75)	
15	RINGO STARR	62 – 76
	(with Beatles: 62 – 70 & 76. Solo: 71 – 75)	
14	MICK JAGGER	63 – 76
	(with Rolling Stones: 63 – 69 & 71 – 76. Solo: 70)	

Paul Weller

13	MORRISSEY	83 – 95
	(with Smiths: 83 – 87. Solo: 88 – 95)	
13	PAUL WELLER	77 – 89
	(with Jam: 77 – 83. With Style Council: 84 – 89. Weller's solo career started in 1991 and he has hit every year since)	
12	GEORGE MICHAEL	82 – 93
	(with Wham!: 82 – 85. Solo: 86 – 93)	
11	STING	78 – 88
	(with Police: 78 – 81 & 83 – 84. Solo: 82 & 85 – 88)	
11	LIONEL RICHIE	77 – 87
	(with Commodores: 77 – 80. Solo: 81 – 87)	
11	BRYAN FERRY	72 – 82
	(solo: 73 – 78. With Roxy Music: 72, 79 – 82)	
10	BELINDA CARLISLE	87 – 96
	(solo: 87 – 94, 96. With Go-Gos: 95)	
10	FREDDIE MERCURY	84 – 93
	(with Queen: 84 – 86 & 89 – 92. Solo: 87 – 88 & 93)	
10	GEORGE HARRISON	62 – 71
	(with Beatles: 62 – 70. Solo 71)	
10	DUSTY SPRINGFIELD	63 – 70
	(with Springfields: 61 – 62. Solo: 63 – 70)	

Paul Weller has charted in one form or another every year since 1977, except 1990.

most weeks

most weeks on chart in each year

The acts who spent the most time on the charts in each year are:

Bill Haley's record of 110 weeks in one calendar year had stood for 40 years before being trounced by Oasis.

year	act	weeks
1952	Vera Lynn	10
1953	Frankie Laine	84
1954	Frankie Laine	67
1955	Ruby Murray	80
1956	Bill Haley and his Comets	110
1957	Elvis Presley	108
1958	Elvis Presley	70
1959	Russ Conway	79
1960	Cliff Richard	79
1961	Elvis Presley	88
1962	Chubby Checker	73
1963	Beatles	68
1964	Jim Reeves	73
1965	Seekers	51
1966	Dave Dee, Dozy, Beaky, Mick and Tich	50
1967	Engelbert Humperdinck	97
1968	Tom Jones	58
1969	Marvin Gaye	60
1970	Elvis Presley	59
1971	Elvis Presley	66
1972	T. Rex	58
1973	David Bowie	55
1974	Wombles	65
1975	Mud	45
1976	Rod Stewart	48
1977	Elvis Presley	51
1978	John Travolta	60
1979	Donna Summer	46
1980	Madness	46
1981	Adam and the Ants	91
1982	Soft Cell	49
1983	Michael Jackson	60
1984	Frankie Goes To Hollywood	68
1985	Madonna	84
1986	Madonna	59
1987	Madonna	41
1988	Kylie Minogue	54
1989	Bobby Brown	52
1990	New Kids On The Block	56
1991	R.E.M.	36
1992	Michael Jackson	38
1993	Whitney Houston	50
1994	Mariah Carey	45
1995	Oasis	65
1996	Oasis	134

Frankie Laine's 1953 total includes 16 weeks in duet with Jimmy Boyd and two with Doris Day. Chubby Checker's 1962 total includes three weeks in duet with Bobby Rydell. The Beatles' 1963 total includes one week backing Tony Sheridan. Marvin Gaye's 1969 total includes 29 weeks in duet with Tammi Terrell. John Travolta's 1978 total includes 42 weeks in duet with Olivia Newton-John. Donna Summer's 1979 total includes nine weeks in duet with Barbra Streisand. Michael Jackson's 1983 total includes 14 weeks in duet with Paul McCartney. Kylie Minogue's 1988 total includes four weeks with Jason Donovan. Mariah Carey's 1994 total includes ten weeks in duet with Luther Vandross. Oasis' 1995 total includes two weeks for an interview disc credited to Oas*s.

Oasis

most weeks on chart in one year (by artist)

weeks	act	year
134	Oasis	1996
110	Bill Haley and his Comets	1956
108	Elvis Presley	1957
97	Engelbert Humperdinck	1967
91	Adam and the Ants	1981
88	Elvis Presley	1961
84	Frankie Laine	1953
84	Pat Boone	1957
80	Madonna	1985
80	Ruby Murray	1955
79	Russ Conway	1959
78	Cliff Richard	1960
77	Adam Faith	1960
73	Chubby Checker	1962
73	Jim Reeves	1964
72	Beatles	1964
71	Mr Acker Bilk	1962
70	Bachelors	1964
70	Elvis Presley	1958

most weeks on chart in 1995

65	OASIS
42	CELINE DION
40	OUTHERE BROTHERS
39	BON JOVI
34	EAST 17
34	MICHAEL JACKSON
33	JANET JACKSON
33	WET WET WET
29	BOYZONE
29	MADONNA
29	MN8
29	JIMMY NAIL
29	WHIGFIELD

For the first time since Frankie Goes To Hollywood hit the charts in 1984, a British act carried off the singles chart championship. In 1995 Oasis became only the tenth UK group to top the top ten year-end list, while their much publicised rivals, Blur, failed to make the year end top ten altogether. Strangely, in a year that was so dominated by news of a revival in British pop, less than half of the year's top acts were homegrown and a record five nations were represented. The last time overseas artists outnumbered indigenous talent in the UK charts was in 1991, a year generally perceived to have been dominated by UK dance groups.

1991 was also the last time Madonna graced the year end top ten. Her appearance this time round was her seventh in total, one more than Michael Jackson, who, sales-wise, enjoyed the best year of his career so far. Despite the adverse publicity of the preceeding two years, he managed to rack up two number ones and a top three hit with his sister, Janet, who herself made it onto this list, one place lower than her elder brother. Holding on from last year were East 17 and Wet Wet Wet. It was East 17's third consecutive year in the top ten and the first time they had been placed higher than arch-rivals Take That.

Liam Gallagher

most weeks on chart in 1996

134	OASIS
43	MICHAEL JACKSON
42	CELINE DION
42	FUGEES
41	MARK MORRISON
39	GEORGE MICHAEL
38	PRODIGY
37	GABRIELLE
35	PETE ANDRE
35	SPICE GIRLS

Apart from a series of large outdoor concerts, 1996 was a quiet year for Oasis. They released no new albums during the period and only one single, 'Don't Look Back In Anger', which reached number one for a sole week in March. To top the year-end weeks tally with such a restricted output is quite an achievement. To do so with the most weeks ever recorded in a calendar year is truly astonishing. Throughout 1996 the entire Oasis back catalogue, nine singles in total, made regular forays into the lower reaches of the chart thanks to a 'three CD singles for £10' marketing promotion by Creation Records. It was a ploy used later in the year, but to lesser effect, by The Prodigy who also managed to make the year-end top ten despite releasing only two new singles in 1996, one of them in late November.

The year's longest running single was, of course, by Oasis. 'Whatever', first released back in 1994, made six separate trips to the top 75 in 1996, adding a further 32 weeks to the 15 racked up in 1994 and 1995. Its total of 47 weeks on chart is the highest posted for any single from the nineties. Three other Oasis hits, 'Wonderwall', 'Cigarettes And Alcohol' and the aforementioned 'Don't Look Back In Anger' also accumulated more than 20 weeks on the chart - all in a year when the average life span of a hit single was growing shorter and shorter. Not only were Oasis the first group ever to become singles chart champions more than once, they also led the way in the album field too. Both 'Definitely Maybe' and '(What's The Story) Morning Glory' spent the entire year on the LP listings and two boxed sets of singles also charted. At the time of writing, '(What's The Story) Morning Glory' had sold nearly four million units in the UK, the second biggest selling album of all time after the Beatles' 'Sgt. Pepper'.

Liam Gallagher gave up vocal duties in favour of his brother Noel on 'Don't Look Back In Anger'. He did, however, sing on the single's B-side, a cover of Slade's 'Cum On Feel The Noize'.

most weeks

most weeks on chart
(by recording)

Total weeks on chart, regardless of the number of re-issues or re-entries. This list shows which recording has appeared on the singles charts for the most weeks. Re-recordings of the same song by the same artist do not count but re-mixes of the same track do.

The Arthur Baker remix of New Order's 'Blue Monday' charted in 1988. The song hit again in 1995, remixed by Hardfloor and Jam & Spoon.

Chart wks	runs	title	artist
124	10	MY WAY	Frank Sinatra
67	8	AMAZING GRACE	Judy Collins
59	3	RELAX*	Frankie Goes To Hollywood
57	8	ROCK AROUND THE CLOCK* . .	Bill Haley and his Comets
56	1	RELEASE ME*	Engelbert Humperdinck
55	1	STRANGER ON THE SHORE . .	Mr Acker Bilk
53	5	BLUE MONDAY	New Order
47	2	I LOVE YOU BECAUSE	Jim Reeves
47	8	WHATEVER	Oasis
46	5	WHITE LINES (DON'T DON'T DO IT) .	Grandmaster Flash and Melle Mel
44	5	ALL RIGHT NOW	Free
44	5	LET'S TWIST AGAIN	Chubby Checker
44	5	TAINTED LOVE*	Soft Cell
43	2	BROWN GIRL IN THE RING	Boney M
41	5	DECK OF CARDS	Wink Martindale
40	1	RIVERS OF BABYLON*	Boney M
40	2	A SCOTTISH SOLDIER	Andy Stewart
40	2	TIE A YELLOW RIBBON ROUND THE OLD OAK TREE*	Dawn
39	3	HE'LL HAVE TO GO	Jim Reeves
38	2	SOMEWHERE MY LOVE	Mike Sammes Singers
37	1	LOVE IS ALL AROUND	Wet Wet Wet
36	1	I BELIEVE*	Frankie Laine
36	1	I PRETEND*	Des O'Connor
36	2	THE POWER OF LOVE*	Jennifer Rush
36	3	SHE LOVES YOU*	Beatles
35	2	ALBATROSS*	Fleetwood Mac
35	2	AND I LOVE YOU SO	Perry Como
35	4	HEARTBREAK HOTEL.	Elvis Presley
35	2	HOUND DOG	Elvis Presley
35	4	LEADER OF THE PACK	Shangri-Las
35	3	LET'S DANCE	Chris Montez

'All Right Now' includes 10 weeks as the lead track on the 'Free EP'.

Only 11 of the 26 records that have spent 35 or more weeks on the chart have reached number one (marked with an asterisk *).

New Order

most weeks on chart
(by a song in all it's recorded versions)

This list shows the most successful songs to hit the charts from 1952 to 1996. Only complete recordings of the song count – parts of songs in medley discs are not included.

weeks	title	number of versions
167	MY WAY	5, all vocal
96	UNCHAINED MELODY	8, 7 vocal, 1 instrumental
94	AMAZING GRACE.	2, one vocal, one instrumental
70	ROCK AROUND THE CLOCK	3, all vocal
68	CAN'T HELP FALLING IN LOVE	5, all vocal
68	I BELIEVE	4, all vocal
66	ONLY YOU	6, all vocal
65	STRANGER ON THE SHORE . . .	2, one vocal, one instrumental
62	THEME FROM 'THE THREEPENNY OPERA'/MACK THE KNIFE	6, all vocal
59	RELAX	1, vocal
58	JE T'AIME... MOI NON PLUS/LOVE AT FIRST SIGHT. . . .	4, 3 vocal, 1 instrumental
58	RELEASE ME	2, both vocal
56	DECK OF CARDS	2, both vocal
56	TRUE LOVE	5, 4 vocal, 1 instrumental
53	BLUE MONDAY	1, vocal
51	IT'S ONLY MAKE BELIEVE	4, all vocal
51	LOVE IS ALL AROUND	2, both vocal
51	WHITE LINES (DON'T DON'T DO IT)	2, both vocal
50	LET'S TWIST AGAIN	2, both vocal
	LIGHT MY FIRE	4, all vocal
	WHEN I FALL IN LOVE	3, all vocal

most collaborations

In this table we list the 20 artists who have had hit collaborations with five or more acts (excluding charity conglomerations):

12 ELTON JOHN
Kiki Dee 1976, 1993
John Lennon 1981
Millie Jackson 1985
Dionne Warwick
& Friends 1985
Cliff Richard 1986
Jennifer Rush 1987
Aretha Franklin 1989
George Michael 1991
Eric Clapton. 1992
RuPaul 1994
Marcella Detroit 1994
Luciano Pavarotti 1996

10 CLIFF RICHARD
Hank Marvin 1969, 1986
Olivia Newton-John . . .1980, 1995
Phil Everly 1983, 1984
London Philharmonic
Orchestra 1983
Sheila Walsh 1983
Young Ones 1986
Sarah Brightman 1986
Elton John. 1986
Van Morrison. 1989
Helen Hobson 1996

7 BOMB THE BASS
Merlin and Antonia. . . . 1988
Lorraine 1988
Maureen 1988
Justin Warfield 1994
Spikey Tee 1994
Carlton 1995
Bernard Fowler 1995

7 SHABBA RANKS
Scritti Politti 1991
Maxi Priest 1991, 1993
Johnny Gill 1992
Eddie Murphy 1993
Queen Latifah 1993
Patra and Terri
& Monica 1995
Mykal Rose 1995

6 BEATMASTERS
Cookie Crew 1988
PP Arnold. 1988
Merlin 1989
Betty Boo 1989
Claudia Fontaine 1989
Elaine Vassell 1992

6 DAVID BOWIE
Queen 1981
Bing Crosby 1982
Pat Metheny 1985

Mick Jagger 1985
Al B. Sure! 1993
Lenny Kravitz. 1993
+ 1 uncredited
Pet Shop Boys. 1996

6 JOCELYN BROWN
Incognito. 1991
Jamestown. 1991
Right Said Fred 1991
Sonic Surfers. 1993
Kym Mazelle 1994
Todd Terry and
Martha Wash 1996

6 ERIC CLAPTON
Delaney & Bonnie
and Friends 1969
Michael Kamen 1986
Tina Turner 1987
Elton John 1992
Sting 1992
Cher, Chrissie Hynde
and Neneh Cherry . . . 1995

6 MAXI PRIEST
Beres Hammond 1988
Jazzie B 1990
Shabba Ranks . . . 1991, 1993
Apache Indian 1992
Lee Ritenour 1993
Shaggy 1996

5 SARAH BRIGHTMAN
Royal Philharmonic
Orchestra. 1983
Paul Miles-Kingston . . . 1985
Steve Harley 1986
Cliff Richard. 1986
José Carreras 1992

5 ARETHA FRANKLIN
George Benson. 1981
Eurythmics 1985
George Michael 1987
Elton John. 1989
Whitney Houston 1989

5 MARVIN GAYE
Mary Wells 1964
Kim Weston 1967
Tammi Terrell 1968, 1969
Diana Ross 1974
Diana Ross,
Smokey Robinson and
Stevie Wonder 1979

5 JAMES INGRAM
Patti Austin 1983
Michael McDonald 1984, 1985
Linda Ronstadt 1987

Quincy Jones,
Al B Sure!
El DeBarge and
Barry White 1990
Dolly Parton 1994

5 MICHAEL JACKSON
Diana Ross 1978
Paul McCartney . . . 1982, 1983
Stevie Wonder 1988
Janet Jackson 1995
3T 1996

5 JELLYBEAN
Catherine Buchanan 1986
Steven Dante 1987
Elisa Fiorillo 1987
Adele Bertei 1988
Richard Darbyshire 1988

5 KYM MAZELLE
Robert Howard 1989
Soul II Soul 1990
Rapination 1992, 1996
Jocelyn Brown 1994
Motiv 8 1995

5 DIANA ROSS
Marvin Gaye 1974
Michael Jackson 1978
Marvin Gaye, Smokey
Robinson and
Stevie Wonder 1979
Lionel Richie 1981
Julio Iglesias 1984

5 ROD STEWART
Jeff Beck 1973, 1992
Scottish Football
Squad 1978
Ronald Isley 1989
Tina Turner 1990
Bryan Adams
and Sting 1994

5 BARBRA STREISAND
Neil Diamond 1978
Donna Summer 1979
Barry Gibb 1980
Don Johnson 1988
Michael Crawford 1994

5 STEVIE WONDER
Diana Ross, Marvin Gaye
and Smokey Robinson . 1979
Paul McCartney 1982
Dionne Warwick &
Friends, featuring
Elton John
and Gladys Knight . . . 1985
Michael Jackson 1988
Julio Iglesias 1988

The two most prolific duettists, Elton John and Cliff Richard, combined in 1986 for the hit 'Slow Rivers'. The single failed to make the top 40, peaking at number 44.

most weeks

Elvis Presley

During Elvis Presley's record breaking run of 144 consecutive weeks on chart he scored 13 hits, nine of them number ones.

most consecutive weeks on chart
(by disc)

wks	disc	artist
56	RELEASE ME	Engelbert Humperdinck
55	STRANGER ON THE SHORE	Mr Acker Bilk
48	RELAX	Frankie Goes To Hollywood
47	MY WAY	Frank Sinatra
40	RIVERS OF BABYLON	Boney M
39	I LOVE YOU BECAUSE	Jim Reeves
39	TIE A YELLOW RIBBON ROUND THE OLD OAK TREE	Dawn
38	A SCOTTISH SOLDIER	Andy Stewart
38	WHITE LINES (DON'T DON'T DO IT)	Grandmaster Flash and Melle Mel
37	LOVE IS ALL AROUND	Wet Wet Wet
36	I BELIEVE	Frankie Laine
36	I PRETEND	Des O'Connor

most consecutive weeks on chart
(by artist)

wks	artist
144	**ELVIS PRESLEY** . . . . 28 Jul 60 to 2 May 63
	(from A Mess Of Blues to One More Broken Heart For Sale)
131	**ELVIS PRESLEY** . . . . 29 Nov 69 to 3 Jun 72
	(from Suspicious Minds to Until It's Time For You To Go)
130	**CLIFF RICHARD** . . . . 19 Oct 61 to 18 Apr 64
	(from When The Girl In Your Arms Is The Girl In Your Heart to Don't Talk To Him (re-entry))
105	**BEATLES** . . . . 11 Oct 62 15 Oct 64
	(from Love Me Do to A Hard Day's Night)
89	**CLIFF RICHARD** . . . . 15 Jan 60 to 28 Sep 61
	(from Expresso Bongo EP to A Girl Like You)
85	**ADAM FAITH** . . . . 20 Nov 59 to 6 Jul 61
	(from What Do You Want to Easy Going Me)
85	**TOM JONES** . . . . 10 Nov 65 to 26 Jun 68
	(from Green Green Grass Of Home to Delilah)
80	**DUANE EDDY** . . . . 19 Feb 60 to 31 Aug 61
	(from Bonnie Come Back to Ring Of Fire)
77	**SHADOWS** . . . . 21 Jul 60 to 11 Jan 62
	(from Apache to The Savage)
74	**MR. ACKER BILK** . . . . 15 Jul 61 to 13 Dec 62
	(from That's My Home to Lonely)
72	**FRANK IFIELD** . . . . 5 Jul 62 to 21 Nov 63
	(from I Remember You to Mule Train)
72	**JIM REEVES** . . . . 20 Feb 64 to 8 Jul 65
	(from I Love You Because to How Long Has It Been)
63	**ENGELBERT HUMPERDINCK** . . . . 26 Jan 67 to 10 Apr 68
	(from Release Me to Am I That Easy To Forget)
61	**ELVIS PRESLEY** . . . . 10 May 57 to 11 Jul 58
	(from Too Much To Wear Your Ring Around My Neck)
60	**EVERLY BROTHERS** . . . . 31 Mar 60 to 25 May 60
	(from Let It Be Me to Walk Right Back)
60	**KYLIE MINOGUE** . . . . . . 23 Jan 88 to 18 Mar 89
	(from I Should Be So Lucky to Especially For You)
59	**CONNIE FRANCIS** . . . . . . 4 Apr 58 to 22 May 59
	(from Who's Sorry Now to My Happiness)
57	**BACHELORS** . . . . 23 Jan 64 to 25 Feb 65
	(from Diane to No Arms Can Ever Hold You)
56	**BILL HALEY AND HIS COMETS** . . . . 9 Mar 56 to 5 Apr 57
	(from See You Later Alligator to Don't Knock The Rock)
56	**BOBBY VEE** . . . . 13 Apr 61 to 10 May 62
	(from More Than I Can Say to Please Don't Ask About Barbara)
53	**SEARCHERS** . . . . 27 Jun 63 to 2 Jul 64
	(from Sweets For My Sweet to Don't Throw Your Love Away)
52	**FREDDIE AND THE DREAMERS** . . . . . 9 May 63 to 7 May 64
	(from If You Gotta Make A Fool Of Somebody to Over You)
52	**BILLY FURY** . . . . 27 Apr 61 to 26 Apr 64
	(from Don't Worry to Letter Full Of Tears)
52	**FRANKIE LAINE** . . . . 3 Apr 53 to 2 Apr 54
	(from I Believe to Granada)
52	**RUBY MURRAY** . . . . 3 Dec 54 to 2 Dec 55
	(from Heartbeat to I'll Come When You Call)

most weeks

longest gap between chart hits

This table shows which acts had to wait the longest between chart hits. The definition of a 'hit' is the same as in other lists in this section, i.e. re-issues and re-entries do not count as new hits. Thus the Righteous Brothers do not feature in this list, as they have had no new hits since 1966. The gap is calculated between the last day of one chart run and the first day of the chart run of the next hit.

The appearance of the **Chipmunks** in 1992 was in collaboration with Billy Ray Cyrus and came over 20 years after the death of their creator Ross Bagdasarian, better known as David Seville. The later Chipmunks were the creation of Seville's son, Ross Bagdasarian Jr.

Five of the acts in the table made their chart comeback in association with more contemporary artists: **PJ Proby** with Marc Almond; **Karl Denver** with Happy Mondays; the **Troggs** with Gladiator Wolf; **Donovan** with the Singing Corner; **Ray Charles** with Quincy Jones and **PP Arnold** with the Beatmasters.

Nat 'King' Cole had a gap of 28 years 338 days between 10 Jan 63 to 14 Dec 91, but the re-issue of 'When I Fall In Love' on 12 Dec 87 disqualified him from this table. Similarly 24 years and 28 days elapsed between the disappearance of Bill Haley's 'Don't Knock The Rock' and 'Haley's Golden Medley' coming onto the chart, but two re-issues of 'Rock Around The Clock' interrupted the gap.

act	time period	date
PEREZ PRADO	36 years 27 days	(7 Nov 58 to 4 Dec 94)
COASTERS	34 years 113 days	(11 Dec 59 to 3 Apr 94)
CHIPMUNKS	33 years 87 days	(18 Sep 59 to 19 Dec 92)
DINAH WASHINGTON	30 years 71 days	(24 Jan 62 to 4 Apr 92)
PJ PROBY	28 years 262 days	(10 Apr 68 to 28 Dec 96)
EARTHA KITT	28 years 170 days	(16 Jun 55 to 3 Dec 83)
RITCHIE VALENS	28 years 142 days	(12 Mar 59 to 1 Aug 87)
JOHN LEE HOOKER	28 years 66 days	(19 Aug 64 to 24 Oct 92)
PATSY CLINE	27 years 340 days	(2 Jan 63 to 8 Dec 90)
BOBBY VINTON	26 years 215 days	(27 Feb 64 to 29 Sep 90)
KARL DENVER	25 years 329 days	(16 Jul 64 to 9 Jun 90)
TROGGS	25 years 217 days	(27 Mar 68 to 30 Oct 93)
FRANK IFIELD	24 years 288 days	(22 Feb 67 to 7 Dec 91)
JIMMY CLIFF	23 years 140 days	(24 Oct 70 to 13 Mar 94)
ROLF HARRIS	22 years 232 days	(20 Jun 70 to 7 Feb 93)
CHELSEA FC	21 years 359 days	(14 May 72 to 8 May 94)
ARSENAL FC	21 years 324 days	(19 Jun 71 to 9 May 93)
DONOVAN	21 years 79 days	(23 Sep 69 to 1 Dec 90)
GLENN MILLER	21 years 312 days	(18 Mar 54 to 24 Jan 76)
RAY CHARLES	21 years 307 days	(2 Oct 68 to 13 Jan 90)
PP ARNOLD	20 years 0 days	(25 Sep 68 to 24 Sep 88)

PJ Proby with Mark Almond

Marc Almond's duet with PJ Proby failed to emulate the success of his collaboration with Gene Pitney, but it did bring the trouser-splitting one back to the chart after a hiatus of more than 28 years.

most hits

Double-sided hits, double singles, EPs and albums only count as one hit each time. Re-issues and re-entries do not count as new hits, nor do re-mixes if the same vocal track is used. If the named act on the label has not gone into the studio (or onto the stage) to make a new record, then there is no new hit.

Act	number of hits

CLIFF RICHARD 118
(includes 2 with Olivia Newton-John, 2 with Phil Everly, 1 with Sheila Walsh, 1 with Young Ones, 1 with Sarah Brightman, 1 with Elton John, 1 with Van Morrison and 1 with Helen Hobson)

The only song to have been a hit for both Cliff Richard and Elvis Presley is 'The Twelfth Of Never'. Cliff's version reached number eight in 1964, while Elvis' version, released posthumously, made number 21 in 1995.

ELVIS PRESLEY 111

ELTON JOHN 70
(includes 2 with Kiki Dee, 1 with John Lennon, 1 with Millie Jackson, 1 with Dionne Warwick & Friends, 1 with Cliff Richard, 1 with Jennifer Rush, 1 with Aretha Franklin, 1 with George Michael, 1 with Eric Clapton, 1 with RuPaul, 1 with Marcella Detroit and 1 with Luciano Pavarotti)

DIANA ROSS 58
(includes 2 with Marvin Gaye, 1 with Michael Jackson, 1 with Marvin Gaye, Smokey Robinson and Stevie Wonder, 1 with Lionel Richie and 1 with Julio Iglesias. + 18 with Supremes and 2 with Supremes and Temptations)

DAVID BOWIE 56
(includes 1 with Queen, 1 with Bing Crosby, 1 with Pat Metheny, 1 with Mick Jagger and 1 with Al B Sure!)

ROD STEWART 54
(includes 2 with Jeff Beck, 1 with Tina Turner, 1 with Bryan Adams and Sting and 1 with the Scottish Euro 96 Squad. + 5 with Faces, 1 with Python Lee Jackson and 1 with Glass Tiger)

STATUS QUO 52
(includes 1 with Beach Boys, 1 with Maddy Prior)

STEVIE WONDER 52
(includes 1 with Diana Ross, 1 with Paul McCartney, 1 with Dionne Warwick and Friends, 1 with Michael Jackson and 1 with Julio Iglesias)

MICHAEL JACKSON 47
(includes 2 with Paul McCartney, 1 with Diana Ross, 1 with Stevie Wonder, 1 with Janet Jackson and 1 with 3T)

PAUL McCARTNEY/WINGS 47
(includes 21 as Wings, 2 with Michael Jackson, 1 with Stevie Wonder and 1 with Christians, Holly Johnson, Gerry Marsden and Stock Aitken Waterman)

QUEEN 47
(includes 1 with David Bowie and 1 with George Michael and Lisa Stansfield)

PRINCE 44
(includes 1 with Sheena Easton)

ROLLING STONES 43

MADONNA 42

UB40 40
(includes 2 with Chrissie Hynde, 1 with Afrika Bambaata and Family, 1 with 808 State and 1 with Robert Palmer)

SHAKIN' STEVENS
(includes 1 with Bonnie Tyler)

DONNA SUMMER 37
(includes 1 with Barbra Streisand)

FRANK SINATRA 36
(includes 1 with Sammy Davis Jr., 1 with Nancy Sinatra and 1 with Bono)

TOM JONES 34
(includes 1 with Art Of Noise)

SLADE 34

TINA TURNER 34
(includes 1 with Rod Stewart, 1 with Bryan Adams, 1 with Eric Clapton and 1 with Barry White)

BEE GEES 33

ROY ORBISON 33
(includes 1 with kd lang)

ELVIS COSTELLO 33
(includes 2 as the Imposter and 1 as the Costello Show)

BEATLES 32
(includes 1 with Tony Sheridan and 1 with Billy Preston)

GARY NUMAN 32
(includes 3 with Sharpe and Numan and 2 with Radio Heart)

SHADOWS 31
(+ 30 with Cliff Richard)

FRANKIE VAUGHAN 31
(includes 2 with Kaye Sisters)

BEACH BOYS 30
(includes 1 with Fat Boys, 1 with Status Quo)

NAT 'KING' COLE 30
(includes 1 with George Shearing)

DEPECHE MODE 30

LONNIE DONEGAN 30

HOLLIES 30

HOT CHOCOLATE 30

CHRIS REA 30
(includes 1 with Shirley Bassey)

SIOUXSIE AND THE BANSHEES . . 30
(includes 1 with Morrissey)

KIM WILDE 30
(includes 1 with Junior and 1 with Mel Smith [Mel and Kim])

ELECTRIC LIGHT ORCHESTRA 29
(includes 1 with Olivia Newton-John)

EVERLY BROTHERS 29
(Phil Everly + 1 solo and 2 with Cliff Richard)

FOUR TOPS 29
(includes 2 with Supremes)

BILLY FURY 29

LEVEL 42 29

ORCHESTRAL MANOEUVRES IN THE DARK 29

SUPREMES 29
(includes 3 with Temptations and 2 with Four Tops)

SHIRLEY BASSEY 28
(includes 1 with Yello and 1 with Chris Rea)

GLORIA ESTEFAN 28
(includes 2 as Miami Sound Machine)

IRON MAIDEN 28

PET SHOP BOYS 28
(includes 1 with Dusty Springfield and 1 as Absolutely Fabulous)

STING 28
(includes 1 with Eric Clapton, 1 with Bryan Adams and Rod Stewart and 1 with Pato Banton)

WHO (+ 1 as High Numbers) 28

PETULA CLARK 27

DURAN DURAN 27

ARETHA FRANKLIN 27
(includes 1 with George Benson, 1 with Eurythmics, 1 with George Michael, 1 with Elton John and 1 with Whitney Houston)

FRANKIE LAINE 27
(includes 1 with Jimmy Boyd, 1 with Doris Day and 1 with Johnnie Ray)

AC/DC 26

BANANARAMA 26
(includes 2 with Fun Boy Three and 1 with La Na Nee Nee Noo Noo)

PAT BOONE 26

KATE BUSH 26
(includes 1 with Peter Gabriel and 1 with
Larry Adler)

CHER 26
(includes 1 with Beavis & Butt-Head.
+ 9 with Sonny and 1 uncredited with
Meat Loaf)

PHIL COLLINS 26
(includes 1 with Philip Bailey, 1 with
Marilyn Martin and 1 with David Crosby)

GENESIS 26

JACKSON 5/JACKSONS 26
(11 as Jackson 5 and 15 as Jacksons)

JIM REEVES 26

SIMPLE MINDS 26

DUSTY SPRINGFIELD 26
(includes 1 with Pet Shop Boys, 1 with
Cilla Black and 1 with Daryl Hall. + 5 as a
Springfield)

TEMPTATIONS 26
(includes 3 with Supremes)

T. REX 26
(includes 2 credited to Marc Bolan)

LUTHER VANDROSS 26
(includes 1 with Gregory Hines, 1 with
Janet Jackson and 1 with Mariah Carey)

ABBA 25

CURE 25

DAVID ESSEX 25
(includes 1 with Catherine Zeta Jones)

JANET JACKSON 25
(includes 1 with Luther Vandross and 1
with Michael Jackson. + 1 uncredited with
Herb Alpert)

MADNESS 25

*Other acts that have had 25 hits or
more under more than one name are:*

PAUL WELLER 49
(13 solo, 18 with Jam, 17 with Style Council
and 1 with Council Collective)

ANNIE LENNOX 39
(8 solo, 1 with Al Green, 1 with Paul Simon,
5 with Tourists, 23 with Eurythmics and 1
with Eurythmics and Aretha Franklin)

MIDGE URE 38
(9 solo, 17 with Ultravox, 7 with Visage,
2 as part of Silk, 1 as a Rich Kid, 1 with
Mick Karn and 1 as leader of Band Aid)

BRYAN FERRY 38
(22 solo, 16 with Roxy Music)

MORRISSEY 38
(20 solo, 1 with Siouxsie and 17 as
a Smith)

MARC ALMOND 35
(20 solo, 1 as Marc and the Mambas,
1 with Bronski Beat, 1 with Gene Pitney,
1 with PJ Proby, 2 as Soft Cell/
Marc Almond and 9 with Soft Cell)

DAVE STEWART 35
(1 solo, 1 with Candy Dulfer, 1 with Spiritual
Cowboys, 5 with Tourists, 23 with
Eurythmics, 1 with Eurythmics and
Aretha Franklin and 3 with Vegas)

LIONEL RICHIE 33
(18 solo, 13 with the Commodores,
1 with Diana Ross and 1 as leader of
USA For Africa)

GEORGE MICHAEL 32
(17 solo, 10 with Wham!, 1 with
Aretha Franklin, 1 with Elton John, 1 with
Queen and Lisa Stansfield and 1 with
Boogie Box High. + 1 uncredited with
Lisa Moorish)

ERIC CLAPTON 31
(15 solo, 7 with Cream, 2 with the
Yardbirds, 1 as Derek and the Dominoes,
1 with Delaney and Bonnie and Friends,
1 with Michael Kamen, 1 with Elton John, 1
with Tina Turner, 1 with Sting and 1 with
Cher, Chrissie Hynde and Neneh Cherry)

ROBERT PALMER 27
(23 solo, 1 with UB40 and 4 with
Power Station)

BOY GEORGE 27
(12 solo, 10 with Culture Club, 4 as
Jesus Loves You and 1 with PM Dawn)

JON BON JOVI 26
(2 solo, 24 with Bon Jovi)

TERRY HALL 26
(3 solo, 7 with Specials, 6 with Fun Boy
Three, 2 with Fun Boy Three and
Bananarama, 4 with Colour Field, 3 with
Vegas and 1 with Nearly God)

JOHN LYDON 25
(11 with Sex Pistols, 12 with Public Image,
1 with Time Zone and 1 with Leftfield)

DONNY OSMOND 25
(11 solo, 10 as an Osmond, 4 as half of
Donny and Marie)

NEW ORDER 25
(22 as New Order, 1 as Englandneworder
and 2 as Joy Division, more or less)

*Madonna and
Prince share the
honours for most
new hits in the
90s so far with
20 each.*

---

most hits in one calender year

The acts who have enjoyed the most hits in one calender year are:

1983	**JAM**	14 hits	. . . .(1 hangover from previous year, 13 re-entries)
1957	**ELVIS PRESLEY**	13 hits	. . . .(10 new hits, 3 hangovers)
1977	**ELVIS PRESLEY**	12 hits	. . . .(3 new hits, 1 hangover, 8 re-issues)
1992	**WEDDING PRESENT** . .	12 hits	. . . .(12 new hits)
1996	**PRODIGY**	10 hits	. . . .(2 new hits, 8 re-entries)
1981	**ADAM AND THE ANTS** .	9 hits	. . . .(6 new hits, 2 hangovers, 1 re-entry)
1956	**BILL HALEY AND HIS COMETS**	9 hits	. . . .(7 new hits, 2 hangovers)
1980	**JAM**	9 hits	. . . .(2 new hits, 1 hangover, 6 re-entries)
1996	**OASIS**	9 hits	. . . .(1 new hit, 4 hangovers, 4 re-entries)
1971	**ELVIS PRESLEY**	9 hits	. . . . . .(5 new hits, 1 hangover, 1 re-entry, 2 re-issues)

This table excludes double A-sides where they were listed separately. Thus **Elvis Presley**'s hit total of 16 in 1957 is reduced to 13 after the omission of three charted B-sides. As can be seen, only the **Wedding Present** have ever managed to chart more than ten new hits in a calendar year. All 12 of their singles in 1992 made the top 30 and, because they were deleted after only one week on sale, none of them spent more than two weeks on the chart.

most top ten hits

The same rules apply as for the MOST HITS list, except that a disc must have made the top ten for at least one week to qualify.

act	number of weeks
CLIFF RICHARD	63

(includes 1 with Phil Everly, 1 with Young Ones and 1 with Sarah Brightman)

ELVIS PRESLEY	55
MADONNA	38
MICHAEL JACKSON	35

(includes 2 with Paul McCartney, 1 with Janet Jackson and 1 with 3T. + 11 as a Jackson)

BEATLES	28
ROD STEWART	25

(includes 1 with Tina Turner, 1 with Bryan Adams and Sting. +3 with Faces, 1 with Python Lee Jackson)

PAUL McCARTNEY/WINGS	24

(includes 12 as Wings, 2 with Michael Jackson, 1 with Stevie Wonder and 1 with Christians, Holly Johnson, Gerry Marsden and Stock Aitken Waterman)

QUEEN	24

(includes 1 with David Bowie and 1 with George Michael and Lisa Stansfield)

DAVID BOWIE	23

(includes 1 with Queen, 1 with Bing Crosby and 1 with Mick Jagger)

ELTON JOHN	23

(includes 2 with Kiki Dee, 1 with George Michael, 1 with RuPaul and 1 with Luciano Pavarotti)

STATUS QUO	22
ROLLING STONES	21
ABBA	19
FRANKIE LAINE	19

(includes 1 with Jimmy Boyd and 1 with Doris Day)

STEVIE WONDER	18

(includes 1 with Paul McCartney and 1 with Julio Iglesias)

BEE GEES	17
LONNIE DONEGAN	17
HOLLIES	17
PET SHOP BOYS	17

(includes 1 with Dusty Springfield and 1 as Absolutely Fabulous)

DIANA ROSS	17

(includes 1 with Marvin Gaye and 1 with Lionel Richie. + 7 with Supremes and 1 with Supremes and Temptations)

MANFRED MANN	16

(includes 3 as Manfred Mann's Earth Band)

KYLIE MINOGUE	16

(includes 1 with Jason Donovan)

SHADOWS	16

(+ 25 backing Cliff Richard)

SLADE	16
UB40	16

(includes 2 with Chrissie Hynde and 1 with Robert Palmer)

ELECTRIC LIGHT ORCHESTRA	15

(includes 1 with Olivia Newton-John)

ERASURE	15
TOM JONES	15

(includes 1 with Art Of Noise)

MADNESS	15
PRINCE	15
SHAKIN' STEVENS	15
U2	15

Also worth mentioning are:

GEORGE MICHAEL	23

(10 solo, 9 with Wham!, 1 with Aretha Franklin, 1 with Elton John, 1 with Queen and Lisa Stansfield and 1 as part of Boogie Box High)

PHIL COLLINS	20

(10 solo, 8 with Genesis, 1 with Philip Bailey and 1 with Marilyn Martin)

PAUL WELLER	19

(3 solo, 9 with Jam and 7 with Style Council)

ANNIE LENNOX	15

(4 solo, 8 as one half of Eurythmics, 2 as a Tourist and 1 as part of Eurythmics and Aretha Franklin)

ROY WOOD	15

(1 solo, 7 with Move, 6 with Wizzard and 1 with Electric Light Orchestra)

The film musical Evita spawned two Top 10 hits for Madonna, 'Don't Cry For Me Argentina' and the new Lloyd Webber/Rice composition 'You Must Love Me'.

Madonna

the top ten

most consecutive top ten hits

wks	artist
32	**MADONNA**
26	**CLIFF RICHARD**
	(11 with the Shadows)
24	**BEATLES** (first 24 releases)
23	**ELVIS PRESLEY** (first 23 RCA releases)
19	**ROLLING STONES**
18	**ABBA**
13	**KYLIE MINOGUE** (first 13 releases, including 1 with Jason Donovan)
12	**SHADOWS** (first 12 hits)
12	**SLADE**
12	**TAKE THAT** (including 1 with Lulu. Gary Barlow, Robbie Williams and Mark Owen have each added 1 Top 10 hit to their run)
11	**MARIAH CAREY**
11	**GARY GLITTER** (first 11 hits)
11	**FRANKIE LAINE**
11	**GUY MITCHELL** (first 11 hits)
11	**T. REX**
10	**BAY CITY ROLLERS** (first 10 hits)
10	**DURAN DURAN**
10	**DAVID WHITFIELD**
10	**U2**

At the start of Elvis Presley's run of 23 consecutive top ten hits, three old HMV releases appeared on the chart, one of which, 'Paralysed', reached the top ten. Three EPs by Elvis also hit the charts without reaching the top ten during the five and a half years in which every Elvis single hit the Top Ten, with 20 of the 23 reaching the top three. 'Holiday' by Madonna reappeared in the top ten twice during her run of 27 top ten hits with consecutive releases. As it was first a top ten hit before the release of 'Lucky Star', her first single to fail to hit the upper reaches, it does not count as one of her consecutive top ten hits. Her re-mixed version of 'Crazy For You', which also hit the top ten, does not count as an extra hit. An import, 'In God's Country', interrupted U2's 10 consecutive top ten hits.

Kylie Minogue's record of 13 consecutive top ten hits with her first 13 releases (including one in duet with Jason Donovan) represents the best start to a chart career by any act ever. The Beatles' first 24 releases all eventually hit the top ten but their first single, 'Love Me Do' only did so as a re-issue 20 years on. Between May 1959 and December 1963, the Shadows released 30 singles, either solo or backing Cliff Richard, all of which hit the top ten.
The Rolling Stones' run of 19 consecutive top ten hits began on 12 March 1964 with 'Not Fade Away', and finished on July 21 1978 when 'Miss You/Far Away Eyes' dropped out of the top ten. This is the longest time span for a run of top ten hits with consecutive releases, none of which were re-mixes or re-issues.

Mariah Carey's string of top ten hits is the longest by an active recording act.

most hits without a top ten hit

Up to the end of 1996, ten acts had amassed at least 15 hits without ever visiting the upper reaches of the chart.

hits	act	highest placed hit, year, position
26	**AC/DC**	Heatseeker, 1988, **12**
16	**ALARM**	68 Guns, 1983, **17**
16	**MISSION**	Wasteland, 1987, **11**
15	**LLOYD COLE** (first 9 with the Commotions)	Lost Weekend, 1985, **17**
15	**JULIAN COPE** (has reached top ten with Teardrop Explodes)	World Shut Your Mouth, 1986, **19**
15	**CULT**	Lil' Devil, 1987, **11**
15	**INSPIRAL CARPETS**	Dragging Me Down, 1992, **12**
15	**KILLING JOKE**	Love Like Blood, 1985, **16**
15	**SAXON**	And The Bands Played On, 1981, **12**
15	**The THE**	Disinfected EP, 1995, **17**

Mark E. Smith has accumulated 13 hits as lead singer of the Fall in addition to his collaborations with D.O.S.E. and the Inspiral Carpets. Of his 15 charted hits, only the Inspiral Carpets pairing, 'I Want You', has made the top twenty, peaking at number 18 in 1994. Luther Vandross has had 23 solo hits without ever straying above position 13, but has twice reached the top ten in duet with Janet Jackson and once with Mariah Carey. That Petrol Emotion have scored an unprecedented seven chart hits without ever making the top 40.

the number one hits

1950's

▲ *Indicates a*
hit that entered
the chart at
number one.

1952 *(Top Twelve – NME Chart)*

14 Nov HERE IN MY HEART Al Martino ▲ 9

1953

16 Jan YOU BELONG TO ME Jo Stafford 1
23 Jan COMES A-LONG A-LOVE Kay Starr 1
30 Jan OUTSIDE OF HEAVEN Eddie Fisher 1
6 Feb DON'T LET THE STARS GET IN YOUR EYES
Perry Como 5
13 Mar SHE WEARS RED FEATHERS Guy Mitchell. . . 4
10 Apr BROKEN WINGS The Stargazers 1
17 Apr (HOW MUCH IS) THAT DOGGIE IN THE
WINDOW Lita Roza 1
24 Apr I BELIEVE Frankie Laine 9
26 Jun I'M WALKING BEHIND YOU Eddie Fisher
featuring Sally Sweetland 1
3 Jul BELIEVE Frankie Laine 6
14 Aug MOULIN ROUGE Mantovani 1
21 Aug I BELIEVE Frankie Laine 3
11 Sep LOOK AT THAT GIRL Guy Mitchell. 6
23 Oct HEY JOE Frankie Laine 2
6 Nov ANSWER ME David Whitfield 1
13 Nov ANSWER ME Frankie Laine 8
(ANSWER ME by David Whitfield returned
to number one for one week to share the
top spot with Frankie Laine's version on
11 Dec 1953)

1954

8 Jan OH MEIN PAPA Eddie Calvert. 9
12 Mar I SEE THE MOON Stargazers 5
16 Apr SECRET LOVE Doris Day 1
23 Apr I SEE THE MOON Stargazers 1
30 Apr SUCH A NIGHT Johnnie Ray 1
7 May SECRET LOVE Doris Day 8
2 Jul CARA MIA David Whitfield, with chorus
and Mantovani and his orchestra. 10
10 Sep LITTLE THINGS MEAN A LOT Kitty Kallen . . . 1
17 Sep THREE COINS IN THE FOUNTAIN
Frank Sinatra. 3

Top Twenty began 1 Oct 1954

8 Oct HOLD MY HAND Don Cornell. 4
5 Nov MY SON MY SON Vera Lynn 2
19 Nov HOLD MY HAND Don Cornell 1

26 Nov THIS OLE HOUSE Rosemary Clooney 1
3 Dec LET'S HAVE ANOTHER PARTY
Winifred Atwell 5

1955

7 Jan FINGER OF SUSPICION Dickie Valentine . . . 1
14 Jan MAMBO ITALIANO Rosemary Clooney 1
21 Jan FINGER OF SUSPICION Dickie Valentine. . . . 2
4 Feb MAMBO ITALIANO Rosemary Clooney 2
18 Feb SOFTLY SOFTLY Ruby Murray. 3
11 Mar GIVE ME YOUR WORD
Tennessee Ernie Ford 7
29 Apr CHERRY PINK AND APPLE BLOSSOM WHITE
Perez Prado. 2
13 May STRANGER IN PARADISE Tony Bennett . . . 2
27 May CHERRY PINK AND APPLE BLOSSOM WHITE
Eddie Calvert. 4
24 Jun UNCHAINED MELODY Jimmy Young 3
15 Jul DREAMBOAT Alma Cogan. 2
29 Jul ROSE MARIE Slim Whitman 11
14 oct THE MAN FROM LARAMIE Jimmy Young. . . . 4
11 Nov HERNANDO'S HIDEAWAY
Johnston Brothers. 2
25 Nov ROCK AROUND THE CLOCK
Bill Haley and his Comets 3
16 Dec CHRISTMAS ALPHABET Dickie Valentine. . . . 3

1956

6 Jan ROCK AROUND THE CLOCK
Bill Haley and his Comets 2
20 Jan SIXTEEN TONS Tennessee Ernie Ford 4
17 Feb MEMORIES ARE MADE OF THIS
Dean Martin 4
16 Mar IT'S ALMOST TOMORROW
Dreamweavers. 2
30 Mar ROCK AND ROLL WALTZ Kay Starr with
the Hugo Winterhalter Orchestra 1
6 Apr IT'S ALMOST TOMORROW Dreamweavers . . 1

Top Thirty began 13 April 1956

13 Apr POOR PEOPLE OF PARIS
Winifred Atwell 3
4 May NO OTHER LOVE Ronnie Hilton 6
15 Jun I'LL BE HOME Pat Boone. 5
20 Jul WHY DO FOOLS FALL IN LOVE Teenagers
featuring Frankie Lymon 3
10 Aug WHATEVER WILL BE WILL BE Doris Day. . . . 6
21 Sep LAY DOWN YOUR ARMS Anne Shelton. 4

19 Oct A WOMAN IN LOVE Frankie Laine 4
16 Nov JUST WALKIN' IN THE RAIN Johnnie Ray . . . 7

1957

4 Jan SINGING THE BLUES Guy Mitchell 1
11 Jan SINGING THE BLUES Tommy Steele and
    the Steelmen 1
18 Jan SINGING THE BLUES Guy Mitchell 1
25 Jan THE GARDEN OF EDEN Frankie Vaughan . . . 4
    (SINGING THE BLUES by Guy Mitchell
    returned to number one for one week to
    share the top spot with GARDEN OF EDEN
    by Frankie Vaughan on 1 Feb 1957)
22 Feb YOUNG LOVE Tab Hunter 7
12 Apr CUMBERLAND GAP Lonnie Donegan 5
17 May ROCK-A-BILLY Guy Mitchell 1
24 May BUTTERFLY Andy Williams 2
7 Jun YES TONIGHT JOSEPHINE Johnnie Ray 3
28 Jun GAMBLIN' MAN/PUTTING ON THE STYLE
    Lonnie Donegan 2
12 Jul ALL SHOOK UP Elvis Presley 7
30 Aug DIANA Paul Anka 9
1 Nov THAT'LL BE THE DAY Crickets 3
22 Nov MARY'S BOY CHILD Harry Belafonte 7

1958

10 Jan GREAT BALLS OF FIRE Jerry Lee Lewis 2
24 Jan JAILHOUSE ROCK Elvis Presley ▲ 3
14 Feb THE STORY OF MY LIFE Michael Holliday . . . 2
28 Feb MAGIC MOMENTS Perry Como 8
25 Apr WHOLE LOTTA WOMAN
    Marvin Rainwater 3
16 May WHO'S SORRY NOW Connie Francis 6
27 Jun ON THE STREET WHERE YOU LIVE
    Vic Damone 2
    (On 4 Jul 1958 ON THE STREET WHERE
    YOU LIVE by Vic Damone and ALL I HAVE
    TO DO IS DREAM/CLAUDETTE by the
    Everly Brothers shared the top spot)
4 Jul ALL I HAVE TO DO IS DREAM/CLAUDETTE
    Everly Brothers 7
22 Aug WHEN Kalin Twins 5
26 Sep CAROLINA MOON/STUPID CUPID
    Connie Francis 6
7 Nov IT'S ALL IN THE GAME Tommy Edwards 3
28 Nov HOOTS MON Lord Rockingham's XI 3
19 Dec IT'S ONLY MAKE BELIEVE Conway Twitty . . 5

1959

23 Jan THE DAY THE RAINS CAME Jane Morgan . . . 1
•30 Jan ONE NIGHT/I GOT STUNG Elvis Presley 3
20 Feb AS I LOVE YOU Shirley Bassey 4
20 Mar SMOKE GETS IN YOUR EYES Platters 1
27 Mar SIDE SADDLE Russ Conway 4
24 Apr IT DOESN'T MATTER ANYMORE
    Buddy Holly 3
15 May A FOOL SUCH AS I/I NEED YOUR
    LOVE TONIGHT Elvis Presley 5
19 Jun ROULETTE Russ Conway 2
3 Jul DREAM LOVER Bobby Darin 4
31 Jul LIVING DOLL Cliff Richard and the
    Drifters 6
11 Sep ONLY SIXTEEN Craig Douglas 4
9 Oct HERE COMES SUMMER Jerry Keller 1
16 Oct MACK THE KNIFE Bobby Darin 2
30 Oct TRAVELLIN' LIGHT Cliff Richard and the
    Shadows 5
4 Dec WHAT DO YOU WANT Adam Faith 3
    (On 18 Dec 1959 WHAT DO YOU WANT by
    Adam Faith and WHAT DO YOU WANT TO
    MAKE THOSE EYES AT ME FOR by Emile Ford
    and the Checkmates shared the top spot)
18 Dec WHAT DO YOU WANT TO MAKE THOSE
    EYES AT ME FOR Emile Ford and
    the Checkmates 6

1960's

1960

29 Jan STARRY EYED Michael Holliday 1
5 Feb WHY Anthony Newley 4
10 Mar POOR ME Adam Faith 1
17 Mar RUNNING BEAR Johnny Preston 2
31 Mar MY OLD MAN'S A DUSTMAN
    Lonnie Donegan 4
28 Apr DO YOU MIND Anthony Newley 1
5 May CATHY'S CLOWN Everly Brothers 7
23 Jun THREE STEPS TO HEAVEN
    Eddie Cochran 2
7 Jul GOOD TIMIN' Jimmy Jones 3
28 Jul PLEASE DON'T TEASE Cliff Richard and
    the Shadows 2
4 Aug SHAKIN' ALL OVER Johnny Kidd and the
    Pirates 1

Record Retailer, now Music Week, began publication of a Top Fifty on 10 Mar 1960. From this point on their charts are used. The final New Musical Express chart used is that of 26 Feb 1960, as the chart published in Record Retailer on 10 Mar 1960 was dated 5 Mar and clearly corresponded with the NME chart of 4 Mar 1960.

the number one hits

▲ *Indicates a hit that entered the chart at number one.*

11 Aug PLEASE DON'T TEASE Cliff Richard and
the Shadows 2
25 Aug APACHE Shadows 5
29 Sep TELL LAURA I LOVE HER Ricky Valance 3
20 Oct ONLY THE LONELY Roy Orbison 2
3 Nov IT'S NOW OR NEVER Elvis Presley 8
29 Dec I LOVE YOU Cliff Richard and
the Shadows 2

1961

12 Jan POETRY IN MOTION Johnny Tillotson 2
26 Jan ARE YOU LONESOME TONIGHT
Elvis Presley 4
23 Feb SAILOR Petula Clark 1
2 Mar WALK RIGHT BACK/EBONY EYES
Everly Brothers 3
23 Mar WOODEN HEART Elvis Presley 6
4 May BLUE MOON Marcels 2
18 May ON THE REBOUND Floyd Cramer 1
25 May YOU'RE DRIVING ME CRAZY
Temperance Seven 1
1 Jun SURRENDER Elvis Presley 4
29 Jun RUNAWAY Del Shannon 3
20 Jul TEMPTATION Everly Brothers 2
3 Aug WELL I ASK YOU Eden Kane 1
10 Aug YOU DON'T KNOW Helen Shapiro 3
31 Aug JOHNNY REMEMBER ME John Leyton 3
21 Sep REACH FOR THE STARS/CLIMB EV'RY
MOUNTAIN Shirley Bassey 1
28 Sep JOHNNY REMEMBER ME John Leyton 1
5 Oct KON-TIKI Shadows 1
12 Oct MICHAEL Highwaymen 1
19 Oct WALKIN' BACK TO HAPPINESS
Helen Shapiro 3
9 Nov LITTLE SISTER/HIS LATEST FLAME
Elvis Presley 4
7 Dec TOWER OF STRENGTH Frankie Vaughan 3
28 Dec MOON RIVER Danny Williams 2

1962

11 Jan THE YOUNG ONES Cliff Richard and the
Shadows ▲ 6
22 Feb ROCK-A-HULA BABY/CAN'T HELP
FALLING IN LOVE Elvis Presley 4
22 Mar WONDERFUL LAND Shadows 8
17 May NUT ROCKER B. Bumble and
the Stingers 1

24 May GOOD LUCK CHARM Elvis Presley 5
28 Jun COME OUTSIDE Mike Sarne with
Wendy Richard 2
12 Jul I CAN'T STOP LOVING YOU Ray Charles 2
26 Jul I REMEMBER YOU Frank Ifield 7
13 Sep SHE'S NOT YOU Elvis Presley 3
4 Oct TELSTAR Tornados 5
8 Nov LOVESICK BLUES Frank Ifield 5
13 Dec RETURN TO SENDER Elvis Presley 3

1963

3 Jan THE NEXT TIME/BACHELOR BOY
Cliff Richard and the Shadows 3
(BACHELOR BOY listed from 10 Jan 63 only)
24 Jan DANCE ON! Shadows 1
31 Jan DIAMONDS Jet Harris and Tony Meehan . . . 3
21 Feb WAYWARD WIND Frank Ifield 3
14 Mar SUMMER HOLIDAY Cliff Richard and the
Shadows 2
28 Mar FOOT TAPPER Shadows 1
4 Apr SUMMER HOLIDAY Cliff Richard and the
Shadows 1
11 Apr HOW DO YOU DO IT Gerry and the
Pacemakers 3
2 May FROM ME TO YOU Beatles 7
20 Jun I LIKE IT Gerry and the Pacemakers 4
18 Jul CONFESSIN' Frank Ifield 2
1 Aug (YOU'RE THE) DEVIL IN DISGUISE
Elvis Presley 1
8 Aug SWEETS FOR MY SWEET Searchers 2
22 Aug BAD TO ME Billy J. Kramer and
the Dakotas 3
12 Sep SHE LOVES YOU Beatles 4
10 Oct DO YOU LOVE ME Brian Poole and the
Tremeloes 3
31 Oct YOU'LL NEVER WALK ALONE Gerry and
the Pacemakers 4
28 Nov SHE LOVES YOU Beatles 2
12 Dec I WANT TO HOLD YOUR HAND Beatles 5

1964

16 Jan GLAD ALL OVER Dave Clark Five 2
30 Jan NEEDLES AND PINS Searchers 3
20 Feb DIANE Bachelors 1
27 Feb ANYONE WHO HAD A HEART Cilla Black . . . 3
19 Mar LITTLE CHILDREN Billy J. Kramer and
the Dakotas 2

Date	Title	Weeks
2 Apr	CANT BUY ME LOVE Beatles	3
23 Apr	WORLD WITHOUT LOVE Peter and Gordon	2
7 May	DON'T THROW YOUR LOVE AWAY Searchers	2
21 May	JULIET Four Pennies	1
28 May	YOU'RE MY WORLD Cilla Black	4
25 Jun	IT'S OVER Roy Orbison	2
9 Jul	HOUSE OF THE RISING SUN Animals	1
16 Jul	IT'S ALL OVER NOW Rolling Stones	1
23 Jul	HARD DAY'S NIGHT Beatles	3
13 Aug	DO WAH DIDDY DIDDY Manfred Mann	2
27 Aug	HAVE I THE RIGHT Honeycombs	2
10 Sep	YOU REALLY GOT ME Kinks	2
24 Sep	I'M INTO SOMETHING GOOD Herman's Hermits	2
8 Oct	OH PRETTY WOMAN Roy Orbison	2
22 Oct	(THERE'S) ALWAYS SOMETHING THERE TO REMIND ME Sandie Shaw	3
12 Nov	OH PRETTY WOMAN Roy Orbison	1
19 Nov	BABY LOVE Supremes	2
3 Dec	LITTLE RED ROOSTER Rolling Stones	1
10 Dec	I FEEL FINE Beatles	5

1965

Date	Title	Weeks
14 Jan	YEH YEH Georgie Fame and the Blue Flames	2
28 Jan	GO NOW Moody Blues	1
4 Feb	YOU'VE LOST THAT LOVIN' FEELIN' Righteous Brothers	2
18 Feb	TIRED OF WAITING FOR YOU Kinks	1
25 Feb	I'LL NEVER FIND ANOTHER YOU Seekers	2
11 Mar	IT'S NOT UNUSUAL Tom Jones	1
18 Mar	THE LAST TIME Rolling Stones	3
8 Apr	CONCRETE AND CLAY Unit Four Plus Two	1
15 Apr	THE MINUTE YOU'RE GONE Cliff Richard	1
22 Apr	TICKET TO RIDE Beatles	3
13 May	KING OF THE ROAD Roger Miller	1
20 May	WHERE ARE YOU NOW (MY LOVE) Jackie Trent	1
27 May	LONG LIVE LOVE Sandie Shaw	3
17 Jun	CRYING IN THE CHAPEL Elvis Presley	1
24 Jun	I'M ALIVE Hollies	1
1 Jul	CRYING IN THE CHAPEL Elvis Presley	1
8 Jul	I'M ALIVE Hollies	2
22 Jul	MR. TAMBOURINE MAN Byrds	2
5 Aug	HELP! Beatles	3
26 Aug	I GOT YOU BABE Sonny and Cher	2

Date	Title	Weeks
9 Sep	(I CAN'T GET NO) SATISFACTION Rolling Stones	2
23 Sep	MAKE IT EASY ON YOURSELF Walker Brothers	1
30 Sep	TEARS Ken Dodd	5
4 Nov	GET OFF OF MY CLOUD Rolling Stones	3
25 Nov	THE CARNIVAL IS OVER Seekers	3
16 Dec	DAY TRIPPER/WE CAN WORK IT OUT Beatles	5

1966

Date	Title	Weeks
20 Jan	KEEP ON RUNNING Spencer Davis Group	1
27 Jan	MICHELLE Overlanders	3
17 Feb	THESE BOOTS ARE MADE FOR WALKIN' Nancy Sinatra	4
17 Mar	THE SUN AIN'T GONNA SHINE ANYMORE Walker Brothers	4
14 Apr	SOMEBODY HELP ME Spencer Davis Group	2
28 Apr	YOU DON'T HAVE TO SAY YOU LOVE ME Dusty Springfield	1
5 May	PRETTY FLAMINGO Manfred Mann	3
26 May	PAINT IT, BLACK Rolling Stones	1
2 Jun	STRANGERS IN THE NIGHT Frank Sinatra	3
23 Jun	PAPERBACK WRITER Beatles	2
7 Jul	SUNNY AFTERNOON Kinks	2
21 Jul	GET AWAY Georgie Fame and the Blue Flames	1
28 Jul	OUT OF TIME Chris Farlowe and the Thunderbirds	1
4 Aug	WITH A GIRL LIKE YOU Troggs	2
18 Aug	YELLOW SUBMARINE/ELEANOR RIGBY Beatles	4
15 Sep	ALL OR NOTHING Small Faces	1
22 Sep	DISTANT DRUMS Jim Reeves	5
27 Oct	REACH OUT I'LL BE THERE Four Tops	3
17 Nov	GOOD VIBRATIONS Beach Boys	2
1 Dec	GREEN GREEN GRASS OF HOME Tom Jones	7

1967

Date	Title	Weeks
19 Jan	I'M A BELIEVER Monkees	4
16 Feb	THIS IS MY SONG Petula Clark	2
2 Mar	RELEASE ME Engelbert Humperdinck	6
13 Apr	SOMETHING STUPID Nancy Sinatra and Frank Sinatra	2
27 Apr	PUPPET ON A STRING Sandie Shaw	3
18 May	SILENCE IS GOLDEN Tremeloes	3

the number one hits

12 Sep TEARS OF A CLOWN Smokey Robinson and
the Miracles 1

19 Sep BAND OF GOLD Freda Payne 6

31 Oct WOODSTOCK
Matthews' Southern Comfort 3

21 Nov VOODOO CHILE Jimi Hendrix Experience . . . 1

28 Nov I HEAR YOU KNOCKIN' Dave Edmunds 6

1971

9 Jan GRANDAD Clive Dunn 3

30 Jan MY SWEET LORD George Harrison 5

6 Mar BABY JUMP Mungo Jerry 2

20 Mar HOT LOVE T. Rex 6

1 May DOUBLE BARREL Dave and Ansil Collins . . . 2

15 May KNOCK THREE TIMES Dawn 5

19 Jun CHIRPY CHIRPY CHEEP CHEEP
Middle Of The Road 5

24 Jul GET IT ON T. Rex 4

21 Aug I'M STILL WAITING Diana Ross 4

18 Sep HEY GIRL DON'T BOTHER ME Tams 3

9 Oct MAGGIE MAY Rod Stewart 5

13 Nov COZ I LUV YOU Slade 4

11 Dec ERNIE (THE FASTEST MILKMAN IN THE
WEST) Benny Hill 4

1972

8 Jan I'D LIKE TO TEACH THE WORLD TO SING
(IN PERFECT HARMONY) New Seekers 4

5 Feb TELEGRAM SAM T. Rex 2

19 Feb SON OF MY FATHER Chicory Tip 3

11 Mar WITHOUT YOU Nilsson 5

15 Apr AMAZING GRACE
The Pipes and Drums and Military Band
of the Royal Scots Dragoon Guards 5

20 May METAL GURU T. Rex 4

17 Jun VINCENT Don McLean 2

1 Jul TAKE ME BAK 'OME Slade 1

8 Jul PUPPY LOVE Donny Osmond 5

12 Aug SCHOOL'S OUT Alice Cooper 3

2 Sep YOU WEAR IT WELL Rod Stewart 1

9 Sep MAMA WEER ALL CRAZEE NOW Slade 3

30 Sep HOW CAN I BE SURE David Cassidy 2

14 Oct MOULDY OLD DOUGH Lieutenant Pigeon . . . 4

11 Nov CLAIR Gilbert O'Sullivan 2

25 Nov MY DING-A-LING Chuck Berry 4

23 Dec LONG HAIRED LOVER FROM LIVERPOOL
Little Jimmy Osmond 5

1973

27 Jan BLOCKBUSTER Sweet 5

3 Mar CUM ON FEEL THE NOIZE Slade ▲ 4

31 Mar TWELFTH OF NEVER Donny Osmond 1

7 Apr GET DOWN Gilbert O'Sullivan 2

21 Apr TIE A YELLOW RIBBON ROUND THE OLD
OAK TREE Dawn featuring Tony Orlando . . 4

19 May SEE MY BABY JIVE Wizzard 4

16 Jun CAN THE CAN Suzi Quatro 1

23 Jun RUBBER BULLETS 10CC 1

30 Jun SKWEEZE ME PLEEZE ME Slade ▲ 3

21 Jul WELCOME HOME Peters and Lee 1

28 Jul I'M THE LEADER OF THE GANG (I AM)
Gary Glitter 4

25 Aug YOUNG LOVE Donny Osmond 4

22 Sep ANGEL FINGERS Wizzard 1

29 Sep EYE LEVEL Simon Park Orchestra 4

27 Oct DAYDREAMER/THE PUPPY SONG
David Cassidy 3

17 Nov I LOVE YOU LOVE ME LOVE Gary Glitter ▲ . 4

15 Dec MERRY XMAS EVERYBODY Slade ▲ 5

1974

19 Jan YOU WON'T FIND ANOTHER FOOL LIKE ME
New Seekers 1

26 Jan TIGER FEET Mud 4

23 Feb DEVIL GATE DRIVE Suzi Quatro 2

9 Mar JEALOUS MIND Alvin Stardust 1

16 Mar BILLY DON'T BE A HERO Paper Lace 3

6 Apr SEASONS IN THE SUN Terry Jacks 4

4 May WATERLOO Abba 2

18 May SUGAR BABY LOVE Rubettes 4

15 Jun THE STREAK Ray Stevens 1

22 Jun ALWAYS YOURS Gary Glitter 1

29 Jun SHE Charles Aznavour 4

27 Jul ROCK YOUR BABY George McCrae 3

17 Aug WHEN WILL I SEE YOU AGAIN Three Degrees . 2

31 Aug LOVE ME FOR A REASON Osmonds 3

21 Sep KUNG FU FIGHTING Carl Douglas 3

12 Oct ANNIE'S SONG John Denver 1

19 Oct SAD SWEET DREAMER Sweet Sensation . . . 1

26 Oct EVERYTHING I OWN Ken Boothe 3

16 Nov GONNA MAKE YOU A STAR David Essex . . . 3

7 Dec YOU'RE THE FIRST THE LAST MY
EVERYTHING Barry White 2

21 Dec LONELY THIS CHRISTMAS Mud 4

the number one hits

1975

Date	Title	Weeks
18 Jan	DOWN DOWN Status Quo	1
25 Jan	MS. GRACE Tymes	1
1 Feb	JANUARY Pilot	3
22 Feb	MAKE ME SMILE (COME UP AND SEE ME) Steve Harley and Cockney Rebel	2
8 Mar	IF Telly Savalas	2
22 Mar	BYE BYE BABY Bay City Rollers	6
3 May	OH BOY Mud	2
17 May	STAND BY YOUR MAN Tammy Wynette	3
7 Jun	WHISPERING GRASS Windsor Davies and Don Estelle	3
28 Jun	I'M NOT IN LOVE 10CC	2
12 Jul	TEARS ON MY PILLOW Johnny Nash	1
19 Jul	GIVE A LITTLE LOVE Bay City Rollers	3
9 Aug	BARBADOS Typically Tropical	1
16 Aug	CAN'T GIVE YOU ANYTHING (BUT MY LOVE) Stylistics	3
6 Sep	SAILING Rod Stewart	4
4 Oct	HOLD ME CLOSE David Essex	3
25 Oct	I ONLY HAVE EYES FOR YOU Art Garfunkel	2
8 Nov	SPACE ODDITY David Bowie	2
22 Nov	D.I.V.O.R.C.E. Billy Connolly	1
29 Nov	BOHEMIAN RHAPSODY Queen	9

1976

Date	Title	Weeks
31 Jan	MAMMA MIA Abba	2
14 Feb	FOREVER AND EVER Slik	1
21 Feb	DECEMBER '63 (OH WHAT A NIGHT) Four Seasons	2
6 Mar	I LOVE TO LOVE (BUT MY BABY LOVES TO DANCE) Tina Charles	3
27 Mar	SAVE YOUR KISSES FOR ME Brotherhood Of Man	6
8 May	FERNANDO Abba	4
5 Jun	NO CHARGE J.J. Barrie	1
12 Jun	COMBINE HARVESTER (BRAND NEW KEY) Wurzels	2
26 Jun	YOU TO ME ARE EVERYTHING Real Thing	3
17 Jul	THE ROUSSOS PHENOMENON (EP) Demis Roussos	1
24 Jul	DON'T GO BREAKING MY HEART Elton John and Kiki Dee	6
4 Sep	DANCING QUEEN Abba	6
11 Oct	MISSISSIPPI Pussycat	4

Date	Title	Weeks
13 Nov	IF YOU LEAVE ME NOW Chicago	3
4 Dec	UNDER THE MOON OF LOVE Showaddywaddy	3
25 Dec	WHEN A CHILD IS BORN (SOLEADO) Johnny Mathis	3

1977

Date	Title	Weeks
15 Jan	DON'T GIVE UP ON US David Soul	4
12 Feb	DON'T CRY FOR ME ARGENTINA Julie Covington	1
19 Feb	WHEN I NEED YOU Leo Sayer	3
12 Mar	CHANSON D'AMOUR Manhatten Transfer	3
2 Apr	KNOWING ME KNOWING YOU Abba	5
7 May	FREE Deniece Williams	2
21 May	I DON'T WANT TO TALK ABOUT IT/ FIRST CUT IS THE DEEPEST Rod Stewart	4
18 Jun	LUCILLE Kenny Rogers	1
25 Jun	SHOW YOU THE WAY TO GO Jacksons	1
2 Jul	SO YOU WIN AGAIN Hot Chocolate	3
23 Jul	I FEEL LOVE Donna Summer	4
20 Aug	ANGELO Brotherhood Of Man	1
27 Aug	FLOAT ON Floaters	1
3 Sep	WAY DOWN Elvis Presley	5
8 Oct	SILVER LADY David Soul	3
29 Oct	YES SIR I CAN BOOGIE Baccara	1
5 Nov	NAME OF THE GAME Abba	4
3 Dec	MULL OF KINTYRE/GIRLS' SCHOOL Wings	9

1978

Date	Title	Weeks
4 Feb	UP TOWN TOP RANKING Althia and Donna	1
11 Feb	FIGARO Brotherhood Of Man	1
18 Feb	TAKE A CHANCE ON ME Abba	3
11 Mar	WUTHERING HEIGHTS Kate Bush	4
8 Apr	MATCHSTALK MEN AND MATCHSTALK CATS AND DOGS Brian and Michael	3
29 Apr	NIGHT FEVER Bee Gees	2

Top 75 began 6 May 1978

Date	Title	Weeks
13 May	RIVERS OF BABYLON Boney M.	5
17 Jun	YOU'RE THE ONE THAT I WANT John Travolta and Olivia Newton-John	9
19 Aug	THREE TIMES A LADY Commodores	5
23 Sep	DREADLOCK HOLIDAY 10CC	1
30 Sep	SUMMER NIGHTS John Travolta and Olivia Newton-John	7
18 Nov	RAT TRAP Boomtown Rats	2
2 Dec	DA YA THINK I'M SEXY Rod Stewart	1

9 Dec MARY'S BOY CHILD - OH MY LORD

Boney M. 4

1979

6 Jan Y.M.C.A. Village People 3

27 Jan HIT ME WITH YOUR RHYTHM STICK

Ian and the Blockheads 1

3 Feb HEART OF GLASS Blondie 4

3 Mar TRAGEDY Bee Gees 2

17 Mar I WILL SURVIVE Gloria Gaynor 4

14 Apr BRIGHT EYES Art Garfunkel 6

26 May SUNDAY GIRL Blondie 3

16 Jun RING MY BELL Anita Ward 2

30 Jun ARE 'FRIENDS' ELECTRIC? Tubeway Army . . . 4

28 Jul I DON'T LIKE MONDAYS Boomtown Rats . . . 4

25 Aug WE DONT TALK ANYMORE Cliff Richard 4

22 Sep CARS Gary Numan 1

29 Sep MESSAGE IN A BOTTLE Police 3

20 Oct VIDEO KILLED THE RADIO STAR Buggles . . . 1

27 Oct ONE DAY AT A TIME Lena Marten 3

17 Nov WHEN YOU'RE IN LOVE WITH A BEAUTIFUL

WOMAN Dr Hook 3

8 Dec WALKING ON THE MOON Police 1

15 Dec ANOTHER BRICK IN THE WALL (PART II)

Pink Floyd 5

1980

19 Jan BRASS IN POCKET Pretenders 2

2 Feb THE SPECIAL AKA LIVE! (EP) Specials 2

16 Feb COWARD OF THE COUNTY Kenny Rogers . . . 2

1 Mar ATOMIC Blondie 2

15 Mar TOGETHER WE ARE BEAUTIFUL

Fern Kinney 1

22 Mar GOING UNDERGROUND/DREAMS OF

CHILDREN Jam ▲ 3

12 Apr WORKING MY WAY BACK TO YOU

Detroit Spinners 2

26 Apr CALL ME Blondie 1

3 May GENO Dexy's Midnight Runners 2

17 May WHAT'S ANOTHER YEAR Johnny Logan 2

31 May THEME FROM M*A*S*H (SUICIDE IS

PAINLESS) Mash 3

21 Jun CRYING Don McLean 3

12 Jul XANADU Olivia Newton-John and

Electric Light Orchestra 2

26 Jul USE IT UP AND WEAR IT OUT Odyssey 2

9 Aug THE WINNER TAKES IT ALL Abba 2

23 Aug ASHES TO ASHES David Bowie 2

6 Sep START Jam 1

13 Sep FEELS LIKE I'M IN LOVE Kelly Marie 2

27 Sep DON'T STAND SO CLOSE TO ME Police ▲ . . 4

25 Oct WOMAN IN LOVE Barbra Streisand 3

15 Nov THE TIDE IS HIGH Blondie 2

29 Nov SUPER TROUPER Abba 3

20 Dec (JUST LIKE) STARTING OVER John Lennon . . 1

27 Dec THERE'S NO-ONE QUITE LIKE GRANDMA

St Winifred's School Choir 2

1981

10 Jan IMAGINE John Lennon 4

7 Feb WOMAN John Lennon 2

21 Feb SHADDAP YOU FACE

Joe Dolce Music Theatre 3

14 Mar JEALOUS GUY Roxy Music 2

28 Mar THIS OLE HOUSE Shakin' Stevens 3

18 Apr MAKING YOUR MIND UP Bucks Fizz 3

9 May STAND AND DELIVER Adam and the Ants ▲ . 5

13 Jun BEING WITH YOU Smokey Robinson 2

27 Jun ONE DAY IN YOUR LIFE Michael Jackson . . . 2

11 Jul GHOST TOWN Specials 3

1 Aug GREEN DOOR Shakin' Stevens 4

29 Aug JAPANESE BOY Aneka 1

5 Sep TAINTED LOVE Soft Cell 2

19 Sep PRINCE CHARMING Adam and the Ants 4

17 Oct IT'S MY PARTY Dave Stewart and

Barbara Gaskin 4

14 Nov EVERY LITTLE THING SHE DOES IS MAGIC

Police 1

21 Nov UNDER PRESSURE

Queen and David Bowie 2

5 Dec BEGIN THE BEGUINE (VOLVER A EMPEZAR)

Julio Iglesias 1

12 Dec DON'T YOU WANT ME Human League 5

1982

16 Jan LAND OF MAKE BELIEVE Bucks Fizz 2

30 Jan OH JULIE Shakin' Stevens 1

6 Feb THE MODEL/COMPUTER LOVE Kraftwerk . . . 1

13 Feb A TOWN CALLED MALICE/PRECIOUS Jam ▲ . 3

6 Mar THE LION SLEEPS TONIGHT Tight Fit 3

27 Mar SEVEN TEARS Goombay Dance Band 3

17 Apr MY CAMERA NEVER LIES Bucks Fizz 1

the number one hits

8 Feb WHEN THE GOING GETS TOUGH, THE
TOUGH GET GOING Billy Ocean. 4

8 Mar CHAIN REACTION Diana Ross 3

29 Mar LIVING DOLL Cliff Richard and the
Young Ones. 3

19 Apr A DIFFERENT CORNER George Michael. 3

10 May ROCK ME AMADEUS Falco 1

17 May THE CHICKEN SONG Spitting Image 3

7 Jun SPIRIT IN THE SKY Doctor and the Medics. . 3

28 Jun THE EDGE OF HEAVEN Wham! 2

12 Jul PAPA DON'T PREACH Madonna 3

2 Aug THE LADY IN RED Chris de Burgh 3

23 Aug I WANT TO WAKE UP WITH YOU
Boris Gardiner 3

13 Sep DON'T LEAVE ME THIS WAY
Communards. 4

11 Oct TRUE BLUE Madonna 1

18 Oct EVERY LOSER WINS Nick Berry 3

8 Nov TAKE MY BREATH AWAY Berlin 4

6 Dec THE FINAL COUNT DOWN Europe 2

20 Dec CARAVAN OF LOVE Housemartins 1

27 Dec REET PETITE Jackie Wilson. 4

1987

24 Jan JACK YOUR BODY Steve 'Silk' Hurley. 2

7 Feb I KNEW YOU WERE WAITING (FOR ME)
Aretha Franklin and George Michael 2

21 Feb STAND BY ME Ben E. King 3

14 Mar EVERYTHING I OWN Boy George. 2

28 Mar RESPECTABLE Mel And Kim 1

4 Apr LET IT BE Ferry Aid ▲ 3

25 Apr LA ISLA BONITA Madonna. 2

9 May NOTHING'S GONNA STOP US NOW
Starship 4

6 Jun I WANNA DANCE WITH SOMEBODY (WHO
LOVES ME) Whitney Houston 2

20 Jun STAR TREKKIN' Firm. 2

4 Jul IT'S A SIN Pet Shop Boys 3

25 Jul WHO'S THAT GIRL Madonna 1

1 Aug LA BAMBA Los Lobos. 2

15 Aug I JUST CAN'T STOP LOVING YOU
Michael Jackson with Siedah Garrett 2

29 Aug NEVER GONNA GIVE YOU UP Rick Astley . . . 5

3 Oct PUMP UP THE VOLUME/ANITINA (THE FIRST
TIME I SEE SHE DANCE) M/A/R/R/S 2

17 Oct YOU WIN AGAIN Bee Gees 4

14 Nov CHINA IN YOUR HAND T'Pau 5

19 Dec ALWAYS ON MY MIND Pet Shop Boys 4

1988

16 Jan HEAVEN IS A PLACE ON EARTH
Belinda Carlisle 2

30 Jan I THINK WE'RE ALONE NOW Tiffany. 3

20 Feb I SHOULD BE SO LUCKY Kylie Minogue 5

26 Mar DON'T TURN AROUND Aswad. 2

9 Apr HEART Pet Shop Boys 3

30 Apr THEME FROM S EXPRESS S Express 2

14 May PERFECT Fairground Attraction 1

21 May WITH A LITTLE HELP FROM MY FRIENDS/
SHE'S LEAVING HOME Wet Wet Wet/
Billy Bragg with Cara Tivey 4

18 Jun DOCTORIN' THE TARDIS Timelords 1

25 Jun I OWE YOU NOTHING Bros 2

9 Jul NOTHING'S GONNA CHANGE MY LOVE
FOR YOU Glenn Medeiros. 4

6 Aug THE ONLY WAY IS UP Yazz and the
Plastic Population 5

10 Sep A GROOVY KIND OF LOVE Phil Collins. 2

24 Sep HE AIN'T HEAVY HE'S MY BROTHER
Hollies 2

8 Oct DESIRE U2 1

15 Oct ONE MOMENT IN TIME Whitney Houston . . 2

29 Oct ORINOCO FLOW Enya. 3

19 Nov FIRST TIME Robin Beck 3

10 Dec MISTLETOE AND WINE Cliff Richard. 4

1989

7 Jan ESPECIALLY FOR YOU Kylie Minogue and
Jason Donovan. 3

28 Jan SOMETHING'S GOTTEN HOLD OF MY HEART
Marc Almond with Gene Pitney. 4

25 Feb BELFAST CHILD Simple Minds 2

11 Mar TOO MANY BROKEN HEARTS
Jason Donovan. 2

25 Mar LIKE A PRAYER Madonna 3

15 Apr ETERNAL FLAME Bangles 4

13 May HAND ON YOUR HEART Kylie Minogue 1

20 May FERRY 'CROSS THE MERSEY Christians,
Holly Johnson, Paul McCartney, Gerry
Marsden and Stock Aitken Waterman ▲. . . 3

10 Jun SEALED WITH A KISS Jason Donovan ▲ . . . 2

24 Jun BACK TO LIFE (HOW EVER DO YOU WANT ME)
Soul II Soul featuring Caron Wheeler. 4

▲ Indicates a hit that entered the chart at number one.

22 Jul YOU'LL NEVER STOP ME LOVING YOU
Sonia 2

5 Aug SWING THE MOOD Jive Bunny and the
Mastermixers 5

9 Sep RIDE ON TIME Black Box 6

21 Oct THAT'S WHAT I LIKE Jive Bunny and the
Mastermixers 3

11 Nov ALL AROUND THE WORLD
Lisa Stansfield 2

25 Nov YOU GOT IT (THE RIGHT STUFF)
New Kids On The Block 3

16 Dec LET'S PARTY Jive Bunny and the
Mastermixers ▲ 1

23 Dec DO THEY KNOW IT'S CHRISTMAS
Band Aid II ▲ 3

1990's

1990

13 Jan HANGIN' TOUGH
New Kids On The Block 2

27 Jan TEARS ON MY PILLOW Kylie Minogue 1

3 Feb NOTHING COMPARES 2 U
Sinead O'Connor 4

3 Mar DUB BE GOOD TO ME Beats International
featuring Lindy Layton 4

31 Mar THE POWER Snap 2

14 Apr VOGUE Madonna 4

12 May KILLER Adamski 4

9 Jun WORLD IN MOTION Englandneworder 2

23 Jun SACRIFICE/HEALING HANDS Elton John 5

28 Jul TURTLE POWER Partners In Kryme 4

25 Aug ITSY BITSY TEENY WEENY YELLOW POLKA
DOT BIKINI Bombalurina 3

15 Sep THE JOKER Steve Miller Band 2

29 Sep SHOW ME HEAVEN Maria McKee 4

27 Oct A LITTLE TIME The Beautiful South 1

3 Nov UNCHAINED MELODY Righteous Brothers . . . 4

1 Dec ICE ICE BABY Vanilla Ice 4

29 Dec SAVIOUR'S DAY Cliff Richard 1

1991

5 Jan BRING YOUR DAUGHTER...TO THE
SLAUGHTER Iron Maiden ▲ 2

19 Jan SADNESS PART I Enigma 1

26 Jan INNUENDO Queen ▲ 1

2 Feb 3 AM ETERNAL KLF featuring Children of

the Revolution 2

16 Feb DO THE BARTMAN Simpsons 3

9 Mar SHOULD I STAY OR SHOULD I GO
Clash 2

23 Mar THE STONK Hale and Pace and
the Stonkers 1

30 Mar THE ONE AND ONLY Chesney Hawkes 5

4 May SHOOP SHOOP SONG (IT'S IN HIS KISS)
Cher 5

8 Jun I WANNA SEX YOU UP Color Me Badd 3

29 Jun ANY DREAM WILL DO Jason Donovan 2

13 Jul (EVERYTHING I DO) I DO IT FOR YOU
Bryan Adams 16

2 Nov THE FLY U2 ▲ 1

9 Nov DIZZY Vic Reeves and the
Wonder Stuff 2

23 Nov BLACK OR WHITE Michael Jackson ▲ 2

7 Dec DON'T LET THE SUN GO DOWN ON ME
George Michael and Elton John ▲ 2

21 Dec BOHEMIAN RHAPSODY/THESE ARE THE
DAYS OF OUR LIVES Queen ▲ 5

1992

25 Jan GOODNIGHT GIRL Wet Wet Wet 4

22 Feb STAY Shakespeare Sister 8

18 Apr DEEPLY DIPPY Right Said Fred 3

9 May PLEASE DON'T GO/GAME BOY KWS 5

13 Jun ABBA-ESQUE (EP) Erasure ▲ 5

18 Jul AIN'T NO DOUBT Jimmy Nail 3

8 Aug RHYTHM IS A DANCER Snap 6

19 Sep EBENEEZER GOODE Shamen 4

17 Oct SLEEPING SATELLITE Tasmin Archer 2

31 Oct END OF THE ROAD Boyz II Men 3

21 Nov WOULD I LIE TO YOU Charles and Eddie . . . 2

5 Dec I WILL ALWAYS LOVE YOU
Whitney Houston 10

1993

13 Feb NO LIMIT 2 Unlimited 5

20 Mar OH CAROLINA Shaggy 2

3 Apr YOUNG AT HEART Bluebells 4

1 May FIVE LIVE EP George Michael and Queen
with Lisa Stansfield ▲ 3

22 May ALL THAT SHE WANTS Ace Of Base 3

12 Jun (I CAN'T HELP) FALLING IN LOVE WITH YOU
UB40 2

26 Jun DREAMS Gabrielle 3

17 Jul   PRAY   Take That ▲. 4
14 Aug   LIVING ON MY OWN   Freddie Mercury 2
28 Aug   MR. VAIN   Culture Beat 4
25 Sep   BOOM! SHAKE THE ROOM   Jazzy Jeff and
       the Fresh Prince. 2
9 Oct   RELIGHT MY FIRE   Take That featuring
       Lulu ▲. 2
23 Oct   I'D DO ANYTHING FOR LOVE (BUT I WON'T
       DO THAT)   Meatloaf 7
11 Dec   MR. BLOBBY   Mr. Blobby 1
18 Dec   BABE   Take That 1
25 Dec   MR. BLOBBY   Mr. Blobby 2

1994

8 Jan   TWIST AND SHOUT   Chaka Demus and
       Pliers with Jack Radics and Taxi Gang 2
22 Jan   THINGS CAN ONLY GET BETTER   D:Ream. . . 4
19 Feb   WITHOUT YOU   Mariah Carey ▲ 4
19 Mar   DOOP   Doop 3
9 Apr   EVERTHING CHANGES   Take That ▲. 2
23 Apr   THE MOST BEAUTIFUL GIRL IN THE WORLD
       Prince. 2
7 May   THE REAL THING   Tony Di Bart 1
14 May   INSIDE   Stiltskin 1
21 May   COME ON YOU REDS
       Manchester United Football Squad 2
4 Jun   LOVE IS ALL AROUND   Wet Wet Wet. 15
17 Sep   SATURDAY NIGHT   Whigfield ▲. 4
15 Oct   SURE   Take That ▲. 2
29 Oct   BABY COME BACK   Pato Banton 4
26 Nov   LET ME BE YOUR FANTASY   Baby D 2
10 Dec   STAY ANOTHER DAY   East 17. 5

1995

14 Jan   COTTON EYE JOE   Rednex 3
4 Feb   THINK TWICE   Celine Dion 7
25 Mar   LOVE CAN BUILD A BRIDGE   Cher,
       Chrissie Hynde and Neneh Cherry with
       Eric Clapton 1
1 Apr   DON'T STOP (WIGGLE WIGGLE)
       Outhere Brothers 1
8 Apr   BACK FOR GOOD   Take That ▲. 4
6 May   SOME MIGHT SAY   Oasis ▲ 1
13 May   DREAMER   Livin' Joy ▲ 1
20 May   UNCHAINED MELODY/(THERE'LL BE BLUE
       BIRDS OVER) THE WHITE CLIFFS OF
       DOVER   Robson Green and Jerome Flynn ▲. 7

8 Jul   BOOM BOOM BOOM   Outhere Brothers 4
5 Aug   NEVER FORGET   Take That ▲ 3
26 Aug   COUNTRY HOUSE   Blur ▲ 2
9 Sep   YOU ARE NOT ALONE   Michael Jackson 2
23 Sep   BOOMBASTIC   Shaggy   ▲ 1
30 Sep   FAIRGROUND   Simply Red ▲ 4
28 Oct   GANGSTA'S PARADISE   Coolio
       featuring LV ▲. 2
11 Nov   I BELIEVE/UP ON THE ROOF
       Robson and Jerome ▲ 4
9 Dec   EARTH SONG   Michael Jackson ▲ 6

1996

20 Jan   JESUS TO A CHILD   George Michael ▲ 1
27 Jan   SPACEMAN   Babylon Zoo ▲. 5
2 Mar   DON'T LOOK BACK IN ANGER   Oasis ▲ . . . 1
9 Mar   HOW DEEP IS YOUR LOVE   Take That ▲. . . 3
30 Mar   FIRESTARTER   Prodigy ▲ 3
20 Apr   RETURN OF THE MACK   Mark Morrison. . . . 2
4 May   FASTLOVE   George Michael ▲ 3
25 May   OOH AAH... JUST A LITTLE BIT   Gina G 1
1 Jun   THREE LIONS (THE OFFICIAL SONG OF THE
       ENGLAND FOOTBALL TEAM)   Baddiel and
       Skinner and the Lightning Seeds ▲ 1
8 Jun   KILLING ME SOFTLY   Fugees ▲ 4
6 Jul   THREE LIONS (THE OFFICIAL SONG OF THE
       ENGLAND FOOTBALL TEAM)   Baddiel and
       Skinner and the Lightning Seeds 1
13 Jul   KILLING ME SOFTLY   Fugees 1
20 Jul   FOREVER LOVE   Gary Barlow ▲. 1
27 Jul   WANNABE   Spice Girls 7
14 Sep   FLAVA   Peter Andre ▲ 1
21 Sep   READY OR NOT   Fugees. 2
5 Oct   BREAKFAST AT TIFFANY'S
       Deep Blue Something 1
12 Oct   SETTING SUN   Chemical Brothers ▲ 1
19 Oct   WORDS   Boyzone ▲. 1
26 Oct   SAY YOU'LL BE THERE   Spice Girls ▲ 2
9 Nov   WHAT BECOMES OF THE BROKEN HEARTED/
       UP ON THE ROOF/YOU'LL NEVER WALK
       ALONE   Robson and Jerome ▲. 2
23 Nov   BREATHE   Prodigy ▲. 2
7 Dec   I FEEL YOU   Peter Andre ▲ 1
14 Dec   A DIFFERENT BEAT   Boyzone ▲ 1
21 Dec   KNOCKIN' ON HEAVEN'S DOOR - THROW
       THESE GUNS AWAY   Dunblane ▲   1
28 Dec   2 BECOME 1   Spice Girls ▲ 3

number one hits

most number one hits
(by artist)

After 755 number one hits in 44 years, only 29 acts have achieved as many as four chart toppers, and only three acts have number one tallys running into double figures. It would seem that Elvis and the Beatles are forever destined to jointly head this list after the Beatles failed to garner an 18th number one with 'Free As A Bird', which narrowly missed the top spot in December 1995.

act	weeks
BEATLES (includes 1 with Billy Preston. Paul McCartney + 4 solo, John Lennon + 3 solo and George Harrison + 1 solo)	17
ELVIS PRESLEY	17
CLIFF RICHARD (includes 1 with Young Ones)	13
ABBA	9
ROLLING STONES (Mick Jagger + 1 with David Bowie)	8
TAKE THAT (Gary Barlow + 1 solo)	8
MADONNA	7
GEORGE MICHAEL (includes 1 with Aretha Franklin and 1 with Queen and Lisa Stansfield. + 4 with Wham!)	7
MICHAEL JACKSON (+ 1 with Jacksons)	6
SLADE	6
ROD STEWART	6
BEE GEES	5
BLONDIE	5
DAVID BOWIE (includes 1 with Queen and 1 with Mick Jagger)	5
POLICE	5
QUEEN (includes 1 with David Bowie and 1 with George Michael and Lisa Stansfield. Freddie Mercury + 1 solo)	5
SHADOWS (+ 7 with Cliff Richard. Hank Marvin + 1 with Cliff Richard and the Young Ones)	5
JASON DONOVAN (includes 1 with Kylie Minogue)	4
EVERLY BROTHERS	4
WHITNEY HOUSTON	4
FRANK IFIELD	4
JAM	4
FRANKIE LAINE	4
PAUL McCARTNEY (includes 1 with Stevie Wonder and 1 with Christians, Holly Johnson, Gerry Marsden and Stock Aitken Waterman. + 17 with Beatles)	4
KYLIE MINOGUE (includes 1 with Jason Donovan)	4
GUY MITCHELL	4

PET SHOP BOYS	4
SHAKIN' STEVENS	4
T. REX	4
WHAM! (George Michael + 7 solo)	4

Also worth mentioning are:

GERRY MARSDEN (3 with Gerry and the Pacemakers, 1 as lead vocalist of the Crowd and 1 with Christians, Holly Johnson, Paul McCartney and Stock Aitken Waterman)	5
HOLLY JOHNSON (3 with Frankie Goes To Hollywood and 1 with Christians, Gerry Marsden, Paul McCartney and Stock Aitken Waterman)	4

most weeks at number one
(by artist)

act	weeks
ELVIS PRESLEY	73
BEATLES (Paul McCartney + 17 solo. John Lennon + m7 solo. George Harrison + 5 solo)	69
CLIFF RICHARD (includes 3 with the Young Ones)	44
FRANKIE LAINE (1 week top equal)	32
ABBA	31
WET WET WET	23
TAKE THAT (Gary Barlow + 1 solo)	21
QUEEN (includes 2 ith David Bowie and 3 with George Michael. Freddie Mercury + 2 solo)	20
SLADE	20
EVERLY BROTHERS (1 week top equal)	19
MADONNA	18
ROLLING STONES (Mick Jagger + 4 with David Bowie)	18
ROD STEWART	18
FRANK IFIELD	17
PAUL McCARTNEY (2 solo, 9 with Wings, 3 with Stevie Wonder and 3 with Christians, Holly Johnson, Gerry Marsden and Stock Aitken, Waterman)	17
GEORGE MICHAEL (includes 3 with Lisa Stansfield and Queen, 2 with Aretha Franklin and 2 with Elton John)	17
BRYAN ADAMS	16
WHITNEY HOUSTON	16

Besides her seven number one singles Madonna has also accumulated six number two hits and seven number threes.

500

SHADOWS (+ 29 backing Cliff Richard. Hank Marvin + 3 more with
Cliff and the Young Ones) 16

T. REX 16

JOHN TRAVOLTA AND OLIVIA NEWTON JOHN
(Olivia Newton-John + 2 with Electric Light Orchestra) 16

DORIS DAY 15

FRANKIE GOES TO HOLLYWOOD (Holly Johnson + 3 with
Christians, Gerry Marsden, Paul McCartney and Stock
Aitken Waterman) 15

MICHAEL JACKSON (+ 1 with Jacksons) 15

Also worth mentioning are:

GERRY MARSDEN (11 with Gerry and the Pacemakers, 3 with
Christians, Holly Johnson, Paul McCartney and Stock Aitken
Waterman and 2 as lead vocalist with the Crowd) 14

most weeks at number one
(by an artist in one calendar year)

year/act	weeks
1953 FRANKIE LAINE (1 week top equal)	27
1961 ELVIS PRESLEY	18
1991 BRYAN ADAMS	16
1963 BEATLES	16
1978 JOHN TRAVOLTA & OLIVIA NEWTON-JOHN	16
1962 ELVIS PRESLEY	15
1984 FRANKE GOES TO HOLLYWOOD	15
1994 WET WET WET	15
1958 CONNIE FRANCES	12
1962 FRANK IFIELD	12
1964 BEATLES	12
1976 ABBA	12

'Love Is All Around' by Wet Wet Wet was overtaken by Whigfield 'Saturday Night', denying the Scottish group the record for most consecutive weeks at the top.

most weeks at number one
(by one disc, in total)

year	disc/act	weeks
1953	I BELIEVE Frankie Laine	18
1991	(EVERYTHING I DO) I DO IT FOR YOU Bryan Adams	16
1994	LOVE IS ALL AROUND Wet Wet Wet	15
1975/6 & 1991/2	BOHEMIAN RHAPSODY Queen	14
1955	ROSE MARIE Slim Whitman	11
1954	CARA MIA David Whitfield	10
1993/4	I WILL ALWAYS LOVE YOU Whitney Houston	10
1952/3	HERE IN MY HEART Al Martino	9
1954	OH MEIN PAPA Eddie Calvert	9
1954	SECRET LOVE Doris Day	9
1957	DIANA Paul Anka	9
1977/8	MULL OF KINTYRE/GIRLS' SCHOOL Wings	9
1978	YOU'RE THE ONE THAT I WANT John Travolta and Olivia Newton-John	9
1984	TWO TRIBES Frankie Goes To Hollywood	9

Wet Wet Wet

number one hits

most weeks at number one
(by one disc, consecutive weeks)

year	disc/act	weeks
1991	(EVERYTHING I DO) I DO IT FOR YOU Bryan Adams	16
1994	LOVE IS ALL AROUND Wet Wet Wet	15
1955	ROSE MARIE Slim Whitman	11
1954	CARA MIA David Whitfield	10
1993/4	I WILL ALWAYS LOVE YOU Whitney Houston	10
1952/3	HERE IN MY HEART Al Martino	9
1953	I BELIEVE Frankie Laine	9
1954	OH MEIN PAPA Eddie Calvert	9
1957	DIANA Paul Anka	9
1975/6	BOHEMIAN RHAPSODY Queen	9
1977/8	MULL OF KINTYRE/GIRLS' SCHOOL Wings	9
1978	YOU'RE THE ONE THAT I WANT John Travolta and Olivia Newton-John	9
1984	TWO TRIBES Frankie Goes To Hollywood	9
1953/4	ANSWER ME Frankie Laine (1 week top equal)	8
1954	SECRET LOVE Doris Day	8
1958	MAGIC MOMENTS Perry Como	8
1960	IT'S NOW OR NEVER Elvis Presley	8
1962	WONDERFUL LAND Shadows	8
1969	SUGAR SUGAR Archies	8
1992	STAY Shakespears Sister	8

'Bohemian Rhapsody' by Queen is the only single to have been a number one hit in four separate years, (1975, 1976, 1991 and 1992).

most weeks at number one
(by one song)

weeks		
22 weeks	I BELIEVE	two versions
16 weeks	(EVERYTHING I DO) I DO IT FOR YOU	one version
15 weeks	LOVE IS ALL AROUND	one version
14 weeks	BOHEMIAN RHAPSODY	one version
14 weeks	UNCHAINED MELODY	three versions
11 weeks	MARY'S BOY CHILD	two versions
11 weeks	ROSE MARIE	one version
11 weeks	YOUNG LOVE	two versions
10 weeks	ANSWER ME	two versions
10 weeks	CARA MIA	one version
10 weeks	I WILL ALWAYS LOVE YOU	one version

most number one hits
(in a year)

Three number ones in a year has been accomplished 13 times, as follows:

1953 **Frankie Lane** (I Believe, Hey Joe, Answer Me)

1963 **Gerry and the Pacemakers** (How Do You Do It, I Like It, You'll Never Walk Alone)

1963 **Beatles** (From Me To You, She Loves You, I Want To Hold Your Hand)

1964 **Beatles** (Can't Buy Me Love, A Hard Day's Night, I Feel Fine)

1965 **Beatles** (Ticket To Ride, Help!, Day Tripper/We Can Work It Out)

1973 **Slade** (Cum On Feel The Noize, Skweeze Me Pleeze Me, Merry Xmas Everybody)

1976 **Abba** (Mamma Mia, Fernando, Dancing Queen)

1980 **Blondie** (Atomic, Call Me, The Tide Is High)

1984 **Frankie Goes To Hollywood** (Relax, Two Tribes, The Power Of Love)

1989 **Jason Donovan** (Especially For You, Too Many Broken Hearts, Sealed With A Kiss)

1989 **Jive Bunny and the Mastermixers** (Swing The Mood, That's What I Like, Let's Party)

1993 **Take That** (Pray, Relight My Fire, Babe)

1996 **Spice Girls** (Wannabe, Say You'll Be There, 2 Become 1)

Four number ones in one year has been achieved twice, by Elvis Presley in 1961 and 1962. His chart-toppers in 1961 were 'Are You Lonesome Tonight' (Jan/Feb), 'Wooden Heart' (Mar/Apr), 'Surrender' (June) and 'Little Sister/His Latest Flame' (Nov/Dec). In 1962 they were 'Rock-A-Hula Baby/Can't Help Falling In Love' (Feb/Mar), 'Good Luck Charm' (May/Jun), 'She's Not You' (Sep) and 'Return To Sender' (Dec).

number one hits

most consecutive number one hits

11 in a row	BEATLES	(from From Me To You through to Yellow Submarine/Eleanor Rigby. 1963 to 1966)
6 in a row	BEATLES	(from All You Need Is Love through to The Ballad Of John And Yoko, 1967 to 1969)
5 in a row	ELVIS PRESLEY	(from Little Sister/His Latest Flame through to Return To Sender, 1961 to 1962)
5 in a row	ROLLING STONES	(from It's All Over Now through to Get Off Of My Cloud, 1964 to 1965)
4 In a row	TAKE THAT	(from Pray through to Everything Changes, 1993 to 1994)
4 in a row	TAKE THAT	(from Sure to How Deep Is Your Love, 1994 to 1996)
3 in a row	FRANK IFIELD	(I Remember You, Lovesick Blues and Wayward Wind, 1962 to 1963)

The first hat-trick by a British artist

3 in a row	GERRY AND THE PACEMAKERS	(How Do You Do It, I Like It and You'll Never Walk Alone, 1963)
3 in a row	ABBA	(Mamma Mia, Fernando and Dancing Queen, 1975 to 1976)
3 in a row	ABBA	(Knowing Me Knowing You, The Name Of The Game and Take A Chance On Me, 1977 to 1978)
3 in a row	POLICE	(Message In A Bottle, Walking On The Moon and Don't Stand So Close To Me, 1979 to 1980)
3 in a row	BLONDIE	(Atomic, Call Me and The Tide Is High, 1980)
3 in a row	JOHN LENNON	(Imagine, (Just Like) Starting Over and Woman, 1980)

Either the fastest or slowest hat-trick depending on whether it started when Imagine first entered the chart in November 1975, or when (Just Like) Starting Over came in late 1980

3 in a row	FRANKIE GOES TO HOLLYWOOD	(Relax, Two Tribes and The Power Of Love, 1984)
3 in a row	JIVE BUNNY AND THE MASTERMIXERS	(Swing The Mood, That's What I LIke and Let's Party, 1989)
3 in a row	ROBSON AND JEROME	(from Unchained Melody/White Cliffs Of Dover to the triple A-sided What Becomes Of The Broken Hearted/Saturday Night At The Movies/You'll Never Walk Alone, 1995 to 1996)
3 in a row	SPICE GIRLS	(from Wannabe, Say You'll Be There and 2 Become 1, 1996)

All of Take That's eight number one hits entered the chart in pole position.

Successive releases are successive official single releases. The Beatles' two runs of number ones were each interrupted by irregular releases. An old single with Tony Sheridan reached number 29 in the midst of their 11 number ones, and their double EP 'Magical Mystery Tour' made number two while 'Hello Goodbye' was becoming the second of their six chart-toppers on the trot. An album track, 'Jeepster', and an old recording, 'Debora/One Inch Rock' were released during T. Rex's run of number ones. An EP by Elvis, 'Follow That Dream', pottered about the lower reaches of the charts during Elvis's run of five consecutive number ones. During Police's hat-trick, one single on another label, one old single re-issued and a six-pack of singles hit the chart. John Lennon's 'Imagine' was the first of the three singles of his hat-trick but the second of the three to reach the top. During his hat-trick, a flood of old Lennon hits swarmed back on to the chart.

Take That

number one hits

first two hits at number one

Only 15 acts in the 44-year history of the chart have reached the top with each of their first two chart hits

act	hits	years
EDDIE CALVERT	Oh Mein Papa; Cherry Pink and Apple Blossom White	1954, 55
ADAM FAITH	What Do You Want; Poor Me	1959, 60
TENNESSEE ERNIE FORD	Give Me Your Word; Sixteen Tons	1955, 56
FRANKIE GOES TO HOLLYWOOD	Relax; Two Tribes	1984
ART GARFUNKEL	I Only Have Eyes For You; Bright Eyes	1975, 79
GERRY AND THE PACEMAKERS	How Do You Do It; I Like It	1963
JIVE BUNNY AND THE MASTERMIXERS	Swing The Mood; That's The Way I Like	1989
GEORGE MICHAEL	Carless Whisper; A Different Corner	1984, 86
MUNGO JERRY	In The Summer Time; Baby Jump	1970, 71
GARY NUMAN/TUBEWAY ARMY	Are 'Friends' Electric?; Cars	1979
NEW KIDS ON THE BLOCK	You Got It (The Right Stuff); Hangin' Tough	1989, 90
OUTHERE BROTHERS	Don't Stop (Wiggle Wiggle); Boom Boom Boom	1995
RIGHTEOUS BROTHERS	You've Lost That Lovin' Feelin'; Unchained Melody	1965, 90
ROBSON AND JEROME	Unchained Melody/White Cliffs Of Dover; I Believe/Up On The Roof	1995
SPICE GIRLS	Wannabe; Say You'll Be There	1996
STARGAZERS	Broken Wings; I See The Moon	1953, 54
ROD STEWART	Maggie May; You Wear It Well	1971, 72
JOHN TRAVOLTA AND OLIVIA NEWTON-JOHN	You're The One That I Want; Summer Nights	1978

It took 25 years for the Righteous Brothers to join this elite list. They finally made it when the re-issued 'You've Lost That Lovin' Feeling' hit number one in 1990.

Of these acts Frankie Goes To Hollywood, Gerry and the Pacemakers, Jive Bunny, George Michael, Mungo Jerry, New Kids On The Block, Outhere Brothers, Robson and Jerome, Spice Girls and John Travolta and Olivia Newton-John hit the top with their first two UK releases. For both the Righteous Brothers and New Kids On The Block, it took a re-issue to push one of their hits to the top. Band Aid and Band Aid II both hit number one with their only releases - the African famine relief singles, 'Do They Know It's Christmas'.

The Spice Girls

first three hits at number one

Five acts have now achieved the feat of taking their first three hits to number one. They are Gerry and the Pacemakers in 1963, Frankie Goes To Hollywood in 1984, Jive Bunny and the Mastermixers in 1989, Robson and Jerome in 1995/96 and the Spice Girls in 1996. No solo artist has ever managed a trio of chart toppers with their first three hits and of the four groups and one duo who have, only the Spice Girls have also gone on to score an American number one.

number one in different versions

17 songs have been number one in two versions:

ANSWER ME ....David Whitfield (1953), Frankie Laine (1953)

BABY COME BACK.....................Equals (1968), Pato Banton (1994)

CAN'T HELP FALLING IN LOVE.... Elvis Presley (1962), UB40 (1993)

CHERRY PINK AND APPLE
   BLOSSOM WHITE...........Perez Prado (1955), Eddie Calvert (1955)

DIZZY ....Tommy Roe (1969), Vic Reeves and the Wonder Stuff (1991)

DO THEY KNOW IT'S
   CHRISTMAS ....Band Aid (1984), Band Aid II (1989)

EVERYTHING I OWN ....Ken Boothe (1974), Boy George (1987)

I BELIEVE ....Frankie Laine (1953), Robson and Jerome (1996)

I GOT YOU BABE ....Sonny and Cher (1965), UB40 with
                                                              Chrissie Hynde (1985)

LIVING DOLL ....Cliff Richard and the Drifters (1959),
                                             Cliff Richard and the Young Ones (1986)

MARY'S BOY CHILD ....Harry Belafonte (1957), Boney M (1978)

SINGING THE BLUES ....Guy Mitchell (1957), Tommy Steele (1957)

SPIRIT IN THE SKY ....Norman Greenbaum (1970),
                                                              Doctor and the Medics (1986)

THIS OLE HOUSE ....Rosemary Clooney (1954), Shakin' Stevens (1981)

WITH A LITTLE HELP FROM
   MY FRIENDS ....Joe Cocker (1968), Wet Wet Wet (1988)

WITHOUT YOU ....Nilsson (1972), Mariah Carey (1994)

YOUNG LOVE ....Tab Hunter (1957), Donny Osmond (1973)

Two songs have been number one in three versions:

UNCHAINED MELODY ....Jimmy Young (1955),
                            Righteous Brothers (1990), Robson and Jerome (1995)

YOU'LL NEVER WALK ALONE ....Gerry and the Pacemakers (1963),
                            Crowd (1985), Robson and Jerome (1996)

Four titles have been used twice for different songs at number one - 'Forever And Ever' (Slik & Demis Roussos), 'The Power Of Love' (Frankie Goes To Hollywood & Jennifer Rush), 'Tears On My Pillow' (Johnny Nash & Kylie Minogue) and 'Woman In Love' (Frankie Laine & Barbra Streisand).

fastest number one

The 15 acts who have hit the top within two weeks are:

0 days	**AL MARTINO**	(14 Nov 52)
0 days	**WHIGFIELD**	(17 Sep 94)
0 days	**ROBSON AND JEROME**	(20 May 95)
0 days	**BABYLON ZOO**	(27 Jan 96)
0 days	**DUNBLANE**	(21 Dec 96)
7 days	**EDISON LIGHTHOUSE**	(24 to 31 Jan 70)
7 days	**MUNGO JERRY**	(6 to 13 Jun 70)
7 days	**DAVE EDMUNDS**	(21 to 28 Nov 70)
7 days	**NICOLE**	(8 to 15 May 82)
7 days	**MUSICAL YOUTH**	(25 Sep to 3 Oct 82)
7 days	**SPITTING IMAGE**	(10 to 17 May 86)
7 days	**SNAP**	(24 to 31 Mar 90)
7 days	**PARTNERS IN KRYME**	(21 to 28 Jul 90)
7 days	**VANILLA ICE**	(24 Nov to 1 Dec 93)
7 days	**GABRIELLE**	(19 to 26 Jun 39)
7 days	**MR. BLOBBY**	(4 to 11 Dec 93)
7 days	**DOOP**	(12 to 19 Mar 94)
7 days	**STILTSKIN**	(7 to 14 May 94)
7 days	**SPICE GIRLS**	(20 to 27 Jul 96)

Of these acts only Mungo Jerry, Snap, Robson and Jerome and Spice Girls have topped the chart again, and only Snap have racked up a total of more than 100 weeks on chart.

Other first-time chart acts, who had already been in the charts under another name who have also had rapid climbs to the top are:

0 days	**BAND AID**	(1984)
0 days	**DAVID BOWIE AND MICK JAGGER**	(1985)
0 days	**FERRY AID**	(1987)
0 days	**CHRISTIANS, HOLLY JOHNSON, PAUL McCARTNEY, GERRY MARSDEN AND STOCK AITKEN AND WATERMAN**	(1989)
0 days	**GARY BARLOW**	(1996)
0 days	**BAND AID II**	(1989)
0 days	**GEORGE MICHAEL AND ELTON JOHN**	(1991)
0 days	**GEORGE MICHAEL, QUEEN AND LISA STANSFIELD**	(1993)
7 days	**GEORGE HARRISON**	(1971)
7 days	**QUEEN AND DAVID BOWIE**	(1981)
7 days	**CAPTAIN SENSIBLE**	(1982)
7 days	**USA FOR AFRICA**	(1985)
7 days	**CLIFF RICHARD AND THE YOUNG ONES**	(1986)
7 days	**ARETHA FRANKLIN AND GEORGE MICHAEL**	(1987)
7 days	**BOY GEORGE**	(1987)
7 days	**ENGLANDNEWORDER**	(1990)
7 days	**CHER, CHRISSIE HYNDE, NENEH CHERRY WITH ERIC CLAPTON**	(1995)

number one hits

slowest number one

If an artist is ever going to have a number one hit, it usually happens within a year or two of that artist's first hit. About half of all the acts who have hit the very top did so with their first chart hit. There are 11 acts whose first number one came more than 15 years after their chart debut.

time between hits		artist	date of hits
29 years	42 days	JACKIE WILSON	(15 Nov 57 to 27 Dec 86)
26 years	19 days	BEN E. KING	(2 Feb 61 to 21 Feb 87)
25 years	259 days	CHER	(19 Aug 65 to 4 May 91)
19 years	151 days	ELTON JOHN	(23 Jan 71 to 23 Jun 90)
18 years	218 days	STEVIE WONDER	(3 Feb 66 to 8 Sep 84)
18 years	216 days	JOHNNY MATHIS	(23 May 58 to 25 Dec 76)
18 years	13 days	MANCHESTER UNITED F.C.	(8 May 76 to 21 May 94)
16 years	218 days	BORIS GARDINER	(17 Jan 70 to 23 Aug 86)
15 years	157 days	CHUCK BERRY	(21 Jun 57 to 25 Nov 72)
15 years	156 days	MEAT LOAF	(20 May 78 to 23 Oct 93)
15 years	127 days	LOUIS ARMSTRONG	(19 Dec 52 to 24 Apr 68)

Of these acts, Cher, Elton John and Stevie Wonder had featured on number ones before their solo successes. Stevie Wonder's first week at number one was his 301st of solo chart action, but Elton John's was his 371st week, the longest wait in chart terms for a number one. It was a re-issue of his 45th and 46th solo hits, the most hits ever achieved by an act before their first number one. Cher, who hit number one in duet with her then husband Sonny in only their third week of chart action, had less luck as a soloist. Hers is the longest wait of all those who finally hit the top with a newly-recorded song. The number one hit by Jackie Wilson was a re-issue of an old recording. Lulu has never had a solo number one, but there was a gap of 29 years and 148 days from her first week on the charts on 14 May 1964 until she topped the charts with Take That on 9 October 1993. Gene Pitney has never had a solo number one, but there was a gap of 27 years and 311 days from his first week on the charts on 23 March 1961 until he topped the charts with Marc Almond on 28 January 1989.

Eric Clapton has also never had a solo chart topper, but there was a gap of 15 years and 95 days between his debut with Delaney and Bonnie and Friends on 20 December 1969 and his first chart topper with Cher, Chrissie Hynde and Neneh Cherry on 25 March 1995. Of course, his very appearance on the chart had been five years earlier in 1964 with the Yardbirds.

Nine recordings have taken longer than five years to hit the top after their first appearance on the chart:

All the records featured in the chart opposite dropped off the charts between their original chart entry and their chart-topping reappearances.

time between hits		hit/artist	date of hits
29 years	42 days	REET PETITE - Jackie Wilson	(15 Nov 57 to 27 Dec 86)
25 years	244 days	STAND BY ME - Ben E. King	(22 Jun 61 to 21 Feb 87)
25 years	83 days	UNCHAINED MELODY - Righteous Brothers	(12 Aug 65 to 3 Nov 90)
18 years	356 days	HE AIN'T HEAVY, HE'S MY BROTHER - Hollies	(4 Oct 69 to 24 Sep 88)
8 years	284 days	YOUNG AT HEART - Bluebells	(23 Jun 84 to 3 Apr 93)
8 years	166 days	SHOULD I STAY OR SHOULD I GO - Clash	(25 Sep 82 to 9 Mar 91)
7 years	327 days	LIVING ON MY OWN - Freddie Mercury	(21 Sep 85 to 14 Aug 93)
6 years	63 days	SPACE ODDITY - David Bowie	(6 Sep 69 to 8 Nov 75)
5 years	70 days	IMAGINE - John Lennon	(1 Nov 75 to 10 Jan 81)

David Bowie

gap between number one hits

Of all the acts that have enjoyed two or more hits, only nine acts have suffered through a gap of more than seven years between number ones, although two of them have, incredibly, done so twice.

During Cliff's second hiatus, he took the top slot in March 1986 with the Young Ones. Queen hit the top with David Bowie in 1981, five years into their wait for a second chart-topper.

25 years	259 days	...	RIGHTEOUS BROTHERS	(11 Feb 65 to 28 Oct 90)
23 years	65 days	...	HOLLIES	(15 Jul 65 to 18 Sep 88)
14 years	363 days	...	QUEEN	(24 Jan 76 to 20 Jan 91)
11 years	172 days	...	DIANA ROSS	(11 Sep 71 to 2 Mar 86)
11 years	238 days	...	FRANK SINATRA	(1 Oct 54 to 27 May 66)
11 years	124 days	...	CLIFF RICHARD	(17 Apr 68 to 19 Aug 79)
9 years	231 days	...	BEE GEES	(4 Sep 68 to 23 Apr 78)
9 years	80 days	...	CLIFF RICHARD	(15 Sep 79 to 4 Dec 88)
8 years	215 days	...	BEE GEES	(10 Mar 79 to 11 Oct 87)
7 years	357 days	...	DON McLEAN	(24 Jun 72 to 15 Jun 80)
7 years	279 days	...	UB40	(31 Aug 85 to 6 Jun 93)

Cher waited for 25 years and 239 days between dropping from number one in duet with her then husband Sonny in 1965 and reaching the top again on her own in 1992.

There was a gap of 21 years and 200 days between Gerry and the Pacemakers' 'You'll Never Walk Alone' and the Crowd's chart topping rendition of the same song with Gerry Marsden again on lead vocals. 16 years and 9 days elapsed between the last day of the final Rolling Stones number one, and Mick Jagger's reappearance at the top with David Bowie.

There was a gap of 14 years and 113 days between Eddy Grant's last day at number one as one of the Equals and his first day on top as a soloist. Elton John's first solo number one hit, 'Sacrifice/Healing Hands', happened 13 years and 293 days after he and Kiki Dee dropped from number one with 'Don't Go Breaking My Heart'.

'Tears Of A Clown' by Smokey Robinson and the Miracles fell from number one 10 years and 268 days before Smokey Robinson's solo hit 'Being With You' reached the top. Chrissie Hynde waited 9 years and 208 days between her number one duet with UB40, 'I Got You Babe', and her collaboration with Cher, Neneh Cherry and Eric Clapton.

The Beatles crammed all of their 17 chart toppers into a period of six years and 54 days.

longest span of number one hits

Five acts have scored number one hits over a period of more than 20 years:

31 years	153 days	...	CLIFF RICHARD	(1959 to 1990)
25 years	286 days	...	RIGHTEOUS BROTHERS	(1965 to 1990)
23 years	105 days	...	HOLLIES	(1965 to 1988)
20 years	87 days	...	ELVIS PRESLEY	(1957 to 1977)
20 years	34 days	...	BEE GEES	(1967 to 1987)

Cher first hit number one as half of Sonny and Cher in August 1965, and dropped from the top after her solo number one in June 1991, almost 26 years later. Diana Ross first hit number one as lead singer for the Supremes in 1964 and dropped off the top for the final time as a soloist in 1986, over 21 years later.

Cliff Richard is the only act to have number one hits in five decades. In the 1950s he hit number one twice, in the 1960s seven times, in the 1970s once, in the 1980s once solo and once more with the Young Ones and Hank Marvin, and so far once in the 1990's. This record is unlikely ever to be equalled.

The only acts, apart from Cliff Richard, to have hit number one in three different decades are Elvis Presley (50s, 60s and 70s) and the Bee Gees (60s, 70s and 80s). Queen hit number one in the 70s and 90s, and also topped the charts in 1981 by teaming up with David Bowie.

the one-hit wonders

Qualification: one number one hit, and nothing else - ever. 35 immortal acts now make up the list.

year	act	hit
1954	KITTY KALLEN	Little Things Mean A Lot
1956	DREAMWEAVERS	It's Almost Tomorrow
1958	KALIN TWINS	When
1959	JERRY KELLER	Here Comes Summer
1960	RICKY VALANCE	Tell Laura I Love Her
1962	B. BUMBLE AND THE STINGERS	Nut Cracker
1966	OVERLANDERS	Michelle
1968	CRAZY WORLD OF ATHOR BROWN	Fire
1969	ZAGER AND EVANS	In The Year 2525
1969	JANE BIRKIN AND SERGE GAINSBOURG	Je T'Aime...Moi Non Plus
1969	ARCHIES	Sugar Sugar
1970	LEE MARVIN	Wand'rin' Star
1970	NORMAN GREENBAUM	Spirit In The Sky
1970	MATTHEWS' SOUTHERN COMFORT	Woodstock
1971	CLIVE DUNN	Grandad
1973	SIMON PARK ORCHESTRA	Eye Level
1975	TYPICALLY TROPICAL	Barbados
1976	J. J. BARRIE	No Charge
1977	FLOATERS	Float On
1978	ALTHIA AND DONNA	Up Town Top Ranking
1978	BRIAN AND MICHAEL	Matchstalk Men And Matchstalk Cats And Dogs
1979	ANITA WARD	Ring My Bell
1979	LENA MARTELL	One Day At A Time
1980	FERN KINNEY	Together We Are Beautiful
1980	MASH	Theme From M*A*S*H
1980	ST WINIFRED'S SCHOOL CHOIR	There's No One Quite Like Grandma
1981	JOE DOLCE MUSIC THEATRE	Shaddap You Face
1982	CHARLENE	I've Never Been To Me
1985	PHYLLIS NELSON	Move Closer
1987	M/A/R/R/S	Pump Up The Volume
1988	ROBIN BECK	First Time
1990	PARTNERS IN KRYME	Turtle Power
1991	HALE & PACE and the STONKERS	The Stonk
1994	DOOP	Doop
1996	DUNBLANE	Knockin' On Heaven's Door Throw These Guns Away

22 other one-hit wonders exist, made up of acts who have had hits in other guises. They are:

year	act/hit
1974	JOHN DENVER *Annie's Song* (has also hit with Placido Domingo)
1980	OLIVIA NEWTON-JOHN AND ELECTRIC LIGHT ORCHESTRA *Xanadu* (both have had solo hits)
1981	QUEEN AND DAVID BOWIE *Under Pressure* (both have had solo number one hits)
1982	PAUL McCARTNEY WITH STEVIE WONDER *Ebony And Ivory* (both have had solo number one hits)
1984	BAND AID *Do They Know It's Christmas?* (a conglomeration of hit-makers)
1985	ELAINE PAGE AND BARBARA DICKSON *I know Him So Well* (both have had solo hits)
1985	USA FOR AMERICA *We Are The World* (another conglomeration of hit-makers)
1985	CROWD *You'll Never Walk Alone* (and another conglomeration)
1985	DAVID BOWIE AND MICK JAGGER *Dancing In The Street* (both have had solo hits)
1986	CLIFF RICHARD AND THE YOUNG ONES WITH HANK MARVIN *Living Doll* (Cliff and the Young Ones (a.k.a. Bad News) have both had solo hits, as has Hank Marvin)
1987	STEVE 'SILK' HURLEY *Jack Your Body* (Steve is one half of the duo J.M. Silk)
1987	ARETHA FRANKLIN AND GEORGE MICHAEL *I Knew You Were Waiting For Me* (both have had solo hits)
1987	FERRY AID *Let It Be* (yet another conglomeration)
1988	TIMELORDS *Doctorin' The Tardis* (subsequently hit as The KLF)
1989	KYLIE MINOGUE AND JASON DONOVAN *Especially For You* (both have had solo number one hits)
1989	CHRISTIANS, HOLLY JOHNSON, PAUL McCARTNEY, GERRY MARSDEN AND STOCK AITKEN WATERMAN *Ferry Cross The Mersey* (charity disc for the Hillsborough Disaster Fund)
1989	BAND AID II *Do They Know It's Christmas?* (another conglomeration - only Keren Woodward and Sarah Dallin of Bananarama appeared on both)
1990	ENGLANDNEWORDER *World In Motion* (a combination of New Order and the England World Cup Squad)
1991	VIC REEVES AND THE WONDER STUFF *Dizzy* (both acts have had separate hits)
1991	GEORGE MICHAEL AND ELTON JOHN *Don't Let The Sun Go Down On Me* (both have had solo number one hits, and other number ones in other duets)
1993	GEORGE MICHAEL AND QUEEN WITH LISA STANSFIELD *Five Live EP* (all three acts have had separate number one hits)
1995	CHER, CHRISSIE HYNDE AND NENEH CHERRY WITH ERIC CLAPTON *Love Can Build A Bridge* (all four have had solo success)

With a total of eight weeks spent at number one, the Archies' 'Sugar Sugar' is the longest running chart topper by a one-hit wonder.

least successful chart act

Since 13 May 1978, when the Top 75 was first published, 27 acts have clocked up a chart career consisting of only one week at number 75. They are:

hit act	date
ADICTS Bad Boy	14 May 83
ANGELWITCH Sweet danger	7 Jun 80
APPLES Eye Wonder	23 Mar 91
BABY JUNE Hey! What's Your Name	15 Aug 92
DANIELLE BRISEBOIS Gimme Little Sign	9 Sep 95
DAYTON The Sound Of Music	10 Dec 83
DEPTH CHARGE Legend Of The Golden Snake	29 Jul 95
DTOX Shattered Glass	21 Nov 92
THULI DUMAKUDE The Funeral	2 Jan 88
EXPOSE I'll Never Get Over You (Getting Over Me)	28 Aug 93
GEORGE FENTON and JONAS GWANGA Cry Freedom	2 Jan 88
GOOD GIRLS Just Call Me	24 Jul 93
GRAND PRIX Keep On Believing	27 Feb 82
HEARTBEAT COUNTRY Heartbeat	31 Dec 94
DAVID HOLMES Gone	6 Apr 96
ANTHONY HOPKINS Distant Star	27 Dec 86
KREUZ Party All Night	8 Jul 95
LA GANZ Like A Playa	9 Nov 96
LOST Techno Funk	22 Jun 91
MICHAEL LOVESMITH Ain't Nothin' Like It	5 Oct 85
MC DUKE I'm Riffin' (English Rasta)	11 Mar 89
PRETTY BOY FLOYD Rock And Roll (Is Gonna Set The Night On Fire)	10 Mar 90
QUENCH Dreams	17 Feb 96
CHERYL PEPSII RILEY Thanks For My Child	28 Jan 89
SEDUCTION Heartbeat	21 Apr 90
SIMONE My family Depends On Me	23 Nov 91
SOULED OUT In My Life	9 May 92

Adicts, Grand Prix, David Holmes and Kreuz have also hit the album charts, with marginally more success. Thuli Dumakude's hit was the flip side of the George Fenton and Jonas Gwanga record. Both tracks were from the soundtrack of the film, Cry Freedom.

There are 11 other acts who have spent one week at number 75 in this particular combination, but they have had hits under other guises.

act hit	date
CILLA BLACK and DUSTY SPRINGFIELD Heart And Soul	30 Oct 93
(both have had number one solo hits, the only artists on this list to have done so)	
JOHNNY CLEGG and SAVUKA Scatterlings Of Africa	16 May 87
(Clegg also hit as part of Juluka)	
NIKKI D Daddy's Little Girl	30 Mar 91
(has hit with Alyson Williams)	
DEJA Serious	29 Aug 87
(Deja were Starlena Young and Curt Jones, who had hits as members of both Aurra and Slave)	
FISH AND TONY BANKS Short Cut To Somewhere	18 Oct 86
(both have had solo hits, as well as with Marillion and Genesis)	
JHELISA Friendly Pressure	1 Jul 95
(Jhelisa Anderson, sister of Carleen, was lead singer of Soul Family Sensation)	
KIRSTY MacCOLL and EVAN DANDO Perfect Day	24 Jun 95
(MacColl has had solo hits, Dando is vocalist with the Lemonheads)	
MELISSA MANCHESTER and AL JARREAU The Music Of Goodbe	5 Apr 86
(Jarreau has had solo hits)	
MONKEY MAFIA featuring PATRA Work Mi Body	10 Aug 96
(Patra has had a solo hit and one with Shabba Ranks)	
JOHN PARISH and POLLY JEAN HARVEY That Was My Veil	23 Nov 96
(PJ Harvey has had solo hits)	
STOP THE VIOLENCE Self Destruction	18 Feb 89
(charity ensemble featuring hitmakers Boogie Down Productions, Public Enemy and Stetasonic)	

From 10 March 1960 to 6 May 1978, when only a top 50 was published, nine acts managed a chart career that consisted of one week at number 50. They were Angels, Chaquito, Jimmy Clanton, Cookies, Tim Hardin, Tony Hatch, Moontrekkers, Hal Paige and the Whalers and Sundragon.

top 100 chart hits

Part 1 of British Hit Singles lists the 20,101 hits that have entered the UK singles chart in the 44 years since its inception in 1952. This final chart of the book gives an indication as to which of those hits have performed best.

The top 100 is based on a sophisticated points system, designed to enable comparison between singles released in the early days of the chart, when only a top 12 was published, and today's top 75. So, for each week a single spends at number one it is awarded 100 points, and for each week the record spends elsewhere in the chart, pro-rata points are given depending on the size of chart at the time. Thus a single at number 10 in a chart of 75 fares better than a single at number 10 in a chart of just 20 titles, as was the case in the 50s.

This methodology benefits those hits whose sales came over a longer period of time rather than those whose sales were concentrated in just a few weeks. There is no room for 'Do They Know It's Christmas' or 'Mull Of Kintyre' - two of Britain's biggest selling singles - as both had chart careers confined exclusively to the Christmas period. Whereas Frank Sinatra's 'My Way', which never climbed higher than number five on the weekly listings, is included here at number two thanks to its record-breaking 167 weeks on the chart.

The final listing delivers up some other surprises - who would have thought that 'The Birdie Song' would be placed higher than 'A Whiter Shade Of Pale' or that Oasis would be outdone by Rolf Harris? Perhaps the most startling fact of all is that the act with the most discs in the chart is not the Beatles or Elvis but gentleman Jim Reeves!

1   RELAX . . . . Frankie Goes To Hollywood
2   MY WAY . . . . Frank Sinatra
3   STRANGER ON THE SHORE . . . . Mr. Acker Bilk
4   (WE'RE GONNA) ROCK AROUND THE CLOCK . Bill Haley and his Comets
5   I BELIEVE . . . . Frankie Laine
6   BLUE MONDAY . . . . New Order
7   I LOVE YOU BECAUSE . . . . Jim Reeves
8   RIVERS OF BABYLON/BROWN GIRL IN THE RING . . . . Boney M
9   LOVE IS ALL AROUND . . . . Wet Wet Wet
10 RELEASE ME . . . . Engelbert Humperdinck
11 SHE LOVES YOU . . . . Beatles
12 BOHEMIAN RHAPSODY . . . . Queen
13 AMAZING GRACE . . . . Judy Collins
14 LET'S TWIST AGAIN . . . . Chubby Checker
15 THINK TWICE . . . . Celine Dion
16 HOUND DOG . . . . Elvis Presley
17 TIE A YELLOW RIBBON ROUND THE OLD
    OAK TREE . . . . Tony Orlando and Dawn
18 ALBATROSS . . . . Fleetwood Mac
19 TAINTED LOVE . . . . Soft Cell
20 ALL RIGHT NOW . . . . Free
21 HEARTBREAK HOTEL . . . . Elvis Presley
22 (EVERYTHING I DO) I DO IT FOR YOU . . . . Bryan Adams
23 GHOSTBUSTERS . . . . Ray Parker Jr.
24 I WILL ALWAYS LOVE YOU . . . . Whitney Houston
25 SECRET LOVE . . . . Doris Day
26 SIDE SADDLE . . . . Russ Conway
27 I REMEMBER YOU . . . . Frank Ifield
28 LET'S DANCE . . . . Chris Montez
29 THE LAST WALTZ . . . . Engelbert Humperdinck
30 THE POWER OF LOVE . . . . Jennifer Rush
31 TAKE MY BREATH AWAY . . . . Berlin
32 RIDE ON TIME . . . . Black Box
33 WHITE LINES (DON'T
    DON'T DO IT) . . . . . . Grandmaster Melle Mel and the Furious Five
34 YOUNG GIRL . . . . Gary Puckett and the Union Gap
35 TEARS . . . . Ken Dodd
36 SAILING . . . . Rod Stewart
37 AS LONG AS HE NEEDS ME . . . . Shirley Bassey
38 YOU'RE THE ONE THAT I WANT
    . . . . John Travolta and Olivia Newton-John
39 REET PETITE . . . . Jackie Wilson
40 CARA MIA . . . . . . David Whitfield with Mantovani and his Orchestra
41 DISTANT DRUMS . . . . Jim Reeves
42 WHAT A WONDERFUL WORLD/CABARET . . . . Louis Armstrong
43 MAGIC MOMENTS/CATCH A FALLING STAR . . . . Perry Como
44 TELSTAR . . . . Tornados
45 LEADER OF THE PACK . . . . Shangri-Las
46 I WON'T FORGET YOU . . . . Jim Reeves
47 I WILL SURVIVE . . . . Gloria Gaynor
48 WHEN I FALL IN LOVE . . . . Nat 'King' Cole
49 TRUE LOVE . . . . Bing Crosby and Grace Kelly

top 100 chart hits

50 **GIVE ME YOUR WORD** . . . . Tennessee Ernie Ford
51 **DIANA** . . . . Paul Anka
52 **DECK OF CARDS** . . . . Wink Martindale
53 **IMAGINE** . . . . John Lennon
54 **HOLIDAY** . . . . Madonna
55 **THE LOCO-MOTION** . . . . Little Eva
56 **SUGAR SUGAR** . . . . Archies
57 **I JUST CALLED TO SAY I LOVE YOU** . . . . . . Stevie Wonder
58 **I FEEL LOVE** . . . . Donna Summer
59 **I'LL BE HOME** . . . . Pat Boone
60 **NIGHTS IN WHITE SATIN** . . . . Moody Blues
61 **AGADOO** . . . . Black Lace
62 **WHAT DO YOU WANT TO MAKE THOSE**
    EYES AT ME FOR . . . . Emile Ford and the Checkmates
63 **WITHOUT YOU** . . . . Nilsson
64 **I PRETEND** . . . . Des O'Connor
65 **WHO'S SORRY NOW** . . . . Connie Francis
66 **THE BIRDIE SONG (BIRDIE DANCE)** . . . . Tweets
67 **TERRY'S THEME FROM LIMELIGHT** . . . . Frank Chacksfield
68 **I GET THE SWEETEST FEELING** . . . . Jackie Wilson
69 **HANDY MAN** . . . . Jimmy Jones
70 **HONEY** . . . . Bobby Goldsboro
71 **SINGING THE BLUES** . . . . Guy Mitchell
72 **A WHITER SHADE OF PALE** . . . . Procul Harum
73 **DOWNTOWN** . . . . Petula Clark
74 **TWO TRIBES** . . . . Frankie Goes To Hollywood
75 **REACH OUT I'LL BE THERE** . . . . Four Tops
76 **AMERICAN PIE** . . . . Don McLean
77 **HE AIN'T HEAVY HE'S MY BROTHER** . . . . Hollies
78 **HE'LL HAVE TO GO** . . . . Jim Reeves
79 **MISSING** . . . . Everything But The Girl
80 **TWO LITTLE BOYS** . . . . Rolf Harris
81 **WONDERWALL** . . . . Oasis
82 **OH CAROL** . . . . Neil Sedaka
83 **UNCHAINED MELODY** . . . . Righteous Brothers
84 **TEMPTATION** . . . . Heaven 17
85 **WHEN A MAN LOVES A WOMAN** . . . . Percy Sledge
86 **LIVING DOLL** . . . . Cliff Richard and the Drifters
87 **LITTLE THINGS MEAN A LOT** . . . . Kitty Kallen
88 **ONLY THE LONELY** . . . . Roy Orbison
89 **FROM ME TO YOU** . . . . Beatles
90 **CRAZY FOR YOU** . . . . Madonna
91 **YOUNG AT HEART** . . . . Bluebells
92 **THERE GOES MY EVERYTHING** . . . . Engelbert Humperdinck
93 **HALFWAY TO PARADISE** . . . . Billy Fury
94 **A WONDERFUL TIME UP THERE/IT'S TOO SOON TO KNOW** . . Pat Boone
95 **YOU TO ME ARE EVERYTHING** . . . . Real Thing
96 **WOODEN HEART** . . . . Elvis Presley
97 **LOST IN MUSIC** . . . . Sister Sledge
98 **A SCOTTISH SOLDIER** . . . . Andy Stewart
99 **LOVE LETTERS IN THE SAND** . . . . Pat Boone
100 **CRAZY FOR YOU** . . . . Let Loose

Frankie Goes To Hollywood

picture credits

Page 15 Alarm - Steve Gillett, Peter Andre - Mushroom Records, Tina Arena - Columbia Records.
Page 21 Joan Armatrading - S.I.N., Ash - Infectious Records, Auteurs - Hut Recordings.
Page 26 Babybird - Echo, Babylon Zoo - Redferns, Beatles - Corbis.
Page 43 Blur - EMI Records, Bone Thugs-N-Harmony - Epic, Boo Radleys - Creation Records.
Page 51 Boyz II Men - Retna, Boyzone - Steve Double/S.I.N., Bucks Fizz - Retna.
Page 58 Buzzcocks - One Stop Music Distribution, Chemical Brothers - Virgin Records, Chi-Lites - Retna.
Page 68 Chicago - Robin Kaplan/Retna, China Crisis - Andrew Catlin/S.I.N., Chubby Checker - Photofest/Retna, Christie - Brian Longley.
Page 77 Clash - Adrian Boot/Retna Edwin Collins - Hazel Maxwell Management, Alice Cooper - Anna Meuer/S.I.N., Cranberries - Island Records.
Page 86 Creedence Clearwater Rivival - Michael Putland/Retna, Crosby Stills Nash & Young - Michael Putland/Retna, Sheryl Crow - A&M Records.
Page 97 Dead Or Alive - Peter Anderson/S.I.N., Dexy's Midnight Runners - Virginia Turbett/S.I.N., Celine Dion - Epic, Divine Comedy - Steve Gillett.
Page 106 Dodgy - A&M Records, Dollar - Nell Matthews/Retna, Donovan - Michael Putland/Retna, Doors - Doors Photo Library/ Retna.
Page 111 Dreadzone - Virgin Records, Dubstar - Andy Willsher/S.I.N., Ian Dury And The Blockheads - Retna.
Page 115 East 17 - London Records, Earth Wind And Fire - Peter Anderson/S.I.N., Enya - WEA Records.
Page 122 - David Essex - Michael Putland/Retna, Eternal, Andy Earl/EMI, Everything But The Girl - Virgin Records.
Page 131 Joe Fagin - ACL Records, Falco - Peter Noble/S.I.N., Eddie Fisher - Fiona Simon/Retna,

Mike Flowers Pops - London Records.
Page 138 Foreigner - Michael Putland/Retna, Fugees - Columbia Records, Fun Boy Three - Steve Rapport/Retna, Billy Fury - King Collection/Retna.
Page 145 Gina G - Steve Gillett, Gabrielle - Go! Discs, Marvin Gaye - Photofest/Retna.
Page 151 Debbie Gibson - Jayne Houghton/S.I.N., Go West (both) - Steve Gillett, Hall And Oates - Virginia Turbett/S.I.N..
Page 158 Rolf Harris - Michael Putland/Retna, George Harrison - Michael Putland/Retna, PJ Harvey - Steve Gillett.
Page 167 Jimi Hendrix Experience - Retna, Hootie And The Blowfish - Roy Tee/S.I.N., Hue And Cry - S.I.N..
Page 178 INXS - Mercury Records, Jam - Peter Noble/S.I.N., Jamiroquai - Sony S2.
Page 186 Jesus Jones - EMI, Jon Of The Pleased Wimmin - East West Records, Kinks - Corbis.
Page 207 Jerry Lee Lewis - Corbis, Lightning Seeds - Epic, Longpigs - Mother Records.
Page 214 Louise - EMI, Lush - 4AD, Sean Maguire - Parlophone, Manfred Mann - G. Hanekrout/ Retna.
Page 227 Manic Street Preachers - Epic, Marmalade - Retna, Richard Marx - Retna, Metallica - Antol Corbijn/Mercury.
Page 240 Robert Miles - Deconstruction Records, Kylie Minogue (with Nick Cave) - Mute Records, Alanis Morissette - WEA Records, Mark Morrison - WEA Records.
Page 247 Musical Youth - Adrian Boot/Retna, Jimmy Nail - East West Records, Olivia Newton-John - Corbis.
Page 258 Gilbert O'Sullivan - Park Records, Ocean Colour Scene - Steve Double/S.I.N., Odyssey - Mick Hudson/Redferns.
Page 264 OMC - Patrick Ford/Redferns, Joan Osborne - Steve Gillett, Ozzy Ozbourne - Katia Natola/S.I.N..
Page 276 Presidents Of The United

States Of America - Lisa Johnson/Columbia, Public Image Ltd - Robert Matchell/Retna, Pulp - Island Records.
Page 284 Prodigy - XL Records, Shabba Ranks - David Corio/S.I.N., Otis Reading - S.I.N., Demis Roussos - Kevin Cummins/Retna.
Page 297 Joan Regan - Hulton Deutsch Collection/Corbis, Alexei Sayle - David Corio/S.I.N., Shampoo - EMI.
Page 312 Shed Seven - Polydor Records, Showaddywaddy - Michael Putland/Retna, Sleeper - Indolent Records.
Page 323 Simply Red - East West Records, Skunk Anansie - One Little Indian, Small Faces - King Collection/Retna.
Page 336 Smashing Pumpkins - Ross Halfin/Retna, Sting - S.I.N., Strawberry Switchblade - Jayne Houghton/S.I.N..
Page 345 Suede - Nude Records, Suggs - WEA Records, Supergrass - Parlophone.
Page 352 Technohead - Inge Bekkers/Road Runner Records, Terrorvision - EMI, TLC - Steve Granitz/Retna.
Page 366 Toyah - Corbis, Tricky - Island Records, Undertones - Peter Noble/S.I.N., Upside Down - Steve Gillett.
Page 378 Luther Vandross - Epic, Pete Whylie - S.I.N., Weezer - Martyn Goodacre/S.I.N., ZZ Top - Steve Gillett.
Page 476 Morrissey - Steve Gillett.
Page 477 Paul Weller - Go! Disks.
Page 478 Oasis - S.I.N.
Page 479 Liam Gallagher - Steve Gillett.
Page 480 New Order - London Records.
Page 482 Elvis Presley - Corbis.
Page 483 PJ Proby with Mark Almond - EMI.
Page 486 Madonna - WEA.
Page 501 Wet Wet Wet - Precious.
Page 503 Take That - RCA.
Page 504 Spice Girls - Ellen Von Untwerth/Virgin Records.
Page 506 David Bowie - RCA.
Page 511 Frankie Goes To Hollywood - ZTT